Career and College Major Application Matrix

Chapter, Page Number, & Description	Education (including Early Childhood, Primary, Secondary & Special Education)	Healthcare (including nursing, physical, speech, & occupational therapy)	Psychology & Sociology	Mental Health & Human Services
Ch.6, p.196: Temperament and how it modulates a child's behavior.	X		X	
Ch.6, pp.197–198, Box: Autism, its causes and treatment.	X	X	X	X
Ch.6, p.201, Fig. 6.2: Pediatric symptom checklist.		X		
Ch.6, p.203, Fig.6.3: How changing demographics of childhood will impact future occupations that service children.	X	X		X
Ch.6, p.205, Box: Social worker, profile.	X		X	X
Ch.6, pp.210–211: How fathers influence children's development.	X		X	X
Ch.6, p.214, Box: Elements of quality childcare.	X			
Ch.6, pp.218–220: Signs of abuse of children.	X	X		X
Ch.6, p.219, Box: Strategies for interacting with infants with disabilities.	X	X		X
Ch.7, pp.228–229: Otitis media: Symptoms and treatment.		X		
Ch.7, pp.230–231: Congenital birth defects, including resources for children with developmental delays.	X	X		X
Ch.7, pp.234–235: Food allergies and their symptoms.	X	X		
Ch.7, pp.236–237: Children with HIV or AIDS. A comprehensive care effort.	X	X		X
Ch.7, pp.238–239: Sleep disturbances in young children.	X	X		X
Ch.7, p.241, Box : Immigrant cultures and customs regarding illnesses.	X	X	X	
Ch.7, pp.246–248: Jean Piaget's theory of preoperational thought on the development of intelligence in infants and children.	X		X	
Ch.7, pp.250–251: How language is acquired and language disorders in young children.	X	X	X	
Ch.7, p.252, Box: Speech therapist, profile.	X	X		
Ch.7, p.254, Table 7.5: Early signs of developmental delay in children.	X	X		
Ch.7, pp.257–259: How Piaget's and Kohlberg's theories promote moral development in children.	X		X	X
Ch.8, pp.265–267: Examples of how "play" influences preschooler's social development.	X		X	
Ch.8, pp.267–268: Examples of cultural differences in children's play.	X		X	
Ch.8, pp.268–270: Examples of how Western, Asian, African, and Hispanic cultures effect children's emotional development.	X		X	X
Ch.8, p.272, Table 8.1: Progression of emotional development, ages 2-6.	X		X	X
Ch.8, pp.273–275: Cognitive and social factors that influence a child's self-esteem.	X		X	X
Ch.8, p.276: Examples of gender biases in Afghanistan culture.			X	X
Ch.8, pp.280–281: Cultural trends affecting families in the U.S.	X		X	X
Ch.8, pp.282, 284–285: Key child-rearing practices.	X			X
Ch.8, pp.283, Box: Easing the transition into kindergarten.	X			
Ch.8, pp.285–287: Behavioral signs of child abuse.	X	X		X
Ch.8, p.290: How to parent more effectively.			X	X
Ch.8, pp.290–293: Alternative American family structures and how they influence children's development.	X		X	X
Ch.8, p.297, Box: Preparing for children with disabilities in early childhood settings.	X	X		
Ch.8, p.300, Box: Brief history and overview of Headstart.	X			X
Ch.8, p.301–302: Media influences on children's behavior (internet, video, and computer games).	X		X	X
Ch.9, p.311: Definition of dyslexia.	X	X		
Ch.9, p.312: Description of genius and gifted children, along with sample enrichment programs.	X		X	
Ch.9, p.312, Table 9.2: Chronic health conditions of children, ages 5 to 11.		X		
Ch.9, pp.313–314: Major causes of obesity in children and related health risks.	X	X		X
Ch.9, pp.314–315: Analysis of middle school children's eating disorders.	X	X		X
Ch.9, pp.315–318, 320: Examples of Piagetian conservation tasks with cross-cultural applications.	X		X	
Ch.9, pp.319, Box: How parents and teachers can foster creative thinking in children.	X		X	
Ch.9, pp.322–324: Comparison of bilingual education programs in U.S. school programs.	X	X		
Ch.9, pp.324–325: Examples of I.Q. tests and their limitations.	X		X	
Ch.9, pp.325, 328: Using "cognitive style" as a teaching/learning strategy	X			
Ch.9, pp.326–327, Box: How culture influences academic achievement in Asian and American children.	X		X	
Ch.9, pp.328–330: Differences between mental retardation and learning disabilities.	X	X	X	X
Ch.9, pp.330–331: Symptoms of ADHD and the health side effects of psychoactive treatment.	X	X		X
Ch.9, pp.332–333 Box: Crucial components of a school Individual Education Plan (IEP) for handicapped students.	X			X
Ch.9, p.334, Box: Special education teacher, profile.	X			

IMPORTANT

HERE IS YOUR REGISTRATION CODE TO ACCESS MCGRAW-HILL PREMIUM CONTENT AND MCGRAW-HILL ONLINE RESOURCES

For key premium online resources you need THIS CODE to gain access. Once the code is entered, you will be able to use the web resources for the length of your course.

Access is provided only if you have purchased a new book.

If the registration code is missing from this book, the registration screen on our website, and within your WebCT or Blackboard course will tell you how to obtain your new code. Your registration code can be used only once to establish access. It is not transferable.

To gain access to these online resources

1. USE your web browser to go to: **http://www.mhhe.com/vzcrandell8**

2. CLICK on "First Time User"

3. ENTER the Registration Code printed on the tear-off bookmark on the right

4. After you have entered your registration code, click on "Register"

5. FOLLOW the instructions to setup your personal UserID and Password

6. WRITE your UserID and Password down for future reference. Keep it in a safe place.

If your course is using WebCT or Blackboard, you'll be able to use this code to access the McGraw-Hill content within your instructor's online course.

To gain access to the McGraw-Hill content in your instructor's WebCT or Blackboard course simply log into the course with the user ID and Password provided by your instructor. Enter the registration code exactly as it appears to the right when prompted by the system. You will only need to use this code the first time you click on McGraw-Hill content.

These instructions are specifically for student access. Instructors are not required to register via the above instructions.

Thank you, and welcome to your McGraw-Hill Online Resources.

13 Digit: 978-0-07-326986-3
10 Digit: 0-07-326986-7
t/a Human Development

9EVT-9XVV-UB37-YJVX-7QQC

REGISTRATION CODE
REGISTRATION CODE

Human Development

EIGHTH EDITION

James W. Vander Zanden
The Ohio State University

**Thomas L. Crandell
and Corinne Haines Crandell**
Broome Community College

Boston   Burr Ridge, IL   Dubuque, IA   Madison, WI   New York   San Francisco   St. Louis
Bangkok   Bogotá   Caracas   Kuala Lumpur   Lisbon   London   Madrid   Mexico City
Milan   Montreal   New Delhi   Santiago   Seoul   Singapore   Sydney   Taipei   Toronto

HUMAN DEVELOPMENT, EIGHTH EDITION

Published by McGraw-Hill, a business unit of The McGraw-Hill Companies, Inc., 1221 Avenue of the Americas, New York, NY 10020. Copyright © 2007, 2003, 2000, 1997, 1993, 1989, 1985, 1981, 1978 by The McGraw-Hill Companies, Inc. All rights reserved. No part of this publication may be reproduced or distributed in any form or by any means, or stored in a database or retrieval system, without the prior written consent of The McGraw-Hill Companies, Inc., including, but not limited to, in any network or other electronic storage or transmission, or broadcast for distance learning.

Some ancillaries, including electronic and print components, may not be available to customers outside the United States.

This book is printed on recycled, acid-free paper containing 10% postconsumer waste.

2 3 4 5 6 7 8 9 0 WCK/WCK 0 9 8 7 6

ISBN-13: 978-0-07-319486-8
ISBN-10: 0-07-319486-7

Editor-in-chief: *Emily Barrosse*
Publisher: *Beth Mejia*
Executive editor: *Mike Sugarman*
Senior marketing manager: *Melissa Caughlin*
Senior development editor: *Judith Kromm*
Senior project manager: *Marilyn Rothenberger*
Lead production supervisor: *Carol Bielski*
Designer: *Marianna Kinigakis*
Photo researcher: *Judy Mason/Nora Agbayani*
Media producer: *Stephanie George*

This book was set in 10/12 Stempel Garamond by EPS, NY, and printed on 45# Pub Matte Plus by Quebecor World, Versailles.

The credits section for this book begins on page C-1 and is considered an extension of the copyright page.

Library of Congress Cataloging-in-Publication Data

Crandell, Thomas L.
    Human development / Thomas L. Crandell, Corrine H. Crandell.— 8th ed.
        p. cm.
    Includes bibliographical references and index.
    ISBN 0-07-319486-7
    1. Developmental psychology. I. Crandell, Corinne Haines. II. Vander Zanden, James Wilfrid. Human development. III. Title.
BF713 .V36 2007
155—dc21

                                                                                2005030980

www.mhhe.com

Contents in Brief

Contents

PART FOUR
Early Childhood: 2 to 6 223

PART SEVEN
Early Adulthood 441

CHAPTER 13 Early Adulthood: Physical and Cognitive Development 442

CHAPTER 14 Early Adulthood: Emotional and Social Development 473

Preface

You, the student, in reading this text, will soon come to realize that human development is emerging as a truly vibrant and relevant field for the twenty-first century—but every text is written from a unique perspective based on the life experiences and professional background of the authors. So, before you read about human development over the next several months, you may ask: "What *are* the unique backgrounds of the authors of this text?"

James Vander Zanden, sociologist and professor emeritus at Ohio State University and original author of this text for 20 years, wrote this text from the perspective of a man who endured abuse from early childhood and subsequently had a troubled childhood and adolescence. He became intrigued by the study of human behavior, decided to make it his career, and became dedicated to the betterment of the human condition. Prior to writing the first edition of this text, James Vander Zanden lost his wife following an illness, and he was left with the awesome responsibility of raising two young sons as a single parent. Leaving the academic environment for a few years, he began researching and writing *Human Development* and assumed the role of a full-time parent to his children. His work in the area of human development over the life span became profoundly helpful in raising his sons. Both young men have earned Ph.D. degrees and are living happy, productive, and rewarding lives.

In U.S. contemporary life, about 4 to 5 percent of men in the United States are single parents, juggling responsibilities between working and raising children. In a poignant revelation, James Vander Zanden admits difficulties "moving ahead" in his professional career during those child-raising years, not unlike the obstacles faced by many employed women who are either single or married mothers and are also devoted to parenting their children. Yet, looking back, James Vander Zanden believes the rewards and satisfaction of parenthood were far greater than those found in academia.

Tom Crandell, an educational psychologist and psychology professor, and Corinne Crandell, an adjunct psychology instructor, continue to build on the foundation of James Vander Zanden's work. We teach developmental psychology classes, conduct research, write about human development, and experience the stages of life across the life span. We bring to this text a wealth of knowledge and understanding about the issues facing divorced and single parents, stepfamilies, families with children with special needs, and families supporting aging relatives. Our third child—our daughter/stepdaughter with Down syndrome—has particularly enriched our lives and has made us appreciate the complexity of human development. Thus, unlike other human development texts, this one includes information about the development of differently-abled children as well as "typical" children. Our other three adult children are now in successful careers and/or raising their four children, our grandchildren, who are a joy. At the same time, our mothers are in late adulthood and need increasing assistance. The richness of life experience is coming full circle for us.

> Every child comes into a family somewhat like a rock thrown into a pond. The ripples caused by the new arrival affect everyone. Nobody in the family remains exactly the same. Everyone changes. (Perske, 1981)

Just as the birth of a new child in a family changes the whole family, so too does newer research about human development add to the expanding collection of classic developmental theories about what is "normal" or what can be "expected" along the trajectory of human life stages. Students reading this text will learn that the study of human development is contingent on a diverse body of knowledge that incorporates a variety of views and theoretical approaches. Developmental psychologists are reaching out to other disciplines and embracing a multidisciplinary, collaborative approach that draws on concepts and contributions from sociology, social psychology, anthropology, gender studies, biology, medicine, social history, demography, criminology, and so forth.

Our cross-cultural knowledge base is expanding, with the Internet providing nearly instant access to published empirical findings from research conducted around the world. The result is that the field has much to offer humans in its global efforts to cope with serious social problems such as poverty and an ever-growing aging and ethnically diverse population.

Although developmentalists recognize individual variation due to genetic influences, they also study the environmental (social and ecological) context in which behavior occurs. Developmentalists are especially concerned with the far-reaching environmental effects of poverty on human development. To investigate contemporary concerns, they are placing greater reliance on time-extended research designs and enlarging the breadth of their research objectives.

We hope that students who read this textbook will find answers to their questions about their own lives, much as we have done in our research and writing of this book. It is our earnest desire that courses in human development and developmental psychology help people move toward Abraham Maslow's ideal and become self-actualized men and women. They should acquire a new vision of the human experience, which can help them lead fuller, richer, and more fruitful lives. For readers who are parents, our goal is to help you to improve your parenting skills.

We share the belief of many people that education is not the sum of 8, 12, 16, or more years of schooling. Instead, it is a lifelong habit, a striving for growth and wise living. Education is something we retain after we have put away our texts, recycled our lecture notes, and forgotten the minutiae we learned for an exam. Therefore, textbooks must present controversy and unanswered questions. Otherwise students will believe that facts are the stuff of education, and they will derive a false sense of security from cramming their heads full of information rather than refining their minds with thoughtful analysis. The stuff of human development is ultimately about real people living their lives in a real world, and many of the boxes in this eighth edition of *Human Development* offer students an opportunity to think critically about social issues and how these issues relate to their personal lives and world.

Organization and Focus of the Eighth Edition

This textbook views human physical, cognitive, emotional, and social growth as blending in an unending, dynamic process. In terms of its approach to the study of the life span, *Human Development* emphasizes development in context. This approach focuses on the development of people within families and the larger ecological context implied by this theme. By examining the groundbreaking work of developmentalists such as Jean Piaget, Erik Erikson, Urie Bronfenbrenner, Lev Vygotsky, K. Warner Schaie, Daniel Levinson, Bernice Neugarten, and Paul and Margret Baltes, students will fully understand the complex network of developmental tasks that shape us as we move through the life span.

Much like the course of human life, this edition reflects both continuity and change. Like previous editions, the eighth edition of *Human Development* features

a chronological approach to studying the life span and consists of 19 chapters. The first two chapters orient the student to the central research methods and the diversity of theories utilized in the study of human development. Chapter 3 examines beginnings: reproduction, heredity and genetics, and the prenatal period. Chapter 4 presents birth and the first two years of infant growth. Chapters 5 and 6 include infant cognitive, language, emotional, and social development. From Chapter 7, "Early Childhood," to Chapter 18, "Late Adulthood," each stage of the life span has been organized into two chapters: Physical, cognitive, and moral development are examined in the opening chapter, and emotional and social development follows in the subsequent chapter. Chapter 19 deals with dying, death, and coping with grief.

Thinking Critically

As we have said, a course on human development should do more than provide students with a body of scientific findings. Rote memorization of definitions and facts does not do justice to the dynamic nature of this subject matter. We must encourage students to think critically and creatively about their own development and how it is shaped by the world around them. This text will provide students with a deeper understanding of the human experience and the variety of factors that directly or indirectly mold their life course.

These new abilities will not be limited only to the classroom, however. The challenging, real-life topics we discuss include newest contraceptive methods and public access, assisted reproductive technologies for infertile couples, genetic counseling and testing, and stem cell research and human cloning (Chapter 3); effects of absentee fathers on children, and early intervention services for infants born at risk and craniosacral therapy (Chapter 4); differing theories of language acquisition, bilingualism, and effects of infant media viewing (Chapter 5); elements of a quality child-care program and rising incidence of autism (Chapter 6); nutrition and health issues for young children such as HIV/AIDS or asthma, early signs of developmental delays in children, and moral development in childhood (Chapter 7); the special needs of gifted and talented children and key child-rearing practices (Chapter 8); typical health issues in middle childhood such as the rising rate of obesity, assessment of children's intelligence (including emotional intelligence), the escalating number of ESL students in American schools, school programs for children at risk, and U.S. schoolchildren's academic achievement in international comparison (Chapter 9); nurturing a healthy self-concept, the impact of divorce on children and the impact of living in a variety of family structures, and out-of-school care and supervision (Chapter 10); adolescent health issues, variations in formal operational thought, use of media and technology for instruction, and high-risk behaviors (Chapter 11); the rising incidence of early teenage sexual behaviors, sexual orientation, shift in teenage autonomy, adolescent career development and choice (Chapter 12); generational expectations and goals, preparing for adulthood and careers (Chapter 13); cohabitation, delayed marriage and family transitions, single-parent families, work significance, and Levinson's stages of a man's or woman's life (Chapter 14); physical and health changes in middle adulthood, sexual functioning in middle adulthood and the increasing risk of AIDS and STIs, maximizing cognitive abilities in middle adulthood, and a schedule of physical checkups at midlife (Chapter 15); adaptation in a stepfamily, job satisfaction, coping with unemployment or forced retirement, and lifelong learning (Chapter 16); theories of aging, exercise and longevity, coping with cognitive changes, and Social Security debate (Chapter 17); social relationship changes and aging, faith and adjustment to aging, policy issues in an aging society (Chapter 18); who makes end-of-life decisions and preparing advance directives, a guide for professionals and families coping with a terminally ill person who requests physician-assisted suicide, warning signs of suicide, and coping with grief (Chapter 19).

bond with children born at risk (Chapter 6); changing demographics and implications for health of minority children (Chapter 7); preparing for children with differences in early childhood settings (Chapter 8); individual differences in children's cognitive development, bilingualism and ESL instruction, and the diversity of family structures and their impact on child development (Chapter 9); adoption of children from other cultures (Chapter 10); cultural practices of female genital mutilation, international comparison of adolescent intellectual performance, and cultural aspects of adolescent identity formation (Chapter 11); adolescent sexual orientation and behaviors (Chapter 12); examination of young adult health across cultures, and young adult gay/lesbian/bisexual attitudes and behaviors (Chapter 13); diversity in adult lifestyle options, lesbian and gay parenting, and arranged marriages or love matches across cultures (Chapter 14); strategies for success for middle-age college students (Chapter 15); life without a middle age (Chapter 16); theories of biological aging and longevity (Chapter 17); ethnic diversity and the aging population, and lesbian and gay elderly adjustment to aging (Chapter 18); faith and facing death, and cross-cultural perspectives on dying, death, and grief (Chapter 19).

Commitment to Diversity

Past editions of *Human Development* have been lauded for their sensitivity and coverage of issues of race, class, gender, and ethnicity. The eighth edition continues this legacy by updating and integrating information on cross-cultural, minority, gender, and individual differences wherever possible. The eighth edition of *Human Development* utilizes an integrative approach to demonstrate our commitment to diversity, as well as addresses some issues in boxes entitled "Human Diversity." This edition, in particular, presents recent findings of developmental research that shed light on important issues for growing populations of Hispanic Americans and Asian Americans. The special needs and mandated services for children born at risk are also presented, and the realities of an inclusive lifestyle for those who are differently-abled are covered across the life course. Also, this edition addresses the development of lesbian and gay individuals from adolescence into late adulthood.

Attention to both classic and emerging issues in human development is a crucial component of our task as teachers and authors. Specific examples of this approach include discussions of psychological research and spiritual traditions (Chapter 2); genetic counseling and testing (Chapter 3); a cross-cultural view of sleeping with an infant (Chapter 4); assisting infants with hearing impairments (Chapter 5); developing an emotional

New to the Eighth Edition

This edition has been reorganized to make it even easier for instructors and students to use. We had six main goals in revising this edition:

1. To reorganize the chapters to achieve greater continuity about development across the life span. Concepts, issues, theories, and research findings are grouped more precisely into physical, cognitive, moral, emotional, or social development for each stage of the life span.
2. To present the textual material and update half of the illustrations in a more readable format, supported by additional applications to real-world situations. The use of critical thinking questions as advance organizers, the placement of headings, and the section of summary questions make the information more easily assimilated and memorable.
3. To present students with the most up-to-date research in the many domains of study across the human life span. Overall, this edition includes more than 1,200 new references. A substantial amount of research was extracted from U.S. Census and National Institutes of Health data reports from 2000 to 2005, which provide a broad view of national issues and concerns that affect the quality of life across generations. More specifically,

every chapter has been updated to incorporate the most recent research findings across all stages of development and relevant cross-cultural studies across the life span whenever pertinent.

4. To provide several "Implications for Practice" boxes to expose readers to careers and professionals who service people in various capacities across the life span.

5. To provide instructor and students with a "Career and College Major Application Matrix." This matrix enables readers to identify and locate specific career applications and examples useful to students pursuing careers in education, health care, psychology and sociology, and mental health and human services.

6. To introduce students to new information and strategies for managing many experiences and challenges that will face them across the life course.

Expanded Section Coverage on Crucial Issues in Life-Span Development

In addition to including coverage of such topics as early intervention services for children born at risk (Chapter 7) and diversity in adult lifestyle options (Chapter 14), the eighth edition of *Human Development* is unrivaled in its detailed coverage of numerous critical issues. Each chapter features new research findings and updates as well as coverage of classic studies in human development. This unique quality manifests our commitment to students' learning and overall breadth of knowledge. We begin by addressing the changing conception of age and aging (Chapter 1). Based on reviewers' comments, Maslow's humanistic theory has been reintroduced (Chapter 2). Information on genetics, assisted reproductive technologies, stem cell research and human cloning has been updated (Chapter 3). The research findings have been updated on the increasing numbers of babies being born at risk due to multiple births from assisted reproductive technologies and substance abuse and the significant impact of poverty (Chapter 4). Findings about the impact of an increasing number of children growing up with absentee fathers are presented (Chapter 4). There is expanded coverage of information pertinent to raising a child with developmental delays—especially pervasive developmental disorders such as autism and attention deficit disorders, as well as understanding the needs of a child who is determined to be intellectually gifted or talented (Chapters 8 and 9). More recently there is a research focus specific to emotional health and its relationship to cognitive growth and job satisfaction, healthy social relationships and family life, and overall life satisfaction (Chapters 6, 8, 16, and 18); the increasing number of Hispanic American and Asian American children who need extensive services from the educational system (Chapters 7 and 9); single parenthood and its association with poverty (Chapters 8, 10, and 14); changing trends in teenage substance abuse, sexual behaviors, sexual orientation, and violence (Chapter 11); adult diversity of lifestyle options and delay of marriage (Chapter 13); demographic changes of four generations of adults, the significance of work, delayed marriage, and delayed parenting (Chapter 14); reproduction after menopause, maximizing cognitive abilities in midlife, staying healthy in midlife (Chapter 15); the increasing number of Americans redefining middle adulthood and late adulthood (Chapters 15 and 17); the "sandwich" generation at midlife, job satisfaction or midlife career changes, and forced retirement or remaining employed (Chapter 16); exercising and longevity of life, varied cognitive functioning, generational tensions including the Social Security debate (Chapter 17); the role of faith, lifestyle, and aging, grandparents parenting grandchildren, policy issues and advocacy in an aging society (Chapter 18); the hospice movement; physician-assisted suicide (Chapter 19); and the worldwide AIDS epidemic (Chapters 11, 13, 15, and 19).

Positive Approach to Adulthood and Aging

The text features an extensive, honest discussion of the aging process, from young adulthood through late adulthood. Topics examined include the latest research and theory on biological aging, Alzheimer's disease, memory and cognitive functioning, Elderhostel programs for the aging, theories of adjustment, sexuality in late adulthood, institutional and adult day care, psychosocial aging, faith and aging, and the bereavement of widows and widowers. Many of the issues on aging are presented with cross-cultural views.

Pedagogy and Design of This Text

We have incorporated a number of in-text learning aids throughout this edition, including chapter previews, critical thinking questions, in-text review questions, key terms, chapter topical summary statements, and a glossary of terms at the end of the book. The design of the text has been updated with a carefully planned color and background schema that enhances student learning.

The chapter preview serves as a cognitive bridge, or advance organizer, between the concepts learned in the previous chapter and the new concepts to be learned in the current chapter. The critical thinking questions were carefully and creatively devised to encourage students to challenge their own beliefs about critical issues of human development relevant to that chapter. In-text review questions were provided at critical intervals to provide students with an opportunity to assess and review what they just read and to serve as a positive reinforcer. Updated illustrations were carefully selected by content and strategically placed to serve as a visual schema and to maintain interest for the learner. The segue at the end of each chapter serves as a post-organizer and helps the readers associate and relate information learned and prepares the students for new information to follow in the next chapter. Topical summary statements provide an organizational framework to help students understand and integrate the material that has been learned. These summary statements can also be used by students who are "top-down" learners and choose to look at the chapter in a holistic fashion, prior to reading the specific content of the chapter. The key terms provide students with the basic vocabulary to be learned in each chapter and are associated with the most important concepts. The lists of Internet Web sites were carefully selected to provide the reader with resources to follow up on issues of interest or discussion. The end-of-the-book glossary provides definitions of the key terms in the text for easy referral.

Past editions of *Human Development* by Vander Zanden, Crandell & Crandell have been lauded for their multidisciplinary approach to the study of human development. Our eighth edition continues with this tradition but in an even more effective way. We have added a "Career and College Major Application" matrix, which highlighs chapter-by-chapter and page-by-page real-world examples that will enable students and instructors to more easily translate developmental theory into practice. The matrix contains a variety of topics that will appeal to students interested in careers in education, healthcare, psychology and sociology, and mental health and human services. The matrix is located on the inside of the front and back covers of this text.

Practical and Informative Boxed Material

In an effort to highlight the most current issues in a comprehensive and accessible manner, three different kinds of boxes are carefully woven into the text narrative. The "More Information You Can Use" boxes provide practical information that can help students make better-informed decisions as they encounter real-life situations. The "Human Diversity" boxes further examine special topics related to issues of race, class, gender, ethnicity, and culture. "Further Developments" boxes take an in-depth look at specific issues across the life span. "Implications for Practice" boxes provide readers exploring careers in human development with helpful information about several professionals working in key occupations.

The Most Current Research and Theory

The eighth edition of *Human Development* includes comprehensive discussions of the ground broken by inspirational researchers and theorists such as Bruner, Vygotsky, Field, Maccoby, Elkind, Gilligan, Ainsworth, Kübler-Ross, Kagan, Belsky, Baumrind, Izard, and many others. The most current findings in research and theory provide evidence of our increased understanding of development over the life span.

New Photo Program

In thumbing through this eighth edition, you will undoubtedly note the beauty and creativity of our updated photo program (with a 50 percent revision). The photos and illustrations in *Human Development* display our continued commitment to clarification of concepts and issues of diversity. Sensitivity to race, class, gender, ethnicity, and ability (or disability) is of tantamount importance, and this is reflected in the photos we have chosen for this edition.

New References

The eighth edition is both a useful teaching tool and a thorough resource for students and instructors. The references in each chapter have been streamlined to allow for easier reading of the text. More than 1,200 new references have been added to this updated edition of *Human Development* and are integrated throughout the text. Additionally, at the conclusion of each chapter, the reader will be able to explore up-to-date research findings and relevant professional organizations by connecting to Web sites on the Internet. These Web sites can be hot-linked through the text's Online Learning Center at www.mhhe.com/vzcrandell8.

Supplements

The supplements listed here may accompany the eighth edition of *Human Development*. Please contact your local McGraw-Hill representative for details concerning policies, prices, and availability as some restrictions may apply. You can find your local representative by using the "Rep Locator" option at www.mhhe.com.

For Instructors

Instructor's Manual
Prepared by Jada Kearns
Valencia Community College

This collection of resources includes tools to benefit any classroom, such as learning objectives, chapter summaries, lecture topics, classroom activities, student projects, updated and expanded video suggestions, and a list of Internet sites. The Instructor's Manual can be found in the Instructor's Edition section of this text's Online Learning Center. It is also available on the Instructor's Resource CD-ROM.

Online Learning Center
www.mhhe.com/vzcrandell8

The Instructor's Edition of the companion Web site includes the Instructor's Manual, a full set of PowerPoint Presentations, suggested links to Internet resources, and an Image Gallery with selected images and tables from the book. Access to the Instructor's Edition is password protected. Instructors can obtain a password by contacting the local McGraw-Hill representative.

Test Bank
Prepared by Ellen Boesenberg
Binghamton University

This resource contains over 1,500 factual, conceptual, and applied multiple-choice questions. It is on the Instructor's Resource CD-ROM in both Word and computerized formats.

Instructor's Resource CD-ROM

This tool offers instructors the opportunity to customize McGraw-Hill materials to create their lecture presentations. Resources included are the Instructor's Manual, PowerPoint presentation slides, the Test Bank, and the Computerized Test Bank, all on one easy-to-carry disk.

McGraw-Hill's Visual Assets Database (VAD) for Life-Span Development

Jasna Jovanovic
University of Illinois—Urbana-Champaign

McGraw-Hill's Visual Assets Database is a password-protected online database of hundreds of multimedia resources for use in classroom presentations, including original video clips, audio clips, photographs, and illustrations—all designed to bring to life concepts in human development. In addition to offering multimedia presentations for every stage of the life span, the VAD's search engine and unique "My Modules" program allows instructors to select from the database's resources to create customized presentations, or "modules." These customized presentations are saved in an instructor's folder on the McGraw-Hill site, and the presentation is then run directly from the VAD to the Internet-equipped classroom. For information about this unique resource, contact your McGraw-Hill representative.

McGraw-Hill Contemporary Learning Series

Taking Sides: Clashing Views on Controversial Issues in Life-Span Development

In this debate-style reader, current controversial issues are presented in a format designed to stimulate student interest and develop critical thinking skills. Each issue is thoughtfully framed with an issue summary, an issue introduction, and a postscript. An instructor's manual with testing material is available for each volume. *Using Taking Sides In The Classroom* is also an excellent instructor resource with practical suggestions on incorporating this effective approach in the classroom. Each *Taking Sides* reader features an annotated listing of selected Web sites and is supported by our student Web site, www.mhcls.com.

Annual Editions: Human Development

This regularly updated collection of articles covers topics related to the latest research and thinking in human development. These editions contain useful features, including a topic guide, an annotated table of contents, unit overviews, and a topical index. An instructor's guide, containing testing materials, is also available.

Notable Sources in Human Development

This resource is a collection of articles, book excerpts, and research studies that have shaped the study of human development and our contemporary understanding of it. The selections are organized topically around major areas of study within human development. Each selection is preceded by a headnote that that establishes the relevance of the article or study and provides biographical information on the author.

For Students

Study Guide
Craig Vivian
Monmouth College

This comprehensive study guide is designed to promote active learning. It includes learning objectives for each major topic covered in the book, as well as true-false, factual and conceptual multiple-choice, matching, and essay questions. An answer key is included so that students can assess their comprehension of the text content.

Online Learning Center
(www.mhhe.com/vzcrandell8)

The companion Web site for *Human Development*, Eighth Edition, offers an array of resources for students, including unique video scenarios accompanied by relevant study questions. Several brief, professionally acted video scenarios, written by Craig Vivian, Monmouth College, depict concepts in human development. Each video is followed by a fill-in-the-blank exercise that helps students match concepts from the book with elements of the video's plot. Students then have the opportunity to either continue with a decision-making scenario or check their understanding of the concepts by completing a set of multiple-choice and critical thinking questions. The Student Edition also provides chapter outlines, learning objectives, links to Internet resources, and multiple-choice quizzes prepared by Jeannette W. Murphey, Meridian Community College.

Multimedia Courseware for Child Development and Multimedia Courseware for Adult Development
Charlotte J. Patterson
University of Virginia

These interactive CD-ROMs include video footage of classic and contemporary experiments, detailed viewing guides, challenging previews, follow-up quizzes, and interactive feedback, graphics, graduated developmental charts, a variety of hands-on projects, related Web sites, and navigation aids. The CD-ROMs are programmed in a modular format. Their content focuses on integrating digital media to better explain physical, cognitive, social, and emotional development throughout childhood, adolescence, and adulthood. It is compatible with both MacIntosh and Windows computers.

Acknowledgments

In truth, authors have but a small part in the production of textbooks. Consider the thousands upon thousands of researchers who have dedicated themselves to the scholarly investigation of human behavior and life-span development. Consider the labors of countless journal editors and reviewers who assist them in fashioning intelligible reports out of their research findings. And consider the enormous effort expended by the personnel of research-grant agencies and reviewers who seek to funnel scarce resources to the most promising studies. Indeed, a vast number of scholars across the generations have contributed to our contemporary reservoir of knowledge regarding human development. Textbook authors simply seek to assemble the research in a coherent and meaningful manner. More specifically, a number of reviewers helped us shape and guide the manuscript into its final form. They appraised the clarity of expression, technical accuracy, and completeness of coverage. Their help was invaluable, and we are deeply indebted to them. For the *Eighth Edition*, we extend thanks to:

Whitney Ann Brosi, Michigan State University
Scott R. Freeman, Valencia Community College
William Fuller, Angelo State University

Jean Gerard, Bowling Green State University
Deborah T. Gold, Duke University Medical Center
Jean Hunt, Cumberland College
Robert B. Lee, Fort Valley State University
James D. Rodgers, Hawkeye Community College
Joan Thomas-Spiegel, Los Angeles Harbor College

In addition, we have continued to build on the foundation provided by reviewers of the previous edition. They are:

Jerry J. Bigner, Colorado State University
Stephen Burgess, Southwestern Oklahoma State University
Deborah M. Cox, Madisonville Community College
Rhoda Cummings, University of Nevada, Reno
Dana H. Davidson, University of Hawaii
Karen L. Freiberg, University of Maryland-Baltimore County
Robert J. Griffore, Michigan State University
Patricia E. Guth, Westmoreland County Community College
Harry W. Hoemann, Bowling Green State University
Russell A. Isabella, University of Utah
Jada D. Kearns, Valencia Community College
Michael S. Kelly, Henderson State University
Joyce Splann Krothe, Indiana University
Kathleen LaVoy, Seattle University
Patsy Lawson, Volunteer State University
Timothy Lehmann, Valencia Community College
Elizabeth A. Lemense, Western Kentucky University
Pamela A. Meinert, Kent State University
Linda W. Morse, Mississippi State University
Joyce Munsch, Texas Tech University
Ana Maria Myers, Polk Community College
Gail Overbey, Southeast Missouri State University
Lisa Pescara-Kovach, University of Toledo
Robert F. Schultz, Fulton Montgomery Community College
Elliot M. Sharpe, Maryville University
Jack P. Shilkret, Anne Arundel Community College
Laurence Simon, Kingsborough Community College
Lynda Szymanski, College of St. Catherine
Robert S. Weisskirch, California State University Fullerton
Peggy Williams-Petersen, Germanna Community College

A special note of thanks to creative writer and researcher Ellen Boesenberg, an instructor and doctoral candidate at Binghamton University, who contributed to many of these chapters. We especially appreciate the up-to-date and relevant information in the fields of education and psychology that Ellen brought to this edition. Karen Pitcher, our dedicated research assistant and information resource specialist, was invaluable in providing us current empirical research findings on topics across the entire life span. She reminded us that attention to detail is paramount. We are grateful for two conscientious honors students who volunteered to help us with several key manuscript features. Josh Peck is interested in majoring in educational psychology and assisted us with the development of the Career and College Major Matrix. Andrew Vazquez assisted by conducting an analysis of the text's photo art program from a gender and diversity perspective. Both assisted with organizing our extensive reference list. Joan Shumin, an extremely competent secretary in our Liberal Arts Division, is dependable and always came through with a smile. Our college's Copy Center professionals, Gary Hitchcock, Howard Nickerson, and Sandi Springstead, contributed to our ability to meet many deadlines and reminded us that laughter is the best medicine. We also appreciate the sunny disposition of our mailroom staff, Joan Drew and Hugh MacCulloch, who prepared documentation for delivery to our various editors across the country and without whom we would not have been able to meet our deliverable dates to get this text ultimately into the hands of the reader.

We are indebted to everyone at McGraw-Hill who helped to produce this book and give special thanks to the following professionals in the domain of publishing: to Mike Sugarman, Executive Editor, for supporting our work and our vision to make the Eighth Edition a human development text that will benefit learners both in their academic and personal lives. He "ran interference" for us whenever we needed him; to Marilyn Rothenberger, project manager, for encouraging us through these long months, for being willing to make the tough decisions, and for overseeing the project through the production process and keeping us on schedule; to our expert copy editor, Beatrice Sussman; to photo editor Judy Mason; and to Permissions Editor Marty Granahan, for securing the necessary permissions from a variety of authors and sources. This project has been a total team undertaking at all times. We sincerely appreciate the encouragement and enthusiasm each person brought to this undertaking and the professional competence each one exhibited in bringing this new edition to fruition.

Finally, we wish to acknowledge our children and their spouses, Jim and Karen, Colleen and Curt, Becky, and Patrick, and our grandchildren, Anna, Jacob, Aidan, and Ava. They continually teach us the real joys of life, and we dedicate this book to them.

Tom Crandell

Thomas L. Crandell, Ph.D.

Corinne Crandell

Corinne H. Crandell, M.S.

About the Authors

We bring an uncommon blend of academic, professional, and personal experiences to this text on your behalf. We have been teaching students from the middle school, high school, community college, and the graduate level in a variety of professional capacities for more than 30 years. During this time, we have seen our student population become more diverse, composed of a blend of traditional and nontraditional learners from rural, urban, suburban, and distant cultures. As our student population began to include more adult learners and students with learning disabilities, we prepared ourselves to understand the individual learning needs of our students.

Thomas L. Crandell   After earning a B.A. from King's College in Wilkes-Barre and an M.A. in counseling psychology from Scranton University, Tom taught a variety of undergraduate psychology courses at Broome Community College and worked in college admissions and then as a college counselor for several years. At age 34, he continued his formal education at Cornell University in pursuit of a Ph.D. in psychology and education. While at Cornell, Tom received a research assistantship sponsored by the Office of Naval Research, and he subsequently helped to initiate and develop one of the most productive reading research programs in the country. His experimental findings on learning styles and instructional design have been adopted by researchers and practitioners worldwide. He first won international recognition when his doctoral dissertation was selected as one of the top five in the country by the International Reading Association.

Tom's focus as a college professor and educational psychologist has been on individual differences in learning and atypical development in children and adults. He takes great pride in a course he developed and teaches on human exceptionalities to over 2,000 undergraduate students who have become special education teachers, psychologists, sociologists, social workers, nurses, physical therapists, speech therapists, occupational therapists, clergy, managers of nonprofit agencies, and informed parents. Students often return to him to tell him that his course has changed their entire career plans and how much they enjoy working with individuals in a wide array of jobs that include a broad understanding of human development.

In addition to being a professor, he has been a consultant in educational, business, and legal settings for the past 30 years and has authored numerous articles on the design of online educational materials for ease of learning and ease of use. Many of these design strategies have been incorporated into the eighth edition of this text. In 1996 he earned the "Distinguished Article of the Year" award in the Frank R. Smith Competition by the *Journal for the Society of Technical Communications.* He is a long-standing member of the American Psychological Association. Tom has also coached youth basketball and soccer and has taught adult religious education courses through his church. He has maintained a healthy lifestyle with a passion for basketball and golf throughout his years of professional growth and development.

Corinne Haines Crandell   She earned a B.S. degree from the University at Albany and an M.S. degree from the State University of New York at Oneonta in counseling and psychology. Corinne has completed additional graduate studies in reading, special education, and learning disabilities. Corinne has had a variety of instructional experiences at the community college level teaching psychology classes for many years, has been a college counselor, has co-authored developmental psychology study guides, instructor's manuals, and computerized study guides and developed the first distance learning course in developmental psychology for the SUNY Learning Network, offered over the Internet since 1997. She also supervised student interns in Broome Community College's human services program at nearly 40 social service agencies. For five years she taught in a middle school and worked with children with learning disabilities in grades 4 through 8. Additionally, she was the coordinator of the gifted and talented program for a private school district with 12 schools. Corinne has coached and judged in the regional Odyssey of the Mind program, was a board member for five years at our local Association for Retarded Citizens, and has taught confirmation classes to high school students for the past ten years.

Part ONE
The Study of Human Development

Studying the process of human development across cultures provides us with an opportunity to improve the human condition as well as, hopefully, to acquire the knowledge needed to live more satisfying lives. We therefore begin with an overview of how diverse social science and life science researchers (collectively known as developmentalists) approach the monumental task of studying humans over the course of the life span. Our discussion includes the goals of the scientific community, the recognized framework for studying the life span, what aspects of development warrant extensive examination, and what scientific methods are used to conduct research with humans. Chapter 2 discusses the major developmental theories over the past 100 years, when social scientists, biologists, and chemists focused on studying discrete aspects of human development. Earlier introspective methods about subconscious experience and contemporary measurable evidence about microscopic genetic codes, neurons, and hormones all contribute to our understanding of the human condition. Many contemporary researchers are focusing on how to integrate theory and scientific findings from across cultures into a more meaningful whole about human development.

Human Development Defined

Critical Thinking Questions

1. Developmental change takes place in three fundamental domains: the physical, the cognitive, and the emotional-social. Which domain has been most important for your becoming who you are? Will any one of the domains become more important as you get older?

2. Make a list of three aspects of yourself that have changed over the last 10 years and three that have remained constant. How do you feel about both the "dynamic" and the "static" aspects of yourself?

3. If someone had researched your personal development over time, where would they have noticed the most change? The least change? If they continued their research, where would they probably see the most and least amount of change over the next 10 years, in your opinion?

4. If we could answer most of the important questions about human development by continuously studying 10 individuals who interact with each other from birth until death, would the knowledge gained from the study justify keeping them isolated from the rest of the world for their entire lives?

Outline

Human development can be described as a process of becoming someone different while remaining in some respects the same person over an extended period of time. Development takes place in three essential areas—physical, cognitive, and emotional-social. In other words, you develop when your body, mind, and social relationships change. But many factors—institutions, society, and family—affect individuals and can help or hinder their personal development.

Age is one of the most important indicators of what an individual should be doing. Over the last century, research on development has focused on several areas, including emotion, cognition, self, behavior, thought, and nature. Research is essential to understanding human development, and there are diverse methods for obtaining analyzable information. Valid research findings often help improve the quality of life over the life span.

3

The Major Concerns of Science

A sign posted in a Western cowboy bar says: "I ain't what I ought to be. I ain't what I'm going to be, but I ain't what I was."

This colloquial thought captures the sentiment that lies behind much contemporary interest in the study of human development. It is hoped that with knowledge, we will be able to lead longer, healthier, and more fruitful lives. Knowledge offers us the opportunity to improve the human condition by helping us to achieve self-identity, freedom, and self-fulfillment.

Continuity and Change in Development

The motto in the bar directs our attention to still another fact—that to live is to change. Indeed, life is never static but always in flux. Nature has no fixed entities, only transition and transformation. According to modern physics—particularly quantum mechanics—the objects you normally see and feel consist of nothing more than patterns of energy that are forever moving and altering. From electrons to galaxies, from amoebas to humans, from families to societies, every phenomenon exists in a state of continual "becoming." The fertilized egg you developed from was smaller than the period at the end of this sentence. All of us undergo dramatic changes as we pass from the embryonic and fetal stages through infancy, childhood, adolescence, adulthood, and old age. We start small, grow up, and grow old, just as countless generations of our forebears have done.

Change occurs across many dimensions—the biological, the psychological, and the social-emotional. Life-span perspectives on human development focus on long-term sequences and patterns of change in human behavior. This perspective is unique in tracing the ways people develop and change across the life span.

Contradictory as it may seem, life also entails continuity. At age 70 we are in many ways the same persons we were at 5 or 25. Many aspects of our biological organism, our gender roles, and our thought processes carry across different life periods. Features of life that are relatively lasting and uninterrupted give us a sense of identity and stability over time. As a consequence of such continuities, most of us experience ourselves not as just so many disjointed bits and pieces but rather as wholes—larger, independent entities that possess a basic oneness—and much of the change in our lives is not accidental or haphazard.

The Study of Human Development

Scientists refer to the elements of change and constancy over the life span as development. **Development** is defined as the orderly and sequential changes that occur with the passage of time as an organism moves from conception to death. Development occurs through processes that are biologically programmed within the organism and processes of interaction with the environment that transform the organism.

Human development over the life span is a process of becoming something different while remaining in some respects the same. Perhaps what is uniquely human is that we remain in an unending state of development. Life is always an unfinished business, and death is its only cessation.

Traditionally life-span development has primarily been the province of psychologists. Most commonly the field is called developmental psychology or, if focused primarily on children, child development or child psychology. Psychology itself is often defined as the scientific study of behavior and mental processes. **Developmental psychology** is the branch of psychology that deals with how individuals change with time while remaining in some respects the same.

The field of life-span development has expanded to include not only infant, child, adolescent, and adult psychology but biology, women's studies, medicine, sociology, gerontology, genetics, anthropology, and cross-cultural psychology. A mulitidisciplinary approach stimulates fresh perespectives and advances in knowledge.

What Are the Goals of Developmental Psychologists?

Scientists who study human development focus on four major goals:

1. *To describe the changes that typically occur across the life span.* When, for instance, do children generally begin to speak? What is the nature of this first speech? Does speech alter with time? In what sequence does the average child link sounds to form words or sentences?
2. *To explain these changes*—to specify the determinants of developmental change. What behaviors, for instance, underlie the child's first use of words? What part does biological "pretuning" or "prewiring" play in the process? What is the role of learning in language acquisition? Can the process be accelerated? What factors produce language and learning difficulties?
3. *To predict developmental changes.* What are the language capabilities of a 6-month-old infant likely to be at 14 months of age? Or what are the expected consequences for language development if a child suffers from an inherited disorder?

4. *To be able to use their knowledge to intervene in the course of events in order to control them* (Kipnis, 1994). For example, researchers have found that if infants are put on a special diet after birth, intellectual impairment from one inherited disorder (phenylketonuria [PKU]) can often be minimized (Welsch et al., 1990).

But even as scientists strive for knowledge and control, they must continually remind themselves of the ethical dangers described by eminent physicist J. Robert Oppenheimer (1955): "The acquisition of knowledge opens up the terrifying prospects of controlling what people do and how they feel." We return to the matter of ethical standards in scientific research later in this chapter. The *Human Diversity* box, "Rethinking Women's Biology" looks at the negative implications for females of the fact that, historically, scientists have mainly been males. The four scientific goals—describing, explaining, predicting, and having the ability to control developmental changes—should be kept in mind as you examine the different domains and theories of human development in this book.

Questions

How is development defined? What are the four main goals of the study of human development?

A Framework for Studying Development

If we are to organize information about human development from a variety of perspectives, we need some sort of framework that is both meaningful and manageable. Studying human development involves considering many details simultaneously. A framework provides us with categories for bringing together bits of information that we believe are related to one another. *Categories* let us simplify and generalize large quantities of information by clustering certain components. A framework helps us find our way in an enormously complex and diverse field. One way to organize information about development is in terms of four basic categories:

- The major domains of development
- The processes of development
- The context of development
- The timing of developmental events

Let's look at each of these categories to see how they fit within a given framework.

Major Domains of Development

Developmental change takes place in three fundamental domains: physical, cognitive, and emotional-social. Think how much you have changed in the years since you first entered school. Your body, the way you think, and how you interact with others are aspects of "you" that have undergone transformations and will continue to do so.

Physical development involves changes that occur in a person's body, including changes in weight and height; in the brain, heart, and other organ structures and processes; and in skeletal, muscular, and neurological features that affect motor skills. Consider, for instance, the physical changes that take place at adolescence, which together are called *puberty*. At puberty young people undergo revolutionary changes in growth and development. Adolescents suddenly catch up with adults in size and strength. Accompanying these changes is the rapid development of the reproductive system and attainment of reproductive capability—the ability to conceive children.

Cognitive development involves changes that occur in mental activity, including changes in sensation, perception, memory, thought, reasoning, and language. Again consider adolescence. Young people gradually acquire several substantial intellectual capacities. Compared with children, for instance, adolescents more ably think about abstract concepts such as democracy, justice, and morality. Young people become capable of dealing with hypothetical situations and achieve the ability to monitor and control their own mental experiences and thought processes.

Emotional-social development includes changes in an individual's personality, emotions, and relationships with others. All societies distinguish between individuals viewed as children and individuals regarded as adults, and our relationships with children are qualitatively different from the relationships we have with adults. Adolescence is a period of social redefinition in which young people undergo changes in their social roles and status. Contemporary society distinguishes between people who are "underage," or minors, and those who have reached the age of majority, or adults. Adults are permitted to drive cars, drink alcohol, serve in the military, and vote. How each of us becomes a unique adult can be seen as the result of interaction between the personal "self" and our social environment. As we will see in Chapter 11, some societies recognize adolescence or entry into adulthood through a special initiation ceremony—a rite of passage.

Although we differentiate these domains of development, we do not want to lose sight of the unitary nature of the individual. Physical, cognitive, and emotional-social

Human Diversity

Rethinking Women's Biology

Over the past 15 years we have seen the emergence of "identity politics." Marginalized groups are staking out claims of equality based on the differences between groups and not on a minority's similarities to dominant social groups (Bem, 1998; Armstrong, 2004). These ideas have also surfaced in academe as researchers are challenged to rethink their approaches to describing the world objectively. As you read this discussion, think about how your own development might have been different if you had not been "pushed" quite as hard by society to become "male" or "female." Then apply some of these ideas to race and class to see the implications of this statement: "It takes a whole village to develop a child."

Women's biology is a social construct and a political concept, not just a scientific matter, and this is meant in at least three ways. The first can be summed up in Simone de Beauvoir's dictum "One isn't born a woman, one becomes a woman." This does not mean that the environment shapes us; rather, it means that the concepts "woman" and "man" are social constructs that little girls and boys try to fit as they grow up. Some of us are better at it than others, but we all try. Our efforts have biological as well as social consequences—in fact, this is a false dichotomy because our biological and social attributes are interrelated. How active we are, what clothes we wear, what games we play, what and how much we eat, what kinds of schools we go to (if allowed), what work we do (solely in home or outside of the home), if we are forced into marriage and childbearing at early ages (or not)—all of these affect our biological and social being in ways we cannot sort out. In this sense, one isn't born a woman or man, one becomes one.

The concept of women's biology is socially constructed, and political, in a second way: Women have not been the dominant definers of their biology. Women's biology has been described mainly by physicians and scientists who, for historical reasons, have been mostly economically privileged, university-educated men; and these men have had strong personal and political interests in describing women in ways that make it appear "natural" for women to play roles that are important for men's well-being, personally and as a group. Men's self-serving, ideological descriptions of women's biology date back at least to Aristotle. Present-day scientists and their theories continue to characterize women as weak, emotional, and at the mercy of raging hormones; they "construct" the female as being centered on the functions of her reproductive organs. No one has suggested that men are valuable only for their reproductive capacity, but throughout history women have been looked on as though they were walking ovaries and wombs. Some cultures of the world today continue to value—or devalue—a woman for

Mary Whiton Calkins, 1863–1930, Early Developmentalist and First Female President of the APA Mary Calkins, from Buffalo, New York, attended Smith College in Massachusetts in 1880. She then trained at Harvard under the direction of William James (though she was not allowed to register as a student) and set up an experimental lab and taught the first experimental psychology course at Wellesley College (which hired only female instructors). Though she wrote a scholarly thesis in 1896 on memory of numerals with color and sat for the Ph.D. exam at Harvard and performed brilliantly, she was denied the degree. She was an early pioneer in human development and is known for her valuable research on both memory and the psychology of the self. She also published a text in introductory psychology, was elected by her colleagues in 1905 as the first female president of the American Psychological Association, and in 1918 was elected the first woman president of the American Philosophical Association.

her ability to produce sons as the father's heirs, and in some cultures women are still considered the "property" of the husband (Armstrong, 2004; Moreau & Yousafzai, 2004).

At the turn of the twentieth century, when American women tried to enroll in colleges and universities, scientists originally claimed that women could not be educated because their brains were too small. When that claim became untenable, scientists granted that women could be educated the same as men but questioned whether women should be—whether it was "good" for women. They based their

continued

concerns on the claim that girls needed to devote much energy to establishing the proper functioning of their ovaries and womb; and if they divert this energy to their brains by studying, their reproductive organs would shrivel, they would become sterile, and the human species would die out. This view was held by most men and women, and women who attempted to develop their intellectual capacities endured obstacles and ridicule while paving the way for other women who followed. Now, a century later, American women earn approximately half of all doctorates in psychology. Even more remarkably, in present-day Afghanistan, after more than 5000 years of strict patriarchal oppression, women are slowly emerging as legal citizens to exercise their human rights of education, health care, the franchise, and occupational pursuits (Armstrong, 2004).

The "scientific" logic that barred women from intellectual and occupational pursuits was steeped in gender and class prejudice. The notion that women's reproductive organs need careful nurturing was used to exclude upper-class girls and young women from higher education. But it was not used to spare the working-class, poor, or ethnic-minority women who were laboring in the factories and homes of the upper class. If anything, these women were said to have too many children. In fact, the poor woman's ability to have many children despite working so hard was taken as evidence that she was less highly evolved than upper-class women.

Question

Historically, how has American society determined the norms (standards of behavior evident in the majority) for how females and males should behave, what they should do, and what they could become?

factors are intertwined in every aspect of development. Scientists are increasingly aware that what happens in any one domain depends largely on what happens in the others.

Processes of Development

Development meets us at every turn. Infants are born. The jacket the 2-year-old wears in the spring is outgrown by winter. At puberty, youth exhibit a marked spurt in size and acquire various secondary sexual characteristics. Individuals commonly leave their parents' homes and set out on careers, establish families of their own, see their own children leave home, retire, and so on. The concepts of growth, maturation, and learning are important to our understanding of these events.

Growth takes place through metabolic processes from within. One of the most noticeable features of early development is the increase in size that occurs with age. The organism takes in a variety of substances, breaks them down into their chemical components, and then reassembles them into new materials. Most organisms get larger as they become older. For some organisms, including humans, growth levels off as they approach sexual

Initiation Ceremonies and Religious Rites of Passage
At age 13 Jewish children become obligated to observe the holy commandments. The bar mitzvah is an optional initiation ceremony that formally marks that transition. Youths say the blessing in Hebrew or recite from the Torah as a sign that they are ready to take on the rights and responsibilities of an adult. Adult rights and responsibilities include participating in religious services, testifying before religious courts, and marrying.

maturity. Others—many plant and fish forms—continue the growth process until they die.

Maturation concerns the more or less automatic unfolding of biological potential in a set, irreversible sequence. Both growth and maturation involve biological change. *Growth* refers to the increase in the number of an individual's cells: *maturation* concerns the development of the individual's organs and limbs in relation to their ability to function and reflects the unfolding of genetically prescribed, or "preprogrammed," patterns of behavior. Such changes are relatively independent of environmental events, as long as environmental conditions remain normal. As we will see in Chapter 4, an infant's motor development after birth follows a regular sequence—grasping, sitting, crawling, standing, and walking. Similarly, at about 10 to 14 years of age, puberty brings many changes, including ovulation in girls and sperm production in boys, providing the potential for reproduction.

Learning is the more or less permanent modification in behavior that results from the individual's experience in the environment. Learning occurs across the entire life span—in the family, among peers, at school, on the job, and in many other spheres. Learning differs from maturation in that maturation typically occurs without any specific experience or practice. Learning, however, depends on both growth and maturation, which underlie a person's readiness for certain kinds of activity, physical and mental. The ability to learn is clearly critical, for it allows each of us to adapt to changing environmental conditions. Hence, learning provides the important element of flexibility in behavior.

As we will emphasize in this text, the biological forces of growth and maturation should not be contrasted with the environmental forces of learning. Too often the nature-nurture controversy is presented as a dichotomy—nature or nurture. Rather, it is the interaction between heredity and environment that gives an individual her or his unique characteristics. As we interact with the world about us—as we act upon, transform, and modify the world—we in turn are shaped and altered by the consequences of our actions (Kegan, 1988; Piaget, 1963; Vygotsky, 1978). We literally change ourselves through our actions. As we pass through life, our biological organism is altered by dietary practices, activity level, alcohol and drug intake, smoking habits, illness, exposure to X rays and radiation, and so on. Furthermore, as many of us enter school, finish school, seek a job, marry, settle on a career, have children, become grandparents, and retire, we arrive at new conceptions of self. In these and many other ways, we are engaged in a lifetime process in which we are forged and shaped as we interact with our environment (Charles & Pasupathi, 2003; Eamon, 2001). In brief, development occurs throughout our lifetime—the prenatal period, infancy, childhood, adolescence, adulthood, and old age.

The Context of Development

To understand human development, we must consider the environmental context in which it occurs. In his **ecological approach** to development, Urie Bronfenbrenner (1917–2005) (1979, 1986, 1995, 1997) asserts that the study of developmental influences must include the person's interaction with the environment, the person's changing physical and social settings, the relationship among those settings, and how the entire process is affected by the society in which the settings are embedded. Bronfenbrenner examines the *mutual* accommodations between the developing person and these changing contexts in terms of four levels of environmental influence: the microsystem, the mesosystem, the exosystem, and the macrosystem (see Figure 1.1).

Consider, for instance, Maria and Jami. Both are seventh-graders who live in a large U.S. city. In many ways their lives and surroundings seem similar. Yet they live in rather different worlds. Keep important differences in mind as you read their scenarios:

Maria Maria is the oldest of three children. Her family immigrated to the United States when she was an infant. Both of her parents work outside the home at full-time jobs, but they are usually able to arrange their schedules so that one parent is home when the children return from school. Should the parents be delayed, the children know to go to a neighbor—a grandmotherly figure—to spend the afternoon. Maria often helps her mother or father prepare a dinner "just like we used to eat in Nicaragua." The family members who do not cook on a given evening are the ones who later clean up. Homework is taken seriously by Maria and her parents. The children are allowed to watch television each night, but only after they have completed their homework. Her parents encourage the children to speak Spanish at home but insist that they speak English outside the home. Maria is enthusiastic about her butterfly collection, and family members help her hunt butterflies on family outings. She is somewhat of a loner but has one very close friend.

Jami Jami is 12 and lives with her parents and an older brother. Both of her parents have full-time jobs that require them to commute more than an hour each way. Pandemonium occurs on weekday mornings as the family members prepare to leave for school and work. Jami is on her own until her parents return home in the evening.

FIGURE 1.1 Bronfenbrenner's Ecological Theory of Development This shows the four levels of environmental influences: the microsystem, the mesosystem, the exosystem, and the macrosystem.

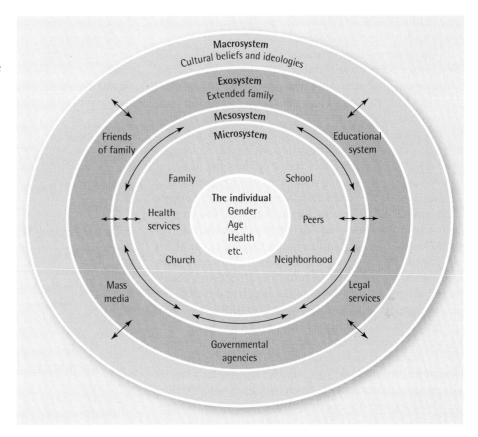

Jami's parents have demanding work schedules, and one of them is usually working on the weekends. Her mother assumes responsibility for a traditional evening meal, but fast food is starting to replace home-cooked meals on a regular basis. Jami's father does not do housework; when he is not working, he can be found with friends at a local bar. Although Jami realizes that getting a good education is important, she has difficulty concentrating in school. She spends a good deal of time with her friends, all of whom enjoy riding the bus downtown to go to the movies. On these occasions they "hang out" and occasionally shoplift or smoke a little marijuana. Her parents disapprove of her friends, so Jami keeps her friends and her parents apart.

In Bronfenbrenner's model, the **microsystem** consists of the network of social relationships and the physical settings in which a person is involved each day. Maria's microsystem consists of her two siblings, mother, father, neighbor, her peers, school, and so on. Likewise, Jami's microsystem consists of her parents, brother, and so on. The **mesosystem** consists of the interrelationships among the various settings in which the developing person is immersed. Both Maria and Jami come from two-parent families in which both parents work. Yet their home environments have substantially different effects on their schooling. Maria's family setting is supportive of academic achievement. Without necessarily being aware of it, Maria's parents are employing a principle of the Russian educator A. S. Makarenko (1967), who was

quite successful in working with wayward adolescents in the 1920s: "The maximum support with the maximum of challenge." Although Jami's parents also stress the importance of doing well at school, Jami is not experiencing the same gentle but firm push that encourages Maria to move on and develop into a capable young adult. Jami's family has dispensed with the amenities of family self-discipline in favor of whatever is easiest. Moreover, Jami is heavily dependent on peers, one of the strongest predictors of problem behavior in adolescence (Eamon, 2001; Tolan, Gorman-Smith, & Henry, 2003).

An environment that is "external" to the developing person is called an exosystem. The **exosystem** consists of social structures that directly or indirectly affect a person's life: school, the world of work, mass media, government agencies, and various social networks. The development of children like Maria and Jami is influenced not only by what happens in their environments but also by what occurs in their parents' settings. Stress in the workplace often carries over to the home, where it has consequences for the parents' marriage. Children who feel rootless or caught in conflict at home find it difficult to pay attention in school. Like Jami, they often look to a group of peers with similar histories, who, having no welcoming place to go and little to do that challenges them, seek excitement on the streets. Despite encountering job stresses somewhat similar to those of Jami's parents, Maria's parents have made a deliberate effort to create arrangements that work against Maria's alienation.

The **macrosystem** consists of the overarching cultural patterns of a society that are expressed in family, educational, economic, political, and religious institutions. We have seen how the world of work contributes to alienation in Jami's family. When we look to the broader societal context, we note that the United States is beginning to catch up with other industrialized nations in providing child-care services and other benefits designed to promote the well-being of families (see Chapters 6 and 8). But only some American parents enjoy such benefits as maternity and paternity leaves, flex time, job-sharing arrangements, and personal leave to care for sick children. Along with most U.S. families today, the families of Maria and Jami are experiencing the unraveling of extended family, neighborhood, and other institutional support systems that in the past were central to the health and well-being of children and their parents.

The ecological approach allows us to view the developing person's environment as a nested arrangement of structures, each contained within the next. The most immediate structure is the setting in which the person currently carries out his or her daily activities; each ensuing structure is progressively more encompassing, until we reach the most inclusive or societal level. These dynamic interlocking structures challenge us to consider the risks and opportunities for development at each level. For instance, such problems as homelessness, child abuse and neglect, school violence, and psychopathology can be insightfully viewed as products of contextual factors that interact with individual and institutional vulnerabilities, particularly the family (Acs & Nelson, 2002; Tolan, Gorman-Smith, & Henry, 2003).

The ecological approach allows us to see people not in some contrived experimental vacuum but actively immersed in a real world of everyday life. Imagine how much more extensive the information gathered would be if a researcher were allowed to record your day-to-day experiences as opposed to interviewing you in a clinical setting. However, this seeming advantage is also the ecological approach's major disadvantage: We usually have enormous difficulty studying people in contexts where a great many factors are operating simultaneously. Because so many factors bear on a person, we find it impractical, indeed impossible, to take them all into account. Only as we control a large array of factors can we secure a "fix" on any one of them. We will have more to say on these matters later in the chapter when we consider the nature of developmental research.

Critiquing his own model, Bronfenbrenner recognized a need to incorporate an investigation of biological, psychological and behavioral aspects of the individual under study. Because of this he now refers to the model as a bioecological theory of development. Further, he saw the need to add the dimension of time to the model and added another system that he called the **chronosystem,** showing that there is change and constancy not only in the individual person but in society as well. As he states, "Not only do persons in the same age group share a life history of common experience, but those of a given age in different generations could have quite diverse experiences, depending on the period in which they live" (Bronfenbrenner, 2005).

Question

Can you give examples of how each of the ecological systems has affected your own development?

The Timing of Developmental Events

Time plays an important role in development. Traditionally, the passage of time has been treated as synonymous with chronological age, emphasizing changes that occur within individuals as they grow older. More recently, social and behavioral scientists have broadened their focus. They consider changes that occur over time, not only within the person but also in the environment, and examine the dynamic relation between these two processes. Paul and Margret Baltes contributed to our understanding of these changes by identifying three sets of influences that mediate through the individual, act and interact to produce development (Baltes & Baltes, 1998; Schulz & Heckhausen, 1996):

1. **Normative age-graded influences** have a strong relation to chronological age. Among youth in early adolescence, like Maria and Jami, these influences include the physical, cognitive, and psychosocial changes discussed earlier. Maria and Jami are entering puberty, a condition associated with biological maturation. But they have also encountered age-graded social influences, such as the abrupt transition from a highly structured elementary school setting to a less structured and more complex middle school or junior high environment.

2. **Normative history-graded influences** concern historical factors. Although there is considerable cultural similarity among the members of a society, each **age cohort** is unique because it is exposed to a unique segment of history. An *age cohort* (also called a *birth cohort*) is a group of persons born in the same time interval. Because society changes over time, the members of different age cohorts age in different ways. Members of each new generation enter and leave childhood, adolescence, adulthood, and old age at a similar point in time, and so they experience certain decisive economic, social, political, and military events at similar junctures. As a consequence of the unique events of the era in which they live out their lives—for instance, the Great Depression of the 1930s, World War II, the

prosperity of the 1950s, the Vietnam War, the age of telecommunications, and September 11, 2001 and global terrorism—each generation fashions a somewhat unique style of thought and life.

3. **Nonnormative life events** involve unique turning points at which people change some direction in their lives. A person might suffer severe injury in an accident, win millions in a lottery, undergo a religious conversion, give birth to multiples of children at one time, secure a divorce, or set out on a new career at midlife or later. Nonnormative influences do not impinge on everyone, nor do they necessarily occur in easily discernible sequences or patterns. Although these determinants have significance for individual life histories, the determinants are not closely associated with either age or history.

Not surprisingly, each age cohort of U.S. youth over the past 80 years has acquired a somewhat different popular image, and each generation confronted an environment different from that faced by earlier generations (see Table 1.1). Awareness of a person's age cohort can help psychologists, social workers and other human service workers to assess the worldviews and particular needs of the individual.

History-graded influences do not operate only in one direction. Consider age cohorts. They are not simply acted on by social and historical forces. Because people of different cohorts age in distinct ways, they contribute to changes in society and alter history's course. As society moves through time, statuses and roles change. Older occupants of social positions are replaced by younger entrants influenced by more recent life experiences. The flow of new generations results in some loss to the cultural inventory, a reevaluation of its components, and the introduction of new elements.

In particular, although parental generations play a crucial part in predisposing their offspring to specific values and behaviors, new generations are not necessarily bound to replicate their elders' views and perspectives. These observations call our attention to the important part that cultural and historical factors play in development. What is true in the United States and other Western societies might not be true in other parts of the world. And what is true for the first decade of the 2000s might not have been true in the 1960s or the 1770s. Accordingly, if social and behavioral scientists wish to determine whether their findings hold in general for human behavior, they must look to other societies and historical periods to test their ideas. Examining behavior from a cross-cultural perspective is a more common approach in psychological research today. Since the advent of telecommunications, we can access relevant documents and publish findings easily in reputable online journals, which commonly feature text, pictures, charts, audio, and video clips. Technological developments in the twenty-first century should aid researchers as they continue to explore human development from a worldwide perspective.

Questions

Look at the pictures in Table 1.1, "Generations," and imagine what the members of each age cohort thought about the times they were living in. What do you think of each era from witnessing it through media such as movies, music, and literature? Is it difficult to understand the experiences of another age cohort?

Nonnormative Life Events
Some people experience a life event that creates a unique turning point or challenge in their lives. What makes these kinds of events so challenging in people's lives?

Table 1.1 Generations

Social demographers suggest that each age cohort consists of people born during the same era of history who experience the same historical, global, and social events and form similar attitudes and values, common tastes (as in clothing, hairstyles, music, entertainment) and defining moments (such as wars or natural disasters).

Age Cohort	History-Graded Event	Demographics	General Traits
b. 1925–1945 Silent Generation		Ages 60 to 80	Lived through the Great Depression years after the stock market crash of 1929 and World War II. Hoboes, soup kitchens, and shelters were common throughout the U.S. They are hard working, economically conservative, and have strong values. A college education was considered a privilege, and ensuring that their children could attend college was essential. An increasing percentage is raising their grandchildren or more involved in their grandchildren's lives.
b. 1946–1964 Baby Boom or Boomers		About 76 million people; by 2030, will surge to 20 percent of the U.S. population	More likely to plan or delay parenting until having achieved their own personal, educational, and professional goals. More women of this generation began to get college degrees. Grew up during the era of "Rock 'n' Roll." Now "sandwiched" between elderly parents and their Millennial children. More involved in the education of their children, and more protective than any other generation. In the late 1960s, this cohort of college students protested against war, curfews, dress codes, gaining more independence and self-governance. Boomers have redefined each life stage they have passed through and are likely to revise views of aging and retirement.
b. 1964–1981 Generation X, Gen Xers, also called "baby busters"		About 60 million	More likely to be raised in day care and were set aside to allow parents to complete their goals. Often considered to be at risk, neglected, aggressive, complainers, self-oriented, slackers, and alienated. Grew up with fewer societal standards amid political, social, economic, and cultural changes, including the emergence of computer technology and the Internet. Many were likely to return to parental homes after college to get established and pay back college loans. More likely to cohabit and marry later, if at all. Less likely to give to charitable organizations.
b. 1982–2002 Millennials, also called Echo Boomers, and Generation Y		More diverse racial and ethnic groups, ranging from about 78 to 80 million (about 1/3 of the American population)	Likely to be first in their family to go to college; described as sheltered, confident, team-oriented, achieving, pressured, and conventional. Tend to respect elders, follow rules, and create positive changes through community service. The most cared for and protected children in U.S. history who have had highly structured childhoods. Tend to come from small families. Demonstrate more traditional values and a return to strong family attachments. Social problems for teens have declined. Higher rates of high school graduation and college attendance. Have technical savvy using wireless Internet, instant messaging, cell phones, DVDs, video games, debit cards, ATMs, online banking, etc.

Source: Donovan, J. (2002-2003). Changing demographics and generational shifts: Understanding and working with the families of today's college students. *Student Affairs in Higher Education,* 12. Retrieved October 17, 2004 from http://www.sahe.colostate.edu/journal_archive.asp.

Partitioning the Life Span: Cultural and Historical Perspectives

The Age-Old Question: Who Am I?

Because nature bestows on everyone a biological cycle that begins with conception and continues through old age and death, all societies must deal with the life cycle. Age is a major dimension of social organization.

For instance, all societies use age to allow or disallow benefits, activities, and endeavors. People are assigned roles independently of their unique abilities or qualities. Like one's sex, age is a master status, which governs entry to many other statuses and makes its own distinct imprint on them. Within the United States, for instance, age operates *directly* as a criterion for driving a car without supervision (recently many states have raised this age from 16 to 18), voting (age 18), becoming president (age 35), and receiving Social Security retirement benefits (age 62). Age also operates *indirectly* as a criterion for certain roles through its linkage with other factors. For example, age linked with reproductive capacity limits entry into the parental role. Age linked with 12 years of elementary and secondary school usually permits entry into college.

Because age is a *master status,* a change in chronological age accompanies most changes in role over a person's life span—entering school, completing school, getting one's first job, marrying, having children, being promoted at work, seeing one's youngest child marry, becoming a grandparent, retiring, and so on. Recent generations have reversed some of these—having babies first and cohabiting or maybe never marrying. Age is a critical dimension by which individuals locate themselves within society and in turn are located by others (Settersten, Furstenberg, & Rumbaut, 2005).

Consider, for example, which activities might or might not attract a nontraditional student at a university. Would a middle-aged parent of two want to join a sorority or fraternity? Would someone in his or her forties be welcome if they did want to join?

Age functions as a reference point that allows people to orient themselves in terms of *what* or *where* they are within various social networks—such as the family, the school, the church, and the world of work. It is one ingredient that provides people with the answer to the question "Who am I?" In brief, it helps people establish their identities.

Cultural Variability

The part that *social definitions* play in dividing the life cycle is highlighted when comparing the cultural practices of different societies. **Culture** refers to the social heritage of a people—those learned patterns of thinking, feeling, and acting transmitted from one generation to the next. Upon the organic age grid, societies weave varying social arrangements. A 14-year-old girl might be expecting to be a junior high school student in one culture, a mother of two children in another; a 45-year-old man might be at the peak of a business career, still moving up in a political career, or retired from a career in major league baseball—or dead and worshipped as an ancestor in some other society. All societies divide biological time into socially relevant units; and although birth, puberty, and death are biological facts of life, *society* gives each its distinctive meaning and assigns each its social consequences.

Viewed this way, all societies are divided into **age strata**—social layers based on time periods in life. Age strata organize people in society in much the same way that the earth's crust is organized by stratified geological layers. Grouping by age strata has certain similarities to class stratification. Both involve the differentiation and ranking of people as superior or inferior, higher or lower. But unlike movement up or down the class ladder, the mobility of individuals through the age strata is not dependent on motivational and recruitment factors. Mobility from one age stratum to the next is largely biologically determined and irreversible.

People's behavior within various age strata is regulated by **social norms** or expectations that specify what constitutes appropriate and inappropriate behavior for individuals at various periods in the life span. In some cases, an informal consensus provides the standards by which people judge each other's behavior. Hence, the notion that you ought to "act your age" pervades many spheres of life. Within the United States, for instance, it is thought that a child of 6 is "too young" to baby-sit for other youngsters. By the same token, a man of 60 is thought to be "too old" to "party." In other cases, laws set floors and ceilings in various institutional spheres. For instance, there are laws regarding marriage without parental consent, entry into the labor force, and eligibility for Social Security and Medicare benefits. We need only think of such terms as childish, juvenile, youth culture, adolescence, senior citizen, and the generation gap to be aware of the potency of age in determining expectations about behavior in our own society. Indeed, we even find apartment dwellings exclusively for a particular age group, such as young singles, and cities designed for a particular age group, such as retired people.

Changing Conceptions of Age

In the United States we commonly think of the life span in terms of prenatal development, infancy, childhood, adolescence, adulthood, middle age, and old age. Yet the

French historian Philippe Ariès (1962) said that in the Middle Ages the concept of childhood was not defined as we know it today. Children were regarded as small adults. Child rearing meant little more than allowing children to participate in adult affairs. Only around the year 1600 did a new concept of childhood emerge.

The past 200 years have witnessed still another revolutionary change in children's lives. School enrollments have risen sharply to the highest level of all time (Federal Interagency Forum on Child and Family Statistics, 2003). In the 70 years between 1870 and 1940, school enrollments rose from about 50 percent to about 95 percent for children age 7 to 13 and to about 79 percent for children age 14 to 17. Simultaneously, the number of days students spent in classrooms doubled. School enrollment today is nearly 100 percent of the child population, aged 5 through 16, because of compulsory attendance requirements. In 2000 more than one-fourth of the U.S. population, or 76 million, were enrolled in an educational setting from preschool through college (U.S. Bureau of the Census 2000) (see Figure 1.2). As children have come to spend larger portions of the year in formal educational settings, they have less time at home with their parents and siblings. Additionally, as more mothers have entered the paid labor force, more younger children are spending substantial portions of their nonweekend days in day-care centers and preschools (see Figure 1.3). The motivating force underlying these major social changes has been parents' desire to alter their family's social and economic status (Acs & Nelson, 2002).

The notion of adolescence is even more recent, dating from the nineteenth and early twentieth centuries in the United States due to compulsory school legislation, child labor laws, and special legal procedures for "juveniles," including additional educational opportunities through high school that made a social fact of adolescence. Now an additional new stage is evolving between adolescence and adulthood called **emerging adulthood** (Arnett, 2000; Furstenberg, 2000). Recent developments—rising prosperity in the 1990s followed by economic downturn in the early 2000s, the increase in educational level, and the enormously high educational demands of a postindustrial society—have prolonged the transition to adulthood (Goldscheider & Goldscheider, 1999; Settersten, Furstenberg, & Rumbaut, 2005).

The notion of "old age" has also undergone change in the Western world. Literary evidence indicates that during the Renaissance men were already considered "old" in their forties. Currently, another division is emerging, one between "young-old" and "old-old." Young-old signifies a postretirement period of physical vigor, new leisure time, and new opportunities for community service and self-fulfillment. In the past old-old characterized an elderly minority in need of special care and support (Neugarten, 1982a, 1982b). Recently, questions have been raised about our "knowledge" of aging in persons over 70. Most of the scientific studies looking at aging have used subjects aged 60 to 70. We might need to differentiate between young-old and old-old when researching those labeled "old" (Baltes & Baltes, 1998).

These emerging distinctions tend to blur many of our assumptions regarding people's rights and responsibilities with respect to social age. All across adulthood, age has increasingly become a poor predictor of the timing of major life events, such as changes in health, work status, family status, interests, and needs. As Bernice L. Neugarten and Dail A. Neugarten (1987) observe: "We have conflicting images rather than stereotypes of age: the 70-year-old in a wheelchair, but also the 70-year-old on the tennis court; the 18-year-old who is married and supporting a family, but also the 18-year-old college student who brings his laundry home to his mother each week" (pp. 30–32).

However, even though some timetables are losing their significance, others are becoming more compelling. Many young people might feel like failures if they have not "made it" in corporate life by age 35. A young

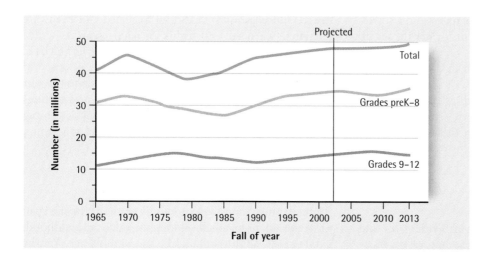

FIGURE 1.2 Public Elementary and Secondary School Enrollment in Prekindergarten Through Grade 12 by Grade Level with Projections: Fall 1965–2013 (Includes Kindergarten and Most Prekindergarten Enrollment)
Much of the recent growth in American school enrollment is driven by the number of births during the period 1981–1994, when the number of births increased to about 4 million annually. What is the projected trend?
Source: U. S. Department of Education. (2003) Projections of education statistics to 2013, Tables 1 and 4. *Digest of Education Statistics 2003.*

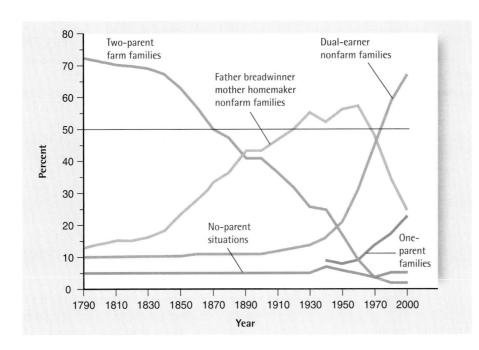

FIGURE 1.3 Types of Families with Children to Age 17: 1790– 2000 Notice the recent dramatic rise in dual-earner nonfarm and one-parent families.
Source: U.S. Bureau of the Census.

woman who has delayed marriage because of her career might feel under enormous pressure to marry and bear a child upon approaching her mid to late thirties—and older. Historical definitions of social age, then, influence the standards we use in giving meaning to the life course, in accommodating to others, and in contemplating the time past and time remaining.

Questions

How does age traditionally factor into the social network of a society? In what way is the notion of becoming an "adult" changing in American culture? What about your idea of what typifies a "senior citizen"?

Connecting Historical "Areas of Concern"

We have chosen three historical points in time—the early years of developmental psychology, the 1950s through the 1960s, and the present era—to show how beliefs about "what research is currently needed" have shifted over the years, while keeping in mind that past developmental issues have served to define today's field of human development.

What Were the Concerns of Early Developmentalists? In the early 1900s, five major areas of research in human development stood out, and these issues are still actively researched today:

Emotional development
Biology and behavior issues

Cognitive development
Conscious and unconscious thought
Role of the self

The Turn of the 20th Century   Researchers of human development were concerned with scientifically discovering and explaining aspects of human development. Remember, science and the scientific method were still relatively new ways of examining phenomenon but were optimistically thought to be the keys that could unlock the secrets of nature and humanity.

Regarding *emotional development*, Charles Darwin wanted to show that emotional expressions were innate, not learned, behaviors. He also wanted to demonstrate that the same biological processes existed in various individuals in diverse cultures. Therefore he collected pictures of individuals from different cultures displaying emotions such as anger, sadness, joy, and surprise to show the similarities across cultures.

A second area that interested researchers was *the biological basis for behavior*. Two issues were hotly debated: the relationship between evolution and development, and the relationship between nature and nurture and their effects on development. Both of these concerns are evident in the work of Darwin and Freud (Cairns, 1983).

A third area in the field's early history was *cognitive development*. As we will see in Chapter 2, Jean Piaget is considered to be the founder of the cognitive development movement. There were, however, other early contributors. One figure who foreshadowed many of Piaget's notions about cognitive development was Alfred Binet. Binet, known as the developer of the first intelligence (IQ) test, also recognized that adult's thinking differed qualitatively from children's thinking. And it was Binet who fashioned ways of testing these differences.

A fourth area was the idea that *conscious* and *unconscious* thought can be differentiated. Both Binet and Freud dealt with this issue. Before Freud articulated his theory, people did not imagine that there were "hidden" areas of the mind guiding their behavior (Cairns, 1983).

A fifth area was the *role of the self* in development. Many of our field's early researchers were preoccupied with the notion of self. None were more focused on this issue than J. Mark Baldwin. His two seminal works, *Mental Development in the Child and the Race* (1895) and *Social and Ethical Interpretations of Mental Development* (1897), were extremely provocative to developmental psychologists at the time. The latter book was the first work by an American psychologist on social-cognitive development in childhood. These themes fell in and out of favor throughout the 50 years that followed.

The 1950s and 1960s   In mid century, John Watson's behavioral theory dominated psychology and in turn shaped the concerns of developmental psychology. Much effort was spent on testing the assumptions of psychoanalytic theory but cast in the language of behavioral theory. Some research was conducted to understand personality and social development across the life span.

Another major interest was in modifying children's behavior. B. F. Skinner, a behaviorist, studied the basic principles of learning in children. The 1950s and 1960s also witnessed the emergence of an intensive investigation of how infants perceive the world.

Contemporary Issues   Researchers today are particularly interested in the biological and chemical bases of behavior, emotional development, the emergence of social relationships, and empirical study of cognitive capacities across the life span.

More attention is also being given to the biological bases of behavior, partly due to advances in the field of *behavioral genetics.* Developmentalists are interested in the role that genetics (biology) plays in the unfolding of behavior across the life span. For example, what genes might be responsible for certain traits in people, such as introversion or extroversion? How do hormones affect behavior, especially during infancy and adolescence?

In the past 30 to 40 years, there has also been more research on the timing of *emotional development* and the role of emotions in social interaction. Recent research on emotions has included studies on self-conscious emotions such as timidity or shyness, guilt, shame, pride, empathy, and envy—emotions Freud considered but that received little attention until recently.

There is a rigorous effort today to explain social interactive processes, particularly the nature of healthy or unhealthy *social relationships,* as demonstrated in parent-infant attachment (bonding) studies (see Chapter 6). The definition of family has been expanded, focusing not only on the mother-infant relationship but also on the roles of fathers, siblings, grandparents, or stepparents in the child's development.

And researchers are returning to issues of the roles played by consciousness, reflection, and motivation in development. Investigators have developed methods that permit examination of the impact of unconscious processes on cognition. These methods are being applied systemically to a range of current topics, from eyewitness testimony to adoption issues.

Since the 1960s researchers have also demonstrated children's remarkable *precocity*—their ability to understand physical and perceptual phenomena at younger ages than formerly believed.

Back to the Future   Why are we returning to the concerns of the past? First, our forebears were farsighted and innovative thinkers. They raised enlightened and enduring questions. Second, as developmentalists established the discipline, they improved it through the use of technologically advanced methods and statistical techniques that enable us to re-pose the earlier questions and address them using modern technology and more sophisticated research methods. In the next section, we will learn more about contemporary methods and techniques used in the study of human development.

> **Questions**
>
> What types of developmental issues being studied a century ago are still under investigation today? What types of human development issues are of more recent concern to social scientists or biologists?

The Nature of Developmental Research

The task of science is to make the world intelligible to us. Albert Einstein once observed that "the whole of science is nothing more than a refinement of everyday thinking." So we do scientific research in much the same way that we ask questions and come to conclusions in our everyday lives. We make guesses and mistakes; we argue our conclusions with one another; we try out our ideas to see what fits, and we get rid of what doesn't. There is one important way scientific inquiry differs from ordinary inquiry: It specifies a systematic and formal process for gathering facts and searching for a logical explanation of them. This process, called the **scientific method**, is a series of steps that allow us to be clear about what we studied, how we studied it, and what our conclusions were. Sufficient detail must be given to allow others to replicate our research and verify our conclusions. These steps of the scientific method provide a framework for objective inquiry: (1) select a researchable problem; (2) formulate a **hypothesis**—a tentative proposition that can be tested; (3) test the hypothesis; (4) draw conclusions about the hypothesis; and (5) make the findings of the study available to the scientific community.

How do we use this method to help us understand and explain human development? First, let's consider some questions we might ask about development: Are there certain measurable factors in childhood predictive of success in different areas of adult life? Which children are more prone to violence, and what can be done to teach these children conflict resolution techniques? Who is likely to be affected by anorexia, and what steps can we take to save this person's life? Does everyone's memory decline with age? What aspects of personality and social competency are related to longevity? Are there peaks in the frequency of sexual activity for men and women, or does it generally increase or decrease with age? It is easy to choose any one of these questions and come up with a researchable problem. Perhaps through your reading and life experience you could suggest a hypothesis—a proposition that can be tested scientifically—that might answer one of these questions. Next you need to test your hypothesis. To do that requires choosing a *research design* that will provide valid (accurate) and reliable (consistent) information to support or reject your hypothesis.

Research Design

In developmental psychology, research focuses on change that occurs over time or with age. Three basic kinds of designs are used: (1) longitudinal, (2) cross-sectional, and (3) sequential. Experimental designs, although powerful, are seldom used in developmental studies because usually it is not possible to exercise the control necessary for experimental design; interesting variables such as **spatial ability** (the ability to mentally manipulate images in different dimensions), memory, and physical characteristics cannot be assigned to groups of individuals or manipulated in terms of quantity or quality presented. Other methods used in developmental research include case studies, observational methods, surveys and cross-cultural studies (see Table 1.2).

The Longitudinal Design

The **longitudinal design** is used to study the same individuals at different points in their lives. We can then compare the group at these regular intervals and describe their behavior and characteristics of interest. This method allows us to look at change sequentially

and offers insight into why people turn out similarly or differently in adulthood.

The Terman Life-Cycle Study, a classic longitudinal study—indeed, the grandparent of life-course research—was begun by psychologist Lewis Terman in 1921–1922 (Cravens, 1992; Friedman & Brownell, 1995). Terman followed 1,528 gifted boys and girls from California public schools—who later nicknamed themselves "Termites"—and a control group of children of average intelligence from preadolescence through adulthood. These subjects were studied at 5- to 10-year intervals ever since. The 856 boys and 672 girls were selected on the basis of their intelligence quotients, or IQs (between 135 and 200 on the Stanford-Binet scale), which were said to represent the top 1 percent of the population. He found that the gifted ones were generally taller, heavier, and stronger than youngsters with average IQs. Moreover, they tended to be more active socially and to mature faster than average children (Terman & Merrill, 1937). One of the effects of the study has been to dispel the belief that the acceleration of bright children in school is harmful.

After Terman's death, other psychologists continued the project and their research has provided longitudinal data on religion and politics, health, marriage, emotional development, family history and careers, longevity, and cause of death (Holahan & Chapman, 2002; Martin & Friedman, 2000; Tucker et al., 1999). One notable recent finding is that "Termites" whose parents divorced had a greater risk of early death (the average age of death for men was 76, compared with age 80 for those whose parents remained married; for women the corresponding ages of death were 82 and 86 years). Researchers speculate that the stress and anxiety associated with their parents' strife took its toll in earlier mortality (Martin & Friedman, 2000).

Limitations of the Longitudinal Design   Although the longitudinal design allows us to study development over time, it has a number of disadvantages. Two major problems are selective attrition and dropout. Subjects drop out because they become ill or die, move away and are difficult to locate, or become disinterested in continuing the study. **Selective attrition** means simply that the individuals who drop out tend to be different from those who remain in the study. For example, those who remain might come from the most cooperative and stable families or be more intelligent or successful. These changes can bias the sample of subjects as it becomes smaller over time (surprisingly enough, only 10 percent of the "Termites" were unaccounted for in 1995). Other problems include testing and tester consistency over the length of the study. It is impossible to test every person at every scheduled testing on every test item. People get sick or go on vacation. They

Table 1.2 Research Designs

Type of Research	Advantages	Disadvantages
Longitudinal—*studies the same individual at different points in his/her life*	Allows researchers to describe change sequentially and offers insight into why people turn out similarly or differently in adulthood	Cannot control for nonnormative events Selective attrition Time consuming and costly Testing and tester consistency
Cross-sectional—*compares different groups of people of different ages at the same point in time*	Less costly and time consuming than longitudinal studies	Confounding of age and cohort
Sequential—*measures more than one age cohort over time*	Overcomes the problem of confounding age and cohort	Costly and complex to plan and analyze over time
Experimental—*measures whether a variable (X) is one of the factors that causes or does not cause characteristic (Y) to occur*	One of the most rigorously objective research designs	Difficult to control for some variables Requires adherence to ethical standards Human behavior in lab may not reflect real-life behavior Costly and time consuming

become upset, so that part of the test must be omitted. They might refuse to comply on some items. And children or their parents occasionally forget appointments (Bayley, 1965; Willett, Singer, & Martin, 1998). Comparable data might not be collected from every subject at every time interval. Likewise changes, such as turnover or burnout, in the staff that tests or observes the participants can result in inconsistencies in the measurements taken.

More importantly, longitudinal studies cannot control for unusual events during this group's life span. Effects of such economic and social events can make it difficult to generalize findings from one age cohort to another age cohort born 10 or 20 years later and can distort the amount or direction of the change reported:

> War, depression, changing cultures, and technological advances all make considerable impacts. What are the differential effects on 2-year-olds of depression-caused worries and insecurities, of TV or no TV, of the shifting climate of the baby-experts' advice from strict-diet, let-him-cry, no-pampering schedules to permissive, cuddling, "enriching" loving care? (Bayley, 1965, p. 189)

The time and money required to complete a long-term study can also be prohibitive (Brooks-Gunn, Phelps, & Elder, 1991). For example, 20 national agencies collaborate annually to fund and report research on the well-being of America's children (America's Children, 2004). Finally, there is the problem of finding out tomorrow what relevant factors should have been considered yesterday. Once set in motion the project is difficult to alter even when newer techniques might improve the overall design. For example, computerized testing or a survey on a Web page could make it easier for participants to record their data and would be less expensive than bringing individuals into a research lab, but would the data be comparable to the data collected earlier? What would be the effect of having no tester-participant interaction? Would participants' responses be affected by their computer experience or comfort level working electronically?

Despite these limitations, longitudinal studies can provide us with important information. For example, if our research interest is the effect of aging on a vital life skill called *spatial ability*, we might design the following study: Select a sample of 20-year-olds and measure their spatial ability. Spatial ability tests might measure individual understanding of such qualities as size, distance, volume, order, and time and can include drawing a specific triangle from memory, arranging blocks to re-create a given pattern, or reading a dial, graph, or map (see Figure 1.4). Tests of spatial ability are used as a means of determining vocational skills and to predict success with specific school-related subjects such as principles of geometry, molecular structure of chemicals, illustrations in mechanical drawing, map reading, learning to drive a car through busy city street locations, and so on. (See the *Further Developments* box on page 20, "The Ins and Outs of Spatial Relations.") We would bring this same group (cohort) back to our lab every 10 years and repeat this measurement. Figure 1.4 describes our hypothetical results on the spatial ability tests, the number of participants tested each time, and their age at the time of testing.

Question

Based on the "results" shown in Figure 1.4, what can you say about age and participants' spatial ability over time?

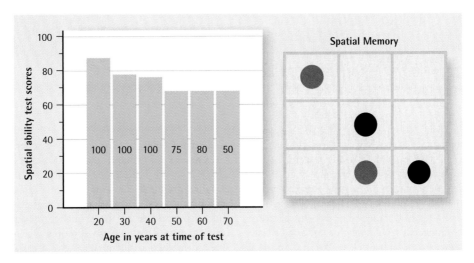

FIGURE 1.4 **Longitudinal Research Study Showing the Effects of Age on Spatial Memory Ability** In this study, the same group of adults was tested at 10-year intervals. Spatial memory is a measure of short-term visual memory for abstract material. The performance task is to view a 3 × 3 grid for 5 seconds and then recreate that same pattern from memory by placing red and black chips on a blank grid. The scores shown here are the average test scores at each age. The number of adults located and tested is indicated inside each bar. What does the graph show about the effects of age on spatial memory?

The Cross-Sectional Design

The hallmark of the longitudinal design is taking successive measurements of the same individuals. In contrast, the **cross-sectional design** investigates development by simultaneously comparing different age groups. Unlike our longitudinal research example just described, we would investigate spatial ability and age by selecting a group of 20-year-olds, a group of 30-year-olds, a group of 40-year-olds, and so on, through our last group, 70-year-olds. We would test the spatial ability of all six groups at the same time. What savings in time and money! You don't have to wait 50 years for the data to be complete, nor do you have to worry about locating your participants and bringing them back for retesting. Staff turnover is not an issue nor in most cases are there problems with participant cooperation and testing inconsistencies. Figure 1.5 summarizes the hypothetical results from the cross-sectional study of spatial ability and age. These findings seem to fit the hypothesis that spatial ability declines with age (see Figure 1.4). But can we really say that? Could there be other differences (besides age) among these selected groups that are affecting spatial ability?

Limitations of the Cross-Sectional Design The confounding of age and cohort is the major disadvantage in cross-sectional research. **Confounding** in research means the elements are mingled so they cannot be distinguished or separated. We can never be sure that the reported age-related differences between participants are not the product of other differences between the groups. For instance, the groups might differ in social environment, intelligence, or diet. So the comparability of the groups can be substantiated only through careful

sampling and measurement techniques. For example, if you were to investigate how many years of formal schooling your grandparents received, versus your parents, versus yourself, you are most likely to determine that your generation has the resources to earn a higher level of education, delaying full-time work status and most likely delaying childbearing. We know that the life experiences of a typical 20-year-old today are much different from those of a 20-year-old in the 1930s or the 1950s.

These problems are highlighted by cross-sectional studies of intelligence. Such studies rather consistently show that average scores on intelligence tests begin to

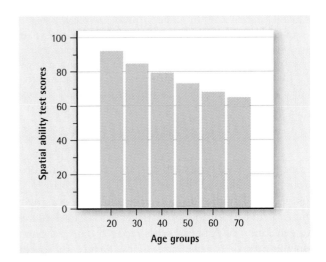

FIGURE 1.5 **Cross-Sectional Study Showing the Effects of Age on Spatial Memory Ability** In this study, adults of various ages were tested on spatial ability. The scores shown here are the average test scores for each age group.

Further Developments

The Ins and Outs of Spatial Relations

So why would someone want to conduct research about spatial relations, you ask? Spatial relations is a quality, a significant complex sense, that develops in infancy and is an integral part of our functioning in the world throughout our lives. Babies use their eyes and hands to begin to recognize the shape, size, position, and distance of objects in relationship to themselves—concepts such as near or far, first or last, top to bottom, up and down, high and low, "so big" and "so small." Spatial skills involve qualities of size, distance, order position, shapes, volume, movement, and time intervals. A baby moves its hands near or far from its face, places small objects in and out of a cup, turns over, crawls across a rug and back, stands up, sits down, wakes up in the morning, goes to sleep in the evening, and so on.

There are two categories of spatial skills—visual-spatial and motor-spatial, and in most instances children learn to coordinate these two skills in completing tasks around them. A toddler and a young child coordinate spatial senses constantly in playing in an ever-expanding world. Walking or running across a room involves both visual and motor skills and recognition of distance. Putting a simple puzzle together successfully involves recognizing the shapes and sizes of pieces, reaching for a specific object, and properly putting pieces in a specific place. Throwing or kicking a ball into a specific space, such as home plate, a baseball mitt, or basketball hoop, involves coordinating these skills.

Other significant spatial skills a child should develop for academic success include printing and then writing the 26 letters of the alphabet, printing numbers 0 to 9, coloring within the lines of a picture, drawing any object, lining up the amounts in an addition problem, recognizing the sequence of letters to read words, writing his or her name, recognizing the hours of the day, days of the week, months of the year, and seasons of the year—to name only a few.

As teens progress through the educational system of high school and college, they are required to visualize internal structures of a plant or organism in biology, the structure and arrangement of molecules in chemistry; recognize, create, and understand geometric shapes (degrees, angles, diagrams, and write logical proofs); understand the rules of English grammar, punctuation, and capitalization in more complex essays (and perhaps in another language as well); memorize and recall the sequence of significant historical events; memorize and use symbols within formulas in advanced mathematics courses; drive a car applying the rules of the road and remember how to navigate through the community and get back home, and so on. Another spatial skill involved with academic success is a sense of order—that is, applying a sense of organization and timeliness to the completion of tasks. Those without a sense of order or timeliness often do not submit assignments on time or completely. Some of us will select careers inherently reliant upon having excellent visual-motor spatial skills, such as professional athletes, biologists, chemists, geneticists, mathematicians, computer programmers, engineers, architects, surgeons, Web developers, graphic designers, and editors in publishing, to name a few.

To try using your own visual-motor spatial skills, go to JigZone.com and try the simplest six-piece jigsaw puzzle (it's timed!) and then return to this page. How did you do? Did you enjoy this brief activity or were you frustrated?

Some children have much more difficulty than others developing and using these spatial skills. Although some are considered to have "weak" spatial skills, others are labeled as having a "dysfunction" or a specific learning disability in visual- or motor-spatial skills. Based on 20 years of research by Linda Silverman (2002) from the Gifted Development Center: www.gifted_development.com (The Gifted Development Center in Denver, Colorado) one can find essential information about learning characteristics of those with strengths in spatial skills versus those who are more challenged in this area.

Source: Silverman, L. K. (2002). *Upside-down brilliance: The visual-spatial learner.* Denver, CO: DeLeon Publishing.

decline around 20 years of age and continue to drop throughout adulthood. But as we will see in Chapter 15, cross-sectional studies do not make allowance for *cohort differences* in performance on intelligence tests. Each successive generation of Americans has received more schooling than the preceding generation. Consequently, the overall performance of each generation of Americans on intelligence tests improves. Improvement caused by increasing education creates the erroneous conclusion that intelligence declines with chronological age (see Chapter 15).

Sequential Design

All **sequential designs** involve measuring more than one cohort over time. This combination of collecting data over time as well as across groups overcomes the age/cohort confounding found in cross-sectional studies as well as the effect of unique events found in longitudinal designs. If we consider our example of age and spatial ability, this time we could select a sample of 25-year-olds and a sample of 35-year-olds, measure their spatial ability and then bring each cohort back for successive measurements at specific time intervals. Figure 1.6 provides some actual data on spatial ability using a sequential design. Spatial ability was measured in adults born in 1930 for the ages 35, 45, 55, and 65. For adults born in 1940, measurements were taken at ages 25, 35, 45, and 55. Each spatial ability score reported in the table is the group average for a particular time interval. First, study the scores of the 1930 group over time and then look at the scores for the 1940 group. Finally, compare the scores of the two groups at a particular age—for example, when both groups were measured at age 35.

Limitations of Sequential Designs   Sequential designs can be complex and difficult to analyze if the groups measured longitudinally (over time) are found to be very different in the variable under study. For example, if 25-year-olds in 1935 have significantly lower spatial ability scores than 25-year-olds in 1965, it is difficult to combine these scores for an overall measurement. Doing so might distort the sequential changes in spatial ability throughout the study. The issues of time and money continue to be a limitation as when any group is followed over a longer period of time.

> **Questions**
>
> Which three research designs are frequently used to describe developmental change across the life span? For each design, can you describe situations where it would be appropriate for researchers to use it?

Year of birth

		1930		1940	
Year of spatial ability measurement	1965	70	(50)	75	(50)
	1975	65	(49)	70	(48)
	1985	60	(45)	65	(45)
	1995	55	(40)	60	(40)

FIGURE 1.6 A Sequential Design Study to Test the Effects of Age on Spatial Memory Ability Spatial ability in two cohorts of adults (one cohort born in 1930 and the other born in 1940) was measured four times at 10-year intervals from 1965 to 1995. The number of participants for each testing is indicated in parentheses. The numbers reported are average scores for each cohort at each time interval. The columns represent cross-sectional data for different subjects, and the rows represent longitudinal data for the same subjects.

The Experimental Design

The **experimental design** is one of the most rigorously objective techniques available to science. An **experiment** is a study in which the investigator manipulates one or more variables and measures the resulting changes in the other variables to attempt to determine the cause of a specific behavior. Experiments are "questions put to nature." They are the only effective technique for establishing a cause-and-effect relationship. This is a relationship in which a particular characteristic or occurrence (X) is one of the factors that causes another characteristic or occurrence (Y). Scientists design an experimental study so that it is possible to determine whether X does or does not cause Y. To say that X causes Y is simply to indicate that whenever X occurs, Y will follow at some later time.

In an experiment, researchers try to find out whether a causal relationship exists between two variables, X and Y. They systematically vary the first variable (X) and observe the effects on the second variable (Y). Factor X, the factor that is under study and is manipulated in an experiment, is the **independent variable.** It is independent of what the participant or participants do. The independent variable is assumed to be the causal factor in the behavior being studied. Researchers must also attempt to control for **extraneous variables,** factors that could confound the outcome of the study; these could include the age and gender of the participants, the time of day the study is conducted, the educational attainment of the subjects, and so on (see Figure 1.7).

The study is planned such that the individuals in the experimental group are administered the independent variable (some refer to this as the "treatment"). In comparison, the **control group** of participants should be identical to the **experimental group** except they will not be administered the independent variable while they perform the same task as the experimental group.

We need to determine if the independent variable has made any difference in the performance of the experimental group of participants. We call the end result of the experiment—the factor that is affected—the **dependent variable,** which is some measure of the participants' behavior. For instance, dependent variables are often administered in the form of paper-and-pencil tests or performance tests, for the researcher must quantify data in some measurable way. The researcher then performs various statistical analyses to be able to compare results and to look for any significant differences (e.g., How did the performance of the experimental group vary from the performance of the control group?).

Let's think back to the relationship between age and spatial ability. In a true experiment we would have to

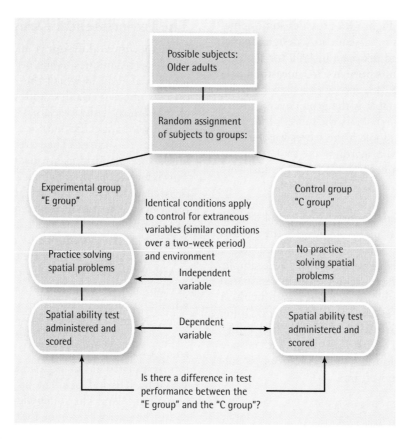

FIGURE 1.7 Sample Experimental Design Elements of a psychological experiment to assess the effects of practicing spatial ability problems on older adults' performance on spatial memory ability.

vary age systematically and measure its effect on spatial ability. The problem is that we can't manipulate age—we cannot assign the same person to different age groups. But what if, after reviewing the literature and the results from our longitudinal and cross-sectional studies, we hypothesize that the decrease in spatial ability in older participants is due, in part, to a lack of recent experience in spatial ability tasks? If we wanted to test that hypothesis, we could design an experiment such as the one presented in Figure 1.7.

In this spatial ability experiment, we would develop a 2-week training and practice course that would give older participants a chance to practice special spatial ability problems. We would randomly assign half of the older participants to the practice course (the experimental group who will receive the training) while the other half of the participants (the control group) would receive a 2-week period of time together to share information and have social conversation. In this example, the training in spatial relations would be the independent variable (practice with spatial relations versus no practice). At

the end of the 2-week period, we would most likely use some type of paper-and-pencil or performance test to measure the dependent variable (spatial ability). If the average spatial ability scores for the group who trained and practiced were significantly higher than the average for the group who did not practice, our hypothesis would be supported.

Experiments must be replicated by other researchers with different groups of subjects to see if there is consistency in results before any major theory can be significantly substantiated.

Limitations of the Experimental Design in Developmental Psychology It is difficult to use an experimental approach in developmental psychology, for several reasons. The first, as indicated earlier, is the inability to assign participants to the variable of interest. Developmental psychologists cannot manipulate many of the variables they study—such as age, gender, abusive family background, or ethnicity. These variables come with the individual along with many other variables that can confuse us when interpreting their effects on the dependent variable. Second, many of the questions we ask involve the effects of stressful or dangerous experiences, such as tobacco or alcohol use, medical procedures, or the withholding of treatments thought to be beneficial. Manipulations of these variables would be unethical, if not impossible. Third, some argue that how people behave or perform in an experimental lab setting is not how they actually behave in a "real-world" setting. Fourth, planning, designing, conducting, and evaluating a true experimental design is very time-consuming and costly, as you can imagine from reflecting on the actual small-group lab experiment illustrated in Figure 1.8.

Questions

Why is the experimental design considered to be the only one that can determine the cause of a specific behavior? Why is experimental design seldom used in most developmental studies?

The Case-Study Method

The **case-study method** is a longitudinal study that focuses on a single individual rather than a group of subjects (see Table 1.3). Its aim is the same as that of other longitudinal approaches—the accumulation of developmental information. An early form of the case-study method was the "baby biography." Over the past two centuries, a small number of parents have kept detailed observational diaries of their children's behavior. Charles Darwin, for example, wrote a biographical account of his infant son.

A good deal of the early work of Jean Piaget, an influential Swiss developmental psychologist, was based on the case-study approach (Gratch & Schatz, 1988; Wallace, Franklin, & Keegan, 1994). Piaget (1952) carefully observed the behavior of his three children—Lucienne, Laurent, and Jacqueline—and used this information to formulate hypotheses about cognitive development. One of his best-known case studies involved his unique technique for studying the mathematical concept of conservation. Piaget would begin with two identical balls of

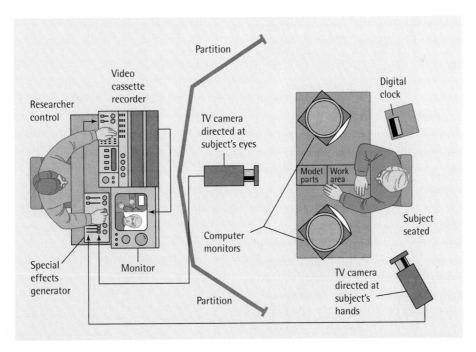

FIGURE 1.8 Experimental Research in a Small-Group Lab Many college campuses provide researchers with special facilities and equipment for conducting experiments and observing participants. This small-group lab consists of two areas separated by a room divider. Researchers at the control console can observe individuals in the experimental area without themselves being observed (and thus do not interfere with the spontaneous behavior of the participants). This small-group laboratory also contains video equipment so the experimenter can view on a television screen the participant's behavior in the experimental area. This format is devised so individuals do not observe and influence one another's perceptions and interpretations of the task to be performed. Moreover, the videotape equipment permits researchers to record behavior. Later the experimenter can analyze the behavior more closely (in this case a second-by-second analysis of the participant's hand actions in an assembly task, an analysis of when the person looked at instructions in picture format or instructions by text and pictures, and analysis of whether the assembly task was performed correctly).

Table 1.3 Research Methods

Type	Limitations
Case study—*a type of longitudinal study that focuses on one individual*	Difficult to generalize data from one individual
	Familiarity of research and subject compromises objectivity
Social survey—*survey of a sample of individuals*	Low response rate
	Bias
Naturalistic—*intensive observation of the behavior of people in their natural setting*	Lack of control
	No independent variable
	Bias
Cross-cultural—*compares data from two or more societies or cultures*	Variability of quality of data
	Research questions may not be applicable
	Seldom provides information on individual differences

clay, show them to the child, and let the child hold and manipulate the balls until the child agreed that the two contained the same amount of clay. Then, in view of the child, Piaget would flatten one ball of clay into a pancake shape. He would then ask the child if both pieces still had the same amount of clay or if the pancake or the ball had more. Between the ages of 4 and 5, children consistently said the ball had more. When tested at the age of 6 or 7, children consistently indicated that the two pieces still contained the same amount of clay, an indication of cognitive maturation (Piaget, 1952).

Case studies have also had a prominent place in the clinical treatment of maladjusted and emotionally disturbed individuals. Sigmund Freud and his followers have stressed the part that early experience plays in mental illness. According to this view, the task of the therapist is to help patients reconstruct their own histories so that, in the process, they can resolve their inner conflicts. An example of a classic case study, published in the late 1950s, is *The Three Faces of Eve*, about a woman with multiple-personality disorder. More recently, the clinical approach has been extended to the study of healthy individuals. Case studies are often used by researchers who study individuals who exhibit behavior that is an exception from the norm, such as a child genius or a serial murderer.

Limitations of the Case-Study Method The case-study method has a number of drawbacks. The data

are recorded on only one individual, and it is difficult to generalize from one case to the whole population of interest. Of course, if the kind of case study is repeated many times, on many individuals, as was the research Piaget did with children, the findings are more valuable. A second problem is the extended interaction between the observer or experimenter and the subject under study. Because case studies normally involve frequent contact between researcher and subject over a long period of time, researchers and subjects become familiar with each other, and the objectivity of the results may be in question. The experimenter might even become a part of the subject's treatment, and the same results would not necessarily be found by a different researcher.

The Social Survey Method

Researchers use the **social survey method** to study the incidence of specific behaviors or attitudes in a large population of people (see Table 1.3). Suppose researchers want to discover the prevalence and characteristics of people who are home-schooling their own children, or the frequency and type of drug use among teenagers, or the impact of a public campaign promoting senior day care. Using the social survey method, researchers ask questions to a sample of individuals who are representative of the population of individuals likely to be affected. These questions can be asked through personal interviews, by phone, by mail, or on the Internet in questionnaire form. When surveys are mailed, the researchers must rely on the people selected to answer the questions and return the document for analysis. For example, in the past several decades in the United States, census takers came to our homes and interviewed us while filling out a very long questionnaire. The national census in 2000 was not conducted in quite the same way, because that has become far too costly and labor intensive, and many people are working during the daytime hours when the census taker would work. Census researchers also must try to interview homeless and institutionalized Americans, as well as immigrants. Social scientists at the Census Bureau have a tremendous logistical task in such a large-scale survey, and it takes years to analyze and report the data collected.

For survey research to produce useful results, the sample of participants must be *representative*, and the questions must be well designed, easy to answer, and clear. For example, open-ended questions that require long answers might have a lower return rate than a simple check-off list. However, open-ended questions might give the researcher more details about a subject's attitude and practice. A survey that is too lengthy or detailed—no matter how significant or timely the questions might be—is likely to get a very poor response rate.

The representativeness of the sample is based on **random sampling.** There are different methods of random sampling, but the basic premise is that each member of the population sampled has an equally likely probability of being chosen. This allows the researcher to generalize her or his findings from the sample to the population of interest. In other words, if we want to be able to talk about the societal issue of teenage pregnancy, we cannot simply interview 500 students from one high school and report the results as representing the national population of teenagers (for instance, students in an urban high school probably are not representative of students in suburban or rural schools). If we interview 100 students from Tampa, 100 from New York City, 100 from Topeka, 100 from Kokomo, and 100 from San Bernardino, perhaps then we can talk about this issue on a national scale. The design and clarity of the questions are particularly important when a document is to be mailed and respondents will not be able to ask for assistance in understanding the questions. Social scientists interested in conducting surveys usually take advanced statistics courses to learn how to design and analyze a reliable survey.

Limitations of the Social Survey Method The greatest concerns in survey research are response rate and bias. Are the individuals who chose to respond (less than a 50 percent return is common) different from the participants who chose not to fill out the survey or agree to be interviewed? This is similar to the problem of *selective attrition* in longitudinal research. In addition, many people who are surveyed give answers they think the researcher expects or that they think will make them seem mature or "good," whereas other respondents might exaggerate when responding. Many adults are sensitive to questions that touch on matters they consider private (such as sexual practices, income, and political or religious beliefs) and are unable or unwilling to give accurate answers on these subjects. Finally, the survey method has limited use with children and cannot be used at all with infants.

The Naturalistic Observation Method

In **naturalistic observation,** researchers intensively watch behavior as it occurs and record it by means of notepad, videotape, or other method (see Table 1.3).

"*Next question: I believe that life is a constant striving for balance, requiring frequent tradeoffs between morality and necessity, within a cyclic pattern of joy and sadness, forging a trail of bittersweet memories until one slips, inevitably, into the jaws of death. Agree or disagree?*"

Survey Questions Should Be Simple and Short to Be Comprehensible

Observers must be careful not to disturb or affect the events under investigation. This method produces more detail and greater depth of insight than the social survey method (Cahill, 1990; Willems & Alexander, 1982), but it is effective only for a smaller range of subjects. For example, naturalistic observation has been used extensively to observe young children's interactions in a nursery or preschool setting, but it would be much harder to use this method to study adults at work. (See the *More Information You Can Use* box, "Tips for Observing Children," on page 26.)

An advantage of naturalistic observation is that it is independent of the participant's ability or willingness to report on given matters. Many people lack

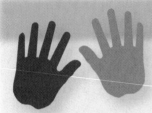

More Information You Can Use

Tips for Observing Children

One of the best ways to learn about children is to observe them. To provide access to the full drama, color, and richness of the world of children, many instructors have their students watch children in the laboratory or in the field. Here are a number of tips that may prove helpful for observing children:

The minimal aids you will need for observation generally include paper, pen, a timepiece, and a writing board.

Record the date, time interval, location, situation, and the age and sex of the subject or subjects.

Most observations take place in nursery school settings. Add diversity to your report by observing children in parks, streets, stores, vacant lots, homes, and swimming pools.

Have the purpose of your research firmly in mind. You should explicitly define and limit in advance the range of situations and behaviors you will observe. Will you watch the entire playground, giving a running account of events? Will you concentrate on one or two individuals? Will you record the activities of an entire group? Or will you focus only on certain types of behavior, such as aggression?

Once the target behavior is identified, describe both the behavior and the social context in which it occurs. Include not only what a child says and does but also what others say and do to the child. Report spoken words, cries, screams, startle responses, jumping, running away, and related behaviors.

Describe the relevant body language—the nonverbal communication of meaning through physical movements and gestures. Body language includes smiles, frowns, scowls, menacing gestures, twisting, and other acts that illuminate the intensity and affect of behavior.

Give descriptions of behavior, not interpretations that generalize about behavior.

Make notes in improvised shorthand. Immediately after an observation session, transcribe your notes into a full report. The longer the interval between your full recording of observations and the events themselves, the less accurate, less detailed, and more biased your report will be.

Limit your periods of observation to half an hour, which is about as long as a researcher can remain alert enough to perceive and remember the multitude of simultaneous and sequential occurrences.

At times, children will notice you are observing them. If they ask what you are doing, be truthful. Explain it openly and frankly. According to Wright and Barker (1950), children under the age of 9 generally display little self-consciousness when being observed.

Keep in mind that one of the greatest sources of unreliability in observation is the researcher's selective perceptions influenced by his or her own needs and values. For example, observers who sharply disapprove of aggressive behaviors tend to over-record these behaviors. Remember at all times that objectivity is your goal.

Use time sampling for some observations. Time your field notes at intervals of a minute or even 30 seconds. You may wish to tally the children's behavior in terms of helping, resistance, submission, giving, and other responses.

Use event sampling of behavioral sequences or episodes for some observations. Helen Dawe's 1934 study of the quarrels of preschool children provides a good model. Dawe made "running notes" on prepared forms that gave space for recording (a) the name, age, and sex of every subject, (b) the duration of the quarrel, (c) what the children were doing at the onset of the quarrel, (d) the reason for the quarrel, (e) the role of each subject, (f) specific motor and verbal behavior, (g) the outcome, and (h) the aftereffects. The advantage of event sampling is that it allows you to structure the field of observation into natural units of behavior.

Naturalistic Observation   What might you be studying in this setting? Would you use time sampling or event sampling? What are some strengths and limitations of this research method?

sufficient self-insight to tell the researcher about certain aspects of their behavior. Or if their behavior is illegal, socially unacceptable, or deviant, they might be reluctant to talk about it.

Using more systematic techniques through observation can provide greater objectivity in collecting and analyzing the data. One technique, **time sampling,** involves counting the occurrence of a specific behavior for a number of time intervals of the same duration. An example would be to count the number of times two children interact during 30-second intervals. Researchers who do not want to lose the sequential flow of events focus on a class of behaviors, such as fighting on a playground, and record the time lapse for each episode; this approach is termed **event sampling.** Still other researchers use precoded behavior categories. They determine beforehand what behaviors they will observe and then record these behaviors using code symbols. Videotaping in observational studies has allowed researchers much greater reliability in coding as well as greater flexibility in choosing events or behaviors observed.

Limitations of Naturalistic Observation Naturalistic observation can provide a rich source of ideas for more extensive future study. But it is not a particularly strong technique for testing hypotheses. The researcher lacks control over the behavior of the individuals being observed. Furthermore, no independent variable is "manipulated." Consequently, the theorizing associated with naturalistic observation (such as trying to figure out why a behavior occurs) tends to be highly speculative. The observer might be biased, have certain expectations, and look for those behaviors to record. Still another problem with this method is that the observer's presence can alter the behavior he or she is observing—all of us tend to act differently when we know we are under close scrutiny. In spite of these shortcomings, there is support for observing behavior as it takes place spontaneously within its natural context. Indeed, some researchers argue that observation of subjects in their natural setting affords greater justice to the rich, genuine, and dynamic quality of human life.

Question
What are the advantages and limitations of each of the following research methods: experimental, case study, social survey, and naturalistic observation?

Cross-Cultural Studies

Have you noticed society (and the world) changing at a rather rapid pace? Have such changes impacted your life, or do you believe there is little impact upon your own personal development, values, or ideologies? For example, when you recently called for computer technical support or ordered merchandise or service, were you speaking with a person from another country? Have you or a loved one recently returned from a tour of duty in Iraq or Afghanistan? Are immigrants moving into your community? Are you planning a semester of study in another country? As a college student, do you have international students as classmates or lab partners?

Since the first publication of this text about 25 years ago, James VanderZanden, a sociologist, incorporated research findings about human development from various societies. Historically, however, for the past century the majority of developmental researchers narrowly focused their interests on Euro-American subjects across the life span, which does not yield an accurate account of human development (Wainryb, 2004). Additionally, much of our present understanding of human development flows from decades of analyses and recommendations of research limited to mainstream members of such Euro-American societies (and for mainly the males of such societies). It has been pointed out that "those with more power within a society have the ability to define what counts as knowledge and to make definitions of knowledge to appear natural rather than artificially constructed" (Gjerde, 2004, p. 145).

At the beginning of the twenty-first century, that power structure is most definitely shifting. The collegial consciousness of diversity issues—necessitated by increasing U.S immigration, corporate and communications globalization, and an ever-changing mix of social, ethnic, and religious groups entering many societies throughout the world—is driving a broader, richer understanding of human development across cultures. Presently, it is exciting to report an acceleration of cross-cultural developmental research, with a broader-based focus on societal, racial, ethnic, gender, education and religious differences and similarities—and among members of ethnic-minority groups within the United States (Chia & Poe, 2004) (see Table 1.3).

Developmentalists use the **cross-cultural method** to discover which theories hold for all societies, which hold for only certain types of societies, and which hold for only one particular society. Societies differ culturally in a good many ways. Consequently, youngsters grow up with different social definitions of the behavior that is and is not appropriate for them as members of particular age groups.

When researchers can compare data from two or more societies and cultures, then culture, rather than individuals, is the subject of analysis. Cross-cultural studies might focus on a single issue, such as child-care practices, puberty rites at adolescence, depression across the life span, living conditions of the elderly, or

New Directions in Development
This young woman was the first to cast a ballot in the 2004 elections in Afghanistan, the first in that country's 5,000-year history. This new cultural practice, a nonnormative event, changed her developmental path, and that of her age cohort, into adulthood. Cross-cultural research and multicultural comparison are current research interests in the field of human development.

a wide variety of behaviors and customs (Denmark, 2004; Harkness, 1992; Nugent, Lester, & Brazelton, 1991). A person's cultural orientation is a powerful influence on his or her view of self, social relationships, values, morals, and developmental path (Wainryb, 2004). Yet McLeod (2004, p. 188) reminds us that within cultures wide variation exists in individual members of a racial or ethnic group, such as "social class, regional identification, country of origin, generational history, recency of immigration, acculturation status, language preference, etc."

Studies dealing with grandparenthood provide a good illustration of cross-cultural research. According to anthropologist A. R. Radcliffe-Brown (1940), tensions between parents and children tend to draw grandparent and grandchild together. To test this hypothesis, a number of researchers examined cross-

cultural data (Apple, 1956; Nadel, 1951). They found close and warm relationships between children and their grandparents only in cultures where grandparents do not serve as disciplinarians. Where grandparents have a disciplinary role, grandparents and grandchildren do not have easy, friendly, playful relations. Other investigators have found strong ethnic differences in grandparenting styles (Ponzetti, 2003). For example, Mexican American grandparents are more likely to live in a three-generational family with their grandchildren, have compassionate, supportive relationships with their grandchildren, and provide more help than Anglo grandparents (Kazdin, 2000; Williams & Torrez, 1998).

Such empirical research is increasingly published in psychological, sociological, educational, medical, scientific, and human services journals and will be relevant to how each of you perform your daily work-related tasks with the diverse populations you serve. Division 45 of the APA, the Society for the Psychological Study of Ethnic Minority Issues, the International Association for Cross Cultural Psychology, and the Center for Cross Cultural Research promote the research mission to broaden understanding of diverse cultural and ethnic groups worldwide. This text incorporates research findings from various societies about cultural practices and values pertaining to prenatal care, birthing and neonatal practices, child rearing, educational and health care practices, gender roles, family structure and work roles, life expectancy and quality of life for the aging, and practices surrounding dying, death, and an afterlife.

Limitations of Cross-Cultural Studies Like other research approaches, the cross-cultural study has limitations. First, the quality of the data varies from casual, unprofessional accounts by explorers and missionaries to the most sophisticated fieldwork by trained anthropologists, sociologists, and psychologists. Second, data for some research problems are lacking for many cultures. Third, the data tend to focus on the typical behaviors and practices of a people but seldom provide information on individual differences among them. Nonetheless, as distinguished anthropologist George Peter Murdock has written, cross-cultural research has demonstrated that it is "unsafe" for the scientist "to generalize his knowledge of Euro-American societies, however profound, to mankind [humankind] in general" (Murdock, 1957, p. 251).

For example, let us say that a social scientist wants to study the prevalence of the personality trait of "shyness" in young children both in the United States and in Japan. How we define "shyness" in children in the United States (embarrassment at being called upon, or being very quiet or meek, and so on) might be a prevalent personality trait of most Japanese children, where modesty, self-discipline, and respect for parents, teachers, and adults are still the norm. To be singled out for the highest grades or the best performance at a task might be an embarrassment or shameful to a Japanese child who has been taught the Confucian philosophy of unity within the group. American society, on the other hand, tends to reward the outspoken, more assertive child, who we say will "get ahead" in life. Cross-cultural researchers must be careful not to impose their own cultural views upon the behavior under study.

Question

What are some of the advantages and limitations of using cross-cultural studies?

Research Analysis

After the research design has been implemented and the subjects chosen and measured, the data are ready to be analyzed statistically. In studies of development we use two broad categories of analysis. First, we can compare different age groups on the variable of interest by simply calculating an average score for each group. We did this informally when we looked at the data on spatial ability using longitudinal and cross-sectional methodologies. We can report sample means and measures of variability and perform various statistical tests to determine how probable it is that the observed differences could have occurred by chance.

Second, we can look at the relationship between two variables using *correlational analysis.* This type of analysis allows us to quantify the association or relationship in terms of strength and direction.

Correlational Analysis

Sometimes social scientists and medical researchers want to know the degree to which two or more behaviors are associated with each other. **Correlational analysis** does not prove causation, but it can be used for predictive purposes (Aronson, Brewer, & Carlsmith, 1985). For example, in American society over the past decade or so, we have heard through the media that there is an association or relationship between eating a high-fat diet and poor health, such as increased incidence of obesity, higher risk of heart attack, and other overall health risks. Likewise, we also have heard that eating fruits and vegetables daily typically can reduce one's level of bad cholesterol, promoting better health. These are examples of relationships. Having a low cholesterol reading by itself is not the cause of excellent health—but it is one of the many factors predictive of better health.

If two conditions occur and rise or fall in value together, then there is some measure of a positive relationship. For example, eating chocolate bars daily is likely to be associated with a higher cholesterol reading. That is, as the first condition (amount of chocolate eaten) increases, the second condition (cholesterol level) also increases. This is an example of a positive correlation. On the other hand, two conditions that tend to occur in opposition to each other—for instance, when people eat more fruits and vegetables, their cholesterol scores tend to decrease—those conditions have a negative correlation. Medical researchers and social scientists are always searching for these types of associations to improve our health.

Plotting the data on a graph or through the use of a mathematical formula can help us determine the extent and direction of these relationships. A **correlation coefficient** (r) is the numerical expression of the degree or extent of relationship between two variables or conditions (note that the word explains itself: co-relation, meaning "with relation"). A correlation coefficient can range from − 1.00 to + 1.00. If it is + 1.00, we say there is a perfect positive relationship between two variables (as one variable increases, the other increases). If it is − 1.00, there is a perfect negative relationship between two variables (as one variable increases, the other decreases). If a correlation is near .00, then there is no relationship between the variables. For example, an educated guess about the relationship between how many chocolate bars we eat daily and our intelligence quotient should lead us to the conclusion that there is most likely no relationship whatsoever (r = .00) (see Figure 1.9).

In social and developmental research, we seldom find perfect correlations, but moderately strong correlations can be found in either a positive or a negative direction and can be helpful in explaining certain relationships. For example, one of the strongest positive correlations examined is that of IQ scores of identical twins. The IQ score of one identical twin is strongly predictive of the IQ score of the other twin. A well-publicized example of a negative correlation is the relationship between the number of hours children watch television and their grades in school: The more hours of TV children watch per day, the lower their grades.

Questions

How would you begin to examine the hypothesis that students who study more get higher grades? What conditions would you need to examine? What type of correlation is this?

Ethical Standards for Human Development Research

Any research on human development involves some risks and raises some ethical questions, yet research on humans is essential to make progress in understanding the developmental process. How can we learn about how people interact, raise their children, and make decisions about marriage and work, and at the same time safeguarding their privacy? Anytime we study humans, we must balance the need to know with the need to protect individuals' personal rights and privacy. The following guidelines and principles established by the American Psychological Association (2003) must be followed any time humans are the participants of our research.

Informed consent: First, the researcher must obtain written consent to participate from each participant. This consent must be voluntary. For example, research

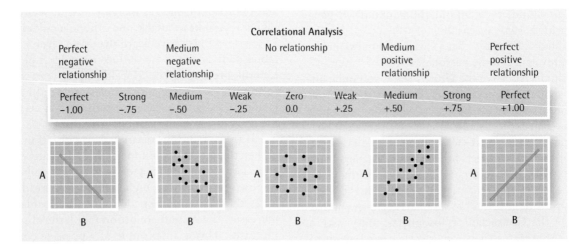

FIGURE 1.9 Degrees of Relationship Using Correlational Analysis The graphs depict a possible range of relationships between two variables. By plotting our data on a scatter diagram, we can actually begin to see something about the strength and direction (+ or −) of the correlation. The graph on the far left is an example of a perfect negative relationship (unlikely or rare in the real world). As one variable increases, the other would have to decrease in the same measure. Notice the direction of the dots—close together and going up to the left. This illustrates a stronger relationship closer to − 1.00. Eating fruits and vegetables to lower bad cholesterol is an example of a negative correlation. With no relationship, the points scatter all over the graph, which tells us the relationship is close to .00. For example, if one plotted the weather and IQ, the chances are great that there is no relationship whatsoever. In a perfect positive relationship, to the far right, as one variable goes up in value, the other variable goes up the same. This would be a + 1.00 correlation. An example of a perfect positive relationship occurs when you get paid for the hours you work: if you work 1 hour at $6 per hour, you will make $6; if you work 2 hours, you will make $12; if you work 5 hours, you will make $30. Perfect relationships are rare in real life (and in reality your take-home paycheck is lower than the full amount: The more you make, the more is taken out).

often takes place on college campuses, and it is easy to imagine participation being linked to grades, extra credit, or even less tangible rewards such as staying in a professor's good graces or a recommendation for graduate school or a job. At any time before, during, or after the research, an individual can withhold her or his consent. Second, the researchers must tell all individuals the purpose of the research and the risks and benefits of participation, emphasize the voluntary nature of participation, and provide them with a way to communicate with a key person involved in the research. Finally, the participants must be able to understand what they are being asked to do, as well as its purpose, risks, benefits, and results. Participants with cognitive disabilities, participants diagnosed with a mental illness, and children and adolescents should have special safeguards to ensure that their rights are protected.

Right to privacy: Participants must be assured that the information they share and all research records of their behaviors will be kept confidential. Any data collected must be coded and reported in such a way that the participant cannot be identified. Even if names are not used, the data should never be reported individually—unless specific permission to do so is given by the participant.

The American Psychological Association updated the guidelines effective June 1, 2003. The new Ethical Principles of Psychologists and Code of Conduct stipulates that with a written release clients' test data must be made available to them. This allows them more autonomy regarding health care decision making. The code also defines "test data" and "test materials" and offers protections for psychology graduate students participating in psychotherapy requirements (Smith, 2003).

The Society for Research in Child Development (SRCD) has also issued a set of guidelines. The SRCD lists all the principles and guidelines on its website at: www. srcd.org in the section Ethical Standards for Research with Children. Research with children raises particularly complex and sensitive issues, because the legal and moral legitimacy of experimentation on human beings depends fundamentally on the participant's consent (Stanley & Sieber, 1992). Children have very limited capacity to give informed consent; very young children have none. Even so, research suggests that many children over 9 years of age are able to make sensible decisions about whether to take part in research (Fields, 1981; Thompson, 1990). Even though parents and legal guardians are empowered to decide whether minors under their control will be used as research subjects, children should not be viewed simply as pawns that can be manipulated at will by their elders. Finally, both the APA and the SRCD state that the experimenter must assume responsibility for detecting and correcting any undesirable results that might follow from an individual's participation in the research.

Along with the rapid increase in the use of the Internet, administering psychological tests and surveys online is increasing as well. There are many new issues and concerns raised by Internet testing. People with little or no access to computers or no prior experience with the Internet may be at a disadvantage when taking an online test. Some ethical issues of Internet testing relate to the lack of control over ensuring a professional context for test administration, appropriate use of the test, qualifications of test, assessors, maintaining security, attaining informed consent, interpreting assessment results, proper release of test data, and use of obsolete tests (Naglieri et al., 2004).

Question

How do we protect humans from unethical studies?

SEGUE

As we have seen, the study of human development is dynamic, and researchers from many disciplines and from many societies contribute to our understanding of the range and depth of human behavior. The growth, learning, and maturation of individuals and groups are examined across cultures, because each society's interpretation of what is and is not normal and natural affects the lives of the individuals within each culture. Developmentalists study the domains, processes, context, and timing of events to understand both changes and continuities of human behavior.

All societies divide the life span in terms of age, defining stages that range from the moment of conception to the moment of death. Societies differ in the prestige they accord various age groupings, particularly young children and the elderly. Also, societies specify expectations for appropriate behavior within each age grouping. The most profound changes that have occurred in families over the past 200 years in Western societies include a shift from rural to urban and suburban life, smaller families, more time spent in formal schooling, more single parents, more women entering the paid labor force, parents and children spending less time together, and a significant increase in the numbers of senior citizens who are living much longer. What developmentalists began studying a century ago is still of prime interest today: the role of biology and behavior, how a person's sense of self develops, how and in what ways a person's environment shapes emotional and social development, maturation in cognitive development, and improvement in the quality of each person's life. Several scientific research methods are used to examine many developmental issues of individuals and groups over the course of the life span.

When we do research with humans, we assume major responsibilities. We must study problems and human behaviors in a rigorous and disciplined way, collect and analyze data objectively, and report our results honestly. At the same time, we have the responsibility to protect the rights and privacy of the individuals we are studying and to protect them from harm.

In Chapter 2, we provide an overview of the strengths and weaknesses of major theories of human cognitive, moral, emotional, and social development over a lifetime.

Summary

The Major Concerns of Science

1. The study of human development involves the exploration of both change and continuity. Scientists who study aspects of human development over the life span are known collectively as developmentalists.
2. The field of human development has four major goals: (a) to describe the changes that occur across the human life span, (b) to explain these changes, (c) to predict developmental changes, and (d) to intervene in the course of events in order to control them.

A Framework for Studying Development

3. Developmental change takes place in three fundamental domains: physical development, cognitive development, and emotional-social development. Yet each of these factors is intertwined in every aspect of human development.
4. The concepts of growth, maturation, and learning are important to our understanding of human development. We must not contrast the biological forces of growth and maturation (nature) with the environmental forces of learning (nurture)—it is the interaction between heredity and environment that gives each individual his or her unique characteristics.
5. Bronfenbrenner's ecological approach to development examines the mutual accommodations between the developing person and four levels of expanding environmental influence: the microsystem consists of the network of social relationships and the physical settings in which a person is involved daily; the mesosystem consists of the interrelationships among the various settings in which the individual is immersed; the exosystem consists of social structures that directly or indirectly affect a person's life; and the macrosystem consists of the overarching cultural patterns of a society that are expressed in family, educational, economic, political, and religious institutions. The chronosystem consists of those aspects of the environment that change and remain constant over time.
6. Timing of life events plays an important role in development. The passage of time has been treated as synonymous with chronological age, but social and behavioral scientists have broadened their focus to take into account the changes that occur over time in the environment—and the dynamic relation between change in the person and change in the environment. These changes are understood in terms of normative age-graded influences, normative history-graded influences, and nonnormative life events. Each individual experiences life events with his or her age cohorts, a generation that moves forward through time together and experiences the same historical life events.

Partitioning the Life Span: Cultural and Historical Perspectives

7. All societies must deal in one fashion or another with the life cycle. They divide this cycle into age strata that reflect social definitions. Such definitions often vary from one culture to another and from one historical period to another.
8. Age is a master status, so most changes in roles over a person's life span are accompanied by a change in chronological age. Age functions as a reference point that allows people to orient themselves where they are within various social networks. Each culture gives distinctive meaning, and assigns social responsibilities, to those in various life stages. Today, as in the past, attitudes toward children and the elderly vary markedly across cultures.
9. All societies are organized into age strata, and people's behavior within various age strata is regulated by the social norms or specific expectations for appropriate and inappropriate behavior.
10. In the United States, we view the life span in terms of prenatal development, infancy, childhood, adolescence, adulthood, and old age. Some developmentalists suggest there is a newer stage of emerging adulthood, following adolescence and before adulthood. Also, because many Americans are living well into their eighties and nineties, old age is evolving into young-old and the old-old.
11. In the early 1900s, researchers investigated emotional development, biology and behavior issues, cognitive development, conscious and unconscious thought, and the role of the self. Contemporary developmentalists are still researching these same topics through the use of technologically advanced methods and statistical techniques. Much classic research is now preserved in archives and databases on the Internet and the data made available for further analysis and investigation.
12. Today's developmentalists are especially interested in the biological, chemical, and genetic bases of behavior, emotional development, emergence of healthy social relationships, and the cognitive capacity of children, teens, and adults of all ages.

The Nature of Developmental Research

13. Using the scientific method, developmental researchers focus on change that occurs over time or with age. The scientific method incorporates these steps: select a researchable problem, formulate a hypothesis, test that hypothesis, draw conclusions about the hypothesis, and make the findings available to the scientific community.

14. In developmental research, three basic designs are used: (1) the longitudinal design (2) the cross-sectional design, and (3) the sequential design.

15. The longitudinal design measures the same individuals at regular intervals between birth and death. It allows researchers to describe change sequentially and offers insight into why people turn out similarly or differently in adulthood, such as the Terman Life-Cycle Study begun in the early 1920s. However, longitudinal studies cannot control for unusual events during the participants' life span, and they are time-consuming and costly.

16. To counteract the limitations of the longitudinal design, the cross-sectional design compares different groups of people of different ages at the same time. However, the confounding of age and cohort is a limitation of the cross-sectional design.

17. The sequential design involves measuring more than one age cohort over time. This combination of collecting data over time as well as across groups overcomes the age/cohort problem found in cross-sectional studies as well as the effect of unique events found in longitudinal designs. Conducting sequential designs can also be costly and complex.

18. The experimental design is one of the most rigorously objective techniques available to science. It offers the only effective technique for establishing cause-and-effect relationships when it is conducted with precision. An experiment is set up to investigate if one variable (X) is one of the factors that causes or does not cause another characteristic (Y) to occur. The factor under study is called the independent variable and is assumed to be the causal factor that affects the results of the comparison between two groups of individuals: the experimental group and the control group. The scores of these two groups are analyzed for statistically significant differences to either prove or disprove whether a causal relationship exists. It is difficult to control for certain variables in an experimental study; high standards of ethics with human subjects must be adhered to; human behavior in a lab may be different from human behavior in the real world, and this type of research is costly and time-consuming.

19. The case-study method is a longitudinal study that describes one individual's experience and behavior over time. This method provides rich detail and description, but its findings cannot easily be generalized to other individuals, other settings, and other time periods. Case studies are often used to examine people with exceptionalities, such as a highly intelligent child.

20. The social survey method uses questionnaires, interviews, and surveys to measure attitudes and behaviors of a sample of people who represent a larger group of the population. The findings of surveys such as the U.S. Census are often used to instigate legislation, or institute policy changes, or change funding for many social programs. It can take years to analyze and disseminate the findings.

21. The naturalistic observation method enables a researcher to study people independently of their ability or willingness to report on themselves. Techniques range from reports on casual, uncontrolled experiences to videotape records taken in a laboratory setting. A limitation of naturalistic observation is the possibility of observer bias.

22. The cross-cultural method allows scientists to specify which theories in human development hold true for all societies, which hold for only certain types of societies, and which hold for only a particular society. Cross-cultural studies might focus on a single issue, such as child-care practices, puberty rites, or living conditions for the elderly. There is a renewed interest in cross-cultural psychology. Researchers must avoid imposing their own cultural views on the behavior under study.

Research Analysis

23. Data collected in human developmental studies can be analyzed descriptively (by group or variable of interest). Correlational analysis quantifies the relationship between two or more variables in terms of strength and direction but does not prove causation. It can be used for prediction, depending on the strength of the positive or negative relationship. A correlation is derived by applying a specific formula, and a correlation coefficient can range only from -1.0 to $+1.0$.

Ethical Standards for Human Development Research

24. A scientist must conduct research with respect for the integrity of the participants and protect their privacy and welfare. Researchers must secure informed consent, assure participants of their safety, and inform participants that their individual performance will be kept confidential. The American Psychological Association and the Society for Research in Child Development have developed strict guidelines that must be followed with research participants.

Key Terms

age cohort (10)

age strata (13)

case-study method (23)

chronosystem (10)

cognitive development (5)

confounding (19)

control group (21)

correlational analysis (27)

correlation coefficient (29)

cross-cultural method (27)

cross-sectional design (19)

culture (13)

dependent variable (21)

development (4)

developmental psychology (4)

ecological approach (8)

emerging adulthood (14)

emotional-social development (5)

event sampling (27)

exosystem (9)

experiment (21)

experimental design (21)

experimental group (21)

extraneous variables (21)

growth (7)

hypothesis (17)

independent variable (21)

informed consent (30)

learning (8)

longitudinal design (17)

macrosystem (10)

maturation (8)

mesosystem (9)

microsystem (9)

naturalistic observation (25)

nonnormative life events (11)

normative age-graded influences (10)

normative history-graded influences (10)

physical development (5)

random sampling (25)

right to privacy (31)

scientific method (16)

selective attrition (17)

sequential design (20)

social norms (13)

social survey method (24)

spatial ability (17)

time sampling (27)

Following Up on the Internet

Web sites for this chapter focus on professional organizations in the field of human development. Please access the text Web site at www.mhhe.com/vzcrandell8 for up-to-date hot-linked Internet addresses for the following organizations and resources:

The American Psychological Association (APA)

APA Division 7: Developmental Psychology

The American Psychological Society

International Association for Cross Cultural Psychology

Galaxy: Social Sciences

Society for Research in Child Development (SRCD)

Theories of Development

Critical Thinking Questions

1. Suppose someone comes up with a new theory of development called the "Food Theory," which states that human development can be explained in terms of the foods we eat. Because no two people eat exactly the same foods, it follows that no two people develop in exactly the same way. Why would you accept or reject this theory?

2. If genetic scientists took one of your cells and cloned you—and then gave the cloned infant to the same caregivers you had—do you think the clone would turn out to be just like you?

3. Do theories of development aid us in understanding by providing a framework, or limit us by forcing connections?

4. In what ways is a theory that tries to explain how humans develop similar to a theory that attempts to explain how the universe developed?

Theories allow us to see the world coherently and to act on the world in a rational way. Many theories have evolved over the past century in Western cultures that attempt to explain how human personality develops, why we behave as we do, what environmental conditions motivate us to act certain ways, and how these factors are interrelated. Some of these theories base their explanations on critical physical and social-emotional circumstances in our earliest years of life; some on the impact of environmental influences of our family, community, and culture; some on our distinct learning and thought processes; some on successful completion of specific developmental "tasks" at each stage over the life span; and some on how a healthy—or unhealthy—sense of self shapes our personality and behaviors. Over the past decade or so, the universal applicability of traditional theoretical models of development has been challenged. Many of the long-standing theories presented in this chapter were formulated by Western white males about Western white males. Some newer theories seek to explain the development of women, nonwhites, and people in non-Western cultures.

Cross-cultural social scientists are putting the older theoretical models to the test on a broader scale in scholarly debates in university settings, in international conferences, and in chat rooms and online discussion groups. This is leading to newer perspectives and understanding on individual development in all domains. More recently, the American Psychological Association established a division, International Psychology, and more than thirty cross-cultural associations are listed on the American Psychological Society Web site that encourage professionals from all disciplines to collaborate and examine human development on a global scale.

Theory: A Definition

Many Americans hold theory in low regard. The word *theory* suggests to them a detached, ivory-tower irrelevance to everyday life. College students often complain, "Why do we have to bother with all these theories? Why not just let the facts speak for themselves!" Unfortunately, facts do not "speak for themselves"; facts are silent. Before facts can speak to us, we have to find relationships among them. For example, you might baby-sit, care for younger brothers or sisters, have children of your own, or anticipate having children. What do you do when they misbehave? Do you scold them, threaten them, spank them, forbid them to engage in a favorite activity, reason with them, ignore them, or demonstrate the behavior you expect? What you do is based on your theory—whether explicit or not—about how children learn. Perhaps the theory is embedded in a proverb or maxim, such as Spare the Rod and Spoil the Child, You Got to Toughen Kids Up for Life, Just Give Them Loads of Love, Spanking Children Causes Emotional Problems, or Children Are to Be Seen and Not Heard. However, the various functions of theory will become more evident as we define the concept of a theory and examine some major types of theories of human development.

A **theory** is a set of interrelated statements that provides an explanation for a class of events. It is "a way of binding together a multitude of facts so that one may comprehend them all at once" (G. A. Kelly, 1955, p. 18). The value of the knowledge yielded by the application of theory lies in the control it gives us over our experience. Theory serves as a guide to action. By formulating a theory, we attempt to make sense of our experiences. We must somehow "catch" fleeting events and find a way to describe and explain them. Only then can we predict and influence the world around us. Theory is the "fabric" we weave to accomplish these ends, just as a fine garment is crafted out of a variety of pieces of fabric and thread, carefully sewn together, and worn for a particular purpose.

More specifically, a theory performs a number of functions. First, it allows us to organize our observations and to deal meaningfully with information that would otherwise be chaotic and useless. As French mathematician Jules-Henri Poincar (1854–1912) observed: "Science is built up with facts, as a house is with stones, but a collection of facts is no more a science than a heap of stones is a house." Second, theory allows us to see relationships among facts and uncover implications that would not otherwise be evident in isolated bits of data. Third, it stimulates inquiry as we search for knowledge about many different and often puzzling aspects of behavior. A theory, then, inspires research that can be used to verify, disprove, or modify that theory. So research continually challenges us to craft new and better theories (see Figure 2.1). In human development, as in other social and behavioral sciences, it is often difficult

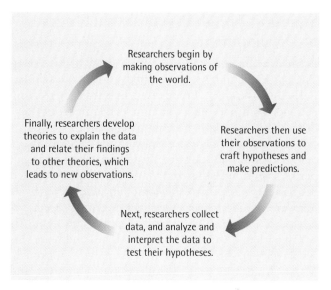

FIGURE 2.1 The Relationships Among Theory, Scientific Method, and Observations of the World

to determine how conclusively the evidence supports a theory, let alone to choose among competing theories. It is a considerably easier task to decide whether the evidence is harmonious with a theory (Lieberson, 1992).

> **Questions**
>
> What is the purpose of a good theory? In what ways is a good theory useful to our lives?

Psychoanalytic Theories

The history of psychology—like the history of the twentieth century—could not be written without discussing the contributions of Sigmund Freud. Both supporters and critics of his theory of personality regard it as a revolutionary milestone in the history of human thought (Macmillan, 1991; Robinson, 1993). His notions of how behavior is motivated have been embedded in the work of a multitude of philosophers, social scientists, psychiatrists, and other mental health practitioners. And characters in countless plays and novels have been built on Freud's view of the individual.

Central to **psychoanalytic theory** is the view that personality is fashioned progressively as the individual passes through various psychosexual stages. He also proposed that people operate from three states of being: the *id*, which seeks self-gratification; the *superego*, which seeks to do what is morally proper; and the *ego*, the rational mediator between the id and superego. Let us turn, then, to a consideration of psychoanalytic theory.

Sigmund Freud: Psychosexual Stages of Development

Freud was born in 1856 and lived most of his life in Vienna. As a child, he was a gifted student and scholar. Early in his career, Freud used hypnosis in treating patients with nervous (which he called neurotic) disorders. But he soon became disenchanted with this method. Some of his patients exhibited nervous disorders that could not be attributed to anything physical, per se. Freud hypothesized that something else caused his patients such distress—something the patient was unaware of. He began experimenting with free association of ideas and with dream analysis and hypnosis to tap patients' "unconscious" thoughts, and from this he developed his famous psychoanalytic approach. Many American and European psychologists and psychiatrists were directly or indirectly influenced by Freud's teachings.

The Role of the Unconscious   Freud stressed the role in our behavior of *unconscious motivation*—stemming from impulses buried below the level of awareness. According to Freud, human behavior arises from a struggle between societal prohibitions and instinctual drives associated with sex and aggression. Because certain behaviors are forbidden and punished, many instinctual impulses are driven out of our awareness early in our lives. Nonetheless, they still affect our behavior. They find new expression in slips of the tongue ("Freudian slips"), dreams, bizarre symptoms of mental disorder, religion, the arts, literature, and myth. For Freud, the early years of childhood have critical importance; what happens to an individual later in life is merely a ripple on the surface of a personality structure fashioned firmly during the child's first five to six years.

Psychosexual Stages   Freud said that all human beings, starting in infancy, pass through a series of **psychosexual stages.** Each stage is dominated by the development of sensitivity in a particular erogenous, or pleasure-giving, zone of the body. The characteristics of Freud's three key psychosexual stages of development—the oral, anal, and phallic stages—are described in detail in Figure 2.2. Each stage poses a unique conflict that individuals must resolve before passing on to the next stage. If they are unsuccessful in resolving the conflict, the resulting frustration becomes chronic and remains a central feature of their psychological makeup. Alternatively, individuals might become so addicted to the pleasures of a given stage that they are unwilling to move on to later stages. As a result of either frustration or overindulgence, they experience fixation, or a com-

Sigmund Freud with his daughter Anna in 1939   Although Freud reached the pinnacle of his fame in the period between 1919 and his death in 1939, he formulated most of the essentials of his psychoanalytic theory between 1893 and 1903. Anna Freud, building on her father's work, pioneered in the psychoanalytic study and treatment of children.

plex, at a particular stage of development. **Fixation** is the tendency to stay at a particular stage: The individual is troubled by the conflict characteristic of the stage and seeks to reduce tension by means of the behavior characteristic of that stage.

Freud also identified two later stages, the *latency* period and the *genital* period. He considered these stages less important to the development of the basic personality structure than the stages from birth to age 7. The latency period corresponds to the middle childhood years. During this phase, Freud thought children suppress most of their sexual feelings and become interested in games, sports, and friendships—boys associate with boys, girls with girls. Sexual reawakening occurs at puberty, launching the genital period. In this stage the equilibrium of the latency period is upset. Young people begin experiencing romantic infatuations, emotional upheavals, and the desire to have a satisfactory sexual relationship.

Appraisal of Freud's Work   For decades Freud's ideas dominated much clinical therapy. To many people Freud seemed to open an entirely new psychological world. His emphasis on environment, not biology or heredity,

Characteristic	Oral	Anal	Phallic
Time period	Birth to approximately 18 months	Approximately 18 months to 3 years	Approximately the third to seventh year
Pleasurable body zones	Mouth, lips, and tongue	Anus, rectum, and bladder	The genitals
Most pleasurable activity	Sucking during the early phase; biting during the later phase	In the early phase, expelling feces and urine; in the later phase, retaining feces and urine	Masturbation
Sources of conflict	Terminating breast-feeding	Toilet training	In boys, the Oedipal complex: boys feel sexual love for the mother and hostile rivalry toward the father, leading them to fear punishment through castration by the father. In girls, the Electra complex: girls feel sexual love for the father and hostile rivalry toward the mother, leading them to conclude that they have been castrated (because they lack a penis). Their sense of castration gives girls a feeling of inferiority that finds expression in "penis envy."
Common problems associated with fixation	An immature, dependent personality with overwhelming and insatiable demands for mothering; a verbally abusive and demanding personality; or a personality characterized by excessive "oral" behaviors, such as alcoholism, smoking, compulsive eating, and nail biting.	A hostile, defiant personality that has difficulty relating to people in positions of authority; a superconformist personality characterized by preoccupation with rules, regulations, rigid routines, compulsive neatness, and orderliness; or a stingy, miserly personality.	Sexual problems in adulthood— impotence or frigidity; homosexuality; inability to handle competitive relationships.
Social relationships	Infants cannot differentiate between self and nonself. Consequently, they are self-centered and preoccupied with their own needs.	Since parents interfere with elimination pleasures, the child develops ambivalent attitudes toward the parents. As children resolve the conflict between their needs for parental love and for instinctual gratification, they evolve lifelong attitudes toward cleanliness, orderliness, punctuality, submissiveness, and defiance.	A successful resolution of phallic conflict leads the child to identify with the parent of the same sex. In this fashion the child achieves a sense of masculinity or femininity and gives up the incestuous desire for the parent of the opposite sex.

FIGURE 2.2 Freud's Key to Psychosexual Stages

as the primary factor in mental health and illness was particularly hopeful. In fact, people were so fascinated with the novelty of Freud's insights that few questioned their truth. Nonetheless, scientists have come to recognize that Freudian theory is difficult to evaluate. It makes few predictions that can be tested by accepted scientific procedures (Colby & Stoller, 1988; Roazen, 1990). Freudians say that only a personal psychoanalysis can reveal the truth of the theory's assertions. Unconscious motivation is, by definition, not in the conscious mind.

Consequently, scientists lack the means to observe and study such motivation objectively.

Freud constructed his developmental stages almost entirely on the basis of inferences from adult patients. Recent historical research has depicted Freud as occasionally claiming cures when there were none and as suppressing or distorting the facts of cases to prove his theoretical points (Crews, 1998). In addition, despite stressing the importance of the early years, Freud rarely worked with children. However, other child psychoanalysts, such as his daughter Anna, did apply his theories to the treatment of children.

Feminist scholars find the psychoanalytic hypothesis of female "penis envy" highly problematic, sexist, and based on the biases of the male-dominated culture of the Victorian era of the late 1800s (Slipp, 1993) (see *Human Diversity:* "Rethinking Women's Biology," in Chapter 1). One feminist scholar finds Freud complicit with the violence of sexual abuse against women and girls (Rush, 1996). Although Freud did acknowledge a link between sexual abuse and neurosis in his earlier *seduction theory,* he then refuted it with later theories that removed the blame from the abuser. Freud's Oedipal and Electra complexes posit children's sexual fantasies as the root of later neuroses, and Rush (1996) argues these are actually a cover-up for the rampant incest and child abuse in Victorian Vienna that Freud encountered with his female patients. This was and continues to be harmful to women because the abuse they suffered was not acknowledged and in effect the victim is blamed.

Freudian theorists tended not only to ignore women's experience but also to blame them for others' psychological difficulties. For example, as recently as the 1950s, Bruno Bettleheim, a Freudian psychoanalyst, claimed that autism resulted from children being raised by a mother devoid of warmth and love, or by what he termed "refrigerator mothers." This conceptualization put a heavy, unnecessary burden on mothers at that time who were attempting to understand a child with such a complex disorder.

Psychiatrist Jean Baker Miller posed her own *relational theory.* In contrast to Freud's views, she feels that relationships are the central need in human life and that problems that develop are caused by relational disconnections. She states that personality growth occurs within relationships and that infants respond to the emotions of caregivers. The goal is to continue to form intimate relationships, not to strive for autonomy and individuation (Miller, 1991; Miller & Striver, 1997).

Finally, critics charge that Freudian theory is a poor guide to healthy personality development because his patients were suffering from emotional difficulties (see the *Human Diversity* box, "Psychological Research and Spiritual Traditions") (Torrey, 1992).

Over the past 35 years, interest in the duration of breast-feeding, severity of weaning, age of toilet training, and other psychoanalytic variables has gradually waned, and the cures expected from psychoanalysis have proven elusive. It is not unusual to encounter someone who has been in psychoanalysis for years. By the early 1970s, a new generation of U.S. psychiatrists was turning to psychobiology, considering defects of nature, not nurture, to be the primary factors in mental illness. These psychiatrists claimed that neurochemical

Jean Baker Miller and Women's Development Dr. Miller, a psychiatrist, expanded on psychoanalytic theory and posed the relational theory of women's development.

factors, not childhood traumas, best explained mental illness and addictions—hence they looked to genes and the biochemistry of the brain, not to bad parenting, to explain how mental illness is transmitted from one generation to another. The shift away from Freudian theory in no way detracts from the revolutionary significance of Freud's work. Perhaps, more than anything else, Freud deserves considerable credit for directing attention to the importance of early social experience in human development and how those experiences impact the later stages of life.

Questions

What are the distinct features of Freud's psychoanalytic theory? What are the strengths and weaknesses of this theory? How is Freud's theory viewed by many contemporary psychologists?

Erik Erikson: Psychosocial Stages of Development

One of Freud's major contributions was to stimulate the work of other theorists and researchers. Erik Erikson was one of the most talented and imaginative of these theorists. A neo-Freudian psychoanalyst of Danish extraction, Erikson (1902–1994) came to the United States in 1933. While acknowledging Freud's genius and monumental contributions, Erikson moved away from the

Human Diversity

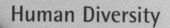

Psychological Research and Spiritual Traditions

What do Tibetan Buddhist monks and Western research psychologists have in common? Maybe more than might be apparent on the surface. In fact, it is precisely what is not apparent—human mental and emotional processes interest both Buddhist monks and psychologists. Many research psychologists are beginning to realize that they have much to learn from the monks, whose centuries-old religious practices offer new directions for their work.

Tibetan Buddhism emphasizes the importance of gaining knowledge through self-examination of one's experiences. As part of their training, Tibetan Buddhist monks practice a type of meditation that involves becoming mindful—that is, the person acknowledges emotions and mental states but controls the reaction to them. The feelings themselves are not controlled, they are recognized and acknowledged. This differs from Western traditions that advise us to control our emotions. "Don't get angry." "Don't feel stressed." Perhaps that advice is easier said than done. What are we supposed to do with these emotions?

Buddhists realize that emotions such as fear and anger are inevitable aspects of human life. But what we can control through *practice of mindfulness* is the reaction that stems from the emotions, or as the Buddhists say, to recognize "the spark before the flame." Research psychologists are proving that this can be done.

In the course of his research, Paul Ekman and Robert Levenson, professors at the University of California, Berkeley, may have found a man who cannot be startled. In a series of yet unpublished experiments, Ekman exposed one Tibetan Buddhist monk to a sudden sound as loud as a firecracker and monitored the participant's blood pressure,

muscle movements, heart rate and skin temperature for signs of startle. The Buddhist monk, possibly due to hours of practice regulating his emotions through meditation, registered "little signs of disturbance." (Dingfelder, 2003)

By studying Buddhist practitioners of meditation, research psychologists can gain important insights into how emotions affect us and how we in turn can work through our emotions. It is a way to practice preventative mental health. This is a different paradigm from the Western model that treats people who are suffering the aftereffects of emotional damage.

Another area of study that interests psychologists is the Tibetan Buddhist monks' practice of creating *mental imagery*. Images such as Buddhist deities and *mandalas* (geometric designs symbolic of order, harmony, and perfect wisdom) are used to calm the mind. "Mental imagery," says Marlene Behrmann, "is critical in a number of tasks besides meditation, from assessing a potential chess move to determining whether a new couch will fit in the living room." She speculates that the current body of research on mental imagery focuses on the skills of amateurs—specifically, Western college sophomores. "By broadening the pool of research participants to include visualization experts such as Tibetan Buddhist monks, psychologists might be able to get an idea of what the upper limits of human visualization look like, says Behrmann" (Dingfelder, 2003). Furthermore, findings from this type of research can be shared with the Buddhist monks to help them to perfect their meditative and visualization techniques as well.

Source: Dingfelder, S. F. (2003, December). Tibetan Buddhism and research psychology: A match made in Nirvana? *Monitor on Psychology, 34*(11), 46–48.

Tibetan Buddhist Monks By studying Tibetan Buddhist monks' centuries-old practice of meditation, psychologists are gaining important insights about how we can work through our emotions to practice preventative mental health.

fatalism implicit in Freudian theory, challenging Freud's notion that the personality is primarily established during the first five to six years of life. He observed that if everything goes back to early childhood, then everything becomes someone else's fault, and this undermines trust in one's own capabilities.

Erikson concluded that the personality continues to develop over the entire life span. His more optimistic view emphasizes success, greatness, and the flowering of human potential. As his work progressed, Erikson also departed from Freud in another respect. He wove the external landscapes provided by culture, society, and history into Freudian notions of the internal dimensions of the mind.

The Nature of Psychosocial Development   Erikson's chief concern is with **psychosocial development,** or development of the person within a social context. In contrast, Freud focused chiefly on the tension occurring as sexual energy sought release, or psychosexual development. Erikson basically formulated eight major stages of development (see Table 2.1), but after his death in 1994, his wife, Joan, published his theory about a ninth stage in very old age (which Erikson himself experienced). Each stage poses a unique developmental task and simultane-

Erik H. Erikson and Joan Erikson   Erikson became a leading figure in the psychosocial study of human growth and development, formulating nine stages, with a "conflict" or "crisis" to be resolved at each stage for healthy development to occur. He and his wife Joan collaborated on writing and refining his theory through his early nineties.

ously confronts individuals with a crisis that they must resolve (Erikson preferred the term *opportunity*). As employed by Erikson (1968a, p. 286), a crisis is not "a threat of catastrophe but a turning point, a crucial period of increased vulnerability and heightened potential." More importantly he said, "remember that conflict and tension are sources of growth, strength, and commitment" (Erikson & Erikson, 1997). He would see great people of history, such as German Reformationist Martin Luther, Indian philosopher and peacekeeper Mohandas Gandhi, former president of South Africa Nelson Mandela, Pope John Paul II, and Mother Teresa of Calcutta as achieving greatness by virtue of the fit between their personal crises and the crises of their times. Their solutions—as expressed in their ideas—become cultural solutions to broader social problems. Some might suggest that former NYC mayor Rudy Giuliani, who helped New Yorkers and the nation through and beyond the September 11, 2001, tragedy, and Oprah Winfrey, media personality and philanthropist, are contemporary self-actualized persons. Perhaps each of you can think of someone in your own community who fits this exceptional profile.

According to Erikson (1959; 1982; Erikson & Erikson, 1997), individuals develop a "healthy personality" by mastering "life's outer and inner dangers." Development follows the **epigenetic principle,** a term he borrowed from biology—"anything that grows has a ground plan, and . . . out of this ground plan the parts arise, each having its time of special ascendancy, until all parts have arisen to form a functioning whole" (Erikson, 1968b, p. 92). Hence, according to Erikson, each part of the personality has a particular time in the life span when it must develop if it is going to develop at all—much like the development of the fetus in the womb, whereby each part of the body must develop when its time approaches. Should a capacity not develop on schedule, the rest of the individual's personality development is unfavorably altered. The individual is then hindered in dealing effectively with reality. However, Erikson did insist that there must be a healthy balance between both sides of each crisis that we encounter. For instance, a healthy mastery of the first stage culminates in a preponderance of *trust,* but also produces a healthy dose of *mistrust:* You cannot trust every person you meet on the street and avoid mishap—you must develop a bit of mistrust to get along in this world. But in the end you should interact with the world from a position rooted in trust, and not mistrust, to further healthy psychosocial development.

Erikson's Nine Stages   Erikson was the first theorist to offer a model of development that extended over the entire life span. Table 2.1 depicts Erikson's nine stages, beginning with "trust vs. mistrust" and ending with "despair vs. hope and faith."

Table 2.1 Erikson's Nine Stages of Psychosocial Development

Stage	Developmental Period	Characteristics of Stage	Favored Outcome
Trust vs. mistrust	Infancy (birth to 1 year)	Come to trust or mistrust themselves and others	Develop trust in self, parents, and the world
Autonomy vs. shame and doubt	2 to 3	With increased mobility, decide whether to assert their will	Develop sense of self-control without loss of self-esteem
Initiative vs. guilt	4 to 5	Are curious and manipulate objects	Learn direction and purpose in activities
Industry vs. inferiority	6 to puberty	Are curious about how things are made and how they work	Develop a sense of mastery and competence
Identity vs. identity confusion	Adolescence	Explore "Who am I?" question	Develop coherent sense of self and ego-identity
Intimacy vs. isolation	Early adulthood	Are able to reach out and connect with others	Become intimate with someone and work toward career
Generativity vs. stagnation	Middle adulthood	Look beyond self to embrace society and future generations	Begin family, develops concern for those outside family
Integrity vs. despair	Late adulthood	Take stock of one's past	Get sense of satisfaction from looking at past
Despair vs. hope and faith	Very old age (late 80s and beyond)	Face new sense of self over failing bodies and need for care	Achieve a new sense of wisdom and transcendance

Appraisal of Erikson's Work Erikson's work provides a welcome balance to traditional Freudian theory. Although not neglecting the powerful effects of childhood experience, Erikson draws our attention to the continual process of personality development that takes place throughout the life span. His view is a more optimistic view than Freud's. Whereas Freud was primarily concerned with pathological outcomes, Erikson holds open the prospect of healthy and positive resolutions of our identity crises. Erikson's portrait of the life cycle allows "second chances" for opportunities missed and paths not taken. It has always been a general tenet of American individualism that people can improve themselves and continually refashion their fate by changing their social situation, so Erikson's perspective has captured the imagination of the U.S. public. The language Erikson provided—"identity," "identity crisis," "the life cycle"—plays a major role in the U.S. way of thinking about adolescence and, beyond this, about the widest range of adult trials and tribulations (Turkle, 1987).

One legitimate criticism of Erikson's work is that all of the subjects of his psychobiographies and most of his case samples were males (Josselson, 1988). However, since the early 1970s, identity development in women has been looked at more closely using Erikson's identity statuses as a base (Marcia, 1991). Josselson (1988) studied women's identity statuses and found that "a woman's identity at the close of adolescence forms the template for her adulthood." The issues most important to her female subjects were social-emotional and religious, not occupational or political. Josselson's findings agree with Jean Baker Miller's relational theory: "Women's sense of self becomes very much organized around being able to make and then to maintain affiliations and relationships" (Josselson, 1988). Gilligan's (1982a; Gilligan, Sullivan & Taylor, 1995) theory also views female identity as rooted in connections to others and in relationships: "Women conceptualize and experience the world in a different voice, and men and women operate with different internal models" (Gilligan, 1982a, p. 7). A comprehensive concept of identity must incorporate both female and male ways of developing (Pescitelli, 1998). (See the *Further Developments* box on page 44, "Theories of Emotions or Playing Mind Games.")

Questions

How does Erikson's theory of psychosocial development differ from Freud's theory of personality development? What crisis/opportunity characterizes each of Erikson's psychosocial stages, and what is the healthy outcome proposed for each stage throughout the life cycle?

Further Developments

Theories of Emotions or Playing Mind Games

Have you recently experienced an emotional high (or low) by winning (or losing) a college scholarship, a large amount of money in a lottery, at a casino, or just playing Texas Hold 'Em in the dorm? Poker has been gaining popularity at campuses across the nation among students and drawing more crowds, and every good poker player knows that opponents can "read" a player's emotional state by his or her facial expressions, especially during "bluffing." A growing list of celebrities are passionate about playing poker, including Ben Affleck, Matthew Perry, Cheryl Hines, and Angela Bassett—all experts at *showing* their emotions! Many of the names of rules of playing Texas Hold 'Em reveal the player's status of his or her emotional behavior, such as *bluff, edge, streak, tells,* and *tilt.*

Moreover, in the public arena of "aging gracefully," more people are using Botox to remove the wrinkles of aging, preventing the person from expressing certain emotions and leaving the individual appearing more *emotionless* (a term used by reporters during John Kerry's presidential campaign). Perhaps, then, it may be advantageous at times to *conceal* our emotions and other times to *reveal* them.

For centuries, philosophers and researchers have tried to understand how our emotions reveal so much about us and if the range of emotional expressions are universal across cultures. Only recently have researchers examined emotions positively and with the same interest as they've shown cognition. One reason emotions have traditionally been given "second status" in academia is that emotions are very hard to quantify and measure. Emotions have also historically been linked to abnormal or irrational behaviors.

Aristotle, for example, endorsed the theory that a balance of bodily fluids determines the individual's temperament. He associated anger with overheated blood and argued that the desire to retaliate for a personal injury or offense will sustain anger indefinitely. Descartes believed that ideas are innate and that the body and mind are distinct entities; he attempted to locate emotions in the nervous system. Spinoza regarded emotions as excessive impulses and promoted rational self-control as the means of freeing the self from

Texas Hold 'Em: An emotional rollercoaster

Source: Chad Woolbert and the Digital Collegian at Penn State.

"emotional bondage." Rousseau insisted that the infant is born with noble emotions, which society adulterates. Kant suggested that innate dispositions are neither good nor bad, and that people need to be guided through life experience and free self-expression to control the emotions produced.

Darwin thought that strong emotions are important for the survival of species—for instance, a strong emotion like fear in response to danger enables one to run away and live to face another day. G. Stanley Hall noted that emotions such as joy, sadness, fear, and anger tend to be expressed more frequently and intensely in childhood and youth. In adolescence, social forces start to redirect the expression of emotions, leading to other manifestations such as violence.

Freud was intrigued with the possibilities of using hypnosis to deal with emotional conflicts in patients. He also attributed fear and anxiety to birth trauma. Later he rejected this view and decided that emotional disturbances were not much different from other neuroses, being much more a matter of degree than difference. William James argued that emotion consists of the feeling or perception of changes occurring in bodily organs—for example, if one sees a dangerous object, one begins to tremble and run and then experience fear, so that the emotion follows the physical movement.

In response to James's theory, several researchers at Harvard in the early twentieth century countered that emotions depend on neural activity in the brain cortex. They removed part of the hypothalamus from a cat and reported that they had eliminated all angry reactions from the cat. John Dewey thought that the brain and all other bodily structures function in harmonious relation to each other, creating a series of feelings, depending on the environment. John Watson concluded from his observations and experiments that fear, rage, and love are inherited or developed shortly after birth, and that all other emotions are learned later through classical conditioning.

More recently, the study of emotions includes the influence of genetic and environmental factors. For more than 40 years, Paul Ekman, from the University of California at San Francisco, researched facial expressions and the physiology of emotions. Ekman investigated universal facial expressions in the United States, Japan, Brazil, and Papua, New Guinea and has authored texts based on his research findings: *Unmasking the Face: A Guide to Recognizing Emotions from Facial Expressions* (2003) and *Emotions Revealed: Recognizing Faces and Feelings to Improve Communication and Emotional Life* (2003). His research has led him to propose that the 10,000 emotional facial expressions are largely universal. Presently he consults on interpersonal deception for the security field to create devices that will allow only classified personnel into high-security areas by matching images of distinctive facial expressions.

Carroll Izard, from the University of Delaware, is also a nationally recognized authority on the emotional development of children—especially aggression in children (Schultz, Izard, & Bear, 2004). His research reveals that everyone feels the basic six emotions: happiness, surprise, fear, sadness, disgust and anger, and 42 muscles in the face are used to express these feelings. He has authored several books, including *The Psychology of Emotions* (2004).

Daniel Goleman, researcher and author, has promoted *Emotional Intelligence: Why It Can Matter More than IQ*, proposing five dimensions of EQ (emotional quotient): self-awareness, managing emotions, motivation, empathy, and social skills (Goleman, 1995). He brought attention to theories of emotional intelligence proposed by other researchers and spurred a profusion of international empirical research.

Source: Originally adapted from Samuel Smith, *Ideas of the Great Psychologists* (1983), and Kirn, W., & Ressner, J. (2004, July 26). Poker's new face: Hot game in town. *Time, 164*(4), p. 30.

Behavioral Theory

Psychoanalytic theory focuses on the mental and emotional processes that shape human personality. The data it uses come largely from the self-observations provided by *introspection.* Behavioral theory contrasts sharply with this approach. As its name suggests, **behavioral theory** is concerned with the observable behavior of people—what they actually do and say. Behavioral psychologists believe that if psychology is to be a science, its data must be directly observable and measurable.

Behavioral theorists have traditionally divided *behavior* into units called **responses** and divided the environment into units called **stimuli.** Behaviorists are especially interested in how people *learn* to behave in particular ways, and hence the approach is also termed *learning theory.* Historically, behaviorism has emphasized two types of learning:(1) *classical,* or respondent,

conditioning and (2) *operant,* or *instrumental,* conditioning (see Figure 2.3).

Classical conditioning is based on the work of Ivan Pavlov (1849–1936), a Russian physiologist. Pavlov gained international renown and a Nobel Prize for his early research dealing with the role of gastric juices in digestion in dogs. Subsequently, Pavlov pursued an observation he made while conducting his gastric experiments with dogs. He noted that a dog would initially salivate only when food was placed in its mouth. With the passage of time, however, the dog's mouth would water *before* it tasted the food. Indeed, the mere sight of the food or even the sound of the experimenter's footsteps would cause salivation.

Pavlov was intrigued by the anticipatory flow of saliva in the dogs, a phenomenon he termed "psychic secretion." He saw the study of "psychic secretions" as a powerful and objective means for investigating the mechanisms by which organisms adapt to their environment.

So Pavlov devised a series of experiments in which he rang a bell immediately before feeding a dog. After doing this a number of times, the dog's mouth would water at the sound of the bell even though food did not follow.

In his experiments, Pavlov dealt with a behavior that is biologically preprogrammed within a dog through genetic inheritance—the salivation reflex. The reflex is an involuntary and unlearned response that is automatically activated by a given stimulus: the presence of food in the animal's mouth. By pairing the sound of the bell with food, Pavlov established a new relationship or connection between a stimulus (the sound of the bell) and a response (salivation) that previously had not existed. This phenomenon is called **classical conditioning**—a process of stimulus substitution in which a new, previously neutral stimulus is substituted for the stimulus that naturally elicits a response. Two illustrations might be helpful: Consider a bright student who develops intense nausea associated with fear when confronted with a test situation. As a child, this student had a teacher who denied recess to youngsters who did poorly on tests and assigned them extra work. Or consider the case of a boy of small size and slender build who develops anxiety about physical education classes after being compelled to compete against bigger and stronger children and knowing he was the likely target of bullies in the class. Perhaps you have opened a cupboard to feed your pet (a stimulus), and your pet runs immediately into the room (response).

Classical conditioning depends on the prior existence of a reflex that can occur in the service of a new stimulus; in other words, you already have some reflex you can work with. But the conditioning of reflexes does not take us very far, because we usually lack some preexisting unconditioned stimulus with which we can link a new stimulus. So psychologists have searched for alternative mechanisms. One of these mechanisms is probably familiar to you if you have seen animals perform tricks. When dolphins perform acrobatic jumps, they are always rewarded with food immediately afterward. In this procedure the dolphin is made to *enact* the behavior and then is rewarded with fish; the food *follows* the response, or the trick, and reinforces that particular behavior. When teaching a dolphin to do tricks, trainers employ **operant conditioning**—a type of learning in which the consequences of a behavior alter the strength of that behavior. *Operants* are behaviors that are susceptible to control by changing the effects that follow them; they are responses that "operate" or act on the environment and generate consequences. So when a dolphin engages in behavior that produces food, the behavior is strengthened by this consequence and therefore is more likely to recur in the future (in contrast to classical conditioning, where the food produces the behavior) (see Figure 2.3).

To summarize, classical conditioning derives from preexisting reflexes; operant conditioning does not. In classical conditioning a stimulus is said to elicit the response, whereas in operant conditioning the response is emitted. In classical conditioning antecedents determine the response probability; in operant conditioning it is determined by *consequences.*

We owe much to the earlier work of behaviorist John Watson (1878–1958), who said that people do not go through distinct stages but do go through a continuous process of behavior changes due to responses to environmental influences (external stimuli). Later, B. F. Skinner (1904–1990), at Harvard University, promoted our understanding of operant conditioning, especially the role of *rewards* and *punishments.* During the 1950s and 1960s no U.S. psychologist enjoyed greater prominence or commanded greater influence than did Skinner. Among the concepts popularized by Skinner is that of **reinforcement**—the process whereby one event strengthens the probability of another event's occurring. Skinner showed that much of life is structured by arranging reinforcing consequences, or "payoffs." For instance, businesses reward appropriate employee work behaviors with wages, commissions, and bonuses; and teachers use a variety of positive praise and rewards to motivate students who are struggling to learn a more difficult concept. Also, psychotherapists lead clients to set goals to reduce ineffective behaviors or increase effective behaviors by having clients select their own rewards that are reinforcers.

Many of the principles of learning have found a use in **behavior modification.** This approach applies learning theory and experimental psychology to the problem of altering maladaptive behavior. According to behaviorists, pathological behavior is acquired just as normal behavior is acquired—through the process of learning. They claim that the simplest technique for eliminating an *unwanted* behavior is usually to stop reinforcing it. Interestingly enough, by attending to a child's inappropriate behavior (e.g., by scolding), we can reinforce exactly what we want to diminish. The next time you are in a grocery store, observe how a parent reacts when his or her child wants a package of candy at the checkout counter. The parent might start out by saying no, then give in to the child's demand to avoid a commotion. Would you care to guess what is going to happen the next time that same child comes to the grocery store checkout line? (Remember, the candy is the reinforcer.)

But behavior modification can also involve more deliberate intervention in the form of rewards or punishments. Rewards, as reinforcers, normally are selected by the individual whose behavior is to be changed. Behavior modification has helped obese people lose weight and has helped people overcome *phobias,* such as fears of high places, taking tests, sexual inadequacy, closed-in spaces, speaking before an audience, and many others.

Our understanding of conditioning has undergone major transformations over the past three decades (Chiesa, 1992; Rosales-Ruiz & Baer, 1997). Psychologists no lon-

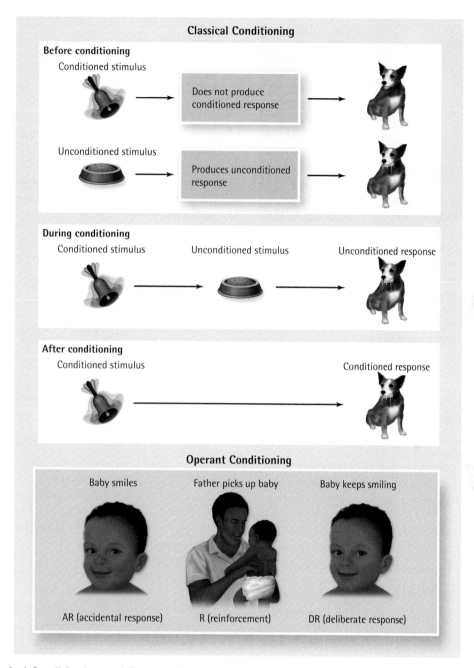

FIGURE 2.3 Classical Conditioning and Operant Conditioning
Operant Conditioning illustrations: From Diane E. Papalia, Sally W. Olds, and Ruth D. Feldman, *Human Development*, 7th edition. Copyright © 1998 by The McGraw-Hill Companies, Inc. Reprinted with permission of The McGraw-Hill Companies, Inc.

ger view conditioning as a simple, mechanical process involving the association of two events that happen to occur rather closely in time. Organisms do not pair events in a vacuum. The environmental context—the overshadowing of some stimuli, the blocking of others, and the highlighting of still others—is critically important. As seen from a cognitive learning perspective, organisms learn only when events violate their expectations (Williams, LoLordo, & Overmier, 1992). Over time, organisms build an image of the external world and continually compare this image with reality, selectively associating the most informative or predictive stimuli with certain events.

For conditioning to occur, a stimulus must tell the organism something useful about events in the world that the organism does not already know. For example, suppose you retrieve a baseball from a bed of poison ivy. A few hours later, your skin becomes red and itchy, and tiny blisters develop. You are unlikely to link the two events. But should a physician, friend, or coworker point out to you that you are allergic to poison ivy, you grasp the relationship between the blisters and the offending plant. You then take care to avoid contact with poison ivy in the future. You have learned!

B. F. Skinner In the 20 years following World War II, B. F. Skinner (above left) was the dominant figure in American psychology. His experimental work with pigeons pioneered many facets of behavioral theory. As a strict behaviorist, Skinner did not concern himself with what goes on inside the organism. Instead, he stressed the significance that learning processes (environmental forces) play in an organism's acquisition of various behaviors. His theories are prevalent in the educational and therapeutic communities today.

Questions

Consider the growing problem of the eating disorder anorexia nervosa, which occurs mainly in younger people. Using the terminology of a behavioral psychologist, how would you explain the development of this condition? Using behavioral principles described in the preceding section, what would you propose as a plan to reduce this harmful behavior?

Humanistic Theory

In the past 40 years or so, a "third force" in psychology has arisen in reaction to the established traditions of psychoanalysis and behaviorism. Commonly termed **humanistic psychology,** it maintains that humans are different from all other organisms in that they actively intervene in the course of events to control their destinies and shape the world around them. Humanistic psychologists, such as Abraham Maslow (1968, 1970) and Carl R. Rogers (1970), share a common concern with maximizing the human potential for self-direction and freedom of choice. They take a **holistic approach,** one that views the human condition in its totality and each person as more than a collection of physical, social and psychological components (Schneider, Bugental, & Pierson, 2002).

One of the key concepts advanced by Maslow is the **hierarchy of needs,** depicted in Figure 2.4. Maslow felt that human beings have certain basic needs that they must meet before they can go on to fulfill their other developmental needs. At the bottom of Maslow's pyramid are fundamental requirements to satisfy physiological needs (including needs for food, water, and sex) and safety needs. Next, Maslow identified a set of psychological needs centering on belongingness (love) needs and self-esteem needs. At the top of the pyramid, he placed the need to realize one's unique potential to the fullest in a process he termed **self-actualization.** To Maslow, such people as Abraham Lincoln, Albert Einstein, Walt Whitman, Eleanor Roosevelt, Reverend Martin Luther King, Reverend Billy Graham, and Dr. Maya Angelou are good examples of self-actualizers. From their lives he constructed what he believed to be a composite picture of self-actualized persons (Maslow, 1970). They

- Have a firm perception of reality.
- Accept themselves, others, and the world for what they are.
- Often are spontaneous in thought and behavior.
- Are problem-centered rather than self-centered.
- Have an air of detachment and a need for privacy.
- Are autonomous and independent.
- Resist mechanical and stereotyped social behaviors, although they are not deliberately or flamboyantly unconventional.
- Are sympathetic to the condition of other human beings and seek to promote the common welfare.
- Establish deep and meaningful relationships with a few people rather than superficial bonds with a great many people.
- Have a democratic world perspective.
- Transcend their environment rather than merely cope with it.
- Have a considerable fund of creativeness.
- Are susceptible to peak experiences marked by rapturous feelings of excitement, insight, and happiness.

Maslow and other humanistic psychologists argue that scientific inquiry should be directed toward helping people achieve freedom, hope, self-fulfillment, and strong identities. The goal of humanistic therapy is to help a person become more self-actualized—that is, to guide the client to self-directed change, building self-esteem along the way (in contrast to psychoanalysis and behavior modification, which are directed more by the therapist). However, many other psychologists are skeptical about their humanistic colleagues. Indeed, important differences characterize their intellectual style (Kimble, 1984). Psychoanalytic and behavioral psychologists see increasing the storehouse of scientific knowledge as their primary task, whereas humanists primarily focus on improving the human condition. Moreover, the former view behavior as determined by underlying

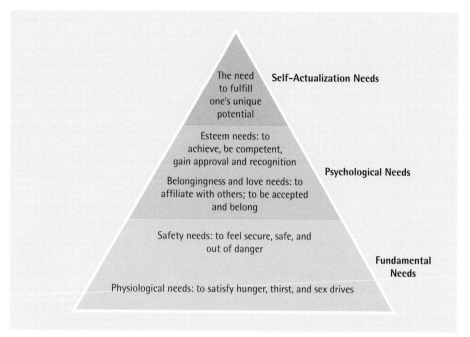

Figure 2.4 Maslow's Hierarchy of Human Needs According to the humanistic psychologists Abraham Maslow and Carl Rogers, fundamental needs must be satisfied before an individual is free to progress to psychological needs, which in turn must be met before the person can realize self-actualization needs.
Source: From Maslow/Frager, *Motivation and Personality*, 3/e, © 1987. Adapted by permission of Pearson Education, Inc., Upper Saddle River, New Jersey.

laws that can be revealed by using the scientific method. Many humanistic psychologists assert that there is nothing lawful about human behavior except perhaps at the level of statistical averages; they investigate behavior by relying on intuition and insight. Additionally, critics charge that humanistic psychology turns people inward, encouraging an intense concern with the self, breeding a narcissistic outlook, one that says that if each of us works on becoming more fully human ourselves, then social ills such as racism, homelessness, hunger, and militarism will flourish.

Questions

What is the primary task of a humanistic psychologist? How might such a psychologist guide someone to change unwanted behavior?

Cognitive Theory

In its early formulations, behaviorism regarded human life as if it were a "black box." Behaviorism's proponents viewed input or stimuli as entering the "box" at one end and coming out the other end as output or responses. They had little concern about what was inside. But over the past 50 years, psychologists have become increasingly

interested in what goes on inside the box. They term these internal factors **cognition**—acts or processes of knowing. **Cognitive theory** takes issue with a number of behaviorist tenets. Cognition involves how we go about representing, organizing, treating, and transforming information as we devise our behavior. It encompasses such phenomena as sensation, perception, imagery, retention, recall, problem solving, reasoning, and thinking.

Cognitive psychologists are especially interested in the cognitive structures and processes that allow a person to mentally represent events that transpire in the environment. The initial impetus to the study of cognition in the United States came from the work of a Swiss developmental psychologist, Jean Piaget (1896–1980).

Jean Piaget: Cognitive Stages in Development

Like Freud, Piaget is recognized as a giant of twentieth-century psychology (Beilin, 1992). Anyone who studies Freud and Piaget will never again see children in quite the same way. Whereas Freud was primarily concerned with *personality development*, Piaget concentrated on changes that occur in the child's *mode of thought*. Central to Piaget's work are the **cognitive stages** in development—sequential periods in the growth or maturing of an individual's ability to think—to gain knowledge, self-awareness, and awareness of the environment.

Adjustment as Process When Piaget began to work with children in the early 1920s, little was known about the process by which thinking develops. To the extent that they considered the matter at all, most psychologists assumed that children reason in essentially the same way as adults. Piaget soon challenged this view. He insisted that the thought of infants and children is not a miniature version of adult thought; it is qualitatively distinct. As children grow up, the form of their thought changes. When they say that their shadow follows them about when they go for a walk or that dreams come through the window, they are not being illogical. Rather, they are operating from a mental framework different from that of adults.

Piaget depicted children as engaged in a continual interaction with their environment. They act on, transform, and modify the world in which they live. In turn, they are shaped and altered by the consequences of their own actions. New experiences interact with an existing structure or mode of thought, thereby altering this structure and making it more adequate. This modified structure in turn influences the child's new perceptions. These new perceptions are then incorporated into a more complex structure. In this fashion, experience modifies structure and structure modifies experience. Hence, Piaget viewed the individual and the environment as engaged in continuing interaction. This interaction leads to new perceptions of the world and new organizations of knowledge (Beilin, 1990, 1992; Brown, 1996).

Basically, Piaget saw development as **adaptation.** Beginning with the simple reflexes they have at birth, children gradually modify their repertoire of behaviors to meet environmental demands. By interacting with their environment during play and other activities, children construct a series of *schemas*—concepts or models—for coping with their world. In Piaget's theory, **schemas** are cognitive structures that people evolve for dealing with specific kinds of situations in their environment. Thus, as portrayed by Piaget, children's thoughts reflect not so much the bits of information that they acquire but the schemas or mental frameworks by which they interpret information from the environment.

As Piaget viewed *adaptation,* it involves two processes: assimilation and accommodation. **Assimilation** is the process of taking in new information and interpreting it so that it conforms to a currently held model of the world. Piaget said that children typically stretch a schema as far as possible to fit new observations. But life periodically confronts them with the inescapable fact that some of their observations simply do not fit their current schemas. Then, *disequilibrium* or imbalance occurs. As a result, children are compelled to reorganize their view of the world to fit new experience. In effect, they are required to invent increasingly better schemas or theories about the world as they grow up. **Accommodation** is the process of changing one's schema to make it better match the world of reality. Unlike assimilation, in which new experiences are fit into existing conceptions of the world, accommodation involves changing a conception to make better sense of the world. To exemplify these concepts, imagine a child who understands that some animals, called fish, live in the ocean (this is *assimilation*). Yet on viewing whales leaping out of the ocean during a whale watch, he discovers that whales are not fish but mammals that need to breathe air. The child makes an *accommodation* in his understanding of the animals that live in the ocean.

A balance between the processes of accommodation and assimilation is **equilibrium.** When in equilibrium, the child assimilates new experiences in terms of the models she or he arrived at through accommodation. But equilibrium eventually gives way again to the process of accommodation and the creation of new schemes or models. Thus, as viewed by Piaget, cognitive development is marked by alternating states of *equilibrium* and *disequilibrium.* Each stage consists of particular sets of schemes that are in a relative stage of equilibrium at some point in a child's development.

In one study, Piaget and other researchers asked children whether they had ever had a bad dream. One 4-year-old said that she had dreamed about a giant and explained, "Yes, I was scared, my tummy was shaking and I cried and told my mommy about the giant." When asked, "Was it a real giant or was it just pretend?" she responded, "It was really there but it left when I woke up. I saw its footprint on the floor" (Kohlberg & Gilligan, 1971, p. 1057).

Jean Piaget at Work Piaget spent more than 50 years observing children in informal settings, and he developed a stage theory of cognitive development. His work convinced him that a child's mind is not a miniature model of the adult's. We often overlook this fact when attempting to teach children by using adult logic.

According to Piaget, this child's response is not to be dismissed as the product of wild imagination. Viewed from the perspective of her current schema, the happenings in dreams are real. As the child matures, she will have new experiences that will cause her to question the schema. She might observe, for instance, that there is not really a footprint on the floor. This assimilation of new information will result in disequilibrium. Through accommodation, she will then change her schema to make it a better fit with reality. She will recognize that dreams are not real events. She will then formulate a new schema that will establish a new equilibrium. In this new schema, a child her age will typically depict dreams as imaginary happenings. She will still believe, however, that her dreams can be seen by other people.

The process of accommodation continues through additional steps of the same sort. Soon after realizing that dreams are not real, the child comes to recognize that they cannot be seen by others. In the next step the child conceives of dreams as internal, but nevertheless material, events. Finally, somewhere between 6 and 8 years of age, the child becomes aware that dreams are thoughts that take place within her mind.

Characteristics of Piaget's Cognitive Stages Piaget contended that biological growth combines with children's interaction with their environment to take them through a series of separate, age-related stages. The stage concept implies that the course of development is divided into steplike levels. Clear-cut changes in behavior occur as children advance up the developmental staircase, with no skipping of stages allowed. Although teaching and experience can speed up or slow down development, Piaget believed that neither can change the basic order of the stages (Piaget, 1970). Piaget distinguished four stages in the development of cognition or intelligence. They are

Table 2.2 Piaget's Stages of Cognitive Development

Developmental Stage	Major Cognitive Capabilities	Example
Sensorimotor stage (birth to 2 years)	Infants discover the relationships between sensations and motor behavior.	They learn that their hands are part of themselves whereas a ball is not.
	Children master the *principle of object permanence.*	Piaget observed that when a baby of 4 or 5 months is playing with a ball and the ball rolls out of sight behind another toy, the child does not look for it even though it remains within reach. Piaget contended that infants do not realize that objects have an independent existence. Around the age of 8 months, the child grasps the fact of object constancy and will search for toys that disappear from view.
Preoperational stage (2 to 7 years)	Children develop the capacity to employ *symbols,* particularly language.	Children use symbols to portray the external world internally—for instance, to talk about a ball and form a mental image of it.
	Egocentrism prevails.	Children of 4 and 5 years consider their own point of view to be the only possible one. They are not yet capable of putting themselves in another's place. A 5-year-old who is asked why it snows will answer by saying, "So children can play in it."
Stage of concrete operations (7 to 11 years)	Children show the beginning of rational activity. They are able to "conserve" mass, weight, number, length, area, and volume.	Youngsters come to master various logical operations, including arithmetic, class and set relationships, measurement, and conceptions of hierarchical structures. Before this stage children do not appreciate that a ball of clay can change to a sausage shape and still be the same amount of clay.
	Children gain the ability to "conserve" quantity.	Before this stage, children cannot understand that when water is poured out of a full glass into a wider glass that the water fills only halfway, the amount of water remains unchanged, Instead, children "concentrate" on only one aspect of reality at a time. They see that the second glass is half empty and conclude that there is less water in it. Now children come to understand that the quantity of water remains the same.
Stage of formal operations (11 years and older)	Youths acquire a greater ability to deal with abstractions.	When younger children are confronted with the problem, "If coal is white, snow is _____," they insist that coal is black. Adolescents, however, respond that snow is black.
	Youths can engage in scientific thought.	At this stage, youths can discuss Newtonian principles about the behavior of spherical objects.

summarized in Table 2.2 and will be treated in greater detail in later chapters concerned with cognitive growth.

Appraisal of Piaget's Work   U.S. scientists largely ignored Piaget's discoveries until about 1960. Today, however, the study of cognitive factors in development is of central interest to U.S. psychologists. For the most part, psychologists credit Piaget with drawing their attention to the possibility that an unsuspected order might underlie some aspects of children's intellectual development (Levin & Druyan, 1993). Nonetheless, many early American followers of Piaget, such as John H. Flavell, have become disenchanted with the Piagetian model. Flavell (1992) says that the notion of stages implies long periods of stability, followed by abrupt change. But he argues that development does not happen this way. The most important changes happen gradually, over months and even years. In short, human cognitive development is too varied in its mechanisms, routes, and rates to be accurately portrayed by an inflexible stage theory. According to Flavell, then, growing up is much less predictable than Piaget thought.

A mounting body of evidence also suggests that Piaget underestimated the cognitive capabilities of infants and young children. For instance, the kinds of memory Piaget found in 18-month-old babies researchers now find in babies at 6 months of age. Of course, Piaget did not have many of the methods now available to scholars, including equipment and procedures to measure the brain's electrical activity. Researchers investigated the role of social feedback (adult responses) to infants' noncrying vocalizations to determine its influence on vocal learning (Goldstein & West, 1999). They concluded that social feedback plays an important role in the development of communication skills by giving social significance to the infants' vocalizations. The operational thinking capabilities of children from 2 to 7 years of age also are considerably greater than Piaget recognized (Novak & Gowin, 1989).

Research on other cultures has revealed both striking similarities and marked differences in children's performance on various cognitive tasks. Certain aspects of cognitive development among children in these cultures seem to differ from particular assumptions of Piagetian theory (Chieh, 2000; Chieh & Nuttall, 1999; Maynard & Greenfield, 2003). We should remember that no theory—particularly one that offers such a comprehensive explanation of development—can be expected to withstand the tests of further investigation without undergoing some criticism (Beilin, 1990; Brown, 1996).

It is too soon to determine the ultimate impact Piaget's theory will have on our understanding of cognitive development. Yet we must recognize that we would not know as much as we do about children's intellectual development without Piaget's monumental contributions. He noted many ways in which children seem to differ from adults, and he shed light on how adults acquire fundamental concepts such as the concepts of

space, time, morality, and causality (Sugarman, 1987). Contemporary researchers have attempted to integrate aspects of Piaget's theory into cognitive learning and information-processing theories, which are discussed in the next section (Brown, 1996; Demtrious, 1988).

> **Questions**
>
> Piaget is often considered to be one of the great "stage" theorists of developmental psychology. In your own words, how would you explain his stage theory of cognitive development? Why have his research findings been criticized recently?

Cognitive Learning

Piaget's work gave a major impetus to cognitive psychology and to research into the part played by inner mental activity in human behavior (Sperry, 1993). Cognitive psychologists view the contents of conscious experience and their subjective qualities as dynamic, emergent properties of *brain activity* (inseparably interfused with and tied to the brain's cellular and biochemical properties and processes). Reversing classical behavioral notions, cognitive theorists affirm that the world we live in is driven not solely by mindless physical forces but also by subjective human attitudes, values, and aims.

These psychologists are finding, for instance, that mental schemes—often called "scripts" or "frames"—function as selective mechanisms that influence the information individuals attend to, how they structure it, how much importance they attach to it, and what they then do with it (Markus, 1977; VanderZanden, 1987). And as we noted earlier in the chapter, psychologists are also finding that learning consists of more than merely bringing two events together. People are not simply acted upon by external stimuli. They actively engage their environment, evaluate different stimuli, and devise their actions accordingly.

Classic behavioral theory also fails to explain many changes in our behavior that result from interactions with people in a social context. Indeed, if we learned solely by direct experience—by the reward or punishment for our actions—most of us would not survive to adulthood. If, for example, we depended on direct experience to learn how to cross the street, most of us would already be traffic fatalities. Similarly, we probably could not develop skill in playing baseball, driving a car, solving mathematical problems, cooking meals, or even brushing our teeth if we were restricted to learning through direct reinforcement. We can avoid tedious, costly, trial-and-error experimentation by imitating the behavior of socially competent models. By watching other people, we learn new responses without first having had the opportunity to make the responses ourselves. This process is termed **cognitive learning.** (It is also termed *observational learning, social learn-*

ing, and *social modeling.*) The approach is represented by the work of theorists such as Albert Bandura (1977, 1986, 1989a), Walter Mischel (1973), and Ted L. Rosenthal and Barry J. Zimmerman (1978).

The cognitive learning theory of Bandura (1989a, 1989b) relies heavily on notions of information-processing theory, which holds that individuals perform a series of discrete mental operations on incoming information and then mentally store the conclusions drawn from the process (Mayer, 1996). Bandura's theory emphasizes how children and adults mentally operate on their social experiences and how these mental operations in turn influence their behavior. People abstract and integrate information that they encounter in the course of their social experiences, including their exposure to models, verbal discussions, and encounters with discipline.

By means of this abstraction and integration, individuals mentally represent their environments and themselves, particularly in terms of the expectations they hold for the outcomes of their behavior and the perceptions they evolve of the actual effectiveness of their actions. Bandura portrayed people not as weather vanes who constantly shift their behavior in accordance with momentary influences but rather as stewards of values, social standards, and commitments. That is, individuals judge and regulate their own behavior. They evolve beliefs about their own specific abilities and characteristics (what Bandura called "self-efficacy") and then use these beliefs in fashioning what they say and do. Moreover, children and adults not only respond to environments, they actively seek out all sorts of environments (Grusec, 1992).

Cognitive learning theorists say that our capacity to use symbols gives us a powerful way to comprehend and deal with our environment. Language and imagery allow us to represent events, analyze our conscious experience, communicate with others, plan, create, imagine, and engage in foresightful action. Symbols are the foundation of reflective thought and enable us to solve problems without first having to enact all the various solutions. Indeed, stimuli and reinforcements exert little impact on our behavior unless we first represent them mentally (Bandura, 1977; Rosenthal & Zimmerman, 1978).

Cognitive theorists reject the portrayal of children as "blank slates" who passively and unselectively imitate whatever the environment presents to them. Rather, they portray children as active, constructive thinkers and learners. Children's cognitive structures and processing strategies lead them to select meaningful information from an array of sensory input and to mentally represent and transform this information. Children actively seek knowledge, develop their own theories about the world around them, and continually subject these theories to knowledge-extending and knowledge-refining tests. So, to a considerable degree, children manufacture their own development as they interact with the environment (Flavell, 1992).

Cognitive learning theories have been criticized for their lack of attention to significant developmental changes that can impact behavior. Bandura attempted to respond to this matter in his later theoretical writings, but he and his associates undertook little accompanying research that specifically addressed developmental issues. Consequently, approaches that emphasize more clearly age-related changes in development have moved to the forefront of interest for many developmental psychologists (Grusec, 1992).

> **Questions**
>
> What are the significant features of cognitive learning theories? Who are some of the prominent theorists associated with these approaches?

Social Modeling Often Influences Child Behavior How little we may be aware that children imitate our behaviors.

Ecological Theory

As mentioned in Chapter 1, Urie Bronfenbrenner (1917–2005), proposes an **ecological theory** that centers on the relationship between the developing individual and the changing environmental systems. These interactions cannot be captured entirely in the laboratory, for, as Bronfenbrenner (1979, p. 27) points out, "Development never takes place in a vacuum; it is always embedded and expressed through behavior in a particular environment." One cannot grasp human development by simply observing and measuring individuals' behavior in clinical settings that are divorced from their relevant social, physical, and cultural environments. Of course, change must occur over time, and so Bronfenbrenner added the concept of the chronosystem to capture the dynamics of development with and across other systems. The **chronosystem** refers to changes within the individual and changes in the environment across time, as well as the relationship between the two processes. For example, if a divorce occurs in a child's family during the preschool period, it will have a different impact than if the child is an adolescent or young adult.

Bronfenbrenner's ideas have been influenced by Freud, Piaget, Vygotsky, and, most importantly, Kurt Lewin. According to Lewin's field theory, the "dialogue" between the person and the environment can be expressed in the formula $B = f(PE)$: *Behavior* is determined by the interaction between the *Person* and the *Environment*. Bronfenbrenner modified the formula to reflect the distinction between behavior and development so that his formula reads $D = f(PE)$: *Development* is the result of the interaction between the *Person* and the *Environment*. By substituting development for behavior in the equation, he highlights the importance of time and, with that, change and the significance of the longitudinal study as essential to understanding the human condition.

In proposing the ecological model as a research tool, Bronfenbrenner wants to move away from the traditional focus that sees either the environment *(E)* or the person *(P)*—instead of the relationship between them—as the most important aspect of development. Furthermore, he wants to focus on the process of development rather than concentrate on isolated variables at a single point in time. Think of someone you know who either dropped out of school or considered dropping out. Bronfenbrenner suggests that an approach focusing solely on factors such as the yearly income of the family, intellectual ability, or ethnicity to explain the student's disengagement from school will miss most of the information relevant to this particular student's situation. Instead of trying to match categories or labels with certain outcomes, researchers must look at the relationships among variables in different environments. If you were to read an article in a research journal that sought to explain your friend's "dropping out" primarily in terms of distinct categories to which she or he belonged, you would probably be dissatisfied with the explanation, knowing that the reasons were much more complex or historical than those offered by the researcher.

Finally, Bronfenbrenner's theory is important as a way of capturing how people make sense of their

circumstances and how their understanding, in turn, influences their behavior. You have probably been in a situation where a number of people reacted differently to the same experience. How each person defined that situation—based on his or her personal history, expectations, feelings, and so forth—determined how he or she behaved. It is important to keep in mind while studying development not only that different people see things differently, but that the same person—as she or he develops cognitively, physically, and psychosocially—will see the same phenomenon differently throughout the life span. For example, a person will probably have very different reactions to a film about war if the same film is seen both before and after the person has fought in a real war.

Question

Every morning when she rises, a woman from the Kiribati Islands in the Pacific pulls one hair from her head, places it in a container, and then goes out to check her fish trap. You need to come up with a reason that explains why she does this. You have two possible ways to collect data and arrive at an understanding of why she does this. You do not speak the language, but you can use an interpreter for one day, or you can observe her for one week without being able to talk to her. Which of the previous theories, in your opinion, comes closest to explaining her behavior? Explain your decision.

Sociocultural Theory

Lev Vygotsky, a Russian psychologist who is credited with creating one of the outstanding schools of Soviet psychology, is known for his **sociocultural theory** of psychological development. The major theses of his work are as follows:

- Development of individuals occurs during the early formative years and has a specifically historical character, content, and form; in other words, development will be different depending on when and where you grow up.
- Development takes place during changes in a person's social situation or during changes in what activities the person undertakes.
- Activities are usually done in groups during social interaction.
- Individuals observe an activity and then internalize the basic form of that activity.
- Systems of signs and symbols (like language) must be available to be able to internalize activities.
- Individuals assimilate the values of a particular culture by interacting with other people in that culture.

It is important to note that Vygotsky assumes that the development of the individual is determined by the *activity of groups.* The child will interact with another person, assimilate the social aspects of the activity, and take that information and internalize it. In this way social values become personal values (Vygotsky, 1978).

Consequently, according to Vygotsky, to understand the mind we must first understand how the functions of the mind are shaped by psychological processes, especially language. Vygotsky's theory provides a developmental perspective on how such mental functions as thinking, reasoning, and remembering are facilitated through *language* and how such functions are anchored in the child's *interpersonal relationships* (Tappan, 1997). The child, according to Vygotsky, will observe something happening between others and then will be able to take that observation and mentally incorporate it. One of Vygotsky's examples is the way children use language.

First, a child will be told "Say please and thank you" by his or her parents. The child will also see people saying "Please" and "Thank you" to each other. Then the child will begin to say these words aloud. By saying "Please" and "Thank you" aloud, the child is internalizing the words and the concepts they stand for in a social setting. Only after assimilating the words' meanings can the child individually start to act in a polite manner. It follows that development is always a social process for Vygotsky, and child–adult interaction plays an important role (Berk & Winsler, 1995). So it should come as no surprise that for Vygotsky, the way to understand development is to observe the individual in a social activity. (See the *More Information You Can Use* box below, "Vygotsky's Insights: Interdependence as a Model of Human Development.")

More Information You Can Use

Vygotsky's Insights: Interdependence as a Model of Human Development

It is quite absurd to think of human development as an individual activity. Yet if one examines the preferred and actual practices of many parents in the United States, it becomes apparent that they are stressing individualism and independence as soon as the child is born. Common wisdom and practice is to place the infant, soon after birth, in a separate room to encourage independence. Parents also reinforce a preference for objects rather than people to be used as means of comforting in times of distress. Children are supplied and rely on "blankies," pacifiers, and stuffed animals rather than parents or other people to console them when they are upset or conflicted. Parents and children become adversaries over sleeping arrangements as children get older. The "terrible twos" revolve around the young child's eventual demand for independence. Furthermore, children are expected and, at times, encouraged to compete with other children both inside and outside the family, in school, and finally with other adults in the workplace.

Child-rearing practices in many other cultures stress *interdependence,* sometimes called *collectivism,* over independence or *individualism,* with the focus on ties to family. Children are socialized to think of themselves as being part of a group or community, rather than an individual at odds with those in the vicinity. For example, in the Pacific Island nation of Kiribati, an infant is in constant contact with some member of the extended family during the first year of life—sleeping with, eating with, and tagging along to work with a family member. These infants are socially involved in all of the day-to-day activities of the mother and father.

Three generations of a family will gather around the baby to sing traditional songs while the infant is initiated into the social and cultural rhythms of the community. Rather than battling parents over issues of independence, the caregivers support the needs of the infant as they carry out the routine activities—there is no battle of the wills.

This view of interdependence is an alternative to the view generally held in the United States—which prizes independence. But interdependence is natural to human activity and offers different trajectories for development and also points to one of the fundamental aspects of Vygotsky's view regarding development: "All of the higher [psychological] functions originate as relations between human individuals" (1978).

Scenario
Later in this text we describe an actual situation that happened in an elementary school in Southern California, where Mexican-American mothers were coming to school to literally spoon feed the free breakfast to their elementary-aged children and to partake of the free breakfast themselves each morning. You recognize that these parents are approaching parenting from an *interdependence* perspective. Hypothetically, as a future elementary teacher or school principal or superintendent, how would you approach this sensitive situation, since the mothers are not eligible for this program, and the teachers want the children to learn to be more responsible and *independent*?

Source: Adapted from Barbara Rogoff. (1990). *Apprenticeship in thinking.* Oxford: Oxford University Press.

Questions

Which prominent theorist proposed sociocultural theory? How does his theory explain how a child learns using such functions as thinking, reasoning, and remembering?

Controversies

Each theory has its proponents and its critics. Yet the theories are not mutually exclusive; we need not accept one and reject the others. As we pointed out at the beginning of this chapter, theories are simply tools—mental constructs that allow us to visualize (that is, to describe and analyze) something. Any theory limits the viewer's experience, presenting a tunnel perspective. But a good theory also extends the horizon of what is seen, functioning like a pair of binoculars. It provides rules of inference through which new relationships can be discovered and suggestions as to how the scope of a theory can be expanded. (See Table 2.3.)

Furthermore, different tasks call for different theories. For instance, behavioral theory helps us understand why U.S. children typically learn English and Russian children learn Russian. At the same time ethological theory, one of the evolutionary adaptation theories, directs our attention to ways in which the human organism is neurally prewired for certain activities, so that, in interaction with an appropriate environment, young children typically find that their acquisition of language comes rather "naturally"—a type of *easy learning*. Simultaneously, psychoanalytic theory alerts us to personality differences and to differing child-rearing practices that influence a child's

learning to talk. Cognitive theory encourages us to consider the stages of development and the mental processes involved in the acquisition of language. Sociocultural theory reminds us of the range of influences that impact individual development—from individual attributes and family characteristics to community and cultural influences. The distinction between mechanistic and organismic models helps to clarify some of these theories.

Mechanistic and Organismic Models

Some psychologists attempt to classify developmental theories in terms of two basic categories: a mechanistic worldview and an organismic worldview (see Table 2.4).

The **mechanistic model** represents the universe as a machine composed of elementary particles in motion. All phenomena, no matter how complex, are viewed as ultimately reducible to these fundamental units and their relationships. Each human being is regarded as a physical object, a kind of elaborate machine. Like other parts of the universal machine, the organism is inherently at rest. It is inherently passive and responds only when an external power source is applied. This view is the *reactive organism model.* In keeping with this worldview, human development is portrayed as a gradual, uninterrupted, chainlike sequence of events. Indeed, one can question whether a machine can be said to "develop"; it changes only when some external agent adds, subtracts, or alters the machine's parts (Sameroff & Cavanagh, 1979). Change cannot occur without influence from the environment. Individual differences are the central focus of mechanistic approaches. Behavioral learning theories fall within this tradition.

Table 2.3 Theories of Human Development

Theory	Theorist(s)	Description
Psychoanalytic theories	Sigmund Freud (psychosexual) Erik Erikson (psychosocial)	Focus on the importance of early experience in forming the personality and the role of unconscious motivation
Behavioral theories	John Watson B. F. Skinner Albert Bandura	Focus on the role that learning in the environment plays in inducing people to act the way they do
Humanistic theory	Abraham Maslow Carl R. Rogers	Focuses on maximizing human potential; states that humans try to control their destinies and shape the world
Cognitive theories (observational learning, social learning, social modeling)	Jean Piaget	Focus on the importance of mental capabilities and problem-solving skills that help people adapt and cope
Ecological theory	Kurt Lewin Urie Bronfenbrenner	Focuses on the interaction of the developing person and the changing environment
Sociocultural theory	Lev Vygotsky	Focuses on the interaction of the individual and others in social settings and how individuals learn cultural meanings

Table 2.4 Mechanistic and Organismic Paradigms

Characteristic	Mechanistic Paradigm	Organismic Paradigm
Metaphor	The machine	The organism
Focus	The parts	The whole
Source of motivation	Intrinsically passive	Intrinsically active
Nature of development	Gradual, uninterrupted adding, subtracting, or altering of parts (continuity)	Discrete, steplike levels or states (discontinuity)

In contrast, the **organismic model** focuses not on elementary particles but on the whole. The distinctive interrelations among the lower-level components are seen as imparting to the whole characteristics not found in the components alone. Hence, the whole differs in kind from its parts. The human being is seen as an organized configuration. The organism is inherently active—it is the source of its own acts rather than being activated by external forces. This view is the *active organism model.* Viewed from this perspective, human development is characterized by discrete, steplike levels or states. Humans are portrayed as developing by constantly restructuring themselves. The new structures that will be formed are determined by the interaction between the environment and the organism (Gottlieb, 1991). The stage theories of Freud, Erikson, and Piaget fall within the organismic tradition.

However, most psychologists prefer an **eclectic approach.** This perspective allows them to select and choose from the various theories and models those aspects that provide the best fit for the descriptive and analytical task at hand. Perhaps we can gain a better understanding and appreciation of these controversies by considering an illustration, continuity and discontinuity in development.

> **Question**
>
> Can you compare and contrast the major premise of mechanistic, organismic, and eclectic views of human development?

Continuity and Discontinuity in Development

Most psychologists agree that development involves orderly sequences of change that depend on growth and maturation as individuals interact with their environment. Other psychologists emphasize discontinuity in sequences of change. Those who support continuity say that development produces smooth, gradual, and incremental change. Those who stress continuity typically fall within the mechanistic camp. Those who accentuate discontinuity usually fall within the organismic camp.

The two different models of development can be clarified by considering two analogies. According to the *continuity model,* human development is analogous to the growth of a leaf. After a leaf sprouts from a seed, it grows by simply becoming larger. The change is gradual and uninterrupted. Psychologists who emphasize the part that learning plays in behavior tend to take this point of view. They see the learning process as lacking sharp developmental states between infancy and adulthood. Learning is cumulative, building on itself.

According to the *discontinuity model,* human development is analogous to the developmental changes that produce a butterfly. Once a caterpillar hatches from an egg, it feeds on vegetation. After a time it fastens itself to a twig and spins a cocoon within which the pupa develops. One day the pupal covering splits open and the butterfly emerges. Psychologists who adopt the discontinuity model see human development as similar to the process of insect metamorphosis. Each individual is seen as passing through a set sequence of stages in which change constitutes a difference of kind rather than merely of degree. Each stage is characterized by a distinct and unique state in ego formation, identity, or thought. The theories of Sigmund Freud, Erik Erikson, and Jean Piaget are of this sort.

How we view development depends in part on our vantage point. To return to our analogies, when we first observe a caterpillar and then a butterfly, we are struck by the dramatic qualitative change. But when we observe the developmental changes that occur within the cocoon, we have a different impression. We see that butterfly-like characteristics are gradually acquired, and consequently we are more likely to describe the process as continuous (Lewis & Starr, 1979). However, if we look at a seed and then a tree, we are impressed by the magnitude of the change that has occurred.

Increasingly, psychologists are less inclined to divide themselves into sharply opposing camps on the issue of continuity and discontinuity in development. They, too, recognize that much depends on one's vantage point and hence see both continuities and discontinuities across the life span (Colombo, 1993; Lewis, 1993). In sum, social and behavioral scientists increasingly have come to see development as residing in a relation between organism and environment—in a transaction or collaboration: People work with and affect their environment and, in turn, it works with and affects them.

Questions

How would you explain the continuity versus discontinuity models of human development over the life span? Which view do you think is more accurate? Why?

Nature Versus Nurture

Time and again it has been officially claimed that heredity-environment questions are dead, that they have been definitely answered for all time. Yet in one fashion or another, each generation resurrects them, thrashes them out once more, and then presumes once again to set them to permanent rest. For example, a prevailing question in contemporary U.S. society is why some of our children and adolescents are so violent. Is the child's tendency to be violent due to an inherited genetic flaw, or due to the type of home environment, or due to a combination of both factors? Some of the difficulties associated with the nature-nurture controversy stem from the fact that investigators often operate from different assumptions. Various schools of thought ask different questions and hence come up with different answers. How we phrase our questions structures the alternatives by which the questions are answered.

Scientists began by asking *which* factor, heredity or environment is responsible for a given trait, such as a mental disorder or a person's level of intelligence. Later, they sought to establish *how much* of the observed differences among people is due to differences in heredity and *how much* to differences in environment. Human intelligence is one trait which the study of genetics has yielded more information than any other. Researchers are eager to use data from the Human Genome Project to identify specific genes that are responsible for the hereditability of intelligence (Plomin & Spinath, 2004). And recently, some scientists have insisted that a more fruitful question is *how* specific hereditary and environmental factors *interact* to influence various characteristics (Anastasi, 1958; Colledge et al., 2002). Each of these questions leads to its own theories, interpretations, and methods of inquiry.

The "Which" Question   Most students can recall debating in a class the question "Which is more important, heredity or environment?" Yet most scientists today reject this formulation. They believe that phrasing the issue in terms of *heredity versus environment* has caused the scientific community, and society at large, untold difficulties. Counterposing heredity to environment is similar in some respects to debating whether sodium or chlorine is more important in ordinary table salt. The point is that we would not have salt if we did not have both sodium and chlorine (see Figure 2.5).

The "How Much" Question   As scientists recognized the inappropriateness of the "which" question, some of

them reformulated the issue. Granting that both heredity and environment are essential for the emergence of any characteristic, they asked, "*How much* of each is required to produce a given trait?" For example, they asked, "What percentage of a person's level of intelligence is attributable to heredity, and how much depends on environment?" The same question could be asked of a given mental disorder.

Scientists have traditionally sought answers to the "how much" question by measuring the resemblance among family members with respect to a particular trait (Segal, 1993). Botanists use similar procedures to discover the separate contributions of heredity and environment by taking cuttings from a single plant and then replanting the parts in different environments: one at sea level, another at an intermediate elevation, and still another in the alpine zone of a mountain range. Each cutting develops into a new plant under different environmental conditions. Because the cuttings are genetically identical, any observed *differences* in vigor, size, leaves, stems, and roots are directly traceable to differences in environment (Dobzhansky, 1962).

Such deliberate experimentation is not possible with humans. Nonetheless, nature occasionally provides us with the makings of a natural experiment. From time to time a fertilized egg, by some accident, gets split into two parts termed *identical* or *monozygotic twins*. Genetically, each is essentially a carbon copy of the other. The study of identical twins reared under different environmental conditions is the closest approach possible to the experiments with plant cuttings (see "The Minnesota Twin Project" later in this chapter).

In contrast to identical twins, *fraternal* or *dizygotic twins* come from two eggs fertilized by two different spermatozoa. They are simply siblings who happen to develop separately in the womb at the same time and are (usually) born at the same time. Important evidence can be obtained and comparisons can be made between identical twins reared apart and fraternal twins reared together. Many scientists believe that such comparisons reveal valuable information about the relative contributions that heredity and environment make to a particular trait or behavior (Boomsma, Busjahn, & Peltonen, 2002).

By studying children who were adopted at birth and reared by foster parents, one can compare some characteristic of the adopted children, such as IQ score or the presence of a particular mental or physical disorder, with that of their biological parents and their foster parents. In this fashion researchers attempt to weigh the relative influences of the genetic factor and the home environment.

The "How" Question   A number of scientists, such as the psychologist Anne Anastasi (1958), believe that the task of science is to discover how hereditary and environmental factors work together to produce behavior. They argue that the "how much" question, like the "which" question, is unproductive. The "how much" question

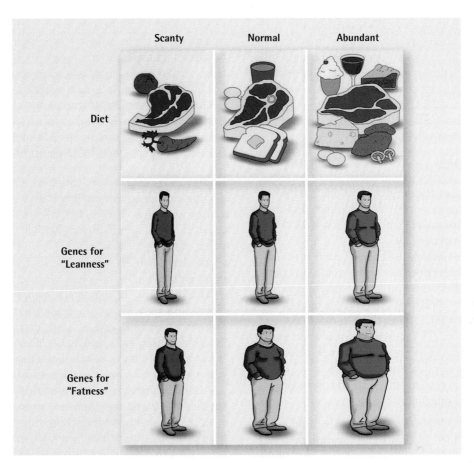

	Scanty	Normal	Abundant

Diet

Genes for "Leanness"

Genes for "Fatness"

FIGURE 2.5 Gene-Environment Interaction Obesity represents one of the most serious health issues, and it develops because of a mismatch between energy intake and expenditure that results from behavior (feeding behavior and time spent active) and physiology (resting metabolism and expenditure when active). Both traits are affected by environmental and genetic factors. A person who has a gene for "fatness" might actually weigh less than one with a gene for "leanness," if the former lives on a scanty diet and the latter on an abundant diet.

Source: From *Mankind Evolving: The Evolution of the Human Species* by Theodosius Dobzhansky. Copyright © 1962 by Yale University. Reprinted by permission of Yale University Press.

assumes that nature and nurture are related in such a way that the contribution of one is *added* to the contribution of the other. This produces a particular behavior.

Anastasi, among others (Lykken et al., 1992; Thelen, 1995), disputes this view. She argues that as applied to human life, neither heredity nor environment exists separately. They are always interconnected, continually interacting. Consequently, Anastasi says, it is a hopeless task to identify "which" of the two factors produces a particular behavior or to determine "how much" each contributes. However, Anastasi recognizes that the role played by hereditary factors is more central in some aspects of development than in others. She thus sets forth the notion of the **continuum of indirectness.** At one end of the continuum are the most direct contributions of heredity—such as physical characteristics like eye color and chromosomal disorders like Down syndrome. At the other end of the continuum are contributions of heredity that are quite indirect—such as social stereotypes members of a given society attach to various categories of skin color and hair texture.

Medawar (1977) also notes that we might not be able to attach exact percentages to the contributions of heredity and environment. Because heredity and environment interact in a relationship of varying dependence, what appears to be a hereditary contribution in one context can be seen as an environmental contribution in another context. An example is provided by *phenylketonuria (PKU),* a severe form of mental retardation that is transmitted genetically. PKU results from the inability of the body to metabolize *phenylalanine,* a common constituent of proteins in our diet necessary for growth. But if a child who has inherited a susceptibility to the disease is given a diet free of phenylalanine, there is no buildup of toxic materials, and the child's development is essentially normal. Hence, PKU can be viewed as entirely environmental in origin, because PKU shows up in the presence of phenylalanine but not in its absence.

Heredity and environment interact in complex ways. Genes influence the kinds of environment we seek, what we attend to, and how much we learn (Plomin & Daniels, 1987; Scarr, 1997). For instance, psychologists Sandra

Scarr and Kathleen McCartney (1983) contend that each stage in a child's psychological development is ushered in by an increment in the child's biological maturation. Only after the child is genetically receptive is the environment able to have any significant effect on her or his behavioral development. Scarr and McCartney believe that children's genetic predispositions tailor their environment in three ways—passively, evocatively, and actively:

- *Passive relationship:* Parents give their children both genes and an environment that are favorable (or unfavorable) to the development of a particular capability. For example, parents gifted in social skills are likely to provide their children with an enriched social environment.
- *Evocative relationship:* A child evokes particular responses from others because of the child's genetically influenced behavior. For instance, socially engaging children typically elicit from other people more social interaction than passive, sober children do.
- *Active relationship:* Children seek out environments that they find compatible with their temperament and genetic propensities. For example, sociable children search for playmates and even create imaginary playmates if real ones are not at hand.

In short, what children experience in any given environment is a function of genetic individuality and developmental status (Phillips et al., 2000; Scarr, 1997). Scientists, then, are increasingly able to apply rigorous measurements to some aspects of the old nature-nurture controversy. In particular, valuable new insights are coming from a rapidly growing field of study that undertakes to embrace, forge, and integrate insights from both psychology and genetics—behavioral genetics.

> **Questions**
>
> Historically, as scientists have studied the heredity-environment debate, what types of questions have they investigated? Where do contemporary researchers stand now?

Behavioral Genetics

Behavioral genetics focuses on individual differences and seeks answers to why individuals within a species exhibit different behaviors. There is much more acceptance in the field of psychology for the influence of genetics on individual difference (Plomin & Colledge, 2001). Interest in the hereditary aspects of behavior had been subdued for nearly half a century by both behaviorism and psychoanalytic theory. The renewed interest in biological factors is due partly to exciting new discoveries in microbiology and genetics (advancing technologies let us examine cell structures both microscopically and chemically) and partly to the failure of social scientists

to document a consistently strong relationship between measures of environmental experience and behavioral outcome. The pendulum seems to be swinging away from the environmentalists toward the side of the biologists. Indeed, some scholars worry that the pendulum is moving too rapidly toward a biological determinism that is as extreme as the earlier loyalty of some social and behavioral scientists to an environmental explanation of behavior (Kagan, 1994; McDonald, 1994).

Jerome Kagan: Timidity Studies   One area of recent investigation is extreme timidity ("shyness"). Jerome Kagan and his associates (Kagan, 1989; Kagan & Snidman, 1991) followed 41 children in longitudinal research for eight years, studying "behavioral inhibition." The researchers found that 10 to 15 percent of those studied seem to be born with a biological predisposition that makes them unusually fearful of unfamiliar people, events, or even objects like toys. These youngsters have intense physical responses to mental stress: Their dilated pupils, faster and more stable heart rates, and higher levels of salivary cortisol (a hormone found in saliva) indicate that their nervous system is accelerated by even mildly stressful conditions.

Other researchers have found that shy biological parents tend to have shy children—even when the youngsters are adopted by socially outgoing parents (Daniels & Plomin, 1985). In addition, shy boys are more likely than their peers to delay entry into marriage, parenthood, and stable careers; to attain less occupational achievement and stability; and—when late in establishing stable careers—to experience marital instability. Shy girls are more likely than their peers to follow a conventional pattern of marriage, childbearing, and homemaking (Caspi, Elder, & Bem, 1988). Although some children are inherently inhibited and "uptight," they can be helped, by good parenting, to cope with their shyness. In other words, a predisposition like that for timidity can be enhanced or reduced, but not eliminated, by nurturing child-rearing experiences. Kagan offers this additional bit of advice: "Look at whether the child is happy. Some shy kids are. And they often end up doing well in school . . . they become computer scientists, historians. We need these people, too" (quoted by Elias, 1989, p. 1D).

> **Question**
>
> Briefly, how would you summarize Kagan's research findings on timidity?

The Minnesota Twin Project   The results of an ongoing project at the University of Minnesota similarly suggest that genetic makeup has a marked impact on appearance, personality, health factors, and intelligence, (Bouchard et al., 1990; Lykken, Bouchard, McGue, & Tellegen, 2004). Researchers put 348 pairs of identical twins, including 44 pairs who were reared apart, through six days of extensive testing that included analysis of their blood, brain waves, intelligence, and allergies. All the twins took several personality tests, answering more than 15,000 questions on subjects ranging from personal interests and values to aggressiveness, aesthetic judgment, and television and reading habits.

Of 11 key personality traits or clusters of traits analyzed in the study, 7 revealed a stronger influence for hereditary factors than for child-rearing factors. The Minnesota researchers found that the cluster that rated highest for heritability was "social potency" (a tendency toward leadership or dominance); "social closeness" (the need for intimacy, comfort, and help) was rated lowest. Although they had not expected "traditionalism" (obedience to authority and strict discipline) to be more an inherited than an acquired trait, it is one of the traits with a strong genetic influence. The Minnesota researchers do not believe that a single gene is responsible for any one of the traits. Instead, each trait seems to be determined by a large number of genes in combination, so that the pattern of inheritance is complex—what is called **polygenic inheritance** (see Chapter 3).

Such findings do not mean that environmental factors are unimportant. It is not full-blown personality traits that are inherited but rather tendencies or predilections. Such family factors as extreme deprivation, incest, or abuse would have a larger impact—though a negative one—than the Minnesota research reveals.

The message for parents is not that it matters little how they care for and rear their children but that it is a mistake to treat all children the same. Children can—and often do—experience the same events differently, and this uniqueness nudges their personalities down different roads. In studies of thousands of children in Colorado, Sweden, and England, researchers found that siblings often respond to the same event (a parent's absence, a burglarized home), and interpret the same behavior (a mother's social preening) in quite different ways (Plomin & Spinath, 2004). Birth order, school experiences, friends, and chance events often add up to very different childhoods for siblings (Leman, 2004; McGuire et al., 1994).

Youngsters perceive events through unique filters, each of which is skewed by how earlier experiences affected them. Because each child carries about her or his own customized version of the environment, it seems that growing up in the same family actually works to make siblings different. Even youngsters as young as 14 months of age are acutely aware of the minute-by-minute differences in parental attention and affection doled out to their brothers and sisters, as evidenced by the skill they display in yanking back the spotlight. Parents who try to be evenhanded are foiled by their own consistency because they cannot control the way children perceive these efforts. So in guiding and shaping children, parents should respect their individuality, adapt to it, and cultivate those qualities that will help each child cope with life. For a timid child good parenting would involve

Identical Twins Separated at Birth Often Reveal Startling Similarities Identical twins raised apart are rare and are very valuable to scientists. Separated as infants from Guadalajara, Mexico, identical twins Adriana Scott and Tamara Rabi both were adopted into families only miles apart in the New York City area. While attending Hofstra, Adriana's classmates continually mistook her for Tamara, attending Adelphi University. While conversing via e-mail, they found out they shared the same birthday, both were adopted, and both were raised as only children. They met each other and were amazed at the uncanny similarities in their behavior and lives: both are 5′ 3 3/4″ tall, both are psychology majors with a B average, both experience difficulty with math, both love music and dancing, and both use similar expressions and gestures, and both lost their adoptive fathers to cancer. They became the subjects of a CBS documentary and met their biological mother, Norma de la Cruz.

providing experiences in which success will encourage the child to take more risks. If another child is fearless, good parenting will involve cultivating qualities that temper risk taking with intelligent caution. Remember, though, that cultures differ in the value they place on such personality traits as risk taking or timidity, so that good parenting will differ from culture to culture.

Some scholars fear that the results of the Minnesota research will be used to blame the poor and downtrodden for their misfortunes. Political liberals have long believed that crime and poverty are primarily the by-products of unhealthy social environments. So they are distrustful of biological or genetic explanations of behavior. Other scholars point out that the research holds promise for preventive medicine. If researchers can find a genetic predisposition for various disorders, we can then work on changing the environment with diet, medication, or other interventions. For example, if offspring of alcoholics are found to have genes that render them susceptible to alcoholism, they could be taught from childhood to avoid alcohol. Scientists can also develop new treatments. For instance, if they find a gene that increases a person's risk for schizophrenia or bipolar disorder (also known as manic-depressive illness), researchers can find the protein that the gene codes for and better understand the basic mechanism of the disease. Once they understand the basic mechanism, they can search for new ways to treat the disease. In sum, the potential dangers of genetic research are large, but so are its potential benefits.

Questions

How would you summarize the major findings of the Minnesota Twin Studies? What do we mean by polygenic inheritance?

Evolutionary Adaptation

It follows that organisms are *genetically prepared* for some responses (Eibl-Eibesfeldt, 1989). For instance, much learning in many insects and higher animals is guided by information inherent in the genetic makeup of the organism (MacDonald, 1992). The organism is preprogrammed to learn particular things and to learn them in particular ways. As we will see in Chapter 5, Noam Chomsky says that the basic structure of human language is biologically channeled by an inborn language-generating mechanism. Such a mechanism helps to explain why we learn speech so much more easily than we learn inherently simpler tasks such as addition and subtraction.

Ethologists, those who study the behavior patterns of organisms from a biological point of view called **ethology,** hold that human babies are biologically preadapted with behavior systems like crying, smiling, and cooing that elicit caring by adults (Zebrowitz, Olson, & Hoffman, 1993). Similarly, babies having attributes of cuteness—with large heads, small bodies, and distinctive facial features—induce others to want to pick them up and cuddle them. Ethologists call these behaviors and features **releasing stimuli.** They function as especially potent activators of parenting. A number of psychologists, among whom John Bowlby (1969) is perhaps the most prominent, compare the development of strong bonds of attachment between human caretakers and their offspring to the process of imprinting encountered among some bird and animal species. **Imprinting** is a process of attachment that occurs only during a relatively short period and is so

resistant to change that the behavior appears to be innate. Konrad Lorenz (1935), the Nobel Prize–winning ethologist, has shown that there is a short period of time early in the lives of goslings and ducklings when they slavishly follow the first moving object they see—their mother, a human being, even a rubber ball. Once this imprinting has occurred, it is irreversible. The object becomes "Mother" to the birds, so that thereafter they prefer it to all others and in fact will follow no other. Imprinting (Lorenz uses his native German word *Prgung,* which literally means "stamping in") differs from other forms of learning in at least two ways. First, imprinting can take place only during a relatively short period, termed a **critical period.** (For example, the peak period for the imprinting effect among domestic chickens occurs about 17 hours after hatching and declines rapidly thereafter.) Second, as already mentioned, imprinting is irreversible; it is highly resistant to change, so that the behavior appears to be innate.

Some developmental psychologists have applied ethological notions to human development. However, many prefer the term *sensitive period* to "critical period," for it implies greater flexibility in the time dimension and greater reversibility in the later structure. According to this concept, particular kinds of experience affect the development of an organism during certain times of life more than they do at other times (Bornstein, 1989). As we

Konrad Lorenz Here, young goslings follow the eminent Austrian ethologist rather than their mother. Because he was the first moving object that they saw during the critical imprinting period, they came to prefer him to all other objects.

saw in our earlier discussion of Freud, the notion of sensitive periods is central to psychoanalytic thought. Freud's view that infancy is the crucial period in molding an individual's personality was the basis of his famous aphorism "No adult neurosis without an infantile neurosis."

However, most life-span developmentalists reject the idea that the first five years of a child's life are all-important. More recent research suggests that the long-term effects of short, traumatic incidents are generally negligible in young children (Werner, 1989). Jerome Kagan (1984) comes to a somewhat similar conclusion on the basis of studies that he and his associates have conducted in Guatemala since 1971.

Questions

Who are ethologists and what contributions have they made to our understanding of human development? How does evolutionary adaptation apply to human development?

SEGUE

In Chapter 2 we have considered several major types of theory dealing with human development:

- Psychoanalytic theories draw our attention to the importance of early experience in fashioning personality and to the role of unconscious motivation.
- Behavioral theories emphasize the part that learning in one's environment plays in prompting people to act as they do.
- Humanistic theories attempt to maximize the human potential for self-direction and freedom of choice, with a goal of self-actualization.
- Cognitive theories highlight the importance of various mental capabilities and problem-solving skills that arm humans with a powerful potential to adapt and cope.
- Ecological theory focuses on the process of development and stresses the importance of the relationship between the developing individual and the changing environment.
- Sociocultural theories focus on the interaction between the individual and others in a social activity and how individuals assimilate and internalize cultural meaning.

With Chapter 3, we will begin to take you on a journey through all of the stages of life, from conception through birth, infancy, early childhood, middle childhood, late childhood, adolescence, early adulthood, middle adulthood, late adulthood, and dying and death. In each of these life stages, you will need to understand the developmental theories presented in Chapter 2.

We have also written this text to help you broaden your understanding of human development from several other perspectives. Throughout the following chapters you will encounter a prudent blending of research findings and theories from the hard sciences of biology, chemistry, and genetics as well as from the social sciences of psychology, sociology, anthropology, history, and political science. In addition, we have incorporated some findings from cross-cultural research. You will come to realize that contemporary developmentalists live and work around the world, conduct research and collaborate on a global scale, and disseminate findings such that the "newest" theories are more easily accessible than in the past. We encourage you to use your critical thinking skills to evaluate the diversity of theories you will undoubtedly encounter, both in our text, in your classroom, and in the online world.

Summary

Theory: A Definition

1. The framework of a theory allows us to organize a large array of facts so that we can understand them. If we understand how nature works, we have the prospect of gaining some control over our destiny.
2. Theories about human development can provide information or serve as a guide to acting on the world in a rational way, and they can inspire or stimulate further inquiry or research about behaviors.
3. Some newer theories seek to explain the development of women and nonwhites.
4. Cross-cultural social scientists are examining the universality of older theoretical models of development in cultures across the world.

Psychoanalytic Theories

5. Sigmund Freud postulated psychoanalytic theory that personality development involves a series of psychosexual stages: oral, anal, phallic, latency, and genital. Each stage is dominated by sensitivity in a particular pleasure-seeking zone of the body and poses a unique conflict that the individual must resolve before passing on to the next stage. Without healthy resolution, the person remains fixated in an earlier stage of personality development.
6. Freud also proposed that people operate from three states of being: the id, which seeks self-gratification; the superego, which seeks what is morally proper; and the ego, which is the rational mediator between the id and superego.
7. Freud used a variety of therapeutic techniques, such as hypnosis, free association, and dream analysis, to tap into the unconscious thoughts of his patients, which he thought was the source of his patients' distress.
8. Critics complain that Freudian theory is difficult to evaluate because it makes predictions about unconscious states that cannot be observed and tested by accepted scientific

procedures. Freud's work is also criticized for concluding early childhood is a significant stage of development, while he studied mainly adult patients with disorders.

9. Freud's daughter Anna continued her father's work, applying psychoanalytic theories to the treatment of children.

10. Contemporary feminist scholars find Freud's work to be problematic for he neglected to study women's development and psychological difficulties within the context of the historical time period. Psychiatrist Jean Baker Miller proposes that women often experience the world from the framework of relationships in their lives.

11. Erik Erikson, a neo-Freudian theorist, identifies nine psychosocial stages over the course of the life span, each of which confronts the individual with a major task (crisis) that the individual must successfully resolve to achieve healthy psychosocial development (see Table 2.1). Erikson's theory draws our attention to the continual process of personality development that takes place throughout a person's life span—even to the completion of the life cycle.

12. Borrowing the epigenetic principle from biology, Erikson proposes that each part of the personality has a particular time span within the full life span when it must develop if it is going to develop at all.

13. Erikson's view of psychosocial development is more optimistic than that of Freud's. However, one major criticism is that his subjects were mainly males and his method of study was mainly psychobiographies. More contemporary researchers propose that female identity is rooted in connections to others and in relationships.

Behavioral Theory

14. Behavioral theory contrasts sharply with psychoanalytic theory. Behavioral proponents, such as Watson and Skinner, believed that if psychology is to be a science, it must look to data that are directly observable and measurable, and not rely on introspection and self-observation by subjects.

15. Behaviorists are especially interested in how people learn to behave in particular ways. People learn to respond to the stimuli in their environment, and in turn their responses shape their behavior. Some learning is based on classical conditioning, using a subject's reflex/innate responses—whereas other learning derives from operant conditioning, where the consequences of the behavior alter the strength of the behavior.

16. Behaviorists deem learning to be a process called "conditioning," whereby individuals, as a result of their experience within an environmental context, establish an association or linkage between two events.

17. Behaviorists use concepts such as reinforcement, which can be either rewards or punishments, to shape desired behavior. Reinforcers strengthen the probability of another event's occurring.

18. Behavior modification is an approach that applies behavioral/learning theory to the problem of altering maladaptive behavior, such as phobias, weight loss or weight gain, test anxiety, addictions, and so on.

Humanistic Theory

19. Humanistic psychology, which is sometimes called the "third force" in psychology, arose in reaction to psychoanalysis and behaviorism. It maintains that human beings are different

from all other organisms in that they actively intervene in the course of events to control their destinies and to shape the world around them. Its proponents seek to maximize the human potential for self-direction and freedom of choice.

Cognitive Theory

20. In direct contrast to behavioral theory, cognitive theory examines internal mental representations such as sensation, perception, imagery, retention, recall, problem solving, reasoning, thinking, and memory. Cognition involves how children and adults go about representing, organizing, treating, and transforming information that in turn alters behavior.

21. For Jean Piaget the critical question in the study of growing children is how they adjust to the world they live in. By playing and interacting with their world, children develop schemas or mental frameworks. Adaptation to one's world includes both assimilation and accommodation of schemas. When in equilibrium, a child assimilates new experiences in terms of the models she or he arrived at through accommodation.

22. Piaget proposed four progressive stages of cognitive development: sensorimotor, preoperational, concrete operations, and formal operations (see Table 2.2).

23. Cognitive learning theorists say that our capacity to use symbols affords us a powerful means for comprehending and dealing with our environment. Verbal and imagined symbols allow us to represent events; analyze our conscious experience; communicate with others; plan, create, imagine; and engage in foresightful action.

24. Some contemporary cognitive psychologists suggest that Piaget underestimated the cognitive capabilities of infants and young children; and cross-cultural studies of cognitive development in children are finding aspects of his stage theory to be less applicable.

25. Cognitive learning and information-processing theorists are building on Piaget's theories, and their research findings suggest that mental "schemas" function as selective mechanisms that influence the information individuals attend to, how they structure information, how important it is to them, and what they do with the information.

26. Through the process of cognitive learning (also called observational learning, social learning, or social modeling), people can learn new responses without first having had the opportunity to make the responses themselves. Humans have a great capacity to use symbols to comprehend and deal with the environment.

Ecological Theory

27. Urie Bronfenbrenner devised an ecological theory that centers on the relationship between the developing individual and four expanding levels of the changing environment, from home and family to the broader cultural context (microsystem, mesosystem, exosystem, and macrosystem) (see Chapter 1).

28. Bronfenbrenner added the concept of the chronosystem to capture the dynamics of development with and across other systems.

Sociocultural Theory

29. Lev Vygotsky proposed sociocultural theory—focusing on the interaction between the individual and others in a

social activity and how individuals assimilate and internalize cultural meanings. Mental functions such as thinking, reasoning, and remembering are facilitated through language, and such functions are anchored in the child's interpersonal relationships during activities such as play.

30. Americans seem to reward independence and individualism in their children, whereas other cultures of the world stress interdependence in child-rearing practices.

Controversies

31. Each developmental theory has its proponents and critics. Yet the theories are not mutually exclusive; we need not accept one and reject the others. Different tasks and components of development simply call for different theories—some are mechanistic (the organism is passive and responds), whereas others are organismic (the organism is inherently active). However, most psychologists prefer an eclectic approach to development.

32. Continuity theories of development suggest that human development is gradual and uninterrupted, whereas discontinuity models suggest humans pass through a set sequence of stages, characterized by distinct states of ego formation, identity, or thought.

33. When scientists recognized the inappropriateness of the "which" question, some of them took a somewhat different approach. They sought to establish "how much" of the observed differences among people are due to heredity and how much to differences in environment. Recently, scientists have insisted that a more fruitful approach is to be found in the question of "how" specific hereditary and environmental factors work together to influence various characteristics.

34. Jerome Kagan and his associates at Harvard have shown the part genetic factors play in extreme timidity. Bouchard and colleagues at the University of Minnesota have similarly examined how the genetic makeup of twins (mainly those separated at birth) impacts personality.

35. Ethologists propose that humans are biologically preadapted (from evolution) with behavior systems like crying, smiling, cooing, and others that elicit care by adults; and these features function as especially important activators of parenting. The concept of a critical (sensitive) period for certain development to occur during the early years of life is being closely examined by some developmentalists, while being rejected by others.

Key Terms

accommodation (50)	critical period (62)	organismic model (57)
adaptation (50)	eclectic approach (57)	polygenic inheritance (61)
assimilation (50)	ecological theory (53)	psychoanalytic theory (37)
behavior modification (46)	epigenetic principle (42)	psychosexual stages (38)
behavioral genetics (60)	equilibrium (50)	psychosocial development (42)
behavioral theory (45)	ethology (62)	reinforcement (46)
chronosystem (54)	fixation (38)	releasing stimuli (62)
classical conditioning (46)	hierarchy of needs (48)	responses (45)
cognition (49)	holistic approach (48)	schemas (50)
cognitive learning (52)	humanistic psychology (48)	self-actualization (48)
cognitive stages (49)	imprinting (62)	sociocultural theory (54)
cognitive theory (49)	mechanistic model (56)	stimuli (45)
continuum of indirectness (59)	operant conditioning (46)	theory (37)

Following Up on the Internet

Web sites for this chapter focus on the historical study of human development and major theories of various aspects of development. Please access the text Web site at www.mhhe.com/vzcrandell8 for up-to-date hot-linked Internet addresses for the following topics:

APA Society for the History of Psychology (Division 26)
Archives of the History of American Psychology
Classics in the History of Psychology

Erikson's Eight Stages of Psychosocial Development
Key Theorists in Psychology
A History of Women in Psychology
A History of Japanese Psychology
A Chronology of Psychology in Great Britain
The Jean Piaget Society
Resources in the History of Psychology
Twin Studies

Part TWO
Beginnings

The biological foundations of heredity, reproduction, and prenatal development are discussed in Chapter 3. Today we think we know much more about the beginnings of life, yet medical research continues to astound us and makes us search for an answer to the question, "When does life begin?" The Human Genome Project, a worldwide collaborative study that has mapped all human genes, will lead to even greater understanding of, and perhaps treatments for, hereditary defects. Chapter 3 explains sophisticated genetic testing and assisted reproductive technologies that have led to advances in fertility. More recent technological advances have led to the possibility of becoming pregnant after menopause. The stages of prenatal development leading up to birth have remained the same, though sophisticated imaging techniques allow us to observe the tiniest humans readying themselves for living outside of the womb.

Reproduction, Heredity, and Prenatal Development

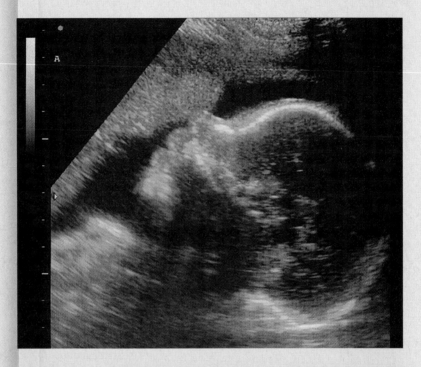

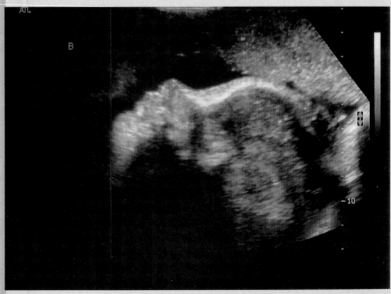

Critical Thinking Questions

1. Can you envision a time in the near future when human reproduction is accomplished primarily using technology to enhance the genetic traits of children and reduce the likelihood of illness and disease? What trait would you like to see copied in your own child?

2. Is there an optimum time during a natural menstrual cycle to conceive or avoid conception—or is it simply a common myth?

3. Why does the law allow people more freedom to destroy fetuses than to create them?

4. What should happen to women who abuse a developing fetus by exposure to some of the known biochemical agents (teratogens) that compromise the health of the developing fetus—when it is going to cost society millions, if not billions, of dollars to treat and care for children with birth defects through adulthood? Is an extensive education campaign enough, or should there be stricter penalties for repeat abusers?

5. A child dies and one parent decides to clone the child from a lock of hair or saved baby teeth—but the other parent doesn't want to do this. Who owns the DNA of the dead child?

Outline

L ike all other living things, the majority of human beings are capable of producing new individuals and thus ensuring the survival of the species. With the use of assisted reproductive technologies (such as artificial fertilization, human egg and sperm donations, cryogenic preservation, implantation techniques) and birth alternatives (such as selected surrogacy, intrauterine surgery, grandmothers bearing their own grandchildren), many humans who were previously deemed infertile can choose to reproduce. Many infertile couples and singles—both women and men—can now choose to have their own biological offspring, instead of adopting a child or remaining childless. In another technological miracle, Japanese researchers unveiled the first artificial "womb tank" in 1997, a technological wonder that could potentially revolutionize the bearing of children and childbirth before 2010. And the idea of human cloning, once merely a futuristic idea in science-fiction novels, is a current—though ethically questionable—possibility.

It's almost as if the idea of woman + man = child is the old-fashioned way to re-create the species. What once was a private experience has now become both public Internet entertainment and big business. For people with the resources, there certainly is a kaleidoscope of opportunities to procreate.

Reproduction

Reproduction is the term biologists use for the process by which organisms create more organisms of their own kind. Biologists depict reproduction as the most important of all life processes.

Two kinds of mature sex cells, or **gametes,** are involved in human reproduction: the male gamete, or **sperm,** and the female gamete, or **ovum** (egg or oocyte). In the process called **fertilization/fusion,** a male sperm enters and unites with a female ovum to form a **zygote** (fertilized egg). Sperm cells are not visible to the naked eye, being only six-hundredths of a millimeter long (.00024 inch). A sperm cell consists of an oval head, a whiplike tail, and a connecting middle piece, or collar, and moves by lashing its tail. A normal adult man's testes might produce as many as 300 million or more mature sperm each day, each of a unique genetic composition.

Ova, on the other hand, are not self-propelled and are moved along by small cilia structures in the woman's reproductive tract (see Table 3.1). During a woman's fertile years between puberty and menopause, typically at least one or perhaps more ova are released each month (Park et al., 2004). Each ovum, too, has a unique composition of genetic material and is about the size of the period at the end of this sentence, which can barely be seen by the naked eye. At most, only some 400 to 500 of the immature ova ultimately reach maturity. The rest degenerate and are absorbed by the body (Nilsson & Hamberger, 1990).

The Male Reproductive System

The primary male reproductive organs are a pair of **testes** normally lying outside the body in a pouchlike structure, the scrotum (see Figure 3.1). Sperm are produced and stay viable at a temperature a little lower than normal body temperature (about 96 degrees Fahrenheit). The scrotum holds and protects the testes and keeps them from being held too close to the man's warmer body. The testes produce sperm and the male sex hormones, called *androgens.* The principal androgens are *testosterone* and *androsterone.* The androgens are responsible for producing masculine secondary sexual characteristics, including facial and body hair, increased muscle mass, and a deeper voice.

Sperm are produced in winding tubules, within each testis. They are then emptied into the *epididymis,* a long, slender, twisted tube, where they are stored. During sexual arousal and ejaculation, the sperm pass from the epididymis along muscular ducts into the *urethra.* On the way they are mixed with secretions (which will nourish the sperm on their journey out of the man's body and into the woman's body) from the *seminal vesicles* and the *prostate gland.* The mixture of the sperm and secretions is termed semen, which will be ejaculated through the male's urethra—a tube that also connects with the bladder—and is surrounded by the man's external reproductive organ, the **penis.**

Sperm production and viability are influenced by many factors, including the man's own physical health, work, and recreational environment—even tight clothing can affect the temperature of the scrotum and harm sperm development. We learned a great deal about the male contribution to fer-

---

Table 3.1 The Sperm and the Ovum

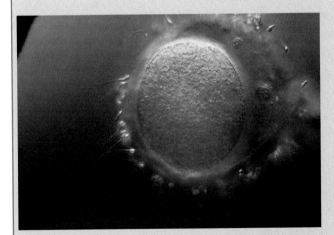

The Sperm and the Ovum The larger ovum is at the center and much smaller sperm surround the ovum, each trying to penetrate the cell wall and deposit its genetic material.

Source: Nilsson, Lennart. (1993). *How was I born?* New York: Dell.

Description

Sperm are unusually small cells with very little cytoplasm. Once sperm are ejaculated with semen into the female's vagina, they make their way through the cervix and the uterus, and then fewer of them move into the fallopian tubes (oviducts). Of the millions of sperm that enter the vagina, only a few hundred complete the journey. After one sperm succeeds in penetrating and entering the ovum, a biochemical change occurs in the ovum's cell wall and prevents penetration by any other sperm. The ovum (egg cell) is the largest human cell, between 0.1 and 0.2 millimeter in diameter.

Vulnerabilities

Gametes (sex cells) from the male and female carry their own unique genetic material. Their genes carry dominant and recessive traits. Trisomy 21 (Down syndrome) is an example of an inherited disorder that occurs at the moment of conception when the sperm and egg begin pairing up genetic material. The man's and woman's sex cells are vulnerable to disease, substance abuse, and biochemical hazards in the workplace and home environment both prior to sexual activity and after fertilization. Infertility can be caused by these factors.

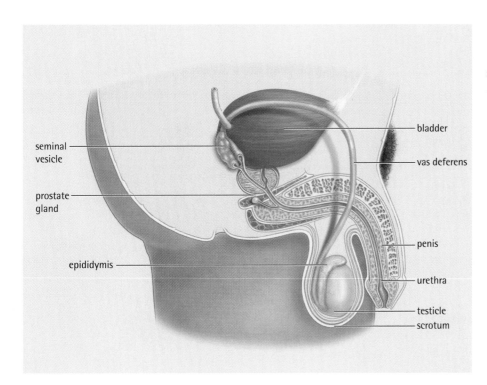

FIGURE 3.1 The Male Reproductive System This Illustration of the male pelvic region shows the organs of reproduction.

Source: Healthwise, Incorporated. PO Box 1989. Boise, ID 83702.

seminal vesicle

prostate gland

epididymis

bladder

vas deferens

penis

urethra

testicle

scrotum

tility and birth defects from Americans who returned from the Vietnam War after being exposed to Agent Orange, a potent chemical defoliant that has been linked to an increase in birth defects by these servicemen and Vietnamese citizens even years later. Americans who served during Desert Storm and are suspected of having been exposed to multiple vaccinations or biological warfare toxins are also being studied for long-term health, neurological, and reproductive effects (Couzin, 2004; Hotopf et al., 2004). We now know that smoking, drinking alcohol, ingesting psychoactive drugs, chemicals, or radiation in a work environment; and unprotected sexual activity can affect the health of a man's reproductive organs and developing sperm. However, men can often improve their health and habits and can be fertile into extreme old age (Perloe & Sills, 1999).

Questions

Can you identify the primary sex organs in males? Can you explain their functions in the process of human reproduction? What types of conditions can harm the male reproductive organs?

The Female Reproductive System

A woman's reproductive system is composed of the organs that produce ova (eggs), are involved in sexual intercourse, allow fertilization of the ovum, nourish and protect the fertilized ovum until it is developed, and are involved in giving birth. The primary female reproductive organs are a pair of **ovaries,** almond-shaped structures that lie in the pelvis (see Figure 3.2). While still in her mother's womb, a female embryo's developing ovaries produce approximately 400,000 immature ova. After puberty, the ovaries produce mature ova and the female sex hormones, *estrogen* and *progesterone.* These hormones are responsible for the development of female secondary characteristics, including breast (mammary gland) development, body hair, and hip development.

One or more ova are expelled from typically one of her ovaries on a monthly schedule. For most women this is approximately every 28 days, though for some women the cycle varies, particularly during the first few, and last few, years of menstruation. **Menstruation** is the periodic discharge of blood and cells from the lining of the uterus, marking the end of one cycle and the beginning of another. **Ovulation** occurs with the discharge of an ovum from a follicle in the ovary, and the ovum is moved through the **fallopian tube,** or oviduct, where it may be fertilized if sperm are present. The fallopian tube is lined with tiny, hairlike projections called *cilia* that propel the ovum along its course through the fallopian tube into the womb, or uterus. This short progression takes a few days; the fallopian tube is about 6 inches long and has the circumference of a human hair (Nilsson & Hamberger, 2004).

The pear-shaped **uterus,** a hollow, thick-walled, muscular organ, will house and nourish what will be called the developing **embryo,** the organism from the time the **blastocyst** implants itself in the uterine wall until the organism develops into a recognizable human fetus. The muscular uterus prepares itself each month

FIGURE 3.2 The Female Reproductive System This Illustration of the female pelvic region shows the organs of reproduction.

Source: Rolin Graphics, Brooklyn Park, MN 55443.

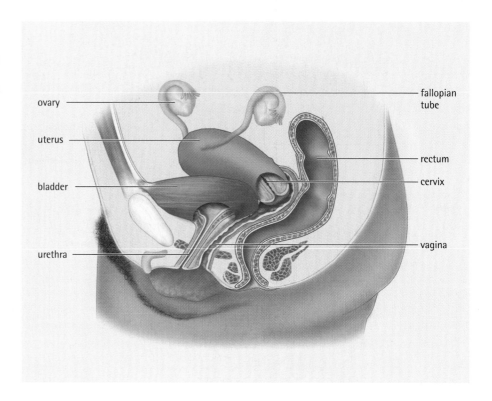

for potential conception with a blood-rich lining, which each month it sheds for four to six days (in menstruation) if conception (fertilization) does not occur. The unfertilized ovum is expelled from the body through the narrow lower end of the uterus, called the *cervix,* which projects into the vagina. The **vagina** is a muscular passageway that is capable of considerable dilation. The penis is inserted into the vagina during sexual intercourse, and the infant passes through the vagina at birth. Surrounding the external opening of the vagina are the *external genitalia,* collectively termed the *vulva.* The vulva contain the fleshy folds, known as the *labia,* and the *clitoris* (a small, highly sensitive erectile structure comparable in some ways to the man's penis).

A woman's home and working environment, nutritional habits, level of exercise, health care, and sexual behaviors have a great impact on the health of her reproductive system, as well as the health of a potential fetus, both before and after conception.

Questions

Can you identify each of the primary female sex organs involved in the process of human reproduction? What types of conditions can harm the female reproductive organs?

How and When Fertilization Occurs

The Menstrual Cycle   The series of changes associated with a woman's **menstrual cycle** begins with menstruation, the maturing of an ovum, ovulation, and the eventual expulsion of an unfertilized ovum from the body through the vagina. A healthy woman's ovaries typically produce at least one mature ovum, or egg cell, every 25 to 32 days, the average being every 28 days (Park et al., 2004).

A woman's health (illness, disease, stress, nutritional deficiencies, or excessive exercise) can affect her menstrual cycle. Variations among women in the length of the ovarian cycle are common and normal. Young women who have just begun menstruating and older women who are approaching or in their forties are quite likely to have irregular cycles or to skip cycles. Day 1 of a cycle is the first day of menstruation. Toward the middle of each menstrual cycle (around days 13 to 15) for a majority of women, typically one ovum reaches maturity in a follicle of an ovary and passes into one of the two passages called the fallopian tubes (also called oviducts) from the ovaries to the uterus. *Fertilization,* if it occurs, typically takes place in the fallopian tubes.

This is commonly considered the most optimum time for conception to occur, because a mature ovum is viable for approximately 24 hours. If there is no fusion with a sperm in the fallopian tube, the ovum begins to degenerate after 24 hours and will be expelled from the body during menstruation. Recently, however, researchers at the National Institute of Environmental Health Sciences have demonstrated in a study of the urine and hormone levels of 213 healthy women what some accidentally pregnant women may have long suspected:

> Only about 30 percent of women actually have their fertile window entirely within the time span for fertility—between days 10 and 17 of their menstrual cycle. In fact, the researchers found, there is hardly a day in the menstrual cycle during which some women are not potentially fertile. Women in this study were of prime reproductive age (most between 25 and 35) when the menstrual cycles are most regular. The window of fertility would be even more unpredictable for teenagers or for women approaching menopause, the NIEHS researchers said. (National Institute of Environmental Health Sciences, 2000)

Ovulation   An ovary contains many follicles, and typically only one undergoes full maturation in each ovarian cycle. However, recent research using high-resolution ultrasound (not blood analysis for hormone levels) with a small sample of adult women revealed that nearly 10 percent produced two mature ova per cycle—whereas about 10 percent did not ovulate at all (Baerwald, Adams, & Pierson, 2003). This explains why some fraternal twins have separate conception days. Also, this finding makes "natural family planning" a challenge. Predicting ovulation by measuring the participants' hormone levels did not match the activity in the ovaries. However, initially a *follicle* in an ovary consists of a single layer of cells; but as it grows, the cells proliferate, producing a fluid-filled sac that surrounds the primitive ovum, which contains the mother's genetic contribution. Most women's ovaries seem to alternate releasing an ovum every other month, though it has been found that when one ovary is diseased or has been removed, the other ovary will ovulate each month.

Through the influence of the *hypothalamus* in the forebrain instructing the *pituitary gland* to release a surge of luteinizing hormone (LH), the maturing follicle in the ovary ruptures, and the ovum is discharged. This discharge of the ovum from the follicle in the ovary is called ovulation. When the mature follicle ruptures, releasing its ovum, it undergoes rapid change. Still a part of the ovary, the follicle transforms itself into the *corpus luteum*, a small growth recognizable by its golden pigment. The corpus luteum secretes *progesterone* (a female hormone), which enters the bloodstream and causes the mucous lining along the inner wall of the uterus to prepare itself for the potential *implantation* of the newly fertilized egg. If conception and implantation do not occur, the corpus luteum degenerates and eventually disappears. If pregnancy occurs, the corpus luteum continues to develop and produces progesterone until the placenta takes over the same

function. The corpus luteum then becomes superfluous and disappears (Nilsson & Hamberger, 1990).

Questions

What is the purpose of menstruation, and what happens during a typical menstrual cycle for most women? Is there an optimum time during this cycle for conception to occur?

Fertilization   At the time of sexual intercourse, a man customarily ejaculates 100 to 500 million sperm into the woman's vagina. Sperm can ascend the *cervical canal* only during those few crucial days when the woman's *cervix* is open and produces strands of mucous that allow some of the sperm to enter the uterus and fallopian tubes. Sperm have a high mortality rate within the female tract because of its high acidity and other factors related to the health of the sperm, yet a small number of sperm are viable up to 48 hours in the female's reproductive tract. The one sperm that fuses with the ovum has won against gigantic odds, several hundred million to one. The union (or fusion) of a sperm and an ovum is called *fertilization,* and when this process is successful, we say that *conception* has occurred. This normally takes place in the upper end of the fallopian tube. When there is a joining of the chromosomes from the sperm and egg, the new structure is called a *zygote,* with its unique genetic makeup (see Table 3.2 on page 74). Even then, however, the new zygote is extremely vulnerable. For various reasons, about one-third of all zygotes die shortly after fertilization (Ellison, 2001).

If fertilization fails to take place, the decreasing levels of ovarian hormones (estrogen and progesterone) typically lead to menstruation about 14 days after ovulation. The thickened layers of tissue lining the uterus are not needed for the support of a zygote, so they deteriorate and are shed over a three- to seven-day period, when the debris from the wall of the uterus, a small amount of blood, and other fluids are discharged from the vagina. Before the end of a menstrual flow, the pituitary gland secretes luteinizing hormone (LH) into the bloodstream that direct one of the ovarian follicles to begin rapid growth. As a consequence, the cycle starts anew.

Questions

How and where does the process of fertilization occur? What are some factors that inhibit or prevent fertilization? What happens to the ovum if fertilization does not occur?

Multiple Conception   If more than one ovum matures and is released, the woman might conceive multiple, nonidentical siblings (**dizygotic** or fraternal twins). Identical

Table 3.2 Conception

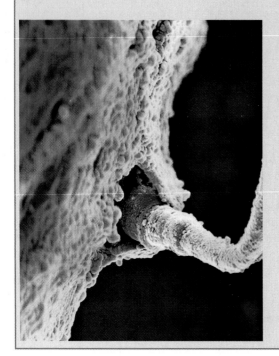

Description	Vulnerabilities
Fertilization occurs when the two gametes, ovum (egg) and sperm, have fused. Their DNA has joined, creating a new structure called a zygote. Additional sperm that did not penetrate the cell wall of the egg (normally nearly 100 or so) continue to attempt to penetrate the cell wall of the ovum. This action, plus the movement of the cilia of the tubal lining, promotes a counterclockwise motion of the zygote. The zygote will proceed down the fallopian tube, a journey of approximately 6 inches that will take 3 to 4 days.	The fallopian tube has about the same circumference as a human hair. If the fallopian tube is scarred or blocked, the zygote will be unable to proceed. Damage or obstruction to the fallopian tube can occur because of such factors as pelvic inflammatory disease (PID), sexually transmitted infections (STIs), and endometreosis, to name a few. There is potential for incomplete fusion if the sperm is defective or if the biochemistry of the cell wall of the ovum is not functioning properly.

Conception   The photo shows a sperm, its tail thrashing, burrowing into an ovum, just before depositing its genetic material.

Source: Nilsson, Lennart. (1990). *A child is born.* New York: Dell.

twins (**monozygotic** twins) result from one fertilized egg splitting into two identical parts after conception. Triplets and higher order multiples may occur as a combination of single and/or dizygotic or monozygotic twins but are more likely with assisted reproduction.

For couples selecting assisted reproduction methods, multiple conceptions also occur in a petri dish in a medical laboratory. After the resultant embryos (usually several) grow for a few days, some are transplanted into a woman's uterus in hopes that at least one will implant itself into the uterine wall and continue to develop. Since 1980 the rate of twin births has risen 65 percent; for triplets and higher-order multiples, the rate has increased more than 400 percent. The rapid rise in multiple births is associated with advances in fertility therapies and with older ages of childbearing in the United States and in other industrialized countries (see Figure 3.3) (Martin et al., 2003).

Reduction of Higher-Order Multiple Pregnancy

Multiple pregnancy of an order higher than twins involves far greater risks for the woman's health and also for her fetuses, which are likely to be miscarried or to be delivered prematurely with a high risk of either dying or having birth defects. In such circumstances it may be considered ethically acceptable to use *selective reduction* procedures to reduce the number of embryos than to do nothing. The procedure is usually performed between 9 and 11 weeks of pregnancy.

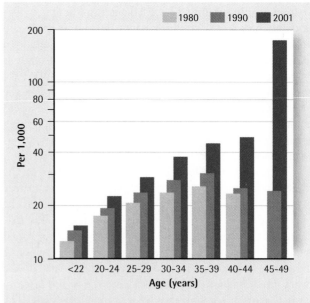

NOTE: The birth rate for women 45-49 years of age for 1980 is not shown because of the small number of twin births. Rates are plotted on a log scale.

FIGURE 3.3 Twin Birthrates by Age of Mother: United States, 1980, 1990, and 2001   The birthrate for twins has climbed for all age groups since 1980, and the largest increases continue to be for older mothers, ages 45 to 49.

Source: Martin, J. A. Hamilton, B. E., Ventura, S. J., Menacker F., Park, M. M. & Sutton, P. D. (2002, December 18). Births: Final data for 2001. *National Vital Statistics Reports, 51*(2), 1–103. Retrieved January 6, 2005 from http://www.cdc.gov/nchs/data/nvsr/nvsr51/nvsr51_02.pdf.

It is very important that such selective reduction should not be considered as an alternative to very careful monitoring of infertility treatment. If this is done, higher-order multiple pregnancies should occur very infrequently ("Recommendations on Ethical Issues in Obstetrics and Gynecology," 2000). Although medical professionals in the fertility business do not view this as an abortion procedure—because the intention of the mother is that the pregnancy continues—others can't bring themselves to consent to eliminating any baby and simply leave it in the hands of a higher authority. Whatever the choice made by the parents, it is one of life's most difficult decisions (O'Brien, 2001). (See page 112 photo of the McCaughey Septuplets—the parents decided not to undergo selective reduction.)

> **Questions**
>
> What is the difference between dizygotic and monozygotic twins? Since 1980, why has the rate of multiple births risen dramatically? What are some potential risks of multiple pregnancy? What does the concept of "selective reduction" mean?

Conceiving or Avoiding Conception

Do you and your partner want to conceive a child in the near future? Or do you and your partner not want to conceive a child right now? Do you know when a woman is most likely to be "fertile"? As previously mentioned, generally at midcycle (for a majority of women, but not all) an ovum in the fallopian tube is viable for approximately 24 hours. Sperm are viable for fertilization for approximately 48 hours once they are introduced into the vagina. Women who have difficulty conceiving must become aware of their optimal time of conception by taking their daily body temperature and/or undergoing a daily high-density ultrasound to determine their days of ovulation.

Recent investigations have discovered optimum times of the calendar year as well. In some regions of the world, people mating during the optimal fertility season have twice the chance of conceiving than they have at other times. The optimal period for conception seems to be when the sun shines for about 12 hours a day, and the temperature hovers between 50 and 70 degrees Fahrenheit. Most likely, an internal biological clock, fine-tuned by the length of daylight, contributes to the seasonal differences (Sperling, 1990). But *infertility rates* in industrialized countries have been rising for the past three decades. It is suspected that this is due to women delaying childbirth (an older woman's ova are less likely to be fertilized than a younger woman's ova), an increase in pelvic inflammatory diseases and other sexually transmitted infections, an increase in uterine cells growing outside the uterus (*endometriosis*), and lower sperm counts in men (Swan et al., 2003; Swan, Elkin, & Fenster, 2000).

> **Question**
>
> Is there an optimum age when conception/fertilization is more likely to occur?

Infertility and Assisted Reproductive Technology

Since 1978 when Louise Brown, the world's first "test-tube baby" was born in England, medical researchers have created many fertility drugs and microscopic and surgical procedures that have dramatically transformed infertility treatments. In the United States alone, it is estimated that one out of every six couples is coping with infertility (Gosden, 2000). Worldwide, the estimate runs into millions of couples with infertility issues. Many of these couples seek **assisted reproductive technologies (ARTs)** to increase their chances of becoming pregnant. The Centers for Disease Control and Prevention (CDC) reports that 107,587 known assisted reproduction cycles were carried out in the United States in 2001 resulting in 26,550 live births—or nearly a 25 percent success rate (Centers for Disease Control and Prevention, 2003a). As of December 2003, there were 421 fertility clinics in the United States and hundreds more around the world. The goal of these fertility clinics is to offer hope to childless couples, single women, same-sex couples, and those who postpone childbearing because of illness, disease, career, or late marriage or remarriage (Centers for Disease Control and Prevention, 2003a; Lemonick, 1997). A woman's ability to conceive declines dramatically after age 35.

Declining Male Fertility   Diagnoses among American couples who had ART procedures in 2001 resulted in the discovery of nearly 20 percent male infertility. Analysis of the data from 101 worldwide studies published between 1934 and 1996 on male reproductive dysfunction revealed declining semen quality (see Figure 3.4), rising infertility, and increasing rates of testicular disorders (Claman, 2004; Swan, Elkin, & Fenster, 2000). Medical researchers are also reporting trends of rapidly declining male semen quality (sperm count) in Great Britain and other countries throughout Asia and Europe, and some demographers are suggesting a new period of rapid population decline (Sobotka, 2004; Yeoh & Chang, 2003). Some researchers are suggesting that postponement of childbearing is a key factor, for sperm motility decreases markedly from one's twenties to one's forties and older (Arnst, 2003; Sobotka, 2004).

Assisted Reproductive Technologies (ARTs)   There are several assisted reproductive technology options because there are many reasons why conception might not occur through sexual intercourse. A man's sperm count might be too low, he might have sustained injury or disease of the testicles, or his sperm might be unhealthy or have slow motility. A woman's fallopian tubes might be blocked, scarred, or missing from disease, injury, or surgery. The follicles in her ovaries might not be producing healthy ova. A woman might have undergone radiation or chemotherapy that destroyed her ova. (With cryopreservation her ova might be kept viable.) The endometrial lining of the uterus might not be able to host a developing embryo. In some instances there is no physiological reason why a couple cannot conceive (see Figure 3.4). And in some cases, same-sex couples wish to have a child.

In vitro fertilization (IVF) is fertilization outside the body in a petri dish in a medical lab environment. In an attempt to accomplish pregnancy, these steps are involved:

1. Stimulate the ovaries to produce several viable eggs using a protocol of follicle-stimulating hormones.
2. Retrieve several eggs from the ovaries.
3. Fertilize several eggs with sperm of spouse or donor in the IVF lab.
4. Let the embryos develop for 3 to 5 days in a special culture in a petri dish; extended embryo culture is proving more successful.
5. Place the "best" embryos into the uterus and wait to see if implantation takes on the wall of the uterus; single versus multiple embryo transfer is proving less risky to the embryo and mother.

GIFT (gamete intrafallopian transfer) utilizes many of the preceding steps, but after the woman's eggs are retrieved from her ovaries, the eggs and sperm are placed into the woman's fallopian tubes to facilitate fertilization in the body.

ZIFT (zygote intrafallopian transfer) is similar to the GIFT procedure, except laboratory-fertilized embryos (zygotes) are placed in a healthy fallopian tube.

ICSI (intracytoplasmic sperm injection) is injection of a sperm directly into an egg using a microscopically fine needle. ICSI is typically used when a man has a low sperm count, but embryos created by this method have higher rates of chromosomal abnormalities and miscarriage (Schultz and Williams, 2002). Researchers from France now suggest that couples undergo individual analysis of their genetic blueprint (called *karyotyping*) prior to using ICSI (Morel et al., 2004).

In vitro fertilization procedures are available for a woman past menopause. These IVF procedures can use the woman's own eggs and her partner's sperm, or donor eggs or donor sperm. In 2004 a 56-year-old woman in the U.S. gave birth to twins using IVF procedures, followed by a 59-year-old woman giving birth to twins (Rubin, 2004). Multiple births, considered to be very high-risk, are on the rise in the United States because of these procedures (see Figure 3.5) (Martin et al., 2003). However, researchers are attempting to improve the chances of having a healthy, full-term fetus by using SET, or *single embryo transfers,* versus implanting multiple embryos.

Preimplantation genetic treatment (PGT) is now available as an alternative to chorionic villus sampling or amniocentesis. PGT is gene screening of embryos created by IVF. Doctors already use various methods to select the "best" specimens from a batch of IVF embryos. But newer procedures can diagnose some inherited genetic or chromosomal disorders from a single cell of an

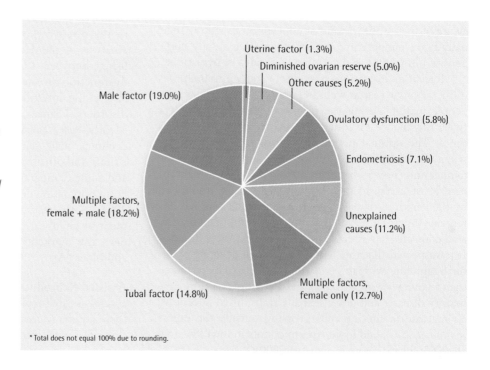

FIGURE 3.4 Diagnoses Among Couples who had ART Cycles Using Fresh Nondonor Eggs or Embryos: 2001* Diagnoses range from one infertility factor in one partner to multiple factors in either one or both partners.

Source: Centers for Disease Control and Prevention and American Society for Reproductive Medicine. (2004, December). 2001 Assisted reproductive technology success rates: National summary and fertility clinic reports. Retrieved November 15, 2004, from http://www.cdc.gov/reproductivehealth/ART01/PDF/ART2001.pdf.

Uterine factor (1.3%)
Diminished ovarian reserve (5.0%)
Other causes (5.2%)
Male factor (19.0%)
Ovulatory dysfunction (5.8%)
Endometriosis (7.1%)
Unexplained causes (11.2%)
Multiple factors, female + male (18.2%)
Multiple factors, female only (12.7%)
Tubal factor (14.8%)

* Total does not equal 100% due to rounding.

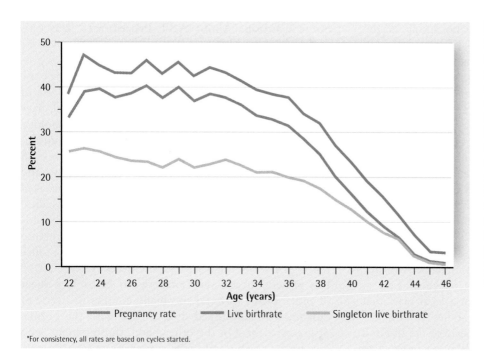

FIGURE 3.5 ART Success Rates Differ Among Woman of Different Ages: 2002[*] A woman's age is the most important factor affecting the chances of a live birth when her own eggs are used. Among women in their twenties, pregnancy rates, live birthrates, and singleton birthrates were relatively stable, but success rates declined steadily from the mid-thirties on as fertility declined with age. Live birthrates and singleton live birthrates differ because of the higher percentage of multiple-birth deliveries counted among total live births.

Source: National Vital Health Statistics. (2004, December). 2002 Assisted reproductive technology success rates: National summary and fertility clinic reports, p. 22.

*For consistency, all rates are based on cycles started.

early embryo, and growth of affected embryos would be terminated (Pearson, 2004).

Sperm sorting (sperm separation) is separation for X-bearing (female) and Y-bearing (male) sperm cells and simple medical insemination and for prevention of sex-linked diseases and family balancing.

Embryo adoption, another fertility option, is accomplished by using embryos donated by another family that has completed an in vitro fertilization process and has excess embryos that they do not intend to use. The recipient parents have the option of legally adopting an embryo to attempt pregnancy. The adopted embryo(s) are then transferred into either the recipient mother or a surrogate mother (Davidson, 2001; "Embryo Adoption," 2001).

Techniques have been developed to retrieve and save viable eggs and sperm for potential future use. The science of *cryopreservation* (a technique for preserving gamete cells or embryos through freezing) is making it possible for people to store eggs, sperm, and embryos, called *frozen embryo transfer (FET)* for an indefinite period for potential future use (Check et al., 2004). For a person with uterine, ovarian, or testicular cancer who requires chemotherapy, radiation, or surgical removal of the reproductive organs, egg or sperm retrieval and storage can be done prior to other treatments. A woman's eggs are more fragile than a man's sperm, but in 1997 a woman gave birth to twin boys conceived from donor eggs that had been frozen for two years. Doctors are also removing ovarian tissue and testicular tissue for later reimplantation, developing methods for longer embryo growth outside the womb, and microscopically transferring chromosomes and/or nuclei from older eggs to younger eggs.

A newer method, *cytoplasm transfer,* is in its early stages. Cytoplasm, the nonnuclear part of a cell, can be removed from the eggs of younger women and injected into the eggs of older women. To date, cytoplasm transfer has met limited success (Opsahl et al., 2002).

Future Assisted Reproductive Technologies The scientific search to help couples conceive has been a worldwide research effort. The first "test-tube baby" was born in England in 1978. Australia claims the first baby born from a frozen embryo. Researchers in a Belgian lab found a way to inject sperm directly into an egg cell (Lemonick, 1997). In 2001 Cornell researchers got embryos to attach to uterine tissue grown in a lab (Moyer, 2001). Researchers at the University of Florida and Temple University are conducting initial studies on synthetic amniotic fluid that keeps tiny premature infants alive (Amniotic Boost, 2004).

And most remarkably, medical researchers at Juntendo University in Japan are developing an artificial uterus (or a "womb tank"), a chamber connected to a machine that brings oxygen and nutrients to the fetus developing inside, but completely outside the woman's body. This new science of **ectogenesis,** the process by which a fetus gestates in an environment external to the mother, may evoke images of Aldous Huxley's *Brave New World*—but researchers estimate that ectogenesis will be a reality within five years (see Figure 3.6) As of this writing, Japanese researchers have developed goats in such a chamber over three months and then healthy goats were "born" (Farooqi, 2003; Zimmerman, 2004).

While critics call such a chamber unnatural and dehumanizing and posing moral, social, and psychological dilemmas, Farooqi (2003) from Texas A&M says, "Ectogenesis is merely an artificial means to sustain life, and, by this definition, it is no different than life support. And while ectogenesis may entail an unnatural delivery, so does a Cesarean section." And as Farooqi and proponents suggest, such an approach to saving very premature infants may end the abortion debate forever. An unwanted fetus could be removed from the biological mother, developed in a life-supporting chamber, and adopted at "birth." Yet critics argue the critical intimate, bonding connection between a developing fetus and the woman's body is gone when such a method is used (Welin, 2004).

From a legal perspective, the courts worldwide may have to decide the legality of such a method. Attorney Michelle Hibbert (2004) from the College of Law at Arizona State University states from a legal view that although an infertile couple (or a single) has freedom and rights to use ART methods, ectogenesis severs the link between the genetic parent and developing fetus. And developing fetuses in "mechanical gestation" may not have constitutional protections.

Babies of the Future

Ectogenesis

Producing babies outside the mother's body in the laboratory. A mother could walk right through her "pregnancy"—because she wouldn't be carrying the baby.

Cloning

Creating identical copies of humans. The danger is that the rich and powerful could run off copies of themselves. Imagine a million-strong army of Hitlers!

Farming women

Dosing women with hormones to stimulate them into multiple ovulation and storing eggs for breeding future generations—one woman produced 44 eggs at one go.

Genetic engineering

Tailoring future offspring to any specifications: color, height, size, intelligence, strength.

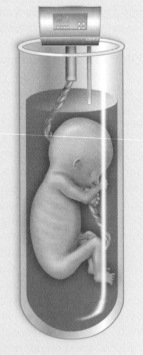

FIGURE 3.6 Ectogenesis: Babies of the Future May Develop Outside the Mother's Womb Reproductive researchers predict that the science of ectogenesis, the process by which a fetus gestates in an environment external to the mother, will be a reality within five years. Such a method is highly controversial at this time.

Source: Squier, S.M. 1994. *Babies in Bottles: Twentieth-Century Visions of Reproductive Technology.* Rutgers Univnisity.

Some Cautions About ART Procedures   It is estimated that between 35 to 70 million couples worldwide who were infertile already sought ART methods to produce a child, and there is an increasing demand for use of ART procedures (Schultz & Williams, 2002). As of 2004 approximately 1 million children worldwide have been born through assisted reproductive technology (Green, 2004). Yet more studies across several countries confirm that rates of miscarriage, prematurity, low birth weight, infant birth defects or developmental delays, and infant mortality are higher than with normally conceived babies (Hansen et al., 2002; Schieve et al., 2002). Medical researchers are improving these techniques, are extending the time for embryo growth before implantation into the mother, and are implanting fewer embryos to reduce the high risks of higher-order multiples (Green, 2004). But present success rates of between 25 to 30 percent of actual births leave far too many couples in a state of despair, with unfulfilled dreams, and with the burden of greater debt. On the other hand, those parents who give birth to twins and higher-order multiples are facing their own unique challenges in managing the emotional demands and expenses of such a large family.

Questions

What percent of couples in the United States are experiencing complications with fertility? What do we know about the success rate of ARTs, especially with advancing age? What are several techniques involved in accomplishing successful IVF?

Developmental Biology and Reproduction in the Twenty-First Century   **Cloning** is a form of *asexual reproduction*, which creates an embryo by a process called *somatic cell nuclear transfer (SCNT)*. The first step is to remove the nucleus from a female egg cell and strip out most of the genetic material—creating a "denucleated egg." The second step is to remove the nucleus from an ordinary body cell (e.g., a skin cell) and insert that nucleus into the denucleated egg—a process called *nuclear transplantation*. The third step is to "shock" the new combined cell with a tiny electrical (or chemical) charge in hopes of stimulating division and growth (normally triggered by the sperm cell). Thus, a new embryo may be created that is nearly a 98 percent genetic replica of the donor body cell—that some call a "clonote" (Hansen, 2004; McHugh, 2004). In *reproductive cloning*, the cloned embryo is placed into a woman's uterus, with hopes that it will implant in the uterine wall and develop into a fetus and be born healthy. Although many biomedical researchers, policy makers, legislators, ethicists, and clergy believe there should be a ban on reproductive cloning, there appears to be less opposition to therapeutic cloning (Ulick, 2004).

In *therapeutic cloning*, the resultant embryo is allowed to grow four to five days to the blastocyst stage.

Then its *stem cells* are extracted and grown to become other body cells or potentially body organs (skin, blood, bone, pancreatic cells, neurons, sperm, eggs, and so on) (see Figure 3.7). Although ardent opponents say such human embryos must not be designed solely for destruction (disrespecting the sanctity of life), zealous proponents say stem cells can be used to cure illness and disease (e.g., cancer, diabetes, Parkinson's, Alzheimer's, spinal cord injuries, and others) (Friedrich, 2004; Weiss, 2004b). But ending such suffering is hypothetical conjecture at this time. (See the *Further Developments* box on page 80, "Stem Cell Research: Making Progress or Opening Pandora's Box?"). It is also hypothesized that a person receiving his or her own cloned tissue cells, or a transplanted body organ, is not likely to experience immunological rejection. Yet other developmental biologists have reservations about not keeping the human gene pool diverse to ward off future viruses that could kill millions of cloned humans (Hansen, 2004).

The goal of earlier cloning research was to create herds of genetically identical animals; now some researchers want to help infertile couples and homosexuals have their own genetic offspring. Others want to conduct research to understand human or animal diseases and perhaps develop cures (Bowring, 2004). Yet the fertility researchers at the Roslin Institute in Great Britain report it took 277 attempts before a "normal" sheep, called Dolly, was born in 1996. Further, 98 percent of the sheep embryos never implanted or died off during gestation or soon after birth. However, since Dolly, other animals were cloned: mice, cats, pigs, goats, a mule, and some endangered species. But with humans it is estimated that biomedical researchers would need millions of women's egg cells—with innumerable failed attempts and grotesque fetal and placental distortions and maternal complications—as animal researchers have witnessed (Hansen, 2004). Yet Great Britain, Canada, Australia, New Zealand, Japan, South Korea, and many European countries are researching therapeutic cloning, and a flurry of daily reports can be found online at the International Society for Stem Cell Research (ISSCR).

Reservations   In 1998, President Clinton called for a U.S. ban on human cloning and convened the National Bioethics Advisory Commission (National Public Radio, 1998). In 2001 and 2003 the U.S. House of Representatives passed the Human Cloning Prohibition Act, making illegal all uses of human somatic cell nuclear transfer (SCNT), banning human cloning, and imposing criminal and civil penalties if convicted of attempting or performing human cloning, or importing products used from human cloning. In 2001 and 2004, President Bush called on the U.S. Senate and the United Nations to authorize a ban on human cloning (but not on private funding in the United States for therapeutic stem cell research), but members of both bodies cannot come to a consensus (Weiss, 2004b). Such biomedi-

cal research is being conducted in labs around the world, but the U.S. National Institutes of Health wants to bring all existing stem cell lines from fertility clinics available to U.S. researchers into one repository. This would allow researchers easier access, lower costs, standardized conditions, uniform quality, and regulatory oversight and review of stem cell and embryonic research (Knight, 2004).

Biological Enterprise   The Raëlians, a religious sect led by Raël (who claims space aliens cloned humans 25,000 years ago) and a French chemist, claim their company Clonaid created the first cloned human baby in 2002 but provide no proof. By 2004, they claim to have successfully cloned at least 14 human babies and are creating another 10 per month. Their newest company, Babytron, claims to have created the first artificial womb, allowing for growth of a baby from conception to birth in a machine outside a woman's body (at least three other labs around the world are claiming the first artificial womb) (McGovern, 2003). Clonaid's other goal is to provide immortality for clients. Two other scientists, one a U.S. fertility expert and an Italian gynecologist (who claims creating three human clones), are publicly offering cloning services to infertile couples and homosexuals. In February 2004, South Korean scientists announced they had created 30 human embryos by cloning and were harvesting stem cells for therapeutic research (Boyce, 2004; Fischer, 2001).

An explosive growth of such research continues. In 2004 scientists at Harvard Medical School and the Boston Children's Hospital announced plans to proceed with stem cell research (and Harvard is petitioning its Ethics Committee also to create cloned embryos) (Cook, 2004). And, as mentioned in the *Further Developments* box on page 80, "Stem Cell Research: Making Progress or Opening Pandora's Box?," in 2004 Californians passed a $3 billion bond act to draw biomedical researchers from all over the world to conduct stem cell research, and other states are quickly following suit, which is certain to lead to reproductive cloning unless the U.S. Congress takes decisive action (McHugh, 2004).

Questions

Can you describe the process of cloning to create a human embryo? Do you think the destruction of human embryos for stem cell research amounts to the killing of babies, or do you think this research will lead to a greater demand by infertile persons? If present regulations allow for cloned embryos to grow only for 14 days in a lab, do you think there will be a "slippery slope" in the future such that cloned embryos will become fetuses used solely for body parts?

Ethical Dilemmas of Baby Making

Most people have a very strong urge to reproduce, and many biomedical researchers believe reproduction by any

Further Developments

Stem Cell Research: Making Progress or Opening Pandora's Box?

S tem cells are those cells that have the capacity to re-produce themselves. Thus they divide and renew themselves for long periods, are unspecialized, and are capable of differentiating into any of the 220 types of human cells or tissues. This research is highly controversial because many researchers propose the best source of stem cells for creating human tissues and organs is human fetal tissue from the blastocyst stage (a preimplantation embryo of 30 to 150 cells) (see Figure 3.7) (Miller, 2001). Such embryonic stem cells (ES) can come from aborted fetal tissue, embryos created by IVF, and leftover or frozen embryos from IVF procedures. However, other stem cells can be found in fetal placenta and umbilical cord tissue, and *adult* stem cells can be found in fat cells, skin, blood, bone marrow, and other body cells (Chapman, Frankel, & Garfinkel, 1999).

Legislation and Regulation

In 2001, President Bush restricted U.S. federal research funding to experiments involving only those cell lines from embryos left over at fertility clinics and designated for disposal. Along with many bioethicists and pro-life advocates, he is concerned about the unregulated creation and destruction of additional embryos and the potential exploitation of women (Goldstein & Allen, 2001). However, private funding of human stem cell research is not regulated or prohibited by law, and the President and Congress support and fund *adult* stem cell research (National Institutes of Health, 2004a). As of late 2003, more than 60 U.S. and international companies with over 1,000 scientists were pursuing some form of ES research for therapeutic product development ("Embryonic Stem Cell Research," 2004).

In November 2004, a divided United Nations rejected a ban on embryonic stem cell research (Arieff, 2004). Most countries in the European Union are rapidly allowing ES research, and other countries—for example, Israel, Australia, New Zealand, China, South Korea, Taiwan, and Japan are already conducting ES research (Hoffman, 2003; "Stem Cell Research," 2003; Tauer, 2004; Wang, 2003).

Pro-Choice

Pro-choice advocates, many biomedical scientists, some afflicted with disease or illness, and some politicians and venture capitalists predict ES research holds the *potential* for curing many human diseases and illnesses—they say this is the first step in changing the face of disease, human suffering, ending infertility, and preventing aging or death (Tauer, 2004). In 2004 Harvard scientists offered other stem cell researchers free access to 17 new human embryonic stem cell lines developed without government money, hoping to boost research (Nano, 2004). Stem Cell Sciences Ltd. from Australia is offering a stem cell line to academics and companies to accelerate research (National Institutes of Health, 2004c).

As of 2004, California voters approved Proposition 71, the *California Stem Cell Research and Cures Initiative*, which will allow that state to fund $3 billion worth of stem cell research through 2014. The approved funding creates the Institute for Regenerative Medicine, which will distribute funds and establish research guidelines. California's state constitution will be amended to guarantee biologists the right to do ES research and protect the institute from interference or supervision by the legislature. Proponents believe this will make the state a global leader in this field, draw

continued

FIGURE 3.7 Harvesting Embryonic Stem Cells for Research and Cures
Worldwide, there is increasing research investigating the use of embryonic stem cells and other body cells, such as skin cells, fat cells, and umbilical cord blood cells to create new human cells and tissues.

Source: From Stephanie Nano, "Scientists Give Free Access to Stem Cell Lines," Associated Press, March 3, 2004. Copyright © 2004 Associated Press. Reprinted by permission.

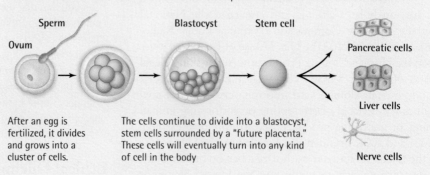

Free access to new stem cell lines

Researchers believe stem cells can be coaxed to form specialized cells needed to cure disease.

Sperm · Ovum · Blastocyst · Stem cell · Pancreatic cells · Liver cells · Nerve cells

After an egg is fertilized, it divides and grows into a cluster of cells.

The cells continue to divide into a blastocyst, stem cells surrounded by a "future placenta." These cells will eventually turn into any kind of cell in the body prominent international biotech researchers to California, and will prove to be economically advantageous. The state of Wisconsin quickly followed with a $750 million initiative to build the *Institute for Discovery* to conduct stem cell research (Seely, 2004). Other states are following. It's a competitive race, with billions of dollars to be made, and many believe such biomedical research is the next "Silicon Valley" (Kotkin, 2004; Spar, 2004).

Stem Cell Reservations

Citizens of various countries hold different religious, philosophical, and ethical beliefs, and some countries forbid the creation of human embryos for research. Supporters of such research downplay any moral reservations, saying ES are a "clump of invisible cells" or "not a real-life person like you." However, other medical scientists, bioethicists and most clergy, politicians, and many Americans believe they cannot support sacrificing one person to extend or improve the life of another person. To them, this is morally wrong since they believe human life begins at conception. The Pope, as leader of the Catholic Church and its millions of followers, "condemns stem-cell research using embryos because they are destroyed in the process but does not oppose other forms of stem cell research where cells are taken from body tissues and life is not threatened" (Owen, 2001).

Use of stem cells from early human embryos, and embryonic germ and fetal stem cells from aborted, fetal tissues, raises ethical, legal, religious, and policy questions: What regulatory agencies will set standards and monitor such research? With a continuous and rising demand for embryos to conduct such research, where will they come from? Will women be paid for

their aborted embryos? Will embryonic stem cells be allowed to develop into the fetal stage and then be destroyed? Will human embryonic cells be joined with other animal cells? Should stem cell lines be treated with any new drug that pharmaceutical companies want to experiment with?

Those opposed agonize over the sale or use of human body parts as a business "commodity" rather than the "miracles" that parents know they are through natural conception, development, and birth (Sandel, 2004). Regulatory laws, commissions, standards and oversight are lacking to prevent human cells from being used irresponsibly, opening the door to new high-tech eugenics.

A Compromise

The Center for Genetics and Society has called for tough public oversight and accountability of the California Stem Cell Initiative to avoid abuses of public monies and to protect the women who will be supplying the eggs for research (Darnovsky, 2004). The debate about ES research is intensely emotional, but various resources indicate that biomedical researchers have been conducting stem cell research with some success for at least a decade. Yet there is no proof that the use of embryonic stem cells will generate other healthy human tissues and organs (Kelly, 2004; Koucheravy, 2004). There is already a rising momentum of research worldwide, and persons on all sides of this issue agree that using other adult stem cells, placental, and umbilical cord stem cells should be used to explore the likelihood of cures and other life-saving advancements. If the predictions of some biomedical researchers come true, humans will be able to have a better quality of life and live much longer by replacing body parts or organs.

means possible is a basic human right. Using refined methods of ARTs, pregnancy rates and normal full-term births have significantly increased, and more than a million babies were born to couples with infertility issues, to same-sex couples, or to singles. Most astonishingly, fertility experts predict *an end* to infertility in the near future. Researchers are using new chemical treatments and microscopic devices, creating new ARTs (including human cloning that would allow anyone to have a baby), and planning to create and design human infants that are free of disease, disorders, or illness. To this end, biomedical researchers are already:

- Improving diagnostics for infertility and determining optimal times for conception
- Improving hormone treatments for natural conception
- Improving IVF techniques and implanting fewer— but healthier—embryos in the uterus to avoid the high risk of multiples
- Making it possible for women born without a uterus, those having undergone chemotherapy and radiation, and more menopausal women to bear children

- Designing synthetic amniotic fluid for life support in artificial wombs
- Creating artificial wombs for embryonic implantation outside of a woman's body
- Creating artificial womb tanks to grow and develop to term aborted or miscarried fetuses in the early or later stages of development (providing an end to abortion or birth defects that occur because of a compromised delivery)
- Improving 3-D and 4-D diagnostic imaging to assess the health of the embryo and fetus during all stages of development prior to birth
- Attempting to remove genetic defects by replacing defective genes at the embryo stage

The most disconcerting of all is *ectogenesis*, which makes use of an artificial womb tank; proponents predict this will end the practice of natural human pregnancy— permitting full-term prenatal development in a technologically monitored, simulated uterine environment and allowing for easy surgical intervention or gene transfer to correct visible defects (Osgood, 2004; Tonti-Filippini, 2003). Parents-to-be will watch their embryo grow into a 40-week fetus with high success rates of a healthy "birth." Will women go for the sales pitch: no maternal "morning sickness," weight gain, or health complications for the mother, no loss of time at work for obstetric checkups or maternity leave, and a "healthier" baby?

Designing "perfect" babies sounds idyllic, but where does the natural bonding of mother to developing baby enter this picture? Where is that sense of awe about a miracle of life? Where is the respect for the human life that a man and woman create together? Yet the same ethical unease arose with the creation of incubators for premature babies in the late 1800s, with the first birth control pills in the 1960s, with the first human heart transplant in 1967 ushering in the age of donor tissues and organ transplants, and with the first baby created by IVF in 1978. Today the public welcomes such life-saving or life-creating procedures. However, as with all new medical "miracles," there must be federal regulation and oversight because there have already been disasters. In 1957 the drug *thalidomide* was sold in Europe and Canada to ease pregnant women's "morning sickness" or insomnia. Tragically for both mothers and children, over 10,000 babies were born with stunted or missing limbs (yet it has reemerged to ease nausea of AIDS and chemotherapy) (Public Affairs Committee, 2000).

Economics, again, is a driving force in improving human reproduction and birth of healthy babies because medical care for premature babies in neonatal intensive care units (NICUs) costs billions of dollars per year—and one cannot assess the emotional toll on anxious parents awaiting the fate of their precious child (March of Dimes, 2004c).

Social scientists, physicians, bioethicists, politicians, clergy, and laypeople raise legitimate questions about ARTs. How long (days or cell divisions) are embryos allowed to develop in a lab? Should embryos be designed to meet certain characteristics? What happens if the recipients change their minds or if an abnormality occurs? Should researchers be allowed to destroy developing embryos or fetuses? Is such destruction a form of eugenics? Will human fetal tissue be grown solely for transplantation (i.e., *xenotransplantation*) (Center for Biology Evaluation and Research, 2004)? Who owns the anonymous embryos developed in a lab? How will children conceived through cloning technologies feel when they find out how they were created? Will development outside a mother's body affect the natural bonding process?

Congress has not passed joint legislation governing ARTs to protect Americans from abuse, despite an opposing range of proposed laws by the House and Senate (Johnson & Williams, 2004). The lack of consistent national or state laws regarding this fast-growing industry leaves the U.S. consumer in a vulnerable situation. One law, *P.L. 108-199*, provides for research using stem cells found in umbilical cord blood by making $10 million available to establish a National Cord Blood Stem Cell Bank (Johnson & Williams, 2004). The Food and Drug Administration (FDA) released a regulation effective May 25, 2005 called *Current Good Tissue Practice for Human Cell, Tissue, and Cellular and Tissue-Based Product Establishments: Inspection and Enforcement*. This regulation governs methods used; facilities and controls used; the manufacture, recordkeeping, and establishment of a quality scientific program—and intends to improve protections of public health while keeping regulatory burdens to a minimum (McKeever, 2004). Some predict the U.S. Supreme Court may enter the policy debate to decide if asexual reproduction is protected by the Constitution. And more U.S. universities, such as Harvard, are getting around President Bush's executive order of 2001 regarding stem cell research by setting up private institutes to get federal funding (Tanne, 2004).

The 57th World Health Assembly met and urged its 192 member nations to implement oversight of "procurement, processing, and transplantation of human cells, tissues, and organs, ensuring accountability for human material for transplantation and its traceability," to "harmonize global practices," to "consider setting up ethics commissions," and to "take measures to protect the poorest and vulnerable groups from . . . the sale of tissues and organs" (Human Organ and Tissue Transplantation 2004, p. 2). Yet many European Union countries, Canada, Australia, China, Japan, South Korea, and some U.S. states are proceeding without such protocol.

The researchers, fertility specialists, politicians, and venture capitalists who support ARTs, including cloning, assert they are not subverting any moral standard. Some say they are bringing humankind closer to God by helping infertile couples fulfill their dream to reproduce or eliminating suffering (Talbot, 2001). Yet many people, especially women, still have moral reservations about redefining motherhood and humanity—and express serious concerns for the future of all humankind.

> **Questions**
>
> What is cloning? What is stem cell research, and why are embryonic stem cells considered to be "the best"? Why are these ARTS so controversial? Where does U.S. legislation stand on these issues of life and death?

Birth Control Methods

Contraception is the leading reason that women first seek care of a **gynecologist** (a physician who specializes in women's reproductive health), and 75 percent see such a physician by the age of 20 (Frankel, 2004). Over the past decade intensive, multipronged approaches to reducing U.S. teen pregnancy and adult unwanted pregnancy have been very successful (see Figure 3.8). After peaking in the early 1990s, births to the youngest teens (ages 10 to 14) are reported to be at their lowest levels in 60 years. Between 1990 and 2002, there was a 43 percent *decline* in the number of births to these very young women, despite the 16 percent rise in young females (Menacker et al., 2004).

Also, in the last decade managed-care insurance plans improved coverage such that by 2002, a majority of plans covered the five leading methods of reversible contraception: diaphragm, one- and three-month injectables, the IUD, and oral contraceptives (Sonfield et al., 2004). Since 1998 the Food and Drug Administration (FDA) has approved at least 14 new contraceptive products for women in the United States. Such essential plans provide reproductive choice for the 60 million U.S. women who are in their childbearing years, and the proportion of women practicing contraception continues to rise ("Facts in Brief," 2004).

Additionally sexually active adolescents and adults are now better informed about other risks of sexual activity, including HIV and AIDS, sexually transmit-

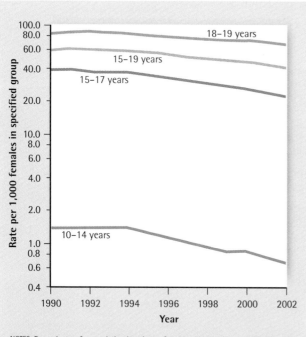

FIGURE 3.8 Birthrates for Females Aged 10–19 Years: United States, 1990–2002 The birthrate among young U.S. adolescents aged 10 to 19 has fallen to the lowest levels in 30 years, and there is continued progress in reducing births to teens of all ages. The 43 percent decline in the number of births since 1990 for the 10- to 14-year-old age group occurred despite the 16 percent increase in the female population aged 10 to 14 years. Births to very young mothers are associated with very high health risks to both the mother and baby.

Source: Menacker, F., Martin, J., MacDorman, M. F., & Ventura, S. J. (2004, November 15). Births to 19–14-year-old mothers 1990–2002: Trends and health outcomes. *National Vital Statistics Reports, 53*(7). Washington, DC: CDC, U.S. Department of Health & Human Services.

ted infections, and lower socioeconomic consequences. They also are more aware of the variety of birth control options to prevent pregnancy and have legal access to abortion to terminate pregnancy.

Contraception There are many contraceptive products and methods that range from reversible to irreversible, but most contraceptives do not protect against HIV or other sexually transmitted infections. Worldwide, various experimental male contraceptives are under clinical trials, including the injection of a liquid plug into the vas deferens and hormonal implants of androgen/progestin in combination, which were successful with a small number of subjects (Turner et al., 2003).

Various advocates of reproductive health choices are working in concert to promote a better informed public, making options more accessible through insurance coverage, and lobbying for more effective means of birth control—including dual-action drugs (e.g., promoting hair growth *and* contraception). (See the *More Information You Can Use* box on page 84, "Contraceptive Products, Plans, and Policymaking: Present and Future.") Also, in some states, a range of health-care providers (PAs, RNs, LPNs, pharmacists, and medical office assistants) are distributing some contraceptives in pharmacies and community clinics. Pharmacists are also being trained to give injections for emergency contraception.

Abstinence Moral values are at the center of the issue of teen pregnancy. Hence, some public health advocates and policy makers agree that *abstinence* is a key ingredient, or the **A** in the **ABCs** of preventing unwanted pregnancy or sexually transmitted infections (**B** is "be faithful to your partner" and **C** is if active, use a condom) (Cohen, 2004). They claim that a major cause of much lower teen pregnancy and abortion rates over the past decade is due to the efforts of "abstinence until marriage" or "abstinence until older" programs as a component of the publicly funded Personal Responsibility and Work Opportunity Reconciliation Act of 1996 (HR 3734). The U.S. Congress continued backing abstinence education in 2005 with $131 million in federal funds (Sherman, 2004).

The abstinence movement, though, is opposed and criticized by those in the public health sector who want to teach a more comprehensive contraception program to prevent pregnancy and sexually transmitted infections (STIs). With this adversarial mindset, early analysis of some abstinence programs has been rather inconclusive or disparaging. A 10-year federal study of "abstinence only" programs is due in 2006. But both sides should be allies and not foes in this public health issue: "Preventing teen pregnancy is as much about moral and religious values as it is about public health," and "the most prevalent reason virgin teen girls give for not engaging in sex is that it is against their religion or morals" (Whitehead, Wilcox, & Rostosky, 2001, pp. 1, 4). Also, faith communities that

More Information You Can Use

Contraceptive Products, Plans, and Policymaking: Present and Future

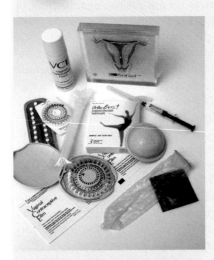

Available Contraceptive Products/ Methods

Reversible Contraception
Abstinence
Cervical cap
Condoms (male and female)
Diaphragm
Implant, *Norplant* (5-year implant)
Injectable, 1-month (*Lunelle*)
Injectable, *Depo-Provera*, 3 months
IUD (intrauterine device)
IUD—*Mirena coil*—5 years
Oral contraceptives–the "pill"
Patch (*Ortho Evra*)
Rhythm method (predicting fertility),
    also called natural family planning
Spermicide creams and gels
Sponge (*Today Sponge*)
Vaginal ring (*NuvaRing*)
Withdrawal (coitus interruptus)

Emergency Contraception
(Plan B) (or *levonorgestrel*)
RU-486 (or *mifepristone*)

Irreversible Contraception
Abortion: surgical or medical
Hysterectomy
Tubal ligation
Vasectomy

Reproductive Health Care Providers

Medical Model (at present)
Physician
Gynecologist/Obstetrician
Planned Parenthood
Community health clinics

**Proposed Pharmacy Access Model
    (5 states have passed legislation)**
Advance prescription for emergency
    contraception
Over-the-counter access
Quick Start on oral contraceptives
Easier, convenient refills
Pharmacists give injectables for
    emergency contraception
Pharmacists write prescriptions for pill,
    patch, and ring
Physician assistants and RNPs write scripts
Expanded support staff training (LPNs, RNs,
    pharmacy clerks, medical office assistants,
    and others)

Community-Based Distribution Model
Health clinics, high schools,
    family planning clinics

Pharmaceutical and Product Manufacturers

Research and development
Conduct clinical trials
New products
Clear regimens
Simple packaging
Simplify instructions
Reasonable cost
Continue research on
    male oral contraceptives

Advocacy, Education, Counseling, and Advertising

Education
Parents
Family planning clinics
Sex education in schools
Improve contraceptive counseling
Public service TV ads
Entertainment television
    (e.g., *Friends* episode)
Provide constructive activities for teens

Proposed
More print media, TV,
    and media information
Update Web health sites
Provider sends e-mail, postcards,
    voicemail messages
Social marketing: beauty salons,
    public bathrooms, bars, churches
Celebrity spokespersons
More consumer research on lifestyle
    and contraception (failed and successful
    strategies)
Better consumer protection and education

Legislation, Insurance, and Policymaking

Insurance Companies
Continue to mandate coverage of a wide range
    of contraceptive methods
Provide affordable coverage

Government
Propose public funding to cover
    contraception for those not covered
    by insurance
Conduct consumer research and evaluation of
    unwanted pregnancy and its effect
    on other social programs
Study products from other countries

Food and Drug Administration (FDA)
Shorter time to market for new products
Better consumer protection to minimize risks
    while preserving benefits
Better labeling of products

Source: Child Trends. Child Trends DataBank Indicator: Late or No Prenatal Care. Retrieved from http://www.childtrendsdatabank.org/figures/25-Figure-1.gif. Reprinted with permission. Original data from National Vital Statistics System.

promote abstinence help teens develop morally and spiritually, provide productive youth development activities, give them confidence and hope for their future, and connect them to caring adults.

In a recent national survey, results from 1,000 teens and 1,000 adults show that most adults (94 percent) and teens (92 percent) said it is important for teens to be given a strong message from society that they should not have sex until out of high school (Albert, 2003). And more young people are cautious about early and casual sex (Albert, 2003; Bernstein, 2004). Teens realize that HIV/AIDS and STIs are big problems, and a growing number of teens, especially those in poor minority neighborhoods, are motivated to go to college and change their lives (Bernstein, 2004). While contemporary teens have greater awareness of, and access to, contraceptive choices, they also want to learn more about relationships, intimacy, love, and communicating with partners (Bernstein, 2004).

Abortion   Contraceptives are not foolproof and nearly 50 percent of pregnancies among American women are unintended, but termination of the pregnancy is a legal option. **Abortion** is the spontaneous or induced expulsion of the fetus prior to the time of viability. Abortion on demand has been a legal medical procedure since the U.S. Supreme Court legalized abortion in *Roe* v. *Wade* in 1973. The majority who undergo abortion are young, unmarried, and likely to obtain an abortion within the first eight weeks of pregnancy when health risks are at their lowest (Strauss et al., 2004). The published statistics are astonishing: from 1973 to 2001 more than 45 million abortions were reported (the total is higher as Alaska, California, and New Hampshire have not reported since 1998). More than 850,000 women had abortions in 2001, yet this reveals a pattern of marked decline since a high in 1990 (Strauss et al., 2004).

The striking reduction in surgical abortions is partially attributed to increasing use of emergency contraception pills sold in the United States, and taking a regimen of pills prevents pregnancy after unprotected intercourse. A few states are experimenting with training pharmacists, nurse practitioners, physician's assistants, and medical residents to distribute such emergency contraception. *Mifeprex* or *methotrexate* prevent a pregnancy by blocking progesterone receptors and preventing the endometrium lining from implanting or nourishing an embryo. It can take a few weeks and miscarriage-like cramping and bleeding before the chemically caused abortion is complete, whereas surgical abortions are finished within an hour ("Induced Abortion," 2003). And such pills work only in early pregnancy. Various advocacy groups are lobbying for campus health centers to be able to provide a full range of reproductive, contraceptive, and emergency contraceptive services.

An especially volatile issue is *partial-birth abortion,* performed toward the last trimester when a fetus could be viable outside the womb. The procedure (called "dilation and extraction," or "D&X") involves bringing the fetus feet-first into the birth canal, puncturing its skull with a sharp instrument and sucking out its brain, then removing it from the mother's body. In 2000 approximately 2,200 such late-term abortions were performed in the United States (Schneider, 2003). Advocates for abortion say that a fetus does not feel pain (Dailard, 2004). However, one might reconsider when viewing the "photo of the 20th century" and the reaction of a 21-week-old fetus Samuel Armas undergoing surgery at www.michaelclancy.com. His mother chose not to abort a fetus with spina bifida and had experimental intrauterine surgery that was successful.

The abortion issue has spawned a bitterly divisive conflict between two large factions of citizens, the pro-life and the pro-choice advocates—and abortion laws vary from state to state, with at least 30 states banning partial-birth abortion (Dailard, 2004).

Pro-Life View   The pro-life advocates point to the extensive loss of human life, the reported lasting psychological harm to the women who have selected this choice, and the moral decay of a society that allows this to happen. The National Right-to-Life Committee and other psychologists have identified "postabortion stress syndrome" as a cluster of symptoms some women experience after the abrupt termination of a pregnancy by elective abortion: depression, a sense of worthlessness, personal relationship disorders, sexual dysfunction, damaged self-esteem, a sense of victimization, and, for a small number of women, suicide (MacNair, 2001; Rue et al., 2004). Presently there are nearly 3,000 Crisis Pregnancy Centers across the United States to help counsel women facing unplanned pregnancy and ready to offer medical, financial, and legal assistance ("Alternatives to Abortion," 2004). The woman who initiated the *Roe* v. *Wade* lawsuit to secure a safe, legal abortion in 1973 is now an outspoken pro-life advocate. Since 1995 the U.S. Congress passed legislation to ban partial-birth abortion that was vetoed by former President Clinton. President Bush signed the *Partial-Birth Abortion Ban Act of 2003,* after the House and Senate passed it. Within hours, three judges signed restraining orders on the law. Critics of the law contend it is vaguely worded and may restrict access to safe, affordable procedures (Greene & Ecker, 2004).

Pro-Choice View   Advocates state that abortion provides many benefits to women and couples who choose not to have or cannot afford a baby and that every woman deserves the right to control what happens to her body. Illegal abortions performed prior to 1973 put women at a much greater health risk than those performed in medical settings today. Couples with a high risk of producing a fetus with genetic defects have a choice to continue or terminate the pregnancy. Pro-choice advocates further state that the abortion procedure, performed during early stages of pregnancy, is statistically safer to the mother than childbirth. In the United States in 2001, only 11 women died from complications after a legal abortion (out of a reported 850,000).

Both sides of this emotional issue are gathering greater force, affecting the outcomes of election campaigns at state and national levels, and impacting the future of our society.

The Expanding Reproductive Years

Of great interest to medical professionals—especially pediatric endocrinologists—is the fact that American and European girls are starting puberty earlier than they did 25 to 30 years ago. In the early 1900s girls did not menstruate until 14 years old, on average. Today some girls begin developing pubic hair and breasts as young as 5 years old and begin menstruating at 8 or 9 years old: the average age is 12.8 for Caucasian girls and 12.2 for African American girls. This has been called "developmental compression," and girls who undergo precocious puberty often struggle with poor self-esteem and social pressures among peers (Ellis & Garber, 2000). For some girls, along with precocious puberty comes earlier sexual activity and early pregnancy. This is a critical societal issue because such young girls do not have the resources to support themselves and the children they are bearing. The health-care system, the social welfare system, the educational system, governing agencies, and American business and industry are collaborating to educate American youth about the risks of teen (or younger) pregnancy.

At this time there is no scientific consensus about the cause of the increasing incidence of earlier puberty, though researchers speculate it is related to earlier weight gain or exposure to chemicals in the food supply that mimic hormones (Kaplowitz et al., 2001). Others suggest that from a psychosocial perspective, stressful family relationships and the presence of a stepfather in the home are contributing factors (Ellis & Garber, 2000). Yet pediatric endocrinologists suggest that onset of pubertal development before the age of 8 years in a girl or 9 years in a boy warrants a clinical and bone age evaluation (Carel, Lahlou, & Chaussain, 2004). The incidence of teen pregnancies for girls ages 10 to 14 had reached an all-time high by the early 1990s but by 2002 were reported to be at their lowest levels in 60 years (Menacker et al., 2004). Yet U.S. teen pregnancy and births remain the highest in the industrialized world (see Figure 3.8) (McNamera, 2004).

Throughout history, a woman's reproductive years have typically ceased after her last menstrual cycle (on average, about age 50) called *menopause.* In a recent European multinational study with a large sample of couples, it was found that women experienced fertility decline in their late twenties with substantial decreases by their late thirties. Male fertility was less affected by age, but male participants showed significant declines in fertility by their late thirties as well

(Dunson, Colombo, & Baird, 2002). Yet with ART methods today, more women are attempting to have a baby during their forties, fifties, or after menopause. Infertile women in their thirties and forties and menopausal women undergo a careful health screening, but some are ineligible for ARTs. Those accepted are at high risk for pregnancy complications, and only a small subgroup of women can afford the cost of assisted reproduction (while some have insurance coverage and costs are tax deductible as medical expenses under current law) (Pratt, 2004). The American Fertility Association and the American Society for Reproductive Medicine have launched an extensive educational campaign targeting those who are waiting to conceive: *Advancing Age Decreases Your Ability to Have Children.* With advancing age, only a small percentage of women are able to get pregnant and produce a healthy child. For example, in 2002 in the United States, women ages 50 to 55 gave birth to 263 children (and some were multiple births) (Heffner, 2004).

A woman past menopause has no viable ova of her own, so donated ova are sought from a woman in her twenties or thirties. The older woman is treated with a regimen of female hormones to stimulate her uterus to be healthy for IVF. Sperm are used from the woman's spouse or from a donor, typically under age 40. Fertilization occurs in a medical lab, and several embryos are grown for a few days before being implanted into the woman's womb. Thus, the risk of multiple conception is high.

Additionally, international commercialization of egg donation and purchase is gaining momentum. A recent survey among 49 countries revealed great disparities about regulations, guidelines, and legislation for ART clinic procedures, procurement, and costs (Jones & Cohen, 2004). Although many in the medical field agree for ethical reasons that a donor should not be paid for her eggs, she can be compensated for her time and the inconvenience of surgical extraction. Egg donors may be paid $7,500 or much higher, and fertility clinics now advertise at top college campuses, may request genetic testing of donors, and yet provide no legal protection for donors (Blackley, 2003). Another major concern is the issue of what genetic traits are being selected by those with the purchasing power. Are couples selecting to have more boys than girls? What heritable traits do consumers hope to have in a child? Heredity makes a significant contribution to what we look like, what our abilities are or what our disabilities or diseases may be, how we might behave, and our life's potential.

Questions

What are some methods of birth control available to women in the United States? How commonly is abortion used as a method of birth control? What are the major arguments of the two contrasting views about abortion, and at what stage of pregnancy do most women seek abortions? How does a woman who has experienced menopause potentially have a baby, and how likely is she to be successful?

Heredity and Genetics

Perhaps at the heart of the debate about ART and the expanding range of reproductive years is our understanding that each person's genetic makeup is very complex and unique, with a range of flaws likely. With normal sexual reproduction, many things often malfunction. What will happen when scientists have free license to re-create the human species—and all its genetic combinations? How many embryos may we create and destroy before accepting the "perfect" one? Is there such a thing as the "perfect baby"? Do we really want to parent a younger physical replica of ourselves?

As mentioned earlier, a major debate in the fields of psychology, psychobiology, and sociobiology involves what contribution hereditary or environmental factors make to our unfolding physical, intellectual, social, and emotional development. This is called the nature (biology) versus nurture (environment) debate. Sociobiologists work to define laws of the evolution and biology of social behavior in many species. Psychologists tend to focus on the nature of psychological mechanisms and adaptability to one's environment. Healthy debate among professionals, including views of bioethicists, contributes to our knowledge about the significant role of biological inheritance.

We now take a look at our biological inheritance, referred to as **heredity,** the genes we inherit from our biological parents. Each of us has inherited a specific genetic code from our biological parents, and fertilization is the major event determining our biological inheritance. We begin life as a single fertilized cell, or *zygote,* that contains all the hereditary material passed on to us from our parents and their ancestors. Precisely blueprinted in this original cell are the 200 billion or so cells that we possess nine months later at birth. **Genetics** is the scientific study of biological inheritance by geneticists, and in 2000 the first draft of the genetic blueprint of humans was accomplished by the Human Genome Project.

The Human Genome Project

In 1990, scientists from the U.S. Department of Energy and the National Institutes of Health began competing in an exciting scientific race with Celera, a private company, to discover the sequencing of the **human genome,** the genetic blueprint of all the *genes* on their appropriate chromosomes within the 6 feet of DNA coiled up in every human cell (Travis, 2000). Since the first draft of the human genome was reported in 2000, hundreds of scientists worldwide collaborated to convert the draft into a genome sequence with high accuracy that is 99 percent complete. There are far fewer genes than expected—only about 20,000 to 25,000 rather than the figure of 100,000 predicted by genetic researchers (International Human Genome Sequencing Consortium, 2004). Humans have only twice as many genes as a fruit fly or a lowly nematode worm. What a surprise!

This sequencing of genes holds the entire set of hereditary instructions for creating, operating, and maintaining an organism, and reproducing the next generation. Each of your body's trillions of cells contains a copy of your genome. More important, a genome is information that affects every aspect of our behavior and physiology. Not only do our genes influence what we look like, but molecular errors in our genes are responsible for an estimated 3,000 to 4,000 clearly hereditary diseases (National Human Genome Research Institute [NHGRI], 1998b).

In short, the genome is divided into chromosomes, chromosomes contain genes, and genes are made of **DNA (deoxyribonucleic acid),** which in turn tells a cell how to make vital proteins. "The way genes influence your traits is by telling your cells which proteins to make, how much, when, and where" (DeWeerdt, 2001). It has been found that human beings are 99.9 percent alike in their genetic sequence—it is the 0.1 percent that gives us our appearance on the outside and on the inside, at a cellular level. So no two people are exactly alike (Eisner, 2000).

The next phase of sophisticated genetic studies continues as the *Genomes to Life* project with visionary goals of (1) sequencing genomes of other animal species, (2) mapping genomes and making datasets publicly available, (3) studying variation within genomes, (4) reducing both computation time and costs for sequencing, and (5) studying specific diseases (Collins et al., 2003). What research scientists learn will eventually help doctors predict, detect, and treat human diseases and conditions—and some of these "corrections" to the human genetic code might be achieved during the embryonic or fetal stages of life.

Questions

How do scientists study heredity and genetics? What have geneticists accomplished with the Human Genome Project to date, and what are their goals in the near future? Approximately how many genes are in the human genome?

What Are Chromosomes and Genes?

Around the early 1900s, the use of microscopes to study cellular tissue led to the discovery of chromosomes. **Chromosomes** are long, threadlike structures made of protein and nucleic acid that contain the hereditary materials found in the nuclei of any cell. Upon fertilization, for humans, the 23 chromosomes of the ovum are combined with the 23 chromosomes of the sperm, for a total of 46 chromosomes, usually referred to as 23 pairs (see the photo on page 88 of the Karyotype of Human Chromosomes). Exceptions to this normal pairing will be discussed later in this section.

Each chromosome contains a linear arrangement of thousands of smaller units that divide it into regions called **genes,** which transmit inherited characteristics passed from biological parents to children. They are like beads on a string, and each gene has its own specific location on the

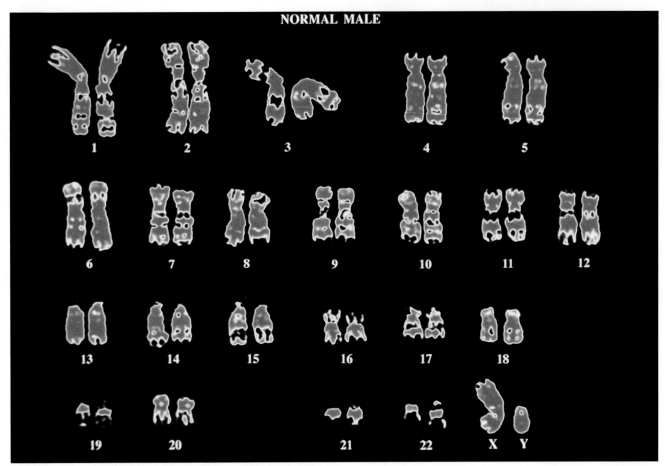

NORMAL MALE

A Karyotype of Human Chromosomes Every cell nucleus contains 23 pairs of chromosomes—two of each type. Each parent provides one member of the pair. Chromosomes differ in size and shape. For convenience in talking about them, scientists arrange the 23 pairs in descending order by size, and number them accordingly. The members of each chromosome pair look alike, with the exception of the 23rd pair in males. As the illustration shows, the 23rd chromosome is the sex-determining chromosome. An XX combination of chromosomes in this pair produces a female; an XY combination would produce a male. The male Y chromosome is much smaller.

Source: Lennart Nilsson & Lars Hamberger. (2004). *A child is born.* 4th Edition, Revised & Updated. New York: Dell, p. 19.

chromosome. Each human cell contains approximately 20,000 to 25,000 genes and 3 billion letters of chemical code, which are composed of DNA. DNA is the active biochemical substance in genes that programs the cells to manufacture vital protein substances, including enzymes, hormones, antibodies, and other structural proteins (National Human Genome Research Institute [NHGRI], 1998a). This DNA code of life is carried in a large molecule shaped like a double helix or twisted rope ladder (see Figure 3.9).

Nearly all cells in the human body are formed through a kind of cell division called **mitosis,** during which every chromosome in the cell splits lengthwise to form a new pair. Through this process of nuclear division, the cell replicates itself by dividing into two "daughter" cells with the same hereditary information. Unlike other cells in the human body, the gametes—ova and sperm—have only 23 chromosomes each, not the usual 23 pairs. Gametes are formed by a more complex kind of cell division called meiosis. **Meiosis** involves two cell divisions during which the chromosomes are reduced to half their original number. Each gamete receives only one chromosome from each pair in every parental cell. This is half the usual number, allowing each parent to contribute half the total number of chromosomes and genetic material at fertilization. Thus, upon fertilization, the newly formed zygote contains 23 pairs of chromosomes (see Figure 3.10).

Each person's human genome is slightly different because of mutations—"mistakes" that occur occasionally in a DNA sequence, and some of these mutations are expressed as diseases and defects in the human organism. Geneticists predict breakthroughs over the next 15 to 20 years in the early detection and treatment of many diseases. The goal of the new science of gene therapy is to correct or replace the altered gene. The gene for cystic fibrosis, the most common lethal hereditary disease among Caucasians, was discovered in 1989, and the first human gene therapy efforts are under way in federally approved clinical trials. Scientists can test for these diseases directly as well as prenatally. About 5 percent of the project's annual budget is spent trying to resolve the ethical, legal, and social issues likely to arise from this research (Collins et al., 2003).

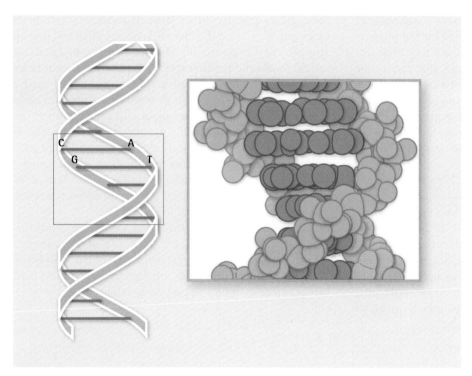

FIGURE 3.9 A Model of the DNA Molecule The double-chained structure of a DNA molecule is coiled in a helix. During cell division the two chains pull apart, or "unzip." Each half is now free to assemble a new complementary half. At the right side of this illustration, we see a larger depiction of genes, which transmit inherited characteristics. DNA in genes programs cells to manufacture vital protein substances.

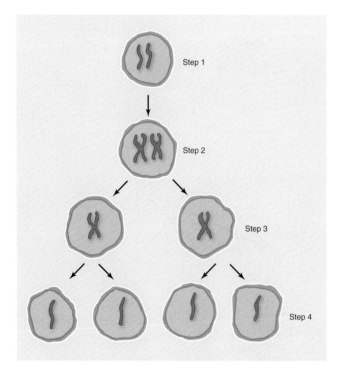

FIGURE 3.10 Meiosis This simplified diagram illustrates how gametes (ova and sperm) are formed through meiosis. In Step 1 each chromosome teams up with its partner. During Step 2 the first meiotic division occurs; both chromosomes of each pair are duplicated. (For simplicity, the figure portrays only one pair, although humans normally have 23 pairs.) Each original chromosome and its exact copy, termed a chromatid, are joined at the center. Step 3 involves a second meiotic division. Each of the two original chromosomes and its copy become a part of an intermediary cell. In Step 4 each chromatid—the original and its copy—segregates into a separate ovum or sperm gamete. Thus, the intermediary cells undergo cell division without chromosome duplication. This process produces four gametes.

Determination of an Embryo's Sex

In many societies, even today, a male child is expected to inherit the family name or carry on the family business or provisional role in a culture. Consequently, in many cultures the birth of a male child is celebrated but the birth of a female child might not be. An extreme example is China. To control population growth, in 1979 China had family-planning laws that allowed only one child per family; some couples aborted female children because

they wanted a male child instead, while some women were fined heavily or underwent forced abortion or sterilization to avoid additional pregnancies. Social scientists studying China's one-child policy report a high ratio of boy babies compared with female babies and projections for future social problems—school closings, fewer workers in a growing economy, and a shortage of marital partners—thus the policy has relaxed in some respects ("China's One Child Rule Risks Social Problems," 2004).

Historical literature records many incidents of women being faulted, divorced, or killed for not producing a male child. However, through the study of genetics we know that it is the male's sperm that carries the chromosome that determines the sex of a child. Of the 46 chromosomes (23 pairs) that each human normally possesses, 22 pairs are similar in size and shape in both men and women that are called **autosomes.** The 23rd pair, the **sex chromosomes**—one from the mother and one from the father—determine the baby's sex. Each of the mother's ova has an X chromosome. However, a sperm can contain either an X chromosome or a Y chromosome. If an ovum with X is fertilized by a sperm with X, then the zygote will be a female (XX). If an ovum with an X is fertilized by a sperm with Y, then the zygote will be a male (XY). The Y chromosome determines that a child will be male. Approximately six to eight weeks into embryonic development, the male embryo starts producing the male hormone testosterone, which promotes the development of male characteristics.

Questions

What are the mechanisms of heredity, and what is their function on the double helix? How many chromosomes does the mother contribute to the genetic makeup of a zygote, and how many chromosomes does the father contribute? How many total chromosomes does each human normally possess? What is the genetic makeup of a female versus a male on the sex chromosome?

Principles of Genetics

Have you ever wondered how your own heredity has influenced your characteristics and development? Much of our original understanding of genes and the science of genetics came from studies conducted by an Austrian monk, Gregor Johann Mendel (1822–1884). By crossing varieties of peas (short, tall; red flowers, white flowers) in his small monastery garden, Mendel was able to formulate the basic principles of heredity. Mendel hypothesized that independent units he called "factors" determined inherited characteristics, and today we call these units *genes.* Mendel reasoned that the genes that control a single hereditary characteristic must exist in pairs. Advances in microbiology and genetics have confirmed Mendel's hunch. Genes occur in pairs, one on a maternal chromosome and the other on the corresponding paternal chromosome. The two genes in a pair occupy a specific position on each chromosome. Recently, each and every human gene was mapped for both its location and function by the Human Genome Project, as cited earlier.

Dominant and Recessive Characteristics   Each member of a pair of genes is called an allele. An **allele,** then, is one member of a pair of genes found on corresponding chromosomes that affect the same trait. There can be only

two alleles per person for any characteristic, one from each parent (one on the maternal chromosome and one on the paternal chromosome). Mendel demonstrated that one allele, the **dominant character,** completely masks or hides the other allele, the **recessive character.** Mendel used a capital letter of the alphabet to signify the dominant allele *(A)* and a lowercase letter to signify the recessive allele *(a).* When both alleles from the parents are the same, this is referred to as a **homozygous** characteristic *(AA)* or *(aa).* When the two paired alleles are different, this is called a **heterozygous** characteristic *(Aa).* The characteristic of the dominant allele *(A)* will be expressed, unless the recessive alleles pair up *(aa)* (see Figure 3.11).

Not all traits are transmitted as simply. Some inherited traits, or defects, are the result of the complex interaction of many genes, which is called **polygenic inheritance.** Personality, intelligence, aptitudes, and abilities are examples of polygenic inheritance.

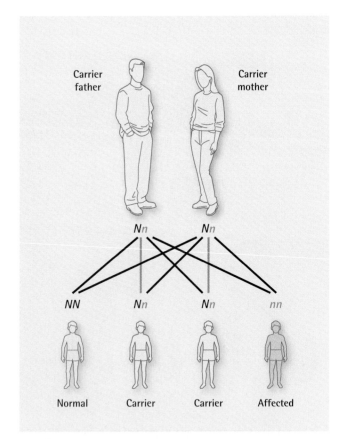

FIGURE 3.11 Transmission of Recessive, Single Gene Defects Both parents, usually themselves unaffected by the faulty gene, carry a normal gene (*N*) that dominates its faulty recessive counterpart *(n).* The odds for each child are (1) a 25 percent chance of being *NN*, normal: inheriting two *N*s and accordingly being free of the faulty recessive gene; (2) a 50 percent chance of being *Nn* and therefore a carrier like both parents; and (3) a 25 percent risk of being *nn*, affected; inheriting a "double dose" of *n* genes, which may cause a serious genetic disease.

Questions

What is an allele, and what is the function of a dominant allele in contrast to a recessive allele? How do you distinguish between a homozygous versus a heterozygous characteristic? What do we mean by polygenic inheritance, and can you give an example?

Phenotypes and Genotypes   By cross-pollinating red-flowered and white-flowered pea plants, Mendel demonstrated the distinction between the **genotype,** the actual genetic makeup of an organism, and the **phenotype,** the observable (or expressed) characteristics of the organism. In human beings, the phenotype includes physical, physiological, and behavioral traits. Humans also possess dominant and recessive genes, as mentioned earlier.

As an illustration, consider your eye color. Brown is the dominant eye color in humans worldwide. Blue and green are recessive eye colors. When looking at your own eyes in a mirror (without colored contact lenses), you are observing the phenotype. Potentially, the underlying genotype could be one of three possibilities for eye color, with *B* representing brown: *BB, Bb,* or *bb.* If you are a brown-eyed person, you have either the *BB* or the *Bb* genotype. If you are a blue-eyed or green-eyed person, you have inherited the two recessive alleles for eye color and have the *bb* genotype. Do you have naturally dark hair or light colored hair (blonde or red)? The observed color of your natural hair is your phenotype. Again, using *B* for brown or black, there are three possible genotypes: *BB, Bb,* or *bb.* If you have naturally dark hair color, your genotype is dominant with either *BB* or *Bb.* If you have naturally light hair color, your genotype is recessive and is *bb.* To modify what a TV comic Flip Wilson used to say: What you see is not necessarily what you get.

Multifactorial Transmission   The recognition that environmental factors interact with genetic factors to produce traits is termed **multifactorial transmission.** If we consider that heredity and genetics provide us with our basic biochemical structure and an unfolding plan over the course of development, what role does our environment (or ecological systems, as Bronfenbrenner would say) play in our development? Are you who you are because of this genetic blueprint that has been passed along to you, or does your environment promote or detract from that blueprint? Do you have any influence on your own life's development?

For example, consider Leann Rimes, who was born with a predisposition toward musical talent. From an early age she loved singing and sang publicly. With her parents' encouragement and support (praise, lessons, time, financial sacrifice, and management), she developed her ability throughout her childhood. By her early teens, she had received recognition and praise from top professionals in the country music field. Her self-motivation and the encouragement from others promoted the development of her natural abilities. Without such encouragement and support through her early years, she might not have developed her singing talent.

Additionally, some physical characteristics are the result of multifactorial transmission. For example, the age for the onset of puberty and the age of menopause are believed to be preprogrammed genetically, but nutrition, physical fitness, stress, illness, and disease can advance or delay these preprogrammed events.

Sex-Linked Inherited Characteristics   Genes are inherited independently only if they are on different chromosomes. Genes that are linked, or appear on the same chromosome, are inherited together. Good examples of linked genes are **sex-linked traits.** The X chromosome, for instance, contains many genes that are not otherwise related to sexual traits. Hemophilia, a hereditary defect that interferes with the normal clotting process of blood, is a sex-linked characteristic carried by the X chromosome. There are about 150 other known sex-linked disorders, including a type of muscular dystrophy, certain forms of night blindness, Hunter's syndrome (a severe form of mental retardation), and juvenile glaucoma (hardening of the fluids within the eyeball).

The vast majority of sex-linked genetic defects occur in men, because men have only one X chromosome. In women, the harmful action of a gene on one X chromosome is usually suppressed by a dominant gene on the other chromosome. Thus, though women themselves normally are unaffected by a given sex-linked disorder, they can be carriers. A man is affected if he receives from his mother an X chromosome bearing the genetic defect (see Figure 3.12). A man cannot receive the abnormal gene from his father. Males transmit an X chromosome only to their daughters, never to their sons, who always receive a father's Y chromosome.

A common example of a sex-linked trait is male-pattern baldness (which begins with thinning hair at the crown of the man's head and can lead to extensive baldness by the late twenties and early thirties). The mother inherits this trait from her father, but she herself is not affected. However, her sons have a 50 percent chance of being affected. Another illustration of a sex-linked trait is red-green color blindness. The majority affected by this are males, who often do not realize they see things "differently" until they start driving and have difficulty recognizing the red and green on traffic lights. To those affected, these two colors look more like a brownish color. Newer traffic lights have a shutterlike clear covering that opens up and closes quickly to emit a pulsing bright light on the red and green so those affected with red-green color blindness can more accurately distinguish the command. Preschool and kindergarten

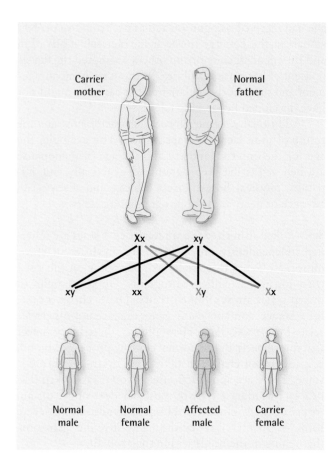

FIGURE 3.12 **Transmission of Sex-Linked Genetic Defects** In most sex-linked genetic disorders, the female sex chromosome of an unaffected mother (a woman who does not herself show the disorder) carries one faulty chromosome (X) and one normal chromosome (x). The father carries normal x and y chromosomes. The statistical odds for each male child are (1) a 50 percent risk of inheriting the faulty (X) chromosome and hence the disorder and (2) a 50 percent chance of inheriting normal x and y chromosomes. For each female child the statistical odds are (1) a 50 percent risk of inheriting one faulty (X) chromosome and hence becoming a carrier like her mother and (2) a 50 percent chance of inheriting no faulty gene.

teachers teaching color recognition are likely to be the first to spot this in affected children.

In rare instances a female can inherit these disorders if the X chromosome she receives from her mother and the X chromosome she receives from her father both bear a gene for a given disease or disorder.

Questions

What is a person's genotype versus his or her phenotype? If a person has eye color of *Bb*, what can you say about his eye color? Can you give an example of multifactorial transmission? Why do the majority of sex-linked defects occur in males?

Genetic Counseling and Testing

Over the past 20 years or so, our increased knowledge of genetics has given rise to the field of **genetic counseling,** a process whereby physicians and specialists counsel couples about concerns they may have about inherited diseases in their family history. (See the *Implications for Practice* box, "Genetic Counselor.") People who are deciding whether to create a child might have concerns about inherited diseases in their family backgrounds and seek genetic counseling to find out the risk of passing along this particular disorder or disease. In some genetic disorders, the disease shows up during the first year of life; in others, the symptoms do not become apparent until much later. Some disorders are much more serious than others. A variety of diagnostic tests are now available to parents with substantiated histories of genetic disease and to couples who, for whatever reason, wish to determine whether a fetus has defects. Some genetic defects are more prevalent in people of certain racial or ethnic backgrounds. For example, sickle-cell anemia occurs among people of African descent, and Tay-Sachs disease occurs in Ashkenazic Jews (see the *Human Diversity* box on page 95, "Genetic Counseling and Testing").

Though genetic counseling can be quite beneficial in many circumstances, ethicists also debate the pros and cons of genetic counseling. How is a decision made that a fetus should live or die? Is our society moving into a disguised eugenics movement? Is genetic information kept private? Is genetic information a reason to excuse certain illegal behaviors in a court of law? What do we do after we test a 2-year-old for a disease and find out the child has inherited a disorder? How much does it cost to raise a child with severe disabilities? What are the hidden emotional and social costs to the family and to society? There are many sides to this issue, and no conclusive answers.

Genetic and Chromosomal Abnormalities

Some disorders are associated with the presence of too few or too many chromosomes (rather than the normal 23 pairs, in humans). One common disorder is Down syndrome, a disorder that occurs in 1 out of every 800 live births (National Down Syndrome Society [NDSS], 2004). In the United States, nearly 350,000 families have a child with Down syndrome. Approximately 5,000 children with Down syndrome are born each year. As the mortality rate associated with Down syndrome is decreasing, the prevalence of individuals with Down syndrome in American society is increasing.

There are three causes of Down syndrome, but in about 95 percent of cases there are three copies of the 21st chromosome, a condition called Trisomy 21. In these individuals the total number of chromosomes is 47 instead of the normal 46. The extra chromosome alters the course of development and causes the characteristics associated with

Implications for Practice

Genetic Counselor
Luba Djurdjinovic, M.S.

I am an executive director/director of genetics programs/genetic counselor at the Ferre Institute. Genetic counseling is the process of helping people understand and adapt to the medical, psychological, and familial implications of genetic contribution to disease. Families pass on a health legacy in terms of lifestyle choices and genetic makeup, and some families wish to understand why and how these conditions are passed down and their options in identifying "at-risk" individuals. A person's genetic makeup provides the initial contribution to the development of common health conditions (heart disease, cancer, stroke, dementia, and others). Some families have many generations with a common health or physical condition.

When first meeting families for genetic risk assessment and counseling, I learn as much as possible about the family's medical history. The family helps me collect family medical records and information. I review their health information to provide a genetic perspective on the family's concerns. I provide such information in a structured educational and psychologically sensitive manner. Individuals and families learn about inheritance, the natural history of the condition, and chance of occurrence or recurrence in the family. Genetic testing options are explored as well as opportunities in managing the condition and any treatment options. Some families are directed to research studies. Counseling is important to assure that informed choices are promoted and appropriate support is provided for adaptation to the risk information and/or genetic condition.

Genetic counselors complete a two- or three-year master of science degree with an emphasis in human genetics. Candidates for admission to a genetic counselor training program are encouraged to have direct experience with persons challenged by disability and demonstrate an ability to appreciate the psychological challenges individuals and families might face. They are encouraged to understand the professional role of genetic counselors through an internship, observation, and discussion with a genetic counselor. Upon completion of training, genetic counselors are encouraged to take a national certification exam, and some states require licensure of genetic counselors. Genetic counselors must complete a clinical rotation at a medical school and/or major medical center in the areas of pediatric genetics, prenatal genetics, cancer genetics, and adult disease genetics. Some seek specialty clinical internships related to neuromuscular disease, blood disorders, craniofacial disorders and others.

Genetic counselors appear to share common characteristics such as curiosity about human dilemma and adaptations to it. Counselors should have strong interpersonal skills and enjoy engaging the client in the genetic counseling process. Clients often feel that scientific information is "above their head," and it is the genetic counselor's role to make every effort to assist the client in learning and applying the new information. The person will be a "lifelong learner," because understanding science and medicine requires ongoing aggressive continuing education.

I enjoy many aspects of my profession, especially meeting families. First, I am amazed at family adaptations to generations of challenges that can come from some inherited conditions. I also value the efforts that families undergo to learn the reasons why a condition has occurred and wish to understand the recurrence. Assisting with each family's experience prepares me to meet the next family and learn about their dilemma. Finally, the community of genetics professionals in the United States is small, and there is a close collegial relationship.

Down syndrome: flat facial profile, upward slanted eyes, protruding lower jaw, poor Moro reflex, hyperflexibility of joints, excess skin on neck, protruding underlip, a small mouth cavity that causes the tongue to protrude, short neck, very short fifth finger on each hand, one long crease across the palm of each hand, typically mild to moderate mental retardation, global developmental delays, and increased incidence of respiratory, cardiovascular, and other manifestations (NDSS, 2004).

Today, early intervention services help children with Down syndrome develop to their full potential. Those who receive good medical care and are included

Young Adults with Down Syndrome: Productive Members of Society Three of these young women have Down syndrome, and they reside in a community residence with professional staff that fully supports their need to be integrated into the community to learn and grow, to become as independent as possible by developing life skills, to make many of their own decisions, to develop their abilities and interests to their full potential, to be employed and contribute to their own support, and to be actively engaged in social and recreational activities. Infants and children with Down syndrome are eligible for early intervention services, mainstreamed in inclusive classrooms, and experience more social acceptance by peers.

in school and community activities can be expected to adapt successfully, develop social skills, find work, participate in decisions that affect them, and make a positive contribution to society. Some adults with Down syndrome are marrying and forming their own families (children of Trisomy 21 parents have a 50 percent chance of having normal intelligence) (NDSS, 2004). Parents of adults with Down syndrome have noted major changes in public acceptance toward individuals with disabilities and an expansion of support services.

Can genetic counseling predict who is likely to have a child with Down syndrome? A few relevant factors are known. Down syndrome affects people of all races and economic levels. The additional chromosome that causes Down syndrome is more likely to originate from the mother (95 percent chance) than from the father (5 percent chance). Older women have a much higher risk of having a child with Down syndrome. A 35-year-old woman has a 1 in 400 chance, a 40-year-old woman has a 1 in 110 chance, and at age 45 the incidence is approximately 1 in 35 (NDSS, 2004). However, younger women also give birth to children with Down syndrome. Some genetic research-

ers suggest that the current statistics are misleading because the total number of older women (over 35) having babies is typically far fewer than the total number of younger women who are having babies. A number of other disorders are linked to sex chromosome abnormalities.

For those who believe they may have a significant chance of bearing a child at risk of a genetic disorder, genetic counseling and testing can determine with a high degree of accuracy whether the fetus has this defect, can help couples prepare for a child with a disability, or can lead to termination of a pregnancy.

> **Questions**
>
> What does a genetic counselor do, and what types of diagnostic tests are available for assessment of embryonic and fetal health? How and when is amniocentesis performed and why? What are some potential outcomes of fetal diagnostics for parents?

Prenatal Development

Whether conception occurs naturally or as a result of an assisted reproductive technique, between conception and birth the human being grows from a single cell, barely visible to the naked eye, to a mass of about 7 pounds containing some 200 billion cells.

The **prenatal period** is the period between conception and birth. It normally averages about 266 days, or 280 days from the last menstrual period. Embryologists divide prenatal development into three stages: The **germinal period** extends from conception to the end of the second week; the second, the **embryonic period** extends from the end of the second week to the end of the eighth week; and the third, the **fetal period** extends from the end of the eighth week until birth. Developmental biology is progressing rapidly, giving us a better understanding of how the body and its specialized organs and tissues are formed (Barinaga, 1994; Visible Embryo Project, 1998).

The Germinal Period

The *germinal period* is characterized by (1) growth of the *zygote* after fertilization and (2) establishment of a linkage between the zygote and the mother's support system. After fertilization, the zygote begins a three- to four-day journey down the fallopian tube toward the uterus (see Figure 3.14 on page 96). The zygote is moved along by the action of the cilia and the active contraction of the walls of the oviduct. Within a few hours of fertilization, growth begins with the initiation of mitosis. In mitosis the zygote divides, forming 2 cells identical in makeup to the first cell. In turn, each of these cells divides, making

Human Diversity

Genetic Counseling and Testing

Prenatal diagnosis employs techniques to determine the health status of an unborn fetus. Congenital anomalies (existing at birth) account for 20 to 25 percent of perinatal deaths. Prenatal diagnosis is helpful for (1) managing the pregnancy, (2) determining pregnancy outcome, (3) planning for birth process complications or newborn health risks, (4) deciding whether to continue a pregnancy, and (5) finding conditions that could affect future pregnancies (Prenatal Diagnosis, 1998).

A **genetic counselor** has a graduate degree, training, and experience in medical genetics and counseling and works with a health-care team, giving information and support to those who may be at risk for an inherited condition. Genetic counselors work in hospitals, medical facilities, universities, corporations (such as pharmaceutical firms or genetic testing companies), HMOs, or in independent practice (National Society of Genetic Counselors, 2004). Genetic testing has been used to detect life-threatening conditions and to treat the fetus while still in the uterus. For example, medical scientists are currently attempting to transplant healthy genes directly into the affected fetus to alter the infant's genetic blueprint. The aim is to treat the condition by editing a defective gene out of the infant's hereditary code.

Invasive and noninvasive techniques help to identify many genetic and chromosomal problems during prenatal development. **Amniocentesis** is an invasive procedure done normally between the 14th to 18th week of gestation. A physician inserts a long, hollow needle through the abdomen into the uterus, drawing out a small amount of amniotic fluid surrounding the fetus. A fetal ultrasound is done prior to and during this procedure to view positions of fetal organs and extremities (see Figure 3.13).

The amniotic fluid contains fetal cells that are grown in a culture and analyzed for various genetic abnormalities. Genetic and chromosomal defects, such as those associated with Down syndrome, spina bifida, and other inherited disorders, can be detected in this manner. With advancing age the risk of a baby with genetic problems is greater than the risk of miscarriage due to the procedure. Risks with amniocentesis are uncommon but, besides miscarriage, can include maternal Rh sensitization that can be treated with RhoGAM. Genetic counselors determine the risk factors involved for each case. Some women say the risk of amniocentesis is too high (Prenatal Diagnosis, 1998).

Ultrasonography determines the size and position of the fetus, the size and position of the placenta, the amount of amniotic fluid, and the appearance of fetal anatomy (an ultrasound image of fraternal twins is on page 68). This noninvasive procedure uses sonar to bounce sound waves off the fetus. The embryo can be visualized by week 6 of prenatal development.

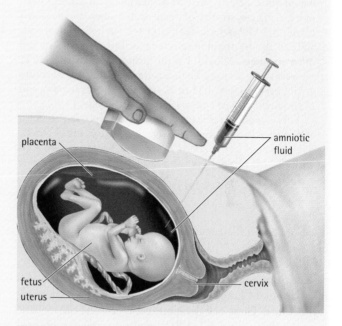

FIGURE 3.13
Amniocentesis Amniocentesis is a procedure for detecting hereditary defects in the fetus. A sterile needle is inserted into the amniotic cavity, and a small amount of amniotic fluid is withdrawn. This sample is centrifuged to separate fetal cells from the fluid. The cells are then grown in a laboratory culture and analyzed for chromosomal and genetic abnormalities.

Source: Yale New Haven Health System, 789 Howard Avenue, New Haven, CT 06519. Yalenewhavenhealth.org.

The result is a picture that is safer for the mother and fetus than that afforded by standard X rays (Prenatal Diagnosis, 1998). Another slightly invasive procedure, **fetoscopy,** allows a physician to view the fetus after 12 weeks through a lens inserted through a very narrow tube into the uterus. This procedure is more risky than amniocentesis.

Another invasive method is **chorionic villus biopsy (CVS),** which can be performed early during pregnancy. The chorionic villi are hairlike projections of the membrane that surrounds the embryo. The physician, guided by ultrasound, inserts a thin catheter either through the abdomen or through the vagina and cervix and into the uterus and, employing suction, removes a small plug of villous tissue. Although the chorion is not an anatomical part of the embryo itself, it is embryonic rather than maternal in origin. The most common test used on cells obtained by CVS is chromosome analysis to determine the karyotype of the fetus. CVS has a 3 to 5 percent risk of miscarriage and might cause maternal Rh sensitization.

continued

With optional **maternal blood sampling** for fetal blood cells, researchers have detected Down syndrome and other common birth defects by analyzing fetal cells shed into the mother's bloodstream. The **maternal serum alpha-fetoprotein (MSAFP) test** analyzes two major blood proteins—albumin and alpha-fetoprotein (AFP). When the fetus has neural tube defects such as anencephaly or spina bifida, more AFP crosses the placenta and reaches the mother's blood. MSAFP detects defects in the fetal abdominal wall and can also be useful in screening for Down syndrome and other trisomies. MSAFP has the greatest sensitivity at 15 to 18 weeks of gestation. The measurement of maternal serum estriol between weeks 15 to 20 will give a general indication of the well-being of a fetus (Prenatal Diagnosis, 1998).

Genetic testing results can bring relief or produce anguish and sorrow. Parents who learn that they are carriers of genetic diseases often feel ashamed and guilty. They are also faced with the difficult decision of whether to have an abortion if the test results indicate a high risk of fetal defects. Parents who learn that the child they are expecting is abnormal can experience psychological problems including denial, severe guilt, depression, termination of sexual relations, marital discord, and divorce. Clearly, some parents need psychological counseling in conjunction with genetic counseling.

The Human Genome Project continues to fund research on how fetal/newborn genetic screening affects public policy decisions and ethics in research in health-care environments (Murray & Baily, 2002–2005). Genetic screening and prenatal diagnosis may create new opportunities for discrimination, and disability rights groups say such tests increase discrimination toward those with disabilities (Davis, 2004; Parens & Asch, 2000). Your genetic profile could be used to determine who you could marry, what jobs you could apply for, and whether insurance companies would consider you a good risk. Another dilemma is whether you would want to know if you had inherited a harmful gene.

4 cells. The 4 cells then divide into 8, 8 into 16, 16 into 32, and so on.

The early mitotic cell divisions in development are called *cleavage* and occur very slowly. The first cleavage takes about 24 hours; each subsequent cleavage takes 10 to 12 hours. These cell divisions soon convert the zygote into a hollow fluid-filled ball of cells termed a *blastocyst* (see Table 3.3). The blastocyst should continue to develop and travel into the uterus. When a blastocyst remains trapped in the fallopian tube, the pregnancy is ectopic or tubal. An *ectopic* pregnancy is dangerous and will cause the mother a great deal of pain. The blastocyst will have to be surgically removed or the fallopian tube will burst, causing hemorrhaging.

Once the blastocyst enters the uterine cavity, it floats freely for 2 or 3 days. When it is about 6 to 7 days old and composed of some 100 cells, the blastocyst makes contact with the endometrium, the wall of the uterus. The endometrium in turn becomes vascular, glandular, and thick. The blastocyst "digests" its way into the endometrium through the action of enzymes and gradually becomes completely buried in it. As a result, the embryo develops within the wall of the uterus and not in its cavity. This invasion of the uterus by the blastocyst creates a small pool of maternal blood. During the germinal period, the organism derives its nourishment from the eroded tissue and maternal blood that flow through spaces in the outer layer of cells of the blastocyst.

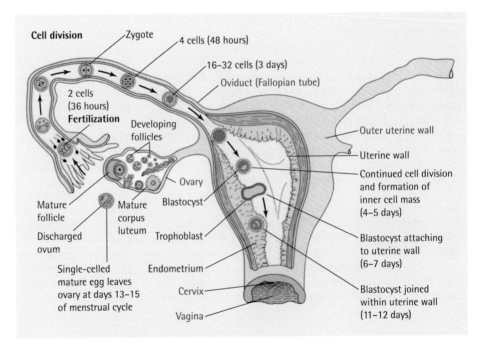

FIGURE 3.14 Early Human Development: The Course of the Ovum and Embryo The drawing depicts the female reproductive system, the fertilization of the ovum, and the early growth of the blastocyst, which will soon become an embryo.

Table 3.3 Blastocyst, Cleavage, and Implantation

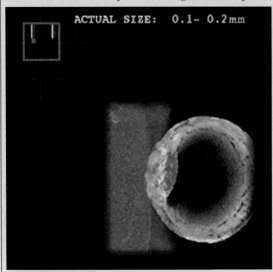

ACTUAL SIZE: 0.1– 0.2 mm

Implantation of Blastocyst Around the 9th to 11th day, the blastocyst implants itself in the nutrient-rich lining of the uterus.

Description	Vulnerabilities
The early process of *mitotic cell division* reduces cell size within the same original structure. During this process, called cleavage, the mass of the embryo remains constant. At the 16-cell stage, cells begin to adhere to each other. At the 100-cell stage, the cell cluster is filled with gel-like fluids, has entered the upper end of the uterus, and is now called a *blastocyst.* The outer layer of cells are the trophoblast, and the inner cluster is called the inner cell mass. By the 9th to 11th day of development, the blastocyst buries itself in the nutrient-rich lining of the mother's uterus (implantation).	During implantation, a variety of chemicals (proteins and hormones) enter the mother's bloodstream from the blastocyst, and a complex interchange of "information" begins. The mother's uterus might reject the blastocyst as a foreign cell (it has its own unique genetic makeup—different from the mother's). If anything goes wrong during this stage, the mother's own immune system might destroy the blastocyst (Nilsson & Hamberger, 1990). If the mother's uterus is diseased from pelvic inflammatory disease or sexually transmitted infections, the blastocyst might not be able to implant itself into the uterine wall and will not survive.

By the 11th day, the blastocyst has completely buried itself in the wall of the uterus, in a process called **implantation** (see Table 3.3). The hormone progesterone from the ovary prepares the uterine lining for implantation. This increase in progesterone is also a signal to the brain that the woman is pregnant, and most pregnant women cease to menstruate (in rare instances, a woman might menstruate and not realize she is pregnant). At this stage in development, the organism is about the size of a pinhead. As of yet, the mother is seldom aware of any symptoms of pregnancy. The blastocyst, now made up of hundreds of cells, is busy surrounding itself with chemicals to prevent the uterine immune system from destroying it, and the cervix has been sealed by a plug of mucus (Nilsson & Hamberger, 1990).

During the implantation process, the blastocyst begins separating into two layers. The outer layer of cells, called the **trophoblast,** is responsible for embedding the embryo in the uterine wall. The inner surface of the trophoblast becomes the nonmaternal portions of the *placenta,* the amnion and chorion. The **amnion** forms a closed sac around the embryo and is filled with a watery amniotic fluid to keep the embryo moist and protect it against shock or adhesions. The **chorion** is a membrane that surrounds the amnion and links the embryo to the placenta. The internal disc or cluster of cells that compose the blastocyst, called the **inner cell mass,** produces the embryo. The entire process is controlled by genes. Some genes turn on rapidly as the embryo develops; others turn on slowly; and still others operate throughout the prenatal period and beyond. The patterns of gene activity are complex and involve many different genes (Nilsson & Hamberger, 1990).

Toward the end of the second week, mitotic cell division proceeds more rapidly. The embryonic portion of the inner cell mass begins to separate into three layers: the **ectoderm** (the outer layer), which is the source of future cells forming the nervous system, the sensory organs, the skin, and the lower part of the rectum; the **mesoderm** (the middle layer), which gives rise to the skeletal, muscular, and circulatory systems and the kidneys; and the **endoderm** (the inner layer), which develops into the digestive tract (including the liver, the pancreas, and the gallbladder), the respiratory system, the bladder, and portions of the reproductive organs (Nilsson & Hamberger, 1990).

The Embryonic Period

The *embryonic period* lasts from the end of the second week to the eighth week. It spans that period of pregnancy from the time the blastocyst completely implants itself in the uterine wall to the time the developing organism becomes a recognizable human fetus. During this period the developing organism is called an *embryo* and normally experiences (1) rapid growth; (2) the establishment of a placental relationship with the mother; (3) the early structural appearance of all the chief organs; and (4) the development, in form at least, of a recognizably human body. All of the major organs are developing now, except the sex organs, which will begin to develop within several weeks; at that point male embryos begin to produce the hormone testosterone, and male sex organs begin to differentiate from female organs.

The embryo becomes attached to the wall of the uterus by means of the placenta. The **placenta** is a partially permeable membrane that does not permit the passage of blood cells between the two organisms. The placenta forms from uterine tissue and the trophoblast of the blastocyst and functions as an exchange terminal that permits entry of food materials, oxygen, and hormones into the embryo from the mother's bloodstream and the exit of carbon dioxide and metabolic wastes from the embryo into the mother's bloodstream. This feature provides a safeguard against the mingling of the mother's blood with that of the embryo. Were the mother's and embryo's blood to intermix, the mother's body would reject the embryo as foreign material.

The transfer between the placenta and the embryo occurs across a web of fingerlike projections, the villi, that extend into blood spaces in the maternal uterus. The villi begin developing during the second week, growing outward from the chorion. When the placenta is fully developed at about the seventh month of pregnancy, it is shaped like a pancake or disc, 1 inch thick and 7 inches in diameter. From the beginning, the **umbilical cord** links the embryo to the placenta and is a conduit carrying two arteries and one vein. This connecting structure, or lifeline, is attached to the middle of the fetal abdomen.

Development that commences with the brain and head areas and then works its way down the body is called **cephalocaudal** development. This direction of development ensures an adequate nervous system to support the proper functioning of other systems. During the early part of the third week, the developing embryo begins to take the shape of a pear, the broad, knobby end of which becomes the head. The cells in the central portion of the embryo also thicken and form a slight ridge that is referred to as the *primitive streak.* The primitive streak divides the developing embryo into right and left halves and eventually becomes the spinal cord. The tissues grow in opposite directions away from the axis of the primitive streak, a process termed **proximodistal** development. Cephalocaudal development and proximodistal development are illustrated in Chapter 4.

By the 28th day, the head region takes up roughly one-third of the embryo's length. Also about this time, a brain and a primitive spinal cord become evident. As development progresses during the second month, the head elevates, the neck emerges, and rudiments of the nose, eyes, mouth, and tongue appear. Another critical system—the circulatory system—also develops early. By the end of the third week, the heart tube has already begun to beat in a halting manner.

Within four weeks of conception, the embryo is about 1/5 inch long—nearly 10,000 times larger than the fertilized egg. About this time the mother usually becomes suspicious that she is pregnant. Her menstrual period is generally two weeks overdue. She might feel a heaviness, fullness, and tingling in her breasts; simultaneously, the nipples and surrounding areolas may enlarge and darken. Also at this time, about one-half to two-thirds of all pregnant women experience a morning queasiness or nauseous feeling. The condition, called "morning sickness," can persist for several weeks or months and varies in intensity from woman to woman.

The developing embryo is particularly sensitive to the invasion of drugs, diseases, and environmental toxins in the mother's body because so many of its major body systems are developing. The mother's excessive use of alcohol, nicotine, or caffeine, and her use of other more potent chemical agents such as methamphetamine, crack cocaine, heroin, and strong prescription medications can certainly harm the development of this embryo's organs and structures. Each organ and structure has a **critical period** during which it is most vulnerable to damaging influences.

The Fetal Period

The final stage in prenatal life—the *fetal period*—begins at the end of the eighth week and ends with birth. During this time the organism is called a **fetus,** and its major organ systems continue to develop and assume their specialized functions. By the end of the eighth week, the organism definitely resembles a human being. It is complete with face, arms, legs, fingers, toes, basic trunk and head muscles, and internal organs. The fetus now builds on this basic form.

Development during the fetal period is less dramatic than that during the embryonic period. Even so,

Embryo with Primitive Streak Barely 6 weeks old and measuring 15 mm (just over 1/2 inch), the embryo has its transparent back turned toward us. The primitive streak, visible through the thin skin, will become its spinal cord. The embryo is encircled by its amniotic sac, with the ragged chorionic villi and the umbilical cord to the right. The yolk sac hovers to the left.

Source: Lennart Nilsson (1990). *A child is born.* New York: Dell.

significant changes occur. By the eighth week the fetal face acquires a truly human appearance. During the third month the fetus develops skeletal and neurological structures that lay the foundation for spontaneous movements of the arms, legs, and fingers. By the fourth month, stimulation of the infant's body surfaces activates a variety of reflex responses. About the beginning of the fifth month, the mother generally begins to feel the spontaneous movements of the fetus (called *quickening,* a sensation like a moving butterfly in the abdominal region). Also during the fifth month, a fine, downy, woolly fuzz *(lanugo hair)* begins to cover the fetal body.

At six months the eyebrows and lashes are well defined; the body is lean but strikingly human in proportions; the skin is wrinkled. At seven months the fetus (now weighing about 2½ pounds and measuring about 15 inches in length) gives the appearance of a dried-up, aged person, with red, wrinkled skin covered by a waxy coating *(vernix).* The fetus is now a viable organism and can cry weakly. At eight months, fat is being deposited around the body, the fetus gains an additional 2 pounds, and its neuromuscular activity increases.

At nine months the dull redness of the skin fades to pink, the limbs become rounded, and the fingernails and toenails are well formed. At full term (40 weeks) the body is plump; the skin has lost most of its lanugo hair, although the body is still covered with vernix; and all the organs necessary to carry on independent life are functioning. The fetus is now ready for birth—which will be discussed in Chapter 4.

The Timing of Birth Recently, reproductive researchers have begun to understand the biochemical changes in the mother, the fetus, and the placenta that work in concert to control the timing of birth. Endocrinologists find that the rate at which the placenta releases a protein called *corticotropin-releasing hormone (CRH)* into the maternal and fetal blood can cause premature, full term, or late labor and delivery (Smith, 1999). Like members of a highly trained orchestra appearing at the same time for a performance, precise levels of critical hormones must be released by the mother, the fetus, and the placenta culminating with delivery. CRH from the placenta acts on the fetal pituitary, which causes fetal adrenal glands to secrete *cortisol,* promoting fetal lung maturation. The fetal pituitary produces specific hormones, and the fetal adrenal glands then secrete hormones—which the placenta converts to estrogen. Rising levels of estrogen cause the uterus and cervix to undergo many changes during the last two weeks of pregnancy—ending with birth and discharge of the placenta.

Presently, about 6 to 8 percent of all newborns are premature and are at greater risk of birth defects (Smith, 1999). Research findings on the genes that trigger the release of CRH and other hormones associated with labor may lead to screening women at risk for premature delivery. Such

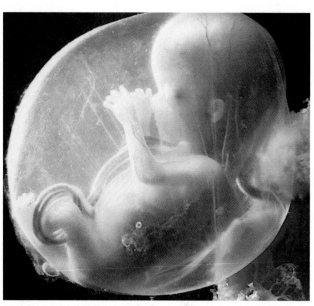

The Fetus at Three Months

At 3 months the fetus is a little more than 3 inches long and weighs nearly an ounce. Its head is disproportionally large and appears increasingly like that of a human. By now the external ears and eyelids have formed. The umbilical cord increases in size to accommodate the growing organism. The fetus is developing the skeletal and neurological structures that provide the foundation for moving in its capsule, where it floats weightlessly much in the manner of an astronaut in space.

Source: From W. J. Robbins. *Growth.* Copyright © 1928. Reprinted by permission of Yale University Press.

women could plan to give birth at a hospital with a neonatal intensive care unit, or scientists predict that in the future a blocking agent could delay labor and delivery until the fetus is mature (Romero, Kuivaniemi, & Tromp, 2002).

> **Questions**
>
> How long is the average prenatal period (length of pregnancy)? What are the three distinct prenatal periods, and what important developments occur during each? What is the role of the placenta? How do you define cephalocaudal development versus proximodistal development?

Loss by Miscarriage

A **miscarriage** occurs when the zygote, embryo, or fetus is naturally expelled from the uterus before it can survive outside the mother's womb. The medical term for miscarriage is **spontaneous abortion,** which is most likely preceded by cramping or bleeding. An estimated 10 to 15 percent of known pregnancies of American women end in miscarriage during the first or early second trimester, but only 1 percent of women experience recurrent pregnancy loss (Carson & Ware-Branch, 2001). Women in developing countries around the world experience much higher rates of pregnancy complications, fetal loss and maternal death, and many organizations are collaborating to improve services for prenatal and obstetric care (Safe Motherhood Initiative, 2004). *All* women who miscarry want to know the cause of their loss.

Approximately 75 percent of miscarriages occur before 12 weeks of development, which normally indicates a problem with the implantation of the embryo into the uterine wall, some form of genetic mutation causing abnormality of the embryo, or exposure to infectious agents (Carson & Ware-Branch, 2001). Later miscarriages are commonly the result of some structural problem with the uterus, problems with implantation, or a cervix that does not stay closed but begins to open (DeFrain, Millspaugh, & Xiaolin, 1996). In some women the cervix is temporarily "sewn" to prevent premature birth. The pregnant woman might also have sustained a serious accident, trauma, or illness that triggers a miscarriage. Additionally, we are just beginning to understand the significant impact of environmental factors on prenatal development or loss as well. Sometimes miscarriage is unpredicted and inexplicable, and of couples who experience recurrent pregnancy loss, more than 50 percent will have no specific diagnosis (Carson & Ware-Branch, 2002).

Substantial research findings document the mother's deep emotional distress for months or even years after a miscarriage, yet Western cultures have no established ritual to mourn the loss of a child by miscarriage. Over the past 20 years, researchers have conducted empirical studies on the psychosocial impact of this loss on mothers, fathers, and other family members (Beutel et al., 1996; Geller, Kerns, & Klier, 2004). The mother and father are greatly in need of social and family support at this time. Despite this, women consistently report unhelpful responses from family, friends, physicians, and other health-care professionals following a miscarriage (Geller, Kerns, & Klier, 2004). Established support groups and visits by the clergy are normally very helpful to the family. Some women need further support by meeting with mental health professionals.

As for any other death of a loved one, grieving can take a long time. Both mothers and fathers report having disturbing nightmares about crying babies, flashbacks over many years, feelings of "going crazy," feelings of guilt and blame, and thoughts of suicide. Most parents resolve the issue after a lengthy period of shock, pain, disorganization, and redefinition (Geller, Kerns, & Klier, 2004). There are sites on the Internet devoted to remembering those special little ones, and many communities offer group support.

Prenatal Environmental Influences

To most of us, the concept of "environment" refers to a human being's surroundings after birth. In truth, environmental influences are operating from the moment of conception, if not actually before with the mother and father's own health. The fertilized ovum undertakes a hazardous week-long journey down the fallopian tube and around the uterus, encountering throughout a highly variable and chemically active medium. We generally think of the uterus as providing a sheltered, warm, and protected environment for prenatal development. But even after implanting itself in the uterus, the embryo is vulnerable to maternal disease, malnutrition, infections, immune disorders, use of cigarettes, prescription drugs and illegal drugs, accidental trauma or biochemical malfunctioning, and exposure to X rays.

Most pregnancies end with the birth of normal, healthy babies. Nonetheless, as previously stated, about 10 to 15 percent of all conceptions in American women result in spontaneous abortion or stillbirths (the baby dies before birth). Another 3 to 4 percent of conceptions lead to babies born with birth defects. The March of Dimes (2004e) defines a birth defect as "an abnormality of structure, function, or metabolism (body chemistry) present at birth that results in physical or mental disabilities, and several thousand different birth defects have been identified." Scientists term any environmental agent that contributes to birth defects or anomalies a **teratogen,** and the field of study of birth defects is called **teratology.**

Maternal Medications   Maternal medications account for 1 to 3 percent of birth defects (Scheinfeld & Davis, 2004). According to medical opinion, pregnant women should not take drugs except for conditions that seriously threaten their health—and then only under the supervision of a physician. The thalidomide tragedy in the early 1960s awakened the medical profession and the public to the potential dangers of drugs for pregnant women. European, Canadian, and Australian women who had been prescribed thalidomide (a sedative) for nausea or "morning sickness" during the embryonic stage of pregnancy gave birth to nearly 10,000 infants with serious teratogenic effects: absence of ears and arms, deafness, facial defects, and malformations in gastrointestinal systems (Rajkumar, 2004) The use of thalidomide has returned in some countries, because it reduces nausea in patients with various health problems. We learned that many drugs and chemical agents cross the placenta and affect the embryonic and fetal systems (Rajkumar, 2004). Quinine (a treatment of malaria caused by a parasite) can cause congenital deafness. Barbiturates (sedating drugs) can affect the oxygen supply to the fetus and result in brain damage. Antihistamines can increase the mother's susceptibility to spontaneous abortion.

Likewise, increased rates of miscarriage and birth defects among coffee drinkers prompted the Food and Drug Administration (FDA) to recommend that women stop or reduce their consumption of caffeinated coffee, tea, chocolate, and cola drinks during pregnancy (Wisborg et al., 2003). Asthmatic women who require systemic steroids are more likely to have complications during pregnancy (Beckmann, 2003).

The most widely used prescription drug for women of child-bearing years is *Accutane* and its generic versions (some sold illegally over the Internet) that are prescribed for persons with severe acne and cause known birth defects (Honein, Paulozzi, & Erickson, 2001). Patients sign informed consent about reproductive outcomes, must take pregnancy tests, and must use birth control while taking Accutane. In December 2004 a federal registry instituted stricter guidelines because fetal deaths and congenital malformations still occur (Krauskopf, 2004). Women of child-bearing years must exercise extreme caution when taking teratogenic prescription drugs.

Maternal Infectious and Noninfectious Diseases

Under some circumstances infections that cause illness in the mother can harm the fetus. Infections can be passed along by certain raw foods (e.g., chicken, hot dogs, fish, sandwich meats), by pets (protect hands when cleaning a cat litter box), and by exposure from people who are infected, especially children. Always wash hands after caring for children or changing baby diapers ("Attention Pregnant Women," 1999). Infections can also be passed along during vaginal, oral, and anal sex. When the mother is directly infected, viruses, bacteria, or malarial parasites might cross the placenta and infect the child. In other cases the fetus can be indirectly affected by a mother's fever or by toxins in the mother's body. The exact time during the fetus's development at which an infection occurs in the mother has an important bearing. As described earlier, the infant's organs and structures emerge according to a fixed sequence and timetable, and each has a critical period during which it is most vulnerable to damaging influences.

Rubella and Other Infectious Agents   If the mother contracts rubella (German measles) in the first three months of pregnancy, there is a substantial risk of blindness, deafness, brain damage, and heart disease in the fetus. In 10 to 20 percent of the pregnancies complicated by rubella, spontaneous abortion or stillbirth ensues. However, should the mother contract the disease in the last trimester, there is usually no major damage. Various other viral, bacterial, and protozoan agents are suspected either of being transmitted to the fetus or otherwise interfering with normal development. These agents include hepatitis, influenza, poliomyelitis, malaria, typhoid, typhus, mumps, smallpox, scarlet fever, gonorrhea, chlamydia, trichomoniasis, syphilis, herpes, and cytomegalovirus infection.

Chlamydia   The most frequently reported sexually transmitted infection (STI) is *chlamydia* caused by bacteria that can damage a woman's reproductive organs or lead to infertility. An estimated 2.8 million Americans are infected annually. Symptoms in women are often mild and unnoticed until infertility is discovered. Having multiple sex partners increases the risk of contracting chlamydia. Noticeable symptoms also include lower abdominal pain, low back pain, nausea, fever, pain during intercourse, or bleeding between menstrual periods. Men with chlamydia may notice signs of discharge from their penis, a burning sensation when urinating, or itching or burning around the tip of the penis. If left untreated, this infection can spread into the uterus or fallopian tubes and cause pelvic inflammatory disease (PID). PID can cause permanent damage to the reproductive organs and surrounding tissues. Women infected with chlamydia are up to five times more likely to become infected with HIV, if exposed. All pregnant women should have a screening for chlamydia, since it can cause premature delivery or be passed from an infected mother to her fetus during vaginal childbirth. Untreated infants may experience conjunctivitis or blindness or pneumonia complications. Chlamydia can be treated with antibiotics (Weinstock, Berman, & Cates, 2004).

Trichomoniasis   This STI is caused by a single-celled parasite, and it is a curable infection that affects both women and men. Women experience vaginal symptoms and men experience urethra infection. Trichomoniasis causes genital inflammation, which can increase a woman's susceptibility to HIV infection if she is exposed to the virus. Trichomoniasis can usually be cured with metronidazole, given by mouth in a single dose. Pregnant women with trichomoniasis may give birth prematurely or have a low birth weight baby (Weinstock, Berman, & Cates, 2004).

Human Papillomavirus (HPV)   In the United States, HPV is also one of the most common STIs, but there are many types of HPV. Some are called low risk, but others are high risk and can lead to genital warts or cancers of the cervix, vulva, vagina, anus, or penis. Health experts predict that 20 million people in this country are already infected. HPV can result in genital warts, which are very contagious and spread during sex with an infected partner. A majority of people who have sex with a partner with genital warts will also develop warts, typically within a few months. Sexually active women should have a regular cervical exam to detect the presence of HPV infection. Scraped cells from the cervix should be examined under a microscope to see if they are cancerous. HPV has no known cure, but genital warts can typically be removed by creams, scraping, surgery, freezing, burning, or use of lasers. A pregnant woman should not use these creams because they are absorbed by her skin and may cause birth defects in a fetus (National Institute of Allergy and Infectious Diseases, 2004b).

Syphilis   Syphilis is a bacterial STI that continues to rise as a serious health problem to both mother and baby, especially for women who are trading sex for drugs or have multiple sex partners (Altman, 2004). Syphilis develops in four progressive stages: a primary stage when genital sores appear; a secondary stage of a skin rash; a latent stage when bacterial infections affect major organs of the body; and a final stage resulting in blood vessel and heart problems, mental disorders, blindness, nerve system problems, and even death ("Syphilis: What Happens," 2004). *Congenital syphilis* occurs when an infected pregnant woman does not seek treatment, and the bacterial infection is passed through the placenta or during delivery of the fetus. If not detected at birth, the disease takes a gradual toll in deterioration of the brain and spinal cord, affecting thought, speech, hearing, and motor abilities, and personality before the child dies (Tramont, 2000).

Many known syphilitic pregnant women do not show clinical evidence of the disease and are not taking penicillin. Thus, all pregnant women should take the Wasserman test for syphilis. Antibiotic treatment with penicillin will usually cure this infection but may not reverse the damage done to the body (Tramont, 2000).

Genital Herpes   Nearly 45 million Americans have acquired *herpes simplex 2 virus, HSV-2,* commonly called genital herpes, but reports of new cases have declined considerably in the early 2000s—especially among teens and men (Altman, 2004). Pregnant women with genital herpes have risk of miscarriage, and babies delivered vaginally are at risk of getting the disease. Because some infected babies die and others suffer permanent brain damage, obstetricians advise cesarean delivery to minimize the risk of infection (Corey et al., 2004). Those infected experience few symptoms to outbreaks of painful sores and itching, flulike symptoms such as fever, headache, and muscle ache, painful urination, and discharge from the vagina or urethra. Those infected are at much higher risk of getting HIV (Randerson, 2003). There is no cure for genital herpes, but the FDA has approved three antiviral medications to alleviate symptoms in men and nonpregnant women: *Zovirax, Famvir,* and *Valtrex.* Medical experts urge that those infected seek treatment to remain healthy, that they fully disclose their status to partners, and practice safe sex to reduce HSV-2 transmission. Condom use alone does not prevent the transmission of herpes. Findings from a large, international study with heterosexual couples show a daily dose of Valtrex cut the transmission of HSV-2 by 50 percent (Corey et al., 2004).

Gonorrhea   Gonorrhea is a treatable bacterial STI, and it is commonly called "the clap." Its symptoms are similar to chlamydia: burning and pain during urination, abnormal discharge from the vagina or penis, pain or swelling of the testicles, and in women, abdominal or back pain, pain during intercourse, bleeding between periods, nausea, or fever, and pain in the rectal or anal area. An infected woman can pass along this infection during delivery, and newborns may experience conjunctivitis (pink eye) or pneumonia complications. Applying silver nitrate or other medications to the eyes immediately after birth can prevent the infection. Treatment for a person with

gonorrhea includes a regimen of antibiotics, although some recent strains of gonorrhea are antibiotic resistant (Brocklehurst, 2004; Workowski & Levine, 2002).

HIV/AIDS   By 2004 health experts worldwide indicate the number of women infected with *human immunodeficiency virus* (HIV/AIDS) continues to increase rapidly to nearly 50 percent of the estimated 40 million affected, with much higher female rates in poorer countries ("HIV Infection in Women," 2004). HIV/AIDS rates have risen to pandemic magnitude in Eastern and Southern Asia, Eastern Europe and Russia, Central Asia, and sub-Saharan Africa ("AIDS Epidemic Update," 2004). In addition to increasingly higher rates of heterosexual transmission, some mothers with HIV/AIDS are drug users at risk of contracting HIV from shared needles (American Academy of Family Physicians, 2002). Many people are unaware of their HIV status, and marriage and long-term monogamous relationships do not protect women from being infected. Perinatal transmission (from mother to child) of HIV accounts for more than 90 percent of all pediatric AIDS cases, and experts estimate that 10 million children worldwide and nearly 10,000 U.S. children are living with HIV/AIDS ("AIDS Epidemic Update," 2004). World Health Organization (WHO) experts estimate more than 500,000 children under age 15 died from HIV/AIDS just in 2004 ("AIDS Epidemic Update," 2004).

Some mothers with HIV show no outward signs of disease, but once diagnosed, health officials report that a three-part regimen of the drug *ZVD (zidovudine)* given during gestation, at birth, and to the infant at 6 weeks after birth has dramatically reduced mother-to-child transmission of HIV (Public Health Service Task Force, 2004). However, those infected experience damaged immune systems, leaving them prey to infections, cancer, and early death. Half to three-quarters of infants infected with HIV have distinct head and face abnormalities. Most prenatally infected babies develop symptoms of the disease within the first 12 months of life, including recurrent bacterial infections, swollen lymph glands, failure to thrive, neurological impairments, and delayed development (Kirton, 2003; Magder et al., 2005). Many mothers with HIV/AIDS are poor, lack medical insurance or prescription coverage, and require financial assistance and social services (often not available in poor regions of the world). As such, poor mothers breastfeed their infants, putting their infants at great risk (Heymann & Phuong, 1999). In the past few years, the World Health Organization has greatly expanded efforts for HIV/AIDS funding, education, treatment, and care (Public Health Service Task Force, 2004).

Health management protocol of pregnant women to determine HIV status has reduced transmission to newborns to 2 percent and includes: (1) informed consent and voluntary early screening of *all* pregnant women and detection of HIV; (2) HIV counseling; (3) antiretroviral therapy (zidovudine) in the health care of women with HIV, reducing fetal transmission; (4) prenatal care and analysis of women's immunologic status to guide treatment options; (5) offering an elective cesarean section delivery at 38 weeks of gestation to decrease risk of fetal transmission at birth; and (6) formula feeding but no breast-feeding after birth (Krist, 2001). In the United States, nearly 40 percent of pregnant women have not been tested, but rapid HIV testing for women in labor is now feasible and accurate (Bulterys et al., 2004; "Rapid HIV Testing of Woman in Labor," 2003).

More than 20 million people worldwide have died since HIV/AIDS was first identified in the early 1980s. However, recent statistics are hopeful regarding new annual U.S. pediatric cases: 952 cases in 1992 but only 92 in 2002, and nearly 10,000 U.S. children infected at birth are still living (Stodgill, 2002). But cases among young heterosexual women of childbearing ages have risen to one-fourth of those affected.

HIV/AIDS, especially perinatal transmission to babies, must be taken very seriously. Since 1981 when the first cases were diagnosed in the homosexual community and later in the heterosexual community, nearly 1 million cases of AIDS have been reported to the U.S. Centers for Disease Control and Prevention, and more than 5,000 American children have died from HIV/AIDS ("HIV/AIDS Surveillance Report," 2004).

Diabetes Diabetes is a metabolic disorder in which the body has problems converting food to energy because of a deficiency of insulin from the pancreas and an excess of sugar in the blood and urine. There are two types that cause serious health complications and require regular monitoring of blood glucose (sugar) and intake of artificial insulin: (1) Type 1 diabetes is usually diagnosed in children and in young adults (formerly called juvenile diabetes), and (2) Type 2 diabetes is associated with excessive weight gain and little exercise (formerly associated with aging). But proper diet and regular exercise can often delay or prevent Type 2 diabetes (Chan et al., 2002). Worldwide, changing population demographics, such as an aging population and increasing numbers of ethnic groups and children more at risk of obesity, are making Type 2 diabetes a major health problem (Barrett, 2004; Eisenberg, 2003).

A woman with gestational diabetes must carefully monitor her condition and administer insulin artificially. Maternal diabetics are at much higher risk of adverse pregnancy outcomes, such as miscarriage, intrauterine death, congenital malformations including neural tube defects, stillbirth, and labor and delivery complications, including neonatal respiratory distress syndrome and fetal obesity (Hampton, 2004; Lauenborg et al., 2003). A woman with gestational diabetes must see her doctor regularly, optimize glucose control, get regular ultrasound exams, and closely monitor the fetal activity level ("Introduction to Diabetes," 2004).

Maternal Sensitization: The Rh Factor Pregnant women should undergo routine screening for their Rh factor in their red blood cells. There is a possible incompatibility of a protein in the mother's and child's blood cells that may produce a serious and often fatal form of anemia and jaundice in the fetus or newborn—a disorder termed *erythroblastosis fetalis*. About 85 percent of all whites have this Rh factor; they are called Rh-positive (Rh+). About 15 percent do not have it; they are Rh-negative (Rh−). The Rh factor is expressed with your blood type, such as O+, O−, or A+, B−, AB+. Among blacks only about 7 percent are Rh−, and among Asians the figure is less than 1 percent (Bowman, 1992). Rh+ blood and Rh− blood are *incompatible* but adverse outcomes are preventable. Each blood factor is transmitted genetically in accordance with Mendelian rules and Rh+ is a dominant trait. Generally, the maternal and fetal blood supplies are separated by the placenta. On occasion, however, a capillary in the placenta ruptures and a small amount of maternal and fetal blood mixes. Likewise, some admixture usually occurs during the "afterbirth," when the placenta separates from the uterine wall.

An incompatibility results between the mother's and the infant's blood when an Rh− mother has a baby with Rh+ blood. Under these conditions, the mother's body produces antibodies that cross the placenta and attack the baby's blood cells. Erythroblastosis fetalis can now be prevented if an Rh− mother is given anti-Rh antibodies (RhoGAM) shortly after the birth of her first child. If an Rh− mother has already been sensitized to Rh+ blood by several pregnancies in the absence of RhoGAM therapy, her infant can be given an interuterine transfusion.

Questions

What maternal factors contribute to a spontaneous abortion, commonly called "miscarriage"? At what time during the prenatal period is a woman at highest risk of miscarriage? What maternal illnesses are known to compromise fetal health?

Major Drug and Chemical Teratogens

Smoking The nicotine in tobacco is a mild stimulant drug. When a pregnant woman smokes, her bloodstream absorbs nicotine that is transmitted through the placenta to the embryo, which increases fetal activity and is associated with prematurity and low birth weight. In a longitudinal study researchers are following the health of more than 1,000 British and Irish severely premature babies into childhood. These children have a higher range of physical and cognitive disabilities than their peers and require many more services during childhood (Hopkin, 2005; Marlow et al., 2005). More congenital abnormalities are prevalent among the infants of women who smoke (Zimmer & Zimmer, 1998).

Alcohol   Alcohol is the leading teratogen to which the fetus is likely to be exposed, and it can result in a preventable form of mental retardation (Fox & Druschel, 2003). FASD (fetal alcohol spectrum disorder) is a cluster of severe physical and mental defects caused by alcohol damage to the developing fetus. Postnatal care cannot erase the growth retardation, head and facial abnormalities, skeletal, heart, and brain damage (MedicineNet, 1997). Recent findings from international studies indicate that 60 percent of women drink at some point during their pregnancy, thus public health care must place more emphasis on education (Gilbert, 2004).

Marijuana   Marijuana, a psychoactive drug, is the most frequently used illicit drug in America, and more than 50 percent of twelfth-graders report using it (Hansen, 2002). It has detrimental health effects on a pregnant woman, altering her mood, memory, motor control, quality of sleep, and other cognitive functions. A body of research shows that marijuana use has injurious effects on fetal development and neonatal behavior, including altered response to visual stimuli, increased activity level, a high-pitched cry, and altered neurological development (Hansen, 2002). Infants exposed to marijuana in utero are sometimes identified at birth and during the neonatal period by low birth weight and size, respiratory problems, slow weight gain, and increased risk of sudden infant death syndrome. It is difficult to isolate the effects of prenatal marijuana exposure from other drug use on pregnancy outcome (Kozer & Koren, 2001).

Oral Contraceptives   Exposure to first-generation oral contraceptives (from the 1960s–1970s) during the first trimester was linked to birth defects (Nora & Nora, 1975). But today's oral contraceptives are third generation with reduced doses of combined estrogen and progesterone. Surprisingly, published research is limited, and your authors found only one study indicating a higher risk of congenital urinary tract anomalies with use of oral contraceptives after conception (Li et al., 1995). There is a consistent message in present research literature that oral contraceptives are safe for most women, but each woman must be monitored carefully by her physician and exercise caution.

Cocaine and Other Hard Drugs   Fetal exposure to heroin, methadone, cocaine and its derivative "crack" produces a wide range of birth deformities (Zimmer & Zimmer, 1998). Newborn infants exposed in utero to heroin are identified by premature birth size and weight, excessive tremulous behavior, profuse sweating, excessive sneezing, excessive yawning, poor sleep patterns, poor swallowing ability, poor sucking or eating ability, and increased risk of SIDS (Calhoun & Alforque, 1996). "Crack babies" are small with low birth weight, have tremulous behavior, nasal stuffiness, prolonged high-pitch crying, high temperature, poor sucking or feeding ability, respiratory problems, regurgitation problems, excessive hyperactivity, and rigidity (Lester, 1997). These newborns experience the same withdrawal symptoms as adults. Recent research suggests that there isn't a "crack syndrome" as such because of prenatal exposure to other drugs and prevalence of maternal STIs, and long-term anomalies mostly affect children exposed during all three trimesters of development (Behnke et al., 2002; Vidaeff & Mastrobattista, 2003). Maternal and neonatal mortality is associated with cocaine use and combined drug/alcohol use. Thus, screening protocols that identify pregnant women abusing illicit drugs, collaboration with drug treatment programs, and follow-up for drug-using women and their children are essential to improve mortality outcomes (Wolfe et al., 2004). Hard drug use is staggering in long-term health effects and cost to society.

Environmental Toxins   Pregnant women often encounter potentially toxic agents in everyday substances, including hair spray, cosmetics, insecticides, cleansers, food preservatives, and polluted air and water. The risks associated with these agents remain to be determined, but chemical defoliants must be avoided. The National Cancer Institute has linked defoliant chemical sprays used in Vietnam with a substantial increase in malformed Vietnamese infants. Miscarriages and birth defects also occur at two to three times average rates in areas of California where water is contaminated by chemicals used in high-tech electronics manufacturing (Miller, 1985).

Workplace Toxins   Medical authorities are concerned over the hazards to the reproductive organs and processes that are found in the places where people work. For instance, studies reveal that continuous exposure to a variety of gaseous anesthetic agents used in hospitals and dental offices is associated with an increase in spontaneous abortions among female workers (Rowland et al., 1995; Sessler & Badgwell, 1998). Their children also have a higher incidence of congenital malformations (Bronson, 1977). The University of Massachusetts School of Public Health has found that women working in so-called clean rooms of semiconductor makers—where computer chips are etched with acids and gases—have a miscarriage rate nearly twice the national average (Meier, 1987). Studies are also under way to determine the risks posed by video display terminals (VDTs) (that emit wavelengths of ionizing radiation) following reports of high miscarriage rates among some VDT users in several industries. Prenatal exposure to the element mercury is associated with neurological and kidney disorders, and women of child-bearing age are advised to follow dietary guidelines for eating fish, a common source of mercury (Centers for Disease Control and Prevention, 2004d).

Sperm cells are as susceptible to harm from environmental toxins as are ova. A body of research in teratology and neurotoxicology reports a link between reproductive anomalies and male exposure to chemicals, radiation, and trace metals (Kalter, 2004). Mercury, solvents, and various pesticides and herbicides can affect the genes in the sperm, the structure and health of the sperm, the epididymis, seminal vesicles, prostate, or be carried in semen causing male infertility, spontaneous abortions, and congenital malformations. In sum, working men and women with potential contact should go through training and follow exposure prevention guidelines: wash hands regularly, wear protective clothing, avoid skin contact, keep the workplace clean, leave contaminated clothes and objects at work, and change into street clothes before leaving.

Maternal Stress The effect of maternal emotions on the unborn infant has long been a subject of folklore. Most of us are well aware that being frightened by a snake, a mouse, a bat, or some other creature will not cause a pregnant woman to give birth to a child with a distinctive personality or birthmark. Medical science does suggest, however, that severe, prolonged anxiety in an expectant mother can have a harmful effect on her child (Couzin, 2002). When the mother is anxious or under stress, various hormones such as *epinephrine* (adrenaline) and *acetylcholine* are released into her bloodstream. These hormones can pass through the placenta and enter the fetus's blood. Should a pregnant woman feel that she is experiencing prolonged and unusual stress, she would be well advised to consult a physician, a trained therapist, or someone in the clergy.

Maternal stress and anxiety are linked with complications of pregnancy, mainly prematurity and low birth weight for gestational age (Mulder et al., 2002). Lou and colleagues (1994) followed more than 3,000 women through pregnancy and obtained results about their stress using the questionnaire method. They found that maternal stress and smoking contributed independently and significantly to a lower gestational age, lower birth weight, smaller head circumference, and poorer scores on the neonatal neurological exam (Lou et al., 1994). Some stress and anxiety are inescapable features of expectant motherhood, but too much stress can have long-term effects on the fetus (Couzin, 2002).

Maternal Age The number of U.S. teen births has declined significantly for all ages 19 and under since 1972, but national data indicates that teens experience high rates of abortion, miscarriage, late or no prenatal care (see Figure 3.15), premature births, very low birth weight and perinatal deaths compared with older women of child-bearing ages (Henshaw, 2004; Rowland & Vasquez, 2002). Black, Hispanic, and Native American teens are more likely to delay seeking prenatal care (Hamilton, Martin, & Sutton, 2004). Such unsafe pregnancy outcomes occur despite the fact that teens are generally in better health, suffer from few chronic diseases, and engage in fewer risky behaviors than older women (Menacker et al., 2004). Because young mothers are often poor and less educated, many experts assumed their living conditions explained their pregnancy problems, but recent data shows that middle-class teenagers are almost twice as likely as older women to deliver premature babies (Stevens-Simon, Beach, & McGregor, 2002). Also, researchers find that teen mothers seem to provide lower-quality parenting. Pregnancy and motherhood are stressful to the adolescent and even more so when her baby is preterm and low birth weight. She is dealing with the demands of parenting concurrent with establishing her own identity and confronting the developmental tasks of adolescence while experiencing educational and economic limitations and complex family problems (Menacker et al., 2004).

The current consensus tends to be that a healthy woman in her thirties or early forties enjoys a good prospect of giving birth to a healthy infant and remaining well herself, provided that she is under medical supervision. This is especially good news since more women are postponing childbirth, while completing an education or establishing a career (Hamilton, Martin, & Sutton, 2004). Women over 35 are at a higher risk for fertility difficulties, diabetes, hypertension and other health issues, miscarriage, fetal chromosomal abnormalities, intrauterine death, and labor and delivery complications (Byrom, 2004; Jacobsson, Ladfors, & Milsom, 2004). Women who elect to have children after menopause (using ARTs) will be under careful study to determine to what extent their health is compromised by pregnancy in later midlife. In 2002, 263 U.S. births were reported in women between 50 and 54 years of age (Heffner, 2004). In 2005, a 67-year-old university professor in Romania gave birth to a baby girl and in 2003 a 65-year-old Indian woman gave birth to a healthy boy (Caplan, 2005).

Maternal Nutrition and Prenatal Care The unborn infant's nourishment comes from the maternal bloodstream through the placenta. Babies of poorly nourished mothers are more likely to be underweight at birth, to die in infancy, to suffer rickets, to have physical and neurological defects, low vitality, and certain forms of mental retardation. Poor maternal nutrition—associated with war, famine, poverty, drug addiction, and poor dietary practice—has long-term insidious effects on brain growth and intelligence (Rowland & Vasquez, 2002). Thus, maternal nutritional deficiencies, particularly severe ones, are reflected in changes in genes, structure, physiology, and metabolism of the child—predisposing such individuals to other diseases in adulthood (Grimm, 2003; Guoyao et al., 2004).

Early and regular prenatal care, taking prenatal vitamins and folic acid, getting moderate exercise, not smoking or not using harmful drugs are significantly correlated with babies born with adequate birth weight and fewer birth complications. Women should make a prenatal visit as soon as they know they are pregnant and attend scheduled visits thereafter. The timeliness of

FIGURE 3.15 Percent of Births to Mothers Receiving Late or No Prenatal Care, Selected Years: 1970–2003* More U.S. women of all races seek early prenatal care. Prenatal care enhances pregnancy outcome by providing health care, advice, and managing chronic and pregnancy-related health conditions. By 2003, 84 percent of mothers-to-be received prenatal care during the first trimester of pregnancy, and the percent of mothers with late or no prenatal care has dropped to only 3.5 percent.

Source: Child Trends Data Bank http://www.childtrendsdatabank.org/indicators/25PrenatalCare.cfm.

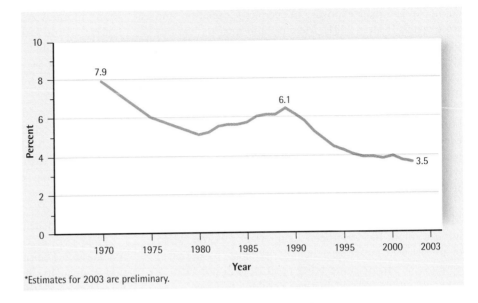

*Estimates for 2003 are preliminary.

prenatal care starting in the first trimester continues to improve since 1990 to nearly 85 percent, but only 3.5 percent of U.S. pregnant women seek third trimester or no care (see Figure 3.15) (Martin et al., 2003). The rates of drug addiction and poor prenatal care are highest for single, young, minority mothers who might decide not to seek prenatal care for fear of losing existing children or being prosecuted. Although state laws vary in protecting fetal rights versus maternal rights, the U.S. Supreme Court ruled in 2001 in *Ferguson* v. *City of Charleston* that secretly testing women for prenatal drug use while seeking care at a public hospital in South Carolina violated their Fourth Amendment rights. No state has laws criminalizing prenatal drug use, but criminal laws about possession, delivering drugs, child abuse and neglect, or manslaughter have been enforced. Thirty-four states have expanded their child welfare policies to address prenatal drug exposure or death under civil laws as child abuse or neglect (Dailard & Nash, 2000; Robbins, 2004).

Research studies over the past 30 years overwhelming confirm that early and regular prenatal care pays off, both in significantly improved health for newborns and their mothers and in lower costs to society (Fiscella, 1995).

Questions

About what percentage of pregnancies end in miscarriage? What are some prenatal environmental influences and known teratogens that are harmful to the development of the zygote, embryo and fetus? What actions can a pregnant woman take to promote a safe pregnancy for herself and optimum health for her baby throughout the prenatal period?

SEGUE

In this chapter we have given you an introduction to the marvelous intricacies and complexities of the female and male reproductive systems. Assisted reproductive technologies (ARTs) have brought hope for those who had previously been classified as infertile. The microscopic hereditary code transferred from both parents to the zygote at conception provides a blueprint for our physical makeup and a timing device for various changes in our body's makeup during our lifetime. It is truly a "miracle of life" to realize that each of us started out with such a complex code and that it was embedded in a fertilized egg smaller than the period at the end of this sentence.

Many structures in the mother's womb must function properly to support the embryo/fetus during its course of development and birth. However, for optimum health of both mother and fetus, the mother-to-be must seek early and regular prenatal care, get proper nutrition and sleep, abstain from smoking cigarettes or using alcohol and other drugs, avoid toxins in the home and work environments, exercise moderately to prepare for labor and delivery, and try to keep stress to a minimum whenever possible.

In Chapter 4, we discuss the variety of approaches employed to prepare for the coming birth of a child, methods used to ease mothers and the fetus through labor and delivery, and the exciting and challenging first two years of infant development.

Summary
Reproduction

1. Many technological advances are available to help more people reproduce—and more assisted reproductive technologies are planned for the near future.

2. Like all other living things, human beings are capable of reproducing new individuals of their own kind. Two kinds of cells called gametes are involved in human reproduction: the female's ovum and the male's sperm. A sperm fuses with an ovum to form a zygote (fertilized egg) in a process called fertilization or commonly called conception. Each ovum and sperm contributes its own unique genetic material to the zygote during fertilization.

3. The male's primary reproductive organs are a pair of testes located in an external pouchlike structure called the scrotum. Healthy sperm are produced daily in the testes at a temperature a little lower than normal body temperature (about 96 degrees). The testes produce the principal male sex hormones, called androgens (testosterone and androsterone), which produce male secondary sex characteristics.

4. During sexual arousal and ejaculation, mature sperm are released from the tubules, emptied into the epididymis, and mixed with nurturant fluids from the prostate gland and seminal vesicles. This mixture is called semen, which is ejaculated out of a man's body through the urethra in the man's penis.

5. A male's sperm production (sperm count and health) can be compromised by illness, sexually transmitted infections, and exposure to biochemical substances in the home, work, or recreational environment.

6. The primary female reproductive organs are a pair of ovaries that lie deep in her pelvic area. Each ovary produces mature eggs (ova) and the female sex hormones estrogen and progesterone. During ovulation and menstruation, a mature egg normally is moved into the fallopian tube (oviduct), then into the uterus (womb), through the cervix, into the vagina, and out of the body through the folds of skin outside of the vagina, called the vulva.

7. An ovary contains many follicles, and normally only one ovum develops to maturity in a cycle. The discharge of the mature ovum from its follicle is called ovulation. Typically a woman's ovaries alternate the release of an ovum monthly.

8. The series of regular hormonal and physical changes associated with producing a mature ovum is called the menstrual cycle. The cycle begins the first day the woman menstruates, and the average length of the cycle is about 28 days (with individual variation). A mature ovum is produced toward the middle of each monthly ovarian cycle (normally between days 13 to 15) when an ovum reaches maturity and passes into one of the fallopian tubes. This window of fertility varies, particularly for teens and perimenopausal women. If sperm are present, fertilization may take place in the fallopian tube.

9. If fertilization does not take place, decreasing levels of female hormones lead to menstruation (shedding of the thickened uterine lining) about 12 to 14 days later. For most women, this menstrual cycle continues for 30 to 40 years, unless pregnancy, disease, illness, stress, or surgical intervention occurs.

10. Fertilization, the union of an ovum and sperm, occurs most often in the upper end of the fallopian tube, and the new organism is called a zygote. A small number of sperm are viable in a woman's reproductive tract for up to 48 hours—but a high percentage will die in the vagina because of its high acidity. A biochemical change in the ovum allows only one sperm to penetrate. About one-third of all zygotes die after fertilization.

11. A woman might conceive dizygotic, fraternal children (nonidentical) if two ova or more are released during the same menstrual cycle. Monozygotic, identical twins are the result of one fertilized egg splitting into two identical parts after conception. Multiple conceptions occur more frequently now due to in vitro fertilization procedures, especially for women in their thirties and older. Such conceptions put the mother and the babies at higher risk.

12. Secretions of progesterone from the corpus luteum prepare the uterus for implantation of the zygote in the lining of the uterus.

13. Many U.S. women are delaying childbirth until their thirties or older, but those 35 and older have a higher rate of infertility. Nearly one out of every six U.S. couples experiences infertility. Medical researchers have created fertility drugs and assisted reproductive technologies (ARTs) over the last 25 years to aid in conception.

14. A common treatment is in vitro fertilization (IVF), where fertilization occurs outside the womb in a medical lab. Embryos develop for a few days and are implanted into the woman's (or surrogate's) uterus for potential implantation and maturation. Ovarian tissue and/or sperm can be cryopreserved for potential later use. Some postmenopausal women are also becoming pregnant. But ART methods such as cloning and stem cell research to produce human embryos for reproduction or experimentation are strongly debated.

15. Reduction of higher-order (multiple) pregnancies is termed selective reduction, and this is a highly complex decision for those that desire to have children.

16. Recent studies have discovered there are optimal times of a menstrual cycle and seasons of the year for conception to occur—yet infertility rates are increasing worldwide. Reasons for increasing infertility rates include low sperm count, injury or disease to the reproductive organs, or surgical removal of reproductive organs. In some cases, there is no identifiable cause. ART success rates remain low around 25 percent.

17. Some biomedical researchers support research on reproductive techniques such as preimplantation genetic treatment to screen embryo health and cloning, growing a baby identical to the parent from a single somatic cell. The U.S. House of Representatives passed a bill banning human cloning in 2001 and 2003. In 2004 California voters passed a bond act to promote stem cell research, which allows embryonic experimentation and may lead to human cloning. Worldwide, such biomedical research is experiencing explosive growth, and one goal is to end infertility. Legislation is lacking to protect couples and embryos.

18. Public education campaigns about birth control methods, including abstinence, are targeting young adolescents, women at risk of HIV and STIs, and those with multiple sex partners. The FDA has approved at least 14 new

contraceptive products. Elective abortion is legal in the United States, and pro-life and pro-choice advocates dispute each other with powerful political efforts. Partial-birth abortion is highly controversial.

19. Women are conceiving at younger and older ages than before. Young teens (or younger) and more postmenopausal women are having babies. The youngest teen pregnancy rate dropped 43 percent since the early 1990s, yet the United States has the highest teen pregnancy rate in the Westernized world. Unwanted pregnancy puts a great financial strain on families and society. While some U.S. women have insurance coverage for birth control, many do not.

Heredity and Genetics

20. Our biological inheritance is called heredity, and genetics is the scientific study of biological inheritance. A major debate among developmentalists is the nature-nurture controversy. Does the genetic "blueprint" in our chromosomes and genes make us who we are? How much do parenting and environment contribute to influencing our personality, motivation, skills, and traits?

21. The Human Genome Project, sponsored by both public and private research, has successfully mapped the human genome, the sequencing of the genetic blueprint of all the genes on their appropriate chromosomes. Our individual genome affects every aspect of our physiology and behavior. Many types of mutations result in hereditary diseases. The genome is divided into chromosomes, chromosomes contain genes, genes are made of DNA, which in turn tells a cell how to make vital proteins. Humans are 99.9 percent alike in their genetic sequence. The Genomes to Life project is under way to map other species.

22. Chromosomes are long threadlike structures made of protein and nucleic acid located in the nucleus of each cell. The chromosome is shaped like a rope ladder (or double helix) and contains about 20,000 to 25,000 hereditary markers called genes (like the beads on a string). Genes are composed of DNA (deoxyribonucleic acid), which actively programs cells to manufacture vital substances for life. Upon normal fertilization, the 23 chromosomes of the ovum and the 23 chromosomes of the sperm combine to create a genetically unique zygote with 46 chromosomes (23 pair).

23. Mitosis is the type of cell division through which nearly all cells of the human body (except the sex cells) replicate themselves. In the cell nucleus, each single chromosome splits lengthwise to form a new pair, called "daughter" cells, which have the same hereditary code as the original. Meiosis is a replication process that takes place in the gametes (the sperm and ovum). Meiosis involves two cell divisions during which the chromosomes are reduced to half their original number. Each gamete receives only 23 chromosomes, not 23 pair as in other cells. Half the usual number allows the sperm and egg to each contribute one-half of the genetic material at fertilization.

24. The male's sperm carries the chromosome that determines the sex of a child. Of the 23 pairs of chromosomes that most humans possess, 22 are similar in size and shape in both men and women and are the autosomes. The 23rd pair, the sex chromosomes (one from the mother and one from the father), determines the baby's sex. The mother's ovum contributes an X chromosome; the sperm contributes either an X (female) or Y (male) chromosome. An ovum (X) fertilized by a sperm with X will produce a female child (XX). An ovum (X) fertilized by a sperm with Y will produce a male (XY). The Y chromosome from the father determines the child will be a male (XY). Approximately 6 to 8 weeks into embryonic development, the male embryo produces the hormone testosterone, which promotes masculinization of the fetus.

25. Each member of a pair of genes at a specific location on the chromosome is called an allele. Mendel demonstrated that one allele can be dominant and hide the traits of the other allele, which is then considered a recessive character. A dominant character is labeled with a capital letter, such as (A), and the recessive character is signified by a lowercase letter (a). When both inherited alleles from parents are the same, this is called a homozygous trait and is represented as either (AA) or (aa). When inherited alleles from parents are different, the trait is heterozygous and represented as (Aa). Not all traits are inherited from a single gene. Some traits, such as personality and intelligence, are the result of the complex interaction of many genes, which is called polygenic inheritance.

26. An organism's genotype is its actual genetic makeup, whereas the phenotype is its observable characteristics. In humans, the phenotype includes physical, physiological, and behavioral traits. Humans also possess dominant and recessive traits. For example, brown hair is a dominant characteristic, whereas red hair is recessive. Brown hair, however, can be either BB or Bb, whereas red hair must be bb. In humans, environmental factors interact with genetic factors to produce traits, and this is called multifactorial transmission.

27. Genes can also be linked together during inheritance. The X chromosome can carry a sex-linked trait such as hemophilia, red-green color blindness, and approximately 150 other traits and disorders. The vast majority of sex-linked genetic defects occur in males. Though a woman can be a carrier of a sex-linked disorder, she herself rarely exhibits that characteristic.

28. The field of genetic counseling and testing has arisen out of genetic research to apply knowledge about genetics on reproduction, health, and well-being. Individuals might be concerned about a family history of inherited disease or ones specific to their ethnic/racial background. Diagnostic tests are available to counsel those who are most likely to be affected. A number of known disorders are linked with the presence of too few or too many chromosomes.

29. Prenatal diagnosis employs techniques to determine the health and condition of an unborn fetus. Amniocentesis is one invasive procedure used in the fourth month of pregnancy to diagnose a number of genetic diseases. Ultrasonography, now available in 3-D or 4-D (showing depth), allows physicians to determine size, position, and appearance of the fetus, placenta, amniotic fluid, and umbilical cord. Fetoscopy allows a direct view of the fetus. Chorionic villus biopsy (CVS) is an invasive sampling of a very small amount of villous tissue in very early embryonic development. Maternal blood sampling might potentially detect some birth defects by analyzing fetal cells shed into the pregnant woman's bloodstream. Down syndrome is a chromosomal disorder with a higher incidence

than some other genetic defects that appears in all cultures of the world. An older pregnant woman has a higher risk of having a child with Down syndrome.

Prenatal Development

30. The prenatal period normally lasts about 266 days, or 280 days from the last menstrual period. Embryologists divide it into three stages: the germinal period, the embryonic period, and the fetal period.

31. The germinal period is characterized by the growth of the zygote (the fertilized egg) and the establishment of an initial linkage between the zygote and the support system of the mother through implantation in the uterine wall. The zygote divides through mitosis. In about six or seven days the more developed structure called the blastocyst begins the process of differentiation into the chorion, trophoblast, and inner cell mass. By the end of the second week, the embryonic portion of the inner cell mass differentiates into three layers: ectoderm, mesoderm, and endoderm.

32. The embryonic period lasts from the end of the second week to the end of the eighth week. The embryo undergoes rapid growth, establishment of a complex physical membrane exchange with the mother through the placenta, differentiation in early structural form of the chief organs, and appearance of recognizable features of a human body. Stem cell researchers harvest cells from the inner mass of the embryo, resulting in the death of the embryo. In the embryonic stage, structures develop based upon two principles: cephalocaudal development (brain and head first down to trunk to the toes) and proximodistal development (tissues grow in opposite directions away from the axis of the primitive streak, the earliest structure of the spinal cord).

33. A woman may be unaware that she is pregnant until about four weeks after conception, when she is unlikely to menstruate (although some women do), her breasts may become tender and swollen, and she may be experiencing a type of nausea, commonly termed "morning sickness," as her body adjusts hormonally to the pregnancy. The early developing embryo is highly sensitive to the mother's ingestion of drugs, medications, and environmental teratogens—which are risky and could affect the development of embryonic organs and structures.

34. The fetal period begins with the ninth week and ends with birth, and now the organism is called a fetus. The differentiation of the major organ systems continues, and the organs become competent to assume their specialized functions. The fetus becomes a sensory aware and active being inside the mother's womb. It can move around, suck its thumb, kick its feet, and hear sounds outside the mother's womb.

35. A miscarriage, or spontaneous abortion, occurs when the zygote, embryo, or fetus is naturally expelled from the uterus before it can survive outside the mother's womb. About 10 to 15 percent of known pregnancies end in miscarriage, and most occur before the 12th week. Parents commonly experience a great deal of emotional distress after miscarriage and need social support. Grief over the loss of the child can last a long time for both parents and siblings. Most pregnancies end with the birth of normal, healthy babies.

36. Toxic environmental substances (collectively called teratogens) in the home, workplace, and social-recreational settings can affect the organism from the moment of conception and throughout the prenatal period—potentially resulting in birth defects. The pregnant woman is highly advised to avoid cigarettes, caffeine, alcohol, and other psychoactive substances, and to protect herself against any sexually transmitted infections. She must get professional prenatal care (especially if she herself has health conditions), get proper nutrition, get plenty of sleep, avoid excessive stress, and exercise moderately to prepare herself for a healthy pregnancy and labor and delivery in nine months.

Key Terms

abortion (85)

allele (90)

amniocentesis (95)

amnion (97)

assisted reproductive technologies (ARTs) (75)

autosomes (90)

blastocyst (71)

cephalocaudal (98)

chorion (97)

chorionic villus biopsy (CVS) (95)

chromosomes (87)

cloning (78)

critical period (98)

deoxyribonucleic acid (DNA) (87)

dizygotic (73)

dominant character (90)

ectoderm (97)

ectogenesis (77)

embryo (71)

embryonic period (94)

endoderm (97)

fallopian tubes (71)

fertilization/fusion (70)

fetal period (94)

fetoscopy (95)

fetus (98)

gametes (70)

genes (87)

genetic counseling (92)

genetic counselor (95)

genetics (87)

genotype (91)

germinal period (94)

gynecologist (82)

heredity (87)

heterozygous (90)

homozygous (90)

human genome (87)

implantation (97)

in vitro fertilization (IVF) (76)

inner cell mass (97)

maternal blood sampling (96)

maternal serum alpha-fetoprotein (MSAFP) test (96)

meiosis (88)

menstrual cycle (72)

menstruation (71)

mesoderm (97)

miscarriage (99)

mitosis (88)

monozygotic (74)

multifactorial transmission (91)

ovaries (71)

ovulation (71)

ovum (70)

penis (70)

phenotype (91)

placenta (97)

polygenic inheritance (90)

prenatal diagnosis (95)

prenatal period (94)

proximodistal (98)

recessive character (90)

reproduction (70)

sex chromosomes (90)

sex-linked traits (91)

sperm (70)

spontaneous abortion (99)

stem cells (80)

teratogen (100)

teratology (100)

testes (70)

trophoblast (97)

ultrasonography (95)

umbilical cord (98)

uterus (71)

vagina (72)

zygote (70)

Following Up on the Internet

Web sites for this chapter focus on heredity, genetics, and human reproduction. Please access the text Web site at www.mhhe.com/vzcrandell8 for up-to-date hot-linked Internet addresses for the following organizations and topics:

American Fertility Association

American Social Health Association

American Society for Reproductive Medicine

The International Society for Stem Cell Research

National Campaign to Prevent Teen Pregnancy

Reproductive Technologies Web at Harvard

Research Ethics and Stem Cells: National Institutes of Health

The Visible Embryo Project

Video Scenario—http://www.mhhe.com/vzcrandell8

In this chapter, you've just read about the biological foundations of heredity, reproduction, and prenatal development. Using the OLC (www.mhhe.com/vzcrandell8), watch how these concepts, such as genetic counseling, come to life as Joe and Gina discuss their pregnancy. Joe and Gina's discussion also introduces some key concepts you'll explore in the next chapter, Birth and Physical Development.

Part THREE
Birth and Infancy
The First Two Years

Chapter 4 describes the preparation of the mother for labor, delivery, and birth of the neonate. We will discuss several birth and delivery methods, including natural, or prepared, childbirth. The significance of early caregiver-infant bonding within increasingly diverse family structures is also examined. Potential birth complications and birth defects are examined as well. Then we will turn to the infant's first two years of physical, motor, and sensory development. In Chapter 5, we examine the processes of cognitive and language development, which allow infants to take greater command of their environment. Chapter 6 describes the emotional and social development of infants, including the significant influences of attachment, temperament, and parenting practices.

Birth and Physical Development

The First Two Years

Critical Thinking Questions

1. If you were to design the "perfect" birth experience, where would you want to be and who would you want to assist you? If you have an older child, would you want to include this child in the experience? Why or why not?

2. Most births result in healthy newborns. Hypothetically, though, if your newborn has a disorder, how do you think you might react, and who would you turn to to cope?

3. Recognizing that parenting styles vary, do you think you might be a "responsive" parent, attending to a crying child's every need, or would you think that approach "spoils the child"?

4. If you were planning to become a child-care provider for young toddlers in your home, what would you plan to do to provide them with physical activity and sensory stimulation?

Extensive research in prenatal development over the past 30 years has revealed that the tiny human demonstrates physical, cognitive, and emotional behaviors. Routine use of noninvasive diagnostic and imaging technologies have made it possible for us to view the developing embryo and fetus in its preparation for birth. The moment of first seeing a fetal ultrasound or hearing the fetal heartbeat is a peak moment in life for many expectant parents.

Touch, the first sense and the cornerstone of human experience and communication, begins in the womb (Montagu, 1986). The first dramatic movement that symbolizes life itself is the first heartbeat at three weeks after conception. Hand-to-head, hand-to-face, hand-to-mouth movements and mouth opening, closing, and swallowing are present at 10 weeks of development (Tajani & Ianniruberto, 1990). The fetus lives in a stimulating environment of sound, vibration, and motion, and when a mother laughs or coughs, her fetus moves within seconds (Chamberlain, 1998). Voices reach the womb, and patterns of pitch and rhythm, as well as music, reach the fetus. A mother's voice is particularly powerful (Shahidullah & Hepper, 1992). The fetus reacts to amniocentesis (usually done between weeks 14 and 16) by shrinking away from the needle, a reaction easily observed on the ultrasound. Rapid eye movement sleep, a manifestation of dreaming, is observed as early as 23 weeks of gestation (although the eyelids remain closed) (Hopson, 1998).

Remarkable as it is, then, most full-term infants arrive at birth with all sensory systems functioning. Newborns are real, separate persons—not the "blank slates" they were thought to be only a few decades ago. Tests made at birth reveal exquisite taste and odor discrimination and definite preferences, and visual tests demonstrate how remarkably a newborn can imitate a variety of facial expressions. When newborns are awake, their eyes constantly seek out the environment (Slater et al., 1991). Throughout the newborn's first two years of life, extraordinary emotional and social developments accompany the maturation of its physical and cognitive systems.

Birth

A Child Is Born into a Family

Today's babies are born into a shifting composition of American families and households, and American families are composed of fewer children (Federal Interagency Forum on Child and Family Statistics, 2004; Whitehead & Popenoe, 2004). Demographic trends in rates of marriage, cohabitation, divorce, fertility, and mortality influence family composition, and all these factors affect the quality of life of our most precious resource—our children. Although a small proportion of men and women choose to remain childless or experience infertility, more than 80 percent of U.S. adults will be the parent of a child by the age of 35 (Child Trends, 2002). The National Center for Health Statistics reports that after annual declines in numbers of births throughout the 1990s, more than 4 million babies were born each year in the United States since 2000 (Hamilton, Martin, & Sutton, 2004).

Significantly, a mother and father's marital status and the structure of a family have a direct impact on the infant's and growing child's economic status, level of support, and overall well-being. Marriage between two biological parents generally provides many resources that benefit child well-being, but the proportion of the population made up of married couples with children, although the majority, continues to decrease (Child Trends, 2002). In 2003, 68 percent of children lived with two married parents. Of the remaining children, 23 percent lived with their mothers, 5 percent lived with their fathers and 4 percent lived in a setting with neither parent. In 2003, more than one-third of all U.S. births were to unmarried women (Federal Interagency Forum on Child and Family Statistics, 2004). About 40 percent of nonmarital births occur to cohabiting couples, yet cohabitation arrangements are often short-lived (Child Trends, 2002). Grandparents play a significant role in child rearing even if a parent is present. Ten percent of children raised by a single mother live in their grandparents' household (Fields, 2003).

For the vast majority of mothers and fathers, raising children is a central focus of their lives, and most adults state that watching their children grow up is life's greatest joy (Child Trends, 2002). However, more new mothers than ever are working outside the home on either a full-time or part-time basis to support their child(ren). Consequently, after birth more newborns than ever will receive child care outside their home in a variety of child-care arrangements. And the quality of infant care is an essential factor in the equation of development because developmentalists have made many discoveries about how an infant's earliest experiences affect the way the brain is organized. But first we turn to the birth of the baby, which will forever transform women into mothers and men into fathers.

Preparing for Childbirth

In the 1940s the English obstetrician Grantly Dick-Read (1944) began popularizing the view that pain in childbirth could be greatly reduced if women understood the birth process and learned to relax properly. Childbirth, he argued, is essentially a normal and natural process. He trained prospective mothers to relax, to breathe correctly, to understand their anatomy and the process of labor, and to develop muscular control of their labor through special exercises. He also advocated training the father as an active participant in both prenatal preparation and delivery.

During the same time, Russian doctors began to apply Pavlov's theories of the conditioned reflex to delivery practices and reasoned that society conditioned women to be tense and fearful during labor. If pain was a response conditioned by society, it could be replaced by a different, more positive response. Accordingly, the **psychoprophylactic method** evolved, which encouraged women to relax and concentrate on the manner in which they breathed when a contraction occurred.

In 1951 Fernand Lamaze (1958), a French obstetrician, visited maternity clinics in the Soviet Union. When he returned to France, he introduced the fundamentals of the psychoprophylactic method. Lamaze emphasized the mother's active participation in every phase of labor. He developed a precise and controlled breathing drill in which women in labor respond to a series of verbal cues by panting, pushing, and blowing. The Lamaze method has proved popular with U.S. physicians and prospective parents who prefer natural childbirth, and nearly every hospital and many private medical organizations offer Lamaze childbirth preparation classes, which encourage participation by the father or a close relative or friend.

Natural Childbirth   For many Americans, the term **natural childbirth** has come to be equated with a variety of approaches that stress the mother's and father's preparation for childbirth and their active involvement in the process. But the term actually refers to an awake, aware, and unmedicated mother-to-be. A woman proceeding through a Lamaze delivery might use a number of cognitive techniques that distract her from the activities of the labor room and provide an additional source of support. These techniques include using visual focus and sucking on hard candies or ice chips (Wideman & Singer, 1984).

Natural childbirth offers a number of advantages. Childbirth education classes can do much to relieve the mother's anxiety and fear; along with natural childbirth classes, prospective parents get to see a birthing room. Many couples find their joint participation in labor and delivery a joyous, rewarding occasion. And the mother takes no medication or is given it only sparingly in the final phase of delivery, at her request. There is con-

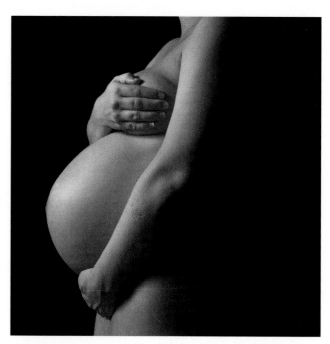

Preparing for Childbirth A woman's body changes dramatically over the nine months of pregnancy, giving her time to prepare herself for the most significant change in her life—motherhood. One century ago a woman could expect to give birth to at least four children, whereas a majority of contemporary American women average two children.

flicting research on the effects of these analgesic and sedative drugs. Some studies show that using particular medications can reduce the need for cesarean sections and reduce delivery time (Votipka, 1997). Other studies show that interventions such as giving emotional support during labor and delivery substantially decreased cesarean section rates, forceps deliveries, the duration of labor, and the use of anesthetics and medications (Bower, 1991). Safe obstetric practice seems to suggest caution in the administration of these drugs, because what passes into the mother's system might affect the baby during labor and delivery.

Medical authorities are increasingly concluding that no mother should ever labor and deliver alone (Collins et al., 1993). Evidence suggests that women who have a friendly companion with them during childbirth have faster, simpler deliveries, have fewer complications, and are more affectionate toward their babies. This insight has led to the reemergence of *doula* services (*doula* is a Greek word meaning "someone who nurtures and cares for new mothers"). Doulas and *midwives*, as acknowledged members of the maternity care team, provide emotional care and physical comfort and are usually licensed and often affiliated with **obstetricians** (physicians who specialize in conception, prenatal development, birth, and the woman's postbirth care). For centuries in European cultures, doulas or midwives attended women in labor and delivery until approximately the 1600s or 1700s. From that time until the late 1960s, physicians in Western societies claimed that labor and delivery came exclusively under their medical domain.

Although natural childbirth clearly offers advantages for many couples, it is more suitable for some couples and some births than others. In some cases the pain becomes so severe that wise and humane practice calls for medication. Although the average intensity of labor pain is quite high, women substantially differ in their experience of it. And despite their pain and discomfort, most women say that childbirth is one of the greatest, if not *the greatest,* experience of their lives (Picard, 1993). However, both proponents and critics of natural, or prepared, childbirth agree that women who are psychologically or physically unprepared for it should not consider themselves inadequate or irresponsible if they resort to conventional practice. Indeed, many practitioners view prepared childbirth training and pain-relief remedies as compatible, complementary procedures.

Birthing Accommodations

With smaller families and more childbirth classes, most couples are seeking an obstetrician and a hospital that view uncomplicated pregnancies as a normal process rather than as an illness. And they are rebelling against regimented and impersonal hospital routines. They do not want the delivery of their babies to be a surgical procedure unless such surgery is necessary or planned. Nevertheless, 99 percent of births in 2001 were delivered in hospitals. Of out-of-hospital births, two-thirds occurred in a residence and nearly one-third were delivered in a community birthing center (Martin et al., 2003).

Although a high majority of all births were delivered by physicians in hospitals, other options exist. Among the maternity care options more widely available is **midwifery** (pronounced "mid-wiff-ery"). The percentage of births attended by midwives has increased from less than 1 percent in 1975 to 8 percent in 2002. Most of this increase is due to the increase in midwife-attended births in hospitals (Martin et al., 2003). All 50 states have legalized the provision of prenatal care and delivery by midwives so long as the practitioners are registered nurses (Friedland, 2000). Midwives who are not nurses are also seeking legal status. The demand for the use of midwives (common until 1940) is now being fueled by middle-class and affluent professional women who prefer a more personal birthing experience and by women who lack access to, or cannot afford the high costs of, traditional obstetrical and gynecological care (Lyndon-Rochelle, 2004).

In response to the home-birth movement, many hospitals have introduced **birthing rooms.** Such rooms have

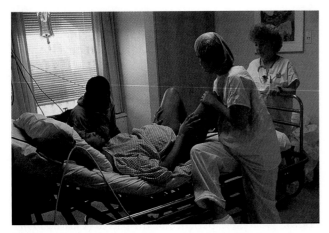

Birthing Room The scene above reflects a family-centered childbirth experience in a birthing room with rooming in for the newborn. How different is this from childbirth up through the 1950s in the United States?

a homelike atmosphere complete with wallpapered walls, window drapes, potted plants, color television, a queen-size bed, and other comforts. Medical equipment is normally out of view. The woman can give birth assisted by a nurse-midwife or an obstetrician and her husband or other partner. Other relatives, friends, or even the baby's brothers and sisters might be present. Should complications arise, the woman can be quickly moved to a regular delivery room. This arrangement allows for a homelike birth with proximity to hospital life-saving equipment. The mother and child might then return home about 6 to 24 hours after an uncomplicated delivery.

Other hospitals, while retaining more traditional childbirth procedures, have introduced family-centered hospital care, in which birth is made a family experience. The plan is usually coupled with rooming in, an arrangement in which the infant stays in a bassinet beside the mother's bed. This practice runs counter to the U.S. hospital tradition of segregating infants in a sterile nursery. **Rooming in** allows the mother to get acquainted with her child and integrates the father early into the child-care process. Under the supervision of the nursing staff, parents gain skill in nursing/feeding, bathing, diapering, and caring for their infant. Women who desire to breast-feed their babies can begin the process with the sympathetic help and support of the trained hospital staff.

Birthing centers are opening in many urban areas. These primary care facilities are used only for low-risk deliveries because they lack high-tech equipment. Should complications arise, patients are transferred to nearby hospitals (DeWitt, 1993). Another recent trend has shortened hospital stays for new mothers and their newborns. In today's cost-conscious climate of managed health care, maternity stays have declined from the week-long sojourn common in the 1950s, and still prevalent in

many European nations, to a national average of about two and a half days. Three days is now typical for cesarean births. Not surprisingly, many health professionals criticize the fact that most health insurance allows only such abbreviated stays, saying that mothers need more hospital time to rest and recover and to acquire basic child-care skills. Although many problems with newborns surface early, some conditions, including jaundice and heart murmurs, tend to appear only after the first six hours, and the mother herself might experience medical complications hours after delivery (Lord, 1994).

> **Questions**
>
> What are the differences among giving birth in a birthing room in a hospital, in a medically supervised birthing center, or in a home delivery with a midwife or doula attending? What are some factors to consider in making this important decision?

Stages of the Birth Process

Birth is the transition between dependent existence in the uterus and life as a separate organism. In less than a day, a radical change occurs. The fetus is catapulted from its warm, fluid, sheltered environment in the womb into the larger world. The infant is compelled to depend exclusively on its own biological systems. Birth, then, is a bridge between two stages of life. Normally around 266 days of prenatal development, some factors, suspected to be hormonal signals including *oxytocin* from the pituitary gland to the blood, prompt uterine contractions and labor. In this section we will explain the stages of the birth process, labor, delivery, and crucial neonatal assessment at birth.

A few weeks before birth, the head of the infant generally turns downward, which ensures that it will be born head first. (A small percentage of babies are born buttocks or feet first, in the *breech position.* This most often requires a surgical delivery.) The uterus simultaneously sinks downward and forward. These changes are termed **lightening.** They "lighten" the mother's discomfort, and she now breathes more easily, because the pressure on her diaphragm and lungs is reduced (see Figure 4.1). At about the same time the mother might begin experiencing mild "tuning-up" contractions (*Braxton-Hicks contractions*), which are a prelude to the more vigorous contractions of labor.

Labor   The birth process consists of three stages: labor, delivery, and afterbirth. Either at the beginning of labor or sometime during it, the *amniotic sac* that surrounds and cushions the fetus ruptures, releasing the amniotic fluid, which should then flow as a clear liquid from the vagina. This "water breaking" is usually the first signal to the mother-to-be that labor is impending. It is imperative that she call her obstetrician, doula, or midwife at this time. Again, a woman should not attempt to deliver alone. The duration of this first stage of labor varies considerably depending on several factors: the age of the mother, her number of prior pregnancies, and potential complications of the pregnancy. During **labor** the strong muscle fibers of the uterus rhythmically contract, pushing the infant downward toward the birth canal (the vagina). Simultaneously, the muscular tissue that forms the thick lower opening of the uterus (the cervix) relaxes, becoming both shortened and widened, which permits the infant's passage (see Figure 4.1).

Normally labor averages about 14 hours for women having their first babies. Women who have already had at least one baby average about 8 hours. Initially, the uterine contractions are spaced about 15 to 20 minutes apart and last for about 25 to 30 seconds. As the intervals shorten to 3 to 5 minutes, the contractions become stronger and last for about 45 seconds or longer. As the mother's uterine contractions increase in intensity and occur more frequently, her cervix opens wider (dilates) (see Figure 4.1). Eventually it will expand enough to allow the baby's head and body to pass through.

Delivery   **Delivery** begins once the infant's head passes through the cervix (the neck of the uterus) and ends when the baby has completed its passage through the birth canal. This stage generally requires 20 to 80 minutes but can be shorter in deliveries of subsequent children.

During delivery, contractions last for 60 to 65 seconds and come at 2- to 3-minute intervals. The mother aids each contraction by "bearing down" (pushing) with her abdominal muscles at recommended times. With each contraction, the baby's head and body emerges more.

Crowning occurs when the widest diameter of the baby's head is at the mother's vulva (the outer entrance to the vagina). If the pain is too intense, an *epidural anesthetic* may be administered to the external surface of the spinal cord, numbing the woman's body from the waist down (see Figure 4.2). The longer the fetus remains *in utero* after drug administration to the mother, the greater the exposure to the fetus's brain and CNS (Golub, 1996). Sometimes an incision called an *episiotomy* is made between the vagina and the rectum if the opening of the vagina does not stretch enough to allow passage of the baby's head. This type of surgical intervention has come under much criticism but might be necessary to prevent complications of delivery in some births. Once the head has passed through the birth canal, the rest of the body quickly follows.

The second stage of labor is now over, unless there are multiple births involved. The doctor or health professional will quickly suction mucus from the baby's throat with a hand-operated suctioning device. The newborn, called the **neonate,** is still connected to the mother by the *umbilical cord,* which will be attended to within a few minutes. The newborn will be quickly assessed for its level of alertness and health and might be placed on the mother's warm body or quickly cleaned of

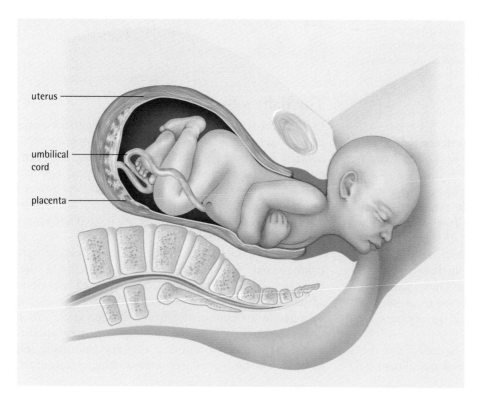

uterus

umbilical
cord

placenta

FIGURE 4.1 Normal Birth The principal movements in the mechanism of normal labor and vaginal delivery. *Source:* Northwestern Memorial Hospital, http://health_info.nmh.org/hwdb/images/hwstd/medical/obgyn/n5551690.jpg

Epidural Anesthetic

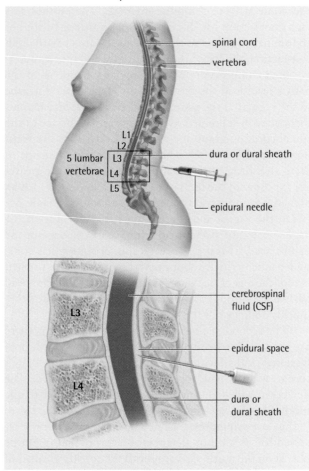

FIGURE 4.2 An Epidural Anesthetic An epidural injection places anti-inflammatory medicine into the epidural space between vertebrae to reduce the pain in the lower body from contractions during labor and birth. It may also be used during a cesarean section delivery.
Source: Reproduced with permission from www.mydr.com.au. Copyright © 2005 CMPMedica Australia.

the *vernix caseosa* (a white, waxy substance that covers its body) and placed into the father's or mother's awaiting arms.

Afterbirth After the baby's birth, the uterus commonly stops its contractions for a few minutes. The contractions then resume, and the placenta and the remaining umbilical cord are expelled from the uterus through the vagina. This process, expelling the **afterbirth,** may last for about 20 minutes. During this process, the father of the baby may choose to assist with the clamping and "cutting the cord" to separate the newborn baby from the mother.

A newer technique may be used to collect and preserve the blood from the placenta and umbilical cord

using *cryopreservation* for potential later transplantation. The "progenitor" cells (normally found in bone marrow) are vital in treating such life-threatening diseases as leukemia, types of cancer, or some immune or genetic disorders. In some hospitals parents have the option of storing the blood from their baby's cord and placenta. After the safe birth of the baby, a five-minute procedure is used to collect the blood contained in the placenta and umbilical cord. Some private blood banking companies urge prospective parents to collect and store umbilical cord blood which is sent to their facilities where it is processed to separate the stem cells. Some medical doctors however discourage the practice ("Cord Blood Banking Industry," 2004).

Most parents cherish the miracle of birth as a peak moment of their lives. However, personal and cultural attitudes can temper reactions to the birth of a baby. Was this baby planned for and wanted? Has the mother's health been compromised in some way? Is the baby's father present at the birth? Is it already known the child has a birth defect? Is the family already overburdened with many children? Is this a young teenager's first pregnancy? Is this baby the product of rape or incest? Is this a surrogate pregnancy? Is there a planned adoption? These types of circumstances certainly impact the mother's and father's level of acceptance and emotional reaction at the first sight of their newborn child.

Questions

What is usually the first indication to a woman that she is about to give birth? What are the events that occur in the progressive stages during labor and delivery culminating with birth and expulsion of the afterbirth?

The Baby's Birth Experience

In 1975 Frederick Leboyer, a French obstetrician, captured popular attention with his best-selling book *Birth without Violence* (1975). Birth for the baby, says Leboyer, is an exceedingly traumatic experience. Leboyer calls for a more gentle entry into the world via lowered sound and light levels in the delivery room, the immediate soothing of the infant through massaging and stroking, and a mild, warm bath for the newborn.

However, claims like Leboyer's are exceedingly controversial. Canadian researchers have found that Leboyer's method offers no special clinical or behavioral advantages to the infant or mother that are not offered by a gentle, conventional delivery (Nelson et al., 1980). Other researchers report that despite surface appearances, the stresses of a normal delivery are usually not harmful. The fetus produces unusually high levels of the stress hormones adrenaline and noradrenaline that equip it to withstand the stress of birth. This surge in hormones protects the infant from asphyxia during delivery and prepares the infant to survive outside the womb. It clears the lungs and changes physiological properties to promote normal breathing and simultaneously ensuring that a rich supply of blood goes to the heart and brain (Lagercrantz & Slotkin, 1986). The shock of birth triggers babies' gasping efforts to breathe for themselves. Some babies breathe on their own prior to the traditional slap on the bottom.

Parents can take comfort from knowing that from the baby's standpoint the stress of labor during normal birth is likely to be less unhappy and more beneficial than common sense might suggest, for the neonate's blood flow must reverse itself, a specific valve in the heart must close, and the baby's lungs must begin to function on their own. By the same token, however, Leboyer fostered a more humane view of childbirth management.

Electronic Fetal Monitoring   Normally during the process of labor and delivery in a hospital setting, a Velcro-type strap connected to an electronic monitor is placed so that it encircles the mother's abdomen and back. The fetal heartbeat is monitored continuously and registered on a strip of paper. The baby's pulse slows down during strong contractions, but it regains its original rate in between. Its heartbeat is likely to be twice as fast as the mother's. Even though normally the baby's body is well prepared to withstand the stress of delivery, surgical intervention can be necessary if the heart-rate monitor indicates that the fetus is in distress. Using this monitor and newer computer devices can be crucial to the survival of some babies.

Newborn Appearance   At the moment of birth, infants are covered with *vernix,* a thick, white, waxy substance. Some newborns still have their *lanugo,* the fetus's fine, woolly facial and body hair, which disappears by age 4 months. The matting of their hair with vernix gives newborns an odd, pasty look.

On the average, a full-term newborn is 19 to 22 inches long and weighs 5½ to 9½ pounds (recently a diabetic Brazilian woman gave birth to a 16.7-pound boy by cesarean section!) (Associated Press, 2005). Their heads are often misshapen and elongated as a product of molding. In *molding* the soft skull "bones" become temporarily distorted to accommodate passage through the birth canal. Babies born by C-section do not have this same elongated look. In most infants the chin recedes and the lower jaw is underdeveloped. Bowleggedness is the rule, and the feet might be pigeon-toed. Even more crucial is the neonate's behavioral status, to which we now turn our attention.

The Apgar Test   The average birth weight for babies is about 7 pounds 6 ounces (3.3 kilograms) (Department of Health and Human Services, 2003a; Hamilton, Martin, & Sutton, 2003). However, weight is only one factor in assessing a neonate's health. The normalcy of the baby's condition at birth is usually appraised by the physician or attending nurse in terms of the **Apgar scoring system,** a method developed by an anesthesiologist, Virginia Apgar (1953). The infant is assessed at one minute and again five minutes after birth on the basis of five conditions: heart rate, respiratory effort, muscle tone, reflex irritability (the infant's response to a catheter placed in its nostril), and body color. Each of the conditions is rated 0, 1, or 2 (see Figure 4.3). The ratings of the five conditions are then summed (the highest possible score is 10). At 60 seconds after birth, about 6 percent of all infants receive scores of 0 to 2, 24 percent have scores of 3 to 7, and 70 percent have scores of 8 to 10. A score of less than 5 indicates the need for prompt diagnosis and medical intervention. Infants with the lowest Apgar scores have the highest mortality rate.

Brazelton Neonatal Behavioral Assessment Scale and The Clinical Neonatal Behavioral Assessment Scale   Dr. T. Berry Brazelton, a noted pediatrician, author, and television and Internet physician, devised the *Neonatal Behavioral Assessment Scale (NBAS)* to be used several hours after birth or during the week after birth. Additionally, it is used by many researchers studying infant development. An examiner uses the 27 subtests of the NBAS to assess four categories of development: physiological, motor, states, and interaction with people (Brazelton, Nugent, & Lester, 1987). A low score might indicate potential cognitive impairment in a neonate or a need for more stimulation as provided by early intervention methods. The *Clinical Neonatal Behavioral Assessment Scale (CNBAS)* is the updated version of Brazelton's original scale. It is a brief interactive scale consisting of 18 behavioral and reflex items, designed to examine the newborn's physiological, motor, state, and social capacities (Brazelton, 2001).

> **Questions**
>
> What do we know about the baby's own birth experience? What is a typical neonate's appearance and activity level at birth? How might a newborn's health be assessed at birth?

Caregiver-Infant Bonding

During most of human history, babies have been placed immediately on their mothers' bodies after birth. According to the studies by anthropologist Meredith Small

The Miracle of Birth This newborn surely earned a high Apgar score.

Source: Kristi Gilleland, ShutterPoint. com.

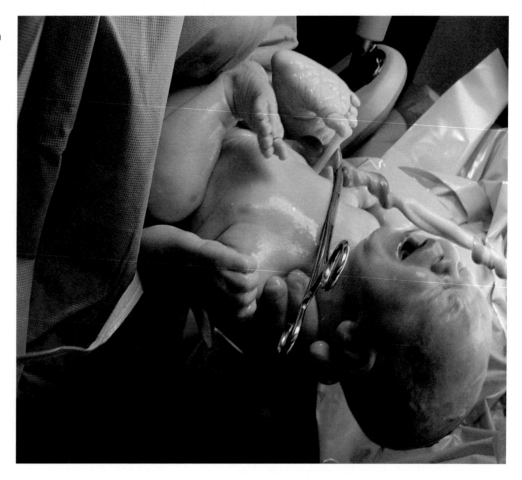

(1998), in most cultures around the world babies are still placed on their mothers this way. However, research on the concept of parental bonding has undergone a drastic change in the last few decades. Although it was studied as a psychological/medical construct in the 1970s, it is now more widely viewed from a cross-cultural perspective. Earlier research focused on European Americans and with an Anglo/Eurocentric perspective. As the findings from cross-cultural studies of caregiving emerge and as previous practices are seen in historical perspective, a different picture emerges. As Rogoff (2003) explains, "The cultural research draws attention to community aspects of infants' and caregivers' attachments to each other, including the health and economic conditions of the community, cultural goals of infant care, and cultural arrangements of family life." For example, a recent study compares cultural models of infant development between rural Africans and urban Europeans (Keller, 2001).

Harry Harlow conducted and published results from his infant monkey attachment experiments, finding infant monkeys preferred to cling to the wire-mother covered in cloth (Harlow, 1971). Bowlby's attachment theory proposes that attachment is a mechanism of evolutionary survival. Later seen in political context it can be understood as a response to the post World War II economy in which women were discouraged from entering the workforce. Ainsworth's "strange situation" research that examined child-mother bonding is criticized for using small samples that were not representative of a wider ethnic, more diverse socioeconomic population. Recent studies also take into account the political context on caretaking beliefs and practices (Ahnert & Lamb, 2001).

The practice of separating babies from their mothers has arisen only in the past 100 years and only in Western cultures after Martin Cooney invented one of the first incubators to aid premature infants and advocated sepa-

Sign	0 Points	1 Point	2 Points
A Activity (muscle tone)	Absent	Arms and legs flexed	Active movement
P Pulse	Absent	Below 100 bpm	Above 100 bpm
G Grimace (reflex irritability)	No response	Grimace	Sneeze, cough, pulls away
A Appearance (skin color)	Blue-gray, pale all over	Normal, except for extremities	Normal over entire body
R Respiration	Absent	Slow, irregular	Good, crying

FIGURE 4.3 Apgar Scoring for Newborns A score is given for each sign at 1 minute and 5 minutes after the birth. If there are problems with the baby, an additional score is given at 10 minutes. A score of 7–10 is considered normal, whereas 4–7 might require some resuscitative measures, and a baby with an Apgar of 3 and below requires immediate resuscitation. *Source:* Adapted from V. A. Apgar, "A proposal for a new method of evaluation of the newborn infant," *Current Researches in Anesthesia and Analgesia*, Vol. 32 (1953), pp. 260–267. Reprinted by permission of Lippincott Williams & Wilkins.

ration of mother and child for health benefits (this was back when microorganisms had first been discovered to exist). By the 1940s incubators for most newborns became standard practice in hospitals, and more mothers chose to give birth in hospitals rather than at home. The new mother, often heavily sedated, was given only a glimpse of her baby before being whisked to the maternity ward to recuperate and the baby was whisked to the nursery (Small, 1998). By the late 1960s, birthing practices began to change in the Western world. In 1976, two obstetricians, Marshall Klaus and John Kennell, theorized that there is a critical early period of sixteen hours for mother-infant bonding. By 1978 the American Medical Association proclaimed as its official policy the promotion of bonding between newborns and their mothers (Small, 1998).

Maternal Bonding The concept of maternal bonding has also undergone change and its role in society is under debate. Evolutionary biologists argue that it is natural (adaptive) for mothers and their newborns to bond; requiring close proximity, constant interaction, and emotional attachment. Bonding is especially necessary in our species, because human infants are dependent beings, who need much care, protection and teaching. Other scholars "believe it fosters unwarranted social stereotypes that portray motherhood as the 'font of emotional support'" (Eyer, 1992; Sluckin, Herbert, & Sluckin, 1983). Most psychologists and medical professionals now recognize that not spending the first few minutes or hours together will not leave a permanent gap in the relationship. **Parent-infant bonding** is considered by most as a *process* of interaction and mutual attention that occurs over time and builds an emotional bond.

Proponents of natural childbirth argue that it facilitates emotional bonding between parents and their child.

This is a time for intimacy, which is only the beginning of parent-infant bonding. It is a time of gentle touching and looking at each other, and some mothers may select to breast-feed their newborn.

Mothers who have cesarean deliveries or parents who adopt children should not conclude that they have missed out on something fundamental to a healthy child-parent relationship. A growing body of research suggests that parents who do not have contact with their infant immediately after delivery typically can bond as strongly with the youngster as parents who do have such contact (Eyer, 1992).

Bonding with several caretakers is required in some societies where there is a style of communal living. Researchers have shown that the Efé forest-dwellers of the Congo have a very flexible practice of child rearing (Ivey, 2000). Infants are cared for by a number of adults in the village. An Efé infant might spend 50 percent of its day with other caretakers and might be nursed by any of several women who are lactating. Yet the baby clearly knows who its mother and father are (Tronick, Morelli, & Ivey, 1992).

Developmentalists also recognize that some mothers and fathers have difficulty forming this attachment. Attachment can be difficult for mothers who have had a particularly complicated labor and birth or whose infants are premature, malformed, or initially unwanted. Because some births are high risk, not every parent-child relationship begins calmly.

Paternal Bonding In many cultures, expectant fathers might experience **couvade syndrome**—complaints of uncomfortable physical symptoms, dietary changes, and weight gain because of their partner's pregnancy (Small, 1998). A study of 147 expectant fathers in the Milwaukee area found that about 90 percent of them experienced "pregnancy" symptoms similar to those of their wives.

Father-Infant Bonding Studies reveal that the presence and involvement of fathers in the nurturing and development of their children confers many benefits to both. Note how a smiling father, Paulo from Dar Es Salaam, Tanzania, carefully holds his infant close, promoting father-infant bonding.

Source: Paige King, ShutterPoint.com.

For instance, the men had nausea in the first trimester and backaches in the last trimester. The majority of the men reported weight gains ranging from 2 to 15 pounds, and they all lost weight in the first four weeks after the babies were born. Couvade could be one way fathers express a bond of sympathy with the expectant mother and a change in social roles (Lewis, 1985). In addition, expectant fathers commonly become more concerned about their ability to provide for and protect an expanding family (Kutner, 1990).

Anthropologists have found that biological fathers have a very important parenting role in societies where family life is strong, women contribute to subsistence, the family is an integrated unit of parents and offspring, and men are not preoccupied with being warriors. Although the degree of fathering across cultures varies, the potential for human males to contribute to infant care is great. There is also more evidence of the importance of father involvement in their children's development (Horn & Sylvester, 2004; Tamis-LeMonda, & Cabrera, 2002).

To their benefit, many contemporary American fathers are visiting the obstetrician with the mother-to-be to hear the baby's heartbeat and to see the first ultrasound or amniocentesis, planning for the baby's arrival, attending childbirth preparation classes, participating in the birth, and helping to care for the baby after birth by changing diapers, feeding, bathing, and so on. Recent research reviews indicate that the father's love and caring is just as important as the mother's for their children's cognitive, emotional, and physical

health (National Fatherhood Initiative, 2001; Rohner & Veneziano, 2001).

After the birth, new fathers and mothers report similar emotions when first viewing the newborn. When given a chance, fathers explore a new baby's body in the same pattern as mothers do: fingers first, then palms of hands, arms, legs, and then trunk (Small, 1998). New fathers, like mothers, also instinctively raise the pitch and cadence of their speech (speaking what is called **"motherese"**) with their newborn. Clearly, the more fathers interact with their babies, the more mutual attachment occurs (Small, 1998).

American Children Living Without Fathers In the United States, extensive research is being conducted about the effects of absentee fathers on the lives of the many children being born to an increasing number of single mothers. The percentage of children living with two parents has been declining among all racial and ethnic groups. While about two-thirds of American children live within a family with a mother and father present, one-third do not. Nearly 24 million children reside in a home without their biological father (National Fatherhood Initiative, 2004). Approximately 5 percent of children reside with a single father (Child Trends, 2002).

Effects of Fatherlessness on Children Unless you come in contact with children in day care, in school, in health care, or in other child-care settings, you may be unaware of the societal impact of this change in the family structure in the United States. Of all single-mother families, 65 percent of them have incomes below $30,000 per year compared with 15 percent of all two-parent families. Although nearly all children living with both parents were covered by health insurance, 86 percent living with single mothers and 82 percent living with single fathers were covered (Fields, 2003). According to a U.S. Bureau of the Census report (2003a):

> Children in two-parent families generally had access to more financial resources and greater amounts of parental time. They also were more likely to participate in extracurricular activities, progress more steadily in school, and have more supervision over their activities such as television watching. The presence of two parents continues to be one of the most important factors in children's lives.

Father Involvement Fathers parent differently than mothers do. Mothers tend to be more verbal with children, whereas fathers tend to be more physical. Fathers often engage in rough-and-tumble play with their sons, which we are discovering serves as practice for boys to develop control over their aggression. The combination of the mother's nurturing and the father's tendency to encourage achievement both contribute to the childhood experience. Fathers usually provide positive role models for daughters as well. Both father and mother love have a significant impact on a child's personality and psychological development, and some evidence suggests that father love is even more strongly associated with some aspects of development (Rhoner & Veniziano, 2001).

Fathers provide a different style of caring, discipline, and parenting; these traits also promote both physically and psychologically healthier children who feel cared about. Studies have shown that the presence and involvement of fathers in the nurturing and development of their children confers benefits that are irreplaceable by any father substitute, where the substitute is the state, a grandparent, a male friend, or a stepparent (Martin, 1998).

Unfortunately, though, some American men (from all racial/ethnic and socioeconomic statuses) have made little or no effort to bond with or support the children they are producing, some lead dysfunctional lives or are abusive, some are incarcerated in prison, and some men father many children by several women without regard to the future welfare of the mothers or babies. There are far-reaching harmful social and economic consequences for many neglected or abandoned children and American society.

Questions

What are some factors that promote caregiver-infant bonding? In what ways might a father bond with his infant? What are the known consequences of fatherlessness for children?

Complications of Pregnancy and Birth

Although most pregnancies and births proceed without complications, there are exceptions. Currently in the United States slightly more than one in seven women experience complications during labor and delivery that are due to conditions existing prior to pregnancy (including diabetes, pelvic abnormalities, hypertension, and infectious diseases) (National Library of Medicine, 1998). During pregnancy or in the labor or birth process, complications can arise that require surgical intervention. The purpose of good prenatal care and diagnostics under medical supervision is to minimize complications. But if complications develop, much can be done through medical intervention to help the mother and save the child. Fetal ultrasounds and other diagnostics should be administered routinely to check for potential complications.

For example, about 1 percent of babies are born with **anoxia,** oxygen deprivation caused by the umbilical cord's having become squeezed or wrapped around the baby's neck during delivery. As mentioned in Chapter 3, in some pregnancies the mother and baby have incom-

patible Rh factors in their blood, and medical procedures can prevent serious complications. Efforts used to be concentrated on saving the mother if there were complications; today saving both the mother and the infant is a high priority.

Technological innovations have decreased infant mortality rates. Larger urban hospitals are likely to have a **neonatology intensive care unit (NICU)** (pronounced "nick-u") staffed with *perinatologists* and *neonatologists* who specialize in managing complicated, high-risk pregnancies, birth, and postbirth experience. The percentage of infants born preterm and with low birth weight continued to rise in 2003, mainly because of the increasing number of multiple births due to ART procedures (Hamilton, Martin, & Sutton, 2004). In 2003, about 90 percent of infants were born within the range of normal birth weight. The next sections discuss some complications of labor and birth, including cesarean delivery and infants born at risk.

Cesarean Section Delivery   Some women who experience complications in labor or delivery will have a surgical delivery called the **cesarean section ("C-section").** In this surgical technique, the physician enters the uterus through an abdominal incision and removes the infant. In 1970 the C-section rate was about 5 percent, and by 2003 the rate reached an all-time high at 27 percent (Hamilton, Martin & Sutton, 2004). The dramatic rise in cesarean deliveries in the United States can be attributed to many factors: older mothers giving birth; higher rates of twins, triplets, and higher-order multiples; bigger babies; improved technology to save high-risk infants; women's choice to schedule a surgical delivery; obstetrician choice to select surgery; concerns over sexual dysfunction; pelvic-floor damage; painful labor; and the rise in malpractice suits.

Sometimes the C-section is a planned surgery if there are known risks to the mother or fetus (as with a mother who is diabetic, has high blood pressure, is HIV positive, or has **placenta previa**—the placenta is lower in the uterus than the fetus' head and would be expelled first). Another condition, **preeclampsia** (also called toxemia), affects about 5 percent of women and includes hypertension (high blood pressure) (March of Dimes, 2005). *Placental abruption* is a serious condition in which the placenta partially or completely separates from the uterine wall and necessitates surgical intervention to save the mother and child. Or it might be discovered during labor and delivery that an emergency cesarean section is necessary—for instance, when the mother's pelvis is too small to allow passage of the infant's head, or when the baby is positioned abnormally, as in *breech* presentation (buttocks or feet first rather than head first) or *transverse* presentation (a sideways or vertical position). Around 4 to 5 percent of all cesareans are done to deliver a breech baby. An obstetrician might attempt a maneuver called "external vision" at about 37 weeks if the baby hasn't turned so it is head first. In skilled hands, 60 to 70 percent of the babies turn—but the procedure is not without risk and could trigger premature labor (Sears & Sears, 1994).

A cesarean is major surgery and entails some risks, especially to the mother. Cesarean delivery can provoke anxiety, especially in women not prepared for it. However, with the use of an *epidural anesthetic* injection into the space between vertebrae, pain sensation is blocked from the waist down (see Figure 4.2). The mother can be awake during delivery, the father can be in the delivery room, and both can share in the moment of birth. When a woman chooses a *general anesthetic,* she will be unaware of the birth, and the father is usually not allowed in the delivery room (though he is likely to hold the infant almost immediately after birth).

Some women who have had cesareans feel "cheated" out of the experience of a natural delivery, but most are grateful for the option to deliver a healthy infant. Women who have had cesareans also typically experience more discomfort and the temporary incapacitation that accompanies recuperation from surgery. As a response to these problems, childbirth classes now usually include units on cesarean birth options, and hospital media materials promote the theme, "Having a Section Is Having a Baby." Additionally, more women now are giving birth vaginally after having had a cesarean delivery in an earlier pregnancy; this is referred to as *VBAC, vaginal birth after cesarean.*

Researchers have found that when a trained woman companion or doula provides constant support during labor and delivery, the need for cesarean sections, forceps deliveries, and other such measures is significantly reduced. However, every mother-to-be should plan for the unexpected in scheduling her place and method of delivery.

At-Risk Infants   Development of at-risk infants is a topic of increasing importance. Advances in medical technology are saving many newborns who previously would not have survived. Concurrently, the number of babies born unusually small is rising in the United States (Hamilton, Martin, & Sutton, 2004).

On an average week in the United States*

    77,341 Babies are born

    9,246 Babies are born preterm

    6,040 Babies are born low birth weight

    529 Babies die before reaching first birthday

Premature Infants   Prematurity seems to be the principal culprit since prematurity/low birth weight is the leading cause of death in the first month of life (March of Dimes, 2003). In 2003, over 12 percent of all U.S.

births were preterm, with an 18 percent prematurity rate for black infants and 11 percent for white infants and a 12 percent rate for Hispanic infants (Hamilton, Martin, & Sutton, 2004). A **premature infant** has been traditionally defined as a baby weighing less than 5 pounds 8 ounces at birth or having a gestational age of less than 37 weeks. Babies classified as *very preterm* are born at less than 32 weeks of gestation. *Very low birth weight* describes babies born weighing less than 3 pounds 4 ounces. Although low birth weight is associated with prematurity, apparently it is developmental immaturity rather than low birth weight per se that is the primary source of the difficulties. More than half the low-birth-weight babies born in the United States are not preterm; **small-for-term infants** whether singletons, twins, or multiple births typically do well. Again, multiple births continue to increase because of in vitro fertilization procedures, and with multiple births there is a higher risk of low birth weight, complications, and premature birth.

For preterm infants, however, survival rate correlates closely with birth weight, with better survival for the larger and more mature infants. Nonetheless, in a number of the nation's better hospitals, physicians are saving 80 to 85 percent of the infants weighing 2.2 to 3.2 pounds and, even more remarkably, 50 to 60 percent of those weighing 1.6 to 2.2 pounds. Amazingly, in September 2004 the world's smallest surviving baby, Rumasia Rahman, was only 8.6 ounces when she was born as a twin three months early (the size of a cell phone) (Donavan, 2004). However, treating premature babies is hardly routine and frequently costs thousands of dollars a day. Significantly, the March of Dimes (2004d) reports that prematurity/low birth weight is the second leading cause of all infant deaths and the leading cause of infant deaths among African Americans (see Table 4.1).

Neonatology intensive-care units (NICUs) for preterm babies are quite foreign to parents who are unprepared to encounter their infant in a see-through incubator (Kolata, 1991). The baby is in an *isolette* and might be receiving oxygen through plastic tubes inserted in the nose or windpipe. Banks of blipping lights, blinking numbers, and beeping alarms of electronic equipment and computerized devices monitor the baby's vital signs.

Another leading cause of death in premature infants is a condition called *respiratory distress syndrome (RDS).* Some 8,000 to 10,000 infant deaths each year are linked with RDS; another 40,000 newborns suffer from it annually. One difficulty is that premature infants lack a substance known as *surfactant,* a lubricant found in the amniotic fluid surrounding a fetus in the womb. Surfactant helps inflate the air sacs in the lungs after birth and prevents the lungs from collapsing or sticking together after each breath. The fetus normally does not develop surfactant until about week 35. Recently, researchers have found that providing premature infants with the

---

Source: March of Dimes, Perinatal Overview: United States, 2003. From the National Center for Health Statistics, period linked infant birth/death data.

Table 4.1 Low Birth Weight by Race/Ethnicity, United States, 2000–2002, Averages

Race/Ethnicity	U.S. Percentages
Hispanic	6.5
White	6.8
Native American	7.1
Asian	7.5
Black	13.2
Average	7.7

Source: March of Dimes, *Peristats.* Retrieved January 19, 2005 from http://www.marchofdimes.com/peristats/. Data from National Center for Health Statistics.

substance can avoid many otherwise fatal complications and can save the babies.

Prematurity, especially very preterm, is associated with a high prevalence of developmental disabilities and neurological problems during infancy and childhood (Marlow et al., 2005). First, the relative immaturity of the premature infant makes it a less viable organism in coping with the stresses of birth and postnatal life and more susceptible to infections. Second, the developmental difficulties shown by the premature infant might be associated with the same prenatal disorders that caused the baby to be born early (such as maternal malnutrition, drug use, sexually transmitted infections, poverty, and maternal diabetes). Some research findings suggest that the long-term status of preterm infants is more likely to be related to the socioeconomic status, education, and supportive home environment than to the preterm status itself. Third, once delivered, the premature infant is often placed in an incubator (isolette) and connected to many tubes and monitoring devices.

To ensure survival of preterm infants, nurses must spend most of their time with "procedural care"—that is, feeding, changing, bathing, taking vital signs, providing respiratory care or needle sticks, and so on. However, research studies over the past 25 years demonstrate that preterm infants are more likely to survive if they have gentle touch and "comfort care"—that is, normal skin contact, massage, and other stimulation, especially from the parents (Harrison, 2001). Thus, a program called "Kangaroo Care" was developed, promoting infant recovery of premature babies through skin-to-skin, chest-to-chest contact between the mother or father and the child while sitting in a quiet, dimly lit NICU (Kangaroo Care, 1998). Health benefits to premature infants from 26 weeks to 33 weeks included decreased levels of motor activity, less oxygen required, less behavioral distress, greater daily weight gain, and fewer blood transfusions (Harrison, 2001).

Most premature infants show no abnormalities or mental retardation. Winston Churchill, former Prime Minister of England who was born prematurely, lived to be 91 and led an active, productive life. Recent advances in the monitoring of premature babies have allowed physicians to anticipate and, in many cases, prevent or minimize some problems through therapeutic interventions. The result has been a reduction in the overall complications and mortality associated with premature birth. Medical science continues to make important and exciting strides in helping preterm babies (Rowland & Vasquez, 2002). For some infants, prematurity can lead to developmental delays, chronic respiratory problems, and vision and hearing impairment in addition to greater risk of infant mortality (March of Dimes, 2003).

A recent longitudinal study compared 23 sets of extremely-low-birth-weight children to their full-term

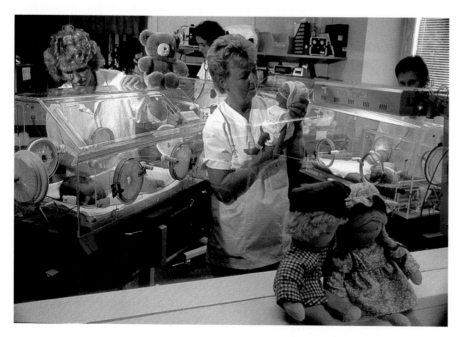

Neonatal Intensive Care The incubator, combined with many other technical advances, has helped to save the lives of many premature babies, enabling many to develop normally. Parents may be a little overwhelmed with the technology at first, but the neonatal professional staff trains the family to help in the care of the newborn.

Source: Lennart Nilsson. (1990). *A child is born.* New York, NY: Dell.

siblings using standardized medical, social, cognitive, motor, and language tests. The results showed that the extremely-low-birth-weight children were lighter, shorter, and had a smaller head circumference. They also had lower IQs, lower scores on some of the Stanford Binet tests, and lower Peabody motor quotients. Higher socioeconomic status was found to have a positive impact on cognitive and language ability scores but did not affect motor scores. The study concluded that preschool-age cognitive and language functioning were affected by both preterm status and socioeconomic variables; however, motor scores were only related to preterm status (Kilbride, Thorstad, & Daily, 2004).

Questions

What are some of the causes of premature birth? What are some other complications that might arise during labor and delivery of the neonate? How does the medical community save many of these babies born at high risk?

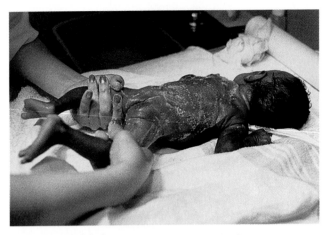

Drug-Exposed Infants Bathing is one of the few ways nurses have found to comfort drug-exposed newborns. Soap and warm water soothe the frantic babies. The bath also removes the sweat that envelops them as they go through withdrawal.

Source: Ken Kobre, Photojournalism Professor, San Francisco State University, California.

Postmature Infants A baby that is delivered more than two weeks after the usual 40 weeks of gestation in the womb is classified as a **postmature infant.** Most postmature babies are healthy, but they must be watched carefully for a few days. Some babies are heavier because their mothers are diabetic or prediabetic, or an extra amount of sugar has crossed the placenta. Such babies might have metabolic problems for the first few days after birth and require closer medical scrutiny. Postmature infants are likely to be larger, posing more complications for both mother and infant during delivery. A mother's options include induced labor and cesarean delivery.

Infants Born with Drug Exposure The majority of babies born are not addicted to any substances. Yet, because of the potential legal penalties ranging from misdemeanors to child abuse to criminal homicide in several states, many pregnant drug addicts have resisted prenatal care. Arizona, California, Hawaii, New York, South Carolina, Texas, and Utah are taking an aggressive stand on pregnant women using drugs ("Prosecutors Focusing on Pregnant Women," 2003). Without prenatal care the fetus is deprived of proper nutrition, blood, and oxygen for normal growth and is exposed to harmful teratogens.

Drug-exposed babies are likely to be premature, have low birth weight, and have smaller-than-normal head size. Over a period of several days to a few weeks, these neonates experience severe pain and withdrawal symptoms, and seizures are perhaps the most striking sign (Crump, 2001). Typically, when held, these babies tend to arch their backs, pull away, and cry in a high shrill cry until they exhaust themselves. Cocaine-exposed infants are more jittery, have more muscle tension, are hard to

move because they are stiff, don't like to be touched, and have difficulty feeding (Turner, 1996).

These behaviors can further influence how the parents or caretakers treat the baby and how the child is likely to grow and learn. However, recent reevaluation of the studies on cocaine use of pregnant women on their babies has not found detrimental long-term effects for the children's development. Perhaps more detrimental is the stigma attached to "crack kids" and the socioeconomic factors that hamper social, emotional, physical, and mental development of these children (Frank et al., 2001).

Babies Born with HIV HIV is the insidious virus that causes AIDS, and here are some startling statistics:

• Worldwide, women account for nearly half of all people living with HIV/AIDS (and in many poor countries, women account for much higher percentages of those infected).

• Experts estimate that 10 million children worldwide and nearly 10,000 U.S. children are living with HIV/AIDS. World Health Organization (WHO) experts estimate more than 500,000 children under age 15 died from HIV/AIDS just in 2004 ("AIDS Epidemic Update," 2004).

• Since AIDS was first identified in the early 1980s, more than 5,000 American children have died from HIV/AIDS ("HIV/AIDS Surveillance Report," 2004).

• By 2004, researchers estimate that more than 15 million children have become orphans because of the AIDS epidemic ("Worldwide HIV & AIDS Epidemic Statistics," 2004).

The U.S. Public Health Service promotes routine, voluntary prenatal HIV testing and *zidovudine* therapy to reduce the transmission of HIV from mother to child. The best recommendation for a pregnant woman with HIV is to see her health-care provider early and often during the pregnancy to maintain her own health and her fetus's health and to plan for the infant's birth and care. Unfortunately, many pregnant women still go untested despite recommendations for testing as part of prenatal care. Another study conducted by Mother Infant Rapid Intervention at Delivery (MIRIAD) the group found that administering *rapid HIV testing* to women in labor allowed for accurate results in about an hour (Bulterys et al., 2004).

A baby can contract HIV during pregnancy, during labor and delivery, or during breast-feeding. Getting treatment with *antiretroviral* medications during pregnancy, labor, and delivery coupled with treatment for the infant called *protease inhibitors* can dramatically reduce the risk of transmission of the virus (U.S. Public Health Service Task Force, 2002). After the U.S. Public Health Service issued its treatment recommendations in 1994, pediatric AIDS cases declined. The good news today is that more than 90 percent of U.S. babies born to HIV-positive mothers do not get HIV. The estimated number of new pediatric AIDS cases (cases among individuals younger than age 13) in the United States fell to only 92 in 2002 ("HIV/AIDS Surveillance Report," 2004).

All babies of women with HIV will test positive for the HIV antibodies at first, but this doesn't mean the baby is infected. A baby who is not infected will lose the mother's antibodies between 6 and 18 months of age and start to test negative for HIV. The baby who is infected with HIV will continue to test positive for HIV (National Institute of Allergy and Infectious Disease, 1997). Babies born infected with HIV appear normal at birth, but 10 to 20 percent develop AIDS and die by the age of 2. With early diagnosis and early medical treatment, a high percentage of children with HIV are living much longer, many into adolescence and adulthood (Storm et al., 2005).

Since the 1980s more than 1,500 children who were born to HIV-infected mothers in eight European countries were enrolled at birth in a longitudinal study, the *European Collaborative Study.* HIV-infected children grew considerably slower than uninfected children, and severely ill children have poorer growth at all ages. Such stunted growth has adverse effects on a child's quality of life, especially once they reach adolescence (Newell et al., 2003). HIV-infected children often experience functional impairments, behavioral problems, physical symptoms, and limitations in activities and in school performance. They also require comprehensive health care to maximize their potential as they move into adolescence and adulthood (Storm et al., 2005). The International Association for Physicians in AIDS Care and the American International Health Alliance launched a project in many countries to create pediatric resource centers for HIV-positive children, to establish the Global AIDS Learning and Evaluation Network (GALEN), and to promote more extensive pediatric HIV treatment and research initiatives.

After the baby with HIV is born, the parents and caretakers must face not only the emotional strains of caring for a sick baby, but also the financial strains. The National Pediatric and Family HIV Resource Center (NPHRC) offers state-of-the-art information to families and professionals caring for infants and children with HIV/AIDS. Also, the U.S. Department of Health and Human Services offers comprehensive information and guidance to families, researchers, and the medical community at AIDSinfo.nih.gov.

Babies with Fetal Alcohol Spectrum Disorder (FASD)   Research has shown that when the mother-to-be drinks during her pregnancy, not only does the placenta "soak it up like a sponge," but the alcohol remains in the amniotic fluid longer than it does in the mother's system. Drinking as few as two drinks in early pregnancy or four drinks all at once (a binge episode) can kill the baby's developing brain cells and alter developing body organs. Drinking alcohol during pregnancy can lead to a range of effects known under the umbrella term **fetal alcohol spectrum disorders (FASD),** among them fetal alcohol syndrome (FAS) (National Organization on Fetal Alcohol Syndrome, 2004a).

Symptoms of FASD can include growth deficiencies both before and after birth, central nervous system dysfunction resulting in lowered IQ and learning disabilities, physical malformations of the face and cranial areas and growth retardation, and other organ dysfunctions (see Chapter 3). A recent study found that babies born to mothers who drank heavily during pregnancy can suffer permanent nerve damage ("Alcohol Consumption Among Women," 2004). Some children are diagnosed with *FAE, fetal alcohol effects,* which is a manifestation of fewer of these effects. In 2003, FASD cost the United States over $5 billion. An individual afflicted with FASD can incur health-care costs of over $800,000 over their lifetime (National Organization on Fetal Alcohol Syndrome, 2004b). *FASD is the leading known preventable cause of mental retardation,* and it appears in every race, social class, and culture. FASD affects as many as 40,000 infants annually—more than Down syndrome, cerebral palsy, and spina bifida combined (National Organization on Fetal Alcohol Syndrome, 2004b).

In July 1998, South Dakota became the first state to enforce treatment programs for alcoholic pregnant women. Friends and relatives can commit a pregnant alcoholic woman to an emergency detoxification center, and judges can order pregnant alcoholic women into treatment facilities (Zeller, 1998). Like other children born with birth defects, these children are eligible from birth for early intervention services. Parents, caretakers, and teachers should realize that these children may have difficulty staying focused, recognizing and understanding patterns, predicting "commonsense" outcomes, or mastering math and reading. They may have short attention spans, memory problems, and difficulty with problem solving. It is also important to realize that a child does not outgrow FASD (National Organization on Fetal Alcohol Syndrome, 2004b).

Babies with Prenatal Exposure to Chemical Toxicants   According to Hallman and colleagues (2003), over 70,000 of the 697,000 Gulf War veterans have reported to the Gulf War Health Registry since 1992. Many of these veterans have experienced symptoms such as fatigue, muscle and joint pains, rashes, memory loss, and attention problems among others (Hallman et al., 2003). One study found an unusually high incidence of Lou Gehrig's disease—as much as three times more frequently than would be expected in a comparable age group ("ALS More Common," 2004).

These veterans claim they were exposed to a number of different "reproductive toxicants," including the anthrax vaccination, antibotulism medicine, and depleted uranium. A very high percentage of the children born to these veterans after the war are sick or were born with congenital birth defects (multiple deformities that are statistically unlikely to have occurred from chance alone). As reported in *VFW Magazine*, researchers at the Pentagon's Naval Health Research Center found that infants of veterans born after the war had a certain kidney defect not found in their children born before the war ("Gulf War Syndrome Update," 2003). Infants born to male veterans had higher rates of heart valve defects, and male infants born to female veterans had a higher rate of genital-urinary defects.

Affected families have emotional strain, financial drain, and disbelief that their health needs had been unrecognized by the U.S. government military, medical, and insurance systems. However, members of the U.S. House of Representatives presented the *Persian Gulf War Illness Compensation Act of 2001* to clarify the standards for compensation for Persian Gulf veterans suffering from certain undiagnosed illnesses. The press release states, "Americans who fought in the Persian Gulf War may have been exposed to chemical weapons or other harmful chemical or biological agents" (Gallegly, 2001a, p. 1). The U.S. House of Representatives approved the incorporation of the above act into the *Veterans Benefits Act of 2001* (Gallegly, 2001b). However, health-care providers, educators, and mental health professionals need to be aware of the special needs of this population of families who live with chronic illness.

By the mid-1950s in Minimata Bay, Japan, babies, children, and adults had physical deformities and brain damage due to corporate mercury poisoning of the bay that provided contaminated fish that the residents ate. In the early 1960s, American society experienced a similar high incidence of miscarriage and limb deformities with the widespread use of the prescription drug *thalidomide* for pregnant women's "morning sickness." Veterans exposed to Agent Orange during the Vietnam War in the 1960s and 1970s produced many children with birth defects. The high incidence of miscarriages and birth deformities in the 1970s in Love Canal, near Buffalo, New York, were proven to be directly related to air and water contamination. We must not forget how vulnerable a developing embryo or fetus is to what we are exposed to and ingest.

Support for Babies with Disorders   Parents who give birth to an infant diagnosed with any disorder at birth might want to get connected immediately to local professionals and support groups that focus on that disorder. Knowledge can alleviate much fear and anxiety at this early stage and give parents the hope they need to parent this child as normally as possible. There are also thousands of support groups with Internet Web sites for families living in more remote locations or having a child with a rare disorder. Although pediatricians and specialists are learning more about the physiological aspects of many disorders, their medical training often does not include learning about the social and emotional consequences of raising a child with a difficulty. Organizations such as the *National Down Syndrome Society (NDSS)* provide invaluable information, support, research, and a place to connect with other parents who share parents' same concerns.

Public Law 99-457: Early Intervention Services for Infants Born at Risk   Public Law 99-457, originally enacted by the U.S. Congress in October 1986, was designed to provide early intervention services (free education, training, and therapeutic services) to families with children from birth to 5 years that have disabilities and special needs. The program seeks to enhance the development of infants and toddlers with disabilities and their families' ability to meet their needs. There is an infant component for those from birth to age 2, and there is a preschool component for those aged 3 to 5. One goal of early intervention is for fewer children to have a need for special education classes during their formal schooling years. Another goal is for more children to achieve independent living at home and in the community, thus decreasing the need for institutionalization. This law was amended in 1991 and is known as the **Individuals with Disabilities Education Act (IDEA).** Congress and President Bush reauthorized IDEA as the *Individuals with Disabilities Education Improvement Act* (PL-108-446) in 2004. See the *More Information You Can Use* box "Careers in Early Intervention Services."

More Information You Can Use

Careers in Early Intervention Services

Early intervention services are defined under the *Individuals with Disabilities Education Act (IDEA)* as "services that are designed to meet the developmental needs of each child eligible . . . and the needs of the family related to enhancing the child's development." It is significant that the act seeks to involve parents and caregivers to the greatest extent possible. Furthermore, the experts who are trained to assess children for these services are encouraged to do so in the child's natural settings. These assessments must be made from a variety of perspectives and require a multidisciplinary approach (Addison, 2004). In other words, it takes the input of several trained professionals to provide as complete a picture as possible of the child. Some of the personnel involved in this process include audiologists, family therapists, nurses, nutritionists, occupational therapists, physical therapists, and social workers.

Let's take a brief look at some of the services these professionals provide for the assessment of need for intervention services:

- *Audiologist:* Identifies auditory impairment and extent of hearing loss. Makes referrals for medical care and other services. Provides auditory training, rehabilitation, teaches speech reading and use of hearing devices.
- *Family therapist:* Provides family training and counseling. Makes home visits to help the family understand the child's special needs.
- *Nurse:* Assesses the child's health status to determine provision of care and to prevent health problems. Helps the child restore or improve function. Administers prescribed medications.
- *Nutritionist:* Assesses nutritional history, diet, feeding skills, and food habits. Develops dietary plans and monitors nutritional needs.
- *Occupational therapist:* Addresses the child's needs for adaptive development, behavior and play, as well as sensory, motor, and postural development.

Speech-Language Therapy Speech therapists, also called speech pathologists, diagnose, treat, and help to promote correct speech, language, cognition, communication, voice, swallowing, speech fluency, and other related disorders. The Bureau of Labor Statistics projects that employment of speech-language pathologists is expected to grow rapidly. A master's degree is required.

Source: Rainbow-Center.net.

continued

- *Physical therapist:* Evaluates and assesses the child's movement dysfunction. Plans programs for individual and group services to prevent, alleviate, and compensate for the child's movement dysfunction.
- *Social worker:* Evaluates the child's home environment, and parental interaction. Provides individual and family counseling and helps to strengthen social skills. Coordinates and facilitates the use of community resources.

If you are interested in pursuing a career in early intervention services, you can search further in your campus career development center or career placement office. Those offices, your campus library, and Web sites will have a variety of resources, such as the *Dictionary of Occupational Titles (DOT)*, *Occupational Outlook Handbook (OOH)* available online through the U.S. Department of Labor, *Selected Characteristics of Occupations Defined in the Dictionary of Occupational Titles*, *The Worker Traits Data Book*, and the *Handbook for Analyzing Jobs*. Web sites for professional organizations provide a wealth of specific career information and some offer scholarships.

Early Intervention Professional Occupations

Advocacy, legislative	Geneticist	Pediatrics, neurology
Advocacy, special education	Interpreter	Physical education, adaptive
Administrator, special education	Movement therapy	Physical therapy
Art therapy	Music therapy	Psychiatry, adult
Audiology	Neurology	Psychiatry, child
Behavioral therapy	Nursing	Psychoanalysis
Child development, generalist	Nursing, neonatal intensive care	Psychology, child development
Cognitive/behavioral therapy	Nursing, School	Psychology, clinical
Education, elementary	Occupational therapy	Psychology, developmental
Education, preschool	Pediatrics, behavioral	Recreational therapy
Education, special	Pediatrics, developmental	Social work
Family practice	Pediatrics, general	Speech and language therapy

Infant Mortality   Babies are not supposed to die; it feels contrary to the natural order of life. Consequently, the death of an infant is a traumatic experience—most say it is the worst experience in life. Parents, family, and friends will go through a period of grief and mourning, just as when an older loved one dies. **Infant mortality** is the death of an infant within the first year of life. In 2001 more than 27,000 infants died in the first year of life. While the Centers for Disease Control and Prevention issued a report that stated the infant mortality rate reached a record low average of 6.8 per 1,000 live births in 2001, the infant mortality average rate rose to 7.0 in 2002 but is double that rate to 14.0 per 1,000 for black infants ("Infant Deaths Up in U.S.," 2004). The major reason for the 2001 decline is the significant reduction in *sudden infant death syndrome (SIDS)*, which dropped 11 percent from 2000 to 2001 but still accounts for about 3,000 infant deaths within the first year of life (National Center for Health Statistics, 2004a). The unexpected rise in infant deaths in 2002 is attributed to an increase in premature births.

In the United States, in 2002, the leading causes of infant death were birth defects, premature birth and low birth weight, sudden infant death syndrome, maternal complications of pregnancy, and cord and placenta complications (see Figure 4.4) (National Center for Health Statistics, 2003a). Infant mortality rates are highest for women under 20 years of age and lowest for women between the ages of 30 and 39 (March of Dimes, 2004d). In addition to age of the mother, infant mortality rates were higher for women who did not receive prenatal care, women who smoked during pregnancy, and women with less education. Infant mortality rates were higher for male infants, multiple births, preterm, and low-birth-weight infants (National Center for Health Statistics, 2003a).

Questions

What are some serious conditions that can compromise a neonate's health during and after birth? What are some of the leading causes of infant mortality in the United States? What is an early intervention program, and which babies and families are eligible for these services?

Postpartum Experience for Mom and Dad

Whether a newborn is born healthy or at risk, every new mother needs time to adjust and adapt, both physi-

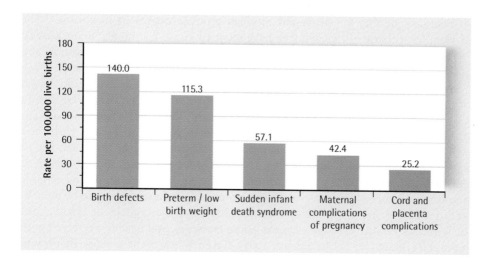

FIGURE 4.4 Infant Deaths by Cause of Death: United States, 2002 The leading causes of infant death in the United States include birth defects, prematurity/low birth weight, sudden infant death syndrome (SIDS), maternal complications of pregnancy, and cord and placenta complications.
Source: March of Dimes, *PeriStats.* Retrieved January 19, 2005 from http://www.marchofdimes.com/peristats/. Reprinted with permission. Data from National Center for Health Statistics.

cally and emotionally, after delivery of her child. Society and the media perpetuate the myth that motherhood is equated with total fulfillment and joy. These myths create unrealistic expectations for women. Normally the *postpartum period* lasts several weeks. However, some women need several months to adapt. Each woman experiences a range of hormone fluctuations after giving birth, especially a woman who was pregnant with twins or multiples. Her progesterone levels were elevated during the course of her pregnancy (and some women say they feel their best when they are pregnant). Now her highly active endocrine system is attempting to bring her body back to some type of prepregnancy balance, and this can promote mood swings. Mothers of babies born prematurely experience a higher level of postpartum depression than mothers who deliver full term, and mothers of twins or multiples have a higher risk for anxiety and depression during the prenatal and postpartum periods.

Most women, no matter what their discomfort, want their babies with them as often as possible during their hospital stay. However, the many postpartum variables can cause a woman to feel quite fatigued and apprehensive about meeting her responsibilities as new mother, wife or partner, and possibly mother to other children. "How can I cope with all of this?" might be on her mind.

Some women choose to leave the hospital with their newborn a few hours after giving birth; others stay several days to recuperate from surgery or complications. The postpartum period is a time of adjustment for the father, too. He is most likely trying to manage at home and work while beginning to adapt to his role as "Dad" to the new baby. The mother is going to need his help more than ever, especially if she is recuperating from surgery or if the baby was born at risk. Some women (and men) seem to need much more time to adapt, both physically and emotionally. Although a high percentage of new moms experience what is called the "baby blues," including anxiety and insomnia, and weepiness, approximately 10 percent of new mothers experience what is called **postpartum depression (PPD).** PPD has a biochemical basis and includes feelings of being unable

The Postpartum Period Is a Time of Adjustment for the New Mother and Father
Source: For Better or for Worse © 1997 Lynn Johnston Productions. Dist. By Universal Press Syndicate. Reprinted with permission. All rights reserved.

to cope, thoughts of not wanting to take care of the baby, unrealistic fears, or thoughts of wanting to harm the baby.

Newborns demand a great deal of time and attention, both night and day, and might spend quite a bit of time crying—*I am hungry. I need to be changed. I am sleepy. I am cold. I need comfort. I am sick. I want attention* (Harnish, Dodge, & Valenti, 1995). Most of us have never had anyone else be as dependent on us as a newborn! If a mother exhibits signs of postpartum depression, she needs to seek professional counseling from her gynecologist, medical doctor, and/or a therapist familiar with PPD, and social support from family and friends (most cities have some form of Women's Health Clinic through a local hospital or community agency). The National Association of Neonatal Nurses recommends clinicians conduct screening to identify women most at risk of PPD, and they recommend the *Postpartum Depression Predictors Inventory (PDPI) Revised* be administered to all mothers of infants in NICU. This inventory covers such variables as marital status, socioeconomic status, self-esteem, prenatal depression, prenatal anxiety, unplanned/unwanted pregnancy, previous depression history, social support, marital satisfaction, and infant temperament ("Recognizing and Screening for PPD," 2003).

If the new mother's depression goes untreated, it can linger, affecting her family—especially the children, who are at higher risk of developing depression themselves (Abrams et al., 1995; DeAngelis, 1997b). Performer Marie Osmond suffered PPD and is speaking out about coping with the anguish and emptiness she experienced. Andrea Yates, a woman from Houston, admitted drowning her five children (ages 6 months to 7 years) and was pronounced mentally fit to stand trial and was sentenced to life in prison. Her attorneys say she suffered a *psychotic form of severe PPD* that began after the birth of her fourth child. At the time of the crime, she was also taking antidepressants and an antipsychotic drug (Thomas et al., 2001). Although some experts question the use of PPD as a defense, the National Organization for Women (NOW) came to her defense, hoping to bring greater attention to women who suffer from varying degrees of PPD.

A woman who already has depressive symptoms before giving birth is at increased risk for having difficulty adjusting to her new role as a mother. There is increased risk for not developing secure attachment with the child, as well as problem behaviors and delays in acquiring competencies for the child. A recent study of mothers and newborns in Pakistan linked maternal depression to high rates of malnutrition and failure to thrive (Bower, 2004).

Developmental psychologist Dr. Tiffany Field has been researching the effects of maternal depression on newborns, infants, and children and has found that depressed mothers produce depressed newborns. "The newborns have elevated stress hormones, brain activity suggestive of depression, show little facial expression, and have other depressive symptoms as well" (Field, 1998). Depressed infants are slower to learn to walk, weigh less, and are less responsive than other babies. Dr. Field's intervention strategy with these mothers and infants includes coaching the mothers into interacting with their babies and massaging the full body of the infant for 15 minutes per day. Such touch provides mutual benefits.

In addition to physical care, we know that infants have cognitive, emotional, and social needs to be met. To develop normally, they need eye contact, need to be spoken to, need gentle massages, and need to be played with (Lamberg, 1999). Recently researchers in Sweden found evidence in a small sample that a child's depressed state may remain beyond the period of the mother's depressed mood (Edhborg et al., 2001). Therefore, it is very important to examine whether the mother has preexisting conditions and to understand the context of environmental risks related to depression (Carter et al., 2001).

> **Questions**
>
> How does a mother come to bond with her newborn? What are some signs of postpartum depression, and what should a mother do if she experiences these symptoms? How does the infant of a depressed mother typically behave? What might you suggest as an intervention strategy for a new mother who is experiencing depressive symptoms?

Development of Basic Competencies

To the watchful observer, newborns continue to communicate their perceptions and abilities. Newborns tell us what they hear, see, and feel in the same ways other organisms do—through systematic responses to stimulating events. In brief, newborns are active human beings who are eager to understand and engage their physical and social world. The hallmark of the first two years of life—the period called **infancy**—is the enormous amount of energy children spend exploring, learning about, and mastering their world. Once infants are walking, they are often referred to as "toddlers." Few characteristics of infants are more striking than their relentless and persistent pursuit of competence. They continually initiate activities by which they can interact effectively with the environment. Healthy children are active creatures. They seek stimulation from the world around them. In turn, they act on their world, chiefly on caretakers, to achieve the satisfaction of their needs.

According to sleep researcher James McKenna (quoted in Small, 1998, p. 35), "There is no such thing as a baby: there is a baby and someone." McKenna and other infant researchers have discovered that infant biology is intimately connected to the biology of the adults who are responsible for their care. This symbiotic relationship, called **entrainment,** is "a kind of biological feedback system across two organisms, in which the movement of one influences the other . . . the physiology of the two individuals is so entwined that, in a biological sense, where one goes, the other follows, and vice versa" (Small, 1998, p. 35). Entrainment is first and foremost a physical relationship (touching, nursing, cleaning, massaging, etc.). The connection is also visual and auditory: A newborn recognizes its mother's voice (and usually its father's voice, too) and prefers it over other sounds.

Child development expert Edward Tronick points out that a baby's most powerful, adaptive, and necessary skill is the ability to engage an adult on a social level to meet its needs (Small, 1998). Some infant researchers refer to entrainment as a type of synchronicity, a physical reaction, between a baby and its caretakers. Child expert Dr. Brazelton (1998) says that this synchronicity of movements and physical reactions between parents and infant is vital to infant development. He further suggests that infants who fail to thrive lack this physical engagement with their mother (as can happen when the baby is institutionalized, or the mother is severely depressed or addicted to drugs and doesn't attend to the infant's needs). An infant with **failure to thrive (FTT)** does not take nourishment and therefore is severely underweight for its age and gender. Failure to thrive can stem from any number of causes, among them inherited physiological and biochemical anomalies, virus infections, size of parents, food allergies or intolerance to certain foods such as *celiac disease,* or the result of a condition like obstructive sleep apnea syndrome (Chan, Edman, & Koltai, 2004; Core, 2003; Sanderson, 2004).

Newborn States

Interest in neonate sleeping patterns has been closely linked with interest in newborn states. The term **states,** according to Peter H. Wolff (1966), refers to a continuum of alertness ranging from regular sleep to vigorous activity (see Table 4.2). The noted pediatrician T. Berry Brazelton (1978) says that states are the infant's first line of defense. By means of changing state, infants can shut out certain stimuli and thereby inhibit their responses. A change in state is also the way infants set the stage for actively responding (Blass & Ciaramitaro, 1994). Consequently, the newborn's use of various states reflects a high order of nervous system control (Korner et al., 1988). The *Brazelton Neonatal Behavioral Assessment Scale* evaluates a neonate's early behavior by assessing

---

Table 4.2 Infant States

Regular sleep: Infants are at full rest; little or no motor activity occurs; facial muscles are relaxed; spontaneous eye movement is absent; respirations are regular and even.

Irregular sleep: Infants engage in spurts of gentle limb movements and more general stirring, squirming, and twisting; eye movement is occasional and rapid; facial grimaces (smiling, sneering, frowning, puckering, and pouting) are frequent; the rhythm of respiration is irregular and faster than in regular sleep.

Drowsiness: Infants are relatively inactive; on occasion they squirm and twist their bodies; they open and close their eyes intermittently; respiratory patterns are regular but faster than in regular sleep.

Alert inactivity: Although infants are inactive, their eyes are open and have a bright, shining quality; respirations are regular but faster than during regular sleep.

Waking activity: Infants may be silent or moan, grunt, or whimper; spurts of diffuse motor activity are frequent; their faces may be relaxed or pinched, as when crying; their rate of respiration is irregular.

Crying: Vocalizations are strong and intense; motor activities are vigorous; the babies' faces are contorted; their bodies are flushed bright red. In some infants, tears can be observed as early as 24 hours after birth.

---

how the baby moves from sleep states to alert states of consciousness (Brazelton, Nugent, & Lester, 1987).

Reflexes   The newborn comes equipped with a number of behavioral systems, or reflexes, that are ready to be activated. A **reflex** is a relatively simple, involuntary, and unlearned response to a stimulus. In other words, it is a response that is triggered automatically through built-in circuits. Some reflexes, such as coughing, blinking, and yawning, last throughout life. Others disappear over the first weeks and reappear as learned voluntary behaviors as the infant's brain and body develop. Reflexes are the evolutionary remains of actions seen in animals lower in the phylogenic scale (Cratty, 1970). Reflexes are good indicators of neurological development in infants. Researchers estimate that the human is born with at least 70 reflexes. Table 4.3 illustrates some of these.

Sleeping   The major "activity" of newborns is sleeping. Newborns normally sleep 16 or more hours per day, in seven or eight naps. Sleep and wakefulness alternate roughly in 4-hour cycles—3 hours in sleep and 1 hour awake. Unless they are ill or uncomfortable, neonates will sleep wherever they are (in a crib, a stroller, or cradled in Mom or Dad's arms). By six weeks the naps become longer, with infants taking only two to four naps during the day. Around this age, many begin to

Table 4.3 Some Newborn Reflexes

Reflex	Description
Sucking reflex 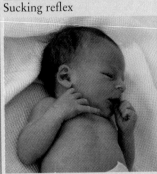	When a newborn's mouth or lips are touched, she automatically sucks on the object in her mouth.
Stepping reflex 	When the baby is held upright with the soles of the feet touching a firm surface, he will deliberately take "steps," as if walking. This behavior disappears after the first week then reappears in several months as learned, voluntary behavior.
Tonic neck (fencer's pose)	When the baby's head is turned to one side, her arm on that side will straighten and the other arm will bend as in a fencing position.
Palmer grasp	When an object is placed on the baby's palm, he will close his hand around it and grasp it firmly.

sleep through most of the night, though others will not sleep through the night for many months yet. "Lack of sleep, and more especially broken sleep, is the very worst part of parenting for many people," states British psychologist Penelope Leach (1998, p. 109) in her book *Your Baby and Child.* As the infant matures into a 1- to 2-year-old toddler, sleep time is usually reduced to one naptime during the day and an extended sleep at night. (See the *Human Diversity* box on page 135, "Co-Sleeping, a Cross-Cultural View.")

Sudden Infant Death Syndrome (SIDS) The rate of **sudden infant death syndrome (SIDS)** deaths has been on the decline (see Figure 4.5) since the start of the national *Back to Sleep* campaign through the 1990s, but it remains one of the leading causes of postneonatal death in the United States and is most likely to occur between 2 and 4 months of age ("Sudden Infant Death Syndrome," 2004). The mortality rate from SIDS in 2002 was 57.1 per 100,000 live births (see Figure 4.4) (MacDorman et al., 2005). SIDS occurs most often during the third or fourth month of life, although it can happen up to a year old. Parents put their seemingly healthy baby down to sleep and return to find that the infant has died. There is typically no warning. SIDS is one of the leading causes of infant death (after birth defects and accidents). It is one of medicine's unsolved mysteries, and considerable money is being spent researching the cause.

Although overall SIDS rates declined markedly in the last decade, the incidence of SIDS is highest in Native American and African American groups, and rates are lowest among Mexicans and Hispanics (U.S. Department of Health and Human Services, 2004b). Several measures to prevent SIDS include: get regular prenatal care, good nutrition, refrain from smoking and using drugs, avoid teen pregnancy (especially multiple teen births), and wait at least a year between births. Caregivers should be sure to put the infant on its back to sleep, use a firm mattress with nothing in the bed, avoid overheating the baby's room, avoid exposing the baby to tobacco smoke and

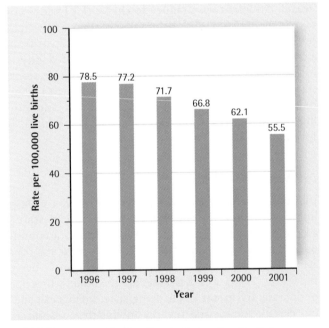

FIGURE 4.5 SIDS Infant Death Rates Are Declining: United States, 1996–2001 Because of the national Back to Sleep campaign, infant survival rates for the first year of development are improving.
Source: March of Dimes, *PeriStats.* Retrieved January 23, 2005 from http://www.marchofdimes/peristats/. Reprinted with permission. Data from National Center for Health Services.

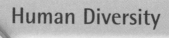

Human Diversity

Co-Sleeping, a Cross-Cultural View

Cultural Attitudes Toward Infant Sleep Arrangements

Ethnopediatricians (social scientists influenced by Vygotsky's view that child development is inseparable from society and culture) now focus on the importance of the sleep environment because they believe that the sleep environment is crucial to infant health and development. Moreover, anthropologists studying cultures around the world have discovered that for most of human history, babies and children have slept with their mothers, or perhaps with both parents, because of the physical nature of their huts and one-room dwellings. Worldwide, most people live and sleep in one-room dwellings, with dwellings of more than one room for the affluent only (Small, 1998). Culture, customs, and traditions handed down through the generations influence how we sleep, with whom we sleep, and where we sleep. One study of 186 non-industrial societies revealed that in two-thirds of the cultures, children sleep in the company of others. More significantly, in all 186 societies, infants slept with a parent or parents until at least 1 year old (Small, 1998). "The United States consistently stands out as the only society in which babies are routinely placed in their own beds and in their own rooms" (Small, 1998, p. 112). Babies in other cultures sleep in various environments—in a swaddling cloth on their mother's back, in a hanging basket, in a hammock made of skin or fiber, on a futon, on a mattress made of bamboo, and so on.

Anthropologist Gilda Morelli and colleagues (1992) studied the sleeping arrangements of parents and babies in the United States and in a group of Mayan Indians in Guatemala. The Mayan babies always slept with their mothers for the first year and sometimes the second. Mayan mothers reported no sleep difficulties because they turned and nursed their babies whenever the babies cried with hunger. Mayan mothers also view the mother and child as one unit. In the American sample, no babies slept with their parents. Seventeen of the 18 mothers reported having to wake up and get up for nighttime feedings. Mayan mothers expressed shock and disapproval when they discovered how American babies were put to bed. They saw closeness at night between mother and baby as what all parents should do for their children (Morelli et al., 1992). Americans in the study reported that co-sleeping was worrisome and somehow emotionally and psychologically unhealthy. Typically, American mothers are advised by pediatricians and child-care experts that sleeping alone is safer for the baby.

Co-sleeping is socially acceptable in Korean society and is considered a natural part of parenting (Yang & Hahn, 2002). Koreans sleep either on a bed above the floor or on the floor on a futonlike mattress called a "yo." "Even sleeping on separate single-size yo, people may sleep next to each other within arm's reach and so be able to touch physically. . . . Even if parents sleep on a bed, a yo is placed near the bed to enable physical contact between parents and

Customs and Baby Sleep Arrangements Culture, customs, and traditions influence whether a baby sleeps swaddled on a mother's back, in a woven basket, in a hammock, on a futon, on a mattress made of bamboo, in a crib in a separate room, or co-sleeps with parents.

continued

child, so bed sharing and room sharing have about the same meaning in Korea" (Yang & Hahn, 2002).

Japanese mothers are given pamphlets that tell them they should be "responsive and gentle and communicate frequently with their babies, to entwine the infant to its mother and bring the baby into the family fold" (Wolf et al., 1996). Japanese babies and children are placed on futons in the parental bedroom, for the Japanese concept of family includes sharing the night. Japanese mothers are not interested in making their infants become independent, but rather in making sure they become part of the mother, a connected social being (Small, 1998).

The non-Western view of co-sleeping appears to be to promote attachment with the infant, whereas Western cultures value independence and self-sufficiency in their children (Gordon, 2002). The ideology of privacy when sleeping appeared in the United States during the 1800s, when housing expanded. American parents are taught that it is morally correct for infants to sleep alone (Small, 1998). A few other industrialized nations have set sleep expectations for children, too. Dutch parents believe children should be regulated in sleep and all other matters. Babies and children are put to sleep at the same time every night, and if they wake up, they are expected to entertain themselves. A regular routine for the infant is a must in the Dutch family (Small, 1998).

Helping the Baby Sleep Through the Night

American parents often struggle to get their infant to sleep through the night. Some of their strategies to induce sleep include placing a pacifier in the baby's mouth, rocking the baby, placing in the crib devices or stuffed animals that play a mother's recorded heartbeat, taking car rides, using automatic infant swings, and playing "white noise" machines or quiet music to mask other noises in the home. In American culture, sleeping patterns have become a marker of infant maturity and development: *Is the infant sleeping through the night yet?* Newborns have short sleep patterns, but typically by 3 or 4 months of age, the infant brain has matured enough to develop a *circadian rhythm*—brain recognition of day and night that it did not experience while in the womb (Rivkees, 2003). James McKenna (1996), sleep researcher, has discovered that babies, like adults, sleep different amounts, and each culture helps determine how much that sleep should progress.

McKenna has also conducted co-sleeping experiments in a sleep lab environment with mothers and infants. He found that co-sleepers are physiologically entwined and react to each other's movements and breathing. Because babies are born neurologically immature, they have episodes of breathing lapses. Co-sleeping babies respond more to the patterns and rhythms of the mother's breathing, and McKenna suggests that this is a way of teaching infants how to regulate breathing. Co-sleeping mothers pay much more attention to their infants (kissing, touching, repositioning). To McKenna (1996), "it is no coincidence that management of breathing ability comes developmentally at three to four months of age—just at the same period when babies are most vulnerable to SIDS."

persons with respiratory ailments, avoid overdressing the baby, and consider using a baby monitor (American SIDS Institute, 2004).

Crying Crying in the newborn is an unlearned, involuntary, highly adaptive response that incites the parents to caretaking activities. Humans find few sounds more disconcerting and unnerving than the infant's cry. Physiological studies reveal that the sound of a baby's cry triggers an increase in parents' blood pressure and heart rate (Donate-Bartfield & Passman, 1985). Some parents feel rejected because of the crying and reject the child in turn. But simply because caretakers have difficulty getting babies to stop crying does not mean they are doing a bad job. Crying is the chief way that babies communicate. Different cries—each with distinctive pitch, rhythm, and duration—convey different messages.

The Language of Crying Most parents typically learn the "language" of crying rather quickly (Bisping et al., 1990). Babies have one cry that means hunger, one that means discomfort, one that means it needs attention, one that means frustration, and others for such problems as pain or illness. Children's cries become more complex over time. Around the second month, the irregular or fussy cry appears (Fogel & Thelen, 1987). At about 9 months, the child's cry becomes less persistent and more punctuated by pauses while the youngster checks how the cry is affecting a caregiver (Bruner, 1983).

Babies exposed prenatally to cocaine and other drugs by their mothers present special problems. These newborns commonly experience withdrawal symptoms consisting of irritability and incessant shrill crying, inability to sleep, restlessness, hyperactive reflexes, tremors, and occasionally convulsions. Some of these symptoms subside after the infant has gone through withdrawal (Hawley & Disney, 1992). In non-Westernized cultures, if babies are wrapped tightly next to the mother's front or back during the day, they exhibit less crying and are more subdued than American babies tend to be (Small, 1998).

Shaken Baby Syndrome If they cannot get the baby to stop crying, some parents or caretakers wind up feeling distraught and helpless and act out angrily toward the baby. Until more recently, **shaken baby syndrome (SBS)** was a medical diagnosis that few of us knew about. This syndrome occurs when a baby's head is violently shaken

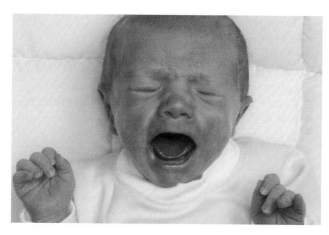

Newborn States A baby's major job is to regulate its internal states, which include sleeping, feeding, eliminating, and communicating with caregivers.

back and forth or strikes something, resulting in bruising or bleeding of the brain, spinal cord injury, and eye damage. Health-care and child-care professionals look for a glassy-eyed look or lethargy in an infant if they suspect the baby has been shaken or abused. Bruises and vomiting can also indicate SBS (Duhaime et al., 1998). Infants less than 6 months old are particularly vulnerable to SBS. Of those diagnosed each year, one-third die, one-third suffer brain damage, and one-third recover.

Researchers have found that men (fathers or boyfriends) are more likely to inflict this injury, followed by female baby-sitters, then mothers (Duhaime et al., 1998). Boy babies are more likely to be the victims of this abuse than girl babies (Duhaime et al., 1998). SBS usually results from an impulsive, angry response to an infant's crying. Parents should take extra precaution to select baby-sitters carefully and to never leave a child with a stranger. Younger babies may accept a new sitter more easily; however, most infants by 7 to 8 months develop a fear of strangers called "stranger anxiety" and are more apt to cry for long periods of time when left with a strange caretaker.

What if a parent feels frustrated by a baby's incessant crying? First, check the infant to make sure nothing is wrong (see the next section, "Soothing the Infant"). If the child's physical and comfort needs have been met, the parent who fears hurting the child should leave the room, shut the door, go to another room, and calm down. Calling a trusted family member or friend to come help might provide some relief. The infant is trying to communicate its discomfort, and crying is the only way she can communicate with you. If this happens regularly, the infant needs to be examined carefully by a pediatrician to check for **colic**—a condition of discomfort, of unknown cause, in which the baby cries for an hour or more, typically every day at about the same time, for up to several weeks.

Soothing the Infant   Meeting physical and emotional needs is likely to soothe a crying baby. If a baby is crying because it is hungry or sleepy, it is likely that it will briefly soothe itself by sucking its own fingers. A baby who contents himself this way might not need a pacifier. There are pros and cons to giving a baby a pacifier. Infants who can learn to comfort themselves are learning to meet their own needs, compared with those that learn to howl until someone puts a pacifier in their mouth.

The first order of business is to try to determine why the baby is crying. Newborns often are comforted by being swaddled in a light blanket. Has the baby eaten enough? Is he warm enough? Is her diaper wet? Has the caretaker given comforting touches and words recently? Many older infants like to have a comfort object, such as a specific blanket or stuffed animal, at naptimes or at particularly stressful times. Some infants like rhythmical behaviors, such as rocking in a chair or riding in a stroller. In many cultures of the world, babies spend most of their time carried in a sling on the back or side of an adult, which is warm as well as physically soothing (see the *Human Diversity* box on page 135, "Co-Sleeping, a Cross Cultural View."). Most importantly, parents should try to remain calm and not show anger and stress around babies, for the infant's behavior often mirrors its caretakers' behavior (recall the "synchronicity" concept between child and caretaker mentioned earlier in this chapter).

Feeding   The first few weeks of feeding a newborn can be worrisome, because a baby will feed only when its internal state signals that it needs nutrition. After a few weeks, the caretaker will be more aware of this particular baby's pattern of feeding. When fully awake, neonates spend a good deal of time feeding. Indeed, their hunger and sleep patterns are closely linked. Newborns might feed 8 to 14 times during the day. Some infants prefer to feed at short intervals, perhaps every 90 minutes, all day. Others have intervals of 3 to 4 hours or longer.

Fortunately, infants come to require fewer daily feedings as they grow older. Most seem to eat three to five meals a day by the time they are 1 year old. As they grow into toddlers, all babies begin to vary in how much they will eat at one time and what they will eat. A child who earlier ate very little might begin to eat a lot more, or one that ate well might now eat very little. Child health experts suggest that this is normal and that young children experience "growth spurts," occasional periods of time when they need considerably more energy to accommodate their bodies' growth.

On-Demand Feeding Versus Scheduled Feeding   Several decades ago, doctors recommended strict feeding schedules for infants. But some pediatricians recognize that babies differ markedly, and they encourage parents to feed their baby when it is hungry—let the infant pick its own times in the 24-hour cycle to feed, in on-demand feeding. Typically, pediatricians recommend scheduled feedings for twins and multiples. Whatever schedule parents and caretakers follow, they must decide whether the baby will be breast-fed or bottle-fed. Before 1900 the vast majority of mothers breast-fed their babies or employed a "wet nurse" to do this (a wet nurse is a lactating woman employed to nurse others' babies). But in the ensuing years, as women began to leave homes to work in factories, bottle-feeding with infant formulas became increasingly popular, so that by 1946 only 38 percent of women left the hospital with a nursing baby. This figure dropped to 20 percent by 1956. Since then, breast-feeding has gained in popularity. By 2001, two-thirds of U.S. babies were breast-fed for some time after birth (Li et al., 2003).

Breast-Feeding   There is a large body of evidence that breast-feeding the infant for the first several months of life is best (Haynes et al., 2000). The mother's, baby's, and father's brains release a beneficial chemical messenger, *oxytocin,* into their bloodstream before, during, and after birth that promotes the instinctive cues and desire for touching and bonding. Oxytocin also promotes release of the mother's breast milk. In turn, nursing causes the continued release of oxytocin, which then causes a mother to be more relaxed, caring, and attentive to her child's physical, emotional, and social needs (Flower, 2004; Palmer, 2002, 2004). "Frequent proximity and touch between baby and parents can create powerful family bonding with many long-term benefits" (Palmer, 2002). The release of oxytocin during breast-feeding also causes the woman's uterus to shrink back to normal size. Since the early 1990s, the number of American women breast-feeding after delivery has increased substantially, but many have stopped before six months postpartum. Breast-feeding offers other advantages for mother and baby:

- Mother's milk for the first three to five days provides **colostrum,** a substance that provides antibodies that build up the newborn's immune system, protecting the infant from a variety of infectious and noninfectious diseases.
- Breast milk is the most complete form of nutrition for infants.
- Other benefits attributed to breast-feeding include a reduced chance of developing allergies or asthma and fewer ear infections.
- The newborn can normally digest breast milk easily, because it is more watery than formula-based milk.
- A baby's stools will be of a more liquid consistency, and elimination might be easier than if formula-fed, reducing discomfort of cramping and constipation.
- Breast-feeding is also less costly and less time-consuming than purchasing and preparing formula.

The mother's milk is always ready and at the proper temperature.
- Breast-feeding improves maternal health by reducing postpartum bleeding and may lower the risk of premenopausal breast cancer and ovarian cancer. Also, mothers are likely to return to their prepregnancy weight more rapidly.
- Today, many American women and those from non-Westernized cultures believe that the intimate contact afforded by breast-feeding creates a sense of security and well-being in the infant and that this favorably influences its later personality.

The chief drawback of breast-feeding is that the mother must be available to the infant every few hours, night and day. It is more difficult to do if she has to return to work, unless she expresses her milk and stores it in bottles so that the father and other caretakers can feed the child. Today there are breast pumps that allow the mother to release her milk and refrigerate it for later feedings. Another disadvantage of breast-feeding might be that the mother does not know how much milk the baby is getting than if she were feeding the baby formula from precisely measured bottles. However, a breast-feeding baby who is gaining weight and eliminating several times daily is getting adequate nutrition. Another drawback to breast-feeding is that the mother may need to limit her intake of caffeine (e.g., in coffee, sodas, chocolate, alcohol, and medications), which is a mild stimulant. Other foods such as broccoli, cauliflower, cabbage, and spicy foods can also affect the baby's developing gastrointestinal system and cause crying, crankiness, or irritability. Also, if the mother herself has a preexisting illness, such as AIDS, or is taking medications, she might not be able to breast-feed.

Formula (Bottle) Feeding   The advantage of bottle (formula) feeding is that it gives mothers physical freedom and easily lets fathers and other caretakers become involved in feeding the infant. Also, mothers who are taking medications (e.g., antidepressants, anticonvulsants, insulin, AZT) can still feed their infants. Commercial formulas tend to fill babies up more, so they can go longer between feedings. Mothers who bottle-feed can continue to provide nurturing contact with the baby. One drawback is that formula-fed babies tend to pass bulkier stools and are more likely to experience the discomfort of constipation than a breast-fed baby.

Additional Cautions Regarding Infant Nutrition Breast-feeding infants should be monitored regularly by a health-care professional if the mother is taking medications or drugs. As stated earlier, a mother with HIV should not breast-feed her baby, because the virus might be transmitted to the baby in the breast milk.

However, in some developing countries breast milk might be the only available food for an infant. Also, the Committee on Nutrition of the American Academy of Pediatrics recommends that breast-fed infants be given certain supplements such as vitamin D, iron, and fluoride.

Mothers in developing countries, who are now targeted by suppliers of infant formula, might inadvertently prepare formula with contaminated water—putting the baby's health at risk ("Spotlight on the Baby Milk Industry," 1998). Pediatricians have more recently discovered evidence that cow enzymes and antibodies are likely factors in infant colic, because babies' immature digestive and excretory systems are unable to process these enzymes and antibodies. Formulas with a soy base (vegetable base) do not contain such agents. Some infants cannot digest milk-based or soy-based formulas and need a special pediatric formula to sustain their nutritional needs for development.

Graduating to "Regular" Foods Over the course of the first two years of development, a child will gradually begin to eat "regular" table foods and beverages, such as breads and cereals, mashed vegetables and fruits, juices, and eventually small portions of meats. Pediatricians presently recommend breast-feeding for the first six months followed by introducing mashed vegetables before sweet cereals or fruit. An adequate, balanced diet is extremely important for continued health and brain growth. Two developmental milestones occur when a child can pick up food using the forefinger and thumb and hold a cup and drink from it unaided by adults. It is highly recommended that parents use moderation in giving the child sweetened foods and beverages, since the child's baby teeth could begin to decay. All infants exhibit "likes" and "dislikes" when it comes to the flavors and textures of foods, but it is a good idea to introduce a variety of tastes and textures (such as solid foods, soft foods, liquid foods) into the child's diet during the first few years. How much a child can eat at one time varies from child to child and from age to age in development.

Mastering Toilet Training By about 1½ to 2 years of age, or later, most young children show an interest in toilet training. This is an especially important developmental milestone in American families, because many of our youngsters are taken into public settings, such as child care and preschool, for long periods of time each day.

Along with other muscles in the body that are developing and allowing the child to walk, climb, or run, the muscles in the toddler's anal and urinary tract are developing. When these are strong enough, the child will let a caretaker know that he or she is ready to be toilet trained. When the child begins to demonstrate such understanding, providing "big boy" or "big girl" underpants and praising success reward the child's efforts. No young child should be forced to sit on a toilet for long periods of time nor left alone on the toilet. Freud said in his psychoanalytic theory that attitudes toward one's sexuality form during toilet-training times, and shaming a child for something he or she cannot yet control does a great deal of harm. Words used to identify body parts and elimination of waste vary from culture to culture, within cultures, and within families.

Infant Checkups and Immunizations Regularly scheduled medical checkups are essential so each infant can get proper medical care and immunizations (see Figure 4.6). All children must get several more shots before entering child care, preschool, or public and private school settings. Most local health clinics administer checkups and required vaccinations for free or for a minimal fee. Vaccinations provide immunity to a disease before it has a chance to make the child sick by helping a child's immune system function effectively. Some infants should get their first shot (hepatitis B) after birth before leaving the hospital. Other vaccinations begin at 2 months of age.

Recently, controversy erupted over the safety of some vaccines. Implicated in this controversy is a preservative called *thimerosal*, which contains mercury. A link was made between thimerosal and neurodevelopmental disorders such as autism. This preservative, however, is not widely used anymore in vaccines and it is unlikely that a child will receive a vaccination with thimerosal ("Link between neurodevelopmental disorders and thimerosal remains unclear," 2001).

Questions

What are several states that babies are learning to regulate during the first few years of life? In what ways does an infant begin to regulate its internal states and take in nutrition for growth and development? What do we know about infant sleep states? Are there some other factors that promote or detract from a child's healthy growth and development over the first two years?

Brain Growth and Development

Infants do grow at a surprising rate and change in wonderful ways. Their development is especially dramatic during the first two years of life. Indeed, the change from the dependent newborn to the walking, talking, socially functioning child whom we meet hardly 600 days later is awesome. These maturational changes take

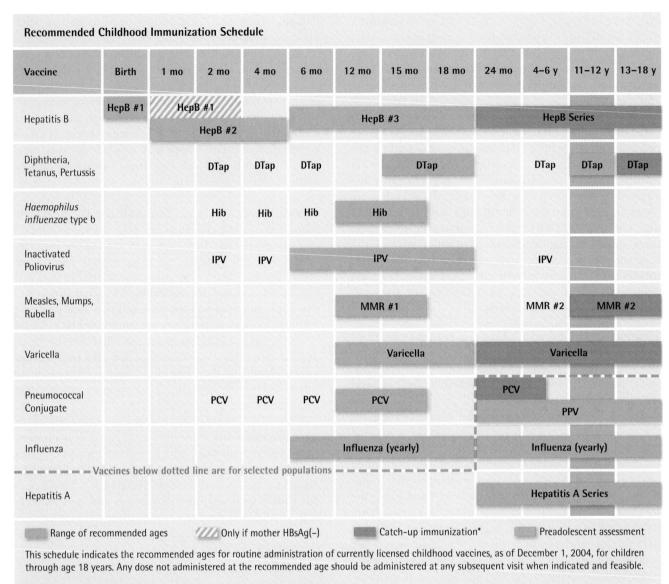

FIGURE 4.6 Recommended Childhood and Adolescent Immunization Schedule (birth–age 18), United States, 2005
Source: Centers for Disease Control and Prevention. (2005, January 7). Recommended Childhood and Adolescent Immunization Schedule—United States, 2005, MMWR, *53*(51), Q1–Q3. Department of Health and Human Services.

place because of growth in key systems of the body. The pituitary gland, in conjunction with the hypothalamus (a structure at the base of the brain composed of a tightly packed cluster of nerve cells), secretes hormones that play a critical part in regulating children's growth (Guillemin, 1982). Too little of the growth hormones creates a dwarf, and too much creates a giant.

Predictable changes occur at various age levels. Many investigators have analyzed the developmental sequence of various characteristics and skills (Gesell,

1928; Meredith, 1973). From these studies psychologists have evolved standards, called **norms,** for evaluating a child's developmental progress relative to the average of the child's age group. Although children differ considerably in their individual rate of maturation, they show broad similarities in the sequence of developmental change. Among infants, length and weight are the indices most strongly correlated with behavioral development and performance (see Figures 4.7 and 4.8 in the *Further Developments* box on pages

Further Developments

Growth Charts for Children, Ages 0 to 3

Birth to 36 months: Boys
Length and weight

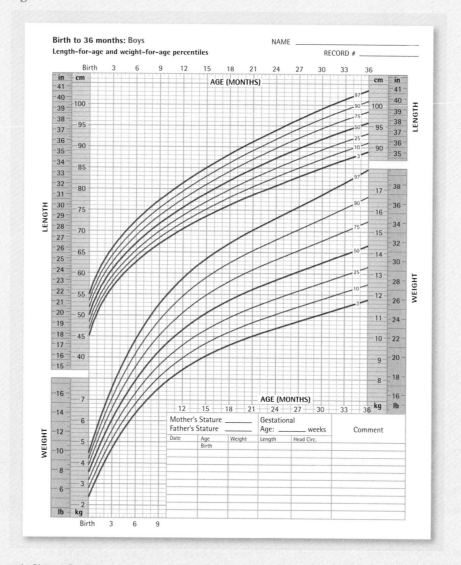

FIGURE 4.7 Growth Charts for Boys, Ages 0 to 3 Among infants, length and weight are the factors most strongly associated with behavioral development and performance.
Source: Centers for Disease Control and Prevention, National Center for Health Statistics: Clinical Growth Charts, modified 4/20/2001, at www.cdc.gov/growthcharts

continued

141, 142, "Growth Charts for Children, Ages 0 to 3") (Lasky et al., 1981).

Charts in pediatricians' offices that are based on norms show relatively smooth continuous curves of growth, suggesting that youngsters grow in a steady, slow fashion. In contrast, parents often say that their growing child "shot up overnight." Intriguing findings by Michelle Lampl and her colleagues seemingly show

Birth to 36 months: Girls
Length and weight

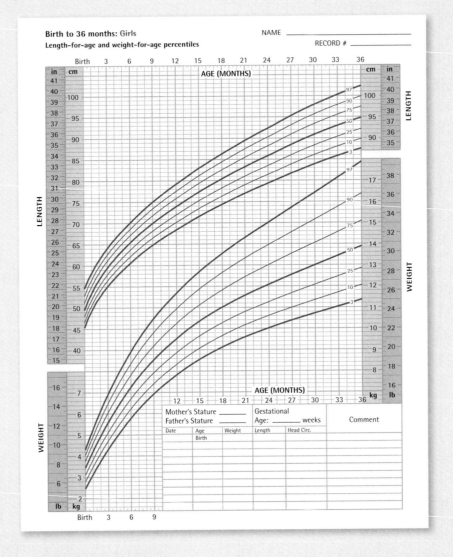

FIGURE 4.8 Growth Charts for Girls, Ages 0 to 3
Source: Centers for Disease Control and Prevention, National Center for Health Statistics: Clinical Growth Charts, modified 4/20/2001, at www.cdc.gov/growthcharts

that babies grow in fits and starts, with long intervals between growth spikes (Kolata, 1992a; Lampl et al., 1995). They find that babies remain the same size for 2 to 63 days and then spurt up by from 1/5 to 1 full inch in less than 24 hours. Additionally, it seems that a few days prior to growing, youngsters often become hungry, out of sorts, fussy, agitated, and sleepy. This research suggests that growth operates in an on/off fashion, much like a light switch. However, other researchers challenge the findings, insisting that human growth occurs continuously (Heinrichs et al., 1995).

The Rate of Growth of Key Systems and the Brain

Not all parts of the body grow at the same rate. The growth curve for lymphoid tissue—the thymus and lymph nodes—is quite different from that for tissue in the rest of the body. At 12 years of age, lymphoid tissue is more than double the level it will reach in adulthood; after age 12 it declines until maturity. In contrast, the reproductive system grows very slowly until adolescence, at which point its growth accelerates. The internal organs, including the kidneys, liver, spleen, lungs, and stomach, keep pace with the growth in the skeletal system, and these systems therefore show the same two growth spurts in infancy and adolescence.

The Newborn and Brain Development The nervous system develops more rapidly than other systems. At birth the brain already weighs about 350 grams; at 1 year it is about 1,400 grams; by 7 years of age, the brain is almost adult in weight and size (Restak, 1984). The circumference of the baby's skull is measured to verify continued cerebral cortex growth with ultrasound imaging while in the womb, at birth, and at every scheduled medical checkup during childhood. Those parts of the hindbrain that control basic processes such as circulation, respiration, and consciousness are operative at birth.

Most neonatal reflexes, like sucking, rooting, and grasping, are organized at the subcortical level (the part of the brain that guides basic biological functioning, including sleeping, heart rate, hunger, and digestion). The parts that control processes less critical to immediate survival, including physical mobility and language, mature after birth. The rapid growth of the brain during the first two years of life is associated with the development of neural pathways and connections among nerve cells, particularly in the cerebral cortex (the part of the brain responsible for learning, thinking, reading, and problem solving). More efficient brains are characterized by a complexity of neuronal interactions and a richness of synaptic connections (see Figure 4.9), and this is why essential nutrition and extensive sensory experience and stimulation play a vital role in brain maturation and cognitive functioning. The rapid development of the cortex during the first 12 months provides the foundation for children's less stereotyped and more flexible behavior (Chugani & Phelps, 1986).

Recent research suggests that even small amounts of chemical exposure of the fetus at a crucial stage of development can lead to the destruction of neurons.

Different chemicals and different exposure times can destroy different areas of the brain. Although fetal alcohol syndrome is now well documented, researchers are finding that even low levels of alcohol can kill neurons; this is especially critical in the second half of pregnancy. Researchers are also studying a possible link between a fetus' exposure to high levels of lead in the womb and the later onset of schizophrenia (Marchant, 2004). Scientists are also working on understanding how the mother's hormones affect fetal brain development ("Maternal T3 and T4 levels in early pregnancy," 2004)

Diagnostics and Imaging PET (positron emission tomography) scanners are providing evidence that the biological or metabolic activity of the brain undergoes substantial change between birth and adulthood. Neuroscientists using PET scans have found that the metabolic rate of the baby's brain is about two-thirds that of the adult's. By the age of 2 the rate approximates that of the adult's, with rapid increases occurring in the activity of the cerebral cortex. By age 3 or 4 the metabolic rate of the child's brain is about twice that of the adult's. The brain stays supercharged until the age of 10 or 11. Metabolic rate then tapers off, reaching the adult rate at about age 13 or 14 (Blakeslee, 1986). Thanks to new scanning and imaging technologies, including powerful brain scans, scientists are now able to form a much clearer picture of the brain's inner workings. This has allowed greater insight into early development.

Environmental Stimulation Factor Researchers now confirm that the way parents interact with children in the early years, and the experiences they provide, have a big impact on an infant's emotional development, learning abilities, and later functioning ("Brain Facts," 1999; Yarrow et al., 1984). A baby is born with an unfinished brain, one that lets the child develop neural pathways in direct response to its world. From birth, the baby's brain

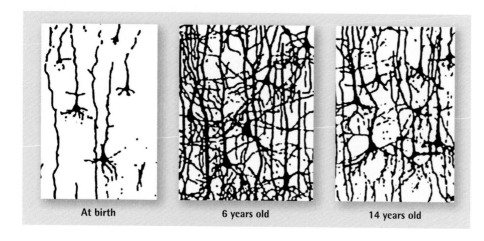

At birth   **6 years old**   **14 years old**

FIGURE 4.9 Synaptic Density in the Human Brain A single neuron can connect with as many as 15,000 other neurons. The incredibly complex network of connections that results is often referred to as the brain's "wiring" or "circuitry." Proper nutrition, experience, and environmental stimulation shape the way circuits are made in the brain.

is rapidly creating neural connections. Researchers are finding that the quality of caregiving has an even greater effect on brain development than most people previously suspected. Of course, heredity also plays a role.

Recent research suggests that the expression of parental love affects the way the brain forms its complex connections: Looking into the baby's eyes and holding and stroking the baby stimulates the brain to release hormones that promote growth; singing and talking to a baby stimulates the sense of hearing ("Brain Facts," 1999). Some researchers refer to this as "emotional intelligence." If an infant's brain is not exposed to visual or auditory experiences, the child will have difficulty mastering language and will have difficulty with visual and auditory tasks ("Brain Facts," 1999; Thompson, 2001). Every caregiver, as well as every family member, is potentially a source of love, learning, comfort, and stimulation that in turn promotes brain growth.

Principles of Development As mentioned earlier, human development proceeds according to two major principles. Development according to the **cephalocaudal principle** proceeds from the head to the feet. Improvements in structure and function come first in the head region, then in the trunk, and finally in the leg region. At birth the head is disproportionately large. In adults the head makes up only about one-tenth to one-twelfth of the body, but in newborns it is about one-fourth of the body. In contrast, the arms and legs of newborns are disproportionately short.

From birth to adulthood the head doubles in size, the trunk trebles, the arms and hands quadruple in length, and the legs and feet grow fivefold (Bayley, 1956). Motor development likewise follows the cephalocaudal principle. Infants first learn to control the muscles of the head and neck. Then, they learn to control the arms, the abdomen, and, last, the legs. Thus, when they begin to crawl, they use the upper body to propel themselves, dragging the legs passively behind. Only later do they begin to use the legs as an aid in crawling. Similarly, babies learn to hold their heads up before they acquire the ability to sit, and they learn to sit before they learn to walk (Bayley, 1935; 1936).

The other major pattern of human development follows the **proximodistal principle**: development from near to far, outward from the central axis of the body toward the extremities. Early in infancy, babies must move their head and trunk to orient their hands when grasping an object. Only later can they use their arms and legs independently, and it is still longer before they can make refined movements with their wrists and fingers. On the whole, control over movement travels down the arm as children become able to perform increasingly precise and sophisticated manual and grasping operations. Another way of expressing the same principle is to say that, in general, large-muscle control precedes fine-muscle control. Thus, the child's ability to jump, climb, and run (activities involving the use of large muscles) develops ahead of the ability to draw or write (activities involving smaller muscles).

Motor Development

Reaching, grasping, crawling, and walking—behaviors that infants become able to perform with considerable

The Cephalocaudal Principle of Development Physical development and motor development come first in the head and neck region, than in the trunk and upper body, and finally in the legs and feet. Thus, when infants begin to crawl, they use their upper body to propel themselves, dragging their legs behind. Then they get up on all fours, using the legs to aid in crawling.

proficiency—have proven to be highly complex and problematic tasks to engineers who design computers and robots that can perform these tasks. And in laboratory tests professional athletes have become exhausted from mimicking baby movements. Not surprisingly, much of the early psychological research devoted to motor development was primarily descriptive, much as we might describe the mechanical activities of a computer or robot (Halverson, 1931; McGraw, 1935).

To crawl, walk, climb, and grasp objects with precision, babies must have reached certain levels of skeletal and muscular development. As their heads become smaller relative to their bodies, their balance improves (imagine how difficult it must be to move around with a head that is one-fourth of one's total size). As children's legs become stronger and longer, they can master various locomotive activities. As their shoulders widen and their arms lengthen, their manual and mechanical capacities increase. Motor development occurs in accordance with maturational processes that are built into the human organism and are activated by a child's interaction with the environment (Thelen, 1981, 1986, 1995).

Rhythmic Behaviors Probably the most interesting motor behavior displayed by young infants involves bursts of rapid, repeated movements of the limbs, torso, or head (Thelen, 1981, 1995). Infants kick, rock, bounce, bang, rub, thrust, and twist. They seem to follow the dictum "If you can move it at all, move it rhythmically." Such behaviors are closely related to motor development and provide the foundation for the more skilled behaviors that will come later. Hence, rhythmical patterns that involve the legs, like kicking, gradually increase at about 1 month, peak immediately prior to a child's initiation of crawling at about 6 months, and then taper off. Likewise, rhythmical hand and arm movements appear before complex manual skills. Thus, bouts of rhythmic movement seem to be transitional behaviors between uncoordinated activity and complex voluntary motor control. They represent a state in motor maturation that is more complex than that found in simple reflexes yet less variable and flexible than that found in later, cortically controlled behavior.

Locomotion The infant's ability to walk, which typically evolves among U.S. youngsters between 11 and 15 months of age, is the climax of a long series of developments (Thelen, 1986, 1995). These developments progress in a sequence that follows the cephalocaudal principle. First, children gain the ability to lift up the head and, later, the chest. Next, they achieve command of the trunk region, which enables them to sit up. Finally, they achieve mastery of their legs as they learn to stand and to walk. For most infants the seventh month brings a surge in motor development. Usually, children begin by *crawling*—moving with the abdomen in contact with the floor. They maneuver by twisting the body and pulling and tugging with the arms. Next, they may progress to *creeping*—moving on hands and knees while the body is parallel with the floor. Some children also employ *hitching*—sitting and sliding along the floor by "digging in" and pushing themselves backward with the heels. In this form of **locomotion** they often use the arms to aid in propulsion. Indeed, an occasional infant varies the procedure by sitting and then, employing each arm as a pendulum, bouncing across the floor on its buttocks.

By 7 or 8 months children resemble perpetual-motion machines, as they relentlessly tackle new tasks. At 8 months they pull themselves to a *standing* position but usually have difficulty getting back down again. Often they fall over backward but, undaunted, keep practicing. The urge to master new motor skills is so powerful in infants at this age that bumps, spills, falls, and other obstacles only momentarily discourage them. Before age 1, many infants are *cruising* (standing and walking while holding on to furniture).

New sights, sounds, and experiences challenge cognitive structures that in turn lead the child to develop new motor skills. For example, the first time children discover they can crawl up the stairs, they will not forget, and they will continually go back to the stairs to repeat the process over and over; however, it will most likely be weeks before they will know how to get back down the stairs, and they will need parental supervision with such developmental tasks. A major milestone of motor development that brings both excitement and caution is when an infant begins walking unaided—on average around 1 year of age.

The stages and the timing of motor development are based largely on studies of infants from Western cultures. But the possibility that there are considerable differences among cultures in the timing of motor development has been raised by a number of studies of African infants (Ainsworth, 1967; Keefer et al., 1982). Marcelle Geber and R. F. Dean (1957a, 1957b) tested nearly 300 infants living in an urban area of Uganda. They found that these babies were clearly accelerated in motor development relative to American white infants. The Ugandan infants' precocity is greatest during the first six months of life, after which the gap between the two groups tends to decrease. It closes by the end of the second year. Cultural variables play a part in the differences between groups' developmental milestones timetables. As Rogoff (2003) explains, "In some communities walking sooner is valued; in others, it is not desired. In Wogeo, New Guinea, infants were not allowed to crawl and discouraged from

Walking Unaided Walking is one of the most thrilling developmental milestones (for both child and parents) occurring around the toddler's first birthday or later. This culmination of physical and motor development brings with it greater independence and mobility in her environment. Caregivers are cautioned to get down to child level and childproof the environment for hazards, such as sharp corners on furniture, open electrical switchplates, plants with poisonous leaves or flowers, household cleaning agents, open access to stairways, and loose electrical cords attached to larger devices. Accidents are a major cause of serious injury to young children.

walking until nearly 2 years of age so that they know how to take care of themselves and avoid dangers before moving about freely" (p. 159).

Manual Skills The child's development of manual skills proceeds through a series of orderly stages in accordance with the proximodistal principle—from the center of the body toward the periphery. At 2 months of age infants merely make swiping movements toward objects with the upper body and arms; they do not attempt to grasp objects. At 3 months of age their reaching consists of clumsy shoulder and elbow movements. Their aim is poor, and their hands are fisted. After about 16 weeks children approach an object with hands open. Around this same time, infants spend a considerable amount of time looking at their own hands. Around 20 weeks children become capable of touching an object in one quick, direct motion of the hand; occasionally, some of them succeed in grasping it in an awkward manner.

Infants of 24 weeks employ a corralling and scooping approach with the palm and fingers. At 28 weeks they begin to oppose the thumb to the palm and other fingers. At 36 weeks they coordinate their grasp with the tips of the thumb and forefinger. Caretakers must take extra precautions once infants can pick up small objects, because infants seem to put all objects in their mouth for the next several months. By about 52 weeks infants master a more sophisticated forefinger grasp (Ausubel & Sullivan, 1970; Halverson, 1931). By the age of 24 months, most children can hold and use such items as eating utensils, a crayon or paintbrush, a ball, or a toothbrush.

Questions

What is the typical developmental progression of physical and motor skills from newborn to 2 years of age? If you worked on staff with a local pediatrician, how would you explain to a concerned parent her healthy infant's not walking by 14 months of age?

Sensory Development

What is the world like to the infant? Increasingly, sophisticated monitoring equipment is permitting us to pinpoint what the infant sees, hears, smells, tastes, and feels. Social and behavioral scientists now recognize that infants are capable of doing much more, and doing it much earlier, than was believed possible even 20 years ago. Indeed, these new techniques and the insights they have given us have been hailed by some psychologists as "a scientific revolution."

During the first six months of life, there is a considerable discrepancy between infants' vast sensory capabilities and their relatively sluggish motor development. Their sensory apparatus yields perceptual input far beyond their capacity to use it. As a result of maturation, experience, and practice, they have already acquired the ability to extract information from the environment at a phenomenal rate. The child surges ahead in an awesome fashion when these perceptual abilities become linked with the big spurt in motor development that begins around the seventh month. Hence, 10 to 11 months later, at 18 months of age, the child is an accomplished social being. Let us consider the processes of sensation and perception. Sensation refers to the reception of information by our sense organs. Perception concerns the interpretation or meaning that we assign to sensation.

Vision   A full-term newborn is equipped at birth with a functional and intact visual apparatus. However, the eyes are immature. The retina and the optic nerve, for instance, are not fully developed (Abramov et al., 1982). Neonates also seem to lack visual accommodation. The muscles that control the lenses are not fully developed. As a result, their eyes sometimes focus too close and sometimes too far. In contrast to earlier research findings that suggested infants see from 7 to 10 inches in front of their face best, more recent research suggests that "infants are generally farsighted at birth" outgrowing it over the first years of life (Hamer & Skoczenski, 2001). As one would expect, infants' visual scanning capabilities become progressively more sophisticated with the passage of time (Bronson, 1994, 1997; Granrud, 1993). Let us take a closer look at the developing visual capabilities of infants by examining a number of specific components (Hamer & Skoczenski, 2001):

- *Visual acuity* (detail vision). By about 2 to 3 months of age, most infants can focus accurately (Hamer & Skoczenski, 2001). By 8 months of age, the infant's nervous system has matured so it is nearly as good as normal adult acuity (nearly 20/20).
- *Contrast sensitivity.* After birth, an infant can see the contrast in large black-and-white stripes, and by 9 weeks of age, infant sensitivity is significantly better. They can then see many subtle shadings of a face or objects in their environment.
- *Eye coordination.* A newborn infant's eyes are not perfectly coordinated, and eyes may wander, even in different directions. By 3 months of age, generally, an infant's eyes are well coordinated.
- *Ability to follow (tracking).* Newborns can follow objects, often with jerky motions. By 3 months, infants can normally follow objects more smoothly.
- *Color vision.* Infants as young as 2 weeks of age have color vision, distinguishing red from green. Infants can also see large colored patterns and black-and-white patterns.
- *Object and face recognition.* At birth an infant's eyes tend to be attracted to the borders of objects, although they have enough detail vision to see the larger features of a face. Newborns ranging from 12 to 36 hours of age produce significantly more sucking responses in order to see an image of their mothers' faces than they do to see an image of strangers' faces (Walton, Bower, & Bower, 1992). Among the indicators that investigators have used are changes in the infant's eye orientation, sucking rate, body movements, skin conductance, heart rate, and con-

ditioned responses. Infants can tell the difference between a mother's or caretaker's face and that of a stranger between 3 and 5 months of age. By the sixth to seventh month, infants come to recognize individual faces (Caron et al., 1973; Gibson, 1969).
- *Visual constancy.* Three- to 5-month-old infants are able to recognize object boundaries and object unity by detecting surface separations or contours (Spelke, von Hofsten, & Kestenbaum, 1989).
- *Depth perception.* At birth it appears that infants have two-dimensional vision—not three-dimensional. Three-dimensional vision requires good muscle coordination of the eyes, sufficient brain and nerve cell maturation, and lots of visual experience. Infants' binocular vision—the ability to tell the distances of various objects and to experience the world three-dimensionally—undergoes a sudden burst between 3 and 5 months of age (Yonas, Granrud, & Pettersen, 1985). The fact that the ability arises quite suddenly and rapidly suggests to some psychologists that it represents a change in the visual cortex, the portion of the brain responsible for vision. Apparently, these developmental changes result in the two eyes working in concert and allow the brain to extract reliable three-dimensional information from perceptual processes.

A family vacation to the Grand Canyon led Eleanor Gibson to undertake a *visual cliff experiment* with the assistance of one of her students, Richard D. Walk (Gibson & Walk, 1960). They devised a technique where an infant is placed on a center board between two glass surfaces on which the child can crawl (see Figure 4.10). The shallow side is covered on the underside with a checkered material. At the deep side an illusion of a cliff is created with a checkered material placed several feet below the glass. The infant's mother stands alternately at the shallow and deep sides and coaxes the infant to crawl toward her. If infants can perceive depth, they should be willing to cross the shallow side but not the cliff side, because the cliff side looks like a chasm.

Gibson and Walk tested 36 infants between 6½ and 14 months of age. Twenty-seven of the infants ventured off the center board and crawled across the shallow side toward their mothers. Only three, however, could be enticed to cross the cliff side. A number of infants actually crawled away from their mothers when beckoned from the deep side; others cried, presumably because they could not reach their mothers without crossing the chasm. Some patted the glass on the deep side, ascertaining that it was solid, but nonetheless backed away. Apparently, they were more dependent on the visual evidence than on the evidence provided by their sense

FIGURE 4.10 The Visual Cliff Experiment In the visual cliff experiment, the child is placed on a center board that has a sheet of glass extending outward on either side. A checkered material is placed on one side about 40 inches below the glass, thus providing the illusion of depth. Despite its mother's coaxing and the presence of a safe glass surface, a 6-month-old infant generally will not crawl across the "chasm." The infant will, however, venture across the shallow side of the apparatus to reach its mother.
Source: Adapted from E. J. Gibson and R. D. Walk, "The Visual Cliff," *Scientific American,* Vol. 202 (1960), p. 65.

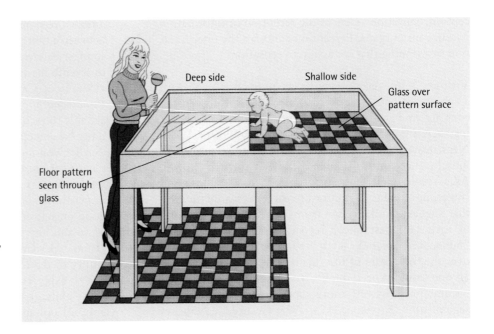

of touch. This research suggests that the vast majority of babies can perceive a dropoff and avoid it by the time they become capable of creeping.

Karen Adolph (2000) studied 9-month-old infants and found that avoiding a cliff does not depend solely on depth perception. Her participants were tested in both an experienced sitting posture and a crawling posture in an adjustable gap apparatus, similar to the device in Figure 4.10 (using repeated trials over time and in a replicated experiment). However, in these trials the gap was open and variable—and the experimenter was poised to catch each infant as he or she reached or crawled across the gap to touch a colorful toy. These infants attempted all gap distances in the crawling posture but showed more fine-tuned avoidance responses in the sitting posture. Each week the infants' bodies and skills in balancing themselves changed considerably, and their responses improved. The results of this study demonstrate that experience promotes learning about balance, control, and various postural milestones (sitting, crawling, and walking) involve "different regions of postural sway for different key pivots around which the body rotates" (Adolph, 2000, p. 291).

In sum, we see that infants have already developed rather sophisticated visual-perceptual capabilities by the time they reach 6 to 8 months of age (Younger, 1992).

Hearing   At the time of birth, normally the hearing apparatus of the neonate is remarkably well developed. Indeed, the human fetus can hear noises three months before birth (Shahidullah, Scott, & Hepper, 1993). However, for several hours or even days after delivery, the ne-

onate's hearing might be somewhat impaired. Vernix and amniotic fluid frequently stop up the external ear passage, while mucus clogs the middle ear. These mechanical blockages disappear rapidly after birth. Yet, on average, each day in the United States, 33 babies (12,000 annually) are born with permanent hearing loss, and four or five per thousand have a hearing impairment ("Fact Sheet," 2005). *It is imperative to identify hearing-impaired babies as early as possible,* and 42 states and the District of Columbia have early hearing detection and intervention laws that screen the hearing of more than 85 percent of those infants born in a hospital or birthing clinic (American Speech-Language Association, 2005). This is a safe, simple, painless assessment, and an infant who is identified will be referred to a pediatric audiologist.

Ear infections are the second most common ailment in infancy (after colds) and are caused by a variety of factors. The most obvious sign of ear infection is persistent high-pitched crying—often after the infant has been lying down for a while. If an infant doesn't respond to a parent's voice or to loud noises by showing a startle reflex or by crying, or doesn't make babbling or cooing sounds within the first few months of life, the infant should be checked immediately for a hearing problem. An infant who cannot hear will not acquire the sounds of human language nor the cognitive or social skills that provide the foundation for success in later schooling without professional intervention. Hearing-impaired and deaf infants are eligible for early intervention services. Clearly, parents will also want to learn sign language to communicate with their baby. Some caregivers use specific baby sign language (gesturing) with babies

Newborn Hearing Assessment Before Leaving the Hospital
Hearing screening by an audiologist is safe, simple, and painless. It is imperative to identify hearing-impaired infants as soon as possible.

with no hearing impairment to teach babies to communicate prior to language development ("Signing with Your Baby," 2005).

Educators have long recognized that hearing plays a crucial part in the process by which children acquire language. But research by Condon and Sander (1974a, 1974b), purporting to show that newborns are attuned to the fine elements of adult speech, surprised the scientific community. The researchers videotaped interactions between neonates and adults and analyzed them frame by frame. To ordinary viewers, the hands, feet, and head of an infant appear uncoordinated, clumsily flexing, twitching, and moving about in all directions. But Condon and Sander say closer analysis reveals that infant movements are synchronized with the sound patterns of the adult's speech. For example, if an infant is squirming about when an adult begins to talk, the infant coordinates the movements of brows, eyes, limbs, elbows, hips, and mouth to start, stop, and change with the boundaries of the adult's speech segments (phonemes, syllables, or words). The newborns, who were from 12 hours to 2 days old, were equally capable of synchronizing their movements with Chinese or English. Condon and Sander conclude that if infants, from birth, move in precise, shared rhythm with the speech patterns of their culture, then they participate

in millions of repetitions of linguistic forms long before they employ them in communication.

However, other researchers have not been able to replicate the Condon-Sander findings. Indeed, John M. Dowd and Edward Z. Tronick (1986) conclude that speech-movement synchrony requires reaction times inconsistent with an infant's limited motor abilities and that the methodology used by Condon and Sander is flawed in many ways. So again we encounter considerable controversy surrounding the question "How much do infants know, and when do they know it?"

Taste and Smell   Both taste (gustation) and smell (olfaction) are present at birth. Infant taste preferences can be determined by measuring sucking behavior (Blass & Ciaramitaro, 1994). Young infants relax and suck contentedly when provided with sweet solutions, although they prefer sucrose over glucose (Engen, Lipsitt, & Peck, 1974). Infants react to sour and bitter solutions by grimacing and breathing irregularly (Jensen, 1932; Rosenstein & Oster, 1988). The findings for salt perception is less clear; some researchers find that newborns do not discriminate a salty solution from nonsalty water, whereas other investigators find that salt is a negative experience for newborns (Bernstein, 1990).

Charles K. Crook and Lewis P. Lipsitt (1976) found that newborns decrease their sucking speed when receiving sweet fluid, which suggests that they savor the liquid for the pleasurable taste. This would indicate that the hedonistic aspects of tasting are present at birth (Acredolo & Hake, 1982).

The olfactory system is unique both in what it responds to and in how it responds. As an environmental monitor, it seems to operate rather cautiously and prefers the familiar to the novel. Much of the time the olfactory system monitors the environment without the organism being aware of the process. The familiar simply fades into the background. But should novel odors come into sensory range, the system promptly brings them to conscious awareness. It is this feature—alerting the organism to potential danger and so increasing the organism's chances for survival—that accounts for the system's evolutionary value (Engen, 1991).

Infants respond to different odors, and the vigor of the response corresponds to the intensity and quality of the stimulant. Engen, Lipsitt, and Kaye (1963) tested olfaction in 2-day-old infants. At regular intervals they held a cotton swab saturated with anise oil (which has a licorice smell) or asafetida (which smells like boiling onions) under an infant's nose. A polygraph recorded the babies' bodily movements, respiration, and heart rate. When they first detected an odor, infants moved their limbs, their breathing quickened, and their heart rate increased. With repeated exposure, however, infants gradually came to disregard the stimulant. The olfactory thresholds decreased drastically over the first few days of life, meaning that the neonates became increasingly sensitive to nasal stimulants. Other researchers have confirmed that neonates possess well-developed olfactory abilities (Rieser, Yonas, & Wikner, 1976).

Cutaneous Senses Heat, cold, pressure, and pain—the four major cutaneous sensations—are present in neonates (Humphrey, 1978). Kai Jensen (1932) found that a bottle of hot or cold milk (above 124 degrees Fahrenheit or below 72 degrees Fahrenheit) caused an irregular sucking rhythm in neonates. On the whole, however, neonates are relatively insensitive to small differences in thermal stimuli. Neonates also respond to body pressure. Touching activates many of the reflexes discussed earlier in the chapter. Finally, we infer from infants' responses that they experience sensations of pain. For instance, observation of neonate and infant behavior suggests that gastrointestinal upsets are a major source of discomfort. As infants receive required vaccination injections during the first few years of life, it is quite obvious that they sense pain and discomfort (Izard, Hembree, & Huebner, 1987). And male infants increase their crying during circumcision, providing additional evidence that neonates are sensitive to pain.

Circumcision Each year within a few days of birth, more than 1 million U.S. male newborns undergo an operation that many medical professionals now believe is unnecessary. Circumcision is the surgical removal of the foreskin (prepuce) that covers the tip (glans) of the penis. Through the centuries this procedure has been a religious rite for Jews and Muslims. Among some African and South Pacific peoples, circumcision is performed at puberty to mark the passage of a youth to adulthood. In contrast, circumcision has never been common in Europe. Until about 20 years ago, U.S. physicians promoted circumcision as a health measure and a protection against cancer of the penis (and, in female sexual partners, cancer of the cervix). The procedure is also viewed as a means to prevent venereal disease and urinary tract infections. Because physicians now maintain that there are few valid medical indications for routine circumcision of the newborn, the practice has been on the decline. It is up to parents to make this decision.

Interconnections Among the Senses Our sensory systems commonly operate in concert with one another. We expect to see things we hear, feel things we see, and smell things we taste. We often employ information we gain from one sensory system to "inform" our other systems (Acredolo & Hake, 1982). For instance, even newborns move both their head and their eyes in efforts to locate the source of sounds, especially when the sounds are patterned and sustained.

Developmental psychologists, psychobiologists, and comparative psychologists have advanced two opposing theories about how the interconnections among systems evolve. Take the development of sensory and motor coordination in infants. One viewpoint holds that infants only gradually achieve an integration of eye-hand activities as they interact with their environment. In the process of adapting to the larger world, infants are seen as progressively forging a closer and sharper coordination between their sensory and motor systems. According to Jean Piaget, infants initially lack cognitive structures for knowing the external world. Consequently, they must actively construct mental schemas that will allow them to structure their experience.

The opposing theory holds that eye-hand coordination is biologically prewired in the infant's nervous system at birth and emerges according to a maturational schedule. This interpretation is favored by T. G. R. Bower (1976). Bower finds that newborn infants engage in visually initiated reaching. Apparently, when neonates look at an object and reach out for it, both the looking and the reaching are part of the same response by which the infants orient themselves toward the object (von Hofsten, 1982).

In ensuing months, however, an increase in visual guidance occurs during the approach phase of reaching

(Ashmead et al., 1993). Perhaps a cautious conclusion to be drawn from this research is that the eye-hand coordination of newborns and very young infants is biologically prewired. But visual guidance in eye-hand coordination becomes more important as older babies monitor and progressively reduce the "gap" between the seen target and the seen hand (McKenzie et al., 1993). So for this later sort of reaching, the youngster must attend to its hand. In sum, eye-hand coordination changes early in life from using the felt hand to using the seen hand (Bushnell, 1985). Development is often characterized by patterns of skill acquisition, loss, and reacquisition on new foundations and levels.

Questions

Which if any sensory systems are already functioning well at birth? What can you tell new parents about when their infant will see visibly, hear acutely, and distinguish qualities of smell, taste, and touch? How do infant senses interconnect?

SEGUE

As any parent knows, infants actively search out and respond to their environment. Scientific research of infants' developing motor and sensory abilities bears out the truth of this observation. Children have a natural endowment that predisposes them to begin learning how the world operates around them. As they mature, they refine their ability to take information from one sense and transfer it to another. All the senses, including seeing, hearing, smell, taste, and touch, create a system that is a whole. Information gained from multiple systems is often more important than that gained from one sense, precisely because it is interactive. A growing body of contemporary research points to the multicausal, fluid, contextual, and self-organizing nature of developmental change, the unity of motor behavior and perception, and the role of exploration and selection in the emergence of new behavior (Smith & Thelen, 2003).

In Chapter 5 we will turn our attention to cognition and maturing intellectual abilities, such as use of language, which grows from the roots in motor behavior, sensation, perception, caretaker attachment behaviors, and experiential factors that we have discussed in this chapter.

Summary

Birth

1. Over 4 million babies were born in the U.S. each year since 2000—the highest increase in a decade—into a shifting composition of families and households. Although still a majority, there are fewer married couples raising children and more single parents who have never married or are divorced. On average, families have only two children. More mothers are working, and newborns today are likely to receive child care outside of their homes.

2. The birth of the newborn, called a neonate, transforms women into mothers and men into fathers.

3. A variety of psychoprophylactic or natural childbirth approaches help a mother prepare for delivery. Lamaze classes help the mother-to-be prepare for an unmedicated delivery. Other women know they have to schedule a cesarean delivery because of their own preexisting health condition, such as diabetes or AIDS. More women are using the services of nurse-midwives and doulas that provide emotional care during pregnancy and through the birth process.

4. Some women choose to deliver in hospital birthing rooms, in birthing centers, or in home delivery with an experienced midwife or doula attending. The majority of American women are attended by obstetricians who specialize in prenatal care, birth, and postnatal care.

5. Most American hospitals and birthing centers offer family-centered hospital care in which childbirth can be a family experience. Natural (prepared) childbirth and rooming in are common features of these programs.

6. The period of gestation for a human baby from conception to birth is around 266 days, nearly 9 months, from the first day of the last menstrual cycle.

7. A few weeks before birth, the majority of fetuses normally position themselves head downward and lower in the uterus, in turn lightening some of the mother's discomfort. Fetal diagnostics at this later stage may indicate abnormal fetal positions that warrant surgical delivery. A hormonal signal from the brain through the blood prompts the beginnings of labor. Most women experience mild "tuning up" contractions for a few weeks prior to birth.

8. The birth process consists of three stages: labor, delivery, and afterbirth. At the beginning of labor, the amniotic sac ruptures, releasing the amniotic fluid that has cushioned the fetus. During the several hours of labor, the strong muscle fibers of the mother's uterus contract rhythmically,

pushing the baby toward the birth canal. The first periodic contractions are about 15 to 20 minutes apart and come more quickly and intensely as delivery nears. Delivery begins when crowning occurs, and the baby's head passes through the cervix and ends with the passage of the baby through the birth canal. Birth concludes when the mother's body expels the afterbirth, the remaining umbilical cord and placenta.

9. More mothers are choosing to store the blood from their baby's umbilical cord and placenta, which may be used for stem cell research and other medical uses.

10. The Leboyer method of birth advocates that infants need a gentler delivery, lower sound and light levels, a warmer delivery room, newborn massage, and a warm bath. Yet most obstetricians believe that ordinary stresses of birth do not exceed the infant's physical or neurological capacity.

11. In a hospital setting, electronic fetal monitoring and computers continually assess the pulse and heartbeat of the fetus to determine whether the fetus is in distress and needs surgical delivery.

12. On average, a full-term neonate is 19 to 22 inches long and weighs 5½ to 9½ pounds and is covered with a waxy substance called vernix. Many still have a fine body hair called lanugo. Natural delivery newborns have longer, more "pointy" heads for a few weeks than those who arrive by C-section delivery.

13. Other health factors are assessed at 1 minute and 5 minutes after birth using the Apgar scoring system: heart rate, respiratory effort, muscle tone, reflex irritability, and skin tone. Other scales, such as the Brazelton Neonatal Behavioral Assessment Scale (NBAS) and the newer CNBAS, might be used during the first week to assess physical behaviors, reflexes, and social capacities.

14. The newborn is now called a neonate, and the first several weeks of life are called the neonatal period.

15. Parent-infant bonding is a process of interaction and mutual attention between parents and their infant. Attachment occurs over time with close proximity, constant interaction, and emotional attachment whether the child is delivered by natural birth, delivered by cesarean, or adopted.

16. The birth rate for never-married women has risen dramatically since the early 1980s, and there's evidence that many of these mothers and infants are highly likely to experience the deleterious effects of poverty. The number of parents living with a child is generally linked to the amount and quality of human communication and resources available to the child.

17. Extensive research has been and continues to be conducted on the contribution of fathers and the effects of fatherlessness on infants and children. In most instances, both mothers and fathers can contribute significantly to the parenting role.

18. In a small percentage of cases, complications arise during pregnancy and childbirth. If complications develop, much can be done through medical intervention and technology to help the mother and infant. Among the possible complications at birth are anoxia, oxygen deprivation at birth, Rh factor incompatibility, premature birth, or other complications that require surgical cesarean delivery. Larger

hospitals today have neonatology units to help premature, very-low-birth-weight, or at-risk infants survive, resulting in lower rates of infant mortality.

19. Postmature infants, those delivered more than two weeks after the usual 40 weeks of gestation in the womb, are usually larger and healthy. Birth options include induced labor or cesarean delivery.

20. Although the majority of American infants are born without complications, a small percentage of them are born as premature infants, or small for term. Others are born with drug addictions and experience withdrawal. These include "crack babies" and those with fetal alcohol syndrome (FAS). A smaller percentage of babies are born with HIV. Some are born with genetic disorders, birth defects from prenatal chemical toxicant exposure, or experience birth complications.

21. Infants who are determined to be at risk from birth or during the neonatal period are eligible by law for early-intervention services from birth through preschool age. There are many support groups, resources, and Internet sites for parents who have a child with a disorder. Also, many professional occupations today support these special infants, children, and their parents.

22. Fewer neonates experience mortality or die shortly after birth. Infant mortality occurs because of such conditions as birth defects, prematurity or low birth weight, sudden infant death syndrome (SIDS), maternal pregnancy complications, and cord and placenta complications.

23. After birth, some mothers experience postpartum depression (PPD), which might include crying spells, depression, sleep changes, appetite changes, anxiety, and thoughts of not being able to cope with taking care of the baby. The depressed mother should seek professional support and care for herself because maternal depression has a significant impact on the infant's behavior, emotional responsiveness, and cognitive development.

Development of Basic Competencies

24. The first years of life after birth are called infancy. Some infant researchers have discovered that infant biology is intimately connected to the biology of the adults responsible for infant care. This symbiotic relationship is called entrainment, which is first and foremost a physical relationship (touching, nursing, cleaning, and massaging) and includes synchronicity of movements and reactions between parent and infant. A small number of infants are classified with failure to thrive and are likely to be missing this synchronicity and engagement with caretakers.

25. Sleeping, crying, feeding, and eliminating are the newborn's chief behaviors. An infant's responses at any given time are related to its states. These infant states have been identified: regular sleep, irregular sleep, drowsiness, alert inactivity, waking activity, and crying. Also, neonates are born with good indicators of neurological development called reflex behaviors, which are simple, involuntary, unlearned responses, such as sucking, coughing, blinking, yawning, stepping, and others.

26. The major activity of newborns is sleeping, perhaps 16 or more hours per day, typically in four-hour cycles. It

may be weeks or months before infants sleep through the night and normally take one nap a day. Pediatricians and social scientists are examining attitudes toward co-sleeping with infants and the setting for infant sleep, which depends on culture, customs, and traditions. Co-sleeping infants respond more to the patterns and rhythms of their mothers' breathing.

27. Annually, nearly 3,000 U.S. families experience the devastating tragedy and agony of sudden infant death syndrome (SIDS) or crib death. The decline in SIDS deaths over the past decade is attributed to the national education campaign to place the infant on its back to sleep and avoid smoking around a baby. Several theories have been posed as the cause, but there is no one answer.

28. Crying is the language of the newborn and is an unlearned, involuntary, highly adaptive response that incites the parents to caretaking activities. Different cries have distinctive pitch, rhythm, and duration and convey different messages to caretakers. Infants born ill from drug exposure often cry incessantly and with a high pitch as they experience withdrawal symptoms.

29. Some caretakers become so annoyed with infant cries that they harm the infant out of frustration, causing shaken baby syndrome. If a baby's head is violently shaken back and forth, causing bruising and bleeding of the brain and spinal cord, this could result in brain damage and cause mental retardation, brain death, or infant death. Parents are cautioned to never leave a child with a total stranger. A child's incessant crying could be a sign of colic, a condition of lengthy crying for an unknown cause, which might last for several weeks.

30. Newborns spend much of their waking time feeding, and pediatricians encourage parents to feed their baby when it is hungry, called on-demand feeding. Breast-feeding and formula-feeding both offer advantages and disadvantages. Extensive research suggests that breast-feeding is best for healthy mothers and infants. Over the first two years, infants will gradually begin to eat regular table foods and beverages, and there are a lot of individual differences in taste and food preferences.

31. Along with typical physical and motor development, the muscles of the anal and urinary tract are developing, allowing children to be toilet trained over a variable period of time.

32. Parents should schedule regular medical checkups and vaccinations to help a growing child's immune system function effectively. Proof of vaccinations is required for entry into child care, preschool, and kindergarten.

33. Not all body systems grow at the same rate, but infant researchers have come up with predictable changes that occur at various age levels and have established standards of growth and maturation, called norms, or averages of the child's age group.

34. Not all parts of the body grow at the same rate: (a) The nervous system grows more rapidly than other systems. Environmental stimulation and emotional comfort stimulate brain growth. (b) At 12 years of age, a child's lymphoid tissue is more than double the level it will reach in adulthood; after 12 it declines until maturity. (c) The reproductive system grows very slowly until adolescence, at which point its growth accelerates. (d) The skeletal and internal organ systems show two spurts, one in early infancy and the other at adolescence.

35. Normal development follows two patterns: the cephalocaudal principle and proximodistal principle. Infants gain motor skills first over the head muscles, then the trunk muscles, and finally the leg muscles. The child's development of manual skills proceeds through a series of orderly stages in accordance with the proximodistal principle—from the center of the body toward the extremities (out to the fingertips). On the whole, large-muscle control precedes fine-muscle control.

36. Young infants display bursts of rapid, repeated, rhythmic movements of the limbs, torso, and head. The behaviors are closely related to motor development and provide the foundation for later, more skilled actions.

37. The development of locomotion proceeds in a specific sequence, but children vary in their rate of development. First they lift the head and then the chest; then they sit, crawl, and creep; then stand and cruise around furniture; and eventually they walk unaided, on average around a year old, but later for some infants.

38. Sensation refers to the reception of information (stimuli) by our sensory organs, whereas perception concerns our interpretation or meaning that we give to that stimulus. Healthy infants are born with their sensory systems functioning, but over the course of the first several months of life, these systems and the brain are constantly growing, adapting, and adjusting to clearly interpret sensations of their new world.

39. At birth a neonate's eyes are immature. It will be several months before infant eyes can focus clearly and work in coordination. A neonate can see in shades of black, white, and gray; within a few months the cells of the retina will develop so that colors and contrasts will be more evident. The visual cliff experiment reveals that children possess depth perception by several months of age. More recently, research shows that experience with each milestone of posture, such as sitting, crawling, and standing, promotes learning about balance control and depth perception. Infants typically undergo a patterned sequence of changes in their method of focusing and organizing visual events.

40. At birth neonate hearing is normally well developed, and it is known that the fetus can hear before birth. Hearing plays a very important role in the process by which infants acquire language. Although some researchers suggest infants coordinate their movements to the sounds, pitch, and speed of adult caretaker speech, others dispute this finding. Ear infections are the second most common ailment in infancy (after colds) and are caused by a variety of factors.

41. Taste and smell are present at birth, and infants show distinct preferences. Skin/cutaneous senses of heat, cold, pressure, and pain are also present at birth. The practice of routine circumcision for infant boys is declining.

42. Infants are actively searching out and responding to their environment. Information gained from their senses is interactive with environmental experiences and the quality of caretaker involvement.

Key Terms

afterbirth (118)

anoxia (123)

Apgar scoring system (119)

birth (116)

birthing centers (116)

birthing rooms (115)

cephalocaudal principle (144)

cesarean section
 (C-section) (123)

colic (137)

colostrum (138)

couvade syndrome (121)

crowning (117)

delivery (117)

entrainment (133)

failure to thrive (FTT) (133)

fetal alcohol spectrum disorder (FASD)
 (127)

Individuals with Disabilities Education
 Act (IDEA) (128)

infancy (132)

infant mortality (130)

labor (117)

lightening (116)

locomotion (145)

midwifery (115)

motherese (122)

natural childbirth (114)

neonate (117)

neonatology intensive care unit (NICU)
 (123)

norms (140)

obstetricians (115)

parent-infant bonding (121)

placenta previa (123)

postmature infant (126)

postpartum depression (PPD) (131)

preeclampsia (123)

premature infant (124)

proximodistal principle (144)

psychoprophylactic method (114)

reflex (133)

rooming in (116)

shaken baby syndrome (SBS) (136)

small-for-term infant (124)

states (133)

sudden infant death syndrome (SIDS)
 (134)

Following Up on the Internet

Websites for this chapter focus on preparation for birth and delivery, neonate assessment, infant development, and parent-infant attachment. Please access the text Web site at www.mhhe.com/vzcrandell8 for up-to-date hot-linked Internet addresses for the following organizations and resources:

Association of Women's Health, Obstetric and Neonatal Nurses

Childbirth.org

Depression After Delivery

March of Dimes Perinatal Center

National Center for Cultural Competence

National Newborn Screen and Genetics Resource Center

National SIDS Center

Neonatology on the Web

Parenthood.Com Helping Families Grow

Video Scenario—http://www.mhhe.com/vzcrandell8

In this chapter, you've just read about labor, delivery, and birth of the neonate, including information about various delivery methods. Using the OLC (www.mhhe.com/vzcrandell8), re-visit Joe and Gina's discussion regarding their pregnancy and listen in on their decision-making process with regard to the birth of their baby.

Infancy
Cognitive and Language Development

Critical Thinking Questions

1. Learning is defined in terms of three criteria: There must be some change in behavior, this change must be relatively stable, and the change must result from experience. Can learning take place if only two of the three conditions are present? Why or why not?

2. A researcher in Japan developed a handheld electronic gadget called the "Bow-lingual" that he claims can translate a dog's barking into six basic categories of "emotions." "Happy," "fun, "annoyed," and "frustrated" are just a few of the options. The invention, which uses a microphone on the dog's collar to record the bark, relays up to 200 words to the owner about the dog's "feelings" together with the relevant pictures. Do you think it will be possible for researchers to invent a device that translates the variety of cries of human babies into human language? Why or why not?

3. Most U.S. children learn to comprehend more than 14,000 words between the ages of 2 and 6; they average 6 to 9 new words per day. Why do they learn at that rate, and why don't we continue to learn at that rate when we are older?

4. Speech develops through a series of stages, ending in the construction of two- and three-word sentences for the beginning language learner. Do you think you could learn a second language easier and faster today if you went through a similar process?

Our cognitive and language abilities are probably our most distinctive features as human beings. Cognitive skills enable us to gain knowledge of our social and physical environment. Language enables us to communicate with one another. Without either, human social organization would be impossible. Even if we lacked these abilities, we might still have families, for the family organization is not peculiar to humans—it appears elsewhere in the animal kingdom. But without cognitive and language abilities, our families would probably not have the structure we recognize as typically human. We would lack rules about incest, marriage, divorce, inheritance, and adoption. We would have no political, religious, economic, or military organizations; no codes of morality; no science, theology, art, or literature. We would have virtually no tools. In sum, we would be without culture, and we would not be human (White, 1949). This chapter surveys the processes by which cognition and language develop during the early years of infancy, from birth through age 2.

Cognitive Development

As discussed in Chapter 2, **cognition** refers to the process of knowing and encompasses such phenomena as sensation, perception, imagery, retention, memory, recall, problem solving, reasoning, and thinking. We receive raw sensory information and transform, elaborate, store, recover, and use this information in our daily activities (Neisser, 1967). Some infants exhibit early superior abilities to communicate using their native language in comparison to the majority of infants who are on-time with communication skills. Others are identified as having specific language impairments (SLIs)—that is, those with hearing impairments or deafness, mental retardation, neglect or caretaker deprivation and abuse, and **autism,** a disorder that typically appears in early childhood and is characterized by marked deficits in communication and social interaction.

Making Connections

Mental activity allows us to "make something" out of our perceptions. We do so by relating some happening to other events or objects in our experience. We use information from our environment and our memories to make decisions about what we say and do. Because these decisions are based on available information and on our ability to process the information intelligently, we view them as rational (Anderson, 1990). This capacity allows us to intervene in the course of events with conscious deliberation.

For instance, if we show youngsters aged 13 to 24 months the simple steps involved in "making spaghetti" with clay, a garlic press, and a plastic knife and then allow them to undertake the task for themselves, they are able to recall the sequence of events and repeat them—sometimes eight months later. Clearly, these youngsters are obtaining knowledge from their senses, imitating others' actions, and remembering the information—all evidence of higher cognitive functioning. Indeed, a mounting body of evidence suggests that 16- and 20-month-olds are capable of organizing their recall of novel events around causal relations—they know that "what happens" occurs in such a way that one event ordinarily follows another event and that this same sequence of events will again unfold in the same manner in the future (Bauer & Mandler, 1989; Oakes, 1994).

Psychologists, neuroscientists, pediatricians, and other developmentalists are increasingly coming to view infants as very complex creatures who are capable of experiencing, thinking about, and processing enormous amounts of information (Phillips, 2004; Linnell, 2002). Building on the developing competencies detailed in Chapter 4, infants begin to form associations between their own behavior and events in the external world in the early months of their lives. As they do so, they progressively gain a conception of the world as an environment that possesses stable, recurrent, and reliable components and patterns. Such conceptions allow them to begin functioning as effective beings who cause events to happen in the world about them and who evoke social responses from others (Henry, 2001). Let us begin our exploration of these matters with a consideration of infant learning.

Learning: A Definition

Learning is a fundamental human process. It permits us to adapt to our environment by building on previous experience. Psychologists have traditionally defined learning in terms of three criteria:

- There must be some change in behavior.
- This change must be relatively stable.
- The change must result from experience.

Learning, then, involves a relatively permanent change in a capability or behavior that results from experience. As we discussed in Chapter 2, theories of learning fall into three broad categories:

1. Behavioral theories emphasize that people can be conditioned by positive or negative reinforcers.
2. Cognitive theories focus on how to fashion the cognitive structures by which individuals think about their environment.
3. Social learning theories stress the need to provide models for people to imitate.

These three kinds of theories highlight some of the common influences on individuals that facilitate learning.

How Soon Do Infants Start Learning?

A growing body of research, worldwide, confirms that fetuses in the last trimester are learning while in the womb. Psychologist Anthony DeCasper and other researchers have investigated fetal and infant auditory perception (DeCasper et al., 1994). They found evidence that fetuses can discriminate between low-pitched notes that are within the range of normal human speech, and they propose that it is possible that fetuses can sense the mother's emotions by differentiating different types of speech patterns, such as those produced by anger or happiness (Henry, 2001; LeCanuet et al., 2000). They believe that some kind of learning is occurring, although they do not know its exact mechanism. The researchers devised a nipple apparatus that activates a tape recorder. By sucking in one pattern, newborns would hear their own mother's voice; by sucking in another pattern, they would hear another woman's voice. The babies (some just hours old) tended to suck in a way that would allow them to hear their mother's voice. The researchers concluded that the infants' preferences were affected by their auditory experiences before birth.

In earlier tests, 16 pregnant women read Dr. Seuss's *The Cat in the Hat* to their unborn children twice a day for the last six weeks of gestation—for a total of about five hours. After they were born, the infants were allowed to choose, by means of their sucking behavior, to hear either a recording of their mother reading *The Cat in the Hat* or a recording of their mother reading stories by other authors having a different meter. By means of their sucking responses, the infants chose to hear *The Cat in the Hat*. Since this initial research, other studies have indicated that by the 30th week of pregnancy the fetus can hear and distinguish sounds and demonstrate physiological responses, such as accelerated or lowered pulse, to those familiar sounds after birth (Kisilevsky, 1995; LeCanuet et al., 2000).

In similar cross-cultural research, Kisilevsky and colleagues (2003) studied 60 fetuses in China for auditory perception of language and found that fetal heartbeat rates increased when a recording of the mother's voice was played near the mother's abdomen. The fetuses got "excited" as they recognized their mothers' voice, and they clearly distinguished her voice over the voices of strangers. This research confirms that a fetus is learning in the womb, is capable of memory, and can sustain attention (Kisilevsky et al., 2003). Fetal auditory perception for music was also studied during the last two trimesters of pregnancy. Fetal responses to 5-minute piano recordings of Brahms' *Lullaby* varied from younger fetuses to older fetuses. Fetuses older than 33 weeks of gestation

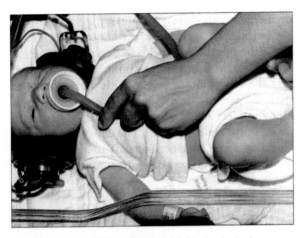

Can a Fetus Learn? This baby is participating in Anthony DeCasper's research on learning in fetuses and newborns. The infant sucks to hear a tape recording of his mother reading a story that she read aloud, on a regular basis, while pregnant. The rate of sucking is much higher for the familiar story than for another one and when a mother reads the story rather than a stranger.

showed sustained acceleration in heart rate, and those over 35 weeks showed changes in body movements as well as changes in attention (Kisilevsky et al., 2004).

It appears that infants are born with an innate perception of the *prosody* of music—that is, the rhythm and intonation (Saffran & Thiesssen, 2003). Jónsdóttir notes (2001) by the beginning of the third trimester, fetuses are sensitive to music and clearly hear the *whoosh* and flow of the womb, the mother's heartbeat, and her digestive and breathing sounds. Some suggest that language develops from this innate musical knowledge, since linguists have classified spoken languages according to their rhythmic properties (Loewy, 2004; Ramus, Nespor, & Mehler, 1999). Some parents interpret these findings to mean that they can give their infants a developmental head start by reading to them or playing classical music before they are born.

The findings of DeCasper and others (DeCasper et al., 1994) have prompted research about the development of premature babies and exposure to the many sounds in neonatal intensive care units (NICUs), such as beeping machines and the hum of conversations of strangers. Music therapists continue to study infant crying, babbling, and language development to devise early intervention methods for those children with delayed language. Although many parents believe that educational programming on electronic media can accelerate a baby's learning language and cognitive development, the American Academy of Pediatrics (2001) issued a policy statement that parents not allow infant viewing and listening to television for the first two years (see the *Further Developments* box on pages 159–161, "Babies in Diapers, Media Viewing, and Cognitive and Language Outcomes?"). Only 25 years ago we gave fetuses and newborns little credit for having cognitive and learning capabilities. Many of the responses that babies show are adaptations to specific stimuli for which newborns appear to be biologically prepared (Sameroff & Cavanagh, 1979), so in a moment we will take another look at Piaget's work, particularly his notions regarding the sensorimotor period.

Newborn Learning Developmental psychologists have long been interested in knowing whether newborns can learn—or, more particularly, whether they can adjust their behavior according to whether it succeeds or fails. Arnold J. Sameroff (1968) conducted a study on infant learning involving neonatal sucking techniques and tentatively suggests that the answer is yes. It is generally recognized that two nursing methods are available to newborns—*expression* involves pressing the nipple against the roof of the mouth with the tongue and squeezing milk out of it, and *suction* involves creating a partial vacuum by reducing the pressure inside the mouth and thus pulling the milk from the nipple.

Further Developments

Babies in Diapers, Media Viewing, and Cognitive and Language Outcomes?

Do you watch television or play DVDs in your home with babies or young children present? As you hold your infant in your arms, are you watching *Monday Night Football? The Nightly News?* or *Desperate Housewives?* Or are you watching *Blues Clues, Dora the Explorer, Teletubbies,* or Bill Cosby's newest venture, *Little Bill?* What do you know about the effects of a steady "diet" of heavy television viewing (and hearing) on the cognitive and language development of infants under age 2? Do you think that your child's television viewing will enhance your child's language ability or comprehension? Are we placing our infants and toddlers at risk by saturating their home environments with home theaters and large HDTV screens with surround sound systems (Anderson & Pempek, 2005)?

Caution: Baby on Board

The American Academy of Pediatrics (AAP) (1999) recommends that caregivers not expose children under age 2 to media presented on electronic screens—for example, television, videos, DVDs, CDs, computer games, or large-screen movies. This policy was the result of empirical findings in the 1990s on the harmful effects of aggression and violence in media on older children, evidence that children have less interaction with caregivers when media is used in the home or in child-care-settings, and evidence that more children are obese due to sedentary behaviors such as watching TV and playing video/computer games. Nevertheless, since this recommendation, more television programs, home videos,

and computer software are being produced for infants and toddlers, such as *Baby Einstein* products. Until recently, few researchers were investigating the developmental impact of media exposure in infants from birth to age 2.

This Generation's Pathway to Communication Is Electronic

Babies typically learn language and vocabulary from such "environmental stimuli" as parents, siblings, other family members, caregivers, and television or other media (Shonkoff & Phillips, 2000). Whereas infants from earlier generations were introduced to language through adult and sibling communication and print media, the current generation of babies is being raised with a full range of electronic media. Woodward and Gridina (2000) surveyed more than 1,000 parents nationally in 1999 and found nearly all homes had two or more TVs, and nearly half had a VCR and DVD, video game equipment, a computer, and an Internet subscription.

What Parents Report

In a national phone survey in 2003, more than 1,000 parents revealed that infants and toddlers are spending an *average* of more than 2 hours daily with screens (television, video, or computer). Responses ranged from no media viewing to as much as 18 hours a day of infant TV viewing. Surprisingly, more than one-fourth of American children under age 2 have a television in their bedrooms, and *two-thirds* of these infants watch TV *every day.* Fewer parents are monitoring children's TV viewing time or content; only about 20 percent of parents believe their children watch too much TV, and they believe educational programming is good for their baby's intellectual development (see Figure 5.1) (Rideout, Vandewater, & Wartella, 2003).

Yet critical questions remain about what infants and toddlers are able to learn from television in a home environment or whether television affects infant communication abilities. In Linebarger and Walker's (2005) longitudinal study with a modest sample of 51 infant participants, parents kept a daily log of infant viewing patterns, and the infants were assessed on various measures of cognition, vocabulary, and expressive language. Parents reported that infants first showed interest in watching television at 9 months of age, with an acceleration of viewing time at 18 months (1½ years). Television viewing increased with the child's age, but viewing child entertainment programs and adult programming were not significantly related to vocabulary growth (expressive language production). By age 30 months (2½ years), the average child had a parent-reported production of 438 words.

Caution: Baby on Board More young children from birth to age 2 are being exposed to electronic media despite the recommendation of the American Academy of Pediatrics that caregivers not expose children under age 2 to media presented on electronic screens.

continued

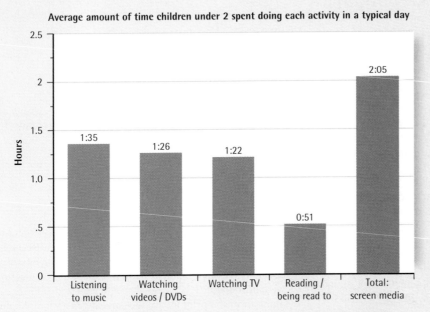

Average amount of time children under 2 spent doing each activity in a typical day

NOTE: The sample of children under 2 who use a computer or play video games in a typical day is too small for reliable data on time spent with those media.

FIGURE 5.1 Daily Activities and Infants Results of a recent parent survey revealed that children under age 2 spend about 2 hours per day, on average, viewing and listening to electronic media on screens. Some parents report no television viewing, whereas some parents report infant viewing up to 18 hours per day.
Source: From Rideout, V. J., Vandewater, E. A., & Wartella, E. A., *Zero to Six: Electronic Media in the Lives of Infants, Toddlers and Preschoolers* (#3378), The Henry J. Kaiser Family Foundation, Fall 2003. This information was reprinted with permission of The Henry J. Kaiser Family Foundation. The Kaiser Family Foundation, based in Menlo Park, California, is a non-profit, independent national health care philanthropy and is not associated with Kaiser Permanente or Kaiser Industries.

Program Content Matters

Children who watched *Dora the Explorer* and *Blue's Clues* and those who watched *Arthur* and *Clifford* used more single- and multiple-word utterances compared with nonviewers. Children watching *Sesame Street* and *Teletubbies* produced fewer single- and multiple-word utterances. Watching Disney videos was unrelated to single- or multiple-word utterances. Each of these TV programs has specific strategies embedded into curricula to inhibit or promote expressive language and vocabulary. For example, *Blue's Clues* and *Dora the Explorer* have characters speaking directly to the child, actively eliciting participation, labeling objects, and providing opportunities for the child to respond—thus promoting expressive language and vocabulary growth. *Arthur, Clifford,* and *Dragon Tales* use a visually appealing storybook format with vocabulary and definitions, and there are already known positive relationships between vocabulary and language production and reading storybooks. Viewing *Teletubbies* was negatively associated with vocabulary acquisition and use of expressive language. Thus, appropriate program content matters.

Foreground Versus Background Television

A few researchers make a critical distinction between foreground and background television. *Foreground television* is programming in which children attend in a sustained manner; it is designed for young children, and it is presumably comprehensible to young children, though *looking at a TV* and *comprehending* are two different things. Foreground television for young children is likely to have lively music and bright colors. With *background television,* young children pay little overt attention—it is not produced for chil-

dren, and it is mainly incomprehensible to them. Much of the TV that is on in most homes is background television to a young child, and a large percentage of American infants under age 2 are exposed to many hours of background television. Very young children initially pay little attention to televised programs, and the amount of TV that is in the foreground increases with their development (Anderson & Pempek, 2005). Additional studies found that constant background television diminished both lengths of infant play times and the degree of focused attention during play times, and that interactions between parents and children are substantially decreased by more than 20 percent in the presence of background television (Anderson & Pempek, 2005).

Video Viewing Deficits

Anderson and Pempek (2005) conducted a review of the research literature on children's television viewing, comprehension, and learning and found that 12- to 30-month-olds have little difficulty imitating live demonstrations but have much more difficulty imitating a video demonstration. Three-year-olds do well on a hiding-search task viewed on a video, but 2-year-olds do poorly on such an object-retrieval task. Children 2 years and older can learn vocabulary from television and from video. Ten- and 12-month-olds exposed to an actress in a video talking in both a positive way and then a fearful way about certain objects became fearful of specific objects. Overall, infants have great difficulty learning from video programming.

An Important Case Study

It is known already that caregivers cannot rely solely on television programming to teach language to children. In a classic study by Sachs, Bard, and Johnson (1981), a 3-year-old boy with deaf parents was exposed to the English language only by television. By age 3 he had acquired some vocabulary but his grammar was dysfunctional.

Parental Factors

In the 2003 Kaiser Family Foundation survey with more than 1,000 parents, those with less education were more likely to have heavy television viewing with children in the home, and parents with more education were more likely to have books available at home, to engage in reading, and to value reading (Anand & Krosnick, 2005). Lower-income households exposed children to television for greater periods of time, perhaps owing to having less income for alternative entertainment. Preschool boys were more likely to watch TV, play video games, and play computer games more than preschool girls. Children of married parents watched less TV than did the children of single parents, but children and parents sometimes watch TV together (Anand & Krosnick, 2005).

This research itself is in its infancy, and more longitudinal studies need to be conducted with baby participants.

Sameroff devised an experimental nipple that permitted him to regulate the supply of milk an infant received. He provided one group of babies with milk only when they used the expressive method (squeezing the nipple); he gave the second group milk only when they used the suction method.

He found that the infants adapted their responses according to which technique was reinforced. For instance, the group that was given milk when they used the expressive method diminished their suction responses—indeed, in many cases they abandoned the suction method during the training period. In a second experiment Sameroff (1968) was able to induce the babies, again through reinforcement, to express milk at one of two different pressure levels. These results suggest that learning can occur among 2- to 5-day-old, full-term infants. Newborns can also categorize varieties of speech rhythm and can discriminate sounds between two languages (Ramus, 2002). There appears to be a link between rhythm, phonemes (basic units of sound such as *ba*), syllable structure, and eventual word learning (Houston, Jusczyk, & Jusczyk, 2003; Ramus et al., 2000). When we first hear a foreign language, we cannot detect the boundaries between words. *Itisasifeverythingrunstogether.* (It's as if everything runs together.) Yet we perceive word boundaries when listening to a language *we have learned*. This is part of the pacing and rhythm of an infant's native language (see Table 5.1 and Figure 5.2 on page 162).

Question

In what ways have researchers demonstrated that a fetus and a neonate can learn?

Piaget: The Sensorimotor Period

As we saw in Chapter 2, the Swiss developmental psychologist Jean Piaget contributed a great deal to our understanding of how children think, reason, and solve problems. Perhaps more than any other person, Piaget was responsible for the rapid growth of interest in cognitive development over the past 50 years. In many respects the breadth, imagination, and originality of his work overshadowed other research in the field.

Piaget charted a developmental sequence of stages during which the child constructs increasingly complex notions of the world, and he described how the child acts at each level and how this activity leads to the next level. His most detailed analysis was of the first two years of life, which he calls the "sensorimotor period." In Piaget's terminology, *sensorimotor* refers to the coordination of motor activities with sensory inputs (perceptions), which is the major task of the **sensorimotor period.** In this period of development, babies develop the capacity to look at what they are listening to and learn to guide their grasping and walking by visual, auditory, or tactile cues. In sum, the infant comes to integrate the motor and perceptual systems. This integration lays the foundation for the development of new adaptive behaviors.

A second characteristic of the sensorimotor period is that babies develop the capacity to view the external world as a permanent place. Infants fashion a notion of **object permanence**—they come to view a thing as having a reality of its own that extends beyond their immediate perception of it. As adults, we take this notion for granted. However, infants do not necessarily do so during the first six to nine months in the sensorimotor period. Sometime after six to nine months, a baby becomes capable of searching for an object that an adult has hidden under a cloth. The child will search for it on the basis of information about where the object went. In so doing, the infant understands that the object exists even when it cannot be seen. This developing ability provides a fixed point for constructing conceptions of space, time, and cause.

According to Piaget, a third characteristic of the sensorimotor period is the inability of infants to represent the world to themselves internally. They are limited to the immediate here and now. Because they

Table 5.1 How Do Infants Learn to Distinguish the Sounds of Language?

Researchers believe young infants can distinguish the patterns of sounds within words and at the ends of words. The waveform below is "Where are the silences between words?" At the Infant Learning Lab, Psychology Department at University of Wisconsin, Madison, the infant sits in the parent's lap in a small soundproof room and listens to such sounds playing from audio speakers. The researchers focus on what learning processes underlie the acquisition of words (tone, rhythm, sequence, memory, and word segmentation). The gray lines indicate silent points in the phrase, often occurring in the middle of a word and not between words. Note the silent point in the middle of the word "between" and no silent point at the boundary of "between" and "words." You can hear this waveform at www.waisman.wisc.edu/infantlearning/infantlang.html.

How Do Infants Learn to Distinguish the Sounds of Language? Experimental setup: Rachel Robertson testing a baby.

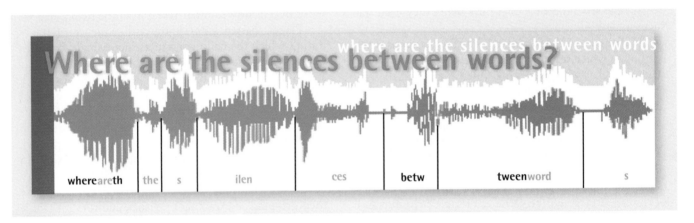

FIGURE 5.2 How Do Human Infants Learn to Use Language?

cannot fashion symbolic mental representations of the world, they "know" the world only through their own perceptions and their own actions on it. For example, children in the sensorimotor stage know food only as something they can eat and manipulate with their fingers, and they cannot conceive of it apart from these activities. Infants have a mental picture of food only insofar as actual sensory input reveals the food's existence. This mental picture disappears when the sensory input ceases.

According to Piaget, infants are unable to form a static mental image of food "in their heads" in the absence of the actual visual display. "Out of sight, out of mind" is an appropriate description of how the infant perceives the external world during the sensorimotor stage. The infant enters the sensorimotor period with more than 70 genetically given reflexes (for instance, give any healthy infant an object and the infant will grab it, and it often ends up in the child's mouth).

In sum, during the sensorimotor period infants coordinate the ways they interact with their environment, give the environment permanence, and begin to "know" the environment, although their knowledge of the environment is limited to their sensory interactions with it. The child then enters into the next developmental period ready to develop language and other symbolic ways of representing the world.

Sensorimotor Development and Craniosacral Therapy The Western understanding of the craniosacral system comes from ancient traditions of healing massage in India, China, the Middle East, and North America. Underlying an infant's ability to develop sensorimotor skills is a critical physiological system in the body called the **craniosacral system**—a closed system involving the pumping or inflow and outflow of cerebrospinal fluid within the membranes around the brain and spinal cord. *Cerebrospinal fluid (CSF)* circulates between cells of the brain and spinal cord and fills the spaces between the cells (*neurons,* as you recall from general psychology). This fluid serves several vital functions: (1) helps the brain float to reduce gravity effects; (2) serves as a shock absorber for sudden movements of or blow to the cranium (the bony portion of the skull enclosing the brain); (3) provides nutrients to the brain and spinal cord and pituitary and pineal glands; (4) washes away metabolic waste products and toxic substances; (5) lubricates between cells of the CNS to prevent friction or damage to cell walls; and (6) helps to maintain the proper concentration of electrolyte substances needed for creating and transmitting nerve impulses that allow for cognitive, emotional, and physical functioning (Upledger, 2004). The volume of fluid within the craniosacral system flows in a constant but rhythmic cycle. Cranial bones make minute adjustments to allow for this rhythmic flow.

The natural birth process allows for a gradual delivery with regular uterine contractions that slowly move the fetus's body and head into changing positions for normal birth. However, injury to a newborn's skull, face, or neck, prior to birth, during birth, or after birth can restrict the natural rhythmic flow of the cerebrospinal fluid—creating excessive or restricted fluid pressure on various areas of the delicate brain or spinal cord. Dr. John Upledger (2004, 2003a, 2003b), a doctor of osteopathy (DO) and professor of biomechanics, discovered that infants may experience craniosacral problems at birth who are born quickly, who are breech birth (feet first), who become "stuck" in the birth canal, who are manually pulled or pushed from the mother's body once the head appears, who are pulled from the body using forceps or vacuum extraction (a suctioning device placed on the fetus's head to make delivery occur faster), who are delivered by C-section, who experience oxygen de-

privation at birth, or whose mouth and nose are heavily suctioned after birth (Upledger, 2003a, b). Neonate cranial bone plates also overlap to allow for easier passage through the birth canal (have you noticed the "pointy head" appearance of most newborns?). This overlap should correct itself within a few days, but in some babies it does not. Other babies that have craniosacral problems are those born with abnormal head shapes, spinal, pelvic, and hip problems.

Here are some symptoms that appear in infants and children that *may be* helped by *craniosacral therapy (CST):* feeding problems (not being able to use the sucking reflex), colic and excessive crying, digestive problems including bowel problems, restlessness, headaches, sinus and ear congestion, motor-coordination impairments, scoliosis (curvature) of the spine, seizure disorder, and in older children learning problems, including attention-deficit hyperactivity disorder, hyperkinetic behaviors, and dyslexia ("Craniosacral Therapy for Children," 2004; Upledger, 2003a, 2001). (CST is known to help a wide range of medical problems associated with pain and dysfunction in adults as well.) Using a hands-on, light-touch method of examining the skull, the base of the skull, the back and pelvis, a skilled therapist monitors the rhythm of the craniosacral system to detect potential restrictions and imbalances of the brain and spinal cord (see Table 5.2 and Figure 5.3).

The goal of craniosacral therapy is to have each child reach his or her optimal functional state—allowing for full sensorimotor development. Ideally, craniosacral therapy would be carried out in the delivery room or within the first few days of life. And doctors of osteopathy, physical therapists, massage therapists, and chiropractors are learning the light-touch massage techniques to help babies and children develop normally. These

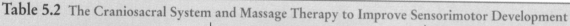

Table 5.2 The Craniosacral System and Massage Therapy to Improve Sensorimotor Development

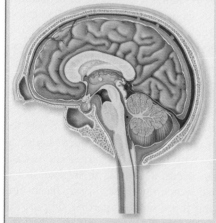

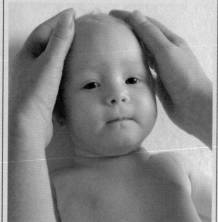

CST facilitates processes that enhance the body's ability for natural healing. Therapy focuses on removing restrictive forces and obstacles to the craniosacral system. Improving fluid motion and exchange within the craniosacral system enhances function of the brain, spinal cord, autonomic nervous system, visual, auditory, olfactory, and gustatory systems, and the immune system.
Source: Upledger, J.E. (2004, August). A look inside the craniosacral system and how CST helps. *Massage Today,* 4(8).

FIGURE 5.3 The Craniosacral System | Craniosacral Therapy (CST)

professionals often work together as part of an early intervention team.

Neo- and Post-Piagetian Research

Piaget's work has stimulated other psychologists to investigate children's cognitive development. They have been intrigued by the idea that infants do not think about objects and events in the same ways adults do, and they have particularly studied object permanence in infants (Johnson et al., 2003). This ongoing work is revising and refining Piaget's insights.

For example, researchers have found that infants possess a set of object search skills more sophisticated than Piaget had imagined (Rochat & Striano, 1998). Many of the errors youngsters make in searching for items do not reflect an absence of basic concepts of objects and space—even by 4 months of age they might understand that an object continues to exist when their view of it is blocked, but they might not yet be capable of coordinating their movements to search for it (Luo et al., 2003).

Playing Is Learning Moreover, developmental psychologists find that children do not develop an interest in objects and object skills in a social vacuum. Rather, caretakers can set the stage for youngsters by "playing" with them, giving babies clues as to what they should do and when they should do it (Bornstein & O'Reilly, 1993; Bruner, 1991). Additionally, by playing with infants, parents provide experiences that youngsters cannot generate by themselves (Vygotsky, 1978). Yet more contemporary parents are substituting media viewing (television, video, and computers) for play time (Anand & Krosnick, 2005).

In the course of such activities, infants acquire and refine their capacities for intersubjectivity, so that by the end of the first year they share attention, emotional feelings, and intentions with others. All the while infants gain a sense of their society's culture and gain some of the skills essential to living in that culture. Caregivers—the curators of culture—transmit the knowledge, attitudes, values, and behaviors essential for effective participation in society, and they help to gradually transform infants into genuine social beings capable of manipulating objects and acting in concert with others. In playing with their youngsters, caretakers provide sociocultural guidance for the children's later cognitive and language performance (Rogoff, 2003). However, this is often not the case with youngsters whose mothers suffer from clinical depression.

Consequences of Maternal Depression Clinically depressed mothers might have such debilitating symptoms that they are virtually incapable of fulfilling their children's needs. Clinical depression is an emotional disorder characterized by a mood drop that can last for months, or

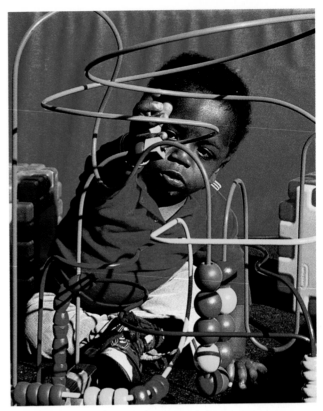

Play Activities Are Essential for Learning Infants coordinate their sensory and motor capabilities during play, and television viewing is not a substitute for play time.

even years. As depression deepens, it commonly involves insomnia, disinterest in work, low energy, loss of appetite, reduced sexual desire, persistent sadness, hopeless feelings, and profound overall emotional despair; even routine tasks become difficult to perform. Additionally, many depressed people report difficulty concentrating, remembering things, and getting their thoughts together. Some also suffer considerable anxiety as part of their depression. Many factors have been implicated in clinical depression. In some women, depression is complicated by drug abuse. Postpartum depression occurs in at least 10 percent of U.S. women, but the rate may be as high as 20 percent. The rate for women with a history of postpartum depression is 25 percent or higher (Clay & Seehusen, 2004).

The children of depressed mothers are susceptible to developmental deficits due to disturbances in the mother-infant interaction (Milgrom, Westley, & Gemmill, 2004). Health professionals report that depressed mothers often appear sad, are given to frequent sighs, fail to interact playfully with their youngsters, seem insensitive to their babies' needs, and focus their gaze downward. Impoverished women with newborns, recent immigrant women, and those without partner support are at a high risk for postpartum depression ("Shades of the Baby Blues," 2004).

Because depressed mothers have a reduced capacity for caregiving, nurturing, and stimulating their infants, their youngsters tend to lag behind in their cognitive adaptations, including emotional, language, and social development. Kaplan, Bachorowski, and Zarlengo-Strouse (1999) observed that mothers suffering from depression are unlikely to use child-directed speech—that is, the sing-song melodic speech considered to be the primary vocal method of engaging and maintaining infant attention. Rather, depressed mothers tend to talk to their infants in a monotone that does not engage the infant's attention.

The babies of depressed women are more withdrawn, unresponsive, and inattentive than other youngsters. They may cry and fuss a good deal, appear apathetic and listless, have problems sleeping and feeding, and fail to grow normally, sometimes diagnosed as **failure to thrive (FTT).** Current thinking about FTT is that there is problematic mother-infant interaction, especially less touching between mother and child. Some researchers suggest, "It is possible that the behavioral characteristics of the infant with failure-to-thrive may be related to underlying physiologic response patterns, specifically, activity of the autonomic nervous system" (Feldman et al., 2004; Steward, Moser, & Ryan-Wenger, 2001, p. 162). Dawson and colleagues (1999) studied patterns of brain activity of a control group of 13- to 15-month-old nondepressed infants with a sample of infants of depressed mothers. In a variety of situations—including interactions with nondepressed adults—the infants of depressed mothers exhibited reduced relative left frontal lobe activity, typically associated with the expression of positive emotions. A longitudinal study of more than 11,000 infants in Great Britain revealed an association between parents' shorter height and babies' slow weight gain, and infants born in a fourth or subsequent pregnancy were twice as likely to exhibit failure to thrive (Blair et al., 2004).

Matters can be complicated by a mother's disciplinary ineptness. For example, depressed mothers might alternately ignore their children and lash out at them with strict prohibitions. Such inconsistent behavior is baffling to youngsters, and they might respond by being negative, challenging limits, resenting punishment, and becoming unusually argumentative. A vicious cycle is likely to ensue wherein this difficult behavior reinforces the mother's depression and sense of parental inadequacy. A study has found that long-term effects are possible if the depression is chronic, the child is a male born at risk, or the family suffers other social risk factors (Kurstjens & Wolke, 2001). Clinical depression is usually a treatable disorder that responds to antidepressant medication and other psychiatric interventions. However, before depression can be treated effectively, it must first be recognized and brought to the attention of appropriate medical personnel who provide close monitoring of medication effects and make recommendations for skilled psychotherapy.

Questions

Why does Piaget call infancy the sensorimotor period, and what are an infant's major cognitive accomplishments during the first two years of life? What is craniosacral therapy and what are some potential health benefits for young children? How does a mother's depression affect an infant's cognitive development?

Bruner on Modes of Cognitive Representation

One of the first U.S. psychologists to appreciate the importance of Piaget's work was Jerome S. Bruner. Bruner is a distinguished psychologist in his own right who has served as president of the American Psychological Association. Many of his research papers show a strong Piagetian influence, especially in the way he treats the stages of cognitive development.

Through the years, however, Bruner and Piaget developed differences of opinion about the roots and nature of intellectual growth. Most particularly, the two disagreed over Bruner's (1970) view that "the foundations of any subject may be taught to anybody at any age in some form." Piaget, in contrast, held to a rigorous stage approach, in which knowledge of certain subjects can be gained only when all the components of that knowledge are present and properly developed.

One of Bruner's primary contributions to our understanding of cognitive development concerns the changes that occur in children's favored modes for representing the world as they grow older (Bruner, 1990; Bruner, Oliver, & Greenfield, 1966). According to Bruner, at first (during the time period that Piaget called the sensorimotor period) the representative process is *enactive:* Children represent the world through their motor acts. In the preschool and kindergarten years, *ikonic representation* prevails: Children use mental images or pictures that are closely linked to perception. In the middle school years, the emphasis shifts to *symbolic representation:* Children use arbitrary and socially standardized representations of things; this enables them to internally manipulate the symbols that are characteristic of abstract and logical thought. Thus, according to Bruner, we "know" something in three ways:

- Through doing it (enactive)
- Through a picture or image of it (ikonic)
- Through some symbolic means such as language (symbolic)

Take, for instance, our "knowing" a knot. We can know the knot by tying it; we can have a mental image of the knot as an object on the order of either a pretzel or "bunny ears" (or a mental "motion picture" of the knot being formed); and we can represent a knot linguistically by combining four alphabetical letters, *k-n-o-t* (or by linking utterances in sentences to describe the process of tying string). Through these three such general means, humans increase their ability to achieve and use knowledge.

Continuity in Cognitive Development from Infancy

Psychologists have long been interested in knowing whether mental competence and intelligence later in life can be predicted from cognitive performance in infancy. Until relatively recently, psychologists believed that there was little continuity between early and later capabilities. But now they are increasingly concluding that individual differences in mental performance in infancy are, to a moderate extent, developmentally continuous across childhood and perhaps beyond (Cronin & Mandich, 2005). Therefore, prevention and early intervention agencies and policies have been established, and efforts for those infants with cognitive and language delays should begin during these early months of life. The concept of cognitive continuity has implications for social policy and future research (Dawson, Ashman, & Carver, 2000).

Decrement and Recovery in Attentiveness Information-processing models of intelligence have contributed to this reassessment. For people to mentally represent and process information concerning the world about them, they must first pay attention to various aspects of their environment. Two components of attention seem most indicative of intelligence in youngsters:

- *Decrement of attention*—losing interest in watching an object or event that is unchanging
- *Recovery of attention*—regaining interest when something new happens

Youngsters who tire more quickly when looking at or hearing the same thing are more efficient processors of information. So are those who prefer the novel over the familiar. These infants typically like more complex tasks, show advanced sensorimotor development, explore their environment rapidly, play in relatively sophisticated ways, and solve problems rapidly. Similarly, the rapidness with which adults learn something is associated with measures of their intelligence. Given equivalent opportunities, more intelligent people learn more than less intelligent people in the same amount of time. Not surprisingly, then, psychologists are finding that decrement and recovery of attention seem to predict childhood cognitive competence more accurately than do more traditional tests of infant development.

The patterns children reveal in attending to information reflect their cognitive capabilities and, more particularly, their ability to construct workable *schemas* (à la Piaget) of what they see and hear. As Harriet L. Rheingold (1985) points out, mental development proceeds through transformations of novelty into familiarity. Each thing in the environment begins as something new, and so development progresses as infants turn something new into something known. In turn, once you know something, it provides a context for recognizing what is new, and so the known provides the foundation for further mental development. Both the familiar and the novel, then, compel attraction and are reciprocal processes central to lifetime adaptation (see the *More Information You Can Use* box, "Reducing Retardation Rates and Boosting Babies' Brain Power").

Questions

Do you agree with Bruner that "the foundation of any subject may be taught to anybody at any age in some form"? And if that's the case, shouldn't all parents make efforts to boost their babies' brain power as early as possible? What research and diagnostic evidence supports early intervention efforts for those infants with physical, cognitive, and language delays?

Language and Thought

Humans are set apart from other animals by their possession of a highly developed system of language communication. This system allows them to acquire and transmit the knowledge and ideas provided by the culture in which they live. To be sure, a number of scientists claim that skills characteristic of the use of language have been developed in a dozen or so chimpanzees (Savage-Rumbaugh et al., 1993). But although the skills exhibited by the chimps are clearly related to human skills, they are hardly equivalent to our intricate and subtle language capacity. And the methods by which chimps typically must be trained are quite different from the spontaneous ways in which children learn a language. Apes learn to deal with signs sluggishly and often only after being plied with bananas, cola, and M&Ms (Gould, 1983).

Language is a structured system of sound patterns (words and sentences) with socially standardized meanings. Language provides a set of symbols that rather thoroughly catalog the objects, events, and processes in the human environment (DeVito, 1970). Humans process and interpret language in the left cerebral cortex (see Figure 5.4).

More Information You Can Use

Reducing Retardation Rates and Boosting Babies' Brain Power

At one time it was thought that the brain is hardwired and that its wiring cannot be changed. However, a mounting body of evidence now suggests that enriched environments can produce physical changes in the developing brain. Imaging studies using techniques like PET scans reveal a positive correlation between positive environmental changes and an increase in synaptic connections among brain cells. "Pushing certain buttons in the brain" through enrichment experiences—good nutrition, toys, playmates, learning opportunities, and parental counseling—can prevent a substantial amount of mental retardation and developmental disability: Early intervention can make the future brighter for many youngsters whose development otherwise would be stunted (Guralnick, 1998).

These findings have led many parents to wonder if they too can boost their baby's intellectual development. Psychologists have long noted that good parenting can have profound and positive consequences for youngsters (Guralnick, 1998). The emotional quality of the parent-infant relationship certainly plays a key part in children's early cognitive and language competence. Parental behaviors affect infants' competence in a number of ways (Olson, Bates, & Bayles, 1984). First, children's learning is directly enhanced if parents provide them with immediate positive feedback when they say or do novel, creative, or adaptive things. Second, children's developmental competence is encouraged when parents provide a nonrestrictive environment that allows them to engage in exploratory behavior. And third, children who are securely attached to their caretakers are more apt than others to undertake competent exploration of their surroundings. Effective parents are aware of their children's developmental needs and guide their own behavior to meet these needs.

These findings have had both positive and negative influences. On the positive side, the research results encourage interventions with infants at risk for delayed cognitive development in areas such as speech and language development. One study in the United Kingdom looked at reading and language impairments of twins from impoverished homes. The key interventions for remediation

Assisting Youngsters Who Have Developmental Delays A new and exciting body of scientific evidence (including brain scanning, such as PET scans) suggests that the connection between the "brain" and the "mind" is a two-way street. For instance, scientists have found that behavioral cognitive therapy techniques not only help some participants with their psychological problems but also change their brains' physical structures. In brief, participants who learn via a series of behavioral techniques to resist various destructive urges end up altering their brains. Such evidence has encouraged others to pursue new research and avenues for assisting children with developmental delays. Modeling behavior helps this child learn appropriate mouth movements for better expressive language skills.

continued

The Functional Importance of Language

Language makes two vital contributions to human life: It enables us to communicate with one another (interindividual communication), and it facilitates individual thinking (intraindividual communication). The first contribution, called **communication,** is the process by which people transmit information, ideas, attitudes, and emotions to one another. This feature of language allows human beings to coordinate complex group activities. They fit their developing lines of activity to the developing actions of others on the basis of the "messages" they provide one another. Thus, language provides the foundation for family and for economic, political, religious, and educational institutions—indeed, for society itself.

"Oh, yes, indeed. We all keep a sharp eye out for those little clues that seem to whisper 'law' or 'medicine.'"

include such strategies such as elicited imitation and modeling (Bishop & Leonard, 2000). On the negative side, the research findings have caused some parents to indulge in what educational psychologists call "hot-housing" or trying to "jump-start" youngsters toward success. The image of a toddler calling out "Five!" when peering at five red dots on a white flash card or reading aloud from *The Cat in the Hat* brings joy to the hearts of many parents. Yet too many parents are pushing very young children too hard to gain academically oriented skills. Thus far, the only proven beneficiaries of preschool programs have been culturally deprived youngsters. Many children who are pressured to learn through inappropriate methods begin to dislike learning.

Young children learn best from their own experience—from self-directed activity, exploring real objects, talking to people, and solving real-life problems, such as how to balance a stack of blocks. And they benefit from having stories read to them on a regular basis. When caretakers intrude in children's self-directed learning and insist on their own priorities for their learning, such as math, reading, or violin, they interfere with children's own impulses and initiative. Parents and caretakers, then, must consider the style of learning appropriate for the very young (Elkind, 1987).

Language has enabled humans, alone of all animals, to transcend biological evolution. Evolutionary processes took millions of years to fashion amphibians—creatures that can live on land or in water. In contrast, a second kind of "amphibians"—astronauts who can live in the earth's atmosphere or in the space outside it—have "evolved" in a comparatively short time (Brown & Herrnstein, 1975). But in the second case, human anatomy did not alter so that it could survive in space—rather, humans increased their knowledge to the point where they could employ it to complement and supplement their anatomy; in this manner they made themselves spaceworthy.

The second contribution of language is that it facilitates *thought* and other cognitive processes. Language enables us to encode our experiences by assigning names to them. It provides us with concepts by which we dissect the world around us and categorize new information. Thus, language helps us to partition the environment into manageable areas relevant to our concerns. Language also allows us to deal with past experiences and to anticipate future experiences through reference. It enlarges the scope of our environment and experience. This second function, the relation of language to thought, has been the subject of intense debate. Let us examine each of these functions more closely.

Thought Shapes Language

Those who hold that thought shapes language argue that thought takes place whether or not there is language. They believe that words are necessary only for conveying thoughts to others. For instance, some types of

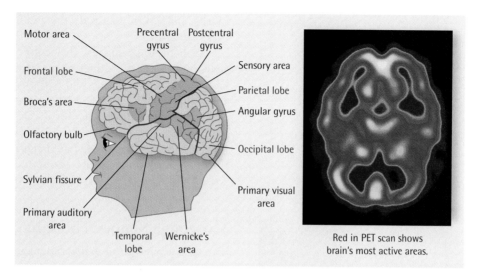

FIGURE 5.4 Where and How Babies Process Sound and Language The drawing at the left shows the left hemisphere of the cerebral cortex. The temporal lobes of each hemisphere interpret the sounds heard by each ear. Often one side is more "dominant" in hearing than the other, though both sides hear a given sound. For most individuals speech-language is located in Broca's and Wernicke's areas. The child is also learning language by observing a speaker's mouth and facial expressions and is also using the visual/occipital cortex. It really becomes a whole brain effort! Note the full brain involvement in language on the PET scan to the right.

An infant's experience with hearing the sounds of a language actively shapes the physical structure of the brain. After a few years of experience hearing one language, a child is able to distinguish the sounds typically heard and loses the ability to distinguish those sounds not used often. In Asian cultures, the sounds for *L* and *R* are likely to give older youth and adults difficulty in distinguishing those sounds. PET scans have shown that such sounds are decoded in distinctly separate parts of the brains of those of us who speak English but in the same part of the brain for those from Asian cultures.

thought are visual images and "feelings." You become aware of language as a vehicle for conveying thought when someone asks you to describe something—your mother, the view from your room, the main street in your hometown. You seek to translate a mental picture into words. But you may find that the task of verbally describing images is complex and difficult.

Piaget (1952, 1962) took the view that structured language presupposes the prior development of other kinds of mental representation. On the basis of his studies, Piaget concluded that language has only a limited role in a young child's mental activity. According to Piaget, children form mental images of objects (water, food, a ball) and events (drinking, sucking, holding) that are based on mental reproduction or imitation, not on word labels. Thus, the child's task in acquiring words is to map language onto her preexisting concepts.

In our discussion in the pages ahead, we will see that Piaget oversimplifies matters. In some areas, representation does precede language. For instance, William Zachry (1978) finds that solid progress in mental representation is necessary for some forms of language production. He suggests that children gain the ability to represent motor schemes (certain generalized activities) internally as images. Thus, the various actions associated with bottles would come to be represented by such mental pictures as holding a bottle, sucking a bottle, pouring from a bottle,

and so on. Later, the child comes to represent the "bottle activities" by the word bottle. The word bottle then becomes a semantic "marker" that represents the qualities associated with a bottle—holdable, suckable, pourable, and so on. In this matter, Zachry says, words come to function as semantic markers for mental pictures.

A review of recent research found that young children have a tendency to search for hidden, nonobvious features when learning the meaning of words (Gelman, 2004). More specifically, children seem predisposed to "whole object" meanings for nouns—they assume that a new noun refers to an entire object rather than to one of its parts. By way of illustration, consider the noun *dog.* Youngsters must learn that dog can refer both to a specific object (for instance, Fido) as well as to the category Dog, yet the word *dog* does not apply to individual aspects of the object (for instance, its nose or tail); relationships between the object and other objects (for example, between a dog and its toy); or the object's behavior (for instance, the dog's eating, barking, or sleeping). Were children to weigh these and countless other possible meanings before arriving at the correct mapping of the word *dog,* they would be overwhelmed by an unmanageable sea of dog-related inputs.

Youngsters need not follow such a laborious route. They bring a bias in thinking with them, one that allows "fast mapping"—the capturing of the basic elements

Acquiring Language An infant learns language from a person speaking directly to him, often saying only one or a few words with exaggerated expression or "parentese," and typically within about 8 to 10 inches of the child's face. When the child makes an effort to repeat the sound, the caregiver is likely to reward the child with a big smile and sounds of pleasure, such as "Good girl!" Some theorists suggest the child already has an internal understanding of the word, whereas others say the child has to learn the word first and then develops a concept for the word. Before 1 year of age, infants demonstrate receptive language skills before being able to speak that word. Ask a child this age to "Go get the ball," and typically he goes to get the ball.

of an experience to the exclusion of other experiences. In addition, children are cognitively biased toward an assumption that words refer to mutually exclusive categories (Taylor & Gelman, 1989). So we see that some aspects of linguistic development are linked to a pre-existing level of conceptual development.

It also seems that infants as young as 4 months of age possess the ability to partition the color spectrum into four basic hues—blue, green, yellow, and red. For example, infants respond differently to two wavelengths selected from adjacent adult hue categories, such as "blue" at 480 millimicrons and "green" at 510 millimicrons. However, infants do not respond differently to two wavelengths selected from the same adult hue category although separated by a similar physical distance (30 millimicrons), such as "blue" at 450 and "blue" at 480 millimicrons. It seems, then, that the mental representations of infants are organized into blue, green, yellow, and red—rather than as exact wavelength codes, which, for adults, makes up the color spectrum (Bornstein &

Marks, 1982). Only later do the children come to name these categories.

Such findings suggest that color organization precedes and is not a product of the categories (the verbal labels *blue, green, yellow,* and *red*) provided by language and culture (Soja, 1994). Additional research confirms that infants spontaneously form categories during the *prelinguistic period* (Roberts, 1988). In some respects, then, children's knowledge of language depends on a prior mastery of concepts about the world to which words will refer (Coldren & Colombo, 1994).

Language Shapes Thought

The second viewpoint is that language develops with, at the same time as, or even prior to the development of thought. According to this viewpoint, language shapes thought. This theory follows in the traditions of George Herbert Mead (1934), Benjamin L. Whorf (1956), and Lev Vygotsky (1962).

This perspective emphasizes the part that concepts play in our thinking. By partitioning stimuli into classifiable units, and into areas relevant to our concerns, life becomes more manageable. Through **conceptualization**—grouping perceptions into categories on the basis of certain similarities—children and adults alike can identify and classify informational input. Without the ability to categorize, life would seem chaotic. By using categories, adults and infants "tune out" certain stimuli and "tune in" others (Needham & Baillargeon, 1998). This allows us to view an object as being the same despite the fact that it varies from perspective to perspective and from moment to moment. And people are able to treat two different but similar objects as equivalent—as being the same kind of thing. Categorization, and making the mental leap from the specific to the general, allows for more advanced cognitive thinking. Significantly, researchers find that language increases the time infants look at objects beyond the time that actual verbal labeling occurs, suggesting infants are biased to look at objects in the presence of language (Baldwin & Markman, 1989).

Concepts also perform a second service. They enable individuals to go beyond the immediate information provided to them. People can mentally manipulate concepts and imaginatively link them to fashion new adaptations. This attribute of concepts allows humans to make additional inferences about the unobserved properties of objects and events (Bruner, Goodnow, & Austin, 1956). Humans have an advantage over other animals in that we can use words in the conceptualization process. Some social and behavioral scientists claim that the activity of naming, or verbally labeling, offers three advantages:

- Facilitating thought by producing linguistic symbols for integrating ideas

- Expediting memory storage and retrieval via a linguistic code
- Influencing perception by sensitizing people to some stimuli and desensitizing them to others

Critics contend, however, that it is easy to oversimplify and overstate the relationship between language and various cognitive processes. Eric H. Lenneberg (1967) and Katherine Nelson (1973) note that a child's first words are often names of preexisting cognitive categories. As pointed out in the previous section, color organization in infants precedes learned categories provided by language. The suggestion here is that language is not the sole source for the internal representation on which thought depends. Nor is language the sole source for the representation of information in memory (Perlmutter & Myers, 1976). And language has at best only a minor impact upon perception.

Even though these perspectives stand in direct contrast, many linguists and psychologists believe that there are many ways to look at the relationship between language and thought. Some theorists believe that language and thought need not be mirror images of each other. Many aspects of language change over time due to cultural forces and interpretation of meaning (Malt, Sloman, & Gennari, 2003).

Question

Historically, there have been two opposing views in scientific circles regarding the relationship between language and thought. The first view is that thought shapes language and the second is that language shapes thought by providing the concepts or categories into which individuals mentally sort their perceptual stimuli. Do you think, then, that someone who is both blind and deaf is without thoughts—or even without language?

Theories of Language Acquisition

How are we to explain the development of speech in children? Is the human organism genetically and biologically "preprogrammed" for language usage? Or is language acquired through learning processes? These questions expose a nerve in the long-standing nature-versus-nurture controversy, with *nativists* (hereditarians) and environmentalists vigorously and heatedly disagreeing on their answers—and the most recent empirical research supports the interplay of both genetic and environmental influences.

Nativist Theories

Youngsters are said to begin life with the underpinnings of later speech perception and comprehension, as they begin life with the specialized anatomy of the vocal tract and the speech centers in the brain. Nativists (hereditarians) contend that human beings are "prewired" by their brain circuitry for language use—that the potential for language acquisition has been "built into" humans by genes and only needs to be elicited by an appropriate "triggering mechanism" in the same way that nutrition triggers growth. They view humans as having evolved in ways that make some kinds of behavior, like language acquisition, easier and more natural than others. And a growing body of empirical findings supports a variety of genetic contributions.

Significantly, recent studies report that there are auditory genes and mutations of genes associated with deafness. Research is progressing rapidly to discover the molecular mechanics underlying hearing and hearing impairments. And there are other exciting genetic studies from Harvard Medical School that are illuminating the mystery of hearing and hearing impairments (Resendes, Williamson, & Morton, 2001). Notably, over the past decade British and American researchers are discovering further details about the role of genes in language production.

Research by Noam Chomsky (1957, 1965, 1968, 1980, 1995), Eric H. Lenneberg (1967, 1969), Peter D. Eimas (1985), and Steven Pinker (1994, 2001) also focuses on the biological endowments that human beings bring to the environmental context of language development.

Noam Chomsky's Nativist Theory Noam Chomsky, a renowned linguist at the Massachusetts Institute of Technology, has provided a nativist theory of language development that has had a major impact on education and psychology over the past 50 years (Chomsky, 1957, 1965, 1968, 1975). Supporters and critics alike acknowledge that Chomsky's theoretical formulations have provided many new directions in the study of linguistics.

Central to Chomsky's position is the observation that mature speakers of a language can understand and produce an infinite set of sentences, even sentences they have never before heard, read, or uttered and therefore could not have learned. The explanation for this, argues Chomsky, is that human beings possess an inborn language-generating mechanism, which he terms the **language acquisition device (LAD)**. Chomsky sees the human brain as wired to simplify the chaos of the auditory world by sorting through incoming frequencies and shunting speech sounds into 42 intelligible **phonemes** (the smallest units of language, such as long *A*, as in bāke) (see Table 5.3). In the process of language acquisition, children merely need to learn the peculiarities of their society's language, not the basic structure of language. Although Chomsky's theory has attracted a good deal of attention as well as controversy, it is difficult to test by established scientific procedures and hence remains neither verified nor disproved.

Table 5.3 Some of the 42 Phonetic Sounds in Modern English

An infant's first "cooing" sounds are simple vowel sounds, with the mouth open and little work done by the tongue or lips.

Phoneme	Spelling(s) and Example Words	Meaningful Names
/A/	a (table), a_e (bake), ai (train), ay (say)	Long *A;* Fonzie's greeting
/E/	e (me), ee (feet), ea (leap), y (baby)	Long *E;* shriek
/I/	i (I), i_e (bite), igh (light), y (sky)	Long *I*
/O/	o (okay), o_e (bone), oa (soap), ow (low)	Long *O;* Oh, I see

In support of his view, Chomsky points out that the world's languages differ in *surface structure*—for example, in the words they use. But they have basic similarities in their composition, which he calls *deep structure.* The most universal features of deep structure include having nouns and verbs and the ability to pose questions, give commands, and express negatives. Chomsky suggests that through preverbal, intuitive rules—*transformational grammar*—individuals turn deep structure into surface structure, and vice versa.

The Twins' Early Development Study Plomin and colleagues (Plomin & Dale, 2000; Plomin & Colledge, 2001; Colledge et al., 2002) have been studying 3,000 twin pairs born in 1994 in England and Wales in the *Twins' Early Development Study (TEDS).* The goal of this longitudinal study in behavioral genetics is to chart a course to identify specific genes in multiple-gene systems responsible for genetic influences on language abilities and disabilities (Colledge et al., 2002; Plomin & Dale, 2000). Extensive data were collected and analyzed on DNA samples and measures of early language delay in these young participants at ages 2, 3, and 4. The results at age 2 for these participants demonstrate substantial differences in the etiology, or cause, of individual differences within the normal range and the low performance range.

Research on a group of 4-year-old twins from the TEDS investigated whether language impairment is as affected by genetic factors as language ability. The results of this study confirmed the findings of four previous twin studies that indicated substantial genetic influence on language impairment. The study found that language disability is more influenced by genetic factors than language ability (Spinath et al., 2004). Another study of 4-year-old twins found that although there is some difference, genetic and environmental influences on language impairment is similar for boys and girls (Viding et al., 2004).

The Cambridge Language and Speech Project British researchers estimate that between 2 and 5 percent of children who are otherwise unimpaired have significant difficulties in acquiring language, despite adequate intelligence and opportunity (Lai et al., 2001). Steven Pinker (2001) and colleagues (Lai et al., 2001) have identified a mutated form of the *FOXP2* gene in a three-generational British family that has a severe speech/language disorder.

Although Pinker does not believe language impairments can be linked to one single gene, in this family this mutation appears to be responsible for their specific language disorder. This gene produces actions on a group of proteins affecting the brain at an early stage in development, leading to abnormality in the brain circuitry needed for normal speech and language. This is the first case of a direct link between a speech/language disorder and a specific gene. Subsequent research findings dispute the linkage between specific language impairments and the *FOXP2* gene (Newbury et al., 2002). However, it has been known that specific language impairments (SLIs) often run in families: "First degree relatives of affected individuals are 7 times as likely to develop SLI as a member of the general population" (Williams et al., 2001, p.1).

According to the International Dyslexia Association, 15 to 20 percent of the population has a reading disability, and the vast majority of them (85 percent) have dyslexia ("What is Dyslexia?" 2000). **Dyslexia** is a learning disability that may manifest itself in several ways. The dyslexic person may have difficulty with reading, spelling, writing, and/or speaking. Many studies are being conducted to determine the causes of dyslexia. One study uses magnetic resonance imaging (MRI) to explore the neural systems of dyslexics for possible disruptions (Shaywitz et al., 2002).

Since 1982 researchers at the Institute for Behavioral Genetics in Boulder have studied over 200 pairs of identical twins and 150 pairs of same-sex fraternal twins in which at least one twin in the pair met the criteria for reading disability (using many performance measures). Significantly, in two-thirds of the pairs of identical twins, both members of the pair are affected, whereas same-sex fraternal twins shared a concordance rate of about one-third (DeFries, 1999).

Applying sophisticated statistical analysis techniques to their data, the researchers discovered significant evidence for genetic influences on reading disability. Additional molecular genetic methods were used to analyze the data for other sets of fraternal twins and siblings who had been genotyped. Evidence for linkage in a small region of chromosome 6 has now been confirmed by three independent groups of investigators (DeFries, 1999; Fisher et al., 1999). This finding provides new information about the primary cause and neurological basis of reading/language disabilities. Eventually the researchers hope to facilitate identification and intervention of preschool children with affected relatives.

International Molecular Genetics Study of Autism
Autism is a neurological disorder that appears in "normal" children at about age 2 who regress and show marked deficits in communication, social interaction, language impairment, preoccupation with fantasy, and unusual repetitive or excessive behaviors. Autism and related disorders occur in as many as 1 in 500 children, and the Autistic Society reports that the incidence of cases is escalating around the world (for example, California has seen a 440 percent increase since 1994) (Hanchette, 2004). Autistic children require speech and language therapy, occupational therapy and adaptive physical education and often life-long supervision and care. School districts report costs of over $50,000 per year per child for education (Choi, 2004). Over the past 20 years, family and twin studies of autism in England, Germany, and the United States have revealed that genes play a significant role in most cases of autism. Furthermore, these studies also suggest that the same genes may be involved in the development of other developmental disorders, such as Asperger's syndrome and other milder difficulties of communication and social interaction. The researchers in this consortium continue to study families with two or more members diagnosed with autism, monozygotic and dizygotic twins, and siblings.

The most recent data reported reveal that autism is influenced by complex, yet strong, genetic factors linked to specific locations on chromosomes 2, 7, and 16 ("A Genome Wide Screen for Autism," 2001). Monozygotic (identical) twins show a relatively high concordance for autism, whereas dizygotic (fraternal) twins show a smaller concordance. The recurrence risk for siblings is far greater than for the general population (Hallmayer et al., 2002). These are just a few of the examples of current research findings that support the nativist view of language/speech development and impairments. The goal of these researchers is to discover the mutated genes, identify those infants and young children most likely to be affected with these auditory/speech/language disorders, and to design medical/pharmacological intervention methods that will improve the children's language/communication skills. Encompassing a broader perspective, researchers at the University of California at Davis are investigating possible genetic, environmental/toxic, or pharmaceutical causes of autism in the CHARGE Study (Childhood Autism Risks from Genetics and the Environment), the first case-controlled study of 2,000 children with autism, children with developmental delay or mental retardation but not autism, and typically developing children (Lowy, 2004).

Most Children Acquire Language with Little Difficulty Even very young children master an incredibly complex and abstract set of rules for transforming strings of sounds into meanings. By way of illustration, consider that there are 3,628,800 ways to rearrange the 10 words in the following sentence:

Try to rearrange any ordinary sentence consisting of ten words.

However, only one arrangement of the words is grammatically meaningful and correct. Nativists say that a youngster's ability to distinguish the one correct sentence from the 3,628,799 incorrect possibilities cannot arise through experience alone (Allman, 1991). Likewise, consider how formidable a foreign language such as Japanese or Arabic seems to you.

Adult Speech Is Inconsistent, Garbled, and Sloppy Reflect for a moment on how a conversation carried on in an unfamiliar language sounds to you; probably more like one giant word than neat packages of words. Or listen to a conversation between two adults; it is full of false starts, "ums," and many "filler phrases" such as "you know." Indeed, linguists have experimentally shown that even in our own language we often cannot make out a word correctly if it is taken out of context. From recorded conversations linguists splice out individual words, play them back to people, and ask the people to identify the words. Listeners can generally understand only about half the words, although the same words were perfectly intelligible to them in the original conversation (Cole, 1979).

Children's Speech Is Not a Mechanical Playback of Adult Speech Children combine words in unique ways and also make up words. Expressions such as "I buyed," "foots," "gooder," "Jimmy hurt hisself," and the like reveal that children do not imitate adult speech in a strict fashion. Rather, according to nativists, children are fitting their speech in underlying language systems with which they are born and so exceptions are not initially mastered.

Concurrent to the exciting findings by geneticists, growing numbers of psychologists and other social scientists are exploring the factors (Werker & Tees, 1999) supporting language environment such as social class (Hoff-Ginsberg, 1991) in which infants and children are reared.

Learning and Interactionist Theories

Some researchers have followed in the tradition of B. F. Skinner (1957), who argued that language is acquired in the same manner as any other behavior, namely, through learning processes of reinforcement (Hayes & Hayes, 1992). Others have studied the interaction between caretakers and youngsters that contributes to the acquisition of language (Baumwell, Tamis-LeMonda, & Bornstein, 1997). Indeed, language use might begin quite early.

As we noted earlier in the chapter, DeCasper's research suggests that babies have a sensitivity to speech that starts even before birth. While they are in the uterus, we believe they hear "the melody of language." After birth this sensitivity provides them with clues about which sounds belong together. The ability of neonates to discriminate between speech samples spoken in their mother's native language and in an unfamiliar language could derive from the unique melodic qualities found in the linguistic signals to which they were exposed prenatally (Fernald, 1990). Young infants respond more calmly to lower-pitched tones in contrast to higher-pitched ones, and they especially seem to enjoy the melody of common lullabies. Every culture has its own renditions of melodies and rhythms that seem to calm a baby. If you haven't heard one lately, take a few seconds and listen to a common lullaby (some can be heard at www.babycenter.com under Lullaby Lyrics) and here is a common one:

> Twinkle, twinkle, little star
> How I wonder what you are!
> Up above the world so high
> Like a diamond in the sky
> Twinkle, twinkle, little star
> How I wonder what you are.

Other researchers suggest that babies intensively tune in to the subtleties of their native language for the first six to eight months before refining their listening practices and that they eventually come to ignore sounds that do not exist in their native language (Werker & Stager, 1997).

Caretaker Speech   Much recent research has focused on caretaker speech. In caretaker speech mothers and fathers systematically modify the language they use with adults when addressing infants and young people. **Caretaker speech** differs from everyday speech in its simplified vocabulary, higher pitch, exaggerated intonation, short simple sentences, and high proportion of questions and imperatives. Parents use caretaker speech with preverbal infants in numerous European languages, Japanese, and Mandarin Chinese (Fernald & Morikawa, 1993; Papousek, Papousek, & Symmes, 1991).

For their part, young infants show a listening preference for caretaker speech with its higher overall pitch, wider pitch excursions, more distinctive pitch contours, slower tempo, longer pauses, and increased emphatic focus (Cooper & Aslin, 1990; Fernald, 1985). Researchers believe levels of auditory recognition in infants are predictive of cognitive abilities in early childhood. One study compared the voice recognition neural pathways of infants born to diabetic mothers and infants born to nondiabetic mothers (deRegnier et al., 2000).

Speech characterized by the first two characteristics of caretaker speech—simplified vocabulary and higher pitch—is termed "baby talk." Baby talk has been documented in numerous languages, from Gilyak and Comanche (languages of small, isolated, preliterate Old World and New World communities) to Arabic and Marathi (languages spoken by people with literary traditions). Furthermore, adults phonologically simplify vocabulary for children—"*wa-wa*" for water, "*choo-choo*" for train, "*tummy*" for stomach, and so on. Baby talk also serves the psychological function of marking speech as affectionate (Moskowitz, 1978).

The Interactional Nature of Caretaker Speech   The interactional nature of caretaker speech actually begins with birth (Rheingold & Adams, 1980). Hospital staff, both men and women, use caretaker speech with the newborns in their care. The speech focuses primarily on the baby's behavior and characteristics and on an adult's own caretaking activities. Moreover, the caretakers speak as though the infants understand them. Their words reveal that they view the newborns as persons with feelings, wants, wishes, and preferences. Similarly, a burp, smile, yawn, cough, or sneeze typically elicits a comment to the infant from the caretaker (Snow, 1977). Often the utterances are in the form of questions, which the caretakers then answer as they imagine the children might respond. If a baby smiles, a parent might say, "You're happy, aren't you?" Or if the child burps, the caretaker might say, "Excuse me!"

Indeed, caretakers impute intention and meaning to infants' earliest behavior, making the babies appear more adept than they in fact are. These imputations facilitate children's language acquisition much in the manner of self-fulfilling prophecies. Infants with depressed mothers are handicapped in this respect because their mothers are less likely to use the exaggerated intonation contours of "motherese" (see below) and because their mothers are slower to respond to their early attempts at vocalization (Bettes, 1988). Recent research in developing countries looks at the relationship of maternal depression to a risk in their infants' health and growth (Rahman, Harrington, & Bunn, 2002).

Motherese or "Parentese"   When infants are still in their babbling phase, adults often address long, complex sentences to them. But when infants begin responding to adults' speech, especially when they start uttering meaningful, identifiable words (at around 12 to 14 months), mothers, fathers, and caretakers invariably speak what is called *motherese* or more recently called **"parentese"** in some research literature—a simplified, redundant, and highly grammatical sort of language.

When speaking parentese, parents tend to restrict their utterances to the present tense, to concrete nouns, and to comments on what the child is doing or experiencing. And they typically focus on what objects are named ("That's a doggie!" or "Johnnie, what's this?"), the color of objects ("Bring me the yellow ball. The yellow ball. No, the yellow ball. That's it. The yellow ball!"), and where objects are located ("Hey, Lisa! Lisa! Where's the kitty? Where's the kitty? See. On the steps. See over there on the steps!"). The pitch of the caretaker's voice is correlated with the child's age: the younger the child, the higher the pitch of speech. In addition, the intonation of infant-directed parentese—the melody inherent in mother speech—offers more reliable cues of a speaker's communicative intent than does speech directed by adults to other adults (Fernald, 1990; Sokolov, 1993). Parentese seems to derive less from parents' intent to provide brief language lessons than from their efforts to communicate to their youngsters. And as we will see later in this chapter, infants also use intonation effectively to express desires and intentions before they master conventional phonetic forms (Lewis, 1936/1951).

Briefly restated, *caretaker speech* is simple, high-pitched, and used to talk to preverbal infants, whereas motherese is employed when the caretaker assumes that the infant can begin to respond and interact with the environment. Motherese is also frequently accompanied by gestures, object motion, and touch, making it a multisensory communication device (Gogate & Bahrick, 2000). In a fascinating observation, infants, even at the one-word stage of language development, spontaneously produce gestures along with their speech (Goldin-Meadow & Mylander, 1998), as do infants with hearing impairments (Goldin-Meadow, 2000; Yoshinaga-Itano, 1999). (See the *Human Diversity* box on page 176, "Helping Infants Who Are Deaf or Hard of Hearing.")

A Resolution of Divergent Theories

Most psychologists agree that language has a biological basis, but they continue to disagree over how much the input from parents and other caretakers matters. The most satisfactory approach seems to be one that looks to the strengths of each theory and focuses on the complex and many-sided aspects of the development of language capabilities. Indeed, language acquisition cannot be understood by examining learning or genetic factors in isolation. No aspect by itself can produce a language-using human. Instead of asking which factor is most important, we need to study the ongoing process by which the factors dynamically come together.

In conclusion, infants are biologically adapted to acquire language. They possess a genetically determined plan that leads them toward language usage. Their attentional and perceptual apparatus seems biologically pretuned to make phonetic distinctions. But simply because human beings possess a biological predisposition for the development of language does not mean that environmental factors play no part in language acquisition. Indeed, language is acquired only in a social context (Huttenlocher et al., 1991). Youngsters' earliest vocalizations, even their cries, are interpreted by caregivers, who in turn use these interpretations to determine how they will respond to the youngsters.

Questions

Nativists insist that human beings possess an inborn language-generating mechanism perhaps linked to genetic codes. Learning/interactionist researchers argue that language is learned within an environmental context. Which position do you take regarding language/speech acquisition? How do infants with hearing impairments come to use a form of communication, and what technological strides are being made to support their language development?

Parentese and Nonverbal Language Male and female caretakers typically speak to infants in a high-pitched, simplified, redundant, and highly grammatical sort of language. Babies communicate to caretakers through their own nonverbal cues and gestures before they can speak any words.

Language Development

What is involved in learning to talk? This question has fascinated people for centuries. The ancient Greek historian Herodotus reports on the research of Psammetichus, ruler of Egypt in the seventh century B.C.—the first attempt at a controlled psychological experiment in recorded history. The king's research was based on the notion that vocabulary is transmitted genetically and that children's babbling sounds are words from the world's first language:

Psammetichus . . . took at random, from an ordinary family, two newly born infants and gave them to a shepherd to be brought up amongst his flocks, under strict orders that no one should utter a word in their presence. They were to be kept by themselves in a lonely cottage, and the shepherd was to bring in goats

Human Diversity

Helping Infants Who Are Deaf or Hard of Hearing

Oral language (speech) is part of the environment for most infants, but typically not for those infants who are born deaf or hard of hearing. Hearing loss is the most common birth defect but with early detection steps can be taken to help the child compensate for this disability. A nationwide effort was begun in 1999 toward the goal of screening every newborn for hearing loss. Currently, forty states have a mandatory screening rate of 90 percent or better (Yoo, 2003).

Prior to universal newborn hearing screening programs, most of the children identified early with hearing loss were those with mild to profound degrees of hearing loss who had disabilities, such as severe/profound cognitive and neurological impairments. For the first time, infants with mild-to-moderate loss with no secondary disabilities are beginning to receive early intervention services (Yoshinaga-Itano, 1999).

For those infants with questionable hearing, a parent-infant facilitator (interventionist) should explain test findings as well as the test limitations and should be assigned to work with the parents and infant for at least the first six months of infancy (Yoshinaga-Itano, 1999). For further information, go to the American Speech-Language Association Web site and read information about a career in speech-language pathology and audiology.

Neonatal Audiology Screenings

Typically, babies born in hospitals are screened for hearing loss before being discharged. Diagnostic methods may include air conduction threshold testing using clicks and/or tone bursts. Neonates diagnosed with **auditory neuropathy** (a disease or abnormality of the auditory system) are often those who spend time in newborn intensive care units. Children with significant hearing loss are beginning to be diagnosed typically between the second and third months.

Cochlear Implants

Recent technological advances in cochlear implants make it possible for a small number of deaf or hard-of-hearing infants as young as 12 months and young children to be able to "awaken" their hearing. Improvements in speech perception and speech production following cochlear implantation are often reported as primary benefits, especially for the youngest children (Kileny, Zwolan, & Ashbaugh, 2001). Therefore, early identification and implantation are critical for optimal speech and language development.

Deaf Infants Use Gestures and Create a Sign Language

However, if cochlear implants are not successful nor an option, it is important to realize that deaf infants manage to create a sign language of their own—stereotyped gestures that refer to objects around them. Susan Goldin-Meadow and Heidi Feldman (1977) studied six deaf children rang-

Learning Sign Language Deaf children pass through the same maturing stages and at the same months of age that are observed in the vocalizations of hearing children. Research with infants in America and China suggests that babbling, whether manual or vocal, is an inherent feature of the maturing brain as it acquires language. Babies can learn signs to communicate as young as about 6 to 8 months.

ing in age from 17 to 49 months. The children's parents had normal hearing. Despite their children's deafness, the parents wanted the children to depend on oral communication. Consequently, they did not expose the children to manual sign language. The researchers observed the children in their homes at periodic intervals. At the time they were studied, the children had learned only a few spoken words. In contrast, each child had individually developed a languagelike system of communication that included priorities found in the language of hearing children.

The children would indicate first the object to be acted on, next the action itself, and finally the recipient of the action (should there be one). For instance, one child pointed at a shoe and then pointed at a table to request that the shoe (the object) be put (the act) on the table (the recipient). Interestingly, even when the children were playing alone,

they employed signs to "talk" to themselves, as hearing children would.

Once the researchers had determined that the children had acquired a sign language, their next task was to discover who had first elaborated the signs, the children or their parents. The researchers concluded that most of each child's communication system originated with the child—not invented by the parents. Some of the children used complex combinations of words before their parents did with them. Moreover, although the parents produced as many different characterizing signs as the children, only about a quarter of the signs were common to both parties. Therefore, gestures might do more than merely reflect understanding: they may be involved in the process of cognitive change itself (Goldin-Meadow, 2000; Goldin-Meadow & Mylander, 1984).

from time to time, to see that the babies had enough milk to drink, and to look after them in any other way that was necessary. All these arrangements were made by Psammetichus because he wished to find out what word the children would first utter. . . . The plan succeeded; two years later the shepherd, who during that time had done everything he had been told to do, happened one day to open the door of the cottage . . . [and both children ran up to him and] pronounced the word "becos." (Herodotus, 1964, pp. 102–103)

When the king learned that the children had said "becos," he undertook to discover the language to which the word belonged. From the information produced by his inquiries, he concluded that "becos" was the Phrygian word for "bread." As a consequence, the Egyptians reluctantly yielded their claim to being the most ancient people and admitted that the Phrygians surpassed them in antiquity.

Communication Processes

Becoming competent in a language is not simply a matter of employing a system of rules for linking sounds and meaning (Ellis, 1992; Feyereisen & de Lannoy, 1991). Language also involves the ability to use such a system for communication and furthermore to keep such systems separate when one has access to two or more.

Nonverbal Communication or Body Language The essence of language is the ability to talk to one another. Yet spoken language is only one channel or form of message transmission. We also communicate by body language (also termed **"kinesics"**), which is the nonverbal communication of meaning through physical movements and gestures. For instance, we wink an eye to demonstrate intimacy; we lift an eyebrow in disbelief; we

tap our fingers to show impatience; or we rub our noses or scratch our heads in puzzlement. Every society develops its own patterns and meanings of such body movements and gestures, thus such communication can be misunderstood when traveling to or moving to another country. Likewise, when immigrant children enter the public school system, there is a lot of confusion about teachers' gestures and nonverbal cues. Some sociologists interested in communication and language have created Web sites devoted to nonverbal communication from cultures around the world.

We also communicate by *gaze:* We look at the eyes and face of another person and make eye contact. One way we use gazing is in the sequencing and coordination of speech. Typically, speakers look away from a listener as they begin to talk, shutting out stimulation and planning what they will say. At the end of the utterance, they look at the listener to signal that they have finished and are yielding the floor; and in between they give the listener brief looks to derive feedback information.

Infants Use Hand Gestures to Communicate This 6-month-old boy is using deliberate gestures. Both hearing-speech-exposed children and children with hearing impairments use a variety of gestures to communicate.

By the end of the second year, most children seem to pattern their eye contact in the way adults in their environment do: looking up when they are done speaking to signal that they are finished and looking up when the other person is through speaking to confirm that the floor is about to be offered back to them. Even so, children show considerable differences in the consistency and frequency of these behaviors (Rutter & Kurkin, 1987). And some groups actually avoid eye contact, such as African Americans, who view staring as aggressive, and Native Americans, who view staring as rude.

Another nonverbal behavior is *pointing.* Pointing can be observed in infants as young as 2 months old, though pointing at such a young age is not an intentional act (Trevarthen, 1977). In contrast, pointing at the end of the first year is an intentional act (Fogel & Thelen, 1987). Pointing is a nonverbal precursor of language. Mothers commonly employ pointing when talking to their youngsters. Children use the gesture to mark out features of a book or to call attention to an activity.

Another form of communication is **paralanguage**— the stress, pitch, and volume of vocalizations by which we communicate expressive meaning. Paralanguage involves *how* something is said, not *what* is said. Tone of voice, pacing of speech, and extralinguistic sounds (such as sighs) are examples of paralanguage. By the late babbling period, infants already control the intonation, or pitch modulation, of their utterances (Moskowitz, 1978). By about 9 months, new social cognitive competencies emerge in joint attention, social referencing, and communicative gestures (Tomasello, 1995).

Most of the research on language development has focused on language production, the ability of children to string together sounds so as to communicate a message in a meaningful fashion. Until recently, little research dealt with **language reception,** the quality of receiving or taking in messages. Yet children's receptive capacities tend to outdistance their productive capabilities. For instance, even very young babies are able to make subtle linguistic discriminations—as between the sounds *p* and *b* (Eimas, 1985).

Older children similarly make finer distinctions in comprehension than they reveal in their own language productions (Bates, Bretherton, & Snyder, 1988). Consider the now somewhat classic conversation the linguist Roger Brown had with a young child (Moskowitz, 1978): The child made reference to *"fis,"* and Brown repeated *"fis."* The child was dissatisfied with Brown's pronunciation of the word. After a number of exchanges between Brown and the child, Brown tried *"fish,"* and the child, finally satisfied, replied, *"Yes, fis."* Although the child was as yet unable to pronounce the distinction between *s* and *sh,* he knew that such a sound difference did exist.

Pointing By 1 year of age, infants use pointing as a nonverbal precursor of language. Parents commonly use pointing when talking to their youngsters. Children often use this gesture to mark out features of a book or to call attention to an activity.

The Sequence of Language Development

Until a couple of decades ago, linguists assumed that children merely spoke an imperfect version of adult language, one that reflected a child's handicaps of limited attention, limited memory span, and other cognitive deficits. However, linguists now generally accept that children speak their own language—a language with characteristic patterns that develop through a series of stages (Brownlee, 1998; Tomasello, 1992).

Children reveal tremendous individual variation in the rate and form of language development (Fenson et al., 1994). Indeed, some children don't begin to talk until well into their third year, whereas others are producing long sentences at this point. Such variations do not appear to have implications for adult language skill, provided that the child is otherwise normal. Table 5.4 summarizes the typical milestones in language development of the "average" child.

From Vocalization to Babbling   Crying is the most noticeable sound uttered by the newborn. As we saw in Chapter 4, variations on the basic rhythm include the "angry" and "pain" cries. Although it serves as the infant's primary means of communication, crying cannot be considered true language (although some mothers say they can easily distinguish meaning among different cries). Young infants also produce a number of other sounds, including yawns, sighs, coughs, sneezes, and belches.

Between the sixth and eighth week, infants diversify their vocalizations and, when playing alone, employ new noises, including "Bronx cheers," gurgling, and tongue noise games. Around their third month, infants begin making cooing sounds and squealing-gurgling noises, which they sustain for 15 to 20 seconds.

Table 5.4 Milestones in Language Development

Age	Characteristic Sounds
1 month	Cries; makes small throaty noises.
2 months	Begins producing vowel-like cooing noises, but the sounds are unlike those of adults.
3 months	Cries less, coos, gurgles at the back of the throat, squeals, and occasionally chuckles.
4 months	Cooing becomes pitch-modulated; vowellike sounds begin to be interspersed with consonantal sounds; smiles and coos when talked to.
6 months	Vowel sounds are interspersed with more consonantal sounds (f, v, th, s, sh, z, sz, and n are common), which produce babbling (one-syllable utterances); displays pleasure with squeals, gurgles, and giggles, and displeasure with growls and grunts.
8 months	Displays adults' intonation in babbling; often uses two-syllable utterances such as "mama" or "baba"; imitates sounds.
10 months	Understands some words and associated gestures (may say "no" and shake head); may pronounce "dada" or "mama" and use holophrases (words with many different meanings).
12 months	Employs more holophrases, such as "baby," "bye-bye," and "hi"; many imitate sounds of objects, such as "bow-wow"; has greater control over intonation patterns; gives signs of understanding some words and simple commands (such as "Show me your nose").
18 months	Possesses a repertoire of 3 to 50 words; may begin using two-word utterances; still babbles, but employs several syllables with intricate intonation pattern.
24 months	Has repertoire of more than 50 words; uses two-word utterances more frequently; displays increasing interest in verbal communication.
30 months	Rapid acceleration in learning new words; speech consists of two or three words and even five words; sentences have characteristic child grammar and rarely are verbatim imitations of adult speech; intelligibility of the speech is poor, although children differ in this regard.
36 months	Has a vocabulary of some 1,000 words; about 80 percent of speech is intelligible, even to strangers; grammatical complexity is roughly comparable to colloquial adult language.
48 months	Language well established; deviations from adult speech are more in style than in grammar.

Adapted from Frank Caplan, ed., *The First Twelve Months of Life*. New York: Grosset & Dunlap, 1973; and Eric H. Lenneberg, *Biological Foundations of Language*. New York: Wiley, 1967, pp. 128–130.

Babbling Around the sixth month, infants in all cultures produce sequences of alternating vowels and consonants that resemble one-syllable utterances, such as "*da-da-da.*" Indeed, infants seem to play with sounds, enjoying the process and exploring their capabilities. Frequently babbled sounds consist of *n, m, y, w, d, t,* or *b,* followed by a vowel such as the *eh* sound in *bet.* It is probably no coincidence that in many languages the words for mother and father begin with these sounds (e.g., *mama, nana, papa, dada, baba*). Consonants such as *l, r, f,* and *v* and consonant clusters such as *st* are rare.

MacNeilage and Davis (2000), researchers at the University of Texas, analyzed audiotapes of several infants from 6 to 18 months and concluded that four patterns of consonant-vowel combinations are common to babies' babbling and first words in several languages. They state these patterns are created by basic open (vowels) and close (consonant) movements of the mouth and jaw during speech—and do not attribute babbling to any genetic or inborn language mechanism—in contrast to the thinking of traditional linguists.

Also, infant *laughter* typically appears around this time.

Deaf infants also go through the *cooing* and *babbling* phase, even though they might have never heard any spoken sounds. They babble in much the same fashion as normal infants, despite the fact that they cannot hear themselves (Lenneberg, 1967; Petitto & Marentette, 1991). This behavior suggests that a hereditary mechanism underlies the early cooing and babbling process. However, later on, deaf babies' babbling sounds have a somewhat more limited range than hearing children's. Furthermore, unless congenitally deaf children are given special training, their language development is retarded (Folven & Bonvillian, 1991).

Recent research conducted by Goldin-Meadow with deaf infants from American and Chinese cultures confirmed that infants have a strong bias to communicate in languagelike ways. The parents in this study differed in their native language, child-rearing practices, and in the way that gesturing is used in relation to speech—yet the children themselves spontaneously introduced languagelike structure into their gestures (Goldin-Meadow & Mylander, 1998).

Early Communication: Cooing Around 3 months of age, infants enjoy making "cooing" sounds. These are usually simple vowel sounds with the mouth open, such as *"ooooh," "eeeeeh,"* and *"ahhhh."* Typically before an infant begins to express harder consonant sounds by around 6 months, he or she will enjoy making "bubbles" with the saliva from the mouth, with simple spitting. The infant is learning to move the tongue and lips in readiness for language.

Other researchers find that deaf babies of deaf parents babble with their hands in the same rhythmic, repetitive fashion as do hearing babies who babble with their voices (Petitto et al., 2001). Sounds such as *"goo-goo"* and *"da-da-da"* that hearing babies make arise around the same time as the babbling signs and motions arise among deaf youngsters. Most of the hand motions of the deaf infants are actual elements of *American Sign Language*—gestures that do not in themselves mean anything but that have the potential to indicate something when pieced together with other gestures.

Significantly, deaf children also pass through the same stages and at the same times that are observed in the vocal babbling of hearing children: They string together signs and motions in much the same way that hearing youngsters string together sounds. Such gestures appear to have the same functional significance as the babble noises of hearing babies, for they are far more systematic and deliberate than the random finger flutters and fist clenches of hearing youngsters (Kyle, McEntee, & Ackerman, 1998). Such findings suggest that language is distinct from speech and that speech is only one of the signal systems available to us for communication with one another. In addition, the research suggests that babbling, whether manual or vocal, is an inherent feature of the maturing brain as it acquires the structure of language.

These observations suggest that although vocal behavior emerges spontaneously, it flourishes only in the presence of adequate environmental stimulation. And deaf babies, of course, are incapable of "talking back," the process of vocal contagion and model imitation noted by Piaget. However, children do not seem to learn language simply by hearing it spoken. A boy with nor-

mal hearing but with deaf parents who communicated by the American Sign Language was exposed daily to television so that he might learn English. He was fluent in sign language but he neither understood nor spoke English. This observation suggests that to learn a language, children must be able to interact with people in that language (Hoff-Ginsberg & Shatz, 1982).

Receptive Vocabulary   Between 6 to 9 months, caretakers will notice that the child understands some words. This is a favorite time for parents, who begin to ask the baby questions: "Where is Mommy's nose?" and the baby points to mommy's nose. Or Daddy might say, "Wave bye-bye to Daddy" as he leaves the house, and the child demonstrates understanding by waving bye-bye. A child who is not yet speaking can respond appropriately when asked to go get things, like his or her toys or the pots and pans in the kitchen. All of these actions demonstrate that children have developed a **receptive vocabulary** long before they speak their first word—that is, long before they have an **expressive vocabulary,** using their own words to effectively convey meaning, feeling, or mood.

Holophrases   The majority of developmental psychologists agree that most children speak their first word at about 10 to 13 months of age. However, the precise age at which a child arrives at this milestone is often difficult to determine. The child's first word is so eagerly anticipated by many parents that they read meaning into the infant's babbling—for instance, they note "mama" and "dada" but ignore "tete" and "roro." Hence, one observer might credit a child with a "first word" where another observer would not. Behavioral theorists suggest that at this time parents reinforce, or reward, the infant with their smiles and encouragement. In turn, the child repeats the same expression over and over, such as "da," which quickly becomes "dada" (or what we interpret to be *daddy*). The *d* sound is easier for the infant to say; the m sound (as in "mama") requires the child to purse the lips together, so it might not be heard for another few months.

Children's first truly linguistic utterances are **holophrases**—single words that convey different meanings depending on the context in which they are used. Using a holophrase, a child can imply a complete thought. G. DeLaguna (1929) first noted the characteristics of holophrases more than 75 years ago:

> It is precisely because the words of the child are so indefinite in meaning, that they can serve such a variety of uses. . . . A child's word does not . . . designate an object or a property or an act; rather it signifies loosely and vaguely the object together with its interesting properties and the acts with which it is commonly associated in the life of the child. . . . Just because the terms of the child's language are themselves so indefinite, it is left to the particular setting and context

to determine the specific meaning for each occasion. In order to understand what the baby is saying, you must see what the baby is doing.

The utterance "mama," not uncommon in the early repertoire of English-language youngsters, is a good illustration of a holophrase. In one situation it may communicate "I want a cookie"; in another, "Let me out of my crib"; and in another, "Don't take my toy away from me." A holophrase is most often a noun, an adjective, or a self-invented word. Only gradually do the factual and emotional components of the infant's early words become clearer and more precise.

Nelson and colleagues (1978) found that children typically pass through three phases in their early learning of language. About 10 to 13 months of age, they become capable of matching a number of words used by adults to already existing concepts, or mental images, such as the concept "bottle" discussed earlier in the chapter. One study reveals that the average child of 13 months understands about 50 words; in contrast, the average child does not speak 50 words until six months later (Benedict, 1976). It is also interesting to note that caretakers have successfully taught preverbal children signs for words such as *more, cat,* and *hungry,* which they use in place of spoken language.

In the second phase, usually occurring between 11 and 15 months of age, children themselves begin to speak a small number of words. These words are closely bonded to a particular context or action.

Overextension In the third phase—from 16 to 20 months—children produce many words, but they tend to *extend* or *overgeneralize* a word beyond its core sense. For instance, one child, Hildegard, first applied the word *tick-tock* to her father's watch, but then she broadened the meaning of the word, first to include all clocks, then all watches, then a gas meter, then a firehose wound on a spool, and then a bathroom scale with a round dial (Moskowitz, 1978). In general, children overextend meanings on the basis of similarities of movement, texture, size, and shape. Overgeneralization apparently derives from discrepancies between comprehension and production. For example, one child, Rachel, overextended *car* in her own verbal productions to include a wide range of vehicles. But she could pick out a motorcycle, a bicycle, a truck, a plane, and a helicopter in response to their correct names. Once her vocabulary expanded—once she acquired the productive labels for these concepts—the various vehicles began to emerge from the car cluster (Rescorla, 1976).

Children tend to first acquire words that relate to their own actions or to events in which they are participants (Shore, 1986). Nelson (1973) noted that children begin by naming objects whose most salient property is change—the objects do things like roll (ball), run (dog, cat, horse), growl (tiger), continually move (clock), go on and off (light), and drive away (car, truck). The most ob-

vious omissions in children's early vocabulary are immobile objects (sofas, tables, chests, sidewalks, trees, grass).

Children also typically produce a holophrase when they are engaged in activities to which the holophrase is related. Marilyn H. Edmonds (1976, p. 188) observed that her subjects

> named the objects they were acting on, saying "ball" as they struggled to remove a ball from a shoe; they named where they placed objects, saying "bed" as they put their dolls to bed; they named their own actions, saying "fall" when they fell, they asserted possession, saying "mine" as they recovered objects appropriated by siblings; they denied the actions of their toys, yelling "no" when a toy cow fell over; and so forth.

Very often, a child's single-word utterances are so closely linked with action that the action and speech appear fused: In a Piagetian sense, a word becomes "assimilated" to an existing sensorimotor *scheme*—the word is fitted or incorporated into the child's existing behavioral or conceptual organization (see Chapter 2). It is as if the child has to produce the word in concert with the action. Edmonds (1976, p. 188) cites the case of a child at 21 months of age who said "car" 41 times in 30 minutes as he played with a toy car.

Two-Word Sentences When they are about 18 to 22 months old, most children begin to use two-word sentences. Examples include "Allgone sticky," said after washing hands; "More page," a request to an adult to continue reading aloud; and "Allgone outside," said after a door is closed behind the child ("allgone" is treated as one word, because "all" and "gone" do not appear separately in these children's speech). Most of the two-word sentences are not acceptable adult English sentences, and most are not imitations of parental speech. Typical constructions are "More wet," "No down," "Not fix," "Me drink," "Allgone lettuce," and "Other fix" (Braine, 1963; Clark, Gelman, & Lane, 1985). Two-word sentences represent attempts by children to express themselves in their own way through their own unique linguistic system.

As with holophrases, one often must interpret children's two-word sentences in terms of the context. Lois Bloom (1970), for instance, observed that one of her young subjects, Kathryn, employed the utterance "Mommy sock" in two different contexts with two different meanings. "Mommy sock" could mean that Mommy was in the act of putting a sock on Kathryn, or it could mean that Kathryn had just found a sock that belonged to Mommy.

Children's actual utterances are simpler than the linguistic structures that underlie them (Brown, 1973). Dan I. Slobin (1972, p. 73) observes that even with a two-word horizon, children can convey a host of meanings:

Identification: "See doggie."

Location: "Book there."

Repetition: "More milk."

Nonexistence: "Allgone thing."

Negation: "Not wolf."

Possession: "My candy."

Attribution: "Big car."

Agent-action: "Mama walk."

Agent-object: "Mama book" (meaning, "Mama read book").

Action-location: "Sit chair."

Action-direct object: "Hit you."

Action-indirect object: "Give papa."

Action-instrument: "Cut knife."

Question: "Where ball?"

Children also use intonation to distinguish meanings, as when a child says "*Baby* chair" to indicate possession and "Baby *chair*" to indicate location.

Telegraphic Speech   Children who begin to use short, precise words in two- or three-word combinations are demonstrating **telegraphic speech** and the first understanding of grammar. The third word frequently fills in the part that was implied in the two-word statement (Slobin, 1972). "Want that" becomes "Jerry wants that" or "Mommy milk" becomes "Mommy drink milk."

Psycholinguist Roger Brown (1973) characterizes the language of 2-year-old children as telegraphic speech. Brown observes that words in a telegram cost money, so that we have good reason to be brief. Take the message "My car has broken down and I have lost my wallet; send money to me at the American Express in Paris." We would word the telegram, "Car broken down; wallet lost; send money American Express Paris." In this manner we omit eleven words: my, has, and, I, have, my, to, me, at, the, in. The omitted words are pronouns, prepositions, articles, conjunctions, and auxiliary verbs. We retain the nouns and verbs:

> The adult user of English when he writes a telegram operates under a constraint on length and the child when he first begins to make sentences also operates under some kind of constraint that limits length. The curious fact is that the sentences the child makes are like adult telegrams in that they are largely made up of nouns and verbs (with a few adjectives and adverbs) and in that they generally do not use prepositions, conjunctions, articles, or auxiliary verbs. (Brown, 1973, pp. 74–75)

Between 12 to 26 months of age, a child is most likely to be using nouns and verbs, with some adjectives and adverbs, such as "Daddy go bye-bye," "Me go out," "Me want drink" (Brown, 1973). Children especially love having parents and caretakers read to them in an exaggerated way.

By 27 to 30 months, a child is starting to form plurals: "Annie want cookies," "Mommy get shoes." The use of articles *a, an,* and *the* are now evident in speech: "The cat goes meow," or "I want a cookie." Some prepositions (indicating placement) are also used: "Jimmy in bed now." Whereas first-language acquisition has predictable milestones, the time course and ultimate attainment of skills in a second language are highly variable ("Reaction Time Studies," 2005).

Bilingualism

Although in overall cognitive capabilities children are less proficient than adults, newborns are language universalists. It seems that normal, healthy infants can learn any sound in any language and distinguish among the vocal sounds that human beings utter (Bjorklund & Green, 1992). In contrast, adults are language specialists. They have considerable difficulty perceiving speech sounds that are not in their native tongue. For instance, Japanese infants can distinguish between the English sounds *la* and *ra*, but Japanese adults cannot because their language does not contrast these sounds (Kuhl et al., 1992).

Some linguists contend there is a critical period of language acquisition and that language learning occurs primarily in childhood. Some aspects of the nervous system seemingly lose their plasticity with age, so that by the onset of puberty the organization of the brain is basically fixed, making the learning of a new language difficult (Lenneberg, 1967). This assumption has recently been challenged by findings that suggest that it is the level of language proficiency and not when the language is learned that leads to bilingual acquisition (Perani et al., 1998).

Given this state of affairs, it is hardly surprising that proficiency in a second language is related to the age at which exposure to the language begins (Stevens, 1999). Put another way, adults who learned a second language early in childhood are more proficient with the language than adults who learn a second language later in life. Similar results are found for older children or adults with hearing deficiencies who learn American Sign Language as their first language (Newport, 1990).

Evidence suggests that, regarding the ability to acquire a second language, there is a gradual decline across childhood rather than a sudden discontinuity at puberty. Indeed, the decline begins very early in life. Patricia K. Kuhl and her colleagues (1992) report that experience alters sound perception by 6 months of age. For instance, experiments with 6-month-old babies in the United States and Sweden reveal that American youngsters routinely ignore the different pronunciations of the *i* sound because in the United States they hear the same sound. But American infants can distinguish slight variation in *y* sounds. The reverse is true of

Swedish babies—they ignore variations in *y* sounds but notice variations in the *i* sound.

These findings have substantial implications for educators. The best time to learn a new language is early in life. The cognitive structures of young children seem especially suited for learning both a first and a second language. This ability is gradually lost across the childhood years. Although adults are able to acquire a second language, they rarely attain the same proficiency as individuals who acquire the language in childhood (Bjorklund & Green, 1992). The sooner bilingual education begins, the better.

As we shall see in later chapters on childhood, the large influx of immigrant children into the United States over the past decade has been cause for a flurry of research on bilingualism. Recent findings from a second language acquisition study suggest that Spanish-speaking children who were identified as "rapid learners" need about three to five years to become proficient in academic settings using English as a second language—however, other children may be much slower in learning English as a second language ("Reaction Time Studies," 2005).

A fundamental challenge in every school district across the country has been whether young children should be taught in their native language while learning the English language over a period of years—or whether non-English-speaking children should be immersed in the English language from the first days in preschool or kindergarten. The state of California recently changed its previous language-support policy in its schools and legislated that English must be the primary language of instruction in the schools.

The Significance of Language Development

Parents anxiously await normal language development in their young children, for in many cultures language expression and understanding are considered indica-

tors of intellectual ability or intellectual delay. Children vary in their timing of their expressive language. Parents and grandparents generally speak constantly to a firstborn child, and firstborns are the most likely to speak early or within the expected range of development. Later-born children with siblings sometimes do not have to speak to get what they want; if older siblings take care of the child and anticipate the child's needs, it is likely that this child will simply delay expressing language. Some children speak very little, and then suddenly they surprise everyone by speaking in short sentences!

However, if caretakers notice that a child does not follow simple instructions or does not speak simple sounds or words according to a normal timetable, they are advised to schedule a checkup with the child's pediatrician. Some children with delayed speech have hearing impairments; others may be eligible for speech therapy to promote normal speech development. We do know that children who have language delays or cannot be understood when they speak are at a risk for later social isolation upon entering group activities, such as child care, preschool, or kindergarten.

Some American parents are enrolling their toddlers in nursery or preschool programs where instruction in a second language is the norm, whereas parents who recently immigrated into this country are struggling to immerse their children in the English-speaking culture. Some children have bilingual parents and seem to learn both languages with ease at home.

Questions

What are the several milestones in infant language development from vocalizations, such as crying, to speaking an actual sentence? Who or what motivates the child to communicate? How easy is it for a young child versus an adult to acquire a second language? Explain your answer.

SEGUE

The issue of the increasing numbers of non-English-speaking young children in the United States has prompted much debate on when language learning should begin, what teaching methods are most effective in the earliest years, what language or languages should be spoken in the child's home, and how all of these programs will be funded. People who work in such areas as health care, social services, teaching, early child care, and criminal justice are particularly aware of

how difficult it is to communicate without a common language. (We encourage readers of this text to learn a second language, for you will find it extremely beneficial when you seek employment.)

In Chapter 6, we discuss the influential role of the home environment and caretakers on the young child's emotional development and the expanding social contexts within which the child's developing sense of self evolves.

Summary

Cognitive Development

1. Chapter 5 surveys the processes of cognitive and language development from late neonatal development through infancy—that is, from birth through age 2. Although some infants exhibit superior abilities in cognitive and language development, others are born with, or develop, cognitive delays and specific language impairments.

2. Cognition refers to the process of knowing and remembering. As infants receive raw sensory information (stimuli), they transform this data into meaningful information in their daily activities and decision making. A mounting body of empirical evidence tells us that a fetus of several months, neonates, and infants can experience and process enormous amounts of sensory information.

3. Learning permits us to adapt to our environment by building on previous experience and is defined as a change in behavior that is stable and results from experience. To facilitate learning, we can condition people, provide a model for them to imitate, or shape and fashion the cognitive structures by which individuals think about their environment.

4. DeCasper and other researchers studying fetal and infant auditory perception found evidence that some types of learning are occurring. An infant's preferences and physiological responses are affected by their auditory experiences before and after birth. A fetus can discriminate sounds of its mother's voice for a few months prior to birth, and it can sense the mother's emotions by differentiating among her speech patterns.

5. Other researchers, such as Sameroff, have demonstrated that newborns can learn. They devised neonatal sucking techniques and reinforcement principles: Neonates can learn to control one of two sucking methods and use different pressure levels for feeding.

6. Jean Piaget characterized children's cognitive development during the first two years of life as the sensorimotor stage. The child's major task during infancy is to integrate the perceptual and motor systems to arrive at progressively more adaptive behavior. Some infants may improve sensorimotor functioning by craniosacral evaluation and therapy methods.

7. Another hallmark of the sensorimotor period is the child's progressive refinement of the notion of object permanence. Six- to 9-month-old infants come to know that objects exist, even when the objects cannot be seen.

8. Piaget's work has stimulated other psychologists to investigate children's cognitive development. Neo-Piagetians are revising and refining Piaget's insights about cognition. They find that infants possess skills more sophisticated than Piaget had imagined. Moreover, youngsters must be provided with experiences that they cannot generate by themselves, such as playing with others.

9. Parents and caregivers transmit to infants the knowledge, attitudes, values, and behaviors essential for later effective participation in society. There is a direct relationship between the severity of a mother's depression and the quality of care she provides. Depressed mothers have a reduced capacity for caregiving, nurturing, stimulation, and talking with their infants. In turn, their infants are more withdrawn, unresponsive, inattentive, and have problems sleeping, eating, and may be diagnosed with failure to thrive. School-age children of depressed mothers often exhibit dysfunctional behaviors. Depressed mothers should see a physician or therapist for antidepressants or other treatment.

10. According to U.S. psychologist Jerome Bruner, the foundations of any subject may be taught to anybody at any age in some form. Children first represent the world through their physical/motor actions, and young children use mental images called ikonic representations (images or pictures), whereas school-age children begin to use symbolic representations (letters, numbers, words), characteristic of logical and abstract thought.

11. Individual differences in mental performance in infancy are most likely developmentally continuous across childhood and beyond. Children's patterns of attending to information reflect their cognitive capabilities, particularly their ability to construct workable schemas of their visual and auditory worlds. Infants who prefer the novel over the familiar are often more efficient processors of information, a feature of higher intelligence.

12. Early intervention enrichment experiences for infants with delayed cognitive development—including good nutrition, toys, playmates, learning opportunities, and effective parenting—can produce physical changes in the developing brain and boost intellectual development. Caretakers need to provide positive feedback about their infant's accomplishments, encourage exploratory behaviors in a safe setting, and make efforts to bond with their infants.

Language and Thought

13. Human beings are set apart from other animals by their highly developed system of language communication. Language allows for communication with one another (interindividual communication) and facilitates thought (intraindividual communication).

14. Historically, there have been two opposing scientific views on the relationship between language and thought: (1) that thought takes place independent of the existence of language, and (2) that language shapes thought by conceptualization, providing the concepts or categories into which individuals mentally sort their perceptual stimuli. Categories are the basis for more advanced cognitive thinking. Naming, or verbally labeling, provides many advantages.

Theories of Language Acquisition

15. Nativists (hereditarians) and learning/interactionist (environmentalists) researchers disagree about the deter-

minants of language. Research is progressing rapidly to discover the genetic, chemical, and molecular mechanics underlying the sense of hearing, hearing impairments, and the production of language. Noam Chomsky and other linguists insist that human beings possess an inborn language-generating mechanism, which is called the language acquisition device (LAD). Recent research in behavioral genetics has supported the nativist/hereditarian view.

16. Plomin and colleagues have been conducting a longitudinal study in behavioral genetics to identify specific genes responsible for influencing language abilities and disabilities in twins at ages 2, 3, and 4. The findings suggest that verbal delay appears to be highly heritable, girls scored significantly higher on verbal measures than boys, and boys and girls scored about the same in nonverbal measures.

17. British researchers estimate that between 2 and 5 percent of children who are otherwise unimpaired have significant difficulties acquiring language, despite adequate intelligence and opportunity. Specific language impairments (SLIs) often run in families. Pinker and colleagues have discovered mutations of specific genes in a three-generation British family that has a severe speech/language disorder.

18. Between 5 to 10 percent of school-age children are affected with developmental dyslexia and have difficulty learning to read and spell despite adequate intelligence and opportunity. Researchers have now discovered significant evidence for genetic influences on reading disability, and they hope to facilitate identification and intervention in preschool children who are affected.

19. Over the past 20 years, family and twin studies in three countries have confirmed that genes on specific chromosomes play a significant role in the disorder of autism and in other developmental disorders. Identical twins show a high concordance for autism.

20. Learning and interactionist researchers (environmentalists) argue that language is learned through the processes of reinforcement. Later-term fetuses and neonates have already learned to differentiate their mothers' voices from those of strangers. Babies "tune in" to the sounds of their native language for the first six to eight months before coming to ignore the sounds that are not in their native language. Parents use caretaker speech patterns when interacting with preverbal infants. When infants begin responding and interacting with their environment, caretakers begin to use a new pattern of speaking called motherese, or "parentese." Babies communicate using sounds, nonverbal cues, and gestures.

21. More, but not all, states are mandating universal newborn hearing screening programs, and a standardized diagnostic protocol is being developed. Prior to these programs, infants with auditory neuropathy were those who were in newborn intensive care units, but now those with mild-to-moderate loss are identified and receiving early intervention services. Cochlear implants can

"awaken" the hearing in year-old infants and preschool children who are affected with hearing impairments. Deaf infants pass through the same maturing stages using their own self-generated gestural sign language and at the same months of age observed in hearing infants.

22. Many scientists have concluded that the acquisition of language cannot be understood by examining either learning or genetic factors in isolation from one another. Complex interactions take place among genetic influences, biochemical processes, maturational factors, learning strategies, and the social environment.

Language Development

23. The essence of language is the ability to understand and transmit messages. Some linguists suggest there is a critical period of language acquisition. Adults who learned a second language early in childhood are more proficient with the language than adults who learn a second language later in life, suggesting the best time to learn a second language is early in life.

24. People, including infants, also communicate through nonverbal body language, which includes gazing, pointing and gesturing, and a variety of stress, pitch, and volume, called paralanguage. By about 9 months of age, new social/cognitive competencies emerge in joint attention, social referencing, and communicative gestures. Although most research has focused on infants' ability to produce language, language reception (the taking in and processing of messages) is receiving greater research scrutiny, and it is known that infants can understand much of what is said to them before they produce language themselves.

25. Linguists now recognize that children speak their own language with its own characteristic patterns. Early communication and speech develop through a series of stages: early vocalizations (primarily crying), cooing and babbling, holophrastic speech, two-word sentences, and three-word sentences. Deaf children and those with hearing impairments pass through the same stages and at the same times observed in vocal babbling infants by stringing together a variety of gestures that are self-produced.

26. Between 6 and 9 months, it is apparent that infants have developed a receptive vocabulary—long before they use expressive vocabulary. Infants' first true words are holophrases, a single word that conveys several different meanings. Two- and three-word combinations demonstrate telegraphic speech and the first use of structure we call grammar. By 27 to 30 months, a child is normally beginning to use plurals, articles, and prepositions.

27. Children vary greatly in the timing of expressing language. Although some speak early, others show signs of delay and may need to be tested by an audiologist or speech-language therapist to be eligible for early intervention services. Other young children may not speak until their third year and speak clearly and in full sentences.

Key Terms

auditory neuropathy (176)

autism (157)

caretaker speech (174)

cognition (157)

communication (167)

conceptualization (170)

craniosacral system (162)

dyslexia (172)

expressive vocabulary (180)

failure to thrive (FTT) (165)

holophrases (180)

kinesics (177)

language (166)

language acquisition device (LAD) (171)

language reception (178)

learning (157)

object permanence (161)

parentese (174)

paralanguage (178)

phonemes (171)

receptive vocabulary (180)

sensorimotor period (161)

telegraphic speech (182)

Following Up on the Internet

Web sites for this chapter focus on cognitive and language development in infancy. Please access the text Web site at www.mhhe.com/vzcrandell8 for up-to-date hot-linked Internet addresses for the following organizations, topics, and resources:

Autistic Society

Society for Research in Child Development

Infant Learning Lab at University of Wisconsin, Madison

Jean Piaget Society

Normal Speech Development

National Institute for Deafness and Other Communication Disorders

International Society of Infant Studies

Infancy

*The Development of
Emotional and Social Bonds*

1. How would you feel if your baby consistently preferred to be held by other people instead of you? Would you try to change your baby's preferences?

2. Why do we sometimes experience two emotional states simultaneously? For example, a child will laugh and cry at the same time. Have you ever loved and hated someone at the same time? Is it really possible?

3. Babies are said to have different temperaments: Some are difficult, some are slow to warm up, and some are easygoing. If you and your baby end up at opposite ends of the temperament continuum and one of you needed to change, who would have more difficulty changing—you or the baby? Why?

4. If you could not raise your child in a traditional home environment (i.e., two parents), what would you opt for—an extended family where many adults take care of the child, a single-parent household, or a child-care center? What factors did you consider in arriving at your decision?

Outline

I n Chapters 4 and 5, we focused on the infant as a growing and cognitively developing being. With those areas of development as a foundation, we now examine multiple ways young children are socialized into the larger human group. In America many families have moved away from the three-generational model of child care in the home evident in many other countries.

There is currently an increasing diversity of family structures and fewer two-parent families. Adding to this mix of societal concerns is the changing demographic nature of the United States. And with more mothers than ever employed outside the home, a growing number of families need assistance from the larger community to provide high-quality care and supervision for growing children.

Young children in the United States are supervised, and therefore socialized, by a larger array of people than ever before. A diversity of programs has evolved over the past two decades to assist in the important task of child care. Additionally, television has come to be a powerful socialization influence. This is of great concern to social scientists who study attachment, because many psychologists believe that children's emotional ties in their early years are extremely significant and serve as models for their later relationships. Perhaps most important, the child's own personality and temperament are underlying factors in the successful development of emotional and social bonds.

Emotional Development

Emotions play a critical part in our daily existence. Indeed, if we lacked the ability to experience love, joy, grief, and anger, we would not recognize ourselves as human. Emotions set the tone for much of our lives, and at times they even override our most basic needs: Fear can preempt appetite, anxiety can wreak havoc on a student's performance on an exam, despair can lead a person to a fatal flirtation with a pistol.

Most of us have a gut-level feeling of what we mean by the term emotion, yet we have difficulty putting the feeling into words. Psychologists and other developmental scientists have similar problems. Indeed, they have characterized emotion in different ways. Some have viewed it as a reflection of physiological changes that occur in our bodies, including rapid heartbeat and breathing, muscle tension, perspiration, and a "sinking feeling" in the stomach. Others have portrayed it as the subjective feelings that we experience—the "label" we assign to a state of arousal. Still others have depicted it as the visible expressive behavior that we display, including crying, moaning, laughing, smiling, and frowning.

Yet emotion is best characterized as a combination of all these components. We will say that **emotions** are the physiological changes, subjective experiences, and expressive behaviors involved in feelings such as love, joy, grief, and anger.

The Role of Emotional Competence

Emotions, then, are not simply "feelings," but rather they are processes by which individuals establish, maintain, and terminate relations between themselves and their environment (Campos et al., 1993). For instance, people who are happily involved in a conversation are likely to continue conversing, and their *facial expressions* and *behaviors* signal to others in the conversation that they too should keep up their interaction; sad people tend to feel that they cannot successfully attain some goal, and their sadness signals others that they need help (Bartlett et al., 1999).

Charles Darwin was intrigued by the expression of emotions and proposed an evolutionary theory for them. In *The Expression of Emotions in Man and Animals,* Darwin (1872) contended that many of the ways in which we express emotions are inherited patterns with survival value. He observed, for instance, that dogs, tigers, monkeys, and humans all bare their teeth in the same way during rage. In so doing, they communicate to members of their own and other species important messages regarding their inner dispositions. Contemporary developmental researchers have followed up on Darwin's leads, noting that emotions perform a number of functions (Mayer, Ciarrochi, & Forgas, 2001):

- *Emotions help humans survive and adapt to their environment.* For instance, fear of the dark, fear of being alone, and fear of sudden happenings are adaptive because there is an association between these feared things and potential danger.
- *Emotions serve to guide and motivate human behavior.* That is, our emotions influence whether we categorize events as dangerous or beneficial, and they provide the motivation for patterning our subsequent behavior.
- *Emotions support communication with others.* By reading facial, gestural, postural, and vocal cues of others, we gain indirect access to their emotional states. Knowing that a friend is afraid or sad allows us to more accurately predict the friend's behavior and to respond to it appropriately.

Being able to "read" another person's emotional reactions also permits **social referencing,** the practice whereby an inexperienced person relies on a more experienced person's interpretation of an event to regulate his or her subsequent behavior. Before they are 1 year old, most infants engage in social referencing. They typically look at their parents when confronted with new or unusual events. They then base their behavior on the emotional and informational messages their parents communicate. Their ability to control emotions develops over time as a result of neurophysiological growth (Izard & Abe, 2004; Rosen, Adamson, & Bakeman, 1992).

Meltzoff and Moore (1977, 1983, 1997) have demonstrated that social referencing begins during the first days of infancy, or even hours after birth, with infants' innate ability to imitate their parents' facial expressions of mouth opening and tongue protrusion. Apparently infants care little whether it is their fathers or their mothers who are doing the signaling (Hirshberg & Svejda, 1990).

Youngsters 10 months of age use others' emotional expressions to appraise events like those encountered in visual cliff experiments conducted by Gibson and Walk (1960) and others (see Chapter 4). When they approach the illusory "drop off," they look to their mothers' expressions and modify their own behavior accordingly. When their mothers present an angry or fearful face, most youngsters will not cross the "precipice." But when their mothers present a joyful face, they will cross it. Infants show similar responses to their mothers' vocalizations that convey fear or joy. This research reveals that infants actively seek out information from others to supplement their own information and that they are capable of using this information to override their own perceptions and evaluations of an event (Hertenstein & Campos, 2004).

Emotional Development in Infancy

One thing is clear: Infants have emotions (Klaus & Klaus, 1998; Weinberg & Tronick, 1994). Psychosocial researchers influenced by *ethological theory* have played a central role in the recent growth of studies on the emotional life of children (see Chapter 2).

Gosselin and Larocque (2000) and other researchers in neurobiology have been influenced by Darwin's ideas and the more recent work of Paul Ekman (1972, 1980, 1994) who believe "affective processing [is] an evolutionary antecedent to more complex forms of information processing . . . higher cognition requires the guidance provided by affective processing" (Adolphs & Damasio, 2001, p. 45).

Ekman and other researchers have shown participants from widely different cultures photographs of faces that people from Western societies would judge to display six basic emotions: happiness, sadness, anger, surprise, disgust, and fear. They find that individuals in the United States, Brazil, Argentina, Chile, Japan, and New Guinea label the same faces with the same emotions. Cross-cultural research supports that humans associate specific emotions with specific facial expressions, and such research focuses on identifying body movements and vocalizations in different types of emotional situations (Camras et al., 2002; Rosenberg & Ekman, 2003).

Ekman takes these findings as evidence that the human central nervous system is genetically prewired for the facial expression of emotion: The face provides a window by which other people can gain access to our inner emotional life and by which we gain similar access to their inner life. But the window is not entirely open. Early in life we learn to disguise or inhibit our emotions. We might smile even though we are depressed, look calm when we are irate, and put on a confident face in the presence of danger.

Psychologist Carroll E. Izard has been a central figure in the study of children's emotional development and has introduced his own "differential emotions theory" (Abe & Izard, 1999; Izard, 2002b). Like Ekman, Izard contends that each emotion has its own distinctive facial pattern. Izard says that a person's facial expression colors what the thinking brain "feels." For example, muscular responses associated with smiling make you aware that you are joyful. And when you experience rage, a specific pattern of muscle firings physiologically linked with anger "informs" your brain that you feel rage and not anguish or humiliation. Thus, according to Izard the feedback from sensations generated by your facial and related neuromuscular responses yield the distinctive subjective experiences that you recognize as different types of feeling (see Table 6.1). (*Smile or frown while you read the next paragraph, and see whether it affects how you feel.*)

Izard finds that babies have intense feelings from the moment of birth. But at first their inner feelings are limited to *distress, disgust,* and *interest*. In the course of their maturation, new emotions—one or two feelings at a time—develop in an orderly fashion. Izard says that emotions are preprogrammed on a biological clock: Infants gain the social smile (joy) at around 4 to 6 weeks of age; anger, surprise, and sadness at about 3 to 4 months; fear at 5 to 7 months; shame, shyness, and self-awareness at about 6 to 8 months; and contempt and guilt during the second year. Izard and others continue to study abnormal child emotional expressions and are developing social competence intervention strategies (Izard et al., 2002).

Psychologist Joseph Campos disagrees with Izard (Campos et al., 1993). He argues that all the basic emotions are in place at birth, depending on a prewired process for which neither experience nor social input is required. Campos says that many of an infant's emotions do not become apparent to observers until later, so the

---

Table 6.1   **Ten Fundamental Emotions**

In his book, *The Psychology of Emotions*, Izard (1991, 2004) explains the characteristics of what cross-cultural research reveals as 10 fundamental emotions. Because of high interest on the part of students, Izard also addresses the emotion of *love*, a feeling or state of relatedness with many others (parents, siblings, grandparents, spouse, children, friends) and an emotion that exists on many levels (as in "I just LOVE that music, animal, car . . . ").

Interest
Enjoyment
Surprise
Sadness
Anger
Disgust
Fear
Shyness
Shame
Guilt

How do you Interpret These Babies' Emotions?

first experience of an emotion does not necessarily coincide with its first expression.

Whether emotions are present at birth or emerge only in the course of maturation, we know that infants' emotional expressions become more graded, subtle, and complex beyond the first year of life (Klaus & Klaus, 1998). Moreover, infants show an increasing ability to discriminate among vocal clues and facial expressions, particularly happy, sad, and angry ones, in the first five months of life (Soken & Pick, 1992). Even more significant, infants progressively come to modify their displays of emotion and their behaviors on the basis of their appreciation of their mother's displays of emotion and behaviors (Klaus & Klaus, 1998).

> **Questions**
>
> How do various theorists view the function of emotions, and why has emotional development in infancy come under much greater research scrutiny? What emotions are preprogrammed according to a biological clock, based on Izard's extensive research?

Stages in Children's Emotional Development Child psychiatrist Stanley Greenspan and Nancy Greenspan, former health economist with the federal government (1985), were among the first researchers to propose a model of emotional development of the typical healthy child from birth to age 4. According to the Greenspans' model, even in infancy children are actively constructing and regulating their environments. Their stages and timing of appearance are described in Table 6.2.

Early attachment relationships lead to purposeful communication and then to the toddler's creation of a coherent, positive sense of self. These early accomplishments lay the foundation for the young child's use of language, pretend play, and engagement in "emotional" thinking (Hyson, 1994, p. 58). The Greenspans stress that the more negative factors interfere with a child's mastering of emotional milestones, the more likely the child's intellectual and emotional development will be compromised later on.

For example, those of us who have taught in elementary school can see that a child will have difficulty mastering the A, B, Cs if Mom and Dad have just separated. In "current events" discussions, elementary-age children will express their fears about moving to a new neighborhood, their anxiety about Mom and Dad remarrying and new stepsiblings moving into the home, or Dad's going to jail for selling drugs. Their main concerns are of a personal, emotional nature, and many children are just "bursting" to let them out.

The *Greenspan Functional Emotional Assessment Scale,* a psychometric identification tool for early identification and intervention for children at risk from birth to age 5, as well as Dr. Greenspan's further explanation of typical emotional development from birth through

Table 6.2 Greenspans' Model of Infant and Young Child Emotional Progress

According to Stanley and Nancy Greenspan (1985), the typical healthy child from birth through age 4 should be observed displaying the following emotional behaviors.

Age	Milestones of Emotional Development	Observed Behaviors
0 to 3 months	Self-regulation and interest in the world	Infants learn to calm themselves, and they develop a multisensory interest in the world.
2 to 7 months	"Falling in love"	Infants develop a joyful interest in the human world and engage in cooing, smiling, and hugging.
3 to 10 months	Developing intentional communications	Infants develop a human dialogue with the important people of their lives (for instance, they lift their arms to a caretaker, give and take a toy offered to them, gurgle in response to a caretaker's speech, and enjoy peekaboo games).
9 to 18 months	Emergence of an organized sense of self	Toddlers learn how to integrate their behavior with their emotions, and they begin to acquire an organized sense of self (for example, they will run to greet a parent returning home or lead a caretaker to the refrigerator to show hunger, instead of simply crying for dinner).
18 to 36 months	Creating emotional ideas	Toddlers begin to acquire an ability to create their own mental images of the world and to use ideas to express emotions and regulate their moods.
30 to 48 months	Emotional thinking—the basis for fantasy, reality, and self-esteem	Young children expand these capacities and develop "representational differentiation," or emotional thinking; they distinguish among feelings and understand how they are related; and they learn to tell fantasy from reality.

age 5 can be found at the Interdisciplinary Council on Development and Learning disorders (www.icdl.com).

Stability of Emotional Expression   Izard and others have also turned up evidence of continuity, or stability, of emotional expression in children (Abe & Izard, 1999). The amount of sadness a child shows during a brief separation from his mother seems to predict the amount of sadness the same child shows six months later. And the amount of anger a child shows when receiving a painful inoculation at 2 to 7 months of age predicts the amount of anger the same child displays at 19 months of age (Izard & Malatesta, 1987). Emotional expressions in late infancy also predict maternal ratings of personality in the preschool years (Abe & Izard, 1999).

Izard does not deny that, in some measure, learning conditions and experience modify a child's personality. For instance, a mother's mood affects how her infant feels and acts (DeHaan et al., 2004). When mothers of 9-month-old youngsters display a sad face, their children often display the same facial expression and engage in less vigorous play than when their mothers appear happy. Izard believes that "the interactional model of emotional development is probably correct. Biology provides some thresholds, some limits, but within these limits, the infant is certainly affected by the mother's moods and emotions" (quoted by Trotter, 1987, p. 44).

Indeed, much parental socialization is directed toward teaching children how to modulate their feelings and expressive behavior to conform to cultural norms. Some studies have found that infants and toddlers have much difficulty with emotional self-regulation (Eisenberg et al., 1998). Other studies suggest that typical children as young as 4 years are able to regulate their emotions, depending on the parent or caregiver they are interacting with and the expected outcomes of those emotional expressions (Kochanska, 2001; Zeman et al., 1997).

Emotional Intelligence

From age 1 to age 2, as children shift cognitively from the sensorimotor stage to the preoperational stage, they begin to acquire symbolic functioning, the emergence of self-conscious emotions, and new coping and self-regulatory skills (Vondra et al., 2001).

Emotional intelligence (EI) is a concept originally posed a decade ago by John Mayer and Peter Salovey (1997) and popularized by Daniel Goleman (1995) that has generated popular fascination and a considerable amount of research over the past decade. EI, also named EQ or EIQ, includes such abilities as being able to motivate oneself, persist in the face of frustrations, control impulses and delay gratification, empathize, hope, and regulate one's moods to keep distress from overwhelming one's ability to think (Goleman, 1995; Mayer, Ciar-

rochi, & Forgas, 2001). Research on EI "applies to clinical psychopathology, education, interpersonal relations, to work, to health and finances, and to psychological well-being" (Mayer et al., 2001).

As the human brain evolved, the limbic system, which is the center of emotions, developed over the brain stem. The brain stem controls basic life processes such as blood pressure, the sleep/wake cycle, and respiration. Continued evolution produced the cerebral cortex above and around the limbic system. The cerebral cortex allows us to think, register sensations, analyze, problem solve, and plan ahead. The limbic system is a "go-between" or "switching station" for the brain stem and the cerebral cortex.

Suppose that you are tired as you read this paragraph. "Bottom-up," the brain stem registers that the body is fatigued and requires sleep and forwards those signals to the limbic system. The limbic system communicates "feelings" of weariness or irritability to the cortex, which is the decision maker in the brain. The cortex senses these "feelings" and decides either to continue with this task or stop to sleep. The limbic system is the intermediary between the brain stem and the cerebral cortex.

Or suppose you are driving your car with the radio on. "Top-down," your cerebral cortex "hears" a familiar song of upbeat tempo on your car radio. The cerebral cortex in turn triggers the emotion of happiness and excitement in the limbic system, which then sends a message to the lower brain stem to increase your pulse and respiration as you sing along.

New scanning, imaging, and diagnostic methods that can map process as well as function are daily revealing new information about neural pathways. We once believed that sensory systems sent information directly to specific lobes of the cerebral cortex, then to the limbic system for processing for emotional interpretation and reaction: We sense, then think, then feel, then react. The newest discoveries in neuroscience, however, tell us we sense, then feel, then nearly simultaneously react and think about what we are experiencing. This is demonstrated time and again in life-threatening situations: People simply react to save a life, then think about their actions later, as all of us witnessed in the many firefighters and police officers who gave up their lives saving others in the World Trade Center disaster and United Airlines Flight 93 crash on September 11, 2001.

Normal neural circuitry from the limbic system to the frontal lobes (which interpret and mediate emotional signals) is crucial to effective thought. Signals of strong emotion from the amygdala in the limbic system to the frontal cortex (as can occur with continual fear and dread in child abuse) can create *deficits* in a child's intellectual abilities, crippling the capacity to learn (Izard et al., 2001). We are all familiar with this effect. When we are emotionally upset (e.g., getting an unexpected termination at work) or emotionally overjoyed (e.g., at winning a lottery), we are likely to say, "I just can't think straight!"

Intellectual deficits due to strong emotion are likely to show up in a child's continual agitation and impulsivity. One study gave neuropsychological tests to primary-school boys with above-average IQ scores who were doing poorly in school and found that the boys had impaired frontal cortex functioning (Goleman, 1995). They were impulsive, anxious, and disruptive in class, all of which suggested faulty frontal-cortical control of their limbic system urges. These are the children at highest risk for later problems such as academic failure, alcoholism, and criminality, because their emotional life is impaired. "These emotional circuits are sculpted by experience throughout childhood—and we leave those experiences utterly to chance at our peril" (Goleman, 1995, p. 27). Neurologist and brain researchers posit that feelings are typically indispensable for rational decisions (Adolphs & Damasio, 2001; Goleman, 1995).

"In a sense, we have two brains or two minds—and two different kinds of intelligence: *rational* [assessed by standard IQ measure] and *emotional*. How we do in life is determined by both—it is not just IQ, but emotional intelligence that matters. Indeed, intellect cannot work at its best without emotional intelligence" (Goleman, 1995). Howard Gardner (1983, 1993b), a psychologist at Harvard, in *Frames of Mind*, posited a theory of multiple intelligences (see Chapter 8) that includes emotional intelligence.

*Inter*personal intelligence is the ability to understand other people: what motivates them, how they work, how to work cooperatively with them. Successful salespeople, politicians, teachers, clinicians, and religious leaders are all likely to have high degrees of interpersonal intelligence. *Intra*personal intelligence is a correlative ability, turned inward. It is a capacity to form an accurate, veridical model of oneself and to be able to use that model to operate effectively in life: There is much evidence that people are at an advantage who are emotionally adept at reading and responding to others' feelings (Gardner, 2002). Researchers who support the concept of EI say that these crucial competencies should be learned and improved on by children, especially if we want to reduce the tide of youth aggression and adult violence in American society.

Questions

What are the several milestones of infant emotional development as proposed by the Greenspans? Can we predict a child's emotional stability from earlier emotional expressions in infancy? What infant behaviors are associated with emotional intelligence?

Attachment

Attachment is an affectional bond that one individual forms for another and that endures across time and space (Ainsworth, 1992, 1993, 1995; Klaus & Klaus, 1998). An attachment is expressed in behaviors that promote proximity and contact. Among infants these behaviors include approaching, following, clinging, and signaling (smiling, crying, and calling). Through these activities a child demonstrates that specific people are important, satisfying, and rewarding. Some writers call this constellation of socially oriented reactions "dependency," whereas laypeople refer to it simply as "love."

What Is the Course of Attachment?   Schaffer and Emerson (1964) studied the development of attachment in 60 Scottish infants over their first 18 months of life. They identified three stages in the development of infant social responsiveness:

- During the first two months of life, *infants are aroused by all parts of their environment*. They seek arousal equally from human and nonhuman aspects.
- Around the third month, *infants display indiscriminate attachment*. During this stage, infants become responsive to human beings as a general class of stimuli. They protest the withdrawal of any person's attention, whether the person is familiar or strange.
- When they are about 7 months old, *babies show signs of specific attachment*. They begin displaying a preference for a particular person and, over the next three to four months, make progressively more effort to be near this attachment object.

Children differ greatly in the age at which specific attachment occurs. Among the 60 babies in the Schaffer and Emerson study, 1 showed specific attachment at 22 weeks, whereas 2 did not display it until after their first birthdays. Cross-cultural differences also play a part in this development (Van IJzendoorn & Sagi, 1999).

Mary Ainsworth found that infants in Uganda show specific attachment at about 6 months of age—a month or so earlier than the Scottish infants studied by Schaffer and Emerson (1964). Similarly, it was found that separation protest occurred earlier among infants in Guatemala than among those in the United States (Lester et al., 1974). Researchers attribute the precocity of the Ugandan and Guatemalan infants to cultural factors. Ugandan infants spend most of their time in close physical contact with their mothers (they are carried about on their mother's back), and they are rarely separated from her. In the United States, infants are placed in their own rooms shortly after birth. Such separation is virtually unknown in Guatemala, where most rural families live in a one-room rancho.

More recent research findings with a small sample of Colombian mothers and infants support Ainsworth's concepts of attachment theory (Posada et al., 2004).

Schaffer (1971, 1996) suggests that the onset of separation protest is directly related to a child's level of object permanence. Social attachment depends on the ability of infants to differentiate between their mother and strangers and on their ability to recognize that their mother continues to exist even when she is not visible. In terms of Piaget's cognitive theory, outlined in Chapter 5, these abilities do not appear until late in the sensorimotor stage. Indeed, Silvia M. Bell (1970) finds that in some instances the concept of **person permanence**—the notion that an individual exists independently of immediate visibility—might appear in a child before the concept of object permanence. Studies by other researchers also confirm that protests over parental departures are related to a child's level of cognitive development (Kagan, 1997; Kagan, Kearsley, & Zelazo, 1978; Klaus & Klaus, 1998).

How Do Attachments Form? Psychologists have advanced two explanations of the origins or determinants of attachment, one based on an *ethological* perspective and the other on a *learning* perspective. Psychoanalytically

Fostering Secure Infant-Parent Attachment Close proximity and contact promote affectional bonds that individuals form for one another. Cross-cultural differences play a part in the development of attachment.

oriented ethologist John Bowlby (1969, 1988) said that attachment behaviors have biological underpinnings that can be best understood from a Darwinian evolutionary perspective. For the human species to survive despite an extended period of infant immaturity and vulnerability, both mothers and infants are endowed with innate tendencies to be close to each other. This reciprocal bonding functioned to protect the infant from predators when humans lived in small nomadic groups (Bowlby, 1969, 1988).

According to Bowlby, human infants are biologically preadapted with a number of behavioral systems ready to be activated by appropriate "elicitors" or "releasers" within the environment. For instance, close physical contact—especially holding, caressing, and rocking—serves to soothe and quiet a distressed, fussing infant. Indeed, an infant's crying literally compels attention from a caretaker, and smiles accomplish much the same end (Spangler & Grossmann, 1993). Rheingold observes:

> As aversive as the cry is to hear, just so rewarding is the smile to behold. It has a gentling and relaxing effect on the beholder that causes him to smile in turn. Its effect upon the caretaker cannot be exaggerated. Parents universally report that with the smile the baby now becomes "human." With the smile, too, he begins to count as a person, to take his place as an individual in the family group, and to acquire a personality in their eyes. Furthermore, mothers spontaneously confide that the smile of the baby makes his care worthwhile. In short, the infant learns to use the coin of the social realm. As he grows older and becomes more competent and more discriminating, the smile of recognition appears; reserved for the caretaker, it is a gleeful response, accompanied by vocalizations and embraces. (Rheingold, 1969a, p. 784)

Sucking, clinging, calling, approaching, and following are other kinds of behavior that promote both contact and proximity. Viewed from the evolutionary perspective, a child is genetically programmed to a social world and "in this sense is social from the beginning" (Ainsworth, Bell, & Stayton, 1974). Parents, in turn, are said to be genetically predisposed to respond with behaviors that complement the infant's behaviors (Ainsworth, 1993; Ainsworth et al., 1979; Klaus & Klaus, 1998). The baby's small size, distinctive body proportions, and infantile head shape apparently elicit parental caregiving (Alley, 1983). A recent analysis of genetic and environmental influences on attachment was conducted with twin pairs from England and the Netherlands. Findings showed that genetic transmission was a minor variable in parental-infant attachment behaviors (Bokhorst et al., 2003).

Bowlby was the first researcher to use the term "maternal deprivation," reflecting the damaging effects of inadequate mothering. His theories were instrumental in changing hospital policies allowing for close parental care that helped improve the outcomes for a sick child (MacDonald, 2001).

Programmed to Elicit Parenting? The noted ethologist Konrad Lorenz argued that humans are genetically programmed for parenting behavior and that caretaking tendencies are aroused by "cuteness." When Lorenz compared human infants with kittens and puppies, he noticed that they all seem to display a similar set of sign stimuli that arouse parental response. Apparently, short faces, prominent foreheads, round eyes, and plump cheeks all stir up parental feelings. Infants reward caretakers with smiles and cooing, too!

In contrast to Bowlby's views, learning theorists attribute attachment to socialization processes. According to psychologists such as Robert R. Sears (1963, 1972), Jacob L. Gerwitz (1972), Sidney W. Bijou and Donald M. Baer (1965), the mother is initially a neutral stimulus for her child. She comes to take on rewarding properties, however, as she feeds, warms, dries, and snuggles her baby and otherwise reduces the infant's pain and discomfort. Because the mother is associated with the satisfaction of the infant's needs, she acquires secondary reinforcing properties—her mere physical presence (her talking, smiling, and gestures of affection) becomes valued in its own right. In brief, attachment develops.

Learning theorists stress that the attachment process is a two-way street. The mother also finds gratification

in her ability to terminate the child's piercing cries and with it to allay her own discomfort associated with the nerve-wracking sound. Also, infants reward their caretakers with smiles and coos. Thus, as viewed by learning theorists, the socialization process is reciprocal and derives from a mutually satisfying and reinforcing relationship (Adamson, 1996).

Who Are the Objects of Attachment?   In their study of Scottish infants, Schaffer and Emerson (1964) found that the mother was most commonly (in 65 percent of the cases) the first object of specific attachment. However, in 5 percent of cases the first attachment was to the father or a grandparent. And in 30 percent of cases, initial attachments occurred simultaneously to the mother and another person. Also, the number of a child's attachments increased rapidly. By 18 months only 13 percent displayed attachment to only one person, and almost one-third of the babies had five or more attachment persons. Indeed, the concept of attachment as originally formulated was too narrow (Bronfenbrenner, 1979). Because infants have ongoing relationships with their fathers, grandparents, and siblings, these psychologists suggest the focus of theory and research should fall on the social network, a web of ties to significant others (Stern, 1985).

What Are the Functions of Attachment?   Ethologically-oriented psychologists point out that attachment has adaptive value in keeping infants alive. It promotes proximity between helpless, dependent infants and protective caretakers. But attachment also fosters social and cognitive skills. In a longitudinal study with internationally adopted children, the quality of early mother-infant interactions and attachment behaviors predicted later cognitive and socioemotional development (Stams, Juffer, & Van IJzendoorn, 2002). According to this view, four complementary systems coordinate the behavior of the child and the environment (Lamb & Bornstein, 1987):

- The attachment behavioral system leads to the development and maintenance of proximity and contact with adults.
- The fear-wariness behavioral system encourages youngsters to avoid people, objects, or situations that might be a source of danger to them; this system is often called "stranger wariness" and will be discussed later in the chapter.
- The affiliative behavioral system encourages infants, once the wariness response diminishes, to enter into social relationships with other members of the human species.
- The exploratory behavioral system provides babies with feelings of security that permit them to explore their environment knowing they are safe in the company of trusted and reliable adults (Jones, 1985).

Temperament

Issues of continuity and discontinuity in children's emotional expressions invariably lead investigators to the matter of infant temperament and, more particularly, to differences in temperament among youngsters. Generally, the child's own personality and temperament are underlying factors in the successful development of emotional and social bonds. These connections may be difficult for children with autism, or pervasive developmental disorders, due to their lack of ability to understand social cues (Izard, 2001). (See the *Further Developments* box "Rising Incidence of Autism.")

Temperament refers to the relatively consistent, basic dispositions that underlie and modulate much of a person's behavior. The temperamental qualities that developmental psychologists most often study are those that are obvious to parents. They include irritability, a happy mood, ease of being soothed, motor activity, sociability, attentiveness, adaptability, intensity of arousal, regulation of arousal states, and timidity (Chess & Thomas, 1996; Goldsmith, 1997; Kagan, 1993).

For example, as we noted in Chapter 2, Jerome Kagan (1997) finds that some children are born with a tendency, or "vulnerability," toward extreme *timidity* when faced with an unfamiliar person or situation and that other children are not. This difference persists as they grow up and has profound social consequences. On the first day at school, timid youngsters tend to remain quietly watchful at the outskirts of activity, whereas uninhibited youngsters are all smiles and eager to approach other children.

In American culture, uninhibited people are typically more popular than inhibited ones, and timid youngsters are often pressured by parents and others to be more outgoing. Kagan believes this bias is regrettable. Instead, he says, we should provide our children with an environment that is, within reason, respectful of individual differences. Although uninhibited children might become popular adults, inhibited children might invest more energy in schoolwork and become intellectuals if they are afforded settings that value academic achievement. Kagan notes that although we push our inhibited children toward the uninhibited end of the scale, other cultures, such as China and Japan, tend to view uninhibited behavior as disrespectful and unseemly (Guillen, 1984).

Individuality in Temperament Alexander Thomas and his associates have come to conclusions quite similar to those of Kagan from their studies of more than 200 children (Thomas & Chess, 1987; Thomas et al., 1963). They found that babies show a distinct individuality in temperament during the first weeks of life that is independent of their parents' handling or personality styles. Thomas views temperament as the stylistic component of behav-

ior—the *how* of behavior, as opposed to the *why* of behavior (motivation) or the *what* of behavior (its content). Thomas names three most common types of babies:

Difficult babies. These babies wail and cry a great deal, have violent tantrums, spit out new foods, scream and twist when their faces are washed, eat and sleep in irregular patterns, and are not easy to pacify (10 percent of infants are difficult babies).

Slow-to-warm-up babies. These infants have low activity levels, adapt very slowly, tend to be withdrawn, seem somewhat negative in mood, and show wariness in new situations (15 percent of infants are slow to warm up).

Easy babies. These infants generally have sunny, cheerful dispositions and adapt quickly to new routines, foods, and people (40 percent of all infants are easy babies).

The remaining 35 percent of infants show mixtures of traits that do not readily fit into these categories. Thomas and Chess (1987) also found that all infants possess nine components of temperament that emerge quickly after birth and continue relatively unchanged into adulthood (see Table 6.3).

Questions

What are the various views about how infant attachment occurs, the functions of attachment, and what the expected stages of attachment are for an infant over the first few years of life? What role does the caretaker play in this important process? In what way does the infant's own temperament play a role?

Table 6.3 Nine Components of Temperament

Activity level: The proportion of active versus inactive periods

Rhythmicity: The regularity of hunger, sleep, bowel movements

Distractibility: The degree to which extraneous stimuli alter behavior

Approach/withdrawal: The response to a new person or object

Adaptability: The ease with which a child adapts to changes

Attention span and persistence: The amount of time a child pursues an activity, and whether he or she is easily distracted

Intensity of reaction: The energy of response

Threshold of responsiveness: The degree of stimulation needed to evoke a response

Quality of mood: The amount of pleasant, friendly behavior versus unpleasant and unfriendly behavior

Further Developments

Rising Incidence of Autism

Autism is a complex, lifelong developmental disability typically appearing during the first three years of life as a result of a neurological disorder affecting normal brain development in the areas of social interaction and communication skills (Autism Society of America [ASA], 2005). Autism is one of five disorders grouped under the umbrella term "pervasive developmental disorder," or PDD. It is a classification of neurological disorders characterized by "severe and pervasive impairment in several areas of development" (DSM-IV-TR, 2000). *Autism spectrum disorder* means the impairments in each area can range from mild to severe along a continuum. A child may have communication and social deficits, sensory sensitivities, difficulties with behavioral and emotional control, abnormal movements and repetitive behaviors, attachment to objects, and resistance to change. Individuals with autism usually have a difficult time with verbal and nonverbal communication, forming relationships, and leisure and play activities. Typically they require constant caregiver supervision, which can be very difficult on a family.

Dr. Leo Kanner first described children with autism in 1943, but many people, including medical, educational, and vocational professionals, are still not aware of how autism affects people and how to effectively work with them. In contrast to popular belief, a number of children with autism may make eye contact, display affection, and show different emotions, although it may be in varying degrees (ASA, 2005). Although each person with autism is a unique individual with his or her own personality, there are characteristics common to autism. The Autism Society of America indicates people with autism may exhibit the following traits (from mild to severe):

- Resistance to change
- Difficulty expressing needs; use gestures or pointing instead of words
- Repeating words or phrases in place of normal, responsive language
- Laughing, crying, showing distress for reasons not apparent to others
- Prefer to be alone; aloof manner
- Tantrums
- Difficulty mixing with others
- Sustained odd play; spins objects
- May not want to cuddle or be cuddled
- Little or no eye contact
- Unresponsive to normal teaching methods
- Inappropriate attachments to objects
- Apparent oversensitivity or undersensitivity to pain
- No real fears of danger
- Noticeable physical overactivity or extreme underactivity
- Uneven gross/fine motor skills

- Not responsive to verbal cues; act as if they can't hear despite normal hearing
- Senses may be overactive or underactive

What Causes Autism?

The etiology of autism spectrum disorder is currently unknown, but a number of theories are being explored. It is generally accepted that there are differences in the shape and structure of the brain in autistic versus nonautistic children (ASA, 2005). Researchers are looking into the link between heredity, genetics, and medical problems. In some families there seems to be a pattern of autism supportive of a genetic basis, although no one gene or genes have been identified. For example, concurrent rates of autism in identical twins approach 90 percent (Blaxill, 2004). Rates of inherited genetic disease don't change abruptly in one generation—but autism rates have increased dramatically in the last decade (see Figure 6.1).

Theories on autism are being explored regarding problems during pregnancy or delivery as well as exposure to viral infections, metabolic imbalances, and environmental chemicals. Newly published research has uncovered a unique and consistent metabolic imbalance in autistic children when compared with normal healthy children (James et al., 2004, 2005). Autism tends to occur more often than expected among people with particular medical conditions including fragile X syndrome, tuberous sclerosis, congenital rubella syndrome, and untreated phenylketonuria (PKU) (ASA, 2005).

The possible relationship between vaccines and autism continues to be debated. Several studies are under way looking into the relation between vaccines containing thimerosal and autism, including a study being undertaken by the CDC (Verstraeten, 2004). A number of outdated theories have been dispelled: Autism is not caused by bad parenting and it is not a mental illness. No known psychological factors in a child's development have been shown to cause autism.

How Is Autism Diagnosed?

There is no medical test to indicate the presence of autism with the diagnosis based on the presence or absence of specific behaviors. Because many behaviors associated with autism also are found in other disorders, various medical tests may be indicated to rule out or identify other potential causes. Any child suspected of having autism should be evaluated by a *multidisciplinary team* of trained professionals, including a child psychologist or psychiatrist, speech pathologist, occupational therapist trained in sensory integration, and other professionals including a developmental pediatrician or pediatric neurologist.

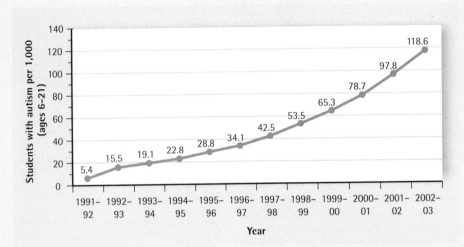

FIGURE 6.1 Children with a Diagnosis of Autism Attending U.S. Schools: 1991–2003 Autism is the most common of the pervasive developmental disorders affecting an estimated 1 in every 166 children (AAP, 2004). U.S. rates of autism increased from fewer than 6 cases per 10,000 children in the 1980s to more than 60 per 10,000 children today (Blaxill, 2004). The number of children diagnosed with autism is growing at a rate of 10 to 17 percent annually, and males make up 70 percent of all autism cases (Kurtz et al., 2003; U.S. Department of Education, 1999).

Source: U.S. Department of Education Annual Reports to Congress (IDEA). In Yazbak, F. E. (2003, Winter). Autism in the United States. *Journal of American Physicians and Surgeons, 8*(4), 103–107.

Effective Approaches for Autism

Diagnosing autistic spectrum disorder in younger children is imperative because the sooner the therapy begins, the more effective it can be. Children from birth to age 3 with the diagnosis of autism are eligible for early intervention services, and after age 3 they get services through their school districts. Various types of therapies are available to children diagnosed with autism including, but not limited to, applied behavioral analysis, auditory integration training, dietary interventions, music therapy, occupational therapy including sensory integration, physical therapy, speech/language therapy, the TEACHH (Treatment and Education of Autistic and related Communi-

cation Handicapped Children) program, vision therapy, and the relationship-development intervention program.

In 2003, the Autism Society of America estimated the cost of treating 1.5 million individuals with autism to be $90 billion a year, rising to $200 to $400 billion by 2010 (ASA, 2003). In addition to the economic costs of treatment, autism impacts the entire family, which must provide care to the loved one affected by this disorder. We are living in a time when many more treatments and therapies are available than only a few years ago. Many parents, doctors, researchers, and educators are working hard every day to find a cause and possible cure for autism; progress is being made, and lives of people with autism are being improved with daily developments in the field.

Theories of Personality Development

Over the past two decades, changes in family structures and stability for many families have precipitated an increasing sense of urgency on both a personal and societal level to discover the "best" parenting practices that promote the healthiest emotional-social development for all infants and children. As more parents become the sole caregiver or are overworked, chronically stressed, overtired, depressed, or unhealthy, there is little time or energy to properly nurture, stimulate, or protect infants and young children.

In contemporary American society there are widespread reports of family violence, chronic neglect, and abuse of young children perpetrated by up to 25 percent

of adults who themselves were victimized as children (Cohn, Salmon, & Stobo, 2002). "Childhood psychosocial dysfunction . . . has become widely acknowledged as the most common, chronic, condition of children and adolescents" (Jellinek & Murphy, 1999a).

Consequently, those of you who are, or plan to become, professionals in health, education, psychology, and human services occupations will play a significant role in ensuring that children at risk and their parents get the help that they need (Cohn, Salmon, & Stobo, 2001). Therefore, next we review major personality theories constructed and researched over the past century. These theories integrate abstract concepts to promote each child's healthy sense of self, including emotional development, the effects of close attachments, a sense of self-awareness, self-regulation and self-control, individual temperament, and a growing sense of social understanding (relating, learning to cooperate, complying with limits of behavior, empathizing with others, and handling frustrations and conflicts).

Beginning in the early 1900s, psychoanalytic and psychosocial scientists began to focus on the long-term developmental impact of healthy emotional development in infancy and early childhood. Later, behavioral and cognitive theories emerged. And more recently, ecological theories have been proposed (Thomas, Chess, & Birch, 1970).

The Psychoanalytic View

In the late 1800s to early 1900s, Sigmund Freud revolutionized the Western view of infancy by stressing the part early infant and childhood experience plays in fashioning the adult personality (see Chapter 2). Central to Freud's thinking was the idea that adult *neurosis* has its roots in childhood conflicts associated with the meeting of instinctual needs, such as sucking, expelling urine and feces, assertion of self, and pleasure (Freud, 1930/1961). Over the past 70 years, Freud's views have had an important influence on child-rearing practices in the United States. According to Freudians, the systems of infant care that produce emotionally healthy personalities include breast-feeding, a prolonged period of nursing, gradual weaning, an on-demand nursing schedule, delayed and patient bowel and bladder training, and freedom from excessive punishment.

Many pediatricians, clinical psychologists, and family counselors have accepted major tenets of Freudian theory, especially as popularized by the late Dr. Benjamin Spock through his best-selling book *Baby and Child Care,* first published in 1946 (and most recently in 1998). Through many revisions and editions, it is said to have sold more copies in 39 languages than any other book worldwide except the Bible.

Freud stated that infants become "fixated" in the oral stage if they are not allowed to continue to nurse at the breast or suck from a bottle until they are physically ready and motivated to drink from a cup. Likewise, Dr. Spock promoted an on-demand feeding schedule during infancy in contrast to a rigid schedule of feeding every two hours as determined by pediatricians. He urged parents to cuddle babies and bestow affection that would only make them happier and more secure. Pediatricians and other experts continue Dr. Spock's legacy at the DrSpock.com site.

Many psychologists, especially those influenced by the Freudian tradition, hold that children's relationships, especially with their mothers, in their early years are extremely significant and serve as prototypes for their later relationships. Viewed from this perspective, the flavor, maturity, and stability of a person's relationships derive from her or his early emotional-social ties. The goal of psychoanalytic therapy is to use therapeutic techniques to discover and discuss any traumatic events from early childhood concealed in the patient's subconscious that might be causing adult personality disturbances.

Psychoanalytic research, however, has produced few empirical findings, relying more on case studies and observational recordings. In an extensive study of child-rearing practices, Sewell and Mussen (1952) found no tie between the types of feeding schoolchildren had received as infants and their oral symptoms such as nail biting, thumb sucking, and stuttering. Many psychologists today believe that children are considerably more resilient and less easily damaged by traumatic events and emotional stress than what Freud thought to be true (Werner, 1990). Nor can parents expect to inoculate their children with love against any future difficulty, misfortune, misery, and psychopathology.

The Psychosocial View

As we noted in Chapter 2, Erikson maintained that the essential task of infancy, the **oral-sensory stage,** is the development of a basic trust in others, which occurs as a caregiver is responsive and consistent in feeding the infant. He argued that during infancy children learn whether the world is a good and satisfying place where one's needs are met by others—or a source of discomfort, frustration, and misery. If the child's basic needs are met with genuine and sensitive care, the child develops a "basic trust" in people and a foundation of self-trust (a sense of being "all right" and a complete self).

In Erikson's view, a baby's first social achievement is the willingness to let its mother move out of sight without undue anxiety or rage, because "she has become an inner certainty as well as an outer predictability" (Erikson, 1963, p. 247). The psychosocial psychologists highlight the importance of resolving progressive conflicts for healthy emotional and social development throughout life.

The Behavioral (Learning) View

The strict behaviorism (also called learning theory) of John Watson in the early 1900s, and later B. F. Skinner, had essentially eliminated the study of emotions from the curriculum of behavioral science during the 1940s and 1950s. Watson claimed he could take a dozen healthy infants and form them into anything he wanted them to be. Behaviorists recognize that infants are endowed with innate emotions (including fear, rage, and love) yet are unconcerned about the child's subconscious or inner feelings. They are more concerned with the outward display of emotions through observable behaviors, then rewarding "appropriate" behaviors or extinguishing "inappropriate" behaviors.

Through keen observation and a system of rewards or punishments, children's behaviors can be shaped or controlled. Reinforcement schedules, time-outs, and other behavioral techniques are used to create desired patterns of behavior and expression of emotions. Most early childhood education programs that follow principles of traditional behavioral theory do not give priority to emotional development (Hyson, 1994). By mastering specific academic and self-regulatory skills, children are supposed to gain positive feelings and self-confidence.

The Cognitive View and Information Processing

Since the 1960s a growing number of developmentalists and cognitive psychologists are focusing their research on components and stages of cognitive growth, building on the legacy of Jean Piaget's body of work on cognitive development in children. Legions of child psychologists and neuroscientists devote their attention to how children reason and solve problems, starting with the infant's experience of sensory stimulation. In the past they have viewed emotion as peripheral, of interest mostly when it interfered with rational thought or found deviant expression in the form of mental illness.

However, over the past decade or so, a renewed interest in the study of emotions is correcting the predominantly behavioral or cognitive view of human development. In the process, information-processing researchers and psychologists are rejecting the image of humankind as simply a "stimulus-response black box" or a "thinking machine" (Goode, 1991; Kagan, 1993). Contemporary theories attempt to examine cognitive, information-processing mechanisms that link affect (emotions) to thinking and behavior (Mayer, Ciarrochi, & Forgas, 2001).

Within the context of an increasing prevalence of behavioral and emotional problems in the United States and other countries, and mounting cross-cultural research on children's emotional well-being, pediatricians are more concerned than ever about identifying and treating children with emotional and/or psychosocial impairments. Because about 13 percent of preschoolers and 12 to 25 percent of all American school-age children display psychosocial problems, many pediatricians argue the *Pediatric Symptom Checklist (PSC)* should become a mandated part of all well-child checkups (Jellinek & Murphy, 1999b). The PSC (Figure 6.2) has been devised to reflect parents' perceptions of their children's psychosocial functioning. Recent findings from a national sample of American children revealed a higher prevalence of behavioral/emotional problems in children who live in poverty, reside in a single-parent family, have a family history of mental illness, or live in foster care (Jellinek & Murphy, 1999b; Rubin et al., 2004).

The Ecological View

Urie Bronfenbrenner's ecological theory (1997) posits that a variety of environmental influences—ranging from the child's family, school, and community experiences through global economic forces—contribute to the emotional and social development of children (see Chapter 2). Naturally the nuclear family, siblings, single parent, grandparent, stepparent, cohabiting partner or main caretaker are going to be major influences, at least initially. As we know, many young children are also in child-care or preschool environments, which means teachers and caretakers exert their influence several hours per day. The availability of high-quality child care, low-cost nutrition programs, and low-cost health care in a community directly affects each child's development. Opportunities for employment in a community can make or break a family—as can the cost of one major illness.

The policies established by state legislators also impact the services offered at a local level to families, especially for education and after-school programs, housing, and health care. Federal decisions to allocate funds to preserve economic stability by helping large corporations generally mean that there will be less funding for programs such as parental leaves of absence for child care. Federal laws can either keep families together or, through welfare incentives or judicial decrees, reward families to keep the father out of the home or involved at a minimal level, leading to even greater effects of poverty.

On a cultural level, a society's views can fluctuate regarding the value of traditional nuclear families, single-parent families, stepfamilies, cohabiting families, same-sex families, or the health and welfare of its youngest citizens. Although some European countries have national parental leave policies with compensation for early child care, the United States does not. In 1993 Congress passed the *Family and Medical Leave Act (FMLA)* that entitles eligible employees to take up to 12 weeks of unpaid, job-protected leave in a 12-month period for specified family and medical reasons and covers employees from public agencies and private-sector businesses that employ 50 or more employees.

A dramatic example of governmental and societal impact on families regards the hotly debated issue of family planning and abortion. The U.S. Supreme Court ruled in 1973 in *Roe* v. *Wade* that women have the right to abortion. As of 2001 at least 45 million abortions were performed legally in the United States (Strauss et al., 2004). The CDC reported a total of about 850,000 for 2001, reflecting significant decline since the early 1990s. Yet these figures reflect data from only 47 states (Strauss et al., 2004). If American women report that nearly half of all pregnancies were unplanned and unwanted—and half of the unwanted babies are aborted—then unintended pregnancy continues to be an issue of personal, social, medical, and economic concern in the United States (Fu et al., 1998). On an international level, as more scientists, medical practitioners, and citizens are urging the use of human embryonic stem cells for "treatment options" and "tissue-replacement therapies," American, European,

Pediatric Symptom Checklist (PSC)

Emotional and physical health go together in children. Because parents are often the first to notice a problem with their child's behavior, emotions or learning, you may help your child get the best care possible by answering these questions. Please indicate which statement best describes your child.

Please mark under the heading that best describes your child:

			NEVER	SOMETIMES	OFTEN
1.	Complains of aches and pains	1	_____	_____	_____
2.	Spends more time alone	2	_____	_____	_____
3.	Tires easily, has little energy	3	_____	_____	_____
4.	Fidgety, unable to sit still	4	_____	_____	_____
5.	Has trouble with teacher (6- to 16-year-old children only)	5	_____	_____	_____
6.	Less interested in school (6- to 16-year-old children only)	6	_____	_____	_____
7.	Acts as if driven by a motor	7	_____	_____	_____
8.	Daydreams too much	8	_____	_____	_____
9.	Distracted easily	9	_____	_____	_____
10.	Is afraid of new situations	10	_____	_____	_____
11.	Feels sad, unhappy	11	_____	_____	_____
12.	Is irritable, angry	12	_____	_____	_____
13.	Feels hopeless	13	_____	_____	_____
14.	Has trouble concentrating	14	_____	_____	_____
15.	Less interested in friends	15	_____	_____	_____
16.	Fights with other children	16	_____	_____	_____
17.	Absent from school (6- to 16-year-old children only)	17	_____	_____	_____
18.	School grades dropping (6- to 16-year-old children only)	18	_____	_____	_____
19.	Is down on him or herself	19	_____	_____	_____
20.	Visits the doctor with doctor finding nothing wrong	20	_____	_____	_____
21.	Has trouble sleeping	21	_____	_____	_____
22.	Worries a lot	22	_____	_____	_____
23.	Wants to be with you more than before	23	_____	_____	_____
24.	Feels he or she is bad	24	_____	_____	_____
25.	Takes unnecessary risks	25	_____	_____	_____
26.	Gets hurt frequently	26	_____	_____	_____
27.	Seems to be having less fun	27	_____	_____	_____
28.	Acts younger than children his or her age	28	_____	_____	_____
29.	Does not listen to rules	29	_____	_____	_____
30.	Does not show feelings	30	_____	_____	_____
31.	Does not understand other people's feelings	31	_____	_____	_____
32.	Teases others	32	_____	_____	_____
33.	Blames others for his or her troubles	33	_____	_____	_____
34.	Takes things that do not belong to him or her	34	_____	_____	_____
35.	Refuses to share	35	_____	_____	_____

Total score _____

Does your child have any emotional or behavioral problems for which she/he needs help? ( ) N ( ) Y

Are there any services that you would like your child to receive for these problems? ( ) N ( ) Y

If yes, what services? _____

FIGURE 6.2 Pediatric Symptom Checklist (available in English and Spanish) This is a parent-completed screening questionnaire, intended to be used as part of routine primary care visits, which would facilitate recognition of children's behavioral/emotional problems. Thirty-five items describe specific behaviors and emotions, and parents rate their child for how true each item is by using the following scale: 0 = not true (as far as you know); 1 = somewhat or sometimes true; 2 = very true or often true. For children aged 2 to 5, the scores on items 5, 6, 17, and 18 are ignored, and a total score based on the 31 remaining items is completed. The cutoff score for young children aged 2 to 5 is 24 or greater. For school-aged children 6 to 16 years, a total score of 28 or higher is taken as an indication of significant and psychosocial impairment. A medical receptionist or clinical aide would tally the scores on the checklist for pediatric follow-up.

Asian, and Australian policies, legislation, and views will continue to change toward the unborn (Darnovsky, 2004). (See *Further Developments:* "Stem Cell Research: Making Progress or Opening Pandora's Box?" in Chapter 3.)

Questions

What is the central focus of healthy personality development during the early years of life for each of the psychoanalytic, psychosocial, behavioral, cognitive, and ecological views? Is there any one personality theory that you believe covers all aspects of infant personality development? Explain your perspective.

Social Development

The Changing Demographics of Childhood

As we enter the twenty-first century, there is an increasing diversity of family structures and fewer two-parent families. Adding to this mix of societal concerns is the changing demographic nature of young children in the United States (see Figure 6.3). The number of young children in the United States has increased significantly since 1950. As of 2002, children made up about 25 percent of the U.S. population. Although the U.S. Census Bureau projects an increase in the number of children under age 19 by 2020, they will represent a smaller proportion of the population because there are well over 200 million and growing in the adult population. With more single parents and mothers employed outside the home than ever, a growing number of families need assistance from the larger community to provide high-quality care, emotional nurturance and stability, and supervision for vulnerable young children (Federal Interagency Forum on Child and Family Statistics, 2004).

What's the Point of All These Statistics?   You might be saying to yourself, who cares about all the numbers in Figure 6.3? This doesn't mean anything to me! Think again. What profession do you plan to pursue? Will there be jobs in your field of choice in 10 years? 20 years? 30 years? A steady increase of infants and preschool children has significant implications for your long-term employment opportunities in professions such as child care, preschool or Head Start, pediatric medicine, nursing, dental hygiene, speech therapy, physical therapy, occupational therapy, audiology, optometry, child psychology, social work, psychiatry, and many social science professorial or consulting occupations—in addition to opportunities for those of you who wish to write books or design software, playgrounds, toys, clothing, and furniture for infants and young children.

Those of you who plan to enter the field of business administration or management should consider the following: Do you plan to offer your future highly skilled employees the benefit of on-site child care, or would you allow more employees who are parents the flexibility to work from home computers? Your expenditure of time, effort, and money today should be examined in light of the population trends of those you wish to serve in the future. We shall revisit this figure in middle childhood and adolescence for those of you who wish to pursue occupations that serve older youth.

The Art of Becoming Human

Above all else, infants are social beings who need to become socialized into their own human group. As Harriet L. Rheingold (1969b, p. 781), a developmental psychologist puts it, "The human infant is born into a social environment; he can remain alive only in a social environment; and from birth he takes his place in that environment." Humanness, then, is a social product (Candland, 1993; O'Connor & Rutter, 2000; Wolff & Fesseha, 1999).

In this chapter you have been studying the typical course of early emotional development and attachment and their effects on what we call the consciousness of being. Yet it has been through the careful study of a number of atypical infants and children who have been isolated, orphaned, abandoned, or institutionalized and experienced severe deprivation and neglect that we have learned that human social contact makes us truly "human." Such intensely emotional experiences can often have far-reaching harmful consequences for those who are victimized.

Case Studies of Severe Early Deprivation   Without social interaction, human infants do not learn to walk upright; do not use a language to communicate needs; do not integrate sensory stimuli into conscious experience; and do not seem to have a sense of self, self-regulation, rational memory, or of any thoughts of the future. Perhaps you have already read the books *A Child Called It* by David Pelzer or his sequel *The Lost Boy.* His stories of extreme childhood neglect and abuse are publicized at a time when professionals are mandated to report such victimization so children are removed from such dangerous settings, but during his childhood and earlier, neglected and abused children, such as David, had nowhere to turn. Let us take a look at a few prominent cases.

Prolonged Neglect, Abuse, and Isolation   Two infants were born at a time in the United States when bearing children out of wedlock was extremely dishonorable: Anna and Isabelle were born illegitimate, and their mothers had hidden them in secluded rooms for years.

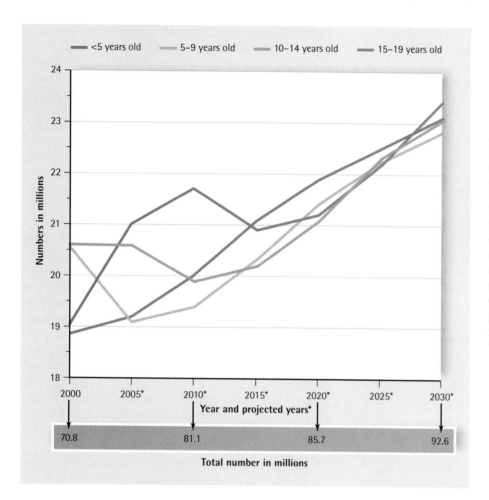

FIGURE 6.3 The Changing Demographics of Childhood: Number of U.S. Children, 19 and Under, Selected Years 2000 and Projected to 2030. Note that the U.S. Census Bureau projects a steady increase in young children under age 5 years over the next 25 years (see red line). Currently, children make up about 25 percent of the U.S. population. Yet children will make up a smaller *proportion* of the total U.S. population, which is well over 200 million adults and increasing as youth become adults. This projected trend has significant implications for all aspects of society and for many occupations that serve infants, young children, and adolescents.
Source: U.S. Bureau of the Census. No. 13, Resident Population Projections by Sex and Age: 2005–2050. *Statistical Abstract of the United States: 2003.*

Both received only enough care to keep them alive. When found, both were extremely retarded, showing few human capabilities or responses. In Anna's case

> [the child] could not talk, walk, or do anything that showed intelligence. She was in an extremely emaciated and undernourished condition . . . completely apathetic, lying in a limp, supine position and remaining immobile, expressionless, and indifferent to everything. Anna was placed in an institution for retarded children, where she died of hemorrhagic jaundice at 10 years of age. (Davis, 1949, pp. 204–205)

However, Isabelle received special training from members of the staff at Ohio State University. Within a week, she attempted her first vocalization. Isabelle rapidly progressed through the stages of social and cultural learning that are considered typical of U.S. children. She finished the sixth grade at age 14 and was judged to be a competent and well-adjusted student. Isabelle completed high school, married, and had her own normal family. A report on the two cases by sociologist Kingsley Davis (1949, pp. 207–208) concluded:

> Isolation up to the age of six, with failure to acquire any form of speech and hence missing the whole world

of cultural meaning, does not preclude the subsequent acquisition of these. . . . Most of the human behavior we regard as somehow given in the species does not occur apart from training and example by others. Most of the mental traits we think of as constituting the human mind are not present unless put there by communicative contact with others.

Thirty years later, near Los Angeles on November 4, 1970, a 13-year-old girl researchers called "Genie" (not her real name) was brought to a social worker, who thought the child was physically disabled, autistic, and about 6 years old. To her dismay she discovered that Genie had been kept naked, arms tied behind her back and harnessed on a potty seat by day and inside a small cage at night for the past 11 years. Her father had locked her up since she was 2 years old to "protect her from the dangers of the outside world." She was not allowed to talk or make noises nor was any family member allowed to talk in her presence—or she was beaten. Her bedroom where she "lived" had no stimuli. The father kept family members under control with a loaded shotgun.

When discovered at age 13, Genie was silent, understood only 20 words and would spit, sniff, and claw at things. She became the subject of intense rehabilitation and research scrutiny in language and behavioral studies. With persistent training from a linguist, Genie learned the names of things, but her use of English syntax (the correct order of words for meaning) was never fully grasped. After several years of residing with her psychologist/researcher, she lived in a series of abusive foster homes. In 1994 she became the subject of an award-winning NOVA documentary, *Secret of the Wild Child.* Currently she resides in a home with retarded adults ("Donation or Coercion?" 2001).

Abandonment and Emotional-Social Deprivation   In the late 1980s another child was found who had experienced severe effects of being orphaned and abandoned at the age of 4 after witnessing the murder of his mother. Several years later women in a rural village in Uganda found John Ssebunya living with a group of vervet monkeys. His remarkable rescue, education, and reintegration into society with a loving missionary couple were documented in a BBC film, *Living Proof* ("The Boy Who Lived with Monkeys," 1999). John made significant strides, and in 1999 at age 14 he flew to America to play soccer in the Special Olympics and to Britain to sing in a children's choir.

Douglas Candland, professor of psychology and animal behavior at Bucknell University and author of *Feral Children and Clever Animals,* examined John and concluded that it was obvious John had spent time living among the animals, but there was no way to know for how long or what they did for him. Since John learned to use basic language skills, then "this is evidence to support the argument that social factors are important to language acquisition" ("Studies of Feral Children," 2001).

Institutionalization and Severe Deprivation   Since the early 1990s many researchers have been studying the physical, emotional, cognitive, and social development of Romanian infants raised in orphanages and later adopted by American, Canadian, and European families—reported to be over 100,000 infants and children. In 1989, after the collapse of the dictatorship and the Romanian economy, it was discovered that thousands of Romanian infants and young children were abandoned to orphanages while older children were abandoned to the streets. The infants, raised in crowded, stark institutions, deprived of normal stimulation and nurturance by any significant caregiver, were considered to be the "lucky" ones because they had food and shelter. Only their basic physical needs were met due to overcrowding and understaffing, and they were severely deprived of cognitive-emotional-social attention (Kaler & Freeman, 1997).

The *English and Romanian Adoptees Study Team* are researching the deleterious impact of severe early deprivation on adopted survivors on a longitudinal

basis. From a pool of Romanian adoptees, two groups of children were randomly selected: those adopted before 24 months of age and those late-placed children adopted between 24 months and 42 months of age. The control group is comprised of within-country, early placed, nondeprived adoptees. The researchers' findings from extensive assessment at age 4 and age 6 indicate that children exposed to longer periods of deprivation exhibited increasingly greater deficits in cognitive, social, physical, and medical well-being (i.e., malnourished, small head circumference, delays in growth). The younger the infant was at adoption, the greater the resiliency following adversity, and psychosocial interventions played a significant role in catching up cognitive skills (O'Connor et al., 2003).

When families undertake late-onset adoptions, it is important that they are aware of the children's risks and vulnerabilities. It is recommended that internationally adopted children, once settled into their new home setting, should have a full multidisciplinary evaluation with subsequent assessments for the first few years after adoption. Early intervention services can target social-emotional, cognitive, motor, speech and sensory-integration issues and provide therapies, as needed (Berger, 2004). See the *Implications for Practice* "Licensed Certified Social Worker."

Reactive Attachment Disorder   Although the majority of these children display remarkable physical and cognitive resilience after being adopted, a subset of these Romanian adoptees are diagnosed with **reactive attachment disorder (RAD).** This clinical diagnosis includes the emotionally withdrawn/inhibited type of child who rarely looks for or reacts to comfort and doesn't show caregiver preference as well as the indiscriminate/disinhibited type of child who will look for affection nonselectively, even from adults who are strangers, and fail to show expected reserve with unfamiliar adults (DSM-IV and ICD 10). Studies of these children, months to years after adoption from Romanian institutions, have shown both patterns of attachment disorder with the disinhibited/indiscrimate type more prevalent (O'Connor et al., 2003; Zeanah, 2000).

Some children who experience multiple primary caregivers (such as living in successive foster homes) are also diagnosed with this disorder (Albus & Dozier, 1999). Infants who are disabled, unwanted, "difficult," lethargic, chronically ill, or experience extended separation from parents run a higher risk for RAD (Tibbits-Kleber and Howell, 1985). Characteristic risk factors for parents/caregivers who raise children with RAD include parental depression, isolation, and lack of social support, as well as extreme deprivation and abuse during their own upbringing (Culbertson & Willis, 1993). Increases in family social problems (i.e., separation, neglect and

Implications for Practice

Licensed Certified Social Worker
Carole A. Rosen, LCSW

I am a licensed certified social worker at the High Risk Birth Clinic in Binghamton, New York, and I presently work with families with children with disabilities or who have had babies born at risk. My main tasks are to complete child and family assessments, provide short-term and crisis intervention counseling, and to act as a liaison with community agencies. I am fluent in American Sign Language—thus I am called in to assist parents who are deaf, who have infants or young children with disabilities, to access necessary services.

I earned a bachelor's degree in sociology and humanities and a master's in social work (MSW). I am certified to practice in New York State (LCSW) and also am an American Certified Social Worker (ACSW). When I was a social worker at a developmental center, I planned, evaluated, and implemented clinical goals for mentally retarded, developmentally disabled, and head-injured clients as well as conducted orientation, training, and supervision of new social workers within the treatment team in counseling and behavior management techniques. I have also worked in a community college in New York, providing individual, vocational and academic counseling; administered a foster-care program for court adjudicated youths in a four-county region of upstate New York; and provided psychotherapy for individuals, couples, and families including play therapy for children in an agency and in private practice.

The characteristics a person should have to enjoy working as a social worker are compassion, patience, and tolerance. Anyone seeking an internship, supervised clinical experience, or work experience needs to enjoy working with families with children of diverse backgrounds, have knowledge of health-related and social issues and developmental disabilities, and have knowledge of community services and the ability to assess individuals and families for treatment. Also, you need to be flexible regarding work settings and family circumstances.

I believe that social work is an absolutely wonderful profession because you can work in so many different settings with such a wide variety of people. It is an exciting field where you are always learning from the people with whom you serve as well from the constant research being done in the field.

---

abuse, or foreign adoptions) may augment the frequency of this disturbance (DeAngelis, 1997a). Some adoptive parents have joined research groups or organized support groups to deal with the severe behavioral effects of their children's earlier physical, emotional, and social neglect (Kaler & Freeman, 1997; O'Connor et al., 2003).

Over the past century, researchers have demonstrated that physical contact and sensory stimulation improve the sensorimotor functioning of children in institutionalized settings (Saltz, 1973; White, 1969). Indeed, even a small amount of extra handling highlights the value of "enrichment," at least over the short term (Wolff & Fesseha, 1999). As pointed out in Chapter 2, although some children show greater resilience than child psychologists believed was the case only a few decades ago, others show greater vulnerability to deprivation experiences (Langmeier & Matějček, 1974; Rutter, 1974, 1998; Rutter et al., 1999). Overall, the research

on institutionalized infants supports the trend toward earlier adoption and the use of foster homes rather than institutions.

Questions

Psychologists stress that children's emotional ties in their early years are extremely significant and serve as models for their later relationships. What have we learned about the effects of severe emotional-social deprivation from the unusual cases of Anna, Isabelle, Genie, and John?

Early Relationships and Social Development

Over the past few decades, many social scientists have been studying the quality of early infant-mother (or infant-caretaker) relationships and various effects on the children's social development.

Maternal Responsiveness and the Strange Situation

Mary Ainsworth and her colleagues devised a procedure called the "Strange Situation" to capture the quality of attachment in the infant-parent relationship (Ainsworth, 1983; Ainsworth & Wittig, 1969). In the **Strange Situation** study, a mother and her infant enter an unfamiliar playroom where they find interesting toys as well as a stranger. After a few minutes, the mother leaves and the youngster is given an opportunity to explore the toys and interact with the unfamiliar adult. When the mother returns, the infant's behavior is observed, and then the procedure is repeated for a total of eight times with slightly different variations. Ainsworth became intrigued by differences in the children's behavior, especially the way they reacted upon reunion with their mothers (Ainsworth & Wittig, 1969):

> When their mother returned to the room, **securely attached infants** (pattern B attachments) would greet her warmly, show little anger, or indicate they wanted to be picked up and comforted by their mother. About 60 percent of the infants used the mother as a secure base from which to explore the unfamiliar environment and as a source of comfort following separation. Securely attached infants seemed to have received consistent, sensitive, and responsive mothering (Ainsworth, Bell, & Stayton, 1974).
>
> **Insecure/avoidant infants** (pattern A attachments), about 20 percent, ignored or avoided the mother on her return. Subsequent studies have repeated and extended the Strange Situation research, suggesting that these infants show little distress at being released from the parent's hold and tend to treat a stranger with a response similar to that given to the parent. Typically these infants are easily consoled by a stranger (Wilson, 2001).
>
> **Insecure/resistant infants** (pattern C attachments), about 10 to 15 percent, were reluctant to explore the new setting when they entered the playroom and would cling to the mother and hide from the stranger. However, when the mother returned after her brief absence, the infant would initially seek contact with the mother only to reject her by squirming, pushing her away, with continued crying. Ainsworth (1993) finds these children display more maladaptive behaviors and tend to be angrier than the infants in the other groups.

Using the Strange Situation method, Main and Solomon (1986) identified another attachment category:

> **Disorganized/disoriented infants** (pattern D attachments). D-pattern youngsters seem to lack coherent coping strategies during separation episodes, and upon parental return, they indicate confusion and apprehension toward their mothers (Jacobsen, Edelstein, & Hofmann, 1994). Moreover, D-pattern youngsters apparently are at greater risk for social maladaptation

in childhood (Lyons-Ruth, Alpern, & Repacholi, 1993; Vondra et al., 2001). D patterns are likely to be linked to parents who suffered from abuse or deep emotional loss and have not yet resolved these issues.

Ainsworth contended that the A, B, and C patterns of attachment behavior in the Strange Situation reflect the quality of maternal caregiving children receive during their first 12 months of life. She traced the origins of the A and C patterns to a disturbed parent-child relationship, one in which the mother was rejecting, interfering, or inconsistent in caring for the child. The mothers would often over- or understimulate their baby; fail to match their behavior to that of the child; be cold, irritable, and insensitive; and afford perfunctory care. Although all children classified as either anxiously or insecurely attached do not suffer from attachment disorders, researchers have found a subgroup of insecurely attached young children as having reactive attachment disorder, described earlier in this chapter (Wilson, 2001).

And even though mothers are influenced by the temperaments of their youngsters (for instance, whether they are irritable and difficult), this factor does not seem to be critical in determining a mother's responsiveness to her child's signals and needs (Belsky & Rovine, 1987). On the whole, other researchers have confirmed the Ainsworth findings, although the relationship is not as strong as Ainsworth initially suggested (Cassidy & Berlin, 1994; Wilson, 2001). Moreover, the quality of a relationship, once formed, is not necessarily permanent (Belsky, 1996a).

Early attachment behaviors are predictive of children's functioning in other areas. Mastery motivation seems to be associated with secure attachment (Yarrow et al., 1984). And some studies report a relationship between attachment security and cognitive development. Recently a longitudinal study was published reporting findings that "maternal responsiveness at both ages (9 and 13 months) predicted the timing of children's achieving language milestones" (Tamis-LeMonda, Bornstein, & Baumwell, 2001). The effects of early attachments similarly carry over to later social relationships (Vondra et al., 2001; Wilson, 2001).

Stranger Anxiety and Separation Anxiety   Wariness of strangers, an expression of the fear-wariness behavior system, usually emerges about a month or so after specific attachment begins. **Stranger anxiety,** a wariness of unknown people, seems to be rather common among 7- to 8-month-old infants, seems to peak at 13 to 15 months, and decreases thereafter. When encountering a strange person, particularly when a trusted caretaker is absent, many youngsters frown, whimper, fuss, look away, and even cry (Morgan & Ricciuti, 1969; Waters, Matas, & Sroufe, 1975). Even at 3 and 4 months of age, some babies stare fixedly at a strange person, and occasionally this prolonged inspection leads to crying (Bronson, 1972).

Another common behavior 8-month-old infants display is **separation anxiety,** distress shown when a familiar caregiver leaves. Parents would do well to introduce grandparents and baby-sitters to an infant during the earlier stages of infancy so there is a caretaker that both the parents and the baby trust when it comes time to go out for an evening together. Sometimes the baby's distress at being left alone with a stranger is so intense that the baby cries the whole time the parents are gone. Most likely those of you who have earned money by baby-sitting can relate to this experience. This can be an extremely volatile situation, because the baby-sitter might not be able to tolerate the noise of loud, prolonged crying and might attempt unhealthy measures to quiet the child. Infant abuse and infant homicide have occurred under these circumstances (see "Shaken Baby Syndrome" in Chapter 4). All local YWCAs, Cooperative Extension, and Red Cross programs provide baby-sitter training, and many high schools offer parenting classes.

Facilitating Secure Attachment

Classifications derived from the Strange Situation predict social functioning in preschool with teachers and peers. Youngsters judged to have secure attachments to their mothers are socially more competent in preschool, sharing more and showing a greater capacity to initiate and sustain interaction. Such children are also more accepting of their mothers' showing attention to their older brothers and sisters, and secure older siblings are more likely to assist and care for their younger brothers and sisters than are insecure older siblings (Teti & Ablard, 1989). And the B-pattern children seem more resilient and robust when placed in stressful or challenging circumstances (Stevenson-Hinde & Shouldice, 1995).

These findings are consistent with the speculations of attachment theorists that young children who enjoy a secure attachment to their parents develop internal "representational models" of their parents as loving and responsive and of themselves as worthy of nurturance, love, and support. By contrast, youngsters with insecure attachments develop "representational models" of the caregiver as unresponsive and unloving and of themselves as unworthy of nurturance, love, and support (Bowlby, 1969, 1988; Vondra et al., 2001). Some evidence suggests that the various patterns of attachment might be transmitted across generations via parents' states of mind, their internal working models of attachment relationships that they subtly communicate to their children (Benoit & Parker, 1994; Bowlby, 1969; Wilson, 2001).

Goodness of Fit

Thomas and Chess (1987) have introduced the notion of "goodness of fit" to refer to the match between the characteristics of infants and their families. In a good match, the opportunities, expectations, and demands of the environment are in accord with the child's temperament. A good match fosters optimal development. Conversely, a poor fit makes for a stormy household and contributes to distorted development and maladaptive functioning. Thomas emphasizes that parents need to take their baby's unique temperament into account in their child-rearing practices. Children do not react in the same ways to the same developmental influences. Domineering, controlling parental behavior can make one child anxious and submissive and lead another to be defiant and antagonistic. As a consequence, Thomas and his colleagues (1963, p. 85) conclude, "There can be no universally valid set of rules that will work equally well for all children everywhere." Parents with difficult babies often feel considerable anxiety and guilt. "What are we doing wrong?" they ask. The knowledge that certain characteristics of their child's development are not primarily due to parental malfunctioning has proven helpful to many parents. A given environment does not have identical functional consequences for all children; if you have siblings, you know this to be true. Babies are individualists from the moment they draw breath. In actuality, pregnant women are likely to notice temperamental differences when the fetus is still in the womb.

Researchers highlight the importance of adjusting child-rearing practices to the needs of individual children, but sometimes caregivers encounter children who overreact to sensory stimulation, are highly excitable, or who have behavioral "meltdowns." A. Jean Ayres, an occupational therapist who worked with children with developmental disabilities, developed sensory integration theory about brain-behavior relationships. **Sensory integration** is "a normal developmental process that allows one to take in, process and organize sensations one receives from one's body and the environment" (Ayres, 1972, p. 11). Although people are familiar with the senses of sight, touch, sound, taste, and smell, most do not know the nervous system also senses movement, the force of gravity and body position (referred to as *vestibular* and *proprioceptive* systems). Not only is it important to a child's well-being that the sensory systems function effectively, but that all of the senses work well together.

A child who is overly sensitive or avoids stimulation can be referred to as *sensory defensive.* Such a child exhibits the fight-or-flight reaction to an otherwise nonthreatening sensation. Thus, a child may perceive touch, sound, taste, or movement as threatening or even painful. A child who underreacts will seek out stimulation in greater intensity and duration than the typical child, sometimes hurting himself (i.e., banging his head or running into walls). These issues may impact on a child's ability to adapt to behavioral demands of daily life within a family, and a referral to an occupational therapist with training and expertise in sensory integration may be appropriate (Bundy, Lane & Murray, 2002).

Children, then, are active agents in the socialization process; they are influenced by, but also influence, their caretakers (Rickman & Davidson, 1994). For instance, even very young infants seek to control their mothers' actions. The infant and the mother might be looking at one another. Should the baby look away and on turning back find the mother's gaze turned away, the baby will start fussing and whimpering. When the mother again gazes at the infant, she or he stops the commotion. Infants quickly learn elaborate means for securing and maintaining their caretaker's attention (Lewis, 1995, 1998).

Indeed, as Harriet L. Rheingold (1968, p. 283) observes: "Of men and women [the infant] makes fathers and mothers." Thus, to a surprising degree, parents are molded by the very children they are trying to rear. Of particular importance in these complex processes are the nature and quality of the emotional bonds or ties that evolve between youngsters and their caretakers—in brief, attachment (Belsky, 1996a, 1996b).

Cultural Differences in Child Rearing

Child-rearing practices differ from one society to another, with greater contrast between industrialized and nonindustrialized countries. In Chapter 4 we learned that in many cultures of the world the mother cradles her baby next to her body during the day—even if working in the fields—and at night, continues to share sleeping quarters for at least a few years. Attachment patterns differ also (Harwood, 1992). A-pattern infants are relatively more prevalent in western European nations and C-pattern infants in Israel and Japan (Van IJzendoorn & Kroonenberg, 1988). West European nations such as Sweden have well-developed and competent national child-care systems, and parents are financially compensated for one year for staying at home to raise children.

Cross-cultural researchers conclude that the quality of the caregiver's sensitivity and emotional availability early in life is critical to the development of an infant's healthy internal representation of the self, the attachment figure, and the external world (Van IJzendoorn & Hubbard, 2000).

Cultural Differences in Attachment An Indonesian mother facilitates physical and social contact with her child by a culturally evolved carrying contrivance. A solid attachment between child and caretaker promotes the youngster's emotional and social development; it eases and forestalls episodes of fussing and crying. Notice, though, that this child appears a little unsure of the photographer.

Questions

Perhaps you, like us, are wondering about how various aspects of attachment theory and "goodness of fit" apply to Osama bin Laden, leader of a terrorist organization known as Al-Qa'edah (the Base) with the explicit aim to wage a jihad against the West, especially the United States. From various accounts, he is one of 50 to 53 children (news accounts say 50; whereas a sister-in-law says 53) by one of his father's four wives (polygamy is culturally acceptable in Saudi Arabia). Read the following quote before continuing:

> The father had very dominating personality. He insisted to keep all his children in one premises. He had a tough discipline and observed all the children with strict religious and social code. He maintained a special daily program and obliged his children to follow. . . . He dealt with his children as big men and demanded them to show confidence at young age. He was very keen not to show any difference in the treatment of his children. . . . Osama lost his father when he was 13 and married at age 17. (*Frontline*, A Biography of Osama bin Laden)

Based on the research and readings about early relationships and social development, what style of early attachment would you say is likely for this man who harbors such anger and hatred? A? B? C? D? Does the concept of "goodness of fit" apply? What cultural factors in child rearing might be involved?

Child Care for Infants and Toddlers

Presently, the U.S. Department of Health and Human Services is conducting the largest longitudinal study ever undertaken, *The National Children's Study,* in which researchers from a consortium of 40 agencies will examine the effects of many environmental influences (including social and emotional) on the health and development of more than 100,000 children from 96 sites. This is the largest-scale study of its kind, following participants from before birth until age 21—with the goal of improving child health and well-being ("Growing Up Healthy," 2004). Child-care arrangements are among the main variables under scrutiny, because early experiences with people shape a child's personality, mind, and behaviors (Phillips & Adams, 2001).

Caregiver-Infant Interaction

Child-care quality is of great concern to social scientists, because they stress that children's emotional ties in their early years are extremely significant for physical, cognitive, and emotional development and serve as models for later relationships. Since the 1970s many American families have moved from the three-generation model of child care in the home evident in many other countries. For example, in Japan, China, and India it is the norm for grandparents to live with their children and help care for their grandchildren. In the United States grandparents and others in the extended family might live nearby, but many live hundreds or thousands of miles away.

Compounding the effects of this unraveling of the traditional family model is the rapid growth in maternal employment to provide economic security for families, high rates of divorce and single parenting, and nonmarital childbearing (Phillips & Adams, 2001).

The U.S. Bureau of Labor Statistics (2004b) data for 2003 shows that more than half (54 percent) of married mothers with children under age 3 were employed either full- or part-time and that more than half (55 percent) of unmarried mothers (never married, divorced, separated, and widowed) with children under age 3 were employed either full- or part-time. This reveals a steep increase in the number of mothers with infants in the workforce since 1975 (34 percent). Thus, young children in the United States are supervised and socialized by fewer parents and are cared for by a larger array of nonfamilial persons than ever before. Child care for infants and toddlers is the most scarce and expensive, and children in working-poor families are at highest risk for poor-quality care. Figure 6.4 sheds light on child-care arrangements (The Urban Institute, 2004).

A diversity of programs, federal policies, and funding subsidies have evolved—and continue to evolve—to

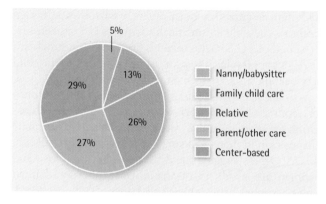

FIGURE 6.4 Child-Care Arrangements for Children Under Age 5 with Employed Mothers, 2002 For mothers who work, many babies are in child care by the age of 3 months—averaging about 28 hours per week, increasing to 35 hours a week by age 2. Infants are more likely to be in other-parent or relative care than older children. Nearly three out of four children younger than 5 with employed mothers are regularly in nonparental child care. *Source:* From *Fast Facts on Welfare Policy.* The Urban Institute, 2002 National Survey of America's Families, http://www.urban.org/uploadedpdf/900706.pdf. Reprinted with permission.

assist in the important task of daily child care for a growing number of babies and toddlers. In 2004, California passed the *Paid Family Leave Act* allowing both female and male employees up to six weeks of *paid* leave to spend time with newborn or newly adopted children, and a recent corporate survey shows that 14 percent of U.S. companies grant paid paternity leave (e.g., Microsoft, IBM, Merrill-Lynch, Eli Lilly, Ikea, and KPMG accounting firm) (Goff, 2004).

The Mother as Caretaker Freudian theory has underlain much research on attachment behaviors, drawing attention to the mother's influence on her developing child. Freud (1940, p. 188) saw the child's relationship to the mother as having lifelong consequences, calling it "unique, without parallel, established unalterably for a whole lifetime as the first and strongest love-object and as the prototype of all later love relations—for both sexes." In keeping with how strongly the psychoanalytic tradition has influenced U.S. life, researchers, clinical psychologists, psychiatrists, sociologists, and the court system have for many decades focused almost exclusively on the mother-child tie. A majority of Americans believe that mothers should be home to care for the very young, yet they also realize that families need child-care assistance to balance employment and child-care responsibilities (K. Sylvester, 2001). The American court system continues to favor the psychoanalytic view that mothers are absolutely critical for child nurturance, are the best parent, and are less likely to abandon their children. In the case of *Nguyen* v. *INS* the Supreme Court upheld an immigration law that explicitly favors the biological mother and penalizes biological fathers: If a child of a

U.S. female citizen is born out of wedlock in a foreign country, the child automatically acquires U.S. citizenship. If a child of a U.S. male citizen is born out of wedlock in a foreign country, legal steps must be taken before the child can become an American citizen (T. Sylvester, 2001).

Some scientists suggest that biological predeterminers contribute to a more nurturant, "maternal" disposition in women and a more instrumental, "paternal" disposition in men (Erikson, 1964; Harlow, 1971; Rossi, 1977). Others suggest the differences between men and women are products of the distinct, socially defined roles assumed by mothers and fathers (Parsons, 1955). Traditionally, a mother's role was to perform general household labor—and child care was simply a component of household labor. Traditionally, a father's role was to be the "breadwinner," to invest time and effort in advancing in his career, and he was not expected to do domestic chores. Today, the roles are merging.

Who Changes the Diapers?   With a high percentage of mothers employed either full-time or part-time, the division of household labor, including child care, for couples is often a point of conflict. Although research studies find that more fathers are doing child care and domestic chores, mothers still do about 80 percent of the child care (Kroska, 2004; Yeung et al., 2001). Often there is a presumption (erroneous as it may be) that working mothers still have more free time than working fathers, who may work longer hours. Thus, typically mothers in two-parent families devote more time to child care than fathers do (Kroska, 2004; Voydanoff, 2004). Recent findings indicate that fathers in intact families spend more

time caring for their older children than for infants and preschoolers (Aldous & Mulligan, 2002). The quality of a marriage is also related to father participation in housework and child care.

Another explanation for the unequal "division of labor" is *human capital theory:* The spouse who earns more money has greater power to avoid doing household or child-care tasks. Obviously, single-parent moms shoulder the full responsibility of earning an income, doing household labor, and managing child care. Only more recently have social scientists examined the significant role that both mothers and fathers play in children's lives, above and beyond financial support.

The Father as Caretaker   Social definitions of fatherhood have alternated over the past century between two poles: fathers as providers and fathers as nurturers (Atkinson & Blackwelder, 1993). In the past decade there has been a revolution in the thinking of social scientists and policymakers about the importance of fathers in young children's emotional, cognitive, and social development (Aldous & Mulligan, 2002).

Increasingly, researchers conclude that fathers are just as good as mothers at taking care of, nurturing, and bonding with children, even in early infancy (Nielsen, 2001). Also, when fathers become involved in caring for their infants, the more likely they are to continue caring for their children five years later. A father caring for his infant is a dynamic in promoting both a healthier child and marital satisfaction (Aldous & Mulligan, 2002).

Parke (1979) observed the behavior of parents of newborns and found that fathers were just as responsive

Fathers Factor Significantly in the Lives of Their Children The presence of a positive father-child relationship improves a child's overall academic achievement and IQ test performance, self-esteem, social competence, and ability to develop self-control and avoid unhealthy behaviors. The federal government is funding community-based education programs to promote involved, responsible, and committed fatherhood for all fathers. Infants also make a considerable contribution to the development of fatherliness through eliciting, evoking, provoking, promoting, and nudging fathering from men.

as mothers to their infants' vocalizations and movements. Fathers touched, looked at, talked to, rocked, and kissed their babies in much the same fashion as mothers do. And fathers, when alone with their infants, are as protective, giving, and stimulating as mothers. Fathers also play more physical games with their children. And they also play more rough-and-tumble games, such as tossing the baby in the air (Parke, 1996, 1998).

Significantly, infants make a considerable contribution to the development of fatherliness through eliciting, evoking, provoking, promoting, and nudging fathering from men (Pruett, 1987). Not surprisingly, John Snarey (1993), drawing from a four-generation, four-decade study of men, finds that fathers who participate actively in child rearing are more likely to become "societally generative" at midlife. Fathers are important in still another respect. Studies show that a mother performs better in the parenting role when the father provides her with emotional support and encouragement (Belsky, 1996a, b). The man who gives warmth, love, and ego gratification to his wife helps her feel good about herself, and she is then more likely to pass on these feelings to their child.

Moreover, being a father contributes to a man's self-concept, personality functioning, and overall satisfaction with life. Men are increasingly recognizing that a close relationship with children is beneficial to both child and adult. In the 1990s more men were "stay-at-home dads," doing much of the child care, while the mother took on the role of earning income. In some families, during the day the mother works and the father stays home with the children—then in the evening the father works and the mother takes over child care (or vice versa). Today, 5 percent of children are living with single-parent fathers (approximately 4 million men) (Fields, 2003).

Absentee Fathers   "The research is clear: Fathers factor significantly in the lives of their children. There is simply no substitute for the love, involvement, and commitment of a responsible father" (Bush, 2001; National Fatherhood Initiative, 2004). Regarding fathering, there seems to be two opposing trends evident in the United States. Although more fathers are providing child care, an increasing number of children are living in homes where their fathers are not present, nor have their fathers invited them to their homes, nor do some children know who their father is. The numbers speak for themselves: 24 million children, one in every three, live in homes where their biological father is absent (T. Sylvester, 2001). These rates are exceptionally high in comparison to only one out of ten in 1960 (T. Sylvester, 2001).

The media has focused attention on unwed fathers: Sensational anecdotes portray them as shiftless and irresponsible, providing neither financial nor psychological support for their children. However, evidence is emerging that challenges such generalizations and shows the diversity of this population (Lerman, 2002). For several years, the *National Fatherhood Initiative* has held national summits on fatherhood, offering information about community-based fatherhood programs in cities across the country that promote involved, responsible, and committed fatherhood for all fathers. The promoters of the fatherhood movement state, "father absence remains the most consequential social problem of our time" (T. Sylvester, 2001, p. 4). Wade Horn, assistant secretary of the U.S. Department of Health and Human Services, states that he oversees 65 different social programs at a cost of $47 billion annually—and the need for such programs is related to the breakup of families, the trend toward single-parent families and absentee fathers (Wetzstein, 2004). Thus, the federal government is funding "healthy marriage and parental relationship" projects in various sites in the country.

The trend in absentee fathers has the utmost social significance, because research shows that fathering is not an unnecessary or superfluous matter. It seems that boys are more affected by the father's absence than girls are (Cooksey & Craig, 1998). Boys from fatherless homes exhibit less well-internalized standards of moral judgment in comparison to boys from intact homes. They tend to evaluate the seriousness of misbehavior according to the probability of detection or punishment rather than in terms of interpersonal relations and social responsibility (Hoffman, 1971).

Research data also reveal that the absence of a positive father-child relationship impairs a child's overall academic achievement and IQ test performance, self-esteem, social competence, and ability to develop self-control and avoid unhealthy behaviors (smoking, substance abuse, early sexual experience, criminal and gang behaviors, abuse from others) (Brotherson, Amamoto, & Acock, 2003; Lamb, 1997). The extent of the impairment is greater the younger the child was when the father left and the longer the father has been absent.

A study of the effect of parental separation on children in their first three years of life showed their psychological development was affected by mother's income, education, ethnicity, beliefs about child rearing, and symptoms of depression and behavior (Clarke-Stewart et al., 2000). Also, recent findings suggest the mother's remarriage, especially if it occurs early in the child's life, appears to be associated with an improvement in intellectual performance (White & Gilbreth, 2001).

Good, Better, Best?   One should not conclude that either mothering or fathering is superior to the other. Each parent affords the child somewhat different kinds of experiences. The ability to nurture is not the property of one sex or the other, and societies can differ considerably in their definitions of the parenting roles. For instance, in a survey of 141 societies, fathers in 45 societies (nearly one-third) maintained a "regular, close" or "frequent, close" proximity with the infant. At the other extreme, in 33 societies (23 percent), fathers rarely or never were in close proximity to the infant (Crano, 1998).

All of this is not to say that mothers and fathers are interchangeable; they make their own contributions to children's care and development. Research suggests that the mother-child and father-child relationships might well be qualitatively different and might have different influences on a child's development (Biller, 1993). Lamb (1977, 1997) finds, for instance, that mothers most often hold babies to perform caretaking functions, whereas fathers spend four to five times as much time playing with their infants as in diapering them, feeding them, washing them, and the like. Today's social scientists are examining children's everyday interactions with both parents. They find that infants learn a good many lessons from the continuities that take place in these early relationships. It seems to be that small moments—not the dramatic episodes or traumas—give rise to most of the expectations that children evolve and bring to their later relationships.

Sibling-Infant Interaction

The birth of a new baby has a significant impact on older siblings. Siblings will have to adjust and accept less attention from their parents, while still getting their needs met within the family situation (Aldous, Mulligan, & Bjarnason, 1998). According to research by Dunn (1993), some siblings become "initiators" with parents to get their needs met, whereas others withdraw and appear to resent the baby more. Wise parents prepare other children in age-appropriate ways for the arrival of a new baby in the family. Some families have older children attend the new sibling's birth; others decide to introduce the new baby to siblings when they bring the baby home from the hospital.

Most siblings display a strong degree of caring, attachment, and protectiveness toward a new child in the family. From the wealth of research on infant cognitive, social, and emotional development over the past 30 years, we know that babies need and appreciate sensory and emotional stimulation, and an older sibling is just the perfect person to assist. Siblings typically spend a great deal of time together, become playmates and companions (depending on age span), and influence social and cognitive learning (Azmitia & Hesser, 1993).

There appears to be cultural differences in the relationship of older siblings to younger ones regarding voluntary responsibility, sharing of a wanted object, and allowing the younger child freedom of choice (Mosier & Rogoff, 2003). Older siblings typically serve as the models for younger siblings, and younger siblings often want to "tag along" with older children. This can create conflict at times, but siblings normally learn to get along

Sibling Interactions and Culture Americans are often shocked to see children care for younger siblings in other cultures, but people from other cultures would be shocked to see that American babies spend so much time alone in infant carriers, cribs, and strollers.

with each other and to share with each other. As we shall see in Chapter 18, we normally have our longest-lasting relationships with siblings (Bank & Kahn, 1997).

Questions

Who is most likely to perform child-care duties in a two-parent family and why? In what ways does a father benefit from starting to take care of his infant from the beginning? If you have siblings, how important were they in your "growing-up" years? What is the quality of your relationship with them now?

Grandparent or Kinship Care

The term **kinship care** has evolved to mean an arrangement in which a relative or someone else emotionally close to a child takes primary responsibility for rearing the child ("Report to the Congress," 2004). Researchers, policymakers, human services professionals, school officials, clergy, and medical professionals noticed a substantial increase in children living with other relatives since the early 1990s, with the greatest growth occurring among grandchildren living with grandparents—and no parent present. In a 1996 survey, the American Association of Retired Persons (AARP) found that American grandparents are raising their grandchildren for the following reasons: drug abuse, child abuse, child abandonment, teen pregnancy, parent illness or death, parent incapable, or incarceration or institutionalization of parent.

Best estimates from the 2002 Census tell us that about 3 million grandparents in the United States are raising one or more grandchildren, more than half of these grandparents are over the age of 50, and most do not have a formal education and are more likely to live in poverty. About one-third of the grandchildren residing with grandparents are under the age of 6 (Fields, 2003; Scarcella, Ehrle, & Geen, 2003). These figures are difficult to extract, because more than 5 million grandchildren reportedly reside with grandparents and parents, yet in other instances, the grandparents and grandchildren reside together with no parent present (Bryson & Casper, 1999). One finding is that African American grandmothers are likely to take on much of the responsibility for children of adolescent parents (Sadler, Anderson, & Sabatelli, 2001). Some of these grandparents are officially foster parents and eligible for financial assistance, whereas others have sought guardianship or legal custody of their grandchildren, and some have no legal status.

Family structure, including information on the marital status and gender of the grandparents—and the presence or absence of parents—helps providers understand the needs of these families and their eligibility for services for the grandchildren (Scarcella, Ehrle, & Geen, 2003). For example, grandchildren living with a grandmother only and no parent present have the highest poverty rate. For those of you who plan to work in public policy, business management, human services, social work, school administration, hospital administration, or gerontology services, you may want to examine the Urban Institute report, *Identifying and Addressing the Needs of Children in Grandparent Care,* to understand the full impact of the different family types on the well-being of both grandparents and young grandchildren.

Raising one's grandchildren has not always been expected to be part of the normal developmental sequence for the majority of American elderly, and many face serious economic hardship on fixed incomes in retirement or they delay retirement (Scarcella, Ehrle, & Geen, 2003). Most are unaware of community resources and may not want to seek public aid, but across the country grandparents are establishing support groups through senior citizen centers and are sharing ideas, resources, and comfort. Although it is natural for grandparents to be upset with their own child for being incapable of parenting the grandchildren, most grandparents find meaning and satisfaction from providing infants and young children with the love, care, stimulation, and security they need for normal emotional and social development (Bryson & Casper, 1999; Waldrop & Weber, 2001).

Early Child-Care Practices

Child-Care Centers Several important social forces have given impetus to the child-care movement in the United States. Families are paying more taxes at all levels of government—forcing mothers and fathers, if present, to work longer hours to support a continued level of economic security. There has been a substantial increase in single-parent families (divorced and never married). Public policy, such as welfare-to-work legislation, also forces mothers living in poorer circumstances to go to work, with a minimal level of subsidized support for child-care assistance. Thus, more than 60 percent of U.S. mothers of preschool-age children are now in the workforce, compared with 29 percent in 1970.

According to the *Gallup Poll Monthly,* nearly half of Americans favored one parent staying home to raise their children (McComb, 2001). When it comes to toddlers, nearly one-half still think that home is best, but one-third prefer child-care centers. However, most infants with working mothers spend the day with relatives in either their own home or another home. As stated earlier, with the passage of the *Family and Medical Leave Act* in 1993, a parent can get 12 weeks of unpaid, job-protected leave from work following childbirth or during serious illness, which has helped alleviate stress, allowing for managing work and family priorities.

Many critics of child care say that children require continuity, stability, and predictability in their care. Followers of the psychoanalytic tradition emphasize that a child's emotional breadth and depth and capacity to love are derived from the experience of love in the early years. Other researchers say emotional competence is a contributor to young children's social success (Campbell, Lamb, & Hwang, 2000; Denham et al., 2001). But in a center children must share the attention of a child-care worker with other youngsters. Add to this vacations and job turnover, and a child ends up with no one special person to be close to.

Much child-care research has been undertaken in centers associated with universities. Such centers have low staff-child ratios and well-designed programs directed at fostering the children's cognitive, emotional, and social development. Many of the childcare workers

More Information You Can Use

Elements of Quality Child Care

Thirteen Indicators of Quality Child Care	
Indicator	**Description**
1. Prevention of child abuse	Fewer instances of abuse occur in child-care programs than in homes or residential facilities. A program can do the following to help curb child abuse: Increase caregiver support, through low child: staff ratios and sufficient breaks; inform caregivers of their legal responsibilities and their rights and protections under the law; focus on positive behavior; evaluate program with feedback to staff; provide sufficient training opportunities; and offer social support, parent networking, child-rearing advice, and informal counseling to troubled parents.
2. Immunizations	Young children in child care face an increased risk of acquiring infectious diseases as compared with older children and adults. Immunizations help protect children both during childhood and for the rest of their lives. Reviewing and monitoring child-care center records increases the reported rate of correctly immunized preschool children. Statewide systems as implemented in Pennsylvania such as ECELS TRAC, developed by the Early Childhood Education Linkage System, are very effective interventions.
3. Staff:child ratio, group size	These are two of the best indicators for determining the quality of a child-care program. They significantly affect many other health and safety issues, such as the transmission of disease, which is greater when there are more children and adults present. These two indicators also improve the caregiving behaviors of staff and the safety of children. Research on mental health and school readiness demonstrate that more secure attachments occur with lower child:staff ratios and smaller group sizes.
4. & 5. Staff—director and teachers— qualifications (two indicators)	Educated and trained caregivers are more likely to promote the physical and mental health, safety, and cognitive development of children in their care. Experienced and educated directors more effectively and appropriately monitor their staff. College-educated caregivers encourage children more, exhibit more teacher direction, and engage in less restrictive behavior. They are more likely to continue in child-care employment, which impacts turnover and helps with attachment and bonding with very young children.
6. Staff training	Directors' and caregivers' training hours in the first year should be 30 hours per year and then 24 hours yearly thereafter. Staff training programs help to reduce the transmission of infectious diseases, reduce the number of accidental injuries in child-care centers, and help to better facilitate a positive learning and socialization environment. Trainings should build on one another and actively involve the participants in learning. Mentoring programs are a good example of this type of training.

are highly motivated and dedicated students preparing for careers as teachers. Yet most of the child care currently available to American parents is not of this type and quality. (See the *More Information You Can Use* box above, "Elements of Quality Child Care.") Regrettably, in most child-care centers, group size is large, the ratio of caretakers to children is high, the staff is untrained or poorly supervised, staff turnover is frequent because of low pay—all of which compromises a child's well-being. In 2002, child-care workers earned $7.86 median hourly wages and salary, much less per hour than elementary school teachers or other workers with the same levels of education (*Occupational Outlook Handbook,* 2004).

Earlier in 2001 the media seized on a preliminary correlation from the first *Study of Early Child Care* associating greater length of time spent in child care

and higher incidence of behavior problems (aggression) by age 4½ (National Institute of Child Health, 2003). Parents, psychologists, and policymakers clamored for an explanation. Upon further examination, you shall see how statistics can be misrepresented. For 10 years a team of researchers commissioned by the National Institute of Child Health and Human Development (NICHD) has been studying more than 1,300 young children (at 10 child-care study sites) to determine how variations in child care for children from birth to age 3 are related to child development. How do child characteristics and child-care characteristics influence developmental outcomes? Here is an important preliminary finding from this ongoing study (Douglas, 2001; "New Research Demonstrates Unique Effects," 2001): 17 percent of the children in the study who spent more than 30 hours a

Thirteen Indicators of Quality Child Care

Indicator	Description
7. Supervision/discipline	Proper supervision will lesson certain behavioral problems, such as being disruptive and unruly, and decrease injury rates. Discipline if used inappropriately—such as controlling behaviors, punishment, verbal reprimands, and corporal punishment—will result in children acting out and being disruptive. These types of behaviors should not be occurring in a child-care program.
8. Fire drills	Children under the age of 5 are twice as likely to die from fire than any other childhood age group. The *Kids Safe* program is an effective way of teaching young children fire safety.
9. Medication administration	Children in child care are more likely to be taking medications because of the increased illnesses associated with being in child care. With over-the-counter medications, written permission of the parent or guardian and instructions from a physician are required. There are many standards and licensing requirements regarding this indicator. A program must have a written policy and clear procedures on giving medicine and on proper storage, as well as designated staff to administer it.
10. Emergency plan/contact	Staff needs to be prepared for emergency situations and injuries by having completed first-aid and CPR training; by having emergency medical policies and procedures in place; and by having critical information on children and staff readily available in an organized, easy-to-use file. At a minimum, accurate contact names and phone numbers, preferred hospitals, copies of insurance, parent/guardian signatures authorizing emergency care, and information on allergies should be kept.
11. Outdoor playground	The majority of child-care injuries occur on outdoor playgrounds. Most injuries are due to falls. Lowering the height of playground equipment and providing more resilient playground surfaces can reduce injury risk in child-care centers.
12. Inaccessibility of toxic substances	Many potentially toxic materials can be found in child-care centers, such as pesticides, art materials, cleaning agents, fuel by-products, cigarette smoke, building materials, improperly fired ceramics, and ground soil. Children differ from adults in susceptibility. Precautionary measures can be taken in the child-care center to minimize the risk of environmental hazards. For example, staff should know the building materials and products used within the center, eliminate hazards regularly, and be familiar with the local health department in the event assistance is needed.
13. Proper hand washing/ diapering	Hand washing is the single most effective way to interrupt the transmission of infectious diseases. Infrequent washing of children's or providers' hands will cause higher frequency of respiratory illness. Child-care programs must provide continuous training, technical assistance, and mentoring assistance in hand-washing procedures.

"13 Indicators of Quality Child Care" from Richard Fiene, "Licensing-Related Indicators of Quality Child Care," *Child Care Bulletin*, Issue 28, Winter 2003, p. 13. U.S. Department of Health & Human Services, Administration for Children & Families. http://www.nccic.org/ccb/issue28.html

week in child care demonstrated some aggressive behaviors between ages 4½ and 6.

As we all know from general psychology, correlation does not mean causation! There could be many other factors at play—for example, the type of parenting in the children's homes, poor nutrition, or lack of sleep because of a demanding work schedule for a mother whose company requires she work four days a week for 10-hour days and take three days off. Or how about those mothers who work in fields such as health care or manufacturing where shift work is required and the infant/toddler experiences a varying schedule of sleep/awake from week to week?

Those with caretaker and parent ratings of some aggressiveness typically fell within the normal range of behavior. (Toddlers aged 2 and 3 typically display some assertiveness as part of their normal development. Two-year-olds' favorite word is no!). Eighty percent of the children in early child care were not exhibiting "problem" behaviors, which the mainstream media did not report!

Caregivers in centers have more training and education than do home-based care providers. Thus, recommendations were made to improve the professional education for teachers in all early education settings. The effects of child care depend to some extent on the amount of time a child spends at a center and, more significantly, on the quality of parent-child interaction when the family is together.

An additional problem with child-care facilities is that they commonly function as networks for spreading a variety of diseases, particularly respiratory infections, hepatitis A, and intestinal illnesses—especially for children under age 2. There is considerable opportunity for the mixing of infected and susceptible children ("Early Child Care," 1998). Medical researchers are also investigating the relationship between early child care and the rising rates of childhood asthma (Christiansen, 2000).

Many social scientists and policymakers have lobbied for higher federal funding, legislation, and guidelines to regulate child-care centers and quality of staffing. Thus, in concert with the federal *No Child Left Behind*

Act for children in public schools, in 2002 a new early childhood initiative began called *Good Start, Grow Smart* to: (1) strengthen Early Head Start and Head Start programs and training for Head Start teachers; (2) create a stronger federal-state partnership in the delivery of quality early childhood programs; and (3) fund $45 million in collaborative research to identify effective prereading and language curricula and teaching strategies. Ultimately, the goal is high-quality training and care for infants and toddlers in *all* care settings. Initial findings from the federally subsidized program Early Head Start for children at risk from birth to age 3 include better performance in cognitive, language, and social-emotional development compared with a control group of children who were not in Early Head Start ("Building Their Futures," 2001).

For now, perhaps the safest conclusion we can draw, based on research, is this: High-quality child care is an acceptable alternative child-care arrangement with possible benefits for both cognitive development and parent-child relationships (NICHD, 2003). Infants around the world are raised under a great variety of conditions; the child-care arrangement is just one of them. And as we have pointed out in previous chapters, home care does not guarantee secure attachments or healthy social and emotional development.

Multiple Mothering   Traditionally in the United States, the preferred arrangement for raising children has been the **nuclear family,** which consists of two parents and their children. The view that mothering should be provided by one figure has been celebrated and extolled by many professionals as the key to good mental health. Yet this view is a culture-bound perspective, for children throughout the world are successfully reared in situations of **multiple mothering**—an arrangement in which responsibility for a child's care is dispersed among several people.

In some cases one major mother figure shares mothering with a variety of mother surrogates, including aunts, grandmothers, older cousins, nonkin neighbors, or co-wives. For instance, within the United States, Jacquelyne Faye Jackson (1993) shows that a multiple caregiver arrangement—based on shared caregiving by a number of parent figures irrespective of maternal marital status—is normative for African American infants. Another example of diffused nurturance is that found among the Ifaluk of Micronesia:

> For the Westerner, the amount of handling the infant receives is almost fantastic. The infant, particularly after it can crawl, is never allowed to remain in the arms of one person. In the course of a half-hour conversation, the baby might change hands ten times, being passed from one person to another. . . . The adults, as well as the older children, love to fondle the babies and to play with them, with the result that the infant does not stay with one person very long. . . . Should an infant cry, it is immediately picked up in an adult's arms, cuddled, consoled or fed. . . . There is little distinction between one's own relatives and "strangers." If he needs something, anyone will try to satisfy his need. Every house is open to him and he never has to learn that some houses are different from others. (Spiro, 1947, pp. 89–97)

Another fascinating approach to child care is found in the collective form of social and economic life in Israeli agricultural settlements (*kibbutzim*). From early infancy children were reared in a nursery by two or three professional caretakers, with communal sleeping at night. Originally, their own mothers visited them regularly, but the concept of communal infant sleeping at night away from parents has been abandoned in favor of sleeping at the parental home (Aviezer, Sagi, & van IJzendoorn, 2002). Despite this arrangement of "concomitant mothering," systematic observation, testing, and clinical assessment have demonstrated that kibbutz children are within the normal range in intelligence, motor development, mental health, and social adjustment (Aviezer et al., 1994; Butler & Ruzany, 1993). The kibbutzim model continues to evolve with the economic success and incorporation of younger workers into this worker cooperative–social engineering experiment (Rosner, 2000).

Children at Risk: Effects of Poverty

Estimates suggest that nearly 13 million children live in poverty in America (Children's Defense Fund, 2003). These children live in environments with an increased risk of lead poisoning, limited learning opportunities, and severe emotional distress due to family disintegration caused by economic strains. Their families cannot afford adequate housing, adequate nutritious food, or quality child care. This means that more than one in five U.S. children suffer in the following ways:

- *Health:* An increased risk of stunted growth, anemia, and less chance that the child will survive to her or his first birthday.
- *Education:* More repeated school years, lower test scores, and less education due to dropping out or expulsion.
- *Work:* Lower wages and lower overall lifetime earnings. In economic terms, the costs of keeping poverty-stricken children in schools longer, as well as having to supply them with free breakfasts and lunches, special education services and tutoring, coupled with large medical expenses due to initial poor health, means that every year that we decide not to address issues of child poverty translates into a monetary loss of as much as $137 billion.

Children raised in poverty are more likely to die from accidents, fire, infectious disease, or other diseases.

Seen from a developmental perspective, children's health, emotional and cognitive growth, and social interactions are all adversely affected by the harsh environments caused by poverty. In short, poverty steals the promise from a child's future, and in the end, it impacts everyone's development (Evans, 2004).

Child Neglect and Abuse   Children are dependent on parents and caregivers to take care of them during childhood, and the majority of American children are well cared for by their parents. However, according to the Center on Child Abuse Prevention Research, during 1999 a case of child neglect or abuse was reported every 10 seconds in the United States—a total of nearly 3.2 million reports and over 1 million confirmed victims in one year—an increasing rate over the previous year (Peddle et al., 2002). Tragically, in 2000 1,356 children, nearly 4 children each day, died of abuse and neglect. Children under 5 account for 80 percent of child fatalities, and infants under 1 year of age account for 40 percent of these fatalities (Peddle & Wang, 2001).

Neglect is defined as the absence of adequate social, emotional, and physical care, and neglect can occur regardless of socioeconomic status. Neglect cases make up approximately 63 percent of the cases in the child protection system (Child Health USA, 2002). **Child abuse** is defined as nonaccidental physical attack on or injury to children by individuals caring for them, and 19 percent of confirmed cases in 2000 were categorized as child abuse (we will consider sexual abuse in Chapter 8). Much of the past research in this area of study has focused on physical abuse and not on sexual abuse, emotional and social neglect, or abandonment.

To generalize about parents who abuse children is difficult. Multiple factors are usually involved, and these vary for different individuals, times, and social environments. Increasingly, however, researchers are looking at child maltreatment from an ecological perspective and examining the complex social context and web in which the behavior is embedded (Baumrind, 1994; Belsky, 1993). Child abuse is not confined to lower-socioeconomic-status households; it is found across the class spectrum. Child abuse is also related to social stress in families. For instance, high levels of marital conflict, interspousal physical violence, and job loss are associated with a higher incidence of child maltreatment (Dodge, Bates, & Pettit, 1990). In addition, child abuse is more common among parents suffering from mental illness and substance addiction (Walker, Downey, & Bergman, 1989). And families that are socially isolated and outside neighborhood support networks are more likely to abuse children than are families with rich social ties (Trickett & Susman, 1988).

Psychiatrists Brandt G. Steele and Carl B. Pollock (1968) made intensive studies of 60 families in which significant child abuse had occurred. The parents came from all segments of the population: from all socioeconomic strata, all levels of intelligence and education, and most religious and ethnic groups. Steele and Pollock found a number of elements common to many child abusers. These parents demanded a great deal from their infants, far more than the babies could understand or respond to. The parents also felt insecure and unsure of being loved, and they looked to the child as a source of reassurance, comfort, and affection. A parent, Kathy, made this poignant statement:

> "I have never felt really loved all my life. When the baby was born, I thought he would love me; but when he cried all the time, it meant he didn't love me, so I hit him." Kenny, age three weeks, was hospitalized with bilateral subdural hematomas [multiple bruises]. (Steele & Pollock, 1968, p. 110)

The Intergenerational Cycle of Violence   Steele and Pollock (1968) found that all 60 child abusers studied had been raised in the same authoritarian style that they were recreating with their own children. Other researchers have confirmed that abusive parents are themselves likely to have been abused or to have witnessed domestic violence when they were children (Moffatt, 2003). Indeed, evidence suggests that the pattern is unwittingly transmitted from parent to child, generation after generation—what researchers and professionals have called a "cycle of violence" and the "intergenerational transmission of violence."

Proponents of social learning theory say that violent, aggressive children have learned that behavior from their parents, who are powerful models for children (Tomison, 1996). Some researchers contend there is a biological or genetic component to aggressive behavior and that aggressiveness is an individual characteristic based on the child's own temperament (Muller, Hunter, & Stollack, 1995)—that is, the child's inherited disposition perpetuates the cycle of maltreatment.

The third explanation for intergenerational transmission of violence is the interaction of environmental (social learning) and biological/genetic factors. Kaufman and Zigler (1993, quoted in Tomison, 1996) suggest that a genetic component for the expression of antisocial behavior puts the individual at risk for expressing violent behavior, and the interaction of both genetic and environmental factors produces the greatest risk for acting violently. It is generally acknowledged that no single factor can explain how maltreatment is transmitted generationally.

Even so, having been abused does not always lead to being abusive; however, the greater the frequency of violence experienced in childhood, the greater the chance that the victim will grow up to be a violent parent (Moffatt, 2003). Corby (2000) found that the vast majority of studies (with the exception of incest research) have

"Quality time . . . quality time . . ."

Social and Emotional Deprivation Occurs Across Socioeconomic Class Lines

focused investigations on mothers' behaviors, despite the fact that men account for more than half of all physical abuse.

Abusing parents usually do not abuse all their children; commonly they select one child to be the victim. Some children appear to be more "at risk for abuse" than other children, including premature infants, those born out of wedlock, those with congenital anomalies or other handicaps, "difficult" babies, or those in stepfamilies. Overall, a child viewed by an abuse-prone parent as being "strange" or "different" is more at risk than are other children (Brenton, 1977). The *Human Diversity* box, "Interaction with Infants with Disabilities," suggests ways to provide good parenting to infants born with disabilities.

Psychiatrists estimate that 90 percent of abusing parents are treatable if they receive competent counseling (Helfer & Kempe, 1984). Most parents want to be good parents. Parent education programs—that teach parenting skills—often help prevent fathers or mothers who have abused their children from doing so again (Peterson & Brown, 1994).

Signs of Abuse and Maltreatment   As mentioned in the *Human Diversity* box, children who are born at risk are more likely to be mistreated. Maltreated children show a variety of symptoms. Because child-care staff and preschool teachers are the only adults outside the family whom many infants or toddlers see with any consistency, they are often in a position to detect signs of child abuse or neglect and to begin to remedy the situation by reporting it to a local child protective services

agency or police department (National Clearinghouse on Child Abuse and Neglect Information, 2003). In fact, most states require teachers and health-care professionals to report cases of child abuse, and the law provides them with legal immunity for erroneous reports made in good faith. Teachers and others in educational settings typically account for the highest percentage of reporting abuse and neglect. The National Clearinghouse on Child Abuse and Neglect publicizes a list of the signs teachers should look for as possible tip-offs of child abuse or neglect, including:

- Does the child have unexplained bruises, welts, or contusions?
- Does the child complain of beatings or maltreatment?
- Does the child frequently arrive early at school or stay late?
- Is the child frequently absent or late?
- Is the child aggressive, disruptive, destructive, shy, withdrawn, passive, or overly compliant and friendly?
- Is the child inadequately dressed for the weather, unkempt, dirty, undernourished, tired, in need of medical attention, or frequently injured?

In addition, being neglected or abused as a child increases an individual's later risk for delinquency, adult criminal behavior, and violent criminal behavior. Almost half of abused and neglected children have had a non-traffic offense arrest (juvenile or adult) and for some subgroups (African Americans and abused and neglected males), almost two-thirds have been arrested as juveniles or adults. A good many other events in children's lives—for instance, their natural abilities, their temperaments, their networks of social support, and their participation in therapy—may mediate the adverse consequences of child abuse and neglect (Widom & Maxfield, 2001).

Neglect puts great burdens on youngsters. Psychologist Byron Egeland's longitudinal study (1993) of children who are at risk because of poor quality of care found that emotionally unresponsive mothers tend to ignore their youngsters when the children are unhappy, uncomfortable, or hurt; they do not share their children's pleasures; and consequently, the children find that they cannot look to their mothers for security and comfort. Both physically abused and emotionally deprived children typically have low self-esteem, poor self-control, and negative feelings about the world. Whereas physically abused youngsters tend to show high levels of rage, frustration, and aggression, those reared by emotionally unavailable mothers tend to be withdrawn and dependent and to exhibit more severe mental and behavioral damage as they get older. Because they come to view and experience the world in deviant ways, many

Human Diversity

Interaction with Infants with Disabilities

I Am Just Like You

Everybody quietly hopes for an exceptional infant, but few parents get one, at least not exceptional in the "gifted" sense. Many people who eventually become great leaders (such as Winston Churchill, Nelson Rockefeller), scientists (such as Albert Einstein, Stephen Hawking), or artists (such as Stevie Wonder) began life with a disability but overcame obstacles to fulfill their potential.

Parents who give birth to a child with a disability often experience a variety of strong emotions, including denial, anguish, pain, guilt, panic, depression, and a deep sense of loss. Some parents of children with special needs confess experiencing all of these feelings. The best advice is to find professionals, advocates, relatives, and friends who will be supportive to you and your child. Professionals in the field of special education and disabilities encourage parents to do the following:

- Love the child exactly as he or she is. Look at your child, touch your child, speak lovingly to your child, and treat your child as normally as possible. Your child is a person first!
- Start early intervention services as soon as possible after birth. You will connect with professionals and advocates knowledgeable about your child's needs. Be aware that we live in a time when there is more professional knowledge than ever before about disorders, birth abnormalities, and children born at risk.
- Get informed and ask questions. If support services are not available in your area, find parental and professional support via professional journals or Web sites. Parents need to know they are not alone. Even parents of a child with a rare diagnosis can connect with someone else in the world who will understand and who is experiencing the same challenge.
- Be aware that the family expends extra energy when a child has a disability, and over time most parents discover untapped energies and resilience to become people they never knew they could become.

- The practice of inclusion allows all children with a disability to be educated in an age-appropriate, regular classroom in the public school system. It is likely that a child with special needs will have his/her preschool programming covered financially by the school district.
- Recognize the main developmental principle that all children, regardless of their abilities, have strengths and skills that will emerge at their own individual rate of growth. Celebrate your child's developmental milestones.
- Recognize that your child can become a positive, contributing member of society.
- Be aware that change can be for the better.

Attachment and Infants with Disabilities Emily, born with a heart condition, has difficulty eating and requires a feeding tube. Her mother views infant massage as a way to enhance her infant's emotional and physical health. Some pediatricians say massage creates emotional contact and attachment between the caregiver and infant.

of them later perpetuate the abusive patterns of their parents and mistreat their own children (Dodge, Bates, & Pettit, 1990).

Breaking the Cycle of Violence Several researchers find there are several factors that seem to "buffer" children from being abused. These include mothers having

strong social support systems; being involved in community activities; having less rigid expectations about what children should be able to do; encountering fewer stressful life events; having a supportive partner/spouse; making a conscious decision not to repeat the history of abuse; having positive school experiences as a child; and having a strong, supportive religious affiliation (Tomison,

1996). Fry (1993) suggests several approaches to breaking the cycle of violence:

- Promote a cultural attitude that physical force is unnecessary and unacceptable (outlawing corporal punishment).
- Train all children in nonviolent conflict resolution and problem solving.
- Train parents in healthy child-rearing techniques.
- Intervene in abusive situations as soon as possible.

Questions

What are the factors associated with incidences of child neglect and abuse? Is there an association between these harmful behaviors and socioeconomic status or parenting style? What social/cultural limits and/or educational policies can be employed to reduce or eliminate child abuse and neglect?

SEGUE

This chapter has documented social and behavioral scientists' long-standing interest in how children's personality development is related to their early emotional and social experiences. Initially social scientists focused upon maternal deprivation, believing that it was enough simply to ask about the mother's influence on the child. As time passed, research began to focus on fathers, and then siblings, grandparents, aunts, uncles, and other extended family members. The circle has widened even further in recent years to child-care providers and preschool teachers.

Sharply divergent views exist among Americans regarding the desirability of child-care facilities. The impulse to decide whether child care is "good" or "bad" has at times seemed more a matter of ideology than an issue for science. In any event, modern societies and social scientists are increasingly confronting this question: How are we to manage the successful care and rearing of future generations of children when parents spend a substantial portion of time at work away from home?

As we examine in the next section, children during the preschool and early elementary school years continue to grow, experience remarkable cognitive development, and experience a diversity of social influences.

Summary

Emotional Development

1. Emotions seem to have evolved as adaptive processes by which humans establish, maintain, and terminate relationships in their environment to enhance survival. Developmental researchers view emotions in differing ways. We define emotions as the physiological changes, subjective experiences, and expressive behaviors involved in feelings such as love and hate. We "read" others' emotions from a combination of their facial, gestural, postural, and vocal cues.

2. Darwin proposed that emotions are inherited patterns for survival, but contemporary researchers suggest that emotions (a) help humans survive and adapt to their environment, (b) serve to guide and motivate human behavior, and (c) support communication with others. Social referencing appears within a few days of birth.

3. Ekman and other ethologists state that the human nervous system is genetically prewired for emotional action and responsiveness, and humans associate specific emotions with specific human facial expressions.

4. Izard studies formulated "differential emotions theory": Emotions result from feedback of sensations generated by facial and neuromuscular responses. Thus, each emotion has its own distinctive facial pattern, and 10 fundamental emotions are found across cultures. Others propose that basic emotions are prewired in an infant's brain and are present at birth (for a fully developed neonate).

5. Maturing infants show an increasing ability to discriminate among vocal cues and facial expressions received, and maturing infants modify their own emotions and behavior.

6. From birth to age 5 infants and children progress through several stages in emotional development. The Greenspan Functional Emotional Assessment Scale identifies children with atypical emotional development.

7. Researchers find continuity and stability of emotional expressiveness in young children. Ratings of infants' emotional expressiveness remain rather stable into children's preschool years, but a caretaker's responsiveness can modify a child's emotions.

8. In the 1990s Mayer and Salovey proposed the concept of emotional intelligence (EI), which Goleman (emotional intelligence) and Gardner (multiple intelligences) have popularized. EI includes interpersonal and intrapersonal skills that lead to social success. Neuroscience shows that we sense, then feel, then nearly simultaneously react and think about what we are experiencing.

9. Emotional circuits in the brain are "sculpted" by experiences in infancy and early childhood. Normal neural circuitry proceeding from the brain stem, through the limbic system, to the cerebral cortex is crucial to effective thought. Maltreatment of infants and young children causes impaired emotional processing, which leads to agitation, impulsivity, and disruptive behaviors.

10. Attachment ("bonding" in the popular vernacular) to a significant person profoundly influences an infant's mind, body, social development, and values. Ainsworth found that infants vary in the timing of attachment (following, clinging, signaling, crying). Close proximity, affection and touching, and responsive eye contact promote secure infant attachment. Infant protests over parental separation are linked to cognitive maturation and person permanence.

11. Bowlby and others state that an infant is biologically pre-adapted for survival into a social world to have its needs met. Infant head shape, body proportion, round eyes, plump cheeks—and its crying, sucking, and clinging elicit immediate response by caregivers. Bowlby's concept of "maternal deprivation" conveys the damaging emotional effects of a mother's lack of responsiveness to her infant.

12. Learning theorists attribute attachment to socialization. In normal attachment, infants and mothers reward and reinforce behaviors in each other. Thus, a mutually satisfying relationship develops called attachment.

13. Most commonly the mother is the object of infant attachment, but it can be the father, grandparent, or other caretaker. With maturation, the number of the child's attachments increases.

14. Differing temperament in infants and young children is associated with variance in emotional expression. The temperamental qualities that are studied most include irritability, mood (disposition), ease of being soothed, activity level, sociability, attentiveness, adaptability, intensity of arousal, self-regulation, and timidity. Cultures place values on different temperamental qualities, such as shyness.

15. Thomas and Chess found that babies show styles of temperament early in life. Most common are (a) difficult, (b) slow-to-warm-up, and (c) easy babies. Some babies have a mixture of traits.

Theories of Personality Development

16. Changes in American family structures and stability have precipitated discovery of the "best" parenting practices offered by a variety of developmental theorists.

17. Freudians stress the psychoanalytic view that the development of an emotionally healthy personality is associated with breast-feeding, a prolonged period of nursing, gradual weaning, a self-demand feeding schedule, delayed and patient bowel and bladder training, and freedom from punishment. Thus the child's relationship with its mother is an extremely strong one. Dr. Benjamin Spock popularized ideas of child-centered care for the past 60 years, but research has provided little empirical support for these views.

18. In the psychosocial view, Erikson stressed an infant's need to develop a basic sense of trust in others, typically with the mother and/or father. The maturing child will need to resolve a series of conflicts during progressive stages of emotional and social development.

19. Behaviorists (learning theorists) observe the outward display of emotions, not the thoughts that caused the emotions. They say a system of rewards and punishments shapes infant behaviors. Caretakers use time-outs, reinforcement schedules, and rewards to promote socially acceptable behaviors or skills to reduce undesirable behaviors.

20. Contemporary cognitive psychologists know that emotions have a significant impact on thoughts and behaviors. They examine the information-processing mechanisms that link emotions to thinking and behaviors.

21. Bronfenbrenner's ecological theory states that a young child's social-emotional development is affected by various levels of environment: the home and family, the neighborhood, the school and church, and community, state, national and international influences.

Social Development

22. The U.S. Census Bureau reports that children are about 25 percent of the U.S. population—projecting a steady increase in children age 0 to 5 by 2020. With fewer two-parent families, there is an urgent need for child-care assistance from the larger community. Those entering professions that service infants and young children have many opportunities.

23. Humanness is a social product that arises as children interact with the significant people in their environment. Proper human stimulation, physical contact, and nurturance are extremely important, but some children experience neglect, abuse, isolation, abandonment, social deprivation, and institutionalization. Reactive attachment disorder (RAD) is applied to at-risk children who show inappropriate or delayed social-cognitive behaviors from severe abuse and neglect, institutionalization, successive foster care, or have handicapping conditions, are "difficult" or chronically ill, or have experienced long parental separation.

24. Early attachment (bonding) patterns predict a child's later functioning and success (peers, academics, marriage, parenting). Ainsworth and colleagues devised the Strange Situation to determine the quality of infant-mother attachment. Three patterns emerged: securely attached (B), insecure/avoidant (A), and insecure/resistant (C). Main and Solomon identified a fourth pattern: disorganized/disoriented (D).

25. Eight-month-old infants typically display stranger anxiety and separation anxiety, expressing distress when a familiar person leaves or a novel person or situation occurs. For several months a baby is likely to show severe distress if left with a stranger, and there is a higher risk of infant abuse.

26. Securely attached (B) infants and children are typically more socially competent in preschool, can initiate and sustain social interaction with others, and are more capable of handling challenging circumstances. Insecurely attached infants come to expect unresponsiveness to their needs, and they come to view themselves as unworthy of love and support.

27. Thomas and Chess propose a "goodness of fit" theory, suggesting that parents take into account their infant's unique temperament in their child-rearing practices. Infants, too, mold and shape their parents.

28. Different cultures vary in child-rearing practices. In non-industrialized countries a mother carries her infant next to her body all day and keeps her infant nearby when sleeping. Western European nations have developed competent national child-care systems and paid compensation for a parent for one year.

Child Care for Infants and Toddlers

29. Young children are supervised and socialized by a larger array of caretakers than before because more mothers are employed, higher rates of divorce, and nonmarital child-bearing. Many infants are in child care by 3 months of age, averaging 28 hours per week. Quality child care for infants and toddlers is scarce and more expensive.

30. The mother-child and father-child relationships are qualitatively different and have a different impact on a child's development. Traditionally, the mother spends more time on child care, and the father is the breadwinner. But many American mothers are employed, and more fathers assist with child care (or are the sole caretaker).

31. In the United States there are high numbers of single mothers and absentee fathers. About 24 million children live in homes with no biological father. Children without fathers are at risk for misbehavior, difficulties in school, poorer academic achievement, and less social responsibility. The quality of the father-child relationship is more important than just his presence.

32. Siblings play an integral part in the emotional, sensory, cognitive, and social development of infants and young children—and siblings play a major role all through our lives. In some cultures older siblings take on the responsibility for younger ones.

33. More grandparents and other kin in the United States are the caretakers of grandchildren. The U.S. Census Bureau reports several different family structures. The main reasons grandchildren are being raised by grandparents include parental drug abuse, child abuse and abandonment, teen pregnancy, parental illness or institutionalization. As caretakers, older adults require financial resources, social support, and child-care assistance.

34. More young children are in child-care settings, from home-based familial care to nonfamilial center care. Half of employed mothers change child-care arrangements often—and cannot afford high-quality care. Young children need continuity, stability, and predictability in their care to develop emotional-social-cognitive competence. Parents are challenging the U.S. government to regulate the child-care industry: raise standards of care, safety, pay and training for child-care workers, and higher subsidies for families.

35. Worldwide, infants are raised under a variety of conditions, including multiple mothering, home care, child day care, and kibbutizm. Research suggests that multiple mothering and high-quality child care are acceptable arrangements.

36. Millions of young children in America experience adverse effects of poverty, including higher incidence of health and safety risks, lower educational attainment, and lower earning capacity for a lifetime. Poverty steals a child's future.

37. The incidence of child abuse and neglect is on the rise and the impact is far reaching. Commonly one child is victimized in such families. Studies show adult abusers were likely abused as children. Much research and new programs are being conducted to institute societal programs to break this cycle of violence. Professionals in child care and supervision are mandated to report neglect and abuse.

38. More babies are being born at risk (due to premature birth, birth defects, or being born into poverty). These infants need to be loved and cherished as any child should. Throughout history, many people who started life with a disability make contributions to society.

Key Terms

attachment (193)

autism (197)

child abuse (217)

disorganized/disoriented infants (206)

emotions (189)

emotional intelligence (EI) (192)

insecure/avoidant infants (206)

insecure/resistant infants (206)

interpersonal intelligence (193)

intrapersonal intelligence (193)

kinship care (212)

multiple mothering (216)

neglect (217)

nuclear family (216)

oral-sensory stage (199)

person permanence (194)

reactive attachment disorder (RAD) (204)

securely attached infants (206)

sensory integration (207)

separation anxiety (207)

social referencing (189)

Strange Situation (206)

stranger anxiety (206)

temperament (196)

Following Up on the Internet

Websites for this chapter focus on emotional and social development in infancy. Please access the text Web site at www.mhhe.com/vzcrandell8 for up-to-date hot-linked Internet addresses for the following organizations, topics, and resources:

Society for Research on Child Development
National Association for the Education of Young Children

National Clearinghouse on Child Abuse & Neglect
Early Childhood News
National Child Care Information Center
Grandparents Raising Grandchildren
Institute for Research on Poverty
Administration on Developmental Disabilities

Part FOUR
Early Childhood
2 to 6

C hapter 7 is the first of two chapters focusing on early childhood, the developmental stage between 2 and 6 years of age. During this period children acquire greater autonomy, evolve new ways of relating to other people, and gain a sense of themselves and their effectiveness in the world. Healthy children experience physical growth, coordination of motor skills, and an energetic zest for play. Proper nutrition, good health, and stimulating sensory experiences provide a foundation for continued cognitive growth and language development. Children also begin to learn a sense of right or wrong based on preoperational thought processes. In Chapter 8, we will examine the young child's growing self-awareness in the domains of emotions and gender. Within the social context of family and friends, child-care settings, and kindergarten, young children acquire a set of guidelines about expressing their emotional needs.

Early Childhood
Physical and Cognitive Development

Critical Thinking Questions

1. How do we know what a young child needs for growth of both brain and body? Why are accidental injuries the leading cause of death in young children?

2. A young girl 5 years old can hear a piece of music once and then sit at the piano and play it perfectly, but she does not know her name and will never learn to read words or music. Is she intelligent? What does it mean to be intelligent, and how do we measure intelligence?

3. Ask a 6-year-old child and a 25-year-old to describe what occurred in their lives the day before. What details will be remembered? In what order will they be remembered? Will the child remember the past the same way an adult will? Any ideas why there might be differences in their recollections and perspectives?

4. Imagine that you are shipwrecked on an island where everyone wears masks so that you cannot see each other's faces. How would you be able to figure out what other people were really thinking? And how do you think your communication would be different?

Between the ages of 2 and 6, children enlarge their repertoire of behaviors. As young children develop physically and cognitively, they become capable beings in their own right. Most are healthy, energetic, and curious about mastering their world. Their growing bodies and increasing strength permit them to climb higher, jump longer, yell louder, and hug harder. For young children, every day is truly a new day. They are expanding their vocabulary, asking questions, and entertaining with their own wit and humor.

As Erikson suggests, young children begin to struggle with their own conflicting needs and rebel against parental controls while acquiring a sense of autonomy or independence. These occasional upheavals are popularly called "the terrible twos," when toddlers begin to assert their own will and have temper tantrums. At the same time, children come to see them-selves as individuals who are separate from their parents, though still dependent on them (Crockenberg & Litman, 1990; Erikson, 1963). How does the young child's mind operate to remember what is significant and what is trivial? We will examine several theories of early cognitive development and memory, as well as physical and moral development.

Physical Development and Health Concerns

Early childhood lays the cognitive and social foundations for the more complex life of the school years. Underpinning these intellectual skills are continued brain growth, physical development, refinement of gross- and fine-motor skills, and maturation of the sensory systems. Among the most encompassing factors that impede both physical and cognitive development in early childhood are the far-reaching outcomes of living in poverty. A special section of this chapter is devoted to health risk factors for many American children, particularly minority children.

Physical Growth and Motor-Skill Development

As we have noted in earlier chapters, growth is unevenly distributed over the first 20 years of life. From birth to age 5, the rate, or velocity, of growth in height declines sharply. You may have heard it said that "young children sprout like weeds," since about twice as much of this growth occurs between the ages of 1 and 3 as between the ages of 3 and 5. Young children maintain the top-heavy look—the head being large relative to the body—until the end of the preschool years, but they become thinner and lose the baby fat that characterizes the infant and toddler. Children under 2 tend to be chubby, whereas children 2 to 6 years old are, for the most part, slim, although you can see that height and weight variations in children stem from both genetic and environmental factors. After age 5, the rate of growth in height levels off and is practically constant until puberty. Additionally, relative to the growth norms of their age group, broadly built children tend to grow faster than average, and slenderly built children slower than average (Tanner, 1971).

One of the most striking and perhaps most fundamental characteristics of growth is what James M. Tanner, a noted authority on the subject, calls its "self-stabilizing" or "target-seeking" quality:

> Children, no less than rockets, have their trajectories, governed by the control systems of their genetical constitution and powered by energy absorbed from the natural environment. Deflect the child from its growth trajectory by acute malnutrition or illness, and a restoring force develops so that as soon as the missing food is supplied or the illness terminated, the child catches up toward its original curve. When it gets there, it slows down again to adjust its path onto the old trajectory once more. (1970, p. 125)

Thus, children display a compensatory or remedial property of "making up" for arrested growth when normal conditions are restored (unless the cause of the interruption is severe or prolonged).

During the preschool and early elementary years, children also become better coordinated physically. Walking, climbing, reaching, grasping, and releasing are no longer simply activities in their own right but have become the means for new endeavors. Their developing skills give children new ways to explore the world and to accomplish new tasks (see Table 7.1).

Gross Motor Skills Healthy young children ages 2 to 6 are constantly active. At this age, children run, jump, or hop every chance they get. Their arm and leg muscles are developing and children in this age group need and benefit from plenty of exercise and activity every day. Caregivers should limit hours of passive activity, such as watching TV, videotapes, DVDs, and playing computer games.

4-Year-Olds Four-year-olds are more comfortable with their bodies and push their physical limits by exploring jungle gyms and other play structures. Coordination between upper and lower body develops, and tasks like running are done much more efficiently. It has been well established that young children go through three distinct stages while learning to walk and reach a mature pattern of walking by approximately 4 years of age (Lee & Chen, 1996).

5-Year-Olds Five-year-olds can be daredevils; they swing, jump, and try acrobatics that cause their parents to hold their breath. It is hard to believe that the 5-year-old who proficiently skates and skips found it difficult to walk very far without falling down just a few years previously. Children with any type of physical disability should still be encouraged to be active so they can develop strength and coordination skills and enjoy the physical act of movement. Recreational therapists and occupational therapists can suggest activities that individual children can accomplish.

- **Recreational therapist:** A recreational therapist works with children providing services that help restore function, improve mobility, relieve pain, and prevent or limit permanent physical disabilities of patients suffering from injuries or disease. The goal of recreational theory is to restore, maintain, and promote overall fitness and health.
- **Occupational therapist:** An occupational therapist helps children not only to improve basic motor functions and reasoning abilities, but also to compensate for permanent loss of function. The goal of occupational therapy is to help people have independent, productive, and satisfying lives.

6-Year-Olds Caretakers need to set boundaries and limits and constantly remind about safety rules and use

Table 7.1 Motor and Skills Development Among Preschoolers, Ages 2 to 5

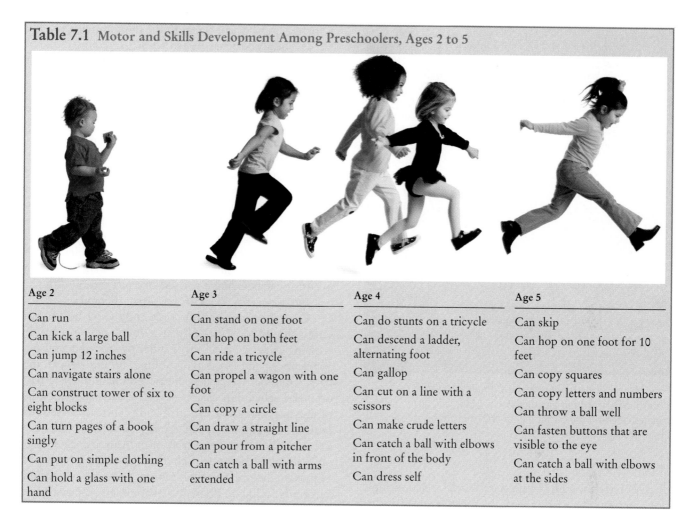

Age 2	Age 3	Age 4	Age 5
Can run	Can stand on one foot	Can do stunts on a tricycle	Can skip
Can kick a large ball	Can hop on both feet	Can descend a ladder, alternating foot	Can hop on one foot for 10 feet
Can jump 12 inches	Can ride a tricycle	Can gallop	Can copy squares
Can navigate stairs alone	Can propel a wagon with one foot	Can cut on a line with a scissors	Can copy letters and numbers
Can construct tower of six to eight blocks	Can copy a circle	Can make crude letters	Can throw a ball well
Can turn pages of a book singly	Can draw a straight line	Can catch a ball with elbows in front of the body	Can fasten buttons that are visible to the eye
Can put on simple clothing	Can pour from a pitcher	Can dress self	Can catch a ball with elbows at the sides
Can hold a glass with one hand	Can catch a ball with arms extended		

of safety equipment, as 6-year-olds actively seek more independence in expanding community environments. Six-year-olds show increased interest in daring adventures and games. They enjoy testing the limits of their bodies by running fast, throwing hard, leaping higher and farther. They enjoy riding bikes, climbing trees and fire escapes, and jumping from higher walls and steps. They may gain (or lose) confidence in their physical abilities as they begin to participate in sports activities in individual or team sports. Parents need to be cautious about demanding coaches and overscheduling a 6-year-old's activities.

Fine-Motor Skills Whereas gross-motor skills are the capabilities involving larger body parts, fine-motor skills involve small body parts. Fine-motor skills develop more slowly than gross motor skills, so 3-year-olds who no longer need to concentrate intensely on the task of running will still require mental energy to stack blocks, construct with Legos, use a paintbrush, sculpt with clay, maneuver a crayon, or tap keys on a computer keyboard. They still tend to force a puzzle piece into the hole or slide and wiggle it until it pops into place. Five-year-olds

normally have their hands, arms, legs, and feet under tight command and are bored with the simple acts of coordination, preferring instead to walk on a balance beam, build high block structures, and begin the task of tying shoelaces. With the use of Velcro on children's footwear, many are delayed in learning the task of tying shoelaces until they are older. Fine-motor skills are required for success in getting dressed, printing the alphabet and numerals, cursive writing, cutting, pasting, coloring within the lines, and putting together puzzles, just to name a few.

Children with Coordination Problems Unfortunately, some 5 percent of youngsters have noticeable difficulties with coordination, and perhaps 50 percent of the children who have these problems at age 5 still have them at age 9. Increasingly, psychologists and teachers are paying attention to these children with poor physical coordination. Assisting less adroit children to become more successful at physical activities can be important. Motor skills form a large part of youngsters' self-concepts and how they perceive others. Researchers find that children with coordination problems are at greater risk for significant social problems later in elementary school because clumsiness

Fine Motor Skills Involve More Complex Hand-Eye Coordination Putting together blocks, beads, and puzzle pieces requires extensive use of fine-motor skills and are favorite activities of young children.

often interferes with youngsters' social relationships. Boys perceived as less adept are most frequently impacted: They tend to have fewer friends than their more coordinated peers (Kutner, 1993). Psychologists and educators are developing ways to help these children improve in areas that initially might seem unrelated.

Question

Why would a pediatrician be concerned if a child's growth or motor skills seemed delayed for the age of the young child, and what services are available for young children diagnosed with physical and motor delays?

Sensory Development

Young children normally love the sensory experiences of various colors and textures of objects—but a small percent experience sensory-integration problems. Most delight in novel experiences and sensations. Toddlers enjoy the sensation of putting objects in the mouth, but preschool children typically will not, although occasionally a child will suck a thumb or fingers as a self-comforting behavior. Along with new sensory experiences, the children are expanding descriptive language to categorize such experiences as slippery sand, crunchy colorful leaves, warm water, fluffy snow flurries, prickly cactus, cuddly kittens, and so forth. As young children mature, they absorb everything about the people in their environment, too.

Visual, Tactile, and Kinesthetic Senses To develop their visual and tactile senses, young children not only explore objects visually but enjoy touching them, especially interesting materials such as sand, water, food, grass, finger paints, Play-Doh, soap, washcloths, and feathers. They use their hands and feet to help them discover all the fascinating differences in the objects in their environment. Some children, however, are more sensitive to sensory experiences (sound, touch, and light may "hurt"), are more clumsy, and have problems with fine-motor skills. Such children would benefit from a professional assessment for sensory integration difficulties and services with an occupational therapist.

Caretakers responsible for a child's eye health and safety should look carefully at a young child's eyes for crossing eyes, a "lazy" or wandering eye and unusual appearance, and excessive rubbing or redness of the eyes. Optometrists and pediatric ophthalmologists recommend scheduling vision exams as early as 6 months of age, for untreated eye problems can lead to serious health, learning, and self-esteem problems. Yet, the Prevent Blindness Organization of America states that only about 14 percent of children get a comprehensive eye exam before entering school ("Children's Vision Screening," 2003). Premature babies are especially at risk for developing an eye disorder called *retinopathy of prematurity (ROP)* and need frequent eye exams. Young children with visual impairments are eligible for early intervention services (see Figure 7.1).

Children are bound to make a mess while exploring, but complex neural connections are developing in the brain because of these stimulating experiences. Yet young children can be taught to pick up after themselves. Sensory experiences help young children to use language skills to classify things (e.g., big or small, hot or cold, wet or dry, smooth or bumpy, loud or soft, pleasant or scary, safe or dangerous). Eventually the young child will be able to throw a ball, use a fork, flush the toilet, open the pages of a book, get dressed, climb up and down stairs easily, and so on, utilizing the maturing visual, tactile, and kinesthetic senses of the muscles for deliberate movements.

Hearing and Language Development A child's language capabilities depend on a healthy auditory system as well as the growth and development of muscles in the mouth, tongue, and larynx. The sounds made by babies less than a year old are considered to be "universal" across cultures, and a child can listen to and learn the sounds of more than one language during this time (Chomsky, 1975). The auditory sense can be temporar-

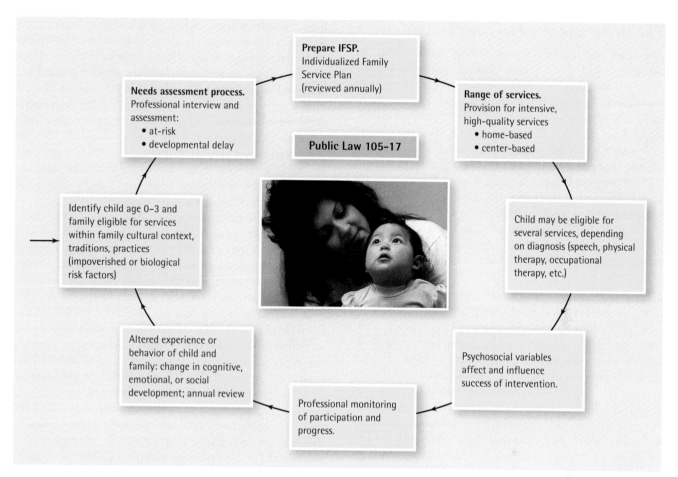

FIGURE 7.1 The Early Intervention Services Process Many young children born at risk or living in poverty conditions are considered eligible for an Individualized Family Service Plan (IFSP) through their local public health department. Seven-month-old Sabrina's 29-year-old mother drank during her pregnancies. Another 3-year-old child in the family also has been diagnosed with FAS (fetal alcohol syndrome).

ily or seriously impaired by colds, ear infections, sinus congestion, sore throats, and allergies (particularly by the phlegm that can block the tubes from the back of the throat to the ears if the child is allergic to dairy products). A common illness of early childhood is **otitis media,** a painful infection in young children that causes fluid buildup in the middle ear with the potential for hearing loss if left untreated. The typical symptom is that the child will be tugging at the ear and crying or screaming in the middle of the night, after lying down for a period of time has caused the fluid to settle painfully in the ear. Typically medication is needed to reduce the fluid accumulation. A child who has a series of ear infections, or for whom medical attention is delayed, might experience hearing loss. Chronic hearing problems interfere with learning and using language and can therefore cause serious delays in cognitive development if left undetected. If a young child does not seem to respond to parental requests or turn in the direction of sounds, a checkup is in order. An *otolaryngologist* (specialist who treats ear, nose, and throat problems) may make a small incision in

the eardrum to drain fluid, or a ventilation tube may be inserted temporarily in the eardrum if there are persistent ear infections. If a child is diagnosed with deafness, there are many accommodations in private and public school environments and a wealth of resources on the Web to help this child develop his or her potential.

Olfactory and Gustatory Sensations Children exhibit a range of responses to smells and tastes of foods and beverages in any culture. Also, children must be taught about what is safe or not safe to put in their mouths. Identifying for children what a smell is (a rose) or what a taste is (strawberry) helps them learn to recognize and cognitively categorize smells and tastes. Because both smell and taste are involved in eating foods, mealtime is when parents notice a "finicky" eater—a small percentage of children are overly sensitive to olfactory or gustatory stimuli or are allergic to specific foods. The combination of the child's developing taste buds and the intensity of new sensations as foods are introduced into the child's diet can make for challenging mealtimes.

The Brain and the Nervous System

The brain and central nervous system (CNS) normally continue rapid development during early childhood. A rich complexity of connections among neurons will continue to develop if the child is stimulated through using his or her senses and through developing social interactions with others. At the age of 5, the child's brain will weigh about 90 percent of its final, adult weight, whereas the child's body will be only about one-third of its final weight. When you see a 6-year-old wearing an adult's hat, you will see that the difference in head size between child and adult is much less than shirt or pant size. Given that children's brains are quickly increasing in size, it is no surprise that their increasingly complex cognitive abilities are impressive.

Children at Risk of Cognitive Delays As children's physical worlds expand, children are confronted with new developmental requirements. They actively seek new opportunities for manipulating and regulating their environment and, in doing so, achieve a sense of their own effectiveness. These processes underlie and stimulate healthy cognitive development. Nevertheless, some young children experience cognitive delays because of congenital birth defects, forms of mental retardation, and other health problems that show up in early childhood, such as attention-deficit hyperactivity disorder or depression, autism, seizure disorders, HIV/AIDS, and other health concerns. However, well-designed early intervention programs can help children who live in high-risk environments or those with developmental disabilities (Shonkoff, 2000).

Congenital Birth Defects Children who are born at risk (e.g., due to premature birth, birth defects, or being born into poverty) are likely to experience slower physical development and slower maturation of their senses and therefore might not get the opportunity to develop to their full potential. These children are eligible for intensive early intervention services, Early Head Start, and an Individualized Family Service Plan (IFSP) will be developed through the young child's health department and public school district (see Figure 7.1).

Autism A child diagnosed with the puzzling neurodevelopmental disorder of autism displays such behaviors before the age of 3—but sadly the child appears to be developing normally before the onset of autism. A child diagnosed with autism typically has few or no language skills, does not initiate or sustain conversation, is unable to interpret the emotional states of others, is hypersensitive to touch and sound, exhibits unusual attachments to inanimate objects, displays odd, repetitive, or self-injurious behaviors, has sleep disturbances, and is more

likely to have epilepsy (Glazer, 2003; Muhle, Trentacoste, & Rapin, 2004). Some children with autism display exceptional intellectual knowledge such as statistics about weather, dates, or birthdates, while a smaller percent are classified as retarded (Goode, 2004). Children with a milder form of autism are classified as having **Asperger's syndrome.** Since the early 1990s, the number of school-age autistic children receiving special education services grew faster than any other disability to 98,000 children by 2001, with more male children affected. In addition 17,000 preschool children aged 3 to 5 were diagnosed with autism in 2001–2002 (Glazer, 2003).

Although autistic spectrum disorders are recognizable, the exact cause has not been determined. The focus of recent research includes genetics, teratology, prenatal or perinatal infection, structural and functional abnormalities in the brain, and pharmacology of vaccines that contain *thimerosal* (DeFossé et al., 2004; Glazer, 2003; Muhle, Trentacoste, & Rapin, 2004; Shastry, 2003). Data from three twin studies indicate the concordance rate for autism among monozygotic twins is 65 percent, whereas for dizygotic twins it is 0 percent (Tager-Flusberg, Joseph, & Folstein, 2001). There is no definitive test to diagnose the disorder and likewise no cure.

Finding the exact causes of autism is not an easy task, but researchers continue to make great strides in devising more behavioral intervention strategies. It is important for caretakers to identify children with early social or language deficits, delays, or regressions as early as possible, refer them for assessment, and advocate for effective treatments (Muhle, Trentacoste, & Rapin, 2004). Children diagnosed with autism or Asperger's are eligible for early intervention services (see Figure 7.1). Behavioral and educational interventions with young children generally improve developmental and behavioral outcomes.

Young Children with Behavior Problems In the United States, about 10 percent of children suffer from mental illness that causes some impairment (Burns et al., 1995; Shaffer et al., 1996). Yet only a small percent of such children receive mental health services (Burns et al., 1995). When a preschool child appears inactive, depressed or troubled, is overly active, or constantly runs, fights, or bites, he or she could have a serious emotional/behavioral problem. A growing number of young children are diagnosed with attention-deficit disorder, severe depression, mood disorders, or reactive attachment disorder (mentioned in Chapter 6).

Researchers studied the data over a ten-year period (1987–1996) from three medical settings in the United States that served over 900,000 children aged 2 to 4 and discovered that psychotropic medications prescribed for preschoolers increased two- to threefold to rates prescribed for adults (Goode, 2000; Zito et al., 2002, 2003,

2005). The medications prescribed in rank order were stimulants, antidepressants, and neuroleptics (used as antipsychotics).

Joseph Coyle of Harvard Medical School provides evidence that the prescription of psychotropic drugs to children under 5 has increased since 1990 in Canada, France, and the United States (2000). However, Coyle cautions that three of four sets of U.S. data analyzed were based on Medicaid recipients rather than a random sample of young children. "Methylphenidate, the commonly prescribed drug in these studies, carries a warning against its use in children younger than 6 years" (Coyle, 2000, p. 1059). **Methylphenidate** (brand name *Ritalin*) is a mild stimulant of the central nervous system used to treat hyperactive behavior disorders in children, or commonly labeled as ADD (attention-deficit disorder) or ADHD (attention-deficit hyperactivity disorder). Newer medications prescribed for ADD and ADHD include *Adderall* and *Concerta* (a reformation of Ritalin). However, Coyle and other doctors say no empirical evidence exists to support psychotropic drug treatment in very young children (Coyle, 2000; Diller, 2002). They believe the pharmaceutical industry has had a profound influence in funding ADHD studies, published drug promotions extensively to doctors, and advertised directly to consumers on television (Diller, 2002).

There are valid concerns that such treatment could have deleterious effects on the developing brain, and extensive studies must be conducted to determine the long-term consequences of the use of psychotropic drugs at this early stage of childhood (Zito et al., 2003). Pediatricians also recommend behavioral therapy, emotional counseling, a healthy diet and nutritional supplements, and early intervention services (see Figure 7.1). The U.S. Surgeon General publicized his 2005 agenda as *The Year of the Healthy Child*, with greater focus on "improving the body, mind, and spirit of the growing child," and special attention on early childhood development and mental health issues ("U.S. Surgeon General," 2005).

Chemical Exposure in Young Children   Caregivers of young children must take precautions to limit exposure to known and questionable toxic substances. Some young children experience compromised physical, motor, health, and brain functioning associated with their exposure to chemical toxicants emitted from industrial factories and old storage facilities, pesticides sprayed on farm crops, toxic chemicals buried in landfills, polluted ponds, streams, and water supplies (à la Erin Brockovich and the Oscar-winning movie).

Pesticides have shown the ability to damage our DNA and genetic structure and are found to seriously weaken the human immune system and have been implicated in some childhood cancers. Significant positive associations were observed for use of pesticides to control

nuisance pests in the home, No-Pest Strips in the home, pesticides to control termites, Kwell shampoo, flea collars on pets, diazinon in the garden or orchard, and herbicides to control weeds in the yard ("Family Pesticide Use Suspected of Causing Child Cancers," 1993). Some young children cannot tolerate color and chemical food additives. Researchers believe that there may be a link between food additives and hyperactivity in children ("Food Additives and Hyperactivity," 2004)

Further Resources for Young Children with Mental Retardation and Other Developmental Delays   Preparing an Individualized Family Service Plan (IFSP) for any eligible young child includes investigating a variety of resources in these areas:

- early identification and assessment of disabling conditions in children
- related services, including transportation
- developmental, corrective, and other supportive services (including speech-language pathology and audiology services)
- psychological services
- physical and occupational therapy, recreation, including therapeutic recreation
- social work services, counseling services, including rehabilitation counseling, orientation and mobility services
- medical services, except that such medical services shall be for diagnostic and evaluation purposes only, as may be required to assist a child with a disability to benefit from special education

Questions

Why is it important for a young child to have many types of sensory experiences? What changes are taking place in healthy children's sensory systems, and what types of sensory disorders impede normal cognitive development? What types of services are available to help those with impairments?

Nutrition and Health Issues

Pediatricians normally recommend that young children eat a "mixed diet." This means a variety of foods and beverages in different combinations so that over time the child will get the proper nourishment (Kleinman, 2004). By the second year of life, toddlers will be able to eat most family foods. At meals they eat much smaller portions than adults; therefore, they need nutritious snacks in between meals.

Small portions of fresh juices, fruits, and vegetables cut up and attractively presented as finger foods are usually quite appealing to young children, although

Further Developments

Growth Charts, Ages 2 to 20

FIGURE 7.2 Growth Charts for Boys, Ages 2 to 20 For comparison with other children, the midline of stature (height) or weight is the 50th percentile, which indicates that 50 percent of the population of boys or girls are taller (or weigh more or less). Weight can be tracked in pounds or kilograms; height can be tracked in inches or centimeters. *Source:* Centers for Disease Control and Prevention, National Center for Health Statistics. CDC growth charts: United States. http://www.cdc.gov/growthcharts/May 30, 2000.

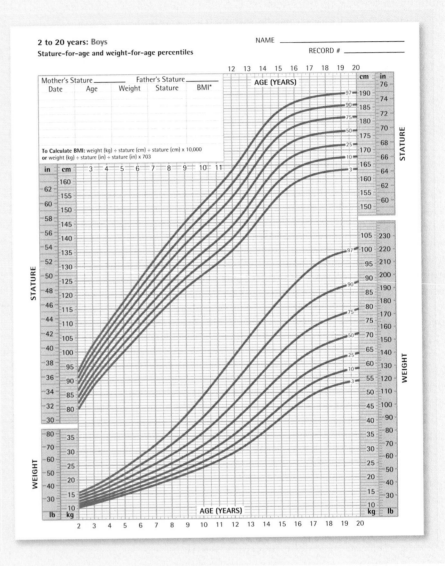

a recent study found that only 16 percent of children entering school ate the recommended daily five servings of vegetables or fruits (Perry et al., 1998). Commercially prepared foods for young children might provide the necessary nutrition, but restaurant and take-out foods tend to be high in sodium, fats, or sugars. Children generally should not be fed highly spiced, fatty foods with artificial colorings, additives, and preservatives.

It is recommended that after the age of 2, children should get most of their calories from grain products, fruits, vegetables, low-fat dairy, beans, lean meat, poultry, fish, and nuts (Dietary Guidelines Advisory Committee,

2005). Most young children do not readily accept spicy, strong-tasting, bitter, or pungent foods. Consequently, pharmaceutical companies add sweeteners to children's medications.

Variability in Eating Behaviors Among Children Like everyone else, young children will feel hungry, their bodies will tell them when to eat, and their hunger might not coincide with the family mealtime. Young children also experience "growth spurts," which coincide with periods of greater hunger. Children can become difficult or disruptive at mealtimes if caregivers impose strict

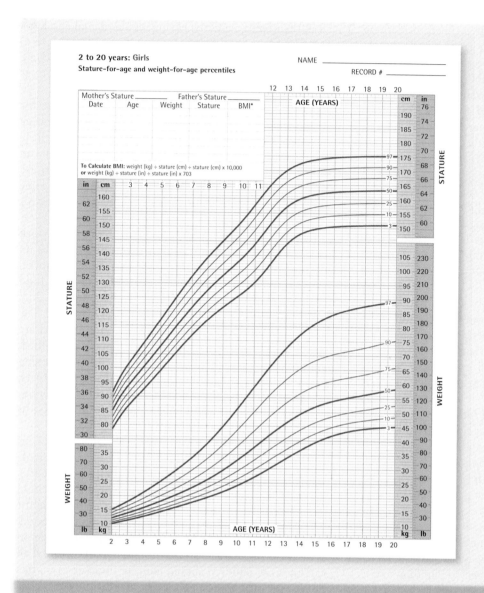

FIGURE 7.3 Growth Charts for Girls, Ages 2 to 20
Source: Centers for Disease Control and Prevention, National Center for Health Statistics. CDC growth charts: United States. http://www.cdc.gov/growthcharts/May 30, 2000.

eating behaviors, such as requiring them to finish all of something and try everything (Satter, 1998). Again, some children react severely to the taste and texture of certain foods, and sensory integration methods might help. Other children have allergies to specific foods, and caregivers must pay special attention to make sure that food is removed from the child's diet.

When a Child Refuses Certain Foods Some foods, like broccoli, cabbage, Brussels sprouts, spinach, cauliflower, olives, and onions, taste very bitter to the sensitive taste buds of young children—and other foods may be rejected because of texture (children often dislike liver, for example). It might be better to reintroduce these foods to the child at several time intervals during development and certainly in tiny portions or substitute with another food from that food group. Leach (1998) cites a research study conducted

at a nursery in London revealing that when children were offered trays of a wide range of suitably cooked and cut-up foods three times each day, they selected for themselves diets that were balanced over the long term. Some would prefer protein one day, fruits other days. Some days they ate more, while some days they ate less.

It is recommended, and soon seen by most parents, that mealtimes should be enjoyable; food should not be used as a reward, punishment, bribe, or threat. It has also been documented that dietary intervention programs can be successful when started early enough (Perry et al., 1998). A routine checkup with a pediatrician will determine whether the young child is growing adequately for gender, age, and body type. Also, a parent or caregiver can track a child's growth with growth charts provided by the CDC. (See Figures 7.2 and 7.3 in the *Further Developments* box above, "Growth Charts, Ages 2 to 20.")

Eating Frequency   Young children need something to eat upon awakening, a midmorning snack, lunch, a midafternoon snack, an evening meal, and maybe a before-bed snack. When hungry children must wait too long to eat, their blood sugar levels will dip, causing energy drain, lack of patience, and a "cranky" attitude. Child-care providers must be prepared to offer children proper nutrition at various times of the day.

Most preschool children and 5- and 6-year-olds in kindergarten classes need the energy boost of the midmorning or midafternoon snack to think clearly and participate in activities (Leach, 1998). Some children are larger or more energetic than others and might need to snack more between mealtimes. Other children are smaller and less energetic and might simply require fewer calories. Cultural background affects what and how much children eat. Children whose families practice fasting to honor religious requirements actually are expected to fast for days or even weeks, eating only one or two meals per day. Gender, ethnicity, and even geographic location have all been examined as influential factors in determining how much energy is needed by children as young as 4 years (Goran et al., 1998).

Dental Health Affects Nutritional Intake   Douglass and colleagues (2004) state that the most common chronic disease of early childhood is *caries* (tooth decay or cavities); thus pediatricians and dentists recommend the first dental visit at the age of 1 year, when teeth erupt. Dentists advocate that primary care physicians examine children's teeth for defects and cavities at every well-child visit (Casamassimo, 2004). To prevent decay of both baby teeth and permanent teeth, children should not be given sweet foods or drinks before they go to bed to sleep. Factors that promote healthy tooth development include limiting sweets in the child's diet, training toddlers and young children to

Young Children Need Nutritious Snacks Energetic young children may need several nutritious snacks a day between meals. These children are in a Montessori preschool where they are encouraged to prepare their own snacks.

clean their teeth regularly, having regular dental checkups and fluoride in local water supplies. Around ages 5 to 6, baby teeth begin to come out, and permanent ones come in. Parents and caregivers should teach and model proper dental hygiene and provide supplies.

Many communities provide free dental checkups for young children at various locations (e.g., a nearby college may have a dental hygiene program that provides free dental services for children). Improper tooth development can impair a child's ability to eat and speak—not to mention affect a child's appearance or health in later years (some children never smile because of decayed or missing teeth).

Allergies   The Food Allergy and Anaphylaxis Network estimates that at least 3 million U.S. children have an allergic reaction to certain foods, which can happen immediately or within hours. For children with food allergies, the organs most affected are the mouth, skin, gastrointestinal tract, and the respiratory system. The foods that most commonly cause allergic reactions are eggs, milk, peanuts, soy, wheat, tree nuts, and shellfish (Sicherer, 1999). Insect stings can also be life threatening to some children, including bees, yellow jackets, hornets, wasps, and fire ants. Some children have serious allergies to animal dander, specific medications, or a reaction to latex ("Information about Anaphylaxis," 2005).

Parents, child-care workers, school nurses, and teachers must know which children have a dramatic multiorgan reaction called **anaphylaxis** (anna-phil-ax-iss), which is life threatening Dr. Sicherer, Mount Sinai School of Medicine (1999), says the foods most responsible for anaphylaxis are peanuts, walnuts, and tree nuts (almond, pecan, cashew, hazelnut, and Brazil nut). The common symptoms of food allergy are noted in Table 7.2, and all caregivers of children should educate themselves on this life-saving information. The only way to prevent an allergen reaction is strict avoidance of the allergy-causing food, animal, insect, or substance (Sicherer, 1999).

Although for generations medical practitioners and dairy advertising convinced parents that children's bones would not grow without daily doses of cow's milk, nowadays, "cow's milk is recognized as a food that some children do better without. . . . The valuable proteins, minerals, and vitamins milk contains are in other foods, too" (Leach, 1998, p. 233). Some children are lactose intolerant (experiencing abdominal pain and cramping or episodes of passing foul-smelling gas or stools shortly after eating dairy foods); they can get the necessary nutrients in soy products, tomatoes, and green and leafy vegetables. Alternative sources of calcium include fresh goat's milk and soy milk (from the soybean plant) and plenty of leafy green vegetables.

A Vegetarian Diet   Children in vegetarian families commonly get their carbohydrates and protein from a range

Table 7.2 Food Allergies May Be Life Threatening

The most common symptoms of food allergies and anaphylaxis are:

- Hives
- Vomiting
- Diarrhea
- Abdominal cramping
- Swelling of the throat, lips, or tongue
- Difficulty breathing or swallowing
- Metallic taste or itching in the mouth
- Generalized flushing, itching, or redness of the skin (hives)
- Nausea
- Increased heart rate
- Plunging blood pressure (and accompanying paleness)
- Sudden feeling of weakness
- Anxiety or an overwhelming sense of doom
- Collapse
- Loss of consciousness

Caregivers must know what foods are common allergens and what to do to save a child's life.

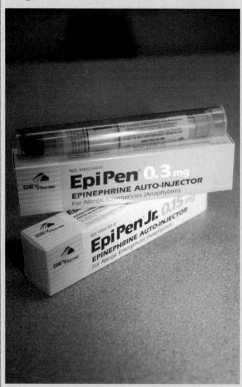

EpiPen site

Caregivers/teachers of a child with a known food allergy should have written parental permission to administer epinephrine from an EpiPen and should be trained in its use.

---

of bean, legume, and nut dishes, and possibly some egg, cheese, or dairy dishes. A strict vegetarian diet for a growing child is questionable, and parents should seek dietary advice from a nutritionist or medical professional. The other trace minerals and vitamins that children need for healthy bones, teeth, blood, and neural growth are usually found in a plentiful fresh fruits and vegetables. On the other hand, fast foods and junk foods are high in fat and have led to an alarming trend of obesity in U.S. children. Obesity rates among children are skyrocketing—double and triple the rates among certain age groups of 30 years ago. Nine million school-age children (about 15 percent of the total) are classified as obese (Arnst & Kiley, 2004).

Good Health Also Means Sufficient Calories Children need an adequate supply of calories daily to keep their bodily functions running smoothly and to provide

the fuel needed for growth of their brain and body systems. Staple carbohydrates, eaten in different forms all over the world, include rice, wheat, potatoes, corn, beans, yams, and sweet potatoes. Children can get an ample supply of protein from meat, fish, poultry, eggs, or foods that contain eggs, cheese, yogurt, peanut butter, and similar foods (Leach, 1998).

In areas of the world with limited food supply, many children develop forms of life-threatening malnutrition called *marasmus* or *kwashiorkor* from diets chronically deficient in carbohydrates, protein, and fat. Malnourished children have little energy, are lethargic, are likely to have a large protuberant abdomen from protein deficiency, and are at high risk of early death (Gehri & Stettler, 2001).

Poverty Effects on Nutrition and Health The term *food security* is used to describe having access at all times

More Information You Can Use

Household Lead Poisoning: Still a Problem

Although overall blood lead level (BLL) rates have been steadily declining over the years, lead poisoning continues to be a major public health issue, especially for young children who are at greater risk by playing near the floor and putting old paint chips into their mouths. The major source of lead exposure is from deteriorating house paint in the form of dust and paint chips and lead pipes (especially houses and buildings built before 1980). Nearly half of all U.S. homes in which children under the age of 6 live still have lead paint, and lead dust is easily spread during renovations, for example (U.S. Department of Housing and Urban Development, 2000). The following symptoms are found with children with lead poisoning: decreased appetite, stomachache, sleeplessness, learning problems, constipation, vomiting, diarrhea, tiredness, lowered IQ, and anemia ("Lead Poisoning," 2005). A pediatrician can order a blood test to determine a child's blood lead levels.

Researchers continue to study the health effects associated with lead exposure. Known harmful effects include brain and nervous system damage, behavioral and learning problems, as well as hormonal effects that delay the process of puberty (Canfield et al., 2003; Selevan et al., 2003).

The health effects of lead exposure appear to be long-term and irreversible. Therapy such as *chelation* does not seem to mitigate the harm to cognitive, behavioral, or neuropsychological function (Rogan & Ware, 2003). Prevention is the only way to protect children from the harmful effects of lead exposure. Homes should be tested for lead paint and repainted frequently to prevent flaking and peeling of old layers of lead paint. Lead can also enter the water supply through contact with lead pipes. Lead pipes should be replaced and water can be filtered to remove some of the lead.

The CDC has changed its threshold level for lead exposure several times as new findings indicated harmful effects at yet lower and lower levels in the blood. The U.S. Department of Health and Human Services set a goal to eliminate BLLs greater than 25μg per deciliter, but that goal was not met. A new target goal was established to eliminate BLLs greater than 10μg per deciliter in children 6 years of age and under by the year 2010. To meet that goal, this issue needs to be addressed by increasing awareness of this public health problem and devoting more funding toward eliminating the sources of exposure. Caregivers who reside in an older residence or work with children in an older building should have the facility and outside soil checked for lead contamination, wash children's toys and hands regularly, dust and wash floors and windowsills regularly, make sure there are no loose paint chips, and avoid exposure to lead dust when remodeling or renovating.

to enough food to support a healthy active life. This means having enough food that is nutritious and safe without having to rely on sources such as food pantries. Because food security is directly related to income and monetary resources, children who live in poverty are much more likely to experience food insecurity. Over 45 percent of children whose household income is below the federal poverty level live in food-insecure situations and rely on community food pantries ("Trends in the Well-Being of America's Children and Youth," 2003).

Safety Practices in a Young Child's Environment   Accidental injuries are the leading cause of child deaths. Thus, all dangerous items, such as sharp knives, matches and lighters, loaded guns, fireworks, and so on, should be kept out of a child's reach, as should plants with poisonous leaves. Put keys in a place so a curious child cannot possibly start the car or lawnmower. When disposing of old appliances, make sure the doors are removed. Drowning is the second cause of death of young children, so adults must always supervise them near water—and that includes a kiddie swimming pool, a Jacuzzi, and the bathtub!

To explore new tastes, young children will try new and different items, many of which are unsafe, such as mothballs, marbles, coins, hard candies, and many household cleansers. Swallowing substances containing lead (e.g., peeling chips of paint) can seriously harm a child's or fetus's developing brain and nervous system. Effects of neurotoxins such as lead include seizure, coma, and death (Centers for Disease Control and Prevention, 2003) (see the *More Information You Can Use* box above, "Household Lead Poisoning: Still a Problem").

Children with HIV or AIDS   Worldwide more than 1,900 children are infected with HIV each day, and HIV infection and AIDS have severely strained child health services (UNAIDS, 2004). Nearly half the 40 million people living with HIV worldwide are women, who in turn may infect their children during pregnancy or birth or leave children orphaned (UNAIDS/UNIFEM/

UNFPA, 2004). One group of affected young children, called *rapid progressors,* develops symptoms and serious complications early in life and often dies before the age of 5. The other group, called *long-term survivors,* develops symptoms much later (some not until their teens) and lives longer. Babies placed in foster care at the time of hospital discharge are eight times more likely to have been born to HIV-infected women, and children in foster care are at risk for sexual abuse, placing them at higher risk for HIV infection (Wilfert et al., 2000b). The American Academy of Pediatrics recommends testing all children in foster care for HIV who have symptoms or physical findings suggestive of HIV infection, been sexually abused, a sibling who is HIV-infected, or a parent who is HIV-infected or is at increased risk of HIV infection (Wilfert et al., 2000a). Foster-care parents need to be educated in the management of all health issues of a child living with HIV or AIDS (Wilfert et al., 2000b).

New antiretroviral treatments and innovative treatment strategies that extend life expectancy for children continue to be developed ("Women, Children, and HIV," 2004). Most children can expect to live longer, healthier lives using active antiretroviral therapy. Comprehensive care for HIV-exposed children requires coordination of care among multiple medical, social service, and education professionals (Wilfert et al., 2000b).

Children with HIV infection can attend school, can participate in activities (sometimes modified as in physical education), and should not be isolated or excluded in an educational setting (Wilfert et al., 2000a). As any child living with a chronic illness, however, they are more likely to get other infections and may require special services, including home instruction and early intervention services (Horn, 1998). When symptoms become more chronic, these children begin to experience cognitive delays and poorer academic performance (Wilfert et al., 2000a).

Because parents usually seek advice from a nurse or pediatrician, they should be familiar with federal disabilities rights laws, such as IDEA and Education of the Handicapped Act Amendments (PL 99-457). Confidentiality about HIV status must be maintained—with parental consent required for disclosure (Wilfert et al., 2000a). Although many breakthroughs have occurred regarding HIV/AIDS treatment, prevention of the infection through vaccination is not yet a reality and might be several years away (Kieny, Excler, & Girard, 2004).

Questions

What types of nutrition and eating behaviors are critical for a child's body growth and brain development, and what are some of the more serious illnesses or diseases affecting young children today? What are the effects of poverty and poor nutrition for growing children?

Self-Care Behaviors

An important aspect of a young child's development is training in self-care behaviors, such as daily bathing and shampooing, cleaning teeth, brushing hair, wiping the nose, wiping the bottom and washing the hands after toileting, hand washing before and after eating, and dressing appropriately for weather conditions (putting on boots, coat, and mittens when it is cold and snowy, for example). Again, cultures differ in how much independence they promote in children regarding self-care behaviors, in the availability of water and supplies for sanitation and self-care, and in the frequency of these behaviors. For example, American soldiers in Iraq started campaigns to provide thousands of Iraqi children with a backpack with toothbrushes and other sanitary supplies.

Toilet Training Elimination training is a big developmental milestone during early childhood, and there is considerable variance in age of mastery. On average, in Westernized cultures children demonstrate self-control of these bodily functions by the third year. In traditional societies, mothers respond compassionately to their child's elimination rhythms by using natural infant hygiene, just as they tune in to the child's other needs (Bauer, 2001).

Parents and caretakers should realize that extreme patience and a sense of humor help both them and the child get through this time of maturation and development. As you shall see in upcoming chapters, though, children who master self-care skills and can self-regulate their own behaviors are likely to develop greater self-esteem and self-confidence, and this can lead to many other positive outcomes as the child matures.

Sleep Cross-sectional studies show that children's sleep patterns and sleep problems are influenced by cultural and social factors (Liu et al., 2005). Parents are often commonly concerned about their young children's sleep behaviors (Thiedke, 2001). Daytime sleep gradually decreases over the first three years, and by age 4 most children no longer require a daytime nap (see Figure 7.4). Night awakenings are common throughout early childhood. "Approximately one child in three up to 4 years of age will continue to awaken during the night and require intervention by a parent to return to sleep" (Thiedke, 2001). There are two camps of thought about young children's sleep habits: (1) children need a daily routine of one early afternoon nap with a reasonable evening bedtime established so the child will get 10 to 12 hours of sleep per night, or (2) the child's sleep schedule can vary at times to meet the parents' needs.

In actuality, sleep schedules are based on parental and caregiver tolerance about sleep habits, the number of caretakers, whether the child goes to child care, and timing

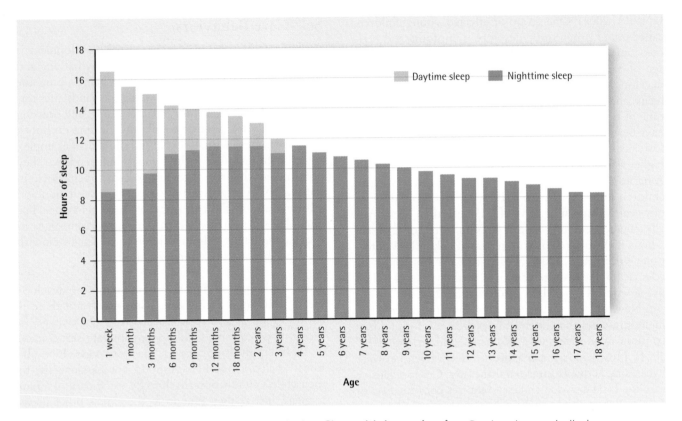

FIGURE 7.4 Change in Hours of Daytime and Nighttime Sleep with Increasing Age Daytime sleep gradually decreases over the first three years, with an increase in nighttime sleep. By age 4 or 5, many children do not take a daytime nap.
Source: Reprinted with the permission of Simon & Schuster Adult Publishing Group, from *Solve Your Child's Sleep Problems* by Richard Ferber. Copyright © 1985 by Richard Ferber, M.D.

of the parents' workday. Today, with over 60 percent of mothers working, many young children awake early, are transported to a child-care center for the day, and return home for only a few hours before bedtime. An overtired child can be whiny and cranky and will probably be difficult or lethargic. It is unfair to punish a child for unruly or uncooperative behavior when the parents are not providing enough rest, relaxation, or sleep time for an energetic, growing child.

Parents who establish a consistent bedtime routine will find it easier than those who reinforce a lot of rocking, getting up many times, walking around, or overplaying. Before bedtime, children are relaxed by having a warm bath, a story read, or a quiet talk. Young children who are allowed to stay up late and run around the house at all hours are likely to be in control of the family over this sleep issue.

Sleep Disturbances in Young Children Two recent cross-cultural studies with large samples of Chinese and American children revealed more sleep problems in the Chinese children. The higher incidence of sleep problems can likely be attributed to Chinese children going to bed, on average, one hour later than American children and also rising about one hour earlier than

American children (Liu et al., 2005). We can predict that children ages 3 to 8 often have sleep problems, though we do not know what causes *nightmares* or *night terrors* ("Sleep Problems: Nightmares," 2001). "Night terrors occur approximately 90 minutes into sleep during stage 3 or 4 NREM sleep. The child suddenly sits bolt upright and screams and is inconsolable for up to 30 minutes before relaxing and falling back to sleep" (Thiedke, 2001, p. 279).

Preschoolers begin to have more problems initiating, maintaining, and resisting sleep. Parents need to set firm limits when the child pleads for one more drink of water or one more story (Thiedke, 2001). A preschool child experiences many daytime stresses or fears—such as attending a new child-care center, the birth of a new sibling, moving to a new home, separation of parents, or death of a significant person or pet—that can trigger bad dreams. Also, young children today are exposed to graphic displays of violence in the media that are very disturbing and can affect sleep quality (Owens et al., 1999).

An estimated 5 to 7 million American children, and a higher percent of boys, experience nocturnal *enuresis* (bed wetting). By 5 years of age, 15 to 25 percent of children wet the bed, and that is when physicians consider an enuretic diagnosis. By age 12 a small percent of boys and girls are still enuretic (Thiedke, 2001, 2003). The causes of enuresis are multifactorial: genetic factors, psychological concerns, bladder problems or infections, and sleep disorders (Thiedke, 2003). A physical exam is in order and a treatment plan is prescribed, including bed-wetting alarms, medication, encouragement and support. Children's self-esteem improved with treatment (Thiedke, 2003).

A young child does not have the vocabulary to understand or express the anxiety she or he is experiencing, and chronic sleep disturbances can be a signal that the child is not coping well. Parents can reassure the child who is experiencing sleep disturbances by giving the child extra love and attention, talking about the child's fears, and being understanding.

Illness and Immunizations   With more children in early childhood education programs or receiving out-of-home care in a nursery, child-care center, preschool, Early Head Start or Head Start, children are continuously in contact with other children and at greater risk for contracting childhood diseases. Most states require proof of immunizations before a young child can be enrolled in child care or public preschool or kindergarten classes. Though some children have more extreme reactions to certain vaccinations, the vast majority will experience better health if their parents maintain the recommended inoculation schedule. The MMR immunization is under close scrutiny by research teams at the Centers for Disease Control and Prevention for its potential association with developmental disorders. For those with questions about the use of certain preservatives in immunizations, parents are advised to confer with their pediatrician about vaccinations and the individual child. These are the recommended vaccinations for children

aged 4 to 6 years ("Recommended Childhood and Adolescent Immunization Schedule," 2005):

- *DtaP*—the fifth booster: diphtheria, tetanus, pertussis
- *IPV*—the fourth booster: poliovirus
- *MMR*—the second shot of measles, mumps, rubella for your child. Also, keep in mind that the second dose is recommended at this time but may be administered if four weeks have passed since the first shot. Both doses must be administered on or after 1 year of age.

Childhood Asthma   Asthma is the leading serious, chronic pediatric disease affecting nearly 9 percent of children, nearly tripling since the early 1990s to more than 6 million children in 2001 (Woodruff et al., 2003). It is the most common reason for child admission to the hospital (see Figure 7.5) and a major cause of school absences ("Chartbook on the Trends in the Health of Americans," 2004). **Asthma** is a chronic lung disease characterized by inflammation and narrowing of small airways in the lungs in response to *allergens,* which trigger the asthma attack. Such "triggers" include pet dander (such as classroom pets), dust and dust mites, molds, infections, exercise, grass, pollens, tobacco smoke, household cleansers, cold air, poor indoor quality, chalk dust, and other respiratory irritants ("Chartbook on the Trends in the Health of Americans," 2004). At least 5 million children in the United States have asthma, and the majority of asthmatic children say they are exposed to cigarette smoke at home ("Smoking Linked to Childhood Asthma," 2001).

Symptoms include coughing, wheezing, shortness of breath, and tightness in the chest, making it very difficult to breathe ("Understanding Allergy and Asthma," 2001). Caretakers must decrease or eliminate a child's exposure

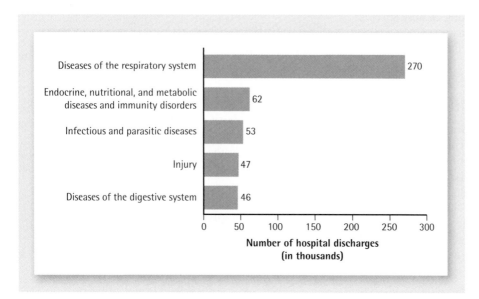

FIGURE 7.5 Major Causes of Hospitalization, Ages 1 to 4: 2000 Diseases of the respiratory system were the major causes of hospitalization for children aged 1 to 4 in 2000.
Source: U.S. Maternal and Child Health Bureau. *Child Health USA 2002.* Washington, DC: U.S. Department of Health and Human Services.

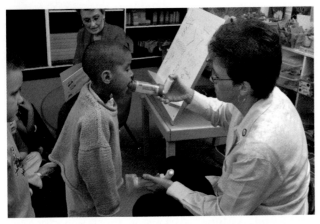

Asthma Is a Main Cause of Child Hospitalizations About 9 percent of American children are diagnosed with asthma, and diseases of the repiratory system were the major causes of hospitalization for children aged 1 to 4 in 2000.

to allergens, thereby decreasing asthma symptoms. After being diagnosed, some children take inhaled medications to improve their breathing (quick-relief drugs), whereas others get regular allergy shots and other medications (long-term control). Families with a child with serious allergies and asthma need to have an emergency *epinephrine* kit available (see Table 7.2) ("Understanding Allergy and Asthma," 2001).

Public School Health Care   Children in the U.S. public school system are checked annually by a health-care professional for physical and health problems, such as malnutrition, obesity, and curvature of the spine; respiratory illnesses such as asthma; sensory capabilities, such as vision and hearing screenings; and overall health and self-care skills, with attention to bathing, body lice, and such. The combination of proper nutrition for growth and development, required sleep for physical maturation and an increased alertness, and childhood immunizations protecting against specific diseases help to lay a healthy foundation for central nervous system development and cognitive functioning.

Demographic Trends and Implications for Child Health

Changes in the populations of specific demographic groups, especially those who may be dependent on services (including children), have implications for how these services are allocated. The total number of children under 18 has increased by over 50 percent since 1950. There were over 72 million children in the United States in 2001, representing about 25 percent of the total population. Although the percentage of children to the total population is projected to remain about the same, the absolute number of children is expected to rise to over 80 million by 2020 ("Trends in the Well-Being," 2003). This larger total number of chil-

dren means that there will be a need for more schools and more services, such as child care and health care.

Table 7.3 shows statistics for 2005 and projections to 2050. Population experts project that the population of Hispanic children under 18 will continue to increase, whereas the black, Asian, and white populations of children will remain relatively stable. The changing demographics in the United States have important implications, not only for the health of the individuals who compose these ethnic and racial groups, but for the overall population (see the *Human Diversity* box "Health Beliefs and Practices Across Cultures"). With increasing numbers of individuals representing diverse groups, there will be large numbers of individuals speaking languages other than English—a great deterrent to getting proper health care. Translation services are needed to ensure that members of minority and racial groups will be able to converse with professionals about their health needs. It is likely they won't seek health care until their health condition has become more serious, thus leading to increased costs of these services and more negative health outcomes.

Child Mortality Rates and Causes

A reduction in both early and late childhood mortality rates in the United States indicates an improvement in the health status of the child population. Even with decreasing mortality rates, since 1960 male children have died at a higher rate than female children (Gardner & Hudson, 1996; "Ten Leading Causes of Death," 2001).

Causes of Death for Young Children   In 2002, among children aged 1 to 4, the deaths of more than 4,800 children were caused by unintentional injuries, congenital birth defects, homicides, malignant neoplasms (cancer), and heart disease ("U.S. Department of Health and Human Services, 2004b). (See Figure 7.6.)

Child Mortality in Minority Communities   Despite overall reductions in childhood mortality, there are also substantial differences across racial and ethnic groups (Kane, 1993). Among Hispanics, for example, Cuban children had lower death rates than their white counterparts, and Puerto Rican and Central and South American children had higher death rates in two recent studies. Asian and Pacific Islanders had significantly lower death rates than all other groups, true for both male and female children.

Browne and colleagues (1997) recommend the following steps to improve health status and outcomes for minority children:

- Expand programs to include courses in culturally sensitive communication and assessment that acknowledge cultural beliefs and values.

Human Diversity

Health Beliefs and Practices Across Cultures

Childhood Checkups and Immunizations

Many childhood diseases are rare in countries where children are routinely protected by immunizations during regularly scheduled checkups with pediatricians and health-care practitioners. However, a majority of the world's children live in countries where preventive immunizations are rare or nonexistent, and families seek their medical care from a person such as a traditional faith healer. Because many young children in the United States today have parents who are immigrants from such countries, health-care and child-care professionals must understand such countries' three basic myths regarding the cause of illness and appropriate cures (which more than likely do not include the concept of immunization) (Lecca et al., 1998):

- *Natural causes:* Illness can be caused by damp and cold. According to Chinese medical practice, illness is caused by the *yin* (female energy) and *yang* (male energy) being out of balance, which is cured with acupuncture or accupressure. Eating things that are poisonous or out of season can cause illness; for instance, many practicing Muslims and Jews do not eat pork, and Muslims fast during the month of Ramadan. Some members of Jehovah's Witness do not want their children to have blood transfusions. Puerto Rican, South American, and Caribbean islanders utilize massage and natural folk and herbal remedies for common illnesses that they classify as *hot* or *cold* illnesses.
- *Supernatural causes:* Illness can be caused by someone, something, or a spiritual energy that is angry with the ill person and puts something bad on that person (hexes, curses, fixes).
- *Religious or spiritual causes:* Illness is caused by thinking or doing evil, by not praying enough, by not having faith, by lying, by cheating, by not respecting elders or religious leaders or God.

The Western medical model of wellness and illness assumes that proper nutrition, sleep, and widespread childhood immunizations prevent most serious illness and potential life-threatening complications. However, more American families travel to countries that do not practice childhood immunization. And as families are moving daily into the United States from all over the world, many—both children and adults—have not been inoculated for childhood diseases and are unaware of, opposed to, or afraid of immunizations. Also, some U.S. families believe that childhood inoculations are not worth the risk, given the possibility that the child could develop a fever, a mild form of the disease, or neurological damage such as autism. Other families neglect taking their children for regular checkups, even though public clinics provide checkups and immunizations free of charge or on a reduced scale.

- Give opportunities to understand the rapidly changing communities that health practitioners work with, along with the cultural barriers to adherence to prevention and treatment programs.
- Create and validate culturally sensitive tools for data collection as well as approaches for interviewing individuals from ethnic and racially diverse populations.
- Encourage minority researchers and students to continue to join in innovative and important research related to the health of women and children.

Table 7.3 Childhood Demographics in the United States—Number of Children Under Age 5 for Hispanics, Blacks, and Non-Hispanic Whites: Years 2000, 2025, and 2050

Children Under Age 5	Year 2000 Actual	Year 2025 Projected	Year 2050 Projected
Hispanics	3,668,905	5,862,000	8,551,000
Blacks	2,744,783	3,345,000	3,982,000
Non-Hispanic whites	11,171,157	12,024,000	12,287,000
Total (all children under age 5)	19,175,798	22,551,000	26,914,000

Note: In July 2003, Hispanic children under age 5 amounted to 4.2 million or 21 percent of the total of 19.8 million children in that age range.

Source: Collins, R., & Ribeiro, R. (2004, Fall). Toward an early care and education agenda for Hispanic children. *Early Childhood Research and Practice (ECRP)*, 6(2). Retrieved February 24, 2005, from http://eerp.uiuc.edu/v6n2/collins.html

FIGURE 7.6 Leading Causes of Death for Children, Ages 1 to 4: 2000 Although child death rates have declined substantially among 1- to 4-year-old children, accidental injuries accounted for 42 percent of all deaths, followed by congenital malformations (birth defects), malignant neoplasms (cancer), homicide, and diseases of the heart.
Source: U.S. Maternal and Child Health Bureau. *Child Health USA 2002*, p. 32 Washington, DC: U.S. Department of Health and Human Services. Retrieved February 24, 2005, from http://www.mchb.hrsa.gov/chusa02/main_pages/page_32.htm

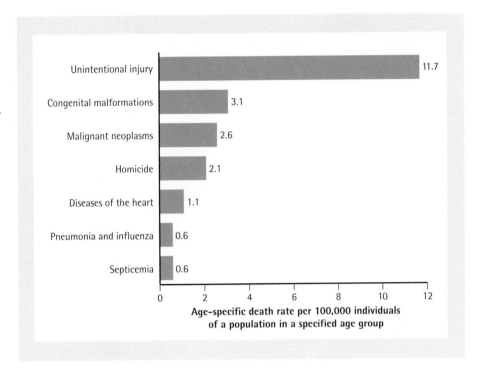

Future Directions Many private and public sector partners are cooperating in a national initiative called the *2010 Express*. Families, child health professionals, state and community representatives, and public and private organizations have come together to produce a *10-Year Action Plan to Achieve Community-Based Service Systems for Children and Youth with Special Health Care Needs and Their Families*. The plan presents strategies for delivering services for children with special health-care needs that can be achieved by 2010.

Questions

What variables will a health-care practitioner examine to determine whether a young child is healthy and developing normally? What are some of the more common childhood disorders and disabilities that compromise healthy development, and what services are available for those affected? What are the main causes of the death of young children?

Cognitive Development

Preschool children who receive adequate nutrition and varied stimulation normally experience a rapid expansion of cognitive abilities. They become more adept at obtaining information, ordering it, and using it. Gradually, these abilities evolve into the attribute called intelligence. Whereas sensorimotor processes largely dominated development during infancy, a significant transition occurs after 18 months toward the more abstract processes of reasoning, inference, and problem solving. Preschool children continue to use their senses to absorb the world around them, and preschool educators use many sensory experiences in teaching about the world (see Table 7.4). By the time children are 7 years old, they have developed a diversified set of cognitive skills functionally related to the elements of adult intelligence (Sternberg, 1990).

Intelligence and Its Assessment

For laypeople and psychologists alike, the concept of intelligence is a rather fuzzy notion (Sternberg, 1990). In some ways intelligence resembles electricity. Like electricity, intelligence "is measurable, and its effect, but not its properties, can be only imprecisely described" (Bischof, 1976, p. 137). Even so, David Wechsler (1896–1981) (1975), a psychologist who devised a number of widely used intelligence tests, has proposed a definition that has won considerable acceptance. He viewed **intelligence** as a global capacity to understand the world, think rationally, and cope resourcefully with the challenges of life. Wechsler saw intelligence as a capacity for acquiring knowledge and functioning rationally and effectively, rather than the possession of a fund of knowledge. Intelligence has captivated the interest of psychologists for a variety of reasons, including a desire to devise ways of teaching people to better understand and increase their intellectual abilities (Sternberg, 1986a).

Table 7.4 Sample Cognitive and Sensorimotor Activities for Preschool, Pre-K Children

Goal	Sensory Experience	Verbal/Math/Motor Activity	Resources
To understand about animals that live in the ocean and have tentacles such as a jellyfish, shrimmp, and an octopus. www.aqua.org/animals/species/jellies.html Take a trip to The Baltimore Aquarium.	**Messy Table Ooey Gooey Jellyfish** A jellyfish is not really a fish. Remember, all fish have backbones and jellyfish have no bones at all. You will need to make up a batch of Jell-o for this activity. Let the children *smoosh* and *gush* the Jell-o, pretending that it is a real jellyfish. You can add small fish to the table for the jellyfish to eat. Explore whale sounds at www.whalesounds.com. Take an online tour of aquarium exhibits with a live web cam and video exhibits at Monterey Bay, California, at www.mbayaq.org/efc.	**Five Scrumptious Shrimp** Five scrumptious shrimp burrowed in the mud Hiding from their predators in the slimy crud Along came a fish as quiet as he could GULP! Four scrumptious shrimp burrowed in the mud. . . . **The Tickle Octopus** by Audrey Wood/Harcourt Brace This is a very funny book. Take the time to let the children repeat the caveman words. **Activity** You can also choose one child to be the tickle octopus. Whenever the tickle octopus comes out, he/she walks around the circle tickling all in the group.	**Jell-O with Swimming Fish (4 servings)** *Ingredients* 1 pkg. blue Jell-O (4-serving size) 3/4 cup boiling water 1/2 cup cold water 1 tray ice cubes 1 pkg. gummy fish *Instructions* Dissolve Jell-O in boiling water. Combine cold water and ice cubes to make 1¼ cups ice and water. Add to Jell-O, stir until slightly thick. Remove any unmelted ice. If it is still too thin, refrigerate for a few minutes. Pour Jell-O into clear glasses. Drop in gummy fish. Refrigerate until set, about 1 hour. Makes 4 servings.

Source: www.creativeprek.com. Reprinted with permission.

Intelligence: Single or Multiple Factors? One recurrent divisive issue among psychologists is whether intelligence is a single, general intellectual capacity or a composite of many special, independent abilities. Alfred Binet (1857–1911), the French psychologist who in 1905 devised the first widely used intelligence test, viewed intelligence as a general capacity for comprehension and reasoning. Although his test used many different types of items, Binet assumed that he was measuring a general ability expressed in the performance of many kinds of tasks.

In England, Charles Spearman (1863–1945) quickly rose to eminence in psychological circles by advancing a somewhat different view. Spearman (1904, 1927) concluded that there is a general intellectual ability, the *g* (for "general") factor, employed for abstract reasoning and problem solving. He viewed the *g* factor as a basic intellectual power that pervades all of a person's mental activity. However, because an individual's performance across various tasks is not perfectly consistent, Spearman identified special factors (*s* factors) peculiar to given tasks, such as arithmetic or spatial relations. This approach is known as the **two-factor theory of intelligence** (see N. Brody,

1992). J. P. Guilford (1967) has carried the tradition further by identifying 120 factors of intelligence. Not all psychologists are happy, however, with such minute distinctions. Many prefer to speak of "general ability"—a mixture of abilities that can be more or less arbitrarily measured by a general-purpose intelligence test.

Multiple Intelligences Psychologist Howard Gardner (1983, 1993a, 1993b, 1997, 1999, 2000a) from Harvard has been conducting research with gifted children for years. On the basis of his research, he proposes that there is not just one factor called intelligence but there are **multiple intelligences (MIs).** That is, humans have at least nine distinctive intelligences that interact (see Figure 7.7): verbal-linguistic, logical-mathematical, visual-spatial, musical, bodily-kinesthetic, interpersonal (knowing how to deal with others), intrapersonal (knowledge of oneself), naturalist (nature smarts), and existentialist (philosophical about existence). Therefore, children have different learning strengths and weaknesses—and Gardner suggests educators vary their instructional and evaluation methods to accommodate

Early Intelligence Testing With the development of IQ tests in the early 1900s, seemingly a scientific instrument was at hand for evaluating the intellectual capabilities of the members of various ethnic groups. Immigrants in the United States from non-English-speaking nations tended to score rather poorly. With a score of about 100 considered "normal," the average score of Jews, Hungarians, Italians, and Poles was about 87. Some psychologists like Henry Goddard concluded that these groups were intellectually inferior—indeed, even "feeble-minded." Decisions were made to allow more Northern Europeans entry into the United States than Southern Europeans, based on early IQ testing.

more than the visual-linguistic and logical-mathematical learners (Gardner, 1999, 2000a).

Gardner not only carves up intelligence into these separate types but also contends that the separate intelligences are located in different areas of the brain (Gardner, 1999). When a person suffers brain damage through a stroke or tumor, all abilities do not break down equally. And youngsters who are *precocious* in one area are often unremarkable in others. In fact, people with retardation whose mental ability is lower in most areas will occasionally exhibit extraordinary ability in a specific area, most commonly mathematical calculation (Treffert, 2001). These observations led Gardner to say that the much-maligned intelligence quotient (IQ) ought to be replaced with an "intellectual profile." Gardner's proposed theory has been embraced by teachers who work daily with children and readily see their different capabilities (Gardner, 1999). But critics such as Sandra Scarr (1985a) dispute Gardner, saying that he is really talking about talents or aptitudes, not intelligences. His critics have difficulty calling "intelligence" what people typically label human abilities or virtues.

Spatial Skills, Music, and Intelligence Gardner defines spatial skills as skills pertaining to the ability to form mental images, visualize graphic representations, and recognize interrelationships among objects (Gardner, 1983, 1997). Spatial skills are used to move objects around (including oneself) in any environment (as in playing sports, strategizing in a game of chess, or becoming skilled at a computer video game) and to solve mathematical and engineering problems later in life.

Along similar lines, psychologist Fran Rauscher (1996) and neuroscientist Dee Joy Coulter (1995) have argued that singing, rhythmical movement, musical games, listening, and early musical instrument training are neurological exercises that introduce children to speech patterns, sensory motor skills, and vital rhythm and movement strategies. All of these nonverbal activities are independent of language, they suggest, and promote brain development in the same neural pathways used for spatial skills (Baney, 1998). Rauscher (1996) conducted a study in 1993 in which ten 3-year-old children took either singing or piano lessons. When tested later, the children's scores improved 46 percent on the Object Assembly Task of the *Wechsler Preschool and Primary Scale of Intelligence–Revised*. In a later study that took place over eight months with three groups of preschool children, the preschoolers taking piano lessons scored a significant 34 percent higher than the other groups not taking piano lessons. Heyge (1996) further states that music is essential to children's lives because it optimizes brain development, enhances multiple intelligences, facilitates genuine bonding between adult and child, builds social/emotional skills, promotes attention to task and inner speech, develops impulse control and motor development, and communicates creativity and joy.

Cultural Bias in Intelligence Testing A "noncultural" or "culture-free" intelligence test is an impossibility. Membership in a particular culture influences what an individual is likely to learn or fail to learn. It would be invalid, for instance, to give these Spanish-speaking youngsters in Mexico the Stanford-Binet intelligence test, designed by and for English-speaking Americans.

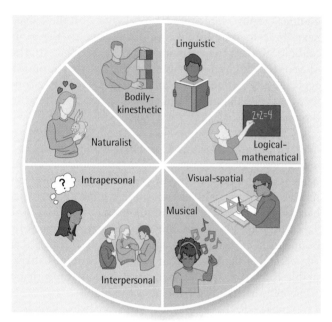

FIGURE 7.7 Multiple Intelligences Howard Gardner proposes that there is not just one factor called intelligence but there are multiple intelligences (MIs). That is, humans have at least nine distinctive intelligences that interact. Thus, children have different learning strengths and weaknesses. Gardner suggests educators vary instructional and evaluation methods to accommodate a variety of learners (Gardner, 1999, 2000a).

In sum, these psychologists and neuroscientists recommend both incorporating music into children's lives as early as possible to build neural connections and revitalizing music programs in the public schools.

Intelligence as Process   Quite different from an "abilities" approach to intelligence are those perspectives that view intelligence as a *process*—they are not so much interested in *what* we know as in *how* we know. Proponents of this approach are less concerned with the "stuff" that allows people to think intelligently and more concerned with the operations involved in thinking. For instance, as we discussed in Chapter 2, Jean Piaget concerned himself with the stages of development during which given modes of thought appear. He focused on the continual and dynamic interplay between children and their environment through which children come to know the world and to modify their understanding of it. Piaget did not view intelligence in set or fixed terms, so he had little interest in the static assessment of individual differences in ability (Piaget, 1952).

Intelligence as Information Processing   More recently, a number of cognitive psychologists have proposed an *information-processing* view of intelligence—a detailed, step-by-step analysis of how we manipulate information (Hunt, 1983; Sternberg, 1984, 1990, 1998). These psychologists are trying to unlock the doors to the mind

by getting "inside" intelligence, seeking to understand the mental processes whereby people solve problems not only on tests but in everyday life. By way of illustration, try this question: If you have black socks and brown socks in your drawer, mixed in a four-to-five ratio, how many socks must you take out to ensure getting a pair of the same color? To find the answer, you must grasp what is important and ignore irrelevant details, a task that requires insight. The color ratio of socks is unimportant. (The answer is three: If the first is black and the second is brown, the third must be one or the other.)

In studying children in grades 4 through 6, Robert J. Sternberg (1986b) and his colleagues compared how children they had identified as gifted and those not so identified approached this problem. Three findings emerged: (1) The gifted children were better able to solve the socks problem because they ignored the irrelevant information regarding ratios; (2) supplying nongifted children with the insights needed to solve this sort of problem increased their performance, whereas it had no effect on the gifted children because they already possessed the insights; and (3) insight skills can be developed by training.

In a five-week training program, both gifted and nongifted youngsters achieved significant improvement in their scores, relative to the scores of an untrained control group. Moreover, these skills were evident in a follow-up study a year later. In short, even though insight skills differentiate between the more and less intelligent, they are trainable in both groups. Sternberg says that this sort of understanding can be achieved only by studying the cognitive processes underlying intelligence—it is not supplied by global intelligence test scores.

> **Questions**
>
> How have various theorists defined the concept of "intelligence" over time? What theory do you think applies to the differences in individual abilities and capacities, such as being classified as "gifted"?

Intelligence and the Nature-Nurture Controversy

Psychologists differ in the relative importance they attribute to heredity and environment, regarding intelligence. As we discussed in Chapter 2, some investigators of the nature-nurture issue have asked the "which" question, others the "how much" question, and still others the "how" question. And because they ask different questions, they come up with different answers.

The Hereditarian Position   Hereditarians tend to phrase the nature-nurture question primarily in terms of the "how much" question and seek answers in family resemblance studies (see Chapter 2) based on intelligence tests (Jensen, 1984). Psychologists have devised tests of intelligence, employing a single number called the **intelligence quotient,** or **IQ,** to measure intelligence. An IQ, let's say 120, is derived from the ratio of tested mental age to chronological age, usually expressed as a quotient multiplied by 100. Today's intelligence tests provide an IQ score based on the test-taker's performance relative to the average performance of other individuals of the same age.

Many psychologists say that the assessment of intellectual abilities is one of their discipline's most significant contributions to society. But other psychologists say that it is a systematic attempt by elitists to "measure" people so that "desirable" ones can be put in the "proper" slots and the others rejected. Research reveals that the median IQ correlation coefficient of separated identical *(monozygotic)* twins in three studies is + .72. The median IQ correlation coefficient of fraternal *(dizygotic)* twins is + .62. In sum, identical twins reared in different homes are much more alike in IQ than the fraternal twins raised together (Jensen, 1972). As the biological kinship between two people increases (gets closer), the correlation between their IQ scores increases. Thus, identical twins, reared together, have the highest correlation of IQ (+ .86) in comparison to other pairs, such as siblings reared together (+ .47), or parent and child of the same sex (+ .40) (Bouchard, & McGue, 1981). On the basis of this and other evidence, hereditarians typically conclude that 60 to 80 percent of the variation in IQ scores in the general population is attributable to genetic differences and the remainder to environmental differences (Herrnstein & Murray, 1994).

The Environmentalist Rebuttal   A number of scientists dispute the claim by Jensen and like-minded psychologists that differences in intelligence are primarily a function of heredity. Some disagree with the formulation of the nature-nurture question in terms of "how much" and insist that the question should be *how* heredity and environment interact to produce intelligence. And others such as Leon J. Kamin (1974, p. 1) go so far as to assert: "There exist no data which should lead a prudent man to accept the hypothesis that IQ test scores are in any degree heritable." Psychologists in agreement with Kamin's view, commonly called *environmentalists,* argue that mental abilities are *learned.* They believe that intellect is increased or decreased according to the degree of enrichment or impoverishment provided by a person's social and cultural environment (Blagg, 1991).

Kamin (1974, 1981, 1994) has vigorously challenged the adoption and identical-twin research that the advocates of heredity use to support their conclusions. He insists that it is improper to speak of individuals as being reared in differing environments simply because they were brought up in different homes. In some cases

identical twins were raised by relatives, or they lived next door to one another, or they went to the same school. Similarly, environmentalists charge that studies of adopted children are biased by the fact that adoption agencies attempt to place children in a social environment that is religiously, ethnically, and racially similar to the one into which they were born.

Contemporary Scientific Consensus   Most social and behavioral scientists believe that any extreme view in the nature-nurture controversy is presently unjustified. Estimates based on twin and adoption studies suggest that hereditary differences account for 40 to 80 percent of the variation found in the intelligence test performance of a population. Bouchard and colleagues (1990) found that 70 percent of the IQ differences among people is attributable to genetic factors, but other experts think that a 70 percent heritability estimate is too high.

Jencks (1972), employing path analysis, which is a statistical technique used to partition the amount of variance within a group, estimated that 45 percent of IQ differences is due to heredity, 35 percent due to environment, and 20 percent due to gene-environment interaction. Jencks introduced the third element of gene-environment interaction because he felt that dividing IQ into only hereditary and environmental components oversimplifies the matter. Similarly, Loehlin and colleagues (1975) contend that we need to consider these three components:

- *Genetic endowment* when intellectual stimulation is held constant
- *Environmental stimulation* when genetic potential is held constant
- *Covariance of heredity and environment*—how these two components vary relative to each other

If genes and environment reinforce each other, then the added component of variance cannot logically be assigned to either nature or nurture. Rather, it is a result of the association of their separate effects.

> ### Questions
>
> What is intelligence? How have the explanations of intelligence changed over time? Why is intelligence difficult to measure? What are the differences between the hereditarian view of intelligence and the environmental view?

Piaget's Theory of Preoperational Thought

Jean Piaget (1896–1980), the Swiss developmental psychologist who pioneered the study of the development of intelligence in infants and children, called the years between 2 and 7 the **preoperational period** (1952, 1963). The principal achievement of that period is children's developing capacity to represent the external world *internally* through the use of symbols. *Symbols* are things that stand for something else. For example: Letters of the alphabet can be symbols, for in English c-a-t represents a four-legged animal. And numbers, such as 3, are symbols for specific quantities of something. Here are some other familiar symbols—do you know what they represent? © σ $:-).

The ability to use symbols frees children from the rigid boundaries of the here and now. Using symbols, they can represent not only present events but past and future ones. The acquisition of language and numeration facilitates children's ability to employ and manipulate symbols.

Difficulties in Solving Conservation Problems   Piaget observed that although children make major strides in cognitive development during the preoperational period, their reasoning and thinking processes have a number of limitations. These limitations can be seen in the difficulties preschool children have when they try to solve conservation problems. **Conservation** refers to the concept that the quantity or amount of something stays the same regardless of changes in its shape or position.

For example, if a ball of clay is shown to a child and then rolled into a long, thin, snakelike shape, the child will say that the amount of clay has changed simply because the shape has changed. Similarly, if we show a child under age 6 two parallel rows of eight evenly spaced pennies and ask which row has more pennies, the child always correctly answers that both rows have the same amount. But if, in full view of the child, we move the pennies in one of the rows farther apart and again ask which row has more pennies, the child will reply that the longer row has more (see Figure 7.8). The child fails to recognize that the number of pennies does not change simply because we made a change in another dimension, the length of the row. Piaget said that the difficulties preschoolers have in solving conservation problems derive from the characteristics of preoperational thought. These characteristics inhibit logical thought by posing obstacles that are associated with centering, transformations, reversibility, and egocentrism.

Centration   Preoperational children concentrate on one feature of a situation and neglect other aspects, a process called **centration.** A preoperational child cannot understand that when the water that fills a tall, thin glass is poured into a short, wide glass, the amount of water remains unchanged. Instead, the child sees that the new glass is half empty and concludes that there is less water than before; the child cannot attend simultaneously to both the amount of water and the shape of the container. To solve the conservation problem correctly, the child must "decenter"—that is, attend simultaneously to both height and width. Likewise, in the case of the pennies, children need to recognize that a change in length is compensated for by a change in the other dimension, density. Thus, there is no change in quantity. Here, too, the ability to decenter—to explore more than one aspect of the stimulus—is said by Piaget to be beyond preoperational children.

States and Transformations   Another characteristic of preoperational thinking is that children pay attention

(a)

(b)

FIGURE 7.8 Conservation Experiment with Pennies Children are first shown two rows of pennies arranged as in *A*. The experimenter asks if both rows contain the same amount of pennies. Then with the children watching, the experimenter spreads out the pennies in the bottom row, as in *B*. Children are once again asked if both rows contain the same number of pennies. Preoperational children will respond that they do not.

to *states* rather than *transformations.* In observing water being poured from one glass into another, preschool children focus on the original state and the final state. The intervening process (the pouring) is lost to them. They do not pay attention to the gradual shift in the height or width of the water in the glasses as the experimenter pours the liquid.

Preoperational thought fixes on static states. It fails to link successive states into a coherent sequence of events. Here's a more common example: If you offer a preoperational child a cookie, and the child complains that it is too small, simply break the cookie into three pieces and place it next to a whole cookie. The odds are the young child will think there is more in the cookie split into three pieces!

Their inability to follow transformations interferes with preschool children's logical thinking. Only by appreciating the continuous and sequential nature of various operations can we be certain that the quantities remain the same. Because preoperational children fail to see the relationship between events, their comparisons between original and final events are incomplete. Thus, according to Piaget, they cannot solve conservation problems.

Nonreversibility   According to Piaget, the most distinguishing characteristic of preoperational thought is the child's failure to recognize the **reversibility of operations**—that a series of operations can be gone through in reverse order to get back to the starting point. After we pour water from a narrow container into a wider container, we can demonstrate that the amount of water remains the same by pouring it back into the narrow container. But preoperational children do not understand that the operation can be reversed. Once they have carried out an entire operation, they cannot mentally regain the original state. Awareness of reversibility is a requirement of logical thought.

Egocentrism   Still another element that interferes with the preschool child's logical understanding of reality is **egocentrism**—lack of awareness that there are viewpoints other than one's own. According to Piaget, preoperational children are so absorbed in their own impressions that they fail to recognize their thoughts and feelings might be different from those of other people. Children simply assume that everyone thinks the same thoughts they do and sees the world from the same perspective that they do.

Both Piaget (1963) and sociologist George Herbert Mead (1934; Aboulafia, 1991) pointed out that children must overcome an egocentric perspective if they are to participate in mature social interaction. For children to play their role properly, they must know something about other roles. Most 3-year-olds can make a doll carry out several role-related activities, revealing that the child has knowledge of a social role—for example, the child can pretend to be a doctor and examine a doll. Four-year-olds can typically act out a role, relating one social role to a reciprocal role—for instance, they can pretend that a patient doll is sick and that a doctor doll examines it, in the course of which both dolls make appropriate responses. During the late preschool years, children become capable of combining roles in more complicated ways—for example, being a doctor and a mother at the same time; most 6-year-olds can pretend to carry out several roles simultaneously.

Critiques of Piaget's Egocentric Child   More recent research by "neo-Piagetians" suggests, however, that although egocentricity is characteristic of preoperational thinking, preschool children are nonetheless capable of recognizing other people's viewpoints on their own terms. Even though, emotionally, toddlers can be quite self-centered, they are not necessarily egocentric in the sense of not understanding other perspectives (Newcombe & Huttenlocher, 1992). Increasingly researchers are uncovering many *sociocentric* (people-oriented) responses in young children. Indeed, some researchers have questioned the characterization of children as egocentric. Consider the following evidence.

Altruism and Prosocial Behavior   Researchers have found evidence of altruistic and prosocial behavior even in very young children. Not uncommon are the following examples: A 2-year-old boy accidentally hits a small girl on the head. He looks aghast. "I hurt your hair. Please don't cry." Another child, a girl of 18 months, sees her grandmother lying down to rest. She goes over to her own crib, takes her own blanket, and covers her grandmother with it (Pines, 1979).

If egocentricity is seen as the inability to psychologically "connect" with someone else, then these examples point to the child's ability to reach out and relate to another individual. If, on the other hand, egocentricity is seen as a "distortive interpretation of other people's experiences, and actions or persons or objects, in terms of one's own schemas" (Beard, 1969), then even these prosocial acts could be labeled "egocentric."

The Montessori Mind   One of the better-known early childhood programs with a set of altruistic priorities different from a traditional preschool is the Montessori "Children's Community" founded in 1907 by Dr. Maria Montessori. Her first school was made up of 60 inner-city children, most of whom came from dysfunctional families. She developed a child-centered philosophy of "education for life" directed toward the development of each child's interests, abilities, and human potential. But her vision expanded beyond an academic curriculum to promote *prosocial behavior* in young children.

Montessori schools today give children the sense of belonging to a family and help them learn how to live with other human beings. By creating bonds among parents, teachers, and children, Montessori sought to create a community where children could learn to be a part of families, where they could learn to care for younger children, learn from each other and older people, trust one another, and find ways to be properly assertive rather than aggressive. Dr. Montessori envisioned her movement as essentially leading to a reconstruction of society. Montessori schools today are found all over the world, including Europe, Central and South America, Australia, New Zealand, India, Sri Lanka, Korea, and Japan (Seldin, 1996).

In sum, newly developing lines of research reveal that, in our efforts to understand children, we have been hampered by adult-centered concepts and by our preoccupation with the adult-child relationship—in other words, by *adult* egocentrism. Moreover, in recent years psychologists have moved increasingly away from Piaget's notion of broad, overarching stages to a more complex view of development (Case, 1991). Rather than searching for major overall transformations, they are scrutinizing separate domains such as causality, memory, creativity, problem solving, and social interaction. Each domain has a somewhat unique and flexible schedule affected not only by age but also by the quality of the environment (Demetriou, Efklides, & Platsidou, 1993; Flavell, 1992). Chapter 9 will consider prosocial behavior at greater length.

Questions

In what ways is Piaget's stage of preoperational thought different from the sensorimotor stage during infancy and the toddler years? What are some criticisms of Piaget's cognitive theory by neo-Piagetians?

The Child's Theory of Mind

Research in the **theory of mind** probes children's developing conceptions of major components of mental activity. When a child begins to comprehend that the mind exists, this paves the way to rudimentary distinctions such as that of being part of the environment while also being separate from it. Furthermore, the child can begin to understand that people can think about objects differently.

For example, a researcher might show a 5-year-old a candy box and ask the youngster what is in it. "Candy," responds the child. But when the youngster opens the box, she is surprised to discover that it contains crayons rather than candy. The researcher then might inquire of the child, "What will the next child who has not opened the box think is in it?" "Candy!" the child answers, grinning at the trick. But when the researcher repeats the same procedure with a 3-year-old, the child typically responds to the first question as expected, "Candy!" but responds to the second, "Crayons!" Significantly, the 3-year-old also says "Crayons" when asked to recall what she herself had initially thought would be found in the box.

Sociocentric Behavior
Developmental psychologists are discovering that young children are considerably less egocentric and more sociocentric than earlier studies indicated. For example, one of the main priorities of a Montessori education is to promote prosocial behaviors.

The 3-year-old, unlike the 5-year-old, fails to understand that people can hold beliefs different from what they know and that are false. The 3-year-old believes that because she knows there is no candy in the box, everyone else automatically knows the same thing to be true (Wellman, 1990). In comparison with older youngsters, the thought of 3-year-olds is still confused. It seems that 3-year-olds struggle with, and typically fail to understand, what 4-year-olds and older children do understand: that people have internal mental states, such as beliefs, that represent or misrepresent the world, and people's actions stem from their mental representation of the world rather than from direct objective reality.

Piaget's sweeping account of children's reasoning was an early attempt to broach the topic of "mind"—the notion of an instrument that can calculate, dream, fantasize, deceive, and evaluate others' thoughts. More recently, research has been done on children's developing understanding of their mental world (Feldman, 1992).

This work has demonstrated that even 3-year-olds can distinguish between the physical and the mental and that they possess some understanding of what it means to imagine, think of, and dream of something (Flavell, 1992). For example, if a 3-year-old is told that one child has ice cream and another child is only thinking of ice cream, then the 3-year-old will be able to say which child's ice cream can be seen by others, as well as touched or eaten. This understanding is facilitated where youngsters enjoy a rich "database" derived from interactions with siblings, caregivers, and peers (Perner, Ruffman, & Leekam, 1994).

Implicit Understanding and Knowledge   Piaget's procedures have also tended to underestimate many of the cognitive capabilities of preschool children. Indeed, recent research has raised an important new issue concerning children's conceptual foundations for learning. Toddlers seem to possess a significant implicit understanding or knowledge of certain principles (Reber, 1993; Seger, 1994). Here we will consider two spheres of conceptual knowledge for illustrative purposes: causality and number concepts.

Causality   Piaget concluded children younger than 7 or 8 fail to grasp cause-and-effect relationships. When he would ask younger children why the sun and the moon move, they would respond that heavenly bodies "follow us about because they are curious" or "in order to look at us." These types of explanations for events led Piaget to emphasize the limitations associated with young children's intellectual operations.

But contemporary developmental psychologists who investigate the thinking of young children find that they already understand a good deal about causality. **Causality** involves our attribution of a cause-and-effect relationship to two paired events that recur in succession. Causality is based on the expectation that when one event occurs, another event, one that ordinarily follows the first, will again follow it. Apparently the rudiments for the causal processing of information are already evident among 3-month-old infants ("If I cry, Mom will come"). And by the time youngsters are 3 to 4 years old, they seem to possess rather sophisticated abilities for discerning cause-and-effect relationships (Gelman & Kremer, 1991).

The versatility of young children grasping causality has led some psychologists to conclude that humans are biologically prewired to understand the existence of cause-and-effect relationships (Pines, 1983). Children appear to operate on an implicit theory of causality. Clearly, the ability to appreciate that a cause must always precede an effect would have enormous survival value in the course of evolution.

Number Concepts   Piaget also deemphasized children's counting capabilities, calling counting "merely verbal knowledge" and asserting that "there is no connection between the acquired ability to count and the actual operations of which the child is capable" (Piaget, 1965, p. 61). Yet young children seem to have an implicit understanding of some number concepts. Preschool youngsters can successfully perform tasks requiring modified versions of counting procedures and can judge whether a puppet's performance in counting demonstrating the concepts of *more* and *less* is correct (Gelman & Meck, 1986). Counting is the first formal computational system children acquire. It allows youngsters to make accurate quantitative assessments of amount, rather than having to rely solely on their perceptual or qualitative judgments. The next time you are near a 2- to 3-year-old, ask, "How old are you?" Invariably the child will hold up fingers and say the number.

> **Questions**
>
> How do we know that a young child is developing preoperational thought processes, according to Piaget? What are some of the other prominent theories about how young children's thought processes develop?

Language Acquisition

Young children oftentimes show a lag between comprehending (which involves *receptive language*) and producing language (which involves *expressive language*). Children younger than 1 year old demonstrate time and again that they understand what we say. Say "Where's Mommy?" and the child looks for Mommy. However, it takes several more months before most children can begin to express their own needs in more than one- or two-word expressions. A 3-year-old might utter the following sentence after knocking on the door, "Is everybody not home?" meaning to inquire, "Is anybody home?" It is important to remember that while children are acquiring language, they understand and use it in ways that represent how and what they know about the world at that particular point in their development.

At this stage of language development, children move beyond two-word sentences such as "Doggy go" and begin to display a real understanding of the rules that govern language as well as master the different sounds within the language, which is known as **phonology.** Past tenses are used (first using "goed" and then "went" as past tense for *go*) as well as plurals ("girls" and "boys") and possessives ("Jim's" and "mine," although at first many children say "mines"), which are all examples of how a word can change form, or what is known as **morphology.**

Around the age of 3, children will begin to properly ask the *wh-* questions (Why? What? Which? When? Who?), which shows an understanding of **syntax,** the ways words must be ordered in a sentence. Using the rules for combining words together meaningfully is called **semantics.** Young children enjoy hearing nonsensical words, such as in Lewis Carroll's poem "Jabberwocky." And between the ages of 3 and 5, children learn what types of language they can use in different social contexts, or the **pragmatics** of language.

Developmental Phonological Disorders   These are language disorders that involve difficulty in learning to use easily understood speech by age 4, and this tends to run in families. The child may be experiencing difficulty storing the sound(s), saying the sound(s), or using the rules of language (Bowen, 1998). Many methods are available to evaluate and treat the many varieties of phonological disorders for most children. (See the *Implications for Practice* box on page 252, "Speech-Language Pathologist.")

Stuttering   Most young children go through periods of *disfluency* as they are learning to speak. However, frequent disruption in the fluency of speech is called *stuttering* or *stammering,* and researchers find that this tends to run in families (Bowen, 2001). Disfluency in the child's speech is typically classified as prolongations ("Mmmm-me too"), periods of silence called blocks ("St—op that"), and repetitions ("N-n-n-n-o") (Bowen, 2001). Geneticists have found stuttering may be inherited and that boys are more susceptible to stuttering (Bowen, 2001). The general guideline today is that parents should seek the help of a pediatrician or a speech-language pathologist if they begin to notice consistent stuttering in a young child (Fraser, 2001). A child who

stutters is eligible for early intervention services, and a variety of scientific approaches are used to help improve the child's fluency.

Language Development in Adopted Chinese Children   As of 2003, more than 44,000 Chinese young children, mainly girls, were adopted into American families, and China has become the largest source of transracial adoption in the United States. Tan and Yang (2005) recently completed an original study investigating the expressive language development of young Chinese girls adopted into American families and having lived with adopted families from 3 to 27 months. All children were exposed to a local dialect prior to adoption into an English-speaking home, yet the adoptees not only caught up after living with adoptive families for an average of 17 months—but surprisingly the adoptees surpassed the normative sample for expressive language. It took about 16 months for the adoptees to catch up with native-speaking children. The researchers speculate that the adoptive families' socioeconomic background and adoptive mother's educational status were responsible for such remarkable expressive language achievement.

Chomsky's Linguistic Theory   Noam Chomsky (1965, 1980) proposes that a linguistic theory ought to be able to adequately explain language structure while taking into account the messy input children receive and from which they construct meaningful sentences. He says that humans are born possessing a **language acquisition device (LAD)** that takes all of the sounds, words, and sentences an infant hears and produces grammar consistent with this data (Lillo-Martin, 1997). Chomsky argues that this must be the case because it would be impossible for an infant to learn language simply by induction—that is, by simply reusing the sentences it had already heard. If that were the case, then a youngster would not be able to utter a novel sentence, but we all know that youngsters come up with some extremely novel sentences.

Late Talkers   Provided the child's hearing is okay and the child is healthy and in an environment to hear speech, there are some reasons why a young child might not use expressive language (words) until 2, 3, or even 4 years of age: The baby is a quiet baby, or was born prematurely and may be experiencing health problems, or is a twin (twins often develop their own private language), or the baby is a boy and boys often talk later, or the baby may be in a bilingual home, or there are older siblings that speak for the child. A study conducted with several hundred same-sex twin pairs with early language delay at ages 2, 3, and 4 revealed that heritability was a factor for a small percent of the children—yet environmental factors shared by both twins was associated with early language delay. Bishop and colleagues (2003) conclude there

Implications for Practice

Speech-Language Pathologist
Aleshia Larson, SLP

I am a speech-language pathologist at The Resource Center, which provides services to persons with disabilities in Chautauqua County. My clients are cognitively impaired, or have suffered a traumatic brain injury, or are children who are behind on speech/language milestones through the early intervention program. I provide language and articulation therapy for people unable to communicate verbally, build communication systems for nonverbal people, and provide swallow evaluations and guidelines for staff to follow to allow a person to eat in the safest manner possible.

I earned an associate's degree in liberal arts from Jamestown Community College in New York, a bachelor's degree in the education of the speech and hearing handicapped from SUNY Fredonia, and a master's degree in speech pathology from SUNY Fredonia. To obtain a provisional teaching license, I had to pass the Liberal Arts and Sciences Test (LAST) and the Elementary and Secondary Assessment of Teaching Skills–Written (ATS–W). To obtain licensure, I passed the *Praxis* examination for speech language pathology.

To enjoy working as a speech-language therapist, a person should be creative, able to think quickly, and be organized but flexible to change as clients will sometimes change the direction of therapy. The populations I work with need hundreds of repetitions to learn something new. *Patience* is an extremely important characteristic. I had supervised clinical experience working at a school, a nursing home, a speech-language clinic, and then at my current position before being hired.

My advice to students considering being an SLP is to keep an open mind about what type of population they want to work with until they have completed all clinical experience. I did not work with the developmentally disabled until my last semester in graduate school, and now I cannot imagine doing anything else. Working with this population is the most rewarding, fun, and fulfilling of all the populations that I have worked with. I really enjoy that each day I get to do new things and really make a difference in people's lives. Through the use of alternative and augmentative communication, I have been part of setting up communication systems with voice output for people in their fifties and sixties who have never been verbal because of physical disabilities. It is extremely fulfilling to help people express their opinions and make choices for the first time and watch their world expand with their new experiences.

is less concern with low expressive language skills with a 2-year-old—unless there is a family history of speech or language impairment. Parents with a child with speech delay should consult their pediatrician, who may refer the child for audiology testing or speech therapy.

Learning to use speech is empowering for children because it enables them to communicate their needs, relate to others, learn about and take command of their environment, and become normal social beings rather than isolates (Sachs, 1987). Thus, an evaluation by an audiologist or speech pathologist may be warranted for children with early language delay. Some children with speech and/or language disabilities make some progress without intervention, but early intervention can dramatically increase the rate of progress (Camarata, 1996).

Vygotsky's Perspective Learning language and furthering cognitive development are not tasks that children can accomplish in the privacy of their cribs—they need to be in a social setting. Lev Vygotsky (1896–1934) first conceived of how language and thought are intertwined with culture and society, thereby proposing that cognitive growth occurs in a sociocultural context dependent on a child's social interactions (Vygotsky, 1962). This led to the well-known concept of the **zone of proximal development (ZPD):** Tasks that are a little too hard for children to accomplish alone can be mastered by children when they are helped by a more skilled partner.

Think back to when you began reading. Your parents or teacher provided encouragement, suggestions, corrections, and praise as you worked through the process of learning to read. Little by little you began to read independently, but it was only through the interaction between you and an older, more accomplished person that you were able to foster this new skill. This same principle applies to learning a sport. Someone usually shows the child how to make a proper arm motion or a specific foot movement, just as the child is on the verge of developing the necessary hand-eye coordination to throw or kick a ball.

Notice that there is a striking difference here between Vygotsky and Piaget: Piaget thought that children learn as independent explorers, whereas Vygotsky asserted that children learn through social interactions. Thus, Vygotsky put forth a sociocultural view that stresses the social aspects of cognitive development that Piaget did not emphasize. Vygotsky asserts that children's minds develop when engaging in activities with more skilled people on tasks that are within the child's ZPD. Furthermore, Vygotsky asserts that when a child and adult are engaged in activities, the child incorporates the language of the adult that pertains to the activity and then reuses that language to transform her or his own thinking.

Language and Emotion

Young children's vocabularies generally are limited, consisting mainly of words that refer to things and action words, with a smaller percentage of words that express *affective* (emotional) states (James, 1990). Research has shown that when children are operating from an emotional state, such as fear, hurt, pain, or stress, they are not able to concentrate on learning tasks. Their energy is concentrated in the processing going on in the limbic (emotional) system of their brains. After reading the next few sentences, stop and try this yourself. Recall a recent hurtful experience. Try to remember the details, picture the faces of the people involved, and feel the emotions you felt when this event occurred. Close your eyes now, and give yourself several minutes.

Now answer this question: *What are the main principles of Chomsky's linguistic theory?* You read about this just a short while ago, but do you now feel a little confused or somewhat overwhelmed, after reliving that hurtful experience? Teachers who have done the exercise you just finished have often commented, "I just can't think" (Rodriguez, 1998). Obviously, then, this happens to children, too.

Some of the healthy ways young children can communicate their feelings are through drawing and physical movement; such activities release the energy built up by the limbic system. This is one of the reasons why child-care centers and preschools usually have a variety of papers, paints, crayons, colored pencils; or small slides and climbing toys; or music time and dance time—to allow children to "express" themselves. Multisensory experiences also allow children to learn to process information from a variety of sources, which helps them develop important skills for advanced learning.

Vygotsky's Zone of Proximal Development (ZPD) Young children often learn from each other. Tasks that are a little too hard for a child to accomplish alone can often be mastered with help from a more skilled partner.

Talking and Communicating Catherine Garvey and Robert Hogan (1973) found that during the greater part of the time that children 3 to 5 years of age spend in nursery school, they interact with others, largely by talking. Furthermore, while some of their speech is **private speech** (directed toward themselves or nobody in particular), most of their speech is mutually responsive and adapted to the speech or nonverbal behavior of a partner (Spilton & Lee, 1977).

Harriet Rheingold, Dale Hay, and Meredith West (1976) have shown that children in their second year of life share with others what they see and find interesting. Preschool, Pre-K, and kindergarten teachers know how to foster this type of social behavior by periodically scheduling a "show-and-tell time" when children bring special objects from home to talk about. Rheingold and her colleagues (1976, p. 1157) concluded:

> In showing an object to another person, the children demonstrate not only that they know that other people can see what they see but also that others will look at what they point to or hold up. We can surmise that they also know that what they see may be remarkable in some way and therefore worthy of another's attention. That children so young share contradicts the egocentricity so often ascribed to them and reveals them instead as already able contributors to social life.

Table 7.5 Early Signs of Developmental Delay in Preschool Children

Language
Pronunciation problems
Slow vocabulary growth
Lack of interest in storytelling

Memory
Trouble recognizing letters or numbers
Difficulty remembering things in sequences (e.g., days of the week)

Attention
Difficulty sitting still or sticking to a task

Motor skills
Problems with self-care skills (fastening buttons, combing hair)
Clumsiness
Reluctance to draw

Other functions
Trouble learning left from right
Difficulty categorizing things
Difficulty "reading" body language and facial expressions

From: Lisa Feder-Feitel, "Does She Have a Learning Problem?" *Child*, February 1997. Copyright © 1997 by Lisa Feder-Feitel. Originally published by Gruner & Jahr USA Publishing in the February 1997 issue of *Child* Magazine. Used with permission.

Disabilities in Cognitive Development Some children are going to experience moderate to severe difficulties and or delays in cognitive development and language skills during early childhood. Children with central nervous system or genetic disorders (such as mental retardation, cerebral palsy, autism), sensory damage (such as blindness or deafness), motor-skill delays (such as muscular dystrophy, paralysis, missing limbs), social neglect (such as abuse, neglect, institutionalization, homelessness, isolation), or serious illness and injuries will progress at a pace slower than is normally expected for their age.

Those who receive early intervention services are likely to make more progress than at-risk children not enrolled in such programs. Additionally, as we mentioned in Chapter 6, children who have experienced social neglect because of moving from foster home to foster home or from community to community (as do many migrant workers' children) or due to deliberate isolation from society are also going to be cognitively delayed and will need extensive stimulation and interaction to develop their potential. Table 7.5 lists some early warning signs of developmental delays.

Questions

How do we know that children from ages 2 to 6 are acquiring language skills in the normal sequence of language development? What language disorders should caretakers be concerned about, and what services are available to help children diagnosed with specific language impairments? Explain Chomsky's and Vygotsky's theories of language development.

Information Processing and Memory

Memory is a critical cognitive ability. Indeed, all learning implies memory. In its broadest sense, **memory** refers to the retention of what has been experienced. Without memory we would react to every event as if we had never before experienced it. Furthermore, we would be incapable of thinking and reasoning—of any sort of intelligent behavior—if we could not use remembered facts. Hence, memory is critical to information processing.

Early Memory

During infancy and childhood, we learn a prodigious amount about the world, yet by adulthood our memories of early experiences have faded (Rovee-Collier, 1987). This phenomenon is called *childhood amnesia*. As adults, generally we remember only fleeting scenes and isolated moments prior to the time we reached 7 or 8 years of age.

Although some individuals have no recollections prior to 8 or 9 years of age, many of us can recall some things that took place between our third and fourth birthdays. Most commonly, first memories involve visual imagery, and most of the imagery is in color. In many cases we visualize ourselves in these memories from afar, as we would look at an actor on a stage (Nelson, 1982).

Just why early memories should wane remains an enigma (Newcombe & Fox, 1994). Freud theorized that we repress or alter childhood memories because of their disturbing sexual and aggressive content. Piagetians and cognitive developmentalists claim that adults have trouble recalling early childhood events because they no longer think as children do—that is, adults typically employ mental habits as aids to memory that young children cannot employ.

Still others say that the brain and nervous system are not entirely formed in the young and do not allow for the development of adequate memory stores and effective retrieval strategies. Then there are those who contend that much learning during the first two years of life occurs in emotion-centered areas of the brain and that this learning is subject to limited recall in later years. Most types of earliest memories we are likely to recall are associated with the emotion of fear. What early experiences do you remember? Do you feel associated emotions?

Finally, Mark Howe and Mary Courage (1993) argue that the problem derives not from memory per se but from the absence of a personal frame of reference for making one's memories uniquely autobiographical (put in other terms, there is no developed "self" present as a cognitive entity). Nonetheless, often our childhood memories remain relatively elusive.

Information Processing

Memory includes recall, recognition, and the facilitation of relearning. In **recall** we remember what we learned earlier, such as the definition of a scientific concept or the lines of a play. (An essay question demands that you recall information.) In **recognition** we experience a feeling of familiarity when we again perceive something that we have previously encountered. (A matching type of quiz requires recognition.) In the *facilitation of relearning,* we find that we can learn material that is already familiar to us more readily than we can learn totally unfamiliar material.

On the whole, children's recognition memory is superior to their recall memory. In recognition the information is already available, and children can simply check their perceptions of an occurrence against their memory. Recall, in contrast, requires them to retrieve all the information from their own memory. When 4-year-olds are asked how many items from a list they think they will remember, they predict they will recall seven items—but they do recall fewer than four (Flavell, Freidrichs, & Hoyt, 1970).

Memory permits us to store information for different periods of time. Some psychologists distinguish sensory information storage, short-term memory, and long-term memory (see Figure 7.9). In **sensory information**

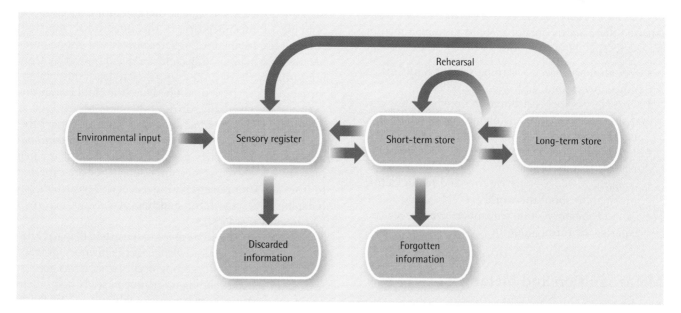

FIGURE 7.9 Simplified Flow Chart of the Three-Store Model of Memory Information flow is represented by three memory stores: the sensory register, the short-term store, and the long-term store. Inputs from the environment enter the sensory register, where they are selectively passed on to short-term storage. Information in the short-term store may be forgotten or copied by the long-term store. In some cases individuals mentally rehearse information to keep it in active awareness in short-term storage. Complicated feedback operations take place among the three storage components.

storage, information from the senses is preserved in the sensory register just long enough to permit the stimuli to be scanned for processing (generally less than 2 seconds). This provides a relatively complete, literal copy of the physical stimulation. For instance, if you tap your finger against your cheek, you note an immediate sensation, which quickly fades away.

Short-Term Memory   Short-term memory is the retention of information for a very brief period, usually not more than 30 seconds. For example, you might look up an e-mail address and remember it just long enough to type it in the address box, whereupon you promptly forget it. Another common short-term memory experience is your introduction to a stranger. How easily do you recall the person's name 10 minutes later? Typically, information is fleeting unless there is some reason or motivation to remember it longer—for example, our nursing students are motivated to do well in their course on human development because they know they must eventually pass a state certification exam for registered nurses that includes questions on human development.

Long-Term Memory   Long-term memory is the retention of information over an extended period of time. A memory might be retained because it arose from a very intense single experience or because it is repeatedly rehearsed. Through yearly repetition and constant media reminders, you come to remember that Memorial Day is in late May, Labor Day is in early September. Researchers have studied memory from many perspectives (Tulving & Craik, 2000). Schacter and Tulving (1994) postulate that there are five major systems of human memory we use to operate in daily life:

- *Procedural memory*—learning various kinds of motor, behavioral, and cognitive skills
- *Working memory*—elaboration on what is known as short-term memory, allowing one to retain information over short periods of time
- *Perceptual representation (PRS)*—used in identifying words and objects
- *Semantic memory*—one acquires and retain factual information about the world
- *Episodic memory*—one remembers events seen or experienced throughout life

Metacognition and Metamemory

As children mature cognitively, they become active agents in their remembering process. The development of memory occurs in two ways: through alteration in the biological structuring of the brain (its "hardware") and through changes in types of information processing (the "software" of acquisition and retrieving). Researchers have observed striking changes as a function of age, both in children's performance on memory tasks and in their use of memory strategies. As they grow older, children acquire complex skills that enable them to control just what they will learn and retain. In short, they come to "know how to know," so that they can engage in *deliberate* remembering (Moore, Bryant, & Furrow, 1989). Individuals' awareness and understanding of their own mental processes is termed **metacognition,** and young children attempt to learn in ways that suit themselves. Listen carefully, and you will hear a young child say, "I can't do that" or the opposite, "Let me do that." These are signs of awareness of their own mental abilities. Overall, memory ability catapults upward from birth through age 5, and then it advances less rapidly through middle childhood and adolescence (Chance & Fischman, 1987).

Humans require more than the factual and strategic information that constitutes a knowledge base. They must also have access to this knowledge base and apply strategies appropriate to task demands (*How am I going to remember to spell this word? to walk home from kindergarten? to throw this ball to home base?*) This flexibility in calibrating solutions to specific problems is the hallmark of intelligence. Flexibility reaches its zenith in the conscious control that adults bring to bear over a broad range of their mental functioning. This conscious control of strategies and awareness or reflection on these strategies continues to expand throughout adolescence and adulthood in both cognitive and socio-moral domains (Schrader, 1988).

Children's awareness and understanding of their memory processes is called **metamemory.** A common example of metamemory is the intentional approach children use to memorize their address and phone number. Because many young children spend time away from home during the day, they are asked to learn this vital information as early as possible. Does the child repeat this over and over verbally, or does the child ask to look at the phone number and address on a sheet of paper? Research reveals that even 3-year-olds engage in *intentional* memory behavior. They appear to understand that when they are told to remember something, they are expected to store and later retrieve it. Indeed, even 2-year-olds can hide, misplace, search for, and find objects on their own (Wellman, 1977, 1990).

By the time children enter kindergarten, they have developed considerable knowledge of the memory process. They are aware that forgetting occurs (that items get lost in memory), that spending more time in study helps them retain information, that it is more difficult to remember many items than a few, that distraction and interference make tasks harder, and that they can employ records, cues, and other people to help them recall things (Fabricius & Wellman, 1983). They also understand such words as *remember, forget,* and *learn* (Lyon & Flavell, 1994).

Memory Strategies

Children (and adults) might employ a variety of strategies to help themselves remember and recall information they are learning or desire to remember. Think about this for a few minutes, prior to reading the next section. If you had to remember the names of five people in your study group you were just introduced to this morning, how would you approach this task? Would you make a list and verbally repeat the list? Would you put names on flashcards and shuffle through the flashcards? Would you make a word out of the first letter of their names, such as taking Harriet, Angela, Paul, Peter, and Yvonne and making the word HAPPY? Then you could think, "We are a *happy* group" to remember their names. Or would you use some other approach?

Rehearsal as a Memory Strategy One strategy that facilitates memory is **rehearsal,** a process in which we repeat information to ourselves. Many individuals adept at remembering people's names cultivate the talent by mentally rehearsing a new name several times to themselves when they are introduced to a person. Researchers have demonstrated that children as young as 3 are capable of various rehearsal strategies. For instance, if 3-year-olds are instructed to remember where an object is hidden, they often prepare for future memory retrieval by extended looking at, touching, or pointing to the hiding place (Wellman, Ritter, & Flavell, 1975). Hide-and-seek activities also help young children develop various memory strategies.

As children grow, their rehearsal mechanisms become more active and effective (Halford et al., 1994). Some researchers believe that the process is facilitated through language, as children become increasingly skillful at verbally labeling stimuli. According to these investigators, the organizing and rehearsing process inherent in naming is a powerful aid to memory (Rosinski, Pellegrino, & Siegel, 1977). As children begin to process information in more sophisticated ways and learn how and when to remember, they become capable of making more decisions for themselves. Parents and teachers can cultivate children's decision-making skills.

Categorization as a Memory Strategy One strategy that facilitates remembering is to sort information into meaningful categories. Sheila Rossi and M. C. Wittrock (1971) found that a developmental progression occurs in the categories children use to organize words for recall. In this experiment children ranging from 2 to 5 years old were read a list of 12 words (*sun, hand, men, fun, leg, work, hat, apple, dogs, fat, peach, bark*). Each child was asked to recall as many words as possible.

The responses were scored in pairs in terms of the order in which a child recalled them: rhyming (*sun-fun,*

hat-fat); syntactical (*men-work, dogs-bark*); clustering (*apple-peach, hand-leg*); or serial ordering (recalling two words serially from the list). Rossi and Wittrock found that rhyming responses peak at 2 years of age, followed by syntactical responses at 3, clustering responses at 4, and serial-ordering responses at 5.

In many respects the progression is consistent with Piaget's theory, which depicts development as proceeding from *concrete* (seeing and touching something) to *abstract* functioning. Other research also confirms that changes occur in children's spontaneous use of categories during the developmental span from age 2 to adolescence (Farrar, Raney & Boyer, 1992). Though children as young as 2 benefit from the presence of categories in recall tasks, older children benefit even more.

For one thing, recall *increases* with age (Farrar & Goodman, 1992). For another, children ages 4 to 6, in comparison with older children, show less categorical grouping of items in recall tasks, fewer subordinate categories in tasks requesting that similar items be grouped together, and lower consistency in the assignment of items to selected categories (Best, 1993). Adolescents adopt even more sophisticated strategies, grouping items into logical categories, such as people, places, and things, or animals, plants, and minerals (Chance & Fischman, 1987).

Questions

What do cognitive scientists tell us about early memory, short-term memory, long-term memory, and children's understanding of their own thought and memory processes? What types of strategies can young children employ to remember, recognize, or recall information or events, and what strategies do you use to remember information?

Moral Development

Social feelings first appear during the preoperational stage. For the first time, feelings can be represented, recalled, and named. The ability to recall feelings makes moral feelings possible. If a child remembers what someone did in the past, and the emotional response linked to the action, the beginnings of moral decision making are in place.

Piaget's Theory

According to Piaget, during the sensorimotor stage, children cannot reconstruct past events and experiences because they lack representation. Once the child has the capacity to reconstruct both the cognitive and affective past, the child can begin to exhibit consistent emotional behavior.

Evolution of Moral Reasoning   When Piaget first studied moral development, he looked at the evolution of moral reasoning in children. He believed that moral feelings in young people pointed to what it was necessary to do and not just what was preferable. He also proposed that moral norms have three characteristics:

- They are generalizable to all situations.
- They last beyond the situations and conditions that engender them.
- They are linked to feelings of autonomy.

But, according to Piaget (1981/1976):

> From two to seven years, none of these conditions is met. To begin with, norms are not generalized but are valid only under particular conditions. For example, the child considers it wrong to lie to his parents and other adults but not to his comrades. Second, instructions remain linked to certain represented situations analogous to perceptual configurations. An instruction, for example, will remain linked to the person who gave it, and finally, there is no autonomy . . . . Good and bad are defined as that which conforms or fails to conform to the instructions one has received.

Reciprocity of Attitudes and Values   Piaget (1981/1976) asserts that reciprocity of attitudes and values is the foundation for social interchange in children. **Reciprocity** leads to each child's valuing the other person in a way that allows him or her to remember the values that the interactions bring forth. The following scenario is an example of how this plays out in children:

> Two young children meet at the park and play. One of the children, Neiko, gives the other child, Kiri, some candy because she obviously wants some. They end up sharing their toys and having a nice time. By labeling Neiko's behavior as "good," Kiri can recall that scene the next time they encounter each other at the park. She might give Neiko something of hers or at least be nice to her owing to the recollection of warm feelings that seeing Neiko conjures up for Kiri.

Playing by the Rules   Piaget based his views on children's moral development by observing local boys playing marbles, which he considered to be a social game with a set of rules. By interviewing these boys, Piaget found two developmental stages in young children's knowledge of rules: the *motor stage* and the *egocentric stage*. In the motor stage, children are not aware of any rules. For example, a young child in this stage might build a nest out of the marbles and pretend to be a mother bird. The game of marbles is not understood. Between the ages of 2 and 5, the egocentric stage, children become aware of the existence of rules and begin to want to play the game with other children (Can you remember the rules of the game *Candyland?*). But the child's egocentrism prevents the child from playing the game socially. The child continues to play alone without trying to compete. For example, a child will throw a marble at the pile and yell, "I won!" At this stage children believe everyone can win. Rules are seen as fixed and as coming from a higher authority.

Intentionality Versus Accident   Piaget (1981/1976) also interviewed children to find out how they viewed *intentionality* versus *accident*. The children found it very difficult to separate the act from the reason for the act. For example, children were told the following two stories:

> Once there was a little girl named Heidi who was playing in her room when her mother called her to come to dinner. Since they were having guests, Heidi decided to help her mother and got a tray and then put 15 cups on the tray so she could carry them into the dining room. As she was walking with the tray, she tripped and fell and broke all of the cups.
>
> Once there was a little girl named Gretchen who was playing in the kitchen. She wanted some jam and her mother was not there. She climbed up on a chair and tried to reach the jam but it was too high. She tried for 10 minutes and became angry. Then she saw a cup on the table so she picked it up and threw it. The cup broke.

Children younger than 7 usually see the first girl as having committed the worse act because Heidi broke more cups than Gretchen. The children judge the act based on the quantitative results of the action, with no appreciation of the intention behind the action. Morality, for preoperational children, is still based mainly on perception. Although young children have the rudiments of moral feelings, they are limited in their ability to comprehend justice as long as they do not understand the intentionality of an action.

Kohlberg's Theory

Lawrence Kohlberg's theory of moral development was influenced by John Dewey's philosophy of development and Jean Piaget's idea that people develop moral reasoning in progressive stages through their social experiences (Gibbs, 2003). Kohlberg was a developmental psychologist who researched the development of moral reasoning by studying differences in children's reasoning about moral dilemmas. According to Kohlberg, preschool children tend to be superficial in their moral judgment because they have difficulty, on a cognitive level, in keeping several pieces of information simultaneously in mind. They begin to be obedient to authority from threat or from punishment, which he categorized as Level 1, the preconventional stage. Kohlberg also held the view that children at this first level of moral reasoning are egocentric and are unable to consider the perspectives of others. He rejected the focus on values and virtues (such as compassion), for he believed such concepts to be too complex for children at this stage. In his view, the child will advance in moral reasoning as he or she goes through progressive stages of moral development within social experiences (Nucci, 1998). Although there has been some critique of Kohlberg's stage theory of moral development for not addressing differences between male and female conceptions of morality, his theory on moral development opened a new path of research in pyschology.

Questions

How are memories of emotion linked to moral reasoning, and what evidence do we have that children are maturing in moral development in early childhood? According to researchers, what healthy attitudes and values should be taught to young children?

Although Piaget and Kohlberg both propose that moral reasoning occurs in progressive stages, what are the differences in their views?

SEGUE

The physical, sensory, and cognitive maturation and skills acquired during the early childhood years have profound implications for children's ability to function fully as members of society (Stipek, Recchia, & McClintic, 1992). We do not develop in isolation. To enter into sustained social interaction with others, we must impute meaning to the people around us. All of us, children and adults alike, confront the social world in terms of categories of people—we classify them as parents, family, cousins, adults, doctors, teachers, teenagers, business people, and so on. Society does not consist merely of so many isolated individuals. It is composed of individuals who are classed as similar because they play similar roles.

And just as we impute meaning to others, we must also attribute meaning to ourselves. We have to develop a sense of ourselves as distinct, bounded, identifiable units. In Chapter 8, we will examine the young child's growing self-awareness in the domains of emotions and gender. Within the social context of family and friends, child-care settings, and kindergarten, young children acquire a set of guidelines about expressing their emotional needs.

Summary

Physical Development and Health Concerns

1. The early childhood years, from ages 2 to 6, encompass physical development, brain growth, the refinement of gross- and fine-motor skills, and sensory system maturation. Growth is unevenly distributed over the first 20 years, and from birth to age 5, the rate of growth declines sharply. The child's body typically becomes slimmer as he or she gets taller. Genes and environment cause variations from the norm. There is a compensatory property of making up for arrested growth (after a prolonged interruption).

2. Preschool children are more coordinated than in earlier years and spend most of their time exploring their environments. Healthy children are very active, developing their arm and leg muscles, which become stronger. Recreational and occupational therapists provide services that improve strength, coordination, sensory capacities, and range of motion for children with physical and motor delays and disabilities.

3. Fine-motor skills develop more slowly, and young children enjoy activities such as playing with small blocks, puzzles, beads, cards, marbles, painting, clay, and crayons—essential skills for later school success. Children with poor motor skills are at risk for poor self-concept and eligible for physical and recreational therapy.

4. Sensory development occurs rapidly at this age, and children enjoy using their senses to learn about the world. Caregivers need to observe children carefully for sensory impairments and seek professional help for diagnoses and early intervention services. Ear infections can impair hearing if left untreated.

5. The brain and CNS normally continue to develop rapidly with rich connectivity of neurons. Sensory stimulation is a key factor in promoting neural growth. By the age of 5, the child's brain will weigh about 90 percent of its final, adult weight.

6. Some young children experience cognitive delays because of congenital birth defects, sensory difficulties, autism, mental retardation, attention-deficit hyperactivity disorder (ADHD), seizures, HIV/AIDS, and other health concerns. Children eligible for early intervention services can improve functioning.

7. A small but increasing number of infants develop autism or one of the pervasive developmental disorders and are eligible for early intervention services.

8. Some professionals advocate the use of psychotropic medications for young children diagnosed with emotional, behavioral, or mood disorders. Methylphenidate (Ritalin) as well as antidepressants and antipsychotics are prescribed for some young children. Many adults are

alarmed by what they consider to be overmedication of children and the potential harm to the developing brain without any empirical studies to support such practices.

9. Caretakers of young children should try to prevent exposing them to neurotoxins, which can impair cognitive development, physical functioning, or cause serious health effects or death. Lead and mercury are two such neurotoxins.

10. Children should consume a variety of foods and beverages to get proper nourishment for brain and body growth. Children demonstrate variability in their eating behaviors, preferences, and frequency. Physical checkups determine if a child is growing adequately for gender, age, and body type. Cultural background affects eating behaviors and preferences.

11. Some children are allergic to specific foods such as nuts, eggs, milk/dairy products, soy, wheat, and fish. Allergic reactions affect various body systems. Some children are severely allergic to specific substances—which can be life threatening if consumed. Such a child should have an EpiPen available.

12. Young children growing up in a vegetarian household should eat a balanced diet with sufficient calories to promote normal physical and cognitive development.

13. Children who live in poverty or in countries with a limited food supply suffer the deleterious effects of malnutrition, causing fatigue and cognitive deficits, as well as a greater risk of illness, disease, and early death.

14. Accidents are the leading cause of death of young children, and caretakers must supervise children and provide a safe environment for playing, eating, and sleeping. Lead exposure can cause serious brain disorders.

15. Worldwide, more young children are diagnosed with HIV/AIDS. Some die before the age of 5; others are long-term survivors. Antiretroviral treatment strategies extend the lives of children. Babies and children in foster care are at higher risk of getting HIV/AIDS. An AIDS vaccine is not available yet.

16. Young children should be taught self-care behaviors that promote cleanliness, healthfulness, self-regulatory skills, and social acceptance. The timing of successful elimination training is variable. Mastering self-care skills increases self-esteem and self-confidence.

17. Ten to 12 hours of sleep and a consistent bedtime routine are recommended for energetic young children. Sleep-deprived children can be difficult, lethargic, inattentive, or accident-prone. From ages 3 to 8, children are prone to sleep disturbances.

18. Children should get immunizations during regularly scheduled checkups with pediatricians and other health-care practitioners. Community health clinics administer free vaccinations for families that meet income eligibility requirements.

19. At least 6 million American children have asthma, the most common pediatric disease and main reason for child hospital admissions. Asthma is a serious, chronic lung disease. Many factors trigger an asthma attack, and prescription medications can relieve symptoms. Caregivers should eliminate the child's exposure to known allergens.

20. Children need proper nutrition, exercise, plenty of sleep, and health care, including childhood immunizations, to support the developing body systems and cognitive functioning. Children in public schools get annual checkups by health-care professionals.

21. Minority children and recent immigrant children may come from families that have alternative perspectives on health, illness, and wellness. However, all children must have vaccinations to enter nursery school, child-care center, preschool, and kindergarten.

22. The leading causes of death among young children are accidents, birth defects, homicides, cancer, and heart disease. More boys die than girls at all ages. Early childhood deaths are decreasing. Children from some minority groups experience higher risk of death.

Cognitive Development

23. When preschool children receive adequate nutrition and sensory stimulation, they experience a rapid expansion of cognitive abilities. Gradually these abilities evolve into intelligence, which includes reasoning, inference, and problem solving. Different models explain what intelligence is.

24. Psychologists differ in the relative importance that they attribute to the roles of heredity and environment in fashioning an individual's intelligence, and different tests have been devised to measure a child's intelligence quotient (IQ). Most social and behavioral scientists say there is interplay between genetic and environmental influences. It is difficult to devise a true "culture-free" IQ test.

25. Jean Piaget pioneered the study of children's cognitive development. He called the years between 2 and 7 the preoperational period, when a child increases the capacity to represent the external world internally through the use of symbols, such as words and numbers. Preschool children have difficulty solving conservation problems. Logical thought is inhibited by obstacles such as centration, transformations, and nonreversibility.

26. Preoperational children operate from egocentrism, are absorbed in their own feelings and thoughts, and are often not able to recognize others' thoughts and feelings. Neo-Piagetians believe that young children do have more reasoning capability and show evidence of prosocial behavior. In the early 1900s Dr. Maria Montessori developed a preschool program centered on children developing prosocial principles within a stimulating, supportive community. Today, Montessori schools are worldwide.

27. Theory of mind research has focused on children's understanding of their own thought processes. From ages 2 to 6 children gain a clearer understanding of their world, people's actions, and their own thought processes, number concepts, and causality of events. These understandings provide the conceptual foundation for children's learning.

28. Children acquire language in a sequence. Infants start with vowel and consonant sounds and progress to single words and two-word combinations. Children from ages 2 to 6 begin to internalize the rules of language: phonology, morphology, syntax, semantics, and pragmatics. Around age 3, children begin to ask What? Why? Which? Who? When? questions, and use different language in social contexts.

29. Learning to use speech enables children to communicate their needs and relate to others socially. Chomsky says babies are born with a natural language acquisition device

(LAD). Yet some young children experience developmental language disorders. Some experience disfluency, called stuttering. Typically children can improve linguistic skills with early speech therapy.

30. Lev Vygotsky said learning takes place in a sociocultural context. Children master tasks that are too hard to accomplish alone with help from a more skilled partner. Children's minds develop as they communicate with others. For those children who cannot communicate well, their thoughts and feelings can be expressed in artwork or physical movements. Multisensory experiences allow a child to process information from many sources.

31. A small number of children experience difficulties in cognitive reasoning and language. Caregivers must watch for signs of atypical development, so a child can be diagnosed and receive appropriate services.

Information Processing and Memory

32. Memory is an integral component of cognition that allows for thinking or reasoning. Information-processing skills include recall, recognition, and the facilitation of relearning. Children's recognition memory is superior to their recall. Our brains store information for different periods of time from a few seconds to short-term memory to long-term memory.

33. As children age, they use higher-order reasoning skills and demonstrate understanding of their own thought processes. Metacognition and metamemory skills demonstrate intentional approaches to memorizing vital information. By kindergarten age, they utilize their own memory strategies, deliberately remembering by using rehearsal and categorization strategies.

Moral Development

34. The ability to recall thoughts and feelings from memory makes moral thought possible. Piaget studied the moral reasoning of children. As young children mature, they come to understand more about attitudes and values and are more aware of the existence of "rules" of accepted behavior. Children under age 7 are limited in their understanding of the intentionality of action versus accident.

35. Kohlberg expanded on Piaget's studies of children's moral reasoning and understanding. He said young children are obedient to authority out of fear from threat or punishment. He called this first stage of moral development the preconventional stage. Kohlberg also thought that young children are egocentric (centered on self) and unable to see the perspective of others.

Key Terms

anaphylaxis (234)

Asperger's syndrome (230)

asthma (239)

causality (250)

centration (247)

conservation (247)

egocentrism (248)

intelligence (242)

intelligence quotient (IQ) (246)

language acquisition device (LAD) (251)

long-term memory (256)

memory (254)

metacognition (256)

metamemory (256)

methylphenidate (231)

morphology (251)

multiple intelligences (MIs) (243)

occupational therapist (226)

otitis media (229)

phonology (251)

pragmatics (251)

preoperational period (247)

private speech (254)

recall (255)

reciprocity (258)

recognition (255)

recreational therapist (226)

rehearsal (257)

reversibility of operations (248)

semantics (251)

sensory information storage (255)

short-term memory (256)

syntax (251)

theory of mind (249)

two-factor theory of intelligence (243)

zone of proximal development (ZPD) (252)

Following Up on the Internet

Web sites for this chapter focus on young children's physical, cognitive, language, and moral development. Please access the text Web site at www.mhhe.com/vzcrandell8 for up-to-date hot-linked Internet addresses for the following organizations and resources:

American Academy of Pediatrics

National Institute for Early Education Research

National Association for the Education of Young Children

Journal of Early Intervention

Early Childhood Education Journal

Early Childhood Research and Practice

Contemporary Issues in Early Childhood

The Food Allergy and Anaphylaxis Network

Early Childhood
Emotional and Social Development

Critical Thinking Questions

1. An American couple adopt a 1-year-old female child from an orphanage in China. Would this young child develop a sense of self and emotional regulation from the Chinese or American culture?

2. How would you explain the parenting style your parents used in raising you? Were they highly restrictive, permissive, or more democratic? In what ways has their approach affected your self-esteem? If you are a parent, do you parent in the same way or differently?

3. When there is a divorce in a family or the death of a parent or sibling or a major move to a new home, people say of a young child, "Oh, she's young, she'll adjust" or "He's young, he's flexible." Do you think this is an accurate appraisal of young children's emotional capabilities?

4. You are the parent of a 3-year-old whose grandmother has baby-sat him for the past year while you work full-time, and the U.S. Congress just passed legislation mandating compulsory all-day prekindergarten for *all* 4-year-olds in the United States beginning the next school year. What are your concerns for the transition of your young child?

Outline

C ognitive factors play an important part in setting the tone for the emotional life of youngsters, and social factors also have an impact on maximizing or minimizing intellectual ability. Through social interactions, children acquire guidelines that mentally or cognitively mediate their inner experience of emotion and their outer expression of it (Demo & Cox, 2000; Wintre & Vallance, 1994). Until the 1980s most American children spent their early years in the confines of home with family members until they entered the social/academic world of school. Thus, much of the classic research studies on the child's emotional regulation, sense of gender identity, and the effectiveness of parenting styles were conducted with mainly intact, middle-class families in the 1950s to 1970s. Today, young children's development occurs within a diversity of home and social environments.

Emotional Development and Adjustment

Since the 1980s there are fewer two-parent families, many more single parents and nonresident fathers, and a major exodus of mothers leaving the home to enter the ranks of the employed. Thus, a record number of young children are being cared for in child-care, preschool, prekindergarten, and full-day kindergarten programs, as well as in nonrelative private homes. Research summarizing the results of three studies found strong evidence of long-term positive outcomes for the use of quality preschool programs in readiness for kindergarten (Bracey & Stellar, 2001). Regardless of time spent with family or in a formal school setting, a substantial body of research indicates that unless children achieve a minimal social competence by age 6, there is a high probability of developing emotional and/or behavioral disorders by adulthood (McClellan & Katz, 2001). Additionally, recent cross-cultural studies of immigrant Hispanic, Asian, and Middle Eastern families are shedding light on how and when young children demonstrate sociocultural standards of emotional self-regulation and conformity to gender roles. It is within this broader context of social influences that we examine the more recent research findings on the emotional and social development of young children from ages 2 to 6.

Thinking Tasks Are Critical to Emotional Development

The process of emotional development and emotional self-regulation might seem slow to parents and caretakers, and young children vary considerably in the display of emotions and self-regulation. Many changes occur in emotional expression and emotional regulation during early childhood, and researchers are attempting to identify factors that promote or inhibit children's social competence and healthy adjustment (Eisenberg et al., 2001).

Emotions Are Central to Children's Lives   Today's child psychologists and early childhood experts believe that children's emotions are central to their lives and should be central to the nursery school, preschool, and early elementary school curriculum. Hyson (1994, p. 2), an early childhood professional, states, "A new generation of emotion researchers [developmental psychologists] has documented emotions' importance as organizers of children's behavior and learning. This knowledge base can provide a solid foundation for rebuilding an emotion-centered early childhood curriculum."

She further states (1994, p. 4) that emotional development and social development are intertwined, and "current theory and research support the belief that all behavior, thought, and interaction are in some way mo-

tivated by and colored by emotions. Thinking is an emotional activity, and emotions provide an essential scaffold for learning. In fact, children's feelings can support or hinder their involvement in and mastery of intellectual content." Shure (1996) agrees that the most important problem-solving skill a child learns is how to think, and it is important that a child learns to generate multiple socially appropriate solutions to interpersonal problems for healthy adjustment.

Teaching Effective Problem-Solving Skills   Youngstrom and colleagues (2000) studied thinking tasks that are integral to social competence and healthy adjustment in a large sample of children in Head Start at age 5 and again at age 7 in first grade. Caregivers, parents, and independent evaluators rated those children at age 5 and age 7 who generated more effective prosocial solutions as more socially competent, showing fewer attention problems and less disruptive behaviors.

In contrast, those children at age 5 and again at age 7 who proposed forceful (e.g., hitting, shouting, grabbing) and ineffective solutions were rated as less socially competent, less attentive, and more disruptive (Youngstrom et al., 2000). However, by age 7, the majority of the children in the sample reported more solutions, used fewer forceful solutions, and generated more prosocial responses (Youngstrom et al., 2000). These researchers conclude that to promote social competence young children must be taught effective problem-solving skills.

Learning Parents' Expression of Emotions   Eisenberg and colleagues (2001) examined the relationship between parental emotional expressivity (toward the child or in general in the home) and children's adjustment and social competence. They defined *expressivity* as "a persistent pattern or style in exhibiting nonverbal and verbal expressions that . . . is usually measured in terms of frequency of occurrence" (Eisenberg et al., 2001, p. 476). The findings from this study suggest that children who display social competence, emotional understanding, prosocial behaviors, higher self-esteem, and security of attachment have parents high in warmth or positive emotion and low in negativity in interactions with their children and in non-child-directed interactions within the home. Further, positive and supportive parents were observed helping their children cope successfully with distressful situations. Thus, it is thought that children from such families are learning to imitate self-regulation and develop appropriate emotional strategies and behaviors. Also these children are likely to be motivated to comply with parental requests out of a sense of trust and reciprocity (Eisenberg et al., 2001).

Some exposure to negative emotions—expressed appropriately and on a limited basis—is important for learning about emotions and how to regulate them. For example, the expression of such nonhostile emotions as sadness, embarrassment, and distress has been positively associated with showing sympathy (Eisenberg et al., 2001). However, children who come from homes where parents display high levels of hostile and hurtful negative emotions (both child-directed or in the home in general) are less likely to comply with parental directives, are more likely to display heightened expressions of negative affect, and are more likely to display problems associated with emotional insecurity (Eisenberg et al., 2001).

Demo and Cox's (2000) research findings also support that those young children who grow up in a more secure family environment are likely to display healthier emotions and earlier self-regulation of emotions, whereas children who were born prematurely, have developmental disabilities, experience maltreatment, or whose parents divorce are more likely to be delayed in self-regulation of emotions and demonstrate poor social competence. We shall discuss parental influence and children's social competence later in this chapter.

Timing and Sequence of Emotional Development

Very young infants express such emotions as happiness, sadness, distress, anger, and surprise (Izard & Malatesta, 1987). Other facial expressions that appear with greater frequency during toddlerhood and preschool years include pride, shame, shyness, embarrassment, contempt, fear, and guilt. These emotional expressions require a certain level of cognitive ability and awareness of cultural values or social standards. Preschool children often display several emotions at once, such as anger and guilt, as when a child is stubbornly refusing to share something with another. With increased physical development, older children have better control of their facial muscles, and they can facially display more complex emotions (Hyson, 1994).

Facial Expressions, Gestures, Body Language, and Voice Quality Much developmental research has focused on the young child's face as the conduit for expressing emotions, yet parents and other child caregivers would be wise to become good "readers" of children's whole body language. Young children can use increased large- and fine-muscle control to express feelings in a more complex, deliberate way. They can jump, wave their arms, clap their hands together, or verbally express their delight (Hyson, 1994). American elementary-school-age children can demonstrate the socially approved action of "thumbs up" or a "high five."

Yet for children from other cultures, these gestures convey different meanings, even insulting or sexual messages. Often the use of simple gestures (such as a teacher's typical waving the hand toward her body to tell

Facial Expressions and Body Language Reveal Emotions
Children require a certain level of physical and cognitive ability to express feelings in a more complex, deliberate way. Most often, young children learn to imitate parental emotional displays!

a young child to "come on") is confusing for immigrant children to learn—it is likely such gestures conflict with their traditional patterns of socialization (Hojat et al., 1999). Understandably, child-care professionals should familiarize themselves with the meanings of such culturally related gestures when attempting to help young immigrant children acculturate into American society.

Psychologists have also discovered that particular voice qualities, such as loudness, pitch, and tempo, can convey specific social-emotional messages, such as fear, anger, happiness, and sadness (Scherer, 1979). As children get older, sound and vocal quality continue to be important tools to convey feelings. Words accompany the emotion as well. "Don't touch my toys!" is conveyed both loudly and emotionally. Words also allow children to convey feelings about themselves and others: "I sad. Daddy make better." With progressive age, children can demonstrate and verbally express their more complex feelings (Ricks, 1979).

Play Behaviors and Emotional-Social Development

Play may be defined as voluntary activities done for enjoyment or recreation that are not performed for any sake beyond themselves. As healthy American children mature from ages 2 to 6, they display an increasingly complex array of emotions, cognitive skills, physical feats, and communication strategies through predictable stages of play (Paludi, 2002):

- *Functional play* is repetitive (rolling a ball or model car around).
- *Constructive play* involves manipulating objects or toys to create something else (using blocks to build a tower).

- *Parallel play* involves solitary play near others (putting a puzzle together alone).
- *Onlooker play* is observational (watching others play a game).
- *Associative play* involves two or more children sharing toys and materials (sharing a box of crayons while they color something separately).
- Ultimately, *cooperative (collaborative) play* involves interacting, communicating, and taking turns (playing board games, jumping rope, or playing a game of kickball).

Thus, during the first two years children's play shifts from the simple manipulation of objects to an exploration of the objects' unique properties and to make-believe play involving ever more complex and cognitively demanding behaviors (Uzgiris & Raeff, 1995). There are many forms of play, including *pretend play, exploration play, games, social play,* and *rough-and-tumble play.* Some of the many benefits of play include getting physical activity, which nourishes the brain and body and relieves stress; appreciating the outdoors; learning to be creative; and learning socialization skills such as following rules, acting cooperatively, trying roles of leading and following, and making friends ("The Case for Elementary School Recess," 2001). Young children often say that play time (or recess) is their favorite time of the day.

The social function of play activities has interested researchers for decades. Mildred B. Parten (1933), an early researcher on social play, studied participation and leadership in preschool play groups as well as the size of the groups, choice of playmates and the social value of play activities, toys, and games. In recent years pretend play has captivated the interest of many psychologists who have viewed make-believe or fantasy behavior as an avenue for exploring the "inner person" of the child and as an indicator of underlying cognitive changes. A young child will pretend with another friend to play "store" or if a friend isn't available, a pet, a stuffed animal, or doll will often be a substitute companion. During this play, the conversation will mimic what parents and caretakers say and do. When young children attend preschool and kindergarten, they imitate the teacher and common interactions of the classroom when playing "school." As might be expected, the proportion of children who engage in pretend play with other youngsters increases with age, especially those children who have stories read to them or who get to explore a variety of environments.

Imaginative Play Is Inexpensive but Priceless   Children learn to be creative by finding things around their home to play with, and they enjoy the discovery of creating things out of common objects, including pots and pans, cardboard, sand, water, string, tape, or pebbles. For example, putting a blanket over the back of two chairs can create a "cave" or secret hiding place that can easily be removed and re-created time and again. A simple large cardboard box can be improvised as a boat, a plane, a cave, a tree house, a car, a dollhouse, or any structure or place the child might imagine! A child can play out self-created dramatic roles using old hats, clothing, and costume jewelry. Far too often parents buy very expensive toys that sit in a corner and are never used.

Imaginary Friends   Between the ages of 3 and 7, many youngsters engage in a form of make-believe play in which they create an **imaginary friend** who becomes a regular part of their daily lives—an invisible character whom they name, refer to in conversations, and play

Pretend Play Young children really enjoy pretend play, also called "make-believe" play, which allows them to try on different roles. Common household items, such as cardboard boxes, stuffed animals, costume jewelry, old hats, shoes, and coats, can serve the child's imagination. Such play is even more fun with a playmate. Many larger communities today have some type of children's museum that allows hands-on role playing with costumes in simulated rooms with a grocery store, restaurant, fire station, doctor's office, farm, and so on.

with in an air of reality that lacks an objective basis (Taylor et al., 2004). Firstborns and very intelligent children often have imaginary friends. Caretakers are advised not to scold children for using their imaginations, and eventually children outgrow their imaginary companion as they interact with real playmates.

Gender Differences in Play One difference in play behavior is that boys tend to select games that require a larger number of participants than those selected by girls—but these differences in the play activities of boys and girls are often fostered by parental and teacher socialization practices. The two genders have somewhat different play styles (Hines, 2004). Boys' play has many rough-and-tumble physical qualities to it and strong overtones of competition and dominance. Girls engage in more intimate play than boys do, and two-person groups are conducive to intimate behavior. Girls are more likely than boys to disclose personal information to a friend and to hold hands and display other signs of affection.

Play Benefits Emotional Well-Being Many early childhood professionals regard play as a primary way

Differences in Play in Boys and Girls In general, boys tend to play in larger groups, to engage in more boisterous, motor activities such as running, jumping, climbing, throwing objects, wrestling—often engaging in play with overtones of competition and dominance. Girls tend to play in two-person groups, to be verbal during play, to hold hands or stay close to each other, and to display other signs of affection.

for children to communicate their deepest feelings (Erikson, 1977). Typically from ages 3 to 5 young children are **egocentric**; that is, their thoughts, words, and feelings are limited in outlook to their own needs, and thus they believe they may have caused something bad to happen (e.g., an argument between parents, illness of a sibling, death of a pet or loved one). Also, preschool and elementary-aged children simply do not know the vocabulary to speak about such feelings as anxiety, depression, jealousy or resentment, rejection or humiliation, or the despair of abandonment or abuse. However, in therapeutic play children demonstrate behaviors, reveal innermost feelings, and express thoughts, which research studies confirm decreases anxiety and aggression, yet increases expression of emotions, social adjustment, and a sense of control (Ray & Bratton, 2001).

Cultural Differences in Play Only more recently have cultural and ethnic differences in play been studied. Thus, known theories about play are based on studies of white, middle-class children from Westernized industrialized societies (Farver, Kim, & Lee, 1995). American parents typically tend to encourage exploration, imagination, and independence in play and are likely to play with their children. Yet more recent cross-cultural studies reveal that parents across cultures have different attitudes about play—although some view play as unnecessary, undesirable, or unsafe, other factors may be lacking such as time, space, materials, or playmates. North American parents view play as essential for development and tend to control their children's play activities (Scarlett et al., 2004).

Yet children in poor countries fill their days with home chores, sibling care, or work and school obligations and are encouraged by parents to work hard, take responsibility, and show initiative. "Play is at best tolerantly accepted by adults, and often it is discouraged or prohibited" (Harkness & Super, 1996, p. 359). Variations in play and social interaction are shaped by what adults believe children need to become productive members of their society.

In a recent study, two Korean American preschool teachers (although having attended U.S. colleges) encouraged traditional Korean values (group harmony and cooperation, de-emphasis on individuality and self-expression), expectations (a highly structured environment with little interaction among children and high parental expectations), and educational goals (perseverance to the task and academic achievement) (Farver, Kim, & Lee, 1995). Chu (1978) states that in Korean culture children are taught it is a virtue to hide one's feelings instead of displaying them outwardly. Thus, the Korean American children under study were observed in more parallel but little pretend or collaborative play, which would promote social skills (Farver, Kim, & Lee, 1995).

Regardless of cultural or ethnic background, the significance of play is recognized in Article 31 of *The United Nations Convention on the Rights of the Child:* "Every child has the right to rest and leisure, to engage in play and recreational activities appropriate to the age of the child and to participate freely in cultural life and the arts" ("The Convention on the Rights of the Child," 2001).

Emotional Response and Self-Regulation

Developmental experts and parents across cultures have different views, values, and beliefs regarding the age at which children are expected to control their own emotions, instead of relying upon external parental/caretaker support (Friedlmeier & Trommsdorff, 1999). Deliberate holding back of feelings is difficult for children until after age 3 (Saarni, 1979). Individual cultural expectations also dictate the norms for the expression or inhibition of emotions by boys or girls. Some believe children should be able to "let their feelings out," whereas others believe children need to learn to hide their feelings.

Emotional self-regulation is a complex task that must be mastered in a healthy way for children to develop a positive relationship with others. At best, self-regulation develops at each child's pace and likely proceeds gradually and unevenly. Children who cry, whine, hit, bite, or scream to get their way certainly will not be well liked; nor will the sad or timid child who sits quietly in a corner away from others. Somewhere there is a healthy balance of emotional self-regulation for each child.

Culture Transmits Expectations   Because of an increasing racial/ethnic mix of U.S. children, contemporary social scientists are studying cross-cultural expectations or unwritten "rules" for expressing emotions. Young children learn by imitation and modeling to convey culturally prescribed emotions through gestures and body language. In Western industrialized cultures, parents tend to support **individualism,** the view that individual autonomy is paramount, thus promoting freedom of expression, independence, individuality, and competition that allow a child to exhibit feelings more openly (Friedlmeier & Trommsdorff, 1999). It is somewhat common to witness a young child crying loudly or having a "temper tantrum" or shouting for joy in public, as examples.

Asian and Pacific Islander (API) Children   In contrast to the individualistic approach, Asian parents traditionally stress **collectivism,** a view that fosters in children a strong emotional bonding and feeling of oneness with parents, denial of individual desires in order to do what is best for the group, obedience to authority, and showing respect to elders (Friedlmeier & Trommsdorff, 1999; Rohner & Pettengill, 1985). Children from Asian cultures are typically encouraged to show a lack of emotion and to have a more compliant nature (Chu, 1978; Lynch & Hansen, 1992).

This growing community in the United States includes three general ethnicities: (1) *East Asians,* including Chinese, Japanese, and Koreans; (2) *Southeast Asians,* largely composed of Indochinese from Vietnam, Thailand (e.g., the Hmong immigrants), Cambodia, Laos, and Burmese and Philippines; and (3) *Pacific Islanders,* mostly Hawaiians, Samoans, and Guamanians (Trueba, Cheng, & Ima, 1993). These groups and their subgroups differ in sociocultural traits, beliefs, and values and each has specific educational needs (Pang & Cheng, 1998). The existence of diverse Asian cultures and the perception of Asian students as the "model minority" have stood in the way of fully understanding the needs of Asian and Asian American students (Gewertz, 2004)

Teachers and other professionals working with young API children need to understand traditional beliefs and values so they don't become an obstacle to effective schooling and emotional well-being for Asian children. A telling example occurred in Stockton, California, in 1989 when a gunman entered a preschool and killed five Cambodian children. The preschool staff responded by revising safety procedures and providing a more secure building so the remaining young children could return with greater assurance of their safety. The Cambodian families refused to send their children to the preschool until the school officials and families performed a traditional religious ritual to comfort the spirits of the dead children (Trueba et al., 1993).

East Asians generally value and promote high educational achievement, and the child's success brings honor and prestige to the family, and failure brings shame to the family (Shen & Mo, 1990). Some immigrant Asian parents have difficulty accepting concepts such as learning disabilities and believe that psychological distress, depression, or mental illnesses are spiritual in origin. Although some Asian families consider having a child with a disability a sign of good fortune, others view it as a punishment of past sins, and some consider it an act of God that cannot be changed (Miles, 1993). A poignant, insightful book about the serious nature of cultural misunderstanding for readers entering the child-care, human services, and health-care fields is *The Spirit Catches You and You Fall Down: A Hmong Child, Her American Doctors, and the Collision of Two Cultures* by journalist Anne Fadiman (check your college library or local bookstore).

The Asian form of communication is more sensitive to nonverbal cues, body movements and gestures, and Asians expect others to be as sensitive to their nonverbal cues. They are typically polite and even submissive in social encounters, use repeated head nodding and lack of eye contact, rarely use the word *no* in order to avoid offending anyone, and are unlikely to respond in a spontaneous way. In the context of an educational environment, teachers take APIs' head-nodding, smiles, and verbal assent as clear indication of consent, when in fact it is likely to be a sign of respect rather than agreement or understanding (Trueba et al., 1993).

Teachers and child-care specialists need to observe Asian children carefully when conversing and looking for social-emotional feedback, and they should consider the context of the situation, for smiles often express confusion and embarrassment rather than pleasure or agreement (Coker, 1988). The stereotypes that *all* Asian children are submissive and academically very bright can create a great deal of anxiety for some children. Traditionally, Asian children have been socialized to listen more than speak, to speak in a soft voice, to be modest in dress and behavior, and to stay close to the mother (or substitute caretaker) or seek her out when exposed to situations that create any negative emotions (Friedlmeier & Trommsdorff, 1999).

The structure of American schooling may undermine their sense of well-being and self-confidence, since U.S. schools promote independence, competition, and individualism. Asian children tend to work more efficiently in a well-structured, quiet environment. They do not like attention drawn to themselves; for example, being called up in front of the class or having one's name put on the board for anything brings distress or a sense of shame (Trueba et al., 1993).

Two- and 3-year-old Japanese children might show greater signs of distress at separating from their mothers because the Japanese culture encourages extreme closeness between mother and child (Hyson, 1994). Lewis (1988) observed children in 15 Japanese nursery schools and learned that Japanese children are allowed to demonstrate anger as long as other children do not get hurt badly. However, as they grow older, Japanese children also encounter more social regulations that promote *ittaikan,* a feeling of oneness with the group (Weisz, Roghbaum, & Blackburn, 1984). Japanese children are prepared for a more rigorous school experience and must pass major exams for promotion to the next grade (Fuligni & Stevenson, 1995; Marlow-Ferguson, 2002).

Hispanic American Expectations   The Hispanic American cultural stereotype for a male child is summed up in the word *macho,* derived from *machismo,* which connotes both positive and negative aspects about the role of a male: to be strong and dominant; to take responsibility for the well-being of his family; to work hard to provide for his family; to treat women with respect; and to be a good son, husband, and father. In contrast, *marianismo* is the Hispanic American cultural stereotype for a female. She is expected to be feminine, to learn self-sacrifice, to provide joy in and take responsibility for her family,

and to subjugate her needs to prepare herself to live in a patriarchal subculture.

Typically there is a strong family cohesion called *familismo,* and children are very unlikely to disclose anything about family situations (Castellanos, 1994; Gil & Vazquez, 1996). Hispanic children also live within a collectivist culture, and family beliefs, values, and traditions are a significant influence on behavior and emotional expression. Here is an example of a conflict between cultural beliefs:

> In one school that has a large population of immigrant Latino students, many mothers were [perceived by teachers and administrators as] "causing a problem" with the federally funded school breakfast program by accompanying their children to school, bringing along younger siblings, and eating breakfast with their children. Some were helping to feed their school-age children. In the eyes of school officials, who were responsible for implementing the federal program, the mothers and siblings were eating food that "belonged" to the children enrolled in the school. . . . In fact, a condition of receiving the federal grant was that breakfasts be provided only to the school children. But teachers and administrators were also greatly concerned that the mothers' behaviors were inhibiting the children's development of independence—a goal of the prevailing U.S. culture in schools. The school addressed the problem by posting signs saying no parents would be allowed in the cafeteria during breakfast. The mothers, who were behaving according to their values of sharing and family unity, had great difficulty understanding the school's perspective and mobilized a protest that caused quite an uproar. (Trumbull, Rothstein-Fisch, & Greenfield, 2000)

African American Expectations   Often African American adults use eye contact and facial expression to discipline their children (King, Sims, & Osher, 2001). Thus, a teacher with a class of African American children may use a certain look that quiets most of the class. However, this is not effective with all African American children (King, Sims, & Osher, 2001). Some are taught by caregivers to refrain from direct eye contact, which people from other cultural backgrounds might misinterpret as shyness or evasiveness (Hyson, 1994).

In her book *I'm Chocolate, You're Vanilla,* Marguerite A. Wright (1998), Harvard-trained clinical and developmental psychologist, states from her research findings that preschool children do not attach any social or emotional meaning to skin color or race, unless their families stress this. García Coll and Magnuson (2000) say race describes a group of people mainly by their physical characteristics, such as skin color, hair type, and other features; in actuality, many Americans are of mixed-race descent. Wright (1998) says that black children, like other children, come to understand gender identity first.

When asked "What color are you?" or asked to match the color of their own skin to a display of color, young children are likely to identify a color of their clothing, or say *chocolate,* or *vanilla,* or *peach.* Wright (1998, p. 14) says that 3- and 4-year-olds' sense of identity comes mainly from their name, gender, and familial relationships, and the concept of "race is the farthest thing from their minds."

She advises parents of light-skinned black children not to be alarmed if their children call themselves white, that it is not a reflection of poor self-image. She says that adults, including parents, child-care staff, and preschool teachers overestimate what young children know about race. When asked to draw a self-portrait, young black children are likely to color themselves "green, blue, yellow, and purple, choices that suggest their actual skin color has little to do with self-image" (Wright, 1998, p. 17). Before children can understand the role race plays in their lives, they must first realize that skin color is permanent. Wright (1998) finds it is normal for black children to talk about wanting to be another skin color, and adults need not shame or demean children for thinking anything is possible. Four-year-olds are likely to believe in a "magical process" to change skin color, which is understandable since many black babies are born with lighter complexions, the palms of their hands are often lighter, and their reasoning is imaginative (Wright, 1998, pp. 20–21).

Preschool children cannot categorize people into different racial groups (e.g., African, Arab, Chinese, and Mexican), they delight in trying on different roles, and they demonstrate a pure appreciation for people as individuals. "White preschoolers share with their black peers an innocence about racial differences" (Wright, 1998, p. 32). Around age 7, children begin to develop the cognitive skills to categorize people into different racial groups, using physical characteristics and social cues. Black children seem to become aware of their race first, biracial children a little later, and white children even later (Wright, 1998). An excellent book illustrating the preceding is entitled *I Am My Body, NOT!,* written and designed by American author Adam Abraham (available in Spanish, Dutch, French, Japanese, and Russian).

Roberts and colleagues (1995, 1997, 1999) began a longitudinal study of 87 African American infants averaging 8 months from nine community-based child-care centers and found that children from more stimulating and responsive homes had larger vocabularies, longer utterances, and used more irregular nouns and verbs. Between 18 and 30 months of age, girls used larger vocabularies, longer sentence lengths, and more irregular nouns and verbs than boys in this sample. Black children are likely to use culturally based speech rhythms, known as "contest" style of speech or "call-and-response" speech after the patterns found in black music—in which black mothers and children volley comments rhythmically back and forth (Hale-Benson, 1990).

American black children come from families with a history of oral tradition in their songs, tales, proverbs, stories, and jokes—preserved and eventually forming the basis of African American music—the Negro spiritual, jazz, the blues, and contemporary rap music. African American language, passed along to young children, uses creativity, poetic beauty, emotional intensity, and rich, colorful imagery ("Parenting Empowerment Project: African American Culture," 2001).

Cross-Cultural Understanding and Effective Teaching, Health Care, and Social Services   Teachers and early intervention specialists need to familiarize themselves with the customs of the young children they work with, learn a few words of that child's language, and create developmentally appropriate, culturally sensitive, and adaptable curriculum and instruction (Feng, 1994). In cross-cultural interactions, "different" does not mean wrong. With greater acculturation into American society, traditional cultural gender-role expectations are being redefined. If the adults in a family do not speak English, the young child who is learning the English language is often called into an adult role as an interpreter. Caretakers of young children and parents who plan to adopt a child from a different background might want to become familiar with the styles of emotional expression prescribed by the child's group of origin.

Ekman (1972) found that preschoolers and school-age children learn about expectations of emotional self-regulation through observation and direct instruction. However, because this is a time of egocentric (centered on self) behavior for preschool children, repeated direct

Fostering a Positive Sense of Identity in All Children
Three- and 4-year-olds' sense of identity comes mainly from their name, gender, and familial relationships. Preschool children delight in trying on different roles, and they share an innocence about racial differences. Around age 7, children develop the cognitive skills to categorize people into different racial groups.

instruction may be necessary. It is common to hear parents of preschoolers and young elementary-age children express frustration: "How many times have I told you to . . . ?" Caretakers of young children need to be patient and persevere by repeatedly explaining and demonstrating the desired behavior. Physical punishment, such as slapping or spanking children, at this stage simply teaches children to use physical measures themselves to control others' behaviors. Most children conform to their appropriate cultural norms over time.

Acquiring Emotional Understanding

Parents often talk to preschoolers about past events ("Remember when we did . . . and . . . happened?"). These reminiscences often are framed within an emotional context (how happy the child was, how much fun some activity was). As children get older and learn more about emotions, they can better match facial pictures with the correct emotion label. Older children also can identify why people feel the way they do—sad, happy, surprised, fearful, or angry (Stein & Jewett, 1986). Even 3-year-olds have their own ideas about what causes fear. Some studies show that preschoolers have difficulty understanding that people can have several emotions at one time (as when a parent says, "I love you, but I'm upset with what you did").

The Link Between Feeling and Thinking When given familiar situations, preschoolers can accurately identify the commonly associated emotion; and when given an emotion, they can easily describe an appropriate eliciting situation (Lagattuta, Wellman, & Flavell, 1997). Although past research proposed that it is not until 8 or 9 years of age that children can begin to understand mental (rather than situational) causes of feelings, more recent research by Lagattuta and colleagues (1997) demonstrates that much younger children can understand the emotional consequences of past experiences when cued cognitively. The findings from these researchers' three recent studies demonstrate that 3- and 4-year-olds have a decided tendency to explain emotions in terms of current external situations, and 4- and 5-year-olds have substantial knowledge about mind and emotion. More specifically, their research with young children demonstrated the following (Lagattuta, Wellman, & Flavell, 1997):

- Young children's prior experiences, desires, beliefs, and thoughts can affect their emotional reactions to current situations (e.g., they can relate to the loss of a pet in a story with photographs and elaborate on why the character in the story is unhappy).
- Young children have the ability to infer mental activity (thinking or remembering), particularly at 4, 5, and 6 years old.

Young Children Often Help Each Other George Mead would say that the child on the left can imagine himself in the role of the child on the right. Young children's prior experiences can affect their emotional reaction to a current situation. By the time children are 4 to 5 years old, they are often motivated to help each other.

- Young children's mental activity can influence their emotional arousal.
- Young children demonstrate knowledge about the sources of their thoughts.
- Young preschoolers can predict that a friend, who had never experienced a character's sad experience, would not feel sad.

Responding to Emotions of Others Toddlers and preschoolers deliberately seek out information about others' emotional reactions. They might appear to be fascinated by "getting a rise out of" their parents and caretakers (what at first might appear to be a game can become irritating to caretakers). By the preschool years, the emotional response to others' distress seems to motivate children to comfort and help their caregivers and peers. As young children develop emotionally, they require help in understanding these emotions in a secure environment, modeling of appropriate emotional response, and support for regulating their emotions (Hyson, 2004).

Forming Emotional Ties Forming emotionally positive relationships with parents and significant others is a key task in the development of a child's sense of self-awareness. Children in child-care settings nowadays have demonstrated that they can also develop close, affectionate bonds with caregivers in these settings (Hyson, 2004). Emotional attachment is demonstrated by such behaviors as clinging, smiling, and crying. As children age, they are able to develop a close attachment to someone without necessarily having physical contact. Young children also

Table 8.1 Progression of Emotional Development, Ages 2 to 6

Age Group	Emotional Expression
2-year-olds	Begin to show facial expressions of shyness, pride, shame, embarrassment, contempt, fear, and guilt.
	Parallel play is common in 2-year-olds—that is, playing independently near others without interaction.
	Play is more likely to be simple manipulation of objects.
	Deliberate holding back of feelings, called emotional self-regulation, is unlikely at this early age.
	Sometimes toddlers deliberately try to elicit emotional responses from caregivers.
	Definitely begin to use the word no.
	Toddlers can also develop close, affectionate bonds with caregivers, demonstrated by smiling, clinging, and crying.
	Two-year-olds demonstrate emergence of the interpersonal self (e.g., reacting happily when mother comes to pick up the child at the end of the day).
	"Watch me do this!"
	Young children conceive of the self strictly in physical terms, pointing to the head, for example.
	Plants and animals also have selves and minds.
	Gifted children master their environment quickly and thoroughly and appear to be self-directed.
3-year-olds	Increased control of large- and fine-muscles to express feelings in a more complex, deliberate way.
	Can now jump, wave arms, clap hands together, and verbally express delight.
	Voice qualities, such as loudness, pitch, and tempo vary, conveying specific feelings, (e.g., "Don't touch my toys!").
	Begin to demonstrate a complexity of emotions through play materials in their environment.
	Associative play is more common, with children beginning to interact with one another and sharing play materials.
	Playing cooperatively begins toward the end of this year.
	Some evidence of emotional self-regulation.
	Learn about expectations of emotional self-regulation from observing others, from modeling behaviors of others, and from direct instruction.
	Gifted children often display leadership qualities and often say "I can do it myself!"
3- to 4-year-olds	Have a tendency to explain feelings in terms of external events ("I sad. He hit me.")
	Are more likely to deliberately elicit emotional responses from caregivers.
	Are likely to want to help with tasks and to help others.
4-year-olds	Have better control of facial muscles and can display more complex emotions at one time.
	Begin to verbally express more complex feelings.
	Can accurately identify a commonly expressed emotion and can describe an eliciting situation.
	Boys seem to prefer to engage in more rough-and-tumble competitive play in larger groups, whereas girls seem to engage in two-person groups with more intimate behaviors, such as talking, holding hands.
	Some children this age have an imaginary friend.
	Four- and 5-year-olds show substantial knowledge about mind and emotion.
	A gender identity is usually established.
5- to 6-year-olds	Greater mastery of thinking and remembering.
	Evidence of an emerging distinction between the mental self and the physical self.
	Evidence of greater variety of temperaments and behaviors in a group.

demonstrate a close bond with siblings and other children in child-care settings (Hyson, 1994).

Emotions are central to children's lives and help them organize their experiences in order to learn from them and develop other behaviors. Though cultures differ in their norms for the expression of feelings by girls and boys, Table 8.1 shows the general progression of emotional development in children from age 2 through age 6.

Questions

In early childhood, how do children acquire emotional understanding and, in turn, increase their ability for emotional self-regulation? What are some examples from cross-cultural studies about the influences on children's emotional development?

The Development of Self-Awareness

As we have seen, emotional development is an essential component of a child's sense of self-awareness. Moreover, a child's own sense of self-worth or self-image is part of the overall dimension called **self-esteem.** Some children develop what is referred to as positive self-esteem; others develop a more negative view of themselves, referred to as low self-esteem.

Enhancing children's self-esteem is an important goal for many parents and most preschool and kindergarten programs, and there is considerable evidence that children's self-esteem can have lifelong effects on their attitudes and behavior, performance in school, relationships with family, and functioning in society (Hong & Perkins, 1997). In this section, we examine the factors that influence a child's developing self-esteem.

The Sense of Self

Among the cognitive and social achievements of the child's early years is a growing self-awareness—the human sense of "I." At any one time, we are confronted with a greater quantity and variety of stimulation than we can attend to and process. Accordingly, we must select what we will notice, learn, infer, or recall. Selection does not occur in a random manner but depends on our use of internal cognitive structures—mental "scripts" or "frames"—for processing information. Of particular importance to us is the cognitive structure that we employ for selecting and processing information about ourselves. This structure is the **self**—the system of concepts we use in defining ourselves. It is the awareness we have of ourselves as separate entities that enables us to think and initiate action.

The self provides us with the capacity to observe, respond to, and direct our own behavior. The sense of self distinguishes each of us as a unique individual, different from others in society. It gives us a feeling of placement in the social and physical world and of continuity across time. And it provides the cognitive basis for our identities (Cross & Markus, 1991).

Neisser (1991) further differentiated between the ecological self and the interpersonal self. The *ecological self* is the self that picks up and acts on the perceptual information presented by objects in the environment (e.g., the family dog nudges the young child to play). The *interpersonal self,* in contrast, is that aspect of self that arises in interactions with other people (e.g., reacting happily when mother comes into the kindergarten room at the end of the day) (Pipp-Siegel & Foltz, 1997). Toddlers' abilities to develop categories of stimuli become more complex. Pipp-Siegel and Foltz (1997) conducted a study with 60 children and mothers at infancy and toddlerhood to determine toddlers' knowledge of self, mother, and inanimate objects. Their research findings show that the complexity of knowledge between knowing self and others changed as a function of age. Two-year-olds demonstrated an emergence of the interpersonal self, with the development of self-conscious emotions and an increased capacity for symbolic play.

The development of a sense of self as separate and distinct from others is a central issue of children's early years (Asendorpf, Warkentin, & Baudonniere, 1996). This fundamental cognitive change facilitates numerous other changes in social development. Youngsters come to view themselves as active agents who produce outcomes. They derive pleasure from being "self-originators" of behavior, and they insist on performing activities independently—resulting in behavior sometimes pejoratively labeled "the terrible twos." All the while toddlers increasingly focus on the outcomes of their activities rather than simply on the activities themselves. A common directive from young children is "Watch me do this!"

Toddlers also gain the ability to monitor their ongoing activities with respect to an anticipated outcome and to use external standards for measuring their task performance. This ability is first evident at about 26 months of age. By 32 months of age, they recognize when they err in performing certain tasks, and they correct their mistakes. For instance, in building a block tower, youngsters are not only better able to avoid errors in stacking blocks but also to manipulate and rearrange the blocks when their first efforts fail (Bullock & Lutkenhaus, 1988).

A concept of the self might also be necessary for self-conscious and self-evaluative emotions, because a notion of self seemingly precedes both self-conscious emotions (such as embarrassment) and self-evaluative emotions (such as pride or shame) (Harris et al., 1992). Having developed self-conscious and self-evaluative emotions—particularly negative emotions when engaging in some transgression—and the ability to evaluate objects and behavior in terms of some standard, youngsters gain the ability to inhibit their behaviors in the absence of caretakers: Social control becomes *self-control* (Stipek, Recchia, & McClintic, 1992).

During the preschool years, young children conceive of the self strictly in physical terms—body parts (the head), material attributes ("I have blue eyes"), and bodily activities ("I walk to the park") (Johnson, 1990). Children view the self and the mind as simply parts of the body (Damon & Hart, 1982). For the most part, children locate the self in the head, although they might also cite other body parts like the chest or the whole body. And they often say that animals, plants, and dead people also have selves and minds.

Between 6 and 8 years of age, children begin to distinguish between the mind and the body (Inagaki & Hatano, 1993). The emerging distinction between the mental and the physical allows children to appreciate the subjective nature of the self. They begin to recognize that people are unique not only because each of us looks different from other people but also because each of us has different feelings and thoughts. Hence, children come to define the self in *internal* rather than *external* terms and to grasp the difference between psychological and physical attributes.

Parents' and caretakers' overall support and unconditional love provide the foundation for a child's ego, or developing self-concept. The **self-concept,** or *self-image,* is defined as the image one has of oneself. One theory is that a child's self-image develops as a reflection of what others think about the child. Parents' facial expressions, tone of voice, and patient or impatient interactions reflect how the parents value each child. Additionally, the child's own personality contributes to the child's growing self-awareness and to the parents' conceptions about the child. For example, a parent might recognize that her child is "shy" or "happy-go-lucky" or "strong-willed"—traits that appear to be inherent in this particular child's nature.

Measuring a Child's Self-Esteem

Sometimes adults recognize a young child's lack of self-esteem by the child's withdrawn, sad, or antisocial behaviors and realize that the child might need intervention to boost self-esteem for better mental health and social functioning. Psychologists have devised a variety of psychometric instruments used to assess the accuracy of such observations. Harter and Pike (1984) developed the *Pictorial Scale of Perceived Competence and Social Acceptance in Young Children.* This has become a commonly used self-report measure, where children are asked to report on their own behavior, with separate scores obtained for cognitive and physical competence, maternal acceptance, and peer acceptance.

An alternate approach to self-esteem measurement is the *Behavioral Rating Scale of Presented Self-Esteem in Young Children,* used to assess inferred self-esteem (Haltiwanger & Harter, 1988). Parents and teachers make inferences about children's self-esteem from observation of their behaviors. Ratings include such behaviors as initiative, preference for challenge, social approach/social avoidance, social-emotional expression, and coping skills. A lower outcome on these self-esteem measures typically associates behavioral difficulties with low self-esteem (Fuchs-Beauchamp, 1996).

Gifted Children and Their Sense of Self

Elizabeth Maxwell (1998) from the Gifted Development Center in Denver, reviewed information on gifted children in early childhood and their sense of self. Anecdotal information was provided by parents of at least 265 children with IQs of 160 or higher, and more than 50 children who scored at 180 or above. Maxwell (1998, p. 245) states, "It is difficult not to notice the assertive drive of gifted and highly gifted young children to master their environment as quickly and as thoroughly as possible, far beyond the age expectations of developmental timetables. They appear to be self-directed, their sense of self-awareness arriving early and thrust in the face of parents and the environment in general." Lovecky (1994) calls this **entelechy,** a particular type of motivation, need for self-determination, and an inner strength and vital force directing life and growth to become all one is capable of being.

Gifted children are active learners with their own agendas, learn remarkably quickly, yet might be difficult to teach or to control. They do not automatically show respect to adults, are likely to see themselves as equal to adults, might demonstrate a strong will, and can present unique challenges to parents and teachers (Maxwell, 1998). On the other hand, many of these young children demonstrate an awareness of their emotional *self-efficacy*—that is, the child's own beliefs and feelings about the degree to which they are able to understand and empathize with others' emotions. They are likely to share easily with others, to have a strong sense of justice, and to display leadership qualities (Maxwell, 1998). A common highly charged directive from precocious children is "I can do it myself!"

> **Questions**
>
> What are some cognitive and social factors that promote a young child's growing self-awareness? What factors/behaviors might a psychologist assess to determine a child's self-esteem?

Gender Identification

One of the attributes of self acquired early in life is **gender,** the state of being male or female. A major developmental task for the child during the first six years of life is to acquire gender identification. All societies appear to have seized on the anatomical differences between women and men to assign **gender roles**—sets of cultural expectations that define the ways in which the members of each sex should behave.

Societies throughout the world display considerable differences in the types of activities assigned to women and men (Ickes, 1993; Murdock, 1935). In many societies, girls are socialized to identify with the mother's nurturant, caregiving role, and boys are prepared to identify with the father's provisional-protector role. In some societies, though, women do most of the manual labor; in others, as in the Marquesas Islands, cooking, housekeeping, and baby-tending are male occupations.

Gender Identity

Most people evolve gender identities reasonably consistent with the gender-role standards of their society. **Gender identity** is the conception that a person has of himor herself as being male or female. Since the 1960s in the Westernized world, a good deal of research has explored the process by which children come to conceive of themselves in *masculine* or *feminine* terms and to adopt the behaviors considered culturally appropriate for them as males or females. It has also activated debate regarding the psychology of gender differences and gender stereotypes. Although a more "gender-neutral" approach was promoted for many years (e.g., dolls for little boys and trains and construction sets for girls and "unisex" clothing), more recently some powerfully influential retailers have done extensive research on buying practices and find that distinct gender-based toys, clothing, television shows, and so forth are in vogue (Bannon, 2000).

Between the ages of 3 and 4, most children have acquired a gender identity through socialization experiences with parents, extended family, preschool experiences, and media influence (Wright, 1998). Between the ages of 4 and 5, children come to understand that their gender is not going to change (Wright, 1998). How children are treated in any culture because of their gender significantly affects how children feel about themselves. You can see how most parents quickly plan to assimilate their child into the appropriate gender role beginning with the fetal ultrasound: What color paint and wallpaper is planned for the baby's room? What color and style of clothing is purchased prior to the birth? What types of toys and stuffed animals are purchased to put in the child's crib? What potential names are selected for the child-to-be? It would be fair to say that, in American society, gender roles have become more versatile over the past 30 years.

Hormonal Influences on Gender Behaviors

Many studies have been conducted to investigate the influence of hormones (chemical messengers of the endo-

crine system) on gender behaviors (Eagly, 1995; Eisenberg et al., 1997). Both sexes have some male and female hormones, though the ratio of each varies in males and females. However, the prevalence of the hormone testosterone tends to make boys more physically active, more aggressive, and less likely to be able to sit still (Maccoby & Jacklin, 1974). Eleanor Maccoby (1980), after repeated reviews of research studies on sex behaviors, concluded: "The tendency of males to be more aggressive than females is perhaps the most firmly established sex difference and is a characteristic that transcends culture." More recent research finds that females are less likely to inhibit aggression when aggression is socially expected and supported—as in school sports, professional teams, and Olympic competition, where females were not allowed until recently (Campbell, 1993). Today, many American communities begin teaching soccer, baseball, or hockey to 5- and 6-year-old boys and girls.

The predominance of either female or male hormones influences the development of the fetal brain. Earlier dissection techniques reported that females tend to have a larger *corpus callosum*, the band of fibers and nerves that connects the two hemispheres and carries messages between the two sides of the brain (Kolata, 1995a, 1995b). It is hypothesized that the slightly increased size of the corpus callosum allows the two hemispheres in female brains to communicate more easily.

In general, boys tend to be more logical, analytical, spatial, and mathematical, whereas females tend to be more verbal at an earlier age, more "emotional," and more social (interested in "people-oriented" activities) (Halpern, 1997). Witness the number of preschool-age boys who enjoy playing video games or sports that are based on spatial relations and the number of little girls who enjoy having a "tea party" or playing "school" and conversing with one another. Also, Halpern (1992) found that males are disproportionately represented among those manifesting **dyslexia** (a learning disorder marked by inability to recognize and comprehend written words) and stuttering problems.

Until many of these studies are replicated, we are not certain whether gender differences in the structuring of particular regions of the brain are the source of differences in gender identity, behavior, sexual orientation, or cognitive processes. Most psychologists agree that it is premature to look only to biology for explanations of gender differences. Certainly each individual child's family experience and cultural socialization patterns also influence gender behaviors.

Social Influences on Gender Behaviors

The fact that hormonal and biological factors sometimes contribute to behavioral differences between men and women does not mean that environmental influences are unimportant. On the basis of his research with hermaph-rodites (individuals having the reproductive organs of both sexes), Money (Money & Tucker, 1975, pp. 86–89) concludes that the most powerful factors in the shaping of gender identity are *environmental:*

> The chances are that society had nothing to do with the turnings you took in the prenatal sex development road, but the minute you were born, society took over. When the drama of your birth reached its climax, you were promptly greeted with the glad ritual cry, "It's a boy!" or "It's a girl!" depending on whether or not those in attendance observed a penis in your crotch.... The label "boy" or "girl," however, has tremendous force as a self-fulfilling prophecy, for it throws the full weight of society to one side or the other as the newborn heads for the gender identity fork [in the road], and the most decisive sex turning point of all.... [At birth you were limited to] something that was ready to become your gender identity. You were wired but not programmed for gender in the same sense that you were wired but not programmed for language.

Clearly, anatomy in itself does not provide us with our gender identity. Because of being labeled "boy" or "girl," a highly stylized treatment of the child is repeated countless times each day (Campbell, 1993). Boys receive more toy action vehicles, sport equipment, machines, toy animals, and military toys; girls receive more dolls, dollhouses, and domestic toys. Boys' rooms are more often decorated with animal motifs; girls' rooms with floral motifs accompanied by lace, fringes, and ruffles. Although the sexual revolution has reshaped many nooks and crannies of U.S. life, it failed to reach very deeply into the toy box. Behind many parents' concerns about the type of toys their children play with are un-expressed fears about homosexuality, yet there is little evidence that children's toy preferences are related to their sexual orientation (Bailey & Zucker, 1995).

Although women give birth and men do not, little evidence exists to support popular notions that some-how biology makes women kinder and gentler beings or that nature equips them specifically for nurturing roles (Whiting & Edwards, 1988). Psychologist Jerome Kagan, who has spent more than 35 years studying chil-dren, speculates that any propensity women might have for caretaking can be traced to an early awareness of their role in procreation:

> Every girl knows, somewhere between the ages of 5 and 10, that she is different from boys and that she will have a child—something that everyone, including children, understands as quintessentially natural. If, in our society, nature stands for the giving of life, nurturance, help, affection, then the girl will conclude unconsciously that those are the qualities she should strive to attain. And the boy won't. And that's exactly what happens. (Kagan, quoted by Shapiro, 1990, p. 59)

Gender and Cultural Distinctions   Perhaps nowhere in the world was the distinction of gender marked as severely, or oppressively, as it was for women and girls in Afghanistan for several years under the rule of the Mus-lim extremist, male-dominated *Taliban.* They cruelly enforced tyrannical dress codes and rules of behavior for women and girls. Women were not allowed to work outside their homes, attend school or universities, seek professional medical care, drive, enter shops run by men, walk outside without a male escort, be seen without the heavy head-to-toe covering called the *burka,* or be seen from outside, so home windows had to be painted dark (Bearak, 2001a, b; Pollitt, 2001). Women were banned from laughing out loud, from wearing makeup, from dancing, from singing, and from playing any music (Mulrine, 2001; Pollitt, 2001).

Public executions of violators of these gender-based restrictions, including hangings, amputations, being shot in the head, or being burned alive, were held nearly every Friday in Kabul's former sports stadium for those who were caught committing such violations (Mulrine, 2001). Thousands of widows, not allowed to work, were forced to become beggars, prostitutes, or to sell their children as slaves, and many women and girls committed suicide (Bearak, 2001a, b; Pollitt, 2001). Although some under-ground schools existed for girls, a generation of young girls in Afghanistan has witnessed brutal atrocities and missed out on an education. The Revolutionary Associa-tion of the Women of Afghanistan (RAWA), established in 1977, continues to fight for the human rights of Af-ghani women and girls. Although women have human rights and can now vote under the new Afghanistan gov-ernment, the Taliban left behind many oppressive ideol-ogies including women are property that can be bought and sold (Jones, 2004; Moreau & Yousafzai, 2004).

Theories Regarding the Acquisition of Gender Identity

Social and behavioral scientists have proposed a number of theories regarding the process by which children psy-chologically become masculine or feminine. Among these theories are the psychoanalytic, psychosocial, cognitive learning, and cognitive developmental approaches.

Psychoanalytic Theory   According to Sigmund Freud, children are psychologically bisexual at birth. They de-velop their gender roles as they resolve their conflicting feelings of love and jealousy in relation to their parents. A young boy develops a strong love attraction for his mother but fears that his father will punish him by cutting off his penis. The usual outcome of this Oedipal situation is for a boy to repress his erotic desire for his mother and identify defensively with the potential aggressor, his father. As a consequence of coming to feel identified with their fathers, boys later erotically seek out females. Meanwhile, Freud said, young girls fall in love with their fathers. A girl blames her mother for her lack of a penis. But she soon comes to realize that she cannot replace her mother in her father's affections. So, most girls resolve their Electra conflicts by identifying with their mothers and later by finding suitable men to love. These complexes are normally resolved by age 5 or 6. Though Freud's theory about gender identity remains controversial, it is common to hear a 4- or 5-year-old child proclaim, "When I'm older, I'm going to marry Daddy (or Mommy)."

Psychosocial Theory Having accepted Freud's psychoanalytic theory of gender identity, Erikson shows how certain gender traits might be assimilated by social interaction. Erikson says that during the ages of 3 to 6, children strive exuberantly to do things and to test developing abilities. Erikson calls this the *locomotor psychosocial stage,* during which time the child attempts to resolve the conflict of **initiative versus guilt** by gaining more independence. Children at this age will attempt to model their behavior after the adults and siblings in their environment. If Daddy is setting the table, then little Jimmy or Jill will want to help. If Daddy approves and lets them help, with supervision, then Erikson would say they are experiencing initiative. If, on the other hand, Jimmy and Jill decide they want to turn on the microwave, they might be scolded that they are too little yet, and they might experience a sense of guilt or inhibition. Erikson would say that there is a balance in this process of always wanting to learn and do and being told "No, you are too little" or "You can't, only grown-ups do this."

Children who learn how to regulate these opposing drives are developing what Erikson called the "virtue of purpose" (Erikson, 1982). Children might begin to say of themselves "I am good" or "I am bad" at this age, depending on the level of encouragement or discouragement they get from their parents and caretakers.

Preschool and kindergarten teachers were asked in a study to describe the behaviors of children with high self-esteem and low self-esteem (Haltiwanger & Harter, 1988). A finding from this study shows that children with high self-esteem are motivated to achieve. In contrast, some children exhibited a "helpless" behavior pattern: They did not attempt new tasks because they anticipated not succeeding, thus they simply did not try. Erikson described this as *inhibitory behavior.* When role-playing with dolls, the children with the "helpless" behavior pattern tended to scold the doll for failure and tell the doll it was "bad" (Burhaus & Dweck, 1995). Children at this age tend to talk with their play things and typically repeat what they themselves have been told.

Cognitive Learning Theory Cognitive learning theorists take the view that children are essentially neutral

at birth and that the biological differences between girls and boys are insufficient to account for later differences in gender identities. They stress the parts that *selective reinforcement* and *imitation* play in the process of acquiring a gender identity. Viewed from this perspective, children reared in a nuclear family setting are rewarded for modeling the behavior of the same-sex parent.

And the larger society later reinforces this type of imitation through systematic rewards and punishments. Boys and girls are actively rewarded and praised, both by adults and by their peers, for what society perceives to be sex-appropriate behavior, and they are ridiculed and punished for behavior inappropriate to their sex (Smetana, 1986). Currently popular among some social and behavioral scientists is the "separate cultures" concept that children learn rules for social interaction from experience in largely sex-segregated peer groups in childhood and then carry this learning into their adult interactions (Maccoby, 1990).

Albert Bandura (1973; Bussey & Bandura, 1984, 1992) gives an additional dimension to cognitive learning theory. He points out that in addition to imitating the behavior of adults, children engage in *observational learning.* According to Bandura, children mentally encode a model's behavior as they watch it, but they will not imitate behavior they have observed unless they believe that it will have a positive outcome for them. He says that children discern which behaviors are appropriate for each sex by watching the behavior of many male and female models. In turn, they employ these abstractions of sex-appropriate behavior as "models" for their own imitative actions.

But not everything learned is performed. Thus, although boys might know how to wear a dress and apply makeup, few boys choose to perform these behaviors. Rather, they are most likely to perform those behaviors that they have coded as appropriate to their own sex. Consequently, the responses children select from their behavioral repertoires depend chiefly on the consequences they anticipate will follow from the behaviors (Bussey & Bandura, 1992).

Cognitive Developmental Theory Still another approach, which is identified with Lawrence Kohlberg (1966; Kohlberg & Ullian, 1974), focuses on the part that cognitive development plays in children's acquisition of gender identities. This theory claims that children first learn to label themselves as "male" or "female" and then attempt to acquire and master the behaviors that fit their gender category. This process is called *self-socialization.* According to Kohlberg, children form stereotyped conceptions of maleness and femaleness—fixed, exaggerated, cartoonlike images—that they use to organize their environment. They select and cultivate behaviors consistent with their gender concepts.

Kohlberg distinguishes between his approach and cognitive learning theory in these terms. According to the cognitive learning model, the following sequence occurs: "I want rewards; I am rewarded for doing boy things; therefore I want to be a boy." In contrast, Kohlberg (1966, p. 89) believes that the sequence goes like this: "I am a boy; therefore I want to do boy things; therefore the opportunity to do boy things (and to gain approval for doing them) is rewarding."

Genital anatomy plays a relatively minor part in young children's thinking about sex differences. Instead, children notice and stereotype a relatively limited set of highly visible traits—hairstyle, clothes, stature, and occupation. Children use *gender schemes* or *models* to actively structure their experiences and to draw inferences and interpretations regarding gender behaviors (Bem, 1993). Viewed in this manner, children develop a rudimentary understanding of gender (*self-labeling*) and in turn invoke gender schemes to process information. These schemes begin developing rather early in life (Poulin-Dubois et al., 1994).

When given a choice of toys, boys more often play with "boy" toys and girls more often play with "girl" toys (Lobel & Menashri, 1993). Apparently, by the time they are 3 years of age, 80 percent of U.S. children are aware of gender differences and can categorize tasks like driving a truck or delivering mail as "masculine" and cooking, cleaning, and sewing as "feminine" tasks (Fagot, Leinbach, & Hagan, 1986). Significantly, children tend to "forget" or distort information that runs counter to their developing gender schemes (Bauer, 1993).

Evaluation of Theories   The theories considered here stress the importance of children's knowledge about **gender stereotypes** (exaggerated generalizations about male or female behaviors) as powerful determinants of sex-typed behavior. Each emphasizes that behavioral differences between the sexes are at least in part perpetuated by the fact that children are more inclined to imitate the behavior of same-sex models than they are to imitate the behavior of opposite-sex models.

Each of the theories has some merit (Jacklin & Reynolds, 1993). Psychoanalytic theory has had historical importance in directing our attention to the significant part that early experience plays in fashioning an individual's gender identity and behavior. Erikson let us know that young children naturally exhibit a drive to act on their world with exuberance (with a purpose), and the word *no* doesn't have to be the only word young children hear if parents and caretakers are willing to supervise them patiently.

Cognitive learning theory has contributed to our knowledge by highlighting the social and cultural components of gender-role development and the importance of imitation in the acquisition of gender behaviors

(Fagot, Leinbach, & Hagan, 1986). And cognitive developmental theory has shown how a gender scheme, or mental model, leads youngsters to sort incoming information on the basis of gender categories and then to adopt the gender-linked characteristics (Bigler & Liben, 1992). So rather than counterposing these theories in an either/or fashion, many psychologists prefer to see them as supplementing and complementing one another.

Mothers, Fathers, and Gender Typing

Social and behavioral scientists suggest that gender stereotypes arise in response to a society's division of labor by sex and serve to rationalize this division by attributing to males and females basic personality differences (Gilmore, 1990). It is hardly surprising, then, that parents typically have clear stereotypes regarding the behaviors they expect from female and male children (Jacobs & Eccles, 1992). Daughters, more often than sons, are described by both their mothers and fathers as "little," "beautiful," "pretty," and "cute." In turn, parents with more traditional gender schemas tend to have children who hold gender-typed views about themselves and others (Tenenbaum & Leaper, 2002).

Furthermore, there are marked and relatively consistent differences in paternal and maternal reactions to female and male infants (Parke, 1995). Fathers are more likely than mothers to describe their sons as "firm," "large-featured," "well-coordinated," "alert," "strong," and "hard." And they are more likely than mothers to describe their daughters as "soft," "fine-featured," "awkward," "inattentive," "weak," and "delicate" (Rubin, Provenzano, & Luria, 1974).

Evidence suggests that in U.S. society, the father plays the critical role in encouraging "femininity" in females and "masculinity" in males in traditional terms (Weinraub et al., 1984). And fathers treat their sons differently from daughters (Lytton & Romney, 1991). Both fathers and mothers are more eager to push their sons toward masculinity than to push their daughters toward femininity. Parents generally express more negative reactions when boys make choices culturally defined as feminine, than when girls make choices culturally defined as masculine (Lewis & Lamb, 2003). Additionally, fathers' fears of homosexuality, in themselves or in their sons, lead many men to inhibit displays of love and tenderness toward their sons (Parke, 1995).

Over the past 40 or so years, the following theory has dominated psychological inquiry and thinking regarding masculinity: Boys learn to be masculine by identifying with their own fathers. Mentally healthy men have a good, firm sense of themselves as masculine beings (Gilmore, 1990). However, because more fathers are now frequently absent from U.S. homes during their children's formative years, larger numbers of boys are

Gender Awareness Mothers and fathers typically react to male and female children in distinct and consistent ways. In American society boys are likely to be described as "big," "strong," and "well coordinated," whereas a girl is likely to be described as "beautiful," "delicate," or "cute." How would you describe this young girl? Children are prepared for their society's gender role from birth and are typically aware by age 4 that their gender does not change.

growing into manhood lacking a secure sense of their masculinity. The opposing view that boys can learn to be masculine through socialization and interaction with other male models, without identifying with their fathers, is being questioned in face of current statistics about the increasing numbers of American children with behavior problems with nonresident or absentee fathers (Lewis & Lamb, 2003).

As mentioned earlier, though, it is difficult to avoid the many confounding effects of poverty when conducting this type of research on families and parenting. These factors cover a broad range of dimensions and reveal that the absence of fathers has far-reaching physical, cognitive, and emotional consequences for individual children as well as society.

Questions

Which biological and sociocultural factors play a role in a child's gender identity? What are the major theoretical views of children's acquisition of gender identity?

Family Influences

Children are newcomers to the human group, strangers in an alien land. Genes do not convey *culture,* the socially standardized lifeways of a people. Clyde Kluckhohn (1960, pp. 21–22), a distinguished anthropologist, provides an illustration of this point:

> Some years ago I met in New York City a young man who did not speak a word of English and was obviously bewildered by American ways. By "blood" he was as American as you or I, for his parents had gone from Indiana to China as missionaries. Orphaned in infancy, he was reared by a Chinese family in a remote village. All who met him found him more Chinese than American. The facts of his blue eyes and light hair were less impressive than a Chinese style of gait, Chinese arm and hand movements, Chinese facial expression, and Chinese modes of thought. The biological heritage was American, but the cultural training had been Chinese. He returned to China.

Families Convey Cultural Standards

The process of transmitting culture, of transforming children into bona fide, functioning members of society, is called **socialization,** through which children acquire the knowledge, skills, and dispositions that enable them to participate effectively in group life. Infants enter a society that is already an ongoing concern, and they need to be fitted to their people's unique social environment. They must come to guide their behavior by the established standards, the accepted dos and don'ts, of their society. Within the family setting, the child is first introduced to the requirements of group life. By the time a child reaches the age of 2, the socialization process has already begun. Developmental psychologists David P. Ausubel and Edmund V. Sullivan (1970, p. 260) observe:

> At this time parents become less deferential and attentive. They comfort the child less and demand more conformity to their own desires and to cultural norms. During this period [in most societies] the child is frequently weaned, is expected to acquire sphincter control, approved habits of eating and cleanliness, and do more things for himself. Parents are less disposed to gratify his demands for immediate gratification, expect more frustration, tolerance, and responsible behavior, and may even require performance of some household chores. They also become less tolerant toward displays of childish aggression.

By their fourth birthday most children have mastered the complicated and abstract structure of their native language, and they can carry on complex social interactions in accordance with their own cultural patterns. At the same time, children are being born into a greater diversity of family environments than ever before in U.S. history. Jay Belsky (1981, 1984, 1990; Belsky & Barends, 2002) studies family sociology and proposes that within the cultural and historical context, the family is a network of interacting individuals functioning as a system, such that a minimum of three dyadic units are interacting: mother-father, mother-child, and father-child. Also, other influences are affecting the family system, including cultural norms, quality of marital relations, parental employment (dual-earner vs. single-earner), division of labor among family members, parenting practices, and infant-child/behavior development.

Cultural Trends Affecting Families

Many researchers are studying how children are being affected by the shifting trends in marriage, divorce, non-marital childbearing, living arrangements such as cohabitation, migration, education, work, income, and poverty (Hetherington & Stanley-Hagan, 2002; Lansford et al., 2001; Wallman, 1998). The trend of increased poverty has critical far-reaching ill effects on the physical, cognitive, social, and emotional well-being of children, as we saw in Chapter 6. These current trends are related to six major demographic transformations over the past 100 years (Hernandez, 1997; Schneider, 1993): (1) the shift from farm to industrial to service work for fathers, (2) a large reduction in family size, (3) greater educational attainment for men and women, (4) women's participation in the labor force, (5) the increase in single-parent families and nonresidential or absentee fathers, and (6) the subsequent rise in childhood poverty.

In addition to these trends, the ethnic diversity of American families and children will continue to increase, with the proportion of Hispanic American children increasing rapidly. It is projected by 2020 that about 53 percent of U.S. children will be non-Hispanic white (see Figure 8.1). These major trends have critical implications for child development in American society today.

Thirty years of research has found troubling evidence that the effect of divorce on kids is more adverse and longer-lasting than parents may realize. According to the Centers for Disease Control and Prevention (CDC) (2003), more than one-fourth of never-married, single mothers are teenagers. Many of their children are born into poverty. Nearly one out of every three children lived with a single parent in 2003. Nearly two-thirds of children go home from school to an empty house, because their parent or parents are at work. What is happening to our children is of concern to us all,

whether or not we are parents. Today's children will bear the responsibility for the next generation of children and a growing population of dependent adults. This state of affairs leads us to take a closer look at the significant role of family influences and parenting.

Determinants of Parenting

Until relatively recently, most socialization research focused on the processes whereby parental child-rearing strategies and behaviors shape and influence children's development. For the most part, psychologists and psychiatrists paid little attention to the parents themselves and the context in which they carried on their parenting. Also neglected was the part children play as active agents in their own socialization and in influencing their caretakers' behavior.

This focus has changed over the past two decades, resulting in a more balanced perspective (Lerner et al., 1995; Lewis & Lamb, 2003; Maccoby, 1992). Jay Belsky (1984) has provided a framework that differentiates among three major determinants of parental functioning: (1) the parents' personality and psychological well-being, (2) the child's characteristics, and (3) the contextual sources of stress and support operating within and upon the family.

The Parents' Characteristics Parenting, like other aspects of human functioning, is influenced by the relatively enduring characteristics, or personality, of a man or woman (Belsky, 1981, 1990). So, as you might expect, troubled parents are more likely to have troubled children (Dix, 1991; Emig, Moore, & Scarupa, 2001). A six-year study of 693 families found that 66 percent of children with emotionally troubled mothers had psychological problems; 47 percent had problems in families where only the father had symptoms; and 72 percent had problems when both parents were disturbed (this was double the rate for children with two healthy parents) (Parker, 1987).

Other researchers find that parental discord or stress can have an adverse effect on children (Crnic & Low, 2002; Lewis & Lamb, 2003). Many studies find that children of depressed mothers suffer adverse effects in childhood and call for effective prevention and intervention strategies to lessen adverse developmental effects in children (Essex et al., 2001). In contrast, children whose parents are happily married have more secure emotional ties to their parents and, as a result, seem to enjoy intellectual and other advantages over children of unhappily married people (Lewis & Lamb, 2003; Wilson & Gottman, 2002). Findings from a recent study investigating family structure and child well-being indicate mothers in two-parent biological families report their children had fewer behavioral problems, and fathers in two-parent

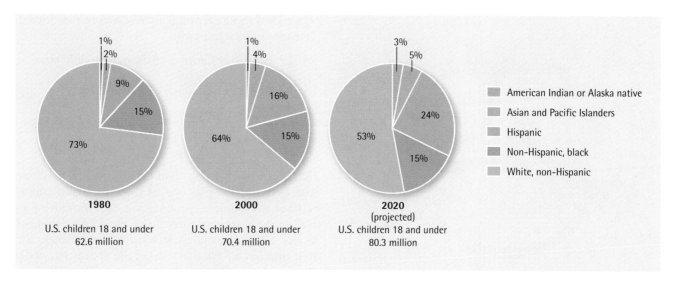

FIGURE 8.1 **Actual and Projected Population and Ethnic Diversity of Children in the United States: 1980–2020** The number of children determines the demand for schools, health care, and other services and facilities that serve children and their families. In 2000, there were more than 70 million children 18 and under in the United States. By 2020, it is projected there will be over 80 million children. Presently, each age group (0 to 5, 6 to 11, and 12 to 17) contains an equal number, about 23 to 25 million children. The proportion of Hispanic American children is increasing rapidly, as the proportion of white non-Hispanic children is decreasing.
Source: Federal Interagency Forum on Child and Family Statistics. (2002, 2003, 2004). *America's Children: Key National Indicators and Well-Being,* U.S. Bureau of the Census, ChildStats.gov.

biological families report spending more time with their children and having higher family cohesion than all other types of family structures (Lansford et al., 2001). Overall, though, these researchers suggest that it is the processes within families that are important determinants of well-being, regardless of family structure (Lewis & Lamb, 2003).

The Child's Characteristics   Children's characteristics influence the parenting they receive (see Figure 8.2) (Sanson & Rothbart, 1995). These characteristics include such variables as age (Fagot & Kavanagh, 1993), gender (Kerig, Cowan, & Cowan, 1993), and temperament (for instance, aggressiveness, passivity, affection, moodiness, and negativity) (Sanson & Rothbart, 1995). And some children are simply more difficult to rear than others (Rubin, Stewart, & Chen, 1995).

Anderson, Lytton, and Romney (1986) observed 32 mothers as they talked to and played with three different boys, ages 6 to 11. Half the mothers had wayward sons who had been referred to a mental health facility and diagnosed with serious behavior problems; the other half were mothers of sons without serious behavior problems. The researchers counted the mothers' positive and negative interactions and the boys' compliance with the mothers in the course of the play sessions. The mothers of the difficult and nondifficult youngsters did not differ in their behavior. The difficult boys were far less compliant than the other boys, regardless of how the mothers behaved or related to them. Overall, evidence suggests

that parents and other adults typically react to disobedient, negative, and highly active youngsters with negative, controlling behavior of their own (Belsky, 1990; Lewis & Lamb, 2003).

Sources of Stress and Support   Parents do not undertake their parenting in a social vacuum. They are immersed in networks of relationships with friends and relatives, and most are employed. These arenas of social interaction can be sources of stress or support, or both. For instance, difficulties at work commonly spill over to the home; arguments at work are likely to be followed by disagreements between a husband and wife (Menaghan & Parcel, 1990). Yet social support, throughout life, has a beneficial effect on each of us irrespective of whether we are under stress (Hashima & Amato, 1994). When we are integrated in social networks and groups, we have access to positive experiences and a set of stable, socially rewarding roles in the community (Cochran & Niego, 1995). See the *More Information You Can Use* box on page 283, "Easing the Transition to Kindergarten."

Not surprisingly, then, research undertaken among Japanese and U.S. mothers shows that the adequacy of a woman's mothering is influenced by the perception she has of her marital relationship (see Figure 8.2). When a woman feels she has her husband's support, she is more likely to involve herself with her infant (Lewis & Lamb, 2003; Wilson & Gottman, 1995). Likewise, researchers find that parents with little social support do a poorer job of parenting than do parents who are integrated in well-

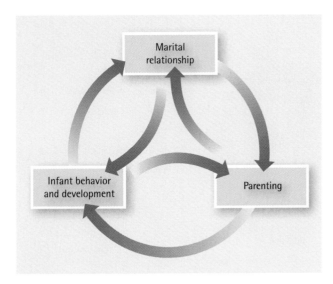

FIGURE 8.2 A Scheme for Integrating the Disciplines of Family Sociology and Developmental Psychology During the infancy years Belsky (1981) proposed an organizational scheme showing the family as a network of interacting individuals functioning as a system—highlighting the possible interrelated influences that marital relations, parenting, and infant/child behavior/development may have on each member of the system. Thus, positive affect (smiling, affection) between the wife and husband influences positive affect toward the infant/child. And negative affect between wife and husband (hostility, verbal criticism) results in negative affect toward the infant/child. Likewise, parenting a child with an "inflexible-explosive" personality, or one with a severe disability, has a major impact on the marital relationship.
From J. Belsky, "Early human experience: A family perspective," *Developmental Psychology*, Vol. 17 (1981), p. 6. Copyright © 1981 by the American Psychological Association. Reprinted with permission of the publisher and the author.

functioning support systems. So let us turn our attention now to the suitability of various parenting practices.

Key Child-Rearing Practices

Most authorities agree that parenting is one of the most rewarding yet difficult tasks any adult faces. Moreover, most parents are well intentioned and desire to succeed at parenting. Because this complex task encompasses many years and consumes much energy, parents have often looked to pediatricians or experts in child psychology to provide them with guidelines for rearing mentally and physically healthy youngsters (Bornstein, 1995). But parents who turn to "authorities" can become immensely frustrated, for they will be confronted with an endless array of child-rearing books, conflicting information, and gimmickry (Young, 1990).

As we have already noted, until relatively recently psychologists assumed that socialization effects flow essentially in one direction—from parent to child. For some 50 years, roughly from 1925 to 1975, they dedicated themselves to the task of uncovering the part that different parenting practices have in shaping a child's

personality and behavior. This research found three dimensions to be significant:

- the *warmth or hostility* of the parent-child relationship
- the *control or autonomy* of the disciplinary approach
- the *consistency or inconsistency* that parents show in using discipline

The Warmth-Hostility Dimension Many psychologists have insisted that one of the most significant aspects of the home environment is the warmth of the relationship between parent and child (Kochanska & Aksan, 1995). Parents show warmth toward their children through affectionate, accepting, approving, understanding, and child-centered behaviors. When disciplining their children, parents who are warm tend to employ frequent explanations, use words of encouragement and praise, and only infrequently resort to physical punishment. Hostility, in contrast, is shown through cold, rejecting, disapproving, self-centered, and highly punitive behaviors (Becker, 1964; Blackson et al., 1999). Wesley C. Becker (1964), in a review of the research on parenting, found that love-oriented techniques tend to promote children's acceptance of responsibility and to foster self-control through inner mechanisms of guilt. In contrast, parental hostility interferes with conscience development and breeds aggressiveness and resistance to authority.

Parents who are substance abusers have a history of aggression, marital conflict, and negative interactions that correlate with behavioral maladjustment in children, especially for boys (Blackson et al., 1999). Additionally, children surviving in such dysfunctional home environments suffer through incidents of physical abuse, neglect, and repeated removal from the home by child protective services (Famularo, Kinscherff, & Fenton, 1992). Blackson and colleagues (1999) are conducting a longitudinal study with young boys until age 30 to examine the long-term impact of family environment, temperamental traits among family members, and the quality of parent-child relationships that escalate boys' behavior problems (conduct disorders and substance abuse).

The Control-Autonomy Dimension The second critical dimension is the range of restrictions that parents place on a child's behavior in such areas as sex play, modesty, table manners, toilet training, neatness, orderliness, care of household furniture, noise, obedience, and aggression toward others (Becker, 1964; Sears, Maccoby, & Levin, 1957). On the whole, psychologists have suggested that highly *restrictive* parenting fosters dependency and interferes with independence training (Bronstein, 1992; Maccoby & Masters, 1970). However, as Becker (1964, p. 197) observes in his review of the research literature,

More Information You Can Use

Easing the Transition to Kindergarten

One of the most significant life-changing experiences for an American family is when their child enters kindergarten, typically mandated by age 5 (or age 6 depending on birth date). Although it is estimated that more than 80 percent of children have had various preschool experiences, kindergarten poses higher academic expectations of children, while direct parent involvement typically decreases. The *Harvard Family Research Project* recently completed a review of current research on the transition to kindergarten, focusing on effective programs and policies that recognize the crucial role that families play in this transition process (Bohan-Baker & Little, 2004).

Often the concept of transition has been tied to the child's readiness skills and abilities. Generally, most schools set up a one-time set of activities at the end of a school year or during the summer before starting kindergarten. School districts typically use developmental checklists for 4- to 6- year-olds and "test" each child to determine "readiness," but early childhood professionals now recommend a transition to kindergarten that includes a broader range of support services from communities, the school districts, teachers, and families (see Figure 8.3). Transition research suggests that school districts need to (1) reach out and link with families and preschools and engage in two-way communication, (2) establish sustained links with families and children prior to the first day of school, and (3) designate a transition coordinator to reach out to create home-school

connections (e.g., news releases, phone calls and letters, and personal contacts or home visits with each child). Once the child enters kindergarten, the door to family communication must remain open and be encouraged (Bohan-Baker & Little, 2004).

Sharon and Craig Ramey (1999) examined many studies that identified characteristics common to children who succeed at school and found that significant adults in a child's life can promote the following 10 characteristics:

Ten Characteristics of Children Who Succeed in School
They love to learn.
They ask questions and they ask for help.
They work hard and know their efforts matter.
They are well-developed socially and emotionally.
They are good at assessing their skills.
Their parents are role models for learning.
They have important adults in their lives who promote learning by "natural" teaching at home.
Their family routines support doing well in school.
Their parents are effective at setting and maintaining limits.
Their schools have high expectations for student achievement, support professional staff development, and communicate frequently with parents.

Source: Bohan-Baker, M. & Little, P. M. D. (2004, April). *The transition to kindergarten: A review of current research and promising practices to involve families.* The Harvard Family Research Project. Retrieved March 5, 2005, from http://www.gse.harvard.edu/~ hfrp/pubs.html

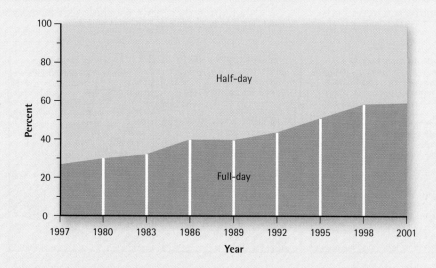

FIGURE 8.3 Trends in Kindergarten Enrollment Among 4- to 6-Year-Olds: 1977–2001 By 2001, with more mothers entering the labor force, 60 percent of U.S. kindergartners attended full-day programs in contrast to 1977, when nearly three-fourths attended only half-day programs. Such full-day enrollment has significant implications for young children, their families, and the availability of educators and community resources to provide for quality education and child care. *Source:* National Center for Education Statistics (NCES). (2004, June). *The Condition of Education 2004 in Brief.* U.S. Department of Education and Institute of Education Sciences. NCES 2004–076.

psychologists have had difficulty coming up with a "perfect" all-purpose set of parental guidelines:

> The consensus of the research suggests that both restrictiveness and permissiveness entail certain risks. Restrictiveness, while fostering well-controlled, socialized behavior, tends also to lead to fearful, dependent, and submissive behaviors, a dulling of intellectual striving and inhibited hostility. Permissiveness on the other hand, while fostering outgoing, sociable, assertive behaviors and intellectual striving, tends also to lead to less persistence and increased aggressiveness.

Combinations of Parenting Approaches   Rather than examine the warmth-hostility and control-autonomy dimensions in isolation from one another, a number of psychologists have explored their four combinations: warmth-control, warmth-autonomy, hostility-control, and hostility-autonomy (Becker, 1964).

Warm but Restrictive Parenting   *Warm but restrictive parenting* is believed to lead to politeness, neatness, obedience, and conformity. It also is thought to be associated with immaturity, dependency, low creativity, blind acceptance of authority, and social withdrawal and ineptness (Becker, 1964; Levy, 1943). Eleanor E. Maccoby (1961) found that 12-year-old boys who had been reared in warm but restrictive homes were strict rule enforcers with their peers. Compared with other children, these boys also displayed less overt aggression, less misbehavior, and greater motivation toward schoolwork.

Warm with Democratic Procedures   Psychologists report that children whose homes combine *warmth with democratic procedures* (autonomy) tend to develop into socially competent, resourceful, friendly, active, and ap-

propriately aggressive individuals (Kagan & Moss, 1962; Lavoie & Looft, 1973). Where parents also encourage self-confidence, independence, and mastery in social and academic situations, the children are likely to show self-reliant, creative, goal-oriented, and responsible behavior. Where parents fail to foster independence, permissiveness often produces self-indulgent children with little impulse control and low academic standards.

Hostile (Rejecting) and Restrictive Parenting   *Hostile (rejecting) and restrictive parenting* is believed to interfere with the child's developing sense of identity and self-esteem. Children come to see the world as dominated by powerful, malignant forces over which they have no control. The combination of hostility and restrictiveness is said to foster resentment and inner rage. These children turn some of the anger against themselves or experience it as internalized turmoil and conflict. This can result in "neurotic problems," self-punishing and suicidal tendencies, depressed affect, and inadequacy in adult role playing (Whitbeck et al., 1992).

Hostile and Permissive Parenting   Parenting that combines *hostility with permissiveness* is thought to be associated with delinquent and aggressive behavior in children. Rejection breeds resentment and hostility, which, when combined with inadequate parental control, can be translated into aggressive and antisocial actions. When such parents do employ discipline, it is usually physical, capricious, and severe. It often reflects parental rage and rejection and hence fails as a constructive instrument for developing appropriate standards of conduct (Becker, 1964).

Discipline   Consistency in discipline is the third dimension of parenting that many psychologists have stressed

Parenting is One of the Most Rewarding but Difficult Tasks Any Adult Faces   Increasingly psychologists are reaching the conclusion that how parents feel about their children makes a greater difference than the specific child-rearing techniques they employ. Parenting is not a matter of magical formulas but one of enjoying children, loving them, and providing guidance and age-appropriate discipline.

Source: For Better or For Worse © 1997 Lynn Johnston Productions. Dist. By Universal Press Syndicate. Reprinted with permission. All rights reserved.

is central to a child's home environment. Effective discipline is consistent and unambiguous. It builds a high degree of predictability into the child's environment. Although it is often difficult to be consistent in how one punishes a child, research by Parke and Deur (1972) reveals that erratic punishment generally fails to inhibit the punished behavior.

In the case of aggression, researchers have found that the most aggressive children have parents who are permissive toward aggression on some occasions but severely punish it on others (Sears, Maccoby, & Levin, 1957). Research suggests that parents who use punishment inconsistently actually create in their children a resistance to future attempts to extinguish the undesirable behavior (Parke, 1974).

Inconsistency can occur when the same parent responds differently at different times to the same behavior. It can also occur when one parent ignores or encourages a behavior that the other parent punishes (Belsky, Crnic, & Gable, 1995; Vaughn, Block, & Block, 1988). On the basis of his observation of family interaction patterns in the homes of 136 middle-class preschool boys, Hugh Lytton (1979) found that mothers typically initiate more actions designed to control their sons' behavior than fathers do. However, the boys were less inclined to obey their mothers than they were their fathers. But when their fathers were present, they were more likely to be responsive to their mothers' commands and prohibitions. Single mothers often experience difficulties disciplining sons.

Child Abuse

Many people have difficulty defining exactly where the line falls between legitimate effective discipline and child abuse. Most Americans define child abuse and neglect as leaving young children home alone, living in a filthy home and lacking food, and hitting a child hard enough to cause bruises. However, many are ambivalent about spanking. Although there are many antispanking and pro-spanking advocates who feel very strongly about this issue, according to a recent survey by Yankelovich (2000), a majority of U.S. adults regard spanking as appropriate as a regular form of punishment.

Psychologists Baumrind and Owens reported controversial findings at the 2001 APA Convention on their longitudinal study revealing that occasional mild spanking does not harm a child's social and emotional development. Their study participants were 168 white, middle-class families assessed from 1968, when their children were preschoolers, to 1980 when the children were age 14. Baumrind and Owens define *spanking* as "striking the child on the buttocks or extremities with an open hand without inflicting physical injury with the intention to modify behavior," but they person-

ally do not advocate spanking (Baumrind & Owens, 2001, p.1).

They, like all social scientists, are in agreement that no parent should use physical punishment abusively, but Baumrind's study failed to find any adverse causal outcomes of "low frequency" spanking by age 14. This study has two limitations: a small sample of predominantly middle-class European American families residing in a liberal community and the possibility that adverse outcomes might emerge in adults who experience "low frequency" spanking in childhood. Yet, recent evidence indicates that undesirable child outcomes are associated with spanking and corporal (harsh) punishment, including higher levels of overall aggression, lower levels of moral internalization, and mental health problems (Baumrind, Larzelere, & Cowan, 2002; Gershoff, 2002; Straus, 2001).

Being poor and being an unmarried mother seemingly increase the likelihood of spanking. Parents who are under stress are more likely to use more severe punishment—and infants and children *under the age of 5* are the most likely of all to be killed by such punishment (Peddle & Wang, 2001).

Child Abuse and Neglect In 2002 an estimated 896,000 American children were reported as victims of child abuse or neglect. The majority of victims experienced neglect, followed by physical abuse, sexual abuse, and emotional abuse with the remainder experiencing unspecified types of abuse (e.g., exploitation, abduction). The highest victimization rates were for the youngest age group (birth to age 3) (see Figure 8.4). An estimated 1,400 American children died from abuse and neglect in 2002. Yet researchers believe that many cases of child abuse and neglect go unreported (Crume et al., 2002; National Clearinghouse on Child Abuse and Neglect Information, 2003). Female parents were the perpetrators of neglect and physical abuse for the highest percentage of child victims. Male parents were identified as the perpetrators of sexual abuse for the highest percentage of victims (Peddle & Wang, 2001).

Sexual Abuse of Children Sexual abuse of children is sexual behavior between a child and an older person that the older person brings about through force, coercion, or deceit (Gelles & Conte, 1990). Sexual abusers of children can be a parent, stepparent, sibling, other relative, trusted friend, neighbor, child-care worker, teacher, coach, or anyone who has access to the child. Males are reported to be the abusers in 80 to 95 percent of cases, with a dramatic increase in adolescent offenders (National Committee to Prevent Child Abuse [NCPCA], 1996a). A national survey found that girls reported being sexually abused three times more often than boys (NCPCA, 1996a), and most research has dealt with the

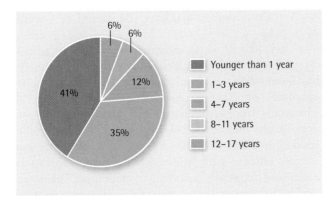

FIGURE 8.4 U.S. Child Abuse and Neglect Fatalities by Age: 2002 Children younger than 4 years of age accounted for 76 percent of all child fatalities in 2002—and most occurred because of neglect. Fatality results from repeated abuse over time (e.g., battered child syndrome), or it may occur because of a single, impulsive incident (e.g., drowning, suffocating, or shaking a baby). Generally a fatality results from a caregiver's failure to act. In 2002 one or both parents were involved in most child abuse or neglect fatalities, followed by nonparent caregivers. Child fatalities represent a small percentage of children experiencing child abuse.
Source: National Clearinghouse on Child Abuse and Neglect Information. (2004). *Child abuse and neglect fatalities: Statistics and interventions.* Washington, DC: U.S. Department of Health and Human Services.

sexual abuse of females. Researchers at the national level cautiously report a 40 percent decline in substantiated child sexual abuse cases over the past decade, partially due to a change in reporting practices, a more conservative approach to identification of abuse, more prevention/awareness programs, and more criminal convictions (Finkelhor & Jones, 2004).

Most of us find the idea that parents use their children (of any age) for sexual gratification so offensive that we prefer not to think about it. In 1974, the federal government adopted a more direct role in child-abuse policies with passage of the *Child Abuse Prevention and Treatment Act* (PL 93-247), which established identification standards, reporting policies, and management policies for these maltreatment cases, while empowering individual states to investigate abuse and provide child protective services (CPS). Public Law 108-36 reauthorized this law (*New Child Abuse Prevention and Treatment Act*). There are many complex problems, issues, and costs to society that arise regarding sexually abused children and the legal system (Bull, 2004).

Sexual contact usually begins when the child is between 5 and 12 years old (though infant and toddler abuse are also reported), and it typically consists at first of fondling and masturbation. The behavior continues over time and might eventually proceed to intercourse or sodomy. One study of incest perpetrators found that almost all of them defined their incestuous impositions as love and care and their behavior as considerate and fair. However, their professed love, care, and sense of

fairness were contradicted in many ways, including their refusal to stop when youngsters wanted them to stop (Gilgun, 1995). Child molesters often disguise themselves as trusted, caring family members, neighbors, and responsible citizens. They spend a lot of time manipulating a family so they will not be suspected of abusing children—who experience confusion, guilt, shame, and fear of revealing the abuse. Thus, child sexual abuse is often unreported.

A review of studies on the effects of sexual abuse on children found greater instances of fears, post traumatic stress disorder, behavior problems, sexualized behaviors, and poor self-esteem among other disorders that afflict sexually abused children (Kendall-Tackett, Williams, & Finkelhor, 1993). Though children might be too young to know the sexual activity is "wrong," they will develop behavioral or physical problems resulting from the inability to cope with the overstimulation. Often there are no obvious physical signs of child abuse, only signs that a physician can detect, such as changes in the genital or anal area. Behavioral signs are likely to include:

- unusual interest in, or avoidance of, all things of a sexual nature
- sleep problems, nightmares, bedwetting
- depression or withdrawal from friends or family
- sexually inappropriate behaviors with others or knowledge beyond the child's years
- statements that their bodies are dirty or fear there is something wrong in the genital area
- refusal to go to school or delinquent behaviors
- aspects of sexual molestation in drawings, games, fantasies
- unusual aggressiveness, secretiveness, suicidal behaviors (even in a younger child), or other severe behavior changes

Sexually abused children are usually afraid to tell others about their experiences because the abuser will control/manipulate the child by saying such things as, "Mommy won't love you anymore" or "Mommy will make you go away if she finds out," or "No one will believe you anyway since you are a child." Wives of men who molest their children usually are passive, have a poor self-image, and are overly dependent on their husbands. They frequently suffer from mental illness, physical disability, or repeated pregnancy.

Although incest commonly involves the oldest daughter, the behavior is often repeated with younger daughters, one after another. Moreover, a father's incestuous behavior places his daughters at greater risk of sexual abuse by other male relatives and family friends. Occasionally in the media there is a report of a drug-addicted parent who prostitutes his or her own child to pay for a drug habit. Female victims tend to show lifetime patterns of psychological shame and stigmatization.

Little is known or written about male victims, since most studies do not differentiate between male and female victims. The available evidence suggests that boys and girls respond differently to sexual victimization. Male victims are less likely to report their abuse. Because boys are socialized to gain control of themselves and their environments, boys might feel their masculinity has been destroyed when they are sexually abused. Or they attempt to "minimize" the importance of the abusive events. Complicating matters, male victims often face the additional problem of stigmatization as homosexual, because the large majority of abusers are male (Bolton, Morris, & MacEachron, 1989).

Sexual abuse should always be reported to authorities, and law enforcement officers, child-care workers, teachers, and medical professionals are mandated to do so. Adults should never dismiss a child's complaint of physical abuse, neglect, or emotional or sexual abuse. All mental health, law enforcement, medical, and child protective services professionals involved in interviewing children suspected of having been abused must be trained in objective, appropriate interview techniques and become knowledgeable about prevention programs and intervention strategies.

Prevention Programs By the 1990s many prevention programs had been designed that employed multiple modes of audiovisual technology (film, video, audiotape, and filmstrip) and format (storybooks, coloring books, songs, plays, and board games). The materials and programs are based on a number of assumptions: Most children do not know what constitutes abusive parenting, children must not tolerate physical or sexual abuse, and children should inform responsible adults upon being sexually touched or physically harmed or neglected by a caretaker. Many nations have responded to the problem of child abuse and offer many perspectives to combat it (Gilbert, 1997).

Questions

What are some effective, healthy child-rearing practices? What are the most common forms of child abuse, and which children are most at risk for severe abuse? What are some behaviors exhibited by children who are victims of sexual abuse, and what can be done to protect them from harm?

Parenting Styles

Diana Baumrind (1971, 1972, 1980, 1996), a developmental psychologist, examines the relationship between parental child-rearing styles and social competence in children of preschool and school age. From 1968 through 1980, she conducted research for *The Family Socialization Project,* examining family socialization practices, parental attitudes, and factors of development at three crucial stages in a child's life: preschool, early childhood, and early adolescence. She included both parents and children from white, middle-class families in her sample and collected data through questionnaires, personal interviews, and videotaped observations of family interactions at home. In her studies of white middle-class nursery-school children, Baumrind (1971) found that different types of parenting tend to be related to quite different behaviors in children. Among other findings in this longitudinal study, she distinguishes among authoritarian, authoritative, permissive, and harmonious parenting.

Authoritarian Parenting The **authoritarian parenting** style attempts to shape, control, and evaluate a child's behavior in accordance with traditional and absolute values and standards of conduct. Obedience is stressed, verbal give-and-take is discouraged, and punitive, forceful discipline is preferred. More commonly, parents using this style of parenting are said to be operating from the *rejecting-demanding dimension.* The offspring of such authoritarian parents tended to be discontented, withdrawn, and distrustful (see Figure 8.5).

Authoritative Parenting The **authoritative parenting** style provides firm direction for a child's overall activities but gives the child considerable freedom within reasonable limits. Parental control is not rigid, punitive, intrusive, or unnecessarily restrictive. The parent provides reasons for given policies and engages in verbal give-and-take with the child, meanwhile responding to the child's wishes and needs. (It may help you to distinguish authorita*tive* from authoritarian by using the mnemonic device of *give*-and-take with authorita*tive.*) Authoritative parenting was often associated with self-reliant, self-controlled, explorative, and contented children. In later research Baumrind (1991, 1994, 1996) found that an authoritative parenting style is especially helpful when parenting adolescents.

Baumrind believes that authoritative parenting gives children a comfortable, supported feeling while they explore the environment and gain interpersonal competence. Such children do not experience the anxiety and fear associated with strict, repressive parenting or the indecision and uncertainty associated with unstructured, permissive parenting. Laurence Steinberg and colleagues (1989) also found that authoritative parenting facilitates school success, encouraging a healthy sense of autonomy and positive attitudes toward work. Adolescents whose parents treat them warmly, acceptingly, democratically, and firmly are more likely than their peers to develop

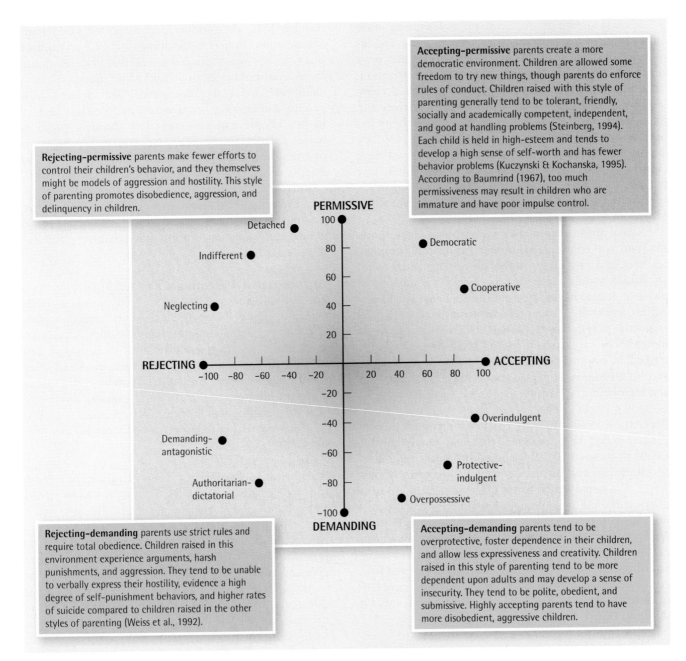

Rejecting-permissive parents make fewer efforts to control their children's behavior, and they themselves might be models of aggression and hostility. This style of parenting promotes disobedience, aggression, and delinquency in children.

Accepting-permissive parents create a more democratic environment. Children are allowed some freedom to try new things, though parents do enforce rules of conduct. Children raised with this style of parenting generally tend to be tolerant, friendly, socially and academically competent, independent, and good at handling problems (Steinberg, 1994). Each child is held in high-esteem and tends to develop a high sense of self-worth and has fewer behavior problems (Kuczynski & Kochanska, 1995). According to Baumrind (1967), too much permissiveness may result in children who are immature and have poor impulse control.

Rejecting-demanding parents use strict rules and require total obedience. Children raised in this environment experience arguments, harsh punishments, and aggression. They tend to be unable to verbally express their hostility, evidence a high degree of self-punishment behaviors, and higher rates of suicide compared to children raised in the other styles of parenting (Weiss et al., 1992).

Accepting-demanding parents tend to be overprotective, foster dependence in their children, and allow less expressiveness and creativity. Children raised in this style of parenting tend to be more dependent upon adults and may develop a sense of insecurity. They tend to be polite, obedient, and submissive. Highly accepting parents tend to have more disobedient, aggressive children.

FIGURE 8.5 Researchers Expand on the Interaction of Parenting Dimensions. Two parenting dimensions have been observed in all societies: the permissive-demanding dimension and the accepting-rejecting dimension (Rohner & Rohner, 1981). Some research findings indicate that parental choice of these dimensions—especially for the demanding style—may be influenced by the parent's genetic makeup; other findings suggest that the parent's own upbringing has a significant bearing on parental practices (Plomin, DeFries, & Fulker, 1988). Research studies also show that each parent is generally consistent in the chosen style of parenting.
Adapted from E.S. Schaefer, "A Circumplex Model for Maternal Behavior," *Journal of Abnormal and Social Psychology*, Vol. 59 (1959), p. 232; and M. L. Hoffman and L. W. Hoffman, *Review of Child Development Research*. Copyright © 1964 Russell Sage Foundation, 112 E. 64th Street, New York, NY 10021. Reprinted with permission.

positive beliefs about their achievement and so are likely to do better in school.

In addition, authoritative fathers and mothers seem more adept than other parents at "scaffolding." **Scaffolding** supports a child's learning through interventions and tutoring that provide helpful task information attuned to the child's current level of functioning (Pratt et al., 1988). On the basis of her research,

Baumrind (1991, 1994, 1996) found a number of parental practices and attitudes that seem to facilitate the development of socially responsible and independent behavior in children:

- Parents who are socially responsible and assertive, and who serve as daily models of these behaviors, foster these characteristics in their children.

- Parents should employ firm enforcement policies geared to reward socially responsible and independent behavior and to punish deviant behavior. This technique uses the reinforcement principles of conditioning. Parents can be even more effective if their demands are accompanied by explanations and if punishment is accompanied by reasons that are consistent with principles the parents themselves live by.
- Parents who are nonrejecting serve as more attractive models and reinforcing agents than rejecting parents do.
- Parents should emphasize and encourage individuality, self-expression, initiative, divergent thinking, and socially appropriate aggressiveness. These values are translated into daily realities as parents make demands upon their children and assign them responsibility.

Parents should provide their children with a complex and stimulating environment that offers challenge and excitement. At the same time, children should experience their environment as providing security and opportunities for rest and relaxation.

Permissive Parenting   The **permissive parenting** style provides a nonpunitive, accepting, and affirmative environment in which the children regulate their own behavior as much as possible. The children are consulted about family policies and decisions. The parents make few demands on the children for household responsibility or orderly behavior. The least self-reliant, explorative, and self-controlled children were those with permissive parents (see Figure 8.5).

Harmonious Parenting   The **harmonious parenting** style seldom exercises direct control over a child. These parents attempt to cultivate an egalitarian relationship, one in which the child is not placed at a power disadvantage. Parents typically emphasize humane values as opposed to the predominantly materialistic and achievement values they view as operating within mainstream society. The harmonious parents identified by Baumrind were only a small group. Of the eight children studied from such families, six were girls and two were boys. The girls were extraordinarily competent, independent, friendly, achievement-oriented, and intelligent. The boys, in contrast, were cooperative but notably submissive, aimless, dependent, and not achievement-oriented. Although the sample was too small to be the basis for definitive conclusions, Baumrind tentatively suggests that these outcomes of harmonious parenting might be sex-related.

Discussion: Control and Autonomy Revisited   Much research confirms Baumrind's findings and insights

(Steinberg et al., 1994). The ability to "achieve one's goals without violating the integrity of the goals of the other" is undoubtedly a major component in the development of social competence (W. Bronson, 1974, p. 280). Clearly, disciplinary encounters between parents and their youngsters provide a crucial context in which children learn strategies for controlling themselves and for controlling others, so parents who model competent strategies are more likely to have children who also are socially competent (Kuczynski & Kochanska, 1995).

By way of illustration, consider Erik Erikson's (1963) notion that how toddlers resolve the stage of *autonomy* versus *shame and doubt* is linked to parental overcontrol. One indication that 2-year-olds are coming to terms with autonomy issues is their ability and willingness to say "No!" to parents. The acquisition of *no* is a spectacular cognitive achievement because it accompanies youngsters' increasing awareness of the "other" and the "self" (Spitz, 1957). *Self-assertion, defiance,* and *compliance* are distinct dimensions of toddler behavior. For instance, if a mother tells her toddler to pick up her toys and place them in a box, and the child says, "No, want to play," the youngster would be asserting herself. If instead the toddler takes more toys from the box or heaves a toy across the room, she would be defying her mother. But if the child follows her mother's instructions, she would be complying.

Susan Crockenberg and Cindy Litman (1990) show that the way parents handle these autonomy issues has profound consequences for their youngsters' behavior. When parents assert their power in the form of *negative control*—threats, criticism, physical intervention, and anger—children are more likely to respond with defiance.

Youngsters are less likely to become defiant when a parent combines a directive with an additional attempt to guide the child's behavior in a desired direction. This latter approach provides the child with information about what the parent wants, while inviting power sharing. For instance, if the parent asks the child to do something ("Would you pick up your toys, please?") or attempts to persuade the child through reasoning ("You made a mess, so now you'll have to clean it up"), the parent implicitly validates for the child that she is a distinct and separate person with her own individual needs.

This approach is consistent with Baumrind's *authoritative* style of parenting and keeps the negotiation process going, allowing the toddler to "decide" to adopt the parent's goal. It seems that children are more willing to accept other people's attempts to influence their behavior if they perceive that they are participating in a reciprocal relationship where their attempts to influence others will also be honored (Kochanska & Aksan, 1995; Parpal & Maccoby, 1985).

Guidance alone seems less effective than guidance combined with control. An invitation to comply ("Could you pick up the toys now?") seems to afford the toddler a choice, and the child might feel free to turn it down in the absence of a clear and firm expression of parental wishes. This approach of guidance without control is consistent with Baumrind's *permissive* style of parenting and seems to be linked to less competent child behavior. When toddlers assert themselves and their parents follow with a power directive ("You better do what I say or I'll spank you!"), the children might interpret the behavior as an assertion of parental power and a diminution of their own autonomy, an approach in keeping with Baumrind's *authoritarian* style of parenting (Crockenberg & Litman, 1990).

Overall, it seems that parents who are most effective in eliciting compliance from their youngsters and deflecting defiance are quite clear about what they want their children to do, yet all the while they are prepared to listen to their children's objections and to make appropriate accommodations in ways that convey respect for their youngsters' individuality and autonomy (Gralinski & Kopp, 1993). At times, the process of achieving compliance can be somewhat extended and complex, with the parent explaining, reasoning, persuading, suggesting, accommodating, and compromising. These parental behaviors encourage and elicit competent behavior from the child (Crockenberg & Litman, 1990). Of course much also depends on the situation and the youngsters' ability to comprehend their parents' instructions (Grusec & Goodnow, 1994).

Questions

According to Diana Baumrind, what are the four main styles of parenting and which is considered most effective? How does each style affect the child's behavior?

Gaining Perspective on Parenting

The parenting dimensions and styles that we have considered thus far have focused on global patterns and practices. But they are much too abstract to capture the subtleties of parent-child interaction. In everyday life parents reveal a great variety of parenting behaviors, depending on many factors: the situation; the child's gender and age; the parents' inferences regarding the child's mood, motives, and intentions; the child's understanding of the situation; the social supports available to the parent; the pressures parents feel from other adults; and so forth (Dix, Ruble, & Zambarano, 1989).

For instance, parents can be warm or cold, restrictive or permissive, and consistent or inconsistent, depending on the setting and circumstances (Clarke-Stewart & Hevey, 1981). The child's response to being disciplined also modifies the parent's behavior and the parent's choice of future disciplinary measures. And the way the child perceives the actions of the parent can be more de-cisive than the parent's actions in themselves (Grusec & Goodnow, 1994). Children are not interchangeable; they do not all respond in identical fashion to the same type of caretaker behavior (Kochanska, 1995).

The Harvard Child-Rearing Study   A follow-up on a classic study helps us clarify some of these matters. In the 1950s three Harvard psychologists carried out one of the most enterprising studies of child rearing ever undertaken in the United States. Robert Sears, Eleanor Maccoby, and Harry Levin (1957) attempted to identify those parenting techniques that make a difference in personality development. They interviewed 379 mothers of kindergartners in the Boston area and rated each mother on about 150 different child-rearing practices. Some 25 years later, a number of Harvard psychologists led by David C. McClelland (McClelland et al., 1978) contacted many of these children, who were then 31 years old, most of them married and with children of their own.

McClelland and his associates interviewed these individuals and administered psychological tests to them. They concluded that not much of what people think and do as adults is determined by the specific techniques of child rearing their parents used during their first five years. Practices associated with breast-feeding, toilet training, and spanking are not all that important. It is how parents feel about their children that does make a difference. What mattered was whether a mother liked her child and enjoyed playing with the child or whether she considered the child a nuisance, with many disagreeable characteristics. Furthermore, children of affectionate fathers were more likely as adults to show tolerance and understanding than were the offspring of other fathers. The Harvard researchers conclude:

> How can parents do right by their children? If they are interested in promoting moral and social maturity in later life, the answer is simple: they should love them, enjoy them, want them around. They should not use their power to maintain a home that is only designed for the self-expression and pleasure of adults. They should not regard their children as disturbances to be controlled at all costs. (McClelland et al., 1978, p. 53)

American Family Structures   According to the report *America's Children in Brief: Key National Indicators of Well-Being, 2004:*

- 68 percent of children currently live with two married parents
- 32 percent of all U.S. children under 18 years of age live in alternative arrangements (23 percent live with mothers; 5 percent live with fathers; 4 percent live with neither parent)

Family structure has an impact on the poverty rate of children. In 2003, female-headed households with

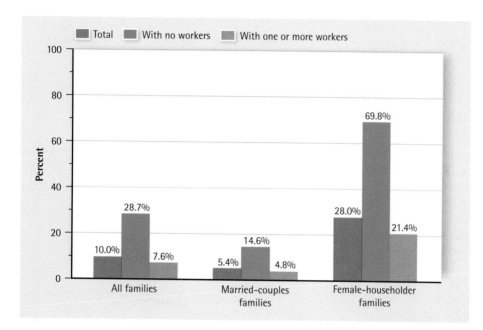

FIGURE 8.6 Poverty Rates by Family Type: 2003 In 2003, the poverty rate for all families was 10 percent. Because poverty status is computed on the family level if one family member works, the poverty status of every family member is affected. However, having a full-time job does not guarantee an escape from poverty. In 2003, the poverty line for a family of four was $18,810; for a family of three, it was $14,680. People in female-householder families had a poverty rate at least four times greater than their counterparts in married-couple families.
Source: DeNavas-Walt, C. Proctor, B. D., & Mills, R. (2004) Income, Poverty, and Health Insurance Coverage in the United States: 2003. Current Population Reports, P60-226, *Poverty in the United States: 2003.* Washington, DC: U.S. Government Printing Office. http://www.census.gov/prod/2004pubs/p60-226.pdf

no father present had poverty rates four times that of two-parent households (Federal Interagency Forum on Child and Family Statistics, 2004). Figure 8.6 provides data on poverty rates by family type. Children in low-income families experience economic insecurity, poor health and/or medical problems, developmental delays, problems learning in school, dropping out of school, becoming single parents, and unemployment as adults (*Child Poverty Fact Sheet [June 2001],* 2001; Federal Interagency Forum, 2004). The total number of children in poverty rose by 2003 to nearly 13 million children. The poverty rate of children also rose to 18 percent and is much higher than the percentages for adults and seniors (U.S. Bureau of the Census, 2004c). Best estimates indicate that 26 million children—or one-third of all children in the United States—live in poverty conditions (National Center for Children in Poverty, 2004).

Divorce   The divorce of a child's parents has a major impact on their lives. The most common family arrangement in the period immediately following a divorce is for the children to live with their single mothers and have only intermittent contact with their fathers. Divorce is a process that begins well before parents separate and continues long afterward (Guttman, 1993). E. Mavis Hetherington and colleagues (1977) did a two-year longitudinal study in which they matched and followed 48 preschool children from a divorced family with 48 children from an intact family. They found that the first year after the divorce was the most stressful.

Many of the stressors that parents experience following divorce and the accompanying changes in their lifestyles are reflected in their relationships with their children (Webster-Stratton, 1989). Hetherington and

colleagues (1976, p. 424) found that the interaction patterns between the divorced parents and their children differed significantly from those encountered in the intact families:

> Divorced parents make fewer maturity demands of their children, communicate less well with their children, tend to be less affectionate with their children and show marked inconsistency in discipline and lack of control over their children in comparison to parents in intact families. Poor parenting seems most marked, particularly for divorced mothers, one year after divorce, which seems to be a peak of stress in parent-child relations. . . . Two years following the divorce, mothers are demanding more . . . [independent and] mature behavior of their children, communicate better and use more explanation and reasoning, are more nurturant and consistent and are better able to control their children than they were the year before. A similar pattern is occurring for divorced fathers in maturity demands, communication and consistency, but they are becoming less nurturant and more detached from their children. . . . Divorced fathers were ignoring their children more and showing less affection [while their extremely permissive and "every day is Christmas" behavior declined].

Hence, many single-parent families had a difficult period of readjustment following the divorce, but the situation generally improved during the second year. Hetherington has found that much depends on the ability of the custodial mother to control her children. Children whose mothers maintain good control show no drop in school performance. Amato (2001) conducted a meta-analysis of 67 studies from the 1990s on divorce effects on children and found that as a group, in contrast with children from intact families, children with divorced parents scored significantly lower on measures of achievement, conduct, adjustment, self-concept, and social relations.

Hetherington also found that when single-parent mothers lose control of their sons, a "coercive cycle" typically appears. The sons tend to become more abusive, demanding, and unaffectionate. The mother responds with depression, low self-esteem, and less control, and her parenting becomes worse (Hetherington & Stanley-Hagan, 2002). In contrast, mothers and daughters in mother-headed families often express considerable satisfaction with their relationships, except for early-maturing girls whose heterosexual and older-peer involvements frequently weaken the mother-child bond (Hetherington, 1989).

More poor, single women are having children or becoming a single head of household with children as a consequence of divorce (see Figure 8.7). The child support system is working hard to establish the paternity of children who receive welfare (or were born outside of marriage), to put legally binding support orders in place, and to use effective enforcement techniques to increase the level of support payments. Yet less than one-fourth of divorced mothers entitled to child support payments are receiving what is due them. Also, the national *Welfare-to-Work* policy imposes a time limit on the receipt of federally funded cash welfare, making the collection of child support payments even more critical to poor families (Doolittle & Lynn, 1998; Martinson, 2000).

Joint-Custody Arrangements   Researchers find that the quality of the child's relationships with *both* parents is the best predictor of her or his postdivorce adjustment (Amato, 1993, 2000). Children who maintain stable, loving relationships with both parents appear to have fewer emotional scars—they exhibit less stress and less aggressive behavior, and their school performance and peer relations are better—than children lacking such relationships (Arditti & Keith, 1993). A meta-analysis of research on joint custody found that children in joint custody arrangements were better adjusted than those in sole-custody arrangements but no different from those in intact family arrangements (Bauserman, 2002).

With **joint custody,** both parents share equally in making significant child-rearing decisions, and both parents share in regular child-care responsibilities. The child lives with each parent a substantial amount of time—for example, the child might spend part of the week or month in one parent's house and part in the other's. Joint custody also eliminates the "winner/loser" character of custodial disposition and much of the sadness, sense of loss, and loneliness that the noncustodial parent frequently feels.

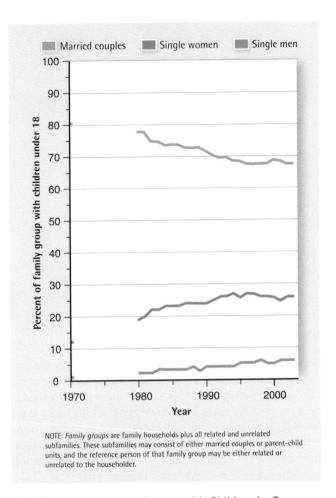

FIGURE 8.7 **U.S. Family Groups with Children by Type of Family Group: 1970–2003** The family is a vital institution in American society and the most significant source of economic and emotional support for children. In 2003, the number of family households were 68 percent of all households (declining from 81 percent of all households in 1970). A noticeable trend is the decline of married-couple households with biological children, from 40 percent in 1970 to 23 percent in 2003. Single-mother families increased from 3 million in 1970 to 10 million in 2003, whereas single-father families grew from less than half a million to 2 million. An increasing number of single parents were never married, and their children are most at risk of the effects of poverty.
Source: Fields, J. (2004, November). *America's Families and Living Arrangements: 2003.* U.S. Census Bureau. Washington, DC: U.S. Department of Commerce. http://www.census.gov/prod/2004pubs/p20-553.pdf

But joint custody is not an answer for all children. Critics point out that parents who cannot agree during marriage cannot reach agreement on rules, discipline, and styles of parenting after divorce. And they say that alternating between homes interferes with a child's need for continuity in his or her life (Simon, 1991). Furthermore, the mobile nature of contemporary society and the likelihood that parents will remarry render a good many joint-custody arrangements vulnerable to collapse (Simon, 1991). So it is not surprising that initial evidence suggests that joint-custody arrangements do not differ from sole-custody arrangements in children's adjustment to divorce (Donnelly & Finkelhor, 1992).

With respect to school achievement, social adjustment, and delinquent behavior, the differences are small or nonexistent between children from one- and two-parent homes of comparable social status (Amato, 2000, 2001). Some research suggests that children and adolescents from single-parent homes show less delinquent behavior, less psychosomatic illness, better adjustment to their parents, and better self-concepts than those from unhappy intact homes (Demo, 1992). Even so, an unhappy marriage or a divorce poses adverse outcomes for children. Each alternative brings its own sets of stressors (Amato, 2000, 2001; Cummings & Davies, 1994).

Psychiatrists and clinical psychologists note that in many cases divorce reduces the amount of friction and unhappiness a child experiences, leading to better behavioral adjustments (White, 1994). Overall, research strongly suggests that the quality of children's relationships with their parents matters much more than the fact of divorce (Hetherington & Stanley-Hagan, 2002).

Society has increasingly come to recognize that the single-parent home is a different, but viable, family form. The nation's public and private schools, communities, and churches are beginning to assist the increasing number of single-parents families with before-school and after-school child-care programs and summer school enrichment or remedial classes for children of all ages. Some school districts have restructured the school day or extended the school year to 12 months with periodic breaks to meet the particular needs of single-parent families.

Young Children with Gay or Lesbian Parents   We do not know how many children have gay or lesbian parents, in part because we lack solid figures on the number of lesbian and gay adults. Usually the children are born to parents in heterosexual marriages who subsequently "come out." Most others are born to lesbians via artificial insemination. And there are increasing numbers of cases of adoption or foster parenting by lesbians and gays.

Until recent years, lesbian and gay parents have been largely invisible, mostly because of harassment and custody concerns, and because they wish to shield their children from turmoil. When lesbian and gay parents do face custody or visitation battles in court, the outcome varies from state to state and from court to court. In 1995, the Virginia Supreme Court denied a lesbian custody of her son, saying she was a poor mother and her live-in lesbian relationship could bring the child "social condemnation." However, there is no convincing evidence that the development of children with lesbian or gay parents is compromised in any significant way.

Recent research questions how prior research has framed this issue (Stacey & Biblarz, 2001). The issue of gay and lesbian parenting is discussed further in Chapter 14.

Summing Up   Clearly, parenting is not a matter of employing a surefire set of recipes or formulas. Cultures differ, parents differ, and children differ. Parents who employ identical "good" child-rearing techniques have children who grow up to be exceedingly different (Bornstein, 1995; Plomin et al., 2001). Furthermore, situations differ, and what works in one setting can boomerang in another. As highlighted by the Harvard research, and the more recent *From Neurons to Neighborhoods,* the essence of parenting is in the parent-child relationship. In their interactions, parents and children evolve ongoing accommodations that reflect each other's needs and desires. Parent-child relationships differ so much, both within the same family and among families, that in many respects each parent-child relationship is unique (Elkind, 1974; Plomin et al., 2001). There is no mysterious, secret method you must master. It is the child that matters, not the technique—but child-rearing experts believe parents should not use severe punishment. On the whole, most parents do very well.

Questions

What types of parenting styles seem to promote emotionally healthy children? In addition to the traditional nuclear family, what are some other types of family structures evident in American society today? What factors are associated with a young child's healthy emotional adjustment to parental divorce?

Sibling Relationships

A child's relationships with sisters and brothers within the family are very important (Dunn, Slomkowski, & Beardsall, 1994). A child's position in the family and the number and sex of his or her siblings are thought to have major consequences for the child's development and socialization (Volling & Belsky, 1992). These factors structure the child's social environment, providing a network of key relationships and roles (E. Brody et al., 1994). An only child, an oldest child, a middle child, and a youngest child all seem to experience a somewhat different world because of the different social webs that encompass their lives, even though they receive the same style of parenting.

Some psychologists contend that these and other environmental influences operate to make two children in the same family as different from each other as are children in different families (Daniels, 1986). These psychologists say that there is a unique *microenvironment* in the family for each child. In this view there is not a single family but, rather, as many "different" families as there are children to experience them. These psychologists conclude that the small degree of similarity in personality found among siblings results almost totally from shared genes rather than from shared experience.

In short, the unique aspects of siblings' experiences in the family are more powerful in shaping their personalities than what the siblings experience in common. Many of the differences in the family environment are more obvious to children than to their parents (McHale et al., 1995), and much depends on how children perceive and interpret parental affection and discipline (Grusec & Goodnow, 1994).

The "pioneering function" of older brothers and sisters can persist throughout life, providing role models for how to cope with bereavement, retirement, or widowhood (Rosenthal, 1992). Indeed, by virtue of today's frequent divorces and remarriages, the sibling bond has been given closer research attention (Sheehan et al., 2004). Sibling relationships typically become more egalitarian but also less intense as youngsters move into later childhood and adolescence (Buhrmester & Furman, 1990).

Children and Birth Order   Worldwide, across many cultures, firstborns are more likely than later-borns to have elaborate birth ceremonies, to become a namesake (paternal name bestowed), to inherit privileges and rank, and to have authority over and respect from siblings. Firstborn sons generally have more control of property, more power in the society, and higher social positions (Herrera et al., 2003; Rosenblatt & Skoogberg, 1974). Moreover, older siblings act as caretakers for their younger siblings in a good many cultures (Dunn, 1983).

Firstborn children continue to be the focus of much research, for they appear to be fortune's favorites (Cicirelli, 1978; 1995; Falbo & Poston, 1993). Firstborns make up a high percentage of students in graduate and professional schools (Goleman, 1985), at the higher-IQ levels (Zajonc, 1976), among National Merit and Rhodes Scholars, in *Who's Who in America* and *American Men and Women of Science,* among Nobel Prize winners (Clark & Rice, 1982), among U.S. presidents (52 percent), among the 102 appointments to the Supreme Court (55 percent were either only children or firstborns), among men and women in Congress, and in the astronaut corps (21 of the first 23 U.S. astronauts were only children or firstborn sons).

Although there has been conflicting research regarding birth-order effects (Ernst & Angst, 1983), Herrera and colleagues (2003) reviewed many birth-order studies to explore the empirical reality of birth-order differences (parental reports, sibling reports, self-reports, and empirical analysis of academic achievement and occupational data) and find relatively consistent patterns of personality traits for firstborn, middle, later-born, and only children and corresponding occupational status. In general, findings from many studies suggest that (1) firstborns are viewed as intelligent, obedient, secure, and responsible; (2) middle children are viewed as ambitious, caring, friendly, and thoughtful; (3) lastborns are believed to be the most creative, emotional, friendly, disobedient, least responsible, and talkative; and (4) only children are viewed as independent and self-centered (Baskett, 1985; Herrera et al., 2003; Musun-Miller, 1993; Nyman, 1995). Jacklin and Reynolds (1993) also find that later-borns seem to possess better social skills than firstborns.

Given that many studies consistently find that firstborns are believed to be more intelligent than other birth ranks, thus more likely to attain higher educational and occupational status, Herrera and colleagues (2003) conducted a survey with two different student populations on beliefs about birth rank and occupational status. Both sets of participants ranked firstborns with occupations of higher prestige, in comparison to lastborns. They ranked firstborns as accountants, astronauts, lawyers, and physicians; but they expected last-borns would become actors, artists, musicians, teachers, photographers, or stunt men. But does expectation meet reality? Herrera and colleagues (2003) then conducted a large representative cross-section sample of the Polish population in 1997 and 1999, examining birth rank, family size, and actual occupational attainment. In fact, their analysis indicated that individuals of higher birth rank and of smaller families actually complete more schooling and attain positions of higher prestige.

Overall, parents and others tend to react differently toward firstborn and later-born children, and in turn reinforce personality stereotypes. Research reveals that parents attach greater importance to their first child (Clausen, 1966). More social, affectionate, and caretaking interactions occur between parents and their firstborn (Cohen & Beckwith, 1977). Thus, firstborns have more exposure to adult models and to adult expectations and pressures (Baskett, 1985).

A second explanation of the differences between first- and later-born children derives from **confluence theory,** a model devised by psychologist Zajonc and colleagues (1986; Zajonc et al., 1991). Confluence theory gets its name from the view that the intellectual development of a family is like a river, with the inputs of each family member flowing into it. According to Zajonc, the oldest sibling experiences a richer intellectual environment than younger siblings do.

Confluence theory has its critics. Thus, a third explanation—the **resource dilution hypothesis**—extends the confluence model to encompass more resources than simply a rich intellectual environment. This theory says that in large families resources get spread thin, to the detriment of all the offspring. In actuality, family resources are finite and status rivalry play in a child's personality formation (Ansbacher & Ansbacher, 1956). Adler viewed the "dethroning" of the firstborn as a crucial event in the development of the first child. With the birth of a sister or brother, the firstborn suddenly loses his or her monopoly on parental attention (Kendrick & Dunn, 1980). This loss, Adler said, arouses a strong lifelong need for recognition, attention, and approval that the child, and later the adult, seeks to acquire through high achievement. An equally critical factor in the development of the later-born child is the competitive race for achievement with older and more accomplished siblings. In many cases the rancor disappears when individuals get older and learn to manage their own careers and married lives (Dunn, 1986).

In sum, many unique genetic and environmental factors intervene in individual families, producing wide differences not just among families but among their members (Heer, 1985).

Questions

In what ways do older siblings influence younger ones in terms of motivation, self-esteem, and social support? In general, how does a child's birth order in a family affect her or his personality?

Sibling Interactions Are Important in All Societies
A child's birth order structures a somewhat different social web or environment for siblings. Indeed, social scientists are increasingly coming to the conclusion that there is not a "single" family but as many "different" families as there are youngsters to experience them. Siblings typically maintain strong bonds throughout life.

including such resources as parental time and encouragement, economic and material goods, and various cultural and social opportunities (music and dance lessons, travel, and college savings). Additional siblings do reduce the share of parental resources, and parental resources do have an important effect on children's educational success and socioemotional development (Downey, 2003).

Sociologists commonly employ the resource dilution hypothesis to explain the relationship they find between the number of siblings and educational attainment: Increases in the number of siblings are associated with the completion of fewer years of schooling and the attainment of fewer educational milestones (positions in student government, on the school newspaper, in drama groups, and so on). In this manner, family size is linked to greater or lesser degrees of achievement (Steelman & Powell, 1989).

A fourth explanation, which was first advanced by Alfred Adler, stresses the part that sibling power

Nonfamilial Social Influences

We have seen that children enter a world of people, an encompassing social network. With time, specific relationships change in form, intensity, and function, but the social network itself stretches across the life span. Yet social and behavioral scientists mostly ignored the rich tapestry of children's social networks until the past two decades. They regarded social intimacy as centering on one relationship, that between the infant and mother, and treated young children's ties with other family members and with age-mates as if they did not exist or had no importance.

However, a growing body of research points to the significance of other relationships in the development of interpersonal competencies. In this section we explore children's peer relationships and friendships. **Peers** are individuals who are approximately the same age. Early friendship is a major source of a youngster's emotional strength, and its lack can pose lifelong risks (Newcomb & Bagwell, 1995).

Peer Relationships and Friendships

From birth to death we find ourselves immersed in countless relationships. Few are as important to us as those we have with our peers and friends (Dunn, 1993; Newcomb & Bagwell, 1995). Children as young as 3 years of age form friendships with other children that are surprisingly similar to those of adults (Verba, 1994). And just as they do for adults, different relationships meet different needs for young children. Some child relationships are reminiscent of strong adult attachments; others, of relationships between adult mentors and protégés; and still others, of the camaraderie of adult coworkers. Although young children lack the reflective understanding that many adults bring to their relationships, they often invest in their friendships with an intense emotional quality (Selman, 1980). Moreover, some young children bring a considerable measure of social competence to their relationships and a high level of give-and-take (Farver & Branstetter, 1994).

As we saw in Chapter 6, attachment theory predicts that the quality of the mother-child tie has implications for the child's close personal relationships. Researchers confirm that preschoolers with secure maternal attachments enjoy more harmonious, less controlling, more responsive, and happier relationships with their peers than do preschoolers with insecure maternal attachments (Turner, 1991). A variety of studies reveal that with increasing age, peer relationships are more likely to be formed and more likely to be successful (Park, Lay, & Ramsey, 1993). Four-year-olds, for instance, spend about two-thirds of the time when they are in contact with other people associating with adults and one-third of the time with peers. Eleven-year-olds, in contrast, spend about an equal amount of time with adults and with peers (Wright, 1967).

Several factors contribute to this shift in interactive patterns: (1) as children grow older, their communication skills improve, facilitating effective interaction (Eckerman & Didow, 1988); (2) children's increasing cognitive competencies enable them to attune themselves more effectively to the roles of others (Verba, 1994); (3) nursery, preschool, pre–K, and elementary school attendance offers increasing opportunities for peer interaction; and (4) increasing motor competencies expand the child's ability to participate in many joint activities.

Children of preschool age assort themselves into same-sex play groups (Maccoby, 1990). In a longitudinal study, Eleanor E. Maccoby and Carol N. Jacklin (1987) found that preschoolers at 4½ years of age spent three times as much time playing with same-sex playmates as they did with opposite-sex playmates. By 6½ years of age, the youngsters were spending eleven times as much time with same-sex as with opposite-sex partners. Moreover, preschool girls tend to interact in small groups, especially two-person groups, whereas boys more often play in larger groups (Eder & Hallinan, 1978).

Peer Reinforcement and Modeling

Children play an important part as reinforcing agents and behavioral models for one another, a fact that adults at times overlook. Much learning takes place as a result of children's interaction with other children (Azmitia, 1988). Here is a typical example (Lewis et al., 1975, p. 27):

> Two four-year-olds are busily engaged in playing with "Playdoh." The room echoes with their glee as they roll out long "snakes." Each child is trying to roll a longer snake than the other. The one-year-old sibling of one of the children, hearing the joyful cries, waddles into the room. She reaches for the Playdoh being used by her sibling. The older child hands the one-year-old some Playdoh, and the child tries to roll her own snake. Unable to carry out the task and frustrated, the one-year-old becomes fussy, at which point the older sibling gives the child a knife. The four-year-old then shows the sibling how to cut the snakes the other children have made.

Indeed, the old one-room school functioned, and functioned well, with the teacher teaching the older children and the older children teaching the younger boys and girls.

Seeing other children behave in certain ways can also affect a child's behavior. By means of imitate-in-turn and follow-the-leader games, youngsters gain a sense of connectedness, of other children being like themselves, and of successfully exerting social control over the behavior of others (Eckerman & Stein, 1990) (see the *Human Diversity* box "Preparing for Children with Disabilities in Early Childhood Settings"). In addition, a study by O'Connor (1969) reveals that severely withdrawn nursery school children engage in considerably more peer interaction after they watch a 20-minute sound film that portrays other children playing together happily. And as we will see in Chapter 9, modeling has proved to be an important tool for helping children to overcome various fears and prepare for new experiences.

Aggression in Children

Aggression is behavior that is socially defined as injurious or destructive, and much human aggression takes place in the context of group activity (Berkowitz, 1993). Even young children display aggression, and with increasing age their aggressive behavior becomes less diffuse and more directed (Feshbach, 1970). The proportion of aggressive acts of an undirected, tempertantrum type decreases gradually during the first three years of life, then shows a sharp decline after the age of 4. In contrast, the relative frequency of retaliatory responses increases with age, especially after children reach their third birthday. Verbal aggression also increases at 2 to 4 years of age (Egeland et al., 1990).

Human Diversity

Preparing for Children with Disabilities in Early Childhood Settings

One of the most fundamental needs of every child is to be accepted and to have a sense of belonging. However, research shows us that children with disabilities or differences are not automatically accepted by their peers unless teachers, child-care workers, and parents take an active role in promoting their acceptance. Early perceptions about people with disabilities or differences lay the groundwork for attitude formation. In fact, by the age of 5, children have already formed perceptions, positive or negative, about youngsters with disabilities (Gifford-Smith & Brownell, 2003). Without thoughtful planning and strategies to promote acceptance, these early attitudes are often negative (Favazza & Odom, 1996). Teachers can address the three key influences in attitude formation by setting up a classroom to promote a positive, accepting attitude on the part of the class and positive self-esteem in children with a disability:

- *Indirect experiences.* Make available photographs, books, displays, and instructional programs that provide information about persons with disabilities. For example, it is not uncommon for children and their uninformed families to misperceive they can "catch" the other child's disability or disease (such as Down syndrome). Children with disabilities need to be visually represented in class settings and community activities, just as all children in the classroom need to be represented in their surroundings. Favazza and Odom (1996) found in a study examining 95 preschool and kindergarten classes that most typically do not have persons with disabilities depicted in displays, books, or curricula that discourage stereotypic views.
- *Direct experiences.* Research has clearly demonstrated that positive experiences with individuals with disabilities can contribute to acceptance. Other children from the class might need to help the child with a disability during playtime or snack time. All children in the group might need to learn sign language, for example. The teacher is crucial in modeling the helping behaviors first. Negative attitudes tend to arise in children who have little or no direct experience with the disability (Gifford-Smith & Brownell, 2003).
- *Primary social group.* The primary social group for a young child is her or his family. Children's attitudes are affected by parental attitudes, including parental silence, which the child experiences negatively. Teachers

and classroom aides must educate themselves about particular children with disabilities. Get to know about disabilities—but also learn the specifics about that child. If possible, make arrangements for a successful adult with this disability to visit the classroom and talk with the children—for instance, invite an adult who is in a wheelchair, or who has a prosthetic limb, or who is working in a sheltered workshop.

Source: Favazza, P. C. (1998, December). Preparing for children with disabilities in early childhood. *Early Childhood Education Journal, 25*(4), 255–258.

All Young Children Enjoy and Benefit from Peer Relationships and Friendships

Girls and boys differ in how they express their aggression toward peers. Boys tend to harm others through physical and verbal aggression (hitting or pushing others and threatening to beat up others); their concerns typically center on getting their way and dominating other youngsters. Girls, in contrast, tend to focus on relational issues (establishing close, intimate connections with one another); they attempt to harm others by damaging their friendships or feelings of peer-group inclusion by such acts as spreading negative rumors, excluding the child from a play group, and purposefully withdrawing friendship or acceptance (Crick & Grotpeter, 1995; Moretti, Odgers, & Jackson, 2004).

The researchers also found that some children entered nursery school with a repertoire of aggressive behaviors; others were passive and unassertive at first. But after the relatively passive children learned to counteraggress and thus end other children's aggressive acts, they themselves began to aggress against new victims. Jay Belsky, child-care expert, says young children spending greater hours in child care and away from parents display escalating aggressiveness is a finding in the *Early Child Care Report,* released by the National Institute of Child Health and Human Development in April 2001. Lead authors of this national study are concerned that parents need to know that 83 percent of the children in child care in the study were not labeled as aggressive, and young children experienced many advantages in high-quality child care (Sweeney, 2001).

Peer Aggression Many aggressive children attribute hostile intentions to their peers even under benign circumstances. Consequently, they are more likely than other children to respond with aggression in interpersonal settings. Boys' acts of aggression are more likely to be of a verbal and physical nature, but girls are more likely to use harmful words, exclusion, or withdrawing friendship.

Even so, some children appear more prone than others to engage in aggressive behavior (Campbell et al., 1994). Some aggression derives from a developmental lag in children's acquisition of role-taking skills (Hazen & Black, 1989), but this is not the entire story. More aggressive children, particularly boys, report that aggression produces tangible rewards and reduces negative treatment by other children (Trachtenberg & Viken, 1994). Additionally, researchers find that youngsters who see and hear angry exchanges among adults become emotionally distressed and respond by aggressing against their peers (Vuchinich, Bank, & Patterson, 1992).

Aggression, hostility, bullying, defiance, and destructiveness are signs of **antisocial behavior,** which involves persistent violations of socially prescribed patterns of behavior (Walker, Colvin, & Ramsey, 1995). Approximately 4 to 6 million children in schools have been identified as antisocial (only some are identified with a behavioral disability), and the numbers are rising (Kazdin, 1993). Research suggests that (Walker, Colvin, & Ramsey, 1995; Walker et al., 2004):

- Aggressive, antisocial behavior among children is not "just a phase" to be outgrown.
- Antisocial behavior in early childhood is the most accurate predictor of delinquency in adolescence.
- Antisocial children can be accurately identified as early as 3 or 4 years of age.
- If an antisocial behavior pattern is not altered by the end of third grade, it can become chronic, only to be "managed" through supports and interventions.
- Prevention and early intervention are the best hopes we have of diverting children from this path.

Questions

What role do early friendships play in a child's emotional development? What are some ways children can be encouraged to accept children with disabilities into the group? What are the research findings on aggressive behaviors in early childhood?

Preschools and Head Start

With a majority of mothers working and with more children being born at risk since the 1990s, increasing numbers of children in the Western world are in early intervention programs, child care, and preschools long before they enter the public school arena (see Figure 8.8). That early childhood programs have a powerful impact on the development of young children is an understatement, and a flurry of research in emotional development of children is being undertaken with renewed vigor.

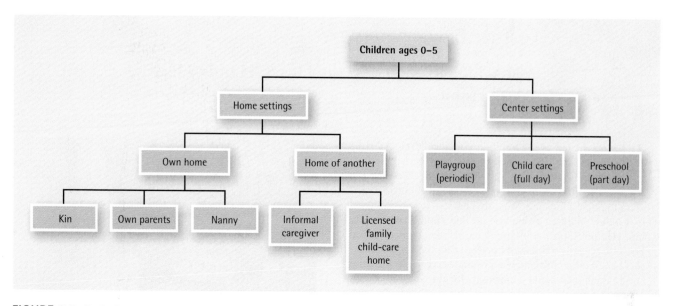

FIGURE 8.8 Early Childhood Care and Education Settings More young children in Westernized societies experience a diversity of child-care settings, some informal and others regulated and licensed. The proportion of young children in out-of-home care while parents are working has risen. By kindergarten, a majority have some preschool experience. Children in high-quality preschool classrooms display greater receptive language ability and premath skills and more advanced social skills. In 2001 more than 900,000 U.S. children were enrolled in Head Start programs, and 822,000 were enrolled in prekindergarten. The availability of quality child care has a direct impact on the employability of mothers.

Source: Adapted from Bairraro, J., & Tietze, W. (1993, October). Early Childhood Services in the European Community: A report submitted to the Commission of the European Community Task Force on Human Resources, Education, Training, and Youth.

Edward Zigler (1994, p. X), says,

Today's children are spending less and less time with their parents, who are forced by economic necessity to work longer hours and to place even their very young children in [nursery and] preschool settings. Thus, the nature of the early childhood curriculum, its developmental appropriateness, and the emotional tone its practice creates are becoming increasingly important.

The children in early childhood settings are just beginning to construct their personal social universes; they are experiencing for the first time many of their own emotional responses and those of others. A healthy goal at this stage of life should be to help young children learn desirable ways of expressing feelings and develop healthy patterns of understanding and regulating their emotions (Hyson, 2004).

Public kindergarten programs were originally established in the 1950s to support and nurture the young child's emotional and social development—to provide a healthy transition time from the emotional support at home for the cognitive tasks ahead. In the mid 1960s, Zigler (1970) directed the earliest days of the *Head Start* program, which had been designed to provide children from low-income families with early intervention education in nursery school settings. Educators believed that appropriate services from outside the family could compensate for the disadvantages these youngsters experienced from the effects of poverty during their early years.

In the 1980s, lawsuits and charges of sexual abuse of young children in preschool and child-care programs forced such programs to focus on the young child's intellectual development, because caretaker displays of touching and physical affection and development of emotional connections with the children had become suspect. Many professionals and parents concerned about child development believe there has been an undue emphasis on formal academics (understanding symbols, time, number, volume, and space), while agreeing that a certain amount of intellectual preparation should be a component of these programs.

Much of what was said in Chapter 6 about child-care centers also holds for preschools. Like child-care programs, the preschool experience has been seen by a number of educators, child psychologists, and political leaders as a possible solution to many of the massive social problems of illiteracy, underachievement, poverty, and racism that confront Western nations.

In recent years, long-term data have become available that reveal that SES-disadvantaged children in such programs do indeed get a head start (Children's Defense Fund, 2003) and benefit from long-term effects as well (see the *Further Developments* box on page 300, "Head Start: Affecting the Heart, Hands, Health, and Home") (Garces, Thomas, & Currie, 2000; Oden et al., 2000).

The payoff of Head Start programs has been not only in education but in dollars, for in the long run its

Further Developments

Head Start: Affecting the Heart, Hands, Health, and Home

Having served over 22 million young children and their families, the *Head Start* program is the largest U.S. school readiness program (Zigler & Styfco, 2004). Begun in 1965, the Head Start program was an offshoot of President Lyndon Johnson's War on Poverty. It was designed to provide children from low-income families with early intervention education by providing literacy, numeracy, and vocabulary skills training in nursery school settings. Educators believed that providing appropriate services to the child and to the family could compensate for the educational disadvantages the children experienced due to poverty. In 1994, Congress created the *Early Head Start* program to address the needs of children younger than 3 and low-income pregnant women (Children's Defense Fund, 2003).

The project has also provided hundreds of thousands of young children with essential health-care services and taught parents better parenting skills (Zigler & Styfco, 2004). A program's effectiveness is increased by involving the parents, strengthening their ties to schools, and bringing them into partnership with the educational enterprise. Many parents have had bad experiences with their own schooling, and these problems need to be addressed before they pass on negative attitudes to their youngsters (Wasik et al., 1990).

Head Start is one of the most researched government-funded programs. However, researchers continue to debate over how to measure the effectiveness of the Head Start program. Although an assessment component is built in to the program, the goals are wide-ranging and appropriate assessment tools have been lacking. "In the fall of 2003, the National Reporting System (NRS) was imposed. The system involves tests of vocabulary, letter recognition, and math skills administered to every kindergarten bound child at the start and end of the Head Start year" (Zigler & Styfco, 2004). Organizations such as the National Black Child Development Institute and the National Council of La Raza have called on Congress to reevaluate this attempt at accountability (Moore & Yzaguirre, 2004). They argue that relying only on cognitive tests of very young children does not reveal the range of developmental progress such as social, emotional, and motor skills development that are hallmarks of school readiness. The implementation of the National Reporting System is slated for review by a panel of experts (Zigler & Styfco, 2004).

Yet long-term data are available that reveal that children in quality preschool programs do indeed get a head start and benefit from long-term effects as well (Garces, Thomas, & Currie, 2000; Oden et al., 2000). In November 2004 a report entitled *Lifetime Effects: The High/Scope Perry Preschool Study Through Age 40* (Schweinhart et al., 2005) was released. This longitudinal study examined the long-term effects of a high-quality preschool program, the Perry Preschool. David Weik-

Quality Preschool and Head Start Programs Make a Difference Quality preschool and Head Start programs have immediate positive effects on children's socioemotional development, including self-esteem, achievement motivation, and social behaviors. Researchers find that quality Head Start programs can make a long-term difference for poor youngsters that extends well beyond the child's school years. Parental Involvement in Head Start also contributes to their own positive growth (Schweinhart et al., 2005).

ert, one of the founders of the preschool, and his colleagues undertook the study in 1962 with 123 children at 3 years of age. Groups were randomly assigned as to who received treatment (preschool) and who did not. They continued collecting data until the participants reached age 40 in 2002.

According to the study findings, the children who received preschool had higher high school graduation rates—65 percent versus 45 percent—than those who did not. The difference is more pronounced for females—84 percent versus 32 percent. The group who received treatment (preschool) had higher employment rates—76 percent versus 62 percent—earned over $5,000 more yearly, were more likely to be homeowners, were likely to be parents raising their own children, and were more likely to have a bank/savings account (Kirp, 2004). These long-term effects are important not only in and of themselves but also for the legacy of benefits from early education and family services for the generations to follow.

Source: Schweinhart, L. J., Montie, J., Xiang, Z., Barnett, W. S., Belfield, C. R., & Nores, M. (2005). *Lifetime effects: The High/Scope Perry Preschool through age 40.* Monographs of the High/Scope Educational Research Foundation, Ypsilanti, MI: High/Scope Press. Retrieved March 1, 2005, from http://www.highscope.org/Research/PerryProject/perrymain.htm

participants are less likely to need remedial programs as children and social support systems like welfare as adults. Apparently, children with preschooling learn how to extract a better education from the school system. Moreover, a program's effectiveness is increased by involving the parents, strengthening their ties to schools, and bringing them into partnership with the educational enterprise (Schweinhart et al., 2005). Finally, as disadvantaged youngsters grow older, they continue to need the same comprehensive services and special attention as Head Start programs provided them in their early years. Our federal government is now providing some monies for Early Head Start programs for children from 0 to 3 and prekindergarten programs, after-school programs, and summer enrichment programs for this group of youngsters to continue developing their competencies to meet the academic curricula and behavioral standards of elementary schools. Additionally, such youth are eligible for high school programs, such as *Gear Up* or *Upward Bound*, that help to prepare them for college success.

Questions

Initially, what was the main goal of public kindergarten programs in the 1950s? Why has that goal changed over the years? What is the purpose of Early Head Start and Head Start, and what population of children is served?

Media Influences

For at least three decades, authorities have expressed concern over the effects of media violence on the behavior of the nation's youth (Kolbert, 1994; Slaby, 1994). In the United States, preschool children watch TV an average of three to four hours per day. Young children observe thousands of murder scenes, beatings, and sexual assaults in both televised and videotaped shows (Seppa, 1997).

Television   Significantly, U.S. youngsters spend more time watching television than in any other activity except sleeping (Gentile & Walsh, 2002), and several studies have linked excessive television viewing with childhood obesity (Robinson, 1999). Furthermore, television has become a major socializing agent of American children, and studies have repeatedly found that television violence is as strongly correlated with aggressive behavior as any other behavioral variable that has been measured. Many studies have found that violence in the media contributes to childhood and adult aggression, especially for those prone to aggressive behavior (Anderson & Bushman, 2002).

Some exceptions include watching educational programs (geared toward very young children) such as *Sesame Street,* which contributes to children's school readiness, letter and number skills, and vocabulary, regardless of parent education, income, native language, or quality of the home environment (Huston and Wright, 1998). Watching prosocial programs such as *Mr. Rogers' Neighborhood* with parent-guided activities increased children's prosocial behaviors (Wright & Huston, 1995). Significantly, children watch such high-quality educational programming less as they get older, and their cartoon and comedy viewing increases with age (Huston et al., 1990). Many of these programs directed toward child audiences are saturated with aggression, mayhem, and violence. For example, *Bugs Bunny* and *Roadrunner* cartoons are typical Saturday-morning fare and average 50 violent acts per hour.

The ability of television to influence youngsters is complex. Until they reach grade school, many children do not comprehend the motives behind the messages promoting products, and preschoolers and toddlers tend to believe what adults tell them. They lack the personal experience and cognitive development to question the accuracy of what they view (Wright et al., 1994). Television rarely portrays the seriously harmful effects of violence in the programs children watch.

A variety of studies reveal that viewing media violence fosters aggressive behavior in a number of ways (Bandura, Ross, & Ross, 1963; Huesmann & Miller, 1994; Kolbert, 1994): (1) media violence provides opportunities for children to learn new aggressive skills; (2) watching violent behavior weakens children's inhibitions against behaving in the same way; (3) television violence affords occasions for vicarious conditioning, in which children acquire aggressive behaviors by imaginatively participating in the violent experiences of another person; and (4) media violence increases children's toleration of aggression in real life—a *habituation effect*—and reinforces the tendency to view the world as a dangerous place.

Longitudinal research that has followed individuals over major portions of their lives, in some cases for up to 22 years, reveals that the viewing of large quantities of television violence by vulnerable youth is one of the best predictors of later violent criminal behavior (Slaby, 1994). In sum, an accumulating body of literature suggests that television provides a variety of entertainment for children but functions as a powerful negative socializer as well (Huesmann & Miller, 1994; Seppa, 1997).

During the preschool years, when viewing habits are established, parents and child-care workers have the most control to influence children's viewing habits (Hughes & Hasbrouck, 1996; Truglio et al., 1996). Research shows if children's parents restrict their viewing, and if their parents spend time encouraging or doing other activities with their children, children will watch less television. Just as significant for child well-being, the nation's pediatricians ask parents to diminish their youngsters' television viewing by half or more because it also contributes to childhood obesity (Robinson, 1999). Educators have also blamed TV for the nation's falling reading scores because they find a strong correlation between the lack of reading skills and excessive amounts of television viewing (Gentile & Walsh, 2002).

Video and Computer Games and the Internet Many of the educational and psychological findings regarding television viewing extend to video games and Internet use. In the early 1970s there was *Pong*, a simple electronic table tennis game. Then came *Pac-Man, Roadrunner, Space Invaders, Asteroids,* and others. By 1980 video games had developed such a considerable following among youngsters that physicians attributed a hand ailment—"space invaders cramp"—to excessive video game playing. A decade later, by 1990, *Nintendo* and *Sega* video games dominated children's play. Nearly one-third of U.S. homes owned a Nintendo or Sega set, and a survey of the 30 top-selling toys found that 20 were video-game related (Provenzo, 1991).

By 2006, many American families owned a personal computer and had access to Internet chat rooms, instant messaging, and the World Wide Web. An Internet link gives a child access to a vast array of educational and entertainment sites, but it also gives the child access to sites that are developmentally inappropriate and can be dangerous for children (for instance, some children have been victimized by pedophiles who logged on to children's chat rooms). "Filtering" software allows parents to "block out" any site that contains the topics they select for blocking, but filters are not a foolproof solution. To top it off, psychologists have now identified a psychological disorder labeled "Internet addiction," which affects children as well as adults.

Many parents are concerned that their child's preoccupation with video games and computers can lead to developmental drawbacks for the child (Hays, 1995; Sheff, 1993). Video games allow youngsters little opportunity to make decisions for themselves, to fashion their own fantasies, or to construct their own resolutions to problems. Most games do not reward individual initiative, creativity, or thought, nor do they allow sufficient freedom for youngsters to experiment with ideas, develop resourcefulness, and use their imaginations.

Critics contend that video games provide very limited cultural and sensory stimulation and that many video games are appallingly violent and stereotypically sexist. Few programmers produce high-quality games such as *Myst*. In addition, children accustomed to the quick gratification that video games provide might be unwilling to put in the effort and long hours of practice that are necessary to play a musical instrument well or to excel at other endeavors.

Yet there is room for optimism when these technologies are used in constructive ways. Video game technology, computer multimedia educational software, and interactive educational Web sites (e.g., *National Geographic Kids Network, The Virtual Smithsonian Online, Monterey Bay Aquarium, WhiteHouseKids.Gov,* pen pal sites, and others) offer educators abundant opportunities for helping children learn and think. Clearly, video games, computers, and Internet access, like television, are phenomena of tremendous import and significance in our society.

The fact that some American children do not have access to learning computer skills to enter the workforce in the next decade demands our serious attention. Social scientists are currently assessing the effects of extended computer use and exposure to various types of computer content on children's (especially young children's) well-being.

Questions

How much do you watch the television or use the computer daily? Do you agree that television is a "silent" socializer? What about video games and computer use, especially chat room dialogue? Do you now spend more time "socializing" online than in actual face-to-face contact with friends?

SEGUE

In this chapter we discussed variables that can promote or detract from a young child's emotional and social development. Each child's whole development—physical, intellectual, emotional, social, and moral—is unique. Even when adults attempt to rush the child from one stage of development to another, these natural developmental processes will move along at the appropriate pace for each young child. A child's emotional self-regulation and self-image are influenced and reflected back by a variety of factors: the child's own developing sense of self; encouragement or discouragement from family members and caregivers; association, acceptance, or dissociation with peers; and, in Western cultures, the extent of media influence. Children need to feel accepted and loved by the significant people in their lives, if they are to maximize their own potential and to have a positive image of themselves. A healthy emotional-social foundation prepares young children for the demands of the middle childhood stage of development, from ages 7 to 12, which we will turn to next in Part 5, Middle Childhood.

Summary

Emotional Development and Adjustment

1. Research on emotions documents that all behavior, thought, and interactions are motivated by emotions. Research reveals variability in paths of emotional development within a diversity of home and social environments. Cross-cultural studies shed light on sociocultural differences in timing and standards of emotional self-regulation.

2. A substantial body of research indicates that children need to achieve minimal social competence by age 6, or risk emotional and behavior disorders by adulthood. Programs are developed to help preschool children develop healthy social-emotional skills.

3. Thinking is an emotional activity, and children's feelings can support or hinder intellectual/academic mastery. Caregivers and teachers rate children with more effective prosocial solutions as more socially competent, with fewer attention problems, and less disruptive behaviors. To promote social competence for young children, parents and caregivers must teach effective problem-solving skills.

4. Parents directly influence social-emotional competence in their children. Children who display social competence, emotional understanding, prosocial behaviors, high self-esteem, and attachment security have parents high in warmth or positive emotion and low in negativity in interactions with children. Children in such families imitate self-regulation and appropriate emotional strategies and behaviors. Exposure to nonhostile emotions such as sadness, embarrassment, and distress are positively associated with sympathy. Children from negative, hostile home environments are least likely to comply with parental directives, and display more negative emotions and emotional insecurity behaviors.

5. Facial expressions, body language, and gestures appear with greater frequency during the preschool years, reflecting greater cognitive ability and awareness of cultural values and standards. Increased large- and fine-muscle control help the child express feelings in more complex ways. Voice qualities convey tempo and specific social-emotional messages.

6. Play allows children to improve cognitive capacities and to communicate their deepest feelings, and there are many cognitive, emotional, and social benefits of play activities. Children mature through predictable, progressively social forms of play: functional, constructive, parallel, onlooker, associative, and cooperative (collaborative) play. Some young children create an imaginary companion. Boys tend to play in larger groups and seem to prefer rough-and-tumble, competitive play, whereas girls tend to prefer two-person groups conducive to verbal interaction and displays of affection. Young children use pretend play to explore their feelings. They use their imaginations and play creatively with objects in their environment.

7. Young children are egocentric, and their thoughts, feelings, and words relate to themselves. They are likely to think they cause bad things to happen. Since they cannot verbally label and discuss their feelings, therapeutic play benefits young children with emotional and behavior disorders by releasing their feelings, thoughts, and aggression. Such play decreases anxiety and aggression and improves social adjustment and emotional well-being.

8. Studies reveal that parents across cultures have many different theories about the role of play. Children in poor countries work long hours each day to support their families' survival. Adults in every society promote play and social interactions that are beneficial to becoming adult members of that society.

9. Cultures and professionals vary in their views on the age at which children should be able to control their emotions. Self-regulation of emotions proceeds gradually at each child's own pace and is unlikely to appear until after age 3. Cultural norms vary for control of boys' and girls' emotions.

10. Parents in Westernized societies encourage exploration, imagination, and independence in play and promote individualism: independence, freedom of expression, and competence. In contrast, Asian and Hispanic societies promote collectivism—fostering strong emotional bonding and feelings of oneness with the family and group. Children are expected to be obedient to authority and show respect to elders.

11. Asian communication is more sensitive to nonverbal cues, body movements, and gestures, so ethnic feedback is different from American understanding and expectations. Hispanic children experience strong family cohesion. A male child is expected to be macho, whereas marianismo emotional-social standards apply for a girl. African American children are taught to use and understand social-emotional facial expressions, sometimes averting direct eye contact. Young children gain a sense of identity from their name, gender, and familial relations and don't classify people by race until around age 7, when they experience cognitive maturation. Typically young children demonstrate an indifference to race and accept peers as individuals. Black children often use culturally based speech rhythms, and American black children often come from homes that use songs and oral traditions with poetic beauty, emotional intensity, and rich imagery.

12. Teachers, child-care professionals, early intervention specialists, and health-care personnel need to familiarize themselves with cross-cultural standards and views as more immigrant children and their families are acculturating into American society.

13. Young children demonstrate extensive understanding of emotional information and reactions. They can develop close, affectionate bonds with family members and other caregivers. One of the main goals of parenting and preschool programs includes enhancing young children's self-esteem.

The Development of Self-Awareness

14. Emotional development is essential to self-awareness. A child's understanding of self as separate from others

continues to develop during the preschool years. Some children develop positive self-esteem; others develop a more negative view of themselves, which has far-reaching life consequences.

15. Children come to view themselves as active agents in socializing with others. Self-control and social control are interrelated. A 2-year-old is likely to view herself in terms of some bodily aspect, whereas a 5- to 6-year-old can distinguish between his mind and his body. Some children need adult intervention to improve their self-esteem and become better socialized.

16. Gifted children demonstrate high motivation and self-determination called entelechy and are likely to be self-directed and possess a more mature self-awareness. Typically, they tend to be active learners, demonstrate a strong will, and are able to empathize with others' feelings and emotional subtleties at earlier ages.

Gender Identification

17. Recognition of one's gender is a major developmental task during the first six years of life. All societies assign males and females specific gender roles. Cultural socialization experiences help a young child develop a gender identity, of being masculine or feminine. Between the ages of 3 and 4, most children acquire a gender identity, and gender roles have become more versatile.

18. Hormones influence the display of gender behaviors. Testosterone tends to make boys more physically active, more aggressive, and less able to sit still. In general, boys also seem to be more logical, analytical, spatial, and mathematical, whereas girls tend to be more verbal, social, and somewhat more expressive emotionally. In addition, each child's cultural socialization patterns and family experience influence gender behaviors. Some researchers propose that environmental factors are a stronger influence on gender identity.

19. Psychoanalytic theory suggests early experience plays a significant role in gender identity. Erikson's psychosocial theory proposes that children attempt to resolve the conflict of initiative versus guilt by acting with purpose on their world. Cognitive learning theory proposes modeling/imitation plays a major role in gender identity. Cognitive developmental theory states children acquire a mental model of a female or male, or traditional gender stereotypes, and then adopt that model's gender-related characteristics. Mothers and fathers tend to treat their sons and daughters differently, promoting masculine or feminine traits. Boys generally learn to be masculine by identifying with their fathers or other male role models. Yet more boys are growing up with nonresident or absentee fathers and lack positive role models.

Family Influences

20. Young children need to be fitted into their society's cultural ways, in a process called socialization. Belsky proposes that within a cultural context, the family is a network of interacting individuals functioning as a dynamic system.

21. Young children are being affected by shifting trends in marriage, divorce, nonmarital childbearing, nonfamilial living arrangements such as cohabitation and foster care, migration of families, higher education standards, work instability and income variability, and the detrimental effects of poverty.

22. Love-oriented parenting techniques tend to promote a child's conscience formation and responsibility. In contrast, hostile and rejecting parents interfere with the child's conscience development and breed aggressiveness and resistance to authority. Children's own personality and temperament characteristics also influence the parenting they receive.

23. Restrictive parenting tends to be associated with well-controlled, fearful, dependent, and submissive behaviors. Permissiveness, while fostering outgoing, sociable, assertive behaviors and intellectual striving, also tends to decrease persistence and increase aggressiveness. Effective discipline is consistent and unambiguous. The most aggressive children have parents who are inconsistent toward aggression.

24. In American society there is strong debate about using spanking as a disciplinary method, with many antispanking and pro-spanking advocates. A well-publicized longitudinal study reported findings suggesting that occasional, mild spanking does not harm a child's emotional-social development. All social scientists agree that no parent should use severe punishment, which causes serious physical, emotional, and behavioral problems in victims. Sexual abuse of children alters a child's cognitive and emotional orientation to the world, causing a loss of control and sense of powerlessness, stigmatization, and a sense of betrayal by a trusted person.

25. All professionals who work with young children are obligated by law to report any suspected child abuse. In 2002 nationwide about 896,000 children were victims of child abuse. Most abused children are neglected. The highest rate of abuse is in the infancy to age 3 group, and child abuse rates decline as children get older. Young children are most likely to be harmed by their mothers. In 2002, over 1,400 American children died from abuse and neglect.

26. Baumrind distinguishes among authoritarian, authoritative, permissive, and harmonious parenting. Authoritative parenting tends to be associated with children having self-reliance, self-control, an eagerness to explore, and contentment. Authoritative parents use scaffolding to support their child's learning. In contrast, the offspring of authoritarian parents tend to be discontented, withdrawn, and distrustful. Permissive parenting promotes the least self-reliant, least explorative, and least self-controlled children.

27. Two-year-olds become more autonomous with their ability and willingness to say "No!" to parents. Parenting styles affect a child's normal self-assertion, defiance, and

compliance. The way parents handle autonomy issues has profound consequences for their youngsters' behavior. Guidance with control appears most effective, yet children in the same family respond differently to the same style of child rearing.

28. In contemporary American society, nearly 68 percent of children (from birth to age 18) live with two parents (both biological or adoptive parents), and 32 percent of children live in alternative arrangements (23 percent live with mothers, 5 percent with fathers, and 4 percent reside with neither parent but live with other relatives, in foster care, detention facilities or other). Over 3 million children reside in homes with a parent who is cohabiting.

29. Family structure impacts the socioeconomic status (SES) of families and children's well-being. There are many known detrimental effects for children living in poverty. Female-headed households had a poverty rate four times that of two-parent households. Nearly 13 million children were reported to live in poverty in 2002.

30. More poor single women are having children living outside of marriage or becoming single head of household with children as a consequence of divorce. Efforts are being made to secure child support payments, which are critical for survival for such families with children, especially since the Welfare-to-Work program imposes a time limit on the receipt of welfare payments.

31. Divorce is a stressful experience for both children and their parents for a period of time. Interactions between divorced parents and their children differ from those in intact families. Children often respond to their parents' divorce by pervasive feelings of sadness, hope for reconciliation, and worries about how to take care of themselves. Parents typically change interaction patterns with their children in contrast to interaction in intact families. There is a two- to three-year adjustment period. Much of the children's well-being depends on the custodial parent's interaction style, time spent with the children, and discipline.

32. With joint custody, parents share in regular child-care responsibilities and decision making. Yet parents often cannot come to agreement. Overall the quality of a child's relationship with both parents is most important. Various societal institutions assist with the needs of single-parent families.

33. A growing number of young children reside in homes with gay and lesbian parent(s). Although some Americans question this lifestyle, there is no convincing evidence that children from such families are compromised in any significant way. Gay and lesbian parenting is discussed in Chapter 14. The essence of successful parenting is in the parent-child relationship.

34. Sibling relationships are normally significant throughout life. Firstborn children often experience more affection, time, and interaction with parents. Some cultures distribute more rights and privileges to a firstborn. Siblings structure a child's social environment, providing key relationships and roles. Family size affects achievement. Confluence theory suggests that each additional child reduces parental interaction. The resource dilution hypothesis proposes that finite resources are less with each additional child, such as economic support, social opportunities, and parental time.

35. Three explanations have been advanced to account for differences between firstborns and later-borns. Adler posed a theory suggesting sibling rivalry plays a role in each child's personality formation, as each child competes for attention and recognition in a family.

Nonfamilial Social Influences

36. Young children enjoy and benefit from peer relationships and friendships, which occur with increasing age. Children serve one another as reinforcing agents and behavioral models, and friendship serves many needs. Preschoolers with close familial attachment tend to enjoy happier relationships with peers. Friendship functions as cognitive stimulation, allows children to self-regulate, provides for socialization, fosters a sense of identity, and enables children to deal with fears. Young children tend to spend more time with same-sex playmates—girls interact in two-person or small groups, but boys often play in larger groups. Young children often model the behavior of others.

37. Children enjoy being with children like themselves. Yet with the inclusive model of education, young children need to prepare to accept and make friends with children with disabilities. Parents, child-care professionals, and teachers need to help young children develop a positive attitude toward children with disabilities.

38. As children grow older, their aggression becomes less diffuse, more directed, more retaliatory, and more verbal. Boys display aggression both physically and verbally, but girls display aggression by using harmful words, exclusion, and withdrawing friendship. The more hours per week young children spend away from parents, the more likely a child will act aggressively. Young children experience many school-readiness advantages in high-quality child care. Children also model aggression witnessed in the home. Currently between 4 and 6 million children have been identified with antisocial behaviors as early as age 3.

39. Children who participate in quality preschool, Early Head Start, and Head Start programs indeed do get a head start. They achieve a higher academic level than children not in preschool. Such quality programs have had positive effects on adolescent and adult outcomes. Parents of children in Head Start also benefit from a guidance and support network.

40. For at least three decades, research findings have suggested that television and video games are major socializing agents of children and that televised violence is highly associated with aggressive behaviors in children. National child health organizations recommend supervision and limitation of young children's television viewing and their use of other media including the Internet.

Key Terms

aggression (296)

antisocial behavior (298)

authoritarian parenting (287)

authoritative parenting (287)

collectivism (268)

confluence theory (294)

dyslexia (275)

egocentric (267)

entelechy (274)

gender (274)

gender identity (275)

gender roles (275)

gender stereotypes (278)

harmonious parenting (289)

imaginary friend (266)

individualism (268)

initiative versus guilt (277)

joint custody (292)

peers (295)

permissive parenting (289)

play (265)

resource dilution hypothesis (294)

scaffolding (288)

self (273)

self-concept (274)

self-esteem (273)

sexual abuse of children (285)

socialization (279)

Following Up on the Internet

Web sites for this chapter focus on early childhood emotional, self-esteem, gender, and identity issues. Please access the text Web site at www.mhhe.com/vzcrandell8 for up-to-date hot-linked Internet addresses for the following organizations, topics, and resources:

**Center on the Emotional and Social Foundations
    for Early Learning**

Child Care and Early Education Research Connections

The Division for Early Childhood

Exceptional Parent

Positive Parenting

**U.S. Administration for Children & Families:
    Child Care Bureau**

Part FIVE
Middle Childhood
7 to 12

Middle childhood, the time during the elementary school years, is a period of slower physical growth but faster intellectual development than what occurred during the preschool years. In Chapter 9 we will see that children experience greater cognitive sophistication, acquire more socialization skills, and understand and cope with their emotions better. Cognitive maturation allows the child to deal with fearful and stressful events or to model prosocial behaviors. In Chapter 10 we will see that children at this stage are industrious, inquisitive, and more socially aware than before. Peer groups begin to exert a stronger influence on preadolescent children than in earlier years. Youth become more aware of social standings such as popularity, acceptance, and rejection. Most children learn to control their emotions in school, in other group settings, or when around peers and friends. Some children, however, need help with academic performance or behavioral control.

Middle Childhood
Physical and Cognitive Development

1. What does it mean to say someone is gifted or a genius? For example, if Mozart had been taken at the age of 20 to a Pacific island where the inhabitants did not know or understand Western music, if he had no musical instruments and no means of expressing his musical talents except by humming or singing, would the islanders have considered him to be a genius? Or would they have thought he was disabled?

2. How do you perceive others? Think back to when you were a child and compare the perception you had of your parents then to the perception you have now. In what ways has your perception of them changed?

3. If you were going to try to teach a "hardened criminal" how to be moral, which of the following approaches would you use, and how would you implement your plan? (1) Place the criminal in a very moral environment and assume that morality would rub off. (2) Teach the criminal the basic principles of morality and then send the person to live in mainstream society. (3) Use examples of crime and deviancy to teach about morality and ethics.

4. Why don't we hold children to adult standards of morality? Why don't we treat adults like children and give them the same treatment for offenses?

In the middle childhood years, children get to rest up a bit after the dramatic physical development of early childhood and prepare for the onset of puberty and adolescence. From a developmental perspective, the changes during this time appear so smooth and uneventful that we might think nothing is happening. The greatest changes will be in cognitive growth, and we will discuss concrete operational thought, intelligence and its measurement, individual differences, and children with special learning needs.

These children capably use complex classifications and enjoy making collections of everything from sports cards to butterflies. They start paying attention to counts and amounts, what is bigger, who has more, and their knowledge of the physical world grows by leaps and bounds. We are also beginning to realize that a significant part of children's work during these years involves learning appropriate cultural and social skills. The patterns and habits of social interaction established now not only will affect the child's adolescence but also will carry into adulthood. We conclude this chapter with an examination of language skills and moral development, two significant issues in contemporary American society.

Physical Development

Writer Robert Paul Smith, in 1957, recalls his elementary years with best friends as a constant whirlwind of play and activity in his book, *"Where Did You Go?" "Out." "What Did You Do?" "Nothing."* Their "doing nothing" included swinging on swings, sliding on slides, going for walks, sitting in boxes, riding bikes, reading on back porches, climbing on roofs, sitting on tree limbs, playing hide-and-seek, standing in the rain and in the snow, skipping, hopping, jumping, galloping, whistling, humming, and screaming. Such carefree experiences with friends are the things we recall with nostalgia as we age. In some ways, childhood today is the same, yet we shall see some differences in how children spend their middle childhood years.

One of those differences is in the increasing numbers of children, ages 5 to 13, who will be passing through elementary and middle schools over the next 45 years (see Table 9.1). Note that there is a 35 percent projected increase of children who will be attending schools, requiring out-of-school supervision, needing medical and dental care, participating in sports or other unsupervised play activities, and growing up in a technically sophisticated world.

As these millions of children grow, there will be individual variations in development, as well as variation due to gender, ethnicity, and socioeconomic status. For example, African American children tend to mature more quickly (as measured by bone growth, percent fat, number of baby teeth) than Americans of European descent. Asian Americans appear to have the slowest rate of physical change and are less likely to show signs of puberty during middle childhood. Although variations in size and maturity are normal, children who fall at one extreme or the other on the continuum can feel deficient because of their physical differences. These feelings are often reinforced by peers who rate attractiveness and popularity on the basis of physical competence and appearance (Jones, 2001).

Growth and Body Changes

Children grow more slowly during the years of middle childhood than in early childhood or in adolescence. With adequate nutrition, the typical child gains about five or six pounds and grows about two inches per year. Girls and boys have similar growth patterns, except that girls tend to have more body fat, and they mature a bit faster than boys. Most children gain small motor skills and hand-eye coordination for writing, getting dressed, tying shoes, and performing other tasks. Gradually, their baby teeth begin to come out and larger permanent ones come in. Children must be taught to perform daily dental care, and periodic dental cleanings should be done. Dental sealants and fluoridated water also help to prevent dental caries. Children who have dental *caries* (cavities) or lose permanent teeth will resist talking, reading aloud, and will become less confident of using language, nor will they smile. Optimal oral health disparities exist because of dental care costs (Goodman et al., 2004). The American Academy of Pediatric Dentistry (2005) recommends that as children participate in contact sports, they should wear mouth guards, helmets, and facial shields to protect permanent teeth and facial bones.

If we look at children during this time period, they appear thinner or slimmer because as they grow taller, their body proportions change. Muscles become bigger and stronger, and children can kick and throw a ball farther than in the earlier years. There is an increase in lung capacity that gives greater endurance and speed, of which children make full use. Some variations in height, strength, and speed are due partly to nutrition, particularly in developing countries, but most of the differences among children are the result of heredity. There are differences not only in size but also in rate of maturation. This is particularly noticeable at the end of middle childhood when some children begin to undergo the changes of puberty and find themselves quite different from their peers in shape, strength, and endurance.

Table 9.1 Projected Population of U.S. Children, Ages 5 to 13: 2005–2050 (in millions)

Year	Projected Population (in millions)
2005	35.4
2010	35.3
2020	38.3
2030	41.3
2040	44.0
2050	47.6

Source: Statistical Abstracts of the U.S.: 2003. Population Projections. No. 13 Resident Population Projections by Sex and Age: 2005 to 2050.

Question

What are the expected growth and body changes for a child during the middle childhood years?

Motor Development

During their middle years, children become more skilled in controlling their bodies. Their rate of physical growth has slowed down temporarily, giving them time to feel comfortable with their bodies (unlike earlier years) and an opportunity to practice their motor skills and increase their coordination. Seven- or 8-year-olds might still have difficulty judging speed and distance, but they have improved their skills sufficiently to be successful in games like soccer and baseball. Jumping rope, skateboarding, rollerblading, and riding bicycles are also activities they can enjoy. Which specific skills are developed depends somewhat on the children's environment (e.g., whether they learn games for snow or the tropics, whether the culture favors soccer or football). Whatever activities children choose, they will lead to greater coordination, speed, and endurance. Gender differences are minimal during this time period, although girls tend to have greater flexibility and boys have greater forearm strength. Age and experience are much more important determinants than gender, and we can see this in team sports where girls and boys are equally likely to score goals or hit home runs and both enjoy doing cartwheels, somersaults, and other gymnastic maneuvers.

Brain Development

As stated in earlier chapters, with regular proper nutrition, health care, and adequate sleep, a child's brain and nervous system will develop by both progressive myelination and regressive pruning processes. During this time period, the capacity, speed, and efficiency of the child's mental processes typically increase as well (De Bellis et al., 2001). Neglect, sensory deprivation, maltreatment, trauma, and being underfed have long-term deleterious consequences for normal brain development and adult potential (Perry, 2002). Memory span increases fairly steadily during the childhood years. One type of improved efficiency is simply faster response time (Kail, 1991). Faster response is due in part to the physical development that occurs in the brain, but also to the fact that children at this age are becoming adept at using more cognitive strategies to help them solve more complex tasks. Using new brain-imaging techniques with healthy boys and girls aged 6 to 17, DeBellis and colleagues (2001) found age-related sex differences in brain maturation processes, such as some increase in interconnecting axons and corpus callosal areas in boys than in girls.

Studies utilizing imaging of the brains of young children have revealed evidence that children's brains appear to be organized differently than adult brains. A stroke in a young child of 6 or 7 might have no subsequent effect on the child's language development, whereas the same kind of stroke in an adult would normally cause permanent loss of language abilities. Studies of children with one hemisphere removed for severe seizure control indicate that these children generally continue to

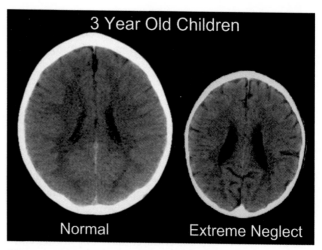

Child Neglect Seriously Affects Brain Development These images illustrate the negative impact of neglect on the developing brain. The CT scan on the left is from a healthy 3-year-old child with an average head size (50th percentile). The image on the right is from a 3-year-old child following severe sensory deprivation and neglect since birth. The brain is significantly smaller than average and has abnormal development of cortical, limbic, and midbrain structures.

display good physical and mental development (Laws & Bertram, 1996; Vining et al., 1997). Perry and other brain researchers are finding trauma, neglect, and abuse can have severe effects on a child's developing brain. Yet plasticity of the brain allows for amelioration of effects if children are placed in a loving, supportive foster care home (Brownlee, 1996; Miller et al., 2000).

Question

What are the typical changes in body growth and brain maturation during these years?

Dyslexia Between 3 to 15 percent of children experience more difficulty with processing visual or auditory information (Bradway et al., 1995). **Dyslexia** is a learning disorder in which an otherwise normally intelligent, healthy child or adult has extreme difficulty recognizing written words affecting reading comprehension and writing. There are more boys with dyslexia than girls (Rutter et al., 2004). Those affected often have an average or above average IQ and tend to learn math skills easier (Rosensweig, 1999). Neuroscientists are studying this brain disorder and so far have discovered from imaging, diagnostics, and limited autopsies of dyslexics that in the language area of the cerebral cortex in the left hemisphere, the layers are disorganized, whirled with primitive, larger cells. Turn this book upside down and try to read the words fluently. This is what reading tasks are like for children with dyslexia, who are at a higher risk of lower achievement in school, poor self-esteem, becoming school dropouts, and limiting their occupational opportunities. Interestingly enough, some of these children are also identified as gifted or talented (Grigorenko et al., 2001).

Genius and Giftedness Neuroscientists and psychobiologists have found that more efficient brains have rich neuronal interactions and a multiplicity of synaptic connections. It has been hypothesized that child geniuses might have more complex synaptic connections in the association areas of the cerebral cortex or that their neurochemical transmissions might be more efficient. The areas in which some children have displayed genius range from piano playing to mathematical problem solving. A standard IQ score of 130 or above, or scoring in the 90th to the 99th percentile in reading or math on standardized achievement tests, usually qualifies a child for a pullout program, in-class enrichment, or advancing a grade.

Children identified as gifted during the middle childhood years of 7 to 12 typically need additional intellectual challenges to avoid boredom in their educational and home environments. Many, but not all, schools provide a special program for these students. Some colleges and universities offer special weekend and summer programs to stimulate the sharp minds of these students. On the East Coast, for example, Johns Hopkins University in Baltimore, Maryland, sponsors the Institute for the Academic Achievement of Youth (IAAY)–Center for Talented Youth (CTY) and conducts annual talent searches. The Johns Hopkins Talent Search Model looks for exceptional mathematical and/or verbal reasoning abilities among second- through eighth-graders to provide opportunities for full development of these children's mathematical and language abilities. Other national and international programs for highly intelligent, creative youth include, among others, the Odyssey of the Mind program, the Science Olympiad, the Invention Convention, National Geographic Kids Network, and MENSA programs. Those of you who are preparing to become educational psychologists, school psychologists, preschool to high school teachers, or future school administrators may want to find out more about the special needs of gifted and talented youth by contacting one of these special programs nearest you.

Health and Fitness Issues

Typically children are much healthier in the middle childhood years than at any time since birth. The rate of illness is lower, with most children in elementary schools reporting four to six acute illnesses in a year. The most common childhood illness is upper respiratory infection, although rates of childhood asthma have been rising, with much higher rates of black and Hispanic youth with asthma seeking care at emergency rooms (Boudreaux et al., 2003). Other chronic health conditions for children from ages 5 to 11 are learning, speech, behavioral, and respiratory problems (see Table 9.2).

Accidents, rather than illness, are the major cause of death or serious injury during this time period, and the most common cause is being killed in a car accident, thus recent stricter seatbelt laws (see Figure 9.1). Table 9.3 shows that mortality rates for children aged 5 to 14 have been decreasing over the years. The good news is that since 1980, overall child mortality rates have been declining for this age group for both male and female children and for all races. However, the mortality rate for black youth is still considerably higher than for white youth.

Children in middle childhood still need adult supervision and care. The greatest number of sports injuries for children in this age group occur when they are playing basketball, football, or baseball, bicycling, and using playground equipment. Injuries from backyard trampolines have become "a national epidemic" (G. Smith, 1998).

There is a growing misperception about violence perpetrated against or by this age group, particularly its older members.

Children under the age of 13 who commit delinquent acts have an increased likelihood (by a factor of 2 to 3) of committing future delinquent acts and are also apt to be delinquent for a longer time period (Loeber & Farrington, 2000). Research on violence indicates that violent or aggressive behavior is often learned early in life, and steps need to be taken in families and communities to help children deal with their emotions without using violence. Consequently, many teacher education programs are training future teachers in conflict resolution methods. One of the strongest findings was that children "do what they see," and the recommendation

Table 9.2 Selected Chronic Health Conditions Causing Limitation of Activity Among Children, Ages 5 to 11: 2001–2002

Chronic Health Condition	Percent Affected
Learning disability	24.8
Speech problem	18.1
Attention-deficit hyperactivity disorder	17.1
Other mental, emotional, or behavioral problem	10.6
Mental retardation and other developmental problem	9.2
Asthma/breathing conditions	7.9

Source: Centers for Disease Control and Prevention, National Center For Health Statistics. *Health, United States, 2004.*

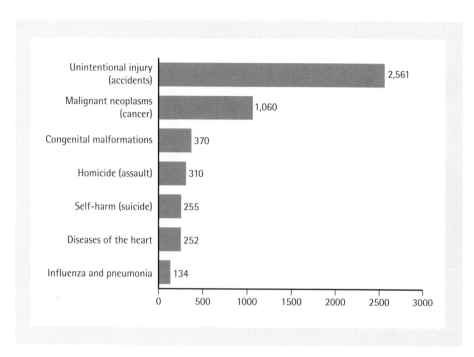

FIGURE 9.1 **Leading Causes of U.S. Child Death, Ages 5 to 14: 2003** Fewer than 7,000 U.S. children, ages 5 to 14, died in 2002, and the major cause was unintentional injuries, with car accidents the main reason. Children in middle childhood experience the fewest deaths of any age group in the life span.

Source: Hoyert, D. L., Kung, H. C., Smith, B. L. (2005, February 28). Deaths: Preliminary Data for 2003. *National Vital Statistics Reports, 53*(15), 1–48. Retrieved March 22, 2005, from http://www.cdc.gov/nchs/data/nvsr/nvsr53/nvsr53_05.pdf

was made that we take care not to be models for violence (American Academy of Pediatrics and American Psychological Association, 1996). Television and realistic video or computer games produce violent images and reward children to be more aggressive (Brink, 2001; Miller, 2001). Some E-rated computer games (suitable for everyone) depict violence, sex, and use of tobacco and alcohol (Thompson & Haninger, 2001).

Obesity   The CDC uses the term *overweight* when referring to children and the term obesity with adults. **Obesity** is defined as having a body mass index (BMI) at or above the 95th percentile for age and gender (see Table 9.4). The percent of overweight children has quadrupled since the 1970s to 16 percent of children ages 6 to 11 by 2002. Thus, doctors refer to the increasing rate of overweight children as an epidemic (Centers for Disease Control and Prevention, 2004h). Major health risks include high cholesterol and blood pressure leading to early cardiovascular disease, higher rate of diabetes mellitus, weight-related orthopedic problems, and skin disorders (Johnson, 2001). Also, being obese can cause depression, a result of negative self-image, low self-esteem, teasing and rejection, and withdrawal from peer interactions (Johnson, 2001). Being overweight as a child greatly increases the risk of being overweight as an adult, and such major health risks shorten adult lives (Crespo et al., 2001).

Obesity is caused by high caloric intake, low activity, and in rare cases hereditary or thyroid hormone factors. Parent and school decisions are related to increasing rates of overweight children: (1) lifestyle changes as moving to suburbs and car-pooling; (2) fears about

child kidnappings and drive-by shootings; (3) increasing work hours for both parents; (4) exercise time limited to organized sports and little or no unstructured play time; (5) fewer physical education classes due to school budget

Table 9.3 Child Mortality Rates Are Decreasing for Children Ages 5 to 14 by Gender and Race, Selected Years 1980 to 2002 (deaths per 100,000 in each group)

Between 1980 and 2002, the death rate declined by more than one-third for children ages 5 to 14. Unintentional injuries (most from motor vehicle traffic accidents) were the leading cause of death, followed by cancer, homicide, and birth defects.

	1980	1985	1990	1995	2002
Total	30.6	26.5	24	22.5	17.4
Gender					
Male	36.7	31.8	28.5	26.7	20.0
Female	24.2	21	19.3	18.2	14.7
Race					
White	29.1	25	22.3	20.6	16.0
Black	39	35.5	34.4	33.4	25.3
Hispanic	*	19.3	20	20.5	15.5
Asian/Pacific Islander	24.2	20.8	16.9	16.8	12.4
American Indian/Alaska Native	*				21.6

*Full data not available.
Source: America's Children: 2004. Table Health 7.B, Centers for Disease Control and Prevention, National Center for Health Statistics, National Vital Statistics System. http://www.childstats.gov/ac2004/toc.asp.html. 2002 data from *National Vital Statistics Reports,* (2004, October 12), 53(5).

Table 9.4 Child Obesity by Gender, Race, and Ethnicity: 1999–2002

Here is the breakdown, by percentage, for children in the U.S. classified as overweight (at or above the 95th percentile in body mass index). Eating high-fat snacks accompanies sedentary activities such as watching TV, playing video games or computer games, and both behaviors are correlated with an increasing rate of children who are overweight.

All Children	Ages 6 to 11	Ages 12 to 19
Boys	**16.9**	**16.7**
White	14.0	14.6
Black	17.0	18.7
Hispanic origin	26.5	24.7
Girls	**14.7**	**15.4**
White	13.1	12.7
Black	22.8	23.6
Hispanic origin	17.1	19.6

Source: Centers for Disease Control and Prevention. (2004h). *Health, United States, 2004.*

constraints; (6) soft drink and snack food vending machines in schools as a source of funding; and (7) more sedentary time spent with TV, video games, and computers (Crespo et al., 2001; Layden, 2004).

We know that obese adults and children take in more calories and exercise less than others of the same age, socioeconomic status, and gender who are not overweight. Studies of twins separated at birth by adoption and reunited in adulthood indicate that children have a genetic tendency toward fatness or thinness. Adult identical twins have much more similar body weights than fraternal twins (Stunkard, 1990). Likewise, adopted children reared by obese parents are not as likely to be obese as are the natural children of these parents. Crespo and colleagues (2001) report that the prevalence of obesity increases for each additional hour of television a child or teenager watches per day. In a study with third- and fifth-grade children, Matheson and colleagues

(2004) found children consume a significant proportion of high-fat foods while watching television.

Adults should act as good role models, provide healthy foods and encourage children to make healthy food choices when at school, promote regular exercise (60 minutes per day for children), and reduce sedentary activities, such as video game and television viewing ("Obesity and Your Child," 2005; Vandewater et al., 2005). If adults live a healthy lifestyle, exercise regularly, and eat low-fat, healthy foods, children usually develop these habits, too.

Nationwide, schools are under criticism for allowing vending machines with soft drinks and high-caloric snacks as a funding source while child health suffers. The Centers for Disease Control and Prevention's *School Health Policies and Programs Study* survey (2000a) concluded that school vending machines, snack bars, or school stores offer high-caloric soft drinks and snacks in 43 percent of elementary schools, 89 percent of middle/junior high, and 98 percent of senior high schools. Some states have enacted legislation to offer healthier lunch options, restrict student access to junk foods, or remove such vending machines. About 20 percent of schools offer fast-food meals to schoolchildren (Layden, 2004).

Eating Disorders   In many countries, a growing number of elementary (as young as 4) and middle school children, mainly girls, are diagnosed with the eating disorders of anorexia and bulimia (Branswell, 2001; Huggins, 2001; Medina, 2001). Mom's nutritional/dieting habits, family environment, Barbie dolls, media portrayal of thin girls and women, and friends are powerful influences on children's eating behaviors (Blinder, 2001; Davison & Birch, 2001). A child's denying regular nourishment causes poor health, fatigue, or even death. It is imperative that parents, teachers, and school nurses learn about the typical physical and behavioral signs and causes of these disorders. Eating disorders are discussed further in Chapter 11.

Role of Play and Exercise   Children who attend public schools are required to participate in physical education classes, unless they have an illness or disability that prevents their participating. However, daily gym class in schools is becoming obsolete due to budgetary constraints and emphasis on raising children's test scores (only Illinois has mandatory daily PE classes in grades K–12). Schools, communities, and policymakers need to provide regular, quality physical education for all youth, activities that can become lifelong habits (Grunbaum et al., 2004). Also, middle schools offer extracurricular sports for both boys and girls, such as indoor and outdoor soccer, basketball, track, football, baseball or softball, volleyball, and tennis. Increased physical activity promotes overall fitness, improves cognitive functioning, improves overall mental health, reduces the effects of stress, and builds self-esteem (Armstrong et al., 1998). All children should develop a regular routine of physical activity and maintain it throughout high school, and throughout life, to keep their immune and cardiovascular systems healthy. Yet recent research reveals age-related declines in physical activity and participation, particularly for girls. Dowda and colleagues (2004) recommend that PE classes be more enjoyable and relevant for girls. Girls report enjoying walking, rollerblading, aerobics, jogging or running, bicycling, swimming, jumping rope (double-dutch), and social dancing; whereas boys report participating in traditional competitive activities. A growing body of research shows that reducing television viewing allows children time for play activities, improving overall health (Crespo et al., 2001, Robinson 2001).

Most children this age love to play, which usually means running and throwing balls as in touch football or dodge ball, wall ball, skateboarding, riding bikes, hopscotch, jumping rope, dancing, and gymnastics. Schools are transitioning from traditional forms of exercise to modern dancing, mountain biking, hiking, in-line skating, cross-country skiing, snowshoeing, climbing walls, and so forth (Layden, 2004). Healthy girls and boys of this age have a difficult time sitting in a classroom all day without being able to expend their tremendous energy. For some—but not all—gym class is their favorite activity of the week because that is where they experience their greatest success!

Healthy Children Enjoy Expending Energy on Sports and Other Play Activities Although many children participate on sports teams, they often spend about 20 minutes a week in a game (others may spend a lot of time sitting on a bench waiting to play). Recreation and health experts recommend turning off the TV and computer and encouraging play activities that children enjoy, such as these youth are doing with double-dutch jump roping. Research indicates that girls enjoy more singular types of energetic endeavors (i.e., walking, jogging, or social dancing), whereas boys typically enjoy competitive sports.

Questions

What are the common causes of childhood illness and death? What factors promote healthy growth and physical and cognitive development?

Cognitive Development

An important feature of the elementary school years is an advance in children's ability to learn about themselves and their environment (Crick & Dodge, 1994). During this period they become more adept at processing information as their reasoning abilities become progressively more rational and logical (Flavell, 1992; Schwanenflugel, Fabricius, & Alexander, 1994).

Cognitive Sophistication

A crucial component of reasoning abilities is being able to distinguish fiction, appearance, and reality (Woolley & Wellman, 1993). Consider, for instance, what happens if you take hold of a joke sponge that looks like a solid piece of granite. Although it looks like a rock, you realize it is a sponge the moment you grasp it. But a 3-year-old is less certain. Very young children often do not grasp the idea that what you see is not necessarily what you get. But by the time they are 6 or 7 years old, most children appreciate the appearance-reality distinction that confronts us in many forms in everyday life (Flavell, Flavell, & Green, 1983).

Children develop **metacognition,** an awareness and understanding of their own mental processes (Lyon & Flavell, 1994). In many respects Piaget's stages constitute **executive strategies.** That is, children come to select, sequence, evaluate, revise, and monitor their problem-solving plans while integrating and orchestrating lower-level cognitive skills. With maturation, strategies used are more complex and powerful. As a learning strategy, metacognition is viewed as a crucial link in performance. A study examining children's mental strategies and solving math problems found metacognition accounts for much of the variance of successful math performance in 8- to 9-year-olds (Despete, 2001).

Piaget's Period of Concrete Operations From Piaget's perspective, there is a qualitative change in children's thinking during middle childhood as children begin to develop a set of rules or strategies for examining the world. Piaget calls middle childhood the **period of concrete operations.** By an "operation" Piaget means an integration of the powerful, abstract, internal schemas such as identity, reversibility, classification, and serial ordering. The child begins to understand that adding something results in more, objects can belong to more than one category, and these categories have logical relationships. Such operations are "concrete" because children during these years are bound by immediate physical reality and cannot transcend the here and now. Consequently, during this period, children still have difficulty dealing with remote, future, or hypothetical (or abstract) matters.

Despite the limitations of concrete operational thought, during these years children make major advances in their cognitive capabilities. For example, in the preoperational period before 6 or 7 years of age, children arrange sticks by size in their proper sequence by physically comparing each pair in succession. But in the period of concrete operations children "mentally" survey the sticks, then quickly place them in order, usually without any actual measurement. Because the activities of preoperational children are dominated by actual perceptions, the task takes them several minutes to complete. Children in the period of concrete operations finish the same project in a matter of seconds, because their actions are directed by internal cognitive processes: They can make the comparisons in their minds and do not have to physically place and see each stick side by side.

Conservation Tasks   The difficulty younger children had solving conservation problems is due to the rigidity of their preoperational thought processes. Let's look at how children use concrete operations to solve these kinds of problems when they are a bit older. **Conservation** requires recognition that the quantity of something stays the same despite changes in appearance. It implies that children are mentally capable of compensating in their minds for various external changes in objects. Elementary school children come to recognize that pouring liquid from a short, wide container into a long, narrow one does not change the quantity of the liquid; they understand that the amount of liquid is conserved. Whereas preoperational children fix ("center") their attention on either the width or the height of the container and ignore the other dimension, concrete operational children decenter, attending simultaneously to both width and height. Furthermore, concrete operational children assimilate transformations, such as to the gradual shift in the height or width of the fluid in the container as it is poured by the experimenter. And most important, according to Piaget, they attain reversibility of operations. They recognize that the initial state can be regained by pouring the water back into the original container. (Decentering, transformations, and reversibility were discussed in Chapter 7.)

Concrete Operational Thought and Conservation Skills
According to Piaget, children in the concrete operational stage of thought can decenter, thus attending simultaneously to both width and height. Furthermore, they assimilate transformations, such as to the gradual shift in the height or width of the fluid in a container as it is poured by the experimenter. Also, they attain reversibility of operations. They recognize that the initial state can be regained by pouring the water back into the original container.

Classification, or the concept of class inclusion, is usually understood by the age of 7 or 8. This development in children can be seen when using a game similar to "20 Questions." Children ages 6 to 11 were shown a group of pictures and were to ask questions to figure out which one the researcher "had in mind." ("Is it alive?" "Is it something you would play with?" etc.) The questions asked were divided into two basic types: strategy (categories) and no strategy (guessing). Six-year-olds typically resorted to guessing particular objects ("Is it a banana?"); older children asked categorical questions ("Is it something that you eat?") (Denney, 1985).

According to Piaget, children in the period of concrete operations develop the ability to use *inductive logic:* Given enough examples or provided with multiple experiences, children can come up with a general principle of how something operates. For example, if they are given enough problems of the form of 3 + 4 = ? and 4 + 3 = ?, they can induce that the order of the numbers in addition is not significant. They know that they will al-

Question

How does the acquisition of concrete operations allow a child to perform Piaget's conservation tasks?

ways get the same answer, 7. On the other hand, they are not very good at moving from the general to the specific, which is *deductive logic*. Starting with a concept or rule and then generating its application is difficult for them because it involves imagining something they might never have experienced. Despite the cognitive advances made in concrete operations, children in this period are still "concrete" and in some degree dependent on their own observations and experiences.

As is true of other cognitive abilities, children acquire some conservation skills earlier, some later (see Figure 9.2). Conservation of discrete quantities (number) occurs somewhat before conservation of substance. Conservation of weight (the heaviness of an object) follows conservation of quantity (length and area) and is in turn followed by conservation of volume (the space that an object occupies). Piaget calls this sequential development, with each skill dependent on the acquisition of earlier skills, *horizontal décalage*.

Horizontal décalage implies that repetition takes place within a single period of development, such as the period of concrete operations. For example, a child acquires the various conservation skills in steps. The principle of conservation is first applied to one task, such as the quantity of matter—the notion that the amount of an object remains unchanged despite changes in its position or shape. But the child does not apply the principle to another task, such as the conservation of weight—the notion that the heaviness of an object remains unchanged regardless of the shape that it assumes. It is not until a year or so later that the child extends the same type of conserving operation to weight.

The general principle is the same with respect to both quantity and weight. In each case children must perform internal mental operations and no longer rely on actual measurement or weighing to determine whether an object is larger or weighs more. However, children typically achieve the notion of the invariance of quantity a year or so before that of the invariance of weight (Flavell, Flavell, & Green, 1983).

Post-Piagetian Criticism The difference in acquisition times does not necessarily fit with Piaget's notion of stages. If, as Piaget says, each stage is a "cohesive whole," then we should find that children of any given age apply similar logic to a wide range of problems. A child who has concrete operations should be able to use operational logic on all tasks presented. Similarly, for children who are capable of operational logic, the amount of particular knowledge they have about the content of a task should not affect their use of these basic operations. But research has found that this is not really the case: It appears to make a difference how much experience or expertise a child has with the objects involved, for children can perform more complex operations on tasks they are

familiar with as opposed to ones that are novel to them (Chi, Hutchinson, & Robin, 1989).

Other research has focused on whether the development of concrete operations can be accelerated, not just by general experience with objects, but through specific training on how to do conservation tasks. Jerome S. Bruner (1970) states: "The foundations of any subject may be taught to anybody at any age in some form." Learning theorists reject Piaget's stage formulations and disagree with Piaget's view that children below the age of 6 cannot benefit from experience in learning conservation because of their cognitive immaturity.

In the early 1960s any number of psychologists attempted to teach young children conservation skills. For the most part, they were unsuccessful. Subsequently, a number of researchers successfully used cognitive learning methods to train children in conservation. Furthermore, psychologists are finding that the content of a task decisively influences how a person thinks (Spinillo & Bryant, 1991). By altering the cognitive properties of a task, one often can elicit preoperational, concrete operational, or formal operational thinking from a child (Chapman & Lindenberger, 1988; Sternberg & Downing, 1982). Issues of this sort have stimulated research in creativity. (For more on this subject, see the *Further Developments* box on page 319, "Creativity.")

Cross-Cultural Evidence Over the past 40 years, children throughout the world have served as subjects for a variety of experiments designed to test Piaget's theory. Research has been conducted in over 100 cultures and subcultures, from Switzerland to Senegal and from Alaska to the Amazon (Feldhusen, Proctor, & Black, 1986). The results show that regardless of culture, individuals do appear to move through Piaget's hierarchical stages of cognitive development—the sensorimotor, preoperational, concrete operational, and formal operational periods—in the same sequence. Some cultural groups do not attain the state of formal operations, though. But cross-cultural research suggests that there is a developmental lag in the acquisition of conservation among children in non-Western, nonindustrialized cultures. Not entirely clear is whether this lag is due to genuine differences among cultures or to flaws in research procedures that use materials and tasks alien to some cultures. For instance, a study of Chinese children performing the Piagetian water-level task found a relationship between cognitive development and the instruction effect (Li, 2000).

The research also raises a question about whether the acquisition of conservation skills in the period of concrete operations occurs in the invariant sequence (horizontal décalage) postulated by Piaget. Children in Western nations, Iran, and Papua, New Guinea, exhibit the expected Piagetian pattern. Thai children, however, appear to develop conservation of quantity and weight

Conservation Skill	Basic Principle	Test for Conservation Skills	
		Step 1	Step 2
Number (Ages 5–7)	The number of units in a collection remains unchanged even though they are rearranged in space.	 Two rows of pennies arranged in one-to-one correspondence	 One of the rows elongated or contracted
Substance (Ages 7–8)	The amount of a malleable, plastic-like material remains unchanged regardless of the shape it assumes.	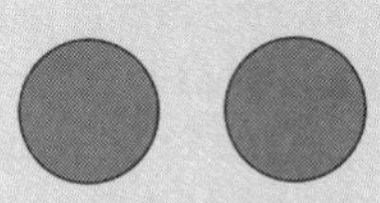 Modeling clay in two balls of the same size	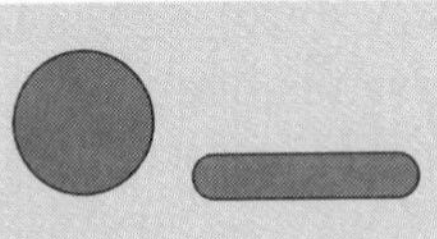 One of the balls rolled into a long, narrow shape
Length (Ages 7–8)	The length of a line or object from one end to the other end remains unchanged regardless of how it is rearranged in space or changed in space.	Strips of cloth placed in a straight line	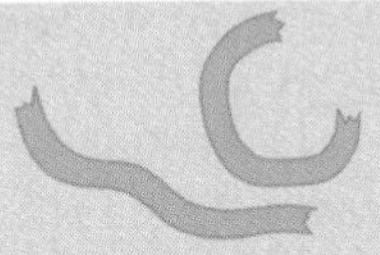 Strips of cloth placed in altered shapes
Area (Ages 8–9)	The total amount of surface covered by a set of plane figures remains unchanged regardless of the position of the figures.	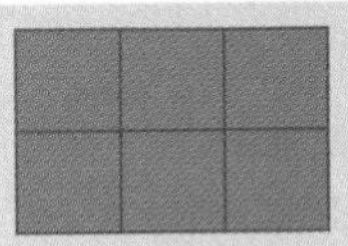 Square units arranged in a rectangle	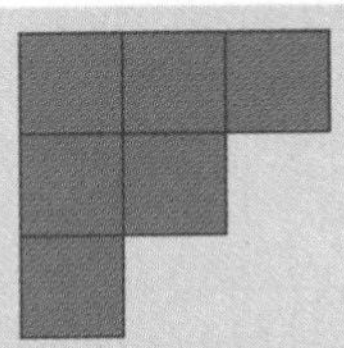 Square units rearranged
Weight (Ages 9–10)	The heaviness of an object remains unchanged regardless of the shape that it assumes.	Units placed on top of each other	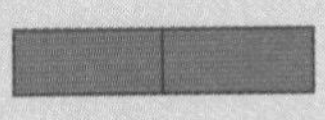 Units placed side by side
Volume (Ages 12–14)	The space occupied by an object remains unchanged regardless of a change in its shape.	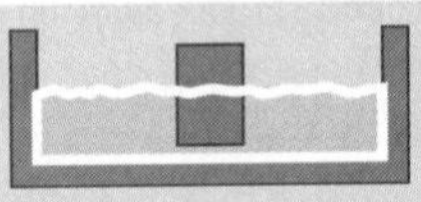 Displacement of water by object placed vertically in the water	 Displacement of water by object placed horizontally in the water

FIGURE 9.2 Sequential Acquisition of Conservation Skills During the period of concrete operations, Piaget says children develop conservation skills in a fixed sequence. For example, they acquire the concept of conservation of number first, then that of substance, and so on.

Further Developments

Creativity

We commonly value creativity as the highest form of mental endeavor and achievement. Whereas intelligence implies quick-wittedness in learning the predictable, **creativity** implies original and useful responses and creations. Often we assume that high intelligence and creativity go hand in hand, yet psychologists find that high intelligence does not ensure creativity, but low intelligence seems to work against it. Above-average intelligence—although not necessarily exceptional intelligence—seems essential for creative achievement (Sternberg, 2001).

In some cases too much brainpower can even get in the way of creativity. Psychologist Dean Keith Simonton (1991) studied renowned creators and leaders of the 1900s and found that the optimal IQ for creativity is about 19 points above the average of people in a given field. Nor is formal education essential. Many famous scientists, philosophers, writers, artists, and composers never complete college. Formal education often instills rote methods for doing things versus offbeat but creative solutions. Albert Einstein describes the stifling effects of formal education: "The hitch in this was the fact that one had to cram all this stuff into one's mind for the examinations, whether one liked it or not. This coercion had such a deterring effect on me that, after I had passed the final examination, I found the consideration of any scientific problem distasteful for an entire year" (Einstein, 1949, p. 17).

Creative people seldom have bland personalities. Psycholinguist Vera John-Steiner (1986) interviewed 100 men and women active in the humanities, arts, and sciences, and she sifted through notebooks, diaries, and biographies of creative individuals such as Albert Einstein and Leo Tolstoy. She finds that scientists and artists mention that their talent and interest were revealed early in life and that they were often encouraged and nurtured by their parents or teachers.

According to one view, creativity requires that a person reorganize a tie or connection with some situation in the world (Sternberg, 2001). Creative accomplishment is exceedingly difficult precisely because it necessitates changing not merely the contents and organization of one's mind but an inclusive system of relationships involving the world, other people, or an established set of cultural concepts (Csikszentmihalyi, 1997). Sometimes it may be easier to stifle creativity than to stimulate it.

Nobel laureate Dr. Salvador E. Luria of MIT, says, "The most important thing is to leave a good person alone" (see Haney, 1985). And although creative people may have innate talent, they must nurture their creativity with discipline and hard work. There are a number of tips that parents and teachers can use to encourage creative thinking and originality in children:

- Respect children's questions and ideas, and their right to initiate their own learning.
- Respect children's right to reject the ideas of caretakers in favor of their own.
- Encourage children's awareness and sensitivity regarding environmental stimuli.
- Confront youngsters with problems, contradictions, ambiguities, and uncertainties.
- Give children opportunities to make something and then do something with it.
- Use provocative and thought-producing questions, and give children opportunities to describe what they learned and accomplished.
- Encourage children's sense of self-esteem, self-worth, and self-respect.

In short, situational, cognitive, motivational, and personality characteristics all play a part in creativity.

Source: Creative Competitions, Inc.

The Gift of Creativity Psychologists agree that a natural gift is not sufficient to produce creative effort. What is required is the convergence of innate talent and a receptive environment, and such talents and interests are revealed early in life. When children are inspired by their own interests and enjoyment, they are more likely to explore unlikely paths, take risks, and in the end produce something unique and useful. Four-year-old artist Marla Olmstead began painting at age 2 and has attracted attention of international art collectors (and a skeptical media). You might enjoy watching her express her creativity at www.marlaolmstead.com.

simultaneously (Boonsong, 1968). And some Arab, Indian, Somali, and Australian aborigine subjects conserve weight before quantity (deLemos, 1969; Hyde, 1959).

Sociocultural factors play a role in children's cognitive development through the interplay of communication and relationships (Hala, 1997). Children of pottery-making families in Mexico performed better on conservation of substance tasks than their peers from other families (Ashton, 1975). And Greenfield (1966) found in her studies of Wolof children in Senegal, West Africa, that it made a difference whether the experimenter or the children poured the water in the Piagetian test involving wide and narrow containers. Two-thirds of children under 8 years old who themselves transferred the water achieved the concept of conservation. Yet only one-fourth of a group who watched the experimenter pour the water realized that the amount of water was the same. The children attributed the experimenter's feat to a "magical action" they did not attribute to their own performance.

> **Questions**
>
> Is there a general consensus among psychologists and educators on how to define creativity? Do creative children tend to follow a single pattern, or do they work in different ways? What elements must be evident for a thought or invention to be considered creative? Do you think U.S. schools foster or stifle creativity?

Information Processing: Another View on Cognitive Development

In Chapter 7, we indicated that some theorists will ask children to report what they are doing intellectually while they perform a task. How does the child process the information she or he is given to solve a problem? How do these intellectual processes change with age? This is quite different from Piagetian theorists who ask what overall structure of logic the child uses and how these structures change over time. According to the information-processing view, we need to understand whether there is a change in the basic processing capacity of the system (hardware), and/or whether there is a change in the type of the programs (software) used to solve a problem. For instance, there are certain limitations to the number of operations a computer can perform at one time and to the speed at which it can perform them. Just like an executive, children at this age might be better at dividing tasks into more manageable segments. For example, with regard to memory, children at this age might become more efficient at using the mnemonic strategies of rehearsal and categorization, as discussed in Chapter 7.

Individual Differences   Much of our thinking so far has centered on how the typical child develops cognitively through this middle childhood period. We have described the changes in the use of concrete operations with advancing age and have shown that the developmental process is predictable to a certain extent, although there is still debate as to what mechanism explains this growth. We have also noticed variations in the rate at which children change and the overall amount of change that takes place in this period. Piaget believed that only 30 to 70 percent of adolescents and adults perform at the formal operation level (Piaget, 1963). Likewise, some children take quite a while to develop operational logic for any task, whereas other children learn some academic skills quite easily and yet struggle with other skills that appear quite similar operationally. School and home environments alone do not seem to account for the individual variability in conceptual ability.

Children's Perception of Others   The elementary school years are a time of rapid growth in children's cognitive understanding of the social world and of the requirements for social interaction (Crick & Dodge, 1994). Consider what is involved when we enter the wider world (Vander Zanden & Pace, 1984). We need to assess certain key statuses of the people we encounter, such as their age and sex. We must also consider their behaviors (walking, eating, reading), their emotional states (happy, sad, angry), their roles (teacher, sales clerk, parent), and social contexts (church, home, restaurant).

Accordingly, when we enter a social setting, we mentally attempt to "locate" people within the broad network of possible social relationships. By scrutinizing them for a variety of clues, we place them in social categories. For instance, if they wear wedding rings, we infer that they are married; if they wear business clothes during working hours, we infer that they are employed in white-collar jobs; if they are in a wheelchair, we infer that they are handicapped. Only in this manner can we decide what to expect of others and what they expect of us. In sum, we activate **stereotypes**—certain inaccurate, rigid, exaggerated cultural images—that guide us in identifying the mutual set of expectations that will govern the social exchange.

Research by W. J. Livesley and D. B. Bromley (1973), based on a sample of 320 English children between 7 and 16 years of age, traced developmental trends in children's perceptions of people. The study reveals that the number of dimensions along which children conceptualize other people grows throughout childhood. The greatest increase in children's ability to distinguish people's characteristics occurs between 7 and 8 years of age. Thereafter, the rate of change is generally much slower; the differences between 7-year-olds and 8-year-olds are often greater than the differences between 8-year-olds and 15-year-olds. This observation leads Livesley and

Bromley (1973, p. 147) to conclude that "the eighth year is a critical period in the developmental psychology of person perception."

Children under 8 years of age describe people largely in terms of external, readily observable attributes. Their conception of people tends to be inclusive, embracing not only personality but also an individual's family, possessions, and physical characteristics. At this age children categorize people in a simple, absolute, moralistic manner and employ vague, global descriptive terms such as good, bad, horrible, and nice. Consider this account by a 7-year-old girl of a woman she likes:

> She is very nice because she gives my friends and me toffee. She lives by the main road. She has fair hair and she wears glasses. She is forty-seven years old. She has an anniversary today. She has been married since she was twenty-one years old. She sometimes gives us flowers. She has a very nice garden and house. (Livesley & Bromley, 1973, p. 214).

When they are about 8 years old, children show rapid growth in their vocabularies for appraising people. Their phrases become more specific and precise. After this age children increasingly come to recognize certain regularities or unchanging qualities in the inner dispositions and overt behaviors of individuals. Here is a description of a boy by a 9-year-old girl:

> David Calder is a boy I know. He goes to this school but he is not in our class. His behavior is very bad, and he is always saying cheeky [impudent] things to people. He fights people of any age and he likes getting into trouble for it. (Livesley & Bromley, 1973, p. 214)

This suggests the rapid development that occurs during middle childhood in children's abilities to make psychological inferences about other people—about their thoughts, feelings, personality attributes, and general behavioral dispositions (Erdley & Dweck, 1993). As children's cognitive ability of "person perception" matures, their vocabulary increases, as does their ability to express their needs and to communicate with others (Livesley & Bromley, 1973, p. 130).

Questions

How does Piaget describe children's cognitive development from age 7 to age 12? Are Piaget's theories about cognitive development applicable to children from other cultures?

Language Development in Middle Childhood

The use of the English language in our schools will be a hurdle to some of our new American schoolchildren,

and our schools and communities must work together with these immigrants and their descendants to assimilate them into our culture. Part of the problem is their resistance to acculturation. Children of Hispanic or Asian origin are more likely to have difficulty speaking English because they are more likely to speak another language at home. It is estimated that nearly 20 percent of children ages 5 to 17 speak a language other than English at home (National Center for Education Statistics, 2003c). This represents at least 2.6 million children—and nearly one-third of American schoolchildren in Western states speak another language at home (Wallman, 2001). Few Hispanic children start elementary school with preschool experience; thus their lack of preparedness and ability to communicate in the classroom puts them at a great disadvantage (Wallman, 2001). These statistics speak to the need to teach all children English language skills in order for them to become more informed and active citizens. Because only a small percent of public school teachers are of minority status or bilingual, more school districts are hiring teachers and classroom paraprofessionals who are bilingual to teach students who do not speak English (Menken & Antunez, 2001).

Learning any language is a lifelong process. Children from the ages 6 to 12 continue to acquire subtle phonological distinctions, vocabulary, semantics, syntax, formal discourse patterns, and complex aspects of pragmatics in their first language (Gleason, 1993). During this time, children are usually in school and add to speech the cognitively complex systems of reading and writing. As they grow older, they grow wiser, and the complexity and cognitive level of their language increases as a reflection of their academic studies and life experiences. Let's take a closer look at the changes in language that take place during middle childhood—in particular, vocabulary, syntax, and pragmatics.

Vocabulary Anglin (1993) reports that a fifth-grader learns as many as 20 new words a day and achieves a vocabulary of nearly 40,000 words by age 11. Some of this increase is basic academic vocabulary, because children spend most of their day in school and are exposed to a wide range of subjects requiring them to understand and use specific new terms. The concrete operational child is also able to learn and understand words that might not be tied to his or her personal experience, such as ecology or discrimination. They are able to describe objects, people, and events in terms of categories and functions rather than just physical features. They are more likely to describe their family dog in terms of its breed, its personality traits, and the kinds of things it can do. They can compare their dog to other dogs and contrast their dog as a pet with other kinds of pets others have. Children begin to understand that words have multiple meanings, and they can use this new skill to tell jokes and ask riddles.

Third-, fourth-, and fifth-grade children typically love to tell and make up their own "knock-knock" jokes. Both in reading and speaking, we see them beginning to make hypotheses about what words mean, using the context of the speaker's situation or, when reading, using pictures or the surrounding known words.

Syntax and Pragmatics   Children now begin studying grammar, for they understand rules apply to language. They might still speak incorrectly, improperly using pronouns and agreement of subject and verb, but they can learn the correct form and can recognize errors in syntax. The structure of their sentences becomes more complex—they use other conjunctions besides, and use adverbs, adjectives, and prepositional phrases. Their cognitive abilities are sufficiently developed to allow the correct use of modal verbs such as *can, must, will, may, might,* and *should* (Nelson, Aksu-Ko, & Johnson, 2001).

A second type of growth occurs in the child's pragmatic language. As discussed in Chapter 7, pragmatic language is use of language in a particular context or situation. In middle childhood, they recognize that they can (and should) modify their voice, volume, and even their vocabulary, depending on the context of the interaction. For example, they will adopt a more formal style of vocabulary and syntax when talking with a teacher or a neighbor, as compared with how they talk to their parents or close friends. This ability of *code switching*, or changing from one form of speech to another, indicates that the child has developed an awareness of the social requirements in a given context. It also allows children a certain freedom in speech when talking with peers, enabling them to express themselves using casual, often emotional words. Think for a minute how you would describe your hectic evening last night to a friend, your boss, or your parents. Research has shown that children of all social strata engage in code switching, and their pronunciation, grammar, and slang all change in this process (Yoon, 1992).

Question
What changes do we see in the way children use and understand language from age 7 to age 12?

Educating Children Whose Communication Skills Are Below Standard   Since the 1980s, dramatically increasing numbers of immigrant children with **limited English proficiency (LEP)** have impacted on U.S. schools. LEP identifies students who were not born in the United States or whose native language is not English and who cannot participate effectively in school because they have difficulty speaking, understanding, reading, and writing English. Educators refer to these children

as **English language learners (ELLs).** Estimates range from 3 to 8 million LEP students nationwide and most speak Spanish (National Center for Education Statistics, 2003a; U.S. Department of Education, 2000, 2001).

In 2002 when the *No Child Left Behind* legislation was signed into law, the National Association for Bilingual Education (NABE) endorsed its passage. However, the law so far has done little to address the needs of ELL children (i.e., limited resources to train teachers, provide instructional materials and programs, and create adequate facilities) (Crawford, 2004).

American educators feel pressured to get LEP students to pass standardized tests, even with the $477 million distributed through the *Title III State Formula Grant Program* in 2003 (U.S. Department of Education, 2005). Research indicates that it takes several years for children to become proficient in a second language.

The first *Bilingual Education Act,* passed in 1968 required schools to "rectify the language deficiency" in LEP children. This act was updated in 1988 and required schools to gather data on the numbers of LEP students and services and to support evaluation and research on the effectiveness of bilingual education programs. One requirement is that each school district present instruction such that non-English speakers have an opportunity to achieve language and math skills equal to that of native-English speakers. More recently, the NCLB in 2001 authorized services to maintain the same goals for LEP students in the *Title III, Language Instruction for Limited English Proficient and Immigrant Students.*

The language of instruction is a critical choice, and we must think about how language is learned and what variables affect speed of acquisition, the relationship of language and thinking, as well as the social context of language (Bialystok, 2001).

Eight approaches are proposed to "rectify the deficiency" and provide mainstream education for children, family literacy, parent outreach, and teacher training programs. The main four approaches are described here (U.S. Department of Education, 2005, p. 25).

English as a Second Language (ESL)   The **English as a second language (ESL) approach** is focused on teaching children English as quickly and efficiently as possible. Thus, children might learn English in a separate class all day, every day, until they reach some standard of proficiency. Then the child will enter the regular classroom and receive full-time instruction in all academic areas in English. We can compare this approach to teaching English with the way foreign languages are taught in U.S. middle and high schools. That is, the child is taught specific vocabulary and the rules of grammar and has practice in speaking and interpreting English. The obvious question then is: When is a child ready to join the mainstream and exit the ESL class?

One important variable is the level of competency and/or formal instruction the child has had in the primary language. If the child's first language is well developed, he might reach age- and grade-level norms in English in 3 to 5 years. If the child has received no formal education in the first language, it can take 7 to 10 years (Collier, 1997; Crawford, 1997). In general, late-exit programs have resulted in higher academic achievement than early-exit programs. Another concern is that these children may come to devalue their first language, refusing to speak it at home and in the community. This limits the quality and quantity of their interactions with their families and excludes their development of cultural identity (Crawford, 1997).

Bilingual Education A second approach, **bilingualism,** provides instruction in both languages by teachers proficient in both. This approach seems ideal to some, who argue that because children receive instruction in their first language, they can continue to acquire both academic skills and language skills. Using their first language (which is more developed), they are able to express more complex ideas, read higher-level texts, and increase their basic vocabulary, which in turn allows them to learn a second language (English) more easily. It has been documented that cognitive and academic development in the first language has an extremely important and positive effect on second-language schooling (Collier, 1992; Garcia, 1994). A great transference of skills (literacy, concept formation, subject knowledge, learning strategies) can take place from the first to the second language, compared with having to learn these in a less developed language (Krashen, 1996; The National Research Council, 1998).

Bilingual programs have consistently shown the greatest gains for children in academic skills and in social and emotional skills. The child is able to interact with family and community with increasing complexity and greater meaning and can feel that her or his first language is on an equal basis with English. When children are tested in their second language, they typically reach and surpass native speakers' performance across all subject areas after 4 to 7 years in a quality bilingual program. Bilingually schooled students typically sustain this level of academic achievement and outperform monolingually schooled students in the upper grades (Collier, 1997).

According to Menken and Antunez (2001), a number of studies have shown bilingual education is effective if children are in well-designed programs and if all teachers have the necessary preparation to work with these children. Such preparation includes learning vocabulary about a culture, people, customs, history, food, and music.

The National Board for Professional Teaching Standards (2004) offers certification in Early and Middle Childhood/English as a New Language to teach children 3 to 12 years old from diverse linguistic and cultural backgrounds. Krashen (1996) argues that bilingual education can be more effective if there are many more books available in both the first and second languages of children enrolled in these programs. He further states that Spanish-speaking LES children have few such books or resources at home, at school, or in school libraries.

Bilingual education programs are controversial and have become a complex issue in nearly all states (Escamilla et al., 2003). California voters approved a referendum in 1998, requiring that teachers teach only in English. Reportedly, about one-third of California school children have low or no proficiency in the English language. Apparently the majority of voters in this state believed the former bilingual approach was not successful and was a too great tax burden. Significantly, many parents did not want their children segregated in schools by bilingual programs. The majority of California voters preferred, instead, an instructional approach called total immersion.

Total Immersion In **total immersion programs,** children are placed in regular classrooms (with or without support in their first language), and English is used for all instruction. This eliminates "separate" education or classes and gives every child an opportunity to observe and learn social communication in English with peers. The theoretical basis of total immersion is that language is best learned not when it is an academic subject but rather when it is useful and that children are motivated to learn the language to understand what is going on around them. However, the process is quite lengthy and learning is directed purposefully during this time to the child's linguistic and cognitive level. That is, we don't teach our 2-year-olds the history of the United States in the colonial period or the language of the scientific method. Immersion programs seem to work best when the children are young and the family has positive feelings about this approach.

During the middle school years, children begin to understand sentence structure and grammar, extend their vocabularies, write coherently, use school, public libraries, or the internet to find information, and give oral presentations in class. They also utilize their language skills in the community through membership in organized clubs and activities or by helping neighbors, working as newspaper carriers, volunteering, and so forth. Children this age learn they have a right to voice their concern about societal issues such as air pollution or recycling, and some write editorials to their local newspaper, to corporate America, or to government representatives. A command of the English language is a symbol of empowerment for both these children and their parents.

Two-Way Bilingual Programs   In **two-way bilingual programs,** both native-speaking students and nonnative speakers receive instruction in English and in another language, for example in Spanish. Participation is on a voluntary basis and instruction is equally divided between the two languages. Students would eventually become proficient in both languages and achieve *biliteracy,* or literacy in two languages. There are about 250 such programs in the United States (Gilroy, 2002). Many view biliteracy as a great advantage in seeking employment opportunites. For such programs to be successful, instruction should begin in the early grades and requires teachers who are competent, inventive, and strong leaders (Glenn, 2002). Massachusetts legislators ensured that children of all ages could continue to enroll in two-way bilingual programs (Zehr, 2003).

Questions

Should children be "allowed" to speak a language besides English in school? Should teachers and other school personnel be required to speak a second language to be able to communicate with the children and parents who are not proficient in English? Should colleges require all teacher education graduates to be proficient in a second language to be able to communicate with an increasingly diverse ethnic population?

English Language Learners There has been a dramatic decline in English and math test scores for children in California—a state that once led the nation. Educators cite many reasons for this change, including a wide array of languages and cultures (1 out of 4 children is learning English) and a lack of state funding to train teachers and provide appropriate instructional materials. In addition, 40 percent of California's children are from low socioeconomic conditions, some districts have to shut down for six weeks when parents return to Mexico as crop workers, and few parents show up on parent-conference night. Many school districts are penalized under No Child Left Behind provisions if scores are low for two years in a row—yet California has a severe budget deficit.

Assessment of Intelligence

When we think about intelligence, we think about the way individuals differ from one another in their ability to understand and express complex ideas, adapt effectively to their environment, learn from experience, and solve problems. (The concept of intelligence was defined in Chapter 7.) Although the children's differences in their ability to do those things may be tremendous, their abilities can also appear to vary due to the time at which we assess them, the methods used, and the specific tasks we ask them to perform (Daniel, 1997). Historically, what we know about differences in school-age children is based on academic performance in school and intelligence testing using psychometric tests. This makes sense because in school these differences play a major role in determining how children learn and what educational programs best meet their cognitive needs. Given that, two questions come to mind. First, what tests should we use to measure their cognitive abilities? Second, how should the information we get from the assessment be used to determine specific educational plans? For a cross-cultural perspective on academic performance, see the *Human Diversity* box, "The Academic Achievement of Asian and U.S. Children."

Types of Intelligence Tests   Intelligence tests come in many forms. Some use only a single type of item or question; examples include the Peabody Picture Vocabulary Test (a measure of children's verbal intelligence) and Raven's Progressive Matrices (a nonverbal, untimed test that requires inductive reasoning about perceptual patterns).

Other tests use several different types of items, including verbal and nonverbal, to measure a wide range of abilities instead of one specific construct such as spatial ability or verbal intelligence. The Wechsler scales and the Stanford-Binet test ask the test-taker to give meanings of words, complete a series of pictures, copy a block design, and complete analogies. Performance on these tests can be measured in several domains (subscores) as well as by an overall score relating to general intelligence. The scores are standardized, with a *mean* of 100 and a *standard deviation* of 15. This permits us to make statements such as 95 percent of the population scored within 2 standard deviations of the mean (between 70 and 130) and compare the person's score to the norming population (the population the test-taker is being compared with).

In contrast to these psychometric tests, other tests give us insight about a person's ability in a specific type of task. If we want to measure spatial ability, we might measure the length of time it takes a person to find a certain place in a new town or unfamiliar setting, or we might measure linguistic ability by asking a person to give an extemporaneous talk.

Schools primarily use the more conventional measurements such as the *Stanford-Binet* or *WISC-III* (*Wechsler Intelligence Scale for Children-III*) because the reliability and validity of such tests are documented, the scores are stable at least for school-age children, and they correlate well with, and are predictive of, academic performance.

The EQ Factor: Emotional Intelligence Learning emotional self-regulation, a component of emotional intelligence, is not an easy task. As we discussed in Chapter 7, the development of emotional intelligence is receiving a great deal of attention from educational psychologists and other researchers concerned with the alarming trend of aggression and violence perpetrated by a growing number of children (and adults) in this country. Some children in middle schools and high schools are bringing weapons to school and concealing them in lockers and book bags. Large urban and suburban schools have resorted to using metal detectors, 24-hour video security systems, and police officers to patrol hallways. When confrontations arise, as they always will, some youth have not been able to control their anger, rage, or fear. A few have taken tragic courses of action, killing innocent peers and school personnel. Drive-by shootings, in which youth in cars randomly shoot innocent children and adults for the thrill of it, have become all too common. Researchers who study emotional intelligence call this a type of "mind-blindness," where the powerful emotional limbic system short-circuits the frontal cerebral cortex, blocking all reasoning. Some psychologists call this "temporary insanity." The traditional intelligence tests that have been used for nearly a century do not begin to tap the social-emotional abilities that can predict success or healthy self-regulatory behaviors—important life skills. However, there are other psychometric instruments that assess the likelihood of deviancy or emotional disturbance in youth and adults.

Limitations of IQ Tests Many times children are included or excluded in specific educational programs based on their intellectual functioning, but the intellectual functioning of children with LEP often cannot be determined. For example, special education services for mental retardation or cognitive impairment are available only to children who are tested using a standard measure of intelligence (IQ test) and obtain a score (full scale) of less than 70 IQ. The intellectual functioning of a child with a score below 70 is assumed to be lower than 97 percent of the population tested. Yet we know without a doubt that a child's academic performance cannot be totally explained by this one score. In fact, other factors, such as the child's motivation, social and language skills, self-concept, and even family and ethnic values, play important roles in the child's success in school.

More recently, some schools have turned to a *multidisciplinary team assessment*. This more comprehensive look at the child might include teacher input on achievement and effort, parent and community reports of how a child functions, observations by a school psychologist of the child in the classroom, review of the child's portfolio or work samples, and recommendations from various professionals and others who have knowledge about the child (e.g., speech therapist, resource room teacher). These additional pieces of information provide a more global understanding of the child's abilities. Nevertheless, it is useful to obtain standard measures as well to prevent bias or prejudice in the child's placement in a special education program.

It is well documented that certain groups of children are identified more frequently as being in need of special education services, even with the use of standard scores. For example, more African American children than white children are being placed in special education classes, even though there is no evidence of underlying differences in their abilities (Coutinho & Oswald, 2000). To ensure proper placement for all children, school psychologists, educational psychologists, and teachers must continue to pursue theoretical as well as practical knowledge about how children learn, the role of intellectual ability, and curriculum and instructional methods that best match children's learning needs.

Individual Cognitive Styles Have you ever felt stupid or out of place in a classroom? Did you feel that you couldn't understand the information being presented, no matter how hard you concentrated? Have you ever wondered why some subjects come easier to you than others? Although intelligence has a role to play in all learning, clearly not everyone learns in the same way. Some people learn best using visual information; others prefer to hear the spoken word. Yet others learn faster and retain the information longer when they involve all of their senses in hands-on learning. Still others, such as some students with autism, "think" in pictures instead of in words, storing images "as if they were on a CD-ROM" (Grandin, 1995). These differences in how individuals organize and process information have come to be called cognitive styles. **Cognitive styles** are powerful heuristics that cut across traditional boundaries between intelligence and personality and influence a person's preferred way of perceiving, remembering, and using information (Crandell, 1979, 1982; Sternberg & Grigorenko, 1997; Witkin, 1964, 1975). Psychologists have been researching cognitive styles for over 50 years and have identified a number of different cognitive style models, including Witkin's field-dependence versus field-independence, Kagan's impulsive versus reflective, and Hill's educational cognitive style (Messick, 1976). Research shows that when students are matched to instruction

Human Diversity

The Academic Achievement of Asian and U.S. Children

International comparisons of academic achievement on tests in mathematics and science are becoming more important as global economic competition becomes more intense. A country's ranking is often viewed as a barometer of its economic strength. Comparisons are often made between the United States and other industrialized nations such as Canada, France, Germany, Italy, Japan, the Russian Federation, and the United Kingdom. Although U.S. students in fourth and eighth grade scored above the international average score in math and science in 2003, the *Trends in International Mathematics and Science Study (TIMSS)* (Gonzales et al., 2004) found that since 1995 they were consistently outperformed by students in several Asian countries: Japan, Singapore, and Hong Kong (see Tables 9.5 and 9.6). Such indicators point toward taking a closer look at successful education practices that support student achievement.

Cultural Differences

Family nurturance and values contribute to differences in school readiness. To solicit child obedience, U.S. mothers assert authority or consequences, whereas Japanese mothers appeal to their children to be polite, loyal, diligent, and respect their elders (Sugiyama, 2001). This Confucian ethical code centers on self-discipline, respect for family, and respect for all forms of learning and infuses many Asian countries (Sugiyama, 2001). Parents strongly support and encourage children, and children work hard to bring honor to their families and approach the classroom with receptiveness and diligence. U.S. mothers rate *ability* rather than effort as a stronger factor in school success, but Japanese, Chinese, and Taiwanese mothers rate *effort* as more important than ability (Sugiyama, 2001; Zhang, 1995). Thus, Asian children expend efforts in the classroom on more productive endeavors than challenging the authority (Zhang, 1995). Achievement consists of hard work and never giving up, states Chinese philosopher Hsun Tzu (pronounced *Sun Zi*) (Zhang, 1995).

School Readiness

Japanese parents have high regard for education and teach children to count to 100 and tell time on clocks before they enroll in elementary school (Sugiyama, 2001). In daily life they expose children to situations that use numbers. Learning the Japanese numeral system is relatively easy: A child learns to count from 1 to 10 and then learns one simple rule and then can easily count to 100 (less to memorize than in the decimal system). By second grade, all Japanese students learn their multiplication facts (*ku ku*), using various songs and mnemonics (Sugiyama, 2001). The Japanese school system has a *no failure policy,* thus teachers must pay special attention to low-achieving students. Such students have higher scores than students from other countries in the TIMSS study (Gonzales et al., 2004). Stevenson and colleagues (1993), in a follow-up study with students from these same cities, determined that Asian children in first grade spend nearly equal amounts of time on language and math instruction, whereas American children spend much more time on language instruction in first grade. American youngsters were more likely to engage in unproductive behaviors, wander around the room, ask irrelevant questions, and talk to peers (Stevenson, Chen, & Lee, 1993).

Are Asian Schools Better than American Schools? Since 1995, Asian schoolchildren performed at the highest levels of math and science on TIMSS, an international assessment with schoolchildren from 46 countries. Asian schools provide a longer school year and a more orderly and focused education than do their American counterparts. Also, Asian teachers of math and science have earned college degrees in those specific content areas and know their content very well. However, many American teachers earn education degrees, with a small percent holding degrees in math or science. Thus, U.S. teacher certification requirements are being upgraded.

Table 9.5 Average Mathematics Scale Scores of Fourth-Grade Students, by Country: 2003

In 2003, U.S. fourth-grade students exceeded the international averages in both math and science, but showed no measurable changes since 1995. Fourth-graders in Hong Kong, Japan, and Singapore outperformed U.S. fourth-graders in both mathematics and science.

Country	2003
Singapore	594
Hong Kong SAR	575
Japan	565
Netherlands	540
Latvia LSS	533
England	531
Hungary	529
United States	**518**
Cyprus	510
Australia	499
New Zealand	496
Scotland	490
Slovenia	479
Norway	451
Iran, Islamic Republic of	389

▨ Average is higher than the U.S. average.
  Average is not measurably different from the U.S. average.
▨ Average is lower than the U.S. average.

Source: Gonzales, P., Guzman, J. C., Partelow, L., Pahlke, E., Jocelyn, L, Kastberg, D., & Williams, T. (2004). *Highlights from the Trends in Mathematics and Science Study (TIMSS) 2003:* U.S. Department of Education, National Center for Education Statistics. Washington, DC: U.S. Government Printing Office. Retrieved March 24, 2005, from http://nces.ed.gov/pubs2005/2005005.pdf, pp. 80 and 91 of report.

Table 9.6 Average Mathematics Scale Scores of Eighth-Grade Students, by Country: 2003

The average math score for U.S. eighth graders increased from 492 in 1995 to 504 in 2003. U.S. eighth-graders were outperformed by eighth-graders in 11 countries, with the highest scores achieved by mainly Asian eighth-graders.

Country	2003
Singapore	605
Korea, Republic of	589
Hong Kong SAR	586
Japan	570
Belgium-Flemish	537
Netherlands	536
Hungary	529
Russian Federation	508
Slovak Republic	508
Latvia-LSS	505
Australia	505
United States	**504**
Lithuania	502
Sweden	499
Scotland	498
New Zealand	494
Slovenia	493
Bulgaria	476
Romania	475
Norway	461
Cyprus	459
Iran, Islamic Republic of	411

▨ Average is higher than the U.S. average.
  Average is not measurably different from the U.S. average.
▨ Average is lower than the U.S. average.

Source: Gonzales, P., Guzman, J. C., Partelow, L., Pahlke, E., Jocelyn, L Kastberg, D., & Williams, T. (2004). *Highlights from the Trends in Mathematics and Science Study (TIMSS) 2003:* U.S. Department of Education, National Center for Education Statistics. Washington, DC: U.S. Government Printing Office. Retrieved March 24, 2005, from http://nces.ed.gov/pubs2005/2005005.pdf, pp. 80 and 91 of report.

Teacher Preparation, Training, and Practice

Han (2001) and the *Before It's Too Late* commission (Glenn, 2000) address differences in teachers' professional training and practices as a crucial component of students' high achievement in math and science. Han (2001) visited public schools in Beijing, China, where she observed teachers whose specialty was math teaching first-grade and second-grade classes. Math teachers have a college degree in mathematics (versus being education majors). Desks in offices are arranged such that math teachers sit together, providing opportunity to share techniques, design effective lessons, and discuss student problems. The teachers' day begins at 8 a.m. and ends around 3:40 p.m., with two long teaching sessions separated by a two-and-one-half hour lunch break. Teachers devote about 4½ hours to preparing lessons, correcting homework, and dealing with student problems. From 3:40 until about 4:40 p.m. students stay after school for an hour-long homework session. Teachers leave around 5 p.m. With no other support personnel, each homeroom teacher is responsible for student achievement and mental development (Han, 2001). Parents can visit the teacher during preparation and planning times.

One half-day is reserved each week for teacher training, conducted by master teachers and in-service training administrators, and there is only one centralized standard curriculum that serves as a guide for daily lesson plans. School administrators also have backgrounds teaching math or science. There are no extra rewards or incentives for attending in-service training, which is standard in an American teacher's contract. Chinese teachers take additional course work at night, weekends, or during summer vacation.

Japanese teachers who specialize in science teach in a consistently structured, effective manner according to an observational analysis of science lessons in 10 Japanese classrooms. They connect student interest and prior knowledge, elicit student ideas through discussion, allow students to guide and conduct investigations, exchange information from findings, analyze and organize information, reflect on original hypotheses, and discuss unanswered questions (Linn et al., 2000).

Student Views

Shimizu (2001), a professor of mathematics at a Tokyo university, asked 80 college students (nonmath majors who were in the 1995 TIMSS study) for their views about why Japanese students excel on international comparative studies. Their responses include high parental expectations, diligence, excellent math teachers, a national curriculum, special schools for those who excel *(juku),* and the importance of academic careers in society.

New Directions

Regardless of the future economic benefits that may accrue, it is important that students receive the best possible education in all subjects. By looking at the cultural and familial values and expectations, school readiness practices, early literacy and numeracy as well as teacher preparation training and practices in other countries, U.S. educators, policymakers, and the general public can gain insight into educational practices that yield successful results.

based on their preferred style of learning, they process the information faster, retain it longer, and are motivated to continue to learn (Dunn, Beaudry, & Klavas, 1989; Messick, 1984). Are you analytical or global? Several features of this book were developed with students' various learning strengths in mind.

Putting theory into practice is difficult because teachers utilize many methods of teaching (speaking, writing on the board or on transparencies, acting or modeling, using manipulatives, showing videos, or using computer instruction, such as PowerPoint, as well as other methods). Teacher education programs are becoming more innovative, developing new delivery and testing strategies, requiring proficiency in a second language, and training in multimedia and multisensory approaches to accommodate the students' differing learning styles. The concept of *portfolio assessment* has been an outgrowth of learning styles: Any student is a whole being, not simply one who writes and speaks and calculates. Some are artistic, some are mechanical, some are musical, and some are quite adept socially. Proponents of portfolio assessment believe that a whole year of a child's academic life should not be reduced to a grade point average. These teachers keep a portfolio of the best of a child's performances for the year. The portfolio might include examples of a child's best work, such as photographs of a class play or sports events, a science fair or a talent show, an original poem, notes on a car the child helped build for *Odyssey of the Mind* competition, in addition to the child's best essays and math exams of the year.

Questions

How do we measure individual differences in cognitive abilities? In what ways is the process of cognitive development universal? Are there individual and group differences in the way people process information? Why do Asian children consistently outperform American children on international assessments in math and science?

Students with Disabilities

The *Education for All Handicapped Children Act*, PL 94-142, enacted in 1975, gave every American school-age child the right to a free, equal, and appropriate education in the least restrictive environment. For the first time, American children with disabilities could attend school and prepare for a meaningful future. This law was reauthorized by the *Individuals with Disabilities Education Act (IDEA)* in 1990. And recently, the *Individuals with Disabilities Education Improvement Act of 2004*, PL 108–446, updated regulations (Learning Disabilities Roundtable, 2005). Today classifications are more specific and include autism, deaf-blindness, emo-

tional disturbance, hearing impairments, mental retardation, multiple disabilities, orthopedic impairments, other health impairments, specific learning disabilities, speech or language impairments, traumatic brain injury, or visual impairments (National Center for Education Statistics, 2002). National data reports state that in 2001–2002, 6.4 million children, ages 3 to 21, with 13 types of disabilities were being served in federally supported education programs—representing a 75 percent increase in children being served since PL 94–142 was enacted in 1975.

Mental Retardation   Children and adults with **mental retardation (MR)** have below average mental functioning and limitations in adaptive skills, and a diagnosis must occur before the child reaches age 18. Since 1976, far fewer children are classified with mental retardation, and in 2002, only about 500,000 were classified with MR—likely because of more refined prenatal diagnostics and more children being classified with learning disabilities. Mental retardation can result from genetic or chromosomal disorders (such as Down syndrome or fragile X), prenatal teratogen effects (such as fetal alcohol syndrome), birth complications, (such as oxygen deprivation), nutritional and/or environmental deprivation after birth, childhood head injuries or exposure to teratogens, and unknown causes. IQ scores are used to classify the severity of retardation into four categories of *mild, moderate, severe,* or *profound.* When both ability and measured intelligence are low, clearly retardation exists. However, when there are discrepancies between ability and measured intelligence, it usually indicates a learning disability. Youth with mental retardation experience limitations in academics, communication, daily life skills, social skills, leisure, and work—although there are more opportunities for development to full potential with many therapeutic services beginning with early intervention at birth.

Learning Disabilities (LDs)   The 2004 law defines a *learning disability* as "a disorder in one or more of the basic psychological processes involved in understanding or in using language, spoken or written, which disorder may manifest itself in an imperfect ability to listen, think, speak, read, write, spell or do mathematical calculations" (Learning Disabilities Roundtable, 2005, p. 10).

Educators employ the term **learning disabilities (LDs)** as an umbrella concept to refer to children, adolescents, college students, and adults who encounter difficulty with school-related or work-related material despite the fact that they appear to have normal intelligence and lack a demonstrable physical, emotional, or social impairment (some prefer the term *differently abled*):

Learning disabilities (LD) is a disorder that affects people's ability to either interpret what they see and hear or to link information with different parts of the brain. These limitations can show up in many ways, as specific difficulties with spoken and written language, coordination, self-control, or attention. . . . Learning disabilities can be lifelong conditions that, in some cases, affect many parts of a person's life: school or work, daily routines, family life, and sometimes even friendship and play. (National Institute of Mental Health, 1993)

In practice, the notion implies that a discrepancy exists between a student's estimated ability and his or her academic performance. Youngsters are usually diagnosed as having a learning disability when their achievement level falls two or more grade levels below their ability, as predicted by a standardized IQ test score (see the hypothetical example in Figure 9.3).

Specific learning disabilities continues to be the most prevalent category of disability among students in elementary through high school, accounting for more than 44 percent of the total (see Figure 9.5) (National Center for Education Statistics, 2004). Nearly four times as many boys as girls are identified with reading disabilities, yet just as many girls have reading disabilities as boys (Lyon, 2000).

Spending for special education for 2.8 million children accounts for about 14 percent of the total education budget of $360.6 billion (see Table 9.7) (U.S. Department of Education, 2002).

A variety of youngsters are designated as "learning disabled." There are some whose eyes see correctly but whose brains improperly receive or process the informational input. Or instead of zeroing in on what is directly in front of their noses, they take a global view (Geiger & Lettvin, 1987). They might get letters mixed up, reading was as "saw" or god as "dog." Others have difficulty selecting the specific stimulus that is relevant to the task at hand from among a mass of sensory information. Still others might hear but fail to remember what they have heard by virtue of an auditory-memory problem. For instance, they might turn to the wrong page in the book or attempt the wrong assignment when they rely

on oral instructions. The sources of such disabilities are varied and include combinations of genetic, social, cognitive, and neuropsychological factors (DeMaria, 2001; Nopola-Hemmi et al., 2001). High-tech brain-imaging techniques, including PET, suggest that signal-processing regions like the thalamus might be implicated. The thalamus is a structure that functions like a telephone switching board; it takes incoming signals from the eyes, ears, and other sensory organs and routes them to different areas of the brain. Whatever the source of the disability, those with a learning disability have problems in reading (*dyslexia*), or writing (*dysgraphia*), or in mathematics (*dyscalcula*), or auditory and visual processing. Students identified as dyslexic make up a large percent of the LD population (Bradford, 2001).

Such disabilities are often called "the invisible handicap" but learning disabilities do not necessarily lead to low achievement. Many accomplished scientists (Thomas Edison and Albert Einstein), political leaders (Woodrow Wilson and Winston Churchill), authors (Hans Christian Andersen), artists (Leonardo da Vinci), sculptors (Auguste Rodin), actors (Tom Cruise and Whoopi Goldberg), Olympic athletes (Bruce Jenner and Greg Louganis), and military figures (George Patton) have had learning disabilities (Schulman, 1986).

The placement of children in a category like "learning disabled" is a serious matter. From a positive perspective, classification provides services that can facilitate learning, improve a sense of self-worth, and foster social integration. But teachers and the public must be aware of the possible harmful effects of labeling so that the labels are not used for obscure, covert, or hurtful purposes (Harris et al., 1992). One thing we can say for sure is that up until 1975, children with disabilities were not offered a public education; most stayed at home with no prospects for the future. Over the past 30 years, the doors of opportunity and progress have opened. Each

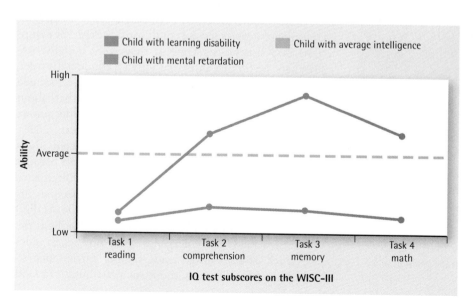

FIGURE 9.3 Hypothetical Profile of a Child with a Learning Disability, a Child with Mental Retardation, and a Child of Average intelligence on the WISC-III IQ Test

Table 9.7 Children Who Were Served by Federally Supported Programs for Students with Learning Disabilities, by Percentage of K–12 Enrollment and by Percentage of All Children with Disabilities, and Number Served: 1977–2002

	1976–1977	1980–1981	1989–1990	1995–1996	2001–2002
Percentage of total public K–12 enrollment	1.8	3.6	5.0	5.6	6.0
Percentage of all disabilities	21.5	35.3	44.6	46.3	44.4
Number served	796,000	1,462,000	2,047,000	2,579,000	2,846,000

Source: U.S. Department of Education, Office of Special Education and Rehabilitative Services, Eighteenth Annual Report to Congress on the Implementation of the Individuals with Disabilities Education Act; and the National Center for Education Statistics, *Digest of Education Statistics, 1996. Digest of Education Statistics, 2000:* Chapter 2. Elementary and Secondary Education. Table 53. Children 3 to 21 years old served in federally supported programs for the disabled, by type of disability: 1976–77 to 1998–99. National Center for Education Statistics, *Digest of Education Statistics, 2003.* Elementary and Secondary Education, Table 52. Retrieved March 24, 2005 from http://nces.ed.gov/

child and her or his family can determine to what extent they will take advantage of this opportunity.

Attention-Deficit Hyperactivity Disorder   A condition that has implications for learning and cognitive

Working with Children in Dyslexia Therapy Programs
Dr. Paula Talla, shown above, finds that a subset of children with reading problems develop severe dyslexia because they have difficulty hearing and generating speech. The youngsters seemingly experience a "language fog." Many of the children can benefit from therapy programs that Talla and her coworkers developed. The therapy entails computer games in which the children practice thousands of sounds during each session.

development is **attention-deficit hyperactivity disorder (ADHD).** ADHD involves a collection of vague and global symptoms. Typically youngsters who are impulsive and cannot stay in their seats, wait their turn, follow instructions, or stick with a task are viewed as having ADHD. Three subtypes of ADHD are recognized: hyperactive-impulsive, inattentive, and combined hyperactive and inattentive (Willingham, 2004/05). The Centers for Disease Control and Prevention (2004c) reports there are nearly 2 million children ages 6 to 11 diagnosed with ADHD. Some of these children also have learning disabilities and some do not. Many children with ADHD and those with both ADHD and a learning disability are often prescribed medication (Centers for Disease Control and Prevention 2004c). Recent research suggests that combining medical and behavioral therapies is an especially effective approach to treating ADHD. However, information on the long-term effects of medications for ADHD in children is lacking. Although research studies are ongoing, prescription drug use for ADHD rose 23 percent from 2000 to 2003 (Zaslow, 2005).

Many adults who had been diagnosed with ADHD continue to experience the condition although the symptoms may not be the same as they were initially. Researchers are finding antisocial activity, conduct disorder, and substance abuse in many adults who were deemed hyperactive in childhood. It is estimated that about 4 percent of the adult population worldwide suffers from ADHD (Wilens, Fararone, & Biederman, 2004). Significantly, clinicians report that some afflicted adults are successful, not in spite of ADHD, but in part because of it. These people, though easily distracted, often have the uncanny ability to "hyperfocus" and can become virtually immune to distractions. Ironically, while ADHD can put those with high IQs and good social skills at the top of their field (e.g., emergency room physicians, sales personnel, stock-market traders, and entrepreneurs), those with ADHD and without such attributes can land in prison given their zeal for risk taking and impulsive behaviors (Barkley, 2001).

There is little consensus on what causes ADHD or even whether it has a single cause. Experts have advanced a variety of theories to explain the disorder, including genetic defects, poor parenting, food additives, spicy foods, allergies, lead poisoning, fluorescent lights, insufficient oxygenation, and too much television watching. An interactive model combining genetic and environmental influences might best explain the development of ADHD in childhood (Barkley, 2001).

Though there are no established laboratory tests for diagnosing ADHD, a 1998 study conducted at Stanford University began to shed some light on brain functioning. The participants underwent magnetic resonance imaging tests (MRI scans) while responding to a response task. Some had ADHD and had not taken *Ritalin* for three days, but some did not have ADHD but were administered Ritalin prior to the MRI. Results indicate that subjects with ADHD experienced increases in blood flow to the attention-regulating basal ganglia (see Figure 9.4) (Rogers, 1998).

Significantly, most nations, such as France and England, still treat unruly youngsters as behavior problems rather than as patients.

Many professionals and members of the public fear that overreliance on prescribing amphetamines to "hyperactive" children has led to abuses and acceptance of drug therapy for children who might not benefit or who might actually be harmed by it. U.S. regulatory agencies and those in Canada disagree over the safety of a particular prescription drug for the treatment of ADHD (Wilde Matthes, Anand, & Davies, 2005). Some children benefit from amphetamine treatment, but the trend toward its indiscriminate use is cause for concern (Accardo & Blondis, 2001). In sum, diagnosing a child as having ADHD, and then prescribing a psychoactive substance with other health side effects, should be carefully determined and monitored on a case-by-case basis.

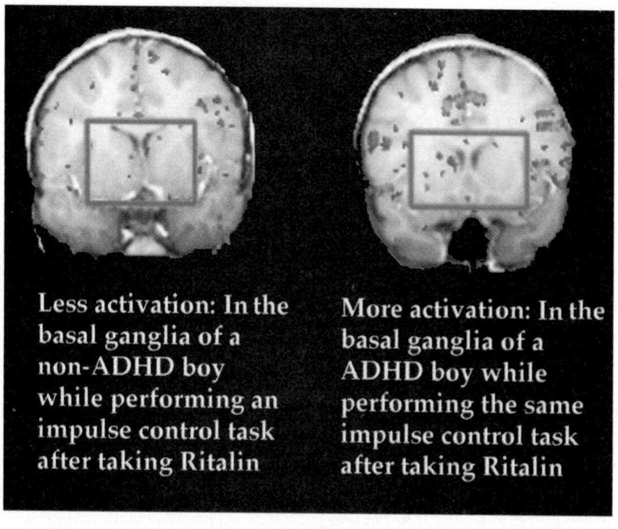

Individual Education Plans (IEPs)   All students classified as having any disability, including a learning disability, are to be provided with an **individualized education plan (IEP)**. This plan, which is developed in a collaborative effort by the school psychologist, the child's teachers, an independent child advocate, and the parent(s) or guardian, is a legal document that ensures that the child with special learning needs will receive the needed educational support services in the least restrictive environment. The child's IEP is updated annually as a result of a formal assessment of the child's yearly academic and social-emotional performance. To see what is involved in developing an IEP, see the *More Information You Can Use* box on page 332, "Individualized Education Plans (IEPs)."

Inclusion   In the past, children with disabilities were schooled at home or in segregated settings. Since 1975 shifts in laws and educational policy formed the basis for inclusive education (Bricker, 2000). Today they have the opportunity of **inclusion**, integration in a range of school placements; full or partial inclusion, integrated activities, and segregated settings (Hanson et al., 2001). Annual placement occurs as a result of appraisal of child characteristics, family expectations and ability to access information, teacher training, availability of services, and supports in the school system. See the *Implications for Practice* box on page 334, "Special Education Teacher." Placement in pre-kindergarten or kindergarten is often fully inclusive yet becomes more restrictive as academics are more challenging in each grade (Hanson et al., 2001). Many have high hopes for inclusion, yet the presence of children with special needs in regular classrooms does not guarantee academic or social success. It works well when leaders are committed to making it work through designing, implementing, and supporting appropriate restructuring of the educational enterprise (Hanson et al., 2001). A recent study found a significant relationship between teachers' prior experience and knowledge of the disabled and their attitudes about inclusion (Burke & Sutherland 2004).

Less activation: In the basal ganglia of a non-ADHD boy while performing an impulse control task after taking Ritalin

More activation: In the basal ganglia of a ADHD boy while performing the same impulse control task after taking Ritalin

FIGURE 9.4 Brain Scans Give New Hope for Diagnosing Individuals with Attention-Deficit Hyperactivity Disorder (ADHD)
Source: Adam Rogers, "Thinking Differently," *Newsweek*, 12/7/98, p. 60.

Questions

What process is used to identify a child as "learning disabled"? Why do some children need an individual education plan? What do we mean by the concept of an inclusive education for children?

More Information You Can Use

Individualized Education Plans (IEPs)

Every day more youngsters are determined to be eligible for an individual education plan (see Figure 9.5). In 2001–2002, 13 percent of public school students had a special education individualized education plan (IEP) (Hoffman, 2002; Snyder & Hoffman, 2002). The IEP planning document is a written description of a program tailored to fit the eligible child's unique educational needs. The IEP is developed jointly by parents, educators, and other professionals. The children themselves may also sit in on the process and contribute to their own plans. Goals and objectives for a child, based on current levels of functioning, are outlined by everyone involved in planning and providing services. The IEP specifies the educational placement, or setting, and the related services necessary to reach those goals and objectives. The IEP also includes the date the services will begin, how long they will last, and the way in which the child's progress will be measured. The IEP is much more than just an outline of, or management tool for, a child's special education program. The development of an IEP gives caregivers the

opportunity to work with educators as equal participants to identify a child's needs. The IEP is a commitment in writing to the educational program and resources the school agrees to provide. Periodic review of the IEP serves as an evaluation of the child's progress toward meeting the educational goals and objectives jointly decided upon by the caregivers and school professionals.

IEP Description

Part 1 of the document describes the child applying for services, including basic information such as the child's name, age, and address, the child's educational level and behavioral performance, and subjective information about the effect of the disability on academic and nonacademic achievements. This section also allows the caregivers to supply information about the child's typical behaviors in question and how the child approaches learning situations. Descriptive statements are essential so that everyone involved in teaching the

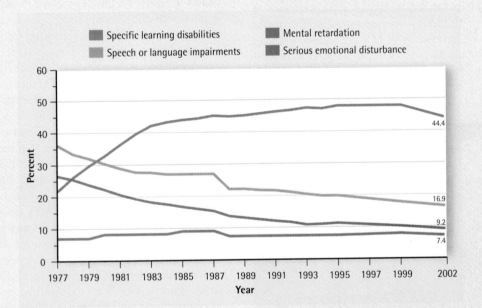

FIGURE 9.5 Children from Age 3 to 21 Who Were Served by Federally Supported Programs for Students with Disabilities, by Type of Disability: Selected School Years Ending 1977–2002 This analysis includes students who were served under Chapter 1 of the Education and Improvement Act (ECIA) and Part B of the Individuals with Disabilities Education Act (IDEA). By 2002, about 45 percent of children with disabilities were classified with specific learning disabilities.
Source: U.S. Department of Education, Office of Special Education and Rehabilitation Services, Eighteenth Annual Report to Congress on the Implementation of the Individuals with Disabilities Education Act; and the National Center for Education Statistics, *Digest of Education Statistics, 1996; in The Condition of Education, 1997; Digest of Education Statistics, 2000,* Chapter 2, Elementary and Secondary Education Table 53: Children 3 to 21 Years Old served in federally supported programs for the disabled, by type of disability: 1976–1977. *Digest of Education Statistics, 2003,* Chapter 2, Elementary and Secondary Education, Table 52. Retrieved March 24, 2005, from http://nces.ed.gov

child has accurate and complete information concerning the child's ability and potential.

Part 2 gives the caregivers and other members of the IEP team a chance to set goals and objectives that will help the child master the skills or behaviors that everyone wishes the child to attain. Goals are an expression of results to be achieved in the long run; objectives are the intermediate steps necessary to reach the long-range goals. Annual goals written on an IEP state what the child is expected to do by the end of the academic year. Each goal must be written as a positive statement that describes an observable event. A poorly written goal is vague (e.g., Truett will learn to write). A well-written goal will answer the questions Who? How? Where? When? (e.g., Truett will write all of the letters of the alphabet unaided by May 7). Caregivers often have questions concerning the goals and objectives put forth by the IEP committee. Common questions are these:

- How will I know if a goal is reasonable or appropriate?
- How do goals and objectives in the IEP relate to the instructional plans of educational personnel?
- Must goals and objectives be written on the IEP for the parts of the child's program in the general education classroom?
- Is it necessary for parents/caregivers to learn to write goals and objectives?
- How much of my child's school day will be spent in pull-out learning activities, such as the Resource Room, rather than with peers?
- What do I do if I don't agree with my school district's plan for my child?

Part 3 describes related services to be provided at no cost to the parent/caregivers. These related services might include assistive technology, audiology, counseling services, medical services, occupational therapy, parent counseling and training, physical therapy, psychological services, recreation, rehabilitative counseling services, school health services, social work services in schools, speech therapy, an aide in the classroom, transportation methods, or out-of-school placement.

Part 4 describes the special education placement provided to the child. Placement refers to the educational setting in which the goals and objectives for the child's special education and related services can appropriately be met. For example, in the past, a child confined to a wheelchair would

be placed in a room with all other children in wheelchairs, regardless of mental ability. Today the IEP guarantees that a child's ability is considered along with the disability.

Part 5 specifies when and for what duration the services will be in place. In general, the long-term duration of services will not exceed one year. This is because the services are reviewed annually to determine if they are still appropriate. In addition to specifying the long-term duration of the child's services, Part 5 of the IEP should include short-term, daily hours for each service (e.g., Jessica will attend individual speech therapy twice a week for 30 minutes each session).

Part 6 is the evaluation process, which allows the people who formulated the IEP to assess whether the IEP is working or needs modification. For example, suppose the short-term objective is this: Kareem will choose two classmates with whom he will cooperatively plan and complete an art project to illustrate a story in the fifth-level reader, by January 10. An evaluation of the child's services and program can occur by asking the following types of questions:

- Was the art project completed on time?
- Did Kareem read and comprehend the story? (There should be an objective, measurable assessment.)
- Did the teacher observe and note incidents to illustrate Kareem's cooperation with classmates?
- What indications show that Kareem made plans for the project?
- How did Kareem demonstrate pleasure in his accomplishments?

The IEP is an important document, and it is hoped that you now have a better understanding of how children with special education needs are able to get the services they require to better succeed in school. Today, students with learning disabilities or other disabilities are: (1) eventually transitioning out to sheltered employment or regular employment; or (2) graduating from high schools; or (3) entering college programs where higher education provides special services to accommodate the student's individual learning needs. In the past these youth were not integrated into the mainstream of society and minimally sustained themselves on social services and welfare. Today, many have become productive, fully integrated members of society.

Source: Anderson, Chitwood, & Hayden. (1997). *Negotiating the Special Education Maze: A Guide for Parents and Teachers.* Bethesda, MD: Woodbine House.

What Do We Know About Effective Schools?

In 1983, *A Nation at Risk,* a report of the National Commission on Excellence in Education, set an alarmist tone that pointed to a "rising tide of mediocrity" in the schools. Other reports, criticisms, and recommendations followed.

Public education performance is not much better than it was two decades ago, yet society demands highly

trained and skilled citizens for twenty-first-century jobs (see the *Human Diversity* box on page 327, "The Academic Achievement of Asian and U.S. Children") (Goldberg, 2001). In December 2001, Congress passed the *No Child Left Behind* education reform plan that addresses creating higher standards and accountability, expanding flexibility and control at the state and local levels for program funding, expanding parental options for disadvantaged children, increasing funding for

Implications for Practice

Special Education, Teacher
James Crandell

I have been a consultant-teacher of special education in the sixth grade at Chenango Forks Central School District for 13 years. Primarily, I am responsible for providing services to 15 students classified with learning disabilities. I also spend time instructing another 35 regular education students.

I wear a lot of hats! My primary role is to develop and deliver classroom lessons that I modify to reflect the various learning preferences and challenges of my students. The remainder of my time is spent on the following: collaborating and planning with my two co-teachers, offering instructional ideas and deciding how our individual lessons will actually be presented; using a variety of behavior modification strategies to provide immediate, predictable, and consistent consequences to those children who have limited self-control; grading various classroom assignments and planning how to assess the content taught so that each child has an equal opportunity for success.

I have a bachelors of science in psychology from SUNY Cortland and a master's degree in special education from Alfred University. Special education teachers are required to complete a student-teaching experience under the guidance of a certified teacher. I was required to pass a state certification exam to qualify for my degree. My previous job experience includes working at a day treatment center with individuals with developmental disabilities.

Foremost, a special education teacher needs to possess a high degree of flexibility. Due to new state regulations regarding the inclusion of students with disabilities in the mainstream classroom, I provide services to my students in other teachers' classrooms. Sometimes it is difficult to work closely with educators who have philosophical differences, but I focus on being helpful because the children are ultimately those who are impacted. Another essential personality trait is patience. These children often make slow progress due to the cycle of failure they experience in their schooling. I am determined to help these students realize that, despite their limitations (i.e., reading-decoding disability), they all have strengths. One of my students is well below grade level in his reading skills, yet he is a phenomenal artist and knows every part of an auto engine. Finally, you must be creative and investigate nontraditional methods for teaching students with special needs. For example, rather than use a vocabulary matching quiz, I ask the child to recognize a picture of the vocabulary term as a way to reflect the child's understanding.

You have to love children to think about being a teacher. Unlike computers, children cannot be programmed—especially middle-schoolers with special needs who are going through major emotional-social developmental changes. Teachers must accept that these feelings may disrupt a well-planned lesson. Skilled teachers know how to provide the students with appropriate ways to express feelings and are able to help children transfer their passion into class work.

The most enjoyable aspects of my job include seeing children be successful, especially those who encounter mostly failure, and relating with my co-teachers who share my love for teaching. I truly enjoy developing a unique strategy for teaching a concept that completely engages the children in the material. I am never bored in my job.

reading instruction, improving teacher quality in every public classroom by 2005, confirming progress by statewide assessments in reading and math biennially, promoting English proficiency for bilingual and immigrant students, and promoting school safety and character education (Kozberg, 2001; U.S. Department of Education, 2001). While school reform, higher achievement expectations for *all* students, teacher training, regular

program evaluation, and accountability are necessary, the education community has many criticisms with the mandates without adequate funding and the emphasis on passing standardized tests (Mathis, 2003).

Some researchers have concluded that successful schools foster expectations that order will prevail and that learning is a serious matter (Johnson, 1994). Much of the success of private and Catholic schools has derived from their ability to provide students with an orderly environment and strong academic demands (Bryk, Lee, & Holland, 1993). Academic achievement is similarly high in the public sector when the policies and resulting behavior are like those in the private sector (McAdoo, 1995). Successful schools, then, possess "coherence"—things work together and have predictable relationships with one another.

Recently, a rural elementary school in Frankford, Delaware, was named a Blue Ribbon School and a National Distinguished Title I School. The principal was honored as a National Distinguished Principal and listed five qualities that she believes are associated with student achievement and school success, beginning with her own high expectations of success and (1) systematic, specific interventions in place for low achievers, including many opportunities for one-on-one support; (2) collaborating teams of teachers that also provide leadership, and to date the teachers have procured $750,000 in grant monies to fully integrate technology instruction into the curriculum; (3) use of data to evaluate programs and drive continuous improvement; (4) gaining extensive support from family and community as mentors; and (5) support for staff development and leadership capacity at all levels (Brittingham, 2005).

"Fed up" with public schools, some parents are turning to evangelical schools, private-tuition schools, charter or magnet schools, and other government-sponsored alternative schools, and homeschooling.

Since 1993, when it became legal to home-school children, the number of children in home schools has risen considerably (Basham, 2001). Nearly 2 million children age 6 to 17 are homeschooled, and numbers rise every year (Bauman, 2001). Basham (2001) reports that a majority of homeschooled children live in two-parent families, and the majority of mothers do not work outside the home. On average, homeschoolers perform at least one grade level above age level (Rudner, 1999). Homeschooled students tend to score above the national average on college admissions tests (Wood, 2003). Homeschooling accounts for a larger portion of the school-age population than private voucher schools and charter schools (Bauman, 2001). We address the strengths of various school models in Chapter 10. One of the main reasons parents choose to home school their children is a concern about character development and family values. We now turn to moral development during the middle childhood years.

Questions

What types of programs are mandated for children with learning or other disabilities? Why do you think more children are being classified as having a learning disability? What types of learning environments in schools have been found to promote effective learning? Why are more children being homeschooled?

Moral Development

As humans, we live our lives in groups. Because we are interdependent, one person's activities can affect others' welfare. Consequently, if we are to live with one another—if society is to be possible—we must share certain conceptions of what is right and what is wrong. Each of us must pursue our interests, be it for food, shelter, clothing, sex, power, or fame, within the context of a moral order governed by rules. Morality involves how we go about distributing the benefits and burdens of a cooperative group existence (Wilson, 1993).

A functioning society also requires that its standards of morality be passed on to children—that moral development takes place in its young. **Moral development** refers to the process by which children adopt principles that lead them to evaluate given behaviors as right and others as wrong and to govern their own actions in terms of these principles. If media interest is any indication, many Americans are quite concerned with the moral status of contemporary youngsters, and they look to the schools to teach values to fill what they deem to be a moral vacuum.

A century ago, Freud believed that children develop a conscience through feeling a sense of guilt for their actions. More recent theories come from the field of cognitive research.

Cognitive Learning Theory

The discussion of cognitive learning theory in Chapter 2 emphasized the important part imitation plays in the socialization process. According to psychologists such as Albert Bandura (1977, 1986, 1999) and Walter Mischel (1977), children acquire moral standards in much the same way they learn any other behavior, and social behavior is variable and dependent on situational contexts. Most actions lead to positive consequences in some situations and not in others. Consequently, individuals develop highly discriminating and specific response patterns that do not generalize across all life circumstances (Bussey, 1992).

Studies carried out by cognitive learning theorists have generally been concerned with the effect that models have on other people's resistance to temptation (Bandura, Ross, & Ross, 1963). In such research, children typically observe a model that either yields or does not yield to temptation. Walters, Leat, and Mezei (1963) conducted such an experiment. One group of boys individually watched a movie in which a child was punished by his mother for playing with some forbidden toys. A second group saw another version of the movie in which the child was rewarded for the same behavior. And a third group, a control group, did not see any movie. The experimenter took each boy to another room and told him not to play with the toys in the room. The experimenter then left the room.

The study revealed that boys who had observed the model being rewarded for disobeying his mother themselves disobeyed the experimenter more quickly and more often than the boys in the other two groups. The boys who had observed the model being punished showed the greatest reluctance of any of the groups to disobey the experimenter. In short, observing the behavior of another person does seem to have a modeling effect on children's obedience or disobedience to social regulations (Speicher, 1994). Of interest, other research reveals that dishonest or deviant models often have a considerably greater impact on children than do honest or nondeviating models (Grusec et al., 1979).

These findings provide a context for evaluating the prevalent notion that violent children's social cognitions, attitudes, and thinking patterns contribute to their violent behavior. Clinical psychologists have often viewed violence as symptomatic of "internal conflicts" or "antisocial personality traits" within individual children. In other words, they assume that the children have deficient or distorted cognitions that contribute to their violent behavior.

"How do you know when the yellow light means slow down and when it means to speed up?"

Children's Models Cognitive learning theorists have generally been concerned with the effect that models have on other people's resistance to temptations. Children are observant of "models" in their environment who either yield or do not yield to temptation.

Source: DENNIS THE MENACE Reprinted with permission of King Features/North American Syndicate.

Cognitive Developmental Theory

Cognitive learning theorists view moral development as a cumulative process that builds on itself gradually and continuously, without any abrupt changes. In sharp contrast to this idea, cognitive developmental theorists like Jean Piaget and Lawrence Kohlberg conceive of moral development as taking place in stages, with clear-cut changes between them, such that a child's morality in a particular stage differs substantially from that child's morality in earlier and later stages. Although the learning and developmental perspectives are frequently counterposed to one another, they nonetheless provide complementary and interdependent analyses of human social interaction (Gibbs & Schnell, 1985).

Jean Piaget   The scientific study of moral development was launched over 60 years ago by Jean Piaget. In his classic study *The Moral Judgment of the Child* (1932), Piaget said that there is an orderly and logical pattern in the development of children's moral judgments. This development is based on the sequential changes associated with children's intellectual growth, especially the stages that are characterized by the emergence of logical thought. In keeping with a constructivist perspective, Piaget argued that moral development occurs as children act on, transform, and modify the world they live in. As they do, they in turn are transformed and modified by the consequences of their actions. Hence, Piaget portrayed children as active participants in their own moral development. In this respect Piaget differed from the cognitive learning theorists, according to whom the environment acts on and modifies children, and children are passive recipients of environmental forces. Cognitive learning theorists picture children as learning from their environment rather than, as Piaget would have insisted, in dynamic interaction with their environment.

Piaget provided a two-stage theory of moral development. The first stage that of **heteronomous morality,** arises from the unequal interaction between children and adults. During the preschool and early elementary school years, children are immersed in an authoritarian environment in which they occupy a position decidedly inferior to that of adults. Piaget said that in this context children develop a conception of moral rules as absolute, unchanging, and rigid.

As children approach and enter adolescence, a new stage emerges in moral development—the stage of **autonomous morality.** Whereas heteronomous morality evolves from the unequal relationships between children and adults, autonomous morality arises from the interaction among status equals—relationships among peers. Such relationships, when coupled with general intellectual growth and a weakening in the constraints of adult authority, create a morality characterized by rationality, flexibility, and social consciousness. Through their peer associations, young people acquire a sense of justice—a concern for the rights of others, for equality, and for reciprocity in human relations. Piaget described autonomous morality as egalitarian and democratic, a morality based on mutual respect and cooperation.

Lawrence Kohlberg Lawrence Kohlberg refined, extended, and revised Piaget's basic theory of the development of moral values. Like Piaget, Kohlberg focused on the development of moral judgments in children rather than on their actions. He saw the child as a "moral philosopher." Like Piaget, Kohlberg gathered his data by asking subjects questions about hypothetical stories. One of these stories has become famous as a classic ethical dilemma:

> In Europe, a woman was near death from a special kind of cancer. There was one drug that the doctors thought might save her. It was a form of radium that a druggist in the same town had recently discovered. The drug was expensive to make, but the druggist was charging ten times what the drug cost him to make. He paid $200 for the radium and charged $2,000 for a small dose of the drug. The sick woman's husband, Heinz, went to everyone he knew to borrow the money, but he could only get together about $1,000, which is half of what it cost. He told the druggist that his wife was dying and asked him to sell it cheaper or let him pay later. But the druggist said, "No, I discovered the drug and I'm going to make money from it." Heinz got desperate and broke into the man's store to steal the drug for his wife. Should the husband have done that? (Kohlberg & Colby, 1990, p. 241)

On the basis of responses to this type of dilemma, Kohlberg identified six stages in the development of moral judgment. He grouped these stages into three major levels:

1. *The preconventional level* (Stages 1 and 2)
2. *The conventional level* (Stages 3 and 4)
3. *The postconventional level* (Stages 5 and 6)

Kohlberg's stages of moral development are summarized in Table 9.8, with typical responses to the story of Heinz. Study the table carefully for a complete overview of Kohlberg's theory. Note that the stages are based not on whether the moral decision about Heinz is pro or con but on what reasoning is used to reach the decision. According to Kohlberg, people in all cultures employ the same basic moral concepts, including justice, equality, love, respect, and authority; furthermore, all individuals, regardless of culture, go through the same stages of reasoning with respect to these concepts and in the same order (Walker, de Vries, & Bichard, 1984). Individuals differ only in how quickly they move through the stage sequence and how far they progress along it. Hence, it

is Kohlberg's view that what is moral is not a matter of taste or opinion—there is a *universal morality.*

Carol Gilligan Research by Carol Gilligan (1982a) suggests that Kohlberg's moral dilemmas capture men's, but not women's, moral development. Gilligan's work reveals that women and men have differing conceptions of morality: Men have a *morality of justice,* the one described by Kohlberg, and women have a *morality of care* (Brown & Gilligan, 1992). Overall, it seems reasonable to conclude that there is considerable merit to Kohlberg's position that the course of moral development tends to follow a regular sequence, particularly in Kohlberg's first four stages. Even so, differences exist among individuals, both in the order and in the rate of attainment of given levels.

Question

What are the major differences between cognitive learning theory, cognitive developmental theory, Piaget's theory, and Kohlberg's theory of moral development?

Correlates of Moral Conduct

As discussed in the previous section, moral conduct tends to vary among individuals and within the same individuals in different situational contexts. Research on morality has focused on developmental transitions and universal processes more than on individual differences. Questions regarding individual differences are somewhat discomforting, for they imply that some people are more moral than others. And most of us are loath to label youngsters as uncaring and unprincipled (Zahn-Waxler, 1990). Even so, a number of researchers have attempted to specify which personal and situational factors are most closely associated with moral behavior (Hart & Chmiel, 1992).

Intelligence Maturity in several of the aspects of moral reasoning described by Piaget and Kohlberg tends to be positively correlated with IQ. The relationship between IQ and honesty disappears or declines when the context is nonacademic or when the risk of getting caught is low. Overall, being smart and being moral are not the same.

Age Research provides little evidence that children become more honest as they grow older. There may be a small correlation between age and honesty, but it seems to be due to other variables that also correlate with increasing age, such as an awareness of risk and an ability to perform the task without the need to cheat (Burton, 1976).

Gender In the United States, girls are commonly stereotyped as being more honest than boys, but research

Table 9.8 Kohlberg's Stages of Moral Development

Level	Stage	Child's Sample Response to Theft of Drug
I Preconventional	1	• Heinz shouldn't steal the drug because he might be caught and go to jail. • Heinz should steal the drug because he wants it.
	2	• Theft is justified because his wife needs the drug and Heinz needs his wife's companionship and help in life. • Theft is condemned because his wife will probably die before Heinz gets out of jail, so it will not do him much good.
II Conventional	3	• Heinz is unselfish in looking after the needs of his wife. • Heinz will feel bad thinking of how he brought dishonor on his family; his family will be ashamed of his act.
	4	• Theft is justified because Heinz would otherwise have been responsible for his wife's death. • Theft is condemned because Heinz is a lawbreaker.
III Postconventional	5	• Theft is justified because the law was not fashioned for situations in which an individual would forfeit life by obeying the rules. • Theft is condemned because others may also have great need.
	6	• Theft is justified because Heinz would not have lived up to the standards of his conscience if he had allowed his wife to die. • Theft is condemned because Heinz did not live up to the standards of his conscience when he engaged in stealing.

Source: Lawrence Kohlberg, "The Development of Children's Orientations toward a Moral Order," *Vita Humana,* Vol. 6 (1963), pp. 11–33; *"Stage and Sequence: The Cognitive-Development Approach to Socialization,"* in D. A. Goslin (ed.), *Handbook of Socialization Theory and Research* (Chicago: Rand McNally, 1969), pp. 347–480; *"Moral Stages and Moralization,"* in T. Lickona (ed.), *Moral Development and Behavior: Theory, Research, and Social Issues* (New York: Holt, Rinehart & Winston, 1976), pp. 31–53.

Do Children of All Cultures Pass Through the Same Stages of Moral Development? Lawrence Kohlberg answers this question affirmatively. Based on the cross-cultural research he and his associates undertook, Kohlberg concluded that all youngsters pass through the same, unvarying sequence of stages. Piaget also believed that autonomous morality arises out of the reciprocal interaction that takes place among peers. Carol Gilligan proposes that men have a morality of justice, whereas women have a morality of care for others. In all cultures, children's moral development is enhanced in different ways by one-on-one games, group competitions, and individual achievements.

fails to confirm this popular notion. Hartshorne and May (1928) found, for instance, that girls tended to cheat more than boys on most of the tests that the researchers observed. Other studies undertaken during the intervening half century show no reliable sex differences in honesty (Burton, 1976).

Group Norms The Hartshorne and May (1928) research revealed that one of the major determinants of honest and dishonest behavior was the group code. When classroom groups were studied over time, the cheating scores of the individual members tended to become increasingly similar. This result suggests that group social norms were becoming more firmly established. Other research confirms the view that groups play an important part in providing guideposts for the behavior of their members and in channeling their members' behavior.

Motivational Factors Motivational factors are a key influence in determining honest or dishonest behavior. Some children have a high achievement need and a considerable fear of failure, and they are likely to cheat if they believe that they are not doing as well on a test as their peers.

Prosocial Behaviors

Moral development, what some call character education, is not simply a matter of learning prohibitions against misbehavior (Schaps, Schaeffer, & McDonnell, 2001). It also involves acquiring **prosocial behaviors**—ways of responding to other people through sympathetic, cooperative, helpful, rescuing, comforting, and giving acts. Some psychologists distinguish between helping and altruism. Helping involves behavior that benefits or assists another person, regardless of the motivation that underlies the behavior. *Altruism,* in contrast, involves behavior carried out to benefit the other person, without the expectation of an external reward. Thus, we label a behavior altruistic only if we are fairly confident that it was not undertaken in anticipation of return benefits. Younger children report more self-oriented motives and older ones more genuine concern with others (Eisenberg, 1992). According to Piaget, a child younger than 6 or 7 is too egocentric to understand another person's point of view.

Although altruistic behaviors appear quite early, not all parents want their children to be Good Samaritans. Parents commonly teach their children not to be too generous and not to give away their toys, clothes, or other possessions. And in public places they might urge their children to ignore and not worry about some nearby person who is suffering or experiencing misfortune.

Research suggests that warm, affectionate parenting is essential for the development of helping and altruistic behaviors in children (Eisenberg, 1992). Yet nurturing parenting is not enough; parents must be able to convey a certain sensitivity regarding their own concern for other living things. If a cat is hit by a car, what matters in the development of a child's prosocial behavior is whether the parent appears to care about the cat—speaks about the cat's suffering and attempts to do something to alleviate it—or seems callous and unconcerned. Or should the child hurt someone else, what matters in the child's development is that the parent describes to the child how the other person feels. Yet there is a fine line between encouraging altruism and fostering guilt; parents should not inject too much intensity into such situations lest their youngsters become overanxious. Moreover, parental warmth and nurturing alone can encourage selfishness. So parents need to provide guidelines and set limits on what youngsters can get away with (see our discussion in Chapter 8 of what Diana Baumrind calls the authoritative style of parenting).

Altruism and helping are often associated with **empathy**—feelings of emotional arousal that lead an individual to take another perspective and to experi-

How Do Children Learn Prosocial Behaviors? Initially, expectations regarding proper and improper behavior are external to children, and some children are very aggressive about getting what they want. As they grow older, and immerse themselves in the life of society, most children will develop self-conceptions that regulate their conduct in accordance with the standards of the group. These expectations pertain not only to prohibited behavior—what children "ought not do" but they also define what children "ought to do" to get along with and not harm others in the group. Moral development involves replacing aggressive or self-serving behaviors with prosocial behaviors—ways of getting along with other children through cooperative, helpful, sympathetic, comforting, rescuing, and giving acts. Children who cannot get along with others or continually harm others may be identified as "emotionally disabled" and may require special intervention services.

ence an event as the other person experiences it. Indeed, some psychologists deem empathy to be the foundation of human morality, particularly in inducing cooperation among strangers and provoking guilt in wrongdoers (Angier, 1995). However, the single most powerful predictor of empathy in adulthood was how much time the children's fathers had spent with them. It seems that youngsters who saw their fathers as sensitive, caring beings were themselves more likely to grow up this way. In addition, mothers' tolerance of their children's dependency—reflecting their nurturance, responsiveness, and acceptance of feelings—was related to higher levels of empathic concern among 31-year-old adults (Koestner, Franz, & Weinberger, 1990).

Although in this section we have examined important personal and situational factors in moral and prosocial behavior, we need to emphasize that human behavior occurs in physical and social settings (see our discussion of the ecological approach in Chapter 1). Historically, when searching for answers to the question of what it takes to get people to live together harmoniously and without violence, sociologists have looked to larger social forces. Beginning with Émile Durkheim

(1893/1964, 1897/1951), sociologists have stressed that people, including children, need to feel part of something. They must bond with some social entity, such as a family, church, neighborhood, or community. Moreover, children require a clear set of standards that tells them what is permissible and impermissible. In sum, children need to feel bonded to a larger social whole. Once they are part of this entity, then standards make a difference to them.

Questions

How does a child develop a conscience and establish prosocial values during middle childhood? Do all children develop these? Why or why not?

SEGUE

Children experience substantial growth in all areas during middle childhood, and in this chapter we have looked at the physical and cognitive aspects of this growth: Children become comfortable with using their bodies and minds in new and exciting ways, and their abilities and skills become more pronounced, as some children are advanced—or delayed—either physically or intellectually in comparison to their peers. Concepts like intelligence and morality start to become important because

children are entering, often without parental or caretaker supervision, into their first social institutions (e.g., sports teams, Girl Scouts, Boy Scouts, YMCA or YWCA, Boys and Girls Club, 4-H, summer camp). Schools, religious institutions, and communities are important sources of interaction for children. Cognition and the ability to interact with others allow children a myriad of possibilities for emotional and social development, and we look at those significant issues in Chapter 10.

Summary

Physical Development

1. Children grow more slowly during middle childhood and become more skilled in controlling their bodies.

2. The brains of young children appear to be organized differently from those of adults. Labels applied to some children during these years include dyslexic, learning disabled, and gifted.

3. This is the period when children are healthiest. Risks include accidents, contagious illness, obesity, eating disorders, and sedentary lifestyles.

Cognitive Development

4. An important feature of the elementary school years is a marked growth in children's cognitive sophistication. During this time, which Piaget calls the period of concrete operations, children achieve mastery of conservation problems. They become capable of decentering, attending to transformations, and recognizing the reversibility of operations.

5. Considerable controversy exists about whether the development of conservation can be accelerated through

training procedures. There is also some question about whether the acquisition of conservation skills in the period of concrete operations occurs in the invariant sequence—horizontal décalage—postulated by Piaget.

6. Using the computer as a model for the brain, information-processing theorists ask whether during childhood there are changes in the basic processing capacity of the system (hardware) or in the type of the programs (software) used to solve a problem.

7. Although the developmental process is somewhat predictable, children vary in their rate and overall amount of change.

8. The number of dimensions along which children conceptualize other people grows throughout childhood. The greatest increase in children's ability to distinguish people's characteristics occurs between 7 and 8 years of age.

9. Children from the ages 6 to 12 continue to acquire subtle phonological distinctions, vocabulary, semantics, syntax, formal discourse patterns, and complex aspects of pragmatics in their first language.

10. For children whose first language is not English, four different approaches have been used in the United States to

open the doors to mainstream education: ESL, bilingualism, total immersion, and two-way bilingualism.

11. Schools primarily use conventional measurements, such as the Stanford-Binet test or WISC-III (Wechsler Intelligence Scale for Children-III), because the reliability and validity of such tests are documented, the scores are stable at least for school-age children, and they correlate well with and are predictive of academic performance.

12. A variety of youngsters are designated as having learning disabilities. LD youngsters have problems in reading (dyslexia), in writing (dysgraphia), or mathematics (dyscalcula), or auditory/visual perception.

Moral Development

13. Cognitive learning theory views moral development as a gradual and continuous process. Children acquire moral standards primarily through imitating the observable values and behavior of others.

14. Cognitive developmental theorists such as Jean Piaget and Lawrence Kohlberg conceive of moral development as taking place in stages, with clear-cut changes distinguishing one stage from the next.

15. A number of researchers have attempted to specify which personal and situational factors are most closely associated with moral behavior. Intelligence, age, and sex differences play only a small part in moral conduct. Group codes and motivational factors have a much larger role.

16. Moral development involves more than simply learning prohibitions against misbehavior. It also involves acquiring prosocial behaviors. Schools, churches, and community organizations promote healthy moral development through character education programs.

Key Terms

attention-deficit hyperactivity disorder (ADHD) (330)

autonomous morality (336)

bilingualism (323)

cognitive styles (325)

conservation (316)

creativity (319)

dyslexia (311)

empathy (339)

English as a second language (ESL) approach (322)

English language learners (ELLs) (322)

executive strategies (315)

heteronomous morality (336)

horizontal décalage (317)

inclusion (331)

individualized education plan (IEP) (331)

learning disabilities (LDs) (328)

limited English proficiency (LEP) (322)

mental retardation (MR) (328)

metacognition (315)

moral development (335)

obesity (313)

period of concrete operations (315)

prosocial behavior (339)

stereotypes (320)

total immersion programs (323)

two-way bilingual programs (324)

Following Up on the Internet

Web sites for this chapter focus on physical, cognitive, and moral development of youth in middle childhood. Please access the text Web site at www.mhhe.com/vzcrandell8 for up-to-date hot-linked Internet addresses for the following organizations, topics, and resources:

Office of English Language Acquisition
ESL for Teachers

National Center for Learning Disabilities
Recording for the Blind and Dyslexic
National Association for Gifted Children (NAGC)
National Board for Professional Teaching Standards
U. S. Office of English Language Acquisition

Middle Childhood
Emotional and Social Development

Critical Thinking Questions

1. Looking back to your childhood, do you remember disliking any particular subject or teacher when you were in elementary or middle school? On the positive side, was there a particular area of study or a teacher that you really liked? Do you remember how you felt when you were in those classes? Have those feelings carried over to how you react when you take courses in those subject areas today?

2. On a scale of 1 to 5 (with 1 being "no impact" and 5 being "most significant"), rate your mother's impact on your becoming who you are as an adult. Now do the same for your father. Is one parent becoming more influential as you get older?

3. Which would have had the greatest effect on altering your sense of self-esteem when you were 12: three friends telling you to "get lost," or your teacher telling you that she had just named her baby after you?

4. Have you experienced prejudice in any form? Do you remember committing prejudiced acts against others? Have these earlier behaviors and actions affected your attitude in any way today? Overall, did your school experience from first grade to sixth grade help or hurt your self-esteem?

As children progress into middle school, ability differences among peers become more apparent. A few excel, others experience difficulty. More immigrant children are in need of services to improve their English communication skills. Children with physical, cognitive, or behavioral problems are assigned to special education services. Schools must meet the demands of inclusion, diversity, higher standards, and discipline.

Over time children engage in activities they enjoy, such as art, music, sports, carpentry, or cooking. For example, basketball legend Magic Johnson, talk show host Jay Leno, clothing designer Tommy Hilfiger, and actors Tom Cruise and Whoopi Goldberg were dyslexic but excelled in other areas. They are successful adults, but their self-esteem was affected during these years.

From the ages of 7 to 12, children form friendships through a variety of pursuits. With more mothers employed, some youth are classified as self-care children, are left on their own, and are vulnerable to victimization. After-school programs might be the only safe haven for these children, but they often find it too restrictive compared with the freedom they are used to. In this chapter we will examine the research on many of these emotional-social issues in middle childhood, many of which are alleviated by a loving, supportive family and economic security.

The Quest for Self-Understanding

In interacting with significant adults and peers, children get clues as to how others appraise their desirability, worth, and status. Through the accepting and rejecting behaviors of others, children continually receive answers to these questions: "Who am I?" "What kind of person am I?" and "Does anyone care about me?" Central to much theory and research in social psychology is the notion that people discover themselves in the behavior of others toward them (Setterlund & Niedenthal, 1993).

Erikson's Stage of Industry Versus Inferiority

According to Erikson's psychosocial model of development, children in middle childhood experience the fourth stage of the life cycle—**industry versus inferiority.** Think back to your own childhood, and you will probably remember this period as the time when you became interested in how things were made or how they worked. Erikson's notion of industry captures children's ability and desire to try their hands at building and working, with activities such as building models, cooking, putting things together and/or taking them apart, and solving problems of all sorts. A child who has difficulty can develop a sense of inferiority if compared with children who easily accomplish tasks. You can imagine two students in a math class: one who always has the right answer and another who tries but cannot come up with the right answer. At the beginning of the school year, the teacher will call on both students, but after a while the student who never gives the right answer will feel academically inferior to the other student and might decide to give up trying at math. In such situations, teachers are very important.

Erikson argued that good teachers were capable of instilling in students a sense of industry rather than a sense of inferiority. Likewise, if children are not given the opportunity to try their hand at constructing, acting, cooking, painting, fixing, and so forth—but are made to watch adults perform these tasks—they will develop a sense of remaining inferior to the adult who is able to accomplish these tasks, while they are relegated to observer status; imagine children who want to help bake a pizza and are told they may only watch because they might make a mess if they were allowed to actively participate. Extracurricular offerings that *encourage* children to "jump right in" and try out a variety of skills include a wide range of sports, clubs, and activities such as Odyssey of the Mind, Science Olympiad, Invention Convention, talent shows, science fairs, the school newspaper, cooking or computer instruction, scouting programs,

and 4-H. Much of children's most exciting learning happens outside of the school classroom!

Self-Image

Self-image is the overall view that children have of themselves. When children are constantly praised or belittled, it is not uncommon for them to internalize this input and start to perceive themselves as "good" or "unworthy." *Self-concept* is a domain-specific assessment that children make about themselves. You might hear a child say, "I am a good athlete," or "I am horrible at math," which is very different from equating poor math performance with being a horrible person. For instance, Theresa is happy, confident, outgoing, and independent. She eagerly accepts new challenges and is not afraid to tackle problems. She thinks she is a nice, intelligent, friendly, caring child. In contrast, Lorri considers herself to be dumb, clumsy, and lacking confidence. She cannot handle being singled out for praise or criticism. She does not actively engage in new projects and tends to watch from the sidelines. Theresa is typical of the child with high self-image, whereas Lorri is a child with low self-image.

Self-Esteem

Since the early 1900s social psychologists and neo-Freudian psychiatrists support that self-conceptions emerge from social interaction with others and that self-conceptions in turn influence and guide our behavior (Cooley, 1902, 1909; Mead, 1934; Sullivan, 1947, 1953). Thus, conventional social-psychological theory states if children are accepted, approved, and respected for who they are, they will most likely acquire positive, healthy **self-esteem,** or a favorable evaluation of themselves. But if the significant people in their lives belittle, neglect, or abuse them, they are likely to evolve low or unhealthy self-esteem. Psychologists further divide self-esteem into earned or global. Children attain *earned self-esteem* as a result of their hard work and actual achievement, and this type is encouraged because it is based on work habits and effort in home and school. *Global self-esteem* is a sense of pride in oneself, likely to be based on inflated opinion or empty praise (Rees, 1998).

Since the 1960s many studies suggested that low self-esteem was the root cause of many U.S. social and economic ills, such as drug abuse, teen pregnancy, spousal abuse, child abuse, poor school or work performance, and higher poverty and crime rates. Then many parents and teachers, armed with routine encouragement and praise, began raising children's global self-esteem (Rees, 1998). However, an evaluation of 9,000 students in grades 1 to 3 who graduated from federal Head Start programs and entered schools promoting self-esteem, schools with traditional instruction, or combination schools found

Self-Appraisals as Reflected Appraisals How we come to perceive ourselves is powerfully influenced by other people's definitions of us—how they respond to us plays a part in how we respond to ourselves. Children who are respected and approved of for what they are have more self-esteem and self-acceptance than children who aren't. This self-confidence is reflected in their achievements.

that schools that provide the tools for academic success are far more effective because students improved in both academic achievement and earned self-esteem (Rees, 1998). Contemporary researchers are finding that self-esteem does not build success; rather, success builds self-esteem.

Although conventional wisdom suggests high self-esteem is desirable, adaptive, and an indicator of emotional well-being, a word of caution is advised: School and athletic programs that superficially bolster a child's ego, with little child effort, promote unstable, high self-esteem often viewed as conceit, pride, or arrogance. In a literature review of violence and self-esteem, Baumeister, Smart, and Boden (1996) found that such extremely inflated self-appraisals are related to interpersonal acts of aggression, bullying, and violence when egos are threatened (as in gang violence).

Stanley Coopersmith (1967) devised the *Coopersmith Self-Esteem Inventory* and studied the kinds of parental attitudes and practices associated with development of healthy levels of self-esteem, using a sample consisting of 85 preadolescent boys. He found that three conditions were correlated with high self-esteem in these children.

• *The parents themselves had high levels of self-esteem and were very accepting toward their children.* The mothers of children with high self-esteem are more loving and have closer relationships with their children than do mothers of children with less self-esteem. . . . The child also appears to interpret her interest and concern as an indication of his significance; basking in these signs of his personal importance, he comes to regard himself favorably.

This is success in its most personal expression—the concern, attention, and time of significant others.

• *Children with high self-esteem tended to have parents who enforced clearly defined limits.* Enforcement of limits gives the child a sense that norms are real and significant, contributes to self-definition, and increases the likelihood that the child will believe that a sense of reality is attainable. Such children are more likely to be independent and creative than those reared under open and permissive conditions.

• *Although parents of children with high self-esteem did set and enforce limits for their children's behavior, they showed respect for the children's rights and opinions.* The parents supported their children's right to have their own points of view and to participate in family decision making.

These findings from Coopersmith's study are reinforced by Baumrind's studies (1967, 1980, 1991, 1996), which found that competent, firm, accepting, and warm parenting is associated with the development of high self-esteem. By providing well-defined limits, parents structure their children's world so that the children have effective standards by which to gauge the appropriateness of their behavior. And by accepting their children, parents convey a warm, approving reflection that allows children to fashion positive self-conceptions.

Adding to the research on self-esteem is the work of Susan Harter (1983), whose *Self-Perception Profile for Children* measures five domains of children's conceptions of self: (1) scholastic competency, (2) athletic competency, (3) physical appearance, (4) social acceptance, and (5) behavioral conduct. Harter asked 8- to 12-year-olds to rate themselves in these domains and to specify how their competence in each domain affected their self-perceptions. What do you think the majority of children listed as most important for their self-esteem? They listed physical appearance as most important, followed by social acceptance.

Gender and Age Trends in Self-Esteem Frost and McKelvie (2004) conducted a cross-sectional study using the *Culture-Free Self Esteem Inventory* with elementary, high school, and university students. Results from their study support emerging trends: Girls under age 13 had higher self-esteem than boys, but adolescent boys have higher self-esteem than adolescent girls. This trend suggests that between childhood and adolescence, girls generally experience a drop in self-esteem, whereas boys experience an increase in self-esteem. Elementary girls had a better body image than elementary boys—across all three age groups, boys wished to gain weight. It appeared that girls' lowered self-esteem and body image with age was specifically related to weight satisfaction.

More Girls Are Participating in Sports Research indicates that sports participation bolsters girls' self-esteem resulting in improved school attendance, higher grades, and more positive body images.

The researchers summarize their findings to say that, in general, when people feel good about their bodies, they may feel good about themselves (Frost & McKelvie, 2004; Sahlstein & Allen, 2002).

Their results coincide with many studies showing that girls involved in sports (school or community youth programs) are more likely to stay healthy, have positive body images, more likely to have higher self-esteem and self-confidence, have higher test scores, more likely to graduate, more likely to attend college, less likely to get pregnant at an early age, and less likely to use drugs or stay in an abusive relationship (Bronston, 1998; Sporting Goods Manufacturers Association [SGMA], 2001; Team Up for Youth, 2005). Since 1987 the number of American girls aged 6 to 11 participating in sports has risen 86 percent, according to the Sporting Goods Manufacturers Association. At the same time more youth are involved in sports, childhood obesity has increased substantially, which is associated with low self-esteem (Strauss, 2002; Swallen et al., 2005). To bolster self-esteem in young girls, the Girl Scouts' program, *GirlSports,* allows girls to earn badges for participation in sports and developed programs linking successful female athletes with girls' sports clinics (e.g., WNBA star Rebecca Lobo and Olympian Jackie Joyner-Kersee were Girl Scouts). The U.S. Department of Health and Human Services also designed its *Girl Power* Web site and informational campaign to boost girls' self-esteem (Bronston, 1998).

The construct of self-esteem appears on a continuum from very low, to healthy levels, to very high levels considered egotistical or narcissistic. Although efforts to raise a child's self-esteem are possible, it is more difficult to teach humility to one with an unfounded sense of superiority over others. In essence, all children's self-esteem will be affected by their own competencies, attributes, and behaviors and by the support they receive from immediate and extended family, friends, and society.

> **Questions**
>
> What factors in an elementary-age child's environment are most likely to influence the child's sense of self-worth? Which of these factors, if any, are found to be more significant for boys or for girls?

Self-Regulated Behaviors

Lying, stealing, fighting, bullying, and other antisocial behaviors are manifestations of emotional and behavioral problems. In educational and expanded societal settings, adults apply higher standards of behavior to fourth- through sixth-grade children than in earlier years. Children are expected to cooperate on the school bus, in classrooms, in gym class, on teams, on the playground, and in extracurricular groups. Children who repeatedly demonstrate they cannot get along with their peers and cannot (or will not) control their overimpulsive or highly aggressive behaviors are likely to be classified by schools as *emotionally disabled,* or *ED.*

Public school district personnel are supposed to identify these youngsters (whom peers and teachers alike are afraid of), conduct an assessment of the child's needs, develop an individualized education plan (IEP), and place the child into an appropriate educational setting where he (and a majority are boys, though fewer are girls) will no longer hurt or intimidate the teacher and classmates. Central to this situation is the child's ability—or inability—to use self-regulatory behaviors. In some children, such as those with *attention-deficit hyperactivity disorder (ADHD)* (see Chapter 9), their biochemistry makes it difficult for them to control behaviors (excessive impulsivity, short attention span, yelling out in class, jumping around, grabbing or hitting others, spilling things). Imagine such a child as being a human jumping bean! Other children have never been taught acceptable social or self-regulatory skills by the significant caregivers in their lives. And some parents encourage an aggressive child, thinking that the aggressiveness shows that the child can handle himself or herself in unpredictable situations—an ability that is often a necessity for survival in inner-city neighborhoods. In any case, these children are at high risk of being rejected by most peers, except those like themselves.

Understanding Emotion and Coping with Anger, Fear, Stress, and Trauma

Cognitive factors also play an important part in setting the tone for the emotional life of youngsters. Recall from Chapter 6 that *emotion* involves the physiological changes, subjective experiences, and expressive behaviors involved in feelings such as love, joy, grief, and rage. As children interact with their mothers, fathers, siblings, classmates, teachers, and others, they acquire guidelines that mentally or cognitively mediate their inner experience of emotion and their outer expression of it (Wintre & Vallance, 1994). For example, our society expects different emotional behavior from girls than from boys. And so parents, by responding more sympathetically to a daughter's sadness than to a son's sadness, encourage boys to suppress their sadness. Or by allowing a son to express his anger but encouraging a daughter to be "nice," parents suppress the daughter's expressiveness of "unladylike" feelings while allowing the boy to speak his mind (Buntaine & Costenbader, 1997).

Questions

What do we mean by emotional self-regulation? Why do parents treat girls and boys differently when they display emotions?

Children's knowledge of their own emotional experiences changes markedly from ages 7 through 12, as they mature cognitively and learn display rules for appropriate expressions of behavior determined by their culture (Buntaine & Costenbader, 1997; Winter & Valence, 1994):

- They come to know the social rules governing the display of emotion.
- They learn to "read" facial expressions with greater precision.
- They better understand that emotional states can be mentally redirected (for instance, thinking happy thoughts when in a sad state).
- They realize that people can simultaneously experience multiple emotions (Levine, 1995).
- They are able to identify their inner states and attach labels, such as anger, fear, or happiness.
- They better understand how other people feel and why they feel as they do, and they become more adept at changing, containing, and hiding their feelings.
- Children also come to realize that the emotions they experience internally need not be automatically turned into overt action, especially if they know there is someone who will listen.

Anger *Anger* is an emotion that is frequently associated with acts of aggression. Boys and girls are equally likely to experience the emotion of anger, but they are socialized to express anger differently (see Figure 10.1). Research on gender and aggression reveals that boys are more likely than girls to react aggressively when they become angry, and this finding occurs across age levels, ethnicity, and socioeconomic status (Buntaine & Costenbader, 1997). Also, when fourth- and fifth-grade boys and girls were posed with hypothetical situations, the girls were better at attending to the behavior's intent (accidental versus deliberate) and attending to the social cues in such situations and thus did not respond as aggressively. One of Buntaine and Costenbader's (1997) major findings was that urban children reported a significantly higher level of total anger than children from suburban or rural schools. The researchers suggest that differential patterns of socialization occur in response to real-life events inherent in the child's inner-city environment. For some children the emotion of anger may lead to displays of repeated aggression—associated with more mental health interventions, delinquency, lower levels of academic achievement, peer rejection, and school dropout (Buntaine & Costenbader, 1997).

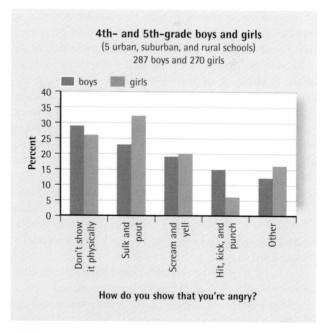

FIGURE 10.1 How Children Express Anger Boys and girls in five urban, suburban, and rural school districts responded to a self-report anger questionnaire that posed hypothetical situations. Boys reported much higher levels of aggressive responses. Under "Other," children wrote responses such as crying, playing music, going to one's room, and making various facial expressions. Boys and girls are socialized to handle their anger differently.
Source: Derived from data in Buntaine, R. L., & Costenbader, V. K. (1997, May). Self-reported differences in the experience and expression of anger between girls and boys. *Sex Roles: A Journal of Research, 36*(9), 625–638.

Fear and Anxiety   Fear plays a protective role in the lives of children of all ages. Psychologists define **fear** as an unpleasant emotion aroused by impending danger, pain, or misfortune, whereas **anxiety** is a state of uneasiness, apprehension, or worry about future uncertainties (Gullone, 2000; LaGreca & Wasserstein, 1995). Distinguishing between fear and anxiety is often difficult, thus the terms are often used interchangeably. Both emotions are normal and involve feelings of apprehension and physiological stress reactions, but normal anxiety is differentiated from *clinical anxiety* by the degree of interference in normal life.

Australian researchers conducted a longitudinal study of more than 300 elementary and high school participants (aged 10 to 18) and found that fears, and the intensity of fears, change as children mature. Younger children report more fears at higher levels of intensity than older children and adolescents, females report more fears with greater intensity than males, but the intensity of fears decreases over time (Gullone, King, & Ollendick, 2002). This finding is consistent with other studies that suggest that as normal children mature they are better able to verbalize their fears and anxieties and learn effective ways of coping. However, children who are nonverbal, those with developmental delays or mental retardation, may not be able to verbalize their concerns.

Psychologists also distinguish between fear and phobia. Whereas fear is viewed as a normal reaction to threatening stimuli, a **phobia** is an excessive, persistent, and maladaptive fear response—usually to benign or ill-defined stimuli, such as a phobia of riding in an elevator or being afraid of snakes. Some children at this age develop what is called *school phobia*. This can occur under a variety of threatening circumstances, such as being victimized by bullies in school, on a school bus, or when walking to and from school. Or if a parent is seriously ill at home, the child might refuse to go to school for fear the parent will die while the child is at school. Occasionally, an insensitive teacher will ridicule or punish a child in front of peers, which can also give rise to phobia. Children who experience school phobia need professional counseling to help them cope with their excessive fear and anxiety and return to school.

As children move through elementary school, their fears change as their cognitive and emotional understanding matures. Gullone (2000) examined a century of cross-national and cross-cultural studies on normal developmental fears. Her review revealed a predictable pattern of developmental fears. She found that:

- Preschool children have fears of being left alone and imaginary fears—of darkness, large animals, and monsters.
- Elementary-aged children have fears of failure and criticism, bodily injury and illness, and supernatural phenomena, such as ghosts.

- Adolescents have more global, abstract, and anticipatory fears such as failure and criticism, social evaluation, economic and political concerns, and violence.
- Throughout all life stages, fears of danger, death, and injury are common.

Cross-cultural findings of normative fear are consistent with the most common fears by developmental age and gender, although cultural norms and practices significantly influence the types and levels of fears reported (i.e., social-evaluative or danger-related) (Gullone, 2000). Recent findings suggest that children seem more anxious than in the past about physical harm or attack by others and about their health and that of their parents (Cook-Cottone, 2004; Gullone, King, & Ollendick, 2002). Unfortunately, their anxiety and fears have intensified because of the September 11, 2001 U.S. terrorist attacks and subsequent elevated warnings of attack, witnessing on TV the widespread tsunami deaths and devastation in southern Asia in January 2005, the destruction by Hurricanes Katrina and Rita, and the direct effects of the death of family members serving in the war in Iraq.

Over the last several years, some researchers have focused on Hispanic American or African American children as participants, mainly those of lower SES. Blakely (1994) interviewed a small sample of parents of Hispanic and non-Hispanic children from New York City. Parents reported that their children's greatest fears relate to social threats, such as kidnapping or sexual molestation. Hispanic children were more fearful than non-Hispanic children, and girls were more fearful than boys. Because it was a small sample and the children were not interviewed, follow-up studies need to be done. Silverman and colleagues (1995) surveyed second-through sixth-graders in an urban school and found that African American children report more fears than white or Hispanic children.

Patricia Owen (1998) examined the fears of nearly 300 children in San Antonio, Texas: Nearly half of the children were either middle-income SES or low SES. All were of either Hispanic/Mexican or Anglo (white) ethnicity, and both girls and boys were sampled. All participants were in third or fourth grade (ages 7 to 9), spoke English, and volunteered for this study. Owen administered the 48-item self-report *Children's Fear Survey Schedule (CFSS)*, with a few additions that were socially relevant (e.g., items on divorce, street drugs, gunshots, gangs, being burned, and drive-by shootings). The findings indicate that children from low SES report a greater number of intense fears than did the middle SES children, though there were no significant ethnic differences. Table 10.1 lists the 10 most common intense fears these children reported, by gender.

In this same study, girls and boys both reported significant fears of social violence. Hispanic and Anglo children differed minimally, and both reported significant fears of social violence. Children from low and mid SES differed little in their fears, which centered on social violence. Fears pertaining to death and social dangers were prominent in this study, which resemble the fears of children in past research. The pervasiveness of real-life fears (drive-by shootings, gangs, street drugs) is affecting American children at younger ages that are growing up in contemporary society. Owen suggests further research on the coping and adaptive behaviors of young children exposed to these real-life dangers.

Although fear can sometimes get out of hand and take on incapacitating and destructive qualities, it does serve an essential "self-preservation" function. If we did not have a healthy fear of fierce animals, fire, and speeding automobiles, few of us would be alive today.

> [The child] learns to anticipate "danger" and prepare for it. And he prepares for "danger" by means of anxiety! From this we immediately recognize that anxiety is not a pathological condition in itself but a necessary and normal physiological and mental preparation for danger. (Fraiberg, 1959, p. 11)

Question

Only 25 years ago, most American children worried about doing well in school, being liked by classmates, and meeting their parents' expectations, though a small number of children developed phobias. In comparison, what types of fears do contemporary American children, aged 7 to 12, report today?

Stress   The image of children in pain and anguish stirs our adult sense of vulnerability, concern, and indignation. We are moved to intercede and attempt to heal—and some of us go into social work, psychology, or medical professions to do just that. Yet all children must confront distressing situations. And, indeed, stress is an inevitable component of human life, so coping with stress is a central feature of human development.

Psychologists view *stress* as a process involving the recognition of and response to a threat or danger, yet stress can accompany upbeat experiences such as graduating to junior high, going to a first dance, competing in a sport, performing in a school concert, or taking home a good report card. We usually talk about stress in terms of physiological effects—"butterflies" in the stomach or stomachache, headache, backache, hives or rashes, short temper, crying jags, dizzy spells, sleepless nights, asthma attacks, and other unpleasant outcomes. Yet without some stress we would find life drab, boring, and purposeless. Stress can be beneficial if it contributes to personal growth and increases our confidence and skills for dealing with future events. (Many students know that stress can mobilize their study efforts the night before a major exam.)

And so it is with children. Hofferth's (1998) nationally representative study finds that for American children ages 3 through 12, parents report that "1 out of 5 children are fearful or anxious, unhappy, sad or depressed, or are withdrawn . . . and about 1 out of 25 have a behavior problem at school." On a positive note, parents also rated nearly half of children in this large sample as excellent in health, friendships, and relationships.

As all of us confront difficult situations, we seek ways for dealing with them. **Coping** involves the responses we make in order to master, tolerate, or reduce stress (Terry, 1994). There are two basic types of coping: problem-focused coping and emotion-focused coping (Folkman & Lazarus, 1985). *Problem-focused coping* changes the troubling situation, whereas *emotion-focused coping* changes one's appraisal of the situation.

As psychologists have come to recognize that children are not miniature adults, they have turned to the study of stress and coping among children (Sorensen, 1993). In conducting this research, psychologists are finding inaccuracies in popular notions. For instance, such events as hospitalization, birth of a sibling, divorce, or war are not necessarily or universally stressful. Children's individual *perceptions* of such events greatly influence their stress reactions. Many stressors long cited by clinical psychologists as very stressful are actually experienced by children as less stressful than such events as being ridiculed, getting lost, or receiving a poor report card (Terry, 1994).

Yet adults and children are alike in that people who feel in *control* of a situation experience a sense of empowerment (Whisman & Kwon, 1993). Individuals with a high sense of mastery believe that they can control most aspects of their lives. But those who are unable to gain mastery, to exert influence over their circumstances, feel helpless. Both children and adults with a low sense of mastery believe that their attempts at control are futile. Apparently a general sense of mastery moderates the negative effects of stress and encourages problem-focused as opposed to emotion-focused coping.

Researchers find that an important moderator of our experience of stress is **locus of control**—our perception of *who* or *what* is responsible for the outcome of events and behaviors in our lives. When people perceive the outcome of an action as the result of luck, chance, fate, or powerful others, they believe in *external control*. When they interpret an outcome as the consequence of their own abilities or efforts, they believe in *internal control* (Weigel, Wertlieb, & Feldstein, 1989). Internal control typically increases with the age of a child. Scores on psychological measures of internal/external control tend to be relatively external at the third grade, with internality increasing by the eighth and tenth grades.

In evaluating matters of stress, coping, and locus of control, three factors stand out in the emerging body of research as being of particular importance: (1) the child's characteristics, (2) developmental factors, and (3) situation-specific factors. Let us examine each of these factors in turn:

- *Dispositional and temperamental differences among children play a central role in influencing their coping responses* (Kagan, 1983). Children differ in their sensitivity to environmental stimuli. Some show signs of greater arousal and distress to events than others, so they must cope with a greater number of stressful situations than do more stress-resistant youngsters. Moreover, children differ in the ways they react once they are aroused or threatened (see Figure 10.1). For example, some become aggressive and enraged, others become withdrawn and pout, and still others resort to daydreaming, fantasizing, or other escapist behaviors. Findings from various studies indicate that girls experience more distress and withdrawn behavior than boys do (Buntaine & Costenbader, 1997; Hofferth, 1998).
- *Developmental factors also play a part.* In middle childhood, children's emerging sense of self makes them more vulnerable to events that threaten their self-esteem than when they were younger. For example, there is research evidence that children who change schools two or more times a year are likely to experience more stress, behavior problems, and problems in school (Crnic & Low, 2002; Hofferth, 1998). Also, as they move into middle school, students with learning problems or mild mental retardation experience even more stressors associated with the increased academic and social challenges for preadolescents (Wenz-Gross & Siperstein, 1998). Additionally, as children get older, their ability to devise strategies for coping with stress improves, and they become more planful (Maccoby, 1983).
- *Situational factors influence how children experience and deal with stress.* Healthy parents often mediate many of the effects of stressful crises (Sorensen, 1993). A caregiver's irritability, anxiety, self-doubt, and feelings of incompetence are likely to intensify a child's fears of hospitalization or moving to a new school. Emotional support from the family and economic security can have a steeling effect, buffering the influence of stressors (White & Rogers, 2000). Children's self-esteem is strengthened when they are accepted by their parents and others despite their difficulties or faults. And resourceful caregivers can help them to understand their problems and find ways to deal with them.

> **Questions**
>
> What types of physical symptoms might a child complain about who is experiencing stressful life events? What is the difference between external control and internal control? What are the three major factors in a child's coping responses to stress?

Trauma It is estimated that 25 percent of children experience a *traumatic event* by the time they reach 16 years old (Cook-Cottone, 2004). A child's emotional and psychological well-being can be harmed by any exceptionally stressful naturally occurring event, such as Hurricanes Katrina and Rita or the tsunami in southern Asia, or human-made events, such as the attack of September 11, 2001. Other events are more personal, such as being abused or neglected; witnessing death of a parent, sibling, friend, or pet; being homeless; witnessing domestic violence; seeing a parent arrested and jailed; witnessing a home burning down; moving repeatedly from foster homes; witnessing a fatal accident such as the space shuttle *Challenger* explosion, and so forth (Graham-Bermann & Levendovsky, 1998). Some children live with chronic health conditions (e.g., asthma, sickle-cell anemia, cancer, HIV): others experience one sudden episode of severe trauma, such as a serious car accident (Cook-Cottone, 2004; O'Maria & Santiago, 1998).

Children clinically classified with **post-traumatic stress disorder (PTSD)** (also called *post-traumatic stress reaction,* or *PTSR*) exhibit a range of physiological stress symptoms and behavioral symptoms including learning and concentration problems; numbness and detachment from others; helplessness; increased irritability and aggressiveness; extreme anxiety, panic, and fears; exaggerated startle response; sleep disturbances; and regressive behaviors such as bed-wetting, clinginess, or school refusal. Preadolescent youth and teens may also present with self-injurious behaviors, suicidal intentions or attempts, conduct problems, or substance abuse (Cook-Cottone, 2004).

To help such children reduce their stress, social workers, school psychologists, teachers, and families need to plan intervention strategies to restore a sense of security, stability, and safety for the child and reintegrate the child into school (Cook-Cottone, 2004). The quality and quantity of assessment tools have increased for clinical and school psychologists to accurately identify PTSD (Cook-Cottone, 2004). Child-trauma experts believe that art therapy and play therapy illuminate a younger child's inner distress, in contrast to conventional adult talk therapies. Some children need long-term therapy before they experience a reduction in distress symptoms, and research findings indicate cognitive behavioral therapy methods are very effective (O'Maria & Santiago, 1998). Cook-Cottone (2004) proposes that school psychologists play a key role in the child's recovery, individualized education plan, and school reintegration. Attentive caregivers and professionals need to understand they are dealing with each individual child's personality and developmental issues as well. To read about helping children with fears, see the *More Information You Can Use* box on page 352, "Helping Children Cope with Disaster and Fear."

Impulsivity and Risk Taking   Youngsters differ in their willingness to take risks. Some children are drawn more to the excitement of risk than others, but we know that young children lack the cognitive awareness of harmful consequences. For example, children with attention-deficit hyperactivity disorder are more prone to impulsivity and injury. Although some youth are more injury prone, others seem to be less sensitive to injury. More boys than girls seek out stimulation in ways that concern their parents, caregivers, and teachers (Morrongiello & Rennie, 1998). Indeed, we tend to categorize children by the frequency and degree of the risks they take, describing a child as cautious or reckless and timid or bold. Risk taking finds different avenues of expression (Boles et al., 2005). Children who excel in athletics, music, art, acting, or leadership routinely take risks that their peers avoid—behaviors we deem "creative" or "courageous." But the pursuit of novelty and excitement can also lead children to seek out unsafe risks such as running away from home, stealing, experimenting with drugs, or setting fires.

Our consideration of emotional development, fear, anxiety, stress, trauma, and risk taking leads us to inquire how children encounter and manage morally relevant social situations, through family influences, a broadening social environment, and the world of school.

Questions

What changes in behavior will a child who has experienced a major trauma likely exhibit? What actions can adults take to help a traumatized child? What behaviors should concern us about a child who is impulsive and takes risks?

Continuing Family Influences

Although it is important to see how children are faring on academic performance measures, as we saw in Chapter 9, children's experiences within family and neighborhood environments are also vital to their emotional well-being and social development. Social scientists at the University of Michigan Institute of Social Research (ISR) have been conducting a longitudinal study on the daily lives of a nationally representative sample of more than 2,000 chil-

dren and their families since 1968 (and their extant 7,000 families with 65,000 individuals still participating in this study) (Hofferth, 1998; Juster, Ono, & Stafford, 2004). How children spend their time provides insight into a variety of issues that directly impact their physical, intellectual, social, emotional, and moral development.

Periodic analysis of "time diaries" reveal how children spend their time is considerably different than just 25 years ago, when children were more active and computer time was nonexistent. Overall, today's children, ages 6 to 17, spend more time in school and more time studying, but they spend almost two hours less a week, on average, on sports and outdoor activities than 25 years ago. Children ages 6 to 11 spend an average of 6 to 7 hours daily in school settings (before school programs, regular school day, and after-school programs). Children's free time, or unstructured play, has declined sharply (see Figure 10.2) (Juster, Ono, & Stafford, 2004).

The frequency of children and parents doing activities together rises slightly as children age. Children's media time (TV, video games, and computer use) has risen to an average of 6.5 hours per day, after attending school—confirmed by a 2005 Kaiser Foundation study that found 75 percent of U.S. homes have three or more TVs (Rideout, Roberts, & Foehr, 2005). Thus, media has significant influence on today's children. Families with more resources and education are more likely to have computers and the Internet, and about 75 percent of children in this study have home access to such technology. On weekly average, children devote little time to reading or being read to outside of school. Gender differences are revealed as well. Girls spend more time on household work, personal care, studying, and passive leisure, whereas boys devote more time to sports, TV, and playing (Juster, Ono, & Stafford, 2004).

Parents in the Michigan Institute of Social Research longitudinal study in 1998 rated 65 percent of the children under age 13 as extremely close or very close to their parents (including those living in stepfamilies, adopted families, and father figures in the home). As children grow older, closeness appears to decline, with parents reporting nearly 60 percent of school-age children as close to them. A majority of parents reported very warm behaviors with their children, though the nature of the relationship changes as children mature and spend more time with peers. Whereas 80 percent of parents reported warmth with preschool children, about 60 percent of parents of school-age children reported warmth factors (hugging, spending time together, joking, playing, talking, etc.) (Hofferth, 1998).

Mothers and Fathers

Public policy (i.e., welfare reform, taxation, family leave, special education, Medicaid, etc.), family resources (SES),

More Information You Can Use

Helping Children Cope with Disaster and Fear

Fear is a normal emotion in reaction to a scary experience. It fosters caution and is an adaptive facet of development, and girls and boys at various ages respond differently (see Table 10.1) (Walsh, 2001). The tragic events of September 11, 2001, Hurricanes Katrina and Rita, the Asian tsunami of 2005, or any disaster experienced, can cause intense, prolonged reactions that interfere with healthy adaptation to life. Very young children cannot tell fantasy from reality, older children have vivid imaginations, and all children sense adult fear and anxiety (Walsh, 2001). Children cannot avoid fears. Rather, children can be encouraged to develop constructive methods for coping with fear. Here are some techniques psychologists have found useful for helping children cope with fear (National Association of School Psychologists, 2001):

As children show signs of stress, expect behavior changes and respond to their feelings. Children show stressful feelings, such as crying, whining, irritability, trembling, clinging, regressive or aggressive or avoidance behaviors, confusion, sleep disturbances, appetite changes, poor concentration, loss of interest in normal activities and school, headaches, stomachaches, and other behaviors ("Recognizing Stress in Children," 2001). Create an accepting situation in which children try to put their fears into words. Help them to see that adults, including you, also have fears, but there are ways to feel better.

Help children feel personally safe. Give extra support and be patient. Establish normal routines that provide stability and security. Inform children of people, places, and schedules that promote safety (i.e., call an employed parent after school, be home before dark).

Find substitute activities to relieve stress. Do not let children dwell on a specific stressor. Plan some enjoyable parent-child activities. Make time to play with children regularly.

Help children gain a sense of control by planning coping strategies. Help children to practice skills that provide specific aid in dealing with the feared situation or object. Children are eager to shed their fears, and when they develop competent skills, stress is relieved. For example, give children afraid of the dark a small night-light that provides minimal lighting.

Help children overcome a specific fear. When it is reasonable and safe, lead children gradually into contact with situations they fear (*desensitization*) and pair the feared stimulus with pleasant activities. This approach is successful in reducing fears of animals, objects, and places (such as swimming pools and fear of water). Permit them to inspect, ignore, approach, or avoid the stimulus as they see fit. Allow a child to observe children enjoying the same feared stimulus (e.g., laughing in a wading pool).

Establish a good line of communication between home and school. If a child has had a major life change, illness, or trauma, let teachers know and then strategize together to help the child cope. Establish consistent expectations for behavior.

Harmful responses such as ignoring, scolding, shaming, ridiculing, coercing, or making fun of children are ineffective, complicate children's difficulties, and increase stress. In sum, caregivers cannot protect children from all fear, but they can help children deal with fear constructively.

Table 10.1 Items with Highest Fear Intensity Rating for Children in San Antonio, Texas, by Gender: 1998

Girls	Boys
1. Drive-by shootings	1. To die
2. Kidnappers	2. Drive-by shootings
3. Gangs	3. Nuclear weapons
4. Gunshots	4. Gangs
5. To die	5. Kidnappers
6. Nuclear weapons	6. Earthquakes
7. Strangers	7. Burned
8. Snakes	8. Death
9. Guns	9. Guns
10. Fire	10. Poison

Source: Patricia R. Owen. (1998, November). Fears of Hispanic and Anglo Children: Real-world fears in the 1990s. *Hispanic Journal of Behavioral Sciences, 20,* 483–491. Copyright © 1998. Reprinted by permission of Sage Publications, Inc.

and family living arrangements (married, single, cohabitation, or foster care) affect the emotional-social relationship that children have with their families. Children learn from interacting with and observing parents and the level of interaction or engagement is generally high, but children are increasingly being affected by demands on their parents' time. According to sociologist Hofferth (1998), two-parent families with a male wage-earner and female homemaker spent an average of 22 hours per week in direct contact with their children. With both parents working in a majority of families, parents spent 19 hours per week with their children. In general, single

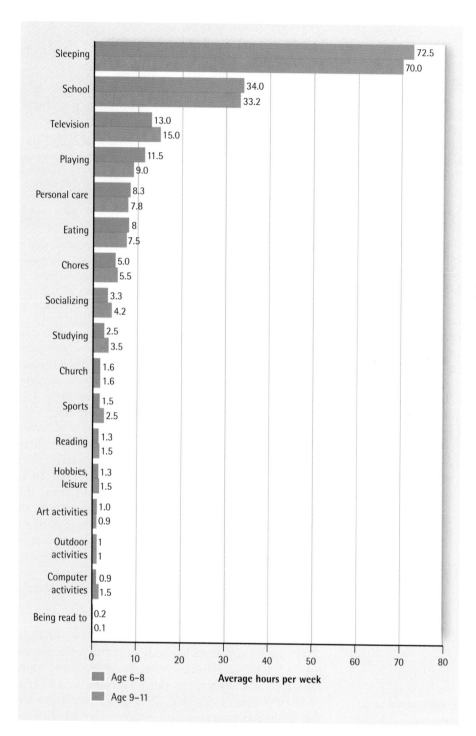

FIGURE 10.2 Weekly Average Time of American Children Ages 6 to 11: 2002–2003 How children spend their time provides insight into a variety of issues that directly impact their physical, intellectual, social, emotional, and moral development. Overall, today's children, ages 6 to 17, spend more time in school and more time studying. After school, television viewing is their most frequent activity—and they spend almost two hours less a week, on average, on sports and outdoor activities than 25 years ago. Children's free time, or unstructured play, has declined sharply.

Source: Juster, F. T., Ono, H., & Stafford, F. P. (2004, November). Changing times of American youth: 1981–2003. Ann Arbor, MI: Institute for Social Research, University of Michigan. Retrieved February 13, 2005, from http://www.umich.edu/news/releases/2004/Nov04/teen_time_report.pdf

mothers spent 9 hours a week with their children, and much of this time together was on weekends. Other major findings on family influences from Hofferth's (1998) study indicated that a warm relationship, parents' expectations for closeness, and parents' expectations for college completion were associated with more positive behaviors in children. Hispanic parents also rated their children more positively than non-Hispanic parents rated their children (Hofferth, 1998).

Employed Mothers Since 1970, maternal employment rates rose markedly for both married and single mothers with children in school, ages 6 to 17. In 2003, more than 10 million married women with school-age children were employed—for 73 percent of married mothers. Nearly 4 million single mothers with school-age children were employed—for 77 percent of single mothers (divorced, separated, or widowed) (U.S. Bureau of the Census, 2004–2005). Thus, it is common for children to either be in other-relative (kin) care, nonrelative care, after-school programming, or in self-care (home alone). Some employed mothers and fathers adjust their work schedule to make sure a child is at home with a parent or older sibling when not in school.

Research shows that mothers who work outside the home have better self-esteem, because they feel more economically secure, more confident in their ability to contribute to society, more competent, and generally more valued (Carlson & Corcoran, 2001). And when a mother feels better about herself and her situation, she is more likely to be better able to nurture her children and will be a more effective parent. Also, Hofferth's (1998) findings indicate that the mother's verbal ability is associated with her children's higher verbal and math achievement scores. Mothers who are warm and close to their children, who do activities with their children, who are involved in their children's schooling, and who expect their children to complete college are most apt to rate their children's behavior more positively (Hofferth, 1998).

However, a common feeling among many working mothers is a sense of guilt—feeling that the child is missing the mother, that the child is not receiving the best "maternal" care, and that the child is being harmed by not being home with the mother after school. On the other hand, children whose mothers work are encouraged to be more independent, and this independence benefits girl especially, as they become more competent, have more self-esteem, and perform better in academics (Bronfenbrenner & Crouter, 1983). Yet families with an employed mother are not all cut from a single mold, and so it is impossible to say that what one family experiences will hold true for all families.

Questions

In general, what types of effects might children experience when their mother is employed? What do children do in their outside-of-school time? How might employment benefit a mother and her children?

Caregiving Fathers Today there is substantial interest in the involvement of fathers, stepfathers, or father figures in the lives of children. Most children still live with a biological father or a stepfather at least part of their childhood, and the presence or absence of a father is considered to be a significant variable affecting a child's well-being and school achievement (Mott, 1994). Recent studies reveal that many men see their family role as being just as important as their working role (Aldous, Mulligan, & Thoroddur, 1998; Cooksey & Fondell, 1996).

A father's time, availability, engagement in shared activities, and warmth are known to be critical to a child's development. Yet many factors have impacted

Children Benefit from Father's Involvement Children and mothers benefit significantly when fathers spend time with their children, and increasing evidence suggests fathers serve as role models for future behaviors.

the role of fathers for U.S. children since the 1980s: the rising divorce rate, which has stabilized recently; the high rates of remarriage (about 75 to 80 percent), the rising rate in childbearing by single women (one of every three children today is born to a single mother); and the rising rates of unmarried couples (cohabiting) with children (with biological fathers or an unrelated father figure). Current estimates suggest that one of every three children will live with a stepparent (usually a stepfather) or a mother's cohabiting partner before age 18. Sociologists Hofferth and Anderson (2003) examined the engagement, availability, participation, and warmth of *residential fathers* with a representative sample of more than 2,500 children. The children's "father" sample was comprised of married biological, unmarried biological, married stepfathers, and unrelated father figures in cohabiting families—reflecting the complexity of contemporary fatherhood.

Biological Fathers Hofferth and Anderson's findings (2003) are consistent with a body of research that shows married, biological fathers generally invest more time, resources, and warmth in their own and in adoptive children (Cooksey & Craig, 1998). Two exceptions are that biological fathers in father-stepmother families report the highest amount of time spent with children, and biological single-parent fathers spend significantly more time with their residential children (about 5 percent of children live with a single father). Biological fathers with daughters only, or only young children, or working long hours engaged in fewer activities with their children. Married biological fathers report higher levels of educational attainment and higher incomes than other "fathers."

When a marital or cohabiting relationship breaks down, some biological fathers disavow or abandon children. This is a heartbreaking emotional and economic loss for children often related to unresolved hostility with the ex-wife or partner, disengagement due to emotional distress, and anguish about developing a new role and identity (often as noncustodial father with support payments) (Baum, 2004). In this study, two-thirds of stepchildren reported minimal or no contact with a nonresident, biological father—but one-third reported frequent contact with a nonresident, biological father. Whereas married biological fathers have legitimate legal protections and obligations to support children, such protections and obligations are ambiguous for other types of "fathers" or father figures.

Stepfathers In Hofferth and Anderson's (2003) study, stepfathers were significantly younger than biological fathers and generally had lower earnings. The younger the children are in a stepfamily, the more likely the stepfather will engage in activities and invest in a warm relationship with them. Stepfathers in this study scored lower on measures of desirable parenting practices and fathering attitudes with stepchildren than married biological fathers, perhaps for two reasons: (1) stepfathers were often committed to providing resources, time, and emotional support to their own biological children from a former marriage or relationship; and (2) if a divorced biological father maintains a close, supportive relationship with his children, a stepfather is less likely to develop a close relationship with stepchild(ren). Stepfathers were least engaged with adolescent stepchildren. Stepfathers, who have no biological children of their own in the household, rated themselves with low amounts of activity or warmth with children. Generally, stepchildren received significantly more time and attention in a *blended family* (mother's children and father's children residing together) than in a nonblended family.

Cohabiting Father Figures In 2002, census data revealed that more than 3 million children lived in nearly 2 million cohabiting families with a father figure. Of all "father" types, a mother's cohabiting partner reported the lowest income. These men reported the least amount of time engaged in activities and warmth with residential children. Thus, children in cohabiting families also reported less warmth and attention from cohabiting father figures than in other "father" types of families, leaving these children vulnerable to other negative influences (Hofferth & Anderson, 2003).

Absentee Fathers The absence of fathers from U.S. children's lives is considered a crisis by those concerned with the welfare of children. Single women bearing children and divorce are the primary causes of father absence in children's lives. In 2002, census data revealed that 24 million U.S. children (34 percent) live absent their biological father. The national study, *Father Facts,*

by the National Fatherhood Initiative (2002) reports that about 40 percent of children in father-absent homes have not seen their father at all during the past year, and 50 percent of these children have never visited their father's homes (many absent fathers live out-of-state). Children who live without fathers are more likely to be poor, to be abused, to be truant from school, to exhibit antisocial and high risk behaviors, and to engage in criminal activity compared with children with involved fathers (National Fatherhood Initiative, 2002).

After reviewing the extensive data on fathers' time, availability, engagement in shared activities, and warmth with children, these sociologists suggest that a father's being married matters to the overall well-being of children. Cooksey and Craig (1998) found that when no "father" was present during the father's own childhood years, men were less likely to report participating in activities with their own children. This suggests a father serves as a significant role model for future behavior. Overall findings indicate that when fathers are involved in children's lives, mothers and children experience many economic and social-emotional benefits (Cooksey & Craig, 1998; Hofferth & Anderson, 2003).

> **Questions**
>
> How does a father's involvement, or lack of it, affect children's lives? In general, in what ways do stepparents and unrelated cohabiting "father figures" react differently to children?

Sibling Relationships

American children today have far fewer siblings than just 25 years ago. Based on U.S. Bureau of the Census (2003b) data on families with children under age 18, 20 percent have one child, 18 percent have two children, and 10 percent have three or more children in the household (with a major decline in families with four or more since 1980). Today 52 percent of families have no children under 18, which include couples having no children and the couples having adult children (U.S. Bureau of the Census, 2004c). However, if you grew up with siblings, you probably remember having a much more intense relationship with them than with your friends. Siblings do not have the luxury of choosing each other, as friends have, and so it is necessary to resolve conflicts and work on cooperation as they live daily life. Likewise, siblings know that an angry confrontation will not bring about an end to the relationship. Even when they temporarily harbor bad feelings for each other, siblings know that they must continue to live together. Sibling relationships are generally described as pleasant, caring, and often supportive (Jones & Costin, 1995). Older siblings normally play a role in helping younger siblings "learn the ropes"—be it with homework, coping with issues such as sex or drugs, or learning the values and morés of society (Cicirelli, 1994). Invariably, some siblings experience conflicts in which aggression or abusive behavior can arise (see Figure 10.1) (Rinaldi & Howe, 1998). Parents play a substantial role in promoting prosocial behaviors in sibling relationships (Perozynski & Kramer, 1999). Sibling relationships often improve when mothers are taught strategies for promoting child sharing and when children are directly taught prosocial-sibling behaviors (Howe, Aquan-Assee, & Bukowski, 2001).

As more diverse family structures have evolved, more children are growing up with stepsiblings, half-brothers and half-sisters, adopted siblings, and non-related "siblings" in cohabiting households—which creates additional stress on families (see the *Human Diversity* box "Adoption and Guardianship"). Sharing personal space and belongings with a sibling can cause conflicts in the best situations, but sharing personal space with children who are unrelated can create added stress for children whose parents are separated or divorced. The adults in a stepfamily or cohabiting family might love each other and the children might come to like each other, but this is not a sure thing. In the meantime, there can be quarrels over discipline, sharing, and distribution of resources.

In many cultures older siblings take on the role of caregiver at an early age and become something of a surrogate parent. With the older sibling taking responsibility for younger siblings, the parents are able to work and pursue other activities (note that relative care, including older siblings, is the main form of after-school care). The firstborn occupies a unique position; initially there are no siblings to share parental attention, but when siblings arrive, this can result in conflict between parents and the firstborn (Dunn, Kendrick, & MacNamee, 1982). Older siblings are generally more aggressive toward younger siblings but they can also be more nurturing at times, whereas younger siblings are less so with their older siblings. Same-sex siblings seem to have more conflict than siblings of different sex.

Question

What are the general findings about the role of siblings in a child's life?

Children of Divorce

Marriage is generally associated with positive outcomes for children, but it is well documented that divorce is associated with harmful outcomes for children (Bramlett & Mosher, 2001). Children experiencing dissolution of a marriage often have more problems in social interac-

tions, behavior, and schoolwork. Although the divorce rate rose in the 1980s and early 1990s, it has stabilized during the last decade. At the same time, there were increasing rates of cohabitation versus marriage, and the outcomes for children who lived in a cohabiting family that dissolved were not included in these earlier studies. Data from the federal study, the *1995 National Survey of Family Growth*, reveal patterns of cohabitation, marriage, divorce, remarriage, and divorce for a representative sample of 11,000 women from ages 15 to 44 (Bramlett & Mosher, 2001).

Age at first marriage is key: first marriages of teens end sooner than those of women who married at age 20 and older, women under age 25 who divorce are likely to remarry, and women younger than 25 who remarry are more likely to experience a second marital disruption. One-fifth of first marriages end within 5 years and one-third ended within 10 years, with higher rates for black women. About 62 percent of the women in this sample have been married. About half of the women in this sample were married, and about 7 percent were cohabiting. About 10 percent reported they were cohabiting after divorce. And 75 percent of divorced women remarried within 10 years—and after 10 years of remarriage at age 25 or older, one-third of remarriages dissolved. Thus, the quality of life for children depends on their parents' marital or nonmarital decisions, especially those made by young women.

Each child reacts differently to the breakup of the family, depending on the child's age and temperament and the parents' competence in handling the situation (Hartup & van Lieshout, 1995). Schlesinger (1998) conducted a longitudinal study of 160 divorcing families with children between 6 and 12 years of age. His major findings suggest that children this age need to know what the separation is about. Their concerns are very different from the concerns of parents—and parents can be too occupied to notice. Children of separation-divorce have loyalty stresses. A national survey finds that high levels of parental conflict have a significant impact on children regardless of family structure (Vandewater & Lansford, 1998). To adjust to the divorce, children need a sense of safety and closeness to their parents and have their basic needs met. Children feel lower levels of conflict when their parents cooperate in matters concerning the children.

Wallerstein and Kelly (1980; Wallerstein, 1987) found that children have six psychological tasks to complete after a divorce, and the ease of completing these tasks is related to how well the parents handle the divorce. These include (1) accepting that the divorce is real; (2) getting back into previous routines like school and other activities; (3) resolving the loss of the family, which means having a "distant" or "absent" parent, restructured family traditions, and loss of security; (4) resolving anger and self-blame, followed by forgiveness; (5) accepting

Human Diversity

Adoption and Guardianship

Improving Child Adoption Policies

One way to create a family with children is to adopt, and federal and state agencies are making it easier for families to adopt. Unlike in the past, most single women today are keeping their babies after birth and fewer babies are available for adoption. Thus some couples or singles pursue adoption through the foster care system or by adopting children from other countries. With the *Adoption and Safe Families Act of 1997,* the federal government provides monetary awards to states increasing adoption of children in the foster care system (Allen, 2001). In 2000 Congress passed legislation to stop illegal adoptions (e.g., some Internet adoptions) and promote legal international adoption and set up a U.S. central authority that accredits adoption agencies and creates a federal database. The *Children's Citizenship Act of 2000* allows internationally adopted children to become citizens when entering the States (Clark & Shute, 2001). The *Hope for Children Act* in 2002 increased the adoption tax credit to $10,000 and increased the employer adoption assistance exclusion to $10,000 (U.S. Congress, 2001). The *Keeping Children and Families Safe Act of 2003* improves child welfare and adoption policies (Horn, 2002/2003). Since 1992, about 120,000 children were adopted annually in the United States (U.S. Department of Health and Human Services, 2004a).

Who Adopts?

About one-fourth of couples with infertility problems attempt to adopt and many turn to private sources (Mosher & Bachrach, 1996). Since the 1970s, U.S. citizens have adopted more than 250,000 children from other countries, with a majority under age 5 (Adoption Institute, 2005). About 53,000 children in foster care were adopted by relatives and foster parents in 2002—although 532,000 children were in the foster care system. Adoptions by single parents have risen to about 30 percent by 2000, and adoptions by lesbian and gay couples are rising (Clark & Shute, 2001). Some families adopt children with special needs who need support from medical, educational, and mental health professionals.

Complex Issues

By best estimates, about 5 million U.S. children are adopted (Hollinger, 1998). Recent years have witnessed significant change in adoption attitudes and issues have become more complex—birth parents versus adoptive parents, biological mothers versus biological fathers, adoption by singles, adoption by gay and lesbian couples, adoptive children with disabilities, adoptive children's rights, surrogacy, racial and religious compatibility, high rate of turnover for child welfare workers, declining recruitment of foster parents, international adoptions, fraudulent adoption agencies (Internet,

national, and international), and lack of legal protections for adoptive families (Bass et al., 2004; Clark & Shute, 2001).

Adoption or Guardianship of Children in Foster Care

Federal and state laws discourage the removal of children from their natural families unless it is needed to ensure the child's safety. For removal, there must be severe family dysfunction: neglect or physical or sexual abuse (U.S. Department of Health and Human Services, 2001). About 260,000 U.S. children enter the foster care system each year. About 60 percent of these children are reunified with parents, but 40 percent remain in the system—and a small percent of these children are adopted (Bass et al., 2004). Some children are more difficult to adopt: older children, minority children, more boys than girls, and those with disabilities or behavioral concerns. From 1980 to 2000 the number of children in the foster care system per year nearly doubled (see Figure 10.3) (U.S. Department of Health & Human Services, 2001). That number has declined as more family members (*kin*) are becoming *legal guardians* for their own grandchildren, nieces, and nephews. With adoption, a child will cut all ties with a biological family and with a familiar neighborhood, school, and friends. But with *legal guardianship,* the child lives with a close family member, maintains familiar emotional ties with extended family and friends, and experiences less trauma and distress. The child may in time be reunited with a natural parent.

Age at Adoption

About 2 percent of unmarried women are voluntarily relinquishing their infants for adoption (Moore et al., 1995). It is primarily infants and young children in foster care who are adopted, and these adoptions are generally more stable. Generally the older the child, the more difficult adoption is for the child and for the adoptive family. Domestic infant adoptions can take several years of wait time, but legal guardianship is accomplished quickly. Other families are turning to international adoptions because of their shorter wait time.

International Adoption

International adoptions are rising, though they are bureaucratic, complicated, and likely to be more fraudulent than domestic adoptions, especially the health assessment of the child (Clark & Shute, 2001). By 2000, 18,000 children from other countries were adopted annually by U.S. families, and the primary countries were China, the Russian Federation, South Korea, Guatemala, and Romania (Clark & Shute, 2001). The costs of international adoptions range from a few thousand dollars to many thousands (Merrill, 1996). Transportation and other fees are additional. Wait time for international adoptions generally ranges from 6 months to 18 months.

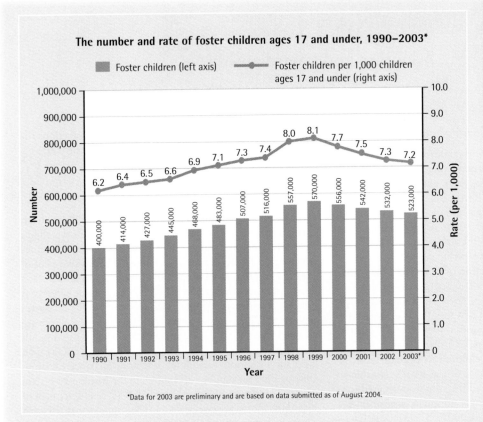

The number and rate of foster children ages 17 and under, 1990–2003*

Foster children (left axis)   Foster children per 1,000 children ages 17 and under (right axis)

*Data for 2003 are preliminary and are based on data submitted as of August 2004.

FIGURE 10.3 Children Living in Foster Care: 1990–2003 Because children enter and exit foster care during the year, the actual number who experience foster care during any year is substantially greater than these estimates. One 1997 source suggests about 700,000 children spent some time in foster care. Many highly fragmented systems are supposed to support this special group of children. The majority is reunited with birth relatives; 20 percent are adopted yearly; and some remain in foster care until reaching adult status.
Source: Art: Child Trends. Child Trends DataBank Indicator: Foster Care. Retrieved from http://www.childtrendsdatabank.org/figures/12-figure-1.gif. Reprinted with permission. Original data from the Adoption and Foster Care Analysis and Reporting System.

Adoption Fees

The cost of adopting can be prohibitive for some families, depending on the type of service used. Public agencies charge either no fee or a minimal fee, though attorney fees must be paid. Religious agencies charge from a few hundred to several thousand dollars. Private domestic agencies typically charge $6,000 to $30,000. Private adoptions can run from a few thousand dollars or much higher if the family pays the medical costs for the pregnant woman. Some U.S. companies offer adoption benefits for employees, typically around $2,000. Some assist with legal fees associated with adoptions, birth mother medical costs, and agency or placement fees (National Adoption Information Clearinghouse, 1996).

Becoming an Adoptive Parent

The root of the word *adopt* means "to choose" and "to take as one's own the creation of another." As Rosenberg (1992, p. 15) observes: "Birth parents are at once birth parents but not rearing parents; adoptive parents are rearing parents but not birth parents; adoptees are their adoptive parents' children but not their birth children, their birth parents' progeny but not their children by rearing." Members of the adoption circle often revisit issues of loss, separation, and insecurity in ways that differ from "regular" families. The traditional closed adoption system encourages birth parents to forget that a child was ever born, while denying any information to adoptees about their birth parents, thereby encouraging the adoptive family to live "as if" all are biologically related. But given conflicting societal messages, some adoptees decide to search for their birth parents, which normally is an emotional and painstaking busi-

ness. The experiences of adult children who are reunited with their birth parents vary from happy reunions to distressing rejections (Lifton, 1994). The adoptive climate in U.S. society is more open than in previous decades, and some states allow for mutual consent registries—permitting parties to an adoption to meet later and allowing for a release of information if both the birth parent and the adult adoptee file formal consents of disclosure of their identities (Hollinger, 1998).

Adoptive Child Well-Being

At one time it was believed that adoption invariably leads to psychological difficulties. But a growing body of evidence reveals that there is no necessary relationship between adoption and psychopathology (Brodzinsky, Schechter, & Henig 1992). Indeed, a federally funded four-year study of several hundred families by the Minneapolis-based Search Institute (1994) revealed that most adoptive families are thriving, and most adoptive adolescents show no signs that adoption has had a negative effect on their mental health. Overall, half of the adoptees said they thought about adoption rarely, 10 percent indicated they thought about adoption every day (10 percent of the adopted adolescents said they thought their parents would love them more if they were biological children, 7 percent said it hurt them to know that they were adopted, and 6 percent indicated they felt unwanted). Yet, some adult adoptees experience identity issues and search for biological family (Brodzinsky, Schechter, & Henig, 1992).

We would do well to remind ourselves that first and foremost all children need and deserve the love and support of a family no matter what their origins in life.

that the divorce will be permanent; and (6) believing in relationships. Many schools offer children of separation-divorce the opportunity to join in a *Banana Splits* program. Children get together in peer groups with a school counselor or school psychologist to share their feelings and experiences and to give and get advice. Such children are taught how to cope with their feelings of loss, helplessness, anxiety, or anger.

Divorce affects children's development in complex ways, with many confounding factors involved. Most children adjust in time but some are troubled years after the divorce. In one study, children were interviewed 10 years after their parents had divorced (children were then ages 6 to 8), and a majority of the girls and boys were well adjusted. Most children lived with their mothers, about 5 percent lived with their fathers, and the rest lived with other kin (often grandparents) or in foster homes. Overall, children who have a stable, loving relationship with both parents have fewer emotional scars (Arditti & Keith, 1993).

Factors that impact the development of children of divorce include:

1. *Age of the child.* Young children respond differently than older children, due to being in a different stage of development.
2. *Level of parental conflict.* High conflict before, during, and after divorce is harmful to children's development.
3. *Gender of the child and custodial parent.* Children living with a same-sex parent were happier, more mature, more independent, and had more self-esteem.
4. *Nature of custody.* Sociologists find that children do better in mother-custody or joint-custody families than in father-custody families, when the mother is employed (Robinson, 1998).
5. *Income.* Often the significant drop in income for mother-custody families creates considerable stress because the family must move to lower-standard housing. The children lose the comfort and security of familiar neighborhoods, friends, and schools, along with losing family routines.

Questions

How do children learn to cope with parental separation and divorce? The stages a child goes through regarding a divorce apparently are similar to the stages of grief and bereavement over the loss of a loved one. How would you describe the stages a child aged 6 to 12 goes through to adapt to the changes in family structure and support?

Single-Parent Families

The family structure is associated with child well-being and with many future outcomes, such as rate of high school completion or dropout, substance abuse, criminal behavior, age at becoming a parent, lifetime earnings, and repeating the parents' marriage or nonmarriage pattern. An extensive amount of research comparing findings from the 1960s through the present suggests that children born to single mothers, regardless of the age of the mother, are more likely to grow up in poverty, to spend their childhood without two parents, and to become single parents themselves (Bramlett & Mosher, 2002). However, child outcomes are likely to be more positive when single mothers are employed. Children growing up in homes with single-parent fathers are likely to fare better because males are more likely to be employed and generally earn higher wages, and single-parent fathers report spending more time in activities with their children (Hofferth & Anderson, 2003). Here are some revealing facts from the study *America's Children in Brief: Key National Indicators of Well-Being, 2004* (Federal Interagency Forum on Child and Family Statistics, 2004):

- By 2003, the proportion of children in two-parent families continued to decrease significantly to 68 percent. The greatest decline is for black children living in two-parent families.
- By 2002, nonmarital childbearing rose significantly among women of all ages to 34 percent (from 5 percent in 1960). Thus, one-third of all births were to unmarried women, and birthrates for single women 20 and older continue to rise. This is correlated with an increase in the number of children living in poverty in 2003, up to 11.6 million.
- In 2003, 32 percent of children lived with a single parent: 23 percent lived with mothers; 5 percent lived with fathers, and 4 percent lived with neither parent (with kin or foster care).
- In 2003, 72 percent of single mothers were employed (but 28 percent were not)—and 84 percent of single-parent fathers with children were employed.

What do these numbers tell us about how living in a single-parent family affects children's development? Research studies on family structure indicate that children raised in a single-parent family headed by an unemployed mother are very likely to have problems in school, get into trouble, and have marital and parenting problems themselves (Kantrowitz & Wingert, 2001).

More recently, though, sociologist Timothy Biblarz from the University of Southern California reported research findings from a study of nearly 23,000 adult men (Robinson, 1998). These males were matched by occupational status, income, and education to the family type in which they were raised. Sons of working single mothers did nearly as well professionally as those reared in two-parent homes. However, the sons of unemployed single mothers were more likely to be in the lowest-paying occupations. Biblarz states, "It seems that success—or lack of it—has more to do with finances than family

A Steep Increase in the Percentage of Single-Parent Families The single-parent family is under close examination by government researchers and social scientists. Single-parent families occur when the mother has never married; the mother is a divorced parent; the mother is widowed, or she has adopted a child. Research suggests that children's well-being is compromised if the single-parent mother is unemployed. Recent findings suggest that sons of employed single mothers do nearly as well professionally as those reared in two-parent homes.

structure" (Robinson, 1998). Children who report having positive interactions with nonresidential fathers or male role models have fewer problems in school and function better in both behavioral and cognitive realms (Coley, 1998). Furthermore, if children have a good relationship with the single parent and income stress is not a factor, they are inclined to be better adjusted than if they remain in a two-parent home that is a divided and hostile environment (Bray & Hetherington, 1993).

Notably, studies examining family-peer linkages have revealed that parenting styles, disciplining methods, parental support, and quality of child-parent attachment definitely influence the children's peer relationships—another key factor that promotes children's self-esteem (Stocker & Dunn, 1994). Also, because the likelihood of remarriage is high, children often enter a stepfamily structure, which can provide greater economic support but sometimes brings higher levels of emotional conflict.

Questions

Nearly every social institution, in Europe as well as in the United States, from the national to the local level, is studying the increasing number of children who live in either never-married single-parent families or divorced single-parent families, the majority of whom are headed by women. In what ways does this family structure affect children? What factors are associated with single parenting and children's well-being?

Stepfamilies

Between 75 and 80 percent of divorced parents remarry (Bramlett & Mosher, 2002). These families are labeled as *reconstituted* or *blended* families, contrasted with intact, biological families. Children often find it difficult to adjust to new parents who have their own children in tow, and the stress from trying to acclimate to the new family dynamics can lead to emotional and behavioral problems. Stepfathers are usually accepted by boys but can come between girls and their mothers. Thus, girls are more likely to reject the stepfather (Bray & Hetherington, 1993). Stepparents usually adopt a *laissez-faire* attitude with stepchildren in regard to discipline and find there are fewer conflicts if the biological parent does the disciplining. A difference can be seen between men and women in the ways they bond with stepchildren, and stepmothers are more likely to slip into the day-to-day activities with their stepchildren, whereas stepfathers are generally less involved with their stepchildren's activities (Hofferth & Anderson, 2003).

As children enter later childhood, no matter the family type or the degree of harmony within the family, they seek peer relationships outside the family to provide a support system associated with resilience and life satisfaction (Nickerson & Nagle, 2004).

Later Childhood: The Broadening Social Environment

Later childhood is a significant time when children enlarge and refine their cognitive and social skills, and social scientists often refer to this time as *preadolescence* or the "tween" years. Preadolescents become increasingly self-directed and begin to choose their own social contacts with peers, and with some they form close friendships. From ages 6 to 14, children's conceptions of friendship show an increasing emphasis on mutual caring, trust, and loyalty (Youniss & Smollar, 1985). Supportive friends are positively correlated with achievement in school, healthy self-esteem, and psychosocial adjustment (Nickerson & Nagle, 2004).

The World of Peer Relationships

During preadolescence, there is a developmental change in what children consider important to know about a friend. Children begin focusing on a friend's preferences, such as her or his favorite games, activities, and people. As they transition to adolescence, young people become increasingly concerned about a friend's internal feelings and personality traits. Hence, there is a progressive shift from concern with the observable and external qualities of a friend (he's my friend because he has a new computer) to concern with a friend's internal psychological world (she's my friend because she and I like the same things, she's fun to be with, and I trust her). Clearly, peer relationships assume a vital role in children's development (Nickerson & Nagle, 2004; Rodkin et al., 2000).

Developmental Functions of Peer Groups

Relationships with peers can help children develop interactional skills, such as communication, perspective taking, reciprocity, and conflict resolution (Dunn, 1993). Public approval or disapproval from peers is linked to self-worth, and as children age, peer friendships take on increasing importance (Harter, 1998). There are many different kinds of peer relationships and groups: a friendship, a school or neighborhood clique, a scout troop, a basketball or soccer team, a gang, and so on. Children may be simultaneously involved in a number of peer relationships, which provide them with a world of children, in contrast to a world of adults. Peer groups serve a variety of functions:

- *Peer groups provide an arena in which children can exercise independence from adult controls.* Because of peer-group support, children gain the courage and confidence they need to weaken their emotional bonds to their parents. The peer culture also operates as a pressure group, by creating peer standards for behavior. The peer group becomes an important agency for extracting concessions for its members on matters as bedtime hours, dress codes, choices of social activities, and amounts of spending money. It affirms children's right to a considerable measure of self-determination. Hence, the peer group furnishes an impetus for young people to seek greater freedom and provides support for behavior they would never dare attempt on their own. Consequently, peer-group affiliations play a significant role in children's school motivation, performance, and adjustment.
- *Peer groups give children experience with relationships in which they are on an equal footing with others.* In the adult world, children often are subordinates, with adults directing, guiding, and controlling their activities. Group membership is characterized by sociability, self-assertion, competition, cooperation, and mutual understanding among equals (Edwards, 1994). By interacting with peers, children learn the functional and reciprocal basis for social rules and regulations. They practice "getting along with others" and subordinating their own interests to group goals. As discussed earlier, Jean Piaget views these relationships among status equals as the foundation for the stage in moral development that he terms *autonomous morality.*
- *The peer group is the only social institution in which the position of children is not marginal.* Children can acquire status and realize an identity in which their own activities and concerns are supreme. Furthermore the "we" feeling—the solidarity associated with group membership—furnishes security, companionship, acceptance, and a general sense of well-being. And it helps children avoid boredom and loneliness during the unstructured, out-of-school hours.
- *Peer groups are agencies for the transmission of informal knowledge, superstitions, folklore, fads, jokes, riddles, games, and secret modes of gratification.* Peer groups are especially appropriate for mastering self-presentation and impression-management skills, because inadequate displays will often be ignored or corrected without severe loss of face. Upstairs, behind the garage, on the street, and in other out-of-the-way places, children acquire and develop many skills essential for the management of adult life.

Obviously, peer relationships are as necessary to children's development as are family relationships. The complexity of social life requires that children be involved in networks both of adults and of peers (Dunn, 1993). Yet some peer groups are in open conflict with adults, as with delinquent gangs. The gang's behavior is oriented toward evading and flouting the rules and regulations of school and the larger adult-dominated society. Also, nondelinquent children find themselves in conflict with parental expectations, as when they argue, "The other kids can stay out late; why can't I?" At the other extreme, the expectations of some peer groups may fully accord with those of adults. This agreement is usually true of youth sports teams, scouting organizations, 4-H, and religious youth groups. Sadly, some children are not accepted by peers and have few, if any, friends—and we shall address potential identification and intervention strategies to help such children in the section "Popularity, Social Acceptance, and Rejection."

Gender Cleavage

A striking feature of peer relationships during the elementary school years is *gender segregation* called **gender cleavage**—the tendency for children to separate themselves into same-sex peer groups. According to a large national study on the well-being of American children, the average child has four friends (Hofferth, 1998). For many children, same-gender friendships are closer and more intense in late childhood and early adolescence than in any other phase of the life span. Although social distance between the genders is present at preschool age, it increases during elementary school years and remains strong through middle childhood (Bukowski et al., 1993). Studies show that when first-grade children are given photos of classmates and asked to point out their best friend, 95 percent select a same-sex child. Whatever characteristics may differentiate the genders, the way boys and girls are socialized in Western countries magnifies the differences greatly. And in the early school years, peers intensify the pressure for gender segregation. A few children might try to play with opposite-sex peers, but they are often rejected. Although first-grade children nearly always name members of their own gender as best friends, girls and boys are observed playing together on playgrounds during recess. By the third grade, though, children divide themselves into two gender camps—with a gender-separation peak around fifth grade. Much of the interaction between boys and girls at the fifth-grade level is bantering, teasing, chasing, name calling, and displays of open hostility. This "them-against-us" view serves to emphasize the differences between the genders and might function as a protective phase in life during which children can fashion a coherent gender-based identity (recall maybe putting a sign on your bedroom door or clubhouse "No Girls Allowed!" or vice versa).

Some evidence suggests that gender segregation could be a universal process in human social development (Edwards & Whiting, 1988). Fifth- and sixth-grade boys are rather disgruntled about the issue of fairness. They are full of healthy energy, boisterous, and louder than most girls at this age. As a result, teachers discipline them more and boys loudly protest that teachers "favor the girls." Girls this age are more verbal and complain to teachers about the boys' behaviors. First-year middle school teachers be forewarned: You may feel that you're spending most of your time settling boys-against-girls disputes!

Gender Cleavage The social distance between the genders, called gender cleavage or gender segregation, increases during the elementary school years and remains strong through middle childhood and peaks around fifth grade. Boys are full of healthy energy, boisterous, and louder than most girls at this age. Maccoby (1988, 1990) contends that rough play and competitive and dominance-oriented behaviors make many girls wary and uncomfortable.

Developmental psychologist Eleanor E. Maccoby (1988, 1990) finds that gender segregation asserts itself in cultural settings in which children are in large enough numbers to permit choice. Indeed, children systematically frustrate adult efforts to diffuse their preferences for interacting with same-gender peers. For example, in coeducational schools, gender segregation is most evident in lunchrooms, playgrounds, on school buses, and other settings that are not structured by adults. We should not assume, however, that gender cleavage is total, even in the preadolescent period. Whether working on class projects or playing tag football, girls and boys intermingle (Thorne, 1993). Moreover, members of both genders show considerable interest in one another. Ten- and 11-year-old boys and girls talk a good deal about each other (for instance, who likes whom) and are often seen closely observing each other's actions.

Maccoby believes two factors give rise to gender segregation. First, boys and girls have differing styles for peer interaction because they find partners of the same gender more compatible. Second, girls have more difficulty influencing boys. Boys engage in a good deal of rough-and-tumble play—teasing, hitting, poking, pouncing, sneaking up on, mock fighting, piling on, chasing, holding, wrestling, and pushing one another. Thus, high levels of competitive and dominance-oriented behaviors, called *proactive aggression*, prevail among boys (Poulin & Boivin, 2000). Boys and men seem to evolve social structures—well-defined roles in games, dominance hierarchies, and team spirit—that allow them to function effectively in their preferred kind of milieu—group settings (Gurian, 1996).

Maccoby contends that rough play and competitive and dominance-oriented behaviors make many girls wary and uncomfortable. For instance, boys are more likely than girls to interrupt one another, use commands and threats, heckle a speaker, tell jokes or suspenseful stories, use "bathroom" humor, try to top another person's story, and call other youngsters names (or pejoratively refer to another boy's mother, a sure way to escalate the mockery). In contrast, girls in groups often engage in "collaborative speech acts"—they express agreement, pause to give another girl a chance to speak, acknowledge a point made by a previous speaker, smile, and provide nonverbal signals of attentiveness. In sum, boys' speech serves egoistic functions and is used to "stake out turf," whereas girls' conversation tends to be a socially binding undertaking. It is not that girls are unassertive among themselves; rather, girls pursue their ends by toning down coercive and dominance-type behaviors and using strategies that facilitate and sustain social relationships.

The prevalence of this childhood gender cleavage provided Sigmund Freud with his concept of the *latency period.* In Freud's view, once children no longer look on the parent of the opposite sex as a love object (thereby resolving their Oedipus or Electra conflict), they reject members of the opposite sex until they reach adolescence. Hence according to Freud, the elementary school years are a kind of developmental plateau, one in which sexual impulses are repressed.

Questions

Did you experience gender cleavage in elementary school? Who were your friends? Why do you think same-gender friends are so prevalent during this stage of life?

Popularity, Social Acceptance, and Rejection

Peer relationships often take on enduring and stable characteristics, in particular the properties of a **group,** defined as two or more people who share a feeling of unity and are bound together in relatively stable patterns of social interaction. Group members have a psychological sense of oneness; they assume that their own inner experiences and emotional reactions are shared by the other members. This sense of oneness gives individuals the feeling that they are not merely *in* the group but *of* the group. A group's awareness of unity is expressed in many ways. One of the most important is through shared **values,** which are the criteria that people use in deciding the relative merit and desirability of things (themselves, other people, objects, events, ideas, acts, and feelings). Values play a critical part in influencing people's social interaction. They function as the standards, the social "yardsticks," that people use to appraise one another. In short, people size up one another

according to various group standards of excellence, which can be prosocial or antisocial.

Peer groups are no exception. Elementary school children arrange themselves in ranked hierarchies with respect to various qualities. Even first-graders have notions of one another's relative popularity or status. Consequently, children differ in the extent to which their peers desire to be associated with them. Recent research has also indicated that if children perceive their peer group to be "different" in some way, the bonds will be much stronger between members (Bigler, Jones, & Lobliner, 1997).

One common measure used for assessing patterns of attraction, rejection, or indifference is *sociometry* (Newcomb, Bukowski, & Pattee, 1993; Ramsey, 1995). In a questionnaire or interview, the person is asked to name the three (or sometimes five) individuals in the group whom they would most like to sit next to (eat with, have as a close friend, live next to, have on their own team, etc.). Researchers also use sociometry to classify children into categories based on their relative status within their peer group. These categories are used to identify children who are at either extreme in status—popular, rejected, neglected, or controversial—or average in status or who differ along an acceptance or friendship continuum (Benenson, Apostolen, & Parnass, 1998). By asking people to name the individuals whom they would least like to interact with in a given context, teachers can identify rejected children who are often social isolates. Because these children are at risk for negative adult developmental problems, social intervention measures can be taken by school counselors or psychologists. The data derived from a sociometric study can be presented in a **sociogram,** which depicts the patterns of choice existing among members of a group at a given time (see Figure 10.4). Sometimes adults overlook the impact of various ecological factors that influence early friendships and sociometric choices, such things as desk arrangements, ability groupings, and the scheduling of classes and recess.

Body Image and Popularity Physical attractiveness is culturally defined and is differently defined by different cultures. Children begin to acquire these cultural definitions by about 6 years of age; by the age of 8, as their thought processes shift to the period of concrete operations, they come to judge physical attractiveness in much the same manner as adults. Can you think why this might be true?

Stereotypes and appraisals of body configurations are also learned relatively early in life. "Lean and muscular," "tall and skinny," and "short and fat" are all bodily evaluations that influence the impressions people form of one another. As mentioned in Chapter 9, negative attitudes toward "fatness" are already well developed among young children. Among boys, a favorable stereotype of the *mesomorph* (the person with an athletic, muscular,

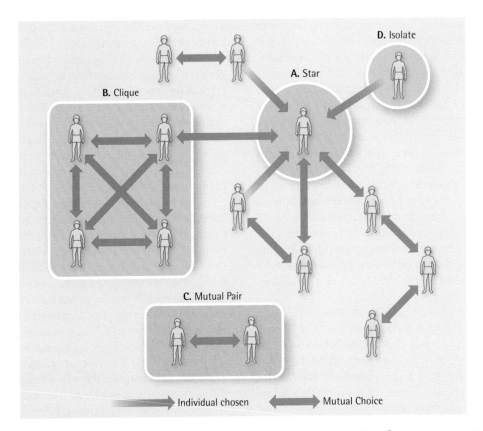

FIGURE 10.4 Sociometry is a Technique Used for Identifying the Social Relations in a Group Each individual is asked to name three (sometimes five) group members with whom he or she would like to participate in a particular activity. The data gathered can be depicted graphically in a sociogram like this one. Different clusters of relationships typically emerge. The male peer group is likely to cluster as one big group of interconnected boys (as in B). The sociogram for girls is likely to be small clusters consisting of two or three close friends (as in C or A). This finding is consistent with observations about children in middle childhood and it appears to extend into adolescence. If a female has more than two best friends, these best friends were generally not best friends with one another. Note also that a few children are likely to be isolates (D) from the group and may need assistance with developing social skills.
Source: From *Sociometry Then and Now: Building on 6 Decades of Measuring Children's Experiences with the Peer Group,* New Directions for Child and Adolescent Development, No. 80, ed. William M. Bukowski and Antonius H. Cillessen. © 1998 by Jossey-Bass, Inc., Publishers. Reprinted with permission of John Wiley & Sons, Inc.

and broad-shouldered build) is evident at age 6. However, boys' desire to look like a mesomorph does not appear until age 7 and is not clearly established until age 8.

Researchers have found many qualities that make children appealing in the eyes of preadolescent and teen peers—and physical development, attractiveness, and body build are their main concerns (Akos & Levitt, 2002). Many studies with teens have consistently reported a significant relationship between physical attractiveness and popularity (Akos & Levitt, 2002). Surprisingly, Phares, Steinberg, and Thompson's (2004) cross-sectional study with elementary and middle school students revealed significant weight and body image concerns—with girls reporting greater body dissatisfaction than boys. Girls as young as 6 in this study had tried to lose weight by dieting, and most children were knowledgeable about weight control methods. Boys typically grow bigger and stronger, which is consistent with cultural ideals for males, so they struggle less with body image dissatisfaction (Maine, 2000). Friedman (1998) reports that at ages 10 and 11, 80 percent of girls are convinced they should be thinner.

In a recent study with 11- to 14-year-old girls, more than one-third reported dieting activity (Byely et al., 2000).

Parents also influence children by transmitting weight-related attitudes and opinions. Mothers placed more emphasis on body image, weight, and dieting than fathers did (Phares, Steinberg, & Thompson, 2004). Teasing by peers and parents about facial features, body weight, or body shape has a strong influence on the development of eating and weight concerns, for boys as well as girls. These researchers found that gender differences concerning body image, physical attractiveness, and weight develop years before any puberty changes—and girls in elementary school report higher levels of body dissatisfaction, depressive symptoms, and lower levels of global self-worth than boys. Thus, these researchers argue it is imperative to address weight and body image concerns well before adolescence (Phares, Steinberg, & Thompson, 2004). Because body dissatisfaction is the single strongest predictor of developing an eating disorder, school counselors suggest intervention strategies, including programs that emphasize health, strength, and self-acceptance; individual counseling; group counseling, peer mentoring, improved library resources, family consultation, and community sponsorship of parks and recreation facilities (Akos & Levitt, 2002).

Behavioral Characteristics A range of behavioral characteristics are related to children's peer acceptance. Both children and teachers tend to describe model popular children as active, outgoing, alert, self-assured, helpful, and friendly. They show interest in others, act in prosocial ways, and are confident but not boastful (Newcomb, Bukowski, & Pattee, 1993). Recent studies of popular boys in grades 4 to 8 find that some preadolescent children consider boys who are "tough" or oppositional to be most popular (Rodkin et al., 2000; Rodkin & Hodges, 2003). Boys of minority groups typically nominate as "most popular" those boys who are low achievers, disobey the rules, put little effort into school, and are good at sports. Thus, both popular-prosocial and popular-antisocial boys are central members of cliques in which they enjoy high levels of prominence. Tough boys have the highest self-perception of their popularity (Rodkin et al., 2000; Rodkin & Hodges, 2003).

In contrast, children who are unpopular with peers have their own distinctive traits (Newcomb, Bukowski, & Pattee, 1993): (1) social isolates are physically listless, lethargic, and apathetic (or they might be experiencing a periodic chronic illness); (2) some children are so psychologically introverted, timid, and withdrawn that they have little contact with peers; and (3) children who are overbearing or aggressively hostile are described by their peers and teachers as noisy, attention-seeking, demanding, rebellious, and arrogant. Other children have been labeled "hyperactive" and prescribed Ritalin to "control" their behavior. Significantly, early peer rejection in the first two months of kindergarten forecasts less favorable school perceptions among youngsters, higher levels of school avoidance, and lower performance levels. Children who experience early rejection are likely to experience serious adjustment problems in later life.

Bullying Behaviors During the preadolescent assimilation to middle school/junior high, youth are more reliant on peers for social support—thus, acceptance and popularity become very important (Espelage, Bosworth & Simon, 2001; Macklem, 2003). Appearance is a central determinant of social status among girls, while for boys, competitive, tough, and aggressive behaviors are often status markers (Eder, 1995). In order to "fit in," some youth resort to bullying. Much of the research on bullying comes from Europe, Canada, Australia, and New Zealand—and it is an increasing problem in schools worldwide (Macklem, 2003; Olweus, 1993). But a national U.S. study with 16,000 students in grades 6 to 10 in public, private, and parochial schools was recently published (Nansel et al., 2001). Nearly one-third

of youth reported moderate to frequent involvement in bullying, as either the aggressor and/or the victim. Bullying behaviors were reported more often in middle school than in high school and in urban schools than in suburban ones (Nansel et al., 2001).

Bullying is deliberate, repeated aggressive behavior that involves *an imbalance of power or strength* toward another person (Nansel et al., 2003; Olweus, 1993). Aggressors might be an individual or a group, and victims might be an individual or a group. Such harmful actions include making faces, using "dirty" gestures, name calling, teasing, pinching, hitting, kicking, restraining actions, threats of harm, stealing money and possessions, harassing sexually, sending mean notes or e-mail, or exclusion from a group. Boys are more likely to be bullied physically, but girls are likely to be the targets of rumors, sexual comments, and social exclusion (Nansel et al., 2001). Victims are likely to be "different" physically, intellectually, racially, socioeconomically, culturally, or by sexual orientation. They are often weaker and younger, are timid and lack confidence, or are not good at sports. An American Association of University Women (AAUW) study, *Hostile Hallways* (2001b), reports four out of five girls experience sexual harassment in school.

The victims, or targets, of bullying experience injurious psychological and physical effects, such as depression, loneliness, anxiety, low self-esteem, stress-related illness, sleep disturbances, headaches, thoughts of suicide, or a final episode of violent revenge or suicide (Limber, 2002). Studies reveal negative outcomes for the aggressor, such as being involved in a fight, theft, drugs, truancy, dropping out of school, later criminal convictions (e.g., gun possession in school), or imprisonment (Nansel et al., 2003). Schools have a legal responsibility to ensure that a safe environment is available to all students, under the provisions of Title IX of the Education Amendments of 1992—and doctors say the effects of bullying have become a public health problem. Several bullying intervention programs for school districts or classroom teachers focus on creating a safe school environment (Espelage & Swearer, 2004).

Unpopular children require early intervention from parents, teachers, and sometimes school psychologists or counselors to acquire more effective social skills, because studies find they maintain the same antisocial behaviors and associate with peers like themselves or remain isolates (Poulin & Boivin, 2000). Generally, the clusters of traits found among popular and unpopular youngsters in the United States hold cross-culturally in industrialized nations (Chen, Rubin, & Sun, 1992).

Social Maturity Children's social maturity increases rapidly during the early school years (French, 1984). In one school system, 50 percent of the first-graders said they would rather play with younger children. This figure dropped to one-third among third-graders.

Standards of Popularity, Bullying, and Exclusion During the preadolescent assimilation to middle school/junior high, children are more reliant on peers for social support—thus, acceptance and popularity become very important. Yet children who might be different in some way—such as physically, intellectually, racially, culturally, or even being quiet or timid—are likely to be talked about, excluded, or bullied. Various intervention programs and strategies can be used to promote acceptance by peers and a safe school climate for all children.

Moreover, whereas one-third of first-graders said they would rather play alone, a small percent of third-graders expressed this preference. And although being with other children bothered one-third of first-graders, fewer third-graders reported this difficulty. In fact, some children go through school with few or no friends. For example, about 6 percent of third- through sixth-grade children in one school system were not selected by any classmate on a sociometric questionnaire. In another study more than 10 percent of children from third through sixth grade reported feelings of loneliness and social dissatisfaction, and these feelings were significantly related to their sociometric status (Renshaw & Brown, 1993). Feelings of loneliness, rejection, and social isolation have profound consequences for child (and adult) self-esteem.

Peer influences operate in many ways. One of the most important is through the pressure that peer groups put on their members to conform to various standards of conduct. Although peer groups constrain the behavior of their members, they also facilitate interaction and communication. They define shared goals and clarify acceptable, or unacceptable, means for pursuing these goals.

Questions

What personality characteristics do a model "popular" child convey versus a "tough popular" child? In contrast, what traits or characteristics are likely to make a child unpopular with the group?

Racial Awareness and Prejudice

A key aspect of many children's peer experiences involves relations with members of different racial and ethnic groups. A growing body of research indicates that children as young as 3 can correctly identify some differences between blacks and whites, and by the age of 7 a majority of children can make such racial identifications accurately (Katz, 2003). Indeed, by age 5 youngsters demonstrate a capacity for strong in-group bias and high levels of same-group cohesion (Aboud, 2003). Children's perceptions and understanding about racial differences follow a developmental sequence similar to that about other stimuli (Wright, 1998). Their own social identities as members of particular ethnic groups evolve slowly with age, as they subjectively identify with a group and assimilate notions of ethnicity and belonging within their self-concepts (Hutnik, 1991). Labeling oneself as a member of an ethnic group is one of the earliest expressions of a child's social identity and typically is acquired by 7 to 8 years of age (Wright, 1998).

However, there is some doubt that children, especially younger grade-school children, show coherent, consistent **prejudice**—a system of negative conceptions, feelings, and actions regarding the members of a particular religious, racial, or ethnic group. It is one thing to demonstrate that in-group bias can develop in young children; it is quite another to say that prejudice is characteristic of young children (Katz, 2003; Wright, 1998). Young children in the preoperational stage classify things and people by the most salient features: big-small, tall-short, or black-white. (You might have been in public with a young child who notices a person with purple hair and the child blurts out, "That girl has purple hair!" Recognizing the obvious feature, the child is not prejudiced toward those with purple hair.)

In another study, kindergartners and third-graders enrolled in a very ethnically and racially diverse laboratory school located on the campus of the University of California at Los Angeles interacted and formed friendships independently of ethnic and racial memberships (Howes & Wu, 1990). At times, what adults perceive to be prejudice in children is instead a preference for other children who share similar subcultural practices and values and hence who offer a more comfortable "relational fit." Moreover, some questions exist as to whether skin color is the principal determinant of racial prejudice (Wright, 1998). Hair and eye characteristics might play an equal or even more important role (Katz, 2003; Wright, 1998).

Much research shows that how people act in an interracial group situation bears little or no relation to how they feel or what they think (Vander Zanden, 1987). The social setting in which individuals find themselves does much to determine their specific responses. Thus, a public show of blatantly racist and discriminatory behavior is commonly defined as counter to American democratic ideals and as

Peer Relationships and Racial Awareness In their relationships with other youngsters of approximately the same age, young people acquire interpersonal skills essential for the management of adult life. Peer groups, including interracial learning teams, provide them with experiences that foster positive interracial contact and friendship.

being "in poor taste." Interracial friendliness is promoted by policies that foster positive interracial contact at early ages in child-care settings, preschool, elementary schools, and neighborhoods. For this reason, to be most effective, integration should begin at the earliest possible time. Many racial and ethnic attitudes are formed early, and adjusting to new environments and avoiding negative stereotypes is more difficult for older students than for younger ones. Indeed, the junior high school and middle school years can be the worst period in which to start integration (Hallinan & Williams, 1989). One successful method for reducing the effects of racism is grouping students into interracial learning teams, which like sport teams, knit members together in common purpose that often leads to interracial friendships (Perdue et al., 1990).

Questions

How do children develop racial or ethnic prejudices? What types of behavioral interventions can be employed, and at what ages, to promote positive views among children with differences?

The World of School

The nature and mission of schools have been disputed through the ages, and Americans are no more in agreement about their schools than the citizens of Rome were

2,000 years ago. Controversy rages—such as the content of school curricula, separation of church and state, teaching approaches, busing to realize better racial and socioeconomic mixes, school financing and taxation, programs for youth with exceptionalities, academic freedom, preparing youth with technological skills, and about school safety.

School is a child's first big step into the larger society for children, and there are choices. Alternative schools include public, private (religious and nonsectarian), charter or magnet schools (more freedom in curriculum design), or home schooling. In 2003, the parents of one-fourth of students reported that they moved to their current neighborhood so their children could attend their school of choice. U.S. homeschooling continues to gain in popularity, with more than 2 million K–12 homeschooled students in 2003. Reasons cited for homeschooling are child safety, chance to provide religious or moral instruction, and dissatisfaction with available public instruction (Princiotta, Bielick, & Chapman, 2004). In Ray's (2003) study with 7,300 homeschooled adults, a high majority are well educated or enrolled in college, employed, and contributing members of their communities.

By 2001 there were a record 45 million children in public schools, and more than 5 million in private schools. Projections to 2013 indicate an increase of 5 percent in enrollment (with an existing shortage now but 2.4 million new teachers needed by 2013) (U.S. Department of Education, 2003). Many U.S. school districts offer incentives such as signing bonuses, subsidized housing, tax breaks, student loan forgiveness, lower mortgage rates, better pension plans, on-site child care, and more (Chaika, 2000).

When they attend school on a regular basis, children are away from family or their neighborhoods for many hours a day, especially for youth in before- and after-school programs while parents work. In school, children encounter a diversity of teachers and children who will pass with them through a series of grades annually, so the school environment has a major impact on the development of a child's personality, self-esteem, intellectual capabilities, interpersonal skills, values, and social behavior ("The Standards: What Teachers Should Know," 1998).

Developmental Functions of Schools

Schools came into existence several thousand years ago to prepare a select few to govern the many and to occupy certain professions. Various models of mass education arose cross-culturally in conjunction with the rise of nation-states, which was closely tied to goals of national development, economic progress, and the formal integration of citizens within a larger social collectivity (Meyer, Ramirez, & Soysal, 1992). Worldwide, schools are often seen as a branch of the state and as serving state purposes. Since 1975, U.S. public schools have become the vehicle by which *all* children have had the opportunity to learn the skills of reading, writing, math, and science that

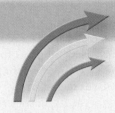

Further Developments

Out-of-School Care and Supervision

The number of American children who routinely spend part of the day unsupervised has been mushrooming. According to the National Institute on Out-of-School Time (2001), about 8 million children ages 5 to 14 spend time without adult supervision on a regular basis when out of school, and most are ages 11 to 14. Although many agencies and schools recognize the need for after-school child supervision, a majority of parents say it is still difficult to find and afford after-school programs (Hofferth & Sandberg, 2001).

The consequences of lack of supervision torment many parents and concern the scientific community, child welfare advocates, and the juvenile justice system. Two factors are under study: the characteristics of families who leave their youngsters unattended and to what extent "self-care" arrangements are associated with increased social, emotional, or cognitive problems in children. It is assumed that families typically use self-care as a last resort and that unsupervised, self-care children are at greater risk for a wide range of health and behavior problems (Hofferth & Sandberg, 2001).

More married and single mothers are employed than ever before, yet many hold minimum-wage jobs—and simply cannot afford after-school care. Federal child-care subsidies help about 10 to 15 percent of families, and such child-care costs consume a large portion of poor or middle-income family wages (Giannarelli & Barsimantov, 2000). Child-care costs for one child average at least $300 per month, which can easily cost $4,000 to $10,000 or more annually depending on where a family resides (Schulman & Blank, 2004).

The majority is in relative care after school (see Figure 10.5), but going home without adult supervision is unsafe. The National Safe Kids Campaign says 4.5 million children 14 and under are injured at home annually, and most injury-related deaths occur when children are unsupervised after school (Karasik, 2000). On school days, between 3 and 6 p.m., serious juvenile crime rates triple—and young children are often victimized (Snyder & Sickmund, 1999). Children's increased television viewing has been associated with lower reading achievement, less homework being done, and increased aggression (Miller, 1995). Some studies report childhood obesity and sleep deprivation have risen because of increased television viewing and less activity (McGowan et al., 2000).

Child-development experts agree that adolescents face more perils than a few decades ago—for example, the increased risks associated with accessibility to addictive drugs and the early age of experimenting with alcohol and sexual activity. As one clinical psychologist observes, "When a six-

an industrial, computer-and-technology, and service-oriented society requires. Moreover, education has become a crucial investment in the economy as well as a major economic resource, and President Bush's proposed $56 billion budget for education is up 33 percent since 2000. (Many U.S. towns survive as "college towns," with the college as the main employer. Further, publishing, software, and educational testing companies are multi-billion-dollar enterprises that market to educators.) Much of the controversial *No Child Left Behind* initiative to raise standards and accountability for K–12 education is driven by the goal of stabilizing or improving the economy and preparing children now for the more technical and sophisticated jobs of the future—jobs we cannot imagine yet!

Elementary schools serve many functions. First, they teach specific cognitive skills, primarily the "core" subjects of language, math, history, and science—all remarkably similar across the world. Yet, overall, U.S. students are falling short in tests of international comparison in some of the core subjects. Also, schools instill general skills, such as being on time, paying attention, sitting quietly, collaborating in classroom activities, and completing assignments and meeting deadlines—preparing youth for future work conditions (Apple & Weis, 1983). Even the school grading system of A to F has its parallel in the merit system of wage and salary scales as a device for motivating individuals.

Second, schools share with the family the responsibility for transmitting any society's dominant cultural goals and values. Like the United States, Japan, China, and Russia stress patriotism, national history, obedience, diligence, personal cleanliness, physical fitness, the correct use of language, and so on in their schools. With respect to basic social norms, values, and beliefs, all education indoctrinates students with the "hidden curriculum" of the times (e.g., today's "tolerance," "diversity," and "pro-choice" agendas).

Third, to one degree or another, schools function as a "sorting and sifting agency" that selects young people for upward social mobility. Some families also influence the careers of their children by socializing them to higher educational and occupational aspirations and by providing them with the support necessary for achieving their goals (Sewell, 1981). Successful elementary and middle-school experiences are particularly important in launching children into this process. Although early academic success does not

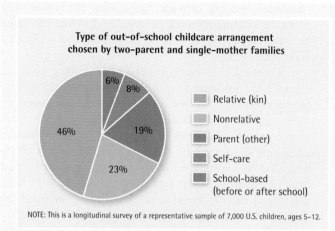

Type of out-of-school childcare arrangement chosen by two-parent and single-mother families

- Relative (kin) — 46%
- Nonrelative — 23%
- Parent (other) — 19%
- Self-care — 8%
- School-based (before or after school) — 6%

NOTE: This is a longitudinal survey of a representative sample of 7,000 U.S. children, ages 5–12.

FIGURE 10.5 Relative Care Is Most Preferred More employed parents (two-parent or single-parent) choose relative care (or *kin* care) than other child-care arrangements for schoolchildren aged 5 to 12. Grandparents, siblings, and other relatives are vital to the health, safety, and supervision of children. Employed Hispanic parents are much more likely to arrange for relative care. School-based care (before or after school) is used the least by employed parents. About 35 percent of children experience more than one child-care setting a week.
Source: Brandon, P. D., & Hofferth, S. L. (2003). Determinants of out-of-school childcare arrangements among children in single-mother and two-parent families. *Social Science Research, 32,* 129–147.

year-old runs away, he gets to the end of the block. When a 16-year-old runs away, she may wind up on Hollywood Boulevard prostituting herself" (Graham, 1995).

Findings from recent studies reveal that children who attend after-school programs experience many benefits, such as better work habits and more homework completed, improved social skills, improved school attendance, higher grades and test scores, fewer hours watching television, more hours in sports and activities, and better conduct in school compared with peers (National Institute on Out-of-School Time, 2001). Consequently, over the past decade many U.S. schools—with federal funding and in partnership with YMCAs, YWCAs, Boys & Girls Clubs, and scouting programs—have established

after-school and summer programs at both the elementary and middle-school levels. These programs provide safety and supervision, nutrition, activities, and adult care for children who would otherwise be unsupervised while parents work.

Although many parents work split shifts, change to part-time work, or stagger their hours of employment to supervise their children, some believe their children are more competent than they really are (Hofferth & Sandberg, 2001). Before making such a decision, they need to consider carefully the child's maturity and the safety of the home and neighborhood. Many well-behaved children are unsupervised at times, but research shows that too many children get into mischief, serious trouble, or harm.

ensure later success, early academic failure strongly predicts later academic failure (Temple & Polk, 1986).

Fourth, schools attempt to help children overcome deficits or difficulties that interfere with adequate social functioning and participation. Schools work in collaboration with parents and guardians, school psychologists, guidance personnel, school nurses, physical therapists, speech therapists, occupational therapists, social services, and the juvenile justice system. Schools also serve a custodial function, providing a day-care service that keeps children out from under the feet of adults and from potential harm on the streets (see the *Further Developments* box "Out-of-School Care and Supervision"). In higher grades they function as a dating and marriage market. And compulsory education, coupled with child labor laws, typically serves to keep younger children out of the labor market and hence out of competition with adults for jobs in the society.

Motivating Students

Most of us assume that people do certain things because the outcomes somehow meet their needs. This premise

underlies the concept of motivation. **Motivation** involves the inner states and processes that prompt, direct, and sustain activity. Motivation influences the rate of student learning, the retention of information, and performance (Owen, 1995). Significantly, a gradual, overall decline occurs in various indicators of academic motivation—attention in class, school attendance, and self-perception of academic competence—as youth move from elementary to middle school or junior high (Eccles, 1999; Wong, Weiss, & Cusick, 2002). Here we will examine a small portion of the topic of motivation that is most relevant to our consideration of the schooling process.

Intrinsic and Extrinsic Motivation   Mark Twain once observed that work consists of whatever we are obligated to do, whereas play consists of whatever we are not obligated to do. Work is a means to an end; play is an end in itself. Many psychologists make a similar distinction between extrinsic motivation and intrinsic motivation. **Extrinsic motivation** involves activity undertaken for some purpose other than its own sake. Rewards such as school grades, honor rolls, scholarships, wages, and promotions are extrinsic because they are independent of the activity itself and are controlled by someone else. **Intrinsic motivation** involves activity undertaken for its own sake. Intrinsic rewards are those inherent to the activity itself and over which we have a high degree of personal control (Schrof, 1993).

As we noted earlier in this chapter, children want to feel effective and self-determining in dealing with their environment. Regrettably, formal education often undermines children's spontaneous curiosity and desire to learn. Children become more extrinsically motivated and less intrinsically motivated to do their schoolwork as they transition into middle and junior high schools. At this same age, many "turn off" to school and education, especially boys and minority youth (Eccles, 1999; Ogbu, 2003). Most psychologists agree that punishment, anxiety or distress, and being ignored impede classroom learning. But they have also become more aware that even rewards can be the enemies of curiosity and exploration (Ginsburg & Bronstein, 1993).

Research by Lepper and Greene (1975) revealed that parents and teachers can unwittingly undermine intrinsic motivations by providing youngsters with extrinsic rewards such as lavish praise, gold stars, money, toys, or treats to undermine children's intrinsic interest in many activities. They suggest that parents and educators should use extrinsic rewards only when necessary to draw children into activities that do not at first attract their interest. But even in these cases, extrinsic rewards should be phased out as quickly as possible.

Attributions of Causality   Closely linked to the matter of rewards is another matter—people's perceptions of the factors that produce given outcomes (Hamilton, Blumenfeld, & Kushler, 1988). Consider the following experience. You have been watching a game involving your favorite football team. With five seconds left in the game and the score tied, a player on your team intercepts a pass and races for the goal line. As the player stumbles into the end zone, the gun sounds, ending the game. Your team has won. Your friend, who favored the other team, says, "Your guys were just lucky!" You respond, "Luck my eye! That was true ability." "Naw," exclaims another friend. "Your guys were more psyched up. They put out more effort." Then a fourth observer interjects, "It was an easy interception. No one was between him and the goal line!" Four people had four different explanations of causality for the same event: luck, ability, effort, and the difficulty of the task (Weiner, 1993).

Youngsters also attribute their academic successes to these differing explanations. And it makes a considerable difference which explanation they employ. Educational psychologists find that when students attribute their successes to high ability, they are more likely to view future success as highly probable as if they attribute their success to other factors. The perception that one has failed because one has low ability is considerably more devastating than the perception that one has failed because of bad luck, lack of effort, or task difficulty (Gardner, 1991).

It seems that both success and failure feed on themselves. Students with histories of performing better than their peers commonly attribute their superior performances to high ability, and so they anticipate future success. Should they encounter periodic episodes of failure, they attribute them to bad luck or lack of effort. But youngsters with histories of low attainment typically attribute their successes to good luck or high effort and their failures to poor ability. Consequently, high attainment leads to attributions that maintain a high self-concept of ability, high academic motivation, and continued high attainment. It is otherwise for those youngsters with low attainment (Carr, Borkowski, & Maxwell, 1991).

Locus of Control   The research on attributions of causality has been influenced by the concept of locus of control. Earlier in this chapter we noted in our discussion of stress that *locus of control* refers to people's perception of who or what is responsible for the outcome of events and behaviors in their lives. Many studies have shown a relationship between locus of control and academic achievement (Smiley & Dweck, 1994). It seems that locus of control plays a crucial role in determining whether students become involved in the pursuit of achievement. Externally controlled youngsters tend to follow the theory that no matter how hard they work, the outcome will be determined by luck or chance; they have little incentive to invest personal effort in their studies, to persist in problem-solving attempts, or to change their behavior to ensure success.

In contrast, internally controlled youngsters believe that their behavior accounts for their academic successes or failures and that they can direct their efforts to succeed in academic tasks. Not surprisingly, pupils with an internal sense of control generally show superior academic performance (Carr, Borkowski, & Maxwell, 1991). The impressive academic success of many Asian Americans seems related to their families' cultural belief that "If I study hard, I can succeed, and education is the best way to succeed" (Sue & Okazaki, 1990). Low educational attainment is often associated with socioeconomic disadvantage and the effects of poverty, a topic that is being given extensive empirical scrutiny by behavioral scientists (Thernstrom & Thernstrom, 2003).

School Performance, Social Class, and Gender Gap

Many studies have shown a close relationship between school performance, SES, and gender (Alexander,

Entwisle, & Olson, 2001). This relationship is evident regardless of the measure employed (occupation of main wage earner, family income, or parents' education). Studies have shown that the higher the SES of children's families, (1) the greater the number of the formal grades the children will complete, the academic honors and awards they will receive, and the effective offices they will hold; (2) the greater their participation in extracurricular activities; (3) the higher their scores on academic achievement tests; and (4) the lower their rates of failure, truancy, suspensions, and premature dropping out of school. Among the hypotheses that have been advanced to explain these facts are the middle-class bias of schools, subcultural differences, a gender gap for boys, and educational self-fulfilling prophecies.

Middle-Class Bias   Boyd McCandless (1970, p. 295) has observed that "schools succeed relatively well with upper- and middle-class youngsters. After all, schools are built for them, staffed by middle-class people, and modeled after middle-class people." Even when teachers are originally from a different social class, they still encourage the development of middle-class values such as thrift, punctuality, respect for property and established authority, sexual morality, ambition, and neatness. More recently, school districts nationwide are hiring teachers and teachers' aides from a diversity of racial, ethnic, and SES backgrounds—especially those who are bilingual—to serve the increasing mix of first-generation immigrant students who are likely to live in poorer neighborhoods.

In some cases middle-class teachers, perhaps unaware of their prejudice, find youth from lower SES different or disobedient. These students sense the lack of acceptance or respect and respond by taking the attitude "If you don't like me, I won't cooperate with you!" The result is that some of these children fail to acquire basic reading, writing, and math skills and become disillusioned with the educational system, which typically is the only avenue available to them to improve their well-being in the long run (Tapia, 1998).

Subcultural Differences   Children of different racial, ethnic, and social classes bring somewhat different experiences and attitudes into the school situation that relate to the "education achievement gap," especially for black and Hispanic students (Ainsworth-Darnell & Downey, 1998; Ogbu, 2003; Zhang & Bennett, 2001). Donald Hernandez (1997), in his extensive historic review of demographic trends of American childhood, states:

> Children in different racial and ethnic groups or with different immigration histories may live in family and neighborhood environments that differ sharply in (1) social organization, (2) economic opportunities and resources, or (3) behaviors, beliefs, and norms,

including those pertaining to parent-child interaction, child-child interaction, nutrition, and child care and development with regard to play, reading, or learning new skills.

Middle-class parents generally make it clear to their children that they are expected to apply themselves to school tasks. But not all groups ascribe to this value, and some directly oppose it (Ogbu, 2003; Thernstrom & Thernstrom, 2003). Therefore, children vary in their level of preparedness for school—for example, in their attitudes regarding a sense of time or punctuality, use of books, pencils, drawing paper numerals and the alphabet, and completing homework.

Perhaps even more important, middle-class children are much more likely than disadvantaged youngsters to possess the conviction that they can affect their environments and their futures. With the common violence in poor neighborhoods, some children are more concerned about making it through the day and are uncertain about their future. Members of social groups that face a job ceiling know that they do, and this knowledge channels and shapes their children's academic behaviors (Thernstrom & Thernstrom, 2003). Moreover, disadvantaged youngsters often find themselves in recurrent school transfers; they fall behind time and again each time they move. Finally, minority-group children who do not speak English are likely to find themselves educationally handicapped in schools where standard English is employed, and some youth drop out of school as early as middle school (Crawford, 1997).

The Gender Gap   It appears that a gender reversal of achievement and engagement in schools has been occurring over the past 30 years, coinciding with myriad efforts, such as Title IX, The Girl Project, American Association of University Women (AAUW) programs for girls, Girl Scouts, to help girls excel at math and science, national take-your-daughter to work days, and so forth. In general, boys are underachieving and disengaging from schools (Coley, 2003; Pollack, 2000). The gender gap begins early: girls' fine-motor skills develop earlier (the nerves on boys' fingers develop later than girls'—thus it is difficult to hold a pencil and write clearly). Girls are better at sitting still, paying attention, abiding by rules, being verbally competent, and dealing with interpersonal relations (Garbarino, 1999). Boys' hormones surge several times a day, causing the urge to move, but they may be lucky to get even one recess to expend that energy (likely to be kept in at recess to catch up or get extra help—or be disciplined for rough behaviors, not paying attention, or interruptions). Boys' female teachers may not know how to help boys harness their energy. Boys comprise more than 70 percent of special education classes, and many are diagnosed with attention-deficit hyperactivity disorder (Bowler, 2003; Conlin, 2003b).

Overall, males achieve higher scores on standardized tests, but more females take advanced placement courses, attend college, and earn 57 percent of bachelor's degrees and 58 percent of master's degrees (Coley, 2001; Sum et al., 2003). Parents, schools, and communities must begin to focus on developmentally appropriate learning for both girls and boys, for this trend affects employment rates, lifetime income, marriage outcomes, and many other socioeconomic factors.

Educational Self-Fulfilling Prophecies Another explanation for social class difference is that children of lower socioeconomic status and minority children are frequently the victims of **educational self-fulfilling prophecies**—or teacher expectation effects (Eccles, 1999). Some children fail to learn because those who are charged with teaching them do not believe that they will learn, do not expect that they can learn, and do not act toward them in ways that motivate them to learn. The hope is that as more college graduates from ethnically diverse backgrounds enter the teaching profession, they will have a better understanding of children's diverse backgrounds and serve as models to the younger generation.

Hence, James Vasquez (1998) writes that children brought up in Hispanic homes come to school with a sense of loyalty to the family, and the family is their basic support group throughout life. This is in direct contrast to the sense of individualism instilled in many other American youth. Consider the differences in these two forms of hypothetical teacher praise: "This is good work, Maria. You should be proud of yourself." Or "Maria, this is good work. I'm going to send it home for your family to see." Vasquez also states that Hispanic youth thrive in an environment of cooperation with the group, which differs significantly from the mainstream value of individual competition and striving to be at the top at someone else's expense. Vasquez (1998) suggests a student-centered, three-step sequence for teachers to develop instructional strategies for adapting instruction to student cultural traits: (1) identify individual student's cultural traits; (2) consider the content to be taught, the context in which it will be taught, and the mode or delivery method; and (3) write down and practice new instructional strategies (see Table 10.2).

"How do you know I'm an underachiever? —Maybe you're just an overdemander!"

Achievement Is Relative
Drawing by Baloo, from *The Wall Street Journal*—Permission, Cartoon Features Syndicate.

Vasquez recommends that teachers avail themselves of educational literature, attend presentations, and read research to enhance their knowledge of the distinctive learning traits of many minority students.

Moreover, communities need to become involved, because schools and school districts do not provide equal learning opportunities, particularly facilities, equipment, and teacher quality. American inner-city school districts often cannot afford to upgrade the infrastructure of the schools because of lack of funds. Black and Hispanic students are often disadvantaged by schools in very much the same ways that their communities are disadvantaged in their interactions with major societal institutions (Ogbu, 2003; Thernstrom & Thernstrom, 2003). To their disadvantage, many minority and low SES youth respond by dropping out of school, and many Hispanic youth as early as middle school (Stern, 2004). As such, a key report, *From Risk to Opportunity: Fulfilling the Educational Needs of Hispanic Americans in the 21st Century*, proposes numerous strategies for improvement: (1) set new and high expectations for children, help parents navigate the educational system, create partnerships that provide options for children, and implement nationwide public awareness and motivation campaign aimed at increasing educational

---

Table 10.2 Three-Step Procedure for Adapting Instruction to Cultural Traits

Step 1: Observe/identify student trait	Step 2: Consider content, context, and mode of delivery	Step 3: Verbalize or write out new instructional strategy
Carlos does better when the material taught involves people interacting in a cooperative way.	*Content:* math concept of making change from $1, $5, and $10 *Context:* people are buying, or trading with each other. *Mode:* student dyads practice using age-appropriate objects	I will have students pair up and practice purchasing items and making change with imitation money and coins.

From: James A. Vasquez, "Distinctive Traits of Hispanic Students." *The Prevention Researcher*, Vol. 5, No. 1.

attainment; (2) support implementation of the No Child Left Behind Act that challenges school standards and accountability to increase fourth graders' proficiency levels; (3) prepare all teachers to address the diverse needs of their students by attracting more Hispanic teachers; (4) conduct research on the educational development of Hispanic Americans across K–college; (5) ensure access to college; and (6) increase accountability and coordination of programs (President's Advisory Commission, 2003).

Schools of the Twenty-First Century Many school reform initiatives have been implemented and are under close scrutiny—in association with research universities and community leadership. Such efforts are put into practice in charter schools, magnet schools, and ventures such as *Atlas Communities, The Modern Red Schoolhouse, Success for All,* Stanford's *Accelerated Schools,* and Yale's *School of the 21st Century (21C)* to create the best possible educational environment for all students. 21C is a comprehensive community model of shared work

dedicated to the healthy growth and development of all children from birth to age 12. To date, 1,300 traditional U.S. schools have converted to year-round multiservice centers accessible to children and parents all day providing guidance and support for parents, including classes in English, preschool programs, before- and after-school and vacation care for children, health education and services for children, networks, and training for community child-care providers, and information and referral for families. A central goal is meeting the needs of the continuing flow of immigrant students and their families (see Figure 10.6) (Finn-Stevenson & Zigler, 1999).

> ### Questions
>
> In what ways do contemporary American schools contribute to a child's overall well-being? In what ways do schools detract from a child's sense of self-worth or motivation? How are U.S. schools changing in the 21st century?

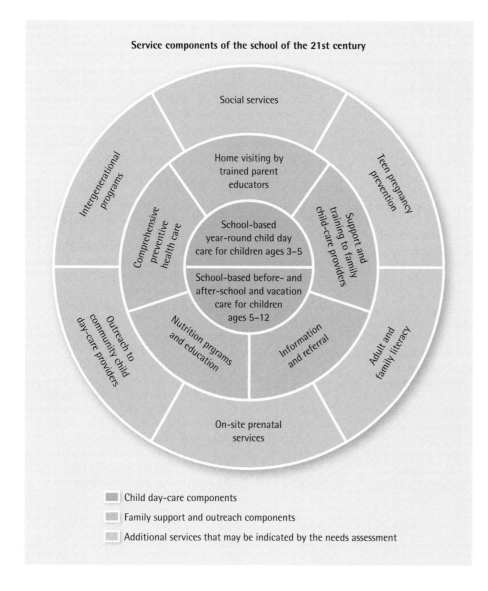

Service components of the school of the 21st century

- Child day-care components
- Family support and outreach components
- Additional services that may be indicated by the needs assessment

FIGURE 10.6 A Model of the School of the Twenty-First Century The school is becoming the central location for providing four comprehensive services that benefit children and their families: education, child care, health care, and social services.
Source: From Zigler, E. F., Finn-Stevenson, M., and Marsland, K. W., "Child day care in the schools: The School of the 21st Century," *Child Welfare,* Vol. 74, No. 6 (November/December 1995), p. 1303. Copyright © 1995 by Child Welfare League of America, Inc. Reproduced with permission of Child Welfare League of America, Inc. via Copyright Clearance Center.

SEGUE

Many interrelated factors are involved in children's healthy physical, cognitive, emotional, and social development throughout the elementary and middle school years. Many middle-class children have protective forces—an intact family structure, economic support, school curriculum and teacher support, friendships, community activities and recreational programs, and supervised after-school programs. Other children, particularly some at a socioeconomic disadvantage, do not develop in a healthy, resilient way because of inconsistent family supervision and the unsupportive nature of the social environments in their lives. The following factors are associated with healthy child development and competency: (1) good self-esteem, (2) optimism and a sense of hope, (3) a sense of resilience, (4) the ability to cope with fears and stress, (5) the ability to experience a range of emotions and self-regulation of emotions, (6) sociability, (7) cognitive abilities to problem-solve, (8) having regular chores at home, and (9) participating in school, church, or extracurricular activities ("Determinants of Health in Children," 1996). These traits provide a solid foundation for thriving in junior high and high school environments during the adolescent stage of development, discussed in Chapter 11.

Summary

The Quest for Self-Understanding

1. Erikson's psychosocial stage during middle childhood is industry versus inferiority. Children desire to try many new things and to develop their abilities. Those who are prevented from trying new activities, don't get the opportunity to try, or don't experience success in comparison to the group are likely to develop low self-esteem.

2. Children's self-concepts develop as they get feedback about their worth or status from the significant people in their lives. Children acquire positive, healthy self-esteem if they are accepted, approved, and respected. Harter identifies five domains that affect children's conceptions of self: scholastic competency, athletic competency, physical appearance, social acceptance, and behavioral conduct. More elementary-age girls are now participating in sports; research findings indicate that girls who participate in sports develop healthier self-concepts.

3. In expanded social settings, children must also learn to regulate their own emotions to get along with the group (classmates, friends in the neighborhood, teammates, relatives). The peer group typically rejects children who cannot self-regulate their behaviors.

4. Children increasingly attribute emotional arousal to internal causes; they come to know the social rules governing the display of emotion; they learn to "read" facial expressions with greater precision; they better understand that emotional states can be mentally redirected; and they realize that people can simultaneously experience multiple emotions.

5. Anger, fear, anxiety, and stress play an important part in the lives of young children. Children aged 5 to 6 often become afraid of imaginary creatures, the dark, and being alone or abandoned. Between 6 and 9 years of age children often fear unrealistic things, such as ghosts and monsters. Research indicates that across gender, ethnicity, and socioeconomic status, older children have more real-life fears of death or harm centered on social violence. Generally, girls experience more fears, anxiety, and stress than boys—especially as they enter middle-school years.

6. All children experience stressful situations in response to perceived threats or dangers, yet they can learn coping strategies to deal with stress. Two important aspects of coping with stress are a child's own sense of mastery and locus of control. Young children often believe the outcome of an action is the result of outside factors, whereas older children come to realize the outcome is moderated by their own efforts and abilities. Supportive caregivers also play a large role in buffering the effects of anxiety and stress.

Continuing Family Influences

7. American children's lives have become more structured as parents' lives have changed. Children's unstructured play time has declined sharply.

8. Research findings indicate that more positive behaviors in children are associated with a warm parental relationship, parents' expectations for closeness, and parents' expectation for college completion.

9. More mothers than ever have become wage earners. Some research finds that women benefit from better economic security and higher self-esteem; other research findings suggest many working women feel guilty about their children spending time in after-school care or self-care situations. But working mothers are not all alike, and there is a great deal of variance in women's beliefs about the significance of working while raising children.

10. Most children still live with a biological father or stepfather during at least part of their childhood. But fathers differ in the amount of time they spend with children, in the activities they share with them, and in the degree to which they take on the responsibilities of parenting.

Fathers in families with biological children spend the most time with children, whereas stepfathers with no biological children report the least amount of time spent with children. When fathers are involved in children's lives, both children and mothers benefit.

11. Results from a national study indicate that, on average, there are three children under 18 in a child's household. Sibling relationships are often more intense than relationships with friends. Siblings normally feel loyalty and support for each other but might also have conflict. Older siblings typically teach younger siblings about the practices and values of a society. More children today are living in stepfamilies. Blended family structures are likely to include stepsiblings, half-siblings, adopted siblings, and unrelated siblings. Sharing and discipline are two emotionally charged issues among siblings. Siblings in other cultures are more likely to take on the responsibility of caregiving at an early age.

12. The American divorce rate has stabilized during the past decade. Children vary in their reactions to divorce, depending on children's age and temperament and parental competence in managing the divorce. Children's concerns about this loss are normally quite different from the parents' concerns. Studies find that children experience less stress when parents cooperate in matters concerning the children.

13. The number of children living in single-parent families has been increasing throughout the 1990s and 2000s. The majority of single-parent families are headed by women, though the number of single-parent families headed by fathers is slowly rising. Single parents include those who have never married, those who are divorced or widowed, and those who have always been single and have adopted. The issue of single parenthood is highly charged in American society today because the parents in these families often need public assistance for the child's well-being. This is a tremendous cost to society, and these children can lack necessary emotional and economic support.

14. Between 75 and 80 percent of divorced parents remarry, creating stepfamilies. Children can find it difficult to adjust to the authority of a new parent, who might or might not bring new children into the reconstituted family. The issue of who disciplines whose children, and how they are to be disciplined, can create frequent conflict in these new marital situations. In many stepfamilies, the divorced parents are also dealing with financial support issues with ex-spouses to adequately care for children. Child-stepparent attachment is likely to be a long, complex process.

Later Childhood: The Broadening Social Environment

15. Peer groups provide children with situations in which they are independent of adult controls, give them experience in egalitarian relationships, furnish them with status in a realm where their own interests reign supreme, and transmit informal knowledge.

16. Gender cleavage reaches its peak at about the fifth-grade level. Although same-gender friendships predominate during the elementary school years, children show a steady and progressive development of cross-gender interests as they advance toward puberty.

17. Elementary school children arrange themselves in hierarchies with regard to various standards, including physical attractiveness, body build, and behavioral characteristics. An observation of peer friendships and of children who are at risk of being social isolates can be done using a sociogram.

18. Children's self-conceptions tend to emerge from others' feedback regarding their desirability, worth, and status. Through their interactions with others and through the effects they produce on their material environment, they derive a sense of their energy, skill, and industry.

19. Over the elementary school years, conformity tends to increase with age in situations in which children are confronted with highly ambiguous tasks. But where the tasks are unambiguous, conformity tends to decline with age.

20. Most children can make accurate racial identifications by 7 years of age. However, whether children, especially younger school children, show coherent, consistent prejudice is doubtful.

The World of School

21. Schools teach specific cognitive skills (primarily the "core" subjects of language, math, history, and science), general skills associated with effective participation in classroom settings, and the society's dominant cultural goals and values. Throughout the 1980s to the present, American schools have been challenged by the increasing enrollment of immigrant and ethnically diverse children, as well as shifting to an inclusive education for children in special education. School buildings are used extensively today for before-school and after-school programs, whereas some children are unsupervised and care for themselves for long hours because more mothers and fathers are working. The issue of quality child care after school has become a priority in American society.

22. Although not all schools are effective, capable teachers can make a difference. Furthermore, effective schools differ from ineffective ones in important ways. Successful schools foster expectations that order will prevail and the view that learning is a serious matter.

23. Motivation influences rate of student learning, retention of information, and performance. Ideally, motivation comes from within (intrinsic motivation).

24. Overall, the higher the social class of children's families, the higher their academic achievement is likely to be. However, cross-cultural research shows that children of different racial and ethnic groups or immigration histories differ in behaviors, beliefs, and norms about children working, playing, reading, or learning new skills.

Key Terms

anxiety (348)

bullying (365)

coping (349)

educational self-fulfilling prophecies (372)

extrinsic motivation (369)

fear (348)

gender cleavage (362)

group (363)

industry versus inferiority (344)

intrinsic motivation (370)

locus of control (349)

motivation (369)

phobia (348)

post-traumatic stress disorder (PTSD) (350)

prejudice (366)

self-image (344)

self-esteem (344)

sociogram (363)

values (363)

Following Up on the Internet

Web sites for this chapter focus on social-emotional issues, family and school influences, and continued identity development of children in middle childhood. Please access the text Web site at www.mhhe.com/vzcrandell8 for up-to-date hot-linked Internet addresses for the following organizations, topics, and resources:

Erikson's Latency Stage

National Center on Fathers and Families

National Home Education Research Institute

U.S. Department of Education and Teacher Loan Forgiveness

NEA's National Bullying Awareness Campaign

National Adoption Institute

Fostering Families Today

Part SIX
Adolescence

A dolescent youth generally experience rapid physical, intellectual, and emotional changes during the time of puberty. Chapter 11 presents maturity issues that accompany the adolescent growth spurt for males and females. Variations in timing of sexual maturation occur and influence both adolescent personality and behavior. Cognitive growth includes the ability to use logical and abstract thought and to plan for the future. Adolescents become more egocentric and influenced by peers than at any other time of development. Social pressures to belong or conform to a group cause some teens to experience anxiety, eating disorders, depression, or attempted suicide. In Chapter 12 we will discuss how teens continue to develop a sense of identity, to establish autonomy, and to explore vocational choices. Some teens begin to question authority, experiment with alcohol or other drugs, become sexually active or pregnant, and are likely to drop out of school. A small number exhibit antisocial behaviors and end up in the juvenile justice system. Most adolescents navigate through adolescence into early adulthood in a healthy fashion.

Adolescence
Physical and Cognitive Development

1. During adolescence some children develop much faster than others. Should we separate students at this age into different schools or tracks based on how much they have developed physically or cognitively?

2. Two lifelong friends accidentally wear the exact same outfits to parties at ages 6, 16, and 60. At which age do you think this will have the most impact on them and why?

3. Think back to when you first became concerned with such things as the environment, your own nudity, politics, and whether you wanted to be seen publicly with your parents. Chances are, your awareness of these issues occurred during adolescence. Why would this be so?

4. If you were forced to get a tattoo tomorrow, but you could choose among (1) a word, (2) a face or a portrait of someone, or (3) an abstract design, which would you choose? Why? Which do you think a 13-year-old would choose: (1) picture of a cartoon character, (2) the "word" *phat*, or (3) a yellow "happy face" symbol? Why? Why would you choose or not choose the same thing?

Outline

For the first time since the 1970s, the number of 12- to 19-year-olds is surging, and this increase is expected to continue until the year 2050 (U.S. Bureau of the Census, 2004g). In the United States, adolescence is depicted mainly as a carefree time of physical attentiveness and attraction, vitality, robust fun, love, enthusiasm, and activity. Although the majority of American teens are managing to get through their adolescent years with relatively few major problems, some find it to be a much more difficult period. In contrast, in much of the world adolescence is not a socially distinct period in the human life span. Although young people everywhere undergo puberty, many assume adult status and responsibility by age 13 or younger.

This chapter focuses on the dramatic physical changes, cognitive growth, and moral challenges that adolescents experience as they make the transition from childhood to adulthood. During this transition they begin to experiment with what they see as "adult" behaviors, such as smoking, drinking, having sex, driving, and working. It is truly an exciting and sometimes frightening time, for it is probably the last time they will experience so many novel emotions and sensations in such a short period of time.

Physical Development

During adolescence young people undergo truly revolutionary changes in growth and development. After a lifetime of inferior size, they suddenly catch up to or surpass many adults in physical size and strength. Females typically mature earlier than males, and this becomes more evident in sixth and seventh grades, when many girls are taller than most boys. Accompanying these changes is the less evident development of the reproductive organs that signals sexual maturity. Remarkable chemical and biological changes are taking place that will, over time, fashion girls into women and boys into men.

Signs of Maturation and Puberty

Puberty is the period in the life cycle when sexual and reproductive maturation becomes evident. Puberty is not a single event or set of events but a crucial phase in a long and complex process of maturation that begins prenatally. However, unlike infants and young children, older children experience the dramatic changes of puberty through a developed sense of consciousness and self-awareness. So not only are they responding to biological changes, but their psychological states also have a significant bearing on those changes (Call, Mortimer, & Shanahan, 1995).

Hormonal Changes During Puberty

The dramatic changes that occur in children at puberty are regulated, integrated, and orchestrated by the central nervous system and glands of the endocrine system. The *pituitary gland*, a pea-sized structure located at the base of the brain, plays a particularly important role. It is called the "master gland" because it secretes into the bloodstream hormones that in turn stimulate other glands to produce their particular kind of hormone. At puberty some type of genetic timing triggers the pituitary gland to step up its production of the growth hormones, stimulates the manufacture of *estrogen* and *progesterone* in females, and stimulates cells of the testes in males to manufacture and secrete the masculinizing sex hormone, *testosterone.* A woman's eggs were created in an immature state while she was a fetus in her mother's womb. However, the hormonal changes of puberty will trigger the ovaries to release one mature egg (ovum) on a "monthly" cycle for about 30 years of her life, typically. Hence, puberty is a time when a system that was established prenatally becomes activated. Unlike females, males first begin to produce sex cells, called sperm, during puberty, and they continue to do so throughout life, unless their testes are affected by illness or are removed.

Biological Change and Cognitive Processes Researchers using neuroimaging find that brain changes in adolescence improve cognitive processes related to formal operational thought (Durston et al., 2001). Although overall brain size remains about the same, pruning processes of gray matter result in regional changes (the principle "use it or lose it" applies): White matter increases (fibers that establish long-distance connections between brain regions); axon diameters and myelination increase, resulting in faster conductivity; the prefrontal cortex, corpus callosum, and temporal lobe structures increase in size, with slight gender variance. These changes improve speed of neural transmission, allowing for improved reasoning, planning, and impulse control (National Institute of Mental Health, 2001b; Paus et al., 1999). Also, studies show adolescents need 8 to 9 hours of sleep daily, but the sleep-wake cycle shifts, and teens naturally fall asleep later and wake up later. Yet with early school hours and busy lives, teens suffer sleep deprivation effects (Graham, 2000; Keller, 2001).

Biological Change and Social Relations Biological factors also have consequences for social relations during adolescence. Researchers have have looked for evidence to support a long-suspected link between hormones and adolescent behavior. Some have found that boys showing a profile of relatively low levels of testosterone and high levels of *androstenedione* are more likely than other boys to exhibit rebelliousness, talking back to adults, and fighting with classmates (Constantino et al., 1993; Schaal et al., 1996). Results of longitudinal data indicate that high testosterone levels in adolescent boys may be associated with social success rather than with aggression, as speculated in earlier studies (Schaal et al., 1996). A study of 400 families looked at the association of testosterone with risk behavior and depression. Looking at testosterone levels in both adolescent boys and girls, it was found that risk behavior and depression were conditional on the quality of the relationship with the parents rather than associated with hormone levels (Booth et al., 2003). Factors to explore for further research in this area are the stability of hormone levels over the course of the day, developmental factors, and taking into consideration that the biological and behavior responses to androgens are context-dependent (Ramirez, 2003).

Even though puberty has a biological foundation, its social and psychological significance is a major determinant of how it is experienced by adolescents. For instance, boys might experience an increase in size and strength that encourages them to use aggression in achieving their goals. Or even though testosterone level is a strong predictor of sexual involvement in young women between the ages of 12 and 16, its effect is reduced or eliminated by having a father in the home or by sports participation;

Adolescent Sleep Needs Change

ZITS. Reprinted with permission of King Features/North American Syndicate.

these environmental factors apparently reduce opportunities for sexual involvement and override hormonal effects on behavior (Udry, 1988). The effect of father absence was found to have an effect on menarche, first sexual intercourse, first pregnancy, and duration of first marriage (Quinlan, 2003). Hormone-level fluctuations in women have been associated with "mood swings," fluctuations that sometimes occur within a month, a week, or even a day. A pleasant, outgoing adolescent girl can become sullen and disagreeable and burst into tears and not even know why. Extreme or rapid changes in female hormone levels have also been linked to depression and unexpected behavior changes, though there is a great deal of individual variability in this.

> ## Questions
>
> What physical changes are expected in girls and in boys during puberty? What triggers the onset of this maturational process?

Ethological Theory   We have seen that biological factors have consequences for teenagers' social relationships. Some developmental psychologists take the argument a step further and contend that timing of onset of puberty, which takes one from the prereproductive to the reproductive phase in the life cycle, has significant ramifications both socially and biologically (Ellis, 2004). Life history theory presents a framework in which to view pubertal timing from an evolutionary developmental perspective. It is focused on the study of survival, growth, development, and reproduction in an ecological context (Coall & Chisholm, 2003).

Extensive research in Western societies demonstrates early pubertal maturation in girls is correlated with a number of negative health and psychosocial outcomes (Ellis, 2004). Girls who mature early are at higher risk later in life for unhealthy weight gain (Adair & Gor-

don-Larsen, 2001); breast cancer (Kelsey, Gammon & John, 1993); and a variety of other cancers affecting the reproductive system (Marshall et al., 1998); have higher teen pregnancy rates and low-birth-weight babies (Coall & Chisholm, 2003); tend to report more emotional concerns such as anxiety and depression and to demonstrate more problem behaviors such as aggression and substance abuse (Ge et al., 2003; Jaffee, 2002).

Jay Belsky (1997, 1999, 2001) has advanced an *ethological theory* that some young mothers are responding to a pattern in human evolution that induces individuals who grow up with insecure attachment to bear children early and often. In so doing, he addresses a matter that has troubled a good many U.S. policymakers, social scientists, and health-care practitioners; namely, the large numbers of teenage mothers in urban areas. The theory draws upon notions derived from *ethology* (see Chapter 2). According to this view, these teenage mothers are implementing a reproductive strategy that, from an evolutionary perspective, makes good sense. Belsky and his associates argue that youngsters growing up in dangerous conditions are "primed" to boost the chances of having their genes survive into the next generation by initiating sex early and entering motherhood early. One element of the theory is that girls reared in homes where there is a good deal of emotional stress, and especially where the father is absent, typically enter puberty at an earlier age than do girls reared in households where care and nurturance are relatively more abundant and predictable. Rather than being a biological given, puberty is said to be partially "set" by early experience. Therefore, human beings, like many other animals, adjust their life histories in response to environmental conditions to enhance their reproductive success. So experience shapes development. Belsky's (1997) theory suggests that young women who grow up under conditions of insecure attachment experience problems that provoke early reproductive readiness, frequent conceptions, but limited parental investment.

In support of their theory, Belsky and his associates cite cross-cultural evidence that girls reared in father-absent households have an earlier onset of puberty than do girls whose fathers are present in the household.

Many developmental psychologists have expressed skepticism regarding ethological formulations. For instance, Eleanor E. Maccoby (1991, 1999) favors a simpler explanation for the earlier pregnancies of girls from troubled homes: They receive less parental supervision. Other dissenters point out that girls tend to enter puberty at the same age as their mothers did by virtue of genetic factors (see Graber, Brooks-Gunn, & Warren, 1995). Girls who develop sexually at earlier ages are more likely to date and marry early, but they are also more likely to make the "worst" marital choices and terminate their marriages with divorce. So the girls whose parents are divorced might simply have had mothers who also tended to have undergone puberty at an earlier age. Significantly, Belsky has recently hinted that this "genetic transmission model may provide a more parsimonious account" than does his *sociobiological model* (Moffitt et al., 1992). Sociologists also distance themselves from these ethological formulations, contending that the more immediate cause of teenage sexuality and pregnancy is to be found in the lack of jobs and the presence of severe poverty in inner-city neighborhoods (Anderson, 1994).

The Adolescent Growth Spurt

During the early adolescent years, most children experience the **adolescent growth spurt,** evidenced by a rapid increase in height and weight. Usually, this spurt occurs in girls two years earlier than in boys. This means that many girls are taller than most boys in late middle school and junior high. The average age at which the peak is reached varies somewhat, depending on the people being studied. Among British and North American children it comes at about age 12 in girls and age 14 in boys. For a year or more, the child's rate of growth approximately doubles. Consequently, children often grow at a rate they last experienced when they were 2 years old. The spurt usually lasts about two years, and during this time girls gain about 6 to 7 inches and boys about 8 to 9 inches in height. By age 17 in girls and age 18 in boys, the majority of young people have reached 98 percent of their final height.

James M. Tanner (1972, p. 5), an authority on adolescent growth, writes that practically all skeletal and muscular dimensions of the body take part in the growth spurt, although not to an equal degree:

> Most of the spurt in height is due to acceleration of trunk length rather than length of legs. There is a fairly regular order in which the dimensions accelerate; leg length as a rule reaches its peak first, followed by the body breadths, with shoulder width last. Thus a boy

stops growing out of his trousers (at least in length) a year before he stops growing out of his jackets. The earliest structures to reach their adult status are the head, hands, and feet. At adolescence, children, particularly girls, sometimes complain of having large hands and feet. They can be reassured that by the time they are fully grown their hands and feet will be a little smaller in proportion to their arms and legs, and considerably smaller in proportion to their trunks.

Physical Growth   Asynchrony refers to the dissimilarity in the growth rates of different parts of the body. As a result of asynchrony, many teenagers have a long-legged or coltish appearance. Asynchrony often results in clumsiness and misjudgments of distances, which can lead to various minor accidents, such as tripping on or knocking over furniture, and to exaggerated self-consciousness and awkwardness in adolescents.

The marked growth of muscle tissue during adolescence contributes to differences between and within the sexes in strength and motor performance (Chumlea, 1982). A muscle's strength—its force when it is contracted—is proportional to its cross-sectional area. Males typically have larger muscles than females, which accounts for the greater strength of most males. Girls' performance on motor tasks involving speed, agility, and balance has generally been found to peak at about 14 years of age, though this statistic is based on past performance and does not reflect the increasing rate of female participation in junior high, high school, college, and professional sport competition. The performance of boys on similar tasks improves throughout adolescence.

At puberty the head shows a small acceleration in growth after remaining almost the same size for six to seven years. The heart grows more rapidly, almost

Adolescent Growth Spurt The rapid increase in height and weight that accompanies early adolescence tends to occur two years earlier in girls than in boys.

doubling in weight. Most children steadily put on subcutaneous fat between 8 years of age and puberty, but the rate drops off when the adolescent growth spurt begins. Indeed, boys actually tend to lose fat at this time; girls simply experience a slowdown in fat accumulation. Overall, the sequence of events in the pubertal process is similar across cultures and ethnicities (Brooks-Gunn & Reiter, 1990).

Maturation in Girls

In addition to incorporating the *adolescent growth spurt,* puberty is characterized by the development of the reproductive system (see Figure 11.1). The complete transition to reproductive maturity takes place over several years and is accompanied by extensive physical changes.

As in the case of the adolescent growth spurt, girls typically begin their sexual development earlier than boys.

When puberty begins in girls, the breasts increase in size. The pigmented area around the nipple (the areola) becomes elevated, and the nipples begin to project forward. This change usually starts at about 9 or 10 years of age and is called the bud stage of breast development. In perhaps half of all girls the appearance of pubic down (soft hair in the pubic region) precedes this bud stage of breast development. Also early in puberty, hormonal action begins to produce an increase in fatty and supportive tissue in the buttocks and hip region. This perfectly normal developmental change prompts some girls in their early teen years to begin dieting or exercising to excess, which can lead to anorexia or bulimia. Many contemporary adolescent girls erroneously think their

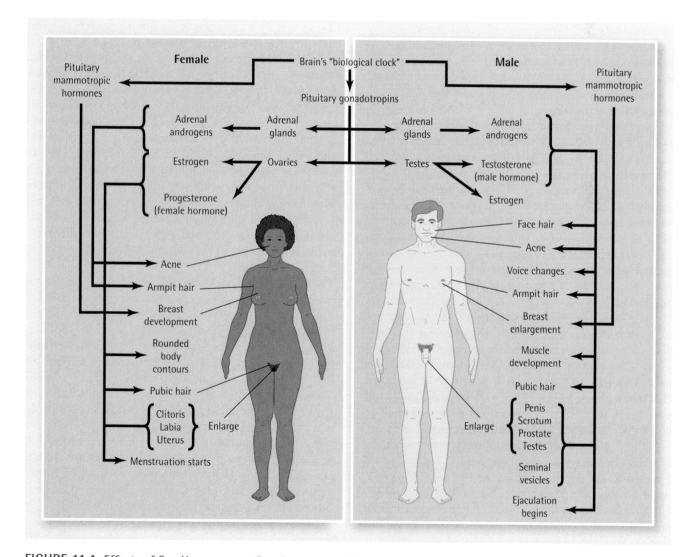

FIGURE 11.1 Effects of Sex Hormones on Development at Puberty At puberty the production of the pituitary gonadotropins (the follicle-stimulating hormone and the luteinizing hormone) stimulates the manufacture and secretion of the sex hormones. The release of these hormones affects a wide range of body tissues and functions.
Source: From John H. Gagnon, *Human Sexualities.* Scott, Foresman, 1977, p. 102. Reprinted by permission of the author.

bodies should be as slender as in their childhood years. Another visible change in puberty is the growth of axillary (underarm) hair.

Menarche   The uterus and vagina mature simultaneously with the development of the breasts. However, **menarche** (me när′ key)—the first menstrual period—occurs relatively late in puberty, usually following the peak of the growth spurt. Early menstrual periods tend to be irregular, perhaps for a year or more. Furthermore, *ovulation* (the release of a mature ovum/egg from an ovary) usually does not take place for 12 to 18 months after the first menstruation; hence, the girl typically remains sterile during this time.

The Earlier Onset of Menarche   Since 1900 in some countries the average age of menarche has declined steadily, and earlier onset appears to be associated with increased caloric consumption and longer life expectancy (Thomas et al., 2001). Tanner's (1972) earlier findings indicated that among well-nourished Western populations the average onset of menarche occurs between 12 and 13 years of age, and in the United States the median age is now 12.4 (Chumlea et al., 2003). However, research within the United States has found that African American girls and Hispanic girls start puberty and menarche significantly earlier than white girls, and the gap between the two has widened over the past two decades (Chumlea et al., 2003; Styne, 2004). The latest menarcheal ages are found among peoples with scarce food resources. Thomas and colleagues' (2001) review of international variability reveals that in countries such as Nepal, Senegal, New Guinea, and Bangladesh, the average age of menarche is about 16. In contrast, the earliest average ages of menarche are in Congo-Brazza, Greece, Italy, Spain, Thailand, and Mexico at around the age of 12.

We should note that a statistical average does not mean that all girls will begin menstruating at that age. More girls today begin menstruating as early as 8 or 9 years old, according to a study involving 17,000 girls aged 3 through 12 from across the United States. In this study nearly 10 percent of subjects were black and 90 percent were white. By 8 years of age, nearly half of black girls and 15 percent of white girls had begun developing breasts, pubic hair, or both (Herman-Giddens et al., 1997). Menstruation occurred at 12.1 years in black girls, 12.2 in Mexican American on average, and at 12.7 in white girls (Wu, Mendota, & Buck, 2002).

Contemporary scientists conducting studies with large, nationally representative samples of girls find that earlier onset of puberty is associated with increased nutrient intake and phytoestrogens, obesity, and low physical activity. Consistent results show strong positive associations of early onset of puberty with obesity (measured as body mass index), with significantly higher incidence in Hispanic and black girls (Adair & Gordon-Larsen, 2001; Kaplowitz et al., 2001; Wolff et al., 2001). Findings from another ethnically diverse sample suggest a gene promoting reduced testosterone levels in girls predicts early onset of puberty—and early puberty is a risk factor for breast cancer (Kadlubar et al., 2001). A pediatric endocrine group has proposed updated guidelines for *precocious puberty* for which girls should be evaluated and considered for medical intervention: in African American girls before age 6, and in white girls before age 7 (Kaplowitz & Oberfield, 1999). Higher proportions of Hispanic and black girls experience early menarche, and a recent study reconfirms that early-maturing black girls in fifth to seventh grade showed patterns of depression along with pubertal changes (Ge et al., 2003). A significantly higher proportion of Asian American girls reach menarche at 14 or later (Adair & Gordon-Larsen, 2001). Menarche is also delayed by strenuous physical exercise; it occurs at about 15 years of age among dancers and athletes in affluent countries (Wyshak & Frisch, 1982).

Rose E. Frisch (1978) advances the hypothesis that menarche requires a critical level of fat stored in the body. She reasons that pregnancy and lactation impose a great caloric drain. Consequently, if fat reserves are inadequate to meet this demand, a woman's brain and body respond by limiting her reproductive ability. Frisch suggests that the improvement in children's nutrition contributes to an earlier onset of menarche because youngsters reach the critical fat/lean ratio, or "metabolic level," sooner. However, not all researchers are convinced that Frisch is correct; instead they speculate that changes in body fat are linked merely temporally rather than causally with menarche (Graber, Brooks-Gunn, & Warren, 1995).

The Significance of Menarche   Menarche is a pivotal event in an adolescent girl's experience. Most girls are both happy and anxious about their first menstruation (Kaplowitz & Oberfield, 1999). It is a symbol of a girl's developing sexual maturity and portends her full-fledged status as a woman. As such, menarche plays an important part in shaping a girl's image of her body and her sense of identity as a woman. Postmenarcheal girls report that they experience themselves as more womanly and that they give greater thought to their reproductive role. However, some researchers report an accentuation of conflict between the mother and the daughter shortly after menarche. This development is not necessarily negative, because it often facilitates the family's adaptation to pubertal change (Holmbeck & Hill, 1991).

One study of 53 women from 34 countries revealed the following common themes concerning menarche: importance of the mother's reaction, difficulties understanding the meanings others attached to it, managing menstrual products, understanding formal education about menstruation, and the age of onset (Uskul, 2004).

Menstruation is often associated with a variety of negative events, including physical discomfort, moodiness, and disruption of activities, especially for girls with precocious puberty aged 6 to 10 (Lemonick, 2000). The Westernized adolescent girl is often led to believe that menstruation is somehow unclean, embarrassing, even shameful, and such negative expectations of menstruation can prove to be self-fulfilling prophecies. See the *Human Diversity* box on page 389, "Cultural Practices of Female Genital Mutilation." Thus, preparedness for menarche is important. Indeed, the better prepared a woman feels she was as a girl, the more positive she rates the experience of menarche and the less likely she is to encounter menstrual distress as an adult (Graber, Brooks-Gunn, & Petersen, 1996).

It seems that most American girls discuss menarche with their mothers, but for the most part the content of the discussions focuses on practical concerns and symptoms rather than feelings. Fathers and daughters seldom, if ever, discuss the daughter's pubertal development. Overall, puberty creates discomfort and embarrassment for many American parents. Moreover, the issues confronting parents as they navigate their own life course influence their response to pubertal children. For instance, mothers might experience more problems with a daughter's menarcheal timing if they themselves are no longer menstruating (Paikoff & Brooks-Gunn, 1991). Cross-cultural studies on menstrual experiences are quite similar around the world, although interpretations, beliefs, and preferences are influenced by socializing factors such as country, customs, religion, literacy, age, work environment, social status, and urban versus rural locale (Severy et al., 1993). A study of Chinese (Hong Kong) girls found that although 85 percent of those surveyed felt annoyed and embarrassed, about two-thirds also felt more grown up, and 40 percent felt more feminine in response to their first menstruation (Tang, Yeung, & Lee, 2003).

Maturation in Boys

Herman-Giddens, Wang, and Koch (2001) recently reported the first study in 30 years on boys' pubertal development, with over 2,000 racially/ethnically diverse participants aged 8 to 19. They found much earlier ages for the onset of pubic hair and genital growth than the 11 to 11.5 years of age in Marshall and Tanner's (1970) study. They also found significant differences by racial/ethnic groups by age 8: Some African American boys began the onset of puberty by age 8, followed by some whites and Mexican American boys 1 to 1.5 years later. By age 15, all boys in this study attained pubertal development, which includes full testes and scrotum growth, penis lengthening and thickening, voice changes as the larynx enlarges and the vocal folds double in length (resulting in

Puberty Rites As part of a four-day Navajo Kinaalda' ceremony (puberty rite), on the last night the tribe's elder women bake *kneel down* bread in the ground. In the morning, the baked bread is shared among those who participate and sing. The songs of the *Blessingway* (Hózhó§ji) are used to bless the "one sung over," to ensure good luck, good health, and blessings for all that pertains to them. The Blessingway ceremony is most closely connected with the *Changing Woman* and also performed for expectant mothers shortly before giving birth. The songs include blessings of beauty, harmony, success, perfection, order, and well-being. The Navajo believe the Changing Woman is closest to being the personification of the earth and of the natural order of the universe (Wyman, 1970).

a boy's voice cracking), and prostate gland fluid that can be ejaculated during orgasm. Mature sperm appear in the ejaculatory fluid about a year later, with wide variation among individuals. By full maturation, boys have "wet dreams," involuntary emissions of *seminal fluid* during sleep. For most males, their first ejaculation elicits both very positive and slightly negative responses. Given open, extensive public education about sexuality and reproduction today, most boys are somewhat prepared for the event.

Axillary and facial hair generally make their first appearance about two years after the beginning of pubic hair growth, though in some males axillary hair appears before pubic hair. The growth of facial hair begins with an increase in the length and pigmentation of the hair at the corners of the upper lip, which spreads to complete the mustache. Next, hair appears on the sides of the face in front of the ears and just below the lower lip, and finally it sprouts on the chin and lower cheeks. Facial hair is downy at first but becomes coarser by late adolescence.

Whereas girls develop fat deposits in the breasts and the hip region, boys acquire additional weight and size in the form of increased muscle mass. Furthermore, whereas the female pelvis undergoes enlargement at puberty, the most striking expansion in males takes place in the shoulders and rib cage (Chumlea, 1982). Some boys and girls experience dramatic body shape changes from junior high through high school, which creates a time of adjustment. American society seems to equate male taller height with popularity, sex appeal, and success. Most boys want to be tall and talk about this a great deal during this growth time. Tall girls, however, might feel more self-conscious about their height during adolescence.

The Impact of Early or Late Maturation

Children show enormous variation in timing and rates of growth and sexual maturation. As Figure 11.2 demonstrates, some children do not begin their growth spurt and the development of secondary sexual characteristics until other children have virtually completed these stages (Tanner, 1973). A recent review of studies in 67 countries revealed the average age of menarche for girls across the world ranged from 12.0 to 16.2 years (Thomas et al., 2001). Thus, one cannot appreciate the facts of physical growth and development without taking account of individual differences.

The majority of young people in the United States move in chronological lockstep through elementary and secondary school. Consequently, fairly standardized criteria are applied to children of the same age with respect to their physical, social, and intellectual development. But because children mature at varying rates, they differ in their ability to meet these standards. Individual differences become most apparent at adolescence. Several studies over the past two decades confirm that adolescents' early or late maturation has important consequences for them in their relationships with both adults and their peers.

Because of different rates of maturation, some adolescents have an advantage in the "ideals" associated with height, strength, physical attractiveness, and athletic prowess (Hayward et al., 1997; Stattin & Magnusson, 1990). Hence, some young people receive more favorable feedback regarding their overall worth and desirability, which in turn influences their self-image and behavior. For example, the value placed on manly appearance and athletic excellence means that early-maturing boys often enjoy the admiration of their peers. In contrast, late-maturing boys often receive negative feedback from their peers, are likely to experience bullying and teasing, and hence can be more susceptible to feelings of inadequacy and insecurity (Meschke & Silbereisen, 1997).

Investigators at the University of California at Berkeley studied the physical and psychological characteristics of a large group of individuals over an extended period of time. On the basis of this work, Mary Cover Jones and Nancy Bayley (1950, p. 146) reached the following conclusion regarding adolescent boys:

> Those [boys] who were physically accelerated are usually accepted and treated by adults and other children as more mature. They appear to have relatively little need to strive for status. From their ranks came the outstanding student-body leaders in senior high school. In contrast, the physically retarded [delayed] boys exhibit many forms of relatively immature behaviors: this may be in part because others tend to treat them as the little boys they appear to be. Furthermore, a fair proportion of these boys give evidence of needing to counteract their physical disadvantage in some way— usually by greater activity in striving for attention, although in some cases by withdrawing.

However, results of a recent longitudinal study reveal that seventh-grade boys who were more physically mature showed more externalized feelings of hostility and more internalized symptoms of distress (Ge, Conger, & Elder, 2001b). Boys who perceived themselves to be late maturing also tended to exhibit feelings of inadequacy, negative self-concept, and feelings of rejection. These feelings were coupled with a rebellious quest for autonomy and freedom from restraint (Mussen & Jones, 1957). Results of a study of college students by Donald Weatherley (1964) largely confirm the findings of Jones and Bayley. Late-maturing boys of college age were less likely than their earlier-maturing peers to have resolved the conflicts attending the transition from childhood to adulthood. They were more inclined to seek attention and affection from others and readier to defy authority and assert unconventional behavior. Research has shown that later maturation for boys is associated with a less positive self- and body-image (Sinkkonen, Anttila, & Siimes, 1998). Interestingly, recent research shows a positive correlation between obesity and late maturation in boys (the opposite is true for girls, where obesity is correlated with early maturation) (Wang, 2002).

A follow-up study of the early- and late-maturing males in the Berkeley sample was conducted when the men were 33 years old. Their behavior patterns were surprisingly similar to the descriptions recorded of them in adolescence (Jones, 1957). The *early maturers* were more poised, relaxed, cooperative, sociable, and conforming. *Late maturers* tended to be more eager, talkative, self-assertive, rebellious, and touchy.

In contrast, research with females has produced nearly the opposite results. Hayward and colleagues (1997) reported the findings of a longitudinal study of growth and development with over 1,400 ethnically diverse girls from San Jose, California. Participants were in sixth to eighth grade when the study began. Using self-report instruments, diagnostic interviews, and psychiatric assessment, the girls were evaluated over several years to determine the

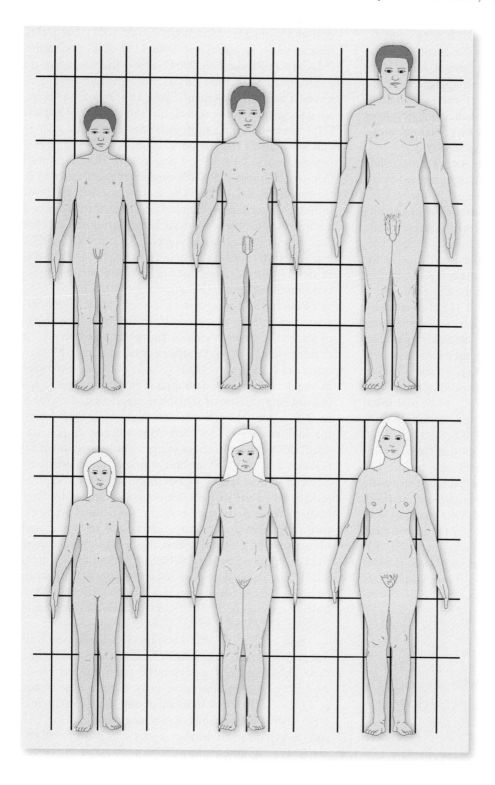

FIGURE 11.2 **Variations in Adolescent Growth** All the girls in the lower row are the same chronological age: 12.75 years. All the boys in the upper row are also the same chronological age: 14.75 years. Some persons of the same sex have completed their growth and sexual maturation when the others are just beginning the process.
Illustration by Tom Prentiss, from J. M. Tanner, "Growing Up," *Scientific American*, Vol. 229 (September 1973), p. 38. Reprinted by permission of Nelson H. Prentiss.

relationship between age of puberty and onset of any internalizing symptoms or disorders. Those girls who were defined as having gone through early puberty (the earliest 25 percent) were twice as likely to develop symptoms such as depression, substance abuse, eating disorders, and disruptive behavior disorders as those girls who matured later. Recent findings further suggest that those girls who go through puberty early remain at increased risk for development of these specific disorders even after they enter high school (Dorn, Hitt, & Rotenstein, 1999).

Still other research across cultures suggests that for both girls and boys, being "on time" is associated with a more positive set of self-perceptions than being "off time"—either early or late (Ge, Conger, & Elder, 2001a;

Graber, Brooks-Gunn, & Petersen, 1996; Graber et al., 1997; Wichstrom, 2000). And then there is the view that the early onset of menarche does not generate uniform reactions among young women; rather it appears to accentuate pretransition differences among them—for instance, stressful transitions merely intensify behavioral problems among girls who were predisposed to behavioral problems earlier in childhood (Hayward et al., 1997).

So what are we to conclude? The answer may reside primarily in the *ecological context:* A dynamic interplay transpires between differing individual temperaments and the social environment to produce substantially differing outcomes among young women (Graber et al., 1997). Additionally, the conflicting findings suggest that the situation for girls is more complicated than that for boys. The findings of more recent research point out the complex nature of variables that interact in producing a girl's reputation during adolescence. The discontinuity between rate of change in evaluations of prestige and rate of physical changes during adolescence means that, for girls, accelerated development is not a sustained asset throughout the adolescent period. A recent study looked at the source of the rating (whether the timing of puberty was rated by the adolescent, the parent, or by a physical exam) as a possible explanation for the variance of findings (Dorn, Susman, & Ponirakis, 2003)

Psychologists also point to still another factor. Early-maturing girls are more likely to be a little heavier and to develop a stocky physique. In contrast, late-maturing girls are more likely to be thin and acquire a slim, slight body build. Thus, over the long run, later maturation in girls may be associated with factors other than maturation itself that function as assets in social adjustment. Knowledge about pubertal timing often has direct implications for adolescent mental health and well-being (McCabe & Ricciardelli, 2004; Stice, Prenell, & Beaman, 2001).

> **Questions**
>
> What are the differences between girls and boys in physical growth and maturation during puberty? What are some of the factors that account for pubertal variability in males and females?

Self-Image and Appearance

The image that adolescents have of themselves is particularly susceptible to peer influences. Adolescents are quick to reject or ridicule age-mates who deviate in some way from the physical norm. Indeed, few words have the capacity to cause as much pleasure—and as much pain—to adolescents as does the word *popularity.* Among U.S. boys, athletic prowess and a muscular body with a large chest but slim waist bring social recogni-

tion and popularity (Kindlundh et al., 2001), but a slim overall body is associated with U.S. girls' popularity (McCabe & Ricciardelli, 2004). To say that teenagers are preoccupied with their physical acceptability and adequacy is an understatement. These concerns arise during adolescence when the nature and significance of friendships are undergoing substantial developmental change and when affect (feeling good about oneself and feeling happy) and self-worth are undergoing change as well (Moneta, Schneider, & Csikszentmihalyi, 2001; Wong & Csikszentmihalyi, 1991). The ability to establish close, intimate friendships becomes more integral to social and emotional adjustment and well-being during adolescence than it was during preadolescence (Buhrmester, 1990). Adolescent friendships have been studied in the context of developmental stage, network of interpersonal relationships, and gender (Buhrmester, 1998).

Puberty brings with it an intensification of gender-related expectations, especially related to physical appearance. Adolescent girls often feel troubled about the development, size, and shape of their breasts. Although estimates vary, more than 130,000 women each year in the United States have breast implant surgery; approximately 1,500 girls under the age of 18 got implants in 2004, even though parental consent is mandatory for such surgery ("The Facts About Breast Augmentation," 2005). Most of these surgeries are for nonmedical reasons, and yet some of these women will become seriously ill with a variety of symptoms caused by implant leakage of saline—or the new silicone gel—into their bodies. Yet experts state it is the third most common surgery in the United States, after nose reshaping and liposuction. In England, breast augmentation is the most frequent type of surgery (Pittet, Montandon, & Pittet, 2005). The original silicone breast implants continue to be banned in the United States because of serious risks of leakage into the body or in some cases deadly outcomes (Neergaard, 2005).

And adolescents, both boys and girls, express considerable concern about their facial features, including their skin and hair. Significantly, the idealized media models (teen magazine cover girls, television actresses, and music idols) tend to be taller and weigh less (many are actually underweight) than young women in general, and the gap between the two is growing (Byrd-Bredbenner & Murray, 2003). Shows such as *Extreme Makeover* do a great disservice to adolescent females and males who are already highly self-critical of their own appearance. As consumers, they do not get the full story.

Weight   A large proportion of adolescents want to change their weight—they perceive themselves as either "too thin" or "too heavy." Indeed, recent research findings from a nationally representative sample of nearly 14,000 adolescents in the *National Longitudinal Study*

Human Diversity

Cultural Practices of Female Genital Mutilation

Millions of young girls worldwide experience serious health risks or death before or during puberty as a result of female genital mutilation. It is estimated that 130 million women have undergone some form of female genital mutilation (FGM), and about 2 million girls are at risk each year for this procedure. The average age of girls who are forced to undergo these procedures is 4 to 12 years old. This traditional practice occurs in 28 countries in Africa as well as parts of the Middle East (Rahman & Tubia, 2000). As more immigrants from these countries enter the United States, their practice of female mutilation continues. Health services professionals in the United States, Europe, and Australia are seeing evidence of this practice on female infants and young daughters of immigrants from Somalia, the Sudan, Ethiopia, Kenya, Nigeria, and some Muslim countries (although it is not sanctioned in the Koran).

Female genital mutilation can take several forms from *clitoridectomy*, where all or part of the clitoris is removed; excision, where all or part of the labia minora are removed; and the most extensive—infibulation.

> Infibulation or pharaonic circumcision [excision with infibulation] means that the entire clitoris and the labia minora are cut away and the two sides of the labia majora are partially sliced off or scraped raw and then sewn together, often with catgut. In Sudan or Somalia, thorns are used to hold the two bleeding sides of the vulva together, or a paste of gum arabic, sugar and egg is used [or horsehair or catgut]. The introitus or entrance to the vagina is thus obliterated which is the purpose of the operation, except for a tiny opening in the back to allow urine, and later menstrual blood, to drain. The legs of the girl are tied together immediately after the operation, and she is immobilized for several weeks until the wound of the vulva has closed, except for a small opening that is created by inserting a splinter of wood or bamboo. (Hosken, 1998).

Bloodborne pathogens such as HIV and hepatitis B virus are easily transmitted during these procedures. Many girls die of hemorrhage or infection. Those who survive often have health complications of urinary tract infections, pelvic inflammatory disease, complications of pregnancy and delivery, or infertility. (An infertile woman can be divorced at will in these cultures and shamed for life.) Many need to undergo deinfibulation because fetal descent is obstructed, which can result in fetal death (Brady, 1998). These centuries-old cultural practices from male-dominated societies are directly related to curbing the girls' developing sexuality and to guaranteeing that the girl is a virgin at marriage. Several reasons are cited for why so many African and Middle Eastern groups still maintain this cruel practice (Hosken, 1998):

- This procedure has been handed down by ancestors to initiate the young girls (and males, in the case of male circumcision) into adult life. Girls must comply to be recognized as adults within their community. Some women view their genital mutilation as a source of pride.
- The girl who has undergone infibulation will bring a higher price as a bride, because her virginity and purity are intact. Payment to the bride's father is still a prevalent practice in these cultures.
- In these cultures, young women are deemed incapable of controlling sexual urges and might bring disgrace to their families. If a girl or young woman refuses to undergo this procedure, in many societies she will be ostracized or considered a prostitute.
- Some men say the external genitalia of women are ugly if they are not removed.
- Others say that cleanliness, or purity, and better health are reasons for undergoing this procedure.
- Religious beliefs are also a significant factor. Generally, Muslims and some Christians in Africa also practice this procedure.
- In West Africa the woman's clitoris represents "maleness" and the prepuce of the male's penis represents "femaleness," and these tissues must be removed before a person is accepted as an adult.

Girls and women who experience the infibulation procedure, which nearly closes up the vaginal opening, will endure this procedure repeatedly during their reproductive lifetime: the scarred tissue will be cut open to allow for intercourse and birth of children, but sewn up again until children are

Young Girls Wait for Female Circumcision These young girls are waiting for their female circumcision in Cooperstown, Liberia.

continued

weaned; then cut open again to allow for intercourse and conception, and then sewn up again; and so on.

There is no doubt that the forced practice of genital mutilation has terrible physical, health, and psychological consequences for these young women, and often death. Hosken (1998), an advisor to the World Health Organization, has witnessed this cruelty firsthand. It is a violation of basic human rights because the procedure is performed on nonconsenting infants, girls, and women who are not anesthetized and are not allowed to heal in sanitary conditions. She protests that FGM is now being carried out more in hospital settings using equipment provided by U.S. taxpayer monies. There seems to be strong agreement that the intense educational campaign must continue to inform African and Middle Eastern families of the serious physical and emotional harm being done to their daughters and wives. More recently, some young women have fled to other countries and sought asylum to avoid such a barbaric practice.

FGM has been outlawed in several Western countries including the United States in 1996. FGM is also punishable by jail terms in 13 African countries but the practice still continues due to long-held beliefs (Rosenberg, 2004).

From: Margaret Brady, "Female genital mutilation." *Nursing 98, 28*(9): 50.

---

of *Adolescent Health* indicate that one-fourth were obese (Adair & Gordon-Larsen, 2001; Popkin & Udry, 1998). Since 1980 the CDC has reported findings from its series of *National Health and Nutrition Examination Surveys* to provide information about overweight children and adolescents. These findings are evidence of a steady increase in the percentage of overweight children and adolescents since the 1970s.

About 25 percent of all boys show a large increase in fatty tissue during early adolescence; another 20 percent show a moderate increase. During the adolescent growth spurt, however, the rate of fat accumulation typically declines in both boys and girls. Whatever the source of obesity, the overweight adolescent is at a personal, health, and social disadvantage. In fact, a stigma is associated with obesity in the United States. Given this state of affairs, particularly for women, it is hardly surprising that adolescent girls are extremely sensitive regarding their body configurations and that even a moderate amount of fat generates intensely negative feelings and distorted self-perceptions. What makes such distortions so cruel is that our body image and our self-esteem are linked, so that if we dislike our bodies, we find it difficult to like ourselves. We examine the highly sensitive issue of weight concerns and obesity in the next section under nutrition and eating disorders.

Questions

Which concerns about appearance or self-image did you have as an adolescent? Do you still worry about some of these things today? If so, which ones and why? Which ones no longer bother you?

Health Issues in Adolescence

What does it mean to be healthy? You might think of yourself as being fairly healthy or as having been a healthy adolescent. Indeed, the majority of adolescents are free of disabilities, weight problems, and chronic illnesses, but a recent health report from the early 2000s indicated that about 6 to 7 percent of children under age 18 suffer from at least one chronic health problem and that many youth are in need of counseling or other health services. Among school-age youth, ages 5 to 17, learning disabilities and attention-deficit hyperactivity disorder were the most common chronic conditions (see Figure 11.3) (National Center for Health Statistics, 2004a).

What sorts of risky behaviors do adolescents engage in that lead to concerns about their health? It is during the adolescent years that many of us drink our first beer, experiment with other psychoactive substances, try smoking, and have our first sexual experiences with members of the opposite sex, same sex, or both sexes. Many adolescents are also stressed by attempting to earn money to help families or save for college by working in part-time jobs, while attending high school full-time. Teens living in poverty are at much higher risk of having chronic health problems, such as asthma and other respiratory illness and developmental disabilities, and it is expected that the general health of adolescents will become worse over the next quarter century simply because more young people will be poor. Some of the negative health factors associated with poverty include premature birth; poor nutrition; lack of or poor-quality medical, dental, and eye care; lack of necessary immunizations; higher risk of exposure to health hazards; and greater incidence of high-risk behaviors.

Many parents become slack about annual checkups for teenage children because they seem so healthy. Parents and caretakers can also be unaware of the recommended immunizations for older children and adolescents (see Figure 4.7, "Recommended Childhood and Adolescent Immunization Schedule"). Of course, adolescents themselves are also likely to refuse to go to the doctor because they associate this with "childhood" behavior. Public school health officials conduct annual hearing and vision exams, and students who participate

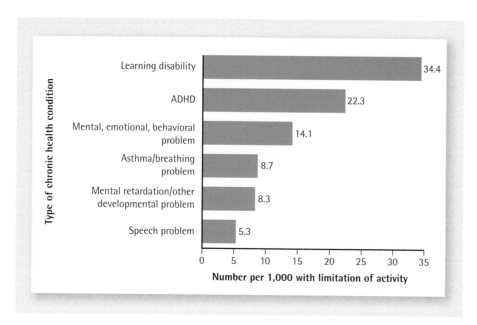

FIGURE 11.3 Chronic Health Conditions among Adolescents, 12 to 17, 2001–2002
Source: Chartbook on Trends in the Health of Americans: *Health, United States, 2004.*

on school sport teams are required to have an annual physical. But a large proportion of adolescents are likely to neglect regular health exams or immunizations. Fortunately, the majority is in excellent health. Many at this age believe that they can take care of themselves, even though they might be participating in risky social behaviors (alcohol or substance abuse, sexual activity, etc.).

As late teens approach the beginning of adulthood, they demand less supervision and more freedom to make their own decisions. They are learning to make more choices for themselves, basically by trial and error; and most are highly influenced by their risk-taking peers and youth-oriented media. Some of the most common health concerns for adolescents are discussed here. Though some people call this stage the beginning of the "age of reason," adolescents make many choices without fully realizing the real-life consequences of their actions.

Nutrition and Eating Disorders

What did you eat for lunch yesterday? A hamburger, a candy bar, pizza, French fries, or chips? Junk food is very tempting for most of us. Owing to our busy schedules, we do not want to sit down, relax, and eat if we can grab a snack or pick up a quick bite to eat. However, most "fast" food has very little nutritional value. Some researchers suggest that culture has a greater influence on family eating habits and the prevalence of developing eating disorders; that is why they believe that eating disorders are more prevalent in white women in Western cultures—which value "thinness" (Williamson et al., 1995). Others suggest that family life and eating behaviors play a far greater role in producing eating disorders, in which a family is preoccupied with perfection,

control, appearance, and weight (Foulkes, 1996). The interactionist view suggests that both culture and family environment are both influential (Haworth-Hoeppner, 2000). Adolescents are usually deficient in calcium, iron, and zinc, which can lead to problems such as thinning of the bones (osteoporosis), anemia, and delayed sexual maturity (Rolfes & DeBruyne, 1997). Typically, three prevalent disorders stem from poor nutritional habits among contemporary American teens: anorexia nervosa, bulimia, and obesity.

Anorexia nervosa   *Anorexia nervosa* is an eating disorder that primarily affects females—at least 10 percent or more of adolescent and adult women report symptoms of eating disorders (Academy for Eating Disorders, 2005), but a small percent of anorexics are males. A person with an eating disorder becomes obsessed with looking thin and terrified of becoming fat. Anorexics perceive food as being a threat to their bodies rather than a source of nutrition and pursue a regimen of self-starvation, often accompanied by excessive exercise. The cause of anorexia is unknown, although scientists are looking at neurochemical imbalance in the brain or genetic causes. Some suspect it involves a disturbance of the hypothalamus; others suggest that its cause might be traced to inadequate coping skills, whereby the person feels that the only thing under her (or in fewer cases, his) control is body weight. One scenario follows:

Jeannette was always a bit chubby until she entered junior high, when she decided one day to lose a little weight. She lost 12 pounds in three weeks and received quite a few compliments from her friends, family, and teachers. She did not stop at 12 pounds and it was soon apparent to her family that something else was going on with their daughter besides her wanting to lose some weight. Her mother describes a meal on a family trip that was undertaken in the hopes that it would divert their daughter's attention away from her constant dieting. "There was the way she would eat her food . . . how she would separate each bit of food, cut it into tiny, precise shapes, and repeatedly calculate calories on a small counter that she clicked. She had that calorie system down to a science, and she would continually pore over what she had on her plate, what she could eat, and how much she would gain." (Sacker & Zimmer, 1987)

Anorexia nervosa is most common in countries where there is no scarcity of food and attractiveness is equated with thinness. About half of the people who have been anorexic will develop bulimia. About 4 percent of college-age women have bulimia. (See the *Further Developments* box "Understanding Anorexia and Bulimia.")

Questions

Why are more teenagers affected by anorexia and bulimia? How does their self-image become distorted and their body shape misperceived? What types of treatments are suggested to help victims become healthier?

Obesity   Obesity is the most common eating disorder in the United States. Overweight adolescents often face social prejudice and peer rejection, and they are likely to experience depression, low self-esteem, health concerns, problematic dietary behaviors, or in some cases, suicide (Kilpatrick, Ohannessian, & Bartholomew, 1999). Results from the *National Health and Nutrition Exam Survey (NHANES)* indicate that 16 percent of U.S. children and adolescents aged 6 to 19 are significantly overweight (National Center for Health Statistics, 2004b). The recent findings for adolescents are of great concern, for overweight adolescents are at increased risk of becoming overweight adults with several obesity-related health conditions (National Center for Health Statistics, 2004b). Obesity is defined several ways, and diverse factors such as body frame, status of adolescent growth spurt, and activity level make it impossible to generalize across the entire population.

How Is Obesity Determined?
Obesity is the excess accumulation of body fat, or *adipose tissue*. A person can be overweight without being obese, as in the case of a bodybuilder with lots of muscle. Medical, government, and research professionals have not come to an exact consensus in their definition of obesity, perhaps because several factors can be examined to make the diagnosis—and overall weight is only one of those factors. One source states that doctors and scientists generally

agree that men with more than 25 percent body fat and women with more than 30 percent body fat are obese (Focus on Obesity, 1998). However, such variables as gender, height, body build, *body mass index (BMI)*, percent of ideal body weight for height from published weight tables, skinfold measurements, and waist-to-hip ratios might also be considered (Gidding et al., 1996). A newer method is *BIA, bioelectrical impedance analysis.* BIA sends a harmless amount of an electrical current through the body, estimating total body water. A trained clinician uses a hand-held impedance monitor and places electrodes on the wrist and ankle. A higher percentage of body water indicates more muscle and lean tissue. A mathematical equation is then used to estimate body fat and lean body mass (Focus on Obesity, 1998). Contemporary research scholars recommend using the BMI assessment, which is weight in kilograms divided by height in meters squared (kg/m^2). Significant obesity in adults has been defined as 130 percent of ideal body weight for height (Gidding et al., 1996). Various measurement findings are compared with normative standards using either percentiles or percentages, which can further confound this vital issue.

Health Consequences
Obesity in adolescents often portends poorly for their health in adulthood:

At 5 feet 6 inches and 216 pounds, Tyshon represents an alarming new health trend: the sharp increase in the number of children with Type 2 diabetes, also known as adult-onset diabetes, an incurable and progressively damaging disease that can cause kidney failure, blindness and poor circulation. . . . Doctors long believed that the disease occurred mostly during middle age or later. "Ten years ago we were teaching medical students that you didn't see this disease in people under 40, and now we're seeing it in people under 10," said Dr. Robin S. Goland, co-director of the Naomi Berrie Diabetes Center. . . . Type 2 diabetes was diagnosed in 10 to 20 percent of the center's new pediatric patients, compared with less than 4 percent in the hospital's clinic five years ago. (Thompson, 1998)

Obese adults are at greater risk for high blood pressure and heart disease, respiratory disease, diabetes, orthopedic disorders, gallbladder problems, breast and colon cancer, depression and other mental health issues, and the high costs of health care. One study has found increased risk for problems associated with high blood pressure, high cholesterol, and insulin resistance in obese children and adolescents (Freedman et al., 1999). Indeed, researchers find that adolescent obesity is even more strongly linked to health risks than being overweight in adult life (Guo et al., 1994). If obesity continues into adulthood, morbidity and mortality are greater than adult onset of obesity (Styne, 2001). Males in the top 25 percent of weight in relation to their height

Further Developments

Understanding Anorexia and Bulimia

Anorexia nervosa is a disorder in which the individual willfully suppresses appetite, resulting in self-starvation. Once considered to be quite rare, the incidence of anorexia nervosa has increased dramatically over the past 30 years. It occurs primarily in adolescent or young adult females of the middle and upper-middle classes. The victims have a fierce desire to succeed in their project of self-starvation; have a morbid terror of having any fat on their bodies; and deny that they are thin or ill, insisting that they have never felt better even when they are so weak they can barely walk. Simultaneously, these people might long for food and even have secret binges of eating (often followed by self-induced vomiting). Anorexia has the highest mortality rate of all mental disorders.

Anorexia and bulimia are usually thought of as psychosocial disorders. Recently however, researchers are finding evidence that links the disorder with genetic factors. By studying chromosomes and family histories, researchers are beginning to see the disorder in a new way (DeAngelis, 2002a). Another contributory explanation for the recent epidemic in cases of anorexia nervosa is the emphasis that Western societies place on slimness. This message reaches society through the mass media, often targeting adolescents and young adults with specific body images deemed to be ideal (Levine, 2000). One antidote to this situation is to teach children media literacy (Morris & Katzman, 2003). From a historical perspective, the preoccupation with weight and thinness, especially among affluent women in the Western world, reflects a relatively recent but growing cultural trend (Attie & Brooks-Gunn, 1987). The development of eating problems apparently is one mode of accommodation that some girls make to pubertal change. As girls mature sexually, they experience a "fat spurt"—that is, they accumulate larger quantities of fat in subcutaneous tissues. Early maturers seem at greater risk for eating problems, partly due to the fact that they are likely to be heavier than their late-maturing peers (Graber et al., 1997). In some cases the refusal to eat is preceded by "normal" dieting, which could be prompted by casual comments by family or friends that the young woman is "putting on weight" or "getting plump." Furthermore, the victim's overestimation/misperception of her body size seems to increase with the severity of the illness. According to this interpretation, the disorder entails self-induced starvation by women who desperately want to be beautiful but end up being grotesquely unattractive.

White and African American young women dramatically differ in how they view their bodies. Whereas a majority of white junior high and high school girls voice dissatisfaction with their weight, a majority of African American girls are satisfied with their bodies (64 percent of African American young women think it is better to be "a little" overweight than under-

weight). It seems that many African American teenagers equate a full figure with health and fertility and believe that women become more beautiful as they age. Significantly, recent studies are finding more African American young women are affected (National Eating Disorders Screening Program, 2001).

Another explanation of the disorder is that it is an attempt to avoid adulthood and adult responsibilities. The young woman with anorexia invariably diets away her secondary sexual characteristics: her breasts diminish, her periods cease entirely (interestingly, menstruation ceases prior to pronounced weight reduction and hence cannot be attributed to starvation), and her body comes to resemble that of a prepubescent child. According to this view, such women are seeking a return to the remembered comfort and safety of childhood (Garner & Garfinkel, 1985).

Approximately two-thirds of victims of anorexia recover or improve, with one-third remaining chronically ill or dying of the disorder. Left untreated anorexia can contribute to osteoporosis, heart problems, infertility, depression, and other medical complications. Most authorities now recognize that anorexia nervosa usually has multiple causes and that it requires a combination of various long-term treatment strategies adjusted to the individual needs of the patient. More recently a short-term, outpatient strategy involving a form of family therapy is proving to be successful as well (DeAngelis, 2002a). A number of psychiatrists have suggested that a subgroup of male athletes—"obligatory runners"—resemble anorexic women (Slay et al., 1998).

Distorted Perceptions Among the Victims of Anorexia
Victims of anorexia nervosa willfully starve themselves, denying that they are actually thin or ill, in the belief that they are too fat.

continued

These men devote their lives to running and are obsessed with the distance they run, their diets, their equipment, and their daily routines while ignoring illness and injury. Both anorexics and obligatory runners lead strict lives that assiduously avoid pleasure. Both groups are concerned about their health, feel uncomfortable with anger, are self-effacing and hard working, and tend to be high achievers from affluent families. And like anorexics, obligatory runners are exceedingly concerned about their weight and feel compelled to maintain a lean body mass.

Bulimia, a disorder often related to anorexia nervosa, is also called *binge eating disorder (BED)*. Bulimia affects about 2 percent of the general population and about 8 percent of people who are obese. Between 1 and 3 percent of adolescent girls suffer from bulimia. Bulimia is characterized by repeated episodes of bingeing, particularly on high-calorie foods like candy bars, cakes, pies, and ice cream. The binge is followed by an attempt to get rid of the food through self-induced vomiting, taking laxatives, enemas, diuretics, or fasting. Bulimic persons do not usually endeavor to become skeletally thin like anorexics, and they are ashamed and depressed about their eating habits and attempt to conceal their eating behaviors. Bulimics are typically within normal weight range and have healthy, outgoing appearances, whereas anorexics are skeletally thin. Bulimia affects a wider range of people. It is more likely to appear in men, African Americans, and across a wider age range than anorexia (Costin, 2002). Young men in activities such as wrestling, male modeling, or acting might engage in similar behavior to squeeze into a lower weight class, look good in photo shoots, or appear more slender on television.

This disorder can produce long-term side effects such as ulcers, hernias, hair loss, dental problems (stomach acid destroys the teeth), and electrolyte imbalance (resulting in heart attacks) (Keel et al., 1999). Like anorexia nervosa, bulimia calls for treatment. Some researchers believe that a hereditary form of depression might underlie some forms of both disorders, and indeed some patients respond to antidepressant medication and behavior therapy (Costin, 2002). Here is an idea of how a bulimic person feels about this compulsion:

> The whole purge process was cleansing. It was a combination of every type of spiritual, sexual, and emotional relief I had ever felt in my life. Purging became the release for me. First, I felt a tremendous rush that you could really call orgasmic. Then, I relaxed completely and fell asleep. After a while, I was hooked. I actually believed I had to purge to fall asleep. (Sacker & Zimmer, 1987)

Anorexia and bulimia are serious eating disorders that have grave health consequences. Researchers and social psychologists are calling on insurance companies to provide better coverage to help address this problem (DeAngelis, 2002a).

are more likely to experience any combination of these health risks before the age of 70. Overweight females are found to be mainly at greater risk of developing arthritis, atherosclerosis, gallbladder disease, breast cancer, and diminished physical abilities in later life (Brody, 1992a; Colditz, 1992).

Obesity also has social and economic consequences: 16-year-old young women who are in the heaviest 10 percent of their age group earn less than do their nonobese peers (Hellmich, 1994). Compared with other women, those who are overweight during their teens and early twenties are less likely to get married, are more socially isolated, are more apt to live in poverty, and get an average of four months less schooling (Bishop, 1993). Thus, that obesity in childhood and adolescence is more common now than in the past is of considerable concern.

How Many Adolescents in the United States Are Obese?
The obesity status of U.S. adolescents continues to increase. In the *National Longitudinal Study of Adolescent Health*, researchers examined a nationally representative sample of more than 13,000 adolescents (from 80 high schools across the United States) and found that one out of four American teenagers are currently obese (Popkin & Udry, 1998). For all groups, more obesity occurs among males than among females, except for blacks (27.4 percent for males and 34.0 percent for females). Asian American and Hispanic adolescents born in the United States are more than twice as likely to be obese as are the first-generation residents of the 50 states (Popkin & Udry, 1998). Results are indicated in Figure 11.4.

Reasons cited for the increase of obesity in American youth include genetic and environmental factors. Studies of families and twins have clearly demonstrated a strong genetic component in resting metabolic rate, feeding behavior, and changes in energy level due to overfeeding. Environmental factors associated with obesity include socioeconomic status, race, region of residence, season, urban living, and being part of a smaller family (Gidding et al., 1996). Diet composition of children does not identify the cause of obesity in youth, because current dietary fat and saturated-fat intake of American children has decreased from previous years. Gidding and colleagues (1996) suggest obesity results, too, from an imbalance between energy intake and energy expenditure.

How Can We Prevent or Reduce Obesity?
Complicating matters, obesity has proven quite difficult to treat (O'Neill, 1995; Wadden & Van Itallic, 1992). In fact, a mounting body of evidence suggests that dieting can make matters worse, leading to counterproductive binge eating and a perpetual cycle of fruitless dieting (National Eating Disorders Screening Program, 2001). Various psychiatrists used to argue that obesity is a response to

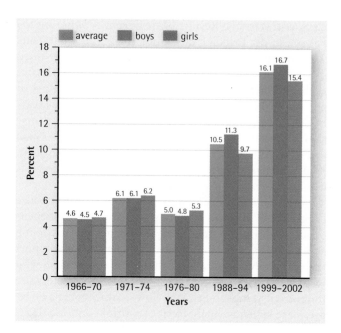

FIGURE 11.4 Prevalence of Overweight U.S. Adolescents, 1966–2002
Source: Centers for Disease Control and Prevention, National Center for Health Statistics. *National Health Examination Survey* and *National Health and Nutrition Exam Survey.*

criticism, derision, and overt discrimination (Wang, Brownell, & Wadden, 2004). Negative attitudes seem to intensify during adolescence, particularly among females. But increasingly, obese people are "fighting back" against discrimination by defining obesity as a disability, in an attempt to make it illegal to discriminate against persons who are obese. Still, medical practitioners are familiar with the long-term effects of obesity and promote getting up, getting regular aerobic activity, changing diet and lifestyle for a higher-quality, longer life. Unfortunately, most school districts across the country are reducing physical education classes to save costs and find more time in the schedule for students to meet higher academic standards.

Question

Why is there an increase in the number of adolescents who have eating disorders, and what are the consequences of entering adulthood with these unhealthy behaviors?

psychological disorders (e.g., women who are fearful of men subconsciously gain weight to create a protective shell and keep men at a distance), but this view has little support among researchers. Another explanation that has attracted considerable interest is that fat babies and fat children develop a permanent excess of fat cells. This excess provides them with a lifelong storehouse of fat cells capable of being filled. When such individuals later become adults, the existing fat cells enlarge but are not thought to increase in number. Still another popular theory postulates the existence of a metabolic regulator or "set point" (Bennett & Gurin, 1982). According to this view, each of us has a built-in control system, a kind of fat thermostat that dictates how much fat we should carry. Some of us have a high setting and tend to be obese; others of us have a low setting and tend to be lean. Even if some lose the weight, long-term studies of weight reduction in children have shown that 95 percent return to their original weight within 5 years (National Eating Disorders Screening Program, 2001). Clinicians treating obesity in children should also screen for hypertension, dyslipidemias (abnormal concentrations of lipoproteins in the blood), orthopedic disorders, sleep disorders, gallbladder disease, and insulin resistance (Barlow & Dietz, 1998).

Today many obese people challenge the prevailing social stereotypes and prejudices. Unlike the physically handicapped, obese people are held responsible for their condition. They are the object of much concern,

Smoking and Tobacco Products

The majority of adolescents who use tobacco do so by smoking cigarettes. Other ways to ingest tobacco include cigars, chewing tobacco, pipes, and *bidis* (leaf-wrapped Indian cigarettes), or *kreteks* (clove cigarettes). The 2004 *National Youth Tobacco Survey* reported that overall use of *any* tobacco products among high school students was 28 percent: 22 percent reported using cigarettes, 13 percent reported using cigars, and 11 percent of males in high school reported using chewing tobacco. Among middle school students, grades 6 to 8, overall use of *any* tobacco products was 12 percent. Eight percent reported using cigarettes, 5 percent used cigars, and 3 percent used chewing tobacco.

The 2004 National Youth Tobacco Survey results show there were only small reductions in smoking rates among either high school or middle school students between 2002 and 2004. Reasons for rates not declining more include heavy media exposure by tobacco marketing campaigns, deep cuts in cigarette prices, state cuts in funding for antismoking campaigns, and teens not having to show proof of age to purchase cigarettes. However, it is recommended that effective antismoking strategies continue to be shown in markets where more teens smoke, and new strategies should be implemented to continue to decrease tobacco use among teens (Hershey et al., 2005). However, some ad campaigns have been very effective because teens used to be pressured into smoking by peers, but now teens are being pressured *not* to smoke since "It's not the cool thing to do" (see Table 11.1). Teens cite being turned off to smoking

Table 11.1 Percentage of Students in Middle School (Grades 6 to 8) and High School (Grades 9 to 12) Who Were Current Users of *Any* Tobacco Product: 2002, 2004

	2002	2004
Grades 6 to 8 Total	13.3	11.7
Male	14.7	12.7
Female	11.7	10.7
Grades 9 to 12 Total	28.2	28.0
Male	32.6	31.5
Female	23.7	24.7

Source: Centers for Disease Control and Prevention (2005c).

because of the antihygienic aspects of smoking, including bad breath, darker teeth, and lingering smoke odors (King, 2005).

Alcohol and Other Substance Abuse

Since 1982, PRIDE, a drug prevention organization, has been gathering information from surveys administered by schools, communities, and states on the drug and alcohol use of students in grades 6 to 12. In 2004, a comprehensive study of more than 114,000 students found slight decreases in alcohol usage for all age groups. In the 2002–2003 school year, 37 percent of junior high students reported having used any alcohol, but in the 2003–2004 school year reported usage went down to 34 percent. Senior high students reported 63 and 62 percent, respectively. Twelfth-graders reported rates of around 70 percent for both time periods (PRIDE Questionnaire Report, 2004).

Alcohol use and binge drinking is highest among 18- to 21-year-olds. Many more males than females reported alcohol use and binge drinking. Adolescent whites and Native Americans or Alaska Natives report the highest rates of alcohol consumption, and Asians and blacks have low rates of alcohol use. Researchers continue to report that regular drug abuse interferes with adolescent educational performance, disengagement from dependence on parents, development of relationships with peers, and important life choices (completing high school, securing and keeping employment, and maintaining family relations).

Substance abuse is the harmful use of various drugs (including prescription drugs) or alcohol, lasting over a prolonged period that puts oneself or others in hazardous situations. Besides alcohol, such drugs include marijuana, ecstasy, amphetamines, methamphetamines, inhalants, cocaine/crack, heroin, LSD and other hallucinogens, narcotics, sedatives (barbiturates), tranquil-

izers, and steroids. Results of the recent *Monitoring the Future* study that surveys more than 50,000 students nationwide show continuing reductions in use of illicit drugs occurring in all grades—except two categories are slightly increasing: inhalants and OxyContin (a class of narcotic) (Johnston et al., 2004). Inhalant use is increasingly more common among eighth-graders because theses substances are easy to obtain and cost less. Such abuse includes breathing fumes from glues, aerosols, paint thinners, butane, and nail polish remover—and this can be deadly.

Although the majority of adolescents do not abuse drugs, those who do run the risk of substance dependency and have a much higher chance of becoming adult drug addicts who often commit crimes to support their addictions. One recent study found that boys who exhibit a cluster of extreme personality characteristics (impulsivity, excitability, and low harm avoidance) by age 6 are far more likely to smoke, drink, and use drugs on reaching adolescence. And adult alcohol abuse is *more than double* in youngsters who begin drinking before age 15. Teens cite other people's homes as the most common setting for drinking ("Underage Drinking," 2005). Moreover, many more adolescent boys than girls use alcohol and drive while intoxicated, and alcohol is a factor in most deaths for 15- to 24-year-olds: traffic accidents, homicides, suicides, and accidental overdoses. In 2002, more than 17,400 people died in auto-crash fatalities by drunk drivers, a number that continues to increase yearly. Beer drinkers cause the majority of auto fatalities. Sadly, the major killer of children ages 2 to 14 is auto accidents. In 2000 about 60 percent of auto fatalities during prom/graduation weekends were alcohol-related for more than 1,200 deaths (Mothers Against Drunk Driving [MADD], 2001). Although state laws set age 21 as the minimum legal drinking age, underage drinking remains America's number-one youth drug problem (Davies, 2004). See the *More Information You Can Use* box.

Therefore, teenage and underage drinking does not just affect the health of adolescents. Fortunately, more chapters of SADD (Students Against Destructive Decisions) have been established to promote better decisions and safe teen driving. The serious issue of peer influence on substance use and abuse is discussed in Chapter 12.

Sexually Transmitted Infections and HIV

Many adolescents frequently engage in sexual intercourse and/or oral sex, and it is not uncommon for sexually active adolescents to have multiple partners. Government statistics show that of the 15 million cases of sexually transmitted infections that are estimated to occur each year, people in the 15- to 24-year-old age bracket account for 10 million of them (Sulak, 2004). By not using condoms, adolescents are vulnerable to **sexually trans-**

More Information You Can Use

A Parent/Teen Contract About Drinking and Driving

This contract is consistent with the vision and mission of MADD. Although this sample contract was originally designed for prom and graduation season, it is well suited for any time of year.

Because it is illegal, I promise not to drink alcohol, particularly during the dangerous prom and graduation season. I commit myself to celebrating in a safe and healthy way. I pledge not to get in a car with someone who has been drinking alcohol. If I find myself in a situation where I feel unsafe or uncomfortable, I promise to call you, my parent or guardian, for a ride home. I commit to this pledge and recognize there are consequences for every decision I make.

_____
Youth Signature

As your parent/guardian, I promise to make myself available to you during this season of celebration. You can count on me any time day or night. I promise that I will agree to pick you up, no immediate questions asked. When we are safe at home, I pledge to respect you and listen to what has happened and help in any way I can.

_____
Parent/Guardian Signature

Source: This information is brought to you courtesy of Mothers Against Drunk Driving—find us online at www.madd.org/. The mission of MADD is to stop drunk driving, support the victims of this violent crime, and prevent underage drinking. Reprinted by permission of MADD.

mitted infections (STIs). Reasons given for not using condoms include these: I was drunk; we decided on the spur of the moment; I was embarrassed to buy them; it spoils the romance. It is not surprising, then, that U.S. teenagers have the highest rates of gonorrhea, syphilis, and chlamydia of the sexually active populations (see Table 11.2) (Mertz et al., 2001).

Table 11.2 Sexually Transmitted Infections (STIs) in the United States

The American Social Health Association (ASHA) estimates there are more than 15 million new cases of sexually transmitted infections in the United States each year.

STI	Annual Incidence*
Human papillomavirus	5,500,000
Trichomoniasis	5,000,000
Chlamydia	3,000,000
Herpes	1,000,000
Gonorrhea	650,000
Hepatitis B	77,000
Syphilis	70,000
HIV	20,000

Number of new cases in a given time period.
Source: Alexander, L. L., Cates, J. R., Herndon, N., & Ratcliffe, J. F. (Eds.). (1998, December). *Sexually transmitted diseases in America: How many cases and at what cost?* 1–27. Research Triangle Park, NC: American Social Health Association (ASHA).

Chlamydia is currently the most prevalent STI in the United States, and few young sexually active females are tested for chlamydia. Left untreated, it can lead to infertility (Ebel, 2005). It is caused by atypical bacteria and can lead to infertility and blindness in women. An infected woman can pass on the chlamydia parasite to her infant as the baby passes through the birth canal. Five percent of female college students have been diagnosed with chlamydia. Fortunately, it is curable. *Syphilis* is a bacterial infection that can be passed on to a fetus through the placenta. Syphilis develops in four phases, beginning with incubation and ending in the final phase some five years later. Death is possible if left untreated. In 2003 women aged 20 to 29 had the highest rates for primary and secondary syphilis. *Gonorrhea* is caused by bacteria and passes from one infected mucous membrane to another. Among women, young women between the ages 15 and 19 have the highest rates of gonorrhea. Among men, the 20- to 24-year-old population had the highest rates of gonorrhea (Centers for Disease Control and Prevention, 2003c).

Other prevalent STIs are *human papillomavirus (HPV)* and *genital herpes simplex,* which is chronic, painful, and extremely contagious. Genital herpes can be fatal to some persons with immune deficiencies and also to infants who contract the disease at birth. There is no cure for genital herpes, and estimates are 45 million are affected in the United States. To further compound the problem, many adolescents are not aware of how they can avoid STIs, cannot identify common symptoms, and do not know what action to take once they show signs of being infected.

Have the national education/health campaigns been effective in informing adolescents to protect themselves against these STIs? Nationally, about two-thirds of high school males and more than half of females who are sexually active report having used a condom at last intercourse (Centers for Disease Control and Prevention, 2003c). These figures indicate that among currently sexually active high school students, condom use has increased significantly from 1999 to 2003 (see Figure 11.5).

This multiyear, national survey by the CDC (Grunbaum et al., 2004) indicates that although fewer stu-

dents are engaging in sexual behaviors that place them at high risk for STIs, AIDS, and pregnancy, many are still practicing high-risk behaviors. The prevalence of condom use continues to increase for students in grades 9 to 12, both for males and females, and overall for all racial/ethnic groups. A dramatic 84 percent decline in U.S. syphilis rates occurred from 1990 to 1999 (after an alarming epidemic from 1986 to 1990). Factors associated with irregular or no contraceptive use include these: low academic skills and aspirations; being a younger teen; a tendency toward risk taking (for instance, alcohol and other drug use); a strained relationship with parents; parental use of corporal punishment; and the absence of a committed relationship (Luster & Small, 1994a, b).

Of more recent concern to health professionals is the high numbers of teens who are having oral sex, their view that oral sex is more acceptable and less risky than vaginal sex, and their lack of understanding about the health, social, and emotional consequences associated with this form of sexual relations. Halpern and colleagues (2005) report findings of the first longitudinal study on teen oral sex with more than 500 ninth-grade males and females (average participant age was 14.5 years). Study participants report oral sex (20 percent) as more prevalent than vaginal sex (14 percent), and they consider it more acceptable and less a threat to their values and beliefs. The truth is that STIs, including HIV, are caused by bacteria and viruses that like warm, moist places such as the mouth and genital area—and STIs can and do spread from the mouth to the genital area and from the genital area to the mouth. It is just as important to talk to a partner about his or her sexual history as you would if you were considering vaginal sex. And use of some type of barrier method is definitely advised.

Most high schools and colleges have a staff nurse who can provide further information and be a safe resource person to those teens who suspect they have contracted a disease, but many youth don't have access to health care. Part of the nature of adolescence is to believe that bad things are not going to happen to you—that you have your whole future ahead. However, contracting or transmitting one of these diseases—particularly HIV—has life-threatening consequences. To further compound matters, teens are still getting pregnant, and the unborn child has a high risk of contracting STIs or HIV if the mother has these diseases (see Chapter 3).

HIV and AIDS   Since the 1980s AIDS has become the most feared sexually transmitted infection. AIDS is caused by the *human immunodeficiency virus (HIV)*, which damages the immune system and prevents the body from fighting infections. Primarily sexual contact with multiple partners and sharing needles for injection drug use spreads this insidious virus. Some individuals carry the virus for up to 10 years before developing

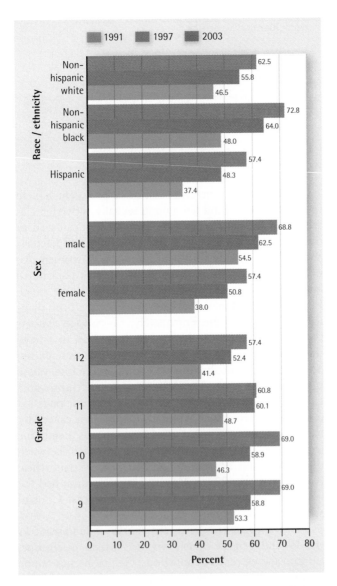

FIGURE 11.5 Percentage of High School Students Who Used a Condom During Their Last Sexual Intercourse, 1991–2003
Source: Grunbaum, J. A., Kann, L, Kinchen, S, Ross, J., Hawkins, J., Lowery, R. et al. (2004, May 21). Youth risk behavior surveillance—United States, 2003. *MMWR, 53* (No. SS-2), 1–96.

AIDS. Most of the early AIDS victims were either gay males or intravenous drug users, but now HIV is spreading rapidly among heterosexuals. Public health experts worry about young people, who are currently the high-risk HIV/AIDS group. It is the seventh leading cause of death among people between the ages of 13 and 24. Although the Centers for Disease Control and Prevention reported over 41,000 cases of AIDS among 13- to 24-year-olds in 2002, the actual number of infected adolescents and young adults may be much higher.

An important risk factor associated with an increase in HIV is the presence of a sexually transmitted infection. About 25 percent of the reported STIs are among teens. A discharge of pus or mucus from chlamydia or gonorrhea increases the risk of HIV transmission three to five times; ulcers from syphilis or genital herpes increase the risk nine times the rate of noninfected individuals (National Institute of Allergy and Infectious Diseases, 2004a). In Chapter 15 we will discuss the increasing rate of HIV in heterosexual middle-aged women.

Millions of teens are part of abstinence-only programs in schools to discourage premarital sex, the spread of various STIs, and unwanted pregnancy and have signed written pledges promising to abstain from sex. Critics of abstinence-only programs say that teens would be better protected by adding a safe-sex component to their educational program.

Rates of abstinence, adolescent sexual experience, types of sexual activity, and effective contraceptive practice are important determinants of adolescent health and well-being, changes in pregnancy rates, and opportunities for an adolescent's future. With sexual experience rates down, multiple-partner rates down, and condom use increasing, we would expect to see a decline in the teenage pregnancy rate.

Questions

What are the current trends in the incidence of sexually transmitted infections in teenagers? Who are the high-risk teens for contracting STIs and HIV? What are some of the reasons you would give teenagers for using condoms?

Teenage Pregnancy

National campaigns to curb teen pregnancy rates over the past 20 years now report significant success. Birthrates have fallen for teens in all age groups to the lowest levels ever reported in the nation, although U.S. teen birthrates are still higher than rates in other developed countries. The birthrate for U.S. teens was 42 births per 1,000 women aged 15 to 19 years (see Figure 11.6) (Hamilton, Martin, & Sutton, 2003). The percentage of

unmarried 15- to 17-year-old women who had ever had sexual intercourse dropped to 30 percent by 2002 and to 31 percent for young men. Also encouraging is that teens are more likely to use contraception; the rate was 79 percent in 1999–2002. Yet despite the decrease in sexual activity and the increase in safer sexual practice, some teens do become parents. The life-changing emotional, social, and socioeconomic consequences of teen pregnancy are discussed in Chapter 12.

Body Art and Tattooing

Young people are currently "body-art" enthusiasts, with more teens and college students getting tattoos and body piercings than any previous American generation. Yet body art has been practiced in every culture for centuries, and the show *Body Art: Marks of Identity* at the American Museum of Natural History confirms its legitimacy (Tanne, 2000). Tattooing, body piercing, and body art are found on people of all ages, occupations, and social classes. Tattoos adorn about 3 to 9 percent of the population, but between 10 and 16 percent of adolescents have tattoos. One study found a link between tattoos and high-risk behavior among adolescents (Roberts & Ryan, 2002). Studies show that adolescents indulge in body art for the following reasons (Greif & Hewitt, 1999):

- To demonstrate social identity, membership, or class
- To commemorate a special event
- To express intimacy (tattooing lover's name)
- To be entertained

Potential health risks from body piercing include hepatitis B, tetanus, as well as skin infections. A poorly placed piercing can cause nerve damage, and a tongue stud can lead to speech problems and chipped teeth. This industry is not well regulated. Having a dermatologist remove a single tattoo can cost $2,000 to $2,500 or more. Recently scarification (cutting), branding, and stretched earlobe holes have made their way into the body art scene; and as adolescents look for novel ways to express themselves, these become even more intriguing. It remains to be seen whether these adornments will be accepted in American work environments. As we recall our own teen years, we recognize that every adolescent cohort finds interesting ways to distinguish itself from the adult generation—including "slang" language, music style, hairstyles, length and fit of clothing, and use of body and facial adornments.

Stress, Anxiety, Depression, and Suicide

Adolescent rates of "seriously considering suicide," or having thoughts about suicide were alarmingly high just

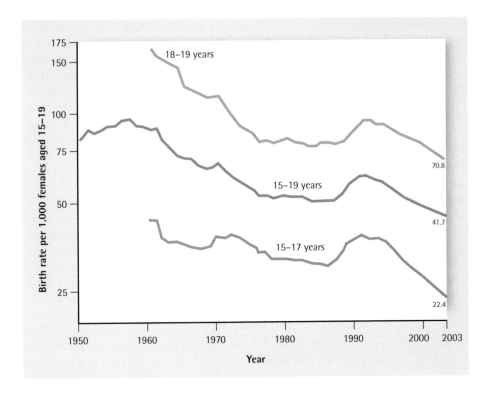

FIGURE 11.6 Birthrates for Teenagers by Age: United States, 1950–2003 Birthrates have fallen significantly for teenagers in all age groups. Over the 40-year period beginning 1960 (when rates for teenagers 15 to 17 and 18 to 19 years were first recorded), teenage birthrates generally declined through the mid-1980s, increased steeply into the early 1990s, and have since fallen steadily. The rate for the youngest teenagers, 10 to 14 years is at the lowest level in more than 30 years. In 2003, births to girls under age 15 years dropped to the lowest number in 45 years.
Source: Hamilton, B. E., Martin, J. A., & Sutton, P. D. (2003). Births: Preliminary data for 2003. *National Vital Statistics Reports, 53*(9), 1–11.

a decade ago (on average, about 29 percent for teens in grades 9 to 12), but overall rates reported in 2003 dropped to 17 percent. Teenage females were much more likely to report considering suicide than males throughout this past decade and up to the present. However, the actual percent of students, overall, who actually attempted suicide rose from 7 percent in 1991 to 8.5 percent in 2003. Moreover, females report attempting suicide at double the rates of males for grades 9 to 12—yet males are four times more likely to end their lives (most often by firearm) (National Center for Health Statistics, 2004a). Suicide is the third leading cause of death of young persons aged 16 to 24 (Hoyert, Kung, & Smith, 2005).

Because stress, anxiety, and depression often occur within the context of adolescent-parent relationships, peer-adolescent relationships, and boyfriend-girlfriend and same-sex relationships, we discuss the range of reactions and coping strategies to anxiety, stress, fear, loss, social isolation, and attacks on self-esteem and self-worth in Chapter 12.

Brain Development and Decision Making As stated earlier, the majority of adolescents are healthy and full of energy, and they typically "squeeze" many physical, academic, social, and family activities into their daily lives, while their sleep-wake cycle shifts to later hours. As we have just seen, they are also at a stage of life when they seek more freedom from parental and adult authority and supervision and have many temptations to take risks or engage in unhealthy behaviors—behaviors they

mistakenly believe are more adultlike and ones where they cannot foresee the outcomes.

When participating in the risky behaviors mentioned earlier, tragically some teens make decisions that will harm them for life or end their lives. Since a majority of teens begin to drive around ages 15 or 16, with little skill and experience, driving accidents are the major cause of death for adolescents (typically both excessive speed and alcohol are factors). Many high schools and parent-teacher organizations now offer extravagant alcohol-free prom nights and graduation events in an attempt to keep every student alive during periods of intense emotional celebration. The other main causes of teen loss of life in descending order are other accidents and injuries, assault (homicide), suicide, cancer, and heart disease (Hoyert, Kung, & Smith, 2005).

As we shall see in the next section on cognitive development, their ability to think, plan, reason, and problem-solve about the consequences of their actions and decisions are also developing, as their brains continue to mature. Neurons make a final growth spurt around the ages of 11 to 13 in the frontal lobes of the brain—the region responsible for reasoning, judgment, planning, and relating emotions. But neuroscientists say it takes a few years to link new neurons to make connections to the rest of the teen's brain (Bowman, 2004). Thus, teen brains *are* different from adult brains and that is evident through MRI (magnetic resonance imaging) scans. The process of *myelinization* (a fatty coating on the long fibers of the neuron) continues, which allows for more efficient and precise communication among neurons and brain regions (Bowman, 2004). One brain disorder that affects some people during later adolescence is *schizophrenia*. Symptoms include disordered thinking, hallucinations, delusions, unusual speech or paranoid behavior, and social withdrawal limiting the ability to interact with others and managing life. Medical intervention is imperative for this disorder.

Also, adolescents do not have the experience to think and make decisions as adults (just as adults we do not always make the "best" decisions, either). Even as 18-year-olds or 19-year-olds, it's as if they have "one foot in childhood and one foot in adulthood." The adjective used to describe high school seniors captures these vacillating behaviors and is called "senioritis." While expressing desire to move on with their lives and leave the parental home, they also have childlike moments and hesitations about handling their own lives. Thus, they often procrastinate about completing college applications, getting reference letters from teachers and employers, or making any plans at all.

Question

Why do many young people choose adolescence as the time to begin experimenting with smoking, drinking, drugs, sex, and other risky behaviors?

Cognitive Development

During adolescence young people gradually acquire several substantial new intellectual capacities. They begin to reflect about themselves; their parents, teachers, and peers; and the world they live in. They develop an increasing ability to use abstract thought—to think about hypothetical and future situations and events. In our society they also must evolve a set of standards regarding family, religion, school, drugs, and sexuality; those who work at jobs during high school must also develop work standards.

Piaget: The Period of Formal Operations

Jean Piaget called adolescence the **period of formal operations,** the final and highest stage in the development of cognitive functioning from infancy to adulthood. This mode of thought has two major attributes. First, adolescents gain the ability to think about their own thinking—to deal efficiently with the complex problems involved in reasoning. Second, they acquire the ability to imagine many possibilities inherent in a situation—to generate mentally many possible outcomes of an event and thus to place less reliance on real objects and events: "If I don't come home at my curfew time with Dad's car,

then . . . or . . . will happen." In sum, adolescents gain the capacity to think in logical and abstract terms.

Formal operational thought so closely parallels scientific thinking that some call it "scientific reasoning." It allows people to mentally restructure information and ideas so that they can make sense out of a new set of data. Through logical operations individuals can transfer the strategic skills they employ in a familiar problem area to an unfamiliar area and thus derive new answers and solutions. In so doing, they generate higher-level analytical abilities to discern relationships among various classes of events.

Formal operational thought is quite different from the concrete operational thought of the previous period. Piaget said that children in the period of concrete operations cannot transcend the immediate. They are limited to solving tangible problems of the present and have difficulty dealing with remote, future, or hypothetical matters. For instance, a 12-year-old will accept and think about the following problem: "All three-legged snakes are purple; I am hiding a three-legged snake; guess its color" (Kagan, 1972, p. 92). In contrast, 7-year-old children are confused by the initial premise because it violates their notion of what is real. Consequently, they can be confused and refuse to cooperate.

Likewise, if adolescents are presented with the problem: "There are three schools, Roosevelt, Kennedy, and Lincoln schools, and three girls, Mary, Sue, and Jane, who go to different schools. Mary goes to the Roosevelt school, Jane to the Kennedy school. Where does Sue go?" they quickly respond "Lincoln." The 7-year-old might excitedly answer, "Sue goes to Roosevelt school, because my sister has a friend called Sue and that's the school she goes to" (Kagan, 1972, p. 93). Similarly, Barbel Inhelder and her mentor, Jean Piaget, found that younger than 12 years of age most children cannot solve this verbal problem (Inhelder & Piaget, 1964, p. 252):

Edith is lighter than Suzanne.
Edith is darker than Lily.
Which is the darkest of the three?

Children under 12 often conclude that both Edith and Suzanne are light-complexioned and that Edith and Lily are dark-complexioned. Accordingly, they say that Lily is the darkest, Suzanne is the lightest, and Edith falls in between. In contrast, adolescents in the stage of formal operations can correctly reason that Suzanne is darker than Edith, that Edith is darker than Lily, and therefore Suzanne is the darkest girl.

Piaget suggested that the transition from concrete operational to formal operational thought takes place as children become increasingly proficient in organizing and structuring input from their environment with concrete operational methods. In so doing, they come to recognize the inadequacies of concrete operational methods for solving problems in the real world—the gaps, uncertainties, and contradictions inherent in concrete operational processes (Labouvie-Vief, 1986).

Not all adolescents, or for that matter all adults, attain full formal operational thought, especially those with mental retardation or developmental disabilities. Therefore, some fail to acquire its associated abilities for logical and abstract thinking and will require social services and additional supports as they transition into adult living. People who score below average on standard intelligence tests show this lack of ability, for instance. Indeed, as judged by Piaget's strict testing standards, less than 50 percent of U.S. adults reach the stage of formal operations. Some evidence suggests that secondary schools can provide students with experiences in mathematics and science that expedite the development of formal operational thought. And some psychologists speculate that various environmental experiences might be necessary to its development (Kitchener et al., 1993).

Furthermore, cross-cultural studies fail to demonstrate the full development of formal operations in all societies. For example, rural villagers in Turkey never seem to reach the formal operational stage, yet urbanized educated Turks do reach it (Kohlberg & Gilligan, 1971). Overall, a growing body of research suggests that full formal operational thinking might not be the rule in adolescence. Even so, considerable research confirms Piaget's view that the thought of adolescents differs from that of young children (Marini & Case, 1994; Pascual-Leone, 1988).

Adolescent Egocentricity

Piaget (1967) said that adolescents produce their own characteristic form of **egocentrism,** a view expanded by the psychologist David Elkind (1970) in terms of two dimensions of egocentric thinking: (1) the *personal fable* and (2) the *imaginary audience.* As adolescents gain the ability to conceptualize their own thought, they also achieve the capacity to conceptualize the thought of others. But adolescents do not always make a clear distinction between the two. In turning their new powers of thought introspectively, adolescents simultaneously assume that their thoughts and actions are equally interesting to others. They conclude that other people are as admiring or critical of them as they are themselves. They tend to view the world as a stage on which they are the principal actors and all the world is the audience. According to Elkind, this characteristic accounts for the fact that teenagers tend to be extremely self-conscious and self-preoccupied: The preoperational child is egocentric in the sense that he is unable to take another person's point of view. The adolescent, on the other hand, takes the other person's point of view to an extreme degree.

As a result, adolescents tend to view themselves as somehow unique and even heroic—as destined for unusual fame and fortune. Elkind dubs this romantic imagery the **personal fable.** The adolescent feels that others cannot possibly understand what she or he is experiencing, and often this leads to the creation of a story or personal fable, which the adolescent tells everyone, although it is a story that is not true. If you have ever thought something like, "They will never understand the pain of unrequited love; only I have been through this torture," then you have created your own personal fable.

The **imaginary audience,** another adolescent creation, refers to the adolescent's belief that everyone in the local environment is primarily concerned with the appearance and behavior of the adolescent. The imaginary audience causes the adolescent to be very self-critical and/or extremely self-admiring. The adolescent really believes that everyone she or he encounters thinks solely about that individual night and day. Remember how devastating a pimple was in high school because you thought every eye would be glued to your affliction? You probably never thought that everyone else was too concerned and preoccupied with their own pimples to notice yours. Elkind believes that adolescents can eventually distinguish between real and imaginary audiences, and he also acknowledges that the adolescent's imaginary audience and personal fable are progressively modified and eventually diminished.

Other psychologists, such as Robert Selman (1980), also find that young adolescents become aware of their own self-awareness, recognizing that they can consciously monitor their own mental experience and control and manipulate their thought processes. However, only later in adolescence do they come to realize that some mental experiences that influence their actions are not accessible to conscious inspection. In brief, they become capable of distinguishing between conscious and nonconscious levels of experience. Hence, although they retain a conception of themselves as self-aware beings, they realize that their ability to control their own thoughts and emotions has limits. This gives them a more sophisticated notion of their mental self and what constitutes self-awareness.

The growing self-awareness of teenagers also finds expression in the increasing differentiation of the self-concept during adolescence. Adolescents provide different self-descriptions in different social contexts. The self-attributes teenagers assign themselves differ depending on whether they are describing their role in relation to their mother, father, close friends, romantic partners, or classmates, or their role as student, employee, or athlete. For instance, the self they depict with their parents might be open, depressed, or sarcastic; with friends—caring, cheerful, or rowdy; and with a romantic partner—fun-loving, self-conscious, or flirtatious. The

Adolescent Egocentrism Teens erroneously believe that everyone is watching and noticing them when they are in a public setting; thus they spend excessive amounts of time on grooming and hygiene. In the early teen years, girls tend to conform to similar hairstyles and clothing. Thus, even though they want to be respected as individuals, they often look and act very much alike.

cognitive-structural advances noted earlier in this chapter permit teenagers to make greater differentiations among role-related attributes. Simultaneously, the differing expectations of significant others in different social contexts compel adolescents progressively to differentiate the self with respect to varying social roles (Harter & Monsour, 1992). We will discuss adolescent egocentricity in its social context in Chapter 12.

Questions

How does a typical adolescent develop cognitively during the junior high to high school years? Why do adolescents tend to be more concerned with themselves than with others?

Educational Issues

For most teenagers, entering high school is a highly anticipated venture from the more structured middle school or junior high. Students get an opportunity to select a few courses and a daily schedule along with enrolling in required state-mandated courses (mathematics, English, social studies, science, and foreign lan-

guage). Students with an aptitude in vocational careers select from courses such as computer science, carpentry, mechanical drawing, auto mechanics, machine shop, child care, veterinary care, food service, cosmetology, horticulture, and prenursing. Many large high schools offer "schools within a school," such as a core of special courses for students who are highly gifted or talented in the fine arts along with a mentoring experience in typically music, drama, or computer art and design.

Of significant interest is the educational performance of those youth in junior high who were in the Head Start programs as preschoolers. Results from the Extended Early Childhood Intervention and School Achievement: Age Thirteen Findings from the *Chicago Longitudinal Study* indicate that at-risk children who participated in follow-up programs for three or more years after early intervention services had significantly higher reading achievement in the seventh grade, had a lower rate of being held back a grade, and were less likely to receive special education services (Reynolds & Temple, 1998). Further investigation connected with this study of childhood intervention indicates other long-term effects such as higher rates of educational attainment and lower rates of juvenile arrest (Reynolds, Suh-Ruu, & Topitzes, 2004).

Students who are high achievers can select advanced courses that challenge their problem-solving and critical thinking skills and allow them to earn college credits while in high school (called advance placement or AP courses). Typically high schools have a variety of extracurricular opportunities that allow adolescents real-world opportunities to try out potential career skills. Such activities might include working on the school newspaper or yearbook, participating on highly competitive sports teams, singing in concert choirs and performing in orchestras, acting in dramas, learning debate skills on mock trial teams, assisting with the operation of an on-campus store for supplies, being an officer of a club, participating on a community service club, or being a class officer.

Adolescents with low or limited intellectual capacity, while being included in some regular high school classes, are eligible to receive life-skills training in specific vocational programs with work experience. Their preparation during high school is called the "aging out" process, and these students are eligible to remain in academic and skills-training until they are 21 years old, should they choose to do so.

Students with high intellectual abilities who have had positive experiences during their school years typically enjoy the challenge of high school and anticipate entering college. However, those who have not experienced academic success or social acceptance in the earlier grades of school seem to begin to transition out, both physically and psychologically—poor or more erratic school attendance, an unmotivated attitude toward schoolwork, disagreements with adults, increased substance abuse, and sometimes trouble with the law. Recent Hispanic/Latino immigrant youth, ages 16 to 19, are more likely to drop out of school than other youth. In 2000, more than 20 percent dropped out of high school, followed by 12 percent of African American youth, and 8 percent of white youth (Fry, 2003a). Hispanic dropouts most likely have very poor English skills and have fewer years in the formal schooling system, yet they are often willing to work very hard and are more likely to get some type of employment (Fry, 2003a). As of 2004, 18 states have passed laws raising compulsory school attendance to age 17 to get more students to complete a high school degree, but enforcement of such laws will certainly be complicated—especially with an existing teacher shortage and knowing the nation will need 2.2 to 2.4 million more teachers in the next ten years (Gormley, 2004).

These youth are highly aware of when they can "quit" school, and some are at risk of dropping out well before the legal age by disappearing into the community or becoming a PINS youth (person in need of supervision). Many communities now have group homes for some of these teenagers, where they receive more structure and supervision than these youth may have experienced before.

Pregnant teenage girls are another group at risk of never earning a high school diploma. The *Even Start* program is federally sponsored and administered through many large urban high schools. The goals of this program are threefold: (1) to help the young mothers earn a high school diploma while learning effective parenting skills; (2) to physically nurture and intellectually stimulate the infants and preschool children of these teenagers in a nearby setting where mothers can interact with their children during the school day; and (3) to nurture the self-esteem of mother and child and provide healthy role models who encourage the teenage mothers to develop their abilities and talents.

Effective Classroom Instruction   Today's classrooms are changing—and secondary education will continue to change dramatically to meet the needs of the ever-increasing population of twenty-first century adolescents (see Figure 11.7). Also, teacher certification requirements are more rigorous to provide a new generation of highly trained educators, especially in math and science (Vail, 2005). Results of two international science and math tests reveal that U.S. students are falling behind other industrialized countries, especially in comparison to the high achievement of students in the Pacific Rim countries and in Europe. Also, in 2004 the average verbal SAT score was 508 (up 1 point from 2003), and the average math score was 518 (down 1 point from 2003). More colleges and businesses report that high school students are not prepared for college nor for the world of work.

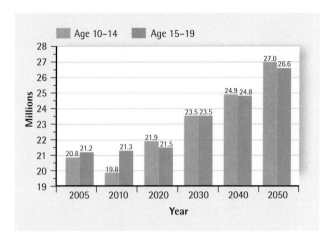

FIGURE 11.7 U.S. Adolescent Population Projections, 2005–2050
Source: U.S. Bureau of the Census. *Statistical Abstract of the United States. 2004–2005.* No. 12. Resident Population Projections 2005–2050.

Student math and English remediation in college are at high levels: two-year public colleges report 63 percent; public four-year colleges report 38 percent, and private four-year colleges report 17 percent are getting remediation to prepare for college-level courses (Hardy, 2005).

Reading textbooks alone does not spark every student's imagination, but computer access opens up a world of active learning. For example, teachers report students are more engaged in assignments and collaborative projects when using wireless laptops (Joyner, 2003). Curriculum-specific expertise and technological preparedness are essential for teachers using CD-ROMs, video laserdiscs, DVDs, multimedia presentations, Internet-based lessons, and distance-learning courses. Technical and computer expertise is needed to plan, develop, and access Internet Web sites to gather and disseminate course information and homework assignments. Teachers also need to learn classroom management and conflict-resolution skills to diffuse potential aggressive or violent behaviors.

Today's students are a much more culturally diverse population, some are more intellectually gifted or challenged than others, some have disabilities, and some have limited English proficiency. More research reveals the great variance among the physical, cognitive, and emotional needs of contemporary teens. Competent and highly qualified teachers must come to the classroom well prepared to stimulate, motivate, educate, and evaluate. And students demand practical relevance to course content they are learning. Roberts, Foehr, and Rideout (2005) surveyed more than 2,000 youth nationwide, ages 8 to 18, who also kept weekly diaries of media use. They report that Millennial-generation students use a record number and variety of electronic devices and media in their homes and bedrooms (see Table 11.3). More stu-

Table 11.3 Time Spent with Media and Selected Nonmedia Activities in a Typical Day

Activity	Time
Watching TV	3:04
Hanging out with parents	2:17
Hanging out with friends*	2:16
Listening to music	1:44
Exercising, sports, etc.	1:25
Watching movies/videos	1:11
Using a computer	1:02
Pursuing hobbies, clubs, etc.	1:00
Talking on the telephone*	0:53
Doing homework*	0:50
Playing video games	0:49
Reading	0:43
Working at a job*	0:35
Doing chores*	0:32

Asked only of 7th- to 12th-graders.

Source: From Roberts, D. F., Foehr, U. G., & Rideout, V., *Generation M: Media in the Lives of 8–18 Year Olds* (#7251), The Henry J. Kaiser Family Foundation, March 2005. This information was reprinted with permission of The Henry J. Kaiser Family Foundation. The Kaiser Family Foundation, based in Menlo Park, California, is a nonprofit, independent national health care philanthropy and is not associated with Kaiser Permanente or Kaiser Industries.

dents are media multitasking, or using several devices at one time while trying to complete homework (for example, downloading music, using instant messaging, while a DVD is playing on the TV). One MIT expert on children, identity, and digital culture says it is common for teens to have up to four media screens on at one time, affecting their ability to pay attention and focus on the task at hand (Turkle, 2003).

Students must come to high school prepared to learn, but few high schools have changed the daily starting schedule to meet the change in adolescent sleep patterns (Keller, 2001). High school classes are not an end in themselves, at least not for most students. High school instruction should be like a springboard, providing a firm foundation while launching the young adult onto new heights. Supporting the classroom teacher to provide the best education for every student are classroom aides, guidance counselors, school psychologists, school nurses, librarians, school administrators, and clerical staff.

Academic Standing and Global Comparisons Even with all this professional and technological support, though, American high school seniors performed well below the international average in mathematics and science literacy in the largest international study of student

achievement ever undertaken—the *Third International Mathematics and Science Study (TIMSS),* released in February 1998 by researchers at Boston College (Forgione, 1998; Sullivan, 1998) (see Table 11.4). This large-scale study included more than 500,000 students from 45 countries, and TIMSS assessed students in their last year in all types of schools and programs (Forgione, 1998). This research is evidence of a downward trend in the math and science skills of American youth in the years following the fourth grade, where American children perform above average when compared with international peers. Since the TIMSS results were issued, U.S. middle schools and high schools require many more math and science courses—and teacher certification requirements are more rigorous. A gender gap was found as well: Boys outperformed girls in math and science literacy in nearly all countries tested.

Students from Hong Kong, Chinese Taipei, South Korea, the Netherlands, and Sweden fared best in overall mathematics and science literacy. French students performed highest in advanced mathematics. Those from Sweden and Norway performed highest in physics. American high school seniors showed sharp declines in math and science skills in comparison to the scores for fourth-graders. Few American students take calculus or physics, compared with students from other countries. Some factors appear to be related to the lower performance of U.S. high school seniors ("Building Knowledge," 1997): (1) more U.S. students work part-time jobs and work more hours than students in countries that scored higher and lower than U.S. students, and (2) U.S. students had fewer hours of mathematics instruction per week.

In 2000, a national commission released its report, *Before It's Too Late,* with specific guidelines to improve

Table 11.4 U.S. Twelfth-Grade Mathematics and Science Achievement in International Context

Subject	Country	Score
Mathematics and Science Literacy (average score of 500)	Netherlands	559
	Sweden	555
	United States	471
Advanced Mathematics (average score of 501)	France	557
	United States	442
Physics (average score of 501)	Norway	581
	United States (the lowest ranking of all 45 countries)	423

Source: Pascal D. Forgione, Jr., U.S. Commissioner of Education Statistics, National Center for Education Statistics (NCES), *Pursuing Excellence: A Study of U.S. Twelfth-Grade Mathematics and Science Achievement in International Context, and The Release of U.S. Reports on Grade 12 Results from the Third International Mathematics and Science Study (TIMSS),* February 24, 1998. http://nces.ed/gov/timss/

the quantity, quality, and working environment for math and science teachers and to raise curriculum and evaluation standards for teaching U.S. children (Glenn, 2000). With the *No Child Left Behind (NCLB)* legislation in 2001, standards have been raised in math and science around the nation. Students are now required to take more rigorous math and science courses. NCLB has its share of criticism, but without such major improvements, American youth will be at a disadvantage for employment in this age of scientific and technological advances.

Use of Media and Computer Technology The exciting diversity and richness of the world is opening up to our youth—and to all of us—through high-speed computer networks. Without a doubt, there is a high rate of job growth and opportunity for today's adolescent in the technology and computer industries. The network wiring of schools was a national goal, but more recently "wireless" networks are the Internet connection of choice, with funds coming from both the public and the private sector. However, some parents and faculty are concerned that computer games, Internet access, and chat rooms are a waste of time taking away from the three Rs or will lead to immoral, or dangerous, activities.

Modes of instruction using the computer, such as distance learning options, are expanding. Such instructional formats allow students with special interests to enroll in online classes that their high school or college might not be able to offer, such as Japanese, Russian, sign language, or Latin. Today all research journals, magazines, and newspaper articles are available via the computer. High school and college libraries are now considered "Information Resource Centers." Many parents have purchased computers for home use and consider this expense an investment in their child's future. It is well known that nearly all occupations today utilize computers: Auto mechanics use computers to evaluate and calibrate auto engines; beauticians use computers to help a customer plan a "new" look; medical personnel use computers for diagnostics and imaging; farmers use computers to plan crops and costs; business personnel use computers to manage every aspect of business; astronauts use computers on the international space station; artists, animators, and musicians use computer software to create cartoons, movies, and music. We must prepare this adolescent cohort for its technologically oriented future.

Questions

Why do you think American high school seniors' academic performance in math and science ranked below average in the international TIMSS study? What would you recommend to improve the academic performance of U.S. teens?

Moral Development

At no other period in life are people as likely to be as concerned with moral values and principles as they are during adolescence. A recurrent theme of American literature, from *Huckleberry Finn* to *Catcher in the Rye*, has been the innocent child who is brought at adolescence to a new awareness of adult reality and who concludes that the adult world is hypocritical, corrupt, and decadent. *Adolescent idealism,* coupled with *adolescent egocentricity,* frequently breeds "egocentric reformers"—adolescents who assume that it is their solemn duty to reform their parents and the world in keeping with their own highly personalized standards.

Some two and a half millennia ago, the Greek philosopher Aristotle came to somewhat similar conclusions about the young people of his time:

> [Youths] have exalted notions, because they have not yet been humbled by life or learned its necessary limitations; moreover, their hopeful disposition makes them think themselves equal to great things—and that means exalted notions. All their mistakes are in the direction of doing things excessively and vehemently. They love too much, hate too much, and the same with everything else.

The Adolescent as a Moral Philosopher

Significantly, young people have played a major role in many social movements that have reshaped the contours of history. In Czarist Russia the schools were "hotbeds of radicalism." In China, students contributed to the downfall of the Manchu dynasty and again to the political turmoil of 1919, the 1930s, and 1988 to 1989. And German students were largely supportive of different forms of right-wing nationalism from the mid-nineteenth century on and showed support in student council elections for the Nazis in the 1930s (Lipset, 1989).

As we saw in Chapter 9, Kohlberg and his colleagues have found that in the course of moral development people tend to pass through an orderly sequence of six stages. These six stages of moral thought are divided into three major levels: the *preconventional,* the *conventional,* and the *postconventional.* Preconventional children are responsive to cultural labels of good and bad out of consideration for the kinds of consequences of their behavior-punishment, reward, or the exchange of favors. Persons at the conventional level view the rules and expectations of their family, group, or nation as valuable in their own right. Individuals who pass to the postconventional level (and Kohlberg says few people do consistently) come to define morality in terms of self-chosen principles that they view as having universal ethical validity and application for the good of all (see Figure 11.8). The impetus for moral development results from increasing cognitive sophistication of the sort

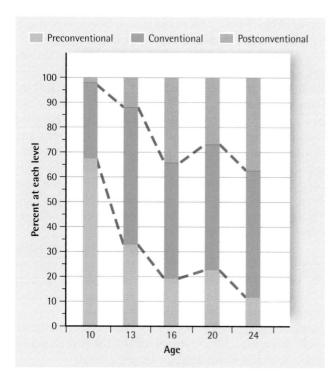

FIGURE 11.8 Age and Level of Moral Development The subjects in this study were urban middle-class male Americans. All percentages are approximate and are extrapolated from charts in the references cited below. The sizes of the samples studied are not stated in the originals.
Source: Daedalus, Journal of the American Academy of Arts and Sciences, from the issue entitled *Twelve to Sixteen: Early Adolescence,* Vol. 100, no. 4, Fall 1971, Cambridge, MA: Lawrence Kohlberg, "Continuities in Childhood and Adult Moral Development Revisited."

described by Piaget. Consequently, postconventional morality becomes possible only with the onset of adolescence and the development of formal operational thought—the ability to think in logical and abstract terms. Thus, postconventional morality depends primarily on changes in the structure of thought, rather than on an increase in the individual's knowledge of cultural values (de Vries & Walker, 1981). In other words, Kohlberg's stages tell us how an individual thinks, not what she or he thinks about given matters.

James Fowler has devised a stage theory based on a broad definition of faith called *faith development theory (FDT).* Older teenagers often begin to struggle with identity issues of "Who am I" and "What is the meaning of life," and "What am I going to do with my life?" Various forms of religiosity often appeal to young people at this stage, whereas for others a quest for spiritual understanding outside of formal religious groups becomes more important. Drawing on the disciplines of philosophy and psychology, Fowler explores the stages of faith and identity development (Fowler & Dell, 2004). Fowler describes several different types of "faithful" people who possess similar patterns in their expression of faith.

Fowler's theory of faith development includes a hierarchy of six stages that are sequential and do not vary. These stages range from an early imaginary, fantasy stage around ages 3 to 6 to various steps in accepting or struggling with conventional religious doctrines (with symbols and rituals) with maturity. Few humans ultimately transcend to what Fowler describes as *universalists* who are "feeling at one with God," willing to sacrifice for their beliefs (Fowler, 2001).

> **Questions**
>
> In what ways is adolescent egocentrism different from the egocentrism of a 4-year-old? How does a typical adolescent's moral development change from sixth grade to twelfth grade?

The Development of Political Thinking

The development of political thinking, like the development of moral values and judgments, depends to a considerable extent on an individual's level of cognitive development. The psychologist Joseph Adelson and his colleagues have interviewed large numbers of adolescents between 11 and 18 years of age. Their aim has been to discover how adolescents of different ages and circumstances think about political matters and organize their political philosophies. Adelson (1972, p. 107) presents adolescents with the following premise:

> Imagine that a thousand people venture to an island in the Pacific to form a new society; once there they must compose a political order, devise a legal system, and in general confront the myriad problems of government.

Each subject is then asked a large number of hypothetical questions dealing with justice, crime, the citizen's rights and obligations, the functions of government, and so on. Adelson (1975, pp. 64–65) summarizes his findings as follows:

> The earliest lesson we learned in our work, and the one we have relearned since, is that neither sex, nor race, nor level of intelligence, nor social class, nor national origin is as potent a factor in determining the course of political thought in adolescence as is the youngster's sheer maturation. From the end of grade school to the end of high school, we witness some truly extraordinary changes in how the child organizes his thinking about society and government.

Adelson finds that the most important change in political thought that occurs during adolescence is the achievement of increasing abstractness. This finding echoes Piaget, who described the hallmarks of formal operational thought in terms of the ability to engage in logical and abstract reasoning. Consider, for example, the answers given by 12- and 13-year-olds when they are asked, "What is the purpose of laws?" (Adelson, 1972, p. 108):

> They do it, like in schools, so that people don't get hurt.
> If we had no laws, people could go around killing people.
> So people don't steal or kill.

Now consider the responses of subjects two or three years older (Adelson, 1972, p. 108):

> To ensure safety and enforce the government.
> To limit what people can do.
> They are basically guidelines for people.
> I mean, like this is wrong and this is right and to help them understand.

An essential difference between the two sets of responses is that the younger adolescents limit their answers to concrete examples such as stealing and killing. Eleven-year-olds have trouble with abstract notions of justice, equality, or liberty. In contrast, older adolescents can usually move back and forth between the concrete and the abstract. In brief (Adelson, 1975, p. 68):

> The young adolescent can imagine a church but not the church; the teacher and the school but not education; the policeman and the judge and the jail but not the law; the public official but not the government.

Another difference between the political thinking of younger and older adolescents is that the former tend to view the political universe in rigid and unchangeable terms. Younger adolescents have difficulty dealing with historical

causes. They fail to understand that actions taken at one time have implications for future decisions and events.

There is also a sharp decline in authoritarian responses as the child moves through adolescence. Preadolescents are more one-sided in their views toward lawbreakers. They see issues in terms of good guys and bad guys, the strong against the weak, and rampant corruption versus repressive cures. They are attracted to one-person rule and favor coercive and even totalitarian modes of government. By late adolescence children generally have become more liberal, humane, and democratic in their political perspectives (Helwig, 1995). Thus, they see many sides to the September 11, 2001 issues—some want war; others want peace.

Adelson finds some national variations among young people of different political cultures. Germans tend to dislike confusion and to admire a strong leader. British adolescents stress the rights of the individual citizen and the government's responsibility to provide an array of goods and services for its citizens. Americans emphasize social harmony, democratic practices, the protection of individual rights, and equality among citizens.

Question

Why and in what ways do adolescents generally become more politically aware as they progress through high school, graduate from high school, and enter college, the military, or the world of work?

SEGUE

We have seen how adolescents enter puberty and have discussed the physical and cognitive changes linked to this period in life. Maturation brings with it certain responsibilities and temptations that many adolescents find difficult to come to terms with; it is no surprise, then, that some adolescents begin to engage in behaviors that adults see as "destructive," although most adolescents come through these years unscathed. A review of the research on physical development and health issues in adolescence reveals that today's teens have

many serious concerns they are dealing with on a daily basis. As we shall see in Chapter 12, at a time when teens are presented with many challenges and choices, they become more reluctant to discuss these significant issues with parents or caretakers and turn to friends for information, advice, support, and comfort. In Chapter 12 we will turn our discussion to the individual adolescent's developing self-concept and self-esteem, family and peer influences, and continuing preparation for a healthy adult life.

Summary

Physical Development

1. During adolescence, young people experience the adolescent growth spurt, a very rapid increase in height and weight. The spurt typically occurs in girls two years earlier than in boys.
2. Adolescence is also characterized by the development of the reproductive system. The complete transition to

reproductive maturity takes place over several years and is accompanied by extensive physical changes.
3. Children of the same chronological age show enormous variations in growth and sexual maturation. Whether they mature early or late has important consequences for them in their relationships with both adults and peers. Because of different rates of maturation, some adoles-

cents have an advantage in height, strength, physical attractiveness, and athletic prowess.

4. Any difference from the peer group in growth and development tends to be a difficult experience for the adolescent, especially if the difference places the individual at a physical disadvantage or in a position of unfavorable contrast to peers.

5. Many teenagers are preoccupied with their physical acceptability and adequacy. These concerns take place during a time of substantial developmental change in the nature and significance of friendships.

Health Issues in Adolescence

6. Three disorders stem from poor nutritional habits: anorexia nervosa, bulimia, and obesity.

7. Substance abuse is the harmful use of drugs or alcohol, lasting over a prolonged period that endangers self or others.

8. Unprotected sex often leads to the spread of STIs. AIDS is caused by a virus that damages the human immune system and prevents the body from fighting infections.

Cognitive Development

9. Jean Piaget called adolescence the period of formal operations. Its hallmarks are logical and abstract reasoning. Neither all adolescents nor all adults, however, attain the stage or acquire its associated abilities for logical and abstract thought.

10. Adolescence produces its own form of egocentrism. In turning their new powers of thought on themselves, adolescents assume that their thoughts and actions are as interesting to others as they are to themselves.

11. Students are divided into different ability groups in school during this period. Special programs help make the transition from school to work less problematic for many adolescents.

Moral Development

12. At no other period of life are individuals as likely to be concerned with moral values and principles as they are during adolescence. Some, but not all, adolescents attain Kohlberg's postconventional level of morality. In the process a number of young people go through a transitional phase of moral relativism. Fowler describes stages of development in his faith development theory.

13. During adolescence young people undergo major changes in the way they organize their thinking about society and government. Maturation appears to be the most potent source of these changes. As children move through adolescence, their political thinking becomes more abstract, less static, and less authoritarian.

Key Terms

adolescent growth spurt (382)

anorexia nervosa (393)

asynchrony (382)

bulimia (394)

egocentrism (402)

imaginary audience (402)

menarche (384)

obesity (392)

period of formal operations (401)

personal fable (402)

puberty (380)

sexually transmitted infections (STIs) (396–397)

substance abuse (396)

Following Up on the Internet

Web sites for this chapter focus on physical, cognitive, and moral maturation in adolescence. Please access the text Web site at www.mhhe.com/vzcrandell8 for up-to-date hot-linked Internet addresses for the following organizations, topics, and resources:

Adolescent Health from the American Medical Association

The Female Genital Mutilation Education Project
Monitoring the Future Surveys
AIDS Prevention Education
TIMSS International Study Center at Boston College
National Teacher Recruitment Clearinghouse

Video Scenario—http://www.mhhe.com/vzcrandell8

In this chapter, you've just read about maturity issues associated with adolescence, adolescent egocentricity, social pressures and anxieties adolescents face as part of this time of life. Using the OLC (www.mhhe.com/vzcrandell8), watch the *Adolescence video scenario and its ending #1* to see how these concepts, such as alcohol and substance abuse and other pressures of the peer group, come to life as Maggie and Aron celebrate together along with their friend, Kevin. Maggie and Aron's scenario also introduces some key concepts regarding peers and parenting that you'll explore in the next chapter, Adolescence: Emotional and Social Development.

Adolescence
Emotional and Social Development

1. When you were an adolescent, who had the most influence on how you saw the world and yourself? Was it your parents, your peers, or a best friend? Who has had the most lasting influence?

2. Are there very different developmental paths for different types of people? For example, does an African American lesbian go through the same developmental stages as a Caucasian heterosexual male? If so, what does this say about any theory?

3. How do you think the media influence adolescent identity formation?

4. What kinds of issues would you expect a teenager's diary to discuss—personal, political, moral, or cultural? What would you expect to find any different in a teenager's diary written in 1900?

Outline

The Western model of segregating youth from the "adult world" has given rise to a kind of youth culture. The obvious features of the youth culture revolve around various peer-group trademarks (such as style of music or the latest electronic gadgets), and the notion of a generation gap oversimplifies the relationship between youth and adults. Some difficult adjustments that teens must make revolve around their lifestyle choices and their sexual identity and expression. As teens begin to enter into the adult environment, they experience many exciting activities for the first time. Adults might encourage part-time employment and discourage sexual activity or substance use.

Most American adolescents make a successful transition into young adulthood. However, some teens are likely to engage in high-risk behaviors, such as substance abuse, eating disorders, indiscriminate sexual activity, pregnancies, abortion, suicide attempts, delinquency, self-mutilation practices, school failure, and little or no transition into employment. On the other hand, teens who continue to experience a high self-concept through tenth grade are likely to finish college, pursue advanced degrees, and continue building a foundation for their adult life.

In this chapter, we examine the influential factors that promote or demote an adolescent's self-worth and how—and with whom—an adolescent successfully navigates through this challenging stage of life.

Development of Identity

Over a period of several years or longer, a teenager spends a good deal of time focusing on the question "Who am I?" Through social interactions with family members, friends, classmates, teammates, teachers, coaches, advisors, and mentors, most adolescents come to a firmer understanding of their abilities and talents. Some want to make their own mark in the world using their unique talents; others decide to follow in a parent's footsteps or enter into a family-owned business. Many decide to enter college or the military, which allows them time to postpone declaring a vocation or career. A smaller number decide to drop out of school and mainstream society to "find themselves," because they need to go to work to help support a family (as is the case with some immigrant youth), or because they are dissatisfied and/or unsuccessful in the school system. Unfortunately, those who do not earn a high school degree put themselves at risk for unemployment, teen pregnancy, teen parenting, health risks, and high poverty. In 2003, 13 percent of persons ages 16 to 24 were neither working nor enrolled in school, and females were more likely than males to be in this situation (Wirt et al., 2004). However, some school dropouts are able to enter the world of work, and we address this issue later in this chapter. As we shall see, there are several theories that attempt to explain why adolescence seems to be a pivotal point in an individual's life.

Hall's Portrayal of "Storm and Stress"

The notion that adolescence is a distinct and turbulent developmental period received impetus in 1904 with the publication of G. Stanley Hall's (1904) monumental work, *Adolescence.* Hall, one of the major figures of early U.S. psychology, depicted adolescence as a stage of **storm and stress,** characterized by inevitable turmoil, maladjustment, tension, rebellion, dependency conflicts, and exaggerated peer-group conformity. This view was subsequently taken up and popularized by Anna Freud (1936) and other psychoanalysts (Blos, 1962). Indeed, Anna Freud (1958) went so far as to assert: "The upholding of a steady equilibrium during the adolescent process is itself abnormal." Viewed from this Western perspective, the adolescent undergoes so many rapid changes (a convergence or "pileup" of life changes) that a restructuring of identity or self-concept is required if these changes are to be properly integrated into the individual's personality. Further complicating matters, biological and hormonal changes are thought to influence the adolescent's sense of emotional and psychological well-being and to generate—in some youth—substantial mood swings, irritability, and restlessness (Buchanan, Eccles, & Becker, 1992). As you can see, adolescence was originally conceived as

the "troubled waters" one had to pass over when voyaging from the more peaceful world of childhood to the demanding "real world" called adulthood. However, to this day non-Western cultures do not recognize an adolescent stage of development between youth and adulthood.

Sullivan's Interpersonal Theory of Development

One of the first theorists to propose that adolescents go through stages of development was Harry Stack Sullivan. He emphasized the importance of relationships and communication for teenagers in *The Interpersonal Theory of Psychiatry* (Sullivan, 1953). Sullivan's theory—in contrast to Freud's—explains the principal forces in human development as being social instead of biological. His social theory is enlightening when used to examine adolescent development and the impact on individuals of peer groups, friendships, peer pressure, and intimacy. In essence, Sullivan states that positive peer relationships during adolescence are essential for healthy development and that negative peer relationships will lead to unhealthy development, such as depression, eating disorders, drug abuse, delinquency, or criminal behavior. We will focus on three periods of Sullivan's theory: preadolescence, early adolescence, and late adolescence.

Preadolescence   Preadolescence (which some now call the "tween" years) begins with a sudden powerful need for an intimate relationship with a same-sex playmate. It ends when the adolescent begins to experience a desire for genital sexuality. During this time personal intimacy involves interpersonal closeness but does not involve genital contact. Best friends, what Sullivan refers to as "chums," most likely have many of the same characteristics (same sex, social status, and age) and will share love, loyalty, intimacy, and the opportunity for self-disclosure—but they will not have a sexual relationship and will not experience what Sullivan calls the "lust dynamism." By having a "chum," the preadolescent gains insight into how others see the world, which helps diminish most forms of egocentric thought.

Early Adolescence   With the onset of puberty, most adolescents experience genital maturation. Sullivan (1953) says the intimate personal relationship that preadolescents had with their same-sex chums is challenged due to the emerging need for sexual intimacy with opposite-sex partners. Because the preadolescent has experienced intimacy with only someone of the same sex, the advent of early adolescence brings with it three separate needs: a need for sexual satisfaction, a continued need for personal intimacy, and a need for personal security (i.e., a need to be seen as socially acceptable by the potential sexual partners).

Security issues include positive self-esteem, value as an individual, and an absence of anxiety. For adolescents the new importance of their genitals as an indicator of their worth is enough to throw them into a state of disequilibrium. Remember what it was like when you first became aware that other people perceived you as a sexual being? If you were to observe young adolescents today in malls or schools, the first thing you would probably notice are their various attempts to catch someone's eye either by teasing, flirting, or some act of bravado. Sullivan says early adolescence leads to late adolescence when individuals have found a way to satisfy the genital drive they have acquired.

Late Adolescence The period of late adolescence begins once the individual has established a method of satisfying sexual needs and ends with the establishment of a relationship that is both sexually and personally intimate. Love is the result of fusing intimacy and lust, and love with another person leads to a stable long-term relationship of adulthood. In late adolescence, the ability to sexually reproduce merges with the capacity for close interpersonal relationships.

Sullivan's theory attempts to get one step closer to the nitty-gritty details of what adolescents do and experience on the journey to sexual adulthood. It also tries to explain why adolescents go through stages of development, in contrast to Hall, who wanted to paint a much more general picture of adolescence as a tumultuous period of life. Hall and Sullivan both wanted to explain certain aspects of adolescence in terms of how the youth makes a transition to becoming an adult. Hall looks at generalities, Sullivan looks at relationships. Neither emphasizes adolescent introspection or young people's psychological task of trying to make sense of the internal and external changes characteristic of adolescence. Erik Erikson, however, looks a little closer at the personal psychosocial tasks that teens struggle with during adolescence.

Erikson: The "Crisis" of Adolescence

Erik Erikson's work has focused attention on the struggle of adolescents to develop and clarify their identity. His view of adolescence is consistent with a long psychological tradition that has portrayed adolescence as a difficult period. As described in Chapter 2, Erikson divides the developmental life-span sequence into nine psychosocial stages. Each stage poses a somewhat different issue or significant challenge during development in which the individual must move in either a positive or a negative direction. A major task in self-development or ego adjustment becomes the focus of each psychosocial stage. Erikson's fifth stage covers the period of adolescence and consists of the search for **identity.** He

suggests that an optimal feeling of identity is experienced as a sense of well-being: "Its most obvious concomitants are a feeling of being at home in one's body, a sense of 'knowing where one is going,' and an inner assuredness of anticipated recognition from those who count" (Erikson, 1968a).

Erikson observes that adolescents, like trapeze artists, must release their safe hold on childhood and reach in midair for a firm grasp on adulthood. The search for identity becomes particularly acute because the adolescent is undergoing rapid physical change while confronting many imminent adult tasks and decisions. Recent empirical research has supported Erikson's view that adolescents do indeed go through identity exploration and a concomitant "crisis" (Makros & McCabe, 2001). The older adolescent must often make an occupational choice or at least decide whether to continue formal schooling, apply for an apprenticeship for various jobs, seek employment, enter the military, or simply drop out. Other environmental aspects provide testing grounds for a concept of self: broadening peer relationships, sexual contacts and roles, moral and ideological commitments, moving out of a parental home and into one's own, and emancipation from adult authority.

Adolescents must synthesize a variety of new roles to come to terms with themselves and their environment. Erikson believes that, because adolescent identities are diffuse, uncrystallized, and fluctuating, adolescents are often at sea with themselves and others. This ambiguity and lack of stable anchorage can lead many adolescents to overcommit themselves to cliques or gangs, allegiances, loves, and social causes: To keep themselves together they temporarily overidentify with the heroes of cliques and crowds, some to the point of apparently completely losing their sense of individuality. Yet in this stage not even falling in love is entirely a sexual matter. Adolescent love can be an attempt to arrive at a definition of one's identity by projecting one's diffused self-image on another and by seeing it reflected back and gradually clarified. This is why so much of young love is conversation. Clarification can also be sought by destructive means. Young people can become remarkably clannish, intolerant, and cruel in their exclusion of others who are different in skin color, cultural background, looks or abilities, in tastes and talents, and often in entirely petty aspects of dress and gesture arbitrarily selected as the signs of being "in" or "out."

According to Erikson, this clannishness explains the appeal that various extremist and totalitarian movements have for some adolescents; in other words, you do not see many 75-year-old "skinheads." In Erikson's view, every adolescent confronts a major danger: that he or she will fail to arrive at a consistent, coherent, and integrated identity. Consequently, adolescents might experience *identity diffusion*—a lack of ability to commit oneself, even in late adolescence, to an occupational or ideological position and to assume a recognizable station in life. Another danger is that adolescents might fashion a **negative identity**—a debased self-image and social role. Still another course taken by some adolescents is formation of a **deviant identity**—a lifestyle at odds with, or at least not supported by, the values and expectations of society. Other researchers have followed Erikson's lead.

James E. Marcia (1966, 1991) examined the development and validation of ego identity status in terms of achievement, moratorium, foreclosure, and diffusion. Marcia interviewed college students to find out how they felt about future occupations, religious ideology, and worldview. From these interviews Marcia found that students could be classified according to four types of identity formation:

1. **Identity diffusion.** A state in which the individual has few, if any, commitments to anyone or to a set of beliefs. Relativistic thought and emphasis on personal gratification are paramount. There is no core to the person that one can point to and state, "This person stands for X, Y, or Z." Those who are identity diffused do not seem to know what they want to do in life or who they want to be. *Example: Henri joins one cause this week and another next week. He is a strict vegetarian this month and an avid carnivore next month. He cannot tell you why he believes what he does except in very vague terms, such as "Because that's the way I am."*

2. **Identity foreclosure.** The avoidance of autonomous choice. Foreclosure is premature identity formation. The adolescent accepts someone else's (such as parent's) values and goals without exploring alternative roles. *Example: Carmen wants to be a doctor and has wanted to be a doctor since her parents suggested it at age 7. Now at 18, she does not think twice about the idea because she has internalized her parents' expectations. You might hear her say, "Mom wants me to go to Harvard, so Harvard here I come!"*

3. **Identity moratorium.** A period of delay, during which adolescents can experiment with or try on various roles, ideologies, and commitments. It is a stage between childhood and adulthood when the individual can explore various dimensions of life without yet having to choose any. Adolescents might start or stop, abandon or postpone, implement or transform given courses of action. *Example: André joined the Peace Corps because he didn't quite know what he wanted to do after college, and he thought this would give him a chance to "find himself."*

4. **Identity achievement.** A period when the individual achieves inner stability that corresponds to

what others perceive that person to be. *Example: Everyone agrees that when Jamella walks into the room she will handle the situation in a professional manner and refuse to divulge confidential information afterward. In fact, this is exactly what happens. Everyone knows that Jamella is trustworthy, and she sees herself in the same light.*

David Elkind (2001), in *The Hurried Child*, has added a view of adolescence in which the harsh realities of the world have increased pressures on adolescents (to have higher school achievement, to complete more sophisticated courses, to become healthy and fit, to be the best in sports, to be attractive and to fit in, to better prepare for the jobs of the twenty-first century, etc.) and therefore identity formation can no longer be put off until late adolescence.

Questions

In what respects do Hall, Sullivan, and Erikson view the developmental tasks of adolescence similarly? In what ways do these theorists differ in their views of adolescent identity formation?

Cultural Aspects of Identity Formation

Any number of social scientists have suggested that few people make the transition from childhood to adulthood more difficult than Western nations do (Chubb & Fertman, 1992; Elkind, 2001; Sebald, 1977). At adolescence boys and girls are expected to stop being children, yet they are not expected to be men and women. They are told to "grow up," but they are still treated like dependents, economically supported by their parents, and frequently viewed by society as untrustworthy and irresponsible. According to this view, conflicting expectations generate an identity crisis among U.S. and European youth.

Many non-Western societies provide rites of passage or **puberty rites**—initiation ceremonies that symbolize the transition from childhood to adulthood (Delaney, 1995). For example, male and female adolescents in African and Middle Eastern countries are subjected to circumcision rituals and ceremonies, which are physically and psychologically harmful (Van Vuuren & deJongh, 1999). Yet most youth endure these rituals in order to enter the status of adulthood in their culture. Rites of passage occur across cultures, have existed throughout human history, and include specific rituals: seclusion from society, instruction from elders, a transition ceremony, and a return to society with recognition of adult status (Delaney, 1995). Ceremonies include physical and spiritual cleansing, prayers and blessings, wearing traditional clothing, offering of traditional foods or fasting, and traditional music. It is not simply the rite but the extensive time contributed by elders that help many adolescents make a healthier transition to adult status (Delaney, 1995). In some cultures, adolescent males and females are then segregated until a later age of arranged marriage.

Western societies provide less obvious rites of passage. Some examples include the Jewish bar mitzvah or bat mitzvah, Christian confirmation, securing a driver's license at age 16 or 17, voting at age 18, graduating from high school and college, or entering the military. Self-initiation is more common among American youth: cigarette smoking, alcohol consumption, sexual activity—changes that occur among peers without adult presence.

Adolescence: Not Necessarily Stormy or Stressful?

Psychologist Albert Bandura (1964) stresses that the stereotyped storm-and-stress portrait of adolescence most closely fits the behavior of "the deviant 10 percent of the adolescent population that appears repeatedly in psychiatric clinics, juvenile probation departments, and in the newspaper headlines." Bandura argues that the "stormy-decade myth" is due more to cultural expectations and the representations of teenagers in movies, literature, and other media than to actual fact. Daniel Offer likewise finds little evidence of "turmoil" or "chaos" in his longitudinal study of a sample of 61 middle-class adolescent boys (Offer, Ostrov, & Howard, 1981). Most were happy, responsible, and well-adjusted boys who respected their parents. Adolescent "disturbance" tended to be limited mostly to bickering with their parents. Like Bandura, Offer concludes that the portrayal of adolescence as a turbulent period comes from the work of such investigators as Erik Erikson who have spent their professional careers primarily studying disturbed adolescents. He concludes (Offer & Offer, 1975, p. 197): "Our data lead us to hypothesize that adolescence, as a stage in life, is not a uniquely stressful period." Offer's more recent study of some 6,000 adolescents in 10 nations (Australia, Bangladesh, Hungary, Israel, Italy, Japan, Taiwan, Turkey, the United States, and West Germany) lends cross-cultural support to this conclusion (Offer et al., 1988; Schlegel & Barry, 1991).

Adolescence can also be overrated as a time of major attitudinal change. Aspirations, self-concepts, and political attitudes from parental modeling and gender attitudes toward household work generally are important to young adult attitude formation. Though differences in these areas show up between individuals who achieve success in education (and later on the job) and those who do not, these differences are already largely established by the tenth grade (Cunningham, 2001; Zimmerman et al., 1997). In other words, young people who enter high school with high aspirations and positive self-concepts

are likely to retain these advantages at least five years beyond high school. Hence, students in graduate and professional schools typically have high self-esteem that mirrors the positive self-images they possessed five years earlier. Similarly, the poor self-images of school dropouts are already established before these adolescents withdraw from school. Such individual differences are quite stable across time (Jessor, Turbin, & Costa, 1998).

Data from longitudinal studies first undertaken with youngsters between 1928 and 1931 by psychologists at the University of California at Berkeley and then followed by researchers for more than 50 years confirm these findings: Competent adolescents have more stable careers and marriages than less competent ones, and they experience less personality change over the adult years (Clausen, 1993). On the whole, many researchers find that the overall self-esteem of most individuals increases with age across the adolescent years (Chubb, Fertman, & Ross, 1997). Of course, there are exceptions. Changes in social environment, including changing schools, can interfere with those forces that otherwise bolster a child's self-esteem. Thus, the transition into a middle or junior high school can have a disturbing effect under certain circumstances, particularly for girls (Seidman et al., 1994). Indeed, the endangered self-esteem of adolescent girls is now the focus of considerable study.

Carol Gilligan: Adolescents and Self-Esteem   Self-esteem in adolescent girls was examined by the American Association of University Women (AAUW, 1992), and findings were reported in *How Schools Shortchange Girls.* Carol Gilligan assisted with this study and states that girls in elementary school generally are more confident, assertive, and feel positively about themselves; but by junior high school and high school most have a poorer self-image, lower expectations, and less confidence about their abilities (Brown & Gilligan, 1992). Notably, few girls were enrolling in rigorous math, science, or computer science courses in high school, which are factors related to college acceptance, scholarship, and employment opportunities in a technologically driven society. This report was a catalyst for change: Girls' enrollments and test scores went up in math and science, but not as much in computer science (Leo, 1999). A recent study, however, found very little difference in the math scores for boys and girls, yet gender stereotypes and socialization keep girls from pursuing math-related jobs (Barnett & Rivers, 2004).

Critics of the Gilligan study contend that from grade school through college, girls earn higher grades, higher class ranking, and more honors than boys (except in science and sports) and that boys experience more behavioral and academic difficulties (Leo, 1999). Yet academic standing is only one domain of global self-esteem. More recently Quatman and Watson (2001) studied gender and global self-esteem of adolescents and found that boys scored significantly higher than girls in six of the eight domains and were equal to girls in two. Some findings are:

- *Perception of peer popularity:* no differences in score
- *Academics:* no differences in score, but girls see themselves as hard workers, conscientious, cooperative, and having better behavior in school than boys
- *Personal security:* boys scored higher
- *Home/parents:* boys scored higher; girls experienced less satisfaction with home life/parents
- *Attractiveness:* boys scored higher; girls were more likely to select "I look ugly"
- *Personal mastery:* boys scored higher; girls were more afraid to make mistakes and were less sure of themselves
- *Psychological reactivity/permeability:* boys scored higher; girls reported more psychosomatic symptoms such as headaches, stomachaches, and getting upset when scolded
- *Athletics:* boys scored higher; girls felt less competent

Gilligan contends that girls are more likely than boys to develop a *collectivist* or *connected* model for the self and are likely to feel good about themselves from being sensitive to, connected to, and interdependent with others. Thus, adolescent girls who attend large junior high or high schools can lose the connectedness that promotes meaningful relationships. In contrast, boys are likely to feel more positively about themselves by being independent, separate, and competitive with others (Quatman & Watson, 2001).

In brief, Gilligan finds that during adolescence girls begin to doubt the authority of their own inner voices and feelings and their commitment to meaningful relationships. Whereas as 11-year-olds they assert themselves and still speak their minds, in adolescence they come to fear rejection and anger, and so they mute their voices and repress their autonomy. Western culture, Gilligan says, calls on young women to buy into the image of the "perfect" or "nice" girl—one who avoids being mean and bossy and instead projects an air of calmness, quietude, and cooperation. Schools contribute to the problem by educating primarily for individuality, competition, and autonomy while negating the pursuit of rewarding relationships.

More recently, Gilligan has turned her attention to developing programs that will help young women write authentic and meaningful scripts for their own lives and prevent them from "going underground" with their feelings. Meanwhile, Gilligan's thesis has not gone unchallenged. For instance, Christina Hoff Sommers (1994) and others attack the credibility of virtually all gender-bias research as itself biased and lacking in substance. A symposium of experts discussed the recent AAUW (2001) report, *Beyond the Gender Wars,* and urged that educators address the needs of all youth by improving instruction in safe schools using multiple learning styles, active learning, and collaborative approaches (Taylor, 2001).

Mary Pipher: Identity Formation in Adolescent Girls   In 1994, clinical psychologist Mary Pipher published a revealing exposé entitled *Reviving Ophelia: Saving the Selves of Adolescent Girls,* based on 20 years of counseling preadolescent and adolescent girls. From observing and documenting the significant changes she has witnessed in young women during the course of her clinical practice, she warns that our culture (schools, media, the advertising industry) is destroying the identity and self-esteem of many adolescent girls, and she provides some recommendations for healthier identity formation. Her work not only supports Gilligan's theories, but she further states that girls now are living in a whole new world. Theirs is a world of life-threatening experiences including living with anorexia; depression; self-mutilation behaviors; STIs including genital herpes, genital warts, and HIV; harassment; sexual violations (including date rape) and violence including stranger rape; early and multiple pregnancies or abortions; earlier and more serious substance abuse; and higher incidences of suicide.

Something dramatic happens to early adolescent girls. Studies show a drop in girls' IQ scores and math and science scores. In early adolescence, girls become less curious and less optimistic; they lose their resiliency and their assertive tomboyish personalities and become more deferential, self-critical, and depressed. Their voices go "underground," their speech is more tentative and less articulate. Many vibrant, confident girls (particularly the brightest and most sensitive ones) become shy, doubting young women. Zimmerman and colleagues (1997), in a longitudinal study, examined identity and self-esteem trajectories in more than 1,000 youth from grades 6 to 10. Their findings indicate a steadily increasing drop in self-esteem for the female group, whereas the male adolescents were in the moderate and rising self-esteem group. In contrast to this finding, another researcher says boys are also at risk during their identity-formation years.

Denner and Dunbar (2004) studied a small sample of Mexican American adolescent girls to begin to study if they, too, move from being confident and outspoken to losing their voice and power during adolescent development. In Mexican families, the traditional concept of *Marianismo* defines expectations that girls will remain committed to a submissive feminine role, will show respect for family, and will remain sexually pure. As these teen girls acculturate into American society, they face gender inequalities at home and in school, but they also value being strong, speaking up for what they believe in, and being protective of younger siblings.

Identity Formation in Adolescent Girls Some recent studies suggest that teenage females develop a poorer self-image and less confidence in themselves and their abilities than they had in late childhood.

For Better or for Worse © 2005 Lynn Johnston Productions. Dist. By Universal Press Syndicate. Reprinted with permission. All rights reserved.

Michael Gurian: Identity Formation in Boys   Michael Gurian is a counselor and therapist who has devoted a great deal of study to the identity development of boys. His 1996 book, *The Wonder of Boys: What Parents, Mentors and Educators Can Do to Shape Boys into Exceptional Men*, describes what he thinks boys need to become strong, responsible, sensitive men. His theory about male identity development is centered on recognizing that brain and hormone differences basically control the way males and females operate. Some of the latest research in the 1990s on brain differences in female and male brains confirms the structural and behavioral differences that Gurian discusses.

Gurian states when a boy reaches puberty, the influence of testosterone on both brain and body increases. A male's body will experience five to seven surges of testosterone a day (Gurian, 1996). A boy can be expected to bump into things a lot, be moody and aggressive, require a great deal of sleep, lose his temper, have a massive sexual fantasy life, and masturbate a lot. Most important, in Gurian's view, is that boys need a primary and extended family, relationships with mentors (wise and skilled persons, such as scouting and organized sports attempt to provide), and intense support from school and community (Zimmerman et al., 1997). When positive role models and adult support are not available in our culture, adolescent boys are prey to gang activity, sexual misconduct, and crime. This is verified by the high rate at which young males are committing crimes (most violent crime is committed by males), being killed, or being incarcerated in our criminal justice system. Gurian states that "boys are acting out against society and parents because neither is providing them with enough modeling, opportunity, and wisdom to act comfortably within society" (Gurian, 1996, p. 54).

Scholars now propose a collaborative approach to examining the maturational challenges of adolescence and healthy self-esteem, no matter what gender, racial, ethnic, or socioeconomic status (AAUW, 2001a). Teens, however, prefer to work on these challenges within a peer group.

Peers and Family

Historically, we have had an image of adolescence as a time when the world of peers and the world of parents are at war with each other. However, we derive a quite different picture from psychological and sociological research. Western industrial societies have not only prolonged the period between childhood and adulthood, they also have tended to segregate young people. The notion of a **generation gap** has been widely popularized, implying misunderstanding, antagonism, and separation between youth and adults. The organization of schools into grades based on age means that students of the same age spend a considerable amount of time together. In both academic and extracurricular activities, the schools form little worlds of their own. Middle-aged and older people also tend to create a kind of psychological segregation through the stereotypes they hold of adolescents. They frequently define adolescence as a unique period in life, one that is somehow set apart from—indeed, even at odds with—the integrated web of human activity. Let us examine these matters more carefully.

The Adolescent Peer Group

To the extent that young people are physically and psychologically segregated, they are encouraged to develop their own unique lifestyles (Brown & Huang, 1995). Some sociologists say that Western societies prolong the transition to adulthood by segregating their youth, giving rise to a **youth culture**—a large body of young people with standardized ways of thinking, feeling, and behaving. The first youth culture, the Baby Boomers, arrived after World

War II (born between 1946 and 1964). Many teens had free time, extra money, and unstructured energy. Football teams, cheerleaders, Elvis, rock 'n roll and jukeboxes, and television appeared (Zoba, 1997). Generation X (born between 1964 and 1981) dominated the college culture and work environment for the past 20 years and is often called the "me" generation that mistrusts authority, is indifferent yet pragmatic, and has had difficulty adapting to technological change.

The Millennials (also called *Generation Y* or the *Echo-Boomers*) is the group born between 1982 and 2002 and expected to extend to 2010; demographics show this is the largest cohort in American history: about 78 to 80 million expected to grow to 100 million. Strauss and Howe, authors of *Millennials Rising,* and others (Alch, 2000; Lovern, 2001) observe the current mass of young college students, military recruits, and workers—as Millennials are:

- showing signs of altruistic values, such as optimism, fairness, morality, renewed spiritual awareness, and appreciating diversity (many are from immigrant families).
- exhibiting a greater sense of social responsibility about community, politics, and service to others (as students, they have learned the value of team work).
- advocating strongly for improving the environment, poverty issues, and global concerns.
- placing a renewed emphasis on manners, modesty, and courtesy toward others, which affects workplace expectations, standards, and appearance.
- demonstrating ambition, drive, and a strong work ethic (in school and at work).
- creating a new work culture characterized by independence, entrepreneurship and collaboration; technological savvy about computers, media, and e-commerce; increased productivity; looking for competent mentors and advisors in work relationships.
- backing away from unprotected sex and teen pregnancies, and returning to more conservative marriage and family values.
- showing signs of rising achievement, such as SAT scores, creating higher college SAT averages and admission standards.
- taking more time for themselves and wanting less structured lives than during their earlier heavily scheduled childhoods.

Collins and Tillson (2001), experienced college professors, observe that as students, this cohort functions best when instructors incorporate technology into learning, provide methods of communication and feedback for support, allow opportunities for collaborative learning, use case methods, recognize and engage multiple senses and learning styles, arrange for service learning in community settings, and foster critical thinking, problem solving, and reasoning.

The most obvious features of the youth culture revolve around various peer-group trademarks: preferred music, dance styles, body art (i.e., tattooing and piercing), and idols; fashionable clothes and hairstyles; and distinctive jargon and slang. These features separate teenagers from adults and identify adolescents who share related feelings. Such trademarks facilitate a **consciousness of oneness**—a sympathetic identification in which group members come to feel that their inner experiences and emotional reactions are similar. Additionally, adolescents feel they lack control over many of the changes occurring in their lives. One way they take back control is by assuming the distinctive trademarks of the peer group: They cannot control getting acne, but they do have control over what music they listen to, what they wear and how they adorn their bodies, and how they wear their hair.

Among the central ingredients in the youth culture are various ideas about the qualities and achievements that reveal an individual's masculinity or femininity. Traditionally, for boys the critical signs of manhood are physical mastery, athletic skill, sexual prowess, risk taking, courage in the face of aggression, and willingness to defend one's honor at all costs. For girls the most admired qualities are physical attractiveness (including popular clothing), behaving properly and obeying rules, the ability to delicately manipulate various sorts of interpersonal relationships, and skill in exercising control over sexual encounters (Pipher, 1994).

Overall, two qualities are essential for obtaining high status in today's adolescent society: (1) the ability to project an air of confidence in one's essential masculinity or femininity; and (2) the ability to deliver a smooth performance in a variety of situations and settings. Part of presenting a "cool" self-image is the display of appropriate status symbols—increasingly in the form of mixing desirable luxury-brand items (i.e., clothing, tech-

A Distinctive Youth Culture Some psychologists and sociologists believe that the educational institution segregates young people within high schools and colleges and affords conditions conducive to a distinctive youth culture.

nology, handbags, shoes, sneakers) with bargain items from value-conscious retailers ("Brand Names Take a Back Seat," 2004). Many contemporary teens have disposable income and are vulnerable to the powerful effects of the marketing industry. Teens spent $155 billion on themselves in 2004 and are more likely to have cable TV, a TiVo, a DVD, and online games (Ingrassia, 2005; Romero, 2001). (See the *Human Diversity* box on page 420, "A Peek into the Online World of Young Teens.")

Still other researchers find there isn't a monolithic youth culture. Instead, as young adolescents move into junior high and high school, their world is typically made up of fewer social isolates but many smaller overlapping peer groups with more distinct beliefs, values, and behaviors (e.g., "the jocks," "the brains," and others). Some scholars believe the concept youth culture overshadows individuality in adolescence, since most are motivated to join a peer group over time so they do not feel isolated (Lashbrook, 2000; Ryan, 2001).

The Developmental Role and Course of Peer Groups

Conformity to peer groups plays a prominent role in the lives of many teenagers, and *peer pressure* is an important mechanism for transmitting group norms and maintaining loyalties among group members. Although peers serve as major socialization agents in adolescence, peer pressure varies in strength and direction across grades. Clique membership seems to take on a growing significance for many sixth-, seventh-, and eighth-graders, but then group membership drops off during high school as the individual aspects of social relationships take on greater importance (Brown & Huang, 1995; Lashbrook, 2000; Ryan, 2001).

However, contemporary teenagers differ in a great many ways. Many of these differences arise from differences in socioeconomic, racial, and ethnic backgrounds (Perkins et al., 1998). Generally, every high school typically has several "crowds"—cliques that are often mutually exclusive. Additionally, a "cycle of popularity" seems to bring some teenagers together within relatively stable cliques (for instance, cheerleaders and athletes). In due course, however, many "outsiders" come to resent and dislike their "popular" counterparts, whom they define as "stuck up." Even so, leading-crowd members tend to exhibit higher self-esteem than "outsiders" do. Self-esteem has been found to have an effect on susceptibility to peer pressure, grades, and alcohol usage (Zimmerman et al., 1997). In sum, our search for similarities among young people should not lead us to overlook the individual differences that also exist among them (Lashbrook, 2000; Ryan, 2001).

Questions

In what ways are peer groups important for identity development in adolescence?

Adolescents and Their Families

The parent-child relationship changes at puberty. The amount of time spent with parents, the sense of emotional closeness, and the yielding to parents in decision making all decline from early adolescence to late adolescence (Updegraff et al., 2004). In intact families, parents the same gender as the teen typically have a greater influence on teen socialization (Updegraff et al., 2001). Other studies have found that mothers continue to engage in more frequent interactions with teens and play a greater role in their adolescents' peer relationships. Fathers' interactions typically continue with teens' scholastic achievement and extracurricular performances (Lewis & Lamb, 2003). As stated in early childhood, the quality of the parents' marital relationship continues to be associated with the parent-child relationship. Those who are warm and accepting tend to have children who are more socially competent (Updegraff et al., 2004). But hostile sibling relationships and coercive, irritable, or inconsistent parenting (or stepparenting or foster parenting) during childhood and early adolescence "play an important role in promoting a developmental trajectory that transforms early noncompliance into antisocial behaviors as well as increases the likelihood of associating with deviant peers" (Kim, Hetherington, & Reiss, 1999, p. 1209). Although the vast majority of children in stepfamilies do not show serious behavior problems and are resilient in coping with family reorganization, antisocial behaviors are higher in older teens with divorced and remarried parents than in nondivorced families (Kim, Hetherington, & Reiss, 1999).

Parental supervision and monitoring of peer relations is increasingly important through the teen years. A higher level of parental monitoring is associated with lower rates of delinquency, substance use, and aggression in a sample of African American adolescents. Whereas boys report less monitoring by parents, they also experience higher levels of delinquency, physical aggression, drug and alcohol use, and criminal offenses than girls (Richards et al., 2004). Thus, parents should maintain close ties to their teenage children, offering them encouragement to make their own decisions to help them develop psychological autonomy and their unique personalities. Parents need to respect their teens' opinions, even if they are not the same as their own, and provide them unconditional love and acceptance ("Parenting Teens," 2000).

Influence in Different Realms of Behavior

Both the family and the peer group are anchors in the lives of most teenagers. Parents and peers provide adolescents with different kinds of experience, and the influence of the two groups varies with the issue at hand. When the issues pertain to finances, education, and career plans,

Human Diversity

A Peek into the Online World of Young Teens

What's on the mind of today's young teens?

Apparently a lot more than most adults and parents realize! Each generation of teens is compelled to be in touch with friends and family (and most of us relied on the hard-wired, regular phone, which is still the top communication device today) (see Figure 12.1). A recent research report entitled *Teens and Technology*, based on a nationwide sample ages 12 to 17, reveals that nearly all teens are communicating with an escalating array of technological devices, online services, and online content features that allow for:

- Instant communication among family members and a wide variety of friends and peers by e-mail, cell phone, landline phone, instant messaging (IM), and chat rooms (nearly 90 percent report using email, and 75 percent report using instant messaging).

- Visitations to entertainment and news web sites (music, movies, sports, games, information sources, and TV)—more than 8 out of 10 teens now report going online to play games.
- Ventures into purchasing goods, getting health information, or inquiring about college issues are all up considerably since 2000.

Nearly 9 out of 10 teens use the Internet

Lenhart, Madden, & Hitlin (2005) in 2004 repeated a large-scale survey conducted in 2000 and were surprised to see so many more teens now use the Internet—87 percent in 2005 versus 73 percent in 2000. More than *50 percent* report going online daily and about *50 percent* of online teens live in homes with broadband Internet access (versus telephone dial-up connections). A majority of teens reported owning at least one personal media device: a cell phone, a desktop or laptop computer, or a personal digital assistant (PDA), and nearly half say they own two or more devices. Nearly one-third of teens with cell phones also report using the text messaging feature. Although still in extensive use, teen use of email appears to be declining somewhat in favor of instant messaging (IM) or text messaging on cell phones (teens say that email is something you use to talk to "old people, institutions, or large groups"). About three-fourths of teens report using the Internet on a more centrally located computer in their family home. More than half of the parents who were interviewed for this study also indicated that they use some type of filtering and monitoring software to check on their teen's web surfing.

Nearly one-half use instant messaging (IM) every day

Instant messaging (IM) has become the mode of choice for today's online teens. Teens use IM to discuss homework assignments, plan activities with or joke around with friends on their IM list, and check in with parents. Yet more teens are using IM to provide links to interesting websites, download photos or documents, or send music of video files to those on their IM list. Increasingly, then, technology plays a critical role in the everyday lives of a majority of American teens.

Source: Lenhart, A., Madden, M., & Hitlin, P. (2005, July 27). *Teens and technology: Youth are leading the transition to a fully wired and mobile nation.* Washington, DC: PEW Internet and American Life Project. Retrieved November 20, 2005, from http://www.pewinternet.org

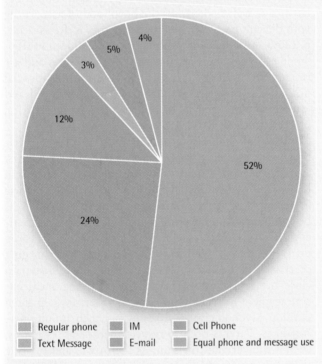

FIGURE 12.1 Today's Teens Use Technology A high majority of American teens use a variety of technological devices to communicate.
Source: Pew Internet & American Life Project, 2005.

adolescents overwhelmingly seek advice and counsel from adults, particularly their parents. Time with parents centers around household activities like eating, shopping, performing chores, and viewing television. And family interaction more closely parallels the goals of socialization dictated by the larger community. Contrary to some psychoanalytic formulations, adolescents do not seem to develop autonomy and identity by severing their ties with their parents. Rather, teenagers benefit in their development by remaining connected with their parents and by using them as important resources in their lives. This effect is most notable when the parenting style is authoritative (Kim, Hetherington, & Reiss, 1999).

For issues involving the specifics of social life—including matters of clothing, hairstyles, personal adornment, dating, drinking, musical tastes, and entertainment idols—teenagers are more attuned to the opinions and standards of their peer group (Lau, Quadrel, & Hartman, 1990). Time with peers is spent hanging out, playing games, joking, and conversing. Teenagers report that they look to interaction with friends to produce "good times" (Larson, 2001). They characterize these positive times as containing an element of "rowdiness": They act "crazy," "out of control," "loud," and even "obnoxious"—deviant behavior that they describe as "fun." Such activities provide a spirited, contagious mood, a group state in which they feel free to do virtually anything. The extent and intimacy of peer relationships increases dramatically between middle childhood and adolescence (Larson, 2000, 2001; Larson et al., 2001).

Much of the similarity found in the attitudes and behaviors of friends is the result of people purposely selecting as friends individuals who are already compatible with them. Not surprisingly, therefore, adoles-cents who share similar political orientations, values, and levels of educational aspiration are more likely to associate with one another and then to influence one another as a result of continued association. Additionally, parents often seek to nudge their youngsters toward "crowds" consistent with their family's values (Brown & Huang, 1995).

More importantly, parents somewhat retain control over their teenager's choice of peers through their selection of the neighborhood in which the family resides or the school (public or private) the youngster attends. The U.S. Census 2000 estimates that 15 million youth, mainly minorities, reside with families in poor neighborhoods. A growing body of research documents that such teens have poorer developmental and life outcomes compared with teens from advantaged neighborhoods. In a recent study, *Moving to Opportunity (MOT) for Fair Housing*, nearly 800 poor families volunteered to be randomly assigned to three types of neighborhoods and were given vouchers to relocate to less poor neighborhoods of their choice or stay in the same poor neighborhood. Leventhal and Brooks-Gunn (2004) report findings from the New York City sample that moved from high-poverty to low-poverty neighborhoods. Adolescent boys' whose families moved to low-poverty neighborhoods spent more hours doing homework, scored much higher on standardized tests, had lower rates of grade retention, and had fewer school suspensions/expulsions than the control group of adolescent peers in high-poverty neighborhoods. Obeidallah and colleagues (2004) found that early-maturing girls who were engaged in violent behavior lived in highly disadvantaged neighborhoods.

For many youth, the right to choose friends is often more important than the choice itself. It signals that their parents recognize their maturity and growing autonomy. Some evidence suggests that adolescents who believe that their parents are not providing them with sufficient space—that their parents are not relaxing their power and restrictiveness—are apt to acquire more extreme peer orientations and to seek out more opportunities for peer advice (Fuligni & Eccles, 1993). Additionally, psychological overcontrol, as well as behavioral undercontrol, places youngsters at greater risk for problem behaviors (Kim, Hetherington, & Reiss, 1999). Disagreements between parents and their teenage offspring occur primarily over differing interpretations of issues and the extent and legitimacy of the youngsters' personal jurisdiction (Larson & Verma, 1999).

The functional constraints provided by the family and the excitement by friends both have their part to play in development (Kim, Hetherington, & Reiss, 1999). Even so, parents and adolescents frequently differ in their perception of the extent to which continuity prevails in values, beliefs, and attitudes across generations.

Teens and Parents Over time, the cohesion or emotional closeness between parent(s) and child ideally becomes transformed from one of dependency to a more balanced connectedness that permits the adolescent to develop as a distinct individual capable of assuming adult status and roles.

Shift in the Family Power Equation   We have seen that from early adolescence to late adolescence, the cohesion or emotional closeness between parent and child ideally becomes transformed from one of considerable dependency to a more balanced connectedness that permits the youngster to develop as a distinct individual capable of assuming adult status and roles. Across adolescence, parents typically make increasingly less use of unilateral power strategies and greater use of strategies that share power with their youngsters—but nearly all young teens report varying degrees of conflict intensity along the path to independence-seeking (Allison & Schultz, 2004). Parents of teens report the most intense conflicts with high school teens with irritating/disruptive behaviors at home, negative personal/moral characteristics, home and school performance, punctuality/curfews, and personal autonomy. Less intense conflicts occur over room care, household chores, inconsiderate behavior, television viewing, personal appearance, and personal hygiene (Allison & Schultz, 2004).

Adolescents and Their Mothers   Mothers typically are more informed and concerned about their adolescents' social relations, because they spend more time monitoring their teens' whereabouts and activities—thus they experience more conflicts (Updegraff et al., 2001). Overall, American adolescent girls receive more mixed messages about their relationship with their mothers than boys do about their fathers. Growing up requires adolescent girls to reject the person with whom they have most closely identified—their mother. Daughters are socialized to fear becoming like their mothers. A great insult to most teenage girls is to say, "Oh, you are just like your mother." Today mothers (and fathers) often don't seem to understand the difficult world their daughters are experiencing. Rosalind Wiseman in *Queen Bees and Wannabes: Helping Your Daughter Survive Cliques, Gossip, Boyfriends, and Other Realities of Adolescence* (2002) states that "many parents do not understand the there is a dangerous hierarchy—from the 'Queen Bee' who dictates rules such as who wears what and who dates whom, to the 'Wannabe' trying to ingratiate herself into a clique or the poor 'Target' of a clique's wrath." African American teens in late adolescence often view their mothers as a source of support and guidance and report more emotional closeness to mothers than to fathers (Smetana, Metzger, & Campione-Barr, 2004).

Clinical psychologist Mary Pipher (1994, p. 107) relates an all-too-common first therapy session with a teenage girl she calls "Jessica," whose mother (a single parent and social worker) had devoted her life to her daughter:

Dr. Pipher: How are you different from your mom?
Jessica: (smirking) "I totally disagree with her about everything. I hate school; she likes school. I hate to work; she likes to work. I like MTV and she hates it. I wear black, and she never does. She wants me

to live up to my potential, and I think she's full of shit. . . . I want to be a model. Mom hates the idea."

Fortunately, it appears that many young women return to closeness with their mothers when they enter young adulthood, particularly after they have had their own children.

Wainright and colleagues (2004) studied a subset of adolescents from the *National Longitudinal Study of Adolescent Health* with opposite-sex parents and same-sex female parents and found that a close parent-child relationship was a more important indicator of psychosocial adjustment and school achievement than family type.

Question

In what areas do teens typically seek out family for advice and support, and when are they likely to seek out friends for advice and support?

Courtship, Love, and Sexuality

One of the most difficult adjustments, and perhaps the most critical, that adolescents must make revolves around their developing sexuality. Biological maturity and social pressures require that adolescents come to terms with awakening sexual impulses. And young teens are being bombarded by the sexualized messages of the culture in movies, advertising, and clothing styles to express their sexuality at even younger ages. Consequently, sexual attraction and sexual considerations become dominant forces in their lives (Longmore, Manning, & Giordano, 2001; Wu & Thomson, 2001). Indeed, first sexual intercourse is a developmental milestone of major personal and social significance and is often viewed as a declaration of independence from parents, an affirmation of sexual identity, and a statement of capacity for interpersonal intimacy.

Adolescent sexuality is a matter that commands considerable societal concern. Since the 1980s rising rates of nonmarital adolescent births and STIs have become symbols of such social ills as poverty, welfare dependence, child neglect and abuse, and AIDS. In the past decade the rates of U.S. teen births have declined by 30 percent to an all-time low with the birthrate for African American teens down 40 percent (Centers for Disease Control and Prevention, 2003d). There are many approaches to further reduce unsafe sexual behaviors among teens:

• The *public health/preventive medicine perspective* sees the issue as a problem of unintended pregnancy that is best addressed by sex education, birth control, and abortion programs and services.
• The *conservative moral view* considers teenage pregnancy to be a problem of precocious sexual activity and advocates abstinence.

- The *economic approach* defines the difficulty as prevalent among ethnic-minority adolescent mothers on welfare who require training to become economically self-sufficient.
- The *social contagion view* considers early sexual initiation as normative behavior among young cohorts, and parents must educate about dangers.

Clearly, the matter of teenage pregnancy is a flash point for intense public passion and debate, exacerbating tensions of gender, race, and class. The matter is further complicated by its linkage to other vexing issues such as abortion, adoption, babies born at risk, special education services, health care for children with disabilities, welfare reform, absentee fathers, and political and taxation policies.

Differing Behavioral Patterns

Youth vary a good deal in the age at which they first experience intercourse (a large proportion of all sexual exposure of females before the age of 14 is involuntary). Contemporary earlier pubertal development applies a downward pressure on the age of sexual debut. Sociologist J. Richard Udry (1988) and his colleagues report strong evidence for a hormonal basis of sexual motivation and behavior, particularly in adolescent males. Interventions that involve parents to reinforce school-based prevention curricula have been found to have an impact on adolescent sexual behavior (Blake et al., 2001). Young people who remain virgins longer than their peers are more likely to value academic achievement, enjoy close ties with their parents, report stricter moral standards, begin dating later, and exhibit more conventional behavior with respect to alcohol and drug use. However, virgins are decidedly not "maladjusted," socially marginal, or otherwise unsuccessful. They report no less satisfaction and no more stress than nonvirgins, and they typically achieve greater educational success than nonvirgins. Furthermore, in many cases teenagers, especially girls, select as their friends individuals whose sexual behavior is similar to their own (Romer et al., 1999).

Aspects of family life also affect adolescent sexual behavior. Generally speaking, the earlier the mother's first sexual experience and first birth, the earlier the daughter's sexual experience. And teenagers with older, sexually active siblings are more likely to begin sexual intercourse at an earlier age (Rodgers & Buster, 1998). Living in poverty also tends to be associated with early sexual activity and early pregnancy. Unwed adolescent pregnancies are several times more likely to occur among youth with poor academic skills and from economically disadvantaged families. Moreover, adolescents, especially daughters, from single-parent households typically begin sexual activity at younger ages than do their peers from two-parent families. A number of factors contribute to the higher rates of sex-

ual activity among teens in single-parent families (Kinsman et al., 1998): (1) there is often less parental supervision in single-parent households; (2) single parents are themselves often dating, and their sexual behavior provides a role model for their youngsters; and (3) adolescents and parents who have experienced divorce tend to have more permissive attitudes about sexual activity outside of marriage.

Adolescent sexual behavior is shaped not only by individual characteristics but also by the surrounding neighborhood context. Communities characterized by limited economic resources, racial and ethnic segregation, and disorganization apparently provide young people with little motivation to avoid early childbearing. The opportunity structures available to many inner-city youth, particularly those relating to education and jobs, often lead youth to conclude that legitimate pathways to social mobility are effectively closed to them. A concentration of poverty, crowded housing conditions, high levels of crime, unemployment, marital dissolution, and inadequate public services engenders a social climate of apathy and fatalism (Romer et al., 1999).

In sum, behavior is shaped by the characteristics of the communities in which teens live with their cohort (Santelli et al., 2000). These communities have fewer adult role models of economic and social success. Where few adult women are able to find stable, sufficient employment, the potential costs of sexual activity in terms of future occupational attainment appear minimal to some female adolescents. Indeed, a variety of social factors encourage teenage girls to become pregnant. For instance, in some ethnic groups having a baby symbolizes maturity and entrance into adulthood (getting one's own apartment, welfare check, and food stamps), and peers often ridicule teens who remain chaste.

Courtship

In the United States, dating traditionally has been the principal vehicle for fostering and developing sexual relations, or "courtship." Dating began with a young man inviting a young woman for an evening's public entertainment at his expense. The first invitation was often given during a nervous conversation on the telephone several days or even weeks in advance. Ideally, the man would call for the woman at the appointed hour in a car and return her by car. Although the traditional pattern has not entirely been replaced, new patterns of courtship swept in on the wave of the youth movements of the late 1960s and early 1970s (Davies & Windle, 2000). The term *dating* itself became too stiff and formal to describe the "just hanging out" and "getting together" that took place among a group of youth (Davies & Windle, 2000). A more relaxed style came to govern the interaction between the sexes, including roving in groups through malls and informal get-togethers. In a recent study of adolescent dating patterns, girls were much more likely than boys to report being in a steady dating relationship (Davies & Windle, 2000).

Many teenage males report that they do not date—or refuse to admit to it. It seems that growing numbers of young men "do not want to look soft" to their friends. This fear, and a desire to demonstrate their manhood, leads many teenage males to abuse or show disrespect to girls (behaviors they carry into young adulthood). Teenage males (and some females) report that they gain popularity by yelling explicit propositions at or fondling females/males who pass by, all the while competing with one another to demonstrate the most flair and audacity in "talking trash" and "making moves." A recent AAUW (2001b) report, *Hostile Hallways: Bullying, Teasing, and Sexual Harassment in School*, reveals a majority of adolescent boys and girls say they experience harassment, but a smaller percentage report being the perpetrators. Additionally, some cohorts of young men view fathering children as a sign of manhood, but one that does not necessarily include marrying the mother or supporting the child.

Love

In the United States nearly everyone is expected to fall in love eventually. Pulp literature, "soap operas," "brides only" and traditional "male" publications, movies, the Internet, and popular music reverberate with themes of

The Concept of Romantic Love Social scientists have found it difficult to define the concept of romantic love. Some say it is recognized by physiological arousal, some say it is a unique chemical reaction that activates the brain's pleasure centers, and others say it is associated with a special transcendent feeling. From a cross-cultural view, the concept of romantic love is not universal.

romantic ecstasy. In sharp contrast to the U.S. arrangement, consider the words of the elders of an African tribe. They were complaining to the 1883 Commission on Native Law and Custom about the problems of "runaway" marriages and illegitimacy:

> It is all this thing called love. We do not understand it at all.
> This thing called love has been introduced.
> (Gluckman, 1955, p. 76)

These elders viewed romantic love as a disruptive force. In their culture marriage did not necessarily involve a feeling of attraction for the spouse-to-be; marriage was not the free choice of the couple marrying; and considerations other than love played the most important part in mate selection. In many non-Western countries of the world, marriage is often preplanned by the parents of the prospective bride and groom, and there is some financial exchange for assurance of the virginity of the bride. Furthermore, in some Middle Eastern, African, and Asian countries, the wife then becomes the property of the husband, a practice abandoned in Western countries early in the 1900s.

Clearly, then, different societies view romantic love quite differently (Gao, 2001; Jankowiak & Fischer, 1992). At one extreme are societies that consider a strong love attraction to be a laughable or tragic aberration. At the other extreme are societies that define marriage without love as shameful. American society tends to insist on love; traditional Japan and China tend to regard it as irrelevant; ancient Greece in the period after Alexander, and ancient Rome during the Roman Empire, fell somewhere in the middle (Goode, 1959). It seems that the capacity for romantic love is universal, but its forms and extent to which the capacity gets translated into everyday life are highly dependent on social and cultural factors (Goleman, 1992, 1995b; Hendrick & Hendrick, 1992).

All of us are familiar with the concept of romantic love, yet social scientists find it exceedingly difficult to define, so it is little wonder that many Americans—especially teenagers—are also uncertain about what love is supposed to feel like and how they can recognize the experience within themselves. Some social psychologists conclude that romantic love is simply an agitated state of physiological arousal that individuals come to define as love. The stimuli producing the agitated state might be sexual arousal, gratitude, anxiety, guilt, loneliness, anger, confusion, or fear. What makes these diffuse physiological reactions love, they say, is that individuals label them as love.

Some researchers reject the notion that love and other states of physiological arousal are interchangeable except for the label we give them. For instance, Michael R. Liebowitz (1983) says that love has a unique chemical basis and that love and romance are among the most powerful activators of the brain's pleasure centers. And they may also contribute to a special transcendent feeling—a sense of being beyond time, space, and one's own body. Intense romantic attractions trigger neurochemical reactions that produce effects much like those produced by psychedelic drugs. Just how such brain chemistry changes are experienced as feelings of love is unknown. What is known, however, is that as a romantic relationship becomes more serious, couples become more passionate, intimate, and committed (Gao, 2001).

> ### Questions
>
> Is the idea of romantic love a universal concept? How does the feeling called love manifest itself in physical, psychological, or emotional ways?

Sexual Attitudes and Behavior

Although we commonly equate adolescent sexuality with heterosexual intercourse, sexual expression takes a good many different forms. Furthermore, sexuality begins early in life and merely takes on more adult forms during adolescence.

Development of Sexual Behavior Both male and female infants show interest in exploring their own bodies, initially in a random and indiscriminate fashion. Even at 4 months of age babies respond to genital stimulation in a manner that suggests that they are experiencing erotic pleasure. When children reach 2 and 3 years of age, they will investigate their playmates' genitals and, if permitted, those of adults as well. But by this time strong social prohibitions come into effect, and children are socialized to restrain these behaviors.

Masturbation, or erotic self-stimulation, is common among children. In many cases children experience their first orgasm through self-stimulation. It might occur through the fondling of the penis or the manual stimulation of the clitoris or by rubbing against a bedcover, mattress, toy, or other object. Boys often learn about masturbation from other boys, whereas girls learn to masturbate primarily through accidental discovery (Kinsey et al., 1953; Kinsey, Pomeroy, & Martin, 1948).

A good many children also engage in some form of sex play with other children prior to adolescence. The activity is usually sporadic and typically does not culminate in orgasm. On the basis of his research in the 1940s and early 1950s, Alfred C. Kinsey and his associates (1948, 1953) found that the peak age for sex play among girls was 9, when about 7 percent engaged in heterosexual play and 9 percent in homosexual play. The peak age for boys was 12, when 23 percent participated in heterosexual play and 30 percent in homosexual play. But Kinsey believed that his reported figures were too low and that about a fifth of all girls and the vast majority of all boys had engaged in sex play with other children before reaching puberty.

Adolescent Sexual Expression Adolescent sexuality finds expression in a number of ways: masturbation, nocturnal orgasm, heterosexual petting, heterosexual intercourse, oral sex, and homosexual activity. Teenage masturbatory behavior is often accompanied by erotic fantasy. One study of 13- to 19-year-olds found that 57 percent of the males and 46 percent of the females reported that they fantasized on most occasions while masturbating; about 20 percent of the males and 10 percent of the females rarely or never fantasized when masturbating (Sorensen, 1973). Many myths have attributed harmful effects to masturbation, but the physiological harmlessness of the practice has now been so thoroughly documented by medical authorities that there is no need to belabor the issue. Even so, some individuals might feel guilty about the practice for social, religious, or moral reasons.

Adolescent boys commonly begin experiencing nocturnal orgasms, or "wet dreams," between ages 13 and 15. Erotic dreams that are accompanied by orgasm and ejaculation occur most commonly among men in their teens and twenties and less frequently later in life. Women also have erotic dreams that culminate in orgasm, but apparently they are less frequent among women than among men.

Petting refers to erotic caressing that may or may not lead to orgasm. If it eventuates in sexual intercourse, petting is more accurately termed "foreplay." Heterosexual and homosexual relations involve petting. Over 50 percent of all adolescents report engaging in petting (Haffner, 1999). Yet those adolescents with higher academic achievement reported postponing any partnered sexual activities—even kissing (Halpern et al., 2000).

A Little History . . . The past 40 years has seen substantial changes in U.S. attitudes toward teenage sexual activity. An American societal change called the *sexual revolution* came about during the Vietnam War years, appearing mainly after 1965, along with availability of the birth control pill. Orgies, partner swapping, and love-ins were implicitly promoted in films, music, and advertising in the late 1960s. The original Woodstock generation symbolized the idea of "free love" and communal living. This period altered the sexual landscape in that sexual attitudes and experimentation became much more relaxed—until the advent of AIDS in the early 1980s.

Today's teens are bombarded with mixed messages about premarital sex. Parents, teachers, politicians, and health professionals promote risk-reducing behaviors, yet the media assail adolescents and adults alike with sexual stimuli on an unprecedented scale. A decreasing proportion of teenagers are sexually active, but a small percentage begins sexual activity at earlier ages. Although the number of very young teens (10- to 14-year-olds) having babies has declined to levels not seen since the 1940s, more than 7,000 gave birth in 2002 (Menacker et al., 2004). According to a national sampling of students grades 9 through 12, nearly half of the country's adolescents have had sexual intercourse (and a small percentage have had multiple sex partners) by the time they are in their senior year of high school (see Tables 12.1 and 12.2) (Grunbaum et al., 2004). Note that these statistics do not include the sexual activity of adolescents who are no longer in the school system.

Adolescent Sexual Activity Rates The rates of teenage sexual experience increased throughout the 1980s but continue to decline since the early 1990s (Ventura et al., 2004). To determine recent trends in sexual risk behaviors among U.S. high school students, the Centers for Disease Control and Prevention (CDC) conducted the *Youth Risk Behavior Surveillance (YRBS), 2003* (Grunbaum et al., 2004). The survey found that about a third of the students surveyed nationwide had engaged in sexual activity three months prior. Of those adolescents, two-thirds reported that they or their partner had used a condom. Results of the survey also indicated that the highest prevalence of sexual activity was among black youth (49 percent), followed by Hispanic youth (37 percent), and white youth (31 percent).

Multiple Sex Partners Social scientists also see a significant downward trend in the number of teens in high school who are engaging in sex with multiple partners (four or more). The same Youth Risk Behavior Surveillance, 2003 reveals that over 14 percent of respondents had had mul-

Table 12.2 Percentage of High School Students Who Have Had Multiple Sex Partners (Four or More Partners During Lifetime), by Grade Level, Sex, and Race/Ethnicity: 1991 and 2003

	1991 (*N*=12,272)	2003 (*N*=15,240)
Grade		
9th	12.5%	10.4%
10th	15.1	12.6
11th	22.1	16.0
12th	25.0	20.3
Sex		
Male	23.4	17.5
Female	13.8	11.2
Race/Ethnicity		
Non-Hispanic white	14.7	10.8
Non-Hispanic black	43.1	28.8
Hispanic	16.8	15.7
Overall Total	**18.7%**	**14.4%**

Source: Centers for Disease Control and Prevention conducted the *Youth Risk Behavior Survey (YRBS)* biannually since 1991. Reported in the *Morbidity and Mortality Weekly Report, 47,* No. 36 (September 18, 1998), p. 751, Table 1. And *Youth Risk Behavior Surveillance—United States, 2003. Morbidity and Mortality Weekly Report, 53,* SS-2 (May 21, 2004), p. 71, Table 42.

Table 12.1 Percentage of High School Students Who Have Had Sexual Intercourse, by Grade Level, Sex, and Race/Ethnicity: 1991 and 2003

	1991 (*N* = 12,272)	2003 (*N* = 15,240)
Grade		
9th	39.0%	32.8%
10th	48.2	44.1
11th	62.4	53.2
12th	66.7	61.6
Sex		
Male	57.4	48.0
Female	50.8	45.3
Race/Ethnicity		
Non-Hispanic white	50.0	41.8
Non-Hispanic black	81.4	67.3
Hispanic	53.1	51.4
Overall Total	**54.1%**	**46.7%**

Source: Centers for Disease Control and Prevention conducted the *Youth Risk Behavior Survey (YRBS)* biannually since 1991. Reported in the *Morbidity and Mortality Weekly Report, 47,* No. 36 (September 18, 1998), p. 751, Table 1. And *Youth Risk Behavior Surveillance—United States, 2003. Morbidity and Mortality Weekly Report, 53,* SS-2 (May 21, 2004), p. 71, Table 42.

tiple partners (see Table 12.2) (Grunbaum et al., 2004). In 2003, nearly one out of five male students reported having multiple sex partners. Prevalence of multiple sex partners is lower among female students (11 percent). The higher rate of multiple sexual partners among American teens compared with teens in other developed countries explains why American teenagers have higher rates of sexually transmitted infections (STIs) (Darroch, Singh, & Frost, 2001).

Teenage Pregnancy

Teenage single parenthood is a major social problem associated with many negative outcomes for the mother, child, and society. According to the National Center for Health Statistics, overall birthrates for adolescents dropped to record lows since the early 1990s (Ventura et al., 2004).

However, one-third of young women still get pregnant at least once before the age of 20. There are about 820,000 pregnancies each year of women under the age of 20. Black women aged 15 to 19 experienced a significant birth rate decline during the 1990s to the present and Hispanic teen birthrates also declined considerably. However, these two groups have higher rates of teen pregnancy and births than other groups. Only about one-third of teen mothers finishes high school and gets a diploma, and only a very small percentage earns a college degree before age 30. A majority of teen mothers end up getting welfare and social services support. It is estimated that the U.S. federal government spends about $7 billion annually on teenage pregnancy and childbearing ("General Facts and Stats," 2002).

Early childbearing also has significant implications for the children of teen parents. The children have lower birth weights, often require early intervention services, and suffer other social risk factors. Inept parenting, poor health care, child neglect, and child abuse are more common among teenage parents. Moreover, children of younger parents tend to score lower than children of older parents on intelligence tests, and they typically do less well in school. The sons of teen mothers are at higher risk of ending up in prison, and the daughters are more likely to become teen parents themselves ("General Facts and Stats," 2002).

Although the U.S. teen birthrate has been falling, it is still much higher than the rates of other industrialized nations—more than twice that of Canada and eight times the rate of Japan (*United Nations Demographic Yearbook 2001*, 2003) (see Figure 12.2). American youth are exposed to conflicting messages about contraception, and there is tremendous controversy about making birth control or

abortion services easily accessible to the nation's teens. Although the majority of teen pregnancies are unintended, some think that having a baby will provide someone who will love them and make them feel grown up. Ultimately, the decision to keep the baby, sign for adoption, or have an abortion is one of the most difficult and consequential a woman faces in her life—and many more teens are deciding to keep the baby, although more than half of teen pregnancies terminate by abortion or miscarriage.

Why Do Teenagers Become Pregnant?   Most teenagers do not consciously plan to become sexually active, and so they do not foresee their first sexual experience. Instead, they often experience their first sexual encounter as something that "just happened." Moreover, most teenagers wait almost a year after becoming sexually active before they seek medically supervised contraceptive care. Adolescents frequently have a sense of invulnerability and fail to associate consequences with actions. Other associative factors for female teenage sexual activity include coercion by male partners (Wulfert & Biglan, 1994); early childhood or physical trauma often leading to early onset

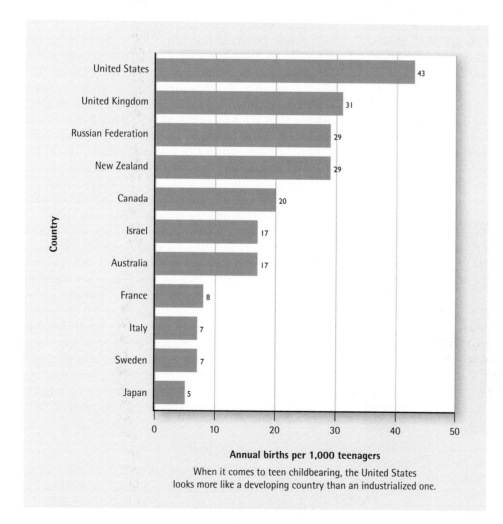

FIGURE 12.2 Early Motherhood in the Industrialized World Although the U.S. adolescent birth rate has fallen, it is still much higher than in other industrialized countries.
Source: United Nations Demographic Yearbook 2001. (2003). New York: United Nations.

When it comes to teen childbearing, the United States looks more like a developing country than an industrialized one.

of illegal drug use, affecting the judgment and increasing incidence of unprotected sex; procrastination about birth control; unrealistic expectations about having a baby; lack of impulse control; a conscious desire to seek welfare dependency; and a low sense of self-esteem or girls not wanting to lose their man (fear of abandonment) (Moore & Chase-Lansdale, 2001; Young et al., 2001).

The Young Teen Mother   The younger a girl is at the onset of sexual activity, the more likely it was due to unwanted or involuntary sex (Menacker et al., 2004). Worldwide, over 13 million teens give birth each year—mostly in developing countries. It is estimated that more than 70,000 girls between the ages of 15 and 19 die each year during pregnancy and childbirth, and infant mortality of children born to teenagers is at least 1 million infants each year (Save the Children, 2004).

Sex Education, "Safe Sex," Contraception, and Abstinence Education   Sex education advocates and parents often operate on the mistaken notion of the "rational teenager" who, when given "the facts," will either abstain from sex or use contraception. These strategies tend to ignore the cognitive qualities of mind that are a prerequisite for making complex interpersonal decisions. When asked why they do not use birth control, teenagers give answers such as "not wanting to," "feels better without it," "don't think about it," or "want to get pregnant." Others give multiple answers involving lack of knowledge or access, being afraid or embarrassed, not expecting to need contraception or not wanting to take the time, and not being worried about pregnancy (Glei, 1999). Significantly, as adolescents become more sexually experienced, they tend to become more consistent contraceptive users.

The Young Teen Mother Although rates of teen sexual activity continue to decline to levels not seen since the 1950s, annually there are still thousands of teenage girls who become pregnant and give birth and decide to keep their babies. Teen motherhood is a life-changing experience, posing many economic, emotional, social, and academic challenges.

Since 1997, federal abstinence-only education programs have been funded with over half a billion dollars. Abstinence-only education requires that educators teach about the social, physiological, and health gains from abstaining from sex (Dailard, 2002). Critics denounce the abstinence approach to sex education, but it is noteworthy that U.S. teen sex and pregnancy rates have declined to levels not seen since the 1950s since a values-added approach was mandated. A majority of teens say they want parents to keep the lines of communication open; media should stop making sex more glamorous than it really is; faith communities should provide more guidance; and all teens should be more responsible ("What Teens Want," 2000).

Polls indicate that most American parents want their children to abstain from sex until they finish high school, yet many also want schools to teach sex education. Advocates of abstinence argue that teaching about "safe sex" is dishonest because condoms do not prevent transmission of several STIs and that teaching about birth control gives teenagers approval to have sex. They also say that decades of teaching our teens about "safe sex" has created a generation of teens who treat sex casually and irresponsibly and promotes easy access to confidential services offering contraceptives and abortions. Critics in the medical community contend that not teaching about "safe sex" leaves our youth defenseless (Koch, 1998). Apparently, the definition of abstinence is misunderstood by many teens. Results of a college undergraduate survey revealed that more than half of students surveyed did not define oral-genital contact as "having sex"—putting them at great risk for STIs (Goodsen et al., 2003). Many professionals agree that parents must play a more active role in combating the national epidemic of teen pregnancies, abortions, and STIs by discussing birth control and contraception.

Abortion   The Centers for Disease Control and Prevention has gathered data on women obtaining abortions since the early 1970s, and since 1990 the number of legally induced abortions for teenagers aged 15 to 19 years has declined significantly (see Figure 12.3) (CDC, 2004a). This decline is due to many factors: More teens are carrying babies to term and keeping their children, attitudes about abortion have changed, contraceptive use has increased, and unintended pregnancies have decreased. Teenage birthrates have decreased, and right-to-life advocates have campaigned rigorously about partial-birth abortion, and abortion laws that affect adolescents (e.g., laws denying parental notification or consent and eliminating mandatory waiting periods) have changed (Koonin et al., 2000).

Sexual Orientation

Because contemporary American society is more open about sexuality issues, research on sexual orientation among adolescents is receiving more attention than in the past. A recent national study of nearly 12,000 students

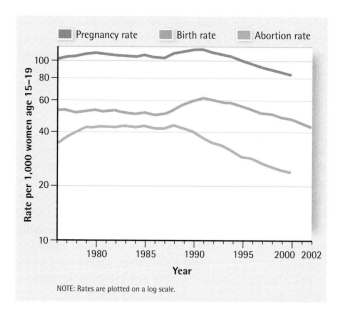

FIGURE 12.3 Pregnancy, Birth, and Abortion Rates for Teenagers 15 to 19 Years Rates have declined significantly over the past decade.
Source: Ventura, S. J., Abma, J. C., Mosher, W. D., & Henshaw, S. (2004). Estimated pregnancy rates for the United States, 1990–2000: An update. *National Vital Statistics Reports, 53*(23). Hyattsville, MD: National Center for Health Statistics.

in grades 9 to 12 found that more than 7 percent of boys and 5 percent of girls reported romantic attraction to same-sex peers, but same-sex relationships were reported by 1 percent of boys and 2 percent of girls (Russell & Joyner, 2001). By age 18, most youth deem themselves to be heterosexual or homosexual, with some 5 percent still "unsure" of their orientation (Russell & Joyner, 2001).

A mounting body of evidence suggests that growing up lesbian or gay is often a difficult journey toward self-acceptance, and research suggests that lesbian teens may be the most distressed (Russell & Joyner, 2001). A recent study found a link between self-harm behaviors and homosexual men and women (Skegg et al., 2003). For youth who are lesbian, gay, or bisexual, the social pressures are intense. To be different is especially difficult during adolescence, when conformity is celebrated and minor differences can mean ostracism. In middle schools and high schools youngsters call one another a great many names, but few labels are more humiliating than a label of "gay." Overall, the victimization of lesbians and gay men through either verbal harassment or physical assault is the most common kind of bias-related violence. Because they are subjected to more social pressures, researchers looked at whether or not suicide rates are higher among sexual-minority youth. This resulted in contradictory findings. One study found that although a small number of sexual-minority youth are at a greater risk for attempted suicide, it is not appropriate to characterize the entire population of sexual-minority youth as at risk (Savin-Williams & Ream, 2003).

Especially troubling is the adolescent's fear of disclosing his or her sexual orientation to family and friends. Thus, many young lesbians and gays keep their feelings hidden. Should they seek out school counselors, clergy, or physicians for help, they are often advised to "go straight." Such sentiments leave lesbians and gays feeling alienated, lonely, depressed, and for some at higher risk of suicide (Russell & Joyner, 2001). Additionally, although heterosexual teenagers learn how to date and establish relationships, lesbian and gay youth are often precluded from such opportunities. Instead, they learn to hide their true feelings. Recent research also indicates that during adolescence children begin to develop gender schemas (perceptions) about heterosexual and homosexual personality traits. It seems that at around the age of 12, heterosexual males and females are seen as more feminine than their gay and lesbian counterparts, a perception that disappears with the advent of adolescence (Mallet, Apostolidis, & Paty, 1997).

A few adolescent homosexual experiences do not necessarily mean a lifetime of homosexuality. Genital exhibition, demonstration of masturbation, group masturbation, and related activities are not uncommon among group-oriented preteen boys (Katchadourian, 1984). This prepubescent homosexual play generally stops at puberty. However, adult homosexuals typically report that their homosexual orientation had already been established before they reached puberty (Mallet et al., 1997). Most teenage boys do not regard their playful sexual contact with other boys as "homosexual" and transition to predominantly heterosexual relationships. In addition to questioning themselves about "Who am I?" most teens in late adolescence are also wrestling with "What am I going to do with the rest of my life?"

Career Development and Vocational Choice

A critical developmental task confronting adolescents involves making a variety of vocational decisions. In the United States, as in other Western societies, the jobs people hold have significant implications for their adult development life course. The positions they assume in the labor force influence their general lifestyle, the quality of the neighborhoods in which they reside, important aspects of their self-concept, their children's life chances, and most of their relationships with others in the community (Link, Lennon, & Dohrenwend, 1993). Additionally, employment ties individuals into the wider social system and give them a sense of purpose and meaning in life.

Preparing for the World of Work

One focus of the transition from childhood to adulthood is preparation for finding and keeping a job in the adult years. Given the importance of the job-entry process, adolescents are ill-prepared for making vocational decisions and for being successful in college to prepare for jobs of the twenty-first century (Achieve, 2005; Greene & Winters, 2005). Most teenagers have only vague ideas about what they are able to do successfully, what they would enjoy doing, what requirements are attached to given jobs, what the current job market is like, and what it will probably be like in the future. Complicating matters, many youth do not see a relationship between their current academic endeavors and their future employment opportunities—until it is too late. Youngsters given to antisocial behaviors are at risk for low academic achievement and school failure, and so they compromise their later job marketability. Of course, many teenagers work—but if they seek and gain work during their teen years, their working can have far-reaching consequences for their relationships with their parents, schooling, acceptance and status among their peers, and standard of living and lifestyle (Lamborn, Dornbusch, & Steinberg, 1996).

Some teens encounter special difficulties in entering the job market—especially females, teens with disabilities, and teens from racial and ethnic minorities. Gender differences surface early, mirroring those of the adult work world (Mau & Kopischke, 2001). Young men are more likely than young women to be employed as manual laborers, newspaper deliverers, and recreation aides, whereas young women are more likely to work as clerical workers, retail sales clerks, child-care workers, health aides, and education aides. Gender segregation also occurs within industries. Among food service workers, young men more often work with things (they cook food, bus tables, and wash dishes), whereas young women more often work with people (they fill orders and serve as waitresses and hostesses).

Changing Employment Trends in the United States

For many U.S. teenagers a steady, decent-paying job is a distant hope. High rates of unemployment have traditionally been the lot of many young people, especially African Americans. Twenty-five years ago young people in the United States could find a job in manufacturing, construction, or sales and expect to make a career of it. But increasingly, young Americans without skills, and often those with them, cannot count on good wages and steady work due to the economic effects of globalization. Even college graduates may be in for more difficult times. Economists have calculated that although skill levels in the workplace rose, the supply of college graduates rose even more rapidly.

Society pays a high price for the unemployment and underemployment of its adolescents and young adults. Adolescents whose jobs supported rather than displaced academic pursuits and provided learning opportunities led to lower rates of school deviance, alcohol use, and arrests among twelfth-graders (Staff & Uggen, 2003).

However, when adolescents take on "intensive" employment, it results in lower grades, lower educational goals, emotional alienation from parents as well as increased delinquency, cigarette smoking, alcohol usage, and marijuana smoking (Paternoster et al., 2003).

Balancing Work and School

Many of today's teens are already working while attending high school (Gehring, 2000). A federally funded study of 12,000 students in grades 7 to 12 conducted by the University of Minnesota and the University of North Carolina shows teens who work 20 hours or more a week during the school year are more likely to be emotionally distressed, drink, smoke, use drugs, and have early sex. About one-third of teens in a recent survey said work limits their participation and achievement in school, sports, and social activities (Gehring, 2000). The bottom line, say counselors, parents, and therapists, is that these youth struggle with balancing daily responsibilities. Good working conditions can boost a teen's morale and motivation to continue an education, but bad working conditions can hurt morale, lower self-esteem, and be a factor in dropping out of high school (Shellenbarger, 1997).

Graduation Rates and Dropout Rates

In 2005 an annual, national high school graduation study conducted by the Manhattan Institute combined state data with U.S. Department of Education data and reported that the overall public high school graduation rate in 2002 was 71 percent. Several states had the highest high school graduation rates at 85 percent each. Several southern states had the lowest high school graduation

Part-Time Employment for Teenagers The jobs that are open to teenagers typically involve repetitive operations that require few skills. Although it is commonly assumed that youth gain on-the-job training, they actually derive very little that is technically useful to them. But they do gain a "work orientation" and practical knowledge of how the business world operates.

rates, each around 50 percent (Greene & Winters, 2005). The findings also indicate a wide disparity in graduation rates of white and minority students. In 2002, about 78 percent of white students graduated from public high schools, compared with just over half of African American and Hispanic students. Official statistics from national government sources report that 87 percent of high school students graduated in 2001—but this data encompass both high school graduates and those who earn their General Education Diploma, or GED (equivalency diploma), by the age of 24 (Federal Interagency Forum on Child and Family Statistics, 2004).

So what is the accurate figure about high school graduation rates—thus revealing dropout data—you might ask. The actual U.S. high school dropout rate is a multifaceted figure to determine because school districts, states, and federal agencies use different definitions, calculations, and jargon (event dropout rate, attrition rate, status rate, and others). States' compulsory school attendance also varies from age 16 to 18. Student mobility from one school district to another is not tracked (except in Texas), nor are districts required to report middle school dropout statistics in the overall picture (Kronholz, 2001). It is difficult to track students who graduate from private high schools, alternative high schools, or earn a GED diploma later. Thus, in reviewing the two recent studies above, it appears that the U.S. high school *dropout rate* is between 13 to 30 percent.

Moreover, dropout rates vary greatly by student socioeconomic status, race/ethnicity (see Figure 12.4), gender, and locale. Students from poor families, more males than females, more minorities, pregnant teens, and those with academic difficulty are likely to leave school (Hood, 2004). In 2002 the federal government mandated higher standards with *No Child Left Behind,* more school accountability, reporting of dropout statistics, and incentives for districts to make gains (Wirt et al., 2004). As such, dropout rates will now be reported to federal agencies, and schools must raise graduation rates or face sanctions. Adding to this complex undertaking are an increasing number of students who are English language learners and the shortage of qualified teachers, especially in math and science, over this next decade (Achieve, 2005; Greene & Winters, 2005). Some studies suggest that too many high schools have consolidated from small, neighborhood schools to large, sprawling facilities that have become impersonal—and fail to meet the needs of a diverse student body. Students feel anonymous in such settings (Hood, 2004).

Because of the technological advances of contemporary society, teens who do not complete high school or who fail to acquire basic reading, writing, and math skills cannot find jobs or must settle for entry-level jobs with limitations for advancement. In 2005 the U.S. governors and business leaders (e.g., Microsoft's Bill Gates) held the first National Education Summit to discuss how to improve the performance of the nation's high schools. Based

on polls from 1,500 high school graduates from 2002, 2003, and 2004, from 400 business CEOs and owners, and 300 college faculty, they derived that 40 percent of today's graduates are not adequately prepared for college work nor entry-level jobs. A small subset of students whose high school and teachers had high expectations of them felt well prepared for, and were doing well in college.

The consensus of the U.S. senators is that the 50-year-old model of high school education must undergo comprehensive reform, reshaping the curricula: High schools must have higher standards, require more core courses (math, science, English), improve career guidance, and get students ready for essential postsecondary education (about 40 percent of college students now take remedial courses). Also, employers and college faculty recommend developing course work that prepares graduates to think analytically, write more, develop good work and study habits, learn to use problem-solving skills, and develop work-related computer skills (Achieve, 2005; Balz, 2005)

Questions

How are adolescents preparing for careers and vocations? Which students are most likely to drop out of high school? Why? What are some recommendations for improving the preparation of high school graduates for the work of the twenty-first century?

Risky Behaviors

Even teenagers who do not perceive themselves as having "problems" might be seen by adult society as engaging in risky or deviant behaviors. Because adults control the channels of power, including legislative agencies, the courts, the police, and the mass media, they are in a better position than adolescents to make their definitions and values "stick" in the realm of everyday life. However, some risky behaviors are common for this age group, including drinking, illicit drug use, suicide, and delinquency. Such behaviors are called risky because typically they interfere with the person's long-term health, safety, and well-being.

Although adolescence is a period affording opportunities for positive development, many young people find themselves in social environments where they are exposed to considerable danger—"high-risk" settings. These youth confront social contexts—family, neighborhood, health-care system, schools, employment training, juvenile justice, and the child-welfare system—that are fragmented and not designed to meet adolescents' unique needs. Poor and minority young people are especially ill-served. They are increasingly found in poor, deteriorating, inner-city neighborhoods riddled with crime, violence, and drugs and with underfunded and poorly designed schools and services.

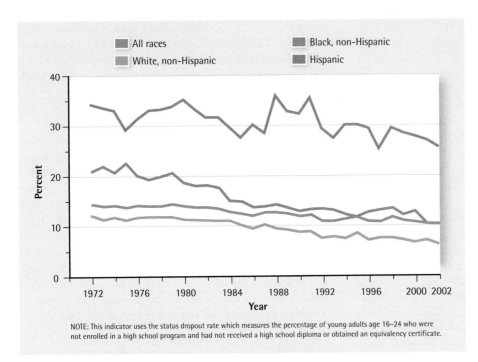

FIGURE 12.4 Dropout Rates Among U.S. Youth Ages 16 to 24 by Race and Hispanic Origin, Selected Years, 1972–2002 High school completion rates up to age 24 include high school diplomas as well as the equivalency GED certificate. National leaders are very concerned about preparing the workforce for the jobs of the twenty-first century.
Source: Child Trends Data Bank. (2004). High School Dropout Rates. Retrieved March 31, 2005, from http://www.childtrendsdatabank.org/indicators/1HighSchoolDropout.cfm Child Trends. Child Trends Databank Indicator: High School Dropout. Retrieved from http://www.childtrendsdatabank.org/figures/1-figure-1.gif. Reprinted with permission. Original data from the Current Population Survey.

NOTE: This indicator uses the status dropout rate which measures the percentage of young adults age 16–24 who were not enrolled in a high school program and had not received a high school diploma or obtained an equivalency certificate.

Social Drinking and Drug Abuse

Nowadays, everyone talks about drugs, but the word itself is imprecise. If we consider a drug to be a chemical, then everything that we ingest is technically a drug. To avoid this difficulty, *drug* is usually arbitrarily defined as a chemical that produces some extraordinary effect beyond the life-sustaining functions associated with food and drink. For instance, a drug might heal, put to sleep, relax, elate, inebriate, produce a mystical experience or a frightening one, and so on. Our society assigns different statuses to different types of drugs. Through the federal Food and Drug Administration, the Bureau of Narcotics, and other agencies, the government takes formal positions on whether a given drug is "good" or "bad," and if "bad," how bad. Sociologists note that some drugs, like caffeine and alcohol, enjoy official approval. Caffeine is a mild stimulant that finds societal approval through the coffee break and coffee shop. Likewise, the consumption of alcohol, a central nervous system depressant, has become so prevalent in recreational and formal business settings that nonusers of the drug are often regarded as somewhat peculiar. And at least until a few years ago, the same held true for the use of nicotine (smoking), a drug usually categorized as a stimulant.

Whether or not they are culturally sanctioned, drugs can be abused. **Drug abuse** refers to the excessive or compulsive use of chemical agents to an extent that it interferes with people's health, their social or vocational functioning, or the functioning of the rest of society. Among adolescents, as among their elders, alcohol is the most frequently abused drug in the United States. According to a 2000 national survey conducted by the National Institute on Drug Abuse, heavy alcohol use was acknowledged by 14 percent

of eighth-graders, 26 percent of tenth-graders, and 30 percent of high school seniors (Wallman, 2001).

Nearly half of all college students engage in **binge drinking** (defined as downing five or more drinks in a row for men, or four or more in a row for women). College and university officials agree that binge drinking is a serious problem. It has far-ranging consequences, including potential death from alcohol poisoning. Binge drinkers are seven to ten times more likely than nonbinge drinkers to have unprotected sex, engage in unplanned sex or be raped while unconscious, get in trouble with campus police, damage property, or become injured or die (Wechsler et al., 2004). Alcohol arrests rose by over 10 percent in 2002, representing the eleventh consecutive year of increases. The increase in arrests is attributed in part to tougher enforcement of law and less tolerance of abuse by peers who are willing to report offenders (Hoover, 2004). The percentage of college women who drink abusively has increased significantly in the last 20 years. Of great concern, a majority of all reported campus violence and rapes occur when alcohol has been used by either the assailant, the victim, or both; many college women get a sexually transmitted infection like herpes or AIDS while intoxicated or under the influence of drugs (Hoover, 2004) (see the *More Information You Can Use* box on page 434, "Determining Whether Someone You Know Has an Alcohol or Drug Problem").

The Centers for Disease Control (Grunbaum et al., 2004) reports in its biannual national survey of high school students that nearly half of high school students nationwide report using marijuana, and about 10 percent or fewer reported using inhalants such as glue or aerosol cans, ecstasy, cocaine, or methamphetamines. Three percent used a needle to inject drugs, and 3 percent had used heroin at least once (Grunbaum et al., 2004).

A growing problem is the use of anabolic steroids by young people, mostly boys, to build their muscles and enhance their athletic performance. The nonmedical use of anabolic steroids is illegal. Nationwide, about 6 percent of students reported using steroid pills or injections (Grunbaum et al., 2004). Medical authorities say adolescents whose bodies are still developing are at special risk for adverse effects from steroids, including stunted growth, mood changes, long-term dependence on steroids, acne, fluid retention, breast development in males, masculinization in females, high blood pressure, and reversible sterility in males. Teenagers might find steroid use appealing because of their concerns about their appearance, peer approval, and "being large and strong enough to make the team" in competitive sports (Petraitis, Flay, & Miller, 1995).

Many psychologists say that coping with the presence of drugs in their social environment is now a developmental task that adolescents must reckon with, just as they must reckon with separation from parents, passing standardized tests, career development, and sexuality. Given the prevalence and availability of marijuana in the peer culture, it may not be surprising that psychologically healthy, sociable, and reasonably inquisitive young people would be tempted to try marijuana. But the findings also show that adolescents who use drugs frequently tend to be maladjusted, showing a distinct personality syndrome marked by increased loneliness, social isolation, poor impulse control, and significant emotional distress, including suicidal thoughts—interfering with problem solving and social-emotional adjustment (Johnson & Gurin, 1994; Petraitis, Flay, & Miller, 1995). For these youngsters, experimentation with drugs is highly destructive and easily leads to pathological functioning.

Why Do Teens Use Drugs?   There are many theories that seek to explain teen substance abuse. One review of several of those theories proposed using a framework that looks at social, attitudinal, and intrapersonal influences (Petraitis, Flay, & Miller, 1995). And heavy drug use impairs competence in the crucial maturational and developmental tasks of adolescence and adulthood by generating premature involvement in work, sexuality, and family roles. In addition, teens see many of their peers using drugs without any apparent harmful effects, creating a climate of disbelief in antidrug campaigns. One place we see the effects of drug abuse is in the size of the nation's prison and jail population, which passed the 2 million mark in 2003. Much of the growth of the total state prison population is due to drug offenses (U.S. Bureau of Justice Statistics, 2003).

A variety of factors have contributed to the illicit use of drugs by young people (Petraitis et al., 1995). The recreational use of illegal drugs has become central to many adolescent peer groups in the past 25 years. Most adolescents who use illegal drugs move in peer groups in

which drugs are a part of daily life. Another contributor in the use of illegal drugs by young people is that they see their parents use drugs—such as alcohol, tranquilizers, barbiturates, and stimulants—and perhaps seeing famous athletes using steroids has led to greater curiosity about and increased teen use of steroids. Nearly all of U.S. adolescents report that their family has a rule against illicit drugs, yet many mimic their parents' drug use and begin taking mood-changing drugs themselves. In this context adolescent drug use is a juvenile manifestation of adult behavior, so it is perhaps more accurate to view drug abuse as a society-wide problem.

Teenage Suicide

In the United States, suicide ranks as the third leading cause of death among young persons aged 15 to 24. Native American and Alaskan Native youth have the highest rates of suicide The overall suicide rate among young people has slowly declined over the past decade. Nearly 4,000 suicides were reported in 2003 for the 15 to 24 age group, and many more males take their own lives than females (Hoyert, Kung, & Smith, 2005). Firearms were used in more than half the total suicides (CDC, 2004e). The self-destructive behavior in these adolescents is alarming and devastating to family and friends left behind. Because stigma is often attached to suicide in Western countries, medical personnel frequently report a suicidal death as an accident or as a death from natural causes.

The national Youth Risk Behavior Surveillance Study (Grunbaum et al., 2004) surveyed more than 15,000 high school students nationally and found that during the previous 12 months 17 percent had seriously thought about attempting suicide and had made a specific plan to attempt suicide, nearly 9 percent had already attempted suicide, and 3 percent had made a suicide attempt that resulted in injury, poisoning, or overdose requiring medical attention.

Comparison by gender reveals that female students were significantly more likely than male students to experience serious depression, to have thought seriously about suicide, to have made a specific plan to attempt suicide, or to have already attempted suicide—but males are more successful at using final methods to end their lives. Comparison by race/ethnicity indicates that Hispanic students were significantly more likely than white students to have attempted suicide and that white students were more likely than black students to have thought seriously about suicide (Grunbaum et al., 2000).

Risk Factors Associated with Suicide A constellation of familial, biological, mental disorder, and environmental factors are associated with youth suicide. These factors include a sense of hopelessness, a family history of suicide, impulsiveness, aggressive behavior, social isolation, previous suicide attempt, easier access to alcohol, use of illicit drugs, low emotional support from a family, negative life events,

More Information You Can Use

Determining Whether Someone You Know Has an Alcohol or Drug Problem

How can I tell if my friend has a drinking or drug problem?

It might be difficult to tell because most people will try to hide their problems, but here is a quiz that you can ask yourself about their behavior (or your own):

1. Do they get drunk or high on a regular basis?
2. Do they lie about how much they drink or do drugs, or do they lie in general?
3. Do they avoid people in order to get drunk or high?
4. Do they give up activities they used to do, such as playing sports or hanging out with friends who do not get drunk or use drugs?
5. Do they plan drinking or taking drugs in advance, perhaps planning the day or activity around the act of drinking or getting high?
6. Do they have to increase the amount of alcohol or drug to maintain the same high?
7. Do they believe that drinking or drugs are necessary to have fun?
8. Are they frequently incapacitated because they are recovering from a "fun night"?
9. Do they pressure others to take drugs or condemn those who do not consume alcohol?
10. Do they take risks, such as careless driving, sexual risks, or otherwise act invincible?

Adolescent Binge Drinking Researchers find that an alarming number of high school and college men and women currently engage in binge drinking with far-reaching social consequences, including unprotected and unplanned sex, rape, traffic accidents and fatalities, encounters with law enforcement agencies, and death.

11. Do they have blackouts where they have no recollection of what happened while they were drunk or high?
12. Do they talk of hopelessness or being depressed or committing suicide?
13. Do they sound selfish or uncaring about other people?

These are signs that a substance is taking control of someone's life. If you see these signs, chances are that your friend or you need help. People with serious drinking or drug problems usually start by saying the experience is great, but addiction can occur very quickly. They can develop serious psychological problems such as depression, suicidal thoughts, thoughts of harming others, and physical problems such as liver damage, brain damage, fetal damage if pregnant, and of course overdose. Being under the influence of substances can cause people to engage in unsafe behaviors, such as driving while intoxicated, having unsafe sex, and trying dangerous "stunts." A young male college senior in our community had been partying all night and was challenged to swim across a river—and tragically he drowned one week before he was to graduate from college.

What would cause my friend to have a problem like this?

Many things can lead to these sorts of problems. Sometimes these problems run in families, similar to heart disease or cancer. If there is a family history of substance abuse, it is more likely that your friend could develop a dependency. Some people take drugs or drink to mask other problems or to avoid things that bother them—stress, work pressures, feelings like they are different from others or they are not worthy, or unhappiness with their situation. They drink or get high to forget their problems. Even though they might forget their problems for a short while, they will more than likely become depressed when the high wears off and they have to face the same problem again and again (Schulenberg et al., 1997).

Why is it hard for individuals to help themselves?

It is very difficult for most people to admit that they have a serious problem. It is even more difficult when you are young and believe that nothing bad can happen to you. Denial and having to hide the problem from friends and family become problems themselves. It can seem easier to cut off everyone and isolate oneself than to constantly hide the evidence of the problem. Once someone withdraws, it is much more difficult to see that there really is a problem.

How can I help my friend?

You have several options:

- Talk to someone you trust—counselor, teacher, doctor, clergy—this will give you another perspective on what you should do.
- Wait until your friend is sober to talk with him or her. Approach him or her in a spirit of support. Encourage your friend to get professional help.
- Try not to accuse or blame your friend. Give examples of what you have noticed that worry you.
- Offer to accompany your friend to seek help.

What does my friend have to do to get help?

First, your friend must admit that there is a problem. This is difficult because it will mean admitting to having wasted part of her or his life. Your friend cannot solve this problem alone but will need professional help. Many people benefit from groups such as Alcoholics Anonymous (AA) or Narcotics Anonymous (NA). Both of these groups often have meetings on campus. Check with your own campus counseling center for meetings times. In the end, it is your friend who must make the decision to get help.

---

and lethal suicide methods (Mohler & Earls, 2001). In many cases psychological depression underlies suicide and suicidal attempts (Mohler & Earls, 2001). **Depression** is an emotional state usually characterized by prolonged feelings of gloom, despair, and futility, profound pessimism, and a tendency toward excessive guilt and self-reproach. Other symptoms of depression include fatigue, insomnia, poor concentration, irritability, anxiety, reduced sexual interest, and overall loss of interest and boredom. At times, depression appears in the guise of other disorders, such as vague pains, headaches, or recurrent nausea. The rate of depression for adolescent girls is twice that of boys. A prime factor is the preoccupation many teenage girls have with their appearance (Ge, Conger, & Elder, 2001a; Halpern et al., 1999). The U.S. Education Department has named depression as a major cause of students' dropping out of college.

Suicide Prevention   The ability to screen for suicide risk is the most important part of suicide prevention. Second is linking at-risk individuals with community mental health services. The potential for suicide is on a continuum from low risk factors to high risk factors.

The strongest risk factor for completed suicide is the presence of a firearm in the home (McKeown et al., 1998). A broader societal focus on reducing substance abuse and poor family functioning includes both community and family interventions, including educating parents and educators (McKeown et al., 1998). Jessor and colleagues (1998) studied nearly 1,500 Hispanic, white, and black high school students in a large, urban school district and found that the following protective psychosocial factors enhance adolescent health: regular physical exercise, healthy eating habits, dental care, safety behaviors, adequate sleep, religiosity, a commitment to school, having friends who take part in conventional youth activities and community volunteer work, an orientation toward parents, positive relationships with adults, church attendance, and involvement in prosocial activities.

Treatment of adolescents with suicidal tendencies usually involves a combination of psychotherapy and

medication for depression (Emslie et al., 1999). The therapist seeks to help the teenager come to terms with his or her problems and acquire more effective techniques for coping with life and stressful circumstances. The therapist also attempts to foster self-understanding, a sense of inner strength, self-confidence, and a positive self-image. Dramatic progress has been made in recent years in the treatment of depression with such medications as *Elavil, Tofranil, Prozac,* and *Paxil* (Keller et al., 2001).

Antisocial Behaviors and Juvenile Delinquency

Youthful "deviance" has been a problem reported by societies throughout human history. The United States is no exception. Young males continue to be responsible for a significant proportion of the nation's crime, and men of this age group are also involved disproportionately with the criminal justice system. However, the number of arrests for young males declined more than 6 percent and 3 percent for females under age 18 over the past decade (U.S. Bureau of Justice Statistics, 2004). Relatively few teens committed felony crimes. In 2003, more than 900,000 males under age 18 were arrested for a broad range of crimes, with highest rates for property crimes and larceny-theft. About 350,000 females under 18 were arrested, with highest arrests for the same crimes as males. In 2003, female juveniles accounted for 20 percent of female arrests (Federal Bureau of Investigation, 2004).

Further examination of the data indicates that serious crimes such as murder, rape, aggravated assault, and robbery are down for males under age 18. Yet the arrest rates for drug abuse violations, embezzlement, offenses against family and children, and driving under the influence have increased. The rates of females under age 18 being arrested for prostitution, drug abuse violations, driving under the influence and drunkenness, embezzlement, offenses against family and children, and assaults have increased. After reaching its highest level in 1993, rates of serious violent crime victimization have dropped 74 percent by 2002. In this same decade, rates of serious violent crime offending rates dropped significantly for youth ages 12 to 17 (Federal Interagency Forum on Child and Family Statistics, 2004)

The media has sensationalized school shootings by male students, leading the public to believe youth crime is on the rise, but youth crime rates have declined significantly, except for arrests for substance abuse. The wider availability of firearms gives a few emotionally disturbed males a lethal weapon that kills a larger number of victims. And there is mounting controversy about imprisoning an increasing number of juveniles for substance abuse and possession with criminals who have committed serious felony crimes. Psychologists, sociologists, and criminologists are increasingly coming to the conclusion that more responsible parenting, closer home and school supervision, and rehabilitation programs—not the police and jails—could reduce most youth crime. For some thoughts on reduction of teen fatalities, see the *Further Developments* box "What Can We Do to Protect Our Youth from Guns and Violence?"

Youth Violence   The youth of this nation remains the largest group to be both victims and perpetrators of violent acts of any subgroup (see Figure 12.5). From 1997 through the present, there were several instances where young male students opened fire on fellow students and teachers, in all cases killing or wounding several people before killing themselves or being subdued—with several fatalities at Columbine High School in 1999 and Red Lake High School in 2005. Such senseless, violent crimes perpetrated by young males on innocent victims were highly sensationalized with every graphic detail. These lurid images leave

the entire nation with the misperception that youth crime is high, even in our own communities. Youth crime and vicitmization can decline further with continued interventions by government, criminal justice, social, and school security programs. Although overall adolescent crime has decreased, firearm deaths continue to be high among, and are perpetrated by, African American males, and this is the leading cause of death for blacks aged 15 to 24 (National Center for Health Statistics, 2004a).

In 2000 more than 81,000 teenagers under age 18 were legally classified as "runaways," and many of these youth are forced into a life of crime to survive. If and when these youth become violent juvenile offenders, they pose a challenge to both the general public and the juvenile justice system (Wallman, 2001).

The majority of adolescents are law-abiding citizens, but adolescent antisocial behaviors, such as delinquency, conduct disorders, driving while intoxicated, substance abuse, and assaults are linked to a wide variety of troublesome adult behaviors, including criminality, drug addiction, economic dependency, educational failure, employment instability, marital discord, and child abuse. Even so, some juvenile delinquents later become law-abiding citizens. Apparently, they realize that what was "fun" as a teenager is no longer accepted behavior for an adult (Sampson & Laub, 1990).

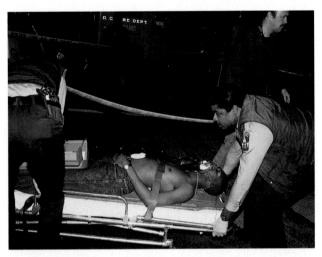

Violence Among American Youth   Young African American males face especially difficult circumstances. The problems for young people are compounded by a deindustrializing economy where well-paying, secure jobs are scarce. Anger and defiance are readily translated into violence in an environment of labor market marginality. The leading cause of death among African American youth is homicide. Indeed, African American young men in New York City's Harlem are less likely to reach the age of 40 than are young men in Bangladesh.

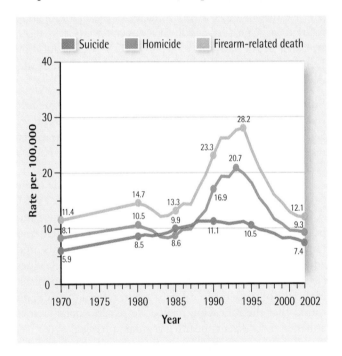

FIGURE 12.5 Death Rates (per 100,000) for Homicide, Suicide, and Firearm-Related Deaths of Youth Ages 15 to 19, Selected Years, 1970–2002
Source: Centers for Disease Control and Prevention. (2004). *Health, United States, 2004, with Chartbook on Trends in the Health of Americans.* U.S. Department of Health and Human Services. Washington, DC: Government Printing Office. Art: Child Trends. Child Trends DataBank Indicator: Teen Homicide, Suicide, and Firearm Death. Retrieved from http://www.childtrendsdatabank.org/figures/70-figure-1.gif. Reprinted with permission. Original data from National Vital Statistics System.

Further Developments

What Can We Do to Protect Our Youth from Guns and Violence?

First we need to ask how youth are getting guns. Most of the firearms used in unintentional shootings of children come from the victim's own home, the home of a relative, friend, or parent of the victim's friend. It was reported that 1.4 million homes had firearms that were stored either unlocked and loaded or unlocked and stored with ammunition. Ensuring safe gun storage is associated with decreased suicide rates for children 14 to 17 years old (Children's Defense Fund, 2005).

In 1994 the federal Assault Weapons Ban went into effect. In the years before the ban went into effect, the numbers of children and teenagers who died from gunfire was on the increase, but in 2002 the death rate was 50 percent lower than it had been in 1994. However, in 2004 Congress allowed the Assault Weapons Ban to expire. This made it legal once again for Americans to buy rapid-fire, military-style weapons designed to kill large numbers of people in a very short time (Children's Defense Fund, 2005).

Educationally, there are programs that emphasize conflict resolution and street survival skills. We can also call for a tightening of security and protection in schools and mandatory sentences for crimes committed with a gun. Long-term solutions include reducing youth access to firearms. This will be difficult, given that so many U.S. homes have guns. Only one-fourth of firearm homicides

are committed in the course of a felony or by a suspected felon, and two-thirds of U.S. felons admitted that their firearms came from friends, family, or acquaintances. This suggests that if private citizens possessed far fewer firearms, criminal access to guns would be greatly reduced. The Children's Defense Fund (2005) has several suggestions for keeping children and teens safe:

1. Support responsible gun control measures.
2. Remove guns from your home.
3. Foster a climate of nonviolent conflict resolution in your home, congregation, school, and community.
4. Encourage nonviolent conflict resolution courses for all students, including the youngest.
5. Do not let children watch violent television shows or play violent electronic games.
6. Help focus public attention on child gun deaths.
7. Engage in Child Watch Visitation programs: Visit hospital trauma units and talk with the families who have lost children.
8. Provide children with positive alternatives to the streets so that they can feel safe and protected.

Source: Centers for Disease Control and Prevention. (2004). *Health, United States, 2004, with Chartbook on Trends in the Health of Americans.* Table 47: Death rates for firearm-related injuries according to sex, race, Hispanic origin, and age: United States, selected years 1970–2002, p. 200.

SEGUE

In the United States the social boundaries of adolescence are rather ill-defined. By tradition, the shift from elementary school to junior high school signaled entry into adolescence. But with the advent of the middle school, the transition became blurred. Nor is it entirely clear when a person leaves adolescence. Roughly speaking, adolescence is regarded as having ended when the individual assumes one or more adult roles, such as marriage, parenthood, full-time employment, military enlistment, or financial independence.

The extension of adolescence and youth has posed two related problems for society and for young people. Society has the problem of providing the young with a bridge to adult roles through appropriate socialization and role allocation.

As we shall discuss in Chapter 13, young adults have the problem of establishing a stable identity, achieving independence, and deciding on future alternatives. Many Western industrialized nations have put off entrance into adulthood for economic, educational, and other reasons. Today, college postpones full adult status for many socially and economically advantaged young people. Unemployment and underemployment produce a somewhat similar effect among less advantaged groups. At the same time, children are reaching puberty earlier than children did a century ago. Thus, physically mature people are told that they must wait 10 or more years before they can assume the full rights and obligations of adulthood.

Summary

Development of Identity

1. Hall's view is that adolescence is characterized by inevitable turmoil, maladjustment, tension, rebellion, dependency conflicts, and exaggerated peer-group conformity. Some social scientists believe this storm-and-stress view has been exaggerated by media influences and is not accurate today.

2. Sullivan's theory, in contrast to Freud's, explains the principal forces in human development as being social instead of biological. The three periods of Sullivan's theory are preadolescence, early adolescence, and late adolescence.

3. The crisis in Erikson's fifth stage of psychosocial development is the search for identity. Erikson suggests that an optimal feeling of identity is experienced as a sense of well-being.

4. Marcia proposes that identity formation can be further classified in terms of four different statuses: achievement, moratorium, foreclosure, and diffusion.

5. The United States and other Western countries seem to promote an extended adolescence. According to this view, conflicting expectations generate an identity crisis among U.S. and European youth. On the other hand, many non-Western societies mark the period of adolescence more clearly. They ease the shift in status by providing puberty rites—initiation ceremonies that socially symbolize the transition from childhood to adulthood. Some circumcision rituals marking adulthood are under attack by international human rights organizations as violating human rights.

6. An AAUW study released in 1992 indicated that females emerge from adolescence with a poorer self-image, relatively lower expectations for life, and considerably less confidence in themselves and their abilities. Other recent studies find similar results. But today girls' enrollments and test scores are up in math and science.

7. Gurian has studied identity development in boys and proposes accepting their biological differences and providing adolescent males with role models and opportunities to learn to act responsibly.

8. Western societies, by prolonging the transition to adulthood and by segregating their youth, have given rise to a kind of institutionalized adolescence or youth culture—more or less standardized ways of thinking, feeling, and acting that are characteristic of a large body of young people.

Peers and Family

9. Both the family and the peer group are anchors in the lives of most teenagers. However, the relative influence of the two groups varies with the issue. Adolescents, who are more segregated by age in high schools, are normally not at war with their parents. Teens often benefit from ties with their parents and seek advice from them on issues of finance, education, and careers.

10. Teens, who seem to develop a consciousness of oneness with their group members, seek advice from peers on topics such as clothes, hairstyle, dating, and music.

11. High status in adolescent society requires being able to project an air of confidence and a "cool" self-image in a variety of situations.

12. Conformity to a peer group and peer pressure play a prominent role in the lives of most teenagers. However, there are many different types of teen groups. A small number of adolescents are at risk from social isolation.

13. For adolescents, the demand to make their own choices is a signal of maturation and growth. The majority of conflicts between teens and parents arise over chores and appearance rather than over substantive issues. Teens desire more open communication with parents.

14. Pipher proposes that girls get mixed messages about modeling their behavior after that of their mothers. Adolescent girls are socialized to psychologically distance themselves from their mothers at a time when they need their guidance and support the most.

Courtship, Love, and Sexuality

15. One of the most difficult adjustments adolescents must make as they make the transition into adulthood revolves around their sexuality, sexual orientation, and sexual expression. Sexual attraction and sexual considerations become dominant forces in their lives. Adolescent sexuality has received considerable public attention because it is associated with many negative individual and societal outcomes that have lifelong consequences.

16. Youth vary a good deal in the age at which they first experience intercourse. Adolescent sexual behavior can be shaped by less parental supervision and by peer group pressures.

17. Social scientists find it difficult to define romantic love, and cross-cultural studies suggest it is not a universal concept.

18. Adolescent sexuality finds expression in a number of ways, including masturbation, nocturnal orgasm, heterosexual petting, oral sex, heterosexual intercourse, homosexual activity, and bisexual activity.

19. The rates of teenage sexual experience increased throughout the 1980s, plateaued by the early 1990s, and declined by high school grade level, by gender, and by race and ethnicity by the late 1990s. Rates of having multiple sex partners have also declined by all grade levels and races and ethnic categories during this decade. As teens become more sexually experienced, they become more consistent contraceptive users. More teens are abstaining from sex.

20. Although teenage birthrates have been declining, childbearing by unwed teens is still very high and is associated with many negative outcomes for the mother, the child, and society.

21. Approximately 7 percent of boys and 5 percent of girls in high school report same-sex attraction. By age 18, most youth deem themselves to be heterosexual or homosexual, with perhaps some 5 percent still "unsure" of their orientation.

Career Development and Vocational Choice

22. Adolescents are confronted with career development and vocational choice. College allows teens an opportunity to explore options and delay vocational decisions. Employment is associated with many positive outcomes as adults, but employment in high school can complicate the picture for teens. The high school dropout rate is higher among the poor, minorities, and pregnant teens; yet there are fewer employment opportunities for this group of teens and the likelihood of lifetime poverty. Determination of high school dropout rates is now mandated by law.

Risky Behaviors

23. Some risk behaviors common for this age group are drinking, illicit drug use, suicide, and delinquency. Such behaviors are called "risky" because typically they interfere with a person's immediate or long-term health, safety, and well-being. The popularity of "binge drinking" puts many high school and college students at a high risk for death as well as victimizes many innocent people. Teen drug use is increasing.

24. Familial, biological, mental disorder, and environmental factors are associated with substance abuse and suicide among youth. These factors include a history of child abuse or sexual abuse, a family history of depression or suicide, impulsiveness, aggressive behavior, social isolation, previous suicide attempt, easier access to alcohol, use of illicit drugs, low emotional support from a family, negative life events, and lethal suicide methods.

25. Childhood antisocial behavior, such as juvenile delinquency, conduct disorder, assaults, and violent outbursts, is linked to a wide variety of troublesome adult behaviors, including criminality, drug addiction, economic dependency, educational failure, employment instability, marital discord, and child abuse. The majority of adolescents are law-abiding citizens.

26. The boundary between adolescence and early adulthood is unclear—until the person assumes a specific adult role.

Key Terms

binge drinking (432)	generation gap (417)	identity moratorium (414)
consciousness of oneness (418)	identity (413)	negative identity (414)
depression (435)	identity achievement (414)	puberty rites (414)
deviant identity (414)	identity diffusion (414)	storm and stress (412)
drug abuse (432)	identity foreclosure (414)	youth culture (417)

Following Up on the Internet

Web sites for this chapter focus on emotional and social issues, career development, and risky behaviors during adolescence. Please access the text Web site at www.mhhe.com/vzcrandell8 for up-to-date hot-linked Internet addresses for the following organizations, topics, and resources:

Adolescence: Erikson's Psychosocial Development
Child Trends Data Bank: Teens

Teen Pregnancy
Healthy Schools, Healthy Youth
Youth Risk Behavior Surveillance
Understanding Adolescent Depression and Suicide
Life Course (by Millennials Rising)

Video Scenario—http://www.mhhe.com/vzcrandell8

In this chapter, you've just read about adolescents' development of identity, establishment of autonomy, and in some cases their questioning of authority. Using the OLC (www.mhhe.com/vzcrandell8), select the *Adolescence video ending 2* and watch how these concepts, such as identity diffusion and imaginary audience, come to life as Maggie and Aron's evening continues—and gets more complicated as Maggie's parents become involved in the plot. Don't forget to test your knowledge of these concepts by trying the fill-in-the-blank and critical thinking question that follow this segment.

Part SEVEN
Early Adulthood

C hapters 13 and 14 focus on the dynamic life stage of young adulthood, which extends from the late teens until the mid-forties, and discuss various theories of adult development. Contemporary young adults in the United States are ethnically diverse, better educated, and likely to delay marriage by cohabiting or living at home longer while establishing careers. Most young adults are physically active and more health conscious than ever. Recent findings suggest most are sexually conservative and are protecting themselves from AIDS and STIs. A smaller number engage in unhealthy behaviors, such as alcohol, drug abuse, or unprotected sexual activity with multiple partners, which leads to a higher risk of AIDS. Most are planning and preparing for their future by training for specific careers, attending college, joining the military, or going to work. Friendships and social relationships are of prime importance to young adults, who are searching for a compatible, intimate partner during this stage of life. Cohabitation prior to marriage is more common; the average age at marriage is now in the mid-twenties. Though the media focus on teen pregnancies, most young adults today are delaying childbearing while establishing careers.

Early Adulthood
Physical and Cognitive Development

Today in American society, there is less demarcation between adolescence and adulthood than a few decades ago. Some social scientists have suggested that adolescence extends well into the twenties, with more young adults living at home with parents during their expensive college years and when launching a career, or returning home after a short-lived marriage or as a single parent. Many middle-class young adults expect to maintain a lifestyle equivalent to or better than that of their parents while struggling through these early adult years.

Following the earlier lead of psychologists such as Erik Erikson, Charlotte Bühler, Carl Jung, Sidney Pressey, Robert Kegan, and others, the social science community has come to recognize that adulthood is not a single monolithic stage, not an undifferentiated phase of life between adolescence and old age. Developmentalists increasingly see individuals as undergoing change across the entire life span. The contemporary notion is of a *process of becoming.* Thus, adulthood is now seen as an adventure that involves negotiating ups and downs and changing direction to surmount obstacles. In this chapter, we examine several views of the stage called early adult development, typical physical and cognitive changes, the differing moral domains of men and women, and the impact of the diversity of values adults impose on society.

Developmental Perspectives

The category *adulthood* lacks the concrete boundaries of *infancy, childhood,* and *adolescence.* Even in the scientific literature it has functioned as a kind of catchall category for everything that happens to individuals after they "grow up." Sigmund Freud, for instance, viewed adult life as merely a ripple on the surface of an already set personality structure; Jean Piaget assumed that no additional cognitive changes occur after adolescence; and Lawrence Kohlberg saw moral development as reaching a lifetime plateau after early adulthood. Many middle-aged American parents are asking themselves: *When is my son or daughter going to be an adult, capable of working and living independently of our resources?* There is no firm answer to their question today, and it seems to be quite an individual matter (Goldscheider, Thornton, & Yang, 2001).

In the United States, adulthood generally begins when a person leaves high school, attends college, takes a full-time job, enters the military, gets married, or becomes a parent. Yet becoming an adult is a rather different matter for various segments of each society. In Western societies, men have traditionally emphasized such issues in development as autonomy, independence, and identity. In contrast, women, some ethnic minorities, and non-Western societies have typically assigned greater importance to issues of relatedness, such as closeness within a family (Guisinger & Blatt, 1994). Recently, Arnett (2000) proposed a distinct developmental stage from about ages 18 to 25 called *emerging adulthood,* a time that for many allows greater exploration of life's possibilities in work, love, and worldviews and lays a foundation for the remainder of adult life.

Demographic Aspects of Adulthood

People's feelings, attitudes, and beliefs about adulthood are influenced by the relative proportion of individuals who are adults and their life perspectives. In the United States, major population or demographic changes are under way that will have important social and economic consequences. The confluence of all adults in the United States is presently comprised of five generations—but *early adulthood,* the focus of this chapter, is comprised of the youngest three generations. The oldest U.S. generation of adults born in 1900 to 1925 are called the GI generation and experienced World War I, prohibition, and suffragettes getting a constitutional amendment for women to vote. Many were Ellis Island immigrants that came to America to work in industries because of economic hardships in Europe. In 2003, fewer than 5 million are alive. (Web

sites at the end of this chapter lead to more information for those of you who plan to work with the elderly.) The next oldest segment of the U.S. adult population is known as the Silent Generation, born between 1925 and 1945. These adults lived through the Depression years of the 1930s and World War II (see *Human Diversity* box on pages 446–447, "The Confluence of Four Generations.") We address the needs of these two generations more specifically in the late adulthood chapters of this text.

The *baby-boom generation* (born 1946 to 1964), now called the "boomers," represents more than 78 million graying adults and an "age lump" passing through the population, a sort of demographic tidal wave. In the 1950s the baby boomers made the United States a child-oriented society full of new schools, suburbs, shopping malls, and station wagons. The baby boomers born before 1955 provided the nation with rock 'n roll, went to Vietnam and Woodstock, attended co-ed colleges in masses, and fueled various societal changes such as civil rights, the women's liberation movement, and peace movements against Vietnam of the 1960s to 1970s. Later, as the baby boomers first entered middle age, the contemplation—even celebration—of the middle years found expression in popular culture. It is no coincidence that sitcoms such as *The Mary Tyler Moore Show* of the 1970s focused on a single woman living on her own and developing her professional career. Or that *All in the Family* sharply contrasted the liberal views of young boomers "Meathead" and Gloria with traditional middle-aged Edith and Archie. Similarly, family situation comedy was popular in *The Cosby Show* and *Family Ties,* which dominated TV ratings in the 1980s. Television sitcoms about singles such as *Murphy Brown, Seinfeld,* and *Friends,* and *Sex and the City* were popular in the 1990s. What do you observe about the message of contemporary TV shows, such as the long-running *Simpsons*—or *Survivor, Fear Factor,* or *Extreme Makeover,* now that Generation X and the Millennials are coming on strong?

The boomers have brought about a rapid expansion of the nation's skilled labor force. The bumper crop of boomers are now in middle adulthood and number about 58 million adults. The "tail-end" of the boomers are in early adulthood, now ages 40 to 44, and presently comprise about 23 million adults. As the boomers have moved into their middle years, they have become more productive (many having attended college and acquired additional skills). Additionally, they earn more money and save more money—all of which will likely give a competitive edge to the United States in the world economic arenas in the 2000s. As the last of the baby-boom generation passes into middle adulthood, the next two generations of young adults have come of age (see Figure 13.1).

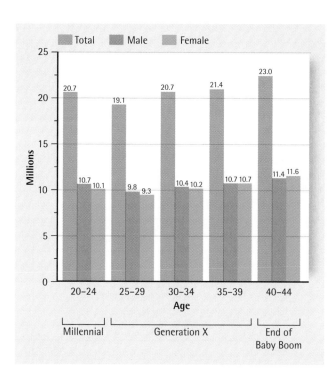

FIGURE 13.1 U.S. Early Adult Population, Ages 20 to 44: 2003

Source: U.S. Bureau of the Census. *Statistical Abstract of the United States: 2004–2005.* Table 11, p. 12.

Question

Think of your favorite television shows—who are the main characters and what issues are explored that demonstrate the values and characteristics of this contemporary generation?

Generation X

The cohort of people aged 25 to 35 comprise about 40 million Americans and are sandwiched between the larger baby-boom and Millennial generations. Generation X is more ethnically diverse than previous generations, and this cohort shares an appreciation for individuality and an acceptance of diversity in race, ethnicity, family structure, sexual orientation, and lifestyle (Stoneman, 1998). They have been raised in a variety of family structures often with both parents working outside the home. More than 40 percent of Gen Xers spent time in a single-parent home by the age of 16 because the divorce rate doubled between the years 1965 and 1977 (O'Bannon, 2001). The *National Survey of Children,* a longitudinal study of people born in the late 1960s, found that one-fourth of this generation had received psychological treatment for either emotional, learning, or behavioral problems by the time they reached adulthood. Yet Gen Xers are generally self-reliant and independent, having grown up with less parental supervision.

Gen Xers share some attributes with the Millennials because they grew up in a computer-oriented society. They are technologically literate and expect the immediate gratification of quick and easy access to people and information via the Internet, Palm-pilots, and cell phones. Translating their independence and technological savvy into careers, many Gen Xers were involved in creating and working in the *dot.com* industry. Although some were characterized as "slackers," others are realizing their ambitious dreams. Many seek greater monetary success and new experiences by hopping from job to job. Having tasted quick success, some Gen Xers in fields of finance and technology lived lavish lifestyles only to have them curtailed when the dot.com industry went bust (Conlin, 2003a). Additionally, Gen Xers are now beginning to face a future in which they must support an aging baby-boom population while maintaining their own lifestyle and paying for their own children's rising educational costs (Reynolds, 2004). Add to this the uncertainty of the future of Social Security, and society can only hope that Gen Xers continue to draw on their problem-solving and creative abilities in the future.

The Millennial Generation

The largest adult cohort in recent history is defined as the group of people born between the early 1980s and the early 2000s. The main reason for the large size of this generation is the fact that many baby boomers decided to delay childbirth. This also accounts for the much

A Young Couple Graduating from College More young adults than ever are attending college and staying in college longer waiting for a better employment picture or to attain better skills to be competitive in the workplace. For the past decade, young women's enrollment and college completion exceeds that of young men.

Human Diversity

The Confluence of Four Generations

Here you will find a general perspective on life for members of each generation, each influenced by cultural, economic, political, and historical events of their early years. Certainly not everyone in each generation shares all of these views, but as an adult cohort, they tend to share many of the same perspectives. Those born early or late in a generation may find they have mixed views and have more in common with another generation.

Born	Silent 1925–1945	Boomer 1946–1964	Gen X 1964–1981	Millennial Early 1980s–Early 2000s
Size	52 million	About 76 million	About 60 million	About 78 to 80 million (depending on end year)
Other Names		Consciousness generation "Me" generation	Modern "Lost" generation "Slacker" generation	Generation Y Echo Boomers Generation Next
Heroes	GI generation	Themselves	Antiheroes	Parents
Family Life	Earliest marrying and babying generation	Religious and/or spiritually-oriented	Adult-oriented from an early age	"Special"—eagerly anticipated
	Silent women divorced in record numbers	Health-oriented	"Antichild" movement	Lowest parent-to-child ratio ever
	Large numbers of women in workforce later in the generational cycle	Wait until later in life to have children	Less parental supervision than ever before	Universally protected
		The "sandwich" generation	Little peer interaction in childhood	Sheltered
Work	Large increase in number of people in "helping professions" in 1960s	Workaholics Career focused	First to seek work/life balance	3 out of 4 work more than 31 hours per week
			Not constrained by time and/or place	More discretionary income than any previous group

smaller size of Generation X. The Millennial generation has several subsets of children but the older portion is now college age. As they come of age, the Millennials are interacting with boomers and Gen Xers who may be their college professors, employers, and workmates. Even as they interact, each generation exhibits its own characteristic traits (see the *Human Diversity* box, "The Confluence of Four Generations").

As children of boomers who consciously decided to delay having children, Millennials are characterized as being wanted, sheltered, and made to feel worthy (recall the advent of "Baby on Board" signs and legislation for baby car seats). They share the technical expertise and ambition of the Gen Xers, but they differ from them in their sense of being a team player. Although feeling more pressured to live up to their parents' expectations, they also tend to be more achievement-oriented and conventional. According to Howe and Strauss (2000):

The old youth angst, cynicism, and alienation are all giving way to a new confidence about the future and

a new trust in parents and authorities. Rates of youth crime, school violence, teen pregnancy, suicide, and the worst forms of substance abuse are all heading down, while measures of teen optimism, achievement, and sense of peer solidarity are all heading up.

The longer process of leaving a parental home remains an important part of the transition for Generation X and the Millennials. Whereas in the past leaving home was frequently associated with the event of marriage, now moving out of the parental home might come from becoming a single parent or from a desire to be independent:

I want material success, but I also want balance in my life. My real dream is to live life as an entrepreneur. Not necessarily to start my own business, but to have this entrepreneurial focus in all aspects of my life. To really build my life and my lifestyle on my own terms, with my own skills, resources, and competencies. (Stoneman, 1998)

In 2003 more than half of men aged 18 to 24 (close to 8 million) lived at home with one or both parents (U.S. Bureau of the Census, 2004b). For women of this age, slightly

Born	Silent 1925–1945	Boomer 1946–1964	Gen X 1964–1981	Millennial Early 1980s–Early 2000s
School Life	Described in college as: Withdrawn Cautious Unimaginative Unadventurous	Grade inflation at an all-time high Overall SAT scores decreased from 1946–1960 Enjoy learning for learning's sake	Grade inflation decreased First generation to be less educated than their parents by both choice and circumstance Largest segment of online learners is in Gen X cohort	Grade inflation on the rise again; are readers Expect active learning in classrooms but study less than any previous generation Volunteerism as part of graduation requirements
Significant Events	Depression of 1930s Sexual revolution occurred while this generation in midlife Korean War	Vietnam Conflict Sexual revolution Kent State shooting Women entering college and many male-dominated professions	Berlin Wall comes down *Challenger* explosion Gulf War	Columbine High School shootings September 11, 2001 Second Gulf War Political strife "Liberals" versus "Conservatives"
Notes	Generation of jealousies and role reversals Focused on previous generation while young and subsequent generation in adulthood	Intense attention focused on this group for the entire boomer lifespan Self-aware and self-centered (largest number of self-help books)	Mired in an age of death: AIDS; homicides/drug-related deaths increased; suicidal (at a near record rate of almost 5,000/year in mid 1980s)	Optimistic Conventional Racially diverse Pressured

Source: Baker College: Effective Teaching and Learning Department. pp. 25–26. Flint, MI: Baker College. Retrieved April 6, 2005, from http://www.baker.edu/departments/instructech/resources/TAG%20document.

doc and DeBard, R. (2004, Summer). Millennials coming to college. *New Directions for Student Services,* 106, 33–45. and "Teaching Across Generations." (2005, January 28).

less than half lived at home with one or both parents. Thus, today's young adults are delaying marriage in contrast to previous generations. Although the median marriage age is rising in the United States, Arnett (2000) points out that marriage age is better understood as a factor of cultural practices and is influenced by socioeconomic status as well. For example, Hispanic females tend to marry early, and the Mormons encourage early marriage. In Gambia, age at marriage is reported to be as early as 10 years (Jeng & Taylor-Thomas, 1985). In Ghana puberty rites signal marriagability to ensure chastity (Bulley, 1984). The age of marriage for women has a significant impact on their living conditions, ability to complete an education and support themselves and their children, and their overall quality of life. Table 13.1 shows the difference of median marriage age among different countries. Note that the more industrialized countries have higher medians, although the trend in the less prosperous countries is also on the rise, especially for men whose employment opportunities have been diminishing.

Question

How would you concisely summarize the general traits and values of Generation X and the Millennial generation in contrast to the previous generation of adults from the baby-boom generation, mostly now in middle adulthood?

Conceptions of Age Periods

Historical evidence suggests that age distinctions were more blurred, and chronological age played a less important role in the organization of U.S. society prior to 1850, compared with today. It seems that age consciousness has grown over the past 155 years in response to developments in education, psychology, and medicine (including the psychology of advertising). Public school systems used to impose strict age criteria for each grade.

Table 13.1 Median Marriage Age of Women in Selected Countries

Industrialized Countries	Age	Developing Countries	Age
United States	25.2	Egypt	21.9
Canada	26.0	Morocco	22.3
Germany	26.2	Ghana	21.1
France	26.1	Nigeria	18.7
Italy	25.8	India	20.0
Japan	26.9	Indonesia	21.1
Australia	26.0	Brazil	22.6

Data are from *The World's Youth,* by J. Noble, J. Cover, and M. Yanagishita, 1996, Washington, DC: Population Reference Bureau. Copyright 1996 by the Population Reference Bureau. Reprinted with permission.

Psychological theories of development afforded a rationale for age legislation regarding child labor, school attendance, and pension benefits. And in medicine, *pediatrics* emerged as a specialty, whereas old age became identified as *gerontology*. Popular culture, as expressed in the media, song lyrics, birthday celebrations, and advice columns of popular magazines, picked up and helped disseminate the notion that there are appropriate ages for experiencing various life events.

For the most part Americans perceive adults of all ages favorably. Nevertheless, older adults are viewed less favorably and as less desirable to be around than younger adults (unless you are an older adult, in which case you may prefer to be around people your own age). Such attitudes are influenced by a variety of factors. Adults who have had more formal education and more experience with a range of older adults have more positive attitudes toward older people than is true of the population generally. Adults who encounter burdens or conflicts associated with the elderly have more negative attitudes toward them.

College students tend to see young people as more adaptable, more capable of pursuing goals, and more active than older people. Overall, age, in and of itself seems to be less important in determining people's attitudes toward the elderly than other types of information such as their personality traits. However, age groups differ on such issues as how old is old, whether they would like to be 100 years old, and how old they expect to live to be. People also evaluate the stages of the life cycle differently depending on their current age. It surprises many young people that their elders look back on the teenage years with little enthusiasm. And many older people see their retirement years as their best years.

Americans have some difficulty specifying the age at which an average man or woman becomes old. Much depends on the person's health, activity level, and related circumstances. Americans have little difficulty characterizing a person as a young adult or an elderly adult, but the boundaries between adjacent age categories are vague (Krueger, 1992). For instance, regarding the transition period between middle age and elderliness, the placing of an individual is only weakly connected to the chronological age of the person being judged. Even so, older adults hold more elaborate conceptions about development (its richness and differentiation) throughout the adult years than younger adults do.

A national survey of American's perceptions of aging found that older people believed "old age" begins at later ages than younger people, women viewed old age as beginning later than men, and whites dated "old age" later than nonwhites (O'Brien et al., 2001).

According to surveys of adult Americans, two-thirds perceive themselves as being younger than they actually are, though those under 30 years of age often perceive themselves as being older than they actually are (Riley & Staimer, 1993). It seems that younger people desire to be grown up and to dissociate themselves from potential social stigmas and disadvantages attached to being "too young." Once individuals reach middle age, however, they think of themselves as being 5 to 15 years younger than they are. Indeed, people frequently say that they feel about 30 or 35 years old, regardless of their actual age. The thirties seem to have eternal appeal. In addition, consistent with the notion that "you're only as old as you feel," aging people's own conceptions of their age seem to be better predictors of their mental and physical functioning than their chronological age is.

> **Question**
>
> Historically, how did social scientists come to distinguish various life stages during adulthood, and what are those stages?

Age Norms and the Social Clock

We commonly associate adulthood with **aging**—biological and social change across the life span. **Biological aging** refers to changes in the structure and functioning of the human organism over time. **Social aging** refers to changes in an individual's assumption and relinquishment of roles over time. Therefore, the life course of individuals is punctuated by **transition points**—the relinquishment of familiar roles and the assumption of new ones.

Age, as reckoned by each society or community, is a set of behavioral expectations associated with given points in the life span. Many behaviors are prescribed for us in terms of society's "dos and don'ts." Conformity with these expectations generally has favorable results; violation, unpleasant ones. Such dos and don'ts are termed **social norms**—standards of behavior that members of a group share and to which they are expected to conform, such as the unacceptability of pushing and shoving when entering or exiting a subway car. Social norms are enforced by positive and negative sanctions. For example, even though the expected U.S. social norm of marrying before having children has relaxed, many single-parent mothers and children still experience many negative outcomes related to living without a husband to help with parenting and chores and living in poverty.

Social norms that define what is appropriate for people to be and to do at various ages are termed **age norms**. Age norms tend to define the "best age" for a man or woman to marry, to have babies, to finish school, to settle on a career, to hold a top job, to become a grandparent, and to be ready to retire. Individuals tend to set their personal "watches" (their internalized age norms) by society's "Big Ben" (Kimmel, 1980). Examples are compulsory school attendance laws, the minimum voting age in election laws, the age at which youth may purchase alcoholic beverages, the age for military service, and the age at which individuals retire and become eligible for Social Security benefits. However, as Sadler (2000) observes, the average U.S. life span is increasing (near age 80 now), and America is experiencing a longevity revolution that is already creating a shift in age norms. As examples, young adults are leaving home later, couples are marrying later, women are having babies much later, and retiring later.

Age norms can also represent informal expectations about the kinds of roles appropriate for people of various ages. At times, such expectations are only vague notions about who is "too old," "too young," or "the right age" for certain activities. The appeal "Act your age!" pervades a great many aspects of life. Variations on this theme are often heard in such remarks as, "She's too young to wear that style of clothing" and "That's a strange thing for a man of his age to say." Do you have any difficulty accepting the reality of 11-year-olds having babies or 63-year-old women having babies?

Age grading at the social level—the arranging of people in social layers that are based on periods in the life cycle—creates a **social clock,** a set of internalized concepts that regulate our progression through the age-related milestones of the adult years. The social clock sets the standards that individuals use in assessing their conformity to age-appropriate expectations. Likewise, people describe what personality characteristics are salient in particular age periods. For example, they think it appropriate to be impulsive in adolescence but not in middle age. And they readily report whether they themselves are "early," "late," or "on time" with regard to family and occupational events. Such an internal sense of social timing can act as a "prod" to speed up accomplishment of a goal or as a "brake" to slow down passage through age-related roles. Not being "on time" can have differing outcomes. For instance, World War II brought substantial social disruptions as men went off to war for years, and these disruptions were associated with an increased risk of adverse change in the trajectories of the men's health across the adult years (Elder, Shanahan, & Clipp, 1994). In contrast, compared with "on time" fathers, "late" fathers are more involved with their youngsters and have more positive feelings about their involvement.

Staudinger (2001) distinguishes between *life review* (a process typically associated with older adults who are reflecting on the past) and *life reflection* (a social cognitive process that begins in adolescence and continues across the life span). Exposure to death has the power to evoke life reflection, even when one's death does not

Changing Notions of the "Right Time" for Life Events What each society determines is appropriate for people to be and to do at various ages are termed *age norms.* To some extent, age norms are variable regarding the "best age" for a woman to have babies. Yet a woman's biological aging affects natural conception, and fertility for women begins to decline by the late twenties. This woman was 57 when she conceived her twin daughters by infertility treatments.

appear imminent. Serious illness—one's own or that of another—can also instigate life reflection.

Although the members of a society tend to share similar expectations about their life cycle, some variations do occur. *Social class* is one important factor. The lower the socioeconomic status, the more rapid the pacing of the social clock tends to be. The higher the social class, the later individuals generally leave school, acquire their first job, get married, begin parenthood, secure their top job, and begin grandparenthood. And new generations believe they can reset the social clock. For instance, young women currently prefer earlier ages for educational and occupational events and later ages for family events than did women of earlier generations. It is not uncommon today for professional women to wait until their late thirties or even their forties to have a first child (as did actress Jane Seymour and performer Madonna). Yet many women who wait until their early thirties or beyond have higher rates of miscarriage, ectopic pregnancy, having a baby with a chromosomal abnormality, or find they must use assisted-reproductive technologies—very expensive and intrusive procedures that may prove futile (Gibbs, 2002).

Neugarten and Neugarten (1987) believe that the distinctions between life periods are blurring in the United States. They note the appearance of the category "young-old," retirees and their spouses who are healthy and vigorous, relatively well off financially, and well integrated within community life. A young-old person could be 55 or 90—visit Jack LaLanne's Web site for inspiration to live well to age 90! The line between middle age and old age is no longer clear. What was once considered "old" now characterizes a minority of elderly people—the "old-old," a particularly vulnerable group who often are in need of special support and care. The Neugartens (1987) observe that increasingly we have conflicting images rather than firm stereotypes of age: the 18-year-old who is married and supporting a family, but also the 18-year-old college student who still lives at home; and the 70-year-old in a wheelchair, but also the 70-year-old running a marathon.

A more fluid life cycle affords new freedoms for many people. But even though some timetables may be losing their significance, others are becoming more compelling. Young adults might feel they are failures if they have not "made it" in a corporation or law office by the time they are 35. And a young woman might delay marriage or childbearing in the interests of a career but then hurry to catch up with parenthood in her late forties or even early fifties today, even though she might expect to live to her late seventies or early eighties.

> **Question**
> What evidence do we see that traditional age-grade norms seem to be "blurring," as Neugarten states?

Age-Grade Systems

In a number of African societies, age norms are embodied in an age-grade system (Foner & Kertzer, 1978). Members of each grade are alike in chronological age or life stage and have certain roles that are age-specific. For instance, the Latuka people of Sudan distinguish among five age grades: children, youths, rulers of the village, retired elders, and the very old. In such societies the individuals of each age grade are viewed as a corporate body and move as a unit from one age grade to another. For example, among the African Tiriki, uninitiated boys may not engage in sexual intercourse, they must eat with other children and with women, and they are permitted to play in the women's section of the hut. After initiation they may engage in sexual intercourse, are expected to eat with other men, and are forbidden to enter the women's section of the hut. In India, young women who marry become the caretakers of everyone in the household, and the older mother or mother-in-law in the home finally enjoys higher social status and a more leisurely life.

Furthermore, age grades differ in the access they afford their members to highly rewarded economic and political roles. In Western societies, in contrast, people's chronological age is but a partial clue to their social locations. Socioeconomic class and ethnic factors cut across lines of age stratification and provide additional sources of identity.

On the surface, societies with age-grade systems seem to provide an orderly method for role allocation and reallocation. But in practice, the transition process is often less than orderly. Conflicts frequently arise between age grades, essentially a version of the time-honored struggle between the "ins" and the "outs." The desire of people to gain access to or hold on to various privileges and rewards fuels social discord and individual grievances. The rules governing transition might not be clear. Even when they seem to be unambiguous, the rules are always open to different interpretations and to "bending" in one or another group's favor. The continuing debate in the United States over Social Security funding and medical benefits reflects this type of tugging between the young and the elderly.

All societies are faced with the fact that aging is inevitable and continuous. Hence, they all must make provision for the perpetual flow of one cohort after another by fitting each age group into an appropriate array of social roles. Societies with age-grade systems attempt to achieve the transition by establishing points in the life course (such as puberty) for entering roles and leaving them. Another solution, more closely approximated in Western societies, is to allow "natural" forces to operate: Younger people assume adult roles when they are ready to do so, whereas older people give up roles when they are ready to do so or when they become ill or die.

In the United States no collective rituals mark the passage from one age grade to another. High school and college graduation ceremonies are an exception, but even here not all individuals in a cohort graduate from either high school or college. And there is some flexibility in the operation of the age system, in that intellectually gifted children skip grades in elementary school and bright youths are allowed to enter college after only two or three years of high school. At the older age levels, too, flexibility often operates within some companies and some occupations with regard to early retirement; for instance, one can retire from the police work or the military after 20 years of service. With corporate downsizing, outsourcing, the dot.com debacle, and the 2000–2001 recession, however, it is more common to see more middle-aged college students retraining for a second career in the workforce. Nevertheless, age norms serve as a counterpart of the age-grade system in broadly defining what is appropriate for people to be and to do at various ages.

Life Events

People locate themselves across the life span in terms of social timetables. They also do so in terms of **life events.** But some events are considered nonnormative—that is largely independent of age or stage, including losing a

Distinctions Between Life Periods Are Blurring It is quite common for contemporary middle-aged Americans to be attending college to upgrade their skills or to earn a first or an advanced degree. Do you have notions concerning the "best age" at which to graduate from college, settle on a career, marry, have children, advance in a job, become a grandparent, or retire?

limb in an automobile accident, winning a lottery, undergoing a "born again" conversion, or being alive when Pearl Harbor was attacked or feeling the awe when Neil Armstrong became the first man to walk on the Moon, or personally experiencing the horror of September 11, 2001. We often employ major events as reference points or time markers in our lives, speaking of "the time I left home for school," "the day I had my heart attack," and "after the World Trade Center attack." Such life events define transitions. Events that produce traumatic or reflective consequences include the death of a loved one, divorce, being fired from a job, or being the victim of a traumatic crime such as rape. These life events cause one to ask questions about oneself or society. Some of the effects of rape on the lives of women are discussed in the *Further Developments* box on page 452, "The Effects of a Violent Crime."

Life events may be examined in a great many ways (Suedfeld & Bluck, 1993). For instance, some are associated with internal growth or aging factors like puberty or old age. Others, including wars, national economic crises, revolutions, and events such as terrorist attacks and the anthrax scare are the consequences of living in society. And still others derive from events in the physical world such as fires, storms, tidal waves, earthquakes, or avalanches. And there are those events with a strong inner or psychological component, including a profound religious experience, the realization that one has reached the zenith of one's career, or the decision to leave one's spouse. Any of these events we might view as good or bad, a gain or a loss, controllable or uncontrollable, and stressful or unstressful.

Often in thinking about a life event, we ask ourselves three questions: *Will it happen to me? If so, when will it occur?* and *If it happens, will others also experience it or will I be the only one?* The first question concerns the probability of an event, such as getting married or being injured playing football. If we believe that the probability of an event's occurring is low, we are unlikely to attend to or anticipate it in advance. For instance, most of us are more likely to devote thought and preparation to marriage than to a serious football injury. The second question involves the correlation between chronological age and an event, such as the death of one's spouse or the suffering of a heart attack. Age-relatedness matters because it influences whether or not we are caught unexpectedly by the event. The third question concerns the social distribution of an event, whether everyone will experience it or just one or a few persons. This question is important because it will largely determine whether people will organize social support systems to assist us in buffering the change. In the United States, for example, we have extensive, organized social support systems for ushering children through formal schooling, for getting and staying employed, for getting married, and for making the transition to retirement.

The Search for Periods in Adult Development

Many psychologists have undertaken the search for regular, sequential periods and transitions in the life cycle. They depict adulthood as being, like childhood, a sort of stairway, a series of discrete, steplike levels. The metaphor of the life course as being divided into stages or "seasons" has captured the imagination of philosophers and poets as well as other writers. One of the most popular versions of the stage approach is contained in Gail Sheehy's best-selling books *Passages* (1976) and *New Passages* (1995). She views each stage as posing problems that must be resolved before the individual can successfully advance to the next stage. In these passages from one stage to the next, each person acquires new strengths and evolves an authentic identity. Such an identity has many of the qualities that Abraham Maslow associates with the self-actualized person.

Other psychologists have taken exception to the stage approach. Some believe that an individual's identity is fairly well established during the formative years and does not fundamentally change much in adulthood. According to this view, people might change jobs, addresses, even faces, but their personalities persist, much like adult height and weight do, with only minor changes. As we noted in our treatment of developmental continuity and discontinuity in Chapter 2, this approach views aging as a continuous yet dynamic process. The discontinuity

Further Developments

The Effects of a Violent Crime

Rape is commonly defined as sexual relations obtained through physical force, threats, or intimidation. About one in four women report that a man they were dating persisted in attempting to force sex on them despite their crying, pleading, screaming, or other resistance (Celis, 1991). In 2003, nearly 200,000 rapes were reported, but fewer than half of victims report a rape (see Figure 13.2). In a large Harvard study of 119 U.S. colleges, 1 in 20 women reported being raped, and most were intoxicated or under the influence of drugs at the time (Mohler-Kuo et al., 2004).

Although each rape and coping experience is unique, there are common outcomes in such stressful life events. For instance, researchers find that victims show a significant increase in health-related problems in the year following the rape. Victims may also experience long-term effects such as chronic fear, anxiety, depression and lowered self-esteem. One study found that the severity of the attack and having been victimized previously were related to lowered self-esteem through avoidance as a coping strategy (Neville et al., 2004). Moreover, the vast majority of rape victims blame themselves (Frazier, 1990; King & Webb, 1981). Controversy rages, however, as to whether self-blame is a healthy or unhealthy response.

Societal attention to the problems that surround rape is a recent phenomenon. It seems that behavior in which some people are victimized is accorded public concern only when the victims have enough power to demand attention. Indeed, for centuries rape was a crime in which the victims were stigmatized for their victimization (a "fallen woman") and blamed for their participation in the act (Allison & Wrightsman, 1993; Fairstein, 1993). Marital rape was viewed as legal, acquaintance rape was typically unrecognized, and women's accusations of rape were generally presumed to be unreliable. And when military histories have been written, the plight of raped women as casualties of war has been deemed not serious enough for inclusion in scholarly works (Brownmiller, 1993). Yet rape during war is commonplace and considered an act of the victors. Significantly, the current concern with rape has paralleled the emergence of the women's movement.

The threat of rape affects women whether or not they are its actual victims, limiting their freedom, keeping them off the streets at night, and at times imprisoning them in their homes. Women who carry the highest burden of fear are those with the fewest resources—the elderly, ethnic minorities, and those with low incomes.

Most rapes (80 percent) are committed by an acquaintance of the victim. Women between the ages of 16 and 25 are three times more likely to be raped than women in other age groups. Many of the victims of sexual assault are college women. Fisher and colleagues (2000) from the U.S. Department of Justice issued a report on the sexual victimization of college women, which noted that 3 percent of their sample had been a victim of a completed or attempted rape. The report explains that although the percentage seems low, when other factors are considered, such as the fact that a student spends only about seven months per year in college and that most students' college careers last five years, the actual victimization rate is closer to 20 to 25 percent. Almost half of college women who were victims of attacks that met the Justice Department study's definition of rape did not consider

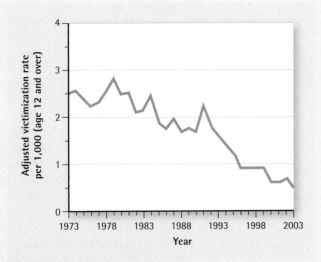

FIGURE 13.2 Reported Rape Rates: 1973–2003 In 2003, national *reports* of forcible rape declined 3 percent but still accounted for more than 93,000 assaults, with 26,350 arrests for forcible rape. Ninety-eight percent of rapes are reported by women, and 2 percent by men. Based on FBI statistics, forcible rape is reported highest in southern states, in very large cities, and also during May to September each year (Federal Bureau of Investigation, 2004). Obviously, women who were raped and murdered were never able to report the crime, thus statistics are actually higher and reported under another category of violent crime. *Source:* U.S. Bureau of Justice Statistics (2005). *National Crime Victimization Survey Violent Crime Trends, 1973–2004:* Adjusted violent victimization rates, Number of victimizations per 1,000 population age 12 and over. Retrieved November 30, 2005, from http://www.ojp.usdoj.gov/bjs/glance/rape.htm

what happened to them to be rape. This in part explains the underreporting of sexual assault to authorities. Some people only consider an attack by a stranger to be rape. Sometimes the victim has a misplaced sense of guilt, feeling that she is to blame, not the attacker.

In the case of acquaintance rape, the majority of male and female students had been drinking heavily or using drugs at the time of the assault. Other high-risk factors associated with rape were being under 21 years old, living in sorority houses, being in a strange environment such as a study

abroad program, and high school drug use and binge drinking (Mohler-Kuo et al., 2004). Rape is a stressful event with lifelong consequences. Many campuses and rape crisis centers now sponsor alcohol prevention programs that address sexual assault, educate men about what constitutes rape, and advise men and women about date rape drugs such as GHB (gamma-hydroxybutyrate), and how to avoid or get out of risky situations. Those few women who falsely accuse a man of rape do a great injustice to the man involved but also leave real victims of rape more vulnerable to being disbelieved.

---

approach stresses the differences between stages and the uniqueness of the issues for each stage.

> **Question**
>
> How does the stage perspective of adult development differ from the view that adult development is a continual process of change over the life course?

Physical Changes and Health

Our physical organism changes across the life span. But in and of themselves such changes may be less important than what people make of them. As we pointed out earlier, cultural stereotypes and social attitudes have a profound effect on our perceptions of biological change and our experience of it. Whereas the physical changes associated with puberty are comparatively easy to identify, later changes (with the possible exceptions of prostate problems or menopause) are less easy to pinpoint as marking stages in adulthood.

Physical Performance

Most individuals believe that getting older means losing a measure of physical attractiveness, vigor, and strength. Yet although physical changes take place throughout adulthood, for the most part they have only minimal implications for an individual's daily life in early adulthood. The years from 18 to about 30 are peak years for speed and agility. Most Olympic athletes fall between these ages, although exceptions include Lance Armstrong, two-time Olympian and seven-time winner of the Tour de France (age 34 at this writing), basketball superstar Michael Jordan who retired at age 36, and Cal Ripkin, who retired from professional baseball at age 41. TV's first physical fitness expert, motivational speaker, and inventor of fitness machines, Jack LaLanne, turned 90 this year and exercises every day. Findings of a study of muscle

function in men and women 20 to 84 years old show that age-related decline of muscle strength is associated with the deterioration of muscle mass in both genders but that it may also be related to neural factors in men (Akima et al., 2001). Some research suggests that hand-grip strength in the thirties is 95 percent of what it was in the twenties, falling to 91 percent in the forties, 87 percent in the fifties, and 79 percent in the sixties. Back strength also diminishes to about 97 percent in the forties, 93 percent in the fifties, and 85 percent in the sixties. But such averages mask the considerable variation found among individuals. A recent study found a relationship between age and a decrease in perceptual motor adaptability (Guan & Wade, 2000).

One area in which individuals in early and middle adulthood are most likely to note changes is in their vision. Between 30 and 45 years of age, individuals tend to experience some loss in the power and elasticity of their eye lenses. Through early and middle adulthood, individuals who are nearsighted tend to become more nearsighted, and those who are farsighted tend to become more farsighted. Aging also produces deterioration in the human auditory and vocal systems, but these changes are generally of little consequence for those in early adulthood.

Physical Health

Adult health is a function of a wide variety of factors, including heredity, nutrition, exercise, prior illness, access to health insurance, and the demands and constraints of the social environment. For the most part we assess people's health by how well they are able to function in their daily lives and adapt to a changing environment. Health, then, has a somewhat different meaning for a young pregnant woman, a nursing home resident, a college professor, a presidential candidate, a high school basketball player, an airline pilot, a construction worker, and a surgeon (Van Mechelen et al., 1996).

Many people living in the United States lack health insurance (at least 44 million or 15 percent of the population, with projections up to 53 million by 2006). Among those most likely to comprise the uninsured are young adults aged 18 to 24, minorities, an increasing number of part-time workers, the unemployed, and immigrants from other countries (National Coalition on Health Care, 2004). Businesses are raising employee health insurance premiums—health costs are soaring—or they are cutting such benefits for new or retired employees. The number of uninsured adults continues to increase substantially. (See the *Implications for Practice* box "Family Nurse Practitioner.") One quarter of all uninsured women are low-income mothers (Lambrew, 2001). Although the federal Medicaid program insures millions of poor persons or those with disabilities, there are millions of others who live at or just above the "poverty line" who are not eligible for coverage. Uninsured persons often avoid seeking health care, or they go to a high-cost emergency room or health clinic. In 2001, the United States spent $99 *billion* in health care for such uninsured citizens, and most states are experiencing large budget deficits due to providing medical care for the uninsured (National Coalition on Health Care, 2004). Hospitals in the southwestern states are going bankrupt and closing because they must treat all persons, including illegal immigrants, without health insurance.

About 14 percent—or 4 million single adult women—have no health insurance coverage. One-third of single women rely solely upon Medicaid coverage. The *Personal Responsibility and Work Opportunity Reconciliation Act of 1996* set a five-year time limit for recipients to leave welfare. The result was that many families lost entitlements such as food stamps and Medicaid. It was believed that full-time employment would provide workers with health-care coverage, but full-time employment no longer guarantees essential health-care coverage.

The vast majority of young adults enjoy good to excellent health, but college graduates are much more likely to be in excellent health than peers who did not attend college (Barnes, Adams, & Schiller, 2003). Recently, many colleges and universities have upgraded gymnasiums into recreation, fitness, and wellness centers for students, staff, and community members. Comprehensive offerings include expanded intramural programs, fitness assessment, personal training, and individualized exercise programs and goals (Blumenthal, 2004). Yet when young adults become ill, their most common illnesses are infectious diseases—particularly colds, upper respiratory infections, and sexually transmitted infections. Employers can expect to lose more work days due to sickness among young adults than among older adults. Among adults ages 20 to 44, limitations of activity are highest for arthritis and other musculoskeletal conditions, followed by mental health conditions (see Table 13.2) (National Center for Health Statistics, 2004). Auto accidents take the highest toll in accidental death and disfigurement among young adults than among other age groups. Most of the other leading causes of death of young adults are associated with unhealthy habits and behaviors—

Implications for Practice

Family Nurse Practitioner
Ronald Dingwell

I am a family nurse practitioner (FNP), and I work in a hospital setting as well as in private practice. I work with both children and adults. My main job tasks are to provide primary and emergency care to an inner-city population of uninsured minorities.

I earned my bachelor's degree in nursing (BSN) from Queen's College in New York City, my master's degree in nursing (MSN) from SUNY Downstate, and my family nurse practitioner (FNP) degree from SUNY Stonybrook on Long Island. Prior to becoming an FNP, I worked as an emergency room nurse for seven years. For students interested in entering this profession, you need to get clinical experience with both primary care (office practice setting) and in acute care (hospital setting). Prior experience as a nurse is valuable in such settings as an ICU (intensive care unit), ER (emergency room), or pediatrics. Such experience will help you determine where your competency or comfort level is as an FNP.

I believe that to enjoy working as a family nurse practitioner, you need to be self-motivated, to have a desire to serve society, and to have the ability to practice independently. What I enjoy most about my profession is helping patients who otherwise would not be able to afford or access health care.

Table 13.2 Main Chronic Health Conditions Causing Limitation of Activity Among U.S. Working-Age Adults, 18 to 44 Years: 2000–2002

Note that persons may report more than one chronic health condition as the cause of their activity limitation.

Condition	Number of Persons per 1,000 Population
Arthritis/other skeletal	21.1
Mental illness	11.8
Fractures/joint injury	6.5
Heart and other circulatory	6.0
Lung disorders/other respiratory	5.2
Diabetes	2.8

Source: Centers for Disease Control and Prevention. (2004). *Chartbook on Trends in the Health of Americans, Health, United States, 2004.* Figure 20. Washington, DC: National Center for Health Statistics.

behaviors that public health practitioners continually warn us to change (see Figure 13.3). For adults of any age concerned with both physical and mental health, exercise affords both physical and psychological benefits.

Dieting, Exercise, and Obesity Being healthy is not something that just happens to you, especially as you get older. Having and maintaining good health consists of personally choosing certain patterns of behavior and avoiding others. Diet and proper exercise are two important components of staying healthy, and these have become daily obsessions for many Americans. After completing high school, most young adults enter into new routines that affect how active they are—some enter into environments that include time for exercise, whereas others take on responsibilities that prevent them from being as active as they were during adolescence. Today, more people walk, jog, cycle, rollerblade, swim, use treadmills and elliptical machines and do weight training than in the last 40 years. Young adult women report that walking and

swimming are their two most common physical activities. And it is therefore no surprise that most people today understand the word *aerobic,* related to cardiovascular fitness, whereas few people would have recognized the word in 1960 (see Table 13.3 for examples of moderate and strenuous activities that raise aerobic levels). Of great concern for many young adults today is the ever-increasing waistline. American adults weigh about 25 pounds more now than they did in 1960, but adults are also about one inch taller than they were then (see Figure 13.4).

Physical Activity and Health Across Cultures Public health programs throughout the Western world have goals to promote the health and well-being of the general public. To achieve this goal, people must increase physical activity to become more fit, engage in better eating habits, and reduce detrimental behaviors like smoking, drinking, using drugs, and having indiscriminate, unprotected sex. A survey of university students from 13 European countries was conducted in 1990 and again in 2000. The survey assessed smoking, exercise, fruit and fat intake, beliefs about the importance of behaviors related to health, and awareness of the influence of behaviors on the risk of heart disease (Steptoe et al., 2002).

The study found that the prevalence of smoking had increased and fruit consumption had decreased from 1990 to 2000, but physical exercise and fat intake did not change much. Awareness of the health effects of smoking and other behaviors was stable over the decade, and knowledge about the effects of fat intake had increased. The study found much variation between country samples. However, changes in beliefs correlated with changes in behavior. Yet the researchers were disappointed in the results of the two survey years in the health behaviors, beliefs, and risk awareness in this young, educated sample of Europeans (Steptoe et al., 2002). Another study of leisure-time activity of university students concluded that physical activity is below optimal levels in a large portion of students. It also found that level of activity is related to cultural factors and degree of economic development of the student's country (Haase et al., 2004).

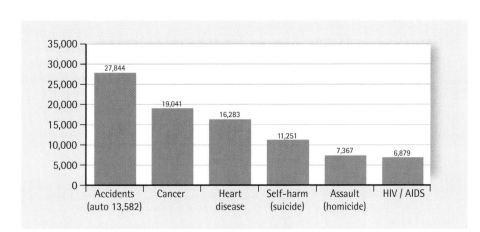

FIGURE 13.3 Leading Causes of Death in Early Adulthood, Ages 25 to 44: 2003 Many causes of death during early adulthood are preventable and are directly related to making poor decisions or taking risks.
Source: National Vital Statistics Reports. (2005, February 28), *53*(15), Table 7, p. 28.

Table 13.3 Examples of Moderate and Strenuous Exercise

Moderate (Activities That Raise Aerobic Levels to 3 to 6 Times Nonactive Levels)	Strenuous (Activities That Raise Aerobic Levels to More Than 6 Times Nonactive Levels)
Walking at 3–4 mph	Walking at 3–4 mph or uphill 5 times a week
Easy cycling	Fast cycling for 1 hour
Leisure swimming	Swimming laps 3 times a week
Golf without cart	Stair-climber 2–3 hours a week
Table tennis	Tennis or racquetball 3 days a week
Canoeing 2–4 mph	Canoeing faster than 4 mph
Mowing yard with power mower	Mowing yard with push mower

Some individuals combine their exercise program with dieting; others use dieting as the primary means of maintaining health. What we eat can affect us in many ways, but most commonly our diet affects how we look and feel and how prone we are to sickness. Several studies also link cholesterol levels to risks of heart disease and confirm the benefits of eating a diet low in saturated fat, cholesterol, and trans fats. Eating an abundance of fruits, vegetables, and whole grains can help maintain a healthy heart (Hu & Willett, 2002; Neville, 2001). Simple ways to lower cholesterol are to eat fiber found in beans, fruits, and vegetables; eat fewer eggs; cut down on saturated fats found in milk, cheese, and meat; and cook with polyunsaturated fats such as sunflower, safflower, or olive oil.

Recent interest in low-carb diets such as *Atkins, South Beach,* and the *Zone* diet has increased tremendously. Currently, one of every six households has a low-carb dieter (Raloff, 2004). Although the results of low-carb dieting may be fast and dramatic, the long-term health effects are in dispute (Kadlec et al., 2004). Perhaps a better guideline to follow for sustained weight loss and overall better health is to follow a diet low in refined simple carbohydrates (e.g., white bread, processed baked goods, and sugar-laden soft drinks) and high in unrefined complex carbohydrates (e.g., brown rice; whole grains; and whole-grain breads, cereals, and baked goods).

Adolescents are, for the most part, active and resilient. Only after they begin the transition to adulthood and the concomitant changes in lifestyle do the effects of poor diet and little exercise begin to show. It is therefore no coincidence that dieting is common in the United States (as one European was overheard remarking to another, "I think all Americans are on a diet"). A national survey revealed that a majority of men and women were either dieting to reduce weight or watching their food intake to prevent weight gain (Kolata, 2000). One major concern regarding diets is the constant on-again, off-again pattern of weight loss/gain that dieting produces. And as discussed in Chapter 11, dieting might lead to obsessive eating disorders such as bulimia or anorexia.

In contrast to many other societies of the world, Western societies put a premium on being thin; and being overweight, or even perceiving oneself as overweight, can place a Westerner in a precarious emotional state. Added to the emotional stress of being overweight are the potential physical problems of high blood pressure, high cholesterol, gallstones, diabetes, stroke, and heart disease ("Executive Summary," 1998). Approximately 70 percent of adults aged 25 to 50 are over their ideal weight. One-third of these are considered *obese* (generally considered to mean being more than 20 percent over the ideal body weight for one's sex, body frame, and age). Because our *metabolism* slows down and the likelihood that we will gain weight increases as we age, preventative measures in the early adult years play a significant role in keeping us healthy as we grow older. (See the *More Information You Can Use* box "Benefits of Aerobic Exercise.")

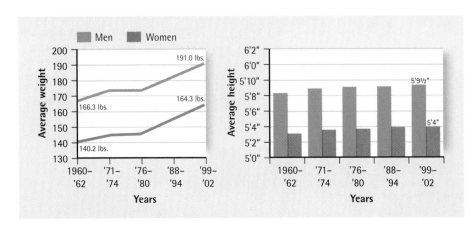

FIGURE 13.4 America's Waistline Is Expanding American adults are nearly 25 pounds heavier and roughly an inch taller than they were in 1960, according to a new report from the National Center for Health Statistics.

Source: Ogden, C. L., Fryar, C. D., Carroll, M. D., & Flegal, K. M. (2004, October 27). Mean body weight, height, and body mass index, United States 1960–2002. *Advance Data from Vital Health Statistics,* No. 3475, Hyattsville; MD: National Center for Health Statistics.
Art: From *Press & Sun-Bulletin* (Binghamton, NY), October 28, 2004. Copyright © 2004 Associated Press. Reprinted by permission.

More Information You Can Use

Benefits of Aerobic Exercise

Most health experts agree that your cardiovascular fitness is best promoted by engaging in exercise that raises your heart rate to 60 percent of your maximum heart rate a minimum of three times a week. To find out what your maximum heart rate is, simply subtract your current age from 220 and then multiply by 0.6. A few sample ages are shown in Table 13.4.

Some experts contend that high-quality exercise on a regular basis significantly reduces the chances of heart attack. The amount of exercise recommended for these results include swimming or running for 25 minutes each day, cycling for 50 minutes at greater than 10 mph, walking for 45 minutes at 4 mph pace, or doing aerobics for 30 minutes. According to the American Heart Association (1998), exercise also benefits us in the following ways:

- Maintains desired body weight
- Strengthens heart and lungs
- Protects against stroke, diabetes, cancer, and osteoporosis
- Lowers blood pressure
- Relieves anxiety

But too much of even a good thing can be bad; overexertion does not produce extra benefits and can even be harmful. If you are just beginning to exercise or want to start an exercise program, consult your physician and ease into exercise slowly. In a survey, awareness of the benefits of exercise was consistently associated with engaging in physical exercise and having a desire to lose weight. Also, 52 percent of men and 54 percent of women were aware that exercise decreases the risk for heart disease (Steptoe et al., 1997). About 37 percent of American adults exercise strenuously at least three times a week. For some examples of moderate and strenuous exercises, see Table 13.3.

Health and Exercise The physical and mental health benefits of regular aerobic exercise and strength training are well known, and college students typically are more fit than their counterparts who are not in college.

Table 13.4 Sample Calculations of Target Heart Rate During Exercise

Current Age	220 - Current Age	Multiply by 0.6	Heart Rate During Exercise
20	220 - 20 = 200	200 × 0.6 = 120	120
30	220 - 30 = 190	190 × 0.6 = 114	114
40	220 - 40 = 180	180 × 0.6 = 108	108
50	220 - 50 = 170	170 × 0.6 = 102	102

Contraception Methods to Prevent Pregnancy, STIs, and HIV According to the Joint United Nations Programme on HIV/AIDS (UNAIDS), the majority of HIV infections for U.S. men occur during injecting drug use and men having sex with men, yet heterosexual sex is the most dominant mode of HIV transmission among women (UNAIDS/WHO, 2004). In many regions of the world, such as Eastern Europe, Asia, Latin America, and sub-Saharan Africa, more than half of those infected are women and girls (UNAIDS/WHO, 2004). In one U.S. study, 20 percent of men having sex with men also report having female sex partners (Harawa et al., 2004). African American and Hispanic women are also at a higher risk

of contracting the HIV virus and other sexually transmitted infections (STIs), and contraceptive practices and family planning are crucial to women's health.

Data about contraceptive use reveals whether adults are using methods to prevent STIs or HIV infections. Findings from personal interviews with a recent representative sample of men and women aged 15 to 44 in the *National Survey of Family Growth* indicate that 98 percent of sexually active women have used at least one contraceptive method, with a majority using the birth control pill, which by itself does not prevent infections (Mosher et al., 2004). But 90 percent report that their partner has used a condom. However, African American and Hispanic women are more likely to use the three-month contraceptive injectable, *DepoProvera*, and female sterilization is much more common among women aged 35 to 44. About 10 percent of the female respondents report using more than one method of contraception. One serious finding was that the percentage of sexually active women not using any contraception increased from 5.4 percent to 7.4 percent from 1995 to 2002. Some of the reasons these women were not using contraception include being pregnant or trying to get pregnant, partner is sterile, or not having intercourse recently. In 2004, about half of young adult women received family-planning medical services—a significant increase since 1995.

Practicing Safer Sex   Many individuals falsely believe that various forms of birth control protect them against STIs and HIV/AIDS transmission. Some young adults believe that requesting condom use is awkward and indicates a belief that the partner may carry an STI. Recent research shows, however, that women who identify themselves as using condoms to prevent pregnancy were more likely to use a condom at last intercourse than were other women (Critelli & Suire, 1998). Research findings also suggest that once a relationship becomes established and partners trust one another, condom use is replaced by oral contraceptives, which seem more convenient but are not effective in providing a barrier for infections (Feinleib & Michael, 1998). Monogamy is frequently cited as a reason for not using condoms, but many young adults consider monogamy to be an effective way to prevent transmission of STIs. Yet many relationships between young adults do not last. Short-term, serial monogamy is not an effective way to prevent transmission of STIs, especially given that in a survey of college men, about 25 percent reported that they lie about their sexual history to obtain sex (Fischer, 1996). Knowledge of risks does not necessarily lead to changed behaviors (Gupta & First, 1998).

Studies of individual responses to the threat of HIV/AIDS and other STIs have found substantial evidence of behavioral changes in high-risk groups (e.g., males having sex with males, intravenous drug users, pregnant mothers, and STI patients). Those with only one sexual partner during their lifetime typically are not changing their behaviors, whereas those who have had multiple partners were more likely to reduce the number of partners. Findings indicate that younger male unmarried adults, nonwhites, and those living in urban areas were more likely to have changed their behaviors because of the threat of HIV/AIDS, including partner reduction, condom use, staying with one partner, or abstaining from sex (Feinleib & Michael, 1998). Still, some of those with the greatest exposure to risk report making no changes in their sexual behaviors (Feinleib & Michael, 1998). This subset of young adults constitutes a major concern for U.S. health practitioners. (See Table 13.5.)

Table 13.5 AIDS Cases in Early Adulthood, United States, by Gender and Race: 1985, 2003

Note that young adults, ages 20 to 39, comprise the majority of newly diagnosed cases of AIDS for both males and females over this time period. Nearly 60 percent of males diagnosed for all reporting years since the early 1980s are in this age bracket, and 63 percent of females diagnosed for all reporting years are within the ages of 20 to 39. Also note the *significant increase* in the number of newly diagnosed young black and Hispanic males and females since 1985. Thus, young adults need to take better preventive measures to avoid HIV sexual transmission.

Age at Diagnosis	1985 (Number)	2003 (Number)	% All Years (% Distribution)
Males			
20 to 29	1,497	3,570	15.2
30 to 39	3,575	12,214	44.4
White males	4,473	11,069	47.1
Black males	1,695	13,820	35.7
Hispanic males	989	6,344	15.8
Asian males	47	458	0.8
Females			
20 to 29	175	1,774	20.2
30 to 39	230	4,075	43.1
White females	143	1,923	21.5
Black females	275	7,373	61.4
Hispanic females	98	1,776	15.9
Asian females	1	105	0.6

Source: Centers for Disease Control and Prevention (2004). *Health, United States, 2004:* Table 52, p. 208. Washington, DC: U.S. Department of Health and Human Services.

The Worldwide Epidemic of AIDS   Although health issues of paramount importance vary across cultures, HIV/AIDS has reached epidemic proportions in all developing regions. In 2004, the UNAIDS program estimated nearly *40 million* children and adults worldwide are living with AIDS, with the highest numbers in the poorest regions: sub-Saharan Africa, nearly 26 million; southern and southeastern Asia with 7 million; Latin America with nearly 2 million; eastern Asia with 1 million; the United States with 1 million; western Europe with more than 600,000; northern Africa with more than 540,000; and the Caribbean countries with more than 440,000 (UNAIDS, 2004). Rates of HIV/AIDS transmission and death are very high in African countries, where many myths about transmission of the disease abound, and condoms and medicines to curb the disease and prolong life are often unaccepted or unavailable. Millions of children in sub-Saharan Africa alone have become orphaned (UNAIDS, 2004). Also, cultural female and male circumcisions are often conducted on groups of adolescents at one time using one unsterilized "surgical" device (Duke, 1999). (See *Human Diversity:* "Cultural Practices of Female Genital Mutilation," in Chapter 11.)

Socioeconomic Status, Ethnicity, and Gender

In the United States, people who are poor and lack higher education have a higher death rate than people who are wealthy and better educated (Stevens, 1996). The reasons are not surprising—poverty increases the likelihood that one will experience inadequate or poor nutrition, poor housing, insufficient or no prenatal care, limited access to health-care facilities, and less education. And many studies confirm that racial and ethnic minorities and single parents are more likely to live in poverty. Poor people who do not have health insurance cannot afford good medical care, and it has been shown that with less education one is more susceptible to heart disease, hypertension, and other health ailments (Pincus & Callahan, 1994). Does this mean that if someone living in poverty won the lottery tomorrow, good health would follow? Better medical care would be within reach with the boost in income, but poor habits with respect to eating, smoking, using drugs, drinking, and having sex at early ages have social links—and these might remain entrenched in the person's lifestyle.

We all know that women have a longer life expectancy than men, but it is not clear how this is related to specific health problems. It has been suggested that women's greater longevity is due to women's having two X chromosomes and larger amounts of the hormone estrogen. But as women's patterns of work and recreation have become more like men's, their health patterns and concerns have become similar. Decreases in smoking among women lag behind the decreases among men. According to the American Cancer Society (2005), more women have died each year since 1987 from lung cancer than from what had been the major cause of cancer death in women—breast cancer. Yet breast cancer is the most frequently diagnosed cancer among women, with much higher rates than lung cancer; but preventative diagnostics, treatments, and survival rates have improved remarkably for breast cancer (American Cancer Society, 2005). Smoking remains the most preventable cause of cancer, and it is a behavior that can be changed. On a positive note, tobacco use among adults and youth has decreased considerably by the early 2000s, and the American Cancer Society (2005) reports that only about 20 percent of women smoke and about 25 percent of men. Smoking among college students has declined markedly to only 12 percent, but non-college peers have a rate of about 30 percent.

The National Mental Health Association (2003) estimates that depression affects nearly 19 million Americans each year and affects the ability to sleep, eat, study, and enjoy life. Also, there is an association between gender and depression, and women experience depression at much higher rates than men. Women who experience greater stress, responsibility, and pressure, such as single parents, also have higher rates of depression. And many young adults do not have insurance coverage for treatment over time—if they seek treatment at all. Women also tend to resort to more dysfunctional ways of coping such as self-blame, venting anger on others, and seeking comfort in sweets or alcohol (Hänninen & Aro, 1996). No one can forget the Andrea Yates tragedy—a former valedictorian, honor society member, and a registered nurse who as a young mother was overwhelmed with raising five young children and experienced severe depression leading to severe mental health problems. Studies suggest black males and white males are affected nearly equally with depression (about 12 percent), but black males have far fewer resources to seek treatment. Mental health experts believe one of the reasons so many young adult black men are incarcerated is because of untreated depression and other mental illness ("Many Black Men Go Untreated for Depression," 2005). Another recent study reports that adults who were foster children also experience higher rates of depression and post-traumatic stress disorder ("Study: Foster Kids Face Mental Illnesses in Adulthood," 2005). Kang and Hyams (2005) also report about 20 percent of veterans returning from combat in Iraq and Afghanistan are experiencing depression and post-traumatic stress disorder.

Research suggests that the gender gap with respect to depression relates to gender inequities in numerous areas of adult life, such as employment opportunities, pay and authority in the workplace, the burden of child care and housework, and conflictual relational situations that women and men often find themselves in as young adults. One reason the gap is not disappearing is that generally men get more pay outside the home, while the balance of power within the home still rests with men (Mirowsky & Ross, 2003). Because women have substantially increased their educational attainment over the past 30 years, some are moving into executive, administrative, medical, engineering, and professional positions with higher incomes. But more women are in service industries that pay minimum wage with few, if any, medical benefits (Chao & Utgoff, 2004). Interestingly, the same Bureau of Labor Statistics report shows that, on average, women contributed 26 percent of the family income in 1970 and now contribute about 34 percent of the family income.

The real median earnings for full-time male workers in 2003 was $40,668 compared with $30,724 for real median earnings for women working full time—about 75 percent of men's income (DeNavas-Walt, Proctor,

& Mills, 2004). With greater pressure today in most families to provide an ever-increasing income to raise a family, a higher proportion of single female parents, and a greater number of single young adults trying to survive on their own, young adults are attending college in record numbers to later secure higher paying jobs. "The labor market is increasingly rewarding individuals with the skills acquired in college," says Andrew Sum, from Northeastern University's Center for Labor Market Studies and lead author of a study on the growing gender gaps in college enrollment and degree attainment. Since 1993, women have outpaced men in college enrollment and degree attainment—that includes more women than men enrolled in college across all age groups and racial and ethnic groups. And there are typically substantial economic and social advantages to acquiring a degree. Women have earned more associate's and bachelor's degrees in all 50 states, and they are closing the gap in earning professional and doctoral degrees (Sum et al., 2003).

Regardless of gender or ethnic background, in 2004 a male college graduate earned, on average, $63,000 annually, compared with $33,000 for men with a high school diploma or GED. A female college graduate earned more than $38,000, compared with almost $22,000 for a high school graduate (see Figure 13.5) (Armas, 2005). Significantly, in October 2004, the unemployment rate for high school dropouts was nearly 40 percent, and the unemployment rate for high school graduates not enrolled in college was 20 percent (see Table 13.6) (U.S. Bureau of Labor Statistics, 2005). However, there are some who turn to ineffective and self-destructive behaviors to cope.

Changes in Drug and Alcohol Use over Time

The end of high school is a major transition period for most adolescents as they enter into the world of young adulthood. The usual roles that young adults take on include college student, civilian employee, and member of the armed forces—though approximately 10 percent of young adults simply "drop out" of mainstream society (some are incarcerated, institutionalized, chronically ill, or disabled). Traditionally, common experiences for young adults have included completing college, securing full-time employment, being promoted in the workplace, marrying, working toward advanced degrees, and parenting. Each of these experiences affects substance or alcohol use during the post high school years, so it is useful to consider the timing of these experiences during young adulthood and how they are interrelated. National data collected from high school classes between 1976 and 1997 indicate that one of the most fundamental choices facing young adults as they leave high school is whether they should go on to college (Johnston, Bachman, & O'Malley, 1997). At least 66 percent of the high school class of 2004 (1.8 million) are attending college—near record highs (U.S. Bureau of Labor Statistics, 2005). High school graduates not going to college, as young adults, are more likely to:

- continue to live at home for a while
- marry at younger ages
- be employed at low-paying jobs
- be homemakers or single-parent moms, for females

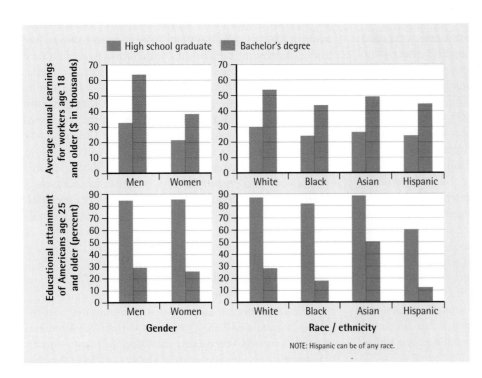

FIGURE 13.5 College-Educated Workers Earn More Figures from a 2004 U.S. Bureau of the Census survey reinforce the value of a college education, showing workers with a bachelor's degree earn more than those with only a high school diploma.
Source: From Genaro C. Armas, "Black, Asian Women with College Degree Outearn White Women," *The Seattle Times,* March 28, 2005. Copyright © 2005 Associated Press. Reprinted with permission.

Table 13.6 Unemployment Rates for 2004 High School Graduates and 2003–2004 High School Dropouts, October 2004

Graduate Status	% Unemployed
High school graduates, enrolled in college	13.3
High school graduates, not enrolled in college	20.0
High school dropouts	39.9

Source: Bureau of Labor Statistics. (2005, March 25). College enrollment and work activity of 2004 high school graduates. *Current Population Survey, USDL 05-487.* Washington, DC: U.S. Department of Labor. Retrieved April 8, 2005, from http://www.bls.gov/news.release/hsgec.nr0.htm

How do these differences compare in terms of new freedoms and responsibilities? College students must learn to manage time and deal with the pressures of exams and school requirements, while they also have more flexibility in their schedules, housing arrangements, and day-to-day lives. It is important to note that these differences do translate into how frequently individuals—especially those not not gainfully employed—use drugs during young adulthood. Mapped over time, data on annual marijuana use and marital status show the following:

- Overall, women use marijuana less than men do.
- Married individuals use marijuana less than single individuals do.
- Young individuals use marijuana more than older individuals do.

Among married men and women, those under age 20 were most likely to use marijuana. These findings show that getting married strongly correlates with a lower rate of use of marijuana. Although this survey did give reasons for this trend, perhaps you can suggest some.

A related problem that has recently received national attention is binge drinking on college campuses. **Binge drinking** is defined as having five consecutive drinks for men, four for women. A Harvard School of Public Health study found that more than 80 percent drink, and about half of those students admitted that they had engaged in binge drinking (Weitzman, 2004). Young adults are dying of alcohol poisoning and alcohol-related accidents, and binge drinking in college continues to make headlines. Tragically, about 1,400 students die from alcohol-related accidents each year. College students also spend more on alcohol than they spend on textbooks, soft drinks, tea, milk, juice and coffee combined—currently $5.5 billion a year (Nelson et al., 2005).

Although drinking had always been part of the college scene, the reason for the increase in bingeing is probably due to the greater social acceptance of drinking over drugs. It is speculated that even though the legal drinking age has been raised, this has only served to function as a new type of prohibition—one that college-age people wanted to breach. Because of the recent attention this problem has received, many college campuses have begun to address this issue. "Young or 'emergent' adulthood is a time of great opportunity, risk and social developmental transition for young people," said Weitzman (2004). The period of young adulthood, ages 18 to 24, coincides with the peak years for onset of the most common mental health and addiction problems among young adults—those associated with alcohol, tobacco and other drug use, depression and anxiety disorders, and suicide.

Questions

Is there any particular segment of the young adult cohort that is most at risk for negative health outcomes? What are some recommendations to maintain or improve physical health during this period of the life span?

Mental Health

Mental health is also a matter of concern at any age. We know that poor health, alcohol and drug use, depression, and ultimately joblessness and family dysfunction are generally interrelated.

It is estimated that about 20 percent of Americans 18 and older (about one in five adults) suffer from a diagnosable mental disorder in any given year (Eaton et al., 2004). Of these, about one-third seek professional help, and general medical practitioners rather than psychiatrists or other psychotherapists treat the bulk of those individuals. In a given year, close to 9 million Americans develop a mental health problem for the first time; another 8 million suffer a relapse; and another 35 million experience continuing symptoms.

Overall, two elements stand out in any consideration of mental health. First, from a social perspective, mental health involves people's ability to function effectively in their social roles and to carry out the requirements of group living. Second, from a psychological perspective, mental health involves a subjective sense of well-being—happiness, contentment, and satisfaction. Yet adequate social functioning and a sense of psychological well-being are not so much states of being as processes. Mental health requires that people continually change and adapt to life experiences, and people who have good mental health are commonly taken to have found a comfortable fit between themselves and the world—they "have it all together." People who do not "have it all together" can experience anxiety, stress, or depression. Let's take a closer look at these issues.

In intensive interviews with 20,000 men and women from households selected to represent the entire population, diagnosed mental disorders ranged from mild impairments like a phobia of heights or enclosed places to incapacitating bouts of depression or chronic problems like schizophrenia. Some 20 million Americans report having at least one phobia severe enough to interfere with their daily functioning. Alcoholism is also prevalent, with close to 14 million Americans reporting an alcohol problem. Many people report having more than one disorder; for instance, 6 million people report having a substance-abuse disorder along with one or more other mental disorders (Hankin et al., 1998).

Some 19 million Americans suffer from some form of depression each year (National Mental Health Association, 2003). And cross-cultural studies consistently find that twice as many adult women as men are depressed, particularly women aged 18 to 24 (Hankin et al., 1998). Findings suggest that women experience more depression because they tend to resort to emotion-focused coping instead of problem-solving coping. In a study conducted by Hänninen and Aro (1996) in Finland with nearly 1,700 young adult females and males, the focus was on functional versus dysfunctional coping strategies. An effective strategy among women was "thinking the problem over with a friend," whereas men tended to use effective coping strategies such as "trying to find something relaxing to do," "tackling the problem more persistently than before," and reassuring themselves that "there's no reason to get upset." Women were more likely to engage in dysfunctional coping strategies, such as "venting anger on other people," "blaming oneself for what happened," and "seeking comfort in sweets." Men were more likely to resort to a dysfunctional approach of "going out for a few beers." Overall, dysfunctional ways of coping with stress exacerbate stress and depression.

A variety of studies reveal that depression and other mental illnesses become more prevalent with low income and low education levels (Hankin et al., 1998). Additionally, young adults between the ages of 25 and 34 report a higher incidence of psychiatric disorder than do elderly people. One partial explanation seems to be that older people sometimes overlook the mental difficulties they had earlier in life. But it is also true that many contemporary young adults face substantial stressors, such as drugs, alcohol, eating disorders, competition in the academic and work world, single parenthood, and fear about the future (Miller, 1994).

Lifetime alcohol use (a central nervous system depressant) increases the risk for major depression for both men and women across studies. Both cultural and acculturation factors appear to play a role in alcohol use, drug use, and depression, according to findings from a recent study with young adult males from Puerto Rico, the Dominican Republic, and Colombia (Zayas, Rojas, & Malgady, 1998). Johnson and Gurin (1994) reported that among Puerto Rican men, depression is strongly associated with alcohol consumption. Research findings are mixed from examining the association between the strains of Hispanic acculturation to American society and alcohol use and mental health problems: Some findings indicate a positive relationship, others find a negative relationship. Some studies, however, suggest that Hispanic men begin heavy alcohol consumption in their early and mid-twenties and drink more heavily than men in the general population (Johnson & Gallo-Treacy, 1993). A study of young adult Hispanic males found that Mexican American and Puerto Rican men between the ages of 25 and 34 years old report more alcohol consumption than do older men (Black & Markides, 1994). More community-based research is needed to understand the associations among immigration experience, sociocultural norms of drinking or drug use, and acculturation experiences (Zayas, Rojas, & Malgady, 1998).

Psychological disorders and disturbances result from both individual vulnerability and environmental stresses. Some people are genetically so susceptible that it is exceedingly difficult for them to find an environment sufficiently low in stress to prevent them from having a breakdown. Hereditary predisposition most commonly takes the form of a defect in the metabolism of one or more neurotransmitters. At the other end of the continuum are people so resilient and resistant to stress that few, if any, environments would trigger severe disturbance in them. For example, some political or military prisoners, despite years of torture and solitary confinement, manage to retain their sanity. In sum, people differ greatly in their vulnerability to mental disorder and disturbance (Wiebe, 1991).

Stress In the course of our daily lives, most of us experience one or more demands that place physical and emotional pressure on us. We commonly term these experiences "stress." The circumstances that lead to stress are many and varied. A study of young adults between the ages 18 and 25 looked at the experiences of those having difficulty obtaining and keeping a job in parts of Europe that were undergoing economic changes. The research explored the effects of choice and uncertainty on the survey respondents' lives (Behrens & Evans, 2002). Adults who say that they feel stress often report that they get only six hours of sleep each night. This compares to adults who sleep seven hours and say they feel stress rarely or never. A recent poll found that one in six Americans reported getting only five hours of sleep per night, and another 55 percent reported getting six or seven hours of sleep (Moore, 2002). Of course, some of these young adults are also parents of newborns and infants, and sleep deprivation for weeks or months is the norm, as difficult as it may be. What are the implications of a largely sleep-deprived society? How does the amount of sleep you get affect your own life?

Gender Differences in Stress A variety of research studies conducted over the past two decades consistently find that women are more likely to feel—or at least to admit to feeling—stress than men are (though men might

Early Parenthood Years Are Most Stressful Because of Sleep Deprivation The circumstances that lead to stress are many and varied. But today's new parents, both of whom are likely employed as well, are often the most sleep deprived and might seek social support to ease that stress.

Source: For Better or for Worse © 2004 Lynn Johnston Productions. Dist. By Universal Press Syndicate. Reprinted with permission. All rights reserved.

be less likely to report being distressed because they want to present themselves in a better light) (Almeida & Kessler, 1998; Nolen-Hoecksema, 2001). There appear to be two major views about this gender difference. *Rumination theory* states that women are more likely to ruminate on (dwell on) their negative emotions, thereby prolonging their distress. Men, on the other hand, tend to respond to distress in a behavioral fashion, distracting themselves from the stress (Nolen-Hoeksema, Morrow, & Frederickson, 1993). The gender-role perspective, however, suggests that women are more distressed than men because their roles as nurturant, empathic caretakers expose them to more daily stressors in contrast to male roles, which are generally more instrumental (Mirowsky & Ross, 1989). Several studies confirm that women were more distressed over family events, and men were more distressed by financial or work-related problems (Almeida & Kessler, 1998; Conger et al., 1993).

Nolen-Hoecksema (2001) found that women from adolescence through adulthood were twice as likely to experience depression as men. The difference may be attributable to differences in stress responses and exposure to certain stressors. This is not surprising, because women in contemporary American society are likely to be wage earners, caretakers of family members, housekeepers, chauffeurs for child activities, PTA participants, and caretakers of elderly relatives. Women also are more likely than men to openly admit that stress has affected their health (Daley et al., 1998). In fact, stressful life events impact heavily on all aspects of anyone's routines, and there is documented evidence of increased accidents or injuries when an individual is under psychological stress (Almeida & Kessler, 1998).

Stress Reported by Nontraditional Versus Traditional College Students Nontraditional students have entered college in record numbers over the past decade. A

nontraditional student is defined as a student with major multiple roles (e.g., spouse, parent, employee, student) and at least a one-year hiatus between high school and college. The average reported absence time between high school and college entry is 10 years. Traditional college students are typically 18 to 23 years old and have come to college directly from high school. The *Digest of Education* ("Postsecondary Education," 2003) reported that in 2001 more than one-third of all college students were 25 years or older, which means many are of nontraditional status. Nontraditional students typically report role strains because of lack of time and the pressure of more role demands. Dill and Henley (1998) recently conducted a study in which nontraditional and traditional students completed a survey on major and daily life events that they perceived to be stressful (positive, neutral, and negative life events). Their findings suggest that in comparison to nontraditional students, *traditional students* are likely to:

- attend class more often
- belong to campus organizations and find social and peer events more important
- report more problems with roommates
- worry more about their academic performance
- spend more time relaxing with friends, though their friends often drink and use drugs
- be happy about becoming independent, though a social network is very important
- feel more pressure about expectations from their parents

In contrast to traditional students, *nontraditional students* are likely to:

- find doing homework more desirable
- experience a greater impact from bad classes or poor teaching

- report more responsibility and obligations at home and have little time for friends
- report concerns about family or friends recovering from illness
- indicate they enjoy going to classes but find that other responsibilities interfere sometimes
- have overall satisfaction with their role as student
- have specific financial aid problems

Overall, both groups of students experience stress, but high levels of stress are more common among nontraditional students. Most colleges have established clubs for nontraditional students, but many cannot find the time to participate. Some colleges have Web sites and offer distance learning courses specifically to meet the needs of nontraditional students.

Stages of Stress Reaction According to a classic study undertaken by Hans Selye (1956), our bodies respond to stress in several stages. The first stage is the *alarm reaction*. The nervous system is activated; digestion slows; heartbeat, blood pressure, and breathing rate increase; and the level of blood sugar rises. In brief, the body pulsates with energy. Then, the *stage of resistance* sets in. The body mobilizes its resources to overcome the stress. During this phase the heart and breathing rates often return to normal. But the appearance of normality is superficial, because adrenocorticotropic hormone (ACTH), produced by the pituitary, remains at high levels. Finally, if some measure of equilibrium is not restored, a *stage of exhaustion* is reached. The body's capacity to handle stress becomes progressively undermined, physiological functioning is impaired, and eventually the organism dies.

By virtue of having been linked to various disorders, including heart disease, high blood pressure, ulcers, asthma, and migraine headaches, stress has acquired a bad name. Yet stress is a factor in everyone's life. Indeed, without some stress we would find life quite drab, boring, and stagnant. Therefore, psychologists are increasingly concluding that stress, in and of itself, is not necessarily bad. Much depends on the knowledge or experience we have to problem solve effectively or cope with the various stresses in our lives. Even so, we can agree that some events are more stressful than others, such as serious illness or disability, the death of a loved one, divorce, and unemployment being the most severe.

More often than not, stress resides neither in the individual nor in the situation alone but in how the person perceives a particular event (Terry, 1994). Not surprisingly, some individuals seem to be more stress-resistant than others by virtue of the attitudes they bring to their lives, and consequently they enjoy better health (Wiebe, 1991). Psychologists find that *hardiness* is associated with an openness to change, a feeling of involvement

in what one is doing, and a sense of control over events (Kobasa, Maddi, & Kahn, 1982). Take the matter of a person's attitude toward change. Should a man lose his job, for example, he can view it as a catastrophe or as an opportunity to begin a new career more to his liking. Likewise, stress-resistant individuals get involved in life rather than hanging back on its fringes: They immerse themselves in meaningful activity. Furthermore, psychologically hardy people believe that they can actively influence many of the events in their lives and that they have an impact on their surroundings. Other researchers also find that good self-esteem and a sense of control are important buffers against the harmful effects of stress (Brandtstadter & Rothermund, 1994).

Because we are social beings, the quality of our lives depends in large measure on our interpersonal relationships. A particular strength of the human condition is our propensity for giving and receiving support from one another under stressful circumstances. Social support consists of the exchange of resources among people, based on their interpersonal ties. Group and community supports affect how we respond to stress through their health-sustaining and stress-buffering functions. Those of us with strong support systems appear better able to cope with major life changes and daily hassles. As we will see in Chapters 18 and 19, people with strong social ties live longer and have better health than those without such ties. Studies covering a range of illnesses, from depression to arthritis to heart disease, reveal that the presence of social support helps people fend off illness, and the absence of such support makes poor health more likely (Turner, Wheaton, & Lloyd, 1995). Social support cushions stress in a number of ways: Friends, relatives, and coworkers may let us know that they value us. Our self-esteem is strengthened when we feel accepted by others despite our faults and difficulties. Other people often provide us with informational support. They help us to define and understand our problems and find solutions to them. We typically find social companionship supportive. Engaging in leisure-time and recreational activities with others helps us to meet our social needs, simultaneously distracting us from our worries and troubles. Other people may give us instrumental support—financial aid, material resources, and needed services—that reduce stress by helping us resolve and cope with our problems.

Adults who say they feel little or no stress tend to be regular exercisers and nonsmokers and to be in good health on the whole. Additional factors affect a person's reaction to stress, because much stress is associated with relationships (family, coworkers, friends, neighbors, and others).

Suicide in Young Adulthood The CDC reports that the suicide rate for young African American males ages 10 to 19 has more than doubled since 1980, rising from a rate of 2 to 4.5 per 100,000—a rate much higher than for young white males. And these numbers may not reflect the actual number of suicides, because they are reported as homicides or accidents. One phenomenon is known as "suicide by cop," whereby young men deliberately engage in gun battle or other life-threatening behaviors. Psychologist Alvin Poussaint in *Lay My Burden Down: Unraveling Suicide and the Mental Health Crisis Among African-Americans* says: "We have data telling us that this is a trend (suicide among young African Americans) on the rise, but we have no data telling us about the socioeconomic background or personal histories of these young men that would help up determine why this trend is on the rise" (Whitaker, 2001, p. 142). Gibbs (1997) suggests young adults should make every effort to graduate from high school, go to college or enroll in job training, apprenticeship, or internship programs, and increase their opportunities for employment to mitigate the effects of the stress and depression in their lives.

Rates of attempted suicide among adolescents and young adults are higher than at other life stages, but men have higher rates of completed suicide than women. Other risk factors for completed suicides include being a male with lower education, lower income, living alone, having divorced, and being unemployed. Having at least one psychiatric admission, having previously attempted suicide, having been sexually abused, being homosexual and having same-sex attraction, having a family member or close friend who commits suicide, or having a history of drug use are other significant risk factors for young adults (Eaton et al., 2004). Also, men and women over age 65 are at a higher risk. According to the CDC (2004e), the highest numbers are among Native Americans or Alaska Native males in the 15- to 24-year-old age group. The rate of suicide for this group is nearly 28 per 100,000 as compared with Asian or Pacific Islander males whose rate is 9 per 100,000. Again, protective factors against suicide include religious beliefs, a close connection to caring friends, close family connectedness (including having one's own children), and gainful employment, which provides economic security and feelings of positive self-worth.

Questions

It is common for all of us to experience greater stress or depression about some issue at a few points in our lives, but which young adults are most likely to experience more serious bouts of depression and mental illness? What types of activities are known to mitigate the effects of significant stress, depression, and other mental illness?

Sexuality

As we all make, or made, the transition to young adulthood, sexuality takes on added importance because we need to position ourselves as competent, independent, caring individuals. "How do I fulfill my sexual needs?" and "How does sexuality fit in with my idea of who I am?" are some of the questions we ask when we are deciding whether sexual relations for us will be casual, monogamous, or simply another form of "fun." At this time, gender roles are likely to become more complex and challenging. Also, the impact of AIDS has given rise to more serious caution and changes in sexual behaviors for a majority of young adults.

Heterosexuality   Many young adults become sexually active in their college years. According to the recent results of an online survey, more than half of college students who live away from home are sexually active, and three-fourths of sexually active students reported that they are engaging in unprotected sex. Yet a majority of those having unprotected sex do not believe that they are at risk for disease (Bjerklie, 2003).

Furthermore, by age 22, 9 out of 10 young adults have engaged in sex, and a majority of these adults have had multiple partners. Gender differences have all but disappeared with regard to premarital sex, with females having almost as many premarital sexual experiences as males. Also, there are no gender differences in attitudes about homosexuality, masturbation, or sexual satisfaction. Promiscuity does not appear to be rampant; the majority of young adults claim that they have had only one partner during the last year. Many of these young adults report having changed their sexual behaviors owing to the threat of AIDS. Some of the recent modifications include having casual sex less frequently, having fewer partners, being monogamous, or practicing abstinence.

Gay, Lesbian, and Bisexual Attitudes and Behaviors Sexual orientation is no longer thought of in terms of either/or—individuals need not be locked into the

Sexual Orientation Studies indicate that lesbian couples tend to be committed to their relationship and endorse a high degree of equality between partners.

categories heterosexual or homosexual. Bisexuality is a case in point, and in recent surveys around 5 percent of males and 2 percent of females describe themselves as homosexual (Kurdek, 1998). In recent history homosexuality had been seen as an aberration, and it was only in the mid-1970s that the American Psychiatric Association declassified homosexuality as being a disorder. The APA now has guidelines for psychotherapy with lesbian, gay, and bisexual clients.

Recently the legality of marriage between same-sex adults has come to the forefront of American culture as same-sex couples have tested and challenged practices that have prohibited it and the privileges associated with marriage. However, as of this writing, in all 17 states that presented constitutional amendments about the definition of marriage to the electorate, a high majority of the citizens voted that marriage should be between a man and a woman. Twenty-three states already define marriage as heterosexual (Knickerbocker, 2005). Younger voters, age 30 and under, express less opposition than older voters, according to a national poll (Kohut & Doherty, 2004). Yet several crucial issues related to same-sex unions have emerged and entered the judicial and corporate arena, such as parenting leaves from employment, property rights, adoption, inheritance, and health coverage. The right for benefits of those couples in *civil unions* and *domestic partnerships* are recognized by more businesses, industries and colleges, however.

The realization that gender is a social "construction" has led many people to question the rigid gender roles that males and females have traditionally held. The new option "transgendered" is now available for those uncomfortable with the limitations of being a "woman" or a "man." Some reject the notion of a singular gender identity as being able to account for how a person experiences the world. They accept a much more fluid conception of gender containing aspects of what have traditionally been called male and female characteristics.

How do gay men and lesbians manage in the United States when they are given minority status and the majority insists on defining them? During the 1960s and 1970s, collectives of men and women created new social structures that were characterized as "open communities" and became havens for people who chose not to define themselves by narrow definitions of sexuality. The gay man made a transition from queen, fairy, closet, to clone, hot man, and dancer (Chauncey, 1994). The 1970s portrayed gay men as bar hoppers looking for hot, quick sex. The caring professional who was looking for a stable committed relationship was not seen as a legitimate role for gay men, until recently. As more studies on sexual minorities are conducted, a clearer picture begins to emerge. For instance, some studies have found that sexual minorities have higher rates of some mental disorders, whereas another study found that lesbians reported rates of mental

health similar to those of heterosexual women in addition to higher levels of self-esteem (DeAngelis, 2002b).

In short, there are many more similarities than differences in human relationships, regardless of sexual preference.

Question

What is social science research finding out about the range of sexual behaviors and changes in sexual attitudes of the current generation of young adults?

Cognitive Development

The varied experiences of adult life pose new challenges and require that we continually refine our reasoning capabilities and problem-solving techniques. Be it in the realm of interpersonal relationships, working, parenting, managing homes, or participating in church or community volunteerism—or even when vacationing—we confront new circumstances, uncertainties, and difficulties that call for decision making and resourceful thought. Consequently, we must learn to identify problems, analyze them by breaking them down into their relevant components, and devise effective coping strategies. The following is a true story of a vacation that challenged the problem-solving and critical thinking skills of two of your authors and demonstrates how well stressful events become etched in our memories. One of the things we learn when things go wrong is what we would do differently the next time the situation arises. We're sure you have your own version of our misadventure:

> One year, we decided to vacation at a rental condo in sunny Myrtle Beach during spring break. While packing the rental car, which was supposed to be a three-seat station wagon, we discovered there was no third seat and that the car could not accommodate everyone. The rental car dealer said he "thought" there was a third seat when he rented the car to us—not to worry, though, because a passenger van will be there in the morning. When picking up the van, we discover it has about 110,000 miles on it, and there's no time to service it. The embarrassed dealer gives us the van for free. Off we go a day later than planned to start our much-needed vacation. Driving well into the night in extremely high winds, we arrive at a motel in the Carolinas. The next morning the motel has no power because the high winds knocked out some lines. With four hungry, irritable teenagers in tow, we attempt to get something to eat and discover that the rental van now will drive only in reverse! After driving around the parking lot in reverse in a van that resembles a large brown elephant, we call the dealer to see what he wants us to do with his van. He says he will reimburse us for repairs. It is Saturday, and most garages are closed.

Luckily, about three hours later a mechanic arrives, fixes the problem and we're on our way. Our first night in a beautiful new condo, at 3 A.M., the fire alarm goes off, and all of the pajama-clad residents have to evacuate the building into the parking lot while firemen check the building. Some teenager thought that setting off the alarm was a fun prank! As adults, we are never on "vacation" from utilizing our reasoning and critical thinking skills! Also, a dose of laughter helped us cope.

Post-Formal Operations

For Jean Piaget, the stage of formal operations constituted the last stage in cognitive development. Piaget depicted adolescence as opening a new horizon in thought. During this period adolescents gain the ability to think about their own mental processes, to imagine multiple possibilities in a situation, and to mentally generate numerous hypothetical outcomes. In brief, adolescence opens to teenagers the prospect of thinking in logical, abstract, and creative ways.

A number of psychologists have speculated about whether a fifth and qualitatively higher level of thought follows formal operations (Demetriou, 1988; Soldz, 1988). Common to the various formulations is the notion that **post-formal operational thought** is characterized by these three features:

- First, adults come to realize that knowledge is not absolute but relativistic. They recognize that there are no such things as facts, pure and simple, but deem facts to be constructed realities—attributes we impute to experience and construe by the activities of the mind. (There are many times in the world of work when people have different visions about a project and need to learn to collaborate.)
- Second, adults come to accept the contradictions contained in life and the existence of mutually incompatible systems of knowledge. This understanding is fostered by the adult's expanding social world. In the larger community the adult is confronted by differing viewpoints, contrary people, and incompatible roles. And she or he is constantly required to select a course of action from among a multitude of possibilities. (There are times when we must respect and do what our older in-laws tell us to do—even if we believe it might not be the best course of action.)
- Third, because they recognize that contradiction is inherent in life, adults must find some encompassing whole by which to organize their experience. In other words, adults must integrate or synthesize information, interpreting it as part of a larger totality. (Sometimes we have to look at the larger picture and realize we need to work to support ourselves and our families—even if we are not satisfied with the atmosphere at work.)

Here, then, is a working model of post-formal operational thought. Future research will be needed to determine the appropriateness of models that set forth a fifth stage in cognitive development.

Or perhaps future research will show that a Piagetian model has limited usefulness. Critics of Piaget are increasingly challenging the assumptions underlying his theory. For instance, evidence suggests that younger and older adults might merely differ in their cognitive competencies. Younger adults seem to place greater reliance on rational and formal modes of thinking; older adults seem to develop a greater measure of subjectivity in their reasoning, and they place greater reliance on intuition and the social context in which they find themselves (Labouvie-Vief, DeVoe, & Bulka, 1989). Further, more complex cognitive tasks place greater demands on working-memory resources that decline with increased age (Salthouse, 1992). In any event, most psychologists now acknowledge that cognitive development is a lifelong process, a viewpoint that has gained widespread acceptance only in the past 40 years.

Thought and Information Processing

Adult thinking is a complex process. We would be little more than glorified cameras and projectors if information handling were limited to storage and retrieval. Psychologist Robert J. Sternberg (1997) has studied how we think by examining what is involved in information processing. He views **information processing** as the step-by-step mental operations that we use in tackling intellectual tasks. He examines what happens to information from the time we perceive it until the time we act on it. The various stages or components of this process are highlighted by an analogy problem: *Washington is to one as Lincoln is to (a) five, (b) ten, (c) fifteen, (d) fifty.*

In approaching this problem, we first encode the items, identifying each one and retrieving from our long-term memory store any information that might be relevant to its solution. For instance, we might encode for "Washington" such attributes as "president," "depicted on paper currency," and "Revolutionary War leader." Encodings for "Lincoln" might include "president," "depicted on paper currency," and "Civil War leader." *Encoding* is a critical operation. In this example, our failure to encode either individual as having his portrait on paper currency will preclude our solving the problem.

Next, we must infer the relationship between the first two terms of the analogy: "Washington" and "one." We might infer that "one" makes reference to Washington having been the first president or to his being portrayed on the one-dollar bill. Should we make the first linkage and fail to make the second, we will again be stymied in solving the problem.

Then, we must examine the second half of the analogy, which concerns "Lincoln." We must map the higher-order relationship that links "Washington" to "Lincoln." On all three dimensions the men share similarities: both were presidents, both are depicted on currency, and both were war leaders. Should we fail to make the connection that both Washington and Lincoln are portrayed on currency, we will not find the correct answer.

In the next step we must apply the relation that we infer between the first two items ("Washington" and "one") and the third item ("Lincoln") to each of the four alternative answers. Of course, Washington appears on the one-dollar bill and Lincoln on the five-dollar bill. Here we could fail to recognize the relationship because we make a faulty application (we might mistakenly recall Lincoln as appearing on the fifty-dollar bill).

We then attempt to justify our answer. We check our answer for errors of omission or commission. We might recall that Lincoln was the sixteenth president, but if we are uncertain, we might select "fifteen," figuring we are somewhat amiss in our recollection. Finally, we respond with the answer that we conclude is most appropriate.

Sternberg (1998) finds that the best problem solvers are not necessarily those who are quickest at executing each of the above steps. In fact, the best problem solvers spend more time on "encoding" than poor problem solvers do. Good problem solvers take care to put in place the relevant information that they might need later for solving the problem. Consequently, they have the information that they require in later stages. Thus, expert physicists spend more time encoding a physics problem than beginners do, and they are repaid by their increased likelihood of finding the correct solution.

Cognitive Development in College Students

It is important that college professors—and college students—understand that students reason differently depending on their level of experience and intellectual development. Over the past few decades several social scientists have spent time examining how college students mature intellectually over time. They observed that social interactions with faculty, peers, parents, and other adults especially influenced student's cognitive development from the freshman to the senior year. William Perry (1968, 1981) studied male students at Harvard at two time intervals in 1971 and 1979. Though his theory is criticized because his subjects were all males, others who have conducted similar studies with both genders find there is some validity in his theory, in which he attempted to extend Piaget's theories of cognitive development. Perry theorized that freshmen college students generally use more dualistic thinking, as in labeling things "right or wrong" or "good or bad." When asked for an opinion, they were likely to say to the professor: "You tell us. You're the teacher." Over time and with a variety of experiences in college, they begin to use "multiplicity" in their thought. That is,

Working Adults and Problem Solving These young adults are working together as a team to analyze, diagnose, and problem solve. With their high level of intelligence, formal education, and practical experience, they continually gather relevant information and spend more time encoding to find the best solutions. Note also that more women and minorities than ever before are entering technical and engineering professions.

they begin to recognize that there are diverse perspectives on the same subject, and they become willing to listen to them. As they continue to develop cognitively, they transition to "relativistic" thought. Using this type of thinking, they realize that they—and others—must support and defend their position in some rational way. This happens as students move into their junior and senior years, making more commitments, as they integrate knowledge, personal experience, and self-reflection. Students demonstrate commitment when declaring a major, planning a career, choosing a religion, firming up relationships, taking a stand in politics, securing jobs, and so forth.

The *Developmental Instruction Model* proposed by Knefelkamp (1984) aided in operationalizing Perry's model. Their model of college student cognitive development involves four components of challenge and support: structure, diversity, experiential learning, and personalism. Each exists within a continuum, such as more structure to less structure, less diversity to more diversity, low involvement in learning to experiential learning, and moderate levels of personalism to high levels of personalism in instruction. College freshman typically appreciate more structure and social support during their first year, and they are more likely to call home for advice, rely on others, and learn through traditional classroom instruction. This model has implications for instructional methods, because it suggests that freshmen might not be ready to "discuss their views" in a class—they might feel they are supposed to be told what to think, unlike a senior, who is definitely ready for this type of cognitive challenge. As students progress through college, they cognitively transition into making and defending their own decisions, appreciating diverse views, experiencing internships in their field, and interacting with professors and mentors for more personalized instruction. This model suggests that colleges and universities must provide students with resources and materials to be able to support and extend their cognitive growth over time.

Questions

What features characterize maturing adult cognition? In light of the above information about adult thought and problem solving (encoding), should time components for tests such as the SAT and the GRE be modified?

Moral Reasoning

As we saw in Chapter 9, Lawrence Kohlberg identified six stages in the development of moral reasoning and grouped them into three levels:

1. *Preconventional* (Stages 1 and 2)
2. *Conventional* (Stages 3 and 4)
3. *Postconventional* (Stages 5 and 6)

Of particular significance, Kohlberg's cognitive-developmental theory stresses the notion that all people go through the stages in the same order, similar to the stages described by Piaget. Yet not everyone is capable of thinking at Kohlberg's highest levels of moral reasoning Even Kohlberg thought his sixth stage, *Universal Principles,* characterized by noble ideals of brotherhood and the community good—is a lofty ideal that people often do not reach consistently (Kincheloe & Steinberg, 1993). Kohlberg said that in the Postconventional Stage 5, *Social Contract and Individual Rights,* most people begin to think about society in a very theoretical way, considering the rights and values that a society ought to uphold for the good of all. He said, "a good society is best conceived as a social contract into which people freely enter to work toward the benefit of all." While different groups within a society have different values, he believed that all rational people would agree they would all want certain basic *rights,* such as liberty and life, to be protected. Also, they would want some *democratic* procedures for improving society and changing unfair laws (Crain, 1985). In his classic moral dilemma, Kohlberg poses a hypothetical situation about a husband, Heinz, stealing a drug he could not afford to save the life of his wife with cancer. Kohlberg believed a person was at Stage 5 of moral reasoning who said that, "From a moral standpoint Heinz should save the life of even a stranger, since to be consistent, the value of a life means any life" (Crain, 1985).

At the highest level of moral reasoning, Stage 6, *Universal Principles,* Kohlberg said that there were universal principles of *justice*—based on an equal respect for all. Has anyone ever said to you, "Walk a mile in my shoes" to gain understanding from the other person's perspective? Kohlberg argued that participants of a moral dilemma should do just that to come to an understanding about such universal principles. As such, Kohlberg himself reasoned that parties capable of Stage 6 reasoning would all agree that Heinz's wife must be saved—this would be the fair solution (Crain, 1985). Kohlberg also posited that some great moral leaders and philosophers have at times advocated civil disobedience to advance the cause of universal ethical principles—certainly persons such as Mohandas Gandhi from India, a lawyer who gave up all he had to become the embodiment of human rights and change by peaceful protest, and Reverend Martin Luther King, Jr., who was also the embodiment of human rights and peaceful protest to change the face of civil rights in the United States. Ironically, both men's lives were abruptly ended by assassins.

In March 2005, Americans struggled with a moral dilemma that will undoubtedly concern more of society in the future: the sanctioning of *euthanasia*—by court-ordered starvation of a 41-year-old (young adult) healthy but disabled woman with brain damage, named Terri Schindler Schiavo. The court accepted the husband's hearsay testimony that she "wished to die rather than live like that" and ordered a simple feeding tube removed. Of note is that she required no other "life support mechanisms," simply food, just as you and I require to live. Had her own wishes been known in writing in a living will—to live or die in a brain-damaged state—it would not have become such a public, contentious issue.

Various parties viewed this from many moral perspectives: the right of the law and judiciary to supersede the wishes of loving parents who wanted to care for their daughter the rest of her natural days; the legal right of a spouse to supersede the biological parental wishes; the rights of a legal spouse over a partner who could not speak for herself; the right of an individual to be able to move on with his life after 15 years of struggle with legal battles; the right of a spouse to deny rehabilitation efforts; the medical community's own disagreement about the level of brain damage and value of a person with brain damage; rights for all Americans that Thomas Jefferson wrote into the Declaration of Independence to "life, liberty, and the pursuit of happiness"; and the personal definition of "quality of life" which causes some people to decide to die by assisted suicide.

After reading Kohlberg's reasoning at Stages 5 and 6, how do you think he would have reasoned out a "just" solution? With the "slippery slope" effect, will the court decision in Florida spread further into the burgeoning numbers of nursing home residents with Alzheimer's disease, developmental centers that house more persons with brain damage, or neonatal units with babies born with severe disabilities? As you will read in later chapters, if we live long enough, each of us will become disabled in some way, such as living with hearing loss, immobility, intellectual and memory decline, vision loss, and so on, and then our personal perspective on "quality of life" may change.

For more than two decades, Carol Gilligan (1982a; Gilligan, Sullivan, & Taylor, 1995) has conducted thoughtful and systematic research involving Kohlberg's framework. She finds that as they move through their young adult years, men and women take somewhat different approaches to the moral dilemmas employed by Kohlberg in his research. Indeed, women tend to score lower than men on Kohlberg's scale of moral development. Gilligan contends that the lower scores result from bias in Kohlberg's approach, since Kohlberg used only male participants in formulating his theory.

According to Gilligan, men and women have different moral domains. Men define moral problems in terms of right and rules—the "ethic of justice." In contrast, women perceive morality as an obligation to exercise care and to avoid hurt—the "ethic of care." Men deem autonomy and competition to be central to life, so they depict morality as a system of rules for taming aggression and adjudicating rights. Women consider relationships to be central to life, so they portray morality as protecting the integrity of relationships and maintaining human bonding. In sum, whereas men view development as a means of separating from others and achieving independence and autonomy, women view it as a means of integrating oneself within the larger human enterprise.

These two ethical views provide somewhat different bases for finding one's identity and integrating the self. Gilligan calls on developmental psychologists to recognize that the feminine moral construction is as credible and mature as its masculine counterpart. The full response to Gilligan's proposal is not in yet. Not all researchers support her contention that women and men differ in their orientation for moral reasoning. Some researchers have found only limited support for Gilligan's assertion that women are more attuned to issues of care in moral conflicts and men more attuned to issues of justice (Pratt et al., 1991). Still others stress that the realm of care is not an exclusively female realm, nor are justice and autonomy exclusively in the male realm. Indeed, orientations toward justice and care are frequently complementary (Gilgun, 1995).

Question

What are some major differences between Kohlberg's and Gilligan's views of moral reasoning?

SEGUE

In this chapter we have examined the physical and cognitive changes that young adults go through upon graduating from high school (or not) and embarking on the road to adulthood. It is a time when young adults are beginning to understand that there are age norms and to explore the dos and don'ts of this stage. Young adulthood is considered to be a time of increased stressors, including having to make "adult" choices such as whether to drink, smoke, or have sex. The young adult needs to worry about other aspects of healthy development, including regular exercise, proper nutrition, and safe sex. How these changes and choices affect the individual we will see in Chapter 14, when we look at the emotional and social dimensions of becoming an adult—most importantly Erikson's idea that becoming intimate with another is the "crisis" of young adulthood.

Summary

Developmental Perspectives

1. People's feelings, attitudes, and beliefs about adulthood are influenced by the relative proportion of individuals who are adults. At the present time the post–World War II baby-boom generation has brought about a rapid expansion in the nation's labor force. Their children have become a surplus of well-educated individuals in keen competition for managerial and professional positions.

2. The contemporary generation of young adults has been given such labels as Generation X and the Millennials. Studies indicate these are cohorts interested in video entertainment and less exercise, a college education, wealth and home businesses, stability in relationships (though more are cohabiting), less sex because of the threat of STIs, more accepting of the diversity around them, and more willing to live at home longer to fin-

ish college, establish a career, or raise a child as a single parent.

3. For the most part, people in the United States perceive adults of all ages favorably. Age norms may also represent informal expectations about the kinds of roles appropriate for people of various ages. Also, age grading is blurring.

4. People pass through a socially regulated cycle from birth to death just as surely as they pass through the biological cycle.

5. Turning points are times at which individuals change direction in the course of their lives. Some life events are related to social clocks, including entering school, graduating from school, starting to work, marrying, and having children. Other life events are unexpected and individualistic, such as winning the lottery or being the victim of a crime.

Physical Changes and Health

6. The majority of young adults in the United States indicate they are in good health.

7. Factors such as socioeconomic status, ethnicity, and gender might not seem obviously connected, but they interrelate to impact on health. People who live in poverty generally experience more negative health outcomes. Men are more likely than women to choose exercise as a leisure activity. Everyone benefits from regular exercise.

8. The most common mental disorders range from mildly impairing problems like a phobia of heights or enclosed places to incapacitating bouts of depression or chronic problems like schizophrenia. The rate of depression for women generally is twice that for men. Suicide rates for young black and Native American men are rising. Black and Asian women have the lowest rates of suicide.

9. In the course of our daily lives, most of us experience one or more demands that place physical and emotional pressure on us. We commonly call these experiences "stress." Nontraditional students typically experience more stressors than traditional college students. One buffer against stress is having a supportive social network of friends and family.

10. In the transition to young adulthood, sexuality takes on added significance, because we need to position ourselves as competent, independent, caring individuals. "What is sex for me?" and "How does sexuality fit with my idea of who I am?" are some of the questions we ask when we are deciding whether sexual relations for us will be casual, monogamous, or simply another form of fun. At this time, gender roles are likely to become more complex and challenging. Most people define themselves as heterosexual, homosexual, or bisexual.

Cognitive Development

11. Some psychologists have speculated about whether a fifth, and qualitatively higher, level of thought follows formal operations. Common to the various formulations is the notion that post-formal operational thought is characterized by three features: accepting that knowledge is not absolute but relativistic; accepting the contradictions contained in life and the existence of mutually incompatible systems of knowledge; and finding an encompassing whole by which to organize experience.

12. College students typically progress in their cognitive development as they proceed through the college years and into graduate school. As they progress, they learn to make important decisions, support and defend their positions, experience internships and fieldwork, and accept that there is a diversity of views on any one issue. College students progress in cognitive maturity from freshmen to senior years and graduate school. Students at all levels generally benefit from personalized instruction.

Moral Reasoning

13. The two main theories of moral reasoning are Kohlberg's and Gilligan's. Kohlberg's is based on a justice orientation, defining moral problems in terms of right, rules, and a sense of justice for all of society. Gilligan argues that Kohlberg's theory reflects male moral reasoning and that women, in contrast, perceive morality as an obligation to exercise care and to avoid hurting others—the "ethic of care."

Key Terms

age grading (449)

age norms (448)

aging (448)

binge drinking (461)

biological aging (448)

information processing (467)

life events (450)

post-formal operational thought (467)

rape (452)

social aging (448)

social clock (449)

social norms (448)

transition points (448)

Following Up on the Internet

Web sites for this chapter focus on generational characteristics, physical changes, and health issues of early adulthood. Please access the text Web site at www.mhhe.com/vzcrandell8 for up-to-date hot-linked Internet addresses for the following organizations, topics, and resources:

American Generations

Millennials Rising

On the Frontier of Adulthood

American Obesity Association

Harvard's School of Public Health College Alcohol Study

Office of Victim Assistance

American Social Health Association

National Institute of Mental Health

Video Scenario—http://www.mhhe.com/vzcrandell8

In this chapter, you've just read about topics relating to early adulthood, including age and social norms, the social clock, and the concept of post-formal operations. Using the OLC (www.mhhe.com/vzcrandell8), watch the *Early Adulthood video scenario* to see how Chris and Lindsay—a young couple moving back home—and Lindsay's parents work through a variety of life events. Lindsay and Chris's scenario, in particular, introduces some key concepts relating to intimate relationships and emotional development that you'll explore in the next chapter, Early Adulthood: Emotional and Social Development.

Early Adulthood
Emotional and Social Development

1. Which would be the more difficult way for you to spend the rest of your life—living with one person you love and not being able to work, or working with stimulating people at a job you love without ever finding someone to love?

2. Do you believe people can fall in love with someone over the Internet without meeting face to face?

3. Would you be willing to marry someone your parents chose for you as a life partner if you thought that you would fall in love with the person after about 10 years of marriage?

4. Which of your personal characteristics would you most want to hide from your partner? Boss? Parents?

Outline

The process of leaving the parental home during early adulthood has become increasingly complex and variable, with many young people experiencing numerous living arrangements in the course of assuming adult status. Contemporary young men and women are also more open than in the past concerning their sexual orientation and behaviors. For the first time, nuclear families dropped below 25 percent of households, reflecting the trend in American society that has granted greater latitude to those individuals whose lifestyle is less constrained by the "traditional" standards of a nuclear family with one man, one woman, and 2.3 children. For most young adults, the period from the late teens until the mid-forties is a time of establishing intimate relationships, preparing for and building up a position in the work world, and looking forward with hopes and dreams for the future.

Theories of Emotional-Social Development

Central to any lifestyle are the bonds we forge with other people. Much of our identity is linked with our relationships with other people—in relatively stable sets of expectations that sociologists term **social relationships.** For example, if someone asks you who you are, you might answer, "I am the daughter (or son) of _____," or "I am the husband (or wife) of _____," or "I am an employee of _____." Two common types of bonds are expressive ties and instrumental ties. An **expressive tie** is a social link formed when we invest ourselves in and commit ourselves to another person. Many of our needs can be satisfied only in this fashion. Through association with people who are meaningful to us, we gain a sense of security, love, acceptance, companionship, and personal worth. Social interactions that rest on expressive ties are termed **primary relationships.** We view these relationships—with friends, family, and lovers—as ends in themselves, valuable in their own right. Such relationships tend to be personal, intimate, and cohesive. For example, one of the longest-lasting primary relationships people normally have is with siblings.

In contrast, an **instrumental tie** is a social link formed when we cooperate with another person to achieve a limited goal. At times, this relationship can mean working with people we disagree with, as in the old political saying, "Politics makes strange bedfellows." More commonly, it merely means that we find ourselves integrated in complex networks of diverse people, such as the division of labor extending from farmers who grow grain, to grocers who sell bread, to those who serve us sandwiches. Social interactions that rest on instrumental ties are called **secondary relationships.** We view such relationships as means to ends rather than as ends in their own right. Examples are our casual contacts with the cashier at the supermarket, the clerk in the registrar's office, or a gas station attendant. Secondary relationships are everyday touch-and-go contacts in which individuals need have little or no knowledge of one another. As we progress through our adulthood, our days are filled with social contacts among our primary and instrumental ties.

Question

Are the ties you have with family expressive or instrumental?

Psychosocial Stages

As we saw in Chapters 2 and 13, some social scientists have undertaken the search for regular, sequential stages and transitions in the life cycle. Erik Erikson, who pioneered a theory of the psychosocial stages of development, identified nine life-span stages, four of which apply to adulthood: early adulthood, which involves intimacy versus isolation; middle adulthood, which involves generativity versus stagnation; late adulthood, which involves integrity versus despair; and very old age, which involves despair versus hope and faith.

The principal developmental task confronting young adults in the stage of **intimacy versus isolation** is to reach out and make connections with other people. Erikson refers to this stage as the first stage "beyond identity," which was the stage associated with adolescence. Individuals must cultivate the ability to enter into and establish close and intimate relationships with others. Should they fail to accomplish this task, they confront the hazards of leading more isolated lives devoid of society-sanctioned, meaningful bonds (e.g., they might join the ranks of young adult gang members, prisoners, the institutionalized, the unemployed, prostitutes, cults, the homeless, the drug-addicted).

In young adulthood, should the individual fail to come to terms with the critical developmental task of the previous identity stage, the person might temporarily drop out of college or settle for a highly stereotyped interpersonal relationship. Erikson expanded on Freud's succinct dictum "To love and to work," explaining that by love he meant the generosity of intimacy as well as genital pleasure. A general work productiveness should not preoccupy the individual to the extent that there would be a loss in one's right or capacity to be a sexual and a loving being. Isolation is the inability to take chances with one's identity by sharing true intimacy, and such inhibition is often reinforced by fears of the outcomes of intimacy, such as having children. Researchers are finding some young adults who mainly connect and communicate with others through the Internet to alleviate loneliness or social isolation (Matanda, Jenvey, & Phillips, 2004).

The experience of loneliness is not reserved for singles. Research studies have found that there is a cultural component as well as a gender component to the experience of loneliness. Personal inadequacies, lack of social contacts, unfulfilling intimate relationships, relocation or significant separation, and social marginality are major factors promoting loneliness (Rokach, 1998). Additionally, Sadler (1978) presents a model of loneliness that many first-generation American immigrants must be experiencing—that of **cultural dislocation,** defined as a feeling of homelessness and alienation from a traditional way of life. Immigrants from South American and Asian cultures typically value family and extended family for personal support; in contrast North Americans emphasize self-reliance, competitiveness, independence, and autonomy (Jylha & Jokela, 1990). Additionally, immigrants who settle in large metropolitan areas often experience unemployment, fear of crime, social prejudice, and large apartment complex living—all of which promote reluctance to interact or get involved with others (Rokach, 1998). Rokach (1998) found that women across cultures tend to derive most of their self-worth from family and offspring, and if they do not have these kinds of relationships, they can become lonely. However, men often invest heavily in their work.

The psychiatrist George E. Vaillant and his associates (Vaillant & Milofsky, 1980) found support for Erikson's formulations when they followed up a group of 392 white lower-class youth and 94 highly educated men who were first studied in the 1940s as subjects in the *Grant Study*. They concluded, as Erikson contends, that the postchildhood stages of an individual's life cycle must be passed through sequentially. Failure to master one of Erikson's stages typically precluded mastery of later stages. However, the men varied enormously in the age at which they mastered a given stage. In fact, one man in six was still struggling in his forties with issues characteristic of adolescence, such as "What do I want to be when I grow up?" When the researchers examined subsequent employment patterns, the men who had been least emotionally mature as boys were much more likely to have experienced significant unemployment by the time they had reached their mid-forties. Clearly, then, people do not march in lockstep across the life span in developing their identities—optimal psychological functioning is a lifelong challenge (Pulkkinen & Ronka, 1994).

Question

What constitutes a meaningful adult life, according to Erikson?

Phases in Adult Male Development

A number of Yale researchers, led by psychologist Daniel Levinson, have also approached adulthood from a stage perspective. Levinson and his colleagues (1978) constructed a framework for defining phases in the life-span development of adult males. They studied 40 men in their mid-thirties to mid-forties who were blue- and white-collar workers in industry, business executives, academic biologists, and novelists and concluded that men go through six periods from their late teens or early twenties to their late forties. Levinson and his associates say that the overriding task throughout a man's adulthood is the creation of a life structure. A man must periodically restructure his life by creating a new structure or reappraising an old one. He must formulate goals, work out means to achieve them, modify long-held assumptions, memories, and perceptions regarding himself and

the world, and then initiate the appropriate goal-seeking behaviors. Transition periods tend to loom within two or three years of, and on either side of, the symbolically significant birthdays—20, 30, 40, and 50. At age 60, famed German writer Goethe noted that "each ten years of a man's life has its own fortunes, its own hopes, its own desires" (Goethe, 1809). The man and his environment interact to move him developmentally through a series of new levels of life organization. This approach focuses on the underlying set of developmental tasks confronting men rather than on the timing of major life events. Following are summaries of the levels, which are depicted in Figure 14.1.

Leaving the Family   The process begins in the individual's late teens or early twenties when he leaves the family. This phase is a period of transition between his adolescent life, which was centered in the family, and his entry into the adult world. Young men might choose a transitional institution, such as the military or college, to start them on their way, or they might work while continuing to live at home. During this period a roughly equal balance exists between "being in" the family and "moving out." Crossing the family boundary is the major developmental task. He must become less financially dependent, enter new roles and living arrangements, and achieve greater autonomy and responsibility. Levinson said this period lasts about three to five years. But today's young men are more likely to delay leaving home because of the higher cost of a college education in preparation for a career or perhaps periods of unemployment.

Entering the Adult World   This period begins with a man's shifting away from his family of origin. Through adult friendships, sexual relationships, working toward advanced graduate and professional degrees, getting internships or apprenticeships or long-term work experiences, or extended military service, he arrives at an initial definition of himself as an adult. This definition allows him to fashion a temporary life structure that links him to the wider society. During this period men explore and tentatively begin committing themselves to adult roles, responsibilities, and relationships that reflect their evolving set of priorities. A man might lay the groundwork for a career; he might develop one career and then discard it; or he might drift aimlessly, precipitating a crisis at about age 30, when the pressures become strong to achieve more order and stability within his life.

Results from the annual *National Marriage Project* of Rutgers University indicate that contemporary young men are much more likely to contemplate finishing school or training, obtaining full-time employment, being financially independent, and then contemplating marriage. In 1970 the median age for men to marry was 23—today it is 27. Moreover, the median age of marriage

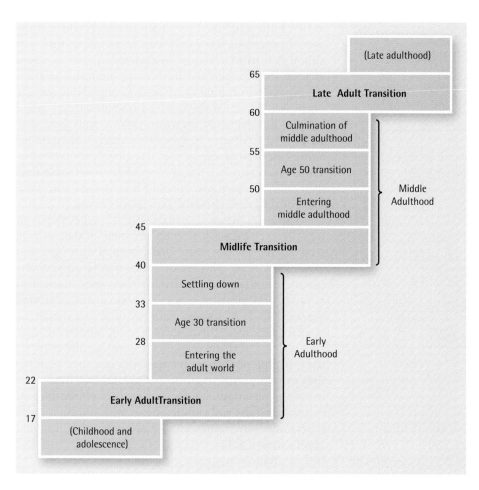

FIGURE 14.1 Periods in Adult Male and Female Development
Daniel Levinson and colleagues conceive of adult development as a succession of periods requiring the restructuring of critical aspects of a person's assumptions regarding self and the world. Levinson's initial study, *Seasons of a Man's Life*, was done with male subjects, but in 1996 similar findings on adult female development were published in *Seasons of a Woman's Life*.
From *The Seasons of a Man's Life* by Daniel Levinson. Copyright © 1978 by Daniel J. Levinson. Used by permission of Alfred A. Knopf, a division of Random House, Inc., and SLL/Sterling Lord Literistic, Inc.

for college educated men is at least a year or two older (Whitehead & Popenoe, 2004). Along the way to marriage, though, more young men are likely to be in one or more cohabiting relationships, which often do not end up in marriage. About 20 percent of young men do not want to marry and hold negative views about marriage. There are signs of a small increase in lifelong singlehood. Based on past data, virtually all persons who are going to marry were married during early adulthood; that is, by age 45.

Settling Down   This period usually begins in the early thirties. The man establishes his niche in society, digs in, builds a nest, and makes and pursues longer-range plans and goals. By this time he has often evolved a dream, a vision of his own future. In succeeding years there can be a major shift in life direction, when he revives the dream and experiences a sense of betrayal, disillusionment, or compromise with respect to it. Careers such as those of professional athletes can interfere with satisfying the developmental tasks associated with this phase. Being "on the road" to compete does not allow most professional athletes opportunities to develop meaningful intimate relationships; and their high-profile status makes them targets of close scrutiny by the media. Though

they might enjoy the limelight, the status, and the high salaries, they are likely to have fewer friendships and to lack a strong intimate relationship with someone. As we all know, several high-profile athletes have admitted to having hundreds of "one-night" stands and are now experiencing the consequences of such a life.

Becoming One's Own Man   This period tends to occur in the mid-to-late thirties. It is the high point of early adulthood and the beginning of what lies beyond. A man frequently feels that no matter what he has accomplished so far, he is not sufficiently independent. He might long to get out from under the authority of those over him. He commonly believes that his superiors control too much and delegate too little; he impatiently awaits the time when he will be able to make his own decisions and get the enterprise "really going." If a man has a **mentor**—a teacher, experienced coworker, boss, or the like—he will often give him up now. At this time, men want to be affirmed by society in the roles that they most value. They will try for a crucial promotion or some other form of recognition. Work and family have traditionally been separate spheres of living for most men, and traditionally many men invested much of their lives in their work role. Because of the

Table 14.1 Percentage of All U.S. Persons Age 15 and Older Who Were Married, by Sex and Race, Is Declining: 1960–2003[a]

	Total Males	Black Males	White Males	Total Females	Black Females	White Females
1960	69.3	60.9	70.2	65.9	59.8	66.6
1970	66.7	56.9	68.0	61.9	54.1	62.8
1980	63.2	48.8	65.0	58.9	44.6	60.7
1990	60.7	45.1	62.8	56.9	40.2	59.1
2000	57.9	42.8	60.0	54.7	36.2	57.4
2003[b]	57.1	42.5	59.3	54.0	36.4	56.6

[a] *Includes races other than black and white.*

[b] *In 2003, the U.S. Bureau of the Census expanded its racial categories to permit respondents to identify themselves as belonging to more than one race. This means that racial data computations beginning in 2003 may not be strictly comparable with those of prior years.*

Source: From Popenoe, David and Barbara Dafoe Whitehead. *The State of Our Unions: The Social Health of Marriage in America, 2004.* The National Marriage Project at Rutgers University, New Brunswick, NJ, 2004. Copyright © 2004 Barbara Dafoe Whitehead and David Popenoe. Used with permission.

2001 American recession and massive layoffs due to a sputtering economy, some men have come to a more balanced understanding of their life priorities—which is not surprising, given that many have arrived at work to find a termination slip and a cleaned-out desk, even after 25 to 30 years of dedicated service. We shall explain more about Levinson's male developmental theory in midlife and late adulthood in Chapter 16.

Stages in a Woman's Life

Although there is a growing interest in adult development, studies dealing with phases in adult female development have lagged behind studies of men (Gilligan, Rogers, & Tolman, 1991; Guisinger & Blatt, 1994). Such research is clearly called for. For example, although Erik Erikson (1968a) says the formation of identity in adolescence is followed by the capacity for intimacy in early adulthood, many women describe the opposite progression, with the sense of identity developing more strongly in midlife (Baruch & Barnett, 1983; Kahn et al., 1985). Women have a longer life span than men, they are increasing their educational attainments, and perhaps three-fourths of women participating in the labor force made obsolete much of previous research and theory.

Levinson received much criticism for not including women in his original study, so he and his colleagues embarked on another study that resulted in the book *Seasons of a Woman's Life* (1996). These studies confirm that entry into adulthood is similar for men and women, in that both faced the four developmental tasks and the *age-30 transition*. Levinson was surprised to find that although men see themselves tied to a future in terms of their job, women are much more interested in finding ways to combine work and family. None of the professional women they studied found that they could balance the demands of work, family, and their own well-being satisfactorily, feeling that they had sacrificed either career or family in the struggle to maintain both. The women also stated that they had more trouble than men finding someone "special" who would stay with them during their personal and career growth.

The age-30 transition marked another developmental difference between women and men, in that women tend to reprioritize their goals around this age. For example, women who began a career early on gravitate toward marriage and family, and those who started off as wives and mothers entered into occupations around the age of 30. Growing numbers of women enter or reenter the labor force, change jobs, undertake new careers, or return to school. Of equal significance are the growing numbers of women who rear their children first in two-parent, then in one-parent, and then again in two-parent households. Numerous combinations of career, marriage, and children occur with respect to both timing and commitment, and each pattern has different ramifications. Some variations in life arrangements also include returning to the parental home for a period. Most poignantly, Daniel Levinson passed away while completing the manuscript for *Seasons of a Woman's Life*, but his wife, Judy D. Levinson, assisted in bringing her husband's life work to the public.

Question

According to Levinson's findings, what is a major difference in the stages of a woman's life versus a man's life?

New Social Definitions for Women

Until the past few decades in the United States, a woman's life was seen primarily in terms of her reproductive role—bearing and rearing children, menopause, and "the empty nest" being the major events of the woman's adult years. In many countries of the world, this view of women has not changed. Indeed, people commonly equate the female life cycle with the family life cycle. Not surprisingly, the major psychosocial transitions in the lives of contemporary U.S. women now aged 60 and over were more likely to be associated with phases of the family cycle than with chronological age (Moen, 2003; Moen, Dempster-McClain, & Williams, 1992). But today, with 90 percent of all women working for pay at some point in their lives, employment outside the home is playing an increasingly important role in women's self-esteem and identity. Although the participation of white and nonwhite women in the labor force has increased from 1890 to the present, proportionately more nonwhite women have been employed outside their own homes than white women. Figure 14.2 provides data on the increasing employment of American women.

Family and Work An accumulating body of evidence corroborates Levinson's conclusions that women differ from men in the ways they approach tasks and the outcomes they achieve. In large measure these differences derive from the greater complexity of women's visions for their future and the difficulties they encounter in carrying them out. Unlike men, most women do not report dreams in which careers stand out as the primary component; women are more likely to view a career as insurance against not marrying or a bad marriage and difficult economic circumstances. Instead, most women's dreams contain an image in which they are immersed in a world centered in relationships with others, particularly husbands, children, friends, and colleagues. Yet today there are variable pathways for young women to fulfill a role as a marriage partner, since more young men are delaying marriage until older. More young women and men are cohabiting, which may or may not lead to marriage. Some young men and women express strong negative views

about marriage; some simply choose to remain single. However, more young women find themselves as single parents with children, without the benefits of marriage.

Most American women say they have attempted to balance work and family. Even today, many single mothers and married women tend to work only in the economic interest of the family and only after all the other needs of its members have been addressed. Unlike men, whose likelihood of marrying and having a family correlates with career success, more successful women are less likely to marry and have a family (Bagilhole & Goode, 2001). Clearly, that a choice must be made between work and family is more apparent for women. Consequently, many women struggle to maintain a balance between the demands of their career and the needs of their family.

The struggle for greater equality between the sexes has increased women's roles and workloads (Gjerdingen et al., 2000). Consequently, some women have difficulty fulfilling all their work and family obligations, giving rise to role conflict and role overload. **Role conflict** ensues when they experience pressures within one role that are incompatible with the pressures that arise within another role, such as the conflicting demands made on them as a parent, spouse, and paid worker. **Role overload** occurs when there are too many role demands and too little time to fulfill them. Women who encounter these types of role strains—and not all women do—are more likely to experience a diminished sense of well-being and a

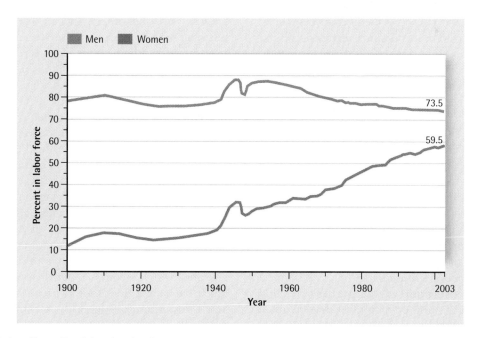

FIGURE 14.2 Labor Force Participation by Sex, 1900–2003 Over the course of the twentieth century and into the 2000s, the labor force participation rate has increased dramatically for women and declined slightly for men. Longer lives, the opportunities of advanced education, and smaller families have enabled more women to enter the workforce. Contemporary employed women and men with children or aging parents are seeking more flexibility in work arrangements to be able to meet the variable needs of their families over time.

Source: U.S. Bureau of the Census, *Historical Statistics of the United States;* U.S. Bureau of Labor Statistics, *Employment and Earnings* (annual summaries). Decennial data 1900–1940, annual data since 1940. Data for noninstitutional population 14 and over through 1965, 16 and over thereafter. U.S. Bureau of the Census (2004). *Statistical Abstract of the United States, 2004–2005.* Civilian Labor Force and Participation Rates With Projections 1980–2012.

decrease in work and marital satisfaction (Tiedje et al., 1990). We should emphasize, however, that most women manage their multiple responsibilities quite well and derive many benefits from participation in the labor force, especially if they receive social support on the job and at home. It is also hypothesized that those women who view themselves as being "feminine and committed to marriage" do not anticipate experiencing the role conflict that many women face (Livingston, Burley, & Springer, 1996). Single-parent families headed by a female, however, face dramatic socioeconomic and psychosocial challenges that dual-earner families do not.

Reentering the Paid Labor Force   Levinson finds that around age 40 men reconsider some of their commitments and often attempt to free themselves from a previously central male mentor. Levinson labeled this the BOOM (Becoming One's Own Man) phenomenon. In contrast, some women enter the world of work, then leave full-time employment entirely while raising children or work part-time, and then reenter full-time employment in their late thirties or early forties. Recent findings suggest that many contemporary women have more mentors, either male or female, to help them navigate to upper administrative positions in their careers (Van Collie, 1998). Mentoring relationships are important in academia and in fields that are traditionally male-dominated. One study looked at the relation between gender roles and mentoring and explored alternative mentorships including peer, multiple, and collective mentoring (Chesler & Chesler, 2002). Furthermore, despite current legal and social trends, there is still evidence of job discrimination against women, particularly middle-aged women, who might have stayed at home to raise children or support their husband's career.

Stocktaking   Psychiatrist Kathleen M. Mogul (1979) also finds that the "stocktaking," or the reevaluation of the situation that might lead to personal questions and changes that men do in their forties, can occur earlier among women. Childless women in their late thirties, forties, and now some in their early fifties often have a "last chance" feeling with regard to motherhood, and options for contemporary women include adoption, in vitro fertilization, or remaining childless. On the other hand, those who became mothers earlier experience a decrease in their absorption of the burdens of child care. And the larger number of middle-aged women who are having children and simultaneously work outside the home also begin to reflect on their coming life pattern.

Differing Adult Experiences   Some psychologists and sociologists believe that the adult experience is different for women than for men (Gilligan, 1982a, 1982b;

Pugliesi, 1995). As we noted in Chapter 11, Gilligan questions the traditional psychological assumption that boys and girls both struggle to define a distinct identity for themselves during adolescence. Instead, she contends that girls must struggle to resist the loss of psychological strengths and positive conceptions of themselves that they had possessed in childhood. Therefore, a woman's development is not necessarily a steady progression; women tend to recover in adulthood the confidence, assertiveness, and positive sense of self that Western society pressured them to compromise during their adolescence (Gilligan, 1982a, 1982b). This is evident in that today more women than men are attending college and earning degrees at all levels except the doctorate, whereas more young men are going to work, are incarcerated, or have "dropped out" (Bowler, 2003; Sum et al., 2003). Economic data suggests that a bachelor's degree, on average, adds about $1.3 million to a man's lifetime earnings and about $650,000 to a woman's—and college-educated women typically want to marry college-educated men (Bowler, 2003; Coley, 2001).

Part of the difficulty, Gilligan says, is that women often find it difficult to commit themselves to competitive success because they are socialized toward the achievement of cooperation, mutuality, and consensus. Many women focus on preserving rather than using relationships. It was otherwise for the men interviewed by Levinson, for whom "friendship was largely noticeable by its absence," and work typically fostered distance between self and others. Indeed, life in contemporary bureaucracies and corporations frequently rewards those who relate to others not as persons but as objects to be manipulated to get ahead. (Think of the recent impersonal vocabulary of corporate firings, such as "downsizing," "takeovers," and "resource actions.") Significantly, the ten most popular sports for men are mostly competitive activities, such as softball, basketball, billiards, and pool, whereas women's top ten tend to be noncompetitive sports, such as walking, swimming, aerobics, running, hiking, and calisthenics.

According to Deborah Tannen (1994), Western nations socialize the two genders differently (also see Chapter 7). Males often gather in hierarchical groups and teach boys how to dominate and jockey for the spotlight, often by versing boys in displays of ridicule and putdowns. In contrast, female groups are structured chiefly around pairs of good friends who share secrets and forge intimacy—basically the same social pattern we see both girls and boys engage in from the preschool years. In large institutional settings such as companies, universities, hospitals, and government agencies, women tend to be consensus builders. So when found in positions of authority, they are inclined to ask others for their opinions. Tannen says that men often misinterpret this behavior as a show of indecisiveness. Moreover, women tend to hesitate to call attention to their accomplishments or seek recognition. Yet Tannen also challenges the notions that women are more indirect than men and that tentativeness reflects low confidence. She notes a parallel in Japanese culture, where it is deemed boorish for a higher-status person to be direct or to be singled out for praise and recognition over others.

Yet it is easy to overstate the differences between women and men. There is neither the "normative (or interchangeable) woman" nor the "normative (or interchangeable) man." Gender is intertwined with race, class, sexual orientation, and countless other variables of human identity (Riger, 1992; Spelman, 1988). Indeed, women and men are more similar than different, and most of their apparent differences are culturally and socially produced.

> **Question**
>
> What are some of the differing career and relationship experiences for contemporary women and men?

A Critique of the Stage Approach

Any stage theory of adult development suggests basic principles for identifying orderly changes that occur in people's lives as well as individual variations from these broad tendencies. However, one drawback of earlier investigations of stage theory was that the subjects were predominantly male, white, and upper-middle class and were born before and during the Great Depression of the 1930s. What held for these Depression Era males often does not hold for today's 50-year-old men and women who were born in the more optimistic years following World War II or those twenty-somethings entering young adulthood today.

Furthermore, even chance events play a large part in shaping adult lives. American careers and marriages often result from the happenstance of meeting the right, or wrong, person at the right, or wrong, time. Coming of age at a certain point in time and experiencing certain decisive economic, social, political, or military events has a profound impact on people's lives. But even though the events could be random, their consequences are not—think of the changes in people's attitude toward life since September 11, 2001 (Kelly, 2001). For example, in non-Western cultures, such as India, China, Japan, and countries of the Middle East and Africa, many marriages are arranged by families to remove the element of chance. And many psychologists and sociologists reject the notion that one must resolve certain developmental tasks in one stage before going on to the next (Rosenfeld & Stark, 1987), pointing out that critical transitions—"passages" or "turning points"—need not be characterized by

"crisis," stress, and turmoil. We actively welcome and embrace some new roles. Consider, for instance, the excitement associated with one's first "real" job, serious love, or first child.

For his part, Levinson acknowledged that a life-cycle theory does not mean that adults, any more than children, march in lockstep through a series of stages. He recognized that the pace and degree of change in a person's life are influenced by personality and environmental factors (war, a death in the family, poor health, a sudden windfall). Hence, Levinson did not deny that very wide variations occur among people in any one life period. He used the analogy of fingerprints. If we have a theory of fingerprints, we have a basis for order, in that we can identify individuals because we know the basic principles around which fingerprints vary. Let's now turn to the ways young adult relationships vary to resolve the "crisis" of intimacy versus isolation.

> **Question**
>
> What are some drawbacks of Levinson's stage theories regarding women and men?

Establishing Intimacy in Relationships

As Tolstoy suggested in 1856, "One can live magnificently in this world, if one knows how to work and how to love." Thus, love and work provide the central themes of adult life. Both love and work place us in a complex web of relationships with others. Indeed, we can experience our humanness only within our relationships with other people. Of equal significance, our humanness must also be sustained through such relationships, and fairly steadily so. Like other periods of human life, young adulthood, from the late teens until the late thirties or early forties, can be understood only within the social context in which it occurs. In addition to relationships in our immediate family, our earliest social relationships are those we have with friends.

Friendships

What is a friend? One old saying goes, "A friend: One soul, two bodies." Think of your friends and see if the following descriptors are true for you—

- You like to spend time with your friends.
- You accept your friends for who they are, and you are not overly concerned to change them.
- You trust your friends.
- You respect your friends.

- You would help your friends and would expect your friends to help you.
- You can confide in your friends.
- You can let down your guard with friends because you do not feel vulnerable with them.

Our friends become our major source of socializing and support during our adult years. We tend to want to spend our free time with those who are experiencing many of the same life events as we are. Women who have babies and young children tend to develop friendships with other women who have babies and young children, often at work, in the neighborhood, or through our children's schools or activities. Single friends might begin to feel "left out" and will gravitate toward finding new friends who are single and share common interests. Men tend to develop friendships within the spheres of work and recreation, and often the topics of their conversations revolve around such events.

And with the growing use of the Internet at work and at home, more studies are focusing on the isolation of our young adult "technocrat" generation, who develop "friendships" in chat rooms in cyberspace rather than across the aisle in a college classroom or across the hall in an apartment building (Matanda, Jenvey, & Phillips, 2004). Despite the many advantages the Internet provides, it is still the face-to-face interaction with friends that provides us with much-needed social support when life gets us down.

Intimacy in Relationships The concept of romantic love is not universally recognized, as some cultures practice arranged marriages between people who have never even met. Many couples from Western cultures describe themselves as being "in love" when they marry. Ideally, the person we love becomes our best friend, intimate partner, and main source of socialization and support during our adult years.

Love

As mentioned earlier, the concept of romantic love is not universal, as is evident in the practice of arranging marriages between people who have never even met before or only know each other superficially. Yet many Westerners describe themselves as being "in love" when they marry, so what do they mean? Why are certain marriages and relationships happier and longer lasting than others? Is being in love significant for happiness and satisfaction in marriage?

Traditionally, love has been divided into what are known as romantic and companionate types of love. **Romantic love** is what we think typically of when we say we are "in love" with someone. **Companionate love** is usually understood as the kind of love you have for a very close friend. The latter is usually manifested in the words, "I love you . . . as a friend, but nothing more." Even though most people can differentiate between the two types of love, psychologists have tried to measure companionate love using a variety of measurements.

Sternberg's Triangular Theory of Love Robert J. Sternberg has proposed that companionate love consists of two other types of love: intimacy and commitment

(Aron & Westbay, 1996; Sternberg, 1988b). According to his **triangular theory of love** (see Figure 14.3), love is made up of these three elements:

- *Passion* (sexual as well as physical attraction to someone)
- *Intimacy* (having a close, warm and caring relationship)
- *Commitment* (intent and ability to maintain the relationship over an extended period of time and under adverse conditions)

A relationship that does not have all three components of a complete, consummate love—passion, intimacy, and commitment—is, says Sternberg, an emotional attachment of one of these seven kinds:

- *Infatuation*—only passion is evoked
- *Fatuous love*—a relationship that has passion and commitment, but not intimacy
- *Companionate love*—a relationship having intimacy and commitment, without passion
- *Romantic love*—a relationship with intimacy and passion, but lacking commitment
- *Nonlove*—none of the three components are present

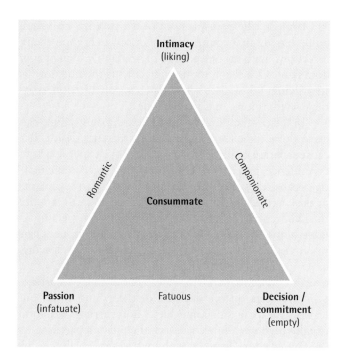

FIGURE 14.3 Sternberg's Triangular Theory of Love According to Sternberg's theory, consummate love is made up of passion (sexual as well as physical attraction to someone); intimacy (having a close, warm and caring relationship); and commitment (intent and ability to maintain the relationship over an extended period of time and under adverse conditions). Many close relationships are comprised of only some of these factors.
Source: Adapted from Janet Shibley Hyde and John D. DeLamater, *Understanding Human Sexuality*, 6th edition. Copyright © 1997 by The McGraw-Hill Companies, Inc. Used with permission of The McGraw-Hill Companies.

- *Liking someone*—intimacy is present, but passion and commitment are absent
- *Empty love*—a relationship consisting only of commitment

However, when all three aspects of his triangular model exist in a relationship, Sternberg calls the emotional bond **consummate love** (Sternberg & Hojjat, 1997). This theory is best thought of as an attempt to explain the real complexities involved in initiating and maintaining a meaningful relationship with another person. Research indicates that lovers' definitions and communications of commitment, intimacy, and passion remain stable among different age cohorts (Reeder, 1996).

Significance of Romantic Love   In a study on the significance of romantic love for relationship quality and duration, Willi (1997) surveyed more than 600 adults in Switzerland and Austria, ranging in age from 18 to 82. Most were married, some were single, some were divorced, and a few were widowed. Based on the following definition of romantic love, most indicated they had fallen in love 2 to 5 times, some indicated 6 to 15 times; 2 percent indicated

they had never been in love; and 1 percent indicated they had been in love more than 16 times:

> Being in love does not simply mean a fleeting or simplistic feeling, but something that for a longer period of time leads to an intensive, erotic attraction and inner fulfillment through the idealization of the relationship with the partner. (Willi, 1997, p. 172)

In this study, men did not fall in love more frequently than women, and being in love did not lead more frequently to a relationship for men (contrary to popular thought). An interesting finding was that for one-third of the sample, a relationship developed with one's great love but did not lead to living together. The married individuals in this study indicated most frequently that they had lived or continue living with their great love (62 percent). For 13.5 percent, the greatest love of their life did not lead to a relationship, mainly because their love was not reciprocated. Those who were married to their great love described themselves as significantly happier than other married respondents did, and their divorce rate was the lowest (6 percent). On a scale of 1 to 5 (1 = not happy, 5 = very happy), those married without children rated themselves significantly happier (4.4) than did those married with children (3.9) (Willi, 1997).

The greatest satisfaction was reported for all groups in the areas of sexual fidelity as well as in the security of the partnership. The least amount of satisfaction overall for marrieds was reported in the areas of tenderness, sex life, and conversation. Singles with stable partnerships and those who were divorced and with new partners were more satisfied with their communication than were marrieds. Overall, 76 percent of the married respondents characterized their partnership as happy to very happy. There were no gender differences in frequency and intensity of being in love, though women were more likely to admit that they had been more intensely in love with someone else than they were with their current partner.

In sum, being in love seems to be a special relationship that clearly distinguishes itself from other kinds of relationships, but it does not necessarily lead to the relationship that one might expect. Recent findings indicate that being in love on the first day or at "first sight" tends to happen to those under the age of 20 (Knox, Schacht, & Zusman, 1999). Also, one does not necessarily need to have married one's great love in order to be happy or satisfied in a relationship, though marrying one's great love is associated with marital duration.

> **Questions**
>
> What are the characteristics of the triangular theory of love? How would you assess a current "love" relationship?

Diversity in Lifestyle Options

People in modern complex societies typically enjoy some options in selecting and changing their lifestyles. A **lifestyle**—the overall pattern of living whereby we attempt to meet our biological, social, and emotional needs—provides the context in which we come to terms with many of the issues discussed in Chapter 13. More particularly, lifestyle affords the framework by which we work out the issues of intimacy versus isolation that Erik Erikson described. **Intimacy** involves our ability to experience a trusting, supportive, and tender relationship with another person. It implies a capacity for mutual empathy and for both giving and receiving pleasure within an intimate context. Comfort and companionship are among the ultimate rewards to be found in a close relationship.

A striking aspect of American society over the past 35 years has been the rapid expansion in alternative lifestyles. Much of the turmoil of the late 1960s revolved around living arrangements, including communal living and cohabitation. From the various liberation movements (African American, Hispanic, Native American, women's, gay, lesbian, feminist, and youth), there has come a broader acceptance of pluralistic standards for judging behavior. Overall, it appears that some elements of society and the media permit citizens greater latitude in tailoring for themselves lifestyles less constrained by traditional standards. Of course, many religious institutions and their followers maintain traditional standards for acceptable and unacceptable behaviors for men and women.

Leaving Home

Leaving home is a major step in the transition to adulthood. Prior to this transition, the two generations typically form a single family. For many decades, marriage was the major reason for leaving home—young people left their parent's home to form a new family, signaling their attainment of adulthood. But over the past two or three decades, the process of leaving the parental home has become increasingly complex, with many young people experiencing numerous living arrangements in the course of assuming adult status (Goldsheider, Thornton, & Yang, 2001). Typically in the past, young Americans left the parental home between the ages of 15 and 23. About this age, nonfamily living occurs with greater frequency. Living in college dormitories and military barracks spikes sharply around age 18, followed by a sharp upturn in housemate living around ages 19 and 20. However, in the United States, Germany, Denmark, Australia, and Great Britain, contemporary young people are leaving home later. Significantly, the parental home remains the primary residence for many young people aged 18 to 34 (Fields & Casper, 2001).

Even so, the pathways out of the parental home are quite varied, and young adults fan out in a good many directions, with no one pattern of nonfamily living being dominant. Other common arrangements include dormitory living, housemate arrangements, cohabitation, marriage, civil unions, and living alone.

In the contemporary United States, young adults can leave home whenever they or their parents desire. Because separate residences are usually more expensive than coresidence, parents often have a strong voice in the matter because they can subsidize new housing arrangements or they can withhold financial assistance. In most families the children are "ahead" of their parents in expecting to leave home. Consequently, parents can and do use their resources in influencing their children's nest leaving, either to forestall departures that are "too early" or to expedite those that are "too late." The timing of marriage typically rests on the decision of the young adult, but leaving the parental home for a nonmarriage situation usually involves a joint decision of child and parents.

Two factors have contributed to making living arrangements negotiable between maturing children and their parents. First, the growth of premarital residential independence has been spurred by an increased emphasis on autonomy and individualism that has led some young people to deem the various costs of leaving home well "worth it." Second, young people are marrying at later ages (between 1970 and 2000, the median age at first marriage rose from 20 to 27 years for men and from 20 to 25 years for women). The negotiations between generations can be problematic because, given the rapid social and economic change of recent years, the experiences of parents and their children are likely to be quite different. Expectations about parental support of their adult children vary as well (Goldscheider, Thornton, & Yang, 2001). Parents might not understand the current trend of being an undergraduate for five or more years interrupted by, or followed immediately by, a trip to Europe. Significantly, there are ethnic and religious variations in leaving home. Hispanic Americans are much more likely than non-Hispanic whites to live at home until marriage. The same pattern prevails among Asian American families. Protestant fundamentalists and students who attended Catholic schools are also more likely to live at home until they marry (Goldscheider, Thornton, & Yang, 2001).

Some sociologists believe that the transition to adulthood is particularly problematic for today's young people. They argue that the amount and duration of parental support have been increased by such factors as postponed careers, recurrent recessions, low beginning salaries, rising housing costs, high divorce rates, high levels of nonmarital childbearing, damaged lives resulting from drug abuse and overindulgent parenting practices of baby boomers (Paul, 2003). These factors complicate

College Attendance Is One Path Toward Leaving Home Contemporary young adults take many paths when leaving the parental home. College attendance and dormitory or apartment living are becoming more common as a transition to independent living for many young adults. Others might seek employment or an apprenticeship, enter the military, join the Job Corps or Peace Corps, travel, remain in the parental home longer, or simply "drop out" with friends. Fewer young adults marry as the means to leaving the parental home.

the many transitions that often are associated with young adulthood. Indeed, rates of childbearing, first marriage, divorce, remarriage, and relocating for family reasons are higher during this period than at any other time in life (Goldscheider, Thornton, & Yang, 2001). Moreover, the early years of a career are frequently unstable, requiring job changes and moving for job-related reasons. Given these circumstances, significant numbers of young adults remain dependent on their parents in many ways well into their late twenties or even later.

Living at Home

In U.S. and English textile communities in the late 1800s and early 1900s, different generations often resided in the same household, providing a good deal of assistance to one another (Hareven, 1987). This extended family arrangement is still common in many Asian and Latin American families (Fuligni & Pedersen, 2002). Then, societal norms began to change in mid–twentieth century, such that U.S. youth were encouraged to leave home and make their own way in the world. Indeed, three decades ago it was not deemed acceptable to live at home after one reached 20 years of age. The goal of raising independent children was grounded historically in the expanding employment opportunities that prevailed in the United States for much of the twentieth century (Goldscheider et al., 1999).

Nowadays, many young people remain in the parental home or return home when circumstances become difficult. But economic pressures need not be severe: Some youth merely wish to save the rent money and instead spend it on a car or save it to purchase a house.

Among the middle classes, comfort is another reason to live in the parental nest. The young people can support themselves, but not in their own home with a comparable standard of living. So instead they borrow a slice of their parent's prosperity. In addition, some young people, particularly men, get another advantage—"maid service" from their mothers. Women are less likely to be doted on by their mothers, and both parents are likely to keep a "shorter leash" on their daughters than on their sons, if they live at the parents' home. Even so, contemporary young adults experience greater equality while living with parents than previous generations did.

Living with parents can be anywhere from highly successful to disastrous (Goldscheider, Thornton, & Yang, 2001). There is a sense of warmth, closeness, and emotional support at a time of widespread personal alienation. But the most common complaint voiced by members of both generations concerns the loss of privacy. Couples report that they feel uncomfortable fighting in front of family members. Young adults, especially the unmarried, complain that parents cramp their sex lives or their music playing, treat them like children, and reduce their independence. Parents often grumble that their peace and quiet is disturbed, the phone rings at odd hours, they lie awake at night worrying and listening for the adult child to return home, meals are rarely eaten together because of conflicting schedules, and too much of the burden of baby-sitting falls on them. Higher expenses might compel parents to relinquish long-awaited vacations, and a need for space means they must postpone a move to a smaller, less expensive townhouse, apartment, or retirement home.

Usually, the happiest refilled nests are those with ample space and open, trusting communication. Those that are most difficult involve grown children who are immature, who have drug or mental health problems, or who become disabled. Parents might treat such a 28-year-old like a 15-year-old, and the 28-year-old behaves like one. Family therapists express concern that those who stay at home do not have opportunities to fully develop their sense of individuality. Staying at home tends to aggravate tendencies toward excessive protectiveness in parents and toward a lack of self-confidence in youth. The resulting tensions lead some families to seek professional counseling.

Staying Single

Recent census data reveal that single status among both men and women under 35 years of age has sharply increased in recent years. More than 60 percent of the male population aged 18 to 34 has never been married and half of the female population age 18 to 34 has never been married. These large percentages reflect the tendency of young people to postpone marriage, to remain in a cohabiting situation, or to choose singlehood. The percentage of never-married and divorced people comprised a larger portion of the population than it did in 1970 (U.S. Bureau of the Census, 2004–2005). This same societal phenomenon is occurring in Japan as well, as a broad spectrum of college-educated adult women are spending time pursuing a career before settling down to marry. Japanese women are marrying later and less often, a reflection of longer school enrollment and awareness of a cultural trend that married Japanese women are to stay home and raise the children (Raymo, 2003).

According to the 2003 *Current Population Survey,* more than one-fourth of the 105 million U.S. households consisted of one person, up from 17 percent in 1970 (see Figure 14.5). However, the singles population is not a monolithic group.

A variety of factors have fueled the increase in single households: the deferral of marriage among young adults, a high rate of divorce and separation, and the ability of the elderly to maintain their own homes alone. Singlehood is also a reclaimable state. A person may be single, then choose to marry or cohabit, and perhaps later divorce and become single again (Bramlett & Mosher, 2001).

Until a few decades ago, social stigma was attached to the terms *spinster* and *bachelor,* and remaining single was actively discouraged. Over the past generation, the notion that individuals must marry if they are to achieve maximum happiness and well-being has been increasingly questioned (Coontz, 2000). Many Americans no longer view "singlehood" as a residual category for the unchosen and lonely. Even so, in Western culture the

Variable Residential Settings After Leaving Home Many young adults take up residence by themselves, as has this young man. Yet other young adults remain in the parental home while finishing college or establishing a career until their late twenties or early thirties. Others are returning home after a college graduation, divorce or separation, or periods of employment/unemployment or cohabitation.

nuclear family composed of a husband, a wife, and their offspring continues to be the measure or standard against which other family forms and lifestyles are judged (Thornton & Young-DeMarco, 2001).

Single individuals (both never-married and divorced or separated) find that as their numbers have grown, singles communities have arisen in most metropolitan areas. Single adults can move into a singles apartment complex, go to a singles bar, take a singles trip or cruise, join a singles social group online, and so on. If they choose, they can lead an active sex life without acquiring an unwanted mate, child, or reputation. About 55 percent of one-person householders were homeowners (U.S. Bureau of the Census, 2004f). Although staying single can offer greater freedom and independence than married life does, it can also mean greater loneliness. The impersonal nature of singles bars has led them to be labeled "meat racks," "body works," and other nicknames that signify a sexual marketplace. Still, many singles remain wary about marriage and look to their work and other interests for their primary life satisfactions. Note the variety of television shows and online dating services that promote singles meeting other singles (*Seinfeld, Friends, The Bachelor,* e-Harmony.com, and many others).

Cohabiting

In 2002 there were nearly 5 million households that were classified as unmarried-partner households in the United States (see Figure 14.4) (Whitehead & Popenoe, 2004). Marriage is distinguished from other types of intimate relationships by its state-sanctioned, and often church-

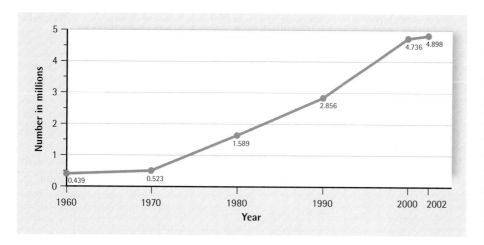

FIGURE 14.4 Cohabiting, Unmarried, Adult Couples of Opposite Sex, 1960–2002 In 2003, there were over 4.8 million households that were classified as unmarried-partner households in the United States. The number of unmarried couples with children has increased more than ninefold from 197,000 in 1960 to over 1.8 million in 2003 (U.S. Bureau of the Census, 2004b).
Source: From Popenoe, David and Barbara Dafoe Whitehead. *The State of Our Unions: The Social Health of Marriage in America, 2004.* The National Marriage Project at Rutgers University, New Brunswick, NJ, 2004. Copyright © 2004 Barbara Dafoe Whitehead and David Popenoe. Used with permission.

sanctioned, status (U.S. Department of Commerce, 1998). Black and white cohabitants also differ in their union outcomes: "Blacks are only half as likely as are whites to marry their cohabiting partner" (Brown, 2000, p. 833). It is easier for unmarried couples to live together today because of more permissive codes of morality, whereas in the recent past cohabitation was looked on as morally wrong. Now university officials, landlords, the media, and other agents of the establishment tend to ignore the matter. Yet there are other traditionalists, clergy, and some social scientists who do not share this view, for research does not support the notion that cohabitation before marriage is associated with getting married nor with later marital success. It seems that the people who flout convention by cohabiting also tend to flout traditional conventions regarding marital behavior, have a lower commitment to marriage as an institution, and are more likely to disregard the stigma of divorce (Brown, 2000; Wu & Pollard, 2000).

As we continue into the new millennium, alternatives to marriage are multiplying. The rise in cohabitation is associated with the decline in marriage and seems most attractive to young adults and to those who are divorced or separated. Cohabitation rates have increased tremendously since 1960 when there were only about 400,000 cohabitating couples. The main increase in cohabitation has occurred since 1970 when the number was still under 1 million (Seltzer, 2004). Both heterosexual and homosexual couples are having children outside of marriage. Reproductive techniques such as sperm and egg donation and surrogate motherhood arrangements, together with cohabiting trends, have strained the strong link that previously existed between being married and raising children (Coontz, 2000). In fact—as occurs with many marriages—biological children have been found to exert a stabilizing influence on a cohabiting relationship (Brown & Booth, 1996).

Although the media have at times labeled cohabiters "unmarried marrieds" and their relationships "trial marriages," the couples usually do not see themselves in this category. College students typically view cohabitation as part of the courtship process rather than as a long-term alternative to marriage. In many cases living together as an alternative to marriage is not radically different from marriage (Brown, 2000; Wu & Pollard, 2000). The partners typically fall into traditional gender roles and engage in many of the same activities that married couples do. Like married men, cohabiting men are more likely to initiate sexual activity, make most of the spending decisions, and do far less of the housework than their working women partners (Brown, 2000). Moreover, cohabiting couples typically encounter many of the same sorts of problems found among married couples. Surprisingly, the incidence of interpersonal disagreements, fights, and violence is higher among cohabiting than among married couples (Brown, 2000). Commonly, the cohabiting couples view themselves as less securely anchored, so they feel more tentative about their capacity to endure difficult periods, and they are less likely than married couples to practice fidelity (Steinhauer, 1995). The average cohabitation lasts about two years and ends either through dissolution or through marriage.

Many cohabitors intend to marry, but of those who have no plans to marry, typically at least one of the partners is poor marriage material. That is, typically they exist on low incomes, receive welfare, or have resident children. Previously married cohabitors are also less likely to report plans to marry than are their never-married counterparts (Brown, 2000). Reasons young men give for cohabiting include: getting sex without marriage, enjoying the benefits of having a "wife" without being married, wanting to avoid divorce, wanting to wait until older to have children, fear of too many changes in marriage, waiting for the perfect soul mate, few social pressures to marry, reluctance to enter marriage with a woman with children, saving for a house, or wanting to enjoy single life as long as possible (Lyon, 2002).

Separating is not as easy for an unmarried couple as popular belief has it. The emotional trauma can be every bit as severe as among married couples undergoing divorce. And in some cases there are legal complications associated with apartment leases, jointly owned property, child custody and visitations, and inheritances. Overall, the dissolution of cohabitation resembles divorce in that the partners experience similar processes of disengagement, emotional distress, and adjustment, especially when there are children involved and no legal mechanism to require support of such children (Wu & Pollard, 2000).

Question

What differentiates cohabiting couples from married couples?

Living as a Lesbian or Gay Couple

As mentioned in Chapter 13, *sexual orientation* refers to whether an individual is more strongly aroused sexually by members of his or her own sex (homosexual), the opposite sex (heterosexual), or both sexes (bisexual). Most people assume that there are two kinds of people, whom they label "heterosexual" and "homosexual." In reality, however, a more accurate view is that a heterosexual orientation and a homosexual orientation are on a continuum (in other words, one could be "more heterosexual" or "more homosexual"). Some individuals show varying degrees of orientation, including a bisexual orientation (Weinberg, Williams, & Pryor, 1994). In brief, human sexuality is quite versatile.

Because there are so many gradations in sexual orientation and practice, some experts on sexuality take the position that there are various sexual behaviors—female-female (lesbian), male-male (gay), and male-female (heterosexual)—not heterosexual or homosexual individuals per se (Kitzinger & Wilkinson, 1995). Complicating matters, some evidence suggests that some women seem to broaden their sexual experience as they get older, so that some heterosexual women become lesbian and some lesbians become heterosexual (Kitzinger & Wilkinson, 1995).

Additionally, we should distinguish between "orientation" and "behavior"—between erotic attraction and what a person actually does. A gay, lesbian, bisexual, or heterosexual person might or might not elect to engage in sexual behavior. How common are homosexual behaviors? In his early data from the late 1940s, Alfred Kinsey found that among single males 20 to 35 years old, those who had exclusively homosexual experience ranged in various samples from 3 to 16 percent, and among females that age, from 1 to 3 percent (Kinsey et al., 1953). However, surveys by the National Opinion Research Center (NORC) in 1970 and 1988 suggest that the percentage of U.S. men who have had at least one homosexual experience is lower than Kinsey's estimates.

Other studies carried out between 1970 and 1994 show the proportion of men describing themselves as gay or bisexual is around 3 percent. In all studies, however, the proportion of persons who are exclusively homosexual throughout their entire lives is quite small (perhaps from 1 to 2 percent of adults) (Demo, 2000).

In the Western world, individuals practicing homosexual behavior have experienced a history of oppression by a culture that has long regarded the behavior as deviant. Indeed, until 1973, the American Psychiatric Association included homosexuality in its manual of pathological behaviors. As a result, many people who were erotically attracted to the same sex remained "in the closet," hiding their sexual orientation. In 1975, the American Psychiatric Association reversed its position. Today the issue of whether or not sexual orientation is a matter of individual choice occupies center stage and is hotly debated by psychiatrists, clinical psychologists, biologists, and others. The public is also divided on the issue, particularly with the issue of civil unions, domestic partnerships, same-sex marriages, and adoption by gay men or lesbians. Based on polls, Americans continue to be nearly equally divided about whether homosexuality should be considered an acceptable lifestyle (Loftus, 2001). However, acceptance of lesbians is greater than acceptance of gay men. Among the heterosexual population, women tended to be more accepting of gays and lesbians (Herek, 2002).

Lesbians and gay men are a varied group (Hewitt, 1998). They come from all racial and ethnic backgrounds, work in all occupational fields, have varied political outlooks, and have varied religious affiliations. There is no such thing as a "heterosexual lifestyle," nor such a thing as a "lesbian lifestyle" or "gay lifestyle." Some lesbians and gay men "pass" for heterosexuals, are married, have children, and in many respects seem indistinguishable from the larger population. Lesbians tend to form more lasting ties than gay men do, and they are less often detected and harassed—though over the past few years the news media have sensationalized child custody cases involving the "fitness" of lesbian mothers.

The 2000 Census provided the option to answer "Unmarried Partner" in relation to other persons in the respondents' households. If the two were of the same sex, it could be inferred that it denoted a gay or lesbian household. Although it is most likely underreported, the number of gay and lesbian households in the U.S. is at least 600,000 ("Survey Says . . . ," 2005). Researchers examined the social and psychological adjustment of a sample of nearly a thousand gay men and lesbians living in the San Francisco Bay area. Overall, they found that adults practicing homosexual behavior resemble adults practicing heterosexual behavior in their reports about their physical health and their feelings of happiness or unhappiness. Overall, the quality of relationships has been the same for

Same-Sex Couples Lesbians and gay men are a varied group. They come from all racial and ethnic backgrounds, work in all occupational fields, have varied political outlooks, and have varied religious affiliations. Overall, the quality of homosexual relationships is similar to heterosexual couples across time when one looks at intimacy, autonomy, problem solving, commitment, and equality. Presently, there is an equal rights movement to legalize civil unions and marriage.

heterosexual and homosexual couples across time when one looks at intimacy, autonomy, problem solving, commitment, and equality (Kurdek, 2004).

Fidelity typically is defined not by sexual behavior but rather by the partners' emotional commitment to each other. For many couples the passion of the sexual encounter dwindles rapidly after two or three years, and outside sexual activity increases. Gay male couples are more likely to break up over incompatibility issues, such as how money is spent, than over the issue of sexual faithfulness. Household duties tend to be sorted out according to partners' skills and preferences and seldom on the basis of stereotyped roles of "husband" and "wife" (Kurdek, 2004).

In recent years a marked decrease in casual sex has occurred among individuals practicing either homosexual or heterosexual behavior (recall the significant declines noted in the chapters on adolescence). The AIDS epidemic has created anxiety and caution within gay male communities throughout the world because many victims of the lethal disease have been gay men. By 2004 an estimated 32 million persons have died from AIDS, with 40 million more still living with AIDS, and 5 million new cases diagnosed in 2004, mainly in developing countries (U.S. AID Health, 2005). In contrast, lesbians have a low incidence of any kind of sexually transmitted infection and are not among the high-risk groups for AIDS. This disease renders the body's immune system ineffective, leaving the victim susceptible to cancers, various infections, and eventually to an early death—though regimens of new medicines are, in general, prolonging the lives of AIDS patients. Gay communities have responded by practicing safer-sex methods to prevent the

transmission of HIV. However, heterosexuals of all ages were mistaken to think this disease affects only those in the homosexual community. Today, the highest numbers of new cases are among heterosexual teenage girls and middle-aged women.

By virtue of some continuing hostility from the larger community, individuals practicing homosexual behavior have often had to live double lives, "gay" at home and "straight" on the job. But shifts in public attitudes and gay rights laws have prompted many to live openly, particularly in large cities such as San Francisco, Los Angeles, and New York. The same acceptance does not hold true in many smaller communities. Furthermore, gay and lesbian organizations and political caucuses have been vigorously championing gay and lesbian rights measures, particularly the right to be covered under a partner's health insurance, the right to adopt, and the right to marry. An extension of this effort is the creation of gay and lesbian clubs on many college campuses and in high schools, in response to which a small number of students has protested that student activity fees should not pay for such activities. Additionally, more colleges are offering—and requiring students in social science majors to take—courses on gay and lesbian issues.

The National Debate on Same-Sex Marriage   In 2004, the issue of same-sex marriage came to the forefront of society in several cities and small towns as a contentious debate between civil rights and state laws (Dignan & Sanchez, 2004). As of 2005, California, Hawaii, Maine, and New Jersey maintain "domestic partner" registries; Vermont and Connecticut sanction civil unions; and in 2004, Massachusetts, by judicial decision, began granting marriage rights to same-sex couples (Ryan, 2004). Marital and "civil union" status to same-sex partners provides economic, medical, inheritance, and legal benefits—and hospital visitation rights. Yet at this writing, as many as 40 states have some form of law or referendum passed by a majority of voters recognizing marriage as between a man and a woman and some ban "civil unions" or "domestic partnerships." Such laws are being litigated in state courts as denying equal rights to same-sex couples, especially as legally married same-sex couples reside, travel, or work in all states.

Question

In what ways have same-sex relationships come to the forefront of society?

Getting Married

A lifestyle practice that apparently exists in all societies is **marriage**—a socially and/or religiously sanctioned union between a woman and a man with the expectation

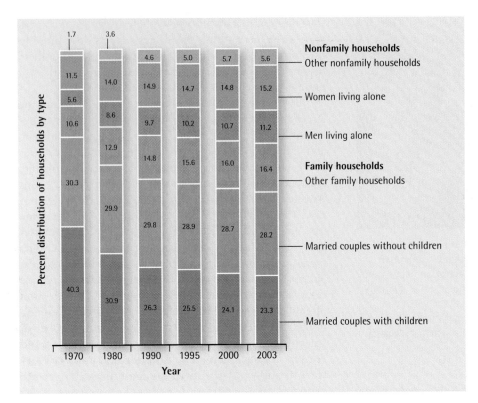

FIGURE 14.5 Household Compositions: 1970–2003 The U.S. Bureau of the Census expects nonfamily households, singles, and cohabiting couples to continue to grow mainly among young adults. Fairly high divorce rates and marriages at later ages are cited as factors. An increasingly elderly population of widows, who often outlive their husbands, continue to contribute to the growth of singles households.
Source: Fields, J. (2004, November). America's Families and Living Arrangements: 2003. Current Population Reports, P20-553. Washington, DC: U.S. Bureau of the Census. Retrieved March 12, 2005, from http://www.census.gov/prod/2004pubs/p20-553.pdf

that they will perform the mutually supportive roles of wife and husband. After studying extensive cross-cultural data, anthropologist George P. Murdock (1949) concluded that reproduction, sexual relations, economic cooperation, and the socialization of offspring are functions of families throughout the world.

Societies differ in how they structure marriage relationships. Four patterns are found: *monogamy* (one husband and one wife), *polygyny (polygamy)* (one husband and two or more wives), *polyandry* (two or more husbands and one wife), and *group marriage* (two or more husbands and two or more wives). Although monogamy exists in all societies, Murdock discovered that in some societies other forms are not only allowed but preferred. Of 238 societies in his sample, only about one-fifth was strictly monogamous.

Polygyny (polygamy) has been widely practiced throughout the world. The Old Testament reports that both King David and King Solomon had several wives. In his cross-cultural sample of 238 societies, Murdock found that 193 (an overwhelming majority) permitted husbands to take several wives. In one-third of these polygynous societies, however, less than one-fifth of the married men had more than one wife. Usually only the rich men in a society can afford to support more than one family (Sanderson, 2001).

In contrast with polygyny, polyandry is rare among the world's societies. And in practice, polyandry has not usually allowed freedom of mate selection for women—it

has often meant simply that younger brothers have sexual access to the wife of an older brother. For example, in some cultures, the father must pay a fee to secure a virginal bride for his son; if the father is unable to afford wives for each of his sons, he might secure a wife for only his oldest son. Consider this account of polyandrous practices among the Todas, a non-Hindu tribe of India:

The Todas have a completely organized and definite system of polyandry. When a woman marries a man, it is understood that she becomes the wife of his brothers at the same time. When a boy is married to a girl, not only are his brothers usually regarded as also the husbands of the girl, but any brother born later will similarly be regarded as sharing his older brother's right. . . . The brothers live together, and my informants seemed to regard it as a ridiculous idea that there should even be disputes or jealousies of the kind that might be expected in such a household. . . . Instead of adultery being regarded as immoral . . . according to the Toda idea, immorality attaches rather to the man who grudges his wife to another. (Rivers, 1906, p. 515)

Anthropologists disagree on whether group marriage genuinely exists in any society as a normatively encouraged lifestyle. There is some evidence that it might take place among the Marquesans of the South Pacific, the Chukchee of Asia (men make wife-lending contracts with each other), the Kaingang of Brazil, and the Todas and Dahari of India. The Ibo and Yoruba of Nigeria consider polygyny a sign of wealth. On occasion, as among

Fraternal Polyandry Ethnic Tibetans along the Tibet-Nepal border in central Asia practice polyandry. A number of brothers jointly take a wife. Although the eldest brother is typically the dominant figure in the household, all the brothers share the work and participate as sexual partners with the wife. Here a 12-year-old bride stands with three of her five husbands-to-be. The grooms, ages 19, 17, and 7, are brothers. Two other brothers, ages 14 and 21, were away. The cultural ideal calls on the wife to show these brothers equal affection and sexual accommodation.

Marriage Young adults are postponing marriage despite a broad range of research that finds that children and adults in married families generally fare better on economic, health, educational, psychological, and social-emotional measures.

the Todas of India, polyandry slides into group marriage when a number of brothers share more than one wife.

Many of the contemporary household arrangements and social realities such as dual-income families, stepfamilies, cohabitating singles, cohabiting families, single parenthood, and high divorce rates are not new in human history. What is new is that these social realities are all coexisting in the United States with greater opportunities for financial independence and improved legal status for women as well as technological innovations that affect women's reproductive lives. These factors along with the option for same-sex marriage have converged in an attempt to transform cultural thought about marriage (Coontz, 2004).

Although some social scientists argue that marriage may be on the decline, demographic trends in the past decade reveal a different picture. As said earlier, many young adults are postponing marriage and are cohabiting prior to marriage—but eventually most do get married. Census information (U.S. Bureau of the Census, 2004b) revealed that the percentage of married couple families with children has now leveled off to about 68 percent, with divorce statistics stabilizing. Also, there are millions of married couples without children. Other factors include increases in the number of immigrant populations such as Asians and Hispanics who comprise more traditional "married with children" households (Frey, 2003). The vast majority of men and women in 2003 had married by their 35th birthday (U.S. Bureau of the Census, 2004b). In addition, events like the September 11, 2001 tragedy and deployment to the Iraq war led some couples to formalize their commitments to each other.

In sum, Western countries have not given up on marriage (Coontz, 2000). Indeed, history reveals marriage to be a very resilient institutional arrangement. Not surprisingly, marriage (with or without children) is the most prevalent American lifestyle (see Figure 14.5), although increasing numbers of Americans have come to define marriage as something that can be ended and reentered. Surveys show that American and European adults depend very heavily on their marriages for their psychological well-being, and, in fact, married couples who described themselves as "in love with their great love" were very satisfied with their relationship (Coontz, 2000; Willi, 1997). In cross-cultural studies of arranged and love marriages, marital satisfaction was higher in love marriages (see the *Human Diversity* box on page 492, "Arranged Marriages or Love Matches"). A resurgence of religious ideals and family values post September 11, 2001 suggests a return to more traditional family values, including a commitment to life-long marriage (Kelly, 2001). Moreover, marriages differ. Marriage encompasses a wide range of interaction patterns, each of which involves a somewhat different lifestyle. (See the *More Information You Can Use* box on page 494, "Research Findings on Marriage and Choosing a Marriage Partner.") Both U.S. federal and state governments have recently enacted marriage promotion initiatives to promote healthy marriages because a broad range of research finds that children and adults in married families generally fare better on economic, health, educational, psychological, and social-emotional measures (Wherry & Finegold, 2004). The U.S. Department of Health and Human Services administers 65 different social programs for children and families at a cost of $47 billion a year—and these programs were created because of the breakup of families or marriages (Wetzstein, 2004). We will return to the significance of marital relationships in Chapters 16 and 18.

Human Diversity

Arranged Marriages or Love Matches

Before the concept of courtly (romantic) love was developed, arranged marriages served to maintain community cohesiveness, consolidate family wealth, and ensure individuals' social status through family connections. It was to be another 400 years before Western society began to accept the idea that passionate love was a legitimate reason for marriage. Historically, owing to the belief that love and marriage did not belong under the same roof, parents wielded great power in that they chose mates for their children through arranged marriages. Think about Romeo and Juliet—the problem for those two lovers was that the families objected to their uniting as a couple. Even today in some countries of the world, girls as young as 11 or 12 are married off by their parents to eligible males for reasons of social and religious custom as well as economic considerations.

Following the Islamic custom of prearranged marriages, Houston Rockets' star Hakeem Olajuwon wed 18-year-old Dalia Asafi in a traditional ceremony in Houston in 1996. "There is no dating process, no boyfriends and girlfriends in Islam," Olajuwon said. "Families meet, talk, get to know one another. Then the marriage is arranged" (Thomas, 1996). The justification given for arranging marriages is that children are too young to understand the real purpose of marriage—an alliance between families. But even in arranged marriages, love can sometimes be taken into consideration, and the extent to which this occurs can be seen if one looks at contemporary marriage arrangement practices around the world. For example in some cultures:

- Parents choose the partner, no discussion or objection allowed.
- Parents choose the partner, discussion or objection is allowed.
- Parents, child, relatives, and friends come to a group decision.
- Child chooses prospective partner and parents give their approval.
- Arranged or love marriages are both options.

Those who favor marriage or relationship based on love argue that it is cruel to force young people to enter into relationships with people they do not love or even like. Furthermore, only the individual can know who that perfect someone will be. Those in favor of arranged marriages argue that love is a kind of madness (a type of irrational thought) that interferes with one's ability to make a good choice for the future. They also point out that "love" is not as discerning as some would like to believe—most people fall in love with someone they meet in the tiny circle of individuals they are acquainted with. Look at what some young people in India said about the pros and cons of arranged marriages (Sprecher & Chandak, 1992):

Arranged Marriages

Advantages
1. Support from families
2. Quality and stability of marriage
3. Compatible or desirable backgrounds
4. Time to learn to adjust to marriage
5. Happiness of parents and family
6. Approval of society
7. Easy to meet a partner
8. Excitement of the unknown
9. Parents know best

Disadvantages
1. Not knowing each other well
2. Problems with dowry
3. Incompatibility/unhappiness
4. Limited choice
5. Family and in-law problems

Arranged marriages may serve the interests of community and family but how do the individuals involved feel about this practice? One effect that had been hidden until recently is the practice of suicide by rural Chinese women who were distressed over their arranged marriages. China is the only country in the world where the suicide rate for women exceeds that of men. In rural areas where there is easy access to dangerous pesticides and access to medical care is difficult, most suicide attempts are successful. As reported in *The Economist,* suicide had been used as a form of social protest and "women are reported to have collectively killed themselves rather than face arranged marriages" ("The Horrible Exception," 2001). In Bangladesh, where arranged marriages are common, women who try to leave unhappy marriages risk death and disfigurement. According to the Women's International Network News, there were 338 acid attacks (throwing acid on the woman's face and body) in 2001. Although acid attacks are punishable by death in Bangladesh, most perpetrators are not punished ("Bangladesh: Acid Attacks Increase Despite Death Penalty," 2002). Although these cases represent the most severe reactions against the practice, young women who are living in Western countries as a result of emigration may experience uncertainty, confusion, and feel torn between traditional family values and Western social values (Zaidi & Shuraydi, 2002).

Another form of the arranged marriage is the so-called *mail-order bride.* In this situation a woman agrees to marry a man after exchanging some correspondence usually through a broker. It is estimated that this industry nets about $2 million annually in profit. In most cases impoverished women from countries in Asia (many are Filipina), Russia, and South America agree to the marriage to help their families back home, further their educations, and start a new life. The U.S. Immigration and Naturalization Service estimates the number of mail-order marriages at 4,000 to 6,000 each year (McClelland, 2002; Tamincioglu, 2001).

However awful arranged marriages might seem in comparison to individual choice and marrying for love, how much choice do you believe there really is? How likely is it that a person from "high society" would marry someone out-side of their social and economic class? Are people more or less likely to marry within their religious group? What about the tendency of family and friends to play matchmaker? What are the factors that impact your marriage choice? Who should make the decisions regarding marriage?

From: S. Sprecher and R. Chandak. Attitude About Arranged Marriages and Dating Among Men and Women from India. *Free Inquiry in Creative Sociology, 20,* 1–11.

Questions

How does the structure of "marriage" vary across cultures? Is marriage as an American institution less stable than it was previously?

Family Transitions

We hear a good deal nowadays about the "demise of the American family." Yet for many Americans the family remains a central and vital institution (see the *Further Developments* box on page 496, "Is the U.S. Family Dis-integrating or Merely Changing?"). Over the course of their lives, most Americans find themselves members of two family groups. First, a person belongs to a nuclear family that often consists of oneself and one's father, mother, and siblings. This group is called the individual's *family of orientation.* Second, because over 90 percent of Americans marry at least once, the vast majority of American adults are members of a nuclear family in which they are one of the parents. This group is called the individual's *family of procreation.*

Various psychologists and sociologists have sought to find a framework for describing the transitions that occur across a person's life span that are related to these shifts in family patterns (Cowan & Hetherington, 1991). One tool that they have devised is the concept of the **family life cycle**—the sequential changes and realignments that occur in the structure and relationships of family life between the time of marriage and the death of one or both spouses. The family life-cycle model views families, like individuals, as undergoing development that is characterized by identifiable phases or stages.

The Family Life Cycle

In the United States, families have traditionally had a fairly predictable natural history. Major changes in expectations and requirements are imposed on a husband and wife as their children are born and grow up. The sociologist Reuben Hill (1964) describes the major milestones in a nine-stage family life cycle:

1. Establishment—newly married, childless
2. New parents—until first infant is 3 years old
3. Preschool family—oldest child is 3 to 6 years old, possibly younger siblings
4. School-age family—oldest child is 6 to 12 years old, possibly younger siblings
5. Family with adolescent—oldest child is 13 to 19 years old, possibly younger siblings
6. Family with young adult—oldest child is 20 years old or more, until first child leaves home
7. Family as launching center—from departure of first child to departure of last child
8. Postparental family—after children have left home, until father (and/or mother) retires
9. Aging family—after retirement of father (and/or mother)

As viewed by Hill and other sociologists, the family begins with the husband-wife pair and becomes increasingly complex as members are added, creating new roles and multiplying the number of interpersonal relations. The family then stabilizes for a brief period, after which it begins shrinking as each of the adult children is launched. Finally, the family returns once again to the husband-wife pair and then terminates with the death of a spouse. However, in the contemporary United States some individuals do not form families, and many families do not pass through these stages. Because this view of the family life cycle revolves around the reproductive process, the approach is not particularly helpful in understanding childless couples. Nor does the family life-cycle approach apply to single-parent families, divorced couples, and stepfamilies (Hill, 1986). Significantly, in its original formulation, the family life-cycle approach made no reference at all to the mother's participation in the paid labor force. Newer versions of the scheme have recognized that a career woman and mother are increasingly one and the same person.

Critics such as Glenn H. Elder, Jr. (1974, 1985) contend that in contemporary society, many behaviors do not occur at the usual ages or in the typical sequence

More Information You Can Use

Research Findings on Marriage and Choosing a Marriage Partner: Helpful Facts for Young Adults

1. **Marrying as a teenager is the highest known risk factor for divorce.** People who marry in their teens are two to three times more likely to divorce than people who marry in their twenties or older.

2. **The most likely way to find a future marriage partner is through an introduction by family, friends, or acquaintances.** Despite the romantic notion that people meet and fall in love through chance or fate, the evidence suggests that social networks are important in bringing together individuals of similar interests and backgrounds, especially when it comes to selecting a marriage partner. According to a large-scale national survey of sexuality, almost 60 percent of married people were introduced by family, friends, co-workers or other acquaintances.

3. **The more similar people are in their values, backgrounds, and life goals, the more likely they are to have a successful marriage.** Opposites may attract but they may not live together harmoniously as married couples. People who share common backgrounds and similar social networks are better suited as marriage partners than people who are very different in their backgrounds and networks.

4. **Women have a significantly better chance of marrying if they do not become single parents before marrying.** Having a child out of wedlock reduces the chances of ever marrying. Despite the growing numbers of potential marriage partners with children, one study noted, "Having children is still one of the least desirable characteristics a potential marriage partner can possess." The only partner characteristic men and women rank as even less desirable than having children is the inability to hold a steady job.

5. **Both women and men who are college educated are more likely to marry, and less likely to divorce, than people with lower levels of education.** Despite occasional news stories predicting lifelong singlehood for college-educated women, these predictions have proven false. Though the first generation of college-educated women (those who earned baccalaureate degrees in the 1920s) married less frequently than their less well-educated peers, the reverse is true today. College-educated women's chances of marrying are better than less well-educated women. However, the growing gender gap in college education may make it more difficult for college women to find similarly well-educated men in the future. This is already a problem for African American female college graduates, who greatly outnumber African American male college graduates.

6. **Living together before marriage has not proved useful as a "trial marriage."** People who have multiple cohabiting relationships before marriage are more likely to experience marital conflict, marital unhappiness, and eventual divorce than people who do not cohabit before marriage. Researchers attribute some but not all of these differences to the differing characteristics of people who cohabit, the so-called "selection effect," rather than to the experience of cohabiting itself. It has been hypothesized that the negative effects of cohabitation on future marital success may diminish as living together becomes a common experience among today's young adults. However, according to one recent study of couples who were married between 1981 and 1997, the negative effects persist among younger cohorts, supporting the view that the cohabitation experience itself contributes to problems in marriage.

7. **Marriage helps people to generate income and wealth.** Compared with those who merely live together, people who marry become economically better off. Men become more productive after marriage; they earn between 10 and 40 percent more than do single men with similar education and job histories. Marital social norms that encourage healthy, productive behavior and wealth accumulation play a role. Some of the greater wealth of married couples results from their more efficient specialization and pooling of resources, and because they save more. Married people also receive more money from family members than the unmarried (including cohabiting couples), probably because families consider marriage more permanent and more binding than a living-together union.

8. **People who are married are more likely to have emotionally and physically satisfying sex lives than single people or those who just live together.** Contrary to the popular belief that married sex is boring and infrequent, married people report higher levels of sexual satisfaction than both sexually active singles and cohabiting couples, according to the most comprehensive and recent survey of sexuality. Forty-two percent of wives said that they found sex extremely emotionally and physically satisfying, compared with just 31 percent of single women who had a sex partner. And 48 percent of husbands said sex was extremely satisfying emotionally, compared with just 37 percent of cohabiting men. The higher level of commitment in marriage is probably the reason for the high level of reported sexual satisfaction; marital commitment contributes to a greater sense of trust and security, less drug and alcohol-infused sex, and more mutual communication between the couple.

9. **People who grow up in a family broken by divorce are slightly less likely to marry, and much more likely to divorce when they do marry.** According to one study,

the divorce risk nearly triples if one marries someone who also comes from a broken home. The increased risk is much lower, however, if the marital partner is someone who grew up in a happy, intact family.

10. **For large segments of the population, the risk of divorce is far below 50 percent.** Although the overall divorce rate in America remains close to 50 percent of all marriages, it has been dropping gradually over the past two decades. Also, the risk of divorce is far

below 50 percent for educated people going into their first marriage, and lower still for people who wait to marry at least until their mid-twenties, haven't lived with many different partners prior to marriage, or are strongly religious and marry someone of the same faith.

Source: From Whitehead, Barbara Dafoe and David Popenoe, "Ten Important Research Findings on Marriage and Choosing a Marriage Partner: Helpful Facts for Young Adults," The National Marriage Project at Rutgers University, New Brunswick, NJ, 2004. Copyright © 2004 Barbara Dafoe Whitehead and David Popenoe. Used with permission

assumed by the family life-cycle model. At times, decisive economic, social, political, or military events intervene to alter the normal course of events. In addition, it is important whether parents are in their early twenties or their late thirties during the childbearing stage of the cycle. And a mentally retarded or handicapped child often stays with the family long after the normatively established "launching" period.

But despite its shortcomings, the family life-cycle model provides a clear picture of family change, particularly for families that remain intact and in which children are present. Each change in the roles of one family member affects all other family members, because they are bound together in a network of complementary roles—a set of mutually contingent relationships. Consequently, each stage in the family life cycle requires new adaptations and adjustments. Of particular importance are the events surrounding parenthood. Accordingly, let us examine more closely the significance of pregnancy and parenthood for young adults.

Pregnancy

Within the life cycle of a couple, particularly a woman, the first pregnancy is an event of unparalleled importance (Ruble et al., 1990). The first pregnancy signals that a couple is entering into the family cycle, bringing about new role requirements. As such, the first pregnancy functions as a major marker or transition and confronts a couple with new developmental tasks. Recall from Chapter 3 that more women from Westernized countries are postponing childbearing, and an increasing number of women are experiencing infertility and are seeking assisted reproductive technologies to become pregnant.

Pregnancy requires a woman to marshal her resources and adjust to a good many changes. Unfortunately, in many cases a woman's earliest experiences of pregnancy might be somewhat negative; she might be an unmarried, young adolescent; she might have morning sickness, vomiting, and fatigue. Pregnancy can also compel a woman to reflect on her long-term life plans, particularly as they relate to marriage and a career. And

pregnancy can cause her to reconsider her sense of identity. Many women seek out information on birth and motherhood to help them prepare for the new role. The woman's partner faces many of these same concerns. He might have to reappraise his conception of age, responsibility, and autonomy. Similarly, pregnancy contributes to changes in the couple's sexual behavior. Few events equal pregnancy in suddenness or significance, and many couples experience the initial phase of pregnancy as being somewhat disruptive, requiring marital adjustments.

On the broader social level, relatives, friends, and acquaintances commonly offer judgments on numerous matters, including whether the woman stands in a proper social relationship with the father-to-be (or will remain a single parent). An employed woman may have to confront changing relationships at work, as her employer and colleagues reappraise their ties with her. If the mother-to-be should withdraw from the paid workforce in preparation for childbirth, she could find that her domestic situation also alters. The more egalitarian values and role patterns of dual-career couples tend to give way to the stereotyped gender-role responsibilities found in traditional nuclear families.

Researchers have identified four major developmental tasks confronting a pregnant woman. First, she must come to accept her pregnancy. She must define herself as a parent-to-be and incorporate into her life frame a sense of impending parenthood. This process requires developing an emotional attachment to her unborn child, something that is now easier to do earlier in the pregnancy, due to the marvels of fetal ultrasound. Women typically become preoccupied with the developing fetus and, especially around the time that they begin to detect clear movements of the child in the uterus, ascribe personal characteristics to it.

Second, as a woman's pregnancy progresses, she must come to differentiate herself from the fetus and establish a distinct sense of self. She might accomplish this task by reflecting on a name for the infant and imagining what the baby will look like and how it will behave. This process is expedited when her increasing size brings about alterations in her clothing and she assumes a "pregnancy identity."

Third, a pregnant woman typically reflects on and reevaluates her relationship with her own mother. This

Further Developments

Is the U.S. Family Disintegrating or Merely Changing?

Some 90 percent of U.S. men and women consider marriage the best way to live. So concern about the future of the family is hardly surprising, given the directions in which family life has been moving in recent decades. However, opinions differ as to the significance and meaning of the changes. There are those who say that the family is a durable feature of the human experience, a resilient institution rooted in our social and animal nature. But because the institutional structure of society is always changing, the family also changes. Indeed, there are some feminists who argue that the traditional family is no longer appropriate for modern times because they see the traditional family structure as flawed by unhealthy conformity and male domination. Others contend that the family is in crisis and they fear its impending demise—noting that divorce rates have risen but stabilized, birthrates have fallen, the number of unwed mothers has increased, single-parent households have proliferated, mothers of young children have entered the labor force in large numbers, and the elderly and some segments of the younger adult population are relying more on the government than on the family for financial support.

Not surprisingly, family issues have entered the political arena with a vengeance. Conservatives usually decry what

Reports of the Death of the American Family Are Greatly Exaggerated Throughout human history the family has proven itself to be an adaptive, resilient institution that satisfies the needs of many people. Although new challenges confront today's families, it seems that people continue to prefer and vitally need the kinds of relationships that a healthy family life can provide.

they see as the lack of traditional family values and issue urgent calls for their revival. All the while, liberals endorse the proliferation and flexibility in family structures and call for additional government assistance programs. As sociologist and former U.S. Senator Daniel Patrick Moynihan (1985) noted, conservatives—fearing government intervention and interference—like to talk about family values but not new government initiatives, whereas liberals prefer to talk about public policy initiatives but not family values.

Much of the debate over the "state of the American family" might be misinformed and misguided because it uses a stereotyped image of the white middle-class family of the 1950s and 1960s as its point of departure for either praise or criticism of subsequent changes. The notion that family life is disintegrating implies that at an earlier time in history the family was a more stable and harmonious institution. Yet historians have never located a golden age of the family (Coontz, 1992, 2000). Their research reveals that the marriages of seventeenth-century England and New England were based on family and property needs, not on choice and affection. Loveless marriages, the tyranny of husbands, and the beating and abuse of children were commonplace (Shorter, 1975). Additionally, families were riddled by desertion and death to an unimaginable degree. Within many families of the eighteenth and nineteenth centuries, subordination to the male head of household was the norm, sometimes enforced by violence (Coontz, 2000).

The idea that families should consist of a breadwinner husband, a homemaker wife, and their dependent children is more recent. In the late 1890s, the rural, preindustrial family was a largely self-sufficient unit, meeting most of its consumer needs. Husbands, wives, children, and lodgers were all expected to participate in gainful work. Later, with the onset of industrialization, more and more family members sought work for wages in factories and workshops. Throughout the Western world the nascent labor movement pressed for a "living wage," an income sufficient for a male breadwinner to support a wife and children in modest comfort.

Americans began sorting jobs into male and female categories during the 1800s. The domestic sphere was defined as the "special place" of women. If women were in the labor force outside the home, it was expected that they would stop working after marriage or make a lifetime commitment of celibacy as a nanny, domestic, nurse, schoolteacher, or nun. The restriction of large numbers of married women to domestic activities took place only after industrialization was well established (Carlson, 1986). Family life prior to the 1950s was hardly orderly, and children were expected to leave school, postpone leaving home, or put off marriage to help the family meet an unexpected economic crisis or a parental death (Coontz, 2000). By the early 1900s, young people married relatively late because they were often obligated to support their parents and siblings. The economic prosperity of the post–World War II years contributed to a much younger age at which marriage occurred. Today's young adults, however, are reversing the trend and marrying at later ages (U.S. Bureau of the Census, 2004–2005). The development of affectionate and private bonds within a small nuclear family were accelerated in the early 1900s with the decline in the boarding and lodging of extended family and nonfamily members, the growing tendency for unmarried adults to leave home, and the fall in fertility (Laslett, 1973).

All in all, reports of the death of the U.S. family may not reflect recent demographic trends. After a decline in the proportion of married with children families, recent census data show a leveling off to about 68 percent over the last decade (U.S. Bureau of the Census, 2004c). This change is a reflection of stabilizing divorce rates and lower birthrates among teenagers. This number will rise further with the inclusion of same-sex marriages with children as these unions become recognized. In some ways our understandings about what constitutes a "family" have changed dramatically; yet a traditional family life still holds significant meaning for many people, especially those who grew up in an intact traditional family. Overall, even though family life normally presents challenges and frustrations, it is something that most people vitally need, particularly when many other spheres of life are becoming "depersonalized." In sum, for most Americans the family remains a vital, adaptive, resilient human institution (Thornton & Young-DeMarco, 2001).

process often entails the woman's reconciliation with her mother and the working through of numerous feelings, memories, and identifications.

Fourth, a woman must come to terms with the issue of dependency. Her pregnancy and impending motherhood often arouse anxiety concerning her loss of certain freedoms and her reliance on others for some measure of support, maintenance, and help. Such concerns are frequently centered on her relationship with her husband or partner.

The accomplishment of these developmental tasks is often expedited by childbirth-training classes, which teach women what to expect during pregnancy and labor. The knowledge and techniques the pregnant woman gains from the classes give her a measure of "active control" and self-help. Finally, when husbands or partners also participate in the training classes, mothers-to-be find additional social support and assistance. Both preparation in pregnancy and a partner's presence are positively associated with the quality of a woman's birth experience. Indeed, much that happens before birth influences what transpires between parent and child after birth. What a woman experiences during her months of pregnancy is covered in detail in Chapter 3.

Transition to Parenthood

Psychologists and sociologists who view the family as an integrated system of roles and statuses have often depicted the onset of parenthood as a "crisis" because it involves a shift from a two-person to a three-person system (Rubenstein, 1989). The three-person system is thought to be inherently more stressful than the two-person system. Sociologists also find other reasons the transition to parenthood could pose a crisis:

> The birth of a child is not followed by any gradual taking on of responsibility, as in the case of a professional work role. It is as if the woman shifted from a graduate student to a full professor with little intervening apprenticeship experience of slowly increasing responsibility. The new mother starts out immediately on 24-hour duty, with responsibility for a fragile and mysterious infant totally dependent on her care. (Alice S. Rossi, 1968, p. 35)

We should note that not all marriages change in exactly the same way, and important individual differences surface in the ways spouses respond to parenthood (Alexander & Higgins, 1993; Levy-Shiff, 1994). A continuing study of more than 250 families by Jay Belsky and his colleagues is providing a rich array of insights about the transition to adulthood and parenthood (Belsky & Rovine, 1990; Jaffee et al., 2001). This research shows that having children does not turn good marriages into bad ones or bad marriages into good ones. Yet overall, after the birth of a baby, couples typically experience a modest decline in the overall quality and intimacy of their marital life. Husbands and wives often have less time to show each other affection, and they share fewer leisure activities (especially the growing number of couples who are having multiple births). The decline in marital satisfaction tends to be greater for wives than for husbands. But on the positive side, there is an increase in a couple's sense of partnership and mutual caretaking. And with the addition of a second child, fathers often become more involved in the work of the home, taking on more household tasks and significantly increasing their interaction with the firstborn youngster (Stewart, 1990). One father observes, "It took only one child to make my wife a mother, but two to make me a father" (Stewart, 1990, p. 213).

Couples who are most likely to report marital problems in early parenthood are those who held the most unrealistic expectations of parenthood. Belsky believes the most successful couples seemingly shift to rose-colored glasses, focusing on what is going well

The Transition to Parenthood After the birth of a baby, a shared division of responsibilities and adequate sleep are especially important for marital satisfaction. New parents can cope with stress by developing a network of supportive people.

rather than on what is going poorly; for instance, they downplay the fact that she has not lost all the weight or that he does not help out enough. One of the biggest postbirth stumbling blocks is the division of labor. Overall, parents typically move to more stereotyped gender roles after the arrival of a baby. Consequently, the wife frequently assumes a heavily disproportionate share of the division of household chores, and this can lead her to have negative feelings toward her husband. It seems that role consensus and a shared division of responsibilities between husband and wife are especially important for the maintenance of ongoing intimate relationships and marital satisfaction (Goldberg & Perry-Jenkins, 2004). A large body of research finds family routines and rituals are embedded in the cultural context of family life and are found to be related to parenting competence, child adjustment, and marital satisfaction. Family rituals include highly stylized religious observances, a certain type of greeting when the spouse returns home, a routine dinnertime, a special weekend activity, or an annual vacation (Fiese et al., 2002).

Although having a baby might not save a marriage, a study by researchers associated with the Rand Corporation found that a first baby can stabilize marriages (Waite, Haggstrom, & Kanouse, 1985). The researchers followed more than 5,000 new parents and more than 5,000 nonparents for three years; the couples were matched on such factors as age and years married. The study showed that by the time their children were 2 years of age, the parents had a divorce rate under 8 percent. The nonparents had a rate of more than 20 percent. But why should babies make a marriage more stable? The Rand researchers speculate that people who decide to have children might be happier together to begin with, that children are a deterrent to divorce because they add complexity and expense to a breakup, and that parents acquire a bond with their partners through their children.

Postpartum Depression About two or three days after delivery, some new mothers experience what is commonly called **postpartum depression (PPD),** or the *postpartum blues.* Symptoms include irritability, waves of sadness, frequent crying spells, difficulty sleeping, diminished appetite, and feelings of helplessness and hopelessness. Generally, the episode is mild and lasts only a short time, up to a few weeks. Similar symptoms often appear in women who adopt a child, and some new fathers also report that they feel "down in the dumps." One study reported that nearly all new mothers experienced some symptoms that have been traditionally associated with the postpartum depression, and more than 60 percent of the fathers had similar symptoms (Collins et al., 1993). Further, if a woman has had a postpartum depression, she is 50 percent more likely to have another case with the next baby (Wisner & Wheeler, 1994).

Some medical experts believe that a woman's hormonal changes associated with childbirth and metabolic readjustment to a nonpregnant state influence her emotional and psychological state. Following childbirth, dramatic changes occur in the levels of various hormones, and changes can occur in thyroid and adrenal hormones. Such changes contribute to depressive reactions (Brody, 1994b). Other explanations emphasize the psychological adjustments required of a woman in her new role as a mother (Mauthner, 1999). Some women experience a sense of loss of independence, of being tied down and trapped by the new infant. Other women feel guilty about the anger and helplessness they feel when their infants cry and cannot be comforted. And others feel overwhelmed by the responsibility of caring for, rearing, and shaping the behavior of another human being. Women with temperamentally difficult babies find that child care severely taxes their emotional and psychological resources, contributing to depression. Although mothers cannot alter their infant's basic temperament, they can cope with stress by developing a network of supportive people (Ritter et al., 2000).

In a small number of cases, the birth of a child can catalyze severe mental illness in women who are predisposed to *schizophrenia* or *bipolar* (manic-depressive) disorder. Women who have the more devastating forms of mental illness might even commit infanticide or suicide (e.g., Andrea Yates). Women should not be afraid or feel ashamed to seek help. Treatment options include psychotherapy, antidepressant medication, participation in a support group, family counseling, and, if circumstances warrant, hospitalization (Brody, 1994b).

> **Question**
>
> How does parenthood change the nature of a marriage in both positive and negative ways?

Lesbian Parenthood

It has been estimated that 1 to 5 million lesbians have had children in the context of past heterosexual relationships, although these percentages are still highly debatable (Parks, 1998). Lesbians also choose other pathways to parenthood, including donor insemination, adoption, and stepparenting. But many lesbian mothers are hesitant to be open about their sexual orientation for fear of losing their children in custody disputes, and it is still common that lesbian mothers in custody disputes often are unsuccessful in keeping their children (Morton, 1998). In many courts of law, lesbian mothers have been deemed "unfit" as parents on a number of grounds (Arnup, 1995). But in fact there is no evidence that lesbian mothers are emotionally unstable or that they might sexually abuse their children. In fact as studies indicate, the majority of child molesters are heterosexual males who are partners of a close relative of the child (Jenny, Roesker, & Poyer, 1994).

Research shows that there are few differences between heterosexual and lesbian mothers, as it is motherhood—not sexuality—that emerges as the dominant identity marker for these women (Demo, 2000). Lesbian women choose to become parents for many of the same reasons as heterosexual parents. But they face certain issues that heterosexual mothers do not face, such as homophobia and societal disapproval (Gartrell et al., 2000). Both of these factors place additional stress on the lesbian mother that can lead her to develop feelings of self-doubt, ambivalence, or a sense of having to overachieve. Lesbian couples with children reported greater sexual and interpersonal satisfaction than those lesbian couples who remained childless. Furthermore, lesbian couples tend to divide housework and child care more equitably than other couples (Parks, 1998).

Even though lesbian parents face social stigma, legal battles, and economic disadvantages, research indicates that both parents and children are healthy, secure, and effective in coping with the challenges they face in their years together (Parks, 1998). In 1986 the *National Lesbian Family Study* was launched to broaden understanding of lesbian families and their children over 25 years. The children in the study at age 5 were healthy, developing normally, and were relating well to peers. Although many birth mothers and co-mothers expressed that having a child strengthened their relationship, about one-third of the participants had "divorced" by the time the child was age 5 (Gartrell et al., 1996, 1999, 2000). A limitation of the existing body of research is that the majority of studies have relied on lesbian mothers who have volunteered for research versus a representative sample of lesbian mothers with children. Yet findings from Golombok and colleague's (2003) British longitudinal study of the psychological well-being of children raised to adulthood in lesbian homes indicate positive mother-child relationships and well-adjusted children:

- These children are no more likely to have a gay or lesbian sexual orientation as adults than are their peers raised by heterosexual parents.
- Men and women raised by lesbian mothers were no more likely to experience anxiety or depression than were their peers raised in heterosexual homes.
- Fear of group stigmatization and the experience of being teased or bullied are central elements of how children feel about growing up in a lesbian-mother family.

> **Question**
>
> What are the findings of the first longitudinal study on the psychological effects of parenting for lesbians and for children growing up in a lesbian-parent home?

Employed Mothers

One aspect of motherhood that some women experience as a challenge is balancing motherhood and career. Despite the "sexual revolution," employed women still bear the brunt of being the primary parent and the primary housekeeper (McLaughlin, Gardner, & Lichter, 1999). Economist Sylvia Ann Newlett notes (quoted in Castro, 1991, p. 10):

> In the U.S. we have confused equal rights with identical treatment, ignoring the realities of family life. After all, only women can bear children. And in this country, women must still carry most of the burden of raising them. We think that we are being fair to everyone by stressing identical opportunities, but in fact we are punishing women and children.

The United States is experiencing radical transformations in the nature of family, work, and careers. Today's workforce is more heterogeneous than ever before. In addition, most working husbands have working wives; most children have working mothers; and almost half the workforce is now female. The most striking change in the latter half of the twentieth century and the beginning of the twenty-first century has been in women's life paths, as mothers and wives continue to enter, exit, reenter, and remain in the workforce in unprecedented numbers. A hundred years ago, only one in five American women was in the paid workforce. About three out of five women are now working for pay (see Figure 14.2; U.S. Bureau of the Census, 2004f). The proportion of working mothers of young children has also more than quadrupled. Although American women were entering the labor force well before the turn of the last century, it is only recently that the employment of mothers of preschoolers—including infants—has become common. Today, almost two-thirds of mothers of preschoolers are in the workforce (Fields & Casper, 2001). Even among mothers of infants, over half are back at work before their baby celebrates a first birthday (Bachu, 2000). All the while, rising educational levels for women have increased both their ability and motivation to obtain employment outside the home. Moreover, a great many families find it an economic necessity that the woman be employed; most divorced, single-parent, and widowed mothers must work to avoid poverty. Even two-parent families find a second income is often required to maintain an acceptable standard of living.

Serious concern is frequently voiced about the future of U.S. children as more and more mothers enter the workforce. Many people fear that the children of a working mother suffer a loss in terms of supervision, love, and cognitive enrichment. Much of the earlier research on maternal employment and juvenile delinquency was based on this assumption: Mothers were working, children were unsupervised, and thus, they became delinquents. But the matter is not that simple. In a classic study of lower-class boys, Sheldon and Eleanor Glueck (1957) found that sons of regularly employed mothers were no more likely to be delinquent than sons of unemployed mothers.

Research findings are contradictory regarding the effects of maternal employment during a child's first year, with some studies reporting negative cognitive and social outcomes (Baydar & Brooks-Gunn, 1991; Belsky & Eggebeen, 1991) and others finding only minimal negative outcomes (Parcel & Menaghan, 1994a). A positive outcome is that mothers' working provides positive role models for children. For older youngsters, however, an accumulating body of research suggests that there is little difference in the development of children whose mothers work and that of children whose mothers remain at home (Polatnick, 2000).

Much depends on whether the mother, regardless of employment, is satisfied in her situation. Budig and England (2001) conclude that the working mother who obtains personal satisfaction from employment, does not feel excessive guilt, has high-quality child care, and has adequate household arrangements is likely to perform as well as or better than the unemployed mother. Mothers who are not working and would like to, and working mothers whose lives are beset by harassment and strain, are the ones whose children are most likely to show maladjustment and behavioral problems. How much time parents spend with their children is not so predictive of young children's development as are the attitudes and behaviors their parents take toward them.

Clearly, contemporary youngsters are affected by the father's as well as the mother's working. Further, having two working parents impacts youngsters in many direct and interactive ways. For instance, parents who have heavy work schedules are less able to spend time with their children fostering the development of their cognitive and social skills.

Separation and Divorce

Divorce is widespread, and a divorce affects everyone involved with the family. The experience does not affect all couples in the same ways; for instance, some spouses continue to have sex even after they are separated or divorced and get along fairly well. But for most, the effects are negative. People who have gone through separation or divorce have increased chances of psychiatric disorders, depression, alcoholism, weight loss or weight gain, and sleep disorders. The effects on young children can also continue into young adulthood, with children of divorce having a decreased capacity for intimacy (Westervelt & Vandenberg, 1997). And parental divorce is associated with an increased risk of offspring divorce, especially when wives or both spouses have gone through the experience of their parents' divorce (Amato & DeBoer, 2000). Traditionally, women are granted either sole custody or joint custody of children and might be awarded a regular child-support stipend by the courts, which might or might not be paid.

Well-Being of Children and Young Adults Whose Parents Have Divorced   Gohm, Oishi, and Darlington (1998) conducted a multinational study investigating the effects of parental divorce on the subjective well-being of adult children. They collected international data from 1995 to 1996 as part of a larger study of issues related to cultural differences in subjective well-being. Participants were several thousand college students from 39 countries (14 Asian countries, 13 European countries, 5 African countries, 4 South American countries, plus Australia, the United States, and Puerto Rico). In some

Employed Mothers A job in the workplace permits participation in the larger society and compensation for one's skills. However, a shared division of responsibilities between husband and wife improves marital satisfaction.

cases, parental divorce increased the well-being of adult offspring, and for some being raised in a second marriage was better than being raised by a single parent (Chase-Lansdale, Cherlin, & Kiernan, 1995). Family stress theory suggests, however, that remarriage is probably beneficial if the remarriage does not result in high levels of marital conflict. Analysis of 37 studies of young adult offspring found no support for gender differences in the impact of divorce (Amato & Keith, 1991). However, "within original family marriages, marital conflict has clear, long-term, negative consequences for the well-being of offspring . . . and is consistent across gender" (Gohm, Oishi, & Darlington, 1998).

Offspring raised in a remarried household where parental conflict is low report life satisfaction similar to that of offspring from average marriages and of offspring from single-parent, divorced homes. Offspring raised in divorced, single-parent households report greater life satisfaction and more positive emotional life (higher subjective well-being) than offspring raised in high-conflict marriages—though this finding varied across cultures (Gohm, Oishi, & Darlington, 1998). "The subjective

well-being of offspring in remarried households is not much greater than that of offspring in a high-conflict marriage, and sometimes it is lower" (Gohm, Oishi, & Darlington, 1998). In fact, Wilson and Daly (1997) report a considerably higher incidence of child abuse and homicide in remarriage families, particularly for children under age 3, in comparison to statistics for intact families. Cherlin (2004) proposes that Americans lack norms of behavior about the way members of stepfamilies should act toward each other. Cherlin (2004) finds the high incidence of divorce and remarriage have contributed to the deinstitutionalization of first marriage. Changes in norms include the changing division of labor in the home, childbearing outside of marriage, cohabitation, and domestic partnerships. The extended social network found in collectivist cultures (those with extended kinship patterns) appears to provide greater psychological and emotional support for children experiencing the trauma of marital conflict and divorce.

Single-Parent Mothers

The percentage of persons living alone is increasing. From 1970 to 2003, the percentage of adults who lived alone increased significantly from 12 percent to 15 percent for women and from 6 percent to 11 percent for men. The proportion of births to unmarried women increased in 2003, comprising 35 percent of all annual births (Hamilton, Martin, & Sutton, 2004). Additionally, increasing numbers of women in Western nations are bearing children outside of marriage (see Figure 14.6). Single parenthood is evident at all socioeconomic levels. Though the numbers are highest for women who live in poverty and among African American women, the most rapid rate increase is seen in nonmarried motherhood among women who have attended college for at least a year and among women with professional or managerial jobs. As women become more financially independent and are able to rely on other relatives for child care, it becomes more feasible to be a single mother or adoptive parent. Significantly, nonmarried childbirth, divorce, and various cohabiting arrangements have also changed the meaning of "family." As noted earlier in this chapter, the traditional nuclear family is currently less a reality for a growing number of Americans.

In single-parent families the responsibilities fall on one adult rather than two, so single parents must allocate their time to cover both their own and their children's physical, social, and psychological needs. The matter is complicated by the fact that many schools and workplaces have inflexible hours, and these hours do not coincide—though more businesses now have flex-time scheduling or on-site child care and more U.S. schools are providing both before-school care and after-school care, as well as all-day summer programs for youth. Single mothers

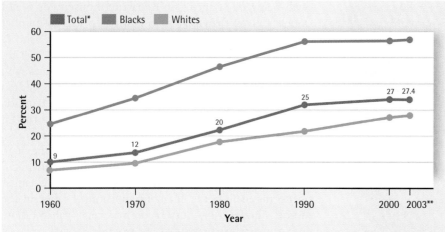

FIGURE 14.6 Single Parenthood Is on the Rise More American children currently live in single-parent households—and the proportion is steadily rising. The United States lags behind other industrialized nations in making available safe and accessible child care to employed single parents. Some large corporations have on-site child care, and many public schools offer before-school and after-school programs, as well as summer supervision. Many single-parent mothers live at a lower socioeconomic status than single-parent fathers.
Source: From Popenoe, David and Barbara Dafoe Whitehead. *The State of Our Unions: The Social Health of Marriage in America, 2004.* The National Marriage Project at Rutgers University, New Brunswick, NJ, 2004. Copyright © 2004 Barbara Dafoe Whitehead and David Popenoe. Used with permission.

* Total includes blacks, whites, and all other racial and ethnic groupings. Over these decades an additional 3–4% of children (not indicated in these groups) were classified as living with no parent.

** In 2003, the U.S. Census Bureau expanded its racial categories to permit respondents to identify themselves as belonging to more than one race. This means that racial data computations beginning in 2003 may not be strictly comparable to those of prior years.

frequently suffer from a lack of free time, spiraling child-care costs, loneliness, and the unrelenting pressures of attempting to meet the demands posed by both home and work, and, for some, college classes as well. Being a single parent calls for a somewhat different kind of parenting. Frequently, single parents find themselves making "the speech," as one mother termed it, explaining:

> I sat down with my three children and said, "Look. Things are going to have to be different. We're all in this together and we're going to have to be partners. I'm earning a living for us now. I'm doing it all. I need your help, if this household is going to work." (McCoy, 1982, p. 21)

Women heading single-parent families often have lower levels of education, lower incomes, and lower levels of social support than women in two-parent families, leading to greater stress. One study found that financial strain resulted in higher levels of depressive symptoms, which in turn had a negative effect on parenting (Jackson et al., 2000). Disruptions due to substantial income changes, residential relocation, unpredictable financial support from an ex-spouse, and household composition changes are more likely. Not surprisingly, female heads generally report much lower self-esteem, a lower sense of effectiveness, and less optimism about the future than women in two-parent settings. However, recently divorced, separated, and widowed women experience more major life-event disruptions than women who have been single for three or more years. And though many women do not choose single parenting, most are proud of their ability to survive under adverse circumstances (DeAngelis, 2001).

For many single mothers, kin networks are important sources of financial, emotional, and child-care support (Oliker, 2000). Many single mothers are dependent on government programs, local charitable organizations, and churches for survival. More recently federal *Welfare to Work* legislation is providing job training for healthy single mothers to become employed within a recommended time period (Oliker, 2000). However, preliminary research findings by social scientists reveal that while about two-thirds of women have left welfare and are earning more money than before, these women and their families face significant psychological and economic challenges. In many respects a single father is in a better position than a single mother, because he is frequently viewed as a person who is doing something extraordinary.

According to the U.S. Bureau of the Census (Grail, 2000), about 56 percent of women raising children without the children's father have been awarded child support. In the United States, divorce courts often demand the father's monetary obligation but not his presence, though more courts are awarding joint custody. And as men start seeing their children less, they often start paying less. Among never-married mothers, only a small number get any financial help from their children's father. It is hardly surprising, then, that nearly three-fourths of never-married young mothers live in poverty.

Some families headed by women survive these hardships with few ill effects. But a disturbing number of children and parents are saddled with problems (McLaughlin, Gardner, & Lichter, 1999). Children living in single-parent families are much more likely to be enrolled below the grade that is modal for their age and to be experiencing school difficulties than are children living with both parents. Some studies also show that juvenile delinquency rates are twice as high for children from single-parent households as they are for children from two-parent households. Lack of parental supervision and chronic social, health, and psychological strains are often associated with poverty (Bank et al., 1993).

Social isolation can create a sense of vulnerability for single mothers. Yet most women report having a partner, boyfriend, friends, or relatives who provide them with assistance on a fairly regular basis. In nearly half of all single-parent families, the parent marries within five years. This new marriage results in a "blended" or "reconstituted" family, which can produce complicated kinship networks (see Chapter 16). Where both partners have been previously married, each has to deal with the former spouse of the current partner as well as with his or her own former spouse and several sets of grandparents (some of them being ex-in-laws). Adding to the difficulties are stepparent-stepchildren relationships, one's own children's reactions to the current spouse, one's own reactions to the current spouse's children, and the children's reactions to one another.

Single-Parent Fathers

The movie *Kramer vs. Kramer* broke new ground in the 1970s by portraying what is now becoming a way of life for increasing numbers of U.S. men: men rearing children alone. In 2003, there were 2.26 million father-child families in the United States. The number of men who become single parents as a result of their wife's death has declined. But overall the number of single fathers has grown slowly, as more men are awarded custody of children in divorce proceedings. Indeed, 25 years ago a father was awarded custody only if he could demonstrate in court that the mother was totally "unfit" for parenthood, and single men adopting children was out of the question.

Although the expectations attached to the father role in a two-parent family are fairly explicit, they are not so explicit for a father in the single-parent family. A number of studies have shown that even though single fathers are confronted with adjustment requirements, most of them raise their children successfully (Heath & Orthner, 1999). But juggling work and child care commonly poses difficulties for single fathers, as it does for single mothers, especially for those with preschool youngsters. Compared with single mothers, however, fathers often make more money and have greater economic security and job flexibility (Amato & DeBoer, 2000). Overall, the single father is neither the extraordinary human being nor the bumbling "Mr. Mom" depicted in popular stereotypes. Concerning child supervision, fathers tend to gravitate toward nurseries and child-care centers, where they feel that the staff has a professional commitment to children.

Generally, single fathers seem better prepared for the physical aspects of parenting—shopping, cooking, cleaning, taking the child to the doctor, and the like—than for dealing with their children's emotional needs. Men who adeptly juggle work schedules to stay home and nurse a sick child report that they fall apart in the face of a healthy temper tantrum. They view their children's strong displays of emotion as "irrational," especially when they cannot trace those emotions to some specific event in the children's lives. Single fathers also tend to express more anxiety over the sexual behavior of their daughters than that of their sons. And many are concerned about the absence of adult female role models within the home. Many single fathers admit that they have had to learn to deal with their children's emotional needs and to develop their own nurturing skills (Lehr & Macmillan, 2001).

Some suggest that the main difficulty for many fathers in making the transition to becoming a single parent is losing companionship rather than becoming a single parent (Stern, 2001). Though dating is often an important part of the single father's lifestyle, he is in no hurry to marry again. Indeed, half were uncertain if they want to remarry and were committed to remaining single for the present. In sum, single-parent fathers and single-parent mothers both find that their greatest difficulties lie in balancing the demands of work and parenthood. Let's now examine the role that work plays in the lives of adults.

> **Questions**
>
> What are the proposed stages of a traditional family life cycle? What do we know about the status of single-parent mothers and fathers raising children?

Work

The central portion of the adult life span for both men and women today is spent at work, and nowadays Americans are working longer than ever. Economist Juliet B. Schor (1998) finds that over the past 20 years the time Americans spend on the job has been rising—a reversal of a century-long trend toward a shorter workday. According to the International Labour Organization in 2001, Americans worked an average of 1,979 hours per year—significantly more than the second place Mexicans at 1,863 hours and the Japanese who averaged 1,842 hours per year. Schor (1998) contends that Americans are working longer to achieve the equivalent of a 1970 standard of living. The net result for Americans is a decline in their happiness and an erosion of their collective ability to care for children, cook, sleep, visit, and enjoy life (Moen, 2003; Schor, 1998). Americans are merging work and family life marked by conflicting career goals and personal needs. Moen and Roehling (2005) find that a majority of men and women would prefer to work fewer hours than they do. Some resolve this conflict by adapting to the job requirements, thus delaying having children. Others opt to meet their families' needs by varying work schedules, working from home, working part-time, or by exiting the workforce, with ramifications for future employment.

Americans' work experience has also undergone a significant change over the past 185 years. More than 70 percent of the U.S. labor force worked on the farm in 1820; today less than 5 percent are engaged in agriculture. Employment in the service industries is about 70 percent now, the same percentage as for farming over a century and a half ago.

For a majority of young Americans, the transition to adult occupational roles is postponed by college. Most youth view a college education primarily as a means to a better job rather than as a vehicle for broadening their intellectual horizons. One of the most significant developments in higher education in recent years is that U.S. colleges are enrolling more adult "nontraditional" students, those who have been out of high school for a year or more, are over 23, and have put off getting a degree. Over the past 20 years the number of nontraditional students enrolled in colleges and universities grew by over 70 percent. The adult nontraditional students are more likely to come from working-class backgrounds, have family and work responsibilities, do not want to waste any time in getting a degree, and strive to do their best. These adults aspire to prepare themselves for a better job or a career.

The Significance of Work for Women and Men

People work for a great many reasons. "Self-interest" in its broadest sense, including the interests of one's family and friends, is an underlying motivation of work in all societies. However, self-interest is not simply the accumulation of wealth. For instance, among the Maori, a Polynesian people of the Pacific, a desire for approval, a sense of duty, a wish to conform to custom, a feeling of emulation, and a pleasure in craftsmanship also contribute to economic activity (Hsu, 1943).

Even in the United States, few activities seriously compete with work in providing basic life satisfaction (Moen & Roehling, 2005; Schor, 1998). In a study conducted more than 50 years ago (Morse & Weiss, 1955) and since replicated several times, a representative sample of U.S. men were asked whether they would continue working if they inherited enough money to live comfortably (Gallup Poll Monthly, 1991; Opinion Roundup, 1980). About 80 percent said they would. The reasons are not difficult to discover. Work, in addition to its economic functions, structures time, provides a context in which to relate to other people, offers an escape from boredom, and sustains a sense of identity and self-worth. Perhaps not surprisingly, then, only one in four million-dollar lottery winners quits working after

hitting the jackpot. Sociologist Harry Levinson (1964, p. 20) has commented:

> Work has quite a few social meanings: When a man works he has a contributing place in society. He earns the right to be the partner of other men. . . . A man's work . . . is a major social device for his identification as an adult. Much of who he is, to himself and others, is interwoven with how he earns his livelihood.

Much the same assessment has been made regarding the meaning of work for women. Although paid work is becoming an economic necessity for an increasing number of women, one of the central themes of the women's movement has been the symbolic meaning of a paid job. For many, though not all, contemporary women, exclusive commitment to the unpaid work of homemaker and mother implies being cut off from the full possibilities of self-fulfillment. Some women view parenting children as the most important job of all and are willing to make sacrifices to continue as full-time homemakers, but a paid job has increasingly come to be seen as the "price of admission" to independence in the greater society and as a symbol of self-worth (Lewin, 1995).

The *Americans with Disabilities Act (ADA)* legislation (P.L.101-336) passed by Congress in 1990 recognizes the significance of work for all adults and opens the doors for more meaningful participation in higher education, work, and society for adults with disabilities. Corporations, municipalities, industries, and colleges are making buildings more accessible; transit companies are providing buses with wheelchair lifts and rescheduling routes to get people to school or a job; and communities across the United States are redesigning buildings, doorways, restrooms, and sidewalks for adults with disabilities. American corporations that receive federal contracts must demonstrate that they have hired persons with disabilities, and everyone benefits from providing meaningful participation in society for this segment of our adult population.

For all of us, our work is an important socializing experience that influences who and what we are. Sociologists Kohn and colleagues (1990) found that college-educated people are more likely to acquire jobs that require independent judgment and lead to higher rankings in the socioeconomic system. By virtue of the intellectual demands of their work, the college-educated evolve an intellectual prowess that carries over to their private lives. They might even seek out intellectually demanding activities in their leisure pursuits (such as community theater, coaching, mentoring, or serving on boards of agencies). Typically, people who engage in self-directed work come to value self-direction more highly, to be more open to new ideas, and to be less authoritarian in their relationships with others. As parents, they pass these characteristics on to their children.

In the United States a strong work ethic permeates the culture. Idleness seems to perpetuate a sense of hopelessness. We have witnessed this with the thousands of skilled, college-educated, but unemployed workers in their thirties, forties, and fifties who lost their jobs in the early to mid 1990s because of corporate takeovers, layoffs, and downsizing. The longer a person is unemployed, cannot find a job, and cannot support a family, the more worthless (or depressed) that person feels, whether man or woman. To be unemployed—especially for a man, whom society views as the main wage earner—is to be a social outcast. Anthropologist Elliot Liebow (1967), in a study of "street-corner men" living in a Washington, D.C., ghetto, found that the inability to gain steady, remunerative, and meaningful employment undermines an individual's self-respect and self-worth. Liebow concludes that the street-corner man is attempting to achieve the goals and values of the larger society, and when he fails to do so, he tries to conceal this failure as best he can from himself and others, often by escaping through alcoholism or substance abuse. In essence, for most people work is a truly defining activity necessary for their healthy development.

Question
What kind of meaning do people derive from their work?

SEGUE

We have looked at love and the institutional extension of love—marriage—as they affect different adults. As individuals go through changes, or stages, they reevaluate themselves, the interactions they have with others, and the meanings that love and work have for them at the moment. For some people this evaluation can lead to transitions like marriage, parenting, divorce, quitting a job, sexual reorientation, cohabitation, and, more likely than not, remarriage. Early adulthood is seen as the time when individuals start out on their first truly independent journey—it is a time when they are able to leave parents to explore what they "really want to do." But we have also seen that sometimes, as society changes, individuals make changes—perhaps postponing their dreams, or at least modifying them. Also, these changes lead to physical and cognitive changes, as adults in their middle years become more sedentary, experience midlife changes, and reassess their life satisfaction. We will explore these significant issues in Chapter 15.

Summary

Theories of Emotional-Social Development

1. Love and work are the central themes of adult life. Both place us in a complex web of relationships with others. Relationships derive from two types of bonds: expressive ties and instrumental ties. Relationships that rest on expressive ties are called primary relationships; those that rest on instrumental ties are called secondary relationships.
2. The metaphor of the life course as being divided into stages or "seasons" has captured the imagination of philosophers and poets as well as other writers. Theorists tend to be divided over the idea that development is divided into predictable, discrete intervals.
3. Erikson's first stage of adult development is called the crisis of intimacy versus isolation.
4. Levinson and his associates say that the overriding task throughout adulthood is the creation of a life structure. Men and women must periodically restructure their lives by creating a new structure or reappraising an old one.
5. Stage theory typically has four characteristics. First, qualitative differences in structure are said to take place at given points in development. Second, the theory posits an invariant sequence or order. Third, the various ingredients making up a distinct structure appear as an integrated cluster of typical responses to life events. And fourth, higher stages displace or reintegrate the structures found at lower stages.

Establishing Intimacy in Relationships

6. Friends become our major source of socializing and support during our adult years. Research on love attempts to explain the real complexities involved in initiating and maintaining a meaningful, intimate relationship with another person.

Diversity in Lifestyle Options

7. Individuals in modern complex societies generally enjoy some options in selecting and changing their lifestyles. A striking aspect of U.S. society over the past 35 years has been the rapid expansion in lifestyles. Greater latitude is permitted individuals in tailoring for themselves lifestyles less constrained by traditional standards of what a "respectable" person should be like.
8. Leaving home is a major step in the transition to adulthood. For a good many decades, marriage was the major reason for leaving home. But over the past few decades, the process of leaving the parental home has become increasingly

complex, and many young people experience numerous living arrangements in the course of assuming adult status.

9. Norms have dictated that U.S. youth leave home and make their own way in the world. But lately adult children have been making their way back to the parental home in increasing numbers. Family therapists express concern that those who stay at home or return home do not have opportunities to fully develop their sense of individuality. The practices aggravate tendencies toward excessive protectiveness in parents and aggravate tendencies toward a lack of self-confidence in youth.

10. Census data reveal a sharp increase in the percentage of men and women under 35 years of age who are single. This increase has resulted in part from the tendency of young people to postpone marriage. A majority of adult singles live with someone else, such as a friend, a relative, or a "spouse equivalent."

11. The number of couples who are not married but live together has increased substantially over the past two to three decades, and those who follow this lifestyle do so more openly than they used to. Cohabitation is not restricted to the younger generation. It is becoming increasingly prevalent among the middle-aged and elderly who are divorced or widowed.

12. Sexual orientation refers to whether an individual is more strongly aroused sexually (erotic attraction) by members of his or her own sex (homosexual), the opposite sex (heterosexual), or both sexes (bisexual). Individuals show varying degrees of orientation, so homosexuals (lesbians and gay males) are a varied group.

13. Marriage is a lifestyle found in all societies. It remains the dominant lifestyle in the United States. About close to 50 percent of all marriages end in divorce, but a majority of Americans remarry.

Family Transitions

14. Families, like individuals, undergo development. In the United States most families have traditionally had a fairly predictable natural history, but today there is more variability. Major changes in expectations and requirements are imposed on a husband and wife as their children are born and grow up.

15. Within the life cycle of a couple, particularly for the woman, the first pregnancy is an event of unparalleled importance. It signals that a couple is entering the family life cycle, bringing about new role requirements. As such, the first pregnancy functions as a major marker or transition and confronts a couple with new developmental tasks.

16. Many psychologists and sociologists who view the family as an integrated system of roles and statuses depict the onset of parenthood as a "crisis" because it involves a shift from a two-person to a three-person system. But some researchers have questioned this perspective. Their research suggests that relatively few couples view the onset of parenthood as especially stressful.

17. There are few differences between heterosexual and lesbian mothers, as motherhood, and not sexuality, is the dominant identity marker for these women. Although lesbian women choose to become parents for many of the same reasons as heterosexual women, they face certain issues that heterosexual women do not face: homophobia, societal disapproval, and fear of losing their children.

18. One aspect of motherhood that appears particularly stressful is balancing motherhood and career. Many people fear that the children of an employed mother will suffer a loss in terms of supervision, love, and cognitive enrichment. But researchers are finding that the employed mother who obtains personal satisfaction from her job, does not feel excessive guilt, and has adequate child care and household arrangements is likely to perform as well as or better than the nonworking mother.

19. Unfortunately, divorce is widespread and affects everyone involved. It does not affect all couples in the same ways, but most effects are negative.

20. Single-parent mothers frequently suffer from a lack of free time, spiraling child-care costs, loneliness, and the unrelenting pressures of attempting to fill the demands posed by both home and work. Not uncommonly, most find themselves in difficult economic circumstances. Nearly three-fourths of never-married young mothers live below the poverty level.

21. Increasing numbers of men are becoming single-parent fathers. Studies show that even though single fathers are confronted with some unique adjustment requirements, most are successful in raising their children. Like single-parent mothers, single-parent fathers find that one of their greatest difficulties is balancing the demands of work and parenthood.

Work

22. Work plays an important part in the lives of all adults, not only because of the money it brings in but also because people's self-definitions and sense of self-worth are tied to their work.

23. Americans are working longer and more women, and those who are mothers, are employed than ever before. Work hours, maternity and paternity leave policies, and corporate on-site child care are becoming more flexible to meet the needs of today's families.

Key Terms

companionate love (482)	intimacy versus isolation (475)	role overload (479)
consummate love (483)	lifestyle (484)	romantic love (482)
cultural dislocation (475)	marriage (489)	secondary relationship (475)
expressive tie (475)	mentor (477)	social relationship (475)
family life cycle (493)	postpartum depression (PPD) (498)	triangular theory of love (482)
instrumental tie (475)	primary relationship (475)	
intimacy (484)	role conflict (479)	

Following Up on the Internet

Web sites for this chapter focus on the diverse social and work roles of contemporary young adults. Please access the text Web site at www.mhhe.com/vzcrandell8 for up-to-date hot-linked Internet addresses for the following organizations, topics, and resources:

Erikson and Young Adulthood
All About Cohabitation

Parents Without Partners, Inc.
Unmarried Couples and the Law (Cohabitation)
Family Education
Father Magazine
American's with Disabilities Act—PL101-336, 1990
Occupational Outlook Handbook on Careers

Video Scenario—http://www.mhhe.com/vzcrandell8

In this chapter, you've just read about early adulthood and relationships, including topics like sexual orientation, cohabitation, living at home, and the transition to parenthood. Using the OLC (www.mhhe.com/vzcrandell8), revisit the *Early Adult-* *hood video scenario* to watch how all of these concepts come to life as part of Lindsay and Chris's move home. Don't forget to test your knowledge of these concepts by trying the fill-in-the-blank and critical thinking question that follow this segment.

Part EIGHT
Middle Adulthood

I f we think of middle age as roughly the years between 45 and 65, middle-aged Americans compose about a fifth of the population. Some were born during World War II. But the majority were born shortly before or during the 1950s and lived out their youth during the Korean War, the Elvis–Bob Dylan–Beatles era of rock 'n roll, the space race, the cold war, school integration, the Vietnam conflict, the women's liberation movement, "free love" and the birth control pill, the original Woodstock, and an era of opportunities for a college education. They entered the job market and made their way in the labor force during the economic golden years of the late 1960s and early 1970s. Each one is experiencing midlife changes, and many are feeling the psychological pressures associated with the shift from the smokestack industrial age to the age of the information superhighway. As a majority of the large baby-boom cohort now occupies middle age, the results of a major national study, *Midlife in the United States,* indicate that middle adulthood is being redefined.

Middle Adulthood
Physical and Cognitive Development

Critical Thinking Questions

1. If you temporarily lost your sight for a week and had no way of knowing how you looked to others, would you feel comfortable in public?

2. Would you feel comfortable knowing that your partner was going to tell an interviewer (anonymously) all of the details of your sex life together? Would you want to listen to a recording of the interview?

3. Wisdom is defined as (1) knowing the truth and acting justly and (2) questioning a truth as well as one's actions. Which of these two approaches seems wiser to you?

4. Assume you have just retired and money is no problem—what would you truly want to do with your time? Would you pursue some creative or new endeavor, or would you accept your life just as it is?

Outline

U ntil recently the middle years, from about age 45 through age 65, were a time of peak earnings and well-being for many adults. Middle-aged Americans were often portrayed as being the settled "establishment" of our society, the power brokers and decision makers. However, this scenario does not depict those middle-aged Americans living in poverty or from ethnic minority communities who have experienced many more difficulties. Additionally, with the changing U.S. socioeconomic conditions (due to corporate mergers, downsizing, international relocations, and outsourcing), newly unemployed men and women are returning to college in ever-larger numbers to retrain in new areas of expertise or to become entrepreneurs. Others are being forced into early retirement. And some are becoming parents for the first time. Having learned to cope with the many contingencies of childhood, adolescence, and young adulthood, middle-aged women and men have a substantial repertoire of strategies for dealing with the physical and intellectual challenges of middle adulthood.

Defining (or Defying) Middle Age

As of 2003, the average life expectancy for U.S. women has risen to 80 years, and for males it is 74.8. Thus, the *average* life expectancy of Americans is now 77.6 years. Although the middle of life falls statistically around age 39, we typically consider middle age as much later (Hoyert, Kung, & Smith, 2005). Indeed, most of us have difficulty identifying which years of life are the middle years. Does middle age begin at 40, 45, or 50? And does middle age end at 60, 65, or 70? The boundaries of midlife have become fluid for the 68 million Americans now at "midlife." It seems that chronological age had a more definitive meaning several decades ago. For instance, in 1900 Americans could expect to live, on average, to age 47; only 3 percent of the population lived past 65. Millions of Americans are living much longer today, and note that women already outlive men by middle age (see Figure 15.1).

By analogy to machines, a human body that has been functioning for a number of decades tends to work less efficiently than it did when it was "new." At age 50 or 60, the kidneys, lungs, heart, and other sensory organs are less efficient than they were at 20. Yet across middle adulthood the physical and cognitive changes that typically occur are, for the most part, not precipitous.

Sensory and Physical Changes

In most cases sensory and physical changes in midlife are so gradual that people are often not aware of any

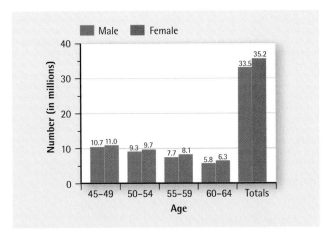

FIGURE 15.1 Middle-Aged Adults in the United States, by Age and Gender: 2003 The majority of the baby-boom generation are now in middle adulthood. The boundaries of midlife have become fluid for the 68 million Americans now at midlife. Millions of Americans are living much longer today, and note that women already outlive men by middle age.
Source: U.S. Bureau of the Census (2004). *Statistical Abstract of the United States: 2004–2005.* Table No. 11. Resident Population by Age and Sex: 1980–2003.

changes until they take stock on a birthday, at the wedding of a child, the first time they are called "Grandma" or "Grandpa," at a retirement celebration, at the death of a parent, or at some other significant life event. After adolescence, most integrated bodily functions decline at the rate of about 1 percent a year. Overall, middle-aged individuals report that they are not appreciably different from what they were in their early thirties. They mention that their hair has grayed (and often thinned), they have more wrinkles, they are paunchier, they may have "lost a step," they tire more easily, and they rebound less quickly. By middle age some individuals overextend themselves physically at work, at home, or during recreational pursuits and require professional assistance for rehabilitation (see the *Implications for Practice* box "Occupational/Physical therapist"). Even so, except for those in poor health, they find that, on the whole, they carry on in much the same manner that they did in their younger years. The best preventatives against loss of strength and vitality and some minor sensory changes are an engaged lifestyle, proper nutrition, and regular exercise, along with a healthy dose of humor about how life marches along.

Vision

At least 75 million Americans over age 40 are experiencing **presbyopia,** a normal condition in which the lens of the eye starts to harden, losing its ability to accommodate as quickly as it did in youth (*presbys* is Greek for "old man" or "elder"). Symptoms include getting headaches or "tired" eyes while doing close work. With the majority of baby boomers now occupying middle age, more people find they need contacts, bifocals, or half glasses to read the newspaper, computer screens, restaurant menus, or small printed numbers on price tags, wristwatches, and prescription dosages. If this problem is not corrected, people find they can read printed material only by holding it farther and farther away from their eyes, until eventually they cannot see to read even at arm's length. In 2001, eye doctors announced a few new laser techniques to treat vision problems after diagnosis of presbyopia and aging eyes ("Eye M.D.s Discuss Breakthroughs," 2001). Adaptation to darkness and recovery from glare also take longer, making night driving somewhat more taxing. Distance acuity, contrast sensitivity, visual search, and pattern recognition are also diminished (Madden, 1990; "Learning to See," 1998).

A number of disorders that affect sight become more common with the normal aging process. **Glaucoma,** increased pressure caused by fluid buildup in the eye, can damage the optic nerve and lead to blindness, if left untreated. The disorder has no symptoms in the early stages and can be detected only by a professional eye examination. **Cataracts,** or clouding of the lens, typically occur in 30 to 50 percent of people over age 65, but

Implications for Practice

Occupational/Physical Therapist
Merida R. Padro

I am the chief occupational/physical therapist at Broome Developmental Center (a division of the New York State Office of Mental Retardation and Developmental Disabilities, OMRDD). My main job tasks include being the department chief for the physical and occupational departments and consultant for the pediatric-geriatric community-based population in our region. I provide staff with in-service training in areas such as back safety, cerebral palsy, handling-positioning, therapeutic dining, blind-sensory awareness, and sensory integration/modulation issues.

I hold a bachelor's of science degree, PT/OT bachelor's, premedical degree of Puerto Rico, and master's degree in occupational therapy in developmental disabilities from New York University. For the past 24 years, I have worked with the cerebral palsy population in Spain, the severe cord injury unit at the Veterans Health Administration Veterans' Hospital, the burn/hand amputee unit in Puerto Rico, the pediatric cerebral palsy population in Laredo, Texas, and the Broome Developmental Center.

To become an occupational or physical therapist, you need to earn an education from an accredited college in either an occupational therapy or physical therapy program. Students must complete field work for six to nine months. In most states you also must pass a state licensure exam in either OT/PT. After earning state licensure, you apply for jobs based on your preference for clinical settings. Occupational and physical therapists might specialize in helping adults adjust to sensory and physical injuries by providing services that restore function, improve mobility, relieve pain, and prevent or limit permanent physical disabilities. To work with individuals who are mentally retarded or developmentally disabled, you need to have a great respect for people, value each one, and have compassion and understanding for every person. You need to be able to be comfortable making eye contact, enjoy smiling at each individual, and focus on small efforts rather than big changes. In a supervisory role, you need to have knowledge, experience, and personal skills to hire, supervise, train, or terminate staff. Also, you need to motivate and train staff as professionals to enhance the quality of services for the special population you serve.

in some instances they appear among individuals in their late fifties and early sixties. The condition can usually be remedied by surgical removal of the affected lens. Then this vision impairment can be corrected by eyeglasses, a contact lens, or an artificial lens placed in the eye at the time of the operation. **Floaters,** annoying floating spots, are particles suspended in the gel-like fluid that fills the eyeball, and generally they do not impair vision. However, a severe "floating" problem accompanied by flashes of light could indicate the more serious problem of retinal detachment, which if detected early enough can be treated with laser surgery. **Dry eye,** stemming from diminished tear production, can be uncomfortable and can usually be eased with drops. Those who look at computer screens or read documents for long hours are more likely to experience this discomfort.

The leading cause of late-onset visual impairment and legal blindness in people over age 50 is called age-related **macular degeneration (AMD).** AMD is caused by the thinning of the layers of the retina (the photosensitive cells at the back of the eye responsible for vision and color perception) and/or rupturing of tiny blood vessels. The first signs of this vision disorder are faded, distorted, or blurred central vision (Browder, 1997). In a University of Wisconsin study, men and women aged 45 to 84 who ate the most saturated fat were 80 percent more apt to show early signs of age-related eye degeneration. Just as saturated fat contributes to clogged arteries and reduces blood flow to the heart, it might reduce the amount of blood reaching the eye. A diet rich in fresh fruits and vegetables helps preserve vision (Browder, 1997). In a large British study with participants age 75

Macular Degeneration One of the eye disorders midlife and older adults might experience is macular degeneration, the first sign of which is faded, distorted, or blurred central vision. Eating plenty of fruits and vegetables and reducing fats in the diet can promote clarity of vision and overall health of the eyes.

and older, smoking doubled the risk of developing macular degeneration (Evans, Fletcher, & Wormald, 2005).

Hearing

More than 5 million people between the ages of 45 and 54 are living with mild-to-moderate hearing loss—and the number is rapidly growing. Changes in hearing usually begin about age 30. In **presbycusis** typically the ability to hear high-pitched sounds, such as speech, declines, but the magnitude of the change varies appreciably among individuals. There appears to be a genetic predisposition to hearing loss, because age-related hearing loss tends to run in families. The baby boomers (including former President Clinton) were the first generation to listen to highly amplified music over a period of years and are now experiencing premature hearing loss requiring hearing aids (Cleveland, 1998). By age 50 about one in every three men and one in every four women have difficulty understanding a whisper. However, only a small number of the age-50 population have substantial hearing problems, but hearing impairments increase from one's fifties to the seventies, such that it is estimated that 40 percent of those over age 75 have a hearing impairment (Rutherford, 2001).

Some of the more common causes of conductive hearing loss include cochlear damage due to prolonged exposure to loud noise, lack of good muscle tone in the middle ear (caused by stress or poor diet), and overgrowth of the cochlear bone, which results in the stapes (stirrup) bone becoming fixed. People with jobs associated with high noise levels—such as miners, truck drivers, heavy equipment operators, air-hammer operators, some industrial workers, and rock concert performers—are particularly at risk. Also, some individuals in their sixties report that they "take in" information more slowly than they did earlier in life. **Audiology testing** done by audiologists determines the extent and type of hearing loss (conduction problems to sensorineural deafness). To conduct a simple test, rub your fingers together next to each ear. If you cannot hear this slight sound, you might have the beginning of hearing loss. Another sign of hearing loss is not being able to hear women's and children's voices, which are at a higher pitch compared to male voices.

A treatment regimen might include getting ears cleaned by a medical practitioner, using an amplification device (hearing aid), or surgical intervention. A standard hearing aid for one ear can cost $500 to $3,000 or more, and Medicare does not cover hearing aids nor do most insurers. Individuals deny hearing loss because it often occurs gradually, they fear the change in lifestyle and the cost, and they are often vain and embarrassed to wear one or two hearing aids (Rutherford, 2001). But hearing loss reduces quality of life, limits the ability to communicate or to drive safely, and can lead to depression. However, family members who live with those affected are aware of the loss, as the TV blares louder and louder (Rutherford, 2001).

Taste and Smell

Taste buds, which detect salty, sweet, sour, and bitter tastes, normally are replaced nearly every 10 days. However, in people who are in their forties, taste buds are replaced at a slower rate, and smell receptors begin to deteriorate, affecting the sense of taste. Women have a better sense of taste than men do because they generally have more taste buds, and scientists believe estrogen increases a woman's taste sensitivity. Salty and sweet are the first tastes to change, and one's appetite may become especially partial to sweet and salty foods (Chaikivsky, 1997).

From age 50 on, the sense of smell typically starts to decline. Probably half of all people who are 65 have had a noticeable loss of their sense of smell. Tastes and flavors are almost entirely detected in the nose, so food won't taste as delicious. Valery Duffy, a taste-and-smell researcher at the University of Connecticut at Storrs, observes that women with a weakened sense of smell are more likely to gain weight as they attempt to satisfy their yearning for flavors or compensate for the loss of flavors with the gratifying texture of fat. One can compensate for the loss of flavors by holding food in the mouth longer or cooking with more flavorful seasonings. Dr. Duffy also suggests as a preventative measure that people get the flu shot each year, because each time one catches the flu, the virus can diminish one's sense of smell (Browder, 1997).

Question

What are some of the typical changes in the senses in midlife?

Appearance

Losing teeth or loosening teeth might sound trivial, yet it takes time to become comfortable with a new facial appearance created by extensive dental work—and these procedures are quite costly.

During midlife, the gums of the teeth begin to recede, which for some leads to a condition called **periodontal disease.** This in turn leads to loss of teeth, and caps, bridges, and false teeth might become necessary. Those who cannot afford dental work are likely to have difficulty eating nutritious foods, and their health might decline (Browder, 1997; Chaikivsky, 1997). Some dental experts suggest that regular flossing and brushing and scheduled dental visits can help people keep their own teeth into their nineties.

As one ages, the skin becomes dryer, thinner, and less elastic after years of exposure to ultraviolet rays. As the skin loses collagen, fat, and oil glands, it becomes more wrinkled. Skin cells grow more slowly with age, and the outer layer of skin is not shed and replaced at the same rate as in younger years. With aging, cells lose some of their ability to retain water, causing dryness. Soaps, antiperspirants, perfumes, and hot baths can aggravate this condition or cause itching. As the skin loses tone and elasticity, it sags and wrinkles, especially in areas where there is frequent movement, such as the face, neck, and joints. Some people also develop "droopy" eyelids as a result. Additionally, darker patches of skin ("age spots") caused by many years of exposure to the sun begin to appear before the age of 60 (Dickinson, 1997).

Scaly patches of skin and any changes in skin color should be checked by a dermatologist, because these could be signs of **basal-cell carcinoma,** which can be treated. However, a study of 37,000 patients with basal-cell carcinoma researchers at the Danish Epidemiology Science Center suggests that this malady could be a marker for **melanoma,** a more serious cancer. A melanoma is a tumor of the skin (which may bleed, darken in color, or itch) that can spread quickly to other body parts. If left untreated, it will be deadly. If caught early, it may be removed surgically, followed by radiotherapy and chemotherapy. Melanomas are caused by chronic sunlight exposure, blistering sunburns, and a family history of skin cancer. Regular head-to-toe examinations of the skin, which is the largest organ of the body, should be conducted by a medical professional as a necessary component of a checkup.

The facial appearance of aging men and women in American society is part of the so-called "double standard of aging." People who smoke tend to have more wrinkles than nonsmokers of the same age, complexion,

and history of sun exposure (National Institute on Aging, 1996b). As men age, they are often considered "mature" or "sophisticated" or more attractive than when they were younger. However, there are very few kind expressions for the way many older women look. American men and women spend billions of dollars each year on "wrinkle creams," bleaching products, skin lotions, facials, and electrolysis for unwanted hair removal and other dermatology procedures (National Institute on Aging, 1996b).

Women vary greatly in how they respond to looking older. There are indications that those who were hugged, kissed, and cuddled when younger tend to accept their bodies as they are. Also, women whose families provided opportunities for physical activity or who were athletes in high school and college feel more positive about their looks than women without such experiences. When self-esteem is high, body image is often positive. Considering the relationship between athletics and self-esteem, it is no surprise that studies show that men tend to overrate their body image, whereas women tend to underrate theirs. A woman who was considered unusually attractive when younger may find it more difficult as she begins to look older, as compared with a woman who never set great store on her looks. Women who are concerned about looking older seem to experience this concern up to their middle and late sixties. In fact, some women like getting older; they feel freer and more confident. What they don't like is looking older (Doress-Worters & Siegal, 1994). In general, compared with women, men have better-looking skin as they age. As men take whiskers from their face each day, they also slough off dead skin cells, leaving a more youthful facial appearance.

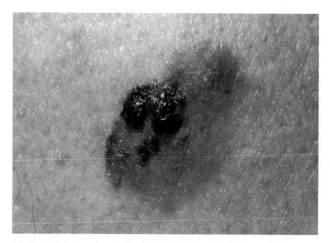

Melanoma A melanoma is a serious skin cancer caused by tumors of pigment-producing cells in the epidermis. It often starts in a mole and is induced by ultraviolet radiation in sunlight, blistering sunburns, and a family history of skin cancer. Early treatment is crucial. An overall skin exam should be conducted by a medical doctor or a dermatologist, who specializes in treating skin conditions.

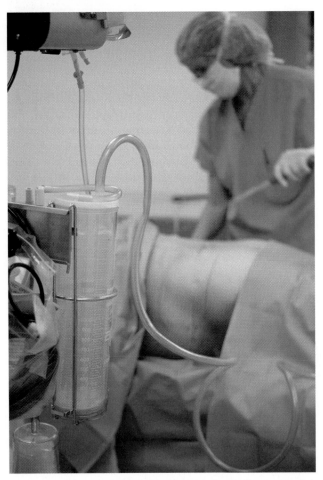

Liposuction Various forms of cosmetic procedures and surgeries remove or lift unwanted wrinkles, excess fat, or sculpt the body. Such procedures are popular among millions of people today to delay the effects of aging. TV programs have popularized these procedures, which are expensive and are not always effective methods of weight loss.

There are many socioeconomic and behavioral implications of the aging of skin. A new cosmetic industry is cropping up that is catering to the needs of black Americans. Sam Fine—makeup artist to black actors, actresses, and musicians—and Julia Chance recently published *Fine Beauty: Beauty Basics and Beyond for African-American Women* (1998). He states that there are 40 to 50 skin shades in African American women alone. Fine has developed a line of cosmetic products to help this segment of the American population become more comfortable with their aging skin (Belluck, 1998).

More American women and men are taking advantage of a European health habit: having facials and full body massages to maintain a healthier, more youthful appearance. Use of cosmetic surgery (face lifts, tummy tucks, breast lifts, and liposuction) by both men and women has also increased as baby boomers have entered their middle years. Wearing hats, long sleeves, and long pants, using more protective sunscreens, using a humidifier in the home, and staying out of the hottest sun of the day from 11 A.M. through 2 P.M. are all highly preventative measures to avoid skin damage. Millions of retirees migrate to southern and western states with sunny climates, where skin cancer rates are high. Proper nutrition and plenty of drinking water, regular exercise, cosmetics and creams such as those that contain **alpha hydroxy,** and limited sun exposure can help keep the skin more supple and healthy (Atkins, 1996).

Hair color change to gray or white is usually the obvious physical change that marks the change in chronological age. During midlife or sooner, the color, thickness, and texture of hair undergo changes, which can include thinning, balding, and graying. Thinning hair is often associated with aging males, many of whom develop hair loss and balding. Many women are also likely to find their hair thinning as they experience perimenopausal symptoms and hormonal changes.

Some hair products, such as *Rogaine,* are marketed as stimulating the scalp to prevent hair loss. Hair coloring and hair restoration techniques can help maintain a more youthful appearance. Many women and men in middle adulthood who are at the prime of their professions want to look their best and consider it essential to retain a more youthful appearance. On the other hand, a growing number of adults in midlife are very accepting of their changing looks and find emotional comfort and satisfaction in this transitional stage of life. Many are so satisfied with their busy new social roles of grandmother and grandfather, mentor at work, and community or church volunteer that they barely focus on "looks."

Body Composition

One of the major concerns of some individuals in midlife is body composition, or proportion of muscle to fat. Around age 30, muscles begin to atrophy, which can diminish strength, agility, and endurance. Men are less likely to notice this because their muscles tend to be larger. By the time a person reaches the fifties, muscle loss is likely to become more evident—and weight gain more pronounced. According to the *Baltimore Longitudinal Study of Aging,* muscle mass declines, on average, 5 to 10 percent each decade. This can become more evident in daily activities like carrying groceries or getting out of a chair. Muscle loss also leads to an increase in body fat. By age 50, one should eat 240 fewer calories a day to maintain the same weight carried at age 30 (Doress-Worters & Siegal, 1994).

Americans are preoccupied with weight because currently in this culture "thin is in." Emphasis on "ideal" weight on weight charts creates damaging pressure on women (and men) to be thin. What seems to be overlooked is that each person has a unique size, shape, and body chemistry strongly determined by heredity. One's

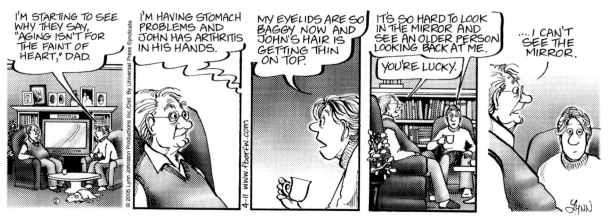

Awareness of Midlife Sensory and Physical Changes In middle adulthood, people often become aware of gradual sensory and physical changes. However, proper nutrition and regular exercise, and an appreciation of life become even more vital to normal functioning.
Source: For Better or for Worse © 2005 Lynn Johnston Productions. Dist. By Universal Press Syndicate. Reprinted with permission. All rights reserved.

weight is a function of several additional factors: energy input (food consumption), energy used (activity level), and the body's rate of using that energy (metabolism). Dieting to lose weight can become an unhealthy way of life. Each time a person goes on a low-calorie diet, the body reacts as if it is being starved and tries to preserve energy by decreasing metabolism. Rate of metabolism slows each time a person diets. After a diet, unless the person dramatically increases exercise, the body adds more fat to protect itself from food deprivation. This explains why 90 to 99 percent of dieters regain their weight, and perhaps gain back more, within five years.

Thin people, who are more likely to be malnourished, are also more susceptible to certain diseases, including lung diseases, osteoporosis, fatal infections, ulcers, and anemia. As more baby boomers join the ranks of the middle-aged population, it is likely that two more severe eating disorders will be prevalent. *Anorexia nervosa*, common among young women, might be increasing among older women. *Bulimia nervosa* seems to be found among all age groups. According to Doress-Worters and Siegal in *The New Ourselves, Growing Older* (1994), the extent of eating disorders among middle-aged and older women is not known, and funding for research on this topic has been cut. Studies show that older people who are "significantly underweight" die sooner than those who are not (Doress-Worters & Siegal, 1994).

Americans appear obsessed with dieting programs and cosmetic procedures and plastic surgeries. In 2004, U.S. surgical and nonsurgical cosmetic procedures (such as Botox or chemical peels) increased by 44 percent, and women had 90 percent of the procedures ("Cosmetic Procedures Increased," 2005). Goodman (1996) examined the social, psychological, and developmental factors that precipitated cosmetic surgery with subjects ranging in age from 29 to 75. She found that age, or cohort membership,

differentiated women's attitudes and behaviors regarding their bodies. Younger women (ages 29 to 49) were uniformly preoccupied with their bodies, the classic area of discontent being breast size—either too big or too small. Older women (over age 50) assigned more importance to their faces than to their figures; their classic complaints involved normal aging—wrinkles, "saggy" jowls, and "droopy" eyelids. Davis (1990) has suggested that media images ushered in the age of "commercialized femininity" for women growing up in the 1950s. Women were encouraged to have an "ivory" complexion, blonde Breck-girl hair, and a Marilyn Monroe figure. (Marilyn Monroe, by the way, was a perfect size 12. Today's models are size 6.) Breasts and cleavage became focal points in media imagery of women, evident in contemporary shows such as *Desperate Housewives* and *Extreme Makeover*.

On a more realistic note, scientists now know that most muscle aging is preventable and reversible with a regular exercise program of resistance training, toning, or weight lifting. In a Tufts University study, women in their sixties increased muscle strength in their legs, backs, abdomens, and buttocks by 35 to 76 percent. After one year of strength training, these women emerged both physiologically stronger by 15 to 20 years and psychologically more youthful (Browder, 1997). A middle-aged person with an active lifestyle can still take advantage of fitness programs that support these health-oriented goals.

Question

What are some of the aspects of natural aging that the baby-boom generation has challenged?

With the normal aging process after age 35, bones become less supple and more brittle and begin to lose their density. It is generally held that women are at greater risk of **osteoporosis** (a disorder of thinning bone mass and microarchitectural deterioration of bone tissue) than men because men have 30 percent more bone mass at age 35 than women, and they lose bone more slowly as they age. Age-related decreases in bone density accelerate with menopause in women, so the earlier a woman experiences menopause, the higher the risk. Osteoporosis is a complex condition. Usually it takes years for it to advance to the stage where it can be detected, because the skeletal structure is not visible and one does not feel the slowing in the replacement of older bone cells with newer bone cells. About 25 million Americans are affected by this type of bone degeneration, and it is estimated that 1.5 million bone fractures each year are a result of osteoporosis (Rohr et al., 2004). As with muscle mass, men start out with greater bone density than women. Consequently, women are likely to experience bone fractures up to a decade earlier than men. A main contributing factor to bone loss in women is the major decline in the production of the hormone estrogen as a woman experiences perimenopause, menopause, and postmenopause. Most physicians today recommend that, as a preventative measure, women perform weight-bearing exercises, avoid cigarettes and excessive alcohol consumption, and begin taking calcium supplements by the time they are 35 years old. And a painless medical test, using a scan of the spine or hip, is now suggested for adults in middle age or older. One should add calcium and vitamin D to one's diet by eating more milk products, egg yolks, leafy green vegetables, certain shellfish, tofu, other soybean products, or add calcium supplements. For people who are lactose intolerant and cannot digest milk products, other foods can supply the additional calcium. We shall discuss the serious health consequences of bone loss for elderly adults in Chapter 17.

Adequate body weight and fat tissue offer some protection from osteoporosis. Bones that carry body weight must work to produce new bone tissue, and fat tissue helps maintain some estrogen in the body after menopause. **Diuretics** such as caffeine and alcohol can cause loss of calcium and zinc in the urine. It is also suspected that smoking interferes with the body's production of estrogen, which in turn affects the onset of osteoporosis. Weight-bearing exercises such as walking, jogging, jumping rope, and dancing make bones work harder, strengthen the muscles and ligaments supporting the skeleton, and slow bone loss. For a person at a higher risk of osteoporosis, a nutritionist can help plan a preventive diet tailored to individual needs, and a physical therapist can suggest an exercise program to strengthen muscles and ligaments at any age.

Many studies are being conducted to examine risk of osteoporosis across cultures. Black women have 10 percent more bone mass than white women, and they might

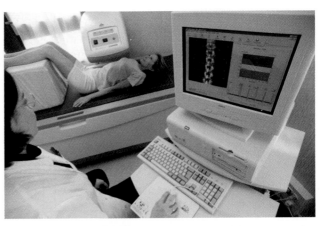

Osteoporosis and Densitometry A densitometer measures the density of a patient's bones and is a quick, painless procedure. Bone loss is a natural part of aging and is caused by loss of the protein matrix in bones, and calcium supplementation is vital. Postmenopausal women are affected due to loss of the hormone estrogen, but men in middle age also lose bone mass. The bones become more porous and brittle, weak and liable to fracture. The vertebrae of the spine begin to crush; over time the adult gets shorter and has a curved upper back.

have more **calcitonin,** the hormone that strengthens bones. However, the consequences of a hip fracture for blacks are far greater, possibly because of the effects of more poverty, inadequate resources for health care, and the greater likelihood of other underlying disease. One study found that groups at high risk for low *bone mass density (BMD)* are not being evaluated and treated at a rate that would prevent further bone density loss and bone fractures (Rohr et al., 2004).

Another disorder that surfaces in middle age is **rheumatoid arthritis,** an inflammatory disease that causes pain, swelling, stiffness, and loss of function of the joints (shoulder, knee, hip, hands, etc.) (National Institutes of Health, 1998). People with this condition may experience fatigue and occasional fever in addition to the typical symptoms. Arthritis symptoms vary from person to person and can last a few months and then disappear for years. Some people have mild forms of this disease; others live with serious disability. Scientists classify rheumatoid arthritis as an autoimmune disease—the person's own immune system attacks her or his own body tissue. Although there is no single test for this disease, especially in its early stages, lab tests and X rays can determine the extent of bone damage and monitor disease progression.

The Centers for Disease Control and Prevention conducted a survey which revealed that there are differences in the prevalence and impact of arthritis. It was found that African Americans had higher incidences of arthritis than whites (CDC, 2005d). The Arthritis Foundation (2004) recommends moderate exercise to reduce joint pain and stiffness, build muscle around the joints, and increase flexibility and endurance. In addition, exercise has other health benefits—overall fitness, better sleep, more energy and better mood, and increased self-esteem.

Hormones

Human growth hormone (HGH), a powerful hormone that has been used to treat children afflicted by dwarfism, has become a controversial antiaging treatment. Hormones are protein messengers of the endocrine system that circulate throughout the body to all organs causing natural reactions, affecting not only ovaries and testes but many other glandular and life functions like memory, protein synthesis, cell repair, metabolism, ability to sleep, body temperature, water balance, and sexual functioning. In its "off label" usage HGH is known as one of a class of *biomedical enhancement drugs* (Conrad & Potter, 2004). Currently, the National Institute on Aging is funding medical studies to investigate earlier findings that HGH and other hormones can slow, stop, or possibly reverse the changes associated with aging. HGH, also known as *somatotropin,* is the most abundant hormone secreted by the pituitary gland and consequently impacts the production of all other endocrine hormones in the body. Daily HGH secretion diminishes with age; a 60-year-old might secrete 25 percent of the HGH secreted by a 20-year-old. Daniel Rudman, an **endocrinologist,** pioneered the original research on HGH in 1985, hypothesizing that the changes in body composition that become apparent around age 35 had to do with declining hormone levels (Rudman et al., 1991).

The physicians administering these hormones call themselves "antiaging specialists." The American Academy of Anti-Aging Medicine, founded in 1993, currently boasts a membership of more than 4,300 U.S. doctors who specialize in youth preservation. Their president states, "We're not about growing old gracefully. We're about never growing old" (Kuczynski, 1998). Daniel Rudman, M.D., in a 1990 study, found that some men over the age of 60 given HGH for six months had improved energy, less body fat, and more muscle mass. It was reported that other studies found side effects such as joint pain, stiffness, and swelling connected with its use (Conrad & Potter, 2004).

Owen Wolkowitz, M.D., of the University of California at San Francisco, administered another hormone—**DHEA (dehydroepiandrosterone)**—to a small group of depressed men and women between the ages of 50 and 75. The findings suggest that the hormone not only lifted depression but improved memory as well. Some researchers also believe that DHEA blocks the decline of the body's immune system. Like HGH, DHEA is abundant in the body when one is age 20, but it con-

tinues to decrease with time. At 80 years of age, humans usually produce only 10 to 20 percent of DHEA produced in a 20-year-old (DHEA Center, 1997; "DHEA Prohormone Complex," 1997). There appears to be a great deal of conflicting information available about the benefits and drawbacks of DHEA, and the traditional medical community urges caution in using this substance until it can be further researched.

The thyroid gland, shaped like a butterfly that wraps around the windpipe, is behind the "Adam's apple" area of the neck. It produces essential hormones that help to get oxygen into cells, stimulating metabolism, growth, and the body's capacity to process calories. With aging, more women than men are affected by an underactive thyroid gland, causing **hypothyroidism.** Symptoms include weight gain, hair loss, fatigue greater than normal, depression, muscle and joint pains, dry skin, and constipation, among other symptoms. Hypothyroidism is also associated with increased levels of LDL (low-density lipoprotein), the "bad" cholesterol, and a higher risk of cardiovascular disease or a heart attack in an aging population (Hak et al., 2000). At a medical checkup, or a visit to an endocrinologist, a simple blood test (TSH or thyroid-stimulating hormone) can detect hypothyroidism. Proper medications and treatments can make a big difference in mood and energy levels and help to reduce weight. Thyroid imbalance is an inherited condition, and research studies estimate more than 25 million Americans are affected—most are living with an undiagnosed chronic condition (Shomon, 2005).

> **Question**
>
> Under what circumstances might a doctor recommend HGH or DHEA to a patient?

Menopause and Female Midlife Change

In 2003, there were over 45 million women over the age of 50 in the United States. It is estimated that by 2010, there will be over 53 million U.S. women over 50 (U.S. Bureau of the Census, 2004–2005). Worldwide, there may be more than 470 million women aged 50-plus, and 30 percent are expected to live to age 80 (North American Menopause Society, 2001). A majority of women born during the baby boom have experienced perimenopause or **menopause**—a process resulting from the decline of ovarian function. Menopause is completed after a year without menstrual activity (Segal & Mastroianni, 2003).

Menopause is the culminating sign of the **climacteric,** characterized by changes in the ovaries and in the various hormonal processes over two to five years prior to complete cessation of menstruation. Probably the most significant change is the profound drop in the production of the female hormones (particularly *estrogen*) by the ovaries. The cessation of menstruation typically takes two to four years, with intermittent periods and the extension of the intervals between periods. This time period is referred to as **perimenopause.** A woman is said to have gone through menopause, or is in **postmenopause,** when she no longer menstruates for one year. Many American women, known as "midlife mommies," are racing the biological clock to have children before their bodies cease to produce mature, viable eggs.

In Western countries, the average age range for complete cessation of menses is between 45 and 55, and the average age is about 51, but it can occur as early as the thirties or as late as the sixties (Sheehy, 1998). A cross-cultural study with nearly 20,000 women from Europe, the Americas, Asia, Australia, and Africa found the median age of natural menopause to range from 49 to 52 years (Morabia & Costanza, 1998). A longitudinal study in the Netherlands found heritable components from mother to daughter largely determine the natural age of menopause (van Asselt et al., 2004).

Bromberger (1997) reported study findings that black women enter menopause sooner than white women: blacks at an average age of 49.3, whites at an average age of 51.5. However, she states that stress might be a factor. Younger women also undergo an early menopause if their ovaries are removed by a surgical procedure called **hysterectomy. Premature menopause,** naturally occurring or induced by surgery or chemotherapy before age 40, affects about 4 percent of the female population (Midlife Passages, 1998b).

Women in Japan and other Asian countries rarely complain about menopausal symptoms. A possible explanation has emerged, pointing to a dietary approach to treating menopausal symptoms: Soybeans and products made from soybeans—such as tofu, soymilk, and soy chips—are rich in large amounts of chemicals in plants that produce natural estrogen. Dietary habits in Asian countries might also account for their lower rates of heart disease and breast cancer. The dietary approach appeals to many women who seek a more "natural" alternative to hormone replacement therapy (Brody, 1997).

Aging changes that can accompany the hormonal changes of menopause include *incontinence* (involuntary leaking of urine), heart disease, and *osteoporosis* (bone thinning). These changes are considered normal reactions to the body's reduced production of sex hormones. Every woman's experience with menopause is different, and most have minimal symptoms and continue to function quite well. Most effects can be reduced with regular exercise and diet modifications, disappear with treatment, or diminish over time. Menopause reminds a woman to continue with a good health program as she ages.

Much controversy surrounds **hormone replacement therapy (HRT),** a regimen often recommended to menopausal women by physicians to maintain cardiovascular fitness, slow bone loss, slow memory loss, and maintain sexual desire. A recent study suggests that between 30 to 50 percent of menopausal women experience sexual dysfunction, related to estrogen reduction (Berman, Lazarus-Jaureguy, & Santos, 2004). Many women are skeptical about taking the hormone treatment advice of their physicians because their mothers or grandmothers were subjects of *estrogen replacement therapy (ERT)* treatment in the 1960s to 1970s, and many developed cancer of the ovaries or uterus, leading to early deaths. The *Women's Health Initiative (WHI)* was established in 1993 and it conducted clinical trials on hormone replacement therapy (Love, 2005). In July of 2002, the part of the Women's Health Initiative study examining the effects of long-term use of hormone therapy was halted. Preliminary results found that postmenopausal women who were using *Prempro* (an estrogen/progestin medication) had slightly higher risk of breast cancer, heart disease, stroke, and blood clots. In March of 2004 investigators halted the part of the WHI study of *Premarin* (estrogen-only medication) because results showed slightly higher risk of stroke. Yet some researchers maintain that low doses of hormone therapy are appropriate for some women with significant menopausal symptoms (National Women's Health Resource Center, 2004).

Clearly, women face a conflict with respect to HRT. In its position statement, the North American Menopause Society (2004) calls for further research with regard to the timing of the start of hormone therapy, formulations, regimens, and dosage of estrogens and progestogens, and assessing the risks and benefits of hormone therapy cessation. Critics of hormone therapies contend that the medical and drug establishment has turned a normal aging event into a "disease" requiring medication, a phenomenon they call "the medicalization of menopause"; the powerful pharmaceutical industry, they argue, has much to gain by making every woman feel that she is "diseased" instead of aging normally (Brody, 1995a). Researchers take a variety of perspectives to understand and manage menopause (Love, 2003).

Today women openly discuss this normal aging event and share information on alternative approaches, the media is educating the public, and discussion of issues is available through Internet newsgroups. Contrary to popular belief, in a poll of 1,000 women over the age of 50, the National Center on Women and Aging at Brandeis University found that more than half of the respondents said that getting older was much better than they expected (Winik, 2004). Many women are relieved that they no longer have to worry about pregnancy, and some report an improvement in their sex lives. And when menopause occurs on time during midlife, it is not likely to be a source of psychological distress (Lennon, 1982; Reichman, 1996). Although conventional wisdom has linked menopause with depression, scientific studies have failed to establish a causal relationship between them. Indeed, research surveys consistently reveal that women are considerably more likely to suffer from depression in their twenties and thirties than at midlife (Elias, 1993).

Women are more likely to feel upset if they view menopause as signaling the end of their attractiveness, usefulness, and sexuality. Such feelings can be heightened by our youth-oriented culture, which tends to devalue older people. From cross-cultural studies, we know that physical and emotional symptoms of menopause are rarer in societies such as Japan and India, where postmenopausal women gain greater power and heightened social status than they enjoyed during their reproductive years (Elias, 1993).

Evidence suggests that the climacteric typically does not cause problems that were not already present in a woman's life. Women with preexisting or long-standing difficulties might be more susceptible to problems and react more adversely during the climacteric than less vulnerable women (Greene, 1984). Many women express satisfaction that their children are grown and have left home, opening all sorts of new possibilities for them (Goleman, 1990b; Reichman, 1996). As Judith Reichman, M.D. (1996), notes, "Menopause is the completion of a life cycle that started before we were born. It does not constitute a stop but actually is the start of the next phase of our lives."

One of the largest and already beneficial studies being conducted, the Women's Health Initiative is studying 164,500 women of various ages and racial and ethnic backgrounds across the United States. The results of this scientific investigation—to find out whether a low-fat diet, HRT, calcium, and vitamin D might prevent heart disease, breast and colorectal cancers, bone fractures, and memory loss—are starting to become available. Thus far it has been shown that dietary changes can be maintained over several years and are having a positive impact on health (Frost & Sullivan, 2004).

Reproduction After Menopause

In just the past decade (excluding the biblical account of Sarah's giving birth when she was over 80 years old), some women have been able to "conceive" and carry a baby to term after menopause. This reproductive process involves a special regimen of hormone injections over time to build up the woman's uterus to provide a viable home for an implanted embryo. A postmenopausal woman no longer has any eggs (ova), so she must seek out a donor to provide healthy eggs. Then her husband's (or donated) sperm is used to fertilize an egg to create a zygote, which will be grown into an embryo before it is transplanted into the woman's uterus in an **in vitro fertilization** procedure. In an exciting new procedure,

a 32-year-old woman's own cryopreserved ovarian tissue was reimplanted, she became pregnant, and she gave birth to a baby girl—after chemotherapy-induced menopause (Donnez et al., 2004).

That a woman gave birth at age 63 was sensationalized in all the media in 1997. The woman had lied about her age, and the California infertility clinic had an upper limit of 55 years old. It was also reported that this couple spent over $50,000 and a great deal of time and effort to have this child (Kolata, 1997a). Paulson and colleagues (2002) reported that women in their sixties are able to conceive with donated eggs (oocyte donation) and that there is no medical reason for excluding these women from becoming pregnant based only on their age. However, a study of more than 1.5 million U.S. births over 15 years reveals higher rates of risk to pregnant women 45 and older: preterm birth, gestational diabetes, preeclampsia, intrauterine fatality, and the mother's perinatal mortality (Hollander, 2004; Jacobsson, Ladfors, & Milsom, 2004).

Worldwide, several thousand postmenopausal women have borne children using this method of procreation. In 2002 there were 263 births reported to U.S. women between 50 and 54 years of age (Heffner, 2004). The age of the mother has become a controversial issue, whereas the age of the father is rarely discussed. Yet research is beginning to delve into this issue (Thacker, 2004). When men in their seventies and eighties father children, they are lauded for their virility. Medical ethicists are debating such questions as these: Are older mothers clutching at eternal youth? Are they a laudable example of the way technology can overcome the barriers of age? Is there something inherently wrong in creating a pregnancy that would not have occurred naturally? Will the children created so late in their parents' lives be able to have a childhood, or will they as teenagers become responsible for aging, possibly senile parents? Will the parents live long enough to raise this child? (Kolata, 1997a, b). Byrom (2004), in a comprehensive review of the existing research, finds that women delaying childbearing will experience physical, psychological, and sociological impacts on their health.

Questions

What is menopause, what are its signs, and how does it affect the woman's life? How might a woman reproduce after menopause?

Male Midlife Change

Men obviously do not undergo menopause, but in midlife they may experience a diminished sex drive, erectile dysfunction, fatigue, and depression—sometimes referred to as *male menopause* or *andropause* (Peate, 2003; Tan & Shou-Jin Pu, 2004). In addition men are likely to experience an enlargement of the **prostate gland,** a walnut-sized gland at the base of the urethra (the tube that emerges from the bladder and carries urine outside the body via the penis). About 10 percent of men aged 40 already have recognizable enlargement of the prostate; the condition is virtually universal in men at age 60. The exact reasons for the enlargement of this gland are unclear, but research is being conducted to shed some light on this in the next few years (National Cancer Institute, 1998a). Hormonal changes associated with aging, such as reduction in testosterone production along with a high-fat diet low in fruit and vegetables, are thought to be implicated in the process (Giovannucci et al., 1993). As the prostate enlarges, it puts pressure on the urethra, which contributes to decreased force in the urinary stream, difficulty in beginning urination, and an increased urge to urinate. Although the condition is not dangerous itself, it can contribute to bladder and kidney disorders and infections and urges to urinate that interrupt sleep. Should serious obstruction to the outflow of urine occur, the tissue causing the enlargement of the prostate can be removed. Only rarely does a patient become impotent after the operation.

Some men experience a condition called **prostatitis,** an inflammation of the prostate gland that may be accompanied by discomfort, pain, frequent urination, infrequent urination, and sometimes fever. In addition to an annual physical examination that includes blood, urine, and possibly other laboratory tests, the National Cancer Institute and the American Cancer Society suggest talking with a physician (most likely a urologist). The physician conducts a digital exam, feeling for any unusual bumps or lumps. Also, the **PSA test** will be conducted, which measures a substance called *prostate-specific antigen (PSA),* which is made by the prostate. It is normal to find small quantities of PSA in the blood. PSA levels differ according to age and tend to rise gradually in men over age 60. PSA may become elevated due to infection (prostatitis), enlargement of the prostate, or cancer. In those questionable cases, other imaging techniques or biopsy may be used for diagnostic purposes. Males age 50 and older should have their prostate checked annually.

A more serious problem is cancer of the prostate. The National Cancer Institute reports that "prostate cancer is the most common malignant cancer in North American men," and it is now the second leading cause of cancer death in men, claiming nearly 40,000 lives each year (National Cancer Institute, 1998b). This type of cancer is rarely seen in men under 50; incidence increases with each decade of life. Japanese men have a low incidence of prostate cancer, however, perhaps due to dietary, genetic, or screening factors. Black males have

been found to have a higher incidence of prostate cancer than white males, although any male with a family history of prostate cancer is at an increased risk of this disease (Jones, 2001). Other lifestyle factors associated with this disease include alcohol consumption, vitamin or mineral interactions, dietary habits, promiscuity, and genital warts (National Cancer Institute, 1998b). A recent double-blind study conducted with U.S. males found that those with a higher intake of selenium (a trace nutrient in grains, fish, and meat) apparently had a lower risk of prostate cancer—but NIH researchers caution that further research needs to be conducted (Giovannucci, 1998).

A major risk with prostate cancer that is not discovered and treated early is that it will metastasize and spread to the bones. Men with higher incomes and education levels appear more likely than less-advantaged men to be screened for prostate cancer, study findings suggest. Current screening methods include the DRE (digital rectal exam) and PSA test, which are conducted during physical checkups for middle-aged and elderly males. Fortunately, most cancers of the prostate, particularly in older men, grow at a slow pace. By age 80 the majority of men have prostate cancer but most outlive it and die from something else.

Although women's levels of the female hormone estrogen plunge during the climacteric, men experience a much slower drop over a period of many years in levels of the male sex hormones—primarily **testosterone** (see Figure 15.2). With a decline in testosterone levels, men may experience a variety of physical and psychosocial symptoms. During this period of male hormonal decline, a typical man loses 12 to 20 pounds of muscle, 15 percent of bone mass, and nearly 2 inches of height between the ages of 40 and 70 (Kessenich & Cichon, 2001). Cultural stereotypes have frequently depicted men in their forties and fifties as suddenly undergoing psychological disturbances, leaving their wives for women young enough to be their daughters, quitting their jobs to become beachcombers, or beginning to drink to excess. Such difficulties are commonly attributed to a "male menopause," which according to psychotherapist and author Jed Diamond is a multidimensional life transition that can only be treated effectively by focusing on the physical, hormonal, psychological, social, spiritual, and sexual changes that occur in men's lives, generally between the ages of 40 and 55.

What part hormonal changes could play in a male midlife crisis that only some men experience is a matter of lively and sometimes heated medical controversy (Angier, 1992). Some authorities attribute a decline in testosterone levels with a concomitant decrease in muscle mass and strength, the buildup of body fat, the loss of bone density, flagging energy, lowered sperm output, decreasing strength and mobility, fading virility, and heightened

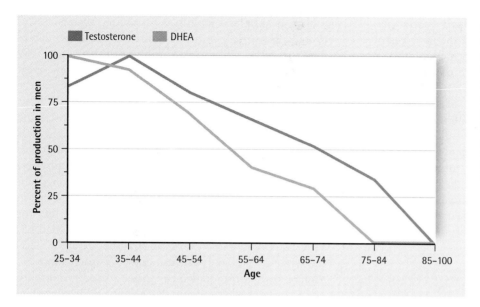

FIGURE 15.2 Testosterone Production in Men Men experience a gradual drop in testosterone production over a period of many years in middle age, in contrast to women, who experience the climacteric around age 50. This graph also shows the drop in DHEA in men.

Source: From Geoffrey Cowley, "Attention: Aging Men," *Newsweek,* September 16, 1996, p. 68. Copyright © 1996 Newsweek, Inc. All rights reserved. Reprinted by permission.

mood swings. But human growth hormone also influences these functions and declines with age. Researchers find it difficult to sort out which hormone plays which role, or, as is most likely, how the two hormones combine to affect men's vigor. Older men also typically lose the circadian rhythms that affect testosterone fluxes in their younger counterparts, in whom hormone levels usually peak prior to rising in the morning, which is one reason why young men often awake with erections.

Although most medical authorities currently do not believe that men undergo a hormonal midlife change comparable to menopause, some nonetheless speculate that as the baby-boom generation enters midlife, interest in treating aging men for profit will encourage the definition of a "clinical syndrome" and its "medical treatment" (Angier, 1992). Researchers at Yale also find that men's concerns about sexuality are a major problem area; such concerns include worries about waning virility and declining physical attractiveness. A rather high incidence of **impotence,** the inability to have or sustain an erection, can reinforce their concerns.

Male Potency   "There is a profound psychological meaning behind sexual activity—it reaffirms self-esteem, attractiveness, and gender identity" (Wincze, 1999). One recent federally funded study carried out in Massachusetts found that about half of American men over age 40 experience potency problems. Although aging can contribute to declining male virility, impotence often results from drugs, medical conditions such as diabetes, cardiovascular disorders, and cancer, and social habits including smoking, alcohol consumption, and lack of exercise. Stress, depression, grief, illness, and accidents can also give rise to temporary impotence (Altman, 1993). The jury is still out on the male impotence drug Viagra,

which sold 200,000 new prescriptions in the first four weeks it was on the market. According to the *New York Times,* about 6 million men in the United States have taken Viagra since it first came on the market in 1998 and a million more have taken either *Evitra* or *Cialis* (Tuller, 2004). Despite a potential market of 30 million men and extensive advertising, sales of these drugs are less than had been expected. Sales of these drugs amounted to about $2.7 billion in 2004—a billion dollars short of drug industry predictions (Schmit, 2005). A troubling trend has recently emerged—the recreational use of erectile dysfunction drugs by men without erectile dysfunction who sometimes mix them with Ecstasy and crystal methamphetamine (Kirby, 2004).

Many psychologists and sociologists believe that the medical model has gained unwarranted predominance over the male body, taking too simplistic a view of male sexuality (Potts et al., 2003). Others dismiss notions of a male menopause and erectile dysfunction as a social myth deriving from an overmedicated culture pathologically fearful of aging and death. They look for social and psychological explanations for understanding changes in a man's life that produce a crisis in his self-concept (Stamler, 2004). However, at present, the validity of male hormonal changes at midlife is under close research scrutiny. The middle years call for physical and emotional readjustments and reassessments, some of which can be unpleasant. Most commonly, troubling events are spread over one or two decades.

Researchers have followed a sample of unusually accomplished, self-reliant, and healthy young men from their first year as Harvard University students, mostly from the classes of 1942 to 1944, until their late forties. The men judged to have had the best outcomes in their late forties regarded the period from 35 to 49 as the happiest in their lives and the seemingly calmer period from 21 to 35 as the least happy. But the men least well adapted at midlife longed for the relative calm of young adulthood and regarded the storms of midlife as unusually painful (Rosenfeld & Stark, 1987).

Men's responses to middle age are varied. Many seem to move calmly through it; others have a stormy passage. For men, it can be a time of developmental defeat, leading to such problems as depression, alcoholism, obesity, and a chronic sense of futility and failure (Sheehy, 1998). Middle age can be a time of new personality growth, a period when a man moves toward a new kind of intimacy in his marriage, greater fulfillment in his work, and more realistic and satisfying relationships with his children.

> **Question**
>
> Is there any validity to the notion of a "male menopause" or midlife change?

Health Changes

The incidence of various health problems increases with age. The National Center for Health Statistics (2004a) reports that the main chronic health conditions of adults from age 45 to 64 are arthritis and other musculoskeletal problems, heart conditions, diabetes, mental health issues, fractures and joint injuries, and lung and respiratory problems. However, people can maximize their chances for

leading healthy and long lives by altering their lifestyles to include a variety of health-conscious practices such as regular exercise and eating a healthy diet. Nazario's 1989 study of the experience of 10,000 devout Mormons residing in California is illuminating. The individuals observe lifestyle habits recommended by the Church of Jesus Christ of Latter-Day Saints, which include abstaining from tobacco, alcohol, caffeine and drugs, eating meat sparingly, consuming plenty of herbs, fruits, and grains, securing ample sleep, and engaging in regular physical activity. Middle-aged Mormon men have a cancer death rate only 34 percent of that of middle-aged non-Mormon white men and only 14 percent of their death rate for cardiovascular disease. A 25-year-old Mormon man has a life expectancy of 85 years, whereas the average American white 25-year-old male can expect to reach about 75. Middle-aged Mormon women have a cancer mortality rate 55 percent of that of middle-aged non-Mormon white women and a death rate only 34 percent of theirs for cardiovascular disease. A 25-year-old Mormon woman has a life expectancy of 86 years; a non-Mormon white female has a life expectancy of 80 years. Studies of other nonsmoking, health-conscious religious groups such as the Seventh-Day Adventists also show low rates of mortality from cancer and heart disease (Nazario, 1989). Of course, health-promoting habits afford no guarantees but merely weight the odds in a person's favor.

Social habits and lifestyles affect our health in many ways. C. Everett Koop, former Surgeon General, estimated that half of U.S. deaths in 1990 were caused by smoking, drinking, sexually transmitted infections, drug

Varied Responses by Males to Midlife Many men navigate through middle adulthood with a healthy lifestyle, seeming to be years younger than they are. Some, however, find it more difficult to adapt, particularly if they lead a less engaged lifestyle.

Changing Unhealthy Habits A nutritious diet and regular exercise are keys to healthy living at all stages of life. At midlife, one's metabolism slows, often leading to weight gain unless one reduces caloric intake or increases activity level. Although many Americans recognize the importance of these factors, some have considerable difficulty changing unhealthy habits. Many programs assist people in achieving behavioral changes to reach their health goals.

abuse, poor nutrition, guns, and motor vehicles. He observed that many of the old epidemics of the eighteenth century have been replaced by "self-induced diseases." Moreover, a mounting body of evidence suggests that strong social ties are conducive to health (Wolf & Bruhn, 1993). Groups provide the structure by which we involve ourselves in the daily affairs of life. Not surprisingly, therefore, living alone can be hazardous to one's health. For example, men and women who lack social and emotional support are more than twice as likely to die following a heart attack as are people with a caring family and friends (Friend, 1995).

Social support can be of tremendous help when we are ill. For instance, patients are far more likely to live at least six months after heart surgery if they draw strength from religion and participation in social groups (Elias, 1995). Religious beliefs typically take on much more significance for middle-aged adults and the elderly. Research studies have shown that patients who have faith that they will heal often do heal more quickly than those who despair over their illness (Elias, 1995). Fortunately, more adults are smoking less, eating more sensibly, and exercising more. Yet many continue their unhealthy ways. The *More Information You Can Use* box on page 526, "A Schedule of Checkups for Midlife Women and Men," highlights potential bodily changes and gives a time schedule for diagnostic exams to help maintain a healthy, active life.

Sleep

Lack of sleep often peaks at midlife, when the demands of work and family are high. The average working person gets 90 minutes less sleep per night than she or he needs, according to Dr. William Dement, founder of a sleep disorder center at Stanford University, California, and author of *The Promise of Sleep*. Compounding the problem is the fact that many people think erroneously that as they get older they need less sleep. However, as one proceeds through middle adulthood, additional factors can also affect the length and quality of sleep.

Use of mild stimulant drugs, such as caffeine and nicotine, can interfere with sleep needs, as can prescription and over-the-counter drugs such as pain relievers, cold remedies, antihistamines, appetite suppressants, decongestants, and drugs for asthma, high blood pressure, and heart and thyroid problems. Even common foods containing sugar (especially eaten late at night) and common beverages, such as alcohol, soft drinks, cocoa, and tea, and not getting enough protein in one's diet can keep one awake or prevent sleep for an extended period of time. Insomnia can also result from worry or depression. Changes in one's circadian rhythms during midlife can affect sleep patterns as well. It is quite common to be able to go to sleep when desired but to wake up only a few hours later and not be able to get back to sleep.

Women experiencing perimenopause often experience this pattern, accompanied by "night sweats," because of ongoing changes in their biochemistry (Doress-Worters & Siegal, 1994). Another factor interfering with sleep for many midlife adults is the "waiting-up-for-teenagers-to-get-home-safely" syndrome!

Medications formulated to help induce sleep, including sleeping pills, tranquilizers, and antianxiety drugs, can actually cause more sleeplessness after discontinuation of their use. Additionally, these types of medications can become addictive. Because they also are central nervous system depressants, their use is likely to affect alertness, aggravate memory loss, and make a person unsteady on arising, which could increase the likelihood of falls or more severe injury. Use of sleeping pills for a shorter duration or situationally is not likely to become addictive. Anyone with serious sleep disturbances should consult a sleep clinic at a local hospital for assistance.

Cardiovascular Fitness

Several risk factors are associated with **cardiovascular** (heart and circulatory system) health, including high

Coming to Terms with Physical Changes in Middle Age
Though anyone can develop high blood pressure and high cholesterol readings, some Americans are more at risk for these effects and need to maintain a healthy weight, follow a high-fiber, low-fat diet, increase their activity level, eat less salt, drink alcohol only in moderation, and learn stress management skills. The southeastern United States has high rates of adult hypertension.

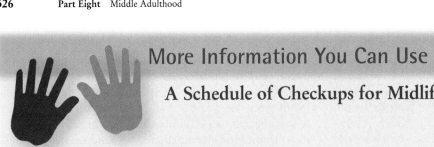

More Information You Can Use

A Schedule of Checkups for Midlife Women and Men

Health Checkups	Diagnosis or Potential Health Concerns	Recommendations
Vision	Presbyopia, glaucoma, cataracts, macular degeneration, dry eyes, watery eyes, "droopy" eyes, other eye conditions.	*If 40 or over,* do you have to hold this book farther and farther away to be able to read this print? *Over 60,* have an eye exam at *least once every 2 years.* This should include dilating the pupils to get a good view of the retina and optic nerve, essential in detecting diseases of the eye.
Hearing	Presbycusis, nerve deafness, or other hearing disorders. About 35% of adults age 65 and older have a hearing loss. It is estimated that 50% of those 75 and older have a hearing loss.	*Check yourself:* Can you hear a bird chirping nearby? Can you hear the telephone ringing? Are you asking others to repeat themselves? Do you have difficulty hearing in a crowded room? Can you hear the sound of rubbing your fingers together near each ear? What is the typical sound level of your work environment? Do you have a familial background of hearing loss? An audiology exam may be in order.
Skin Appearance	Look for patches of dry, scaly skin, darkening of a mole, or other skin protrusion; any bleeding or discharge from skin, sunburn.	The American Academy of Dermatology suggests that people, especially those who live in warm climates, *have a yearly skin exam* as part of a regular checkup. In between checkups, be alert for any changes in your skin.
Dental Health	Cleaning and examination; X rays for periodontal disease.	*Minimum once per year* for teeth cleaning and *every few years for dental X rays.*
Weight	Sources vary on recommendations. Some say 20% over, others say 30% over recommended weight for body size puts a person at a higher risk of heart disease, cancer, and other illnesses.	Look at muscle-to-fat ratio; consider body frame and lifestyle. Start physician-monitored exercise regimen if overweight. Make an appointment with a nutritionist.
Bone Density	Osteoporosis and other bone disorders can be diagnosed with a painless bone densitometry scan. *Osteoporosis is preventable.* Follow a diet rich in calcium and vitamin D and a lifestyle of regular weight-bearing exercise. *Those at higher risk:* small body frame, low body weight, sedentary lifestyle, anorexics and dieters.	Men and women aged 25 to 65 should have 1,000 mg calcium daily. Women near menopause or postmenopause should have 1,500 mg calcium daily. Calcium-rich foods include low-fat dairy products (cheese, yogurt, milk); canned fish with edible bones, such as salmon and sardines; dark leafy-green vegetables such as kale, broccoli, collard greens; breads made with calcium-fortified flour; juices fortified with calcium; calcium supplements with vitamin D as needed.
Cervical Cancer (women)	A Pap *smear,* or cervical biopsy if at higher risk.	A Pap smear every 1 to 3 years to detect cervical cancer. Request lab where a person examines smear; some are examined electronically. Should be done more often if at higher risk: multiple sex partners, sequential sex partners, IV drug user, have unprotected sex, previous history of STI(s), familial history of cancer, heavy smoker, postmenopausal and on HRT.
Menopause (women)	Blood test for level of FSH (follicle-stimulating hormone); begins in only 4% of women under 40. Typical age range is 45 to 55; average age is 51.	Typically if female age 40 or over and if menses are irregular or atypical, or if any other signs of menopause are indicated (hot flashes or hot flushes, sleep irregularities, etc.).
Type 2 Diabetes	In Type 2 diabetes, either the body does not produce enough insulin or the cells ignore the insulin. Insulin is necessary for the body to be able to use sugar and takes the sugar from the blood into the cells. When glucose builds up in the blood instead of going into cells, cells may be starved for energy and high blood sugar levels hurt eyes, kidneys, nerves, or heart.	The goal of treatment is to lower your blood sugar and improve your body's use of insulin with meal planning, exercise, and weight loss. There are many factors involved in controlling blood sugar levels, including diet, exercise and monitoring your blood sugar regularly. Controlling your diabetes is important to reduce the risk of long-term complications.

Health Checkups	Diagnosis or Potential Health Concerns	Recommendations
Breast Cancer (can affect both females and males)	Self-exam. Mammogram: an X-ray picture of the breast, which takes only a few seconds per breast. With aging after 40, the chances of getting breast cancer get higher. After skin cancer, breast cancer is the most frequently diagnosed cancer in U.S. women.	If you are in your forties or older, *having a mammogram every 1 to 2 years could save your life.* Look for any unusual lump or swelling lasting for a period of time; some lumps (cysts) normally occur at a certain time each month; check breasts monthly while in the shower by running hands over breasts lightly to detect any changes or lumps; also check nearby lymph glands for changes. A doctor should do an annual breast exam. Mammograms are recommended once every 2 years after 40 years old or more frequently if there is a familial or personal history of breast cancer. There is a genetic test for those with a higher familial risk of breast cancer.
Cardiovascular Fitness (age 18 and older)	Hypertension or high blood pressure. 		Systolic	Diastolic
Normal	<120	<80
Prehypertension	120–139	80–89
High		
Stage 1	140–159	90–99
Stage 2	≥160	≥100		Have blood pressure taken regularly if overweight or have familial or personal history of hypertension. *To lower blood pressure:* • Maintain healthy weight (lose weight if overweight) • Be more physically active. • Choose foods low in salt (sodium). • Drink alcoholic beverages only in moderation.
Blood Cholesterol	High 240+ Borderline high 200–239 Desirable below 200.	A blood test to check for LDL and HDL for everyone aged 20 and older, every 5 years; men with no risk factors can wait until age 35; women with no risk factors can wait until age 45 (see Table 15.1).
HIV/AIDS	Blood tests to confirm absence or presence of HIV virus; gynecological cervical tests in women.	*Higher-risk factors* include unprotected sexual behaviors, homosexual male sexual behaviors, history of sexual abuse (rape), history of multiple partners, history of sequential partners, IV drug user sharing needles, history of STI(s), extreme fatigue, recurrent female pelvic diseases, female over 50 having unprotected sexual relations.
Prostate Gland (men)	Prostatitis can be caused by several types of bacteria. Symptoms include burning sensation, discharge, difficulty beginning a stream of urine. Treatment regimen is antibiotics. Prostate enlargement is more typical beginning in late 40s and symptoms are similar to prostatitis. Prostate cancer is detected by biopsy.	See a physician (a urologist perhaps, depending upon the severity of the symptoms). The physician inserts a gloved finger into the rectum to feel the prostate through the wall of the bowel. This exam is part of a *routine physical for men over* 40 to detect signs of prostatic cancer—a slow-growing cancer that almost never affects young men but is seen in most elderly men (Nickel, 1997).
Testicular Cancer (men)	Testicular cancer usually affects men between the ages of 15 and 35. If testicular cancer is detected early, it is very curable.	A monthly testicular self-exam (TSE) is performed to identify a number of conditions, but primarily cancer. Regularly examine the testes during a warm shower when the heat of the shower can relax the scrotum. Rotate each testicle between the thumb and forefinger, feeling for a round, firm surface. If you discover a small, painless lump on the surface of the testicle that does not appear to be epididymis, consult a physician immediately. Testicular cancer is almost always painless, so do not wait for the lump to grow or pain to develop.
Colon Cancer (also called colorectal cancer)	Among the most common cancers in the U.S. and most often occurs in men and women over 50. Associated with diets high in fat and calories and low in fiber. First-degree relatives of a person who has had colorectal cancer are somewhat more likely to develop this type of cancer themselves. Ulcerative colitis increases risk. Some types of polyps increase the risk.	Prevention requires early detection and removal of polyps. Also studies suggest a diet low in fat and calories and high in fiber for prevention. Several detection tests are used: a digital rectal exam (DRE) and a fecal occult blood test (FOBT) are used to check for hidden blood in the stool. A double contrast barium enema (DCBE) is a series of x-rays of the colon and rectum. A sigmoidoscopy is an examination of the rectum and lower colon (sigmoid colon) using a lighted instrument. A colonoscopy is an examination of the rectum and entire colon using a colonoscope.

blood pressure, smoking, a family history of heart disease, being male, being diabetic, and being obese. Two cardiovascular diseases are heart disease, the number one cause of death in the United States, and stroke, the third most common cause of death. Blood pressure readings and cholesterol screenings are predictors of cardiovascular fitness.

Blood Pressure   About one in every four American adults has high blood pressure, called **hypertension,** which is a risk factor for other diseases affecting the heart, kidneys, and brain. Hypertension has no warning signs or symptoms. Blood pressure is the force of the blood pushing against the walls of arteries. Each time the heart beats (about 60 to 70 times a minute at rest), it pumps out blood to the arteries. Blood pressure is at its greatest when the heart contracts and is pumping the blood, which is called **systolic pressure.** When the heart is at rest, in between beats, blood pressure falls, which is **diastolic pressure.** Blood pressure is always noted as these two numbers, and both are important. They are usually written one above or before the other, such as 120/80, with the top number systolic and the bottom diastolic. A reading of 140/90 is considered high; 120/80 is normal for the heart and blood vessels (National Institute of Health [NIH], 1996). Blood pressure can fluctuate during a regular day, depending on activity level. During sleep, for instance, blood pressure goes down. Some people have blood pressure that stays up all or most of the time; if left untreated, this can lead to serious medical problems such as arteriosclerosis (hardening of the arteries), heart attack (reduced blood flow that reduces oxygen supply to the heart), enlarged heart, kidney damage, or stroke (NIH, 1996).

Who Is at Risk?   Anyone can develop high blood pressure, but it is more common in African Americans than in whites. In the early and middle adult years, men have high blood pressure more often than women; but as men and women age, more women have high blood pressure than men. After menopause, women have high blood pressure as often as men of the same age. The percentage of men and women with hypertension increases rapidly in older age groups. Some midlife adults have hypertension; more than half of all Americans over age 60 have high blood pressure. Heredity can make some individuals more prone to developing high blood pressure, and some children have hypertension (NIH, 2004b).

The NIH (2004b) promotes several lifestyle changes to help prevent or control hypertension, including these:

- Eating healthy foods that include fruits, vegetables, and low-fat dairy products
- Cutting down on salt and sodium in the diet
- Losing excess weight and staying at a healthy weight
- Staying physically active (e.g., walking for 30 minutes a day)
- Limiting alcohol intake
- Quitting smoking

Medications can help reduce high blood pressure. Regular blood pressure screenings several times a year are recommended during middle adulthood and are available for free in many community settings, such as neighborhood clinics, pharmacies, churches, and schools. Adults with a high risk for hypertension can purchase diagnostic instruments to take their blood pressure readings at home. Following the DASH (Dietary Approaches to Stop Hypertension) eating plan which emphasizes fresh fruits and vegetables, low-fat dairy, whole grains, fish, poultry, and nuts has been shown to have a positive effect on blood pressure ("Facts About the DASH Eating Plan," 2003).

Cholesterol is a white, waxy fat that occurs naturally in the body and is used to build the cell walls and make certain hormones. Cholesterol has been the "buzz word" in health for the past 15 years. Too much of it in one's diet can clog arteries and eventually choke off the supply of blood to the heart. High cholesterol is a leading risk factor for heart disease. The National Cholesterol Education Program suggests being tested from age 20 on, with men 35 and older and women 45 and older being tested every five years. Cholesterol level can be determined with a simple, inexpensive blood test. HDL is

Table 15.1 Blood Cholesterol Levels

ATP III classification of LDL, total, and HDL cholesterol (mg/dL) (Obtain Complete Lipoprotein Profile After 9- to 12-Hour Fast)

LDL Cholesterol—Primary Target of Therapy	
<100	Optimal
100–129	Near optimal/above optimal
130–159	Borderline high
160–189	High
≥190	Very high
Total Cholesterol	
<200	Desirable
200–239	Borderline high
≥240	High
HDL Cholesterol	
<40	Low
≥60	High

Source: National Cholesterol Education Program. (2001, May). *NIH Publication No. 01-3305.* Bethesda, MD: National Institutes of Health.

considered the "good" cholesterol that cleans the blood vessels; LDL is the "bad" cholesterol that builds up and clogs arteries. See Table 15.1 for blood cholesterol levels (NIH, 2004b). The National Cholesterol Education Program (NCEP) has recently updated its guidelines regarding LDL cholesterol, lowering the number to indicate healthy levels (Mitka, 2004). The NCEP has a calculator in its website that allows you to assess your risk for having a heart attack (National Cholesterol Education Program, 2005).

Changing one's diet to reduce consumption of saturated fats and increasing activity level by exercising regularly (brisk walking, running, swimming, cycling, dancing, jumping rope, skating, aerobics) can raise the beneficial HDL cholesterol and lower the damaging LDL cholesterol.

Smoking, especially over a long period of time, can lead to many health deficits. Many empirical studies have documented that smoking can lead to heart disease, lung disease, kidney and bladder disease, and many types of cancers. A variety of smoke-reduction programs (and medications) are available to those who wish to make this lifestyle change to promote better health and well-being, not just for oneself but for one's family as well, since a great deal of research has documented that secondhand smoke is possibly even more harmful than ever believed (American Cancer Society, 1997). Cigarette packages are now required to be labeled "This product is likely to be harmful to your health." People who have quit at any age usually state that food tastes better, breathing is easier, endurance for activity is better, and they feel more energetic—and, as a boon to people around them, they no longer reek of stale smoke. It is never too late to quit. Smoking-related illnesses and diseases cost Americans billions of dollars in medical costs every year, along with the emotional devastation associated with the loss of loved ones who would not give up the habit.

Inflammation, Metabolic Syndrome, and Heart Disease
Recent studies are pointing to inflammation as a factor that may be as important as cholesterol level in causing heart attacks and strokes (LeWine, 2005). Endocrinologists are exploring the links between cellular inflammation and heart attack and diabetes. Researchers have shown that inflamed monocytes and lymphocytes are present in obese people who are at greater risk for heart disease and diabetes. These inflamed cells are also linked to atherosclerosis or insulin resistance and can enter the brain ("Cellular Inflammation Precursor to Heart Disease," 2005). *Metabolic syndrome* (sometimes called syndrome X) is a group of risk factors for heart disease. Some of the risk factors include overweight, high blood pressure, high levels of LDL cholesterol, and high blood sugar levels. Improving the diet and increasing exercise levels are important ways to reduce the symptoms of metabolic syndrome (Deen, 2004). Metabolic syndrome and cardiovascular risk factors have also been found to have an impact on the development of Alzheimer's disease and vascular dementia (Yaffe et al., 2004). Even borderline levels of risk factors such as blood pressure, cholesterol, glucose intolerance, and smoking should be considered for treatment to prevent heart disease (Vasan, & Sullivan, 2005). According to Neighborhood Heart Watch, another risk factor for heart disease is the presence of gum disease (Watch & Update, 2005).

> **Question**
>
> How do smoking, cholesterol, and hypertension contribute to cardiovascular disease and other health deficits?

Cancer

For women between the ages of 40 and 60, breast cancer is the leading cause of death. Colon cancer and lung cancer are also leading causes of death for both males and females. Researchers estimate that over 180,000 women are diagnosed with breast cancer each year in the United States. Ovarian and cervical cancer are also more prevalent at this stage of life (Midlife Passages, 1998a). Some inborn factors might predispose a person to developing cancer, but virtually all experts agree that about 80 percent of all cancers are caused by environmental factors such as toxic substances in cigarettes, air, water, and food, medical treatment, and workplace hazards (Doress-Worters & Siegal, 1994).

Smoking is the number one controllable cause of cancer, causing at least 30 percent of cancer deaths (Doress-Worters & Siegal, 1994). Anyone who has a history of cancer is at a higher risk for developing further cancers. Other risk factors are these:

- *Poverty.* Of persons diagnosed with cancer, those who have financial resources live longer compared with poorer people.
- *Longevity.* Those who live longer have a greater likelihood of getting some type of cancer. Cancer incidence begins to rise at about age 35 for women and a little later for men.
- *Gender and race.* More men than women, and more blacks than whites, die from cancer.
- *Family.* Heredity plays a role in the incidence and types of cancers diagnosed. Inform any health provider of a familial disposition to cancer (Doress-Worters & Siegal, 1994).

As compared with many years ago when cancer was whispered to be "the C word," many communities now have cancer support groups available to help cancer patients and their families cope with this serious ordeal.

Researchers around the world are making scientific breakthroughs every day in the search to understand and cure cancer.

The Brain

The *Baltimore Longitudinal Study of Aging* found that more than 25 percent of persons in their seventies showed no decline in memory or reasoning skills, and many showed little decline into their eighties (Browder, 1997). Recent research suggests that people can slow the process of brain cell loss by staying intellectually active, continuing to problem-solve, and using challenging thought processes. People in midlife should continue the path of active learning: learn and use new words, play games of Scrabble, compete along with *Jeopardy* and *Who Wants to Be a Millionaire* contestants, demonstrate creativity, try a new hobby, take a college course or continue education in some other fashion, mentor someone, join a speakers' group, join an Elderhostel program—in other words anything to keep yourself intellectually engaged with the world.

A **stroke,** or "brain attack," occurs when blood circulation to the brain fails. Brain cells can die from decreased blood flow and the resulting lack of oxygen. Both blockage and bleeding can be involved. Stroke is the third leading killer of Americans and is the most common cause of disability. Each year more than 500,000 Americans have a stroke, with about 160,000 dying. Strokes occur in all age groups, in both sexes, and in all races of every country. For African Americans the death rate from stroke is almost twice that of the white population. High blood pressure, cigarette smoking, heart disease, history of stroke, and diabetes are considered risk factors for stroke (National Institute of Neurological Disorders and Stroke [NINDS], 2004). This brain disorder will be discussed in more detail in Chapter 17.

Parkinson's disease belongs to a group of motor system disorders that are likely to show up in late middle age, usually affecting people over 50. The average age of onset is 60 years old. The four primary symptoms are tremor or trembling in hands, arms, legs, jaw, and face; rigidity or stiffness of limbs and trunk; slowness of movement; and postural instability or impaired balance and coordination. About 50,000 Americans are diagnosed with Parkinson's disease each year. Actor Michael J. Fox is a prominent spokesperson for Parkinson's disease research. Parkinson's affects men and women in nearly equal numbers, and it knows no social, economic, or geographic boundaries. Some studies show that African Americans and Asians are less likely than whites to develop this disease. There is no cure at this time for Parkinson's, but a variety of medications can provide dramatic relief (NINDS, 2005).

Alzheimer's disease (AD) sometimes develops in middle adulthood, but this brain disorder is more likely to show up after age 65. AD begins slowly, and at first the only symptom could be mild forgetfulness. Minimal memory loss is also a symptom of the complex hormonal changes many women experience during menopause, and many middle-aged women worry that they are developing Alzheimer's when they find themselves forgetting things. This form of dementia and memory loss is addressed in more detail in Chapter 17.

Consumption of alcohol (a depressant) at any age slows down brain activity, which in turn affects alertness, judgment, coordination, and reaction time. It is well known that drinking increases the risk of accidents and injury. Some research has shown that it takes less alcohol to affect older people than younger ones. Over time, heavy drinking damages the brain and central nervous system, as well as the liver, heart, kidneys, and stomach. Alcohol is often harmful (even fatal) when mixed with prescription or over-the-counter medications. An older body cannot absorb or dispose of alcohol or other drugs as easily as a younger body. Some people are likely to develop a drinking problem later in life because of situational factors, such as a job layoff, forced retirement, failing health, breakup of a marriage, or loss of friends and loved ones. However, chronic drinkers have been drinking for many years. Once a person decides he or she needs help, there are many treatment avenues available to help change this brain-destroying behavior (National Institute on Aging, 1998).

Question

What are some potential cancers or brain disorders associated with aging, and why are they so life threatening?

Midlife Men and Women at Risk for HIV/AIDS

Fact: Since the AIDS epidemic began in 1981, *about 900,000 Americans have been diagnosed with AIDS*—and AIDS is rising faster in middle age and in older people than in people under age 40 (National Center for Health Statistics, 2004a). However, the actual number of AIDS-infected Americans may be 950,000, since many do not know they are infected. This epidemic is growing most rapidly among minority populations and is the leading killer of African American men and women between 25 and 44 (National Institutes of Health, 2005).

For many years, homosexual males and intravenous drug users seemed to be the most affected populations. Then the virus spread to the heterosexual population, especially to sexually active adolescents. The number of cases among midlife and older women has been steadily increasing, mainly among postmenopausal women who no longer use birth control (see the *Further Developments* box on page 532, "More Midlife Women Are Contracting HIV/AIDS").

Women are becoming increasingly affected by HIV. Approximately 47 percent, or 16.4 million, of the 35 million adults living with HIV or AIDS worldwide are women. Worldwide, as of 2000 an estimated 22 million people had died from AIDS since the epidemic began; 17.5 million were adults, including 9 million women; 4.3 million were children under 15 (CDC, 2000b).

Risk Factors   A link between child sexual abuse and risk for HIV infection has been proposed by several researchers, and recent findings strongly confirm that association (Cassese, 1993; Paone & Chavkin, 1993). In the Women's Interagency HIV Study (WIHS), data from more than 1,500 women in New York City; Chicago; Washington, D.C.; and Los Angeles revealed that 40 percent reported a history of child sexual abuse (Cook, 1997). For these women, a history of sexual abuse, physical abuse, or domestic abuse was highly correlated with engaging in behavior that put them at risk for HIV. Significantly, childhood sexual abuse was associated with use of IV drugs, exchange of sex for drugs, paying money for shelter, multiple sexual partners, and having sex with a person at high risk for HIV. Another risk factor is adolescent or adult sexual assault. It is estimated that more than 30 percent of all females and nearly 15 percent of all males in the United States have been victims of childhood sexual abuse. Sexual violence against women and girls has become a major problem in areas of the world experiencing war and conflict.

A United Nations report on Rwanda estimated that a quarter million women and girls were raped during the genocide. In rural areas of Rwanda the HIV prevalence rate was about 1 percent in 1994 before the conflict started and jumped to 11 percent in 1997. One survey of Rwandan women who survived the genocide found 17 percent to be HIV-positive (World Health Organization, 2004).

Female-to-Male Transmission of HIV/AIDS   Of men and women engaging in heterosexual sex, the women are much more likely than the men to become infected by an HIV-positive partner, according to a 10-year study conducted by researchers at the University of California, San Francisco. The probability of HIV-positive women infecting their male partners with the virus was found to be significantly low. The risk factors for HIV infection among heterosexuals are: (1) unprotected anal receptive sex; (2) lack of condom use; (3) injection drug use; (4) sharing of tainted injection equipment; and (5) the presence of a sexually transmitted infection (STI) (Padian et al., 1997).

Female-to-Female Transmission of HIV/AIDS   Most published studies of sexually transmitted infections and HIV do not examine women who have sex with women (WSW) as a distinct category. Therefore, this group is not well understood in terms of disease transmission (Fethers et al., 2000). Through December 1996, 85,500 women were reported with HIV/AIDS. Of these more than 1,600 were reported to have had sex with women. However, the vast majority had other risks—such as injection drug use, sex with high-risk men, receipt of blood or blood products, alternative insemination, and needle use for piercing and tattooing (Denenberg, 1997). Of the 333 (out of 1,648) who were reported to have had sex only with women, 97 percent of these women also had another risk—injection drug use. Information on whether the woman had sex with women is missing in half of the 85,500 case reports, possibly because the physician did not elicit the information or the woman did not volunteer it (Centers for Disease Control and Prevention [CDC], 1997a). Although female-to-female transmission of HIV is apparently rare, female sexual contact should be considered a possible means of transmission among women who are having sexual relations with women. Women who are lesbian need to know that exposure of a mucous membrane to vaginal secretions and menstrual blood is potentially infectious. A major preventative is accurate knowledge of a partner's HIV status and use of effective barriers (CDC, 1997b).

The focus of research at present is to develop women-initiated methods to avoid sexually transmitted infections, including HIV. Technical products for safer sex are referred to as "barriers," and women and men need to learn the nature of each type of barrier, its relative effectiveness and availability, and how to use it. Mechanical barriers (such as male and female condoms, the diaphragm, the cervical cap) and chemical barriers (such as bacteria- and virus-killing microbicides) can be used alone or in combination. The Food and Drug Administration proposed putting warning labels on vaginal contraceptives that contain spermicide after studies found that nonoxynol 9 can actually increase the risk of infection because it is a vaginal irritant ("FDA Recommends Warning Labels for Nonoxynol 9," 2003). Two microbicides developed to prevent sexually transmitted infections are being tested in Africa and the United States. The microbicides are applied to the surface of the vagina as a preventative measure against infection (National Institute of Allergy and Infectious Diseases, 2005).

The demographics associated with HIV/AIDS is changing. It is rapidly becoming a problem in the middle-aged and older adult populations. During the 1990s, the number of Americans over age 50 with HIV quintupled. Much of the increase is due to the success of antiretroviral drugs that enable people with the virus to live longer; however, new cases are also emerging. Treating older

Further Developments

More Midlife Women Are Contracting HIV/AIDS

Although AIDS is thought of as a disease of the young, in the United States it is rapidly becoming one of the middle-aged and even the old. The number of Americans over age 50 infected with the virus that causes AIDS quintupled during the 1990s, "and a conservative estimate would be that there are more than 100,000 now," said Dr. Marcia G. Ory, a professor of public health at Texas A&M University and co-author of a 2003 report for the CDC on AIDS in older Americans. "Unless there is a new explosion of the disease among teenagers, demographers estimate, the majority of cases by the end of the decade will be in people over 50" (McNeil, 2004).

For a number of reasons, HIV/AIDS is becoming more prevalent in the middle-aged population (see Table 15.2). One reason is that it has become much rarer that newborns are infected, and so the percentages of people with the infection have shifted. Another reason is that people who had become infected are living longer. The less obvious cause is that some people contract the infection later in life. Because it seems less likely to occur, people are often not aware that they can contract it later in life (especially those in long-term marital relationships). When they do become aware of it, their symptoms have already progressed in severity. Middle-aged women have some particular risk factors for contracting the infection.

Postmenopausal women often see themselves as free from the responsibility of birth control—and therefore, mistakenly, as free from needing to protect themselves from disease. Certain biological changes that accompany aging make midlife and older women particularly vulnerable to HIV transmission. During menopause, the vaginal wall becomes thinner and more likely to tear. As women age, vaginal acidity decreases leaving women more vulnerable to urinary tract infections and to contracting HIV as well. Changes in the immune system also contribute to increased vulnerability to HIV.

Drug use, thought to be primarily a behavior of younger people, also occurs among older men and women. The cohort that is now middle aged grew up in the late 1950s and 1960s during the era of "free love" and an American culture more accepting of drug use. As reported in the *New York Times,*

Patricia Shelton, who is nearly 60 years old, has known of her HIV-positive status since 1990. In her twenties and thirties she was a "closet heroin addict," keeping a Wall Street secretarial job, raising her children, not losing control. "A lot of us who had a past are happy housewives now, are mothers and grandmothers, are productive members of society," she said.

Once HIV/AIDS is diagnosed, older women experience further problems in getting the care they need. Many HIV-positive women report changes in menstrual cycles, including longer, shorter, heavier, irregular, or painful periods. Amenorrhea, the absence of a menstrual cycle, is three times more likely to occur in HIV-positive women. Originally this was thought to be premature menopause in which ovarian function wanes and eventually ceases. However, the levels of FSH (follicle-stimulating hormone) detected in HIV-positive women experiencing amenorrhea do not indicate true menopause (Marks, 1998).

HIV Manifestations in Women

Studies have found that the most common reasons infected women first sought medical attention were recurrent vaginal yeast infections, enlarged lymph nodes, and extreme fatigue, followed by bacterial pneumonia. Cervical cancer was added to the list of AIDS-defining conditions in 1993. A Pap smear is typically used to detect cellular changes in the cervix that can indicate a risk of developing cancer. HIV-positive women have a 30 to 40 percent chance of having an abnormal Pap smear after testing positive. Invasive cervical cancer is usually more serious in women who are HIV-positive than it is in HIV-negative women.

On a psychological level, midlife or older women who are HIV-positive are likely to keep this diagnosis to themselves until they become seriously ill. Some cannot afford the medical care or adequate services or believe that they do not have the time to take care of themselves if they are already involved in caring for others. Dr. Alexandra Levine, with the *Women's Interagency HIV Study,* says that American women are very likely to experience a sense of profound isolation as a result of knowing they are HIV-positive (Marks, 1998). In her study with 2,000 participants, a significant number said they had never met or spoken to another woman living with AIDS. To compound matters, people with HIV or AIDS who need elder care might face discrimination in facilities such as nursing homes. Most must rely on in-home care, which for some is not an option either. Also, based on cross-cultural studies of attitudes and health, it is likely that many ethnic minority adults infected with HIV are likely to seek support from each other and not request assistance from health agencies or community resources.

Table 15.2 Women in Middle Adulthood with AIDS: United States: 1985–2003

Age	% Distribution (Out of Total Population with AIDS)	All Years	1985 (Number)	1995 (Number)	2003 (Number)
40 to 49	24.7	38,685	45	3,055	3,547
50 to 59	7.3	11,483	26	818	1,253
60 and over	3.3	5,221	38	335	439

adults with the virus is a challenge because they tend to have interference from other prescription drugs for heart disease, diabetes, and cholesterol that they may be taking. Doctors may also misdiagnose infected individuals because their symptoms may be attributed to other causes such as menopause, congestive heart failure, or Alzheimer's disease. Older adults may be more reluctant to divulge their sexual histories. Women past menopause may feel that they no longer need to take protective measures during sexual activity and hence they become more vulnerable (McNeil, 2004).

Question

Why is HIV/AIDS becoming more prevalent among the middle aged, especially among women?

Stress and Depression

Midlife is often associated with change and adaptation—children leaving home, elderly parents moving in, potential divorce or remarriage, change of jobs, retirement, relocation, children returning home with grandchildren, and so on. Midlife is also associated with losses—forced early retirement, traditional retirement, physical changes or health decline, death of a spouse, parents' loss of physical well-being or death, and so forth. Samuels (1997) reports in *Midlife Crisis: Helping Patients Cope with Stress, Anxiety, and Depression* that depression and substance abuse are common but often underrecognized and undertreated in middle-aged adults. According to Samuels, major depression in midlife is common; approximately 2 percent of midlife adults experience major depression. Depression in older life is associated with increased mortality or suicide, even after controlling for physical illness and disability. Dr. Samuels recommends that physicians pay attention to change and loss in a patient's life as serious predictors of depression, by using various rating scales during a checkup, because suicide risk increases with age, particularly in adult males.

People with mood disorders are likely to self-medicate with alcohol or other substances of abuse (about one in eight older adults has a problem related to alcohol abuse), and one-third of these develop alcohol problems late in life that are related to the psychological stress of aging (Samuels, 1997). An analysis of the adult's history, a full physical, and neurological and mental status examinations can help assess whether a patient is suffering from multiple stressors and depression. An individualized treatment regimen should be established, which might include changes in lifestyle or antidepressant medications. The goal is to give the patient a renewed sense of control and to eliminate stressors or develop coping strategies for those that cannot be eliminated. Depression is a treatable illness, and many organizations provide support and educational materials for midlife patients faced with complex problems.

Research suggests a U-shaped curve with respect to rates of depression in adulthood. High rates occur in young adulthood and then again in later life. This distribution is found to hold for African Americans as well as for white Americans (Turnbull & Mui, 1995). It is important to point out, however, that the majority of research on depression in adulthood is cross-sectional in nature. This method is not well suited for explaining age-related or generational differences because it confounds the effects of aging and cohort (Paludi, 2002).

Sexual Functioning

Americans have well-established stereotypes regarding the sexual lives of various age groups (Laumann et al., 1994). They think of young adults as the most sexually active—as desiring, attempting, and achieving the most sex. They view the middle aged as the most sexually knowledgeable and skilled, but they consider the old as asexual or sexless. A display of erotic interest by older people is considered unnatural and undignified. For example, what our youth-oriented society considers virility in a 20-year-old male it views as lechery in a 65-year-old, who is likely to be labeled a "dirty old man." Despite such stereotypes, classic research on human sexuality by William H. Masters and Virginia E. Johnson (1966) revealed that sexual effectiveness need not disappear as humans age. Like their other activities, people's sexual performance might not have the same physical energy in the later years of life as in the earlier years. But Masters and Johnson found that many healthy men and women do function sexually into their eighties or beyond. Although time takes its toll, it need not eliminate sexual desire nor bar its fulfillment.

Sexual arousal in humans is the product of a complex interaction of affective, cognitive, and physiological processes (Marx, 1988; Morokoff, 1985). But what happens in far too many cases is that older people come to accept social definitions of their sexlessness; they become victims of the myth. Believing they will lose their sexual effectiveness becomes a self-fulfilling prophecy, and some older people do lose it even though their bodies have not lost the capacity for sexual responsiveness. The belief that they are sexless may be reinforced in some men when they are unable to attain or maintain an erection during a number of sexual attempts. This is a common occurrence among men of any age group and can be associated with stress, illness, or overindulgence in alcohol. Indeed, fear of failure is not uncommon among older men. Often, a woman is unaware of her partner's fears, and she mistakes his caution for disinterest.

Changes nonetheless do occur with age. Men over 50 find that it takes longer for them to achieve an erection.

The Sexual Behavior of Middle-Aged Americans There is a stereotypical view that aging men and women are sexless, but research indicates that many men and women are sexually active well into middle age and older years, though frequency of sexual activity often declines with advancing age. Married and cohabiting couples have the most sex. However, drug treatments for certain medical problems can have side effects that affect sexuality.

The erection of older men, particularly those over 60, is generally not as firm or full as when they were younger, and maximum erection is achieved only just before orgasm. With advancing age comes a reduction in the production of sperm and seminal fluid, in the number of orgasmic contractions, and in the force of the ejaculation. And the frequency of sexual activity typically declines with advancing age. Yet Painter (1992) reports findings that 61 percent of married couples in their fifties have sex at least once a week.

Overall, researchers find that the general level of sexual activity of the individuals when they were between 20 and 39 years of age correlated highly with the frequency of their sexual activity in later life (Elias, 1992; Tsitouras, Martin, & Harman, 1982). Hence, if men have maintained elevated levels of sexual activity from their earlier years, and if acute or chronic ill health does not intervene, they are able to continue some form of active sexual expression into advanced age. However, if aging males are not stimulated over long periods of time, their responsiveness can be permanently lost (Masters & Johnson, 1966). Physicians find that many medical problems manifest themselves sexually. Medical problems that affect male sexual performance include diabetes, which occurs in about 10 percent of men over age 50.

Peyronie's disease, a scarring of the tissue inside the shaft of the penis, is more common with men who have diabetes or high blood pressure. Psychological depression is also associated with a decrease in sexual desire. In recent years physicians have become aware of the sexual side effects of medications for heart disease, high blood pressure, and coronary artery disease. Blocking agents used to control high blood pressure, for instance, reduce the flow of blood into the pelvic area. In a younger person it might not matter much, but in older men the result is often impotence (see Figure 15.3).

Masters and Johnson (1966) also found no reason that menopause or advancing age should interfere with the sexual capacity, performance, or drive of women. Basically, older women respond as they did when they were younger, and they continue to be capable of sexual activity and orgasm. Older women tend to lubricate more slowly than they did earlier in life, and the vaginal walls become thinner, which means that the tissues can be easily irritated and torn with forceful sexual activity. Male gentleness and the use of artificial vaginal lubricants can do much to minimize this difficulty. Like aging men, older women also typically have fewer orgasmic contractions; younger women average 5 to 10 contractions, whereas older women average 3 to 5 contractions).

It appears that American men are becoming more aware of their own sensitivity and humanness. Privately, they are increasingly coming to recognize, and even approve of, their feelings of tenderness, dependence, weakness, pain, and so on. But a good many of them, especially older men, are not yet able to talk freely about these traditionally "unmasculine" emotions. Many men are becoming more aware of their own sensitivity and humanness; over the past two decades women have become more aware of their own sexuality. A growing number of women are tired of the traditional pattern of sexual relations, which focused on male erection, male penetration, and male orgasm. Women are increasingly admitting to themselves what they like sexually and are asking their partners for it.

The need to learn about the prevalence of various sexual behaviors and about how the prevalence varies with age and other factors is not strictly an academic issue. Only by studying sexual behavior can we hope to understand and combat the epidemic of sexually transmitted infections, including the AIDS virus. Admittedly, it is difficult to measure many sorts of private behavior, particularly behavior that is potentially awkward or embarrassing to report to others (Barringer, 1993; Lord, 1994). Given this caveat, one of our best sources for data on the sexual behavior of adult Americans is the *National Health and Social Life Survey* conducted in 1992. It contains responses obtained from interviews with a representative sample of over 3,000 men and women, ranging in age from 18 to 59 (Laumann et al., 1994). Among key findings of the survey:

- Married and cohabiting couples had the most sex. Forty percent of marrieds and 56 percent of cohabiting couples had intercourse twice a week or more, and they enjoyed their sex lives more than did singles who lived alone.

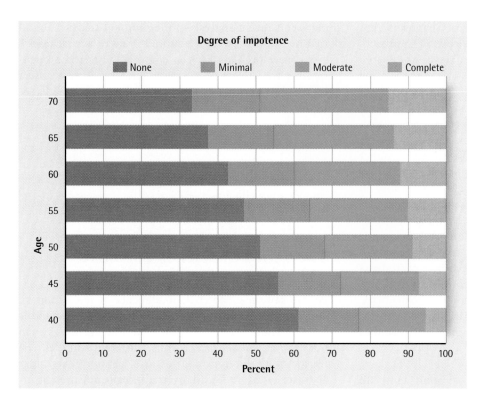

FIGURE 15.3 Aging and Impotence The figure shows the incidence of impotence, by age and degree, in a study carried out among men in Massachusetts who answered a series of questions about their sexual potency during the previous six months.
Source: From Lawrence K. Altman, "Study Suggests High Rate of Impotence: Half of Men over 40 May Have Problem," *The New York Times*, December 22, 1993. Copyright © 1993 by The New York Times Co. Reprinted with permission.

- Only 2.7 percent of men and 1.3 percent of women reported they had homosexual sex over the past year.
- Some 20 percent of men and 31 percent of women have had only one sex partner since age 18; 21 percent of men and 36 percent of women have had 2 to 4 sex partners; 23 percent of men and 20 percent of women have had 5 to 10 sex partners; 16 percent of men and 6 percent of women have had 10 to 20 partners; and 17 percent of men and 3 percent of women have had 21 or more partners.
- Extramarital sex is the exception, not the rule, among Americans. Nearly 75 percent of married men and 85 percent of married women say they have never been unfaithful.

Since the 1970s the media has moved sex from the private to the public arena. The "more liberated" career woman depicted in the media also introduced the necessity of competing and succeeding at a job on the basis of sex appeal and changing oneself to match the media image of beauty. The youngest group in the 1992 National Health and Social Life Survey seems to bear the brunt of society's confusion over changing sex roles and orientations, as women are more publicly protesting abuse in the home, sexual harassment or discrimination in the workplace, date rape, and other mistreatment of women. Yet powerful ads continue to erroneously portray men and women as preoccupied with a youthful appearance and sexual gratification (Laumann et al., 1994).

Question

What does research say in general about sexual frequency, sexual performance, and sexual health among middle-aged adults?

Cognitive Functioning

As noted earlier in this chapter, as people age, they change physically in several different ways. Some physical changes, such as graying hair and facial wrinkles, are obvious and can be quickly verified by a nearby mirror. But what about cognition? Are there parallel changes in aging adults' intellectual abilities as well? And if so how, and in what ways? Research studies designed to answer this question have yielded mixed results: yes, no, and it depends.

Research Findings: A Methodological Problem

Most of the data on age-related cognitive differences is based on IQ scores and have been tabulated using a *cross-sectional research* method. Results of studies that have employed the cross-sectional method indicate that overall composite IQ reaches a peak for most people when they are in their twenties, remains stable for a couple of decades, and then takes a dramatic downward drop (Schaie, 1994). Remember from Chapter 1 that cross-sectional studies employ the "snapshot" approach. Researchers administer tests of intelligence to a large group of individuals of different ages at about the same time and compare their performance. Consequently, a major weakness of cross-sectional studies is that "uncertainty regarding comparability" is always a problem. That is, we can never be sure that the reported age-related differences between subjects are not the product of other variables or events. For example, people in their fifties might have a lower average score than those in their twenties—not because of their age difference but because they might have less experience taking standardized tests. Also, many of today's midlife adults are completing college at this stage of life versus the post high school cohort that comprises higher numbers of students in college. Also, for decades American women were underrepresented in college, but now they are the majority. Moreover, women over age 40 make up over 60 percent of today's nontraditional college students with families (Peter, Horn, & Carroll, 2005).

As psychologists Schaie and Willis (1993) have pointed out, cross-sectional studies of adult aging do not allow for generational differences in performance on intelligence tests. Because of increasing educational opportunities and other social changes, successive generations of Americans perform at progressively higher levels. Hence, the measured intelligence (IQ) of the population is increasing. When comparing adults from different generations—80-year-olds with 40-year-olds, for instance—you are comparing people from vastly different environments. Thus, cross-sectional studies tend to confuse generational differences with differences associated with chronological age.

Using the *longitudinal research method,* researchers study the same individuals over a period of years, more like a case history. When this technique is used, the results are quite different: overall or global IQ tends to rise until the mid-fifties and then gradually decline. In fact, most adults do not experience a decline in general intelligence functioning in middle age and show little decline throughout their sixties, seventies, and even beyond. However, the longitudinal method also presents a problem for the researcher. Whereas the cross-sectional method tends to magnify or overestimate the decline in intelligence with age, the longitudinal method tends to minimize or underestimate it. One reason is that some people drop out of the study over time; the probability is higher that the eldest will die over the course of a 10-year study. Generally, the more able, healthy, and intelligent subjects remain in the study, and those who perform poorly on intelligence tests tend to be less available for longitudinal retesting. Consequently, the researchers are left with an increasingly smaller or biased sample as the subjects are retested at each later

period. A recent analysis of longitudinal analyses found that in adults between 18 and 60 years of age, at least 7 years were needed between cognitive tests to compensate for the effects of retesting (i.e., the positive effect of learning from the test itself) (Salthouse, Schroeder, & Ferrer, 2004).

> **Question**
>
> What are the problems with cross-sectional and longitudinal research on intelligence conducted with subjects over the life span?

The Varied Courses of Cognitive Abilities

As we saw in Chapter 7, intelligence is not a unitary concept in the same sense that a chemical compound is a single entity. People do not have intelligence as such but, rather, *intelligences.* Thus, different abilities can follow quite different courses as a person grows older (Neisser et al., 1996). Many traditional measures of intelligence focus on abilities that are useful in academic environments. For instance, tests that measure *verbal* abilities tend to show little or no decline after the age of 60, whereas those that measure *performance* do seem to show a decline (Schaie, 1989):

- *Verbal scores* are usually derived from tests in which people are asked to do something verbally, such as define a series of words, solve arithmetic story problems, or determine similarities between two objects.
- *Performance scores* are commonly based on people's ability to do something physically, such as assemble a puzzle or fill in symbols to correspond to numbers.

Fluid Versus Crystallized Intelligence   Some psychologists distinguish between **fluid intelligence** (the ability to make original adaptations in novel situations) and **crystallized intelligence** (the ability to reuse earlier adaptations on later occasions) (Cattell, 1943, 1971). Fluid intelligence (Horn, 1976) is generally tested by measuring an individual's facility in reasoning, often by means of figures and nonword materials (letter series, matrices, mazes, block designs, and picture arrangements). Presumably, fluid intelligence is "culture-free" and based on the individual's genetic and neurological structures. Crystallized intelligence is commonly measured by testing an individual's awareness of concepts and terms in vocabulary and general-information tests in areas such as science, mathematics, social studies, and English literature. Crystallized intelligence is acquired in the course of social experience. The scores on tests of crystallized intelligence are most influenced by formal education. Often crystallized intelligence increases with age, or at least it does not decline, whereas fluid intelligence declines with age in later life (Gilinsky & Judd, 1994).

In the earliest published account of the theory, Cattell (1943) argued that fluid ability is "a purely general ability to discriminate and perceive relations between any fundamentals, new or old." Fluid ability was hypothesized by Cattell to increase until adolescence and then slowly decline. Further, fluid intelligence was thought to be the cause of the general (g) factor found among ability tests administered to children and among the "speeded or adaptation-requiring" tests administered to adults. Crystallized intelligence, on the other hand, was thought to increase with age. The important psychological distinction in the theory was between process (fluid intelligence) and product (crystallized intelligence) (Cattell, 1963).

So, does intelligence really decline with age? When the data are gathered and examined within a framework of fluid versus crystallized intelligence, the answer is yes and no. It depends on how you define intelligence. In the *Seattle Longitudinal Study*, which tested the mental abilities of more than 5,000 adults over a period of 35 years, results clearly showed no uniform patterns of age-related changes across all intellectual abilities (Schaie, 1994). The majority of participants showed no statistically significant reduction in most abilities until after age 60, and then only in certain abilities. The only tests on which ability declined with age were related to speed of performance. It was found that fluid intelligence tended to decrease in young adulthood, but these deficits were offset by crystallized abilities, which remained stable or increased into middle age, followed by slight declines (Schaie, 1996). Older students returning to college often do very well academically because of their crystallized intelligence—translating theory into practice using their life experiences (see the *Human Diversity* box on page 538, "Strategies for Midlife College Students"). The Seattle Longitudinal Study was expanded to investigate influences such as cognitive styles, personality traits, lifestyles, and family environments on cognitive aging (Schaie et al., 2004).

Maximizing Cognitive Abilities

Until recently, exceptional performance among healthy adults had not been extensively studied by researchers. However, in the last several years, interest in exceptional achievement and performance has proliferated (Gardner, 1993a, 2000a; Schultz & Heckhausen, 1996). Differing approaches are being employed to explore the behavior of expert performers. One approach is to study the individual characteristics of exceptional performers. This approach is being spearheaded by Howard Gardner (1993b), whose work on multiple intelligences was discussed earlier in Chapter 7. Gardner contends that the importance of multiple intelligences does not decline as a person ages, but merely that these intelligences are more internalized and less visible (Gardner, 1999). Gardner proposes that exceptional performance in later life is dependent on early identification of talent and nurturing of that talent by providing the individual with task-related practice over long periods of time (Gardner, 1993a). Much of Gardner's research findings are based on advances in brain physiology and achievements of savants, prodigies, and geniuses in specific domains. The important aspect of talent, according to Gardner (1983), is not the innate ability of the individual, but rather the capacity to learn material relevant to one of the nine intelligences. Gardner believes that innate intellectual abilities, in order to persist throughout life, must be exercised or practiced regularly and over long periods of time.

Maintaining Expert Performance   Most elite or expert performers in most domains are engaged in their domain of expertise essentially full-time from childhood to late adulthood. For example, millions of people are active in sports, music, visual arts, and chess, but only a small number reach the highest levels of performance—these are distinguished by the length of time and duration they commit to practicing their skill.

Performers rarely reach their optimal performance before adulthood, but it has been found that performance does not necessarily continue to improve in those who keep exercising their skills across the life span. Rather, as Leman (1953) first noted, peak ages for performance seem to fall in the twenties, thirties, and forties. In vigorous sports, such as professional basketball, it is rare for elite athletes above age 30 to reach their personal best. Michael Jordan, Cal Ripkin, and Mark McGuire are noted exceptions to this rule. Similar age distributions, centered around age 30, are also found for fine-motor skills and some cognitive activities (Simonton, 1988). Typically the probability of producing an outstanding work declines with age. However, in novel writing, history, and philosophy the optimal ages are in the forties and fifties. One common hypothesis on aging and expertise is that experts generally age more slowly than other performers. Recent research on expert performance has shown this not to be the case in chess (Charness & Gerchak, 1996), typing (Bosman, 1993), and music (Krampe, 1994). The superior performance of older experts is found to be restricted to relevant tasks in their preferred domains of expertise.

The Role of Deliberate Practice   The most marked age-related decline is generally observed in perceptual-motor

Human Diversity

Strategies for Midlife College Students

Preparation and planning are half the battle of being a successful college student. Midlife students might save some time, money, and frustration when pursuing a college education if they will read the following suggestions, which are based on years of professionally counseling and advising nontraditional college students:

Investigate Your Career Options

Do you need to complete a degree, or is there a one-year certificate program that will prepare you for the job market or launch you into a new career? Have you taken a career interest inventory to see if your interests match those of people who are currently working in a specific field?

Visit the College's Career Placement Office

Start here first. This is a valuable college resource, but most students don't make use of its resources until graduation. This office has your chosen career's employment statistics and employment outlook. Will there be jobs in your locale in a few years? Is your area flooded with certain profession-

als? When there is a surplus of workers for a field, starting salaries are low and it is difficult to secure a job. Are you willing to move to a new locale? This office has data from professional organizations in your field. Look at the "bigger picture" of national or international trends. Is this job being outsourced or taken over by computers? You might need to reevaluate your plans or plan a dual major. This office has annual statistics on job placement of graduates in academic departments. How many transferred for advanced degrees or became employed after graduation? Check with a Chamber of Commerce for employment data, too.

Make an Appointment with Someone Working in Your Field of Choice

Find out how a successful person in the field managed the educational path. Will you need an associate's degree (two years), a bachelor's degree (four years), or graduate school training? Plan ahead to reach your goal. Is there an internship or field experience required for entrance into this field? Is it a paid or volunteer experience? Actual work experience makes a person more competitive when job hunting the next time around. Does this career require passing a state certification exam before you can be hired for a job?

Minimize the Financial Strain of Career Preparation

There are Web sites, books, and consultants that will help you find sources of grants and scholarships (money you do not have to pay back) and loans (money to be paid back in the future). Start with the financial aid office at the college. Funding is available if you take the time to search. Private colleges offer grants, scholarships, or work-study monies if you meet the criteria. Just ask! Funding is available for minorities (women included here), those with disabilities, retraining, and so forth. Do the organizations you are currently affiliated with offer any scholarships? If you are retraining in the same career area, ask if there is a subsidy. Adopt the philosophy "Where there's a will, there's a way!"

Have Your Eyes Checked

You are going to use your eyes for extensive reading, watching videos, reading information on the board, peering through microscopes, and reading from computer screens.

Begin or Maintain a Regular Exercise Regimen

Top researchers on aging and the brain have discovered that "there's a simple way to ward off slowness, stay in shape"

Midlife Learners Over the past two decades, American women made great progress in gaining access to and completing postsecondary education. Among all undergraduates enrolled since 1990, women have made up more than 60 percent of students age 40 or older each year. The majority are single parents, working part-time, and likely to have dependent children.

(Jaret, 1996). With no exercise and a sedentary lifestyle, neurons get less nourishment and can't move electrical impulses as fast—the mind slows, leading to memory problems. Exercise energizes! As an American college student, you can take physical education classes or at least utilize the fitness center on campus that you have paid to use when you paid your tuition. Many fitness centers and P.E. departments offer swimming classes, line dancing, Tai Chi, low-impact aerobics, ballroom dancing, and similar activities. By committing to this exercise regimen as part of your college schedule, you are more likely to stick with it! Hot line for exercisers—American Council on Exercise: 1-800-825-3636. Here you can get help with choosing a program that suits your lifestyle and level of fitness.

Be Aware of the Role of Previous Experience and Expertise

Start with courses on subjects you have some familiarity with. Jumping into courses or full programs in subjects in which you have no background can be overwhelming—not that it can't be done. Scenario: Suppose you are an interior decorator and you have decided to become an engineer. Start with some liberal arts courses to experience some success, then start taking on engineering courses. If you have been technically oriented for the past 25 years, the opposite is true. Start with a course similar to your background training, such as a formal computer course or a drafting or design course. Then work your way into the liberal arts arena.

Get Organized

Make your transition in over a period of time, if possible. Do not take on too much too soon. Become familiar with the physical campus territory as well as the academic program and the requirements outlined in the college catalog. Make an appointment with the chairperson of your department to find out if you are on the right track and in the right degree program. Be sure to sign up for prerequisite courses first (e.g., take general psychology before taking developmental psychology). Organize and save all official paperwork in one place.

Save Your College Catalog and Transcripts

Be sure to get and keep your own copy of the college catalog. It is your contract with the college for your degree program. You might need to show course descriptions and degree requirements to someone at the next college you attend or to state certification personnel. Hint: Most colleges have a disclaimer statement in the catalog stating that you, the student, are responsible for following the degree plan printed in the catalog.

Get Connected with Other Middle-Aged Adult Learners

Is there a group or club on campus for adult students? If not, start one with the midlife students in your classes. Social support has been proven to promote mental, physical, and emotional health. You will also give each other important advice. Many adults who have come from the work world are used to feeling connected to a network of support.

Find Out About Distance Learning Classes

If you have a minimal amount of time to take courses, are a disciplined and dedicated student, or if you are commuting a great distance to take classes, you might be able to sign up for classes you can take using a home computer, saving both time and money! Check with your campus registrar.

Learn to Use a Computer—This Is Essential

Most colleges have minicourses on computer operating systems, software programs, or using e-mail and the Internet. Credit courses can teach you how to use the computer to do spreadsheets, word processing, database, art, Internet, and other information retrieval.

Do Not Focus on Short-Term Losses—Look at the Bigger Picture of Where You Are Going

Don't let a low grade on a quiz or test get you down. As with any new venture, there are peaks and valleys. If you are having difficulty, sign up in your learning assistance center for a free tutor (a student who can help you through the "bumps in the road"). None of us excel at everything. Adult learners tend to be very hard on themselves and tend to expect all A's. Relax a little. If you tend to be an auditory learner and like working in small groups, set up a discussion group with other students in a class before major exams. Use your text, class notes, and the study guide that accompanies your text if you are a visual learner. Ask the instructor for a copy of an old exam so you can benefit from the practice effect.

---

performance as displayed in different sports. High levels of practice are necessary to attain the physical readiness found in mature performers, and the effects of practice appear to be particularly large when intense practice overlaps with physical development during childhood and adolescence. Most of these adaptations require that practice be maintained. When older master athletes are compared with young athletes at a similar level, many physiological measurements do not differ between them. However, at least some physiological functions, such as maximum heart rate, show an age-related decline independent of past or current practice. The ability to retain superior performance in some domains appears to depend critically on maintaining practice during adulthood and into old age (Ericsson, 2000).

Evidence on the role of early and maintained practice in retaining cognitive aspects of expertise is much less extensive. Some abilities, such as the acquisition of a second language, especially accents and pronunciation, appear easier to acquire at young rather than adult ages. Expert performance continues to improve well into adult years, typically reaching its peak between the ages of 30 and 50 (Ericsson, 2000).

The traditional view of talent, which concludes that successful individuals have special innate abilities and basic capacities, is not consistent with the reviewed evidence. Efforts to specify and measure characteristics of talent that allow early identification and successful prediction of adult performance have failed. Differences between expert and less-accomplished performers reflect acquired knowledge and skills or physiological adaptations developed through training (Ericsson & Charness, 1994). Consequently, there is no reason to believe that developed expertise in human performance is limited to traditional domains, such as sports. Through systematic practice and training, similar changes can be expected in several everyday activities, such as thinking, problem solving, and communication (Jaret, 1996). What it takes is desire, practice, and commitment, whether in a sport, such as tennis, or in an academic pursuit, such as taking a human development course in a college continuing education program. A successful life course is achieved when adults continue to stay both physically and mentally active (Schwarz & Knaeuper, 2000).

Cognition and Dialectical Thinking

If we look at cognition instead of intelligence, we see that a slightly different debate has emerged over the years concerning the existence of post-formal operations. Recall that Piaget maintained that cognitive development stops around the age of 15 with what he called formal operations, the ability to perform abstract reasoning. Critics assert that the thought processes of adults are qualitatively different from the logical problem-solving characteristics upon which Piaget focused. These post-formal operations let adults enter the realm of dialectical thought, which does not insist on a single correct answer to any given problem or dilemma, instead searching for complex and changing understandings of the processes or elements involved in the problem.

One proponent of **dialectical thinking** sums it up this way: Dialectical thinking is an organized approach to analyzing and making sense of the world one experiences that differs fundamentally from formal analysis. The latter involves the effort to find fundamental fixed realities—basic elements and immutable laws; the former

attempts to describe the fundamental process of change and the dynamic relationship through which the change occurs (Basseches, 1980). An example of post-formal thought would be the understanding that a family quarrel might be nobody's "fault" and that the solution does not involve one of the parties "giving in" or changing their view of the situation. Instead, the dialectical approach consists of understanding the merits of different or opposing points of view and looks at the possibility of integrating them into a workable solution. This dialectical approach to problem solving is apparent when you think of situations where you have been on both sides of the same issue—for example being a child arguing with your parents, and then being a parent arguing with your child. One reason why post-formal operations are attributed to older individuals is that life experience is probably necessary to see the "bigger" picture. Schaie has proposed a four-stage model of cognitive development that is quite different from Piaget's in that it covers the entire life span and is not confined to preadulthood. Schaie's (1994) four stages are as follows:

1. *Acquisitive stage.* What should I know? (childhood-adolescence)
2. *Achieving stage.* How should I use what I know in career and love? (young adult)
3. *Responsible/executive stage.* How should I use my knowledge in social and family responsibilities? (middle adulthood)
4. *Reintegrative stage.* What should I know? (old age)

Even though the questions in Stages 1 and 4 are worded the same, in Stage 4 the acquisition of information is guided by one's interests, attitudes, and values. An older adult is willing to expend effort on a problem she or he faces in everyday life.

This interest in problem solving might shed light on another aspect of cognition—creativity. J. P. Guilford (1967) distinguished two sorts of thinking—convergent and divergent. **Convergent thinking** is very much like formal operations—the application of logic and reasoning to arrive at a single correct answer to a problem. **Divergent thinking** is more open-ended, and multiple solutions are sought, examined, and probed, thereby leading to what are deemed creative responses on measures of creativity. Creativity goes beyond problem solving and penetrates into problem generation. A creative person not only solves problems but sees problems of which others are not yet even aware. Creativity seems to demand imagination, motivation, and a supportive environment—characteristics that probably do not gel for the individual until middle adulthood. This might explain why it is during middle adulthood that the peak period of creative productivity occurs (Kastenbaum, 1993; Schultz & Salthouse, 1999). The major problem with assessing creativity is the difficulty in defining cri-

Middle Age and Divergent Thinking Divergent thinking leads to creative responses, which demand imagination, motivation, and a supportive environment. Middle adulthood is considered the peak period of creative productivity. Creative experience is described as the "flow," where people become absorbed in an activity.

teria that capture creativity as well as originality, utility, and productivity (Aiken, 1998). The history of science and art indicates that Michelangelo, Verdi, Goethe, Picasso, and Monet created highly original work throughout the life span. From a psychological perspective, creativity results in flow: "the state in which people are so involved in an activity that nothing else seems to matter: the experience itself is so enjoyable that people will do it at great cost, for the sheer sake of doing it" (Csikszentmihalyi, 1993). During such "flow" experiences, people become so absorbed in an activity they disregard distracting concerns such as matters of the self, material gain, security, or personal advancement. Think of artists slaving away day and night, going without food or sleep in order to finish a masterpiece. It is almost as if they are possessed by the activity, unable to see beyond or outside of it.

Question
How can middle-age adults maximize cognitive abilities?

Moral Commitments

Moral development in certain individuals leads to something akin to flow, in that they become committed to doing "good" activities to the extent that, like saints, they have "dedicated the totality of their psychic energy into an all-encompassing goal [which they] follow unto death" (Csikszentmihalyi, 1997). Recently, two of Lawrence Kohlberg's colleagues set out to find individuals dedicated to acts of morality who they designated as **moral exemplars** (Colby & Damon, 1992).

After an extensive search throughout the United States, they found 23 people who demonstrated all of the following characteristics:

- A sustained commitment to moral ideals that include respect for humanity
- Consistency between ideals and actions
- A willingness to risk one's self-interest for the sake of one's moral values
- Being an inspirational force for others, who then became active in moral work
- Humility about one's work and importance, unconcerned with ego

Most of the moral exemplars were in their forties, fifties, and sixties, and they were a diverse collection of individuals. Five of the exemplars were chosen to be interviewed in depth to discover what makes a moral exemplar "tick." Of the five:

- Two did not finish high school, one had a bit of college, one finished college, and one had a Ph.D.
- All were religious.
- Politically they were conservative (1), moderate (2), and liberal (2).
- Vocationally there were a minister, a businessperson, an innkeeper, a civil rights advocate, and a charity worker.

While interviewing these exemplars, Colby and Damon found that they showed enormous ability to critically examine old habits and assumptions and adopt new strategies for dealing with problems, and they constantly took up new and interesting challenges—while maintaining a lasting dedication to their particular values, goals, and moral projects. This amounted to the ability to remain morally stable without becoming cognitively or behaviorally stagnant. Reverend Charleszetta Waddles is one of the exemplars, and through her activities you can get a hint of how moral acts affect people on a day-to-day basis.

Mother Waddles, as she liked to be called, ran the Perpetual Mission for Saving Souls of All Nations in Detroit. The mission serves 100,000 people a year by offering food, clothing, legal services, tutoring, and emergency assistance among other services. Her ultimate goals were to lift the poor out of their condition, help them believe in themselves, and encourage them to take full responsibility for their lives. She did whatever was in her power to help anyone who came to her mission—be it a woman who needed money for an eye operation, a young girl who needed advice about her pregnancy, or a man who lost everything in a fire and had no place to go. Oftentimes she used most of her $900 monthly income to pay for these services herself when she was unable to find resources elsewhere. Mother Waddles, with an eighth-grade education, ran her mission for 30 years and during that time she raised ten children (Colby & Damon, 1992). Mother Waddles died in 2001 at age 88, but her Perpetual Mission continues.

Based on Mother Waddles and other exemplars' experiences, Colby and Damon (1992) have suggested that it is moral commitment that develops in adulthood—as opposed to moral cognition, as might be expected from looking at Kohlberg's thesis. Interestingly enough, Colby and Damon found that most of the exemplars were between the third and fourth stages in Kohlberg's model of moral development (see Chapter 9). In essence, the development of moral commitment results when adults are socially influenced to transform their personal goals, especially when they have a "sense of continued openness to change and growth, an openness that is not the usual expectation in most adult lives" (Colby & Damon, 1992). This capacity to change while keeping a sense of personal stability harks back to the dialectical approach to cognition. It seems that adults have an easier time, perhaps owing to life experience, being able to engage in the dialectical thinking that allows personal aspirations and social needs to inform each other. We will see in Chapter 19 that often the impetus for this dialogue between the self and "other" comes from religious affiliations.

SEGUE

Significantly, today's baby boomers are looking, acting, and feeling younger at middle age than did prior generations. Indeed, the defining characteristics of middle age are starting later and lasting longer, so that age 50 has taken on the connotations that age 40 had only a few decades ago. T-shirts proclaim "50 Never Looked So Good!" Many prominent persons over age 50 continue to lead, inform, or entertain, such as President George W. Bush, Diane Sawyer, Barbara Walters, Tina Turner, Meryl Streep, Susan Sarandon, Dan Rather, Harrison Ford, Al Pacino, Jack Nicholson, and the Rolling Stones. Midlife baby boomers are actively revolutionizing cultural attitudes toward how the "middle-aged" are viewed—not unlike how this generation of Americans initiated sweeping social, political, and cultural changes in the 1960s. In Chapter 16 we will examine the changing self-concept of adults in midlife, who are often reevaluating intimate relationships, reestablishing life priorities, becoming grandparents, shifting occupational ventures, or preparing for retirement.

Summary

Defining (or Defying) Middle Age

1. The boundaries for the age range of midlife have become more fluid in contrast to a century ago. In 1900 Americans could expect to live to about age 47, whereas today Americans can expect to live until their late seventies. Some developmentalists suggest that middle age may range from one's early forties through late sixties.

2. By midlife, the body's organs and systems are functioning less efficiently than they did in early adulthood, although the decline is gradual.

Sensory and Physical Changes

3. The human body, after functioning for a number of decades, tends to work less efficiently than it did when it was "new." Seventy-five million Americans over age 40 are experiencing presbyopia, a normal condition in which the lens of the eye starts to harden, losing its ability to accommodate as quickly as it did in youth. Other symptoms of ocular "wear and tear" include glaucoma, cataracts, floaters, dry eye, and macular degeneration.

4. By age 50 about one in every three men and one in every four women have difficulty understanding a whisper. However, only a small number of the age-50 population can be deemed to have substantial hearing problems.

5. By the forties, one may notice a gradual drop in the ability to taste because taste buds are replaced at a slower rate, affecting the sense of taste. Half of those who reach the age of 65 are predicted to have a noticeable loss of the sense of smell.

6. The appearance of aging men and women in American society is part of the so-called double standard of aging. As many men age, they are considered "mature" or "sophisticated" or even more attractive than when they were younger. However, this is not the case for middle-aged women, who are likely to seek beauty treatments to make them look more youthful, such as massage, Botox treatments, or cosmetic surgeries. Some middle-aged men, especially those in the media and in "power" positions are also using these services.

7. One of the major concerns of some midlife adults is body composition, or proportion of muscle to fat. Muscle mass declines an average of 5 to 10 percent each decade, generally resulting in more body fat. Although obesity is associated with several health risks, so is low body weight. Thin people, who are likely to be malnourished, are also more susceptible to diseases, such as osteoporosis, anemia, and infections.

8. The hormone HGH (human growth hormone), which was developed to treat children afflicted with dwarfism,

has become a trendy antiaging potion. Physicians administering hormones are called "antiaging" specialists. The baby-boomer generation is challenging all aspects of natural aging, and people in their fifties and sixties typically look and act much younger than in past generations.

9. Menopause is one of the most readily identifiable signs of the climacteric, characterized by changes in the ovaries and in the various biochemical processes associated with these changes. Probably the most significant change is the profound drop in the production of the female hormones (particularly estrogen) by the ovaries. The average age at complete cessation of menses ranges between 45 and 55 years in Western countries. There are three stages of this process, which typically takes a few years: perimenopause, menopause, and postmenopause. About 4 percent of women experience premature menopause. Contrary to popular myth, many menopausal women neither have extreme symptoms nor lose their desire for sex. Hormone replacement therapy (HRT) is a medical regimen to ease symptoms of menopause that is being carefully researched in longitudinal studies. Alternative medical approaches, such as eating more foods with soy and calcium, exercising regularly, getting adequate sleep, and using stress-reduction exercises are recommended.

10. Reproduction after menopause is now possible by using hormone injections, donated ova, sperm from a partner or donor, and in vitro fertilization procedures. Creating babies at the middle stage of life has become a biomedical controversy.

11. By age 40, 10 percent of males experience enlargement of the prostate gland, and by age 60, a majority of males are likely to experience prostate problems, such as a decreasing force to the urinary stream, more frequent urgency to urinate, yet more difficulty in urinating (often interfering with sleep needs). A middle-aged male should have regular physical checkups, and the physician should conduct a digital exam and a PSA test for diagnostic purposes. In questionable cases, other imaging techniques and biopsy might be conducted. Prostate cancer is the most common malignant cancer in North American males, and with early detection and treatment, males are likely to live many more years.

12. Cultural stereotypes have frequently depicted men in their forties and fifties as suddenly undergoing a "midlife crisis," leaving their wives for women young enough to be their daughters, quitting their jobs for an entirely different lifestyle, or beginning drinking to excess. Their difficulties are commonly attributed to a "male menopause." Although some psychologists and sociologists typically dismiss notions of a male menopause, other developmentalists suggest that middle-age males do undergo gradual testosterone changes that may cause loss of strength and endurance and higher incidence of depression, obesity, fatigue, sexual dysfunction or impotence, alcohol problems, or actual physical ailments. Men's responses to middle-age changes are varied.

Health Changes

13. Millions of Americans have disabilities ranging from arthritis, diabetes, and emphysema, to mental disorders.

However, people can maximize their chances for leading healthy and long lives by altering their lifestyles to include a variety of health-conscious practices, such as exercising regularly, eating a healthy diet, getting adequate sleep, stopping smoking, reducing stress, drinking in moderation, and practicing healthy social habits.

14. Several risk factors are associated with cardiovascular (heart and blood vessel) fitness or lack of fitness. Heart disease is one of the leading causes of death. Risk factors include high blood pressure (hypertension), smoking, high cholesterol, a family history of heart disease, being male, being diabetic, or being obese. After menopause, women are likely to have high blood pressure at the same rate as men.

15. For women between the ages of 40 and 60, breast cancer is the leading cause of death. Ovarian and cervical cancers are also more prevalent during midlife. Colon cancer and lung cancer are also leading causes of death for midlife males and females. Smoking, environmental factors, poverty, and hereditary factors are associated with a higher risk of cancer.

16. A stroke, or "brain attack," occurs when blood circulation to the brain fails. Brain cells can die from decreased blood flow and the resulting lack of oxygen. Both blockage and bleeding can be involved. Stroke is the third leading killer of Americans and is the most common cause of disability. Each year more than 500,000 Americans have a stroke, with about 160,000 dying. Strokes occur in all age groups, in both sexes, and in all races of every country. Alzheimer's disease, a severe form of memory loss and dementia, is more likely to show up after age 65.

17. Women are much more likely than men to become infected by an HIV-positive heterosexual partner, and the rate of middle-aged women becoming HIV-positive is on the rise.

18. Major life changes are likely to occur in middle age, including loss of friends and loved ones. Consequently, depression and substance abuse are common but are often underrecognized and undertreated in middle-aged adults. Depression in older life is associated with increased mortality (or suicide), even after controlling for physical illness and disability.

19. Far too many older people accept social stereotypes of themselves as sexless; they become victims of the myth. Believing that they will lose their sexual effectiveness becomes a self-fulfilling prophecy, and some older people do lose their desire for sexual activity even though their bodies have not lost the capacity for sex. The baby-boom generation is likely to change this myth. Married and cohabiting couples have the highest frequency of sex.

Cognitive Functioning

20. Tests that measure verbal abilities tend to show little or no decline after the age of 60, whereas those that measure performance do show a decline. Most of the data on cognitive functioning in middle age have come from cross-sectional research studies that do not allow for generational differences in IQ scores, showing IQ scores lowering with advancing age. Results of longitudinal research studies find that overall IQ tends to rise until the mid-fifties and then gradually decline.

21. Psychologists distinguish between fluid intelligence (the ability to make original adaptations in novel situations) and crystallized intelligence (the ability to reuse earlier adaptations on later occasions). A debate has emerged over the years concerning the existence of post-formal operations, contrary to Piaget's model of cognitive development over the life course.

22. Midlife adults can maximize their cognitive abilities by practicing them regularly over time. Even experts must be committed to practice in their domains of expertise. Schaie proposed a model of cognitive development over the life span that includes the acquisitive stage, the achieving stage, the responsible/executive stage, and the reintegrative stage. Guilford distinguishes between convergent thinking (using standard logic and reasoning) and divergent thinking (creative). Further, middle adulthood is considered the peak time of creative thinking.

23. Some people in their forties, fifties, and sixties have been identified as moral exemplars; that is, they consistently demonstrate sustained commitment to moral ideals that include respect for humanity and doing good for others.

Key Terms

alpha hydroxy (516)

audiology testing (514)

basal-cell carcinoma (515)

calcitonin (518)

cardiovascular (525)

cataracts (512)

cholesterol (528)

climacteric (519)

convergent thinking (540)

crystallized intelligence (536)

DHEA (dehydroepiandrosterone) (519)

dialectical thinking (540)

diastolic pressure (528)

diuretics (518)

divergent thinking (540)

dry eye (513)

endocrinologist (519)

floaters (513)

fluid intelligence (536)

glaucoma (512)

hormone replacement therapy (HRT) (520)

human growth hormone (HGH) (519)

hypertension (528)

hypothyroidism (519)

hysterectomy (520)

impotence (523)

in vitro fertilization (521)

macular degeneration (AMD) (513)

melanoma (515)

menopause (519)

moral exemplars (541)

osteoporosis (518)

perimenopause (520)

periodontal disease (515)

postmenopause (520)

premature menopause (520)

presbycusis (514)

presbyopia (512)

prostate gland (522)

prostatitis (522)

PSA test (522)

rheumatoid arthritis (518)

stroke (530)

systolic pressure (528)

testosterone (522)

Following Up on the Internet

Web sites for this chapter focus on physical and health changes, cognitive functioning, and moral commitments common to those in middle adulthood. Please access the text Web site at www.mhhe.com/vzcrandell8 for up-to-date hot-linked Internet addresses for the following organizations, topics, and resources:

Office of Men's Health

Office of Women's Health

Early Menopause

North American Menopause Society

Dr. Susan Love's Site on Breast Cancer

National Institute on Aging

Senior Health

AARP Policy and Research

International Federation on Aging

Video Scenario—http://www.mhhe.com/vzcrandell8

In this chapter, you've just read about health changes, cognitive functioning, and moral commitment associated with middle adulthood. Using the OLC (www.mhhe.com/vzcrandell8), watch the *Middle Adulthood video scenario* to see how these concepts, such as menopause, empty nest syndrome, and male midlife development, come to life as Lisa and Lewis respond to changes in their own lives. This scenario also introduces some key concepts regarding job satisfaction and Erikson's stage of generativity vs. stagnation that you'll explore in the next chapter, Middle Adulthood: Emotional and Social Development.

Middle Adulthood
Emotional and Social Development

Critical Thinking Questions

1. Suppose that each stage of a person's life could be defined in terms of a consuming purpose. For instance, suppose that the child's purpose is to play, the adolescent's purpose is to explore, and the young adult's purpose is to settle. What would the middle-aged adult's consuming purpose be?

2. What would you think if your 55-year-old doctor had her or his tongue pierced? Would you judge this person to be acting immaturely?

3. Who do you think is happier in midlife—people who are married with a job and now raising grandchildren, or people who remained single and have the resources and time to do whatever they desire? Why?

4. Suppose that pay were inversely related to job popularity. Would you collect garbage for $150,000 a year or be a surgeon for $47,000 a year? When thinking of a career in this way, what would motivate you more—economic security or job satisfaction?

Outline

Transition and adaptation are central features in middle adulthood, as they are in other phases of life. Midlife is a time of looking back and at the same time looking forward. Some of the changing aspects of middle age are associated with the family life cycle (see Chapter 14). Many, but not all, parents at midlife today enter the "empty nest" period of life. Some couples at midlife are just beginning their families and are raising young children.

Others are caring for both growing children or grandchildren and elderly parents, and we refer to these as the "sandwich generation." There have also been changes in the workplace. Because of advances in technology and international competition, job obsolescence confronts many blue-collar workers, and studies find this has had a particularly negative economic impact on African American and Hispanic American adults in midlife. Most midlife adults in white-collar and professional occupations are reaching the upper limits of their careers and realizing that they now must settle for lateral occupational shifts. Others at midlife must find new inner resources to deal with unemployment, early retirement, declining health, loss of a spouse—or for a majority a loss of parents. In this chapter we examine the changing emotional-social context of middle adulthood from individual, social, occupational, and cultural perspectives.

Theories of the Self in Transition

Traditionally, developmental psychologists have focused their attention on the many changes that occur during infancy, childhood, and adolescence. Presently, middle age is garnering a great deal of research attention because the huge baby-boom generation has entered middle age and is commanding many resources from, and is in turn changing, society (Lachman, 2004). Underlying most of their research focus, however, is the notion that each individual has a relatively unique and enduring set of psychological tendencies and reveals them in the course of interacting with others and the environment. Only more recently has middle adulthood been examined to determine how and in what ways adults continue to develop and mature (Brim, 1992). Much of the available research on the midlife experience typically focused on physical and intellectual changes in the white middle-class population, was limited by its use of cross-sectional data, and focused on clinical populations (those who were having physical or mental health problems). Until more recently, only a few studies centered on emotional and social development of a diversity of adults in midlife, often identified as 45 to 65 years old (Lachman, 2004). With the increase in longevity in the United States, other European nations, and Japan, many of the events that used to occur in old age (e.g., grandparenthood, retirement) now occur during midlife.

> Now in their fifties, many American men and women are confronted with the fact that there are time limits to their lives. A powerful reminder is the symbolic meaning attached to the number 50. In terms of the life span, age 50 is roughly two-thirds of the way through life, but because 50 marks a half century, the 50th birthday carries a strong symbolic connotation that many men and women see as marking their entry into the "last half of life." . . . They begin counting the number of birthdays left to them rather than how many they have reached. So the fifties become a time for more introspective reflection and stock taking. (Sheehy, 1998)

Significantly, in recent years a life-span perspective of development has emerged that views middle adulthood as a period of both continuity and transition in which individuals must adapt to new life situations and make a variety of role transitions—in the family, at work, in the community, and so on. Recent cross-cultural and gender development research shows that there are multiple paths that individuals take during this transitional time before late adulthood (Lachman, 2004; Plaut, Markus, & Lachman, 2002). That is why it is more common today to see two 48-year-olds who are at different phases of their life cycle—one a first-time parent and the other a grandparent or one launching a new career and the other retired. Consequently, Helson (1997, p. 23) says that "middle age has different meanings in different times and places for different individuals." With this recent perspective in mind, we examine some research that is multidisciplinary, some that address midlife from a gender perspective, and some that look at the issues of midlife for adults in other cultures. Interestingly enough, we also learn from recent findings that adults in some societies experience neither a "middle adulthood" stage nor a "midlife crisis" (Lachman & James, 1997).

Maturity and Self-Concept

Most personality theorists emphasize the importance of maturity to individuals as they move through life. **Maturity** is our capacity to undergo continual change to adapt successfully and cope flexibly with the demands and responsibilities of life. Maturity is not some sort of plateau or final state but a lifetime process of becoming (Waterman, 1993). It is a never-ending search for a meaningful and comfortable fit between ourselves and the world—a struggle to "get it all together." Gordon W. Allport (1961, p. 307) identifies six criteria that psychologists commonly employ for assessing individual personalities:

> The mature personality will have a widely extended sense of self; be able to relate warmly to others in both intimate and nonintimate contacts; possess a fundamental emotional security and accept himself [sic]; perceive, think, and act with zest in accordance with outer reality; be capable of self-objectification, of insight and humor; and live in harmony with a unifying philosophy of life.

Underlying these elements of the mature personality is a positive self-concept (Hattie, 1992; Ross, 1992). **Self-concept** is the view we have of ourselves through time as "the real me" or "I myself as I really am." Self-concept has considerable impact on behavior (Dunning & Cohen, 1992; Greenberg et al., 1992). Indeed, much of our significant behavior can be understood as an attempt to approach or avoid various of our "possible selves" (Cross & Markus, 1991). For instance, a middle-aged man whose feared self includes being a heart attack victim, and who worries about how to avoid becoming that self, might undertake an exercise and diet regimen. The human ability to preserve, enhance, promote, defend, and revise notions about the self (our self-schemas) helps us to explain how older people, experiencing the frailties of advancing age, nonetheless function so well, especially on the subjective level. It seems that aging people do not simply react to aging processes but instead make cognitive shifts and behavioral adjustments that preserve their mental health and behavioral functioning despite their losses (Heidrich & Ryff, 1993).

Mounting evidence suggests that sad people and happy people are each biased in their basic perceptions of themselves and the world (Baumgardner, 1990).

People bring to the world somewhat different cognitive templates or filters through which they view their experiences (Feist et al., 1995). And the way they structure their experiences determines their mood and behavior. If we see things as negative, we are likely to feel and act depressed. If we see things as positive, we are likely to feel and act happy. That is why some view middle age as a time of feeling secure and settled, whereas others view it as a time of being bored or in a rut (Helson, 1997; Lachman, 2004). Such perceptions tend to reinforce and even intensify people's feelings about their self-worth and their adequacy in the larger world. It is how individuals take the idea of self and interact in social situations that interest the theorists we will next encounter.

Stage Models

Erikson posits that the midlife years are devoted to resolving the "crisis" of **generativity versus stagnation.** Erikson (1968b, p. 267) views **generativity** as "primarily the concern in establishing and guiding the next generation." Adults express generativity through nurturing, teaching, mentoring, and leading—by promoting the overall interests of the next generation while contributing to the world of politics, art, culture, and community. As a group, they seek to benefit the larger society and facilitate its continuity across generations. To do otherwise is to become self-centered and to turn inward, resulting in "psychological invalidism," which leads to rejectivity and the unwillingness to care for others. McAdams and de St. Aubin (1992) also see generativity as springing from two deeply rooted desires: the communal need to be nurturant and the personal desire to do something or be something that transcends death. You will recognize the two poles of this particular crisis in stereotypical portrayals of adults. The generative teacher thinks of each pupil as "one of my own children" and tries to generate a love of life in each of the students. The individual

whose resolution is weighted toward stagnation is usually depicted as a "humbug" sort, Scrooge being probably the best-known example. Stories that show an "old grump" turning into an avuncular, caring person depict the transition from stagnation to generativity.

Erikson's "crisis" view has been criticized by others, such as Costa and McCrae (1980). In their studies they find no evidence that psychological disturbance is any more common during midlife than during other periods of life. Other critics of this normative stage approach say midlife is more accurately characterized as a time of productivity and altruism, not a time of turmoil.

Various psychologists have elaborated on Erikson's formulations. Robert C. Peck (1968) has taken a closer look at midlife and suggests that it is useful to identify more precisely the tasks confronting midlife individuals. Peck defines these four tasks:

- *Valuing wisdom versus valuing physical powers.* As we saw in Chapter 15, when individuals progress through middle age, they experience a decline in their physical strength. Even more importantly, in a culture that emphasizes looking youthful, people lose much of their edge in physical attractiveness. But they also enjoy new advantages. The sheer experience of longer living brings with it an increase in accumulated knowledge and greater powers of judgment. Rather than relying primarily on their "hands" and physical capabilities, they must now more often employ their maturity and wisdom in coping with life. In Japanese and Chinese cultures this is definitely the case, and it is not uncommon for well-respected public officials to be in their seventies and eighties.
- *Socializing versus sexualizing in human relationships.* Allied to midlife physical decline, although in some ways separate from it, is the sexual climacteric. In their interpersonal lives individuals must now

People View Their Experiences Through Somewhat Different Cognitive Filters

cultivate greater understanding and compassion. They must come to value others as personalities in their own right rather than chiefly as sex objects.

- *Cathectic flexibility versus cathectic impoverishment.* This task concerns the ability to become emotionally flexible. In doing so, people find the capacity to shift emotional investments from one person to another and from one activity to another. Many middle-aged individuals confront the death of their parents and the departure of their children from the home, and they must widen their circle of acquaintances to embrace new people in the community. And they must try on and cultivate new roles to replace those that they are relinquishing. Those who do not are likely to experience a sense of isolation and loneliness.

- *Mental flexibility versus mental rigidity.* As they grow older, some people too often become "set in their ways." They might become "closed-minded" or unreceptive to new ideas. Those who have reached their peak in status and power are tempted to forgo the search for novel solutions to problems. But what worked in the past might not work in the future. Hence, they must strive for mental flexibility and, on an ongoing basis, cultivate new perspectives as provisional guidelines to tackling problems.

Peck's formulations provide a more positive, dynamic image of middle age than those portraying midlife as a time of turmoil and crisis as people reevaluate their lives. Most adult Americans also see middle age as a time when people deepen their relationships and intensify their acts of caring. A variety of studies confirm that people in their fifties become more altruistic and community-oriented than they were at age 25; for instance, many volunteer to serve on the boards of schools, universities, and community agencies. This might be seen as striving for symbolic immortality by furthering a worthy cause or group, catalyzed by an awakened confrontation with one's own mortality. In general, those individuals who have consolidated their marriages and careers have a secure base from which to reach out to assist others (McAdams, de St. Aubin, & Logan, 1993; Peterson & Klohnen, 1995). Those without a secure base are likely to flounder and experience dissatisfaction with middle age.

Question

How is Erikson's stage theory different from Peck's task theory of midlife personality development?

Trait Models

Until relatively recently, most psychologists believed that personality patterns are established during childhood and adolescence and then remain relatively stable over the rest of the life span. This view largely derived from Sigmund Freud's psychoanalytic theory. As described in Chapter 2, Freud traced the roots of behavior to personality components formed in infancy and childhood—needs, defenses, identifications, and so on. He deemed any changes that occur in adulthood to simply be variations on established themes, for he believed that an individual's character structure is relatively fixed by late childhood.

Likewise, clinical psychologists and personality theorists have typically assumed that an individual gradually forms certain characteristics that become progressively resistant to change with the passage of time. These patterns are usually regarded as reflections of inner traits, cognitive structures, dispositions, habits, or needs. Indeed, almost all forms of personality assessment assume that the individual has stable traits (stylistic consistencies in behavior) that the investigator is attempting to describe (Goldberg, 1993). For example, developmentalists Robert McCrae and Paul Costa, Jr. (1990) found that a few dimensions recur across their many investigations, thereby proposing that the "big five" traits—extraversion, neuroticism, openness, agreeableness, and conscientiousness—constitute the core of personality. Most models concur on the existence of extraversion-introversion and neuroticism (emotional stability/instability), although there is less agreement on what narrower traits constitute these dimensions. What lies beyond extraversion and neuroticism, however, is a more perplexing and contentious issue, with some theorists identifying 5, 11, and even 16 factors (Block, 1995).

Moreover, we all typically view ourselves as having a measure of consistency, and we anticipate and adapt to many events without appreciably changing our picture of the entirety of our lives. So we see ourselves as essentially stable even though we assume somewhat different roles in response to changing life circumstances (Tomkins, 1986).

Situational Models

The trait approach to personality views a person's behavior in terms of recurring patterns. In contrast, proponents of situational models view a person's behavior as the outcome of the characteristics of the situation in which the person is momentarily located. Cognitive learning theorist Walter Mischel (1969, 1977, 1985), provides a forthright statement of the situational position. Mischel says that behavioral consistency is in the eye of the beholder and hence is more illusory than real. Indeed, he wonders if it makes sense to speak of "personality" at all, suggesting that human beings might not have personalities. Mischel concludes that we are motivated to believe that the world around us is orderly and patterned because only in this manner can we take aspects of our daily lives for granted and view them as predictable. Consequently, we perceive our own behavior and that of other people as having continuity. Even so, Mischel admits that a fair degree of consistency exists in people's performance on certain intellectual and cognitive tasks. However, he notes that the correlation between personality test scores and behavior seems to reach a maximum of about .30, not a particularly high figure. People's behavior across situations is highly consistent only when the situations in which the behavior is tested are quite similar. When circumstances vary, little similarity is apparent.

Interactionist Models

In recent years psychologists have come to recognize the inadequacies of both trait and situational models. Instead, they have come to favor an interactionist approach to personality (Field, 1991). They claim that behavior is always a joint product of the person and the situation. Moreover, people seek out congenial environments—selecting settings, activities, and associates that provide a comfortable context and fit—and thereby reinforce their preexisting bents (Setterlund & Niedenthal, 1993). And through their actions, individuals create as well as select environments (Rausch, 1977). By fashioning their own circumstances, they produce some measure of stability in their behavior (Heidrich & Ryff, 1993).

Psychologists have employed a variety of approaches for specifying the form of interaction that transpires between a person and a situation. One approach is to distinguish between those people for whom a given trait predicts behavior across situations and those people for whom that trait is not predictive of behavior. For example, individuals who report that their behavior is consistent across situations with respect to friendliness and conscientiousness do indeed exhibit these traits in their behavior. In contrast, individuals who report that their behavior is inconsistent across situations with respect to these qualities reveal little consistency in their behavior with regard to them (Bem & Allen, 1974). Moreover, people vary in their consistency on different traits (Funder & Colvin, 1991). Hence, if we are asked to characterize a friend, we typically do not run through a rigid set of traits that we use to inventory all people. Instead, we select a small number of traits that strike us as particularly pertinent and discard as irrelevant the hundreds or so other traits. Usually, the friendship traits—such as trustworthiness, kindness, and acceptance—that we select are those that we find hold for the person across a variety of situations.

> ### Question
> Which theory—trait, situational, or interactionist—explains why you might not mind waiting in a slow movie line one day but might become agitated doing so another time?

Gender and Personality at Midlife

In recent years many psychologists have moved away from the traditional assumption that masculinity and femininity are inversely related characteristics of personality and behavior. A variety of studies have examined the dynamics of gender and personality traits during middle adulthood.

Levinson's Theory of Male Midlife Development   Psychologist Daniel J. Levinson (1986) and his associates at Yale University studied stages of male adult development and formed their life structure theory (Levinson et al., 1978; see pp. 463–465). Central to this theory are the roles of family and one's occupation in life. Analysis of their subjects' intensive biographies, described in *The Seasons of a Man's Life* (Levinson et al., 1978) led them to conclude that men often experience a turning point in their lives between the ages of 35 and 45. More recently, Levinson concluded that men's inner struggles occur with renewed intensity in the mid-fifties (Goleman, 1989a). These Yale researchers believe that a man cannot go through his middle adult years unchanged, because he encounters the first indisputable signs of aging and reaches a point at which he is compelled to reassess the fantasies and illusions he has held about himself. Levinson identified several substages from 40 to 65 in his initial study with men in the early 1970s (and with women in the early 1980s) with both beginnings and endings:

- *Midlife transition (age 40 to 45).* This is a developmental bridge between early adulthood and middle adulthood. People come to terms with the end of their youth in the late thirties and try to create a new young-old way of being. Working at individuation at midlife is an especially important task. Initiation into midlife involves making choices.
- *Entry life structure for middle adulthood (age 45 to 50).* People establish an initial place in a new generation and a new season of life. Even if they are in the same job, marriage, or community, they create important differences in these relationships. They try to establish a new place in midlife.
- *Age 50 transition (age 50 to 55).* This is a time to reappraise and explore one's self within this new midlife structure. Developmental crises are common in this period, especially for persons who have made few life changes in the previous 10 to 15 years.
- *Culminating life structure for middle adulthood (age 55 to 60).* It is a time for realizing midlife aspirations and goals.
- *Late adult transition (age 60 to 65).* This requires a profound reappraisal of the past and a readiness for the next era of adulthood. This involves termination of midlife and readiness for late adulthood.

The realization that the career elevator is not going up any longer, and might indeed be about to descend, can add to a man's frustrations and stresses. There is historical evidence that in the early 1900s in the United States, management arbitrarily, and overnight, replaced men in their forties and fifties with younger men; and it was then impossible for these older men to find another job. Thus, the fears that many midlife men have about losing their jobs or being replaced in their jobs is legitimate today, as corporations continue to "merge," "outsource," and "downsize." A man who has not accomplished what he had hoped to with his life now becomes keenly aware that he does not have much more time or many more chances to do it. And even many who have reached their career goals—say, owning their own company, having a high executive position, or earning a full professorship—often find that what they have achieved is less rewarding than they had anticipated. A man might ask himself, "If I am making so much money and doing so well, how come I don't feel better and my life seems so empty?" On the other hand, a blue-collar worker of more modest means might ask, "How much longer am I going to have to put up with this dull job?" Even so, research shows that, for most people, aspirations gradually come to match attainments without severe upset and turmoil (Bridgman, 1984).

Levinson concluded that this age-graded sequence of periods in adult development violates conventional wisdom and the findings that there are no comparable sequences of periods for personality development, cognitive development, and family development. However, based on his research findings, he concludes that this sequence exists. He further states it is a much more complex matter to determine the "satisfactoriness" of individual lives within these stages (Levinson, 1996, p. 29). A developmental crisis occurs when someone is having great difficulty in meeting the tasks in each stage (e.g., makes an abrupt career change, gets divorced, has an affair, or "acts like an adolescent"). Levinson concluded prior to his death in 1994 that though the genders experience different life circumstances, and women work on the developmental tasks of each period with different resources than men have, women and men both go through these life stages.

Male Midlife Developmental Transition Men and women typically work on the developmental tasks of transitioning through midlife with different resources. Two men age 60+ that your authors know bought motorcycles and toured the United States for a year. Another friend was a cowboy for two weeks at a "dude ranch" in Montana. Another bought a large sailboat. Another competed in an American road rally in a classic car. These men fulfilled lifelong dreams.

Question

According to Levinson's research findings, what are the stages of a man's life?

Levinson's Theory of Women's Midlife Development

A white-male-centered view of adult life has been dominant since the earliest of psychological and sociological studies, and before that in the history and literature of various cultures. Though Levinson chose to study adult male development in his initial study in the 1970s, he said that one couldn't study one gender without studying the other, for both influence each other in complex ways (e.g., relationships of husbands and wives, fathers and daughters, mothers and sons, ex-husbands and ex-wives). From 1980 to 1982, Levinson used the method of intensive biographical interviewing with 45 females, ranging in age from 35 to 45. The subjects, selected randomly, constituted three equal groups: (1) primarily homemakers; (2) women with careers in the corporate world; and (3) women with careers in the academic world. The research findings indicate there were apparent gender differences in adult life and development, particularly in the realms of domestic and public life, within a marriage, in the division of "women's work" and "men's work," and in the male and female psyche. Let's look at some of Levinson's findings.

Primarily Homemakers Women who live primarily as homemakers in a traditional marriage are likely to center their lives in the domestic sphere, to engage solely in women's work, and to accept and value themselves and other women as "feminine." These women are also more likely to be marginal to the public world, to be limited as "provisioners" and authorities in the family, and to have difficulty engaging in "men's work." Men's lives are usually centered in the public sphere (their territory, under their control), whereas women typically participate in the public sphere in more segregated, marginal, and subordinate ways (e.g., as secretary to a lawyer, nurse attending a physician—not their territory, not under their control), (obviously many more women have entered the male-dominated professions since this study was conducted in the early 1980s) (see Figure 16.1). The domestic sphere consists of a household and its surrounding social world. In most societies of the world, women's lives continue to be centered in the domestic sphere. The home is the key source of their identity, meaning, and satisfaction.

Traditional Marriage   In many societies, love is not the primary motivating factor for marriage. It is, "first of all, about building an enterprise in which the partners can have a good life" and "take care of each other" in their own fashion (Levinson, 1996). Arranged marriages are still common in many countries. In a **traditional marriage,** the women are homemakers and the men are *provisioners* (involving themselves much more in their work world than in their family). *Patriarchy,* the rule of the father or husband, is a universal theme to some degree in most societies of the world. Consequently, the man is still the dominant authority over the family members. A wife has the responsibility of the housekeeping, family life, and care of the children and husband. A wife might enter the public sphere marginally in her attempts to further her

husband's career (e.g., entertain colleagues), work on the family farm or for the business, or contribute time to the local school, church, or community. In the United States a prime example of this is the thousands of hardworking farm wives who were never employed outside the farm, have not personally contributed to Social Security, and are ineligible for Social Security benefits. Women who have lived their lives in a traditional marriage and then become divorced or widowed during midlife are often faced with a major transition:

> "I knew from the beginning that when he was gone [her husband of 39 years, dying of emphysema], I'd have to go to work," she says. That wasn't a comforting thought. The emotions she felt at the prospect of losing her husband were devastating enough; the idea of having to construct a life on her own was often overwhelming. . . . Work was not a part of the blueprint Vinita had drawn for herself. [Widowed at 56, Vinita Justus, long a homemaker, faced the daunting necessity of joining the workforce]. (Coburn, 1996, p. 57)

As homemaker, women get to create their own home base as center for their lives. It becomes the place where they rest, play, love, enjoy privacy and leisure, and have strong affectional relationships with family members. Domestic work can be hard, though, particularly as women age and are still facing endless household, child-care, eldercare, and husband-care responsibilities (see the *Human Diversity* box "Life Without a Middle Age"). However, taking care of each other has different meanings for men and women in a traditional marriage. A man readily accepts nourishment and support from his wife the homemaker, but he has much more difficulty discussing with her his possible inadequacies at work, and she might find his work world quite alien to her own. And a woman is dependent on her husband to provide for the family. The traditional homemaker and spouse are in a mutual-care arrangement.

Questions

According to Levinson's findings, what are a woman's needs at midlife? What does Levinson mean by the traditional mutual-care arrangement between a husband and a wife?

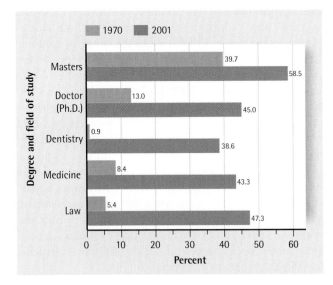

FIGURE 16.1 Percent of Master's, Doctor's, and First Professional Degrees Conferred to U.S. Women: 1970, 2001 Thirty-five years ago a majority of today's midlife women were expected to engage in "women's work" in the domestic sphere or in service occupations. Although women began attending college in greater numbers by the early 1970s, very few were admitted into prestigious, male-dominated professions. In 1970 one of your authors worked at a large U.S. medical center with a medical college—and one woman (from China) was admitted for a medical degree. Note the significant gains.
Source: Freeman, C. E. (2004, November). *Trends in Education Equity of Girls and Women: 2004.* National Center for Education Statistics. NCES 2005-016. Washington, DC: U.S. Department of Health and Human Services.

However, many cultural changes since the 1940s and 1950s in the United States have reduced women's involvement in the family and increased their involvement in the outside world. Today, homemaking is not a permanent, full-time occupation for most American women. Many young women live with the awareness that they will become the primary provisioner for themselves and their children. Those who want to remain homemakers experience social pressures from dominant

Human Diversity

Life Without a Middle Age

Perceptions of age are always mediated by cultural models of the life course, and the Western view of middle age differs significantly from the views of those in non-Western cultures.

India

For centuries in India, well-defined extended family structures in each caste system identified the roles of family members throughout life. The three-generation family life was the norm. When a woman married, she became the person of lowest status in her in-laws' home, with her mother-in-law becoming the "keeper of the traditions" and controlling the behavior of the younger family members. The young bride was expected to take over all household responsibilities, while the elder mother-in-law could now spend more time with her friends and attend to more religious obligations. The elders in the home were to be accorded respect, care, and support by the young. The young were to defer to the elders and care for them during their declining years. With this age-old view of growing older, those in middle adulthood looked forward to receiving respect and care and relinquishing home responsibilities. Tikoo (1996) says it is difficult to give a definite age at which one is middle-aged in India, because the average life expectancy in India is only 58 years; "middle age" in that context would be younger than American middle age. However, Adler (1989) grouped their Indian subjects into "young" (16 to 35), "middle" (34 to 54), and "old" (55 to 80).

In India, aging is not unwelcome, and much folklore highlights the significance of gray hair and wrinkles as signs of one's wisdom and experience (Tikoo, 1996). Tikoo and colleagues surveyed 56 adult men and women (Hindu) with the 97-item self-report *Men's Adult Life Experience Survey.* Findings in 11 developmentally related domains suggested very few gender or age differences, "raising questions as to the meaning or relevance of midlife crisis in India" (Tikoo, 1996). Yet other findings indicate that along with modernization in certain locales in India, there has been an evident decline in extended family life, including a decline in the respect, prestige, and care given the elderly by the young (Kumar & Suryanarayna, 1989). Young adults in India are more mobile today, and some elderly no longer receive the care and support they would have commanded in earlier years.

Japan

In Japan the three-generation household still exists in nearly 20 percent of homes. Women are trained to be good wives and mothers and are formally educated for their role in society (Lock, 1998, p. 59). The dominant image of females is nurturer. Formerly about 98 percent of Japanese women

married; by 1998, that rate had dropped to 88 percent. Traditionally women were expected to marry in their mid-twenties and produce two children within five or six years. By their mid-thirties, their families were expected to be complete. Birth control pills are not available in Japan, but women have access to other birth control devices. Women who remain unmarried by age 25 are described as "unsold merchandise" (*urenoki*) or "overripe fruit" (*tô ga tatsu*), not unlike the U.S. concept of the "old maid."

However, a new demographic trend has emerged in Japan since 1980's called *hikon jidai* (age of nonmarriage). This trend is the result of a declining marriage rate, increasing divorce rate, and a postponement of marriage. In 2002 the marriage rate declined by 6 percent while the divorce rate reached its highest number, almost doubling in two decades. Although the birthrate is the lowest in the world at 1.32 per woman, there is an increasing social acceptance of single

Women from Kashmir, India

continued

motherhood and expanded lifestyle choices for women. In part the gender inequality and stereotypical expectations for women have dissuaded women from marrying and having children (Hirota, 2004). Another factor that has stemmed the rate of first marriages is a rising income for Japanese women (Ono, 2003).

Nevertheless, the traditional perception of the ideal life course of the people of a village, region, or the nation is age-graded—that is, "the life cycle is predominantly a social process involving community rituals in which people born the same year participate together" (Lock, 1998). Biological aging has always been subordinate to social maturation of a family and a community. The female's life cycle has been shaped more by biology than a male's. Middle age, referred to as the *prime of life (sônen)*, is simply a part of the life cycle that begins with marriage and ends at the ritual of turning 60—old age. There is no word in Japanese for menopause, nor is menopause noted by the family or community, though the end of a woman's reproductive cycle (*tenki*) has traditionally been recognized to occur in the "seventh stage" in a woman's life. Japanese physicians have not adopted the "disease" approach to managing menopause. Hormone replacement therapy is not available, but women do use herbal remedies. Japanese women in midlife also have low rates of osteoporosis and heart disease (Lock, 1998, p. 63).

Interviews with midlife Japanese women reveal that many spend time and energy cultivating various art forms (e.g., dance, flower arranging, classical poetry, calligraphy, archery). These traditional art forms are thought to be paths to spiritual awareness, self-development, and self-discipline. Lifelong socialization "is based on an ideology that accepts the possibility of human perfectibility over time, a condition that transcends and continues beyond the unavoidable decline in the body" (Lock, 1998). A woman is recognized as fully mature—a complete adult—after she has raised her own children to adulthood. Grandmothers devote a good deal of time monitoring households, caring for and educating grandchildren, and caring for aging in-laws. *Confucianism* encourages respect for the elderly in life and in the afterlife. To the Japanese, age denotes wisdom and authority. Overall, people strive for a cooperative life in which the "self" is subordinate or nonexistent. In Buddhist thinking, individual discipline fosters a path to maturity and otherworldly transcendence, which can take many incarnations to accomplish. Individual aging therefore is not viewed as a bad thing or a disease, though caring for growing numbers of bed-ridden elderly has become a more pressing social problem.

From: Margaret Lock, "Deconstructing the Change: Female Maturation in Japan and North America," in Richard A. Shweder, ed., *Welcome to Middle Age!* Chicago, IL: University of Chicago Press, 1998.

---

cultural values to become educated and employed. Many women have chosen, or have been forced by divorce or widowhood, to be employed as caregivers: in child care, teaching, nursing, social work, psychology, clerical, service, clergy, and sales (Utz et al., 2004). Only since the 1970s in this country have women been able to enter the higher-status, higher-salaried occupations. Women's entry into the occupational sphere has changed the division of labor and has violated the traditional division of authority in the home. For many midlife women, balancing their investments in a career and a family has become very difficult.

New Beginnings at Midlife   For some people, midlife offers opportunities to explore new career avenues or resume educational goals that were deferred due to marriage and child-care responsibilities. Now freed of some of the familial and financial responsibilities of younger adults, middle-aged adults, more than half of which are women, are returning to college (Rimer, 2000). Advances in technology have allowed many midlife adults to use experience gained in their homemaking and job careers to forge their own home-based ventures. Dedication to healthy lifestyles allows midlife adults to enjoy sport and adventure activities.

Midlife Transition Career Women   Today's midlife women also bought the myth in the late 1960s and 1970s

that a woman could have any career she wanted, as well as marry, have children, and have time for recreation and leisure. These women earned advanced degrees in record numbers, all while caring for home and family or supporting themselves. When something has had to "give" in the family, it has usually been the woman's career. Many midlife women today have made transitions in and out of employment, or have accepted adjunct or temporary work positions, depending on demands of birthing, caring for children, and caring for elderly parents. These same women thought their so-called equality in the workplace also meant equality at home, as in sharing domestic and child-care chores equally. But there has been a great imbalance in the division of labor at home. Women still perform most of the domestic chores for their needy family while they work at a demanding job. Levinson's study revealed that each woman in midlife transition recognized that her efforts to combine love and marriage, motherhood, and full-time career had not given her as much satisfaction as she had hoped. These women are exploring new ways to live in middle adulthood.

The career women and female faculty members in Levinson's study in their early forties went through a major reappraisal of their careers and made significant changes in career and other aspects of their lives. A major component of this struggle was coming to terms with the myth of the successful career woman. Two of the seven female faculty members that were interviewed were not full professors, though they had attained a doctorate by the age of 40. The full professors found that there were even more demands placed upon them to continue teaching, conduct scholarly work and administrative work, to contribute to professional organizations and activities in their field, and so on. All of the female midlife subjects reported a sexist attitude at work (both in education and in business settings).

> Debra (44): My primary dissatisfaction in my life now is my job, and I ought to look for a change in my job situation. I am very ambitious, and so much of my present frustration in my life really has to do with the feeling now of getting nowhere with my career. I'm very unhappy with my work, but I stay because of the money. It enables my family to live a certain lifestyle that I'm not totally prepared to give up, especially with my children about to go to college. I feel trapped in my job economically. (Levinson, 1996, p. 381)

Although women manage multiple demands of career preparation and family, it takes several years of course work and research to get tenure or senior partnerships. Many have to interrupt their careers to manage family priorities. When they attempt to return to collegiate pursuits, they are passed over for promotions. Presently, the percentage of women with professorial status is still only 22 percent across American colleges (Halpern, 2004).

Levinson says that the traditional roles of men and women in marriage have been split, and no clear alternative has yet been established. Thus, several alternative lifestyles have emerged. With one out of every two marriages ending in divorce, many women are finding themselves to be single parents who have to be both provisioner and homemaker. And men are also confused and uncomfortable with their changing roles; changing diapers as first-time (or second-family) dads in midlife was not in their "blueprint" either. Critics of Levinson's work cite the small sample of subjects (approximately 45 in each study). They point out that men or women in their fifties and sixties were not interviewed, though his life structure theory extends to these ages, and they say it is unlikely that such a midlife "crisis" occurs within the narrow age range of 40 to 45.

Ravenna Helson and the Mills Longitudinal Study Subjects at Midlife Helson and Wink (1992) studied personality change of middle-aged women who were subjects in the *Mills Longitudinal Study* (women born in the late 1930s who graduated from a private college between 1958 and 1960). Findings indicate that these women experienced turmoil in their early forties, followed by an increase in stability by age 52. Over this same decade, the women had decreased negative emotions, increased decisiveness, and increased comfort and

Midlife Career Transition Women Midlife offers women opportunities to explore new career avenues or resume educational goals that were deferred due to marriage and child-care responsibilities. Some are returning to college, others use experience gained in their homemaking and job careers to forge their own home-based ventures. Sheehy (1992) calls this postmenopausal zest.

stability through adherence to personal and social standards. By age 52 they had fewer caregiving responsibilities toward their children and more toward their elderly parents. Three-fourths of this sample were menopausal or postmenopausal (Helson, 1997, p. 26).

Helson's findings support those of Neugarten and Datan (1974). Their study in the 1970s found that middle-aged men reported that their period of greatest productivity and reward was after they turned 50. Women homemakers experienced more adjustments as children departed home and were more likely to describe middle age as a period of "mellowness and serenity." But blue-collar workers, both men and women, were likely to report this as a time of decline. (Time, place, and socioeconomic status are factors here, because women who were traditional homemakers did not have a role in the occupational world, whereas some blue-collar women were wage earners at this stage.) Mitchell and Helson (1990) describe women's *prime of life* as being in their early fifties, with a sense of accomplishment from occupational achievement and/or launching of children, convergence of personality resources, and a new, freer lifestyle.

Continuity and Discontinuity in Gender Characteristics Carl Jung (1933, 1960), the influential Swiss psychoanalyst, was one of the first to suggest that gender differences tend to diminish or even "cross over" in later life. Some research confirms that men and women move in *opposite* directions across the life span with respect to assertiveness and aggressiveness, so that patterns of a later-life "unisex" tend to emerge (Hyde, Krajnik, & Skuldt-Niederberger, 1991).

David Gutmann (1987) pursued this possibility by comparing the male subjects in Neugarten's Kansas City study with men in a number of other cultures: the subsistence, village-dwelling, lowland and highland Maya of Mexico; the migratory Navajo herdsmen of the high-desert plateau of northeastern Arizona; and the village-dwelling Galilean Druze herdsmen and farmers of Israel. Gutmann found that the younger men (aged 35 to 54) in all four cultures relied on and relished their own internal energy and creative capabilities. They tended to be competitive, aggressive, and independent. On the other hand, the older men (aged 55 and over) tended to be more passive and self-centered. They relied on supplication and accommodation to influence others. Gutmann concluded that this change from active to passive mastery seems to be more age- than culture-related. Other researchers similarly report that, on the whole, older men are more reflective, sensual, and mellow than younger men (Zube, 1982).

Gutmann (1987) has continued to study personality and aging in a wide range of cultures. In subsequent research he reports that his earlier finding has been confirmed—that around age 55, men begin to use passive instead of active techniques in dealing with the demands of their environment. Women, however, appear to move in the opposite direction, from passive to active mastery. They tend to become more forceful, domineering, managerial, and independent. Those who study the effects of lowered levels of estrogen and progesterone—and thus an increasing influence of testosterone—in postmenopausal women are beginning to document similar findings. Sheehy writes (1992) about women's *postmenopausal zest*:

> Today's pioneering women in postmenopause in advanced societies eventually give up the futile gallantry of trying to remain the same younger self. Coming through the passage of menopause, they reach a new plateau of contentment and self-acceptance, along with a broader view of the world that not only enriches one's personality but gives one a new perspective on life and humankind. Such women—and there are more and more of them today—find a potent new burst of energy by their mid-fifties. (p. 237)

Gutmann's approach to gender behaviors—a functional, role-based theory—is controversial. It has been criticized on theoretical and methodological grounds (McGee & Wells, 1982). Even so, it has provided a starting point for research on gender-role orientation across the life span. The findings of Gutmann and other researchers seem to suggest that in later life people tend toward androgynous responses—thought to be associated with increased flexibility and adaptability and hence with successful aging (Wink & Helson, 1993). The incorporation of both male-typed and female-typed characteristics within a single personality, called **androgyny,** provides an alternative perspective. Androgynous individuals do not restrict their behavior to that embodied in cultural stereotypes of masculinity and femininity.

Questions

What do we know about men's and women's lives and transition through middle adulthood? Do studies of midlife development include ethnic minorities and those who are not of the middle class?

Personality Continuity and Discontinuity

As noted earlier, Robert R. McCrae and Paul T. Costa, Jr. (1990) find considerable continuity in a person's personality across the adult years. They have tracked individuals' scores over time on standardized self-report personality scales. On such personality dimensions as warmth, impulsiveness, gregariousness, assertiveness, anxiety, and disposition to depression, a high correlation exists in the ordering of persons from one decade to another. An assertive 19-year-old is typically an assertive 40-year-old and later an assertive 80-year-old. Likewise, "neurotics" are likely to be "complainers" throughout life (they might complain about their love life in early adulthood and decry their poor health in late adulthood). Although people can "mellow" with age or become less impulsive by the time they are in their sixties, the relation of individuals to one another regarding a given trait remains much the same; when tested most persons drop the same few standard points.

In sum, for many facets of our personality there is strong evidence of continuity across the adult years (Caspi, Elder, & Bem, 1987; Costa, McCrae, & Arenberg, 1980). This element of stability makes us adaptive; we know what we are like and hence can make more intelligent choices regarding our living arrangements, careers, spouses, and friends. If our personality changed continually and erratically, we would have a hard time mapping our future and making wise decisions.

This conclusion is supported by much of the work exploring Erikson's thesis regarding generativity (Peterson & Klohnen, 1995). As the Neugartens note (1987), the psychological realities confronting the individual shift with time. Middle age, for instance, often brings with it multiple responsibilities for jobs and careers, as well as caring for one's children and aging parents (Marks, 1998). Often these duties weigh more heavily on women (Dautzenberg et al., 1999). With these obligations comes the awareness of oneself as the bridge between the generations—the so-called **sandwich generation** (see the *Further Developments* box on page 568, "The Sandwich Generation"). As the sandwich generation tries to fulfill the needs of their children and parents, their own needs may become less prominent yet perhaps more important than ever before (see Table 16.1). As a perceptive woman observed in Neugarten's study of middle age (1968, p. 98):

> It is as if there are two mirrors before me, each held at a partial angle. I see part of myself in my mother who is growing old, and part of her in me. In the other mirror, I see part of myself in my daughter. I have had some dramatic insights, just from looking in those mirrors. . . . It is a set of revelations that I suppose can only come when you are in the middle of three generations.

In a sense, individuals in their forties and fifties are catching up with their own parents, so they might experience increased identification with them and a greater awareness of their own approaching senescence (Stein et al., 1978). Some of the issues of middle age are related to increased stocktaking, in which individuals come to restructure their time perspective in terms of time-left-to-live rather than time-since-birth.

The Social Milieu

Close and meaningful social relationships play a vital part in human health and happiness. Through our association with others—family, friends, acquaintances, and co-workers—we achieve a sense of worth, acceptance, and psychological well-being. This social network is often referred to as a **social convoy,** the company of other people who travel with us from birth to death. As you look at the opening photo for this chapter on page 545, some midlife women have formed local chapters of the "Red Hat Society," to fulfill meaningful social relationships. Levinson (1996) said:

> To study an individual life, we must include all aspects of living. A life involves significant interpersonal relationships—with friends and lovers, parents and siblings, spouses and children, bosses, colleagues, and mentors. It also involves significant relationships with groups and institutions of all kinds: family, occupational world, religion, and community.

Familial Relations

As we noted in Chapter 14, the vast majority of adult Americans have a profound wish to be part of a couple and to make the relationship work. Maintaining a healthy family life continues as a top priority for most adults in middle age (Lachman, 2004).

Married Couples   The 2003 Census figures reveal that over 72 percent of people in middle adulthood are married (see Table 16.2). This represents 3 out of 10 couples of all married people over 18 years old. This statistic does not reveal how many were remarriages, but marriage seemed to be the relationship of choice for a high majority of middle-aged adults. Many couples still have children living at home, since they had started their families later than their parents did (as this was the first generation to use the birth control pill to delay childbearing).

Table 16.1 The Sandwich Generation: Caught in the Middle—The Needs of Middle-Aged Adults, Their Children, and Their Aging Parents

What Kids Want and Need	What Middle-Aged Adults Want and Need	What Aging Parents Want and Need
Independence	Help	Acceptance
Respect	Appreciation	Independence
Sounding board	Pressure off	Respect
Separate entity	"My turn"	Control
Patience	Independence	Sharing
Guidelines	Listening ear	Involvement
Flexibility	Acceptance	Emotional support
Acceptance	Time with my own generation	Interpersonal relationships
Security	Solitude	Interaction
Money	Space	Inclusion
Support	Unconditional love	Control of one's own life
Make choices	Control of one's own life	
Unconditional love		
Control of one's own life		

Source: Herbert G. Lingren and Jayne Decker, *The Sandwich Generation: A Cluttered Nest.* Cooperative Extension, Institute of Agriculture and Natural Resources, University of Nebraska–Lincoln, December 1992, issued online August 1996, http://ianrpubs.unl.edu/family/g1117.htm.

Table 16.2 Marital Status of Americans 45 to 64 Years Old: 2003

	Ages 45 to 54 (Percent)	Ages 55 to 64 Percent
Married	71	79
Divorced	15	13
Never married	12	6
Widowed	2	2

Source: U.S. Bureau of the Census. (2004–2005). *Statistical Abstract of the United States: 2004–2005.* Marital Status of the Population by Sex and Age, Table No. 53, p. 12.

Most were better educated, were employed full-time and in decent financial shape, and seemed to be happy with their sex lives (Lachman, 2004). Many middle-aged adults report that they now had sex less often but that sex was now better. Among both men and women religion now takes on a significant role as a source of community, spirituality, and comfort. Many feel they have a personal responsibility to make the world a better place.

As they have grown older, these first boomers have found themselves to be more conservative in their views, and overall most enjoy material success and comforts. They look forward to spending leisure time with their spouses. Still, the majority is concerned about developing health problems, about the health of their aging parents, about maintaining their lifestyle after retirement, and some worry about not being able to retire. Most indicate they don't feel their age—that they feel much younger (Callum, 1996).

An earlier study of 12,000 U.S. couples was undertaken by sociologists Blumstein and Schwartz (1983). They surveyed a nationally representative sample of adults in four types of couple relationships: married, cohabiting, gay male, and lesbian. Three hundred couples were then selected for in-depth interviews and were interviewed again 18 months later. As with most studies of the early 1980s, this sample was composed of white, well-educated couples. These couples turned out to be more conventional than the researchers had initially expected. Although 60 percent of the wives worked outside the home, only 30 percent of the men and 39 percent of the women believed that both spouses should work. Wives with full-time jobs still did most of the housework. In general, husbands so objected to doing housework that the more they did of it, the more unhappy they were. If the man did not contribute what the woman felt was his fair share of the housework, the relationship was sometimes imperiled. Much of the same pattern held for cohabiting couples (Huston & Geis, 1993; Suitor, 1991).

Men, both straight and gay, placed a considerable premium on power and dominance. Heterosexual men ap-

parently took pleasure in their partner's success only if it was not superior to their own. Gay males likewise tended to be competitive about their career success. In contrast, lesbians did not feel themselves particularly threatened by their partner's achievements, perhaps because women are not socialized to link their self-esteem so highly with success in the workplace (Kurdek, 1994a).

Most married couples in this large sample pooled their money, though some wives did not pool their money. Regardless of how much the wife earned, married couples measured their financial success by the husband's income. In contrast, cohabitors and gay couples appraised their economic status individually rather than as a unit. Findings by Forste and Tanfer (1996) concur with previous studies that found that cohabitors are more likely to value independence and equality.

Typically, one partner in a marriage expressed a desire for "private time." Early in marriage, husbands were more likely than wives to assert that they needed more time on their own. But in long-standing marriages, it was the wives who more often asserted that they needed more time to themselves. Women with retired husbands who "hung around" the house were especially troubled by the constant presence of their partner.

Sociologists Jeanette Lauer and Robert Lauer (1985) looked into the question of what makes successful marriages. They surveyed 300 happily married couples, asking why their marriages survived. The most frequently cited reason was having a positive attitude toward one's spouse. The partners often said, "My spouse is my best friend" and "I like my spouse as a person." A second key to a lasting marriage was a belief that marriage is a long-term commitment and a sacred institution. Marriage itself increases commitment between partners, regardless of prior cohabitation status (Forste & Tanfer, 1996).

Question

What are some of the factors associated with long-lasting and satisfying marriages of middle-aged men and women?

Extramarital Sexual Relations   Traditionally, Western society has strongly disapproved of extramarital sexual relations (referred to now as "EMS"). Opposition has mainly been the result of two beliefs: that marriage provides a sexual outlet and therefore the married person is not sexually deprived and that extramarital involvement threatens the marriage relationship and therefore imperils the family institution. These beliefs find expression in religious values that brand extramarital sexual activity as sinful and label it adultery.

In comparison to Kinsey and colleagues' (1953) studies, rates of EMS reported in the 1970s, 1980s, and

Table 16.3 Extramarital Sex (EMS): Prevalence in U.S. National Surveys, 1953–1997

Research Studies on EMS Using Large-Scale Samples of Respondents (Self-Report and Face-to-Face Interview Methods Used)	Percentage of Married Male Respondents Who Reported Engaging in EMS	Percentage of Married Female Respondents Who Reported Engaging in EMS
Kinsey et al. (1953), p. 417	33	20
Laumann et al. (1994) national survey; lifetime experience of engaging in EMS	24.5	15
Clements (1994) *Parade Magazine* telephone survey of 1,049 adults, ages 18 to 65	19	15

From M. W. Wiederman, "Extramarital Sex: Prevalence and Correlates in a National Survey," *Journal of Sex Research*, Vol. 34, No. 2 (1997), pp. 167–174.

early 1990s have varied (see Table 16.3) (some studies investigated incidence of EMS over the past year; others investigated incidence of EMS over a lifetime). It appears men are more likely to have engaged in extramarital sexual relations over a lifetime. A recent study that examined extramarital relations and the marriage relationship concludes that EMS is both cause and effect in the deterioration of the marriage relationship (Previti & Amato, 2004). Another factor to consider, however, is that more couples are "cohabiting" in long-term arrangements and would not be considered "married" for these national "representative" surveys. We do not know their degree of "faithfulness" to each other in these less formal arrangements.

The prevalence of EMS over the lifetime varies according to sex. Lifetime prevalence of EMS appeared to increase with age among men up to the oldest age group (age 70 and older), at which point it decreased. Laumann and colleagues (1994, p. 216) found that lifetime prevalence of EMS increased steadily with age for men but showed a curvilinear relationship for women, for whom the highest incidence was among women in their forties. Women 60 and older were least likely to report ever having engaged in EMS. The large majority of currently married men (78 percent) and women (88 percent) consistently denied EMS both during the past year and during their lifetime (Wiederman, 1997). Lifetime rates of EMS were twice as high among those who had been divorced or legally separated, compared with respondents who had never divorced or separated (at a statistically significant level).

Sex is not the only lure for extramarital affairs. Affairs are often initiated to fill emotional needs. Emotional infidelity occurs when a person consistently shares feelings and emotional intimacies with someone other than the spouse (Neuman, 2001). Additionally, many people report that they seek a new partner because they crave companionship and someone to make them feel special (Hall, 1987). For their part, evolutionary psychologists contend that human beings are designed to fall in love but not to stay in love. According to this view, males are "programmed" to maximize the spread of their genes into the future by copulating with many women; women, in contrast, are more given to fidelity because they can have only one offspring a year (Wright, 1994).

Separation and Divorce Many Americans follow a path leading from marriage to divorce, remarriage, and widowhood. Marital separation, divorce, and remarriage have also become more common for those in midlife and older as well. Apparently, women currently around the age of 50 are a somewhat unique group. Their generation was the trendsetters, attending college and entering the workforce in extraordinary numbers and shaping new social standards. These changes had vast consequences for traditional husband-wife relationships. According to 2003 U.S. Census data, women in the age cohort 45 to 54 have the highest numbers for divorce of any age group (U.S. Bureau of the Census, 2004–2005).

The first two-decade empirical study of women at midlife—the *National Longitudinal Survey of Mature Women*—was conducted with several thousand women from 1967 through 1989. Hiedemann, Suhomlinova, and O'Rand (1998) examined the data on the 2,000 women who remained in a first marriage and were biological mothers and looked at risk factors for separation and divorce. On average, the women had been married for 17 years. Hiedemann and colleagues' analysis finds an association between the following factors and the risk of separation or divorce:

- Educational attainment reflects the wife's economic independence and the couple's economic status. College-educated wives are more likely to remain married. Women who do not have a high school diploma face higher risks of marital disruption.
- Marriage at young ages increases the risk of marital disruption.
- The longer a marriage survives, the less likely it is to be disrupted.
- A larger family and purchase of a home tend to indicate greater emotional investment in a marriage.
- Controlling for education and work experience, an increase in a wife's economic independence in the form of employment or wages appears to increase the probability of marital disruption.

- The last child's departure from the home has a strong effect on marital stability. The empty-nest experience increases marital disruption for those who reach this phase early in their marriage (around 20 years), but it tends to decrease disruption for those who reach this phase later in their marriage (30 years or more).

Hiedemann and colleagues (1998) suggest that because the baby-boom cohort is expected to live longer after they experience the empty nest, the study of their marriage status should continue.

Friedberg (1998) conducted a 50-state analysis of divorce rates from 1960 to 1990. She examined the rates of divorce from the early 1960s—a time when one had to prove "grounds for divorce" (adultery or cruelty); liberal "no fault" and "unilateral" divorce legislation passed in nearly all states in the early 1970s. She has determined from her study that divorce rates would have been about 6 percent lower if states had not adopted such liberal policies, accounting for 17 percent of the overall increase between 1968 and 1988. Proponents of tightening the current divorce requirements argue that making divorce more difficult will strengthen families, whereas opponents argue that it could damage individuals who remain in dysfunctional family situations. Three states have recently enacted covenant marriage laws that allow married couples to enter into a contract that requires them to submit to counseling before undertaking separation or divorce (Drewianka, 2004).

There is little doubt, from reviewing many research studies conducted over the past 20 to 30 years, that the place of marriage in family life has declined. Cohabitation outside of marriage has become common, and rates of separation and divorce are still high. But divorce rates have stabilized since 1995. Household types also vary among ethnic groups. In 2003, 82 percent of white households were married couple households, with 80 percent of Asian, 68 percent of Hispanic, and 47 percent of African American households comprised of married couples (U.S. Bureau of the Census, 2004b). Socioeconomic factors such as lower incomes, higher rates of unemployment, and lower education are suspected to be the major sources of this racial difference.

Though some African Americans have long, stable marriages, they are the minority and are among the more prosperous (Cherlin, 1998). These intact families are often unreported in the discussions of African Americans and poverty effects, and the strengths of African American families are often overlooked. Extended kinship ties in three-generation African American families are common, and grandparents are very involved in the upbringing of grandchildren. The older generations are an important source of value transmission and have an impact on socialization outcomes of children (McWright, 2002).

The Role of Grandparents With single parenthood, separation, divorce, and remarriage rates high, grandparents provide stability and support in grandchildren's lives. Reliance on extended kinship ties is more common in ethnic minority families.

Questions

What is the status of marriage at midlife? Why do some adults at midlife separate or divorce?

Life as a Single Although returning to single life after divorce has become more common, it is a very difficult experience. In many cases divorce exacts a greater emotional and physical toll than almost any other life stressor, including the death of a spouse (Kurdek, 1991). Studies over the past 20 years document that, compared with married, never-married, and widowed adults, both parties to a divorce have more financial strain, social isolation, physical distress, and increased parenting responsibilities (Wu & Penning, 1997). Study after study documents that divorced or separated individuals are overrepresented among psychiatric patients, compared with those who are married and living with their spouses (Stack, 1990).

The trauma of divorce tends to be the greatest for older women who have been married longer, have two or more children, whose husband initiated the divorce, and who still have positive feelings for their husband or want to punish him. Some middle-aged and older women lack the educational background, skills, and employment experience to reenter or advance within the paid labor market (Wu & Penning, 1997). Additionally, the older the woman is at the time of divorce, the more likely it is that she will not remarry and that she will live many years without support and assistance in her elderly years (Wu & Penning, 1997).

Some women at midlife are single by choice and have never married. However, more midlife women with the resources have adopted children over recent years or have had children by in vitro fertilization. As stated in Chapter 15, in 2002 there were 263 births reported to U.S. women between 50 and 54 years of age (Heffner, 2004). Thus, some women are becoming mothers for the first time in their forties and fifties who are living complex lives as new parents during middle adulthood.

The **displaced homemaker** is a woman whose primary activity has been homemaking and who has lost her main source of income because of divorce from, or death of, her husband. Most of the displaced homemakers who are 65 and older are widowed, whereas most of the displaced homemakers under age 35 are divorced or separated and many have children living with them who are under age 18 (for older women, the children might be grandchildren). Some displaced homemakers work part-time or seasonally, and some do not work at all. Many of these women find themselves ill-equipped to deal with the financial consequences of divorce. They frequently find themselves cut off from their former husband's private pension plan and from medical insurance. Although many live near the poverty line, recent changes in the welfare laws are pushing many displaced homemakers into the workforce.

Divorce affects midlife men and women differently. Men tend to become depressed and have lower achievement goals; women become more outgoing and action-oriented (Elias, 1999; Lachman, 2004). Many women report that they have a more positive self-image and higher self-esteem than they did during their dissatisfying marriage. And nearly two-thirds say that the process helped them gain control for the first time in their lives (in marriage, they report, they had to "knuckle under"). Nor are the women necessarily lonely, because most have supportive female friends. Moreover, many find new activities and careers (Peterson, 1993).

In contrast, men seem to be unwilling converts to single life (Gross, 1992). Overall, divorced men have much narrower support networks than do divorced women. Even when they have ample money, many men find it difficult to put together new lives that can sustain them.

Single Mothers at Midlife A growing number of single women in middle adulthood are bearing children and becoming first-time parents because of assisted reproductive technologies. Thus, the responsibilities and developmental challenges for some in middle adulthood have become more expansive.

American men have typically depended on women to create social lives for them. Not only do men suffer from want of regular companionship, they miss the amenities of established domestic life. And some men begin questioning their worth and competence. Although men might find it easier than women to remarry (statistics favor men), they still do not find it easy to find love, comfort, and a feeling of at-homeness. If men do not remarry, their rates of car accidents, drug abuse, alcoholism, and emotional problems tend to rise, especially five to six years after their divorce. Whereas a decade or so ago many Americans were willing to take a chance on divorce, in recent years they have become more conservative and more realistic in their marital expectations. More and more couples are finding it better to make up than to break up.

As women become better educated and establish occupational and economic independence, the gap of well-being between marrieds and singles is diminishing. For example, the factor of economic strain due to remaining single or returning to single status can become less of an issue. Some even suggest that the stigma of being single might be decreasing, with more unmarried persons engaging in sexual relationships without negative social stigma attached. One study found that regardless of gender, adjustment to divorce was positively related to income, remarriage or a new steady relationship, favorable attitudes regarding marital dissolution before the divorce, and being the one who initiated the divorce (Wang & Amato, 2000).

Remarriage   Many divorced people eventually remarry. About five of every six divorced men and three of every four divorced women marry again. In fact, nearly half of all recent marriages are remarriages for one or both partners. And some of these remarriages are third and fourth marriages. This social pattern is known as "conjugal succession" or "serial marriage." Although lifelong marriage still remains an ideal, in practice marriage has become for most Americans a conditional contract (Bumpass, Sweet, & Martin, 1990). The net result is that only about half of adult Americans are currently married to their first spouses; the others are single, cohabiting, or remarried. The findings of a recent study suggest that remarried couples in middle and later life might indeed have lower risks of marital disruption, particularly if both couples have been previously married (Wu & Penning, 1997).

Men are more likely than women to remarry, for a number of reasons. For one thing, men typically marry younger women, and thus they have a larger pool of potential partners from which to choose. Moreover, men are more likely to marry someone who was not previously married and often marry women with less education than themselves. The likelihood that a woman will remarry declines with age and with increasing levels of education.

A recent Canadian study found that a majority of couples who had previously been cohabitators preferred serial cohabitation to marriage after cohabitation. This compares with previously married people who chose remarriage at a rate of about 20 percent. However, former cohabitators have a higher likelihood of repartnering compared to previously married people (Wu & Schimmele, 2005).

Stepfamilies   According to the Step-family Association of America, at least one-third of all new marriages in the United States involve divorced or widowed parents with children under the age of 18 living in the home ("New Wedding Ceremony Includes Children," 2000). For the first time the 2000 Census included a category for adopted and stepchildren. It reported 2.1 million adopted children and 4.4 million stepchildren, which accounted for about 8 percent of all sons and daughters (Kreider, 2003). These circumstances create what is known as "blended families." Stepparents are probably the most overlooked

Remarriage at Midlife   A majority of divorced adults remarry. The findings of a recent study suggest that remarried couples in middle and later life might indeed have lower risks of marital disruption, particularly if both couples have been previously married.

group of parents in the United States (Pasley & Ihinger-Tallman, 1994). Professionals have by and large studied intact, original families or single-parent families. And for their part, a good number of stepparents feel stigmatized. Images of wicked stepmothers, cruel stepbrothers and stepsisters, and victimized stepchildren found in such tales as *Cinderella* still abound (Dainton, 1993). Stepparents vary widely in terms of their involvement with their stepchildren (Svare, Jay, & Mason, 2004).

Children typically approach a parent's remarriage with apprehension rather than joy. Remarriage shatters their fantasy that their mother and father will get together again someday. And the new spouse may seem to threaten the special bond that often forms between a child and a single parent. Moreover, after having dealt with divorce or separation and single parenthood, children are again confronted with new upheaval and adjustment. Matters are complicated because people often expect instant love in the new arrangement. Many women assume, "I love my new husband, so I will love his children and they will love me, and we all will find happiness overnight." Such notions invite disappointment because relationships take time to develop (Hetherington, Stanley-Hagan, & Anderson, 1989). Complicated scenarios arise, like the following, which would not occur in a traditional family (Fishman, 1983, p. 365):

> My ex-husband has money and he bought our son Ricky a car. That's great! But when my stepson David needs transportation, he is not permitted to borrow Ricky's car because my ex is adamant about not wanting to support someone else's child. Ricky would love to share the car with his stepbrother, but he can't risk angering his father. Besides, David is sensitive about being the "poor" brother and would not drive it anyway. It just burned us up [her and her current husband]. So we scraped together some money we could ill afford and bought an old junker for David. Of course, we fixed it up so it runs safely, and now we've put that problem behind us.

Most stepparents attempt to recreate an intact-family setting because it is the only model they have. Remarriages with complex social systems (for instance, stepsiblings, stepgrandparents, and in-laws from a previous marriage) are more likely to experience difficulties. One woman in a stepfamily with seven children tells of this experience:

> Our first-grader had a hard time explaining to his teacher whether he had two sisters or four, since two of them weren't living in our home. The teacher said, "Justin seems unusually confused about his family situation," and we told her, "He's absolutely right to be confused. That's how it is." (Collins, 1983, p. 21)

With stepfamilies there is yet another dimension—the absent natural parent, whose existence can pose loyalty problems for the children. They wonder, "If I love my stepparent, will I betray my real parent?" In most cases children are happier when they can maintain an easy relationship with the absent parent. Not uncommonly, however, ex-husbands resent having lost control over raising their children and fail to maintain strong relationships or make child-support payments.

Given these tensions, it is hardly surprising that stepparents report significantly less satisfaction with their family life than do married couples with their biological children. Remarriages that bring children from the previous marriage into the household have a 50 percent higher rate of dissolution (Tzeng & Mare, 1995). Moreover, one divorce and remarriage does not end the family transitions for a good many youngsters. By 2010, it is projected that more families will be created by remarriage than any other type of family in the United States (Kallemeyn, 1997). To succeed, the stepfamily must develop workable solutions that leave some of the "old" ways of doing things (traditions, rituals, and customs) intact while fashioning new ones that set the stepfamily apart from the previous family. Although some strains are associated with stepfamilies, so is a good deal of positive adaptation

Stepfamilies A growing number of American households are composed of stepfamilies. Because half of all remarried persons are parents, their new partners become stepparents, and the children become stepchildren. Becoming a member of a stepfamily requires adaptation, cooperation, patience, a sense of humor, and a great deal of faith.

(Kurdek, 1994b). To read more about adjusting to life in a stepfamily, see the *More Information You Can Use* box on page 564, "Adaptation in Stepfamilies."

Question

What are some of the particular stressors for adults who remarry into stepfamilies?

Adult Children and Grandchildren The term **empty nest** refers to a household that had children living at home who now have left home to pursue an education and/or their own households. The empty nest household now contains only one or both parents. Yet today, the post–empty nest might not be so empty. Many adult children are living at home longer while attending college, or when establishing their careers, or returning home with grandchildren during a separation or divorce, or through longer periods of unemployment. The generation of parents who are baby boomers and the generation of their children were born into relative economic prosperity when there is a greater emphasis on parenting, therefore neither parent nor child might think it strange to continue their relationship in a household together. Additionally, more middle-aged adults (primarily women) are working and caring for their own elderly parents and/or their in-laws with the assistance of health care aides and adult day care or raising grandchildren whose parents are incapable of parenting. Middle-aged parents of young adults with disabilities (such as mental retardation, head injuries and paralysis, and other multiple handicaps) today have difficult, time-consuming decisions concerning placement of their children into group homes or supported apartments. They also need to become the legal guardians of their adult child and assist with sheltered

More Information You Can Use

Adaptation in Stepfamilies

Each stepfamily presents its own set of problems and requires its own unique solutions because of the complex mix of the members of the blended family. Several matters of everyday living are common sources of conflict for stepfamilies, but a little prudence can go a long way.

Food

Food preferences are quite salient, especially to the stepchildren. Mealtimes are normally times when a family is together, so there are more opportunities during mealtimes for disruptions to occur. Finding out what family members enjoy eating—and their dislikes—can make for a more pleasant experience when dining. Stepparents who cook should be prepared for negative or rejecting comments for a while, because their stepchildren are accustomed to their own parents' cooking. Preparing each child's favorite meal for a birthday or a special occasion is a subtle way of saying to each child: "You are special. I care about you." Table manners and hygiene should be taught carefully over a period of time. A simple "Don't eat your peas with your fingers" can cause a flare-up! A recently popular expression (and the title of a book stepparents might consider reading) is "Don't sweat the small stuff—and it's all small stuff."

Household Chores

To resolve the problem of completing chores, many families find they must prepare charts allocating duties. This practice seems to work. Find out each child's abilities and make tasks age appropriate. Even 2-year-olds enjoy setting the table. Children generally resist biological parents when it comes to chores, so expect friction when a stepparent is too controlling or demanding. The best rule of thumb for teaching chores is to do the chore with them in the beginning. Large tasks might need to be broken down into smaller tasks that are manageable over a few days (picking up dirty clothes one day, vacuuming the next). Stepchildren who are in the home only on the weekend or during vacations still need to have responsibilities—it actually gives them a sense of belonging ("I had to clean *my* room at Dad's"). Typically, children develop more confidence the more capable they become. Biological parents who miss their children all week might have a tendency to want to do everything for their children—but a child of 6 who gets away with no responsibility becomes a 16-year-old adolescent who can be impossible to live with. A home is not a hotel. A stepparent is not a "servant," nor is a stepchild.

Personal Territory

Changes in living arrangements pose turf problems. The stepparent who has moved into the spouse's home finds that areas of the house are already designated for use and intrusions are deeply resented. This matter is more easily handled by moving to a new house or making personal spaces within the old one. New paint, fresh curtains, a new rug selected by children can personalize their space. If possible, enlist the children's opinions in these decisions. Bring something from the other home to put in his or her new room. Even new husbands and wives do not like sitting in the ex-spouse's chair or sleeping in the ex-spouse's bed. Even biological siblings fight over what belongs to whom, so expect these types of spats among stepsiblings. In the beginning, it is best if the biological parent manages discipline in this area. Stepchildren, even young ones, seem to feel in the beginning that stepparents have no right to tell them what to do (any more than we like a stranger telling us what to do). Expect to hear "You're not my Mom (or Dad)!" Be prepared to discuss the underlying feelings behind any sharp remarks. Acknowledge those feelings and get them into the open for age-appropriate discussions ("I know you're angry that I'm asking you to put your clothes away. It isn't easy having to pack and unpack every weekend, is it? I understand it's a lot of work for you. Perhaps we could do this together.")

Financial Matters

The biological parent might be making alimony and/or child-support payments to an ex-spouse, so there are often financial strains in supporting the "new" family. Where monies come from, and for whom and how funds are allocated, are matters that must be mutually decided. Stepfamily money practices often come under close scrutiny by outsiders, such as lawyers, courts, the social services system, and the IRS. The family must keep track of medical expenses, insurance monies, orthodonture payments, clothing and school-related expenses, and so on. Over time, the ex-spouse is likely to initiate court-ordered audits of a family's income for support readjustment (mainly if there is a bonus or raise in pay). Or a tax audit might be required—dependents are often split equally between ex-spouses by the courts for tax purposes. Limited financial resources require careful management. Use of a computer software program for managing family finances can make the chore of recording and tracking income and expenses easier. You will have an easier time in court if your records are organized and documented. This can save thousands of dollars for a family. The demands of an ex-spouse might seem unreasonable, but this is generally up to the courts to decide (although mediation methods exist). Make sure separation and divorce documents are precise about who is responsible for what expenses. There are legal consequences if a biological parent does not follow through with court-ordered support payments.

Discipline

This is likely to be the area of most disputes between parent and stepparent. Children accustomed to one type of discipline have to adjust to another—often on a weekly basis. Most professionals agree that the parents must yield to compromise so that the children are presented with a united front. Children must not learn to pit one parent against the other. In natural families, parenting techniques evolve gradually as the parents and children move through the family life cycle. But in blended families there is no time for such evolution. A solid understanding of child and adolescent development helps parents communicate effectively. Whatever forms of discipline are decided on, such approaches are best discussed prior to the marriage vows. As stated earlier, discipline should be administered as promptly after the infraction as possible, especially for young children who cannot remember what they did earlier, and the type and degree of discipline should match the misbehavior. As in any family, fairness should prevail. The most effective discipline teaches the child what she or he should do rather than focuses on what was done wrong. ("You didn't pick up your room, so you will have to do it now rather than go to your friend's house" instead of "You are grounded for the weekend!") Fathers in an intact family do not always notice whether bedrooms are clean, chores are done, homework is done, children have brushed their teeth and showered, and so forth. These tasks have traditionally been considered within the mother's domain. Stepmoms, like most mothers, tend to pick up on such details of child care, which fathers might overlook. The stepfamily must reevaluate what is really important in the family over the long run.

Changes over Time

As children become teenagers, they naturally want to spend more time with friends. Both sets of parents need to support the adolescent's interests in school and outside activities. Adolescence is a time when teens need to express themselves and experience some independence, and parents who force children to adhere to a rigid visitation schedule spend much of their time with an unhappy teen. Allow teens to make more choices, just as they do in intact families. Do not, however, let the teen get away with less supervision. At this stage, manipulation of both sets of parents is more likely. A child who has two homes might think, "I can always go to the other home." Try not to dwell on the negative; that type of attention is a reinforcer for some children. Look for and praise the positive. Make them be responsible and learn from the consequences of their actions.

Support Groups

More communities now have support groups for stepparents. Those who are more experienced with this type of family arrangement can understand the special stresses and emotions that young stepparents experience. Many school districts also have support groups for children of divorce or in blended families. Children in intact families often say, "I love you, Mom [or Dad]." It can be years before a stepparent hears anything close to this. Recognize that children do not realize the sacrifices parents make to raise them (until they themselves become parents).

From: L. K. White and A. Booth, "The Quality and Stability of Remarriages: The Role of Stepchildren," *American Sociological Review,* Vol. 50, No. 5 (October 1985), 689–698.

employment or supervised employment. These are often difficult, heart-wrenching decisions for aging parents. We normally expect that our adult children will be capable of making their own life decisions.

But for some older married couples, the nest stays empty after the children depart. This can be especially stressful for a woman who has been a traditional homemaker, for whom being a mother has been a central ingredient in her life and identity. Clinical psychologists and psychiatrists have emphasized the emotional difficulties women face when their children leave home, dubbing the problems the **empty-nest syndrome** (Bart, 1972). A parent who has found her or his meaning in life primarily in the children often experiences a profound sense of loss when the children are no longer around. One mother who had been completely wrapped up in a selfless nurturing of her four children told one of your authors a few months after the last child had left home for college, "I feel such a hole in my life, such a void. It is like I'm a rock inside. Just a vast, solid emptiness. Really, I have nothing to look forward to. It is all downhill from here on!"

Some women object to the overemphasis on physical changes and the "empty nest" in women's midlife maturation. Recent cross-sectional and longitudinal studies find that many women do not regret the end of fertility, experience minimal menopausal symptoms, feel happy when their children are successfully launched, and feel satisfaction when their children continue to stay in touch with them (Helson in Lachman & James, 1997, p. 29). Couples often report that they view the empty-nest period "as a time of new freedom." One 42-year-old woman whose two children were off at college and who had returned to Ohio State University to secure her degree in accounting told one of your authors:

> Sure, I experienced a throb or two when Ida [her youngest child] left home. But, you know, I had expected it to be a lot worse. I really like the freedom I have now. I can do the things I want to do when I want to do them, and I don't have to worry about getting home to make dinner or to do household chores. I'm now back in school, and I love it.

Often, both parents and children adjust to the empty nest on a gradual basis. Children might live at home for a period after securing their first job. Or they might go off to college and return home for semester breaks. Most parents adapt to the empty-nest period quite well. A sample of midlife parents confirmed that parents' self-evaluations are influenced by the perceptions they have of the lives of their grown children (Brim, Ryff, & Kessler, 2004). Overall, midlife adults' sense of self-acceptance, purpose in life, and environmental mastery was strongly linked with their assessments of their children's adjustment.

Caring for Elderly Parents   Psychologists call middle-aged adults the *sandwich generation* because many find themselves with responsibilities for their own children on the one side and for their elderly parents on the other. At the very time when they are launching their own children and looking forward to having more time for themselves, many encounter new demands from their parents. Some midlife couples find that they no sooner reach the empty-nest stage of the family life cycle than the nest is refilled with either an elderly parent or a grown son or daughter who returns home after a divorce or the loss of a job (see Chapter 14). Studies show that 30 to 40 percent of Americans in their fifties help their children, and a third help their parents financially or in other ways (Kolata, 1993). The average U.S. woman will spend on average 17 years raising children and perhaps the same number of years helping aged parents. Since many U.S. couples delayed childbirth during the 1980s, more couples will find themselves "sandwiched" between child care and elder care (McNeil, 2004).

Aging parents sometimes require increased time, emotional energy, and financial aid from their adult children. Despite the profound changes in the roles of family members, the grown children (particularly the daughters and daughters-in-law) still bear the primary responsibility for their aged parents (Brody et al., 1994). The sense of obligation is strong even when the emotional ties between the parent and child were previously weak (Cicirelli, 1992). In 80 percent of cases, any care an elderly person will require will be provided by her or his family. This assistance might be supplemented by help with income and health care costs through Social Security, Medicare, and Medicaid programs; however, changes in reimbursements, stipulated by the Balanced Budget Act of 1997 have led to significant reductions in Medicare support for home health care (Cohen et al., 2001). Despite the fact that the vast majority of adult children provide help to their parents, Americans continue to echo the myth that "nowadays, adult children do not take as much care of their parents as they did in past generations."

Not surprisingly, many "women in the middle" are subjected to role-overload stresses similar to those ex-

The Sandwich Generation   Middle age often brings with it responsibilities for one's own children, grandchildren, and aging parents. The tasks fall disproportionately upon women who, in the American gender division of labor, are the persons assigned primary responsibility for family caretaking.

perienced by younger women in relation to work, child care, and other household responsibilities. Their difficulties are often compounded by their own age-related circumstances, such as lower energy levels, the onset of chronic ailments, and family losses (E. M. Brody, 1990). We might expect that middle-aged women will end up caring for their husbands as they age. Some believe these facts in part explain the appeal that religion has for many middle-aged and elderly women. One 60-year-old woman, whose 90-year-old father shares her home along with her husband and her 30-year-old daughter who moved back home to save money, says:

> At a time of my life I should have less to do, I have greater demands put on me. I have my own getting older to cope with. Sometimes I get angry, not at him [her father], but at what age brings with it. Whenever he gets ill, I panic: now what? Still I couldn't live with myself if I resorted to a nursing home. (Langway, 1982, p. 61)

Despite the changing roles of women, when it comes to the elderly, the old maxim still seems to hold: "A son's a son till he takes a wife, but a daughter's a daughter for the rest of her life." Thus, adult daughters and daughters-in-law often face complex time-allocation pressures. They must juggle competing role demands of employed worker, homemaker, wife, mother, grandmother, and caregiving daughter.

The motivations, expectations, and aspirations of the middle-aged and the elderly differ to some extent because of their different life periods and cohort memberships. At times these differences can be a source of intergenerational strain (Scharlach, 1987). However, resentment and hostility are usually less where the financial independence of the generations enables them to maintain separate residences. Both the elderly and their adult offspring seem to prefer intimacy "at a distance" and opt for residing independently as long as possible. Consequently, the elderly parents who need to call on children for assistance are apt to be frail, greatly disabled, gravely ill, or failing mentally. When middle-aged adults express reluctance to take on primary care for an ailing parent, they are not necessarily being "hardhearted." Rather, they recognize that their marriage or emotional health could be endangered by taking on those caretaking responsibilities (Miller & McFall, 1991). Simultaneously, this realization can produce strong feelings of guilt (Pruchno et al., 1994). As noted earlier, most adult children would rather make sacrifices to care for their parents than place them in a nursing home (E. M. Brody, 1990); however, recent statistics indicate that the fastest-growing population is the 85 and older group. As more people face the prospect of caring for the elderly, the more they will search for help with and alternatives to providing that care themselves (see the *Further Developments* box on page 568, "The Sandwich Generation").

On the other hand, female caregivers who find their caregiving role to be satisfying or rewarding can derive positive health benefits from the endeavor. Of course, the outcomes are frequently otherwise for those who find caregiving stressful or unfulfilling (Stephens & Franks, 1995). In contrast to women, most men apparently find caregiving stressful and are likely to invest themselves more in their occupational role (Allen, 1994).

Questions

What is meant by the expression the sandwich generation? How does being in this generation impact the relationships of middle-age adults with their parents, grown children, and grandchildren?

Friendships

Most people distinguish friend from relative and coworker. This does not mean that a relative could not be a friend. Friends are people who seek each others' company and with whom one can talk and share activities and for whom one has warm feelings (Fehr, 1996). As we have noted throughout this text, close and meaningful social relationships play a vital part in human happiness and health. In study after study, researchers report that people who have friends to whom they can turn for affirmation, empathy, advice, assistance, and affection are less likely to develop diseases like cancer and respiratory

illness and more likely to survive health challenges like heart attacks and major surgery. Indeed, it seems it is more important to have at least one person with whom we can share open and honest thoughts and feelings than it is to have a substantial network of superficial friendships (Brody, 1992c).

So what do we know about the baby-boom generation entering midlife and their friendships? Adams and Blieszner (1998) have been studying the generation born between 1946 and 1964 and its patterns of friendship. They find this is the first American cohort to relocate from their home communities in large numbers as they finished college and sought employment in the 1960s to 1970s. Consequently, this cohort has had more opportunities than any other generation to develop a diversity of, and greater tolerance within, friendships. With the development of television, this generation was also the first to have almost instant knowledge of major current events (e.g., the assassination of President Kennedy, our landing on the moon, the civil rights movement, the Vietnam War, the women's movement, 9/11, and the Iraq War) and developed a high level of cohort identity.

Women in midlife are more likely than men to have intimate friendships (Adams & Blieszner, 1998). Men often have many acquaintances with whom they share experiences, but they frequently have few or no friends. The social contacts of many elderly men are restricted to their wives, their children, and their children's families. Male relationships are often limited to group settings involving their sports team, occupational colleagues, or "brothers" in a fraternal group, such as Rotary, VFW, Shriners, or Knights of Columbus. Numerous social constraints limit the development of closeness among men (Weiss, 1990). Men have also tended to disenfranchise themselves from the house, the primary center of security, warmth, and nurturance. They are more likely to construe the house as a "physical structure." In contrast, women tend to define the house more in terms of a "personalized place" affording "relationships with others." Hence, men commonly socialize outside the home.

Moreover, women tend to maintain family contacts and emotionally invest themselves in the family to a greater degree than men do throughout the lifetime of a family. Women's friendships often take up where their marriages leave off. A woman's best friends typically compensate her for the deficits of intimacy she encounters within her marriage. And shared experiences of child rearing promote a moral and social dialogue among women that gives their friendships depth and intimacy. Significantly, women in the baby-boom generation were the first to give friendships equal status with romantic relationships with men and have adopted a "code of loyalty" to their women friends in contrast to the behavior of older women (Adams & Blieszner, 1998). Thus, women's networks of interpersonal ties work to satisfy

Further Developments

The Sandwich Generation

Middle age often brings with it responsibilities for one's own children, grandchildren, and aging parents. The tasks fall disproportionately upon women who, in the American gender division of labor, are the ones assigned primary responsibility for family caretaking. "Anyone who's raised children or cared for an aging parent knows how exhausting and frustrating (if rewarding) either can be. Doing both at once is vastly harder, and very often stretches your resources—emotional, financial and otherwise—to their limits and beyond" (Weisser, 2004, p. 112).

This is the challenge of the "sandwich generation"—the cohort caught between caring for their children (some of whom are delaying or returning to the parental nest) and caring for their aging parents (who are living longer). "Tough questions and tough decisions are falling to this group. Are time and money devoted to your parents shortchanging your kids? Is it wrong to let your parents accept government help intended for the poor when you're not poor? And what about you and your own financial security? Is it selfish to take money that could be spent on your parents' or kids' welfare and save it for your own retirement—let alone spend it on a romantic vacation?"

There are about 68 million people who make up the sandwich generation (ages 45 to 64), but this number is expected to double in the next 20 years. Part of the reason for the increase in the number of people sandwiched between generations is the trend toward postponing marriages and thus starting families later, as well as the fact that people are living longer. As the number of people who find themselves sandwiched and stretched to the limit grows, there are calls for solutions to this difficult situation. Yet there are things that anyone facing this situation can do to alleviate some of the difficulty. And there are some innovative solutions already being tried that can prevent or reduce the chance of an overwhelming dependence by aging parents.

One of the effects of the Terry Schiavo tragedy is that it drew public attention to end-of-life issues such as living wills. Although it may be an uncomfortable subject for many people, having frank and open discussions about one's wishes for medical and legal decisions can also provide relief and comfort. Aging people who realize that such decisions are inevitable may feel relieved that their affairs are in order and that their wishes will be respected and may be comforted to

know that their children will be spared the task of making these decisions later on perhaps during a time of great stress.

Families can make decisions about drawing up a document called a *durable power of attorney,* which gives the designated person the right to make financial and legal decisions for one's parents should they be unable to do so for themselves. The *health-care directive* is similar to a power of attorney but it concerns health-care decisions. It is also known as a *health-care proxy.* These documents can be done with the help of an attorney, with a software kit, or with a form that can be downloaded from the Internet.

Insurance is another safeguard for the care of the elderly. *Medicare* is available to everyone over the age of 65 and it covers hospital care. But some people choose to buy additional insurance to cover what Medicare does not. Long-term care insurance covers assisted-living, nursing home, and home health care. This might be a consideration for people who wish to preserve their assets. *Medicaid,* which is available to income-eligible individuals, covers nursing home care and in some cases assisted-living and home care as well.

Innovative Solutions for Elder Care

In Boston, Beacon Hill Village is a "virtual community" of 50 residences and 150 members. For a yearly fee, members get discounts on a variety of services such as home repair, car service, and nursing care. This can relieve some of the caregiving responsibilities. For people who do not live in close proximity to their elderly parents, they may wish to secure the professional services of *geriatric care managers (GCMs).* GCMs make assessments of the elderly person's health and living situation to help with nursing home or assisted-living placement, and in-home care services. They also act as liaisons with family members. The National Association of Professional Geriatric Care Managers can provide more information.

Another innovative solution to caring for relatives who do not live in close proximity is a program called *Caring from a Distance.* This program matches elderly family members with volunteer caregivers. President of the organization, Ted Patton explains, "Let's say one adult child is living in New York and has a mother in California, and another baby boomer is in California and has a father in New York. The two could offer to be the eyes and ears for each other's fam-

their emotional needs and add coherence to lives pulled in multiple directions by the fragmenting demands of modern life (O'Connor, 1992). The nature and quality of friendships for this generation have implications for their networks of support in old age and the types of

communities they will choose to live in after they retire. As we shall see in the following section, the relationships we establish with co-workers have less stability than in past generations, as significant changes are occurring in the American workplace.

ily member, checking in with them on a regular basis and giving each other updates."

Homesharing can be an option for seniors who may have more space in their homes than they actually need. Seniors can be matched based on compatibility to share a home and expenses. This often provides much needed companionship as well. It can help ease the worry of relatives who are concerned about their loved ones living alone. Such a program is being tried by the Chicago Department of Aging.

Some companies are offering their employees elder-care referrals, which provide in-home assessments and assist with

placements. In addition, the Alzheimer's Foundation of America is promoting the idea of on-site adult day care as part of employee benefits. Yet another solution that is being tried in some states is a program that allows family members of Medicaid recipients to be paid stipends for caring for their elderly relatives. As you see with the present middle-aged baby-boom cohort, they are generating new solutions to managing developmental tasks, as they have always done.

From: Cybele Weisser. (2004, December). The big squeeze, *Money, 33* (12), 112–118; Laura Koss-Feder. (2003, March 17). Providing for parents: The "sandwich generation" looks for new solutions. *Time, 161* (11).

Question

How do women's and men's friendships in midlife differ in value, settings, and purpose?

The Workplace

Today, new currents are at play in the workplace. These currents involve new technologies, new industries, new markets, job migration, population shifts, and continuing education. Employees, especially those in their forties and fifties, experience continual demands to retrain and upgrade their job skills (see Figure 16.2). Today's midlife employee can no longer rely on the foundation of education and training she or he acquired 20 or 30 years ago.

Many nontraditional students in their mid-thirties and mid-forties have experienced corporate "downsizing," "takeovers," and "restructuring." Some have been forced into unemployment, disability, or early retirement; others are making career changes in order to reenter the occupational sphere. A few make dramatic career changes by personal choice. This experience has a significant impact on economic security, retirement planning, and self-esteem. Following the emotional aftermath and economic disruption caused by the World Trade Center disaster, anecdotal evidence suggests that some people have taken stock of their lives and careers and have made changes based on necessity and the feeling that "life is too short" to delay one's dreams and aspirations.

Job Satisfaction

Levinson says that in midlife, employed men and women experience a different relationship with their occupational status. They are asking themselves, "Is my work satisfying?" There is much greater emphasis on self-fulfillment and satisfaction than on the collection of external rewards. Others ask themselves, "In what ways

have I made a contribution or formed a 'legacy' to something outside of myself or my family?" People often want to be appreciated for their contributions at work and are likely to offer to mentor others who are coming up in the ranks. However, not everyone experiences satisfaction in their work, and some take "psychological retirement" (Levinson, 1996, p. 375). Some whose work performance is minimally adequate accept "early retirement." Some with midlife dissatisfaction with work may become depressed, consume more alcohol or other drugs, become accident prone or regularly absent, experience marital and family discord, or search for youthful forms of excitement that typically are considered inappropriate in middle age (Levinson, 1996, p. 375). Those

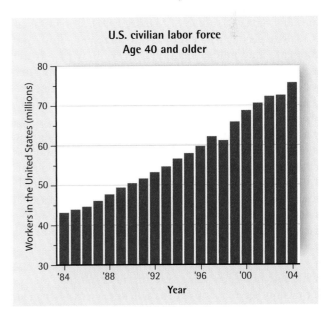

FIGURE 16.2 U.S. Workers Over 40: 1984–2004
Presently, middle-age adults make up more than half of the U.S. labor force. Thus many in midlife are at the top of their careers, productive, and contributing to society—and not retired.
From Hope Yen, "Court Clears Way for More Age Lawsuits," Associated Press, March 31, 2005. Copyright © 2005 Associated Press. Reprinted with permission.

in their early forties might see that the anticipated promotion or advancement isn't coming and make career changes more to their liking. Some today have launched their own consulting businesses. Typically, "the higher one's position [at work], the fewer the attractive alternatives and the greater the potential fall" (Levinson, 1996). French philosopher Albert Camus captures the importance of work in giving meaning and satisfaction to our lives: "Without work, all life goes rotten. But when work is soulless, life stifles and dies."

Significantly, Americans, especially women, have been entering the labor force in ever-increasing numbers since the 1960s, so that today about 67 percent of the working-age population holds jobs or seeks them. Yet work that is not fulfilling can erode and undermine much of our humanness. Some psychologists and sociologists have applied the concept of alienation to such troubles and have sought solutions to these problems in programs designed to decrease alienation. The word **alienation** commonly implies a pervasive sense of powerlessness, meaninglessness, normlessness, isolation, and self-estrangement (Erikson, 1986). Alienation can be expressed in **job burnout.** In terms of psychological effects, the problem that confronts most people in occupational life today is that they cannot gain a sense of self-actualization in their work. Hence, the most potent factors in job satisfaction are those that relate to workers' self-respect, their chance to perform well, their opportunities for achievements and growth, and the chance to contribute something personal and quite unique.

Work affects an individual's personal and family life in many ways (Crouter & Manke, 1994). For instance, jobs that permit occupational self-direction—initiative, thought, and independent judgment in work—foster people's intellectual flexibility. Individuals with such jobs become more open approaching and weighing evidence on current social and economic issues. Individuals who enjoy opportunities for self-direction in their work are more likely to become more self-confident, less authoritarian, less conformist in their ideas, and less fatalistic in their nonwork lives than other individuals are. In turn, these traits lead, in time, to more responsible jobs that allow even greater latitude for occupational self-direction. In sum, the job affects the person and the person affects the job in a reciprocal relationship across adult life (Kohn et al., 1990).

It had been thought that job satisfaction increased with age; however, some researchers argue that the relationship between job satisfaction and age is U-shaped, declining from a moderate level in early years of employment and then steadily increasing up to retirement (Clark, Oswald, & Warr, 1996). Workers just beginning their careers and workers nearing the end of their careers reported being more satisfied than those at the midpoint. As a result, many people at midlife change jobs and even

careers. Midlife women can expect to change jobs nine times now as compared with three times in their lives in the 1970s (Muha, 1999). Two hypotheses might explain this phenomenon. According to one interpretation, younger workers expect a more casual work environment that allows for more worker input and decision making. As this expectation has been found to be profitable in many cases, new companies have adopted this strategy. For example, the work environment at Microsoft is more casual than a more conservative company. Proponents of this view cite as key features of the "new values" a willingness to question authority, a weakening of materialistic standards, and a demand that work be fulfilling and enriching. These values contradict those of an industrial order founded on deference to authority and responsiveness to such traditional rewards as income and promotion.

A second interpretation of age differences in job satisfaction looks to life-cycle effects (Wright & Hamilton, 1978). Proponents of this hypothesis say that older workers are more satisfied with their jobs because on the whole they have better jobs than younger workers do. In the usual career pattern, a person begins at or near the bottom and, where possible, moves up. Young people typically begin their careers when they have relatively few pressing responsibilities. Usually they are unmarried, or without children, or both. They require little more than a start—a job that is "good enough" for the immediate present, supplies sufficient money to meet short-term needs, and affords some opportunity for advancement. But as workers develop new needs (marry, have children, and grow older), they also accumulate the experience, skills, and seniority that allow them to find positions that are progressively more satisfying.

Using data gathered by the University of Michigan's Survey Research Center (based on national surveys of the economically active U.S. labor force), sociologists find age differences in the rewards that workers look for from their jobs and in certain of their work values (Kalleberg & Loscocco, 1983). For instance, older workers seek job security, fringe benefits, and convenient hours, whereas young workers seek promotions and advancement. These differing concerns can be explained by life-cycle effects.

Questions

Are middle-aged workers likely to be satisfied with their jobs? Why or why not?

Midlife Career Change

Most of us start off our careers with the assumption that we will spend our lives in one line of work (chances are, our parents and grandparents did). This perspective is most characteristic of white-collar professionals, such as physicians, lawyers, accountants, engineers, and college professors. Such individuals spend their late adolescence and early adulthood acquiring special skills and credentials. They—and their family, friends, and associates—assume that they will spend their remaining years successfully pursuing a career that constitutes a lifetime commitment. Their work is expected to produce a considerable sense of fulfillment and, with few exceptions, unfold in an orderly progression of steps from an entry position to eventual retirement. Many midlife adults have come to expect that their jobs offer some type of satisfaction—emotional as well as financial. But a recent poll found that less than half of workers of all age groups and income levels were satisfied with their work. Such factors as promotion policies, salary bonuses, education and training, as well as relationships with co-workers influenced workers' job satisfaction levels (Caudron, 2001).

Recent surveys on emotional well-being and aging, and an examination of suicide statistics, have indicated that those who enter "the professions" are also likely to become dissatisfied with their careers, but many feel they cannot change occupations because the financial rewards, security, and prestige are so great. This serious conflict between changing to more satisfying work and living at a different status or remaining in a career that gives no satisfaction might contribute to rise in the suicide rate for people in their forties and older.

The Bureau of Labor Statistics gathers statistics on workers who tell that they are doing different work than they did one year earlier. About one man in eight aged 25 to 34 typically changes his occupation in a year. The same holds true for women, except that women are more likely to change jobs now than in the 1960s. Both men and women switch careers for a variety of reasons. Some find that their career has not provided the fulfillment they had expected or that it no longer challenges them. One professor who left academic life at age 43 for a career in marketing told one of the authors:

> I just got fed up with teaching. It no longer turned me on. I would wake up in the morning and dread the day ahead. When driving over to the university, I would develop waves of nausea. I began thinking to myself, "This is no way to spend the rest of my life." I had always been interested in marketing, and I had done consulting for a number of years before I left the university. It took me about five years before I got the business really rolling but now I'm doing pretty well. I like being my own boss and I like making money—big money. I never could do that as a prof.

At midlife many people take stock of themselves and reassess where they are going and what they are doing with their lives. Some look to formal education to provide them with new skills. Others build on contacts, interests, skills, or hobbies.

Unemployment and Forced Early Retirement

Most people find unemployment a painful experience. As mentioned earlier in this chapter, job insecurity is mounting in the United States, due to automation, corporate downsizing, and outsourcing of jobs to other countries. There has been a rise in the number of workers employment agencies call "contingent workers," "flexible workers," "temporary workers," and "assignment workers"—what some labor economists by contrast call "disposable" and "throwaway" workers (Kilborn, 1993). In fact, a growing percentage of U.S. college faculty are part-time workers (adjuncts), especially at two-year colleges.

Sociologists and psychologists find that unemployment and underemployment have adverse effects on physical and mental health (Feather, 1990). Based on data from the 1970s, M. H. Brenner (1976) of Johns Hopkins University calculated that a rise of 1 percent in the national rate of unemployment, when sustained over a six-year period, is associated with a 4 percent increase in suicide, a 6 percent increase in homicide, and a 4 percent increase in first-time male admissions to state mental institutions. More recent research confirms these findings (Hamilton et al., 1990). The worst psychological effects of job loss, however, can be minimized if opportunities exist for reemployment (Hamilton et al., 1993).

Unemployment also increases the financial and role strains of parents, intensifies conflict between parents and their children, and undermines children's school achievement and health (Conger et al., 1993; Flanagan & Eccles, 1993). George Clem, a 31-year-old unemployed manufacturing worker in Jackson, Michigan, observed: "I've lost everything I ever had—it's all gone. I've lost my job. I've lost my home. I thought I had my future assured, but now I know I have no future." A woman in the same community said: "Emotionally, you begin to feel worthless. Rationally, you know you're not worthless, but the rational and the emotional don't always meet" (Nelson, 1983, p. 8).

National unemployment figures include people who are currently eligible for unemployment benefits. We really do not know the occupational status of people who are no longer eligible for unemployment and are unemployed on a long-term basis. However, studies of workers reveal that their behavioral and emotional reactions to unemployment typically pass through several stages (Kaufman, 1982):

- Initially, they undergo a sequence of shock, relief, and relaxation. Many had expected that they were about to lose their jobs. Hence, when the dismissal comes, they may feel a sense of relief that at last the suspense has ended. On the whole, they remain confident and hopeful that they will find a new job when they are ready. For the first month or two, they maintain normal relationships with their family and friends.

- The second stage centers on a concerted effort to find a new job. If these unemployed persons have been upset or angry about losing their jobs, the feeling tends to evaporate as they marshal their resources and concentrate their energy on finding a new job. This stage can last for up to four months. But individuals who have not found another job during this time move into the next stage.
- The third stage lasts about six weeks. Their self-esteem begins to crumble, and they experience high levels of self-doubt and anxiety. Those nearing retirement age find their outlook particularly bleak (Love & Torrence, 1989).
- The fourth stage finds unemployed workers drifting into a state of resignation and withdrawal. They become exceedingly discouraged and convinced that they are not going to find work, so they either stop looking for work or search for it only halfheartedly and intermittently. Some come through the stage and look back on it as a "cleansing" experience. They might make a conscious decision to change careers or to settle for some other line of work. And they might look for other sources of self-esteem, including their family, friends, and hobbies.

However, individuals who undergo long-term unemployment often find that their family life deteriorates (Larson, Wilson, & Beley, 1994). Health benefits, sick time, vacations, and other benefits end for most Americans when they lose their jobs, and many lose their pensions as well if they did not have enough vested time in the company. Financial pressures mount. They are unable to keep up their mortgage payments, or they fall behind in the rent. They see their cars and furniture repossessed. It is little wonder that they feel that they are losing control of their lives. Weekly visits to charities and food pantries become a necessity. Child abuse, violence, family quarreling, alcoholism, and other evidence of maladjustment mounts. The divorce rate soars among the long-term unemployed. Many men feel emasculated when confronted by an involuntary change of identity and provisioner role in the family, and they lash out with destructive reactions. The unemployment scenario has been more prevalent in African American and other ethnic minority families, especially for unskilled laborers without an education.

Many communities now have career centers where job hunters can search the Internet to get professional assistance in writing and preparing resumes and letters of application, to update and practice interviewing skills, and so on. These services also can help persons with long-term unemployment find retraining opportunities.

> **Question**
>
> Why are many middle-age American workers unemployed or forced into early retirement, and what are these men and women doing about their occupational status?

Dual-Earner Couples

Dual-earner couples accounted for 39 percent of married couples in 1970 and increased to 61 percent in 1993 (Blau, Ferber, & Winkler, 1998). Today various sources report that 70 to 77 percent of adult women work, which means that more than 60 million women are part of the U.S. labor force. In 1950, women made up nearly 25 percent of the labor force (it was socially acceptable for single women to work to support themselves then). Both the women's movement of the 1960s and the passage of Title IX of the Civil Rights Act of 1964 allowed more women to make gains in employment and enter traditionally male-dominated universities and occupations (Barnett, 1997). In 2003, about 60 percent of women age 16 and over were working or looking for work and comprised nearly half of the total labor force (U.S. Bureau of Labor Statistics, 2005).

Men and women typically see and experience inequalities in family work quite differently. Much depends on how fair the man and the woman judge the division of household labor to be (Mederer, 1993). Research by Thoits (1986) and Verbrugge (1989) concludes, however, that there is a positive association between occupying a greater number of roles and increased psychological well-being. These findings are contrary to the traditional belief that multiple roles could not be good for married women with children. More recent studies support the findings that women who are wives and mothers and employees show no more signs of distress than women who occupy fewer of these roles (Barnett, 1997). Moreover, women who have children report increased distress only if they decrease their commitment to the labor force (Barnett, 1997). Examining cross-sectional and longitudinal studies on job distress for men and women, Barnett and colleagues (1995) found that people who report positive job experiences report low psychological distress. If the job experience deteriorates, psychological distress increases. Even today, women who enter male-dominated professions might have to continually fight subtle (or not so subtle) sexism obstacles (Kolbert, 1991). Also, we do know that work has different meanings for men and women (Barnett, 1997).

In 2003, more than 60 percent of married women were in the labor force (U. S. Bureau at the Census, 2004–2005). Though work outside the home creates new sources of conflict for many couples, it also gives them new sources of personal fulfillment (Paden & Buehler,

"I love being a partner Mr. Jenkins! There's just one problem."

Gender Roles Change but Old Ways and Attitudes Might Persist

Source: From *The Wall Street Journal*—Permissions, Cartoon Features Syndicate.

1995). Recent studies also indicate that women's adult career commitments have a positive impact on their children's career goals and aspirations (Vandewater & Stewart, 1997). In addition, workplace policies on parental leave (for child care and parental care) and other institutional arrangements (e.g., flextime policies) that can provide relief to dual-earner couples are becoming top social and political issues.

Choosing Retirement

The traditional definition of *retirement* is "withdrawal from one's position or occupation or from active work life" (*Webster's Dictionary*). With a cohort of more than 68 million adults, there are multiple paths to retirement: Some have already retired, many are contemplating retirement, some have no desire to retire, and those in their late forties are likely planning to retire within the next 10 to 15 years (see Tables 16.4 and 16.5) (Hedge, Borman, & Lammelein, 2004). For many, one spouse is retired and the other is not, which is an important factor in retirement satisfaction (Smith & Moen, 2004). However, Judith Sugar, gerontology and life-span expert, sees this cohort of retirees as changing the definition of retirement, and not falling into the stereotype of a retiree with a drop in self-esteem and life involvement (Sugar & Marinelli, 1997). Many are volunteering, consulting, or working part-time. Sugar says today's retirees are "a pool of talent and abilities that we as a society cannot afford to lose," especially because the cohort in the next generation has barely half the number of adults (Chamberlin, 2004, p. 82).

Table 16.4 Comparison (in Percent) of Labor-Force Early Exits (Retirement), Men and Women Aged 50 to 54, in Germany, Japan, Sweden, and the United States: 1965–1970 and 1990–1995

Years	Germany	Japan	Sweden	United States
Men				
1965–1970	3.1	4.4	4.2	7.1
1990–1995	10.9	.5	10.5	11.9
Women				
1965–1970	5.2	12.3	-3.9*	-4.3*
1990–1995	11.6	14.1	9.3	11.1

*Net accessions rather than net exits. This means more women in the age group were entering the labor force than exiting from it at this time.
Source: Gendell, Murray. (1998). Trends in Retirement Age in Four Countries, 1965–1995. *Monthly Labor Review.* Bureau of Labor Statistics, U.S. Department of Labor. Vol. 121, No. 8, 20–30.

Nancy Schlossberg, psychology professor, author, and consultant on life transitions, says it takes time to get comfortable with a new life in her recent book, *Retire Smart, Retire Happy: Finding Your True Path in Life* (Schlossberg, 2004). Upon retirement, everything changes: relating with a spouse and adult children, separating your identity from your primary profession, and adjusting your daily routines. Some "retirees" fashion whole new careers; others spend more time traveling, volunteering, working part-time, or being with family and grandchildren more (Dittmann, 2004). Schlossberg identifies six types of retirees: (1) *continuers* stay connected with past skills and activities, (2) *adventurers* start new activities or learn new skills, (3) *searchers* are looking for a new niche, (4) *easy gliders* enjoy unscheduled time and "go with the flow," (5) *involved spectators* stay interested in their previous field of work but assume a

Table 16.5 Average Age at Labor Force Exit of Men and Women in Germany, Japan, Sweden, and the United States: 1965–1970 and 1990–1995

Years	Germany	Japan	Sweden	United States
Men				
1965–1970	64.7	66.6	65.7	64.1
1990–1995	60.3	65.2	62.0	62.2
Women				
1965–1970	63.0	63.8	65.5	65.3
1990–1995	59.9	62.9	62.0	62.7

Source: Gendell, Murray. (1998). Trends in Retirement Age in Four Countries, 1965–1995. *Monthly Labor Review.* Bureau of Labor Statistics, US Department of Labor. Vol. 121, No. 8, 20–30.

different role, and (6) *retreaters* become depressed and give up on finding something meaningful to occupy their time and talent (Schlossberg, 2004). Being retired is an evolving state.

For many, planning financial portfolios in middle adulthood has become a priority—while not planning or reflecting on what it is they are going to do to enjoy this new phase of life. Norman Abeles, who helped plan APA's *Office on Aging* suggests a balance of activities to enjoy this new phase of life: exercise, volunteer, and continue your education (Qualls & Abeles, 2000). Sterns and Kaplan (2003) have proposed a model for retirement that suggests considering specific factors before retiring, including reflecting on work satisfaction, sense of satisfaction in community involvement, relationship and degree of family responsibilities (i.e., caregiving for older relatives), and possibilities of new friends and activities as part of a "future self" moving into late adulthood.

SEGUE

Perhaps more than at any other life stage, there are evident, dynamic changes for adults in midlife. This is a time of looking back on one's life and looking forward and making plans for retirement years without the daily structure of an occupation. Our self-esteem and personality traits affect our family and occupational choices and overall happiness at this stage of life. Those who feel overwhelmed with responsibilities of taking care of children, grandchildren, and parents will be psychologically distressed. Those who learn to manage their time and adapt to changing family and occupational responsibilities usually have a positive outlook and are often much happier as

they enter and go through these years of life. Adaptability, flexibility, and a sense of humor all contribute to successful passage through this stage of life. Fewer women nowadays are displaced homemakers because many are engaged in meaningful, satisfying occupational pursuits along with their spouses. Many of those who are dissatisfied with their employment status are taking charge of their careers, going back to college (even in their fifties and sixties), and entering new occupations. Those who are unemployed or experience forced early retirement require more understanding of their emotional distress. They may justifiably feel "old before their time."

Summary

Theories of the Self in Transition

1. Maturity is the capacity to undergo continual change in order to adapt successfully and cope flexibly with the demands and responsibilities of life. Maturity is not some sort of plateau or final state but a lifetime process of becoming.

2. Self-concept is the view we have of ourselves through time as "the real me" or "I myself as I really am." Self-concept in part derives from our social interactions because it is based on feedback from other people.

3. Erik Erikson posits that the midlife years are devoted to resolving the "crisis" of generativity versus stagnation, where generativity is "primarily the concern in establishing and guiding the next generation."

4. Robert C. Peck suggested that midlife individuals confront four tasks: making the transition from valuing physical powers to valuing wisdom; socializing instead of sexualizing relationships; becoming emotionally flexible; becoming "open" rather than "closed minded."

5. Trait models are based on the assumption that an individual gradually develops certain characteristics that become progressively resistant to change with the passage of time.

6. Situational models view a person's behavior as the outcome of the characteristics of the situation in which the person is momentarily located.

7. According to interactionist models of personality, behavior is always a joint product of the person and the situation; people seek out settings, activities, and associates that are congenial for them and thereby reinforce their preexisting bents.

8. According to Levinson's male stage theory, a man cannot go through his middle adult years unchanged, because he encounters the first indisputable signs of aging and is compelled to reassess the illusions he has held about himself.

9. Levinson's study of women in midlife found that combining love/marriage, motherhood, and full-time career had not given women as much satisfaction as they had hoped for, and women were exploring new ways to live in middle adulthood.

10. The women in the Mills Longitudinal Study experienced turmoil in their early forties, followed by an increase in stability by age 52, when they had fewer negative emotions, increased decisiveness, and increased comfort and

stability through adherence to personal and social standards.

11. In later life people tend toward androgynous responses, which are thought to be associated with increased flexibility and adaptability and hence with successful aging. Androgynous individuals do not restrict their behavior to that embodied in cultural stereotypes of masculinity and femininity.

12. On the whole, the greatest consistency in personality appears in various intellectual and cognitive dimensions, such as IQ, cognitive style, and self-concept. The least consistency is found in the realm of interpersonal behavior and attitudes.

The Social Milieu

13. Most American adults in midlife have a desire to be or to remain married. A majority of baby boomers born in 1946 are currently married. Most enjoy spending time with their spouses. Having a positive attitude toward one's spouse is associated with longevity and satisfaction with marriage.

14. Rates of extramarital sexual activity have varied since Kinsey's original self-report sexual behavior surveys in the early 1950s. Peaks of extramarital sexual activity occurred in the 1980s; married couples in the 1990s report less EMS.

15. Although divorce is becoming more common, it is hardly routine. Divorce can exact a greater emotional and physical toll than almost any other life stress, including death of a spouse. Compared with married, never-married, and widowed adults, the divorced have higher rates of psychological difficulties, accidental death, and illness.

16. Many Americans follow a path leading from marriage to divorce, remarriage, and widowhood. Marital separation, divorce, and remarriage have also become more common for those in midlife and older. The effects of divorce are diverse—displaced homemakers, liberated souls, and depressed individuals are all outcomes of divorce.

17. Most divorced people eventually remarry. About five of every six divorced men and about three of every four divorced women marry again.

18. At least one-third of all new marriages in the United States involve divorced or widowed parents with children under the age of 18. A good number of stepparents feel stigmatized. Boys particularly seem to benefit when their mothers remarry.

19. Middle-aged adults constitute a sandwich generation, with responsibilities for their own teenage children on the one side and for their elderly parents on the other side. Eighty percent of care for elderly persons is provided by their families. Responsibility for the elderly falls most commonly on daughters and daughters-in-law.

20. Friendships are very important in middle age. However, women are more likely than men to have intimate friendships in midlife. The nature and quality of friendships for today's generation of middle-aged adults have implications for their networks of support in old age.

The Workplace

21. Work fills many needs. At midlife, some individuals ask themselves, "Is my work satisfying?" and others ask themselves, "In what ways have I made a contribution or formed a 'legacy' to something outside of myself or my family?" Job satisfaction is associated with opportunities to exercise discretion, accept challenges, and make decisions. People appear to thrive on occupational challenges. However, not everyone experiences satisfaction in their work, and some take "psychological retirement."

22. The past three decades have brought considerable economic and social change in the status of women. A majority of women are employed either full-time or part-time today.

23. Career changes are now occurring more often in midlife. Women and men switch careers for a variety of reasons.

24. Unemployment is difficult for many reasons. Financial pressures mount. Child abuse, violence, family quarreling, alcoholism, and other evidences of maladjustment mount. The divorce rate soars among the long-term unemployed.

25. There has been an increase in dual-earner families. Today more than 60 million women are part of the U.S. labor force. In 1950, women made up nearly 25 percent of the labor force.

Key Terms

alienation (570)	generativity (548)	self-concept (547)
androgyny (556)	generativity versus stagnation (548)	social convoy (557)
displaced homemaker (561)	job burnout (570)	traditional marriage (552)
empty nest (563)	maturity (547)	
empty-nest syndrome (565)	sandwich generation (556)	

Following Up on the Internet

Web sites for this chapter focus on successful midlife transitions of middle-age adults. Please access the text Web site at www.mhhe.com/vzcrandell8 for up-to-date hot-linked Internet addresses for the following organizations, topics, and resources:

APA Office on Aging

AARP

Elderhostel

Journals on Aging and Human Development

Positive Aging Newsletter

Financial Literacy for the Sandwich Generation

What Color is My Parachute? (for job hunters and career-changers)

The National Institute on Aging

Video Scenario—http://www.mhhe.com/vzcrandell8

In this chapter, you've just read about issues of emotional and social development in middle adulthood, including information about family roles and social support. Using the OLC (www.mhhe.com/vzcrandell8), revisit Lisa and Lewis's discussion of midlife issues in the *Middle Adulthood video scenario.* Don't forget to test your knowledge of these concepts by trying the fill-in-the-blank and critical thinking questions that follow this segment.

Part NINE
Late Adulthood

Late adulthood brings a broader range of physical, cognitive, and social-emotional changes than any other stage in life. American Sarah Knauss, who until recently was one of the world's oldest persons at 119, headed six generations of descendants, including a daughter who is 95 and a great-great-great-grandson who is 3 (family photo in Chapter 18). In Chapter 17, we will see there is no consensus as to when old age begins and that humans are living longer than ever. Many assume that "old age" starts around retirement or when eligibility for public or private pensions begins. The "beginning of old age" is changing, though, for millions of elderly worldwide are now living well into their eighties and beyond. Recent research disputes the myths that portray old age as an undesirable time of life mainly characterized by debilitation. As we will discuss in Chapter 18, although the elderly experience changes in their cognitive functioning, some of the "oldest old" continue to care for themselves and remain socially engaged into their eighties and older. Many continue to share their maturity and wisdom with members of their extended family. As the elderly experience physical, cognitive, and social changes, most call on their religion and inner reserves of faith and spirituality for comfort and satisfaction with having lived a meaningful life.

CHAPTER

17

Late Adulthood
Physical and Cognitive Development

Outline

This chapter looks at the physical and cognitive functioning of adults in the final stages of life. *Longevity* and *biodemographics* are relatively new areas of study, and we will see where the research stands. Most physical and health changes are due to biological aging, though some 80-year-olds stay active and proclaim they feel like 60-year-olds. Because worldwide more people are living longer, all industrialized countries are experiencing a "graying" of their population and reexamining policies for their citizenry. Issues such as when the elderly should retire, where the funding for old-age pensions is going to come from, how many are working to provide for the elderly, and who is going to pay the bill are serious concerns all over the world. Significantly, antiaging specialists predict that in future years, human life will be extended by many more years.

Though most elderly experience a slowing in physical and cognitive functioning, they also experience a newfound sense of inner peace, finding hope and meaning in their faith and religious rituals. We will examine this last stage, not as the final chapters of a book, but more as an explorer's tentative steps toward the unknown.

Aging: Myth and Reality

Many of us have a half-conscious, irrational fear that some day we will find ourselves old. It is as if we will suddenly fall off a cliff—as if what we will become in old age has little to do with who we are now. But at no point in life do people stop being themselves and suddenly turn into "old people." Aging does not destroy the continuity of what we have been, what we are, and what we will be. In some cultures, such as Japan, aging is viewed positively, but our culture views aging ambivalently, even negatively. The older the old become, especially as they reach quite advanced age, the more likely they are to be unfavorably stereotyped. Take a minute to think about words commonly used to describe people who are in this late stage of life: *slow, tired, frail, miserly, grouchy, eccentric, wise, sweet, doting, serene, incompetent, dependent, disagreeable, stubborn, crotchety, croney,* or *hag.* Hallmark has a successful line of *Maxine* cards, depicting an outspoken, *cantankerous* old woman. Using such words and carrying the stereotype into commercial products contributes to the myths of old age, which tend to become a monolithic misperception about all older people.

The truth about aging is far more optimistic than myths would have us believe. Many losses of function once thought to be age-related, particularly declines in cognitive ability and mobility, are overgeneralized and exaggerated. New research on successful aging suggests that maintaining cognitive function and a positive attitude are crucial. This is based on a new paradigm that purports that memory and cognitive functions do not necessarily decline with age (Volz, 2000). **Ageism** is stereotyping and judging a group of people solely on the basis of their age. Just as sexism or racism denies the variability found in any race or gender, ageism focuses on a narrow range of descriptors of older adults, which are negative for the most part (Perls, 1995).

Negative as well as positive images of older people abound. Research on images of older women tended to focus on nonempirical studies. Sherman (1997) reviews the research literature and presents descriptions of controlled experimental research on images of older women. The review of the empirical research presented a more complex view of aging than the nonempirical studies. Birren (2000) argues that prevailing perceptions about aging do not match the actual longevity, demographic, and social characteristics of the aging population. These outdated notions will gradually disappear as older people become more visible through their increasing numbers and active participation in society.

We will see in this chapter and the next that aging does affect physical, cognitive, emotional, and social development, but we have all heard many inconsistent views on when these changes occur, how much change occurs, and why these changes occur. Ongoing research in **gerontology,** the study of aging and the special problems associated with it, and **geropsychology,** the study of the behavior and needs of the elderly, can help us separate myths from reality. As of 2004, the National Institutes of Health (NIH) has established 13 U.S. Centers on the Demography of Aging at various universities. These centers have been funded $30 million over the next five years to study a broad range of worldwide aging issues, such as biodemography, neuroeconomics, behavior genetics, disease and disability, medical technology, migration and geographic concentration of American elderly, decision making about retirement, pensions, savings, and living arrangements, and health disparities by gender and race (Mjoseth, 2004).

Aging is not a disease, and the ravages of aging are somewhat of a myth, except perhaps for the "oldest old" (Costa, Yang, & McCrae, 1998). Ignorance, superstition, and prejudice have surrounded aging for generations. To dispel some of the mystery, we will look at the demographics of aging and some specific myths in relation to current research.

Older Adults: Who Are They?

The time at which old age is said to begin varies according to period, place, and social rank. One researcher reported, for instance, that the Arawak of Guyana (in South America) seldom lived more than 50 years and that between the thirtieth and fortieth years in the case of men, and even earlier in the case of women, "the body, except the stomach, shrinks, and fat disappears, [and] the skin hangs in hideous folds" (Im Thurn, 1883). Life expectancy for the Andaman Islanders of the Bay of Bengal rarely exceeded 60 years (Portman, 1895), and the Arunta women of Australia were regarded as fortunate to reach 50 (Spencer & Gillen, 1927). In addition, the Creek Indians of North America were considered lucky if they lived to see gray hair on the heads of their children (Adair, 1775). Historically, in 1840 the record for life expectancy was held by Swedish women, who lived on average about 45 years, whereas Japanese women today experience the longest life expectancy—at almost 85 years (Oeppen & Vaupel, 2002).

Future Growth   The U.S. population of people 65 and older was about 36 million in 2003, or more than 12 percent of the total population (see Figure 17.1). Over the twentieth century, those living into late adulthood grew from 3 million to 36 million. The age group 85 and older grew from over 100,000 in 1900 to 4.2 million in 2000. It is projected that the 85-and-older population could reach 21 million by 2050. But it is the baby-boom cohort that will cause a dramatic rise in the 65-and-older

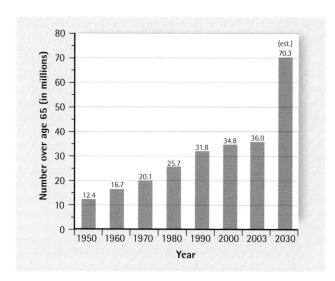

FIGURE 17.1 Americans Age 65 and Over and Projected
From 9 million people over age 65 in 1940, the population over age 65 could nearly double from 2003 to 70 million by the year 2030.
Source: U.S. Bureau of the Census. (2004–2005). *Statistical Abstract of the United States: 2004–2005.* Tables No. 11 and No. 14: Resident Population: 2003.

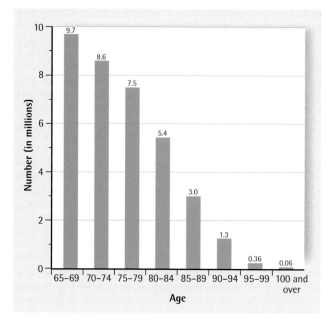

FIGURE 17.2 U.S. Late Adulthood Population by Age: 2003 In 2003, there were nearly 36 million American adults age 65 and older. Note that there were nearly 2 million ages 90 and older and approximately 60,000 centenarians.
Source: U.S. Bureau of the Census. (2004–2005). *Statistical Abstract of the United States: 2004–2005.* Tables No. 11 and No. 14: Resident Population: 2003.

population beginning in 2011 when the first of this cohort reach their sixty-fifth birthdays. It is projected that in 2030 the 65-and-older population will be double the number of 2000 (Federal Interagency Forum on Aging-Related Statistics, 2004).

The growing population of older Americans also differs significantly from current generations of older adults in some important ways (see Figure 17.2). The current population is predominantly female and white. It is projected that the entire white non-Hispanic population will increase from almost 196 million in 2000 (nearly 70 percent of the total population) to over 210 million by 2050 (about 50 percent of the total population). Over the same time, it is projected that the Hispanic population will *increase* by 67 million people. This represents an increase of 188 percent. Hispanic-Americans would then comprise about one-fourth of the total population. The Asian-American population is projected to grow from 11 to 33 million and would then comprise about 8 percent of the total population. The African American population is projected to rise to over 61 million and would be about 15 percent of the total population in 2050 (U. S. Bureau of the Census, 2004a).

These increases in the numbers of elderly Americans will lead to unprecedented increases in health-care costs (medicine, prosthetic devices and medical supplies, physician visits, lab tests, hospitalization, short-term rehabilitation, long-term nursing care, hospice care, home health care, etc.); health-care professionals (physicians, nurses, pharmacists, surgeons, dentists, physical therapists, etc.); residential facilities; and elder-care services

(e.g., social worker, psychologists, gerontologists, Meals on Wheels, clergy, First Alert safety programs, adult day care, senior transit services, financial, legal estate planning, and funeral services, etc.) over the next 30 years (Rice & Fineman, 2004). Significantly, the increase in the minority elderly population will be accompanied by socioeconomic shifts as well. That is, current statistics indicate that rates of poverty are significantly higher for older African Americans and Hispanics compared with whites. The increased risks for illness and disability associated with lower socioeconomic status (SES) will lead to longer hospitalizations, greater home health care and hospice care, and greater per capita health-care expenditures. Not only will there be increases in those subgroups at highest risk for compromised health outcomes, but these populations are least likely to have private health-care insurance and will require public health care (Seeman & Adler, 1998).

Although the United States has a smaller percentage of people over age 65 (12 percent) compared with other developed countries (15 percent in most of Europe and 19 percent in Japan), this is expected to change as the baby boomers reach late adulthood (Federal Interagency Forum on Aging-Related Statistics, 2004). The risks for sensory declines, physical impairment, and disability are higher at older ages for all persons, though a large percentage of older adults report good health and experience little or no functional impairment (Federal Interagency Forum on Aging-Related Statistics, 2004).

Researchers examine demographic characteristics, economic status, lifestyle factors, cognitive ability, personality, family environment, religiosity, and social network structure as predictors of health behaviors (Zanjani, Schaie, & Willis, 2001). A growing body of evidence suggests that the elderly increase their chances for more successful aging through lifestyle choices that include personal control and efficacy, regular exercise, proper nutrition and weight control, a positive attitude, and participation in social activities (Schaie, 1994; Schulz & Heckhausen, 1996). According to Seeman and Adler (1998), the two biggest challenges are: (1) to convince older adults of the value of such behaviors; and (2) to develop programs and policies that not only encourage such lifestyle changes but also promote and facilitate their adoption by all socioeconomic and ethnic segments of the growing population of older Americans. Beyond health-care concerns, Powell and Whitla (1994) predict the likely effects of these population changes will include:

- *An increased dependency ratio in the nation.* In 2005 the midlife workforce comprised nearly 7 out of 10 adult workers, but by 2010 it will decline by an outflow of retirements. This smaller workforce will greatly impact the number of elderly people requiring financial assistance. It is estimated that between the years 2030 and 2080 the annual shortfall of benefits paid to retirees compared to payroll taxes of workers will increase from 3.5 percent to almost 6 percent (Ip, 2005).
- *An increased demand by the aged for various resources* such as Social Security, Medicaid, Medicare, welfare, the Home Energy Assistance Program (HEAP—utility costs), adult day care, public transit, medical and rehabilitative facilities and services, social services, and recreational centers.
- *The emergence of the oldest cohort as a political force and social movement.* The American Association of Retired Persons (AARP) is a powerful lobbying group in Washington, and senior citizens have a history of being politically active. Their interests will command legislative action.

With 13 percent of the 2006 federal budget allocated for Medicare, 8 percent for Medicaid, and 21 percent allocated to Social Security (to $9.5 billion for fiscal 2006), a considerable portion of the budget is used for programs that support the elderly population (Office of Management and Budget, 2005). The *Medicare Prescription Drug Improvement and Modernization Act* will offer Medicare beneficiaries subsidized prescription drug coverage as of January 1, 2006. Those with incomes below 135 percent of the poverty level will pay no monthly premium, no deductible, and a very small co-

pay. These allocations will continue to rise as the elderly population increases. So there is a growing concern over the so-called graying of the budget. Some are concerned that age divisiveness might appear in U.S. politics. See the *Further Developments* box "Generational Tensions: The Social Security Debate" to take a closer look at such highly charged issues.

Myths

The facts of aging are often hidden by a great many myths that have little to do with the actual process of growing old. Let's examine each one in light of recent findings from research.

Myth: Most persons age 65 and over live in hospitals, nursing homes, and other elder-care institutions.

Fact: Only relatively recently have people lived long enough to require long-term care. This increased longevity is primarily due to improved sanitation, nutrition, and medical care (Shute, 1997). Genetic research may also contribute to prolonging the life span. Although Census data reveal that the chances of needing nursing-home care do increase with age, and the actual numbers of nursing-home residents is expected to increase because the population of the elderly is increasing, the rates of nursing-home placements are decreasing.

From 1985 to 1999 the rate of nursing-home residence of people ages 65 to 74 declined by 14 percent; among 75- to 84-year-olds the rate declined by 25 percent; and the rate for those 85 and older declined by 17 percent (Federal Interagency Forum on Aging-Related Statistics, 2004).

Myth: Many of the elderly are incapacitated and spend much of their time in bed because of illness.

Fact: In the United States about 3 percent of the elderly who live at home are bedridden and about 9 percent are housebound. An additional 5 percent are seriously incapacitated, and another 11 to 16 percent are restricted in mobility. By contrast, one-half to three-fifths function without any limitation; more than one-third of those 85 and older report no incapacitating limitation on their activity (Federal Interagency Forum on Aging-Related Statistics, 2004). A person who becomes severely ill or disabled in advanced old age most likely will not linger another four or five years but will enter a relatively short terminal decline of 90 to 120 days. Indeed, given contemporary trends toward greater longevity, many demographers believe that the baby-boom generation will, on average, spend less time in nursing homes and fewer years being severely disabled than did its parents and grandparents (Federal Interagency

Further Developments

Generational Tensions: The Social Security Debate

The proportion of elderly in our society is growing, and this fact will affect every American and every U.S. institution. Over the past several decades, a variety of social policies have been put in place that have allowed the elderly both to disengage from economically productive activities, and to experience an improved standard of living and greater longevity. The Social Security program was created in 1935 and in the beginning provided low benefit payments—to the extent that even into the 1960s one-third of seniors lived below the poverty line. Medicare was enacted in 1965 to provide the elderly with help to pay their health-care costs. In 1972 several amendments were passed to the Social Security Act. While the Supplemental Security Income program provides them with a guaranteed minimum income, the Older Americans Act supports an array of services specifically intended for older persons. Together these programs allow seniors assurance of health care and freedom from dire poverty.

How Does Social Security Work?

The U.S. Treasury oversees four trust funds related to Social Security and Medicare. For Social Security, the Old-Age and Survivors Insurance (OASI) Trust Fund pays retirement and survivors (widows/widowers and their children) benefits. The Disability Insurance (DI) Trust Fund pays disability benefits. Together, these Social Security trust funds are known as (OASDI). For Medicare, the Hospital Insurance (HI) Trust Fund pays for hospital inpatient care and related services. The Supplementary Medical Insurance (SMI) Trust Fund currently pays for physician and outpatient services and in 2006 will begin to provide a prescription drug benefit. These trust funds handle all the incoming revenues collected from taxes on a person's wages (there is an income cap, above which taxes are not collected; nor are taxes collected on investment earnings) as well as the outgoing payments and benefits. Because it is a trust fund, it puts money not needed for the current year in government securities that accumulate interest.

What Is the Issue?

Currently, there is much debate about the future of Social Security, yet according to the Trustees of the Social Security and Medicare Programs (2005), it is Medicare that is in more eminent danger. "The Medicare Hospital Insurance (HI) Trust Fund that pays hospital benefits had negative cash flows in 2004 and annual cash flow deficits are expected to continue and to grow rapidly after 2010 as baby boomers begin to retire." The costs of health care are expected to rise faster than the amount Social Security can pay based on

the taxes it collects from workers' wages (*The 2005 OASDI Trustees Report*, 2005). Why has this issue received less attention than the issue of reforming Social Security?

Social Security currently is running a surplus, and benefit payments are expected to exceed revenues in the year 2018. After 2018 (without any changes) the Social Security trust fund could continue paying scheduled benefits for about 30 years by drawing down on its surplus. According to the Congressional Budget Office, the Social Security trust fund is not expected to run out of money until 2053 (Congressional Quarterly, 2004).

The argument that Social Security is in crisis rests in part on the fact that the ratio of workers supporting beneficiaries is declining (see Figure 17.3). In 1950 there were about 16 workers for every beneficiary. In 2004 there were 3.3 workers and by 2010, there will be 3 workers for each Social Security beneficiary. The reason for this, of course, is the large cohort of baby boomers and a much smaller cohort born 20 years later. In 1965 the number of births dropped below 4 million a year, inaugurating the baby-bust generation. By 2033 the support ratio becomes 2 workers per beneficiary. As the baby boomers begin to pass away, these ratios will change again. The Social Security trustees have predicted that the increased costs associated with the large cohort moving through the system will eventually stabilize by 2038 (Congressional Quarterly, 2004).

Many people do not realize that Social Security was never intended to provide for all their needs when they retired or became disabled. Yet many low-income retirees rely on Social Security for 82 percent of their retirement income. Pension planners typically view Social Security as one leg of a three-legged stool, with private pensions and individual savings providing the other two kinds of support. Critics of the current system contend that most people could do much better if they were able to put their Social Security contributions into a private pension plan. But this argument fails to consider the disability and survivor's benefits that workers or their families might begin drawing at an early age. Moreover, economists say that we cannot make Social Security voluntary. Low-cost people would get out because they could get better investment returns and benefits elsewhere. The high-cost people would stay in, and the system would collapse.

There are many proposals being put forward to stem the looming shortfalls predicted for Social Security. President George W. Bush's 2001 Commission to Strengthen Social Security proposes a plan that would cut back on benefits and establish privatized Social Security accounts. To cut back on benefits, the plan seeks to link baseline benefits to cost-of-living increases rather than as they are currently to

continued

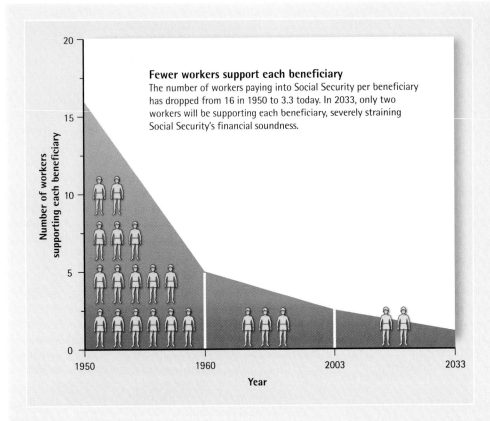

Fewer workers support each beneficiary
The number of workers paying into Social Security per beneficiary has dropped from 16 in 1950 to 3.3 today. In 2033, only two workers will be supporting each beneficiary, severely straining Social Security's financial soundness.

Number of workers supporting each beneficiary

Year

FIGURE 17.3 Fewer Workers per Retiree As the baby-boom generation continues to retire, there will be fewer workers to support Social Security beneficiaries.
From Mary Cooper, "Social Security Reform," *The CQ Researcher,* Vol. 14, No. 33, September 24, 2004, pp. 781–804. Reprinted by permission of CQ Press.

wage rate increases. The other component of the plan would allow workers to put about 3 percent of their taxable wages into private accounts and receive a smaller Social Security benefit (Munnell, 2004a). To benefit from this program,

workers would have to consistently earn more than the amount earned in the trust fund. This would make the plan dependent on the strength of the economy.

Forum on Aging-Related Statistics, 2004; Wilson & Truman, 2004). In sum, notions of gradual aging may well be replaced with perceptions of vigorous adulthood across the life span followed by a brief, precipitous **senescence** (mental decline in old age) or period of physical decline.

Myth: Most elderly people are "prisoners of fear" who are "under house arrest" by virtue of their fear of crime.
Fact: Overall, in 2003 Americans over 65 had the lowest victimization rates of any other age group—only 3 per 1,000 age 65 and over. By far, the highest rate of victimization is among the 16- to 19-year-old age group (Catalano, 2004).

Myth: Most people over 65 find themselves in serious financial straits.
Fact: As a group, Americans over 65 today are in better financial shape than were those who were over 65 three decades ago. Overall, the poverty level for those 65 and older dropped from 35 percent

in 1959 to 10 percent in 2003 (Federal Interagency Forum on Aging-Related Statistics, 2004). Social Security and retirement benefits are the primary sources of income for most elderly persons. Indeed, since 1970, overall income levels of the elderly have climbed relative to the rest of the population because Social Security benefits rose 46 percent, after adjustment for inflation, while the buying power of people earning wages and salaries fell 7 percent. In contrast, the rate of poverty among the nation's children has worsened. Moreover, the elderly pay a smaller share of their income to taxes. So although the elderly might have lower incomes than most U.S. householders, they have a higher net worth—often consisting of home ownership—and they tend to be more satisfied with their financial circumstances than are other Americans.

The economic gap between men and women widens in retirement. Although many women entered the workforce in recent decades, women's average 2003 monthly Social Security benefits were

Increase in Health-Care Costs and Concerns The chances of sensory and physical impairments increase in late adulthood, but life-style choices and social support improve the chance of successful aging.

$798 compared with an average of $1,039 for men (Social Security Administration, 2004). Generally women earn less than men do, and they are more likely to have worked part-time or left the workforce for several years for family reasons. For most women who receive Social Security benefits through their husbands, the benefits—equal to half their husbands' monthly check—are nonetheless more than the amount they would receive on the basis of their own work record. Women comprise 58 percent of Social Security beneficiaries after age 62—and 70 percent of those over 84. For unmarried women (including widows), Social Security comprises about half of their income compared with 35 percent of the income of an elderly couple (Social Security Administration, 2004). Single older women have high levels of poverty. One study reported that nearly one-third of single women over 65 years of age were poor or near poor (125 percent of poverty threshold) in 2000 (Munnell, 2004b). Social security is the *only* source of income for one of every four women 65 and older (Brogan, 2005). In Table 17.1 note that for future planning, the age of retirement is rising to receive full Social Security benefits, although a worker can retire as early as age 62 with a reduction in benefits.

Myth: Most grown children live away from their elderly parents and basically abandon them.
Fact: Most middle-aged children take care of their elderly parents rather than abandon them. According to the National Alliance for Caregiving, nearly one in four American households cares for an elderly relative or friend, helps support their elderly parents financially, or provides other types of support (Cooper, 1998). A follow-up to this study found that caregivers who were 45 and older provided on average eight years of care. Caregivers

helped with expenses for rent, mortgage, and home-care professionals for their elderly relatives between two to six years (Rimer, 1999). By the year 2010, there will be more than 40 million people over the age of 65. The Family Caregiver Alliance estimates

Table 17.1 Social Security Benefits: Normal Retirement

Year of Birth	Normal Retirement Age
1937 and prior	65
1938	65 and 2 months
1939	65 and 4 months
1940	65 and 6 months
1941	65 and 8 months
1942	65 and 10 months
1943–1954	66
1955	66 and 2 months
1956	66 and 4 months
1957	66 and 6 months
1958	66 and 8 months
1959	66 and 10 months
1960 and later	67

Note: Persons born on January 1 of any year should refer to the normal retirement age for the previous year.

A worker can choose to retire as early as age 62. However, if such early retirement is chosen, the worker's benefit will be reduced by a certain percentage. Normal retirement age varies from age 65 to age 67 by year of birth.

Source: U.S. Bureau of the Census. (2005, September 19). *Normal retirement age.* Social Security Administration. Retrieved October 15, 2005, from www.ssa.gov/OACT/progdata/nra.html

that 12 percent of informal caregivers will quit their jobs to provide care to the elderly. As a result, elder-care benefits will increasingly become an employment issue (Ervin, 2000).

Additional myths will be considered in the course of these two chapters. Although the issues cited above are not true for most elderly adults, they are realities for some segments of the older population. But there is a great gap between the actual experiences of most elderly people and the difficulties attributed to them by others. Many of the elderly are resilient and very much alive and not hopeless, inert masses teetering on the edge of senility and death. Generalizations that depict the elderly as an economically and socially deprived group can do them a disservice, for such stereotypes give younger people a clear conscience about distancing themselves from the elderly and treating the elderly as if they have inferior status.

Growth in the size of the older population is not unique to the United States (see Table 17.2). In nearly all industrialized societies, the number of elderly people is growing. The developing countries are projected to grow at even higher rates than the developed countries. Countries including the People's Republic of China, South Korea, India, Egypt, Cambodia, Congo, Brazil, the Philippines, and Turkey are projected to more than double the size of the population aged 65 and older in the year 2025 from the number counted in 2000. Mexico is projected to more than triple its elderly population (U.S. Bureau of the Census, 2001b).

According to the U.S. Bureau of the Census (2004i), the average life expectancy of American women is 79.9 years, whereas men can expect to live to age 74.5. Women outlive men in almost every nation. Life expectancy in the developed countries is comparable to that in the United States, but the figures are different in less developed countries where the life expectancy for women is 66 years and for men 63 years. Part of the difference in life expectancy for women between the developed and less developed countries is due to higher rates of maternal mortality (Jones, 2001). Although the life span for infants is continuing to increase dramatically, the increase in life expectancy for adults, especially males, is less spectacular. A child born in the United States in 2000 could expect to live 77 years, about 30 years longer than a child born in 1900. The major part of the increase in this longevity statistic is due to the fact that the United States has experienced lower death rates for children and young adults. Longevity statistics are averaged to include babies born stillborn or who die at birth, those who die in infancy and childhood, and ages of all adult deaths.

Generally, adults who are 65 or older are considered to be in the final stage of human development. Why should this be so? Considering how much these adults vary in their activities, health, and welfare, it is difficult to say when old age begins. Probably the simplest and safest rule is to consider individuals old whenever they become so regarded and treated by their contemporaries (Golant, 1984). Indeed, although our society is getting older, the old are getting younger. The activities and attitudes of a 70-year-old today closely approximate those of a 50-year-old two decades ago. Their quality of life, especially for the "youngest old," ages 60 to 75, is much greater than that of their parents. A large number remain physically and mentally active, even continuing to work full- or part-time.

Table 17.2 Average Life Expectancy at Birth Across Cultures: 2005			
Country	Age	Country	Age
Japan	81.2	Turkey	72.4
Australia	80.4	China	72.3
Sweden	80.4	Brazil	71.7
Switzerland	80.4	Egypt	71
Iceland	80.2	Philippines	69.9
Canada	80.1	Ukraine	69.7
Italy	79.7	Iraq	68.7
Israel	79.3	Russia	67.1
Germany	78.6	India	64.4
Britain (U.K.)	78.4	Cambodia	58.9
United States	77.7	Congo (Brazzaville)	52.3
Ireland	77.6	Congo (Kinshasa)	51.1
Argentina	75.9	Kenya	48
Mexico	75.2	Angola	38.4

Source: U.S. Bureau of the Census. (2005, April 26). *Summary Demographic Data.* Population Division, International Programs Center. Retrieved April 28, 2005 From www.census.gov/ipc/www/idbsum.html

Questions

How will U.S. population demographics change due to aging of the population? What effect will these changes have on our society's social, health, and economic policies in the next few decades?

Women Live Longer Than Men

The gap between the life expectancy rates for men and women has been increasing since 1920. Although slightly more males are born, the male death rate is consistently higher *at each stage of life* so that by the mid-twenties females begin to outnumber males and continue to do so for all consecutive age groups (U.S. Bureau of the Census, 2000c). Women who turned 65 in 2004 can expect to live on average 20 more years, whereas men who turned 65 can expect to live another 17 years (Social Security Administration, 2004). Women account for 58 percent of the population age 65 and older and 69 percent of the population 85 and older (Federal Interagency Forum on Aging-Related Statistics, 2004). For every 100 women over the age of 65, there are only 71 men in this age group (U.S. Bureau of the Census, 2005).

According to the U.S. Bureau of the Census, in 2000 about one-third of women aged 75 and over needed help with such basics as eating, dressing, bathing, preparing meals, managing money, and getting around outside; in contrast, one-fifth of the men needed such assistance (Cooper, 2004). But men have higher rates of the leading fatal conditions (cancer and heart disease), which parallel their higher mortality. There is some evidence that men also have an incidence of acute illness that is at least equal to that of women when such factors as health-reporting behaviors, environmentally acquired risks, and various psychosocial aspects of illness are taken into account (Verbrugge, 1989).

Genetic differences might play a part in women's greater longevity (Epstein, 1983). Women seem to have an inherent sex-linked resistance to some types of life-threatening diseases. Apparently, a woman's hormones give her a more efficient immune system. Estrogen appears to be protective against cardiovascular disease, because premenopausal women have a substantially lower risk of heart disease than men of comparable ages. Most medical experts believe that smoking accounts for about half of the gender difference in longevity, and now only about 10 percent of elderly American men and women smoke (Federal Interagency Forum on Aging-Related Statistics, 2004).

Another longitudinal study on health, lifestyle, and aging is the *Nun Study* that began in 1986. By studying 678 nuns, who after death will donate their brains to research—biomedical researchers are gaining insights into women's health issues, aging, and factors related to Alzheimer's disease. These women are an excellent resource for medical research because their diet, way of life, and insularity provide the type of research control needed. Early results indicate that positive emotional content in early-life autobiographies was strongly related to longevity decades later (Danner, Snowdon, & Friesen, 2001). Also, initial findings show a correlation between a low rate of Alzheimer's and a high ability in written and oral expression from early in life (Snowdon, 2001). For some of the data on the oldest group of women, see the *Human Diversity* box on page 588, "Women Survivors."

Question

Why do more women than men survive into old age, and how are these women in their eighties, nineties, and centenarians faring?

Health

Although the general public may believe that the elderly suffer poor health, in fact the majority of people 65 and over report their health status as good to excellent. Only about one-fourth reported their health to be fair or poor in 2001, although persons of minority status and older immigrants report more health problems (Heron, Schoeni, & Morales, 2003; Federal Interagency Forum on Aging-Related Statistics, 2004). Indeed, the incidence of self-reported *acute illnesses* (upper respiratory infections, injuries, digestive disorders, varicose veins, and the like) is lower among the elderly than among other segments of the population. However, the incidence of *chronic diseases* (hypertension, heart conditions, arthritis and joint and ligament problems, cancer, diabetes, stroke, respiratory illness, osteoporosis, and so on) rises steadily with advancing years (Federal Interagency Forum on Aging-Related Statistics, 2004).

Despite the higher incidence of chronic health problems among the elderly, most do not consider themselves to be seriously handicapped in pursuing their ordinary activities (only 5 percent reside in some care facility) (National Center for Health Statistics, 2004a). Most of the conditions that create chronic disease increase with advanced age. Over time, it is likely that a person will accumulate more risk factors for a variety of illnesses. As the risk factors increase, the efficiency of the body's systems is reduced by primary aging or the irreversible changes that occur over time. An older adult is more susceptible to disease, will take longer to recuperate from an illness or surgery, and is more likely to have other complications associated with a disease.

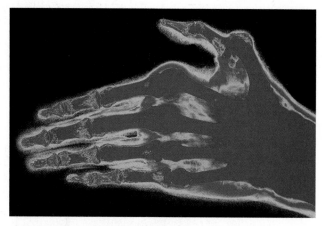

Arthritis This is an X ray of a person's hand with rheumatoid arthritis, a chronic joint disease that causes cartilage destruction, bone erosion, and tendon inflammation. As bones rub together in the joints, there is serious pain, swelling, and stiffness. There are different types of arthritis, and aging men and women are both affected.

Human Diversity

Women Survivors

Jean Calment, a citizen of France and the world's oldest living person at that time, died in August 1997 at the age of 122. She loved wine and candy and smoked until she was 117. She rode her bicycle daily until she was 100 and lived alone until the age of 110, when she entered a nursing home (Neuharth, 1997). Does 122 sound extraordinary to you? Jean Calment reached an old age that antiaging researchers predict many more people will be able to achieve in the next few decades—during your lifetime!

In the mid 1980s the National Institute of Aging began a program to research the oldest population—those over 85—of whom the majority are women (nearly 70 percent in 2004) (see Table 17.3) (Federal Interagency Forum on Aging-Related Statistics, 2004). These older women are extending life to its chronological limit, and they hold the secret of what normal aging is at the extreme of old age. Why do the oldest women live so long? What accounts for their ability to survive? Perls (2004) is trying to find the answers to such remarkable longevity in the *New England Centenarian Study*, because there are between 50,000 to 60,000 Americans 100 and older now, with rapid growth of this population (90 percent females; 10 percent males).

Medical and scientific literature draws attention to genetic solutions, rarely, if at all, acknowledging social and psychological factors. The broad view currently is to describe the oldest women as victims—victims of a system that leaves them with a high risk of disabilities and with neither a husband nor an adequate income. Furthermore, most of these women live alone or in nursing homes. All of these factors—lower income, living alone, disability—lead to a lower quality of life for those who have triumphed in the long journey facing us all. To live through the normal struggles of life and survive into advanced old age is seldom considered heroic or laudable in American culture. Women who live long lives usually are pitied as having unfortunately outlived their friends and family.

What Realities Face These Oldest of the Old?

What about the quality of life of the "oldest old" humans? According to the U.S. Bureau of the Census (2004–2005), more women than men over the age of 75 reported limitation of activity caused by chronic conditions and from limitations on activities such as eating, bathing, dressing and getting around inside their homes. This leads to more women entering nursing homes because of their higher rates of disability and not because they live longer. Longevity often turns women into widows—and many widows suffer financially when their husbands die. Retirement income is set up to reward the primary wage earner and the living spouse. The benefits from Social Security drop by one-third when the husband dies. This drop can be extremely harsh for women, especially if they survive their husbands for many years.

Who Are These Women?

Women who were 90 years old in 2005 were born in 1915, during World War I. This cohort had fewer children than previous cohorts, which means they now have fewer available adult caregivers in old age. Having lived through the Great Depression, followed by World War II, these women endured many hardships. For a large number, their childbearing years were "taken up" by larger social issues, such as World Wars and the Great Depression. African American women have always been part of the labor force, but usually in jobs like private housekeeping and child care that are not covered by Social Security. In rural areas in 1925, education was not a priority for girls, and even if a girl did go to school, eighth grade was considered enough school for almost anyone. The lack of education among today's oldest women diminished their employment opportunities later in life—and made them more vulnerable to the effects of poverty.

Table 17.3 Projected Number of U.S. Centenarians: 2005–2050

Women outlive men in old age, but the quality of life for many elderly women is generally poor. Biomedical researchers suggest that living to 100 and beyond is likely to become typical within this century. *Will you be a centenarian?*

Year	Number
2005	60,000
2010	131,000
2020	214,000
2030	324,000
2040	447,000
2050	834,000

Source: Krach, C. A., & Velkoff, V. A. (1999, July). U. S. Bureau of the Census. Centenarians in the United States, *Current Population Reports*, P23–199RV. Washington, DC: U.S. Government Printing Office.

How Are These Women Situated?

Research shows that this population is quite diverse in terms of physical ability:

- 58 percent needed help getting to the store or doctor's office
- 50 percent were living in their homes, with various levels of disability
- 44 percent lived alone (a majority of these women live in poverty)
- 31 percent lived with relatives (usually daughters)
- 25 percent are in nursing homes
- 25 percent feel "great" and lead independent lives

Few social norms exist for the oldest segment of our population, and their daily lives generally are free of the worries that plague younger individuals. For women who enter the oldest years without severe disability and with adequate financial resources, these years can be a time of independence, personal mastery, and self-assurance. Those without resources are dependent on federal assistance for home health care, nursing care, medical coverage, and so forth. Future research might do well to focus on helping this group of women develop their potential, which should ultimately benefit us all.

Source: Adapted from S. Bould & C. Longino, *Handbook on Women and Aging* (Westport, CT: Greenwood Press, 1997).

The *Baltimore Longitudinal Study,* which began in 1958, has contributed much to our understanding of the health of older Americans (Gunby, 1998). The study follows nearly 2,500 volunteers ranging in age from the early twenties through the late eighties. Every two years the individuals undergo two and a half days of comprehensive physical tests. The study's recent findings that a growing percent of people, especially women, over 65 tend to be overweight causes researchers to be quite concerned. Recent research suggests that higher weights are likely to result in higher death rates, particularly from heart disease (Federal Interagency Forum on Aging-Related Statistics, 2004).

Also, since it has been found that 60 percent of those over age 60 have high blood sugar levels in glucose tolerance tests, medical authorities are questioning many diagnoses of diabetes in older people. Perhaps a reduction in insulin production in the elderly is a normal occurrence and not a sign of disease. As a result of this research, the American Diabetes Association and the World Health Organization have lowered the statistical range used to diagnose diabetes. Observes Dr. Reubin Andres, one of the project's researchers, "Think of it, several million people 'cured' by the stroke of a pen" (Fozard et al., 1994). Proper exercise appropriately and carefully pursued throughout life—even into the eighties and beyond—can significantly deter the deterioration of bodily functions that traditionally accompany aging (see the *More Information You Can Use* box on page 590, "Exercise and Longevity").

Some researchers predict that obesity will impact longevity such that the life expectancy rate which has been steadily increasing for the past two centuries will stop increasing, since obesity causes about 300,000 U.S. deaths annually (Olshansky et al., 2005). Disuse is thought to account for about half the functional decline that typically occurs between ages 30 and 70. The demonstrated benefits of exercise include increased work capacity, improved heart and respiratory function, lower blood pressure, increased muscle strength, denser bones, greater flexibility, quicker reaction times, clearer thinking, improved sleep, and reduced susceptibility to depression. Although exercise by the elderly is not without risk, recent studies show that age-associated declines can be delayed by fitness-promoting exercise.

Nutrition and Health Risks

Good nutrition is another controllable factor contributing to health in old age. Although energy requirements decrease with advancing age, elderly people require just as many nutrients as younger adults. Indeed, they may require more. Recent research suggests that vitamins and minerals are metabolized differently as people age and that the recommended dietary allowances could be inaccurate for elderly persons (Hunter, 1998). Lifestyle differences also contribute to gender differences in life expectancies. The longest-living population is found among Seventh-Day Adventists, nonsmoking vegetarians with religious beliefs (vegetarians eat more fruit, legumes, nuts, vegetables, and whole wheat bread). In a longitudinal study from 1974 to 1988, 34,000 Adventists from California participated in the *Adventist Health Study–1* (Fraser, 2005). Findings showed the Adventists weighed less, had a much lower risk of heart disease, cancer, and prostate problems—in contrast to nonvegetarians. In 2001 *Adventist Health Study–2* began, with a goal of studying lifestyle and aging with more than 100,000 participants from the United States and Canada (Fraser, 2003).

New research suggests that malabsorption of macro nutrients in the elderly is due to disease, not age (Russell, 2001). New recommendations for calcium with vitamin D requirements for the elderly may be double the current required daily allowance (Hunter, 1998). Americans annually suffer more than 275,000 hip fractures, 500,000 vertebral fractures, and 200,000 wrist fractures because of **osteoporosis**—a condition associated with a slow loss

More Information You Can Use

Exercise and Longevity

Many of us think of Juan Ponce de Leon (1460–1521) as the Spaniard who undertook a fruitless search for the fountain of youth. Yet contemporary medical researchers are finding that the explorer might not have failed in his endeavor, although he very likely made the discovery without even realizing it. During the sixteenth century, when few men survived to age 53, Ponce de Leon was hiking Florida's uncharted coastal terrain. Eight years later he suffered a mortal wound from an arrow. Yet historical accounts reveal that Ponce de Leon was a man younger than his years right up to his end (Scheck, 1994).

In the past several decades, study after study has pointed to how modern-day Ponce de Leons are benefiting by staying active during a time in life when they are supposedly past their prime. Medical science has long recognized the rewards to be reaped from exercise by patients with high blood pressure and coronary artery disease. But new information reveals countless other benefits afforded by exercise. With proper counseling, exercise can reduce the risk of falls by restoring coordination and balance and make fractures less likely by strengthening the musculoskeletal system. And physical activity lowers the risk of developing diabetes, osteoporosis, colon cancer, breast cancer, and depression. Exercise and strength training are especially important for women because they have more body fat and less muscle and bone than men, making them more susceptible to fractures and muscle deterioration (Friedrich, 2001).

Exercise gurus have long urged seniors to walk, run, bike, hike, dance, or paddle their way to better endurance and better aerobic capacity (respiratory and circulatory function). But evidence suggests that simply maintaining an independent lifestyle also requires strength. Exercise specialists say that "pumping iron"—lifting weights—can be enormously beneficial. Aerobic activities such as walking, running, and cycling require moving large groups of muscles hundreds of thousands of times against relatively little resistance other than gravity. Strength training entails the working of small groups of muscles only a few times against high, and gradually increasing, resistance. As people enter midlife, their muscles become less bulky as the size and number of their muscle fibers decrease (for instance, from age 30 to age 80, men typically lose 40 percent of their leg muscle strength, and this correlates with a similar loss of muscle mass) (Woollacott, 1993). Exercise cannot replace lost muscle fiber, but it can restore the robustness of the muscles that remain. Young people who are bedridden lose muscle in much the same manner as do the elderly, leading some experts to believe that atrophy is due to disuse as well as age.

Cultivating Healthy Living Habits An accumulating body of scientific evidence points to the important part good habits play in fostering a healthy old age. We are largely responsible for our own old age. Staying active both physically, mentally, and socially contributes to successful aging. Indeed, such practices apparently play a larger role than genes in laying the foundations for a healthy and independent old age.

Strength training can benefit even the very old and frail. Maria A. Fiatarone and her colleagues at the Harvard Medical School analyzed the results of two months of high-intensity workouts by ten frail men and women 86 to 96 years of age. On average, regular conditioning boosted the power of their knee extensors by 174 percent, their heel-to-toe walking speed by 48 percent, and the size of their midthigh muscles by 9 percent (Fiatarone & Evans, 1993).

Does exercise adds years to life? This is still being debated. Medical authorities generally concur that moderate exercise is sufficient to contribute to a healthier life, but recent evidence suggests that exercise must be strenuous to add to the life span. Recent research has found that older adults who participate in moderate exercise for 20 to 30 minutes on most days have better physical function than older persons who are active throughout the day or inactive (Brach et al., 2004). Harvard researchers followed more than 17,000 healthy male alumni over a 26-year period and found that only vigorous exercise increased longevity (Brody, 1995b). The risk of dying for men who expended more than 1,500 calories a week in such activities as running, cycling, and swimming was as much as 25 percent lower than the risk for men who expended fewer than 150 calories a week in such activities (even so, most exercise physiologists believe there is a point at which too much exercise is detrimental to health). The Harvard study defined as vigorous any activity that raised the metabolic rate in a 10-second interval to six or more times the rate at rest. Activities such as the following would achieve the level of caloric expenditure associated with the lowest death rates:

- Walking for 45 minutes at 4 to 5 mph five times a week
- Playing tennis for one hour three times a week
- Swimming laps for three hours a week
- Cycling at 10 mph for one hour four times a week

- Running for 30 minutes at 6 to 7 mph five to six times a week
- In-line skating for two and a half hours a week

In sum, older age is not uniformly associated with declines in physical performance or health. Furthermore, the type of exercise undertaken has an effect on the self-efficacy of older adults (McAuley et al., 1999).

of calcium that results in porous bones. A simple densitometry scan reveals whether a person has low bone mass density (BMD) (see page 518).

Older women are at greater risk for osteoporosis because they have less bone mass and because they lose bone tissue more rapidly after menopause. Thin and small-boned women are also at greater risk. According to recent research, a woman 50 years of age has a 40 percent chance of fracturing a bone over her lifetime and a 19 percent chance of hip fracture (Hubka, 2004). Along with internal bones becoming more "porous" and brittle, the discs between the vertebrae of the spine become less dense, causing vertebrae to form small cracks and become closer to each other. This results in back pain. A person's upper back begins to curve, over a period of years, as he or she loses height. It becomes more difficult for the person to breathe, as the elderly person can no longer stand up straight.

Hip fractures cost close to $13 billion annually in the United States. Such fractures are associated with a one-year mortality of 25 percent in 80-year-old women and have important implications. Long-term bedridden elderly are more prone to getting pneumonia, blood clots, muscle loss—and earlier death. More than 25 percent of affected women must give up their independent status and enter rehab facilities or nursing homes (NIA, 1996a).

Calcium supplements with vitamin D seem to slow or stop bone loss, but they do not increase bone mass. However, bone mass might increase when various prescription drugs are taken with the calcium supplements along with regular weight-bearing exercise (such as walking). Hormone replacement therapy (HRT) has also been found effective if started before or within 10 years of menopause. Any therapeutic regimen should be carefully supervised by a physician. Although there is no absolute cure for osteoporosis, if treatment is begun early, its progress can be slowed and later fractures prevented. Women who remain physically active, keep leg and arm muscles strong, and exercise into the seventh and eighth decade seem to have less of a problem; women who had early menopause, who are very thin, or lead a sedentary

life are more likely to develop the problem. Rohr and colleagues (2004) highly recommend older adults take advantage of screenings and preventive measures for osteoporosis at community senior centers.

Brief blackouts due to lower blood pressure, getting up too quickly, and overmedication are also a major hazard among the elderly that can result in broken hips, bleeding inside the skull, and other fractures and bruises. Medical researchers find that many elderly people have a 20-point drop in their blood pressure when they stand up. Eating also lowers the blood pressure in the elderly for an hour after meals. When the two factors coincide, an elderly person might experience a fainting spell.

Drug Dosages and Absorption Effects Some health problems of older Americans result from overmedicating, mixing medications, skipping medications, and taking incorrect dosage. Elderly persons do not absorb

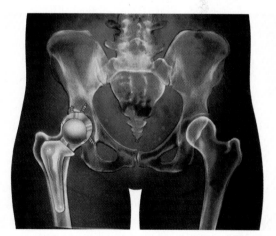

Osteoporosis: Bone Loss and Joint Replacement Osteoporosis is associated with a loss of calcium, resulting in more porous and brittle bones. A daily regimen of calcium with vitamin D, HRT, or prescription drugs can slow the effects of osteoporosis. This colored X ray shows a prosthetic (artificial) hip joint in place for a 72-year-old female. An artificial hip joint is used to replace a diseased hip joint as a result of arthritis or fracture due to osteoporosis. Hip- or knee-joint replacement can dramatically improve joint mobility.

drugs as readily from the intestinal tract, their livers are less efficient in metabolizing medications, and their kidneys are 50 percent less efficient than those of a younger person in excreting chemicals. Hence, a person over age 60 is two to seven times more likely to suffer adverse side effects than a younger patient (Kolata, 1994b).

Although older people might need higher doses of some medications, they need lower doses of others. For instance, the aging brain and nervous system are unusually sensitive to antianxiety drugs such as *Valium* and *Librium,* which can produce confusion and lethargy in the elderly. Sedatives such as *phenobarbital* often have a paradoxical effect on the elderly, inducing excitement and agitation rather than sleep. One U.S. study found that one-fifth of people aged 65 and over received at least one of 33 potentially inappropriate medications (Zhan et al., 2001).

These facts are quite dismaying when we realize that people over 65 take more than 25 percent of all prescription drugs. Indeed, the average healthy elderly person takes at least 11 different prescription medicines in the course of a year. When taken in combination, the medications can produce severe secondary reactions. Some problems arise because the elderly go to various doctors treating them for different conditions, and each doctor prescribes several potent medications—unaware that other medications have been prescribed. Another area of concern is use of sedative medications in elderly nursing home residents (Travis, 2005). Many pharmacy chains now have computerized networks that share information among pharmacies to help prevent harmful mixing of pharmaceuticals, and potential drug effects are now printed out for the patient. Establishing a routine for taking medications as prescribed can be a challenge, for some people resist taking medications at all and others have memory difficulties. There are a variety of inexpensive devices that assist one's failing memory.

Mental Health and Depression Most older adults adapt well to the changes and losses they are confronted with in late adulthood and have good mental health—yet those who live with chronic disease or pain are likely to experience mental health problems. In 2000, for adults 65 and older, about 10 percent of women and 3 percent of men were prescribed antidepressants, and higher rates of antidepressants were prescribed for women and men in middle age (Kobau et al., 2004; National Center for Health Statistics, 2004a). However, a small percentage of elderly people develop symptoms that can lead to more serious depressive disorders or mental illness if not treated or discussed. Symptoms might include loss of energy, fatigue or sleep disorders, loss of appetite, loss of interest in normal activities, or loss of interest in sexual activity. Other risk factors include diagnosis of health problems, cognitive dysfunction, strained interpersonal relations, stressful life events, and inheritance of depression. Depression can result from a physical illness or its treatment. Naturally, people living with chronic pain or a fatal diagnosis have much higher rates of depression and higher incidence of alcoholism, use of drugs, and troubled relationships (National Center for Health Statistics, 2004a).

Generally, women have more depressive disorders than men, though this difference reverses in very old age. At this writing, little research has been done to determine an association between depressive disorders and race, ethnicity, or culture. However, certain factors are associated with depressive disorders and higher rates of suicide: institutionalized and inpatient clients, being male, being 75 years of age or older, substantial health and mobility problems, and cognitive impairment. The suicide rate for adults 75 and over is the highest of any age group—with a much higher rate for males (see Chapter 19) (National Center for Health Statistics, 2004a).

Depressed elderly adults often do not seek treatment. The older adult might not see a physician, or the physician might focus on a physical condition and miss the depressive symptoms, especially if the patient does not mention them. Allowing depression to go untreated until it becomes more severe can lead to use of potent medications, electroconvulsive therapy, or suicide. Recent findings from a longitudinal study suggest that a combination of medications and psychotherapy yielded the best results for elderly patients suffering from major depression (Winslow, 1999). Social support, coping styles, perceived control of life factors, and cognitive appraisals play a protective role against depression (Kasl-Godley et al., 1998). Another protective factor is having a pet as a companion to ease loneliness.

Questions

How do we know there is a relationship between activity and aging? To what extent are the elderly likely to experience depression, and what approaches are suggested to help them cope with this disorder?

Biological Aging

Biological aging refers to changes that occur in the structure and functioning of the human organism over time (see Figure 17.4 on page 594). *Primary aging,* or time-related change, is a continuous process that begins at conception and ceases at death. As humans advance from infancy through young adulthood, biological change typically enables them to make a more efficient and effective adaptation to the environment. Beyond this period, however, biological change generally leads to impairment in the ability to adapt to the environ-

The Elderly with Animal Companions Go to the Doctor Less Psychologist Judith M. Siegel finds that the elderly who have animal companions visit their doctor less often than do those who lack animal companions, and those with dogs have the fewest visits of all. Pets provide companionship and an object of attachment and seem to help their owners in times of stress. Animal companionship is a way of life for nearly one-third of adults age 70 or older.

ment—ultimately, it jeopardizes survival. Improvements in the conditions of health at birth and early childhood and advances in medicine in childhood and adulthood have facilitated longevity and successful aging (Baltes & Smith, 2003; Oeppen & Vaupel, 2002). Those elderly who remain socially involved, mentally stimulated, and physically active increase the likelihood of successful aging (Singer et al., 2003).

Physical Changes Some of the most visible changes associated with aging are in physical characteristics. The hair grows thinner, turns gray, and becomes somewhat coarser. The skin changes texture, loses its elasticity and moistness, and gathers spot pigmentation. By age 40, every man and woman begins losing muscle, which coupled with the loss of the elasticity of the skin, begins to produce skin folds and wrinkling—a condition called *sarcopenia,* or age-related loss of muscle (Raloff, 1996).

Exercises such as yoga, weight training, and *Tai Chi* help to reduce muscle loss, improve balance, and reduce frailty. Note this chapter opens with a recent photo of thousands of older Chinese adults gathered at the Great Wall of China showing their Tai Chi skills—a gentle martial art with graceful exercise sequences used to improve coordination, relieve stress, promote overall well-being and strengthen the immune system (Johnson, 2005). Practicing Tai Chi is reported to have positive effects on various ailments, such as diabetes, arthritis, chronic fatigue, and high blood pressure (Humecky, 2005).

Other changes are noticeable in body height, shape, and weight. As the vertebrae begin to settle closer because the "cushioning" material in between them becomes thinner, reducing the height of the spine, there are also muscular changes that result in a loss of flexibility, making it harder to stand straight. Body-shape changes are primarily the result of the redistribution of fat away from the arms, legs, and face and onto the torso (Overend et al., 1992).

There are also other physiological changes, such as a decline in the capacity for physical work and exercise (sport performance declines after the twenties or early thirties) (Sinaki, 1996). From age 30 to age 70, maximum oxygen intake declines 60 percent, and maximum ventilatory volume declines 57 percent during exercise. Because oxygen is needed to combine with nutrients for the release of chemical building blocks and energy, the older person generally has less staying power and lower reserves. Furthermore, at age 75 the heart pumps about 65 percent as much blood as at age 30; the brain receives 80 percent as much blood; the kidneys only 42 percent as much. However, the nerve fibers that connect directly with the muscles show little decline with age—nerve impulses travel along single fibers in elderly people only 10 to 15 percent slower than in young people. Even so, psychomotor performance is slower and less consistent in the elderly (Kallman, Plato, & Tobin, 1990).

Collagen, a substance that constitutes a very high percentage of the total protein in the body, appears to be implicated in the aging process. Collagen is a basic structural component of connective tissue. Loose connective tissue resembles styrofoam pellet packing material. It supports and holds in place blood vessels, nerves, and internal organs, simultaneously permitting them some freedom of movement. It also holds muscle cells together and binds skin to underlying tissue. Over time, collagen fibers become thicker and less elastic, contributing to a loss of elasticity in the skin, hardening of the arteries, and stiffening of the joints. Thus, over time, collagen speeds the destruction of the organism it helped to build.

Sensory and Functional Changes Our sensory abilities—such as hearing, sight, taste, and smell—also change with age. It is important to understand both the

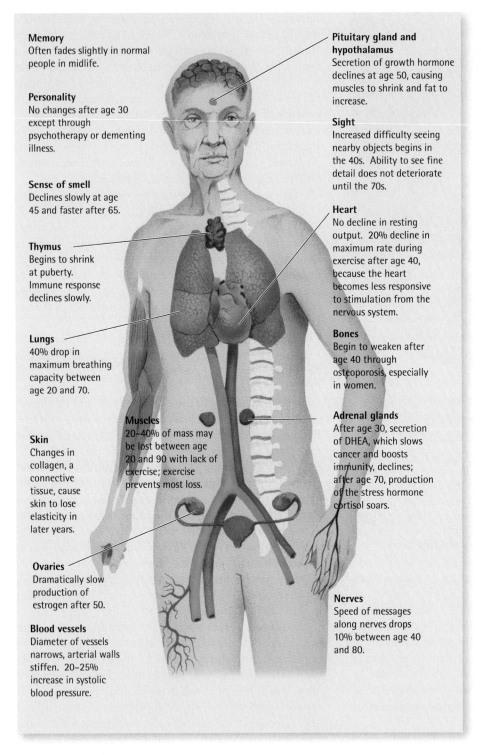

Memory
Often fades slightly in normal people in midlife.

Personality
No changes after age 30 except through psychotherapy or dementing illness.

Sense of smell
Declines slowly at age 45 and faster after 65.

Thymus
Begins to shrink at puberty. Immune response declines slowly.

Lungs
40% drop in maximum breathing capacity between age 20 and 70.

Skin
Changes in collagen, a connective tissue, cause skin to lose elasticity in later years.

Muscles
20–40% of mass may be lost between age 20 and 90 with lack of exercise; exercise prevents most loss.

Ovaries
Dramatically slow production of estrogen after 50.

Blood vessels
Diameter of vessels narrows, arterial walls stiffen. 20–25% increase in systolic blood pressure.

Pituitary gland and hypothalamus
Secretion of growth hormone declines at age 50, causing muscles to shrink and fat to increase.

Sight
Increased difficulty seeing nearby objects begins in the 40s. Ability to see fine detail does not deteriorate until the 70s.

Heart
No decline in resting output. 20% decline in maximum rate during exercise after age 40, because the heart becomes less responsive to stimulation from the nervous system.

Bones
Begin to weaken after age 40 through osteoporosis, especially in women.

Adrenal glands
After age 30, secretion of DHEA, which slows cancer and boosts immunity, declines; after age 70, production of the stress hormone cortisol soars.

Nerves
Speed of messages along nerves drops 10% between age 40 and 80.

FIGURE 17.4 Tendencies in Rates of Aging The rate of aging varies considerably among individuals and even among different organs in the same person. Nonetheless, a number of tendencies in aging occur in a predictable fashion.
© 1992. Reprinted by permission of *The Columbus Dispatch.*

magnitude of the changes and the course of action that can reduce the amount of impairment. Recent studies have shown a strong link between sensory and cognitive functioning in aging. A person whose memory ability has declined with age is more likely to have impaired hearing as well. This relationship does not imply direct causation, but there is connection between these abilities

(Stevens et al., 1998). Baltes and Lindenberger (1997) found comparable links among visual acuity, auditory thresholds, and intelligence.

Vision and Hearing   Some of the visual changes associated with aging begin to unfold during middle age. We saw in Chapter 15 that many adults in their forties need to wear bifocals and develop "dry" eyes, requiring drops of "liquid tears" occasionally. One should have annual eye exams to check for pressure buildup in the fluid of the eye, or *glaucoma,* which must be treated to prevent blindness. Blurred detail vision for most is not a problem until sometime in the seventies or eighties, and this can be a sign of a *cataract,* or hardening of the lens of the eye so that it cannot accommodate as efficiently. Fortunately, cataract surgery has become routine. The "oldest old" are also more prone to *retinal detachment,* a serious condition in which the retinal layer at the back of the eyeball begins to "peel away." If the condition is caught early enough, laser surgery might be able to reattach the retina. A person with other health complications (e.g., high blood pressure, diabetes, or stroke) might find vision difficulties appearing as well.

Hearing loss is a hazard in some occupations, such as working near large engines or motors or working with sound equipment for rock bands. Some hearing loss appears to have a genetic component. Hearing loss occurs in about 25 percent of people aged 65 to 75 years old and in 50 percent of those over age 75. Severe hearing loss or loss of vision diminishes the person's quality of life, making the person more dependent on others to meet even basic needs. Loss of vision or hearing can even lead to one of the most severe things that can happen to an older person—losing his or her driver's license and the freedom of choice and mobility that it allows.

Taste and Smell Older people frequently report that they are losing their ability to enjoy food (de Graaf, Polet, & van Staveren, 1994). This problem is related to a decline in the taste buds (the small protuberances on the surface of the tongue). Persons 70 to 85 years old have, on average, only one-third as many taste buds as young adults (Bartoshuk et al., 1986). Olfactory sensitivity (smell—the ability to distinguish oranges from lemons or chocolate from cheese) also declines among older adults and helps explain why many complain about their food (Ship et al., 1996). Cross-sectional studies reveal that a large number of older individuals have higher detection thresholds for smell, diminished intensities, and an impaired ability to identify and discriminate odors (Ship & Weiffenbach, 1993).

Dental, Swallowing, and Breathing Difficulties Adults who lose teeth and cannot afford dental care are unable to eat a range of foods that provide essential nutrients. Also, they might isolate themselves because of their appearance (Copeland et al., 2004). Older adults also have an increased risk for swallowing disorders (called *dysphagia*) as aging occurs. Many medical conditions can lead to dysphagia, such as stroke, diabetes, alcoholism, head injury, Alzheimer's, multiple sclerosis, Parkinson's, and others. Swallowing is a complex process, and dys-

phagia, if left untreated, can lead to malnutrition, dehydration, respiratory infections, aspiration pneumonia, or even death. One study found that 60 percent of the elderly in long-term care facilities suffer from dysphagia. Assessment includes swallowing tests and other medical diagnostics. Treatment may include swallowing therapy with a speech-language therapist, exercises, medication, or a feeding tube (Prasse & Kikano, 2004). Inability to swallow has a significant impact on a person's health and social-emotional well-being. Late-onset asthma and other respiratory problems affect some seniors. Another condition that results in breathing difficulties is *chronic obstructive pulmonary disease (COPD),* common to those who smoke(d). Allergists and pulmonologists can help to control symptoms (Parkinson, 2005).

Touch and Temperature Sensitivity Hand sensibility (touch/pressure and movement) was found to diminish in older adults on some measures (Desrosier et al., 1996). The elderly are also less sensitive to changes in temperature (Richardson, Tyra, & McCray, 1992). Young adults can detect a temperature drop of only 1 degree Fahrenheit in the surrounding air. Elderly individuals can fail to notice a drop of 9 degrees Fahrenheit. Consequently, older people tend to be susceptible to **hypothermia**—a condition in which body temperature falls more than 4 degrees Fahrenheit and persists for a number of hours. Early symptoms of hypothermia include drowsiness, mental confusion, and eventually a loss of consciousness. This can be life threatening, especially because the aging body becomes less able to maintain an even temperature in winter weather. Social services programs such as HEAP provide funds for elderly who are too poor to pay for the heat in their apartments in the winter months so they do not get hypothermia. Also, thyroid dysfunction among the elderly is common, and one symptom of *hypothyroidism* is always feeling cold (Sidani, 2001). Have you noticed that an elderly relative's thermostat is set at least 10 degrees higher than your own?

Sleep Changes Complaints of sleep difficulties increase with age, as sleep may be disrupted from illness, medications, the physical changes of aging, or moves to hospitals and rehabilitation facilities. More than 50 percent of persons aged 65 and older report problems with sleeping. One disorder common among the elderly is *restless legs syndrome (RLS),* causing unpleasant prickling or tingling sensations in the legs and feet and an urge to move them to get relief. Most frequently, men report difficulties with daytime sleepiness, napping, and nighttime awakenings, whereas women report difficulty in falling asleep, staying asleep, and getting adequate sleep (Middelkoop et al., 1996). Older people do report being sleepy during the day, and they do take naps, so apparently it is not the amount of sleep needed that declines with age but rather the ability to stay asleep. The two main reasons why the ability to sleep decreases with age are changes in circadian rhythms and the presence of sleep disorders (Ancoli-Israel, 1997).

Sleep patterns change across the life span. That is, older people have less Stage 3 and Stage 4 sleep (deep sleep) and less rapid-eye-movement (REM) sleep (dream sleep) (Neubauer, 1999). The sleep/wake cycle is controlled by our biological clock, or circadian rhythm. The average younger adult gets sleepy around 10 or 11 P.M. and sleeps for about 8 to 9 hours, waking between 6 and 8 A.M. As we age, our circadian clock advances, causing *advanced sleep phase syndrome.* People with advanced sleep phase syndrome get sleepy early in the evening; and if they were to go to bed at that time, they would sleep for about 8 hours and wake up at 4 to 5 A.M. But the tendency, of course, is not to go to bed so early, rather delay sleep until the "usual" time of 10 or 11 P.M. The problem is that the person still wakes up at 4 or 5 A.M. Now they have had only 5 or 6 hours sleep, so they will feel tired and maybe nap during the day to "catch up." According to Sonia Ancoli-Israel (1997), director of the Sleep Disorder Clinic, University of California at San Diego, sunlight treatment is the best stabilizer of circadian rhythms, and she recommends bright light exposure in the early evening or late afternoon.

Sleep apnea is a disorder in which the person occasionally stops breathing during sleep. The person gasps for air and might jump up to breathe again. The likelihood of this disorder increases with age (Neubauer, 1999). Treatment is continuous positive airway pressure provided by a machine or a tongue-retaining device in milder cases.

Questions

What are some common physical and sensory changes in late adulthood? How do sleep changes in later years manifest themselves?

Sexuality   "The need for companionship, tenderness, love, intimacy and yes, sex, remains as important as ever, but the rules of the game have changed" (Rimer, 1998, A1). In surveys of older people's attitudes toward sexuality, most felt that sex was important for both physical and emotional health. Wiley and Bortz (1996) found that 92 percent of the men and women as a whole reported that ideally they would wish to have sex at least once per week, and this desire was not diminished with older respondents, but fewer than half the men and women reported having sexual activity as desired. This decrease in activity is well reported, so the question is why sexual activity becomes infrequent (Levine, 1998).

Three major factors are partner availability, difficulty with sexual arousal, and the overall health of older adults. As mentioned earlier, women account for about

70 percent of the 85-and-older population and are likely to be widowed. And older single men tend to choose younger women for companionship. Sexual arousal difficulties occur in both men and women, but male impotence is the frequently occurring problem. Women also experience physical changes after the onset of menopause (less vaginal lubrication, thinning of the walls of the vagina, decreased size of uterus, cervix, and ovaries), which can make sexual intercourse uncomfortable or painful, although medications are available. Other contributing factors are medications that diminish the desire or inhibit erection in males, pain from chronic illness, mobility problems, and lack of privacy in nursing homes (Kennedy, Haque, & Zarankow, 1997). Recent national data (2002) indicate that nearly 11 percent of all cases of AIDS were diagnosed in people 50 and older; thus older adults need education programs to be informed of risk of this disease (Altschuler, Katz & Tynan, 2004).

Questions

What physical changes are considered a normal part of sexual aging for women and men? What are some factors that might account for a decrease in sexual activity?

Sexuality and Intimacy Remain Important A normal part of life for older adults is engaging in sexual intimacy. Four major factors are partner availability, difficulty with sexual arousal, the overall health of older adults, and privacy.

Biological Theories of Aging

Now you might be asking what is driving the changes associated with aging—why do they occur? There are many competing theories to explain the process. We will review several alternative explanations that recently have received the most attention. According to the *wear-and-tear theory*, there is a natural limit to the human life expectancy—about 85 years—and little can be done to push the figure upward. The other view holds that there are no absolute biological limits to how long humans can live. Rheumatologist James Fries (1989, 1997) is the leading proponent of the notion of inborn limits. He contends that the human body is biologically destined to fall apart after 85 years—frailty rather than disease being the primary killer of people at very old ages. Around age 85, give or take seven years, the tiniest insults—a fall that would be trivial to a 20-year-old, a spell of hot weather, or a mild case of the flu—are sufficient to cause death. Fries likens the process to a sun-rotted curtain: You sew up a tear in one place and it promptly tears somewhere else. In the opposing camp are those who argue that old people do die from such causes as osteoporosis or atherosclerosis, but these diseases—once deemed to be the inevitable hallmarks of old age—now can be prevented or delayed.

Forecasting Life Expectancy   As the population becomes generally healthier, people will enter old age in better shape and so life spans can be expected to increase. Biodemographers project that by the year 2070 the average life expectancy for women will be between 92.5 and 101.5 (Oeppen & Vaupel, 2002). Another demographer, S. Jay Olshansky (Olshansky & Carnes, 2001), argues that it will become harder and harder to maintain the pace, so that any major increase is highly unlikely. As in economics, a curve of diminishing returns operates. It is not so much that we are programmed to die, says Olshansky. Rather, we are not programmed to survive very long past the end of our reproductive period. Olshansky calculates that to get an average life expectancy of 85 from today's average of 77.7, we would need to reduce death rates by half at each age interval (equivalent to the complete elimination of heart disease and cancer). And once life expectancy reaches age 85, he says a practical limit is reached because there are too few people over 85 to influence the overall statistics. Yet today's 60,000+ aging American centenarians, as well as increasing numbers worldwide, seem to support Oeppen and Vaupel's theory.

In evaluating these perspectives, it is useful to examine the more prominent theories that seek to explain the biological process of aging. So far researchers have not reached a consensus. Indeed, the process of aging may be too complex for any one-factor explanation.

Genetic Preprogramming   This is also referred to as "mean time to failure." Engineers contend that every machine has a built-in obsolescence and that its lifetime is limited by the wear and tear on the parts. In the same way, aging is viewed as a product of the gradual deterioration of the various organs needed for life (Hayflick, 1980). Most significantly, DNA repair capacity declines with age and DNA damage accumulates (Warner & Price, 1989).

Aging Effects of Hormones   Hormones can promote or inhibit aging, depending on the conditions.

Reducing the secretion of some hormones (e.g., pituitary hormones) in rodents depresses their body metabolism and delays the aging of their tissues. Caloric restrictions likewise seem to slow aging processes. However, a reduction in the secretion of many hormones also occurs with age in rodents and humans. Increasing these hormones (e.g., growth hormone and DHEA) has been found to enhance metabolism and stimulate organ functioning. One study found that replacing the hormone DHEA can play a role in the prevention and treatment of the metabolic syndrome (insulin resistance, diabetes, and atherosclerosis) associated with abdominal obesity (Villareal & Holloszy, 2004).

Accumulation of Copying Errors   According to this theory, human life eventually ends because body cells develop errors in copying. The prints taken from prints are thought to deteriorate in accuracy with the number of recopying events (Busse, 1969; Ferenac et al., 2005).

Error in DNA   Another line of evidence suggests that alterations (mutations) occur in the DNA molecules of the cells—that is, errors creep into the chemical blueprint—that impair cell function and division (Busse, 1969; Hasty, 2005).

Autoimmune Mechanisms   Some scientists believe that aging has a marked impact on the capabilities of the immune system. They are convinced that the body's natural defenses against infection begin to attack normal cells because the information is blurring or because the normal cells are changing in ways that make them appear "foreign" (Miller, 1989; Schmeck et al., 2004).

Accumulation of Metabolic Wastes   Biologists have suggested that organisms age because their cells are slowly poisoned or hampered in functioning by waste products of metabolism. Such waste products accumulate, leading to progressive organic malfunctioning (Carpenter, 1965; Chown, 1972). For instance, researchers have found significant changes with age in the amounts and kinds of metals in certain organs, including the lens of the eye. Additionally, molecules that are the normal by-products of cells' use of oxygen—called "free radicals"—react with virtually every other molecule they encounter, wreaking havoc on vital cellular machinery.

In due course, the injuries are so substantial that cells no longer function properly, organ systems fail, arthritis cripples joints, emphysema undermines lungs, cataracts cloud the eyes, diseases like cancer and heart disease occur, and finally the organism dies (Kolata, 1994a; Merz, 1992). Vitamins C and E and beta carotene are believed by some to be helpful in mopping up free radicals, and so they are taken as dietary supplements. Biologists have identified specific genetic traits associated with the improvement of an organism's defense system against free radicals. This knowledge has allowed them to breed fruit flies that live the human equivalent of 150 years (McDonald & Ruhe, 2003).

Stochastic Processes *Stochastic* implies that the probability of a random happening increases with the number of events. Radiation, for instance, could alter a chromosome through a random "hit" that either kills a cell or produces a mutation in it. The chances for such an event obviously increase, the longer one lives.

Longevity Assurance Theory The theories just outlined focus on cell-destroying mechanisms. In sharp contrast to these approaches, George Sacher (Brues & Sacher, 1965) offers what he terms a "positive" theory of aging because he portrays evolution as having prolonged life among some species. Thus, instead of asking why organisms age and die, he asks why they live as long as they do. Sacher observes that the life spans of mammals vary enormously, from about 2 years for some shrews to more than 60 years for great whales, elephants, and humans. He says that in long-living species natural selection has favored genes that repair cells while weeding out genes that impair cell functioning. Individuals who are the bearers of cell repair genes are more likely to survive and thus pass on their favorable genes to their offspring. Sacher notes that the amount of DNA repair that occurred was in direct proportion to the life span of the species. Because animals with large brains produce small litters, evolution has favored them with longevity genes that lengthen the life span and make up for the losses in reproductive potential (Lewin, 1981).

Given what we know about physical changes in late adulthood, there appear to be three primary ways of slowing the aging process and living longer: (1) individuals can make behavior changes in diet and lifestyle that are known to further life expectancy; (2) medical scientists can develop ways to replace the body's growth factors, hormones, and chemical defense systems that diminish over time and affect youthfulness; and (3) medical scientists can change the genetics of aging with drugs, stem cells, and gene therapies. Clearly, the first option is the principal one currently and readily available to us, although a marketing blitz on HGH and DHEA (not necessarily FDA approved) appears on the Internet.

> **Questions**
>
> What are the major theories about why biological aging occurs? In what ways might we slow the aging process?

Cognitive Functioning

Sooner or later all adults worry about whether they are thinking, remembering, and making decisions with the same sharpness as when they were younger. Even as early as 40, we can begin to notice occasional mental lapses. It could be as simple as having difficulty remembering someone's name, where we parked the car at the mall, where we placed our car keys, trying to remember why we walked into a certain room of our house, or retrieving a certain word or name in conversation. We might wonder if these are normal consequences of aging or if they foretell a more serious process such as Alzheimer's disease. Attitudes or perceptions about aging appear to be important in determining whether people are honored for their wisdom or cast aside for their incompetence. Not all societies value old age in the same way. The Bible celebrates the wisdom of the elderly King Solomon, and Eastern cultures have long revered their elders. We have seen in the United States a less positive attitude, although much depends on the person and the historic period in which she or he lives.

Overall, psychological literature supports the view that aging often brings a decline in intellectual ability (Kennet et al., 2000). However, there is smaller decline—or even little or no decline—for people with favorable lifestyles and good health (Schaie, Willis, & O'Hanlon, 1994). Indeed, a growing body of research suggests that disease, including depression, metabolic disorders, hardening of the arteries, chronic liver and kidney failure, amnesia, or Alzheimer's disease—not age in itself—underlies much of the decline and loss of cognitive and intellectual functioning among the elderly (and medications for chronic conditions might also play a role).

Researchers looking at the physiology of aging brains are surprised at their flexibility and resilience (Cerella et al., 1993). For instance, contrary to what was established scientific opinion only a few years ago, investigators now find that older brains rejuvenate and rewire themselves to compensate for losses. According to Stanley Rapoport, chief of the neurosciences lab at the National Institute on Aging, as brains age, neighboring brain cells (neurons) help pick up the slack; indeed, responsibilities for a task can actually shift from one region to another (Schrof, 1994). Overall, although there is some decline in cognitive functioning for some people in their seventies and more in people in their eighties, many people seem not to be affected. Let's take a closer look at some of these issues.

The Varied Courses of Different Cognitive Abilities

Not only do the declines in cognitive functioning appear later in life than we might have expected, but cognitive abilities vary in how they are affected by aging. The *Seattle Longitudinal Study* (see Chapter 15) found that many abilities start a dramatic downward trend beginning in the twenties, with an even greater one as advanced age is reached. There are important exceptions.

The cross-sectional data for verbal and numeric abilities indicate a peak in midlife with relatively little change into early old age but a significant decline in the eighties. Take a minute to review some weaknesses of a cross-sectional design. The major one, of course, is that you don't know if your groups are comparable. For instance, would your 80-year-olds, if measured at the age of 40, be similar to your current 40-year-olds? In the Seattle study, both longitudinal and cross-sectional data were collected and analyzed.

The only ability that shows profound linear decrement is perceptual speed. This decline is the result of progressive slowing of neural impulses throughout the central nervous system. Another important finding is the extent of individual variation; that is, some very old people are capable of quite quick responses (Powell & Whitla, 1994; Schaie, 1995). Even more interesting is the fact that most other abilities show a gain from young adulthood into midlife. Intellectual competence generally peaks in the forties and fifties, because people continue to gain experience and without significant physiological loss to offset the gain. Speed of numeric computation declines significantly with age when followed longitudinally, but in contrast, verbal ability does not peak until the sixties and declines only modestly after that age.

Some researchers suggest that cognitive functioning should be assessed in less traditional ways than standard intelligence testing. Critics of traditional intelligence testing suggest that aspects of adult functioning, such as social or professional competence and the ability to deal with one's environment, should also be considered (Berg & Sternberg, 1992). Many psychologists are developing new measures of adult intelligence and revising our notions of adult intelligence. Howard Gardner's (1993a, b, 2000a) theories of multiple intelligences also provide insight into adult cognition.

For example, psychologist Gisela Labouvie-Vief (Adams et al., 1990) is investigating how people approach everyday problems in logic. Researchers usually find that the elderly do poorly on measures of formal reasoning ability. But she contends that this poor performance results from differences in the way younger and older adults approach tasks. Older adults tend to personalize the tasks, to consider alternative ways to answer a question, and to examine affective and psychological components associated with a problem solution. She says that reasoning by intuition rather than by principles of formal logic is not an inferior mode of problem solving—merely a different one. In other research (cited in Meer, 1986), Labouvie-Vief has found that when older people are asked to give summaries of fables they have read, they excel at recalling the metaphoric meaning of a passage. In contrast, college students try to remember the text as precisely as they can. Other researchers also find that the lower performance of older people stems from the fact that they might view some things as unimportant and hence selectively ignore what younger people may attempt to capture (Hess & Flannagan, 1992; McDowd & Filion, 1992).

Cognitive functioning depends to some extent on whether the elderly use their abilities. You most likely have heard the expression *"use it or lose it."* For instance, people can perform such complex cognitive tasks as playing chess or the cello well into old age at the same time as they are losing many simpler abilities. Many elderly persons find that what they have been doing, they can keep on doing. John Glenn, in his late seventies, returned to space as an astronaut to conduct research on aging, and Jack LaLanne, who performed the first TV exercise program, is going strong at age 90. Erik Erikson, Jean Piaget, Bernice Neugarten, Dr. Benjamin Spock, Arthur Rubinstein, Eubie Blake, Martha Graham, George Burns, Bob Hope, Andrés Segovia, Pablo Picasso, George Bernard Shaw, Arthur Miller, James Michener, Bertrand Russell, and Senator Strom Thurmond are examples of people who continued to excel at the same high standards of performance well into advanced age. Moreover, Schaie and Willis (1986, 1993) found that individualized training resulted in an improvement in spatial orientation and deductive reasoning for two-thirds of the older adults they studied. Nearly 40 percent of those whose abilities had declined returned to the level they had been at 14 years earlier. In fact, cognitive-training techniques can in many cases reverse declines (Schaie, 1994; Willis & Nesselroade, 1990). In brief, much of our fate is in our own hands, and "use it or lose it" is an underlying principle.

Older adults do slow down in their performance of many tasks (Verhaeghen, Marcoen, & Goossens, 1993), and slower reflexes are a disadvantage in tasks such as driving a car, but for most activities, speed is relatively unimportant (Meer, 1986). Developmentalist K. Warner Schaie (1994, 1996), whose pioneering work has done much to shape our understanding of cognitive functioning across the life span, finds that a variety of factors reduce the risk of cognitive decline in old age: (1) good health and the absence of chronic diseases; (2) environmental circumstances characterized by above-average education, a history of stimulating occupational pursuits, above-average income, and the maintenance of an intact family; (3) a complex and stimulating lifestyle, including extensive reading habits, travel, and a continuing pursuit of educational opportunities; (4) a personality that is flexible and adaptable at midlife; and (5) marriage to a spouse with high cognitive capabilities.

In sum, from a review of the research, these conclusions seem to be the most reasonable: A decline in intellectual ability tends to occur with aging, particularly very late in life. Some aspects of intelligence, mainly those that are measured by tests of performance and fluid ability, appear to be more affected by aging than others. But older people can learn to compensate, and they can still learn what they need to, although it can take them a little longer. Other aspects of intelligence, notably crystallized intelligence, might increase, at least until rather advanced age. There are also considerable differences among people, some faring poorly and others faring quite well. One of the major factors in maintaining or improving mental capabilities is using them. Findings from the *Berlin Aging Study*, the *Kungsholmen Study* (in Sweden), and the *Seattle Longitudinal Study* agree that those who do well in old age seem to remain involved in the world about them, are socially active, and thus do not become ineffective before their time (Palmer et al., 2002; Singer et al., 2003; Vaillant, 2002; Verderber & Song, 2005).

Questions

What factors have been identified with optimal cognitive aging? What can we do to mitigate the decline in certain intellectual abilities?

Overestimating the Effects of Aging

What happens in psychological aging is complex, and we are only beginning to understand it. What is clear, however, is that psychologists have taken too negative a view of the impact of aging on intellectual functioning. One reason for this is that researchers have relied too heavily on cross-sectional studies. As we stated in Chapter 1, cross-sectional studies employ the snapshot approach; they test individuals of different ages and compare their performance. Longitudinal studies, in contrast, are more like case histories; they retest the same individuals over a period of years (Holahan, Sears, & Cronbach, 1995).

Psychologists such as Baltes and Schaie (1976; Schaie, 1994) have pointed out that cross-sectional studies of adult aging do not allow for generational differences in performance on intelligence tests. Because of increasing educational achievement and other social changes, successive generations of Americans perform at progressively higher levels. Hence, the measured intelligence (IQ) of the population is increasing. When individuals who were 50 years old in 1993 are compared with those who were 50 in 1973, the former score higher on almost any kind of cognitive task. But because the people who were 50 years old in 1993 were 30 in 1973,

a cross-sectional study undertaken in 1973 would falsely suggest that they were "brighter" than those who were 50 in 1993. This result would lead to the false conclusion that intelligence declines with age. When you compare people from different generations—80-year-olds with 40-year-olds, for instance—you are comparing people from different environments. Thus, cross-sectional studies tend to confuse generational differences with differences in chronological age.

Other factors have also contributed to an overestimation of the decline in intellectual functioning that occurs with aging. Research suggests that a marked intellectual decline, called the **death drop** or the terminal decline phenomenon, occurs just a short time before a person dies (Johansson & Berg, 1989). Because relatively more people in an older age group can be expected to die within any given span of time, compared with a younger group, the average scores of older age groups are depressed relatively more as a result of the death-drop effect than are the average scores for younger age groups.

Whereas the cross-sectional method tends to magnify or overestimate the decline in intelligence with age, the longitudinal method tends to minimize or underestimate it. One reason is that some people drop out of a longitudinal study over time. Generally it is the more able, healthy, and intelligent subjects who remain available. Those who perform poorly on intelligence tests tend to be less available for longitudinal retesting. Consequently, the researchers are left with an increasingly smaller, biased sample as the subjects are retested at each later period.

Question

What are some reasons cited for the apparent overestimation of declines in intellectual functioning in old age?

Memory and Aging

Growing older is difficult on a personal level for many people. They might have trouble adjusting to changes in how they look or what they can do, and the limitations in daily life, even if minor, can cause them concern. One concern for nearly all older adults is *memory*. No other criterion is used more often to evaluate how we are doing. And for good reason! No other cognitive skill is as pervasive in everything we do, from remembering what we need at the grocery store to remembering how to get there (Cavanaugh, 1998b). Memory loss is also a preoccupation of American culture, reflected in the prevalence of cartoons and jokes about memory and aging. One of the common complaints of middle-aged and older adults is that their memory is "not as good as it used to be."

Samples of adults ranging from 40 to 80 years old suggest that anywhere from about 45 to 80 percent of the respondents say they had experienced some deterioration of memory in the previous year (Aiken, 1998). Clearly, large percentages of middle-aged and older adults believe they have some difficulty with their memory (Lachman, 2004; Lachman & James 1997). But with sufficient motivation, time, instruction, and a suitable environment, older adults can continue to expand their interests, abilities, and outcomes. According to Aiken (1998), these are some of the characteristics of older learners that need to be taken into account in any learning situation for them: (1) preference for a slower instructional pace; (2) inclination to make more errors of omission due to cautiousness; (3) more disrupted by emotional arousal; (4) less attentive; (5) less willing to engage with material that is irrelevant to their own lives; (6) less likely to use imagery.

Older adults often say that the first sign of cognitive aging they noticed was difficulty remembering people's names. As they age, the pool of names they know also becomes larger, so they might have difficulty remembering, not so much because their memories are not as good as they once were, but because they have more things stored in their memory and searching therefore takes longer.

Although the memory for names seems to decline regularly over a lifetime, vocabulary memory remains stable and can even increase slightly (Powell & Whitla, 1994; Schaie, 1994). Moreover, a progressive loss of memory does not always accompany advancing age (see Figure 17.5) (Jennings & Jacoby, 2003). Instead, some memory loss is found with each advance in chronological age, but some elderly retain a sound memory. Nor are all aspects of memory equally affected by aging (Hultsch, Hertzog, & Dixon, 1990; Smith et al., 1990). For instance, age-related decreases are more severe for *recall tasks* than for *recognition tasks*, yet simple *short-term* or *primary memory* shows little decline until late adulthood (Cavanaugh, 1998b) (see Chapter 7). Short-term memory includes remembering such things as whether you took a prescribed pill this morning, whether you just went to the grocery store, and whether a friend just paid a visit. Older adults have more difficulty with short-term memory, particularly if they are taking medications. Younger adults are sometimes amazed by older adults' *long-term memory,* such as remembering something from their youth 85 years ago, reciting poetry they learned in grade school, or remembering specific events, places, and names from childhood.

Question

What types of memory is an older adult likely to retain, and what types of memory is an older adult most likely to have difficulty with?

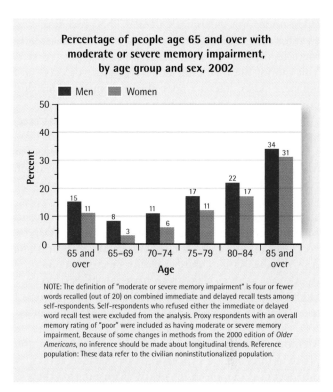

FIGURE 17.5 Aging and Memory Loss Note that some memory loss is natural and increases with aging in both men and women, with the oldest adults experiencing the most impairment. The degree of memory loss is more severe for those with Alzheimer's, which is accompanied by other behavioral, emotional, and psychological changes.
Source: Federal Interagency Forum on Aging-Related Statistics. (2004, November). *Older Americans 2004: Key indicators of well-being.* Washington, DC: U.S. Government Printing Office. Retrieved April 5, 2005, from http://www.agingstats.gov/chartbook2004/OA_2004.pdf

Phases in Information Processing When information is remembered, three things occur: (1) **encoding,** the process by which information is put into the memory system; (2) **storage,** the process by which information is retained in memory until it is needed; and (3) **retrieval,** the process by which information is regathered from memory when it is required. These components are assumed to operate sequentially. Incoming signals are transformed into a "state" (or "trace"). A *trace* is a set of information; it is the residue of an event that remains in memory after the event has vanished. When encoded, the trace is said to be placed in storage. To remember that stored information, the individual actively searches for the stored material (see Figure 7.9, page 255).

Information processing has been likened to a filing system (Vander Zanden & Pace, 1984). Suppose you are a secretary and have the task of filing a company's correspondence. You have a letter from a customer criticizing a major product of your firm. Under what category are you going to file the letter? If the contents of the letter involve a defect in a product, will you decide to create a new category—"product defects"—or will you file the letter under the customer's name? The procedure you used for categorizing the letter must be used consistently for categorizing all other correspondence you receive. You cannot file this letter under "product defects" and the next letter like it under the customer's name and hope to have an efficient system.

Encoding involves perceiving information, abstracting from it one or more characteristics needed for classification, and creating corresponding memory traces for it. As in the case of the filing system, the way in which you encode information has an enormous impact on your ability to retrieve it. If you "file" an item of experience haphazardly, you will have difficulty recalling it. But encoding is not simply a passive process whereby you mechanically register environmental events on some sort of trace. Rather, in information processing you tend to abstract general ideas from material. Hence, you are likely to have a good retention of the meaning, or *gist*, of prose material but poor memory for the specific words.

Memory Failure   Memory failure can occur at any phase in information processing. For instance, difficulty can occur in the *encoding phase*. Returning to the example of the office filing system, you might receive a letter from a customer and accidentally place the letter with trash and discard it. In this case the letter is never encoded because it is not placed in the filing cabinet. It is unavailable because it was never stored. This difficulty is more likely to be experienced by older than by younger people. Older individuals are not as effective as younger ones are in carrying out the elaborate encoding of information that is essential to long-term retention. For instance, the elderly tend to organize new knowledge less well and less completely than they did when they were younger (Hess, Flannagan, & Tate, 1993; Hess & Slaughter, 1990). Thus, overall, older adults process information less effectively than younger adults (Verhaeghen, Marcoen, & Goossens, 1993).

Memory failure can also stem from *storage problems*. For instance, when filing, you might place the letter in the filing cabinet but by mistake put it in the wrong folder. The letter is available but it is not accessible because it was improperly stored. Apparently, this problem occurs more frequently with older adults than with younger adults (Earles & Coon, 1994; Mantyla, 1994). But other factors are also involved. **Decay theory** posits that forgetting is due to deterioration of the memory traces in the brain (Salthouse, 1991). The process is believed to resemble the gradual fading of a photograph over time or the progressive obliteration of the inscription of a tombstone. **Interference theory** says that retrieval of a cue becomes less effective as more and newer items come to be classed or categorized in terms of it (Kausler, Wiley, & Lieberwitz, 1992). For example, as you file more and more letters in the cabinet, more items compete for your

attention, and your ability to find a letter is impaired by all the other folders and letters.

Faulty retrieval of knowledge is a third major cause of memory loss. Older persons can suffer a breakdown in the mechanisms and strategies by which stored information is recalled (Cavanaugh, 1998b). John C. Cavanaugh (1998b) indicates that attention is an important aspect of information processing. The ability to *focus* on what we need to do (selective attention), *perform more than one task at the same time* (divided attention), and *sustain attention* to accomplish long-term tasks all can result in *cue overload*—a state of being overwhelmed or engulfed by excessive stimuli—and failure to process retrieval information effectively. (For instance, you may file a letter under a customer's name but later lack the proper cue to activate the category under which you filed it).

Some researchers suggest that the elderly might be subject to greater inertia or failure of a "selector mechanism" to differentiate between appropriate or inappropriate sets of responses (Allen et al., 1992). Also, retrieval time becomes longer with advancing age (Cavanaugh, 1998b; Salthouse & Babcock, 1991). Overall, older adults have more difficulty with memory than younger adults do. This fact has practical implications. Older people are more likely to be plagued by doubts as to whether or not they carried out particular activities—"Did I mail that letter this morning?" "Did I close the window earlier this evening?" (Kausler & Hakami, 1983). And they are more likely to have difficulty remembering where they placed an item or where buildings are geographically located (Bengston & Schaie, 1999). On a safety level, they may forget they turned on the stove to cook something and then walk away. Or they might forget to take certain medications, which might cause fainting. Or they might forget where they put their $1,200 hearing aid!

> **Question**
>
> What are some of the theories associated with memory difficulties in old age?

Learning and Aging

Psychologists are finding that the distinctions they once made between learning and memory are becoming blurred. Learning parallels the encoding process whereby individuals put into memory material presented to them. Psychologist Endel Tulving (1968) says that learning constitutes an improvement in retention. Hence, he contends, the study of learning is the study of memory. Clearly, all processes of memory have consequences for learning. If people do not learn (encode) well, they have little to recall; if their memory is poor, they show few signs of having learned much. Not surprisingly, therefore, psychologists find that younger adults do better than older adults on various learning tasks (Bengston & Schaie, 1999). This fact has given rise to the old adage "You can't teach an old dog new tricks." But this adage is clearly false. Both older dogs and older humans can and do learn. They would be incapable of adapting to their environment and coping with new circumstances if they did not.

Research suggests that both younger and older individuals benefit when they are given more time to inspect a task. Allowing people ample time gives them more opportunity to rehearse a response and establish a linkage between events, and it increases the probability that they will encode the information in a fashion that facilitates later search and recall. Older adults benefit even more than younger ones when more time is made available for them to learn something.

Older people often give the impression that they have learned less than younger people have because they tend to be more reluctant to venture a response. At times, the elderly do not provide learned responses, especially at a rapid pace, although they can be induced to do so under appropriate incentive conditions. And when tested in a laboratory setting, older adults seem to be less motivated to learn arbitrary materials that appear to be irrelevant and useless to them. Complicating matters, today's young adults are better educated than their older counterparts. Furthermore, another hidden bias is that many elderly individuals take medications that can diminish mental functions. All these factors suggest that we should exercise caution when appraising the learning potential of the elderly, lest we prematurely conclude that they are incapable of learning new things (Singer et al., 2003).

Decline in Cognitive Functioning

Until recently, most everyone, including physicians, accepted the view that senility is natural for people living longer than the Biblical *three score and ten years,* or age 70. **Senility** is typically characterized by progressive mental deterioration, memory loss, and disorientation regarding time and place. Irritability, confusion, inability to use complete sentences, and other marked personality changes usually accompany the intellectual decline. When those affected no longer remember a spouse or children, terror can set in, with screams, because a loved one becomes a total stranger (Cohen et al., 1993):

> My wife refused to believe I was her husband. Every day we went through the same routine: I would tell her we had been married for thirty years, that we had four children. She listened, but she still thought she lived in her hometown with her parents. Every night when I got into bed she'd say, "Who are you?"
>
> (Husband of an Alzheimer's patient)

Aging and Learning Older people continue to learn throughout life, but they might need a little more time than a younger adult might need. They are less motivated to learn irrelevant material. Regularly engaging in mental tasks helps prevent memory decline, and millions of elderly adults enjoy participating in games such as Bingo, poker, bridge, *Jeopardy!* and the like.

Yet findings from the 6-year longitudinal and cross-sectional *Berlin Aging Study* (with participants ages 70 to 104) dispute common thought. Singer and colleagues (2003) report that perceptual speed, fluency, and memory begin to decline with age, but knowledge remained stable up to age 90, with decline thereafter. Rates of decline did not differ between men and women, but women in old age scored higher than men on memory and fluency. Life-history variables, such as higher income, social class, and education, were positively correlated with higher levels of functioning across all four cognitive tasks (Singer et al., 2003). Also adults in their seventies showed less marked decline in the four variables (intelligence, speed, memory, and fluency) than individuals in their eighties and nineties. But declines begin to accelerate among the "old-old" age group (nineties and older), consistent with life-span theory (Singer et al., 2003).

Senility is one of the most serious conditions that a physician can diagnose in a patient. The prognosis is grim, and the effectiveness of current treatments is uncertain. Consequently, it is incumbent upon professionals who treat the elderly to do a full battery of tests to make certain a treatable cause for a patient's symptoms has not been overlooked. Often, underlying physical diseases that can make an elderly person seem senile go unnoticed and untreated. Such individuals are simply dumped into the category of "senile" by families and physicians who have accepted the conventional wisdom that senility is inevitable in the aging process. Common problems often mistakenly diagnosed as senility include tumors, vitamin deficiencies (especially B[12] or folic acid), anemia, depression, such metabolic disorders as hyperthyroidism and chronic liver or kidney failure, and toxic reactions to prescription or over-the-counter drugs (including tranquilizers, anticoagulants, and medications for heart problems and high blood pressure). Many of these conditions can be reversed if they are identified and treated early in the course of the illness.

In persons over 65, about 20 to 25 percent of all senility results from **multiinfarcts** (better known as "little strokes"), each of which destroys a small area of brain cells and often a precursor to a stroke. When a blood vessel that carries nutrients and oxygen to the brain is blocked by a clot or bursts, the person experiences a *stroke,* which might be life-threatening. If part of the brain cannot get blood and oxygen, then cells in the brain die. Since stroke is one of the leading causes of death or severe, long-term disability, it is important to recognize the sudden signs: (1) numbness or weakness of the face, arm or leg, especially on one side of the body; (2) confusion, trouble speaking or understanding; (3) trouble seeing in one or both eyes; (4) trouble walking, dizziness, loss of balance or coordination; and/or (5) severe headache with no known cause. Any of these signs are a medical emergency, and the person needs immediate medical care (American Stroke Association, 2005). If the patient survives, there can be a long period of rehabilitation and recovery in an attempt to regain functioning. Many medical professionals assist in the rehabilitation and recovery process.

Another serious brain disorder is **Alzheimer's disease**—a progressive, degenerative disorder that involves deterioration of brain cells. Autopsies of victims show microscopic changes in brain structure, mainly in the cerebral cortex. Areas involved in cognition, memory, and emotion are riddled with masses of proteins called "plaques" and tangles of nerve cells. The clumps of degenerating nerve cells disrupt the passage of electrochemical signals across the brain and nervous system. The disease reduces production of the neurotransmitters *acetylcholine, norepinephrine, dopamine,* and *serotonin.* Neuronal loss leads to brain atrophy. Serious effects occur in three stages and include memory loss and other cognitive deficits, anxiety, agitation, disorientation, depression, sleep disturbances, irritability, aggression, delusions, hallucinations, and parkinsonian symptoms. In the severe stage, the person is no longer ambulatory, cannot perform self-care tasks, is incontinent, is likely mute but displays psychotic symptoms (Dolin & Evans, 2005).

The disorder has a devastating impact on patient and families. Eventually those diagnosed need skilled nursing care at home and in late stage they need residential facilities (as did former President Ronald Reagan). With many more elderly likely to be affected, families need government insurance programs to pay for care during the prolonged period of deterioration, many more geriatric social workers and nurses, and programs to assist families in coping with the demands of patients (Lyman, 1993). Predictably, the patient and family members caring for Alzheimer's patients are at high risk for depressive disorders (Chesla, Martinson, & Muwaswes, 1994). Families find their loved one progressively regressing, eventually unable to perform simple tasks, or remember a spouse or children. One woman, Marion Roach (1983, p. 22), told of her experiences with her 54-year-old mother, who suffered from the disease:

> In the autumn of 1979, my mother killed the cats. We had seven; one morning, she grabbed four, took them to the vet and had them put to sleep. She said she didn't want to feed them anymore. . . . Day by day, she became more disoriented. She would seem surprised at her surroundings, as if she had just appeared there. She stopped cooking and had difficulty remembering the simplest things. . . . Until she recently began to take sedation, she would hallucinate that the television or the toaster was in flames. She repeats the same few questions and stories over and over again, unable to remember that she has just done so a few moments before.

The disease typically proceeds through three phases (American Psychiatric Association, 2000). At first, in the "forgetfulness phase," individuals forget where things are placed and have difficulty recalling events of the recent past. Later, in the "confusional phase," difficulties in cognitive functioning worsen and can no longer be overlooked. Finally, in the "dementia phase," individuals become severely disoriented. They are likely to confuse a spouse or a close friend with another person. Behavior problems surface: Victims may wander off, roam the house at night or turn on a stove and forget, engage in bizarre actions, hallucinate, and exhibit "rage reactions" of verbal and even physical abuse. In time, they become infantile. The course of the disease, from onset, varies but median survival ranges from five to nine years. Patients usually die of infections (*septicemia*) or pneumonia (Dolin & Evans, 2005).

Alzheimer's researchers resemble the blind men studying the elephant: Each grabs onto a different part of the disease and comes to a different conclusion as to its causes. One popular hypothesis relates Alzheimer's disease to increased levels of a toxic brain chemical—*beta amyloid protein*—that is believed to result from some biochemical blunder. The beta amyloid protein is a major component of the plaques found on the nerve endings of the brain cells in patients suffering from Alzheimer's (Hardy & Higgins, 1992; Marx, 1993). Other researchers believe beta amyloid is a side effect of some other damage.

Another hypothesis looks to a link between zinc and the disease (zinc ions can cause certain brain proteins to convert into an insoluble form that in turn accumulates into plaque clumps) (Kaiser, 1994). Still another hypothesis postulates the existence of a defect in the immune

Alzheimer's Disease Although experts suggest a variety of guidelines to assist with home care for those adults suffering from Alzheimer's disease, the task is exceedingly taxing and stressful over a period of years. More residential care facilities have added special units to accommodate the needs of older adults in the last phases of Alzheimer's disease, which robs an adult of the ability to think, function, and communicate.

system of Alzheimer's victims. And another hypothesis relates Alzheimer's disease to a puzzling infectious agent known as a "slow virus." Such brain disorders as *kuru* and *Creutzfeldt-Jakob disease* are caused by slow viruses and are accompanied by distinctive brain lesions or plaques similar to those that characterize Alzheimer's disease. Kuru, a disease occurring in New Guinea and once believed to be of hereditary origin, is a slow-acting viral infection transmitted from person to person by ritual cannibalism. Medical researchers find that the brains of patients suffering from "slow virus" diseases have a huge deficit in a key enzyme, *choline acetyltransferase,* a substance used in the manufacture of material employed by the brain to transmit nerve signals from cell to cell (Price et al., 1991).

Because Alzheimer's disease tends to run in families, researchers are seeking a genetic source. A family history of Parkinson's disease, which also causes dementia, was found 3½ times more frequently in the families of patients with Alzheimer's disease (Polymeropoulos, Higgins, & Golbe, 1997). Duke University scientists have found a connection between a gene called *apolipoprotein E* and the risk of contracting Alzheimer's; the gene produces proteins necessary to shuttle cholesterol through the bloodstream and that are thought to be essential in protecting brain cells from collapse (Travis, 1993). Additional evidence of genetic or chromosomal factors is found in studies of patients with Down syndrome, showing that many adults with this syndrome eventually succumb to Alzheimer's lesions (National Down Syndrome Society, 1998). Still other researchers have located

on chromosome 14 a genetic defect linked to an inherited form of Alzheimer's that develops unusually early at age 45 (Marx, 1992).

Alzheimer's disease now affects 4.5 million Americans. An estimated 1 percent of 70-year-olds, 3 percent of 80-year-olds, and 8 percent of those 85 and older are affected with this disease (Dolin & Evans, 2005). Earlier onset of Alzheimer's is rare. Alzheimer's is the fourth most common cause of death in the elderly—after cancer, cardiovascular disease, and stroke. Unfortunately, as yet there is no cure for Alzheimer's disease. But new scientific findings offer hope. Pharmaceutical companies are testing more than 100 compounds that might relieve or delay the symptoms of the disease. The drug *tacrine* (also known as THA or Cognex) alleviates some of the cognitive symptoms during the early and middle stages of the disease. Other medications can help control behavioral symptoms such as sleeplessness, agitation, wandering, anxiety, and depression.

A growing body of research finds that the disease is more prevalent in African Americans and Hispanics than it is in whites (Alzheimer's Association, 2003; Dolin & Evans, 2005). Doctors recommend lab tests, neurological exams, and neuroimaging for adults with possible Alzheimer's. They also suggest there might be protective factors in middle age: taking vitamin E and C supplements, remaining physically active, eating a well-balanced diet, and participating in mental activities, such as doing crossword puzzles, playing bridge or poker, learning a new language or a new hobby (Dolin & Evans, 2005).

Parkinson's disease is a progressive disease that occurs when specific neurons die or are damaged in a part of the brain that produce a neurochemical called *dopamine.* This neurochemical allows smooth, coordinated function of the body's muscles and movement. When dopamine-producing cells are damaged, the symptoms of Parkinson's disease appear, which include shaking, stiffness of movement, slowness of movement, and balance difficulties (National Parkinson Foundation, 2005). Actor Michael J. Fox is living with Parkinson's disease, and Parkinson's disease contributed to the death of Pope John Paul II.

Questions

How does Alzheimer's disease affect the person's brain functioning? What are its effects on a person's quality of life? What is Parkinson's disease? What does it mean when a person is classified as "senile"?

Moral Development

Morals, values, and beliefs are often transmitted through formal and informal religious organizations and have varying influences on people's lives. The purpose of organized religions—such as Christianity, Judaism, Islam, Buddhism, Hinduism, Confucianism, and Taoism—is to give spiritual meaning to life. These values, beliefs, and rituals bring people together, provide a source of strength and hope in difficult times, and provide a source of continuity throughout life.

One of the continuous projects facing each of us is the need to make sense of our lives and, above all, to give our lives meaning. If you think back over the major theorists we have reviewed throughout this book, each one is concerned with explaining how our behaviors make sense as we understand the meaning-making system within which they occur. Let us now examine a developmental theory whose locus is faith. We introduce it at this time because it is well documented that the elderly are much more likely to be involved in religion and religious activities than are younger adults (Ellison & Levir, 1998).

Religion and Faith

As people age and their support systems are reduced through loss or tragedy (deaths of their spouse, children, siblings, friends, and neighbors) or movement to a new location (nursing home, living with adult children, or foster care), the elderly might be particularly comforted by the meaningfulness afforded through faith in a higher being outside of the self. Many elderly find strength, solace, and meaning in following religious practices. Those who live into old age often make religion and spirituality an essential part of their lives, attend religious services, and engage in private prayer, and tend to have better health and be more optimistic (Krause, 2005; Ai et al., 2002). The emotional support they find in their religious community is responsible for their closer relationship to God, which in turn leads to greater optimism (Krause, 2005). Vaillant (2002) suggests, from many years of studying the elderly, that successful aging means "giving to others joyously whenever one is able; receiving from others gratefully, whenever one needs it; and being capable of personal development in between." Vaillant (2002) also posits that maturity includes characteristics of forgiveness, gratitude and joy—and staying socially connected. Coincidentally—or perhaps not so coincidentally—Vaillant's findings on successful aging are components of the doctrine of many religions.

James Fowler's Theory of Faith Development   James Fowler, an ordained minister and professor, has attempted to combine theology and developmental psychology to explain the different trajectories that faith takes in individuals. A system of faith continually

The Meaning of Religion and Prayer For adults in old age undergoing physical and cognitive changes and other losses, calling upon their faith and practicing religious customs gives them strength to get through their life changes with an attitude of hopefulness and thanksgiving. This older Mexican woman is praying at the Guadalupe Basilica in Mexico City after the Vatican announced Pope John Paul II had died in April 2005.

changes in response to cognitive development, maturation, and both religious and life experiences. Although Fowler posits seven stages of faith development, we will examine only *Stage 5: Conjunctive Faith and the Interindividual Self* (midlife and beyond), as this stage is most likely to be reached after midlife. The stages are described in Table 17.4.

As we progress through the different stages of faith, we begin and continue to ask the fundamental questions regarding existence: What is life all about? Who is the ultimate authority over my life? How do I give meaning to my life? What is the purpose of my life? Is my life really over when I die? The answers to these questions revolve around what Fowler calls our *Master Story*, which contains the crucial ideas we draw on to give meaning to our

Table 17.4 Fowler's Seven Stages of Faith Development

Stage 0	Primal Faith (birth to age 2)	Really more like a basic trust in caretakers.
Stage 1	Intuitive-Projective Faith (2–8 years)	Beginning to understand cause-and-effect relationships, which are given meaning through the stories and images one gets from caretakers.
Stage 2	Mythic-Literal Faith (childhood and beyond)	Separation of fantasy and real world, but meaning is carried and restricted by the narrative it occurs in.
Stage 3	Synthetic-Conventional Faith (adolescence and beyond)	Belief that everyone has basically the same received beliefs; e.g., that all Catholics understand their religion in the same way. Not yet a personal belief.
Stage 4	Individuative-Reflective Faith (young adulthood and beyond)	A personal faith that can be reflected on.
Stage 5	Conjunctive Faith and the Interindividual Self (midlife and beyond)	Seeks truth of faith in a dialectical, multidimensional manner. (Few people get to this stage.)
Stage 6	Universalizing Faith	Committed to selfless, universal goals. Gandhi and Mother Teresa are examples.

"Seven Stages of Faith Development" from *Stages of Faith: The Psychology of Human Development and The Quest For Meaning* by James W. Fowler. Copyright 1981 by James W. Fowler. Reprinted by permission of HarperCollins Publishers.

lives. The Master Story will become increasingly explicit as we mature, and in many instances can be summed in a few words, such as "It's all about me," or might be in the form of a communal ritual such as the Passover *Haggadah* for the devout Jewish community.

Fowler's seven stages are usually called "soft stages" because they do not involve the strict adherence to logical structures associated with a "hard stage" theory like Piaget's. Furthermore, transitions between stages are usually experienced during developmental milestones such as adolescence, young adulthood, midlife, and old age.

For individuals in mid and late adulthood (who typically are at Fowler's Stage 5), life's paradoxes are numerous and not easily brushed aside. The possibility for appreciating opposites, polarities, and diverse perspectives due to having experienced these aspects of life firsthand contributes to a higher level of meaning-making for some of those in their "winter" years (or what some researchers call the "Fourth Age"). Older adults understand that all narratives point to the existence of a "grand narrative," which in turn suggests that every religious perspective is a "vehicle for grasping truth" (Fowler, 1981). In other words, the individual in Stage 5 realizes that religions are much more similar than they are different—they all have the same seed of truth at the core. The moral aspect of faith becomes apparent if we assume, as Fowler does, that we invest faith in an aggregate of ideas, values, attitudes, and behaviors that are significant to us.

Those at the higher stages of faith development will be more likely to invest in goals focused more on others

and less on self, much like Gandhi, Martin Luther King, Jr., and Mother Teresa did. Fowler worked with Kohlberg for a time, and at one point Kohlberg entertained a seventh stage for his model that reflected an element of faith. Additionally, in 1997 Joan Erikson, at 93 years old, published the last of Erik Erikson's works. Before Erik died (in his early nineties), they collaborated on an update of *The Life Cycle Completed* in which they incorporated a ninth psychosocial stage called "Very Old Age." Their ninth stage outlines the critical role that hope and faith play in the lives of those in their eighties, nineties, and beyond for valuing wisdom.

Studs Terkel, at age 88, distinguished author of *Working* and other oral histories, recently completed *Will the Circle Be Unbroken? Reflections on Death, Rebirth, and Hunger for a Faith*. Terkel was widowed after 60 years of marriage and fondly dedicates this book of wisdom, humanity, and humor to his beloved wife. Sixty-three adults from all walks of life give heartfelt testimony of religious belief, faith, and expectations (or not) of an afterlife. Their life histories reflect an extraordinary range and complexity of experience. And Terkel concludes, "Invariably, those who have a faith, whether it is called religious or spiritual, have an easier time with loss" (Terkel, 2001, p. xix).

Questions

Why do elderly adults become more interested in religious and spiritual observances? How would you explain Fowler's fifth stage of faith development?

SEGUE

In many societies around the world, the "oldest old" are a growing population of adults who are living longer with a higher quality of life than past generations had. Philosophical concerns are being raised about extending life and the allocation of resources for the elderly. Our understanding of biological aging continues to grow, and we now know that longevity is generally associated with healthy genes, a lifestyle of regular exercise, sensible health habits, regular medical checkups, and a network of social support. Recent research on longevity and aging has led to a medical field of antiaging.

Concerning intellectual functioning, those elderly who remain engaged in mental activities are less likely to experience declines in cognitive functioning, though certain types of memory decline before other types.

Though it can take longer for older people to remember recent events, they often are a wealth of information about the past. Additionally, older adults are typically concerned about staying healthy, remaining independent and not dependent on others, and not being left alone in their last years. Eventually, most cope with continual loss—loss of friends and loved ones, loss of health, loss of one's lifelong home, and loss of independence—which can lead to depression and mental illness. For coping with these losses, many find a sense of peace by having or developing a faith in some type of spiritual life after this physical one. And we shall see in Chapter 18, a network of social relationships through family support, social contacts, and adult day care can do a great deal to mediate these losses—improving quality of life.

Summary

Aging: Myth and Reality

1. At no point in life do people stop being themselves and suddenly turn into "old people." Aging does not destroy the continuity between what we have been, what we are, and what we will be.

2. There are a great many myths about aging that have little to do with the actual process of growing old. Included among these myths are those that portray a large proportion of the elderly as abandoned, institutionalized, incapacitated, in serious financial straits, and living in fear of crime.

3. The gap between the life expectancy rates of men and women has been increasing since 1920. On the average, women live several years longer than men. Women seem to be more durable organisms because of an inherent sex-linked resistance to some types of life-threatening disease. Lifestyle differences also contribute to gender differences in life expectancies. A major factor is the higher incidence of smoking among men.

Health

4. Despite the higher incidence of chronic health problems among the elderly, most elderly do not consider themselves to be seriously handicapped in pursuing their ordinary activities. Most of the conditions that create chronic disease increase with advanced age. Some of the health problems experienced by older Americans are the product of side effects associated with medication.

5. Some of the most obvious changes associated with aging are related to an individual's physical characteristics. The hair grows thinner, the skin changes texture, some of the bulk built up during earlier adulthood begins to decrease, and some individuals experience a slight loss in stature. Sensory abilities also decline with age. Aging is likewise accompanied by various physiological changes. One of the most obvious is a decline in the individual's capacity for physical work and exercise. Sleep patterns also change.

6. The incidence of self-reported acute illnesses (upper respiratory infections, varicose veins, injuries, digestive disorders, and the like) is lower among the elderly than among other segments of the population. However, the incidence of chronic diseases (heart conditions, cancer, arthritis, diabetes, osteoporosis, and so on) rises steadily with advancing years.

7. The elderly experience muscle loss, decreases in both size and strength of muscles, a decline in oxygen intake, and reduced heart efficiency.

8. Sensory abilities, such as hearing, sight, taste, and smell, decline with age.

9. Touch and temperature sensitivity also decrease. Some elderly individuals might fail to notice a temperature drop of up to 9 degrees Fahrenheit. Consequently, older people tend to be susceptible to hypothermia—a fall in body temperature of more than 4 degrees Fahrenheit that persists for a number of hours and is potentially fatal.

10. More than 50 percent of persons aged 65 and older report problems with sleep. Older people have less Stage 3 and Stage 4 sleep (deep sleep) and less rapid-eye-movement (REM) sleep (dream sleep). The likelihood of sleep apnea, a disorder in which the person occasionally stops breathing during sleep, increases with age.

11. Some factors leading to decreased sexual activity are difficulty with sexual arousal, the overall health of older adults, and the availability of a partner.

12. Many theories seek to explain the biological process of aging by focusing on cell-destroying mechanisms. Many of the mechanisms overlap. Although the effects of aging are often confounded with the effects of disease, aging is not the same thing as disease.

Cognitive Functioning

13. A decline in adult intelligence becomes more evident after age 60, mainly with slowing of response time and declines in short-term memory. However, different abilities follow quite different courses in aging individuals. Aspects of intelligence that are measured by tests of performance and fluid ability appear to be the most affected by aging.

14. Psychologists have traditionally taken too negative a view of the impact of aging on intellectual functioning, partly because researchers have relied too heavily upon cross-sectional studies.

15. Memory is often affected by aging. But to assume that a progressive loss of memory necessarily accompanies advancing age is incorrect. Memory loss among the elderly has many causes related to the acquisition, retention, and retrieval of knowledge.

16. Senility is typically characterized by progressive mental deterioration, memory loss, and disorientation regarding time and place. Multiinfarcts are responsible for about 20 to 25 percent of all senility in persons over 65. An increasing percent is due to Alzheimer's disease—a progressive, degenerative disorder that involves deterioration of brain cells. The disorder has a devastating impact not only on its victims but also on their relatives.

Moral Development

17. Morals, values, and beliefs are often transmitted to members of society through formal religious organizations. As people age and their support systems (spouse, children, friends, acquaintances) are reduced through loss or movement to a new location (nursing home, living with adult children, foster care), the elderly may be particularly comforted by the meaningfulness afforded through faith in something outside of the self.

18. James Fowler has attempted to combine theology and developmental psychology to explain the different trajectories that faith takes in individuals throughout the life course. His theory involves a seven-stage model of faith development that covers religious as well as nonreligious perspectives. Stages 5 and 6 are predominant in the late adulthood stage of life.

Key Terms

ageism (580)	gerontology (580)	retrieval (601)
Alzheimer's disease (604)	geropsychology (580)	senescence (584)
collagen (593)	hypothermia (595)	senility (603)
death drop (600)	interference theory (602)	sleep apnea (596)
decay theory (602)	multiinfarct (604)	storage (601)
encoding (601)	osteoporosis (589)	

Following Up on the Internet

Web sites for this chapter focus on the changing health needs, declining cognitive functioning, and growing spiritual needs of those in late adulthood. Please access the text Web site at www.mhhe.com/vzcrandell8 for up-to-date hot-linked Internet addresses for the following organizations, topics, and resources:

Administration on Aging
Aging Research Links (international)
Aging Studies Worldwide and Centers
Gerontological Society of America
International Longevity Center
National Academy on Aging Society
Older Americans: 2004 Key Indicators of Well-Being
Adventist Health Studies
The New England Centenarian Study

Late Adulthood
Emotional and Social Development

Critical Thinking Questions

1. Do you think that a 75-year-old and a 25-year-old could fall in love with each other and have a high-quality life together? Why or why not?

2. If society painted an exciting or respectful picture of old age, do you think most elderly individuals would view their own lives differently? How does the media's portrayal of old age affect people's self-perceptions?

3. Nursing homes exist largely because most adults work and cannot take care of those in need on a full-time basis. If the time comes for you to help your elderly parent(s), do you think you would quit your job to support those who sacrificed for you? Why or why not?

4. If, starting tomorrow, you could no longer work, attend school, or have any family or close friends, and you did not know how many more years you had to live—what would you do or think about? How do you think you might feel about living a life "in limbo," away from the mainstream of life?

As Americans are moving further into the new century, we are experiencing a paradigm shift from the Industrial Age to the Information Age, which is significantly impacting individuals, societies, and nations. Advances in medicine, technology, education, the social sciences, and human services allow more people to reach old age with fewer ailments and to live a higher-quality life. Predictions about the rapidly increasing number of elderly foretell a need for major changes in government programs and more options for elder care as well as an increase in products and services aimed at this population so that they can grow older with dignity and vitality (Levine, 2004). In 2003 there were over 36 million Americans age 65 and older comprising over 12 percent of the U.S. population with projections of doubling to over 70 million by 2030 (Federal Interagency Forum on Aging-Related Statistics, 2004).

Significantly, the number of American minority elderly is increasing more rapidly, but many of these elderly hold positions of respect within their ethnic communities and are taken care of by family members. Only about 5 percent of elderly Americans are placed in institutional care facilities to live out their later years if they develop a serious physical or mental health condition, such as Alzheimer's disease. Today home health care and alternative living arrangements are available for elderly persons who need special assistance to maintain independent living and for persons caring for an elderly relative in their home. According to the social model of living, the elderly will have a higher quality of life if they can maintain independence, control, and social engagement.

Social Responses to Aging

It has become increasingly clear that social-emotional and behavioral factors influence the quality of aging, as well as the physical, health, educational, and economic factors discussed in Chapter 17. It is well known that negative emotions such as depression, anxiety, hostility, and anger are associated with illness and disease (Glazer, 2005). More recently, researchers are focusing on positive health factors such as hope, resilience, friendship, and the importance of spirituality in daily life.

Some American elderly are experiencing greater satisfaction in their later years. "Industrialized societies have demonstrated remarkable efficacy and flexibility in extending longevity for many people and in providing the economic and social resources for them to lead a more satisfying life in old age" (Baltes & Baltes, 1998, p.13). Many who are living longer are also staying physically active, mentally engaged, and socially involved longer. Even now, the sight of vigorous people in their eighth and ninth decades is not unusual. Given present trends in mortality, a larger segment of the population is expected to live well into their eighties and beyond, with a high rate of mortality in their mid-eighties. Most people use continuity as a personal goal to guide their individual development (Atchley, 1999). Recent reviews of research results from the *Berlin Aging Study* (Baltes & Smith, 2003) report that the "oldest old" are at the limits of functional capacity, and at the present science and social policy cannot meet their increasing needs. A few research efforts have focused on the cognitive functioning of the "youngest old," those aged 60 to 75. There is a growing body of research worldwide on those 80 and older, particularly in the areas of health, cognition, emotional well-being, and social functioning (Haynie et al, 2001; Isaacowitz & Smith, 2003; Mehta, Yaffee, & Covinsky, 2002; Perls, 2004; Smith et al., 2002; Stek et al., 2005).

Because we know that physical and intellectual declines are common in the elderly, can we predict a constricted range of emotions in elderly adults? If so, what emotional states can we expect the elderly to experience? If not, what life circumstances help some elderly maintain a rich range of emotions, especially those that promote constructive coping? Researchers in Stockholm, Sweden, as part of the *Kungsholmen Project*, reported findings of both positive and negative affect (emotional components of subjective well-being) in 105 people, 90 to 99 years of age, who were not cognitively impaired (Hilleras et al., 1998). *Positive affect* was defined as the extent to which a person feels active, alert, and enthusiastic. *Negative affect* was defined as the extent to which a person feels guilt, anger, and fear. A recent study found that personality and general intelligence were the strongest predictors of positive and negative affect in very old age (Isaacowitz & Smith, 2003).

False Stereotypes

With our culture's preoccupation with youthfulness, many Americans prefer to disregard late adulthood or have distorted notions about it (such as the elderly are suffering and living in pain or living with dementia). Most likely, though, you have heard of "the graying of America," or "the golden years," or "the silent revolution." But specifically to whom do these phrases refer? Gerontologists tend to segment late adulthood into the periods of "young old" (65 to 75 or 80) and "old old" (80 and above) (Baltes & Smith, 1997). Historical gerontologist and chair of the National Council on Aging, W. Andrew Achenbaum (1998) reminds us why we historically have held more negative views of old adulthood:

1. Old age has always been considered to be the last stage of existence before death, and no one wants to be reminded about mortality.
2. Old age is undefined: There are few rites of passage comparable to those celebrated in youth. Not all elderly are married to celebrate golden anniversaries, nor are all grandparents, nor do all elderly retire.
3. There is a growing, diverse composition of elders with varied physical, cognitive, behavioral, and socioeconomic characteristics. Discussion about a "typical" older adult is difficult, yet many are dependent on government entitlements and family support.

These stereotypic views weigh heavily on older adults' self-esteem: A large portion of our elderly have illnesses or impairments associated with physiological aging and are likely to be overmedicated (or in some cases, deliberately sedated). Some suffer from depression and loneliness, and suicide rates are highest among American elderly males. Yet with emerging empirical research on our elderly population, though, we are finding that growing into late adulthood is not necessarily an unhealthy burden. Recall that worldwide the fastest-growing segment of the population is the oldest adult population over 80. Overall, by the year 2030, it is estimated that nearly 20 percent of the U.S. population will be over age 65. While the projected growth of the population aged 65 and older is expected to double by 2030, the population 85 and older could reach about 21 million by 2050 (Federal Interagency Forum on Aging-Related Statistics, 2004). Also, female and Hispanic attitudes about age and aging will become a larger determining factor in American perceptions (Achenbaum, 1998).

Questions

Why has little empirical research been done with the elderly? Why are behavioral scientists studying more issues in late adulthood now?

Positive and Negative Attitudes

A common stereotype is that adults in old age are unhappy, but some research disputes this myth. The findings of a study by Prenda and Lachman (2001) found that future-oriented planning enhanced life satisfaction and the perception of control. These effects were most pronounced for older adults, pointing to the potential for future-oriented planning as an important life management strategy (and transition planning is a new career focus in geropsychology and gerontology). Positive affect is related to favorable life events, positive health status and functional ability, availability of social contacts, and higher levels of educational attainment (Hilleras et al., 1998). However, correlates of positive and negative affect in the very elderly have rarely been researched.

Using the *Positive and Negative Affect Schedule (PANAS)*, Hilleras and colleagues (1998) surveyed their elderly subjects to examine whether similar patterns of positive and negative affect were correlated with personality traits. Factors associated with affect in this study were grouped into categories of personality, social relationship, subjective health, activities, life events, religiousness, and sociodemographic variables.

Factors associated with positive affect included:

- Social relationships, such as contact with friends, living with others, attending religious services, and participating in clubs/society/organizations
- Reading and following news
- An extroverted personality
- Definite beliefs and definite disbeliefs
- Living with other persons

Factors associated with negative affect included:

- Neuroticism
- Own major illness
- Money problems
- Living alone

The Stockholm study also demonstrated that positive affect and negative affect were not correlated with each other. That is, the very elderly who scored high on positive affect (active, alert, and enthusiastic) did not necessarily score low on negative affect (guilt, anger, and fear). This means these elderly subjects responded with a full range of emotions on this scale, not unlike younger adults. One observation, though, was that subjects took a long time to answer each question during the interview process. Findings from this study also underscore that the emotional health of the "oldest old" is quite diverse and that further research is needed on the affective health of this population of adults.

Over the past few decades, researchers in geropsychology, gerontology, and geriatric medicine have posed several theories about personality development and adjustment for those living into the highest ranges of adulthood. Perl's (2004) study of centenarians (a high number from Nova Scotia) shows that many are still active, relatively healthy, self-sufficient, engaged in various activities—and that longevity runs in families. Thus, researchers are now investigating a genetic link to longevity. "Forty percent of centenarians avoid chronic illnesses until they are over 100" (Duenwald, 2003, p. 3). Dr. Barzilai from the Albert Einstein College of Medicine reports similar health findings from more than 200 Ashkenazi Jewish centenarians, who have very high levels of the "good" cholesterol HDL (Duenwald, 2003). Yi and Vaupel's (2002) research findings on the life of the "oldest old" in China confirm similar daily activity, normal cognitive functioning, and life satisfaction, with more decline beginning in their nineties, and with more impairments at age 100 and older.

Self-Concept and Personality Development

Recall from Chapter 17 that genetics, biochemistry, and lifestyle factors are variables that play a large role in physical health and longevity. In this chapter, we continue to examine research findings from social and emotional perspectives: Is there such a thing as an ideal personality type that promotes a high quality of life and longevity? Is there continuity in personality across the life span, or are there dramatic changes along the way?

Psychosocial Theories

Unfortunately, many of the theories proposed on social-emotional development in the earlier years of life never extended to adulthood, especially not to late adulthood. However, as societies around the world are experiencing a similar demographic shift to an older population, many gerontologists, geropsychologists, and sociologists are studying the concepts of "antiaging," "successful aging," "satisfaction with aging," "productive aging," and "optimal aging." There are several proposed psychosocial theories of late adulthood at this time.

Erikson: Integrity Versus Despair   A recurrent theme in Erikson's work is that psychosocial development occurs in stages across the entire life span. According to him, the elderly confront the issue of **integrity versus despair**. In this eighth stage, Erikson says individuals recognize that they are reaching the end of life. Provided they have successfully navigated the previous stages of development, they are capable of facing their later years with optimism and enthusiasm. With retrospection, they can take satisfaction in having led an active, full, and complete life. (See the *More Information You Can Use* box on page 615, "Reminiscence: Conducting a Life Review.") This recognition produces contentment and compensates for decreased physical potency and performance. They find a new unification in their personality, producing a sense of integrity.

In late adulthood, Erikson himself demonstrated a life of ego integrity. At age 87 Erikson wrote and published *Vital Involvements in Old Age,* reporting the results of his personal interviews with American men and women in their eighties and nineties. His last works examined why some elderly live hopeful, productive lives, despite failing health and alertness, and why others, though relatively robust, give in to loneliness, narcissism, and despair (Woodward, 1994). At 92 he was formulating and personally experiencing a last stage of personality development in which each individual confronts his life in relation to existence itself. In 1997, Joan Erikson (in her nineties) published an update of Erikson's *The Life Cycle Completed,* incorporating a ninth stage of psychosocial development. She writes of the challenges of elderly adults facing lost autonomy and more limited life choices. At the end of his life, Erikson viewed hope and faith as playing critical roles in developing *wisdom* in this life stage.

Those who appraise their lives as having been wasted, believing that they missed opportunities they should have taken years ago (a different career path, marrying or marrying a different person, retiring later or sooner, having children) experience a sense of despair. They realize that time is running out and that it is too late to make up for past mistakes. They view their lives with a feeling of disappointment, loss, and purposelessness. Consequently, Erikson says, they approach death with regrets and fear.

Some evidence also suggests that aspects of personality change among the elderly are developmental. The *Berkeley Studies,* a longitudinal study of adults begun in 1928, suggest a decline in extraversion in old age (Field & Millsap, 1991). The decline might reflect a developmental increase in what has variously been termed "inner-directedness" and "interiority" (Field, 1991; Neugarten, 1973). Erikson's notion of wisdom as "a detached concern with life itself, in the face of death itself" suggests a similar inner-directedness (Erikson, Erikson, & Kivnick, 1986). Indeed, some psychologists have wondered whether it is possible to attain Erikson's stage of *ego integrity* without the inward focus associated with interiority (Ryff, 1982).

Question

According to Erikson, what psychosocial tasks confront those in late adulthood?

Peck's Psychosocial Tasks of Later Adulthood Psychologist Robert C. Peck (1968) provides a somewhat related view of personality development during the later years that is more focused than Erikson's. Peck says that old age confronts men and women with three challenges, or tasks, which we will examine here.

Ego Differentiation Versus Work-Role Preoccupation The central issue here is presented by retirement from the workforce. Men and women must redefine their worth in terms of something other than their work roles. They confront this question: "Am I a worthwhile person only insofar as I can do a full-time job; or can I be worthwhile in other, different ways—as a performer of several other roles and also because of the kind of person I am?" (Peck, 1968, p. 90). The ability to see themselves as having multiple dimensions allows individuals to pursue new avenues for finding a sense of satisfaction and being worthwhile.

Body Transcendence Versus Body Preoccupation As people age, they might develop a chronic illness or a substantial decline in their physical capabilities. Those who equate pleasure and comfort with physical well-being can feel that this decrease in health and strength is the gravest of insults. They can either become preoccupied with their bodily health or find new sources of happiness and comfort in life. Many elderly persons suffer considerable pain and physical unease and yet manage to enjoy life greatly. They do not succumb to their physical aches, pains, and disabilities but find human relationships and creative mental activities to be sources of fulfillment. This process of transcendence might prove more difficult for males, who have identified with being strong and placed more reliance on their physical well-being. It is well documented that older males have the highest rates of suicide of anyone in the life span (Hoyert, Kung, & Smith, 2005).

> From age 55 on, you have to focus on what is on the inside, not just what is on the outside. People need to do an internal audit to see what they can improve and what they can throw away. (C. Kermit Phelps, 91, of Kansas City, Missouri, *Monitor on Psychology,* 2000)

Ego Transcendence Versus Ego Preoccupation Younger individuals typically define death as a distant possibility, but this privilege is not accorded the elderly. They must come to terms with their own mortality, and their adaptation need not be one of passive resignation. Rather, the elderly can come to see themselves as living on after death through their children, their work, their contributions to culture or community, and their friendships. Thus, they perceive themselves as transcending a mere

More Information You Can Use

Reminiscence: Conducting a Life Review

For a person in late adulthood, conducting a life review is a significant experience. A **life review** is reminiscence and sharing of family history from one generation to another. This is especially difficult today as more families are geographically separated from one another or have such busy schedules they see each other infrequently. The older person gains feelings of self-worth, continuity in personality, and happiness about preserving family history. During this connection among the generations, individuals discover interesting life experiences and memories about each other, too. "Life reviews affirm the importance of life experiences and achievements and, for some individuals, give new meaning to life" (Moyer & Oliveri, 1996). As Erikson has indicated, adults in this stage of life strive to integrate past psychological themes into a new level of meaning, and they have an individual and wiser perspective on the world and life that is different from the perspective they had when they were younger. A life review allows the older adult to take a look at her or his lifetime as a whole and promotes a sense of integrity.

Sometimes natural reminiscence occurs at family reunions or funerals. However, as people age and significant people in their life move, become disabled, or die, they have fewer contacts that promote natural reminiscence. Reminiscence can be incorporated into private or group settings and sometimes in therapeutic settings. John Kunz (1991) suggests that practitioners who conduct intake interviews at nursing homes, group homes, or adult day-care facilities should be respectful of their elderly interviewees and should expect the interview to take some time, because an elderly person can have more history to tell, and relating that history can be therapeutic. When reminiscence is done in a group, such as an adult day-care setting, those of the same age often benefit from each other, as long as no one or two people dominate the reminiscence.

Taking the time to listen to others helps them know they are important. Here are some suggestions that might spark a reminiscence with someone you love or know.

Items That Prompt Sharing

- Photographs (from childhood, or family reunions, birthdays, anniversaries)
- Family scrapbooks, journals, books
- Newspaper clippings and old magazines
- Mementos from life accomplishments (trophies, badges, ribbons, plaques, etc.)
- Special personal belongings (keepsakes, jewelry, etc.)

Reminiscence: Sharing a Life A life review is a normative process engaged in by anyone, regardless of age, when they are aware that they are approaching death. The person looks back at his or her entire life, tries to resolve issues that were unresolved, tries to accept negative experiences, celebrates the good experiences, and gains a sense of accomplishment and closure with life.

Some Good Communication Skills

- Be an active listener
- Maintain eye contact
- Ask questions that encourage the person to explain or expand on things that seem important
- Watch nonverbal cues for posture, eye contact, and expressions (comfort or discomfort)
- Accept what is said, and allow the person to continue talking without jumping in with your own life experiences
- Realize there may be times of silence or tears (this is normal; allow the person time to regather thoughts and continue)

There are many ways to preserve a life review, including preparing a scrapbook, an audiocassette or videotape, a newspaper article, a letter, or a book for family members or as a contribution to a local museum, historical society, or library. These are forms of remembrance of this special person. The American Association of Retired Persons has an interactive bulletin board on the Internet called "Through the Years," where people can tell the world about their memories of the twentieth century and be a part of history.

Source: Adapted from John Kunz, *Communicating with Older Adults,* 1996, and John S. Kunz, *Reminiscence Approaches Utilized in Counseling Older Adults, in Illness, Crisis, and Loss,* 1991, 48–54.

earthly presence. Note the high number of college scholarships established to allow an elderly person or couple the opportunity to have their good fortune "transcend" time and space in perpetuity for the benefit of others.

Common to the approaches taken to psychosocial development by Erikson, Peck, and many other psychologists is the notion that life is never static and seldom allows a prolonged respite (Shneidman, 1989). Follow-up research on Terman's gifted men and women shows the positive relationship between a self-appraisal of having lived up to one's intellectual potential in midlife and satisfaction with work and family relations as well as joy of living three decades later (Holahan, Holahan, & Wonacott, 1999). Both the individual and the environment constantly change, necessitating new adaptations and new life structures.

Question

What are Robert Peck's views about personality development during late adulthood?

Vaillant's Theory of Emotional Health   As noted earlier regarding findings from the Stockholm study, and from Perl's centenarian study, our personality makes a difference in promoting or detracting from our emotional health and well-being. These recent results support earlier longitudinal research. At five-year intervals, researchers have followed some men who graduated from Harvard University in the early 1940s (Goleman, 1990c). Psychiatrist George Vaillant and colleagues conducted a follow-up study of 173 of these men at age 65 who had participated in the *Grant Study* (Vaillant & Milofsky, 1980).

The project provides insights into which personality factors matter, for better or worse, in later life. The investigators viewed emotional health among the elderly as the "clear ability to play and work and to love" and to achieve satisfaction with life. An ability to handle life's blows without passivity, blame, or bitterness proved especially important. At age 65 the subjects reported that their emotional health was not grounded in a happy childhood, or a satisfying marriage, or professional recognition and accomplishment. Those men who developed a *sense of resilience* to absorb the shocks and changes of life were best able to enjoy life. Their self-awareness allowed them to control their first impulses and to respond calmly using what researchers called mature adaptive mechanisms—instead of lashing out in anger or blame—promoting emotional satisfaction and well-being.

Men who in college were rated by a psychiatrist as being good practical organizers of coursework—rather than as having a theoretical, speculative, or scholarly bent—were among those making the best emotional adjustment in their later years. So were those who as col-

lege sophomores had been described as "steady, stable, dependable, thorough, sincere, and trustworthy." These two traits—*pragmatism* and *dependability*—seemed to matter more than traits such as spontaneity and the ability to make friends easily, which had seemed important for psychological adjustment during the college years. Many factors of early life, even a relatively bleak childhood (such as being poor, orphaned, or a child of divorce), had little effect on well-being at age 65 for the Harvard men. This finding was supported by a four-year study reported by Suh and Diener (1998). They found that emotional well-being is strongly determined by enduring personality characteristics rather than by external life circumstances. In the Grant Study, though, severe psychological depression earlier in life was associated with persistent problems. Being close to one's siblings while in college was strongly linked to later emotional health. As recent research also confirms, the Harvard project revealed that people are extraordinarily resilient and that over a half-century most people retain the capacity to recover from adversity and get on with their lives.

A Trait Theory of Aging

Most of us go about our daily lives "typing" or "pigeonholing" people on the basis of a number of traits that seem particularly prominent in their behavior. They reveal these traits in the course of interacting with others and with the environment. On the basis of this observation, a number of psychologists, including Bernice L. Neugarten, R. J. Havighurst, and S. Tobin (1968), attempted to identify major personality patterns, or traits, that have relevance for the aging process. They studied several hundred persons aged 50 to 80 in the Kansas City area over a six-year period. From their research results, they identified four major personality types:

- Integrated
- Armor-defended
- Passive-dependent
- Disintegrated

The *integrated* elderly are well-functioning individuals who reveal a complex inner life, intact cognitive abilities, and competent egos. They are flexible, mellow, and mature. However, they differ from one another in their activity levels, and the researchers identified three subgroups of integrated elderly. Findings from the 25-year *Okinawa Centenarian Study* suggest that the "oldest old" Japanese are optimistic, easygoing, and adapt to life situations (Willcox, Willcox, & Suzuki, 2000). The *reorganizers* are capable people who place a premium on staying young, remaining active, and refusing to "grow old." As they lose one role in life, they find another, continually reorganizing their patterns of activity. The *focused* elderly display medium levels of activity. They are selective in what they choose to do and center their energy on one or two role areas. The *disengaged* elderly also show integrated personalities and high life satisfaction. But they are self-directed people who pursue their own interests in a calm, withdrawn, and contented fashion, with little need for complex patterns and networks of social interaction.

The *armored-defended* elderly are striving, ambitious, achievement-oriented individuals, with high defenses against anxiety and with the need to retain tight control over events. Here, too, there are differences: The *holders-on* view aging as a threat and relentlessly cling as long as possible to the patterns of middle age. They take the approach "I'll work until I drop dead." They are successful in their adaptation as long as they can continue their old patterns. The *constricted* elderly structure their world to ward off what they regard as an imminent collapse of their rigid defenses. They tend to be preoccupied with "taking care of themselves," but in their preoccupation they close themselves off from other people and experiences.

Passive-dependent elderly form a third group: The *succorance-seeking* have strong dependency needs and elicit responsiveness from others. They appear to do well as long as they have one or two people on whom they can lean and who meet their emotional needs. The *apathetic* elderly are "rocking chair" people who have disengaged from life. They seem to "survive" but with medium to low levels of life satisfaction. Finally, there are those elderly who show a *disintegrated* pattern of aging. They reveal gross defects in psychological functions and an overall deterioration in their thought processes. Their activity levels and life satisfaction levels are low. Neugarten, Havighurst, and Tobin (1968) concluded that personality is an important influence in how people adapt to aging. It has major consequences for predicting their relationships with other people, their level of activity, and their satisfaction with life.

Other Theories of Aging

How successfully people age depends on a complex interaction of variables, including physical and mental health, educational achievement, financial security, and individual and cultural perceptions about aging. Humans also need social settings to develop and express their humanness. Accordingly, psychologists, gerontologists, and sociologists have advanced a number of theories that describe changes in the elderly in the United States in terms of the changes in their self-perception and social environments:

- **Disengagement theory of aging.** A view of aging as a progressive process of physical, psychological, and social withdrawal from the wider world. Consequently, the elderly can face death peacefully,

Differing Responses to Aging Bernice Neugarten identified a number of personality patterns that influence how people respond to the aging process. "Reorganizers" search for settings that permit them to remain integrated by carrying on an active life. This man from China is 105 and is doing a 100-meter run. Being able to engage in favorite activities helps the "oldest old" maintain a zest for life.

knowing that their social ties are minimal, that they have said all their goodbyes, and that nothing more remains for them to do.

- **Activity theory of aging.** The view that the majority of healthy older persons maintain fairly stable levels of activity as long as possible and then find substitutes for the activities they are forced to relinquish. The amount of engagement or disengagement that occurs among the elderly appears to be more a function of past life patterns, socioeconomic status, ability to use the English language, and health than of anything inherent in the aging process.

- **Role exit theory of aging.** The view that retirement and widowhood terminate the participation of the elderly in the principal institutional structures of society—the workforce and the family—diminishing the opportunities open to the elderly for remaining socially useful. The loss of occupational and marital statuses are regarded as particularly devastating, because these positions are master statuses or core roles, anchoring points for adult identity. The social norms that define the behavioral expectations for old age are weak, limited, and ambiguous. Furthermore, the elderly have little motivation to conform to an essentially "roleless role," a socially devalued status.

- **Social exchange theory of aging.** The theory that people enter into social relationships because these provide rewards—economic sustenance, recognition, a sense of security, love, social approval, gratitude, and the like. In the process of seeking such rewards, however, they also incur costs—they have negative, unpleasant experiences (effort, fatigue, embarrassment, etc.), or they are forced to abandon other positive, pleasant experiences in order to pursue the rewarding activity. A relationship tends to persist only as long as both parties receive profit (total reward minus total cost) from it. As applied to old age, social exchange theory suggests that the elderly find themselves in a situation of increasing vulnerability because of the deterioration in their bargaining position (Schulz, Heckhausen, & Locher, 1991). In industrial societies, skills become increasingly outmoded through technological change, and as a consequence of the decline in power available to the elderly, older workers exchange their position in the labor force for the promise of Social Security and Medicare; that is, they "retire."

• **Modernization theory.** The view that the status of the aged tends to be high in traditional societies and lower in urbanized, industrialized societies (Cowgill, 1974, 1986). This theory assumes that the position of the aged in preindustrial, traditional societies is high because the aged tend to accumulate knowledge and control through their years of experience. It is widely believed that *elder respect* continues to be an important aspect of African and Asian cultures (Eyetsemitan, 1997). Ingersoll-Dayton and Saengtienchai (1999) also present a cross-cultural perspective on elder respect in four East Asian countries and show how these attitudes have changed over time.

Although social exchange theory and modernization theory are helpful in drawing attention to elements of exchange that influence the position of the elderly in a society, they fall short of providing a complete explanation (Ishii-Kuntz & Lee, 1987). Van Willigen (2000) studied the perception of physical well-being and the psychological impact of volunteering on elderly persons. The results indicated that older volunteers experienced greater increases in life satisfaction as well as greater positive changes in perceived health than younger adults did. A national survey reveals that about 25 percent of adults age 65 and older are actively volunteering at increasing rates, and nearly half of those volunteers do so through their religious affiliations. Also, more women volunteer than men, and more married persons volunteer compared with singles. Adults with a college education were more likely to provide professional and managerial assistance (see Figure 18.1) (U.S. Bureau of Labor Statistics, 2004c). Volunteering allows the elderly an opportunity to stay actively engaged in a social community and have meaning in their lives. Older people in other cultures often remain engaged in life into old adulthood, where there is no official "retirement" date or age. See the *Human Diversity* box "Elderly Hispanic Americans" for further discussion.

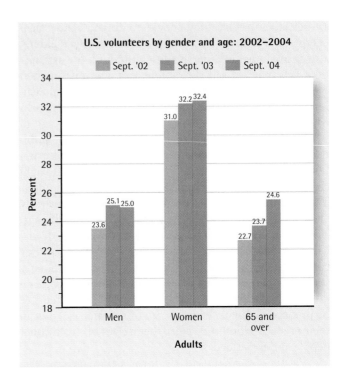

FIGURE 18.1 Volunteerism in Late Adulthood About 25 percent of U.S. adults 65 and older volunteered from September 2003 to September 2004. Note that many more women volunteer than men and that a growing number of persons over age 65 are volunteering as more persons from the baby-boom cohort are retiring.
Source: U.S. Bureau of Labor Statistics. (2004, December 16). *Volunteering in the United States, 2004.* Washington, DC: U.S. Department of Labor.

Question

Which models of aging deal with internal aspects and which deal with external aspects?

Selective Optimization with Compensation

Paul and Margret Baltes endorse the life-span model they call **selective optimization with compensation.** At all stages, and especially in old age, we are adjusting our standards of expectation. A great deal depends on how each elderly person perceives old age. The aging adult who views late adulthood as a time of gaining knowledge and wisdom will have a healthier, more positive self-concept; the aging adult who views old age as a time of physical debilitation and loss of control will form a more negative self-concept. We will enjoy more successful aging if we recognize our capabilities and compensate for losses and limitations. Late adulthood brings many changes in life—that is, we demonstrate "the ability to adjust and to transform reality so that the self continues to operate well if not better than in earlier

Human Diversity

Elderly Hispanic Americans

This is the age of aging" (Fried & Mehrotra, 1998). Until recently, research on aging and late adulthood studied mainly white subjects, who in 1990 made up nearly 90 percent of American elderly. However, the number of ethnic minority elderly is projected to grow much more rapidly than the number of elderly whites over the next 50 years. To date there are limited studies on issues that enhance the lives of our elderly, especially for those of minority backgrounds. It is especially important that we address the needs of our growing, more diverse elderly American population in the related fields of gerontology, gerontological nursing, geropsychology, adult development and aging, human services, health care and health education, public health, health policy, and family studies. Demographic data show that the Hispanic American population is now the largest minority group comprising 12.5 percent of the population according to the 2000 Census (Toussaint-Comeau, 2003). Furthermore, because the number of Hispanic elderly is expected to triple by 2050 (National Hispanic Council on Aging, 2004), we shall focus here on recent research findings regarding the Hispanic American elderly. Hispanics are those persons whose families originated in Central or South America or the Caribbean, and they can be black, white, or Asian—but they share the Spanish language (Fried & Mehrotra, 1998).

Acculturation

The relationship between diversity and psychological distress was studied with immigrant elders from Cuba, Mexico, and Puerto Rico. Using data from the *National Survey of Hispanic People*, Krause and Goldenhar (1992) conducted a phone survey with more than 1,300 elderly and found an association between financial strain and level of acculturation. That is, Hispanic Americans who are more acculturated experience less social isolation, fewer financial problems, and fewer symptoms of depression. Puerto Rican American elderly subjects reported more depressive symptoms than Cuban American subjects.

Mental Health and Well-Being

Minority elders usually seek help for emotional issues from other members of their ethnic group and not from social service agencies. Zamanian and colleagues (1992) surveyed a sample of 159 older Mexican Americans to determine the relationship between depressive symptoms and acculturation. They conclude that "retention of aspects of Mexican culture without concomitant attempts to incorporate aspects of the dominant culture results in the most vulnerable position to depression" (Zamanian et al., 1992). Because there is a relationship between depression and suicide, this is of great

concern. Additionally, minority caregivers are less likely to use agencies offering services for elderly with dementia and Alzheimer's disease (Braun et al., 1995). One study found that knowledge of services and age played a significant role in helping to prepare for the care of the Latino elderly as compared with Anglos (Delgadillo, Sorensen, & Coster, 2004).

Health Care

The Hispanic population in general is at greater risk for diseases such as heart disease, cancer, HIV infection, stroke, pneumonia, diabetes, and influenza (U.S. Food and Drug Administration, 2004). Furthermore, they face the problems of lack of housing, jobs, and the inability to pay for food, clothing, and prescription medicines (National Hispanic Council on Aging, 2004). Gelfand (1994) reminds us that there are large differences among Hispanic American groups in terms of the health of older adults. He cites that Puerto Rican American men have a higher rate of cardiovascular disease than Cuban or Mexican American men; Mexican Americans have the highest rate of cerebrovascular disease, and Cuban Americans have higher rates of cancer. The health beliefs of the Mexican American elderly are more likely to derive from folk medicine than from professional medical practice. One such folk belief system of some Mexican Americans in the Southwest is *curanderismo* (Gafner & Duckett, 1992). This involves a blend of Catholicism, medieval medicine, and the medicine of indigenous Indians. Some of the features of this belief system are (1) the belief that God heals the sick through persons, called *curanderos*, who are blessed with the *don*, a special gift; (2) the reality that a number of conditions can be cured; (3) belief in mystical diseases such as "*susto*, meaning loss of spirit or fright"; (4) the belief that illness and health exist on material, mental, and spiritual levels; and (5) the use of proscribed rituals and herbs for healing (Gafner & Duckett, 1992). *Curanderos* are readily available, do not require medical and insurance forms, and speak the same language and share the same beliefs as the patient.

Providers of Care

Adult children provide the informal help network. A study (Garcia et al., 1992) of four generations of Hispanic American women revealed beliefs that adult children should care for their elderly, children should share their homes with the elderly, and contact should be maintained between children and their elderly parents. Because older Hispanics are viewed as wise, knowledgeable, and deserving of respect, they continue to expect and receive help provided by their adult children and not professional help (Cox & Gelfand, 1987). Latinas were found to view home caregiving as

continued

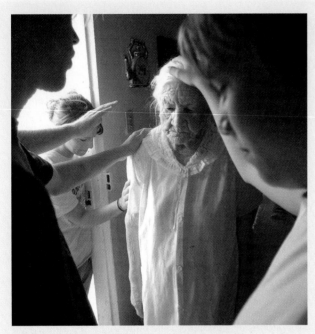

Healing Prayer Mainstream churches now offer "healing prayer" services, while praying or placing hands on the head or shoulders of those in need of healing. In this photo, church missionaries from Texas pray for Maria Jesus Onterverros' bad back. Hispanics in the Southwest are also likely to visit the *curandero*—or traditional healer—who uses herbs, aromas, massage and rituals to treat the whole person and the ills of their body, mind, and spirit (Glazer, 2005).

more beneficial and tended to delay institutionalizing their loved ones suffering from dementia (Mausbach et al., 2004). However, this view is especially burdensome for Hispanic Americans who are caring for elderly with dementia and Alzheimer's disease (Cox & Monk, 1993). A recent study found that Hispanics are more vulnerable to the stresses of caregiving in part due to caring for more impaired relatives, their younger ages, and a comparative lack of expressive support networks (Cox & Monk, 1996). Another recent study found that Latinos received more hours of informal activity of daily living care than whites or African Americans (Weiss et al., 2005). The use of professional services contradicts the norms of filial responsibility, so reaching out for professional care is an extremely difficult choice.

Community Services

Hispanic American elders are likely to differ in their use of community services. Mexican Americans tend to be concen-trated in urban areas, where many live in ghettos. However, they do not typically use senior services such as transportation, senior centers, Meals-on-Wheels, church-based assistance, homemaker assistance, or routine telephone checks. Use of such services increases, though, when Hispanic Americans are involved in the delivery of such services. Leaders of ethnic groups should be involved in the design and implementation of community services so that they do not violate or disrespect cultural values and practices (Fried & Mehrotra, 1998).

Retirement/Standard of Living

Older Mexican Americans tend to have significantly lower incomes than older white Americans. Most Mexican American elderly were unskilled or semiskilled laborers employed for many years on farms or ranches, in factories, or in part-time seasonal jobs (Fried & Mehrotra, 1998). The traditional retirement criteria (age 65, with income from retirement sources, and with a view of oneself as being retired) do not apply to Mexican Americans, who experience "retirement" differently and have access to fewer sources of retirement benefits (Zsembik & Singer, 1990). Some who migrated to the United States late in life are not eligible for Social Security benefits, do not know how to apply for benefits, and might work "under the table" for employers who do not report employee contributions (Garcia, 1993).

Religion and Spirituality

Older Americans of Mexican heritage practice religion that is a blend of different rituals and doctrines from both Aztec and European influences. The Aztecs believed that all things in nature are to be respected and valued. Catholicism is practiced by many elderly Mexican Americans, but there is a trend toward conversion to other religions. Religion remains an important aspect of the lives of these elderly, and many attend weekly services (Villa & Jaime, 1993). Faith, however, represents a way of being and living and is required for spiritual growth. The concept of *fe* (the word *fe* is Spanish for "faith" or "religion") embodies a way of life and incorporates varying degrees of faith, hope, spirituality, beliefs, and cultural values. *Fe* is personally defined by each individual, and *fe* helps individuals cope with poor health, poverty, and death. *Fe* helps elderly Mexican Americans maintain a positive attitude toward life. Anyone who works with this population of elderly needs to understand the significance of *fe* as a valid coping mechanism (Villa & Jaime, 1993).

years. Because of this remarkable power of the self, older adults on average are not at all more depressed or anxious than younger ones" (Baltes & Baltes, 1998). Findings from the recent *Berlin Aging Study* suggest that people aged 70 to 80 continue to have a purpose in life, and for the most part they live in the present with much engagement, mastering the tasks of everyday life (Baltes & Mayer, 1999).

The Third Age Some research indicates that certain aspects of personality actually improve during what the Balteses call the *Third Age*. These include emotional intelligence and wisdom. Emotional intelligence includes the ability to understand the causes of emotions (their expression, underlying feelings, and the associated non-verbal cues). **Wisdom** is "expert knowledge about life in general and good judgment and advice about how to conduct oneself in the face of complex, uncertain circumstances" (Baltes & Baltes, 1998). The Balteses suggest that "our store of wisdom benefits from the ability to engage ourselves with others in discussions of life dilemmas and from having a personality that is open to new experiences and strives toward excellence in matters of human lives" (Baltes & Baltes, 1998, p. 14).

The Balteses propose that on a sociocultural level the elderly have potential that is inactivated. Can we take the adult focus on productivity and transform it into other forms of productivity for society? Are there better ways to prepare for old age? What are the emerging biomedical and genetic interventions to repair body systems and prevent conditions of illness?

The Fourth Age Paul and Margret Baltes advance the theory that as people move into the *Fourth Age* (the late eighties and older), they will face increasingly difficult obstacles and become more vulnerable. People of these advanced ages require more cultural, technical, and behavioral resources to attain and maintain high levels of functioning because they have biological deficits. Baltes and Baltes (1998) point to the findings of the Berlin Aging Study, which focuses on the functioning of those aged 70 to 100. The results indicate that the oldest old do experience more demands and stressors and have fewer mental, emotional, and social reserves to cope with and compensate for these conditions. In the Berlin study, the prevalence of Alzheimer's disease, in particular, was found to be 3 percent in those aged 70 to 80; 10 to 15 percent in those 80 to 90; and about 50 percent in those over 90. But Baltes and Baltes (1998) suggest that in old age people can still find effective strategies for life management. By carefully selecting, optimizing, and compensating, they are able to minimize the negative consequences of old age. They remind us that the indomitable human spirit, when confronted with the challenges of living, comes up with many solutions.

A major challenge of the twenty-first century will be the number of the "oldest" people increasing throughout the world. One study examines several aspects of aging with a focus on the well-being of older adults from different cultures (Antonucci, Okorodudu, & Akiyama, 2003). To date, the person who is documented to have lived the longest is Jeanne Calment, who lived for 122 years in France (1875–1997). She married at age 21 and outlived her husband, daughter, and only grandson. At age 85 she took up fencing, and at age 100, she was still riding her bicycle and living on her own. She enjoyed port wine, olive oil, and chocolate. At age 114 she portrayed herself

Aging and Wisdom Paul and Margret Baltes suggest that a few aspects of personality improve during the "Third Age," including wisdom: having expert knowledge of life in general, and good judgment and advice. Professor and Chairperson Dr. Alan Shalita, Department of Dermatology, SUNY Downstate Medical Center, was named Distinguished Teaching Professor and founded the Department of Dermatology. He is recognized internationally for his skills as a clinician, researcher, and educator. Most importantly, he is a wise, caring mentor to the residents in his program.

in a movie—*Vincent and Me*—she had met Van Gogh at age 14. At 121 she released a CD, *Time's Mistress*, about her life. Although others claim to have lived longer, they do not have official birth certificates or documentation to make the Guinness World Records (2005).

A Life-Span Model of Developmental Regulation

In 1996, Schulz and Heckhausen proposed a life-span theory with the construct of *control* as the central theme for characterizing human development from infancy to old age, a view that they claimed holds true across cultures and historically. Implicit in their view is the thesis that successful aging includes the development of primary control throughout the life course. Schulz and

Heckhausen (1996, p. 708) explain, "Primary control targets the external world and attempts to achieve the effects in the immediate environment external to the individual, whereas secondary control targets the self and attempts to achieve changes directly within the individual."

Both primary and secondary control can involve cognition and action. Schulz and Heckhausen (1996) state that because primary control is directed outward, engaging the external world, it is preferred and has greater adaptive value to the individual. It enables individuals to explore and shape their environment to fit their particular needs and optimize their developmental potential. Primary control also provides the foundation for diversity and selectivity. Adelman says diversity (sampling different performance domains) is optimal throughout the life course: "The principle of diversity has important implications for socializing agents responsible for childhood development. Early in their development, children should be exposed to a variety of domains of functioning so they are challenged, develop diverse skills, and have the opportunity to test their genetic potential" (Adelman, quoted in Schulz & Heckhausen, 1996, p. 706).

The *principle of selectivity* is that individuals must selectively invest time, effort, abilities, and skills—and selectivity must work hand in hand with diversity so that the potential for high levels of functioning in some domains is attained, while other broad, generalizable skills are developed. Some of the major challenges individuals face throughout life involve assessing the trade-offs for a given investment of time and effort and making decisions about whether to continue within a given domain or switch to another (Schulz & Heckhausen, 1996).

For example, as a college student right now, you are investing time and effort by preparing yourself for some career (developing skills in English, perhaps a second language, mathematics, social sciences, life sciences, history, as well as specific courses in your major area of study). At the same time as you are taking a diversity of courses, you are also becoming more selective as you prepare yourself for your chosen profession. During adolescence and early adulthood, we develop a broad range of secondary control strategies (strategies focused inward), including changing aspiration levels, denial, egotistic attributions, and reinterpretation of goals.

Selectivity continues throughout adulthood, and diversity gradually decreases. The trade-off of selectivity over diversity is a hallmark of middle adulthood and old age. For example, most people who can no longer play tennis or basketball because of age are still able to play golf, a sport that does not require the same level of physical exertion. Increasing age-related biological and social challenges to primary control put a premium on secondary (self-directed) control strategies. The older person's own competencies and motivation will lead into experiences of either failure outcomes or positive outcomes. Failure experiences have the potential to undermine their self-concept, and therefore the elderly develop various strategies of *compensation,* such as moving from a two-story home to a residence on one floor and using hearing aids, pill containers, canes, and other adaptive devices. Those elderly who are able to engage and impact their environments for the longest time would be judged most successful.

Associations among personal control, choice, and healthy psychological adjustment have been studied since the early 1900s with younger adults. A study comparing younger and older adults' perceived control of life regrets found that internal control attributions (the way a person adjusts their perceptions about personal responsibility and control) were related to increased feelings of regret and intrusive thoughts in older adults (Wrosh & Heckhausen, 2002). A critique by Gould (1999) argues that the functional primacy of primary control does not hold true across cultures nor is it historically universal. In response to Gould, a review of research from evolutionary, comparative, developmental and cross-cultural psychology finds that primary control does hold functional primacy throughout the life span, across cultures, and throughout historical time periods (Wrosch et al., 2002).

The Impact of Personal Control and Choice

As psychologists since Alfred Adler (1870–1937) have noted, a sense of control over one's fate makes a substantial contribution to most people's mental health. It seems that most individuals prefer and benefit from control most of the time. Psychoanalyst Erich Fromm (1941) argued that a good many people do not wish to be masters of their own fate and hence are attracted to totalitarian leaders and movements. Witness the large number of people (in any culture) who voluntarily sign up for a life in the military, for instance. Perceived control and the desire for control can also decrease with age (Mirowsky, 1995). Lang and Heckhausen (2001) studied the relationship between perceived control over development and subjective well-being. Based on these studies, they conclude that for older adults their perceptions of control are more adaptive when they can be adjusted to different situations and when they reflect a positive evaluation of their abilities. Wahl and colleagues (2004) report a body of research on vision loss in the elderly is associated with higher rates of depression and undermines life plans and expectations because of loss of self-determination. As we shall see, generally those elderly who are forced into institutionalized living arrangements have serious health conditions and lose their sense of control and purpose as others take control over such daily decisions as when to bathe, when to eat, when to sleep, what to eat, and what to wear.

A Sense of Purpose The important contribution that a sense of responsibility, usefulness, and purpose makes to successful aging is highlighted by the research of social psychologists Langer and Rodin (1976). They investigated the impact that feelings of control and personal choice had among residents of a high-quality nursing home in Connecticut. Forty-seven residents on one floor of the home heard a talk by the nursing-home administrator in which he stressed the residents' responsibility for caring for themselves and shaping the home's policies and programs. At the conclusion of his talk, he presented each resident with a plant "to keep and take care of as you'd like." He also informed them that a movie would be shown on two nights, saying, "You should decide which night you'd like to go, if you choose to see it at all." The administrator also gave forty-five residents on another floor of the four-story building a talk. This time, however, he emphasized the responsibility that the staff felt for the residents. He gave them plants with the comment, "The nurses will water and care for them for you." Finally, he told them that they would be seeing a movie the following week and would be notified later about which day they were scheduled to see it.

A trained researcher interviewed the residents individually one week before and again three weeks after the administrator's talk. To prevent bias, the researcher was not told the purpose or the nature of the experiment. The questions she asked the residents dealt with how much control they felt they had over their lives and how happy and active they believed themselves to be. She also rated each resident on an 8-point scale for alertness. On the same two occasions, each member of the nursing staff filled out a questionnaire. The nurses were asked to evaluate each resident in terms of her or his overall activity, happiness, alertness, sociability, and dependence. Like the interviewer, the nurses were not aware of the nature and purpose of the study. According to the various ratings made before the administrator's talks, the two groups of residents were quite similar in their feelings of control, alertness, and satisfaction. Three weeks after the talks, however, the differences were marked.

Despite the high-quality care given them, nearly three-fourths of those in the second group (the group in which the staff retained control and took primary responsibility) were rated as having become more debilitated—over a mere three-week period. In contrast, 93 percent of those in the first group (the group in which the residents were encouraged to make their own decisions and were given decisions to make) showed overall improvement. Langer and Rodin (1976, p. 197) conclude that their findings support the view that "some of the negative consequences of aging may be retarded, reversed, or possibly prevented by returning to the aged the right to make decisions and a feeling of competence." Langer and Rodin (1976) found that the group

of residents who had been given responsibilities during the experimental period were healthier than comparable residents who had been treated in the conventional manner. The two treatment groups also showed different death rates. By the time of the follow-up, twice as many members of the conventional-treatment group, compared with the responsibility-induced group, had died. In sum, medical practitioners would be well-advised to incorporate patient choice in their caregiving.

Question

How do elderly individuals benefit from personal control and choice?

Faith and Adjustment to Aging

Some research studies reveal positive effects of spirituality on health, such as regular attendance at a church, mosque, or synagogue leads to living a longer life (Glazer, 2005). A national survey shows that the vast majority of Americans (95 percent) profess a belief in God or a higher power. Nine out of ten people pray—and most pray every day. The need for religious/spiritual beliefs and practices has always been important in the lives of people across cultures and continues to grow (Glazer, 2005; Mehta, 1997; Miller & Thoresen, 2003). Carter Catlett Williams (1998), as a "Third Ager" and consultant in aging, suggests old age is an adventure to be explored, a God-given mystery, not something to fear or despise. She says there is an "inner life that beckons," remembering the joys and sweet sorrows of the past about people, places, and events that have shaped each one of us and continue to shape who we will become. Dale Matthews (1998) relates findings from hundreds of empirical studies on what he calls the catalyst of the "faith factor" and its powerful benefits to overall well-being and attitude for people of all ages. He says that centuries ago Western cultures separated medicine from religion, but today the medical community recognizes the powerful relationship between the two. Most American medical schools offer courses on spirituality and healing, and some doctors screen patients about their spiritual beliefs or pray with their patients. More hospitals are offering alternative healing centers for meditation and prayer (Glazer, 2005). Medical practitioners and clergy often help patients cope with spiritual crises (e.g., emergency room teams, oncology, cardiology, geriatrics, etc.). In institutional settings, older adults' being able to follow their religious beliefs and practices experience less depression, anxiety, and distress. They derive much comfort from accessibility to support provided from priests, rabbis, and ministers (Fry & Björkqvist, 1996).

Levin (1996) surveyed the research on the "epidemiology of religion," or the evidence of factors (in this case religiosity) that contribute to disease and ill-health. Healthy lifestyles (i.e., abstinence from cigarettes, alcohol, tobacco, and meat) followed by practitioners of some religious groups (such as the Seventh Day Adventists and the order of nuns in the Nun Study) are related to lower incidence of disease and greater longevity (Danner, Snowdon, & Frieson, 2001; Fraser, 2003).

In a study of 760 Midwestern women, those who attended church more than once a month experienced significantly less depression and anxiety than those who attended less frequently or not at all (Hertsgaard & Light, 1984). This finding was confirmed in a study of 451 African American subjects that examined the correlation between regular church attendance and incidence of depression. "People with high levels of religious involvement reported significantly less depression" (Matthews, 1998, p. 25). Several other similar studies confirmed that religious involvement helps prevent depression at particularly stressful times such as severe illness or loss of a loved one. A study by Golsworthy and Coyle (1999) explores the role of spiritual beliefs for older adults who are seeking meaning after the death of a partner. Religious involvement appears to greatly enhance the quality of life for young and old and in many walks of life. Worldwide, researchers find through empirical studies that there is a healing association between religion and health (Murphy, 1997). Starting from the premise that religion and spirituality can and should be studied scientifically, Miller and Thoresen (2003) draw a distinction between the two and call for more research to study the effects of spirituality and religion on health.

Powell, Shahabi, and Thoresen (2003) reviewed the connection of religion or spirituality and health. They examined several hypotheses: church/service attendance protects against death; religion or spirituality protects against cardiovascular disease; religion or spirituality protects against cancer mortality; deeply religious people are protected against death; religion or spirituality protects against disability; religion or spirituality slows the progression of cancer; people who use religion to cope with difficulties live longer; religion or spirituality improves recovery from acute illness; and being prayed for improves physical recovery from acute illness. Among their conclusions is that attending services bestows a generalized protection against mortality. They call for further studies on the factors that produce this "protection." They hypothesize that regular attendance at services may produce positive emotions. Attendees often engage in helping behavior, which confers a sense of self-worth and encourages meaningful social interaction (and about half of U.S. elderly adults volunteer in their religious community, extending those protective benefits) (U.S. Bureau of Labor Statistics, 2004c).

Conversely, elderly people are likely to find needed resources and support through religious institutions.

The most controversial of the hypotheses—the effect of being prayed for, called *intercessory prayer,* has not held up to close scientific scrutiny (Carey, 2004; Krause, 2005; Roberts, Ahmed, & Hall, 2005). Although some conclude that there is a relationship between religion or spirituality and health, others suggest it's simply the "placebo," and others say that spiritually cannot be proven scientifically. However, the link is complex, and further research calls for strong clinical trials.

Question

What do researchers find about the role of religious faith in late adulthood?

Familial Roles: Continuity and Discontinuity

Though the majority of older persons live in a family setting today, the social world of old age differs significantly from that of early and middle adulthood (*Profile of Older Americans,* 1998). Changes in physical vigor and health and in cognitive functioning have social consequences. And shifts in marital roles and work profoundly affect the lives of elderly people through the behavioral expectations and activities that they allow (Smith & Moen, 2004). Hence, the "social life space" of aging adults provides the context in which elderly men and women, like their younger counterparts, define reality, formulate their self-images, and generate their interaction with other individuals.

Throughout history, there has been obvious continuity in intergenerational relations in families: Parents cared for and nurtured children, launched them into independent lives, and typically transferred resources to children and grandchildren upon death. But Pillemer and Suitor (1998) forecast that the contemporary baby-boom generation will experience special issues and challenges, unlike previous generations, due to the plurality of family forms: Divorce, remarriage, single parenting, stepparenting, single lifestyle, cohabitation, civil unions, and alternative family forms create a wide field of kinship bonds. Also, in general younger adults today are more dependent on the labor market for their livelihood than dependent on family resources, so intergenerational support is more a choice than an obligation. However, for elderly who require long-term care, past cultural experience demonstrates that sustained, stable support requires very close kin. In general, the majority of elderly appear to have large resources for stable family support, including greater likelihood of an intact marriage and relatively large numbers of living children and grandchildren (Pillemer & Suitor, 1998).

Intergenerational Support For elderly who are widowed, alone, or require long-term care, cultural experience demonstrates that siblings, adult children, and grandchildren often provide sustained, stable support. Boreddu Casula is 101, a great-grandfather, and is thriving in the care of his extended family in Sardinia. However, in Westernized societies couples are having fewer or no children, which foreshadows more societal care for many elderly in the future.

Love and Marriage

The parents of the baby-boom generation are more likely to still be married because they had the highest rates of marriage for any cohort of the twentieth century (Pillemer et al., 2000). Additionally, caregiving research indicates that the spouse is the first person married elders turn to when they need care. Until age 75 most American householders are part of a married couple (see Figure 18.2). Accordingly, social and behavioral scientists have asked, "What is the nature of marriage in older age?" It seems that most Americans believe that marriages that do not terminate in divorce begin with passionate love and evolve into cooler but closer companionship. However, researchers paint a somewhat different picture. Both marital satisfaction and adjustment begin declining quite early in marriage. The speed and intensity of this decline vary from one study to another. In the middle and later stages of the family life cycle, the evidence is less clear (Vaillant & Vaillant, 1993). Some investigators find a continual decline (Swensen & Trahaug, 1985). Usually, however, they report a U-shaped curve, with a decline in satisfaction during the early years, a leveling off during the middle years, and an increase in satisfaction during the later years (Glenn, 1990).

Sexual activity continues to play an important role in healthy relationships in elderly couples (Zeiss & Kasl-Godley, 2001). However, several issues regarding the sexuality of older adults arise, including physical changes related to aging and compensatory strategies, patterns of change in sexual behavior, psychosocial and cultural aspects of sexuality, sexual dysfunction and issues of cog-

nitively impaired and physically disabled older adults. Though the quality of marriage varies among couples, most elderly husbands and wives report greater happiness and satisfaction with marriage during their later years than at any other time except for the newlywed phase. Carstensen, Gottman, and Levenson (1995) found that older couples expressed more affection toward each other and resolved marital conflicts with less anger than middle-aged couples.

A number of factors appear to contribute to the improvement of marriage in the later years. For one thing, children are launched. The demands of parenthood often add strain to marital relations. Younger couples may experience increased conflict over child-rearing and domestic responsibilities. Furthermore, parents are bearing more and more of the financial costs associated with educating and raising children (Coontz, 1997). In later life, problems with such issues as in-laws, money, and sex have often been resolved or the stresses associated with them have dissipated. And as we have discussed in Chapter 15, older adults tend to be more androgynous in their roles than younger adults are. However, retirement can create new strains for a couple. One retiree points out the following:

> A husband and wife may each have a dream of what retirement would be, but those dreams don't necessarily mesh. They've got to sit down and talk—outline their activities, restructure their time, and define their territories. I discovered that my wife was very afraid that after I retired she'd have to wait on me hand and foot and would lose all her freedom (Brody, 1981, p. 13).

Some women report that they feel "smothered" having their retired husbands about the house so much of the time. Men who attempt to increase their involvement in household tasks might be seen by their wives as intruders. Even so, some wives welcome the participation of their husbands because it relieves them of some responsibilities. The loss of privacy and independence is often offset by opportunities for nurture and companionship. And wives mention having the "time available to do what you want" and the greater flexibility in schedules as advantages of retirement. Yet perhaps the most important factors influencing a wife's satisfaction with her husband's retirement are her own and her husband's good health and adequate finances (Brubaker, 1990).

Over the past few decades, as women have entered the labor force in growing numbers, couples increasingly have had to confront the issue of whether or not the husband and wife will retire at or about the same time (Pienta, Burr, & Mutchler, 1994). A longitudinal study of retirement found that men and women are taking variable paths and timings to retirement and that a couple's decisions are closely interconnected but less predictable and orderly than in the past. Marital satisfaction often

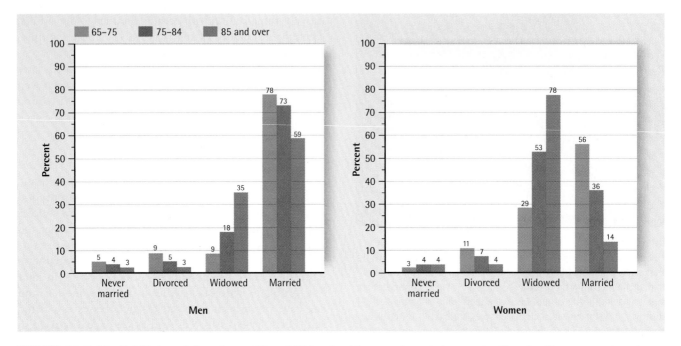

FIGURE 18.2 **Marital Status of Americans, 65 and Older** An older person's marital status significantly affects economic and emotional well-being. Note that many more women than men are widowed and likely to lack economic and emotional support. Note also that even at 85 and older, many more men are married than women in these elder years. Only a small percentage of men and women have never married by late adulthood.

Source: Federal Interagency Forum on Aging-Related Statistics. (2004). *Older Americans 2004: Key indicators of well-being.* Population, p. 5. Retrieved April 18, 2005, from http://www.agingstats.gov/chartbook2004/population.pdf

takes an initial downturn after retirement from a primary career job, and marital quality is most affected when one spouse retires while the other is still working (Moen, Kim, & Hofmeister, 2001). Men report being happier with working part-time after retirement versus fully retiring, whereas retired women often find satisfaction in volunteer activities. When both are retired for a few years, marital quality tends to improve (Moen, Kim, & Hofmeister, 2001). Because retirees are living much longer than in the past, researchers suggest there will be new ideas in policies and practices such as preretirement planning, transitional retirement, part-time retirement, part-year employment/retirement, and so forth.

Marriage also seems to protect people from premature death (Rogers, 1995). Married individuals are healthier than unmarried individuals, and death rates are consistently higher among single and socially isolated people (even after adjustments are made for age, initial health status, smoking, physical activity, and obesity). Significantly, although popular folklore depicts marriage as a blessed state for women and a burdensome trap for men, it is men rather than women who researchers find receive marriage's greatest mental and physical benefits (Anderson & McCulloch, 1993). For instance, women are more likely to be named as confidants by their husbands than they are to name their husbands as confidants. Women are more likely to select as confidants adult daughters and female friends (Antonucci, 1994).

Questions

Why does the happiness of couples who have been married for many years typically have a U-shaped curve? What are the findings about the well-being of elderly singles and elderly couples?

Satisfaction with Marriage Among the Elderly Most elderly couples report greater happiness and satisfaction with marriage than at any time since the newlywed phase. Many say their marriage improved during late adulthood. The couple shown is celebrating their fiftieth wedding anniversary.

Widows and Widowers   A majority of elderly men—about three-fourths—live with their spouses. But because women tend to outlive their husbands, there are far more widows than there are widowers. Fewer than half of elderly women still reside with their husbands. (See Figure 18.3.) This statistic demonstrates particular gender issues that are of great concern worldwide: (1) Elderly women are at much higher risk of living in poverty, especially in nonindustrialized countries where they may have never earned a pension; (2) most are not able to afford adequate health-care services; (3) they are likely to reside with older children; and (4) they are at higher risk for neglect and elder abuse. American women 65 and older were three times as likely as men 65 and older to be widowed (Federal Interagency Forum on Aging-Related Statistics, 2004).

In the *Healthy Sexuality and Vital Aging* study, more older men (60 percent) than women (nearly 40 percent) said they were sexually active (National Council on Aging, 1998). When older people are not sexually active, it is usually due to lack of a partner, or to a medical condition, or lack of privacy. In this same study, 90 percent of the respondents identified a high moral character, a pleasant personality, a good sense of humor, and intelligence as the important qualities in a partner. More women than men were likely to seek financial security from a partner, and more women than men sought a partner who observed a religious faith. Men were more likely to seek a partner who was attractive and interested in sex (Na-

tional Council on Aging, 1998). The National Council on Aging (NCOA) announced its new *Love & Life: A Healthy Approach to Sex for Older Adults* program with four major goals: (1) to educate older adults that sex can be a natural part of life; (2) to educate about sexual dysfunction, disease, and the aging process; (3) to generate discussion between physicians and their elderly patients about sexual needs; and (4) to coordinate education and training on sexuality workshops for older adults.

Remarriage and the Elderly   Remarriage in later life is another recent trend, and research findings suggest that this has profound consequences on a family, especially if it follows a divorce in midlife or later (Pett, Long, & Gander, 1992; Shapiro, 2003). Family rituals get lost and family gatherings become more complex to arrange—and relationships with children and grandchildren are likely to change. Divorce or widowhood in late adulthood often results in coresidence with an adult child, and coresidence is more likely with mothers who are of minority status or with less education. However, divorced fathers have lower rates of contact or coresidence with adult children.

On the other hand, remarriage may improve an older adult's self-esteem and improve relations with adult children (Shapiro, 2003). Nearly half a million people over the age of 65 in the United States remarry each year (U.S. Department of Health and Human Services, 1998). More people are entering late adulthood now—thus it is likely

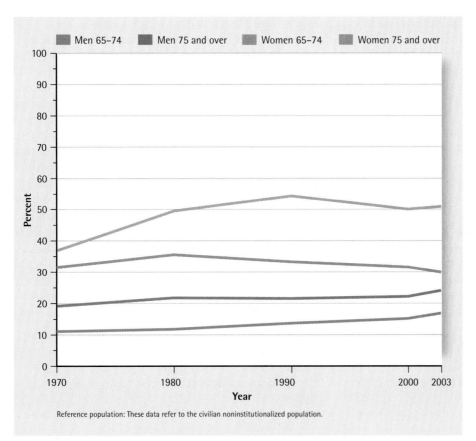

FIGURE 18.3 Population Age 65 and Over Living Alone, by Age and Gender: 1970–2003 With advancing age, rates of widowhood rise and more elderly women live alone—particularly for those 75 and older. Note that a much smaller percentage of elderly men live alone. Older adults who live alone are more likely to live in poverty. Such findings have significant implications for social policy, provision of services, and ability of seniors to maintain their independence.
Source: Federal Interagency Forum on Aging-Related Statistics. (2004). *Older Americans 2004: Key indicators of well-being.* Population, p. 9. Retrieved April 18, 2005, from http://www.aging-stats.gov/chartbook2004/population.pdf

Reference population: These data refer to the civilian noninstitutionalized population.

that more remarriages are occurring. With factors of increased longevity and more later-life remarriages, those currently in middle age could conceivably have several groups to whom they feel obligated: grandparents, parents, children, grandchildren, in-laws, stepchildren, and stepparents. Whereas intergenerational studies have demonstrated that adult children (particularly women) sense obligation toward elderly parents, there is little basis for obligations to extend to stepparents acquired through remarriage. In fact, due to the conditional nature of step relationships that are formed when stepchildren are adults, these adult stepchildren might not be perceived as having responsibilities to help their stepparents (Coleman & Ganong, 2004; Shapiro, 2003).

Singles

The elderly who remain single tend to have more emotional and physical pathology than the married elderly. This appears to be because the married have continuous companionship with a spouse, and spouses normally provide interpersonal closeness, nurturing, emotional gratification, and support in dealing with life's hassles and stress (Venkatraman, 1995). A 17-nation study that relates marital status and happiness found that being married is associated with higher levels of personal well-being, financial support, physical health, and social integration (Stack & Eshleman, 1998).

Studies of intergenerational social supports demonstrate that the people most likely to be listed as key network members at all times are parents and children. If singles that have never married have no children, they are lacking a main component of a significant social network in their later years. If singles have been married and then divorced, their social network can be unstable. As just mentioned, death rates are consistently higher among single and socially isolated people—even after adjustments are made for age, initial health status, smoking, physical activity, and obesity (Pillemer & Suitor, 1998). Males are particularly vulnerable for being socially isolated, which likely contributes to their higher rate of suicide. But older women typically establish a social support network with other females and with family members. With greater numbers of divorced or widowed singles in late life, there are more remarriages, which create elderly stepparent/stepchild relationships. This new family structure can create strain on adult children and less stable intergenerational relationships.

Lesbian and Gay Elderly

Older lesbians, gay men, and bisexuals have been negatively stereotyped as being lonely, isolated, and frustrated. However, in self-report surveys of older gay men and lesbians, they say they are well adjusted and have established social networks. Although they are more likely than heterosexuals to live alone and without a partner, they may have stronger social networks outside the family (Cahill, South, & Spade, 2000). It was erroneously believed in the past that older gay and lesbian adults lead a lonely existence. Berger (1996) reports that gay men tend to build networks of friends—possibly in response to familial rejection. These friendship networks later help gay men cope with aging (Peacock, 2000). One study found that friends and acquaintances provided socializing support, whereas partners, siblings, and other relatives provided emotional support. People who reported more support tended to feel less lonely; those who lived with domestic partners were not only less lonely but also rated their physical and mental health more positively than those who lived alone (Grossman, D'Augelli, & Hershberger, 2000). Quam and Whitford (1992) studied older gay men and lesbians and found that those who maintained a high level of involvement in the gay community had higher levels of life satisfaction and acceptance of the process of aging.

History-graded influences on development have affected different cohorts of lesbians, gay men, and bisexuals (Slater, 1995). For instance, in the past homosexuals were disregarded by social scientists. Yet the gay community has fought for civil rights and protection under the law, such as civil unions, and is continuing to fight for the right to marry with all the benefits of marriage. Lesbians and gay men who are in civil unions seem to get more support from families, but lesbians in civil unions are more likely to be "out" than men in civil unions (Solomon, Rothblum, & Balsam, 2004). One study looked at the economic disadvantage that resulted from not having legal status when the partner of a gay, lesbian, or bisexual dies. For example, although required to pay taxes, the surviving partner would not be entitled to Social Security benefits, would be required to pay taxes on retirement plans such as 401K or IRAs (legally married spouses do not), and would be charged estate taxes on inherited property even if jointly owned (Bennett & Gates, 2004). Researchers continue to study many aspects of policy that affect gay, lesbian, bisexual, and transgendered older adults (Quam, 2004).

Question

Are men or women more likely to be widowed in late adulthood, and do widowed adults tend to remarry or remain single?

Questions

Overall, how do gay and lesbian elderly rate their life satisfaction? What factors contribute to their well-being?

Children or Childlessness

The notion that most elderly people are lonely and isolated from their families and other meaningful social ties is false (Hannson & Carpenter, 1994). Moreover, the elderly are often involved in exchanges of mutual aid with their grown children as both providers and receivers. Many times, the elderly parent helps the adult child by performing child care and other home-related roles, whereas the adult child helps the parent with heavy housework, shopping, bureaucratic mediation, and transportation. Among the American middle class, gifts from living parents play a substantial role in bolstering the living standards of their adult children. For instance, economists have estimated that one in four home buyers receive assistance from their parents or other relatives (Zachary, 1995).

Also, in 80 percent of cases, care for the elderly is provided by their families. This is especially true for elderly ethnic minorities. Despite substantial social change (increased geographic mobility, divorce, and women's participation in the labor force), which has been thought by many to weaken intergenerational family cohesion, adult children, particularly daughters, remain major sources of instrumental support to their parents (Silverstein, Parrott, & Bengtson, 1995). Significantly, older Americans are less likely than their adult children to believe that when elderly parents can no longer take care of themselves, the best solution is for them to move in with their children. The elderly value their privacy and independence (Cherlin & Furstenberg, 1986; Cicirelli, 1992). Those with adult children prefer to live near but not with them, what psychologists term "intimate distance." In sum, most elderly are not so isolated from kin and friendship networks as is commonly believed (Aldous, 1987).

Grandparenting and Great-Grandparenting

Child psychologists emphasize that both children and their grandparents are better off when they spend a good deal of time in each other's company (Smith, 1991). Yet at the turn of the twentieth century, surviving grandparents were in short supply. Now, with the increase in adult life expectancies, more children and adults have living grandparents, stepgrandparents, and great-grandparents. Presently in the United States, grandparents are likely to have five or six grandchildren, on average. Today's grandparents are healthier, more active, and better educated than they used to be, and many have more money and leisure time (Szinovacz, 1998).

Almost 1.3 million children under 18 lived with their grandparents in 2002 (Fields, 2003). Of the total number of children in the U.S. in 2002, 5 percent of them lived with their grandparents. Of the children who live with

their grandparents, 45 percent also live with their mothers in the same household but 35 percent live without the presence of their parents ("Grandchildren Living in the Home of Their Grandparents," 2005). Grandparenthood, for most, is now seen as a sequential phase of life rather than an overlapping phase. In the past, people often became grandparents while still raising their own youngest children, whereas today the youngest has usually left home before people become grandparents (Szinovacz, 1998). Grandmothers outnumber grandfathers because the life expectancy for women is an average of over five years longer than for men at age 65 (U.S. Bureau of the Census, 2004i). However, many middle-aged and older women are working and are unlikely to be available to baby-sit full-time for their grandchildren. Great-grandparents are now more common than grandparents were at the turn of the century.

Another trend over the past few decades is that nearly 25 percent of grandparents will be stepgrandparents, through either their own or their children's divorces (Szinovacz, 1998). The more complex family structures created by multiple divorces involving children have become more common. Overall, 3 percent of grandparents lived in households with grandchildren, and nearly 5 percent live in households with three or

Growing Numbers of U.S. Youngsters Are Raised by Their Grandparents In many contemporary American homes, grandparents play a substantial role in the rearing of their grandchildren. Indeed, in a good many cases, grandparents assume the role of custodial parents or guardians.

Being a Grandparent or Great-Grandparent Regardless of culture, grandparents and great-grandparents can be an important developmental resource for their grandchildren. Both can reap important psychological satisfactions from spending time together.

more generations. Consequently, today's grandparents live through more life transitions than grandparents did in the past, and a majority of grandparents have more roles than grandparents did in the past (Szinovacz, 1998). Of those with children aged 40 and over, nearly 95 percent are grandparents. Over 80 percent of today's families contain three generations, and 16 percent are four-generation families (Szinovacz, 1998).

Despite stereotypes about grandparents, research suggests that grandparents vary considerably in the ways they approach their roles (Silverstein & Marenco, 2001). Much depends on their age and health, their race and ethnic background, and geographic distance. In some cases, due to death, divorce, remarriage, or other family disruption, grandparents are obligated to take on a larger role in the lives of their grandchildren and stepgrandchildren. More than 4 percent of grandparents have either become surrogate parents or assumed primary caretaking responsibility for a grandchild while the mother works (Szinovacz, 1998). The study by Fuller-Thomson and Minkler (2001) points to the policy implications of grandparents that provide child care for their grandchildren. Countless grandparents have stepped into the breach to rescue grandchildren whose parents have faltered due to drugs, abuse, or crime, and these grandparents can find their grandchildren to be a source of much stress (Hayslip & Kaminski, 2005). The American Association of Retired Persons (AARP) has special resources on their Web site for grandparents who have custodial responsibility for grandchildren (see "Following Up on the Internet" at the end of this chapter). So although some grandparents are emotionally or geographically remote, a majority are very closely involved with their grandchildren (Jendrek, 1993).

In contemporary society, the most common kind of relationship between grandparents and grandchildren is companionate, where the grandparent and grandchild are essentially good pals. Grandparents might play, joke, and watch television with their grandchildren, but they are less inclined to discipline them. By the same token, grandparents also want freedom and fulfillment—to spend their leisure time as they please and to have close but not constant association with their children and grandchildren (Hayslip et. al., 1998; Smolowe, 1990). One study looked at the effect of surrogate parenting related to depressive symptoms of grandparents (Szinovacz, 1999).

Although the grandparenting role has different meanings for different people, some themes recur: For many individuals grandparenting is a source of biological renewal or continuity. Being a grandparent instills a sense of extension of self and family into the future and is often a source of emotional self-fulfillment. It generates feelings of companionship and satisfaction between the grandparent and a child that were often absent in the earlier parent-child relationship. A recent study of African American grandparents raising grandchildren found that African American grandmothers in particular were economically vulnerable. The vast majority (80 percent) were living below the poverty line, pointing to the need for more attention to this type of household (Minkler & Fuller-Thomson, 2005). Using a national survey, Szinovacz (1998) presents a demographic profile of grandparents drawing on a variety of racial, ethnic, and gender identities. It explores aspects of grandparenthood such as surrogate parenting, other roles grandparents play, and stepgrandparenthood. In conclusion, the profile recommends that previous descriptions of grandparenthood need to be updated to reflect current realities.

Questions

In what ways has the role of grandparent been redefined over the course of the twentieth century? How do grandparents and grandchildren benefit from a relationship with each other?

ship, followed by the sister-brother and brother-brother relationship (Cicirelli, 2001).

Question

How does the presence or absence of children, grandchildren, and siblings affect the elderly adult's emotional well-being?

Siblings

The longest-lasting relationships people normally have are with siblings. Siblings normally play a significant role in the lives of the elderly (Cicirelli, 2001; Connidis & Campbell, 2001; White, 2001). They provide continuity in family history that is uncommon to most other family relationships—siblings might be the only members of the family of origin that remain. A shared family history frequently affords a foundation for interaction that supplies companionship and a support network as well as validation for an older person's reminiscences of family events. As they advance into old age, many siblings report that they think more often about one another and find that their acceptance, companionship, closeness, and caring for each other increases. The most frequent contact occurs among siblings in relatively close physical proximity. Siblings are especially important kin for those with few or no children (Connidis & Campbell, 2001). Five types of sibling interactions have been identified, ranging from extremely close to distant: congenial, loyal, intimate, apathetic, and hostile (Gold, Woodbury, & George, 1990). The majority of elderly report congenial and loyal relationships with siblings. The sister-sister relationship tends to be the most potent sibling relation-

Social and Cultural Support

Numerous findings from scientific research support the notion that frequent social contact appears to be associated with good health, facilitation of coping with stress, and greater life satisfaction (Cavanaugh, 1998a; Matthews, 1998). A functioning network of social ties is necessary in times of stress, illness, and aging—and includes both emotional support and practical assistance as needed. Indeed, researchers such as Herbert Benson state, "Our need for contact with other human beings is vital" (Matthews, 1998, p. 250).

Friendships

Overall, in terms of companionship, friends are more important and satisfying to older people than their offspring are (Antonucci, Okorodudu, & Akiyama, 2003; Cavanaugh, 1998a). In fact, some research suggests that greater loneliness exists among the single elderly who live with relatives than among those who live alone. An elderly widow who lives with her daughter's family can

Siblings and Social Support The longest lasting relationships we normally have are with our siblings, who provide a continuity in family history that is uncommon to most other family relationships. A shared family history frequently affords a foundation for interaction that supplies companionship, closeness, and a support network as well as a validation for an older person's memories of family events.

be quite lonely if she has little contact with associates her own age. As in other aspects of human affairs, individuals differ greatly in what they view as adequate or inadequate contact with other people. Older adults with physical impairments have fewer opportunities for contact with friends, which results in more social isolation and loneliness (Adams, Blieszner, & Vries, 2000).

Solitude need not be experienced as loneliness, whereas loneliness can be felt in the presence of other people. For instance, persons residing in nursing homes often complain of loneliness, even though they are surrounded by people and, at a superficial level, are interacting with them. *Loneliness* is the "awareness of an absence of meaningful integration with other individuals or groups of individuals, a consciousness of being excluded from the system of opportunities and rewards in which other people participate" (Busse & Pfeiffer, 1969, p. 188).

The quality of a relationship is more important than mere frequency of contact (Field et al., 1993). Overall, maintaining even one meaningful, stable relationship is more closely associated with good mental health and high morale among the elderly than is a high level of social interaction. A confidant serves as a buffer against gradual diminishing of social interaction and against the losses associated with widowhood and retirement (Sugisawa, Liang, & Liu, 1994). For older adults, having contact with friends is more strongly related to social well-being than having contact with adult children (Pinquart & Soerensen, 2000).

Retirement/Employment

Retirement is a relatively recent notion. Indeed, retirement as we understand it today did not exist in preindustrial American society—nor does it exist in some societies today. Older people formerly were not sidelined from mainstream employment, and life expectancies were much shorter. In 1900 the average American male had a life expectancy of 47 years and spent about 3 percent of his lifetime in retirement. Today the average life expectancy of Americans is about 77 years, with retirement averaging more than 10 years, or at least 13 percent of one's lifetime. The proportion of males aged 65 and over who were gainfully employed dropped from 68 percent in 1900, to 42 percent in 1940, to about 18 percent in 2003. Yet in 2003 there were nearly 5 million workers over the age of 65 (see Table 18.1).

Retirement, however, has become a somewhat ambiguous term because it is frequently a transitional process in which a person leaves a "career" job and engages in other paid activities or may become self-employed before withdrawing completely from the labor market (Karoly & Zissimopoulos, 2004). More recently labor force participation rates for men over the age of 55 have been stabilizing and increasing slightly. Labor force participation rates for women over age 55 have been steadily increasing since the 1960s (Federal Interagency Forum on Aging-Related Statistics, 2004). Also about 20 percent of self-employed U.S. workers are age 65 and older, with more men than women choosing self-employment (Karoly & Zissimopoulos, 2004).

Three-fourths of men and more than four-fifths of women retiring on Social Security currently leave their jobs before they are 65, and in companies and public agencies (such as police work and teaching) with high early-retirement pension benefits, the retirement age drops below 60 (Boss, 1998). In government employment, nearly two out of three civil servants retire before the age of 62. Workers who retire at age 60 or 62 can expect to have 15 to 20 years of life remaining. Women

Friendship Older adults are usually retired, no longer rearing children, and have different routines and activities than when they were younger. The availability of time provides opportunities to reestablish old friendships or make new friends. Friends are often more important and satisfying to older people than their offspring. With the oldest adults, physical or cognitive impairments reduce interaction with friends. These BINGO friends met in their 70s and 80s.

Table 18.1 Older Americans Continue in the Labor Force: 2004

Among those aged 55 to 64, about 62 percent work full time. For those 65 and older, about 14 percent work full time—with projections to *20 percent* by 2014. For those 75 and older, 6 percent are working—with projections to *10 percent* by 2014. Many adults transition to part-time work before full retirement, while some start new businesses.

Age Group	Percent in Labor Force
55 to 64	62
65 to 74	22
75 plus	6

Still Working This 90-year-old woman is still working to supplement her Social Security benefits. A college professor from Pennsylvania recently retired at age 104.

Source: Toossi, Mitra. (2005, November). Labor force projections to 2014: Retiring boomers. *Monthly Labor Review, 128*(11), 25–44.

often leave the workforce or work part-time while raising children and have to reenter the labor force later and continue to work in late adulthood to make up for lost income and build a pension. Retirement is a complex decision of mounting significance in the lives of U.S. men and women (see Table 18.1).

People who return to work after trying retirement usually do so rather quickly or not at all. A survey of workers' (aged 50 to 64) intentions for retirement found that over two-thirds of the respondents planned to work for pay after retiring (D. Smith, 2000). Also, self-employment rates begin to rise in middle and late adulthood (Karoly & Zissimopoulos, 2004). Increased longevity and better health also incline workers to continue working past traditional retirement age in their current jobs, whereas some attempt to realize dream jobs that had been deferred (Sherrid, 2000). Of men

aged 55 or older who retire, about one-third return to the workforce. The self-employed, professionals, sales workers, and farm laborers have higher than average rates of returning (Karoly & Zissimopoulos, 2004). But a majority of all those who resume work do so in the first year of retirement; an additional 18 percent join them in the second and third years. About two-thirds of postretirement employment is on a full-time basis (Boss, 1998). At older ages, self-employment may be a form of partial retirement, offering greater satisfaction, flexibility in hours, and earnings that accommodate Social Security limits (Karoly & Zissimopoulos, 2004).

Involuntary Retirement In 1978 Congress passed legislation banning compulsory retirement for most workers before age 70 and in 1986 passed legislation largely abolishing mandatory retirement at any age. Many Americans view the practice of compelling workers to retire as a curtailment of basic rights. Prior to 1978 about half of the nation's employers had policies requiring employees to step down at 65. Business organizations like the U.S. Chamber of Commerce supported forced retirement; they argued that abolishing mandatory retirement would severely disrupt companies' personnel and pension planning and would keep younger people from advancing. However, these fears are unlikely to be realized in the future given the generational demographics. Baby boomers who are now reaching retirement age may be needed to fill jobs that the much smaller age cohorts that follow them cannot. Although baby boomers number about 77 million, Generation Xer's number only 44 million. Nevertheless, high unemployment in many industries (especially in mining and manufacturing), coupled with the prospect of an extended layoff or a difficult search for a new job, has led many older workers to opt for early retirement. And in other cases some older workers have been crowded out of their jobs or have been given special incentives for leaving to make room for younger workers. At the same time, some companies realize that their older employees are a valuable asset—especially given projections of future labor shortages. To accommodate the need for retaining these workers, some researchers are looking toward work design and management models that will meet these needs (Griffiths, 1999).

Contemporary employers, although often pleased with the work habits of older employees, still harbor many negative attitudes toward older workers that are rooted in concerns about higher health insurance costs and older employees' inexperience with new technology such as computers, robotics, and telecommunications. Seemingly, businesses looking to elderly workers to make up for labor shortages might have to offer rather substantial financial inducements to lure some of them out of retirement; many value their free time and independence more than they do the income or other benefits of a job (Parnes & Summers, 1994). A survey conducted by AARP revealed that 80 percent of baby boomers believed that they would work at least part-time during their retirement years. Over one-third of them wish to do so for the interest and enjoyment work provides; one-fourth felt they would need the money (Sherrid, 2000).

Retirement Satisfaction By Western norms, people are integrated into the larger society by their work roles. Work is seen as an important aspect of identity and self-esteem and as providing people with many personal satisfactions, meaningful peer relationships, and opportunities for creativity—in sum, the foundation for enduring life satisfactions. The loss of these satisfactions through retirement has been viewed traditionally as stressful, inherently demoralizing, and leading to major problems in older age (Mowsesian, 1987).

In recent years the negative view of retirement has been challenged. Probably no more than a third of Americans find retirement stressful, either as a transition or as a life stage (Boss, 1998; Midanik et al., 1995). With the trend toward staying in the workforce longer—perhaps working part-time or from the home—and the increased ability to launch new ventures, aging workers can circumvent the feelings of uselessness and lack of stimulation. One longitudinal survey of 5,000 men found that most men who retire for reasons other than poor health are "very happy" in retirement and would, if they had to do it over again, retire at the same age. Only about 13 percent of whites and 17 percent of blacks said they would choose to retire later if they could choose again.

Several studies have looked at the effect of retirement on marriage. One study found that retired men whose wives were still employed and who had had more influence in marital decision making were less satisfied. Similarly, retired women whose husbands remained in the workforce and who had had more influence in marital decision making were also least satisfied (Szinovacz, 2005). Another study examined marital conflict in relation to retirement and found that the effects of the transition to retirement are more subtle than previously thought (Davey & Szinovacz, 2004). Yet another study looked at retirement transition and disability of a spouse on depressive symptoms, finding gender differences related to these factors. Women who felt that their retirement was too early or forced felt more depressed, whereas the same effect was not found in men (Szinovacz & Davey, 2004).

Significantly, more and more retirees are also going back to college. Senior citizens who wish to keep mentally engaged often attend college courses as auditors. In 2004, it was found that the number of auditors had doubled from the previous five years. Because of rising demand to audit courses, some colleges and universities

have imposed caps on the number of auditors. Some universities like Harvard do not permit any auditors of undergraduate courses. On the other hand, some universities have embraced auditors, seeing this as bolstering their image in the community and in the eyes of potential funders. Some campuses offer special retirement learning institutes that cater to seniors. From a consumer point of view, seniors may recommend particular colleges to their grandchildren. Many retirement communities boast proximity to college campuses and their resources as an amenity (Bernstein, 2004).

Social scientists are increasingly coming to recognize that preretirement lifestyle and planning play an important part in retirement satisfaction (Boss, 1998). Positive anticipation of retirement and concrete and realistic planning for this stage in life are related to adjustment in retirement. On the whole, voluntary retirees are more likely to have positive attitudes and higher satisfaction in retirement than those who are forced into early retirement. However, other factors, not always controllable, also influence retirement satisfaction. In sum, those with better health and higher socioeconomic status seem to make a better adjustment to retirement.

Questions

Do the majority of retirees find life after retirement to be stressful? Which elderly are most likely to be dissatisfied with retirement?

A Change in Living Arrangements

A change in living (housing) arrangements represents a major life event for an older person (VandenBos, 1998). And living arrangements for older adults also differ by race, gender, and ethnicity (see Figure 18.4) (Federal Interagency Forum on Aging-Related Statistics, 2004). Older widowed Asian and Hispanic women and men are much more likely to reside with family members. Older men are much more likely to reside with a spouse compared with older females, who are much more likely to be widowed and living alone. Older black men who are single are much more likely to live alone. Note the small percentage of older adults that reside with nonrelatives, in some form of institutional care.

Several factors are likely to initiate a change (or changes) in living arrangements for U.S. elderly, including retirement, change in economic conditions, death of a spouse, remarriage, and declining physical and/or mental capacities. Potential living arrangements include living at home alone, moving to a new location in the case of remarriage, living at home with assisted-living services, living with adult children with adult day-care options, institutional care, retirement communities, group homes and community shelters, adult foster care, or homelessness. Most elderly adults prefer to remain independent in their own homes as long as they can (VandenBos, 1998).

Living Alone at Home and Assisted-Living Services
Nearly 10 million Americans over the age of 65 live alone, but 2 million indicate they have no one to turn to if they need help (see Figure 18.4). Of those living at home, 80 percent are women. Nearly half of those aged 85 and older live alone (*Profile of Older Americans*, 2001). Large numbers of the elderly are now cared for more appropriately, as well as more economically, in their homes—with the help of visiting nurses, social workers, and Meals-on-Wheels volunteers, but many elderly lack a caregiver. At present, there is a shortage of home health aides, and the U.S. Department of Labor lists this job among the fastest growing in the next decade (Horrigan, 2004). Depending on the state, home-care assistance might be available under the following programs: Medicare, Medicaid, the *Older Americans Act,* and Title 20 of Social Security.

Most elderly fear being forced to leave their home because of frailty, illness, widowhood, a decaying neighborhood and crime, or rural isolation and fear of becoming dependent on others. One report on American centenarians suggests that these "oldest old" fear losing their independence and avoid census takers and medical practitioners. Although the philosophy today within the field of aging is to promote independence, many elderly eventually develop physical impairments or cognitive problems that make them unable to safely remain in their homes. Denmark has the leading system of home- and community-based care (Stuart & Weinrich, 2001).

Living with Children and Adult Day Care For the elderly who are living with relatives, senior day-care centers give busy family members a break from caregiving and a chance to work or catch up on tasks. **Adult day care** involves long-term care support to adults who live in the community, providing transportation, health, social, and support services in a protective setting during any part of the day. Socialization, recreation, nutrition, and professional supervision are provided for a few hours or on a daily basis, as needed. Some elderly from ethnic minority families with debilitating illness or dementia expect to live with their adult children, who are then expected to care for their parent or grandparent

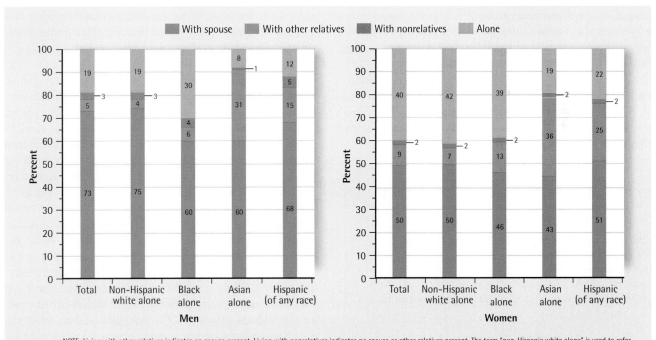

NOTE: Living with other relatives indicates no spouse present. Living with nonrelatives indicates no spouse or other relatives present. The term "non-Hispanic white alone" is used to refer to people who reported being white and no other race and who are not Hispanic. The term "black alone" is used to refer to people who reported being black or African American and no other race, and the term "Asian alone" is used to refer to people who reported Asian as their race. The use of single-race populations in this report does not imply that this is the preferred method of presenting or analyzing data. The U.S. Census Bureau uses a variety of approaches. Reference population: These data refer to the civilian noninstitutionalized population.

FIGURE 18.4 Living Arrangements of Persons 65 and Over, 2003 Older men are much more likely to reside with a spouse than older women, who are much more likely to be widowed. Widowed or single Asian or Hispanic women and men are much more likely to reside with other relatives. Non-Hispanic white women and black women who are widowed have high rates of living alone. Note the very small percentage of elderly adults who reside "with nonrelatives"—that is, institutional care.
Source: Federal Interagency Forum on Aging-Related Statistics. (2004). *Older Americans 2004: Key indicators of well-being.* Retrieved April 18, 2005, from http://www.agingstats. gov/chartbook2004/population.pdf

without seeking assistance from the greater community. To seek help outside of the family would be shameful or indicate failure on the part of the adult child to meet filial obligations (see the *Human Diversity* box on page 619, "Elderly Hispanic Americans"). This puts a great psychological, emotional, and economic burden on the adult children or grandchildren.

Institutional Care   The most recent *National Nursing Home Survey* was conducted in 1999, and the latest survey began in 2004. A 1999 survey of nursing homes revealed that there were 1.63 million U.S. residents in 18,000 nursing homes (Decker, 2005). By 1999, the age of nursing home residents was likely to be 85 and older, with fewer residents between 75 and 84 or younger (see Table 18.2). Other alternative residential care settings and community adult day care have appeared since the early 1990s. As the baby-boom cohort reaches these advancing years, the number needing institutional care will grow substantially. Expenditures for good nursing home care are substantial but are expected to triple by 2030, when the oldest of the baby-boom cohort will reach their mid-eighties (Friedland & Summer, 1999).

Each caregiving environment has its own distinct social climate of care. Some communal climates are friendlier, more oriented toward independence, better organized than others, and provide a range of services within a religious and spiritual context. Certainly many facilities are doing their best to provide the elderly with decent care. U.S. ethnic minorities are significantly underrepresented in nursing homes (Fried & Mehrotra, 1998). Language, monetary, and bureaucratic barriers are often cited as reasons, as well as other cultural norms that enforce intergenerational responsibility.

Even so, nursing homes are hardly "homes." Becoming a resident of a nursing home shifts control of one's life from the individual to the "total institution" and often brings physical and chemical restraint (Mor et al., 1995). Once in a nursing home, the elderly typically become physically, emotionally, and economically dependent on the facility for the rest of their lives (Wolinsky et al., 1992). Staff practices all too often foster patient dependency (Baltes, Neumann, & Zank, 1994). Indeed, some of the characteristics frequently encountered among the institutionalized aged, including depression, feelings of helplessness, and accelerated decline, are partly attributable to the loss of control over their lives (Zarit, Dolan, & Leitsch, 1998). Under such circumstances of forced dependency, the elderly come to see themselves as powerless—as passive objects manipulated and buffeted by the environment. In many nursing homes, the majority of residents shares a small bedroom with others; eat mass-prepared, high-carbohydrate meals in a large, linoleum-floored dining hall; and watching television is common recreation.

Many of the nation's skilled-care nursing homes fail to meet federal standards for clean food and do not administer drugs properly or on a timely basis. Inspection reports on code violations in nursing homes can be difficult to locate, and the decision to place a relative in a nursing home is usually done in a few days under emergency circumstances through recommendations of hospital personnel. Not having enough time to get all the facts to make good decisions about placement, most people select a home nearby so they can visit their loved one. The elderly poor, especially minorities, are often placed in public facilities that generally provide inferior care.

Frail and disabled elderly are often pushed into passive roles; some patients are tied to their beds or wheelchairs or given powerful tranquilizing drugs on the premise that "a quiet patient is a good patient." Research suggests that it is rarely necessary to restrain nursing-home patients suffering from mental confusion or extreme physical weakness (Brody, 1994c). A majority of U.S. nursing homes are privately owned for-profit operations, with a little over one-fourth voluntary non-profit, and 7 percent government operated. European countries are trying a variety of approaches for the care of the elderly (Peck, 2000). For example, in 1987 the Danish government put a moratorium on the construction of nursing homes in preference to assisted-living arrangements to provide long-term care (Valins, 1995).

Inadequate, unskilled staffing is a major problem in many nursing homes. People with little education and minimal skills (and sometimes a criminal record) are often hired as aides, orderlies, janitors, and kitchen help because the jobs are viewed as unattractive, low paying, and rather stressful. With assisting many who may have dementia or multiple care needs, such personnel may

---

Table 18.2 Percent Distribution of U.S. Residents in Nursing Homes: 1977–1999

Based on findings from the National Nursing Home Surveys, 1977–1999, it is evident that the age distribution of residents has changed. By 1999, nearly half of the residents were ages 85 and older and were more likely to be frailer, with more impairment, and requiring a higher level of care. Findings from the 2004 National Nursing Home Survey should be available soon.

Age Group	1977 (Percent)	1985 (Percent)	1999 (Percent)
85 years and over	34.8	40.9	46.5
75–84	36.0	34.4	31.8
65–74	16.2	13.8	12.0
Under 65 years	13.0	10.9	9.7

Source: Decker, F. H. (2005). *Nursing homes, 1977–1999: What has changed, what has not?* Hyattsville, MD: National Center for Health Statistics.

not develop a strong commitment to their jobs or to the nursing home and may abuse the patients (Zarit, Dolan, & Leitsch, 1998).

As the U.S. nursing-home industry has evolved, nursing homes have become a place of last resort for a variety of reasons. They are used by terminally ill patients who require intensive nursing care, by recuperating individuals who need brief convalescence, and by infirm aged who lack the social and financial resources necessary to manage in the community. Consequently, nursing-home residents differ greatly in degree of physical impairment and mental disorientation. Increasingly, the elderly and their children are considering the option of assisted living as an alternative to nursing homes. Assisted living provides a greater measure of privacy with individual apartments yet also provides the care needed through its staff. Shapiro (2001) noted that currently about 800,000 people were served through assisted-living arrangements in the United States.

Government regulations have cast nursing homes in the role of miniature hospitals (Winslow, 1990). The quality of life they afford is largely determined by bureaucratic requirements regarding Medicare and Medicaid and by state licensing standards and mandated regulations. Even chronically ill persons moving into a nursing home continue in a "sick role" long after it is no longer functional, forfeiting independence, autonomy, and quality of life (Cohn & Sugar, 1991). For suggestions on factors to consider when choosing a nursing home, see the *Further Developments* box on page 638, "Selecting a Nursing Home."

Retirement Communities More retirement communities are being developed for middle-class and well-to-do elderly, particularly in the warm southern coastal states and golf resort communities in the Southwest. Of concern to politicians in many northern states is the mass migration of their newly retired elderly, who have been productive citizens and provided a stable tax base in many communities. Some retirement communities are known as "trailer" communities, where the elderly can live comfortably with fewer home-care responsibilities and continue to lead active lives with senior citizens like themselves. Some are townhouses and condos that border lush golf courses and other prime real estate. The nature of such communities, however, is unlike a typical community where people of all ages live side by side. Some elderly especially miss being with children and younger adults daily.

Adult Group Homes More communities are experimenting with newer alternatives such as sheltered housing, assisted-living facilities, and continued-care retirement communities—protected communities arranged in apartment complexes or detached cottages—that provide such supportive services as centrally prepared meals, housekeeping, laundry, transportation, recreational options, and health care (Jeffrey, 1995). This is projected to be a more common living arrangement over the next decade, allowing the elderly to maintain much of their self-reliance while providing a sense of security and support (Zarit, Dolan, & Leitsch, 1998).

> **Questions**
>
> What are some alternatives for assisted-living arrangements for elderly adults who need supervision or care? What are some factors that should be considered when selecting a nursing home?

Elder Abuse

Elder abuse and neglect are both acts of commission and omission that cause unnecessary suffering to older persons (Teaster, 2002). Elder abuse is now internationally recognized as a pervasive and growing problem (Lachs & Pillemer, 2004). It is not known how many older Americans have been abused because there is no uniform reporting system, and it is difficult to collect national data. However, it is estimated that 1 to 2 million Americans age 65 and older are abused by someone on whom they depended for care (National Council on Elder Abuse, 2005). Another study estimates as many as 5 to 6 percent of persons 65 and older have experienced elder abuse. Because most cases go unreported, the full scope of the problem isn't known (Teaster, 2002).

The old stereotype of a younger male abusing a frail elderly female victim is inaccurate. Pillemer and Finkelhor (1988) found that spousal abuse was more prevalent than abuse by adult children—and that finding was confirmed by Teaster's (2002) national study. A spouse with a disability or dementia who is socially isolated is more at risk for such abuse or neglect. Adult protective services are the first responders to vulnerable adults who are being mistreated, neglected, or exploited and unable to protect themselves. In most states, health-care professionals, dentists, lawyers, social workers, clergy, and bankers are mandated reporters of elder abuse and exploitation. Elder abuse is the form of family violence about which we know the least—for it often goes unreported. The legal definitions of abuse include the following:

- *Abuse.* Physical abuse typically means intentionally inflicting, or allowing someone else to intentionally inflict, bodily injury or pain and includes such harmful behaviors as slapping, kicking, biting, pinching, and burning, as well as sexual abuse. It might also include inappropriate use of drugs and physical restraints.

Further Developments

Selecting a Nursing Home

Nursing homes increasingly provide short-term care to residents requiring surgical recuperation and therapy. Long-term or permanent residents have more chronic conditions. As more adults 85 and older are a larger percentage of the nursing home residents, they require more skilled care with daily living tasks. More homes provide care for Alzheimer's patients.

Americans have an enormous fear of growing old, becoming infirm, losing their minds, and being placed in a nursing home, and the vast majority of spouses and adult children typically postpone the arrangement as long as they can (Montgomery & Kosloski, 1994). Placing a spouse or relative in a nursing home can be stressful for the caregiver as well as the patient (Gaugler et al., 2000). Adult children find the decision to be exceedingly excruciating, and they commonly feel ambivalence, shame, and guilt. One 49-year-old East Coast public relations woman tells of her anguish after her 80-year-old mother had suffered a number of small strokes (Moore, 1983, p. 30):

> When it was clear that she couldn't go on living alone, we hired round-the-clock nurses at $400 a week. But first one didn't show up; then my mother didn't like another.... So we brought her to our house for a while, but it was extremely hard on me and the rest of the family. We talked about a nursing home. And though she didn't want to go, it became apparent that it was the only way. She started in a minimum-care facility. But she became more and more confused, so they decided to switch her to their skilled-care facility—a decision in which I had no choice.... It's very sad. She keeps asking: "When can I get out of here and get on with my life?"

Clearly, the prospect of nursing-home care can be traumatic for both the aging parents and their adult children. Should a nursing home be required, the person who is going to be placed there should be involved in the planning, when possible. A number of nursing homes should be visited before a decision is made. A list of licensed nursing homes can generally be secured from the local Social Security office, local hospitals, or a county senior citizen office. Nursing homes often give preference to those who demand the least attention and care, and most good nursing homes have a waiting list. Here are a number of things to look for in a nursing home:

The Facility

- Is the nursing home licensed by a governmental agency? Are recent inspection reports available?
- What arrangements exist for the transfer of a patient to a hospital, should it be required?
- Are the rooms clean, relatively odor-free, and comfortable?
- What are the visiting hours? Who is welcome?
- Does each room have a window, and does the room open to a corridor?

Safety

- Is the building fire-resistant? Does it have a sprinkler system? Are emergency exit routes clearly posted?
- Are there ramps for wheelchairs and handicapped persons?
- Are the hallways well lighted?
- Are the floor coverings nonskid and safe?
- Are there grab bars in appropriate settings, including bathrooms?

Staff

- Are a physician and a registered nurse on call at all times?
- What provision is made for patient dental care?
- Are the staff patient with questions, and are they happy to have visitors inspect the facility?
- Is there a physical therapy program staffed by a certified therapist?
- Are most of the patients out of bed, dressed, and groomed? (Be suspicious if you see many patients physically restrained in their beds or chairs or if they appear to be sedated.)
- Are staff members on the floor actually assisting residents?

Activities

- Does the facility offer a recreation program?
- Are the grounds well maintained, and are patients encouraged to get outdoors when weather permits?
- Are patients left idle and shown no care or interest or are they kept busy?
- Are activities scheduled outside the facility and in the community?

Nursing Home Care More residents are 85 and older, more frail, and with more impairments—requiring a higher level of care.

Food

- Are the meals adequate and appetizing? Are they served at the proper temperature?
- Does a dietician prepare the menu?
- Is the menu posted, and does it accurately describe the meal?
- Does someone notice if a resident is not eating?
- What provision is made for patients who have difficulty feeding themselves?
- What arrangements are made for patients requiring special diets?

Atmosphere

- Are patients accorded privacy in receiving phone calls and visits and in dressing?
- Can residents send and receive mail unopened?
- Are patients allowed to have personal belongings, including items of furniture?
- May residents have plants?
- Is there an outdoor area where residents can sit?

- Do residents of the home recommend it? What do they have to say about it?
- Are patients permitted to wear their own clothing?
- Are the patients well groomed? If they cannot bathe themselves, are they bathed daily and as needed?
- What arrangements are made so that patients can follow their own religious practices?
- Are patients treated with warmth and dignity?

Cost

- Is the facility approved for Medicare/Medicaid reimbursement?
- Will the patient's own insurance policy cover any of the expenses?
- Is the cost quoted inclusive, or are there extra charges for laundry, medicines, and special nursing procedures?
- Are advance payments required? Are the payments refunded should the patient leave the home?

Source: Adapted from W. Andrew Achenbaum, Perceptions of Aging in America, National Forum: *Phi Kappa Phi Journal, 78,* No. 2 (Spring 1998), 30–33; and Nursing Homes: When a Loved One Needs Care, *Consumer Reports, 60* (August 1995), 518–528.

- *Psychological abuse.* This includes verbal harassment, intimidation, denigration, and isolation. It might include repeated threats of abandonment or of physical harm.
- *Neglect.* This includes failure of a caretaker to provide the goods, services, or care necessary to maintain the health or safety of a vulnerable adult. Neglect can be repeated conduct or a single incident that endangers the person's physical or psychological well-being (Morris, 1998).
- *Exploitation.* Taking advantage of an older adult for monetary gain or profit (Lachs et al., 1997).
- *Self-harm.* When an elderly person who lives alone has mental impairments and cannot attend to his or her own nutritional, hygiene, or daily living needs, this is self-harm.

Elder abuse and neglect laws and reporting are inconsistent in many states (Teaster, 2002). Lachs and colleagues reported findings from a 13-year study (1998). Risk factors were analyzed for both reported and verified elder abuse and neglect in a Connecticut cohort of nearly 3,000 adults age 65 and older from diverse ethnic, racial, and social backgrounds. They discovered an association between the following risk factors and elder mistreatment: poverty, minority status, functional and cognitive impairment, worsening cognitive impairment, and living with someone (spouse or family member). With respect to social network factors, living alone was significantly associated with protecting older adults from abuse since most (80 percent) of mistreated subjects lived with someone else (Lachs et al., 1997).

Elder Abuse in the Long-Term-Care Community Providers now recognize that elder abuse and neglect must be prevented—for they have a devastating impact on the victim, the confidence of other residents, their families, and staff morale (see Table 18.3). They also arouse outrage of the public and law enforcement

Table 18.3 Substantiated Reports of Elder Mistreatment/Abuse: 2000

With 44 states responding, 59 percent of the victims were women over age 65. Also, a majority of the victims were non-Hispanic whites. The highest number of substantiated abuse allegations was for victims age 80 and older (46 percent). Considerably more abuse occurred in home settings than in institutional settings, and males or spouses were the perpetrators in a majority of the substantiated cases.

Category	Percent of Total Reports
Self-neglect	41.9
Physical abuse	20.0
Caregiver neglect or abandonment	13.2
Other	10.0
Financial abuse/exploitation	9.8
Emotional/verbal abuse	8.1
Sexual abuse	.08

Source: Adapted from Pamela B. Teaster, *A Response to the Abuse of Vulnerable Adults: The 2000 Survey of State Adult Protective Services.* Washington, DC: The National Center on Elder Abuse, 2002, p. 28. Used by permission of the National Center on Elder Abuse, 2002, p. 28. used by permission of the National Center on Elder Abuse.

officials. The state of Massachusetts has instituted a pilot training program of video training, conferences, and workshops to educate staff on recognizing and preventing elder abuse. The American Health Care Association (AHCA), which represents 11,000 long-term care facilities nationwide, is distributing this video and lobbying Congress for a federal database for CORE (criminal offenders record information) investigations to screen out employment candidates with prior convictions, pending charges of elder abuse, theft, or other serious crimes. In September 1997 in a significant case for patient rights, the Arizona Supreme Court upheld that families of elderly persons who are abused by their caretakers may recover damages for the victims' pain and suffering—even after their deaths (*Denton* v. *American Family Care Corp.*) (Cassens, 1998).

Caregiver Burnout   Caregivers of the elderly with cognitive and functional impairments—even those who are loving and dedicated—are at high risk to experience "caregiver burnout" (Marks & Lambert, 1998). It is most likely that women will become the unappreciated caretakers of disabled elders (Marks & Lambert, 1998). In one study, 20 percent of caregivers said their tasks were so frustrating and difficult that they were afraid they might hurt the patient (Lachs et al., 1998). Pillemer says caregivers must first recognize there's a problem, must not feel guilty, but must seek help. Caretakers should address these questions: "Am I depressed?" "Do I fly off the handle?" "Do I resent my relative?" "Am I denying my relative social activity?" "Do I threaten nursing home placement?" Pillemer (Lachs et al., 1998) recommends the following strategies to cope with caregiving:

- Join a support group that shares the same problems.
- Continue activities you enjoy.
- Seek professional help for parents' physical needs.
- Get more information about caregiver burnout from area agencies on aging.
- Investigate adult day-care or adult respite options in your community.

Questions

In what ways are the elderly victimized by abuse, and who is most likely to perpetrate that abuse? What can be done to prevent elder abuse?

Policy Issues and Advocacy in an Aging Society

The original *Older Americans Act* was passed in 1965, in response to the needs of a growing number of older people. This legislation established the *Administration on Aging (AOA)*, an agency of the U.S. Department of Health and Human Services. This agency advocates and administers programs for senior citizens across the country. Also, it sponsors research and training programs on aging and seeks to educate older people and the public through its regional, state, and area offices about benefits and services available. Nationwide there are 660 Area Agencies on Aging. AOA programs help older persons remain in their homes and offer opportunities for older Americans to enhance their health and remain active in their families and communities through volunteer and employment programs. Supportive services include:

- Information and referral, outreach, case management, escort and transportation
- In-home services, such as personal care, chores, home-delivered meals, home repair
- Community services, such as senior centers, adult day care, elder abuse prevention, congregate meals, health promotion, employment counseling and referral, and fitness
- Caregiver services, such as counseling, education, and respite

In 1992, nearly 70 U.S. behavioral science organizations and federal agencies formulated a national research agenda called the *Human Capital Initiative* to address the serious challenges and opportunities that increasing numbers of diverse elderly pose to our society. In 1993, the *Vitality for Life* proposal was compiled, which called for research in four major aspects of aging: (1) behavior change to prevent damage to body systems and maintain health; (2) psychological health of the oldest old; (3) maximizing and maintaining productivity; and (4) assessing mental health and treating mental disorders. Research, training, and consulting in these areas improves our understanding of the needs of this large group of adults and enhances their quality of life (see the *Implications for Practice* box "Professor and Gerontologist"). Another significant goal is improving life for elderly immigrants assimilating to an "American" way of life. A greater respect and caring for the elderly of all ethnic and cultural backgrounds is surfacing in American society.

In 2000, Congress reauthorized *PL 89-73*, the 1965 *Older American Act* that supports such programs as Meals-on-Wheels and community service jobs. The five-year reauthorization of the Older Americans Act would continue to fund community service job programs that channel funds to organizations including AARP, Green Thumb, and the National Council of Senior Citizens but has created higher performance standards that these organizations must meet to receive this funding. The bill also created a new $125 million National Family Caregiver Support Program that helps families care for

Implications for Practice

Professor and Gerontologist
William C. Lane, Ph.D.

I am an associate professor of sociology at SUNY Cortland and vice president of GoldenLane Associates, Inc., a gerontological consulting firm located in Glenmont, New York. At SUNY Cortland, I teach undergraduates from a number of majors. I created an introduction to social gerontology course for sophomores. I also designed and teach the senior seminar in human services. I started my consulting firm five years ago with a former student. Together, we work with several counties to establish programs to support caregivers for older people as well as for grandparents raising grandchildren. We do training, strategic planning, develop materials and marketing plans, and work on aging policy issues.

As a college professor, I teach students, do academic advisement, and conduct college service programs. I also involve gerontology students in the field by taking them to professional meetings and getting them into settings where they work with older people. Also, I write manuals and training materials, conduct training seminars, do research, conduct marketing focus groups, and work on strategic planning for agencies and service providers. I am the past president of both the New York State Society on Aging (formerly SAGE) and Sigma Phi Omega, the national honor society in gerontology, and past treasurer of the Association for Gerontology in Higher Education.

I received a bachelor's degree in sociology, with a minor in psychology, from Pittsburgh State University (KS). I stayed on for my master's in sociology and was supported by a grant to develop special educational programs for adults 55 and older working with 27 school districts and 6 community colleges in southeast Kansas. That is how I got *hooked* on gerontology. I earned a Ph.D. in sociology at Kansas State University where I was supported by a grant from the Midwest Council for Social Research in Aging, a training program for sociologists. As a professor, I did not have to complete a certification exam, but social workers, nurses, and other professionals complete certification exams for working with older people. My previous careers were as a professional jazz musician and an accountant.

To teach in a college setting, you have to like working with all kinds of students. Some students have a difficulty getting started in their college careers but go on to do exceptionally well in graduate school and excel as professionals. You also have to pay attention to details. As a consultant in gerontology, you need a range of professional experiences.

Internships are essential, for both undergraduate and master's students. Internships and clinical experience help individuals confirm their career direction. I recommend you get a variety of internship, clinical, and volunteer experiences. Such work demonstrates a commitment to the field in which you hope to work. You learn the "language of field" by working with professionals. I have become a better professor, researcher, and consultant from every research project, every board I have served on, and from every group of older people I have encountered.

I enjoy working with college students, but I really like working with older people and with professionals who service this population. I find that service providers of the aging are among the most committed professionals I have encountered. They are sincerely interested in improving the quality of life for older people and their families. And, with the aging of the baby-boom cohort upon us, there will be no shortage of older people to work with over the next 50 years.

the elderly at home by subsidizing respite care, counseling and support groups, and information on obtaining services (Nather, 2000). One major area that needs improvement is a federal system for reporting elder abuse and neglect (Teaster, 2002).

There are many complex decisions ahead for Americans in the near future, as the first of the baby-boom "tidal wave" will turn 65 in 2011. Public policymakers use demographic projections of an aging society to alter public policy and legislation to plan for the collective needs of society. Special challenges include financing government insurance programs of Social Security, Medicare, and Medicaid—with soaring numbers of recipients who are also living much longer (Friedland & Summer, 1999; Rice & Fineman, 2004). An aging, longer-living population will increase both private and public costs—although the baby-boom cohort has more education, better private pension plans, and greater personal wealth than any previous cohort (Rice & Fineman, 2004).

Economists predict that growth of the American economy will affect decisions about tax code configurations, specific regulations, the ability to purchase goods and services, the ability to provide a range of services for the "graying" population, and an alteration to the customary lifestyle of all Americans. Policymakers believe older workers will have to work longer, and age limits will rise for full eligibility for Social Security and other public assistance programs (Wiatrowski, 2001). Also, this demographic shift means an increased need in a skilled geriatric workforce (physicians, surgeons, nurses, therapists, pharmacists, social workers, gerontology professors, and geropsychologists), and more facilities and providers for long-term care (day care, home health, homemaker services, respite care, rehab care, and hospice) (Rice & Fineman, 2004). It is also believed that future scientific, pharmaceutical, and medical breakthroughs (recall stem cell research) will improve health care and extend life expectancy even further.

SEGUE

As you have now read the research findings about the status of America's elderly, note the remarkable progress that has occurred in improving the longevity and the quality of life for our senior citizens. The United States is third after China and India in its numbers of senior citizens. Many of our elderly are reaping the benefits of recent years of research in the physical and social sciences. It seems it was only a few years ago we heard the word *gerontology* for the first time, yet now countless researchers are studying longevity, aging, and the quality of life for all of us when we reach late adulthood. In October 1998 John Glenn reentered the world of space exploration at the age of 77 to provide American scientists with never-before-gathered data on the effects of aging. He passed rigorous physical and cognitive tests to be selected. His research in space aptly symbolizes that the study of aging is truly in its infancy—and "the sky's the limit" for senior citizens living around the world. In our concluding chapter, we shall examine several end-of-life scenarios for people of all ages and the range of coping strategies employed by those loved ones who remain.

Summary

Social Responses to Aging

1. Industrialized societies have extended longevity for many people and provided economic and social resources for them to lead more satisfying lives in old age. Consequently, many of our American elderly are experiencing greater satisfaction in their later years.
2. With our culture's preoccupation with youthfulness, most Americans want to ignore late adulthood or have distorted perceptions of it. These stereotypic views have negative effects on older adults' self-esteem.
3. Among the elderly, positive emotions have been found to be related to favorable life events, positive health status and functional ability, availability of social contacts, and higher levels of educational attainment.

Self-Concept and Personality Development

4. The elderly confront the issue of integrity versus despair. Provided they have successfully navigated the previous stages of development, they are capable of facing their later years with optimism and enthusiasm; those who appraise their lives as having been wasted experience a sense of despair.

5. Peck stresses the changes people go through, from their reflections on retirement, recurring illness, and mortality.
6. Emotional health among the elderly is described as the "clear ability to play and work and to love," and to achieve satisfaction with life. An ability to handle life's blows without passivity, blame, or bitterness is especially important.
7. Neugarten and colleagues identified four major personality types, or traits, related to the aging process: integrated, armored-defended, passive-dependent, and disintegrated.
8. Other theories of aging concentrate on disengagement, activity levels, social usefulness, social exchange, and the modernization of society.
9. Some research indicates that a few aspects of personality, including emotional intelligence and wisdom, actually improve during what the Balteses call the "Third Age," though decline is evident in the "Fourth Age."
10. Research from around the world suggests that there is a healing association between religion and health.

Familial Roles: Continuity and Discontinuity

11. The quality of marriage varies from couple to couple. Most elderly husbands and wives report greater happi-

ness and satisfaction with marriage during their later years than at any other time except for the newlywed phase.

12. Fewer than half of elderly women still reside with their husbands. This statistic demonstrates a particular gender issue that is of great concern worldwide: Elderly women are at much higher risk of living in poverty.

13. A majority of elderly have living children, and the elderly are not so isolated from kin and friendship networks as is commonly believed, due to exchanges of mutual aid and proximity of kin.

14. Child psychologists emphasize that both children and their grandparents are better off when they spend a good deal of time in each other's company.

15. Siblings often play a significant role in the lives of the elderly. They provide a continuity in family history that is uncommon to most other family relationships and might be the only members of the family of origin who are still alive.

Social and Cultural Support

16. Some research suggests that the single elderly who live with relatives are lonelier than those who live alone. An elderly widow who lives with her daughter's family might be quite lonely if she has little contact with associates her own age.

17. Retirement as we understand it today did not exist in preindustrial American society—nor does it exist in some societies today. Older people formerly were not sidelined from mainstream employment. Many of today's workers can expect to have 15 to 20 years of life remaining after retiring.

18. Nearly 10 million Americans over the age of 65 live alone, but 2 million indicate they have no one to turn to if they need help; other arrangements are living with families, nursing homes, retirement communities, and adult group homes.

19. It is estimated that about 1 to 2 million Americans age 65 and older are abused in domestic settings each year. Because most of the cases never come to the attention of the authorities, the full scope of the problem isn't known. A better federal reporting system is recommended.

20. The quality of life for American elderly has been improved by public policy issues, the Older Americans Act, AARP, and other community supports. However, there are some significant policy changes ahead to meet the collective needs of an aging society.

Key Terms

activity theory of aging (617)

adult day care (635)

disengagement theory of aging (617)

elder abuse (637)

integrity versus despair (613)

life review (615)

modernization theory (618)

role exit theory of aging (617)

social exchange theory of aging (617)

selective optimization with compensation (618)

wisdom (621)

Following Up on the Internet

Web sites for this chapter focus on the changing demographics and quality of life for those in late adulthood. Please access the text Web site at www.mhhe.com/vzcrandell8 for up-to-date hot-linked Internet addresses for the following organizations, topics, and resources:

AARP

Workforce Aging in the New Economy

APA Division 20: Adult Development and Aging

National Institute on Aging

Gerontological Society of America

Aging Research and Organizations

Eldercare Locator

National Academy on an Aging Society

Video Scenario—http://www.mhhe.com/vzcrandell8

In this chapter, you've just read about issues of emotional and social development in late adulthood. Using the OLC (www.mhhe.com/vzcrandell8), watch the *Late Adulthood video scenario* to see how these concepts, such as grandparenthood and the issue of integrity vs. despair, come to life as Grandma reflects on people and events in her life. This scenario serves as a capstone to the text as it looks back at many of the stages of human development. Don't forget to test your knowledge of these concepts by trying the fill-in-the-blank and critical thinking questions that follow this segment.

Part TEN
The End of Life

Over the past 50 years, the more recent American practice of "hiding death" has largely been abandoned. With considerable truth it can be said that Western society has "rediscovered" death. An outpouring of scholarly (and not so scholarly) works in sociology, psychology, and thanatology, television documentaries, paperback books, and feature articles in newspapers and magazines have drawn attention to every aspect of the topic. Simultaneously, controversy has swirled in the mass media, in the political arena, in legislative and judicial chambers, in courtrooms across the country, and in our own homes about such matters as the right to die, clinical death, adolescent homicides and suicides, the death penalty, mass suicide, and life after death. People are more willing to discuss dying and death, and such discussions have paved the way for families to experience more meaningful closure to life for loved ones. Our gradual cultural embracing of death as a natural stage of development is leading toward a deeper understanding of the meaning of life.

CHAPTER

19

Dying and Death

I n the cycle of life, each person comes into this world alone and then—typically many years later—exits alone. During the time in between, called a *lifetime*, each of us ponders about this mystery of life and death many times: when experiencing the actual loss of loved ones, when viewing media portrayals of dying and death, or perhaps when conducting one's daily life as a soldier or police officer, fireman, medical professional, clergy, or hospice volunteer.

Throughout the ages, people from every culture have wondered about this great mystery by taking risks and "teasing" death, by wrestling with or writing about their fears, by devising elaborate rituals in preparation, and by building monuments in recognition. Some even welcome or promote their own "final exit." We conclude our final chapter of human development by discussing cultural awareness of issues in thanatology, cross-cultural views of death and grief, the role of religious beliefs, the stages of dying, and adjusting to the death of a loved one. At best, it can be said that facing death is as individual as our own personal philosophies about how we have lived our lives.

The Quest for "Healthy Dying"

Until the late 1800s, in American homes, families typically sat with and talked to their loved one who was dying, prepared the body when the person died, and then "laid out" the deceased in his or her best clothing (or wedding apparel) for a viewing in the parlor of the home. A local carpenter or furniture maker (called an "undertaker") made a wooden casket and brought it to the home for the viewing and in readiness for burial. Often, some of the deceased person's hair was cut and braided into a bracelet to be saved and worn. There were no morticians who embalmed the body, no funeral homes, and no corporations that made expensive caskets. Other family, friends, and community members would come to the house to pay their respects and bring all kinds of food for the "wake." They would "call on" the family (thus funeral "homes" have "calling hours" today).

There were many superstitions about the spiritual state of the deceased—people believed it lingered and they expounded on complimenting the deceased to avoid bad luck or revenge. To allow the spirit to leave, a window was opened, and no one was to stand in a doorway. Often family and friends would sit and talk all night with the deceased and celebrate his or her life. The Irish were known in particular for celebrating and drinking for hours, which often got rowdy and might have involved dancing with the body of the deceased. Dying and death were a natural part of life, and children grew up learning about death. The surviving family performed these mourning rituals to demonstrate their love and respect

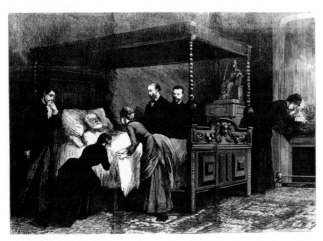

Traditional Rituals of Dying and Death A century ago in Western societies, death was a natural part of everyday life, and family personally attended to the deceased in the home. A widow or widower was expected to sit for calling hours, when visitors brought food, drink and their respects prior to a burial in a simple wooden coffin. Mourning in black apparel for two years was expected. A family's personal preparation and mourning rituals are still common in many parts of the world.

for the deceased, to ease their grief, and to ease their fear of any spirits that might harm them (Kastenbaum, 2004a). A widow or widower was expected to mourn in black apparel for two years. A family's personal preparation, conversation, and celebration is still the ritual in many parts of the world.

By the early 1900s, dying and death gradually were removed from the responsibility of families in Western society. Typically the gravely ill were whisked away to a hospital, and senile relatives and the "oldest old" were sent to "nursing homes" to live out their remaining days. Funeral parlors opened, and morticians retrieved the deceased from hospitals for embalming and viewings. Families were removed from the personal care, cleaning, and dressing of the deceased. Funeral preparations became more impersonal—and costly—conducted by professionals in the funeral industry—and dying, death, and preparation of the body became something to be kept out of sight and out of mind. Over time, family "parlors" in homes became "living rooms," to reflect that the deceased no longer lingered there. Even medical schools avoided the topic of dying and death, and physicians did their best to ignore dealing with dying patients and their families, for their professional oath was and is to maintain and prolong life. Today, some social scientists claim that the United States is a "death-denying culture." Many Americans stress youth, beauty, power, physical fitness, cosmetic surgery, and antiaging. Less than 25 percent have wills, and many are made uncomfortable by discussions of death. Other social scientists claim the United States is a death obsessed culture—with over 45 million abortions to date, the death penalty, the highest rates of murder of any industrialized country in the world, and the state of Oregon allowing euthanasia.

Death confronts us both subtly and blatantly in diseases such as Alzheimer's and cancer and in devastating epidemics, such as AIDS or severe acute respiratory syndrome (SARS). On a nationwide scale, it tore at our hearts, brought us to our knees, and prompted us to action when we heard of the September 11, 2001 attacks, the Oklahoma City bombing, Columbine and other school shootings, the deaths from the War on Terror, the incredible devastation of the 2005 tsunami in Southeast Asia, Hurricanes Katrina and Rita, and other such disasters. We conceal it under a variety of names—abortion, selective reduction, stillbirth, SIDS, mortality, homicide, suicide, suicide bombings, natural disasters, drive-by shootings, schoolyard shootings, occupational fatalities, auto fatalities, terrorism, collateral damage, friendly fire, and so forth.

We are reminded of its inevitability in rituals invoking collective memories, such as memorials commemorating the deaths of famous persons—such as Pope John Paul II, Princess Diana, Mother Teresa, former President Ronald Reagan, Martin Luther King, Jr., and President John Kennedy—that invoke larger moral principles. As the traveling AIDS quilt or the traveling Vietnam Memorial make their way around the country, whole communities come together in deep sorrow for the thousands of lives lost. And most of us experience some forms of preliminary finality in our lives in the "endings" of marriages by divorce or widowhood, the end of careers or group memberships by retirement or resignation, and the end of family traditions such as when the children instead of the parents prepare the annual Thanksgiving meal. If we don't have children, we might decide it is time to go to a community or church Thanksgiving dinner with friends and acquaintances.

Even our everyday conversations are sprinkled with expressions about death: "My back is killing me!" "I was so embarrassed I could have died!" "You scared me to death!" Some people risk death on a daily basis: police, firemen, soldiers, the flag person for a construction crew on a superhighway, stunt people who allow themselves to be set afire or make death-defying leaps out of buildings, those who buy and sell drugs on the street, those who have unprotected sex with multiple partners, and others. Our television movies, popular action films, the evening news, and the local newspapers sensationalize death, making it seem less than real. Death and the true meaning of life have been themes in great literature from the earliest recorded texts, such as the Bible, the *Iliad* and the *Odyssey* to Shakespeare's *Romeo and Juliet* and *Hamlet*. We personify death by giving it names like "the Grim Reaper," "the Gentle Comforter," "the long goodbye," "the last dance," "sacred passage," or the "Gay Deceiver" (Kastenbaum, 1997).

Recently, an A&E reality television show, *Family Plots*, revealed the routines of the staff, the preparation of the deceased, and the grieving families served at a California mortuary. Other recent death themes in literature and the media include the ideas of near-death experiences, past lives, life after death, communicating with the dead, and the presence of angels (e.g., *Medium*, and *Touched by an Angel* television series). Some of these works have made it to best-sellers lists, including *Life After Life* by Dr. Ray Moody, Jr., *Embraced by the Light* by Betty J. Eadie, *Conversations with God* (Book 1, Book 2, and Book 3) by Neale Donald Walsch, and *Talking to Heaven: A Medium's Message of Life After Death* and *Reaching to Heaven* by James Van Praagh. Though they are not grounded empirically, at the very least these works are pricking our consciousness and making us confront what we think about life and death. More sophisticated medical technology has permitted many people to come back from the brink of death. Koerner (1997) reports that nearly one-third of these people—as many as 15 million Americans—report having had metaphysical experiences, with vivid images of an afterlife, when they were near death. Brian L. Weiss—psychiatrist, experimental psychologist, distinguished university chairperson, and author of *Many*

Lives, Many Masters—says that after many years of being immersed in the traditional, conservative aspects of his profession, scientists still have much to learn about the human mind that now seems to be beyond our comprehension. "Rigorous scientific study into the mystery of the mind, the soul, death, continuation of life after death is in its infancy in our society" (Weiss, 1988, p. 11).

> **Question**
>
> Perspectives on the causes and meaning of death have varied throughout history. In contemporary American society, what events are prompting a more open discussion of death and dying?

Thanatology: The Study of Death and Dying

Over the past 30 years, public and professional awareness of the dying person's experience has increased dramatically. "Death with dignity!" has become a major rallying cry. Interest in the field of **thanatology**—the study of death (*thanatos* is the Greek word for "death")—has grown. In recent years university centers were established that study dying, death, grief, and bereavement across cultures. Daniel Leviton and Robert Kastenbaum established one of the first such centers (Strack & Feifel, 2003). Recently, Kastenbaum released his third edition of *The Psychology of Death*, which he first authored 30 years ago. Death awareness advocates assert that the power to control one's own dying process is a basic human right. They point out that in the United States the majority of those who die spend part of their final year in a nursing home or hospital, often in pain and alone. So allowing someone to die naturally often involves a team of professionals who must make a conscious decision whether to continue medical treatment. Some professionals draw a distinction between ordinary and extraordinary treatment, contending that ordinary measures such as nutrition and hydration should be continued, whereas extraordinary treatment such as dialysis with a kidney machine or artificial maintenance of blood circulation may be halted if the case is hopeless. Death-with-dignity advocates insist that aggressive medical care, the norm that life must be maintained at all costs, prevents people from dying quickly and naturally.

The "healthy dying" quest has led some *thanatologists* to expound on the good, acceptable, or self-actualized death (Kastenbaum, 1979, 1997, 2003b). According to this view, it is not sufficient that death be reasonably free of pain and trauma. Instead, it is argued, individuals suffering a terminal illness should be able to select the particular style of exit that they believe to be consistent with their total lifestyle, such as a romantic death, a brave death, or a death that integrates and confirms the person's unique identity (Humphry & Clement, 1998).

Overall, it seems that more and more Americans are trying to take back control of the time, place, and circumstances of their death. We are granting powers of attorney and making advance directives, purchasing cemetery plots and customized gravestones, executing wills and living wills, and so on. Some choose to leave the hospital to die at home. Many are giving family members or close friends the power to terminate medical treatment when they themselves can no longer do so. In a number of states, death-with-dignity advocates have secured the passage of laws that provide for the drawing up of a **living will**—a legal document that states an individual's wishes regarding medical care (such as refusal of "heroic measures" to prolong his or her life in the event of terminal illness) in case the person becomes incapacitated and unable to participate in decisions about his or her medical care (see the *More Information You Can Use* box "An Example of a Living Will").

The 1994 deaths of Jacqueline Kennedy Onassis and Richard Nixon, both of whom rejected medical treatment that could have prolonged their lives, have accelerated changes in Americans' approach to death (Scott, 1994). Other developments—including the substantial sales of Derek Humphry's (1991) do-it-yourself suicide manual *Final Exit* and widespread controversy revolving around Dr. Jack Kevorkian's practice of "assisted suicide"—suggest that some Americans want still more control at the end of life. These people and events then bring more prominence to the right-to-die movement. As with every great moral issue, there are others that oppose the taking of one's life or assisting others, and that perspective is supported by a majority of clergy and others in the right-to-life movement (Smith, 1997).

Questions

How would you describe the study of thanatology, in your own words? Do you believe firmly in the right to die, or the right to life? Why?

The Right-to-Die Movement

"Healthy dying" has become a more prominent issue in the United States, especially when the *New York Times* published an article about a woman named Jo Roman, a 62-year-old artist with terminal cancer who took her own life with an overdose of medication after gathering close friends around her for a celebration prior to her farewell passage (Johnston, 1979). Then, Dr. Jack Kevorkian began to help people with terminal illness end their lives. And most recently the disputes in the Terri Schindler-Schiavo case became headline news in 2005. Gallup polls in 2004 indicated that 65 percent of those

surveyed agreed that physician-assisted suicide should be allowed when a person has an incurable disease and is in great pain. (Perhaps at the heart of the Schiavo controversy was that she had brain damage, needed only a feeding tube to survive, was *not* living in pain, and was not terminally ill.) People who are more educated are more likely to be in favor of physician-assisted suicide with careful review of each individual case. According to a 1997 *Newsweek* poll, 62 percent of college graduates compared with 52 percent of high school graduates were in favor of physician-assisted suicide. According to a *Washington Post* poll conducted in 2000, minorities are much less in favor of the practice, with more than three-fourths of African Americans against it compared with less than half of whites ("Final Request," 2001).

Much criticism is currently leveled at how modern technology is applied to the terminally ill. Critics contend that too much is done for too long a period at too high a cost, all at the expense of basic human considerations and sensitivities, and that the terminally ill become the property of health-care institutions, which override individual autonomy, endurance, dignity, and personhood. Modern medicine has come to be seen by some as the enemy rather than the friend of the terminally ill (Nuland, 1994). Additionally, the argument is often made that ending "futile" medical care for dying patients could be an important cost-saving step in overhauling the nation's health-care system. *Futile care* is sometimes defined as "any clinical circumstance in which the doctor and consultants conclude that further treatment cannot, within a reasonable possibility, cure, palliate, ameliorate, or restore a quality of life that would be satisfactory to the patient" (Snider & Hasson, 1993, p. 1A).

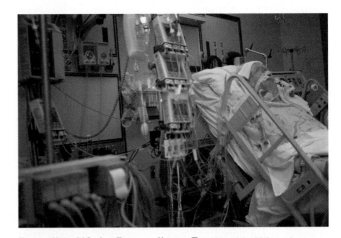

Extending Life by Extraordinary Treatment Although many people claim they would not want their lives extended by extraordinary technological means, others have not declared their wishes should such circumstances arise. Intensive care units (ICUs) and cardiac care units (CCUs) often provide such extraordinary means of survival. Family members often disagree about continuing such extraordinary care for a loved one.

More Information You Can Use

An Example of a Living Will

To my family, my physician, my lawyer and all others whom it may concern: Death is as much a reality as birth, growth, maturity, and old age. It is the one certainty of life. If the time comes when I can no longer take part in decisions for my own future, let this statement stand as an expression of my wishes and directions, while I am still of sound mind.

If at such a time the situation should arise in which there is no reasonable expectation of my recovery from extreme physical or mental disability, I direct that I be allowed to die and not be kept alive by medications, artificial means, or "heroic measures." I do, however, ask that medication be mercifully administered to me to alleviate suffering even though this may shorten my remaining life.

This statement is made after careful consideration and is in accordance with my strong convictions and beliefs. I want the wishes and directions here expressed carried out to the extent permitted by law. Insofar as they are not legally enforceable, I hope that those to whom this Will is addressed will regard themselves morally bound by these provisions.

Signed _____

Date _____

Witness _____

Witness _____

Copies of this request have been given to_____

_____

Source: From Judy Oaks & Gene Ezell, *Dying and Death: Coping, Caring, Understanding* (Scottsdale, AZ: Gorsuch Scarisbrick, 1993), p. 197. Reprinted by permission of Judy Oaks Davidson.

Physician-Assisted Suicide (PAS)   Requests for physician-assisted suicide are not new, and most physicians are likely to face this challenge. Physicians say they have a problem in deciding what medical measures they should undertake. At times, patients and their families are so distraught and frightened that they will not or cannot say what they want done. Cicirelli (1997) reports from a study he conducted with subjects aged 60 to 100 that one-third of the respondents wanted a family member, physician, or close friend to make their end-of-life decision. The decision the family must make often presents an avoidance-avoidance conflict in which people's emotionally charged thoughts tend to freeze: Do we attempt to save our loved one at all costs, even though this person may never regain consciousness or be the person he or she used to be? How can we let this person die whom we love so dearly?

Physicians often withhold antibiotics from terminally ill and senile patients who develop respiratory infections. It is often the nurses who shoulder much of the responsibility for making such decisions. The nurses might decide not to call the physician after the onset of fever, or they might influence the physician to opt for nontreatment. Significantly, the American Hospital Association estimates that 70 percent of the 6,000 deaths occurring in the United States every day are somehow timed or negotiated by patients, families, and doctors who arrive at a private consensus not to do all that they can do and instead allow a dying patient to die (Malcolm, 1990). A national survey of 1,900 physicians (Meier, 1998) found that of those who have been asked by a patient to assist with a suicide, some admit having already assisted a suicide. It was also found that if assisted suicide were legal, more physicians would be willing to assist (Meier, 1998).

Medical personnel who have sped up the death of an incurably ill patient or helped such individuals commit suicide have generally kept silent—although the medical profession typically concedes that throughout history some physicians have helped their patients end their own lives. In recent years, a number of physicians have publicly confided that they have sped up the death of an incurably ill patient or helped such individuals commit suicide (Quill, 1993; Snyder & Quill, 2001). However, such "hidden practices" are risky for patients and can potentially damage a medical practitioner's reputation. By the same token, terminally ill patients who take their own lives often find that they must die alone so as not to place others in legal jeopardy.

Some of the most painful decisions physicians confront concern newborns. With today's neonatal technology, about half the infants born weighing 750 grams (1 pound 10 ounces) can be saved. However, there is a high risk that they will have serious physical and/or mental handicaps. Another dilemma concerns infants born with life-threatening complications, such as a blockage of the intestinal tract or a heart defect, that require surgical correction. A somewhat similar issue is posed by newborns with *meningomyelocele* (me nin go my'e lo cele), a defect in which the spinal cord protrudes outside the body. If untreated by surgery, infants develop a spinal infection and die; if treated, they often suffer paralysis and incontinence. All these cases entail complex bioethical decisions as to whether severely handicapped infants should be treated so that they can survive.

The American Medical Association (AMA) said in 1986 that doctors could ethically withhold all means of life-prolonging medical treatment, including food and water, from patients in irreversible comas even if death were not imminent. The withholding of such therapy should occur only when a patient's coma is beyond doubt irreversible and there are adequate safeguards to confirm the accuracy of the diagnosis. Although the opinion of the 271,000-member association did not make such an action mandatory for doctors, it did open the way for them to withdraw life-prolonging treatment with less fear of being taken to court and to use the opinion as a defense if they are challenged. Two doctors hired by Terri Schiavo's husband agreed she was in an irreversible coma, but many doctors hired by her parents said she was not. Such a diagnosis, then, is complex and not clear-cut. The debate on these issues has spread to the treatment of patients with acquired AIDS and Alzheimer's.

Probably most controversial of all is the issue of **euthanasia,** or "good death," sometimes referred to as "mercy killing." The practice of euthanasia goes back to ancient history. *Passive euthanasia* allows death to occur by withholding or removing treatments that would prolong life. In *involuntary euthanasia,* someone in the family or a legally empowered person decides to withhold or remove medical treatments when the patient is medically considered brain dead. In *voluntary euthanasia,* the patient grants permission to remove treatments that would prolong life. Some people have prepared and signed a legal document known as a "living will" that states the person's wishes about medical treatment in case she or he becomes unable to participate in decisions regarding medical care (see the *More Information You Can Use* box on page 651, "An Example of a Living Will").

In Australia, the Northern Territory became the first state in the world to legalize voluntary active euthanasia under the *Rights of the Terminally Ill Act of 1995.* However, in 1997 their Federal Parliament overturned this legislation. In the Netherlands, euthanasia has been legalized by the Dutch Parliament since 2000 (Howarth & Leaman, 2001). In 2002, Belgium also legalized physician-assisted suicide. In the United States, such measures have usually been defeated; the exception is that Oregon residents passed a *Death with Dignity Act* in October 1997 (Caplan, 1999). Between 1997 to 2004, the Oregon Health Division reported that 208 residents chose to take lethal meds to end their lives (Niemeyer, 2005). Those who chose PAS tended to be divorced or never married, with more formal education, and diagnosed with HIV/AIDS, amyotrophic lateral sclerosis (ALS or Lou Gehrig's disease), or malignant cancer. Loss of autonomy, inability to participate in activities, and loss of dignity were main factors in patients' decisions.

Although Oregonians passed this legislation by 51 percent, many people still oppose physician-assisted suicide. Most religious groups maintain their right-to-life position. For example, the Roman Catholic Church regularly reaffirms its condemnation of euthanasia, while stating that individuals in certain circumstances have the right to renounce extraordinary and burdensome life-support systems (Steinfels, 1992). One quality-of-care result is that Oregonian doctors report that they are more attentive to patient pain and depressive symptoms, and they are more likely to refer terminal patients to hospice care (Niemeyer, 2005).

As you recall, over this half-century there will be much greater numbers of increasingly disabled elderly citizens in countries around the world who will need government-sponsored health care or long-term residential care. Such costs will be an astronomical cost/burden to the younger generation. When any society becomes overburdened with higher taxes to care for these elderly, will the medical community (with their corporate cost-conscious view) decide to terminate the lives of those who are bedridden or disabled and can no longer speak for themselves (*assisted death*) or allow them to live out their natural years? "Mercy killing" of newborns with severe medical conditions is already reported in Holland, France, Great Britain, Italy, Spain, Germany and Sweden (Verhagen & Sauer, 2005). And "mercy killing" of a man in early stages of Alzheimer's and another with dementia was approved in Holland. In 2005, a Dutch "assessment committee" decided that their euthanasia law should apply to those "suffering with living" (Sheldon, 2005). Doctors in the Netherlands proposed the *Groningen Protocol,* whereby a committee of doctors and lawyers is charged with selecting babies and other severely handicapped or disabled people for euthanasia (Hewitt, 2004). American right-to-die advocates in Oregon continue to cite Dutch practices to support and extend their law (Steinbock, 2005). One wonders where this slippery slope might lead?

A number of concerns and attitudes have converged in the right-to-die movement. For one thing, Americans tend to favor a quick transition between life and death. Many people also have a profound fear of being held captive in a state between life and death, as "vegetables" sustained entirely by life-support equipment. Coupled with these concerns are a pervasive fear and intolerance of pain and a growing expectation that one should be without pain in the ordinary course of life; medical staff regularly use pain scales for patients to convey the intensity of pain (Leleszi & Lewandowski, 2005) (see Table 19.1). Some physicians have cautioned that the current preoccupation with the issues of patient autonomy and death with dignity can lead doctors and patients to make clinically inappropriate decisions. They warn of the perils of taking patients at their word. Depressed patients are particularly likely to ask that they be allowed to die. Psychiatric illness, including symptoms of deep despair and hopelessness, can severely distort rational decision making.

Concern has also been expressed that legalizing physician-assisted suicide for the terminally ill would benefit only a few and would open the door to widespread abuse. In actuality, research commissioned by the Dutch government suggests that in more than a thousand cases per year, physicians actively cause or hasten death without the patient's request (Hendin, 1994). Some ethicists fear that most at risk will be patients unable to speak for themselves—the tens of thousands of elderly people suffering from dementia, Alzheimer's, Parkinson's, and other diseases in nursing homes and the severely disabled of all ages.

In 1983 a U.S. presidential commission made a public statement on euthanasia confirming that decisions on whether to continue life-sustaining medical treatment should generally be left to mentally competent patients. Family members would be permitted to make similar decisions for mentally incompetent patients. But the commission said that ending a patient's life intentionally could not be sanctioned on moral grounds. Even so, doctors would be allowed to administer a pain-relieving drug that hastens death provided that the sole reason for giving the drug is to relieve the pain (Schmeck, 1983; Senate Special Committee, 1997). Related developments are "living will" laws that afford protection against dehumanized dying and confer immunity upon physicians and hospital personnel who comply with a patient's wishes. More recently, Linda Emanuel (1998) proposed a model of response to the patient who requests physician-assisted suicide (PAS) (see Table 19.2). She describes a series of steps to assess a patient's competency for such a decision, which include evaluation for depression and other psychiatric conditions and decision-making competence, listing goals of care, providing full information to the patient, physician consultation with professional colleagues, following care plans, removing all unwanted life-support interventions, and securing maximum relief of suffering. The patient would ultimately have the right to decline nutrition and hydration and any regular oral intake (Emanuel, 1998).

Questions

What is our nation's stance on the issues of euthanasia or physician-assisted suicide? What are some other nations' perspectives and practices on this issue?

Suicide In many countries, suicide is one of the leading causes of death (Oaks & Ezell, 1993). Suicide is the second leading cause of death among American college students, and it is the third leading cause of death among all youth ages 15 to 24 (only accidents and homicide claim more young lives) (American Foundation for Suicide

---

Table 19.1 Last-Resort Options for Responding to Intolerable Suffering

Timothy Quill has proposed a form of rubric assessment to help make certain determinations about end-of-life decisions.

Option	Legal Status	Ethical Consensus	Decision Maker
Proportionately intensive symptom management	Legal	Consensus	Patient or surrogate
Stopping or not starting potentially life-sustaining therapy	Legal	Consensus	Patient or surrogate
Sedation to unconsciousness to relieve intractable symptoms	Legal	Uncertain	Patient or surrogate
Voluntarily stopping eating and drinking	Legal	Uncertain	Patient only
Physician-assisted suicide	Illegal (except in Oregon)	Uncertain	Patient only

From Timothy E. Quill, "Dying and Decision Making: Evolution of End-of-Life Options," *New England Journal of Medicine*, Vol. 350, No. 20 (May 13, 2004), p. 2031. Copyright © 2004 Massachusetts Medical Society. All rights reserved.

Table 19.2 Emanuel's Eight-Step Approach to the Patient Who Requests Physician-Assisted Suicide

Step	Suggested Procedure
1	**Assess for depression:** If Yes, then treat for depression. If No, then see Step 2.
2	**Assess for decision-making capacity:** If No, then assess for treatable causes; if none, seek proxy. If Yes, continue with Step 3.
3	**Engage in structural deliberation including advance care planning. Affirm other form of comfort and control:** Request for PAS may be dropped. Provide care as discussed in patient/proxy. Request for PAS may continue. See Step 4.
4	**Establish and treat root cause(s) of request: physical, personal, or social. Hospice philosophy, palliative care skills, as appropriate:** Request dropped. Provide care as discussed in patient/proxy. Request continues. See Step 5.
5	**Ensure full information on consequences, risk, and responsibilities; attempt to dissuade from PAS:** Request dropped. Provide care as discussed with patient/proxy. Request continues. See Step 6.
6	**Involve consultants or institutional committee as appropriate:** Request dropped. Provide care as discussed with patient/proxy. Request continues. See Step 7.
7	**Review adherence to goals and care plan, supporting removal of unwanted intervention and providing full-comfort care:** Request dropped. Provide care as discussed with patient/proxy. Request continues. See Step 8.
8	**Decline PAS (all states except Oregon) explaining why and affirming alternatives.** Provide care as discussed with patient/proxy.

From: Linda Emanual (1998). "Facing Requests for Physician-Assisted Suicide: Toward a Practical and Principled Clinical Skill Set," *Journal of the American Medical Association* (JAMA), Vol. 280, No. 7. Copyright © 1998 American Medical Association. All Rights Reserved.

Prevention, 2005). *Suicidologists* report that in many societies, because of the stigma associated with suicide, many cases are reported as accidents or death from undetermined cause. Tragically, we have become accustomed to hearing about "suicide bombers" in Israel, Afghanistan, Iraq, and other parts of the world—such as bus and subway "suicide bombers" in London—whose intent is also to kill as many innocent persons while committing suicide. In addition to the emotional burden for those left behind, there is an economic burden because most insurance companies do not honor the life insurance policies of those who take their own lives. The social isolation of survivors is also greater than for any other cause of death, as was expressed by a bereaved mother of a child who died from a self-inflicted gunshot wound:

> People I had known for years stopped speaking to me. They couldn't even look me in the eyes in the grocery store. All of a sudden we had no friends. People didn't call, visit, or invite us over. They treated us like we had some dreaded disease. (Oaks & Ezell, 1993, p. 209)

To commit suicide is to intentionally kill oneself. The National Institute of Mental Health (NIMH) has defined three concepts pertaining to suicide (Oaks & Ezell, 1993, p. 209):

- *Suicide ideas.* This pertains to the observation or inference that someone might be moving in the direction of taking his or her life. The subject might seem to be suggesting it, writing about it, talking about it—but does not carry it out.
- *Suicide attempts.* This pertains to the situation in which a person performs an overt life-threatening behavior with the intent of taking his or her own life (e.g., cutting wrists, jumping off a bridge, overdosing on pills). This may become a repetitive behavior with the intent of communicating a message to a loved one and may be a call for help rather than true intent to end one's life.
- *Completed suicide.* This pertains to all persons who were successful in taking their own lives, based on the circumstances surrounding the death.

Various cultural attitudes toward suicide still waver between the extremes of the early Christians, who labeled suicide a sin and denied burial rites to persons who had killed themselves, to considering the victim as insane or weak, to considering suicide the honorable choice when confronted with capture, defeat, or disgrace (e.g., Japanese *kamikaze* pilots in World War II). The idea that suicide is a sin comes from several religious doctrines that state that God made each of us and it is up to God, and only God, to determine our death. Criminologists, on the other hand, are likely to take the position that the person who commits suicide is mentally ill and has a flawed, deviant mind, as in criminal cases when an ex-spouse murders his own family and then takes his own life or terrorists bent on their own destruction as well as others.

Who Commits Suicide and Why?   How do we classify the thousands of suicides committed every year mainly by children, adolescents, and elderly men (see Figure 19.1)? Although more females attempt suicide, more males succeed at suicide (Oaks & Ezell, 1993). Suicide is the tenth leading cause of death in the United States. The death rate in 2002 for suicide of men over 85 is over 50 percent. Elderly males may feel depressed over the loss of physical strength, realize that fewer of their loved ones are left in life, or may recently be diagnosed with a terminal illness or Alzheimer's disease, or might be overmedicated. In 2002, for men ages 15 to 24, death rates for suicide were 16.5 compared with the rate of 2.4 for women ages 15 to 24 (U.S. Bureau of the Census, 2004f). For young males, common causes are pressures associated with peer acceptance (a main factor in the shootings at Columbine High School), job goals, loneliness, and poor health.

> His parents were moving to Houston because the father had been transferred by his employer. He said he was not going with them. He was an honor student, involved in sports and extracurricular activities. He showed his friends his gun, but no one took him seriously enough to tell school personnel. He walked to the front of the classroom, put the gun in his mouth, and pulled the trigger. Postvention assistance included individual counseling for some students and teachers, participation in support groups led by professional counselors, and a memorial service held at the school.

The event was so traumatic, it was weeks before the school atmosphere returned to normal. (Martin & Dixon, 1986, p. 265)

People of Native American heritage (which includes Alaska Natives) have the highest age-adjusted rates of suicide in the U.S. The highest rates of youth suicide occurred in Alaska, and the Aberdeen and Tucson areas with rates six to eight times higher than the national average. Non-Hispanic whites had the second highest rates of suicide. The rates for African American, Hispanic, and Asian people are about half the rates of whites and Native Americans (CDC, 2001a, 2005b). However, the rate of suicide among young Hispanics is of growing concern since Hispanic youth are the fastest-growing segment of the population in the U.S. Suicide is the third leading cause of death among Hispanics aged 10 to 24 (Ikeda et al., 2004)

Suicide rates for white males climb rapidly as men age from their forties into their eighties. A recent study looked at suicide rates within various occupations. Of the 32 occupational groups studied, the results revealed that occupations with higher than average suicide rates included dentists, artists, machinists, auto mechanics, and carpenters. Lower than average suicide rates were found among clerks, elementary school teachers, and cooks (Stack, 2001). It is generally believed that Christmastime and springtime

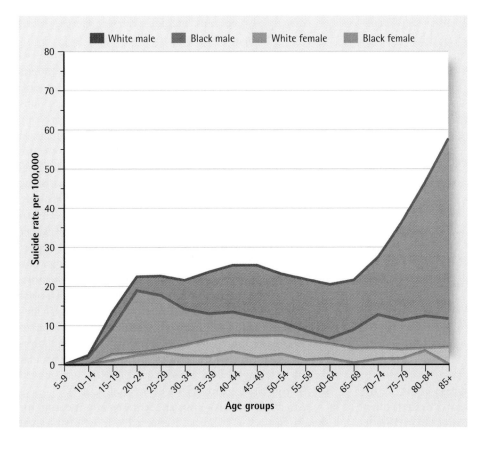

FIGURE 19.1 U.S. Suicide Rates by Age, Gender, and Racial Group, 2000 Suicide rates peak during adolescence and young adulthood and then again in late adulthood, particularly for white males during retirement. *Source:* National Institute of Mental Health, National Center for Health Statistics. (2003). *In Harm's Way: Suicide in America.*

have the highest rates of suicide. However, one study of 678 cases found no correlation between time of year and increase of number of suicides (Bennett & Collins, 2000). Those who are divorced, widowed, and separated commit suicide more than those who remain married and have children. White males commit a much higher number of suicides during their postretirement years in comparison to any other group. Yet since the early 1980s, the rates of teenage suicide have increased significantly.

The U.S. Department of Health and Human Services has identified high-risk areas of the country for the main causes of death. Centers for Disease Control and Prevention (1998) revealed that among whites, suicide rates are highest in the western states and in nonmetropolitan areas throughout the country. Using a firearm is the most common method of suicide in the United States; women are more likely than men to use poison. A research study on the attitudes people hold about suicide reveals a difference in opinions between older and younger respondents. Older adults were found to hold views about suicide that indicated that it was more acceptable, more strongly related to a lack of religious conviction, more lethal, more normal, more permanent, and more strongly related to individual aspects and to demographics (Segal et al., 2004).

Kastenbaum (1991) argues that suicide victims view suicide as a reunion with God or a loved one, as a rest or refuge, as getting back at or hurting someone, as a penalty for failure, as getting attention, or as loss of a life-sustaining drive. Each year over 400,000 people in the United States attempt suicide. In 2002, nearly 29,000 succeeded and left unbelievable shock and grief behind. Suicide peaks during adolescence and during late adulthood. The most vulnerable times are during "rites of passage," such as graduation, anniversaries, birthdays, retirement, or death of a spouse or child. Teens also commit suicide after a "crisis" of rejection or humiliation. About 30 percent of teen suicides are related to issues of sexual identity (Russell & Joyner, 2001). If someone exhibits several of the following signs together, it is time to talk to the person, demonstrate love and concern, convince the person to get counseling, and lock up any weapons in the home. Table 19.3 lists warning signs for suicide.

Questions

What are some common behavioral changes noted prior to suicide? What life events are potential triggers to suicide attempts?

The Hospice Movement

Some have called death the "undiscovered country." At its border, hospice programs provide an affordable alternative for dealing with pain and the end of life in a digni-fied, graceful fashion. In medieval times a hospice was a place where sick and weary travelers could seek comfort and care before continuing on their journey. The **hospice** of today likewise provides comfort and care but with the knowledge that the recipients are nearing the end of their life's journey—that they are dying. (The word *hospice* is Latin for "host" or "guest.") The approach is modeled after St. Christopher's Hospice in England, in operation since 1967. It entails a variety of programs designed to afford an alternative to conventional hospital care for the terminally ill, especially cancer patients:

> Hospice neither hastens nor postpones death. It affirms life, recognizes dying as a part of the normal process of living, and focuses on maintaining the quality of remaining life. (P. North, 1998)

Polls show that most people are less terrified of dying than they are of dying an agonizing, painful, impersonal, and undignified death among machines and strangers. Although few people can be accorded a "perfect death," most can be free of pain; and the fear of terror, isolation, and chaos can be replaced by calm and control. Many hospice proponents believe that rather than debating euthanasia and assisted suicide, the nation should have a national debate about care for the dying (Chase, 1995). There were an estimated 3,300 hospice programs in the United States in 2003 (National Hospice and Palliative Care Organization, 2004). It should be noted that hospice is a concept of care not a place (Hospice Foundation of America, 2005). A typical hospice staff includes nurses, clergy, social workers, physicians, and a host of volunteers.

The hospice program takes a positive attitude toward dying. It does not discontinue such medical treatments as chemotherapy and radiation when they are conducive to the comfort of the patient. But the emphasis falls on "comfort-care" rather than on attempts to prolong life. Comfort-care involves an aggressive treatment of symptoms, both physical and emotional, through the use of psychological, religious, and nutritional counseling, antidepressant medications, and high-dose morphine preparations (designed to free patients from the severe and recurrent pain that frequently accompanies terminal cancer). Significantly, a study of patients at major cancer centers reveals that nearly half are reluctant to report their pain. Others are reluctant to take pain medication for fear that when their pain becomes truly intolerable, it will then be ineffective. And others fear that narcotic painkillers will result in addiction. Many physicians share these misconceptions. Yet much can be done to ease the pain and suffering of patients (and their families) with cancer, AIDS, and degenerative neuromuscular disorders (Lang & Patt, 1994). Children, too, can be well served by hospice care (Himelstein et al., 2004).

Most hospice programs are centered about caring for the dying person at home. Reportedly, most people said

Table 19.3 Warning Signs of Suicide

Signs Among Elderly	Behavioral Signs Typical for Teens	Environmental Signs	Verbal Cues
Severe physical illness	Lack of energy or increased fatigue	Previous suicide attempts by a family member or friend	Direct statements that may need immediate attention:
Chronic pain	Acting bored or disinterested	Problems at school	"I want to die."
Marked change in body image	Tearful sadness	Family violence	"I don't want to live anymore."
Loss of significant emotional ties	Difficulty concentrating or making decisions, confusion	Sexual abuse	"Life sucks and I want to get out."
Decrease in level of socialization	Silent or withdrawn	Major family change	"I won't be a problem much longer."
Lack of a religious faith	Angry and destructive behaviors		"Nothing matters anymore."
Physical disability	Less interest in usual activities		
Cognitive deficiencies	Giving away prized possessions		
Change in or loss of familiar surroundings	Poor school performance		
Isolation	Dwelling on death in creative activities, such as music, poetry, and artwork		
Loss of functional capacities	Difficulty sleeping or change in sleeping patterns		
Reduction of responsibilities	Increased thrill-seeking and risky behaviors		
	Increased use of drugs and alcohol		
	Change in appearance or cleanliness		
	Change in appetite or eating habits		
	Suddenly cheerful after a depression		

From: Gary J. Kennedy, ed., *Suicide and Depression in Late Life*, p. 88. Copyright © 1996 by John Wiley & Sons, Inc. Reprinted by permission of John Wiley & Sons, Inc.

that if they were terminally ill and had only six months to live, they would prefer to receive care and die in their own home or that of a family member. In 2003, of all Americans who died, about 25 percent died at home. For patients under hospice care, 50 percent died at home (National Hospice and Palliative Care Organization, 2004). More hospice services are offered now through hospitals as well as in the patient's home. In a hospital hospice setting, families are included as part of the treatment, visiting hours are unlimited, and day beds are available in the patient's room so family members may stay overnight to be with a loved one as needed. Physicians, nurses, social workers, and volunteers provide emotional and spiritual assistance as well as medical care—either in the patient's home or in this special unit of the hospital.

But the concept of hospice is not so much a place as it is a program or a mode of care. It seeks to give dying patients greater independence and control over their lives so that they do not have to surrender themselves to the care of impersonal bureaucratic organizations. Consequently, hospice services can be quite personal. One hospice had a client whose one wish was to walk again, and so the hospice arranged for a physical therapist that helped the man regain his ability to walk. Another client wanted to make a last trip to Hawaii, and the hospice set it up (Walters, 1991). In sum, the hospice movement undertakes to restore dignity to death.

Advocates of the hospice approach say that it is difficult for physicians and nurses taking care of patients in hospital settings to accept the inevitability of death. Hospitals are geared to curing illness and prolonging life. An incurable case is an embarrassment, evidence of medical failure. Consequently, hospice proponents say, an alternative-care arrangement is required that accepts the inevitability of death and provides for the needs of the dying and their families. Hospice programs hope to

Hospice A hospice provides comfort (including painkillers) and care for terminally ill patients without providing extraordinary measures. Here grandchildren spend time with their grandmother in a hospice setting, which might include being at home.

make dying less emotionally traumatic for both patient and loved ones. Indeed, much effort is directed toward helping family members face the problems that surround terminal illness.

The visiting home-care staff also assists the family with changing bedding, securing all necessary medical equipment, informing the hospice nurse or physician when the patient is in great discomfort and may need to change pain medication, and might sit for long hours with the patient or family members during reminiscence, or discuss many spiritual questions about death and dying. They also give the immediate family members time for a brief respite, if needed. Each patient and family is treated with dignity and warmth. A bereavement follow-up service maintains contact with the family in the period following the loved one's death. Most major health insurance plans, including Medicare, now cover virtually the entire cost of treatment in hospices that meet standards set by the U.S. Department of Health and Human Services. However, there are some patients (and families) who feel anxious about death and dying and opt to be in a typical hospital setting getting aggressive medical treatment for their last days of life.

Question

What is the philosophy of the hospice approach to dying from a terminal illness, and who is most likely to be eligible for these services?

The Dying Process

Throughout history, human societies seemingly have given death their most elaborate and reverent attention

(Ariès, 1978, 1981; Ashenburg, 2002; Rees, 1996). Some of the world's most gigantic constructions, its most splendid works of art, and its most elaborate rituals have been associated with death. Most recently, the elaborate funeral mass and burial of Pope John Paul II at the Vatican in Rome was witnessed by at least 1 billion people via TV, with hundreds of thousands from around the world making the pilgrimage in his honor. More than 500,000 years ago, ceremonial rituals for burying the dead were being employed by Peking Man. And we still are awed by the Egyptian pyramids (and the fascination with King Tut), the huge European burial mound of Silbury Hill, the towering Pyramid Tomb of the High Priest in the Central American Yucatan forest, the beehive tombs at Mycenae, the Taj Mahal, more than 40,000 megalithic burial mounds of northwestern Europe, and areas of Stonehenge in England (once a ritual burial ground for chieftains and leaders) ("English Heritage," 2005).

Monotheistic world religions—Judaism, Christianity, and Islam—put an end to the practice of burying or cremating the elite dead with wives, concubines, slaves, horses, jewels, armor, and other luxuries in hopes of guaranteeing their enjoyment and comfort on their journey to the next world (Ashenburg, 2002). However, in a major shift in thinking, Christianity changed the elaborate rituals surrounding the act of dying, mourning, and funerals with new convictions that every human being was equal in the eyes of God, and death was a release into a better life with God. The same Mass of Christian Burial is said for everyone, rich or poor (Ashenburg, 2002). Such rituals, including many prayers, serve to honor the deceased, help the deceased's soul through a transitional realm of Purgatory to heaven, and reintegrate a family or community after a crisis. The U.S. funeral industry emerged after the Civil War when it also became acceptable to embalm bodies in order that loved ones could view the body for final farewells (Laderman, 2003). Today in industrialized societies we so rarely have personal contact with the deceased because the funeral industry has become a corporate conglomerate of immense proportions and control. Local funeral directors and clergy typically provide loved ones comfort and guidance with specific rituals and religious ceremonies.

Defining Death

To lend a little wit to a morbid topic, comic George Carlin says, "Death is caused by swallowing small amounts of saliva over a long period of time." For centuries, using only sheer observation, some just might have thought that a plausible cause of death. The earliest biblical sources, as well as English common law, considered a person's ability to breathe independently to be the prime index of life. This view coincided with the physiological state of the organism. In the past, absence of spontaneous breath or heartbeat resulted in the prompt death of the brain. Conversely, destruction of the brain produced prompt cessation of respiration and circulation.

Over the past 45 years, technological advances have rendered these traditional definitions of death obsolete. In 1962, Johns Hopkins University physicians developed a coordinated method of resuscitation by artificial ventilation, heart compression (CPR), and electric shock (defibrillation) by which many victims of cardiac arrest can be saved. Another advance has been the invention of the mechanical respirator, which sustains breathing when the brain is no longer sending out the proper signals to the lungs. Still another technological innovation has been the use of an artificial pacemaker to induce regular heartbeat after failure of the heart's own electrical conduction system. And dialysis machines prolong the lives of patients suffering kidney failure. More recently, successful organ transplants have prolonged life because a person diagnosed as "brain dead" has willed his or her organs to be used for transplantation to the life of others (or without such documentation the family decides). As medical procedures are invented that can prolong life, the definition of death becomes more complex (Truog, 2004). (See the *Further Developments* box on page 660, "End of Life—Who Decides.")

These life-extending technologies have compelled courts and legislatures to grapple with new definitions of death. The need to accept brain death as one standard has now been acknowledged in most states and endorsed by the American Medical Association, the American Bar Association, and in 1981 by the President's Commission for the Study of Ethical Problems in Medicine and the *Uniform Determination of Death Act.* **Brain death** occurs when there is no activity in the brain. When the thinking part of the brain (cortex) and the thalamus (which connects the brain stem to the cortex) no longer function, the patient is considered brain dead ("When Does the Brain Go Blank," 2005). The first stage of total brain death is *cerebral death* (the cerebral cortex is no longer functioning). However, the patient might still have a functioning lower brain stem (which regulates breathing, pulse, blood pressure, and other vital functions). A series of landmark court decisions have upheld the validity of the brain-death criterion. Many of these cases involved *transplantation of organs* (such as cornea, kidney, lung, liver, or heart). With organ extraction, the patient's heart is still beating so that the organs still have blood circulating, and it has come to light that the patient's body reacts to the extraction (done without anesthesia because the patient is "brain dead").

As one might expect, definitions as to what constitutes death afford an ethical minefield and have fueled a continuing debate among medical professionals, bioethicists, and legal scholars (Truog, 2004). This is especially true for individuals in **persistent vegetative states,** where the functions of the brainstem, such as breathing and circulation, remain intact, but the person loses the higher functioning of the cerebral cortex. The patient in a persistent vegetative state has periods of sleep and wakefulness and responds to some stimuli such as light and noise. The patient may have gag and swallowing reflexes. Although it might appear to be so, the patient does not have the capability of emotional response, cognition, or willful activity (Quill, 2004). In cases such as Nancy Cruzan, Karen Ann Quinlan, and Terri Schiavo, who were deemed to be legally alive, the courts ruled that families can allow persistent vegetative patients to die by withholding food and water. The case of Terri Schiavo elicited some unprecedented public attention. The general public, right-to-die groups, right-to-life groups, the legal community, medical community, and political community hotly expressed divergent views. The legal battles related to the Schiavo case were brought to public attention by the media and the woman's biological family, spawning further controversy and debate (Annas, 2005). In the end, a judicial decision was upheld, backed by the criminal justice system. However, the patient in this case, being rather young at the time of her collapse, had not prepared any legal documents to inform of her own wishes concerning the manner of death.

Confronting One's Own Death

People differ considerably in the degree to which they are consciously aware of death (Rees, 1997). Some individuals erect formidable defenses to shield themselves from facing the reality that they too must die. The well-to-do investment bankers of stem-cell research in California are hoping to prolong their lives. Three American companies offer human life preservation in a suspended state through *cryonics* life-support technology, and the body of the famous ball player Ted Williams is cryogenically frozen (Sandomir, 2005). Using cryopreservation, a person's body is kept in a state that might be viable and treatable by future medicine. Researchers in biostasis medicine expect that future *nanotechnology* methods will be able to heal at the cellular and molecular levels (Drexler, 1986).

Medical uses: Molecular machine systems will be able to sense and rearrange patterns of molecules in the human body, providing the tools needed to bring about a state of health, regardless of a disease's cause. (MIT Chemist Christine Peterson tells of societal implications in an address to a Congressional committee, 2003)

At present, in one manner or another, everyone must adapt to the fact of their own dying and death. Indeed, a realistic acceptance of death may well be the hallmark of emotional maturity. Its meaning tends to vary from individual to individual. Some elderly visualize death as the dissolution of bodily life and the doorway to a new

Further Developments

End of Life—Who Decides?

Most people wish for a death free of pain and suffering. Yet death is inevitable and the best one can hope for is a "good death." Precisely what this entails varies among individuals. Although some might wish to slip away peacefully in their sleep, others might wish to be conscious and surrounded by loved ones. Yet others may wish to die a heroic death in a flurry of glory or sacrifice. Notwithstanding our wishes, no one of us knows precisely when or how we will die. We each must face death in our own way.

Death, however, is the end point of life. It is dying—the final process of between life and death that raises ethical, religious, medical, legal, social, and cultural questions (Searight & Gafford, 2005). How one dies and who decides are issues that arise when a person faces a terminal illness, or is not competent to make his or her own medical decisions, or has not prepared legal documentation on final wishes. In 2005, Terri Schindler-Schiavo's case, a woman living with brain damage, brought these issues to the forefront of public attention. As the baby-boom cohort faces the end of life, such issues will become paramount.

Having a clear, written statement of one's final wishes can bring a measure of comfort. One might wish to draw up what are called "advance directives," such as a *living will* (see the *More Information You Can Use* box on page 651, "An Example of a Living Will"), an organ donor certificate, a *DNR* (do not resuscitate), or a durable *power of attorney* (designating someone to make medical decisions if the patient is unable). The ethical conclusions one comes to are extremely important and can have a great impact on loved ones, medical personnel, clergy, and the legal system. For clarification, it might be helpful to pose some hypothetical situations.

Let us suppose that a person facing a terminal illness is mentally competent and able to express his wishes. The person is facing real or anticipated suffering as the illness progresses through physical pain and/or incapacitation. Perhaps the first point of decision making would center on the person's moral/religious beliefs as to euthanasia and suicide. The suffering might be a small price to pay compared to committing a sin. A study of 200 older adults' views on end-of-life decisions found that their decisions were greatly influenced by their religiosity, value for the preservation of life as well as for the quality of life, fear of death, and locus of control belief (Cicirelli & MacLean, 2000).

After consideration of the religious/moral perspective, one might consider "How would this affect my family and loved ones?" The legal aspects regarding insurance and other death benefits might also be considered to provide security for one's family. What medical options are available if palliative care should become ineffective? *Palliative care* is the attempt to relieve uncomfortable symptoms and is given in conjunction with treatment for the disease. Hospice care, at home or in the hospital, offers symptom relief.

According to a 2004 Gallup poll, 65 percent of those surveyed agreed that a doctor should be permitted to assist a patient suicide when the person has an incurable disease and is in pain (Schwartz & Estrin, 2005). Physician-assisted suicide (PAS) is legal only in the state of Oregon. In 1997 Oregon enacted its *Death with Dignity Act.* It has been challenged unsuccessfully in court and by referendum (Okie, 2005). The legislation allows doctors to prescribe lethal doses of medications—but the patient must administer them. One study found that more educated adults and single or divorced persons were more likely to use PAS (Wineberg & Werth, 2003). In 2004, 37 Oregonians used PAS (Niemeyer, 2005).

Voluntarily refusing food and fluids is a legal way to end one's life. Nurses were surveyed who have witnessed the deaths of patients who chose self-starvation. In one survey nurses rated the quality of this method of death on a scale from 0 (very bad death) to 9 (very good death) and reported a median score of 8 (Ganzini et al., 2003). However, this method takes several days until death in younger patients, and in some cases it was described as a gruesome way to die (Jacobs, 2003). (Recall current images of starving African children, or victims with severe anorexia, and Holocaust victims in Germany during World War II.) *Terminal sedation* involves having a physician administer medication to induce a coma, along with withholding hydration and nutrition. In 1997 the U.S. Supreme Court decided it was legal, but this practice raises many issues. Physicians, who take an oath to uphold life and do no harm, often find it to be a moral dilemma. Another legal practice is the withholding of life-sustaining treatment. This practice precedes 84 percent of hospital deaths (Gellick, 2004).

Source: Walt Handelsman Copyright 2005, Tribune Media Services. Reprinted with permission.

Any of the decisions involved in end-of-life care are difficult. But with knowledge and forethought, one can make informed decisions—but it is also important to share such wishes with family members to reduce any confusion should such a situation arise. Undoubtedly, there might be debate, but taking the time to reflect on personal beliefs and final wishes can provide comfort to the individual and loved ones left behind.

life, a passing into another world. Those with Western religious convictions often express the belief that in death they will be reunited with loved ones who have died. For such individuals, death is seen as a transition to a better state of being; few say that death will entail punishment. One study using regression analysis found that self-efficacy variables (factors pertaining to a person's perception of being able to achieve desired outcomes in life) were predictors of fear of dying and fear of the unknown after death in older adults. Spiritual health efficacy variables were important predicators for women and instrumental efficacy variables were important for men (Fry, 2003b). Although individuals vary in the extent of their fear of death, it is perhaps quite normal to fear the process of dying:

> No, I'm not afraid to die—it seems to me to be a
> perfectly normal process. But you never know how
> you will feel when it comes to a showdown. I might get
> panicky. (Jeffers & Verwoerdt, 1969, p. 170)

And a 90-year-old man put it this way: "I'm afraid of the unknown, and if I had my druthers, I'd rather not do it" (quoted by Chase, 1995, p. B1). One of the most frequent questions asked of health practitioners about dying (incidentally, also asked about giving birth by mothers about to have a baby) is "How long is it going to take, and is it going to hurt?" Generally, younger people show greater fear of death than persons 65 and over (Riley, 1983).

Physicians caring for the elderly report that patients frequently say, "I am not so much afraid of death as I am of dying." A survey conducted for AARP found that only one-fourth of respondents (Americans over age 18) wanted to live to the age of 100, two-thirds said they did not, and 10 percent did not answer or said they weren't sure. The survey determined that 91 is the average age people wished to reach ("Study Finds Living to be 100 Isn't a Major Goal for Average American," 1999). Furthermore, the survey found that the greatest fear of old age is declining health (46 percent), followed by concerns about having enough money (38 percent), losing mental faculties (13 percent), and dependence on others (12 percent) (Levy, 1999). More than a century ago Canadian physician Sir William Osler, in a study of some 500 deaths, found that only 18 percent of the dying suffered physical pain and only 2 percent felt any great anxiety. Osler concluded: "We speak of death as the king

of terrors, and yet how rarely the act of dying appears to be painful" (Ferris, 1991, p. 44).

A Life Review   Psychologist Robert N. Butler (1971) suggests that the elderly tend to take stock of their lives, to reflect and reminisce about it—a process he calls the **life review.** Often the review proceeds silently without obvious manifestations and provides a positive force in personality reorganization. In some cases, however, it finds pathological expression in intense guilt, self-deprecation, despair, and depression. Reviewing one's life can be a response to crises of various types—such as retirement, the death of one's spouse, or one's own imminent death. In Butler's opinion, the life review is an important element in an individual's overall adjustment to death, a continuation of personality development right to the very end of life. Butler's notions of life review have generally held sway for many years, although some critique exists (Merriam, 1993). Nevertheless, some people are helped along in the life review process if they write autobiographical accounts of their lives or if a close family member (often a grandchild) does a videotaped interview. Life reviews can give new meaning to people's present lives by helping them understand the past more fully (Birren, 1987). To the extent that the elderly are able to achieve a sense of lifetime integrity, competence, and continuity, the life-review process contributes to their successful aging by increasing their self-understanding, personal meaning, self-esteem, and life satisfaction (Staudinger, Smith, & Baltes, 1992). (*Reminiscence* and conducting *a life review* are discussed in detail in Chapter 18.)

Changes Before Death   Various investigators report that systematic psychological changes occur before death, even several months ahead of the event, in what is sometimes called the *death drop.* These changes do not appear to be a simple result of physical illness. Individuals who become seriously ill and recover apparently do not exhibit similar changes. Morton Lieberman and Annie S. Coplan (1970) report, for instance, that individuals whom they later found to be a year or less away from death showed poorer cognitive performance, lower introspective orientation, and a less aggressive and more docile self-image on personality tests than did those who were three or more years away from death. A number of researchers also report a decline in measured intelligence and the complexity of information processing for those who die within a year

as compared with those who die several years later (White & Cunningham, 1988). Psychomotor performance tests, depression scales, and self-report health ratings likewise have predictive value and can alert the physician to the patient's decline (American Geriatrics Society, 1996). Furthermore, research from the *Berlin Aging Study* reveals that those who live into their "Fourth Age" typically experience a critical loss in intellectual functioning, higher incidence of depression, and dementia that is predictive of needing help with survival (Baltes & Smith, 2001).

Not all dying people panic when realizing their death is impending. Some become nostalgic, want to see people they have not seen for a long time, want to patch up differences with loved ones, and become more sensitive to those who will be left behind. Some take the opportunity to enhance relationships and forgive long-held grudges and misunderstandings.

> **Questions**
>
> Is there a universal experience of dying or is it highly individualistic? Do you think there is a cultural component to how one views death?

Near-Death Experiences

The theme of "a beautiful death" has been linked by some with belief in a life hereafter. The "life after life"

movement—supported and researched by Dr. Elisabeth Kübler-Ross, Dr. Ray Moody, Dr. Brian L. Weiss, Dr. Bruce Greyson, Betty Eadie, and others—claims evidence of a spiritual existence beyond death. Greyson (1999) presents criteria for defining near-death experiences. Some persons pronounced clinically dead who have been resuscitated by medical measures or by some miraculous intervention have told of having left their bodies and undergone otherworldly experiences before they were resuscitated. Plato wrote about such an event centuries ago in the *Republic*, says Dr. Bruce Greyson, psychiatrist and NDE researcher, and such reports seem to be prevalent across all cultures (Koerner, 1997). A **near-death experience (NDE)** commonly is precipitated by medical illness, traumatic accident, surgical operation, childbirth, or drug ingestion. An estimated 7 million people have reported near-death experiences ("Brushes with Death," 2002). "I had a floating sensation . . . and I looked back and I could see myself on the bed below (Moody, 1976).

The "typical" report runs along the following lines (Morse, 1992; Rees, 1997): The dying individuals feel themselves leave their bodies and watch, as spectators, from a few yards above their bodies, the resuscitation efforts being made to save them. Then, about a third of them report passing through a tunnel and entering some unearthly realm. "I went through this dark black vacuum at super speed" (Moody, 1976). Half say they see guides or the spirits of departed relatives, a religious figure, or a "being of light." "From the moment the light spoke to me, I felt really good—secure, and loved" (Moody, 1976). Many individuals report having approached a sort of border, seemingly representing the divide between earthly and next-worldly life. But they are told they cannot cross the divide now. They are told they must go back to earth, for the time of their death has not yet arrived. They resist turning back to life, for they are overwhelmed by intense feelings of love, joy, and peace. In some metaphysical manner, they are then reunited with their physical body and they live.

A near-death experience can be a catalyst for spiritual awakening and development in the months and years following the episode. Many individuals develop firmer beliefs in God and an afterlife, become less materialistic and more spiritual, feel a greater love for other people, and spend more time searching for the meaning of life (Rees, 1997). The more NDEs are openly discussed, the more thousands of people claim to have experienced such an otherworldly experience. However, a neuroscientist in a research setting at Laurentian University in Sudbury, Ontario, has induced many of the characteristics of an NDE by stimulating the brain's right temporal lobe, the area of the brain above the right ear that is responsible for perception (Koerner, 1997). A recent study found that the temporal lobe may have an effect on near-death experiences and that people who experience this may have physiological distinctions as well as positive coping styles (Britton & Bootzin, 2004).

Cardiologist Bruce Greyson studied cardiac patients who reported near-death experiences and found that they tend to be younger than other patients and more likely to have lost consciousness; however, they did not differ in sociodemographic variables (Greyson, 2003). Psychologist Ronald K. Siegel (1981) suggests that the visions reported by dying people are virtually identical to the descriptions given by individuals experiencing drug-induced hallucinations, who often report hearing voices and seeing bright lights and tunnel imagery. The episodes, Siegel says, derive from intense arousal of the central nervous system and disorganization of the brain's normal information-processing procedures. Another major skeptic is Daniel Alkon (Koerner, 1997), chief of the Neural Systems Laboratory at the National Institutes of Health, who says *anoxia* (oxygen deprivation to the brain) can induce such mental states. An anesthesiologist attributed reports of bright lights and tunnels to the effect of lack of oxygen on the retina of the eye. He also attributes the sensation of floating or flying to the tensing and relaxing of muscle spindles (the portion of the muscle fiber that transmits these sensations to the brain) (Woerlee, 2004).

In England, Karl Jansen has zeroed in on the shifting levels of a brain neurotransmitter called *ketamine* (Koerner, 1997). A related interpretation holds that at death various forces combine to sever the connections between consciousness and somatic processes while the brain remains active. Dying people who are aware that they are dying may turn their thoughts to the possibility of reuniting with loved ones, and the broader meaning of life. And experiences of intense joy, profound insight, and love may be produced by *endorphins* (molecules that act as both neurotransmitters and hormones), which were designed in the course of evolution to blot out overwhelming pain (Irwin, 1985).

Psychologist Robert Kastenbaum (1977) suggests that the current fascination with "life after life" is simply another "mind trip." He cites cases of some heart-attack victims who, when pronounced clinically dead and then resuscitated, have no recollection of an out-of-body experience. And he tells of people in respiratory failure (choking on a bone or undergoing an acute episode of emphysema) who later report feeling as though they had been in direct hand-to-hand combat with death. Kastenbaum (1977, p. 33) expresses concern lest death be "romanticized" and cautions:

> Death seems to be less demanding, perhaps more friendly, than life. . . . I do not believe the frustrated adolescent, the unemployed worker, the grieving widow or the ailing old person needs to be offered the invitation to suicide on quite so glittering a silver platter.

Hence, there is considerable controversy about near-death experiences, and researchers on both sides of this issue continue to investigate NDEs in as scientific a manner as possible.

Questions

What elements are common in descriptions of near-death experiences? How do scientists explain such sensations?

Religious Beliefs

Notions of life after death have old roots. Ancient Greek philosophy frequently mentioned Hades, the Bible speaks of the "kingdom of Heaven," and Eastern religions speak of realms of life we'll inhabit after this one. Many Eastern religions, such as Hinduism, profess an afterlife and reincarnation of the souls of animals and people and teach their followers not to harm animals or people. Native Americans and the Aborigines of Australia also believe in an afterlife. In the New Testament, Jesus spoke about the kingdom of Heaven as a place of eternal reward:

> I go to prepare a place for you, and if I go to prepare a place for you I will come again, and receive you to myself; that where I am you may be also (John 14:2–3).

Christian theologians traditionally have viewed the book of Revelation as providing the most vivid and familiar biblical images of a mystical heaven: images of "pearly gates and streets of gold, of a vast white throne, and of throngs of saints and angels gathered around God at the culmination of history" (Sheler, 1997). Having ushered in the new millennium, a proliferation of writings about being "born again," the signs of the Apocalypse, the second coming of Christ, and the "Rapture" have a powerful influence on some Christians and others in their views of an afterlife. Strikingly, "nearly 80 percent of Americans—of various religious faiths and of none—say they believe in life after death, and two thirds are certain there is a heaven" (Sheler, 1997). In his book *Teaching Your Children About God*, Rabbi David Wolpe reminds us of the experience of birth into the unknown world of joyous waiting arms, as is the classic view of the afterlife—a birth into a place that we humans can only try to imagine (Sheler, 1997, p. 66). *Agnostics* are unsure about the existence of an afterlife, whereas *atheists* believe that death is the end of their existence.

The Jewish position has been that no one knows the nature of life after death, and therefore speculation is pointless and to be discouraged. Judaism rejects the concept of hell, but Orthodox Jews do believe that in a Messianic era there will be a resurrection—a time when the souls and bodies of the dead will be reunited.

Most Buddhists believe that the body retains "life" for 8 to 12 hours after death, and so it is possible to speak and act in a meaningful way with the deceased. That the person still exists after death has implications for Buddhists because their idea of rebirth hinges on the fact that people experience changes in consciousness every moment. For the Buddhist, every instant involves the death and rebirth of consciousness. In the moment just before death, each person recollects parts of their past lives and glimpses of the future. Then the mind drops into a nonaware state, only to reawaken into one of the six realms of the universe: Hell, Hungry Ghost, Animal, Human, Jealous Gods, or Gods. None of these realms is very desirable, and Buddhism teaches a doctrine of liberation from *karma* into a state of *nirvana*. This detailed picture of the after-death state is very different from the uncertain picture in the West about the nature of afterlife and after-death experience.

Dying

Social scientists observe that modern societies attempt to control death by turning over its management to large, bureaucratic organizations (Rees, 1997). Only a few generations ago, most people in the United States died at home surrounded by family and closest friends. Before the twentieth century, doors on homes were built wide enough to allow a coffin to pass through them, and home parlors were designed to hold mourners. The family assumed the responsibility for laying out the corpse and otherwise preparing for the funeral. Today,

" WELCOME TO THE NEIGHBORHOOD, MR. ROGERS..."

Mr. Rogers' New Neighborhood Writers and artists often depict an afterlife in biblical images of pearly gates, a vast white throne, and of throngs of saints and angels gathered around God at the culmination of history. How befitting it is to imagine America's beloved favorite neighbor for over 30 years (and Presbyterian minister) being greeted so warmly to his new neighborhood.
Source: Bill Schorr. © United Features Syndicate, Inc.

in general, the nursing home or hospital typically cares for the terminally ill and manages the crisis of dying. A mortuary establishment—euphemistically called a "home"—prepares the body and makes the funeral arrangements or undertakes the cremation. The exceptions to this are evident among pockets of immigrants in this country who are unaware that they are required by law to notify various authorities of any death—and some of these families still attempt to manage death and burial according to their cultural customs.

This bureaucratization of death minimizes the average person's exposure to death. The dying and the dead are segregated from others and placed with specialists for whom contact with death has become a routine and impersonal matter (Kamerman, 1988). But as we become increasingly less exposed to death, we have less opportunity to learn and pass along the lessons of how to cope adequately with it. Often neither the person who is dying nor the family and friends understand how to deal with death. These trends concern many thanatologists, who point out that people are often ill-equipped to do the "grief work" so essential to coming to terms with the death of a loved one. Sometimes grief seems to be even more prolonged on a massive scale when a prominent person such as John Kennedy or a celebrity dies an early or tragic death, such as Elvis, Marilyn Monroe, John Lennon, the Mexican-American pop singer Selena, or Princess Diana. Witness the proliferation of Web sites set up in their memory. And they point out that funerals, memorial services, and other forms of grieving rites give continuity to both family and community life.

Stages of Dying Over the past 30 years, Elisabeth Kübler-Ross (1969, 1981) has contributed a good deal to the movement to restore dignity and humanity to death and to reinstate the process of dying to the full course of human life. She noted that when medical personnel and the family attempt to hide the fact that a patient is dying, they create a barrier that prevents everyone from preparing for death. Furthermore, the dying patient generally sees through the make-believe. Kübler-Ross found that it is better for all parties if their genuine emotions are respected and allowed expression. In this fashion, dying can afford a new opportunity for personal growth. Indeed, surveys reveal that four out of five individuals would want to be told if they had an incurable disease. And today, physicians are sharing with patients and their families medical information as to the likely outcome of an illness.

> If you can begin to see death as an invisible, but friendly, companion, on your life's journey—gently reminding you not to wait till tomorrow to do what you mean to do—then you can live your life rather than simply passing through it. (Elisabeth Kübler-Ross (1993, p. 47)

Thanatologists are finding that dying, like living, is a process. Though there are different styles of dying, just as there are different styles of living, some elements are common to the death experience. Kübler-Ross (1969) observed that dying persons typically pass through five stages. Not everyone goes through all the stages, some slip back and forth between stages, and some experience several stages at the same time. According to Dr. Elisabeth Kübler-Ross, who had a series of strokes and died in 2004, these are the five stages:

1. *Denial.* Individuals resist acknowledging the reality of impending death. In effect, they say "No!" to it.
2. *Anger.* Dying people ask the question "Why me?" They might look at the persons around them and feel envy, jealousy, and rage over their health and vigor. During this phase a dying person often makes life difficult for others, criticizing friends, family, and medical personnel with little justification.
3. *Bargaining.* Dying individuals often begin to bargain with God, fate, or the illness itself, hoping to arrange a temporary truce. For instance, a dying person might say, "Just let me live long enough to attend my son's marriage," or "Allow me to get my business in order." In turn the patient promises to be "good" or to do something constructive during his or her remaining time alive. The "bargain" generally is successful for only a short period, because the advance of the illness itself invalidates the "agreement."
4. *Depression.* Dying people begin to mourn their own approaching death, the loss of all the people and things they have found meaningful, and the plans and dreams never to be fulfilled—they experience what Kübler-Ross terms "preparatory grief."
5. *Acceptance.* The dying have by this time mourned their impending loss, and they begin to contemplate the coming of the end with a degree of quiet expectation. In most cases they are tired and quite weak. They no longer struggle against death but make their peace with it.

Says Kübler-Ross about the fifth stage:

> Acceptance should not be mistaken for a happy stage. It is almost void of feelings. It is as if the pain had gone, the struggle is over, and there comes a time for "the final rest before the long journey," as one patient phrased it. (Kübler-Ross, 1969, p. 113)

Although noting the many important contributions of Kübler-Ross's pioneering work on death and dying, conducted over many years with thousands of patients, some believe the linear stage model of grief and bereavement is too confining and requires further study (Corr, 2001).

Kastenbaum's Trajectories of Death Psychologist Robert Kastenbaum (1975) points out that although Kübler-Ross's theory has merit, it neglects certain aspects of the dying process. One of the most important is the nature of the disease itself, which generally determines pain, mobility, the length of the terminal period, and the like:

> Within the realm of cancer alone, for example, the person with head or neck cancer looks and feels different from the person with leukemia. The person with emphysema, subject to terrifying attacks in which each breath of air requires a struggle, experiences his situation differently from the person with advanced renal failure, or with a cardiovascular trajectory [condition]. Although Kübler-Ross's theory directs welcome attention to the universal psychosocial aspects of terminal illness, we also lose much sensitivity if the disease process itself is not fully respected. (Kastenbaum, 1975, p. 43)

Other factors that must be considered are differences in sex, ethnic-group membership, personality, developmental level, and the death environment (a private home or a hospital). Kastenbaum believes that Kübler-Ross's stages are very narrow and subjective interpretations of the dying experience. He claims that her stages are cast with an exaggerated salience and are isolated from the total context of the individual's previous life and current circumstances. And he is concerned lest this stage approach encourage an attitude in which, for instance, medical personnel or the family are able to say, "He is just going through the anger stage," when there may be concrete, realistic factors that are arousing the patient's ire (Kastenbaum & Costa, 1977).

Causes of Death

The most recent comprehensive statistics on causes of death available at the time of publication of this text come from the 1993 National Mortality Followback Survey (NMFS)—the first study since the 1980s to examine detailed patterns of mortality by supplementing the information provided by birth certificates with interviews of next of kin. This survey, published by the Centers for Disease Control and Prevention (1998), allowed for the examination of trends in mortality, differences by income and education, risk factors and causes of death, and health-care utilization in the last year of life. This survey was based on examination of nearly 23,000 records of individuals aged 15 years and older who died in 1993. This sample of subjects was drawn from all states except South Dakota (where state law restricts the use of death certificate information). Here is a summary of the major findings:

Where does death occur?

- 56 percent of deaths occur in a hospital, clinic, or medical center.
- 21 percent of people died at home.
- 19 percent died in a nursing home.

What diseases did people have?

- 25 percent had had a heart attack and about an equal number had angina; more than 40 percent had hypertension.
- Other frequent conditions were cancer and arthritis, each reported for about one-third of decedents.
- 15 percent suffered from memory impairment.

How many smoked or used drugs or alcohol?

- 50+ percent of all decedents smoked cigarettes at some point in their lives.
- About 25 percent of all decedents used alcohol during the last year of their life.
- 29 percent of drinkers used alcohol every day.
- About 2 percent used marijuana during their last year of life.
- Less than 1 percent were reported to have used other types of illicit drugs.

How was their last year of life?

- 58 percent of those with functional limitations received help at home from a spouse.
- 50 percent reported functional limitations due to physical or mental conditions the last year.

- 46 percent had daughters who provided care.
- 39 percent of the decedents took pain medication in the last year of life.
- 31 percent received help from visiting nurses.
- 10 percent were in bed most of their last year of life due to illness or injury.

For those who died of homicide, suicide, or fatal motor vehicle accident:

- 33 percent of decedents involved in fatal vehicle crashes were not wearing seatbelts.
- 19 percent had an alcoholic beverage within 4 hours of death.
- 17 percent had taken drugs or medication within 24 hours of death.
- Of the 36,000 firearm-related deaths, 72 percent involved handguns.

Who gets and pays for health care?

- 75 percent of decedents were covered by Medicare.
- 50+ percent were covered by private insurance or HMOs.
- For 46 percent, Medicare was the principal source of medical payments.
- 20 percent had private medical insurance.
- 10 percent paid for their own medical care.
- 10 percent relied upon Medicaid as the source of payment.
- 10 percent of decedents were reported to have never visited a doctor during the last year of life.
- Nearly 10 percent had made 50 visits or more for health care during the previous year.

Cancer—lung, prostate, and colorectal—has become the leading cause of death of Americans under age 85 (DeNoon, 2005). Other studies reported by the CDC indicate that overall death rates for heart disease, the second highest cause of death but still the main cause of death of those 85 and older, are now higher in the southeastern United States than in the Northeast, which previously was the region with the highest rates. Deaths by heart disease have declined in all areas during the past 30 years. HIV death rates are highest in states on the East and West Coasts and in nearly every urban area of the United States. Homicide, suicide, and motor vehicle injury deaths are also major public health problems in well-defined geographic patterns. Homicide rates are high for young black adults in urban areas, but for young white men the high rates are in southern and southwestern states. For young adults, motor vehicle death rates are higher in the southeastern states and generally in less densely populated areas (Centers for Disease Control and Prevention, 1998).

Other sources indicate that among children, the primary causes of death are in the understudied areas of accidents and injuries, which are now classified as "behavior-related" injuries and under closer research scrutiny (Midlife Passages, 1998a). Table 19.4 lists the major causes of death or disability by various age groups.

Questions

Is there a single major cause of death of adults in the United States? How does the major cause of death change across the life span?

Grief, Bereavement, and Mourning

We know for certain that there is life after death—for the relatives and friends who survive. As they go on with their lives, they must come to terms with the death of the loved one and make many types of adjustment. First, there is psychological coping, often termed "grief work" (mourning, talking about, and acknowledging the loss). Second, there are numerous procedural details that must be attended to, including funeral arrangements and legal routines (dealing with attorneys, settling the estate, filing for insurance, pension, and Social Security benefits, and the like). Third, there is the social void produced by the death of a family member, which requires revising life patterns and family roles (for instance, housekeeping, marketing, securing a livelihood). Where the death of a loved one is anticipated, individuals frequently experience **anticipatory grief**—a "state of emotional limbo, unable to resolve the loss because it has not yet occurred, and unable to avoid the authoritative diagnosis that death will occur" (Stephenson, 1985, p. 163). Life after the death of a loved is still difficult, even when one feels "prepared" for the inevitable.

Adjusting to the Death of a Loved One

Bereavement is a state in which a person has been deprived of a relative or friend by death. **Grief** involves keen mental anguish and sorrow over the death of a loved one. A person in initial grief is often said to be "numb" or in "shock" and likely to want to withdraw from social contact (Ashenburg, 2002). **Mourning** refers to the socially established manner of displaying signs of sorrow over a person's death (for instance, wailing, chanting, wearing black, draping windows and doorways in black, hanging flags at half-mast, writing obituaries, going to a cemetery daily, and the like).

Expressing Anguished Feelings In *Macbeth* Shakespeare proclaims: "Give sorrow words. The grief that does not speak, whispers the o'erfraught heart and bids

---

Table 19.4 Causes of Death in the United States by Developmental Stage: 2003

Causes are rank-ordered, with most frequent cause listed first.[1]

Adolescence (Ages 15 to 24)	Early Adulthood (Ages 25 to 44)	Mid Adulthood (Ages 45 to 64)	Advanced (Ages 65 and over)
Auto accidents	Auto accidents	Cancer (malignant neoplasms)	Heart disease[2]
All other accidents	All other accidents	Heart disease	Cancer (malignant neoplasms)
Assault (homicide)	Cancer (malignant neoplasms)	Auto accidents	Cerebrovascular diseases
Suicide	Heart disease	Other accidents	Chronic lower respiratory diseases
Cancer (malignant neoplasms)	Suicide	Diabetes	Alzheimer's disease
Heart disease	Assault (homicide)	Cerebrovascular disease	Influenza and pneumonia
Congenital malformations	HIV/AIDS disease	Chronic lower respiratory diseases	Diabetes
Influenza and pneumonia	Chronic liver disease and cirrhosis	Chronic liver disease and cirrhosis	Nephritis
Cerebrovascular diseases	Cerebrovascular diseases	Suicide	Motor vehicle accidents
Chronic lower respiratory disease	Diabetes	HIV/AIDS disease	Other accidents
HIV/AIDS disease	Influenza and pneumonia	Septicemia	Septicemia

[1]Note that in 2005 the Centers for Disease Control and Prevention reported that cancer (malignant neoplasms) is now the leading cause of death in adulthood, except for those 85 and older.
[2]Heart disease is still the leading cause of death for the "oldest old."
Source: Hoyert, D. L., Kung, H. C., & Smith, B. L. (2005, February 28). Deaths: Preliminary Data for 2003. *National Vital Statistics Reports, 53*(15), 28–29.

Celebrating a Death: Dr. Benjamin Spock The noted author of the classic book on child rearing died in 1998 at the age of 94. He lived an energetic life and spoke out on important parenting issues as well as other social causes. He requested a "New Orleans style of sendoff" for his own funeral, led by his widow, Mary Morgan. Ashenburg (2002) writes that mourners walking together is a part of all sacred funeral rituals.

it break." And a Turkish proverb declares, "He that conceals his grief finds no remedy for it." Many contemporary clinicians and psychologists agree with these statements. Sympathetic assistance can be all-important in the process of expressing anguished feelings. Rather than uttering platitudes ("She lived a full life"), psychologists suggest, well-meaning individuals can offer emotional support and a ready ear. Today in most communities there are support groups associated with nearly every cause of mortality to help other people go through their grief work. Bereavement is less an intellectual process than one of coming to terms with one's feelings. A social worker who found herself "on the fringe of madness" when her husband died of a heart attack eight years earlier, leaving her with three young children, said: "Being strong and bucking up is a lot of baloney. You don't feel like bucking up. It is a real process that you must be allowed to go through" (Gelman, 1983, p. 120). People who receive the support and comfort of family and friends typically have a lower incidence of mental and physical disorders following bereavement. And for most people the expression of grief following the death of a loved one is an important component in recovery. But there are exceptions. Those whose grief includes an intense yearning for and a high degree of dependency on

the deceased person tend to have a harder time recovering from their loss (Cleiren, 1993).

Culture and Grief Work Sometimes cultural expectations, social values, and community practices interfere with necessary grief work. Dying is often left to medical technology and commonly takes place in a clinical facility outside the home. Funerals are often brief and simplified, and mourning is thought of as a form of mental pathology (the cultural ideal is the self-contained widow who displays a "stiff upper lip"). Yet thanatologists say that expressions of grief and mourning rituals are therapeutic for survivors. Such traditions as the Irish wake and the Jewish *shivah* help the bereaved come to terms with the loss and reconstruct new life patterns with family and friends (see the *Human Diversity* box "A Native American Perspective on Death"). For those with a religious affiliation, church organizations can provide significant support systems (Romanoff & Terenzio, 1998).

In Japan, however, the bereaved are not expected to sever their relationship with the dead by the grief work that is promoted in the West. Japanese culture encourages the survivors to maintain a relationship with the deceased in the form of a family shrine. The family altar can be used to make direct contact with the spirit of the

Human Diversity

A Native American Perspective on Death

The Pulitzer Prize–winning author Studs Terkel has turned his talents to a book on the subject of death. The book, entitled *Will the Circle be Unbroken? Reflections on Death, Rebirth, and Hunger for a Faith,* is based on Turkel's interviews with people of different ages and a variety of backgrounds. The result is a collection of narratives that are personal, poignant, and deeply philosophical. The following is an excerpt from the book.

Vine Deloria: "I'm an old Indian politician, observer of events, and a writer." Deloria's most celebrated book is *Custer Died for Your Sins.* He taught for many years at the University of Colorado and is now retired, though still writing.

I grew up in a border town of about seven hundred people in Martin, South Dakota, right on the Pine Ridge Reservation. I had classmates die, get run over by tractors, drown. A good friend of mine died in those polio epidemics.

On the prairies, death was quite a big event. When I was a child, we had wakes, and they would last quite a while—maybe a couple of days before the actual burial service. A custom they started to do was very comforting: to have a giveaway a year after the funeral. They recognized that you can't observe all that grief in a two- or three-year period, So people set themselves aside for a whole year, and go out of their way to be helpful to other people, and people come in to comfort them. About a year after the person died, they have this big giveaway. They hold a big feast and they give things to everybody in the community. That's to mark the end of the mourning period. They recognize that losing a mate or a family member, a child, is very traumatic. In the old days, they used to cut their hair and gash their skin and go into mourning. Today, they announce that they're going to be mourning for a certain period of time. During that period, you're not supposed to talk harshly to them. Usually, the people in the community will help the grieving family to start accumulating things so they can have a big feast and giveaway a year afterwards. Some people very severely affected by a loss will have giveaways four years in a row.

That was the most comforting thing for me when my father died, looking forward to having a giveaway—that I could feed the people in that community, give them blankets and jackets and scarves and things like that. During the giveaway, I had to pass muster from the medicine man that I knew enough about the culture and language, that I was sincere in what I wanted to do. He used the anniversary of my father's death as an opportunity to tell all of the people what life meant and what death meant. He didn't spend his time talking about my father, so he didn't pull me back into the grief at all. He made me feel like my father, as all the other people who died on that reservation, had moved on. And we should move on, too.

The women up there loved these little blue porcelain, blue enamel bowls. So I just bought all kinds of 'em, handed 'em out. You accumulate goods, but all of your friends also contribute a quilt or a blanket. You basically are celebrating the life of the person who died, and you're thanking the community for their support during this whole year. You're a year away from the immediate shock of losing someone. At these giveaways, they always tell funny stories about funerals, or about someone dying, but they enable you to feel very good that you've really accomplished something by doing this. There's feasting, of course. They cook turkeys, hams, buffalo, whatever.

Just in the last four or five years, people on the reservation have been wanting to be buried up on a scaffold, like the Plains Indians did. They would wrap the body up very carefully and put it up on a scaffold. It would be just a little higher than a person's head. They would let the body disintegrate until it was just bones. They'd visit it every year, make sure that the thing hadn't fallen over. When it was just bones, then they would take the bones and hide them. This comes from the old belief that we are high on the foods. So then we have to return our bodies to the dust, so that the buffalo can feed off us. Scaffolding is coming back among reservation Indians who are reasonably well educated. They see the spiritual connection.

There definitely is a hereafter. There have been numerous near-death experiences, visions, which tell people about the hereafter, with valleys and game and everything. It's painted as a very pleasant place. It's not radically different than the life we have here. You just continue on. Your relatives who have gone before you come and visit. You can stay there for a while and visit them, but you can't drink any of their water and you can't eat any of their food. If you do, you have to stay.

In the old days when they used to kill their favorite horses and dogs to go along with them to the next world, it wasn't just a sacrifice. What they were saying is that the horse and dog are so much a part of me that we all have to go on together. I would be incomplete without them, and they would be incomplete without me. It was a rare occasion because your favorite horse was probably a well-trained buffalo hunter. Your son would get the horse. You wouldn't kill an animal that valuable.

When I was about nine years old, there was a very famous Indian who lived about nine miles west of us, Billy Fire Thunder. He woke up one morning and he said to his wife, "I'm going under the earth tonight at midnight, so I want you to fix my favorite breakfast. And then I want you to take me to town to say good-bye to my friends." He had a nice breakfast and sat and smoked his pipe with a coffee. He went to town and said good-bye to storekeepers and some of the Indians who lived in town. He was very energetic. He didn't say he was going to die, he said, "I'm going on a trip, so I want to say good-bye to you in case I don't come back." Then he went back home and they fed him a real nice meal. And he just took little bites of it, just to get the taste of all these things he liked. Friends from the community came in, and finally, about ten-thirty, he said, "Now I just want my family around because I'm ready to go." He planned out this whole day. It was the talk of the reservation for weeks and

continued

weeks. People just kept saying, "How could a guy know all of this?" Then the old-timers came and said, "Unless you were killed in the war, this is the way you did it. You knew that your end had come." So you made all these last-minute good-byes and "Give my horse to this person"—like that. They said that's the way you're supposed to do it.

When I did my father's memorial, he had left me this beautiful pipe, which is a sacred ceremonial pipe. It had a red buffalo carved on it, with a nice stem and a beaded bag. I had about three pipes, and you're supposed to give the medicine man a pipe when he does the memorial. I'd feel chintzy if I didn't give him the best pipe, my father's. He made this speech and then I gave him this pipe. He's holding the pipe with the bag and he said, "I want to tell people what this means." He said, "When I first looked at it, the bag looked a little familiar." He said, "I made that pipe thirty-two years ago, and I gave it away in a ceremony." And he said, "Look . . . this pipe has never been used." And he said, "This pipe has passed from ceremony to ceremony all these years and now you're giving it back to

me, a pipe I made when I was a young man." I thought it was incredible that no one had ever smoked that pipe, and it had just been a present from one person to another. He's gone, I don't know who has it now—he died this summer. I'm sure he gave it to somebody else. In those ceremonies, those Indians always give the best they have, they don't hold back. 'Cause it was a beautiful pipe. . . . While you're giving it away over here, someone's tapping you on the shoulder to give it to you. It just kept getting given away, all those years. Each time, the person said, "I don't want to give this away, but I can't be a slacker, I can't hold back." So they gave it. No one ever took it out in public and bragged about themselves, "Look at my beautiful pipe," and smoked it. They all treated it with dignity. My father got it—and you'd think once a Christian minister has a pipe, you're never gonna see it again. And then I got the pipe, and I gave it back to the man who made it. The circle of life and death.

From Studs Terkel, *Will the Circle Be Unbroken? Reflections on Death, Rebirth, and Hunger for Faith.* Copyright © 2001. Reprinted by permission of The New Press. www.thenewpress.com.

deceased as though one were calling them on a spiritual "telephone." In this way ancestors can be accessed by all family members and so they continue to have a relationship with those who remain on earth (Rees, 1997).

Consequences of Grief   Bereavement and grief often have a much greater impact than is evident in the period immediately following the death. The survivor is more vulnerable to physical illness and mental illness, even to death, especially if the death was sudden and unexpected. Bereaved people have a higher than average incidence of illness, accidents, mortality, unemployment, and other indices of a damaged life (Kastenbaum & Costa, 1977). Psychological effects, especially depression, are even more serious than the effects on physical health (Bodnar & Kiecolt-Glaser, 1994). Even one year after death, at least one-fourth of bereaved persons are still depressed (Norris & Murrell, 1990). In addition, significant clinical depression at the time of a spouse's death substantially increases the risk for psychological complications during the bereavement process, and survivors of spouses who committed suicide are at even greater risk (Gilewski et al., 1991). An authority on bereavement has this to say about grief:

> It isn't a problem or an illness that can be solved or cured. That's why it is really inappropriate for someone to say: "You can get over this. You can recover." In fact, people can't recover in the sense of going back to the way things were. You must make changes in your life in order to go on. The death and the bereavement wizen you, weather you and make you look at life differently. (Silverman, 1983, p. 65)

Adjusting to Violent and Premature Death   Violent and premature deaths often result in the most severe

grief reactions. Suicide is one of the most difficult types of death for survivors to handle. They may have difficulty acknowledging that the death was a suicide, and even when they do, they can feel guilt and shame that impair normal mourning. Suicide survivors frequently feel that they are somehow to blame—for not seeing the signs and for not fulfilling the stated or unstated needs of the person who died. They also must bear the thought that the dead person did not believe they were worth living for. And their guilt can be intensified if survivors experience a sense of relief after an ordeal of mental illness or of suicide threats and attempts (Murphy et al., 1999).

Adjusting to the Death of a Parent   The bereavement experienced by adult children following the death of an elderly parent has until recently been largely ignored by the media and the academic community—though it has always been of concern of those in the legal profession. A recent study explores the impact of the death of a grandparent on the surviving children and on the family as a whole (Abeles, Victor, & Delano-Wood, 2004). As noted in prior chapters, ties between a parent and an adult child often remain strong across the life span. Giving care to frail older parents, particularly by daughters, tends to extend earlier patterns of intergenerational exchange (Bodnar & Kiecolt-Glaser, 1994).

From an early age youngsters realize that they can lose their parents, and by midlife they have usually seen friends lose parents. Only 1 in 10 children has lost a parent by age 25; but by 54 years of age, 50 percent of adult children have lost both parents, and by 62 years of age, 75 percent have lost both parents (Winsborough, Bumpass, & Aquilino, 1991). Although "anticipatory orphanhood" can acquaint adults with the idea that their parents will die, the sense of preparation is seldom equal to the reality of death (Moss & Moss, 1983–1984). Consequently, the loss of a parent through death can be followed by feelings of considerable distress (Umberson & Chen, 1994).

The bereavement accompanying a parent's death is a complex emotional, cognitive, and behavioral process. Most men and women experience their mother's death as a profound loss. Women seem to be more emotionally affected than men are by the death of their fathers (Douglas, 1990–1991) and by the loss of the last surviving parent (Moss, Rubenstein, & Moss, 1997). Bereavement can be especially difficult for adult children who provided care prior to the parent's death—particularly those who experienced an intensification of their bonds during caregiving (Pratt, Walker, & Wood, 1992). For middle-aged adults, a parental death is often an important personal and symbolic event that heightens a person's awareness of her or his own mortality, and bereavement can stimulate personal growth and development by fostering a greater sense of personal identity and stronger ties to family members (Bass & Bowman, 1990). Yet bereavement feelings are often complicated and contradictory. For instance, caregiving daughters frequently report feeling psychological strength in coping with their mothers' deaths, simultaneously reporting feelings of shock, anger, and guilt (Pratt, Walker, & Wood, 1992).

Bereavement seems to have a three-step progression for healthy adults who have lost a parent, according to a recent study by Petersen and Rafuls (1998). Based on their study of six adults who had recently lost a parent, they suggest that a transition in family values occurs, which they call a model for receiving the scepter of family values. Each new generation takes over the responsibility, role, and authority of the previous generation in this three-step transformation (Petersen & Rafuls, 1998):

Step 1. *Going back to the origins.* Duty and obligation become the most important response the first few days after death, along with an unconscious emotional "moving away" from one's own family.

Step 2. *Reevaluation phase.* A period of preoccupation permeated with a formal sadness, with release in one or two intense periods of crying and very different from depression found with other grief. Participants dealt with this stage quietly, internally, without sharing, yet thought about the deepest meanings of life. Also, within relationships, the most evident consequence during this stage was reduced lovemaking by a couple.

Step 3. *Assuming leadership.* Partners brought the second phase to a conclusion by reminding spouses that they were needed by their own families. These phases seemed to bring about a sense of strength never experienced by these subjects before; they reordered their priorities, and began to appreciate the richness of life around them.

Phases in the Bereavement Process   In standard bereavement by adults, the individual typically passes through a number of phases (Malinak, Hoyt, & Patterson, 1979). The first phase is characterized by shock, numbness, denial, disbelief, and often a need to withdraw (Ashenburg, 2002). The most intense feelings of shock and numbness usually last several days, although the process of struggling with denial and disbelief can persist many days, even months—especially if the death was sudden and unexpected.

The second phase involves pining, yearning, and depression. It usually reaches its peak within 5 to 14 days but can continue longer. Weeping, feelings of hopelessness, a sense of unreality, feelings of emptiness, distance from people, lack of vigor and interest, and preoccupations with the image of the deceased are quite common during this stage. Other symptoms might include anger, irritability, fear, sleeplessness, episodes of impaired recall or concentration, lack of appetite, and weight loss. Not uncommonly, the bereaved might idealize the dead person, maintaining an element of "reverence" despite recognition of the deceased's human faults and failings. In fact, survivors of a bad marriage can become hopelessly stuck in grief. They mourn not only for the marriage that was but also for the marriage that might have been and was not. In cases of pathological grief following the death of a spouse, three factors are typically present: an unexpected death, ambivalence regarding the marriage, and overdependence on the spouse (Rees, 1997). Recovery from grief seems to be quicker and more complete when a marriage was happy.

The third phase of bereavement involves emancipation from the loved one and an adjustment to the new circumstances. In this period the individual mobilizes his or her resources, attempts to become reconnected with people and activities, and seeks to establish a new equilibrium that will permit some element of satisfaction and comfort. Some people may complete the psychological and emotional work of this stage in about six to eight weeks, others in a matter of months; but for still others the process may continue for years.

The fourth phase is characterized by identity reconstruction. The person crystallizes new relationships and assumes new roles without the loved one. At this stage approximately half of the survivors report realizing some benefit or experiencing some growth from bereavement. These gains include an increased sense of self-reliance and strength, a greater caring for friends and loved ones, and a more general quickening to life and deepening appreciation of existence.

Individual Variations in the Bereavement Process
People differ greatly in how they handle the death of a

loved one, their specific symptoms of grief, and the intensity and duration of the symptoms (Johnson, Lund, & Dimond, 1986). Recent criticism of the literature on bereavement points out that there is no consensus on the definitions of normal grief reaction (Bonanno & Kaltman, 2001). The reactions cannot be neatly plotted in a series of well-defined stages, nor is the progression from the time of death to the resolution of bereavement necessarily a straight line. And although shock, anger, and depression are common reactions to loss, not everyone experiences them, no matter how deeply they cared about the person they lost. For instance, a man who lost his wife six months earlier might say he is ready to remarry, and a young mother might laugh with her friends, only days after losing her child. Between a quarter and two-thirds of those who lose a loved one do not show great distress. Indeed, the absence of extreme distress can be a sign of psychological strength and resilience (Goleman, 1989b). New interests and strong social networks seem to promote adjustment (Norris & Murrell, 1990). Although traditional research suggested the importance of working through feelings of grief so as to avoid delayed grief symptoms, more recent research failed to support this contention (Bonanno & Field, 2001).

However, some aspects of grief work do not end for a significant proportion of bereaved individuals. They still feel themselves strongly affected by the deceased person, say they are upset on the yearly anniversary of the person's death, and experience an emotional void in their lives. Their sense of loss may overshadow other experiences, changing the way they interpret even positive events because the events remind them of their loss and their inability to share the experiences with the loved one (Zautra, Reich, & Guarnaccia, 1990). At unguarded moments people can stumble into "little ambushes" of grief. One widower tells of being out driving and spotting a woman with a hairstyle similar to his wife's:

> I said to myself, "There's Nola." Then I laughed out loud and told myself, "How silly of me. Nola is dead." Then my next thought was, "I must go home and tell Nola how silly I just was." It all happened in a fraction of a second. (Gelman, 1983, p. 120)

In sum, we are increasingly coming to realize that there is not a universal prescription for how best to grieve and that people handle grief in a great many different ways (Goleman, 1989b).

Questions

Why do so many people think that the one-year anniversary of the death of a loved one is the time to be "over it"? Is there a standard time frame in many societies when grief work should be over?

Bereavement Ceremonies Throughout the world societies have evolved funerals and other rituals to assist their members in coming to grips with the death of a loved one. The ceremonies highlight the finality of death. Here Hindu mourners prepare a body for their traditional sacred custom of cremation, followed by disposal of ashes into a sacred river.

Widows and Widowers

Nearly three-fourths of American men over age 65 lived with their spouses in 2000. Only about 40 percent of women aged 65 and over are living with a spouse. For women aged 75 and older about one-third lived with a spouse (Administration on Aging, 2001). The proportion of people living with a spouse decreases with age, especially for women. Hence, women 65 and older are much more likely to be widowed than married. This situation results from the fact that the life expectancy of women tends to be five or more years longer than that of men and from the tradition that has ordained that women marry men older than themselves (of interest, women married to men younger than themselves tend to live longer than would otherwise be expected, whereas women married to older men tend to die sooner than would be expected) (Klinger-Vartabedian & Wispe, 1989). Consequently, remarriage tends to be a male prerogative.

Of the more than 800,000 people widowed each year, about one-fourth still suffer serious depression a year or more later. Their eating habits frequently are altered, resulting in poorer health and nutrition (Rosenbloom & Whittington, 1993). Use of alcohol, drugs, and cigarettes rises. Health problems in survivors tend to be worse among those who were already in poor physical or mental health, those who are alcohol or drug abusers, and those who lack a social support network. Survivors with strong social support or who remarry seem to suffer fewer health problems. The responses to widowhood can vary from chronic grief, chronic depression, depression followed by improvement, and resilience according to one study (Bonanno, Wortma, & Nesse, 2004).

The death of a spouse is a traumatic event in a person's life. Although many studies have been conducted regarding the consequences of being a widow or widower, the results have been inconsistent. A study by McCrae and Costa (1993) suggests that there are no significant enduring long-term effects or changes in psychosocial function. On the other hand, other findings suggest that detrimental effects do result after the loss of a spouse (Gallagher-Thompson et al., 1993; Mendes de Leon, Kasl, & Jacobs, 1994). Nevertheless, the fact remains that elderly white widowers have the highest rates of suicide in the nation.

One problem confronted by widowers is the cultural dictate that men are not supposed to feel emotion and pain or say "I need help," due to which men traditionally have had difficulty expressing emotion. Furthermore, many widowers have trouble cooking and caring for themselves. They develop poor eating habits, which, together with other poor health practices and feelings of loneliness and emptiness, often lead to heavy drinking, sleeplessness, and chronic ailments. Overall, older U.S. men seem to have a more difficult time living alone than do U.S. women, they are far less likely to receive help from others, and they have the highest rates of suicide in the life span (National Institute of Mental Health, 2003).

We know quite a bit more about widows than about widowers, largely owing to research by sociologist Helena Lopata (1981). The women studied by Lopata lived in metropolitan Chicago and were interviewed by National Opinion Research Center researchers. Lopata was able to distinguish three categories of widows on the basis of the extent of their involvement in different types of social relationships. At one extreme were women, primarily better educated and belonging to the middle class, who were strongly involved in the role of wife when their husbands were still alive. They built many other roles on the husband's presence as a person, a father, and a partner in leisure-time activities. There was a strong tendency for these women to idealize the late husband, often to the point of sanctification (Futterman et al., 1990). (Former First Lady Nancy Reagan was quoted as saying, "Everything was about Ronnie . . . it was always about him.") At the other extreme were women, primarily lower- or working-class and living in black or ethnic neighborhoods, who belonged to sex-segregated worlds and were immersed in kin, neighboring, or friendship relationships with other women. Between these two extremes were women who led multidimensional lives in which the husband was involved in only part of the total set of relations. The adjustments confronting the women tended to vary with the degree to which their social relationships revolved about or were integrated with those of their husbands.

The main conclusion Lopata drew from her data was that the higher the woman's education and socioeconomic

Widows and Widowers The adjustments confronting widows/widowers tend to vary with the degree to which their social relationships revolved about or were integrated with those of their spouse. Typically, lower socioeconomic status is a significant factor in coping. Children sometimes have greater difficulty coping with the death of a loved one than do adults.

class, the more disorganized her self-identity and life became with her husband's death—but by the same token, the more resources she had to form a new lifestyle once her grief work was accomplished. Other research has suggested that the negative long-term consequences of widowhood seem to derive from socioeconomic deprivation rather than from widowhood itself (Bound et al., 1991).

Of considerable interest, Lopata found that about half of the widows lived entirely alone, and most of these women said they much preferred to do so. Only 10 percent had moved in with their married children. One reason this figure was so low is that the widows cherished their independence, which they did not wish to jeopardize by giving up their own homes and moving into an unfamiliar network of relations. Furthermore, the widows anticipated problems in their role as mothers of grown-up children. They said that if they could not criticize or speak up, they would feel inhibited, but that if they did speak up, their children would become upset. They regarded their relationships with grandchildren as presenting similar problems.

Question

What are the differences in the ways widows and widowers cope with the loss of a spouse?

The Death of a Child

The loss of a child is also associated with deep depression, anger, guilt, and despair. The death of a child is not the natural order of life. Hence, recovery can take a very long time. There are continual reminders of developmental milestones experienced by a dead child's peers of which parents are aware: birthday, anniversary of death, year of graduation from high school, year of graduation from college, likely years of marriage and parenthood, and so forth. Parents must come to recognize the limits of their protective powers. Women who find their primary satisfactions in the mother role might feel useless without someone to care for. Guilt can be especially intense after a death from sudden infant death syndrome (SIDS). Parents of children who die from cancer might find that their grief intensifies during the second year. Parents who feel they did all they could do to care for a child during the final illness seem to recover sooner. Some evidence suggests that parents who chose hospital care rather than home care are more depressed, socially withdrawn, and uncomfortable afterward (Murphy et al., 1999).

Wheeler's (2001) qualitative study showed that parents explore the search for meaning and a renewed sense of purpose after the death of a child. There is a common assumption that a child's death eventually leads to marital breakup, but an empirical study with a nationally representative sample of more than 250 couples reveals only a small percent actually divorce. Most parents in the study sought counseling to cope with their grief (about one-fourth considered divorce but only 9 percent divorced) (Hardt & Carroll, 1999).

Loss by Miscarriage   Parents who have lost a child by miscarriage often receive no recognition of their loss from others, yet their grief work might continue for a lifetime. Support groups may provide comfort to some grieving partners. However, results of a study evaluating perinatal loss support group do not show any statistically significant differences in parents' grief reactions between those who do and those who do not attend such groups (DiMarco, Menke, & McNamara, 2001). Statements such as "At least you can have another one" or "This child wasn't meant to be" do not comfort people experiencing this loss. Every anniversary of the loss is a reminder of the child, who usually has been named and placed in a gravesite but didn't have the opportunity for life. The mother is likely to feel a great deal of guilt, thinking that if only she had done something differently, the child would be here. Most fathers suffer in silence and make efforts to go on with their lives. Repetitive miscarriages can bring about deep depression and feelings of failure in the mother. There are Internet sites devoted to loss by miscarriage or stillbirth that allow parents to commemorate the short life of a child.

Loss by Murder or Violence   Nicholas Green was a 7-year-old American boy on vacation in Italy in 1994 with his parents, Reg and Maggie Green, when he was fatally shot by highway robbers during a night time drive toward their destination. Within hours, his parents made the difficult decision to donate his organs to seven Italian citizens, who survived because of this gift. To this day, Reg Green says he thinks of his son a hundred times a day, and though it does not take away the pain of the loss of his son, he does have a sense of peace knowing that his son helped people in life-threatening situations. John Walsh and his wife lost their son Adam to a vicious child killer, and their lives have never been the same. A recent study comparing the grief of parents whose children died as the result of violence to those who did not found that regardless of cause of death, the timing of grief remained the same, about 3 to 4 years (Bereaved Parents' Outcome . . . ," 2003). The loss of a child is one of life's greatest agonies, even when parents know it is inevitable due to illness or disease; but when someone senselessly takes the life of a child, the bereavement process goes on indefinitely.

A study examined the coping strategies of parents who lost their children to accident, suicide, or homicide (Murphy, Johnson, & Weber, 2002). Some parents start a crusade in honor of their child, such as the campaign for laws for victims' rights, the National Center for Missing and Exploited Children, and the show *America's Most Wanted* that John and Revé Walsh started to honor their 6-year-old son Adam who was brutally murdered. *Megan's Law* now requires that community residents be notified if a released child molester moves into the community. No parents want their child to have lived in vain, and humanitarian efforts—such as organ donation, a national database of convicted child molesters, hot lines and Web sites for teenage runaways, stricter laws and penalties for those who commit the crimes—help these parents keep the memories of their child alive. Often as the result of a tragic event, researchers call for further investigation or expansion of their field of study. The massive deaths that resulted from the events of 9/11 were in part the impetus for a type of study called *macrothanology.* This study focuses on large-scale death, and death resulting from complex and multidomain processes (Kastenbaum, 2004a).

It is with fervent hopefulness that with better understanding of human beings through the study of human development from conception to death, and of the contexts in which we live together, that we can all continue to affirm and enjoy our lives and improve the lives of those with whom we share the planet.

SEGUE

Perhaps the most difficult transition anyone has to make after the death of a loved one is the journey from grief and sorrow to remembrance and honoring. Our loss seems to overwhelm us and, fearing that we will dishonor the one we love by forgetting, we nurture grief, clinging to it with a desperation that comforts us. But in time, this grieving must give away to honoring and remembering. So often are the words "get on with your life" spoken to the one who is left behind, alone. To move on is *not* to forget. It is to remember. It is to remember all that your loved one gave you and all that you shared with your loved one. To move on is to celebrate those gifts and to know your loved one lives on in your memories. It is to realize how deeply he or she touched your life.

Ted Menten, *Gentle Closings: How to Say Goodbye to Someone You Love*, 1991, p. 136

Summary

The Quest for "Healthy Dying"

1. Until very recently, death was a taboo topic in Western society. During the past 40 years, however, this pattern has been reversed. Considerable controversy swirls about such matters as the right to die, clinical death, the death penalty, and life after death.

2. Thanatology is the study of death and dying, and interest has grown in this field.

3. Over the past 30 years, public and professional awareness of the dying person's experience has increased dramatically. "Death with dignity!" has become a major rallying cry. The death awareness movement asserts that a basic human right is the power to control one's own dying process. Much criticism is currently leveled at the way modern technology is applied to the terminally ill. According to this view, too much is done for too long a period at too high a cost, all at the expense of basic human considerations and sensitivities.

4. Cultural attitudes toward suicide still waver among extremes. Early Christians called suicide a sin and denied burial rites to those who killed themselves. Some consider suicide victims to be insane or weak. Others consider suicide the honorable choice when confronted with capture, defeat, disgrace, or severe, prolonged pain.

5. The hospice approach involves a variety of programs designed to provide an alternative to conventional hospital care for the terminally ill, especially cancer patients. The emphasis of the movement falls on "comfort care" rather than on attempts to prolong life. Comfort care involves an aggressive treatment of symptoms, both physical and emotional, through the use of counseling, antidepressive medications, and high-dose morphine preparations. Most hospice programs are centered about caring for the dying person at home.

The Dying Process

6. The earliest biblical sources, as well as English common law, considered a person's ability to breathe independently to be the prime index of life. Over the past 45 years, technological advances have rendered this traditional definition of death obsolete. Such advances have included methods to resuscitate victims of cardiac arrest, mechanical respirators, artificial heart pacemakers, and organ transplants. A growing acceptance in medical and legal circles of the need for an additional criterion of death has resulted in a legal definition that includes the absence of spontaneous brain function.

7. A realistic acceptance of death could well be the hallmark of emotional maturity. People differ considerably, however, in the degree to which they are consciously aware of and think about death. Furthermore, death is a highly personal matter, and its meaning tends to vary from individual to individual. Researchers agree that only a relatively small proportion of the elderly express a fear of death.

8. Elisabeth Kübler-Ross identifies five stages through which dying persons typically pass: denial, anger, bargaining, depression, and acceptance.

9. In some cases persons pronounced clinically dead but then resuscitated by medical measures have told of having left their bodies and undergone otherworldly experiences. Some individuals have interpreted such experiences as scientific evidence of a spiritual existence beyond death. Skeptics rejoin that the visions reported by dying people are hallucinations associated with the intense arousal of the central nervous system and disorganized brain functioning.

Grief, Bereavement, and Mourning

10. Bereavement and grief have a considerably greater impact than is evident in the period immediately following the

death of a loved one. The survivor is more vulnerable to physical and mental illness, even to death. The bereaved adult typically passes through a number of phases. The first phase is characterized by shock, numbness, denial, and disbelief. The second phase entails pining, yearning, and depression. The third phase involves emancipation from the loved one and an adjustment to the new circumstances. The fourth phase is identity reconstruction.

11. Cultures differ in how they perceive death and dying. Every culture has a unique approach for dealing with death, but each will involve an understanding of death, spiritual beliefs, rituals, expectations, and taboos.

12. The major causes of death vary from country to country. Heart disease and cancer are major causes of adult death in the United States. Accidents are the leading cause of child deaths.

13. Women 65 and over are much more likely to be widowed than married. The difficulty women have in adjusting to widowhood tends to vary with the degree to which their social relationships revolved about or were integrated with those of their husbands.

14. Loss of parents, spouse, or children all have a significant impact on a person. Typically parents and adult children retain strong ties throughout life. The loss of a child is one of life's most intensely agonizing experiences, one that many people never quite get over.

Key Terms

anticipatory grief (667)	grief (667)	mourning (667)
bereavement (667)	hospice (656)	near-death experience (NDE) (662)
brain death (659)	life review (661)	persistent vegetative state (659)
euthanasia (652)	living will (650)	thanatology (649)

Following Up on the Internet

Web sites for this chapter focus on controversies about "healthy" dying, the dying process, and the coping of survivors. Please access the text Web site at www.mhhe.com/vz-crandell8 for up-to-date hot-linked Internet addresses for the following organizations, topics, and resources:

Center for Thanatology Research and Education
Sociology of Death and Dying

American Hospice Foundation
American Foundation for Suicide Prevention
American Association of Critical Care Nurses
Near-Death Experiences
Ten Safeguards for End of Living Decisions
Compassionate Friends

Glossary

A

abortion Spontaneous or induced expulsion of the fetus prior to the time of viability, occurring most often during the first 20 weeks of the human gestation period.

accommodation In Piaget's cognitive theory, the process of changing a schema to make it a better match to reality.

activity theory of aging The theory that as an elderly person's level of activity declines, so also do that person's feelings of satisfaction, contentment, and happiness.

adaptation Begins with the single reflexes at birth and continues as a child gradually modifies behaviors to meet environmental demands.

adolescent growth spurt Rapid increase in height and weight during the early adolescent years.

adult day care A program of long-term care and support to adults who live in the community, providing health, social, and support services in a protective setting during any part of the day.

afterbirth Placenta and the remaining umbilical cord expelled from the uterus through the vagina after childbirth.

age cohort (also called cohort or birth cohort) A group of persons born in the same time interval.

age grading Arranging people in social layers based on place in the life cycle.

age norms Social standards that define what is appropriate for people to be and to do at various ages over the life span.

age strata Social layers within societies that are based on chronological age and serve to differentiate people as superior or inferior, higher or lower.

ageism Stereotyping and judging a group of people solely on the basis of their age.

aggression Behavior that is socially defined as injurious or destructive toward a person or a group of persons.

aging The process of biological and social change across the life span.

alienation A pervasive sense of powerlessness, meaninglessness, isolation, and estrangement from others.

allele A pair of genes found on corresponding chromosomes that affect the same trait.

alpha hydroxy An ingredient in skin cream to combat wrinkling.

Alzheimer's disease A progressive, degenerative neurological disorder involving deterioration of brain cells that can occur in late adulthood.

amenorrhea The absence of a menstrual cycle in a female who was normally menstruating, other than during pregnancy. This is more common among females who are anorexic or bulimic and those in perimenopause, and in some females who participate in endurance sports like marathons.

amniocentesis A commonly used invasive procedure conducted between the 14th to 20th week of gestation to determine the genetic status of the fetus, which involves withdrawing and analyzing amniotic fluid.

amnion Forms a closed sac around the embryo and is filled with a watery amniotic fluid to keep the embryo moist and protect it against shock or adhesions.

anaphylaxis A dramatic multiorgan reaction which is life threatening, usually caused by certain foods.

androgyny The presence of both male-typed and female-typed characteristics.

anorexia nervosa A potentially life-threatening eating disorder that affects primarily females, and a smaller percentage of males, in which the person becomes obsessed with looking thin and seriously alters her or his eating behaviors in order to lose weight. Excessive exercise is also associated with anorexia.

anoxia Oxygen deprivation caused when the umbilical cord becomes squeezed or wrapped around the baby's neck during labor and delivery.

anticipatory grief A state of emotional limbo where the death of a loved one is anticipated and individuals feel unable to resolve the loss because it has not yet occurred and are unable to avoid the diagnosis that death will occur.

antisocial behavior A type of behavior that is persistent in violating the socially prescribed patterns of behavior.

anxiety A state of uneasiness, apprehension, or worry about future uncertainties.

Apgar scoring system A standard scoring system developed by anesthesiologist Virginia Apgar to objectively appraise the normalcy of a baby's condition at birth, based on five criteria.

Asperger's syndrome One of the closely related disorders to autism, classified as a PPD (pervasive developmental disorder).

assimilation In Piaget's cognitive theory, the process of taking in new information and interpreting it in such a way that it conforms to a currently held model of the world.

assisted reproductive technologies (ARTs) Scientific technological options used to increase a woman's chance of becoming pregnant when conception does not occur through heterosexual intercourse.

asthma A chronic lung disease characterized by inflammation and constriction of the lower airways.

asynchrony Dissimilarity in the growth rates of different parts of the body. For example, during adolescence the hands, feet, and legs grow before the trunk of the body.

attention-deficit hyperactivity disorder (ADHD) A disorder characterized by impulsivity and the inability to follow instructions, remain seated, and stick with a task. Can be hyperactive-impulsive, inattentive, and combined hyperactive and inattentive.

attachment An affectional bond that one individual forms for another and that endures across time and space.

audiology testing Testing to determine the extent of hearing loss.

auditory neuropathy A disease or abnormality of the auditory system.

authoritarian parenting A parenting style distinguished by attempts to shape, control, and evaluate a child's behavior in accordance with traditional and absolute values and standards of conduct.

authoritative parenting   A parenting style distinguished by firm direction of a child's overall activities but allowing the child freedom to make some decisions within reasonable limits and supervision.

autism   A disorder that typically appears in early childhood and is characterized by marked deficits in communication and social interaction.

autonomous morality   The second stage of Piaget's two-stage theory of moral development which arises from the interaction among status equals relationships among peers.

autosomes   The 22 pairs of chromosomes similar in size and shape that each human being normally possesses in addition to the sex chromosomes.

B

basal-cell carcinoma   The most common form of skin cancer.

behavior modification   The application of learning theory and experimental psychology to alter behavior.

behavioral genetics   The study of genes that cause individuals within a species to exhibit different behaviors.

behavioral theory   A psychological theory that focuses on observable behavior—what people do and say—and how their environment shapes their development across the life span.

bereavement   Being deprived of a relative or friend by death.

bilingualism   Instruction in both first and second languages by teachers proficient in both; proficiency in two or more languages.

binge drinking   Downing five or more alcoholic drinks in a row for men, or four or more in a row for women.

biological aging   Changes in the structure and functioning of the human organism over time.

birth   The fetus's transition from dependent existence inside the woman's uterus to life as a separate organism.

birthing centers   Primary care facilities, other than hospitals, typically located in urban centers, that are used for low-risk childbirth.

birthing rooms   A homelike environment in a hospital or other setting where labor and delivery can occur.

blastocyst   The gel-like fluid-filled ball of cells produced after the zygote goes through early meiotic cell division. The blastocyst gradually moves into the uterus and implants itself into the uterine wall to nourish itself and becomes the embryo.

brain death   Cessation of neural activity when the brain receives insufficient oxygen to function.

bulimia   Also called binge-purge syndrome. A serious eating disorder characterized by repeated episodes of bingeing— particularly on high-calorie foods like candy bars, cakes, pies, and ice cream—and after eating purging by forced vomiting, taking laxatives, enemas, diuretics, or fasting.

bullying   A deliberate, repeated aggressive behavior that involves an imbalance of power and strength toward another person perceived as weaker.

C

calcitonin   The hormone that strengthens bones.

cardiovascular   Heart and circulatory system.

caretaker speech   The simplified form of language used by adults when they are talking to infants and young children.

case-study method   A special type of longitudinal study that focuses on a single individual rather than a group of subjects.

cataracts   A clouding of the lens of the eye that impairs vision, typically seen in older adults; in rarer cases can be found in infants or young people.

causality   A cause-and-effect relationship between two paired events that recur in succession. Piaget concluded that children younger than 7 or 8 fail to grasp cause-and-effect relationships.

centration (centering)   The process whereby preoperational children, ages 2 to 7, concentrate on only one feature of a situation and neglect other aspects. It is characteristic of preoperational thought.

cephalocaudal development (cephalocaudal principle)   Development that proceeds from the head to the feet.

cesarean section (C-section)   A surgical delivery technique by which the physician enters the uterus through an abdominal incision and removes the infant.

child abuse   Intentional neglect, physical attack, or sexual abuse or injury to a child.

cholesterol   A white, waxy substance found naturally in the body that builds the cell walls and makes certain hormones. Certain foods can cause cholesterol buildup in the bloodstream that can cause cardiovascular problems.

chorion   A membrane that surrounds the amnion and links the embryo to the placenta.

chorionic villus biopsy (CVS)   An invasive procedure performed between 9½ and 12½ weeks of gestation to determine genetic characteristics of the fetus. The physician inserts a thin catheter through the vagina and cervix and into the uterus, removing a small plug of villous tissue.

chromosomes   Found in the nuclei of all cells, the long threadlike structures made up of protein and nucleic acid that contain the genes, which transmit hereditary materials.

chronosystem   In Bronfenbrenner's ecological theory, refers to the changes within the individual and changes in the environment across time, as well as the relationship between the two processes.

classical conditioning   A type of learning in which a new, previously neutral stimulus, such as a bell, comes to elicit a response, such as salivation, by repeated pairings with an unconditioned stimulus, such as food.

climacteric   A time in a woman's life characterized by changes in the ovaries and in the various biological processes over two to five years prior to complete cessation of menstruation.

cloning   A form of asexual reproduction, which creates an embryo by a process called "somatic cell nuclear transfer" (SCNT).

cognition   The act or process of knowing, including understanding and reasoning.

cognitive development   A major domain of development that involves changes in mental activity, including sensation, perception, memory, thought, reasoning, and language.

cognitive learning   The process of observing other people and learning new responses or behaviors without first having had the opportunity to make the responses ourselves.

cognitive stages   Sequential periods in the growth or maturation of an individual's ability to think, to gain knowledge, and to be aware of one's self and the environment.

cognitive styles   Consistent individual differences in how a person organizes, processes, recalls, and uses information.

cognitive theory   A theory that attempts to explain how we go about representing, organizing, treating, and transforming information as we modify our behavior.

colic   An uncomfortable condition of unknown origin that can cause a baby to cry for at least an hour or more (typically every day about the same time). Colic typically disappears after the first several months of development.

collagen   A basic structural component of connective tissue in body cells that appears to be implicated in the aging process. During late adulthood the body has less collagen, thus a person's skin appears more wrinkled.

collectivism   A view that fosters in children a strong emotional bonding and feeling of oneness with parents and respect for authority.

colostrum   A substance in mother's milk that provides antibodies that build up the newborn's immune system, protecting the infant from a variety of infectious and noninfectious diseases.

communication   The processes by which people transmit information, ideas, attitudes, and emotions to one another.

companionate love   According to Sternberg, the kind of love a person has for a very close friend.

conceptualization   A grouping of perceptions into classes or categories on the basis of certain similarities. Related ideas can come together to create a concept.

confluence theory   The view that the intellectual development of a family is like a river, with the inputs of each family member flowing into it.

confounding   A variable that may occur in research when the elements under study are mingled so they cannot be distinguished or separated.

consciousness of oneness   A sympathetic identification in which group members come to feel that their inner experiences and emotional reactions are similar.

conservation   Understanding that the quantity or amount of something stays the same regardless of changes in its shape or position. According to Piaget, preoperational children (2 to 7 years old) do not have the concept of conservation. Children are typically in elementary school before they learn this concept.

consummate love   According to Sternberg, the kind of love present when all three aspects of his triangular theory of love exist in a relationship.

continuum of indirectness   The notion that the role played by hereditary factors is more central in some aspects of development than in others.

control group   In an experiment, a group of participants who are similar to the participants in the experimental group but do not receive the independent variable (treatment). The results obtained with the control group are compared with the results of the experimental group.

convergent thinking   The application of logic and reasoning to arrive at a single, correct answer to a problem.

coping   The responses, behaviors, and actions one takes in order to master, tolerate, or reduce stress.

correlation coefficient   The numerical expression of the degree or extent of relationship between two or more variables or conditions.

couvade syndrome   Father's complaints of uncomfortable physical symptoms, dietary changes, and weight gain because of his partner's pregnancy.

craniosacral system   A closed system involving the pumping or inflow and outflow of cerebrospinal fluid within the membranes around the brain and spinal cord that affects the functioning of the nervous system.

creativity   Characterized by originality of useful responses and creations.

critical period   For the developing embryo, the time of development when each organ and structure is most vulnerable to damaging influences. Also a relatively short period of time in which specific development or imprinting normally takes place.

cross-cultural method   A study in which researchers compare data from two or more societies and cultures. Culture, rather than individuals, is the subject of analysis.

cross-sectional method   Investigation of development by simultaneously comparing people from different age groups.

crowning   The stage during childbirth when the widest diameter of the baby's head is at the mother's vulva.

crystallized intelligence   The ability to use knowledge that was acquired earlier in life on later occasions. Crystallized intelligence often shows an increase with age.

cultural dislocation   A sense of homelessness and alienation from a traditional way of life.

culture   The social heritage of a people—those learned patterns of thinking, feeling, and acting that are transmitted from one generation to the next.

D

death drop   A marked intellectual decline that occurs shortly before a person dies.

decay theory   A theory of cognitive decline in which forgetting occurs due to deterioration in the memory traces in the brain.

delivery (childbirth)   The process that begins when the infant's head passes through the mother's cervix and ends when the baby has completed its passage through the birth canal.

deoxyribonucleic acid (DNA)   The active biochemical substance of genes that programs the cells to manufacture vital protein substances.

dependent variable   In an experiment, an objective measure of the subject's behavior—the variable that is affected by the independent variable.

depression   A state of mind characterized by prolonged feelings of gloom, despair, and futility, profound pessimism, and a tendency toward excessive guilt and self-reproach.

development   The orderly and sequential changes that occur with the passage of time as an organism moves from conception to death.

developmental psychology   The branch of psychology that investigates how individuals change over time while remaining in some respects the same.

deviant identity   A lifestyle that is at odds with, or at least not supported by, the values and expectations of society.

DHEA (dehydroepiandrosterone)   A hormone produced by the body that is used to treat depression, improve memory, and block the decline of the body's immune system.

dialectical thinking   An organized approach to analyzing and making sense of the world one experiences that differs fundamentally from formal analysis.

diastolic pressure   Blood pressure when the heart is at rest, in between beats.

disengagement theory of aging   A view of aging as a progressive process of physical, psychological, and social withdrawal from the wider world.

disorganized/disoriented infants   Those who lack coherent coping strategies during separation episodes and indicate confusion and apprehension toward their mothers.

displaced homemaker   A woman whose primary life activity has been homemaking and who has lost her main source of income because of divorce or widowhood.

diuretics   Liquids that cause water loss and also loss of calcium and zinc in the urine.

divergent thinking   Open-ended thought in which multiple solutions are sought, examined, and probed, thereby leading to what are deemed creative responses on measures of creativity.

dizygotic (fraternal twins)   Conception of multiple, nonidentical siblings.

dominant character   In genetics, the property of an allele (gene) that completely masks or hides the other paired allele, as in *AA* or *Aa*.

drug abuse   Excessive or compulsive use of chemical agents to an extent that interferes with an individual's health and social or vocational functioning, or the functioning of the rest of society.

dry eye   Diminished tear production that can be uncomfortable and can usually be eased with eyedrops; typically a condition in late adulthood.

dyslexia   A type of brain dysfunction exhibited by extreme difficulty in learning to read in an otherwise normally intelligent, healthy child or adult.

E

eclectic approach   An approach to studying behavior in which psychologists select from the various theories and models those aspects that provide the best fit for the descriptive and analytical task at hand.

ecological approach   Bronfenbrenner's system of understanding development, according to which the study of developmental influences must include the person's interaction with the environment, the person's changing physical and social settings, the relationship among those settings, and how the entire process is affected by the society in which the settings are embedded.

ecological theory   A theory of development proposed by Bronfenbrenner that proposes that, in order to understand development, researchers must look at the relationship between the developing individual and the changing environment(s).

ectoderm   The cells of the embryo that form the nervous system, the sensory organs, the skin, and the lower part of the rectum.

ectogenesis   The process by which the fetus gestates in an environment external to the mother.

educational self-fulfilling prophecies   Teacher expectation effects whereby some children fail to learn because those who are charged with teaching them do not believe that they will learn, do not expect that they can learn, and do not act toward them in ways that motivate them to learn.

egocentric   Lack of awareness that there are other viewpoints than one's own.

egocentrism   A lack of awareness that there are viewpoints other than one's own. There are two characteristic forms of egocentric thinking in adolescents: the personal fable and the imaginary audience.

elder abuse   Acts of commission and omission that cause unnecessary pain or suffering to older persons.

embryo   The developing organism from the time the blastocyst implants itself in the uterine wall until the organism becomes a recognizable human fetus.

embryonic period   The second stage of prenatal development, the period from the end of the second week to the end of the eighth week of gestation.

emerging adulthood   A stage between adolescence and adulthood.

emotional intelligence (EI)   A relatively new concept, proposed by Goleman, that includes such abilities as being able to motivate oneself, persisting in the face of frustrations, controlling impulses and delaying gratification, empathizing, hoping, and regulating of one's moods to keep distress from overwhelming one's ability to think.

emotional-social development (also called psychosocial development)   A major domain of development that includes changes in an individual's personality, emotions, and relationships with others.

emotions   The physiological changes, subjective experiences, and expressive behaviors that are involved in such feelings as love, joy, grief, anger, and many others.

empathy   Feelings of emotional arousal that lead an individual to take another person's perspective and to experience an event as the other person experiences it.

empty nest   That period of the family life cycle when children have grown up and left home.

empty-nest syndrome   A variety of emotions parents can experience associated with their children growing up and leaving home.

encoding   A cognitive process that involves perceiving information, abstracting from it one or more characteristics needed for classification, and creating corresponding memory traces for it.

endocrinologist   Physician who specializes in treating patients with hormonal disorders.

endoderm   The cells of the embryo that develop into the digestive tract, the respiratory system, the bladder, and portions of the reproductive organs.

endometrial cancer   Estrogen-induced cancer of the endometrium lining of the uterus.

English as a second language (ESL) approach   Instructional methods focused on teaching English to children with limited English proficiency.

English language learners (ELLs)   Refers to students whose native language is not English and who cannot participate effectively in school because they have difficulty speaking, understanding, reading, and writing English.

entelechy   A particular type of motivation, need for self-determination, and an inner strength and vital force directing life and growth to become all one is capable of being.

entrainment   A kind of biological feedback system across two organisms in which the movement of one influences the other.

epigenetic principle   According to Erikson, the principle that each part of the personality has a particular range of time in the life span when it must develop if it is going to develop at all.

equilibrium   In Piaget's theory, this is the result of balance between the processes of assimilation and accommodation.

ethology   The study of the behavior patterns of organisms from a biological perspective.

euthanasia   The act of terminating an ill or injured person's life for reasons of mercy. Also called assisted suicide and mercy killing.

event sampling   A research technique of recording a class of behaviors observed at specific time intervals.

executive strategies   Strategies for integrating and orchestrating lower-level cognitive skills.

exosystem   Bronfenbrenner's third level of environmental influence, consisting of the social structures that directly or indirectly affect a person's life.

experiment   A rigorous study in which the investigator manipulates one or more variables and measures the resulting changes in the other variables in an attempt to determine the cause of a specific behavior.

experimental design   A rigorously objective scientific technique that allows a researcher to attempt to determine the cause of a behavior or event.

experimental group   In an experiment, the group that receives the independent variable (treatment) and then is compared with the control group.

expressive tie   A social link formed when we invest ourselves in and commit ourselves to another person.

expressive vocabulary   Words used by children to effectively convey meaning, feeling, or mood.

extraneous variables   Factors that can confound the outcome of an experiment, such as the age and gender of the subjects, the time of day the study is conducted, the educational levels of the subjects, the setting for the experiment, and so on.

extrinsic motivation   The kind of motivation at work when an activity is undertaken for some reason other than its own sake. Rewards such as school grades, wages, and promotions are examples of extrinsic motivation.

F

failure to thrive (FTT)   An infant or child being severely underweight for its age and sex.

fallopian tubes   Passages from the two ovaries to the uterus that carry the ova from the ovary to the uterus. Fertilization, if it occurs, typically occurs in the fallopian tubes.

family life cycle   The sequential changes and realignments that occur in the structure and relationships of family life between the time of marriage and the death of one or both spouses.

fear   An unpleasant emotion aroused by impending danger, loss, pain, or misfortune.

fertilization/fusion   The union (or fusion) of an ovum and a sperm that usually occurs in the upper end of the fallopian tube and that results in a new structure called the zygote.

fetal alcohol spectrum disorder (FASD)   The range of fetal birth defects caused by drinking alcohol during pregnancy.

fetal period   The third stage of prenatal development, extending from the end of the eighth week until birth.

fetoscopy   A procedure that allows a physician to examine the fetus directly through a lens after inserting a very narrow tube into the uterus.

fetus   The developing organism during the fetal period while in the mother's womb.

fixation   According to psychoanalytic theory, the tendency to stay at a particular psychosexual stage of development.

floaters   Floating spots that actually are particles suspended in the gel-like fluid that fills the eyeball but generally do not impair vision.

fluid intelligence   A cognitive ability to make original adaptations in novel situations. Fluid intelligence is generally tested by measuring an individual's facility in reasoning. Fluid intelligence usually declines with age in later life.

G

gametes   Reproductive cells (sperm and ova).

gender   The state of being male or female.

gender cleavage   The tendency for boys to associate with boys and girls with girls.

gender identity   The conception that people have of themselves as being female or male.

gender roles   A set of cultural expectations that define the ways males and females should behave.

gender stereotypes   Exaggerated generalizations about female or male behaviors.

generation gap   Mutual antagonism, misunderstanding, and separation between youth and adults.

generativity   The concern of an older generation in establishing and guiding the next generation.

generativity versus stagnation   The "crisis" that, according to Erikson, the midlife years are devoted to resolving. Generativity concerns guiding the next generation through nurturing and mentoring. Failure to do otherwise is to become self-centered, which results in psychological invalidism.

genes   Small units of heredity located on chromosomes that transmit inherited characteristics from biological parents to children.

genetic counseling   A process whereby physicians and specialists counsel couples about concerns they may have about inherited diseases in their family history.

genetic counselor   A professional who has a graduate degree, training, and experience in medical genetics and counseling and provides information and support to those who may be at risk for an inherited condition.

genetics   The scientific study of biological inheritance.

genotype   The genetic makeup of an organism.

germinal period   The first stage of prenatal development, which extends from conception to the end of the second week.

gerontology   The study of aging and the special problems associated with it.

geropsychology   The study of the changing behaviors and psychological needs of the elderly.

glaucoma   A condition of vision impairment characterized by increased pressure caused by fluid buildup within the eye that can damage the optic nerve and lead to blindness if left untreated.

grief   An experience involving keen mental anguish and sorrow over the death of a loved one.

group   Two or more people who share a feeling of unity and are bound together in relatively stable patterns of social interaction.

growth   The increase in size that occurs with age.

gynecologist   A physician who specializes in women's reproductive health.

H

harmonious parenting A parenting style distinguished by an unwillingness to exert direct control over children, in an attempt to cultivate an egalitarian relationship.

heredity The genes we inherit from our biological parents, which help shape our physical, intellectual, social, and emotional development.

heteronomous morality The first stage of Piaget's two-stage theory on moral development, which arises from the unequal interaction between children and adults.

heterozygous In biological inheritance, the arrangement in which two paired alleles (genes) are different.

hierarchy of needs A key concept of Abraham Maslow's humanistic theory, which indicates that basic needs must be met before self-development and self-esteem needs can be fulfilled.

holistic approach The humanistic approach according to which the human condition must be viewed in its totality, and each person is a whole rather than a mere collection of physical, social, and psychological components.

holophrase A single word used to convey complete thoughts or sentences; characteristic of the early stages of language acquisition in young children.

homozygous In biological inheritance, the arrangement in which the two paired alleles (genes) are the same.

horizontal décalage According to Piaget, a type of sequential development in which each skill is dependent upon the acquisition of earlier skills.

hormone replacement therapy (HRT) A medical regimen often recommended by physicians to women after menopause to maintain cardiovascular fitness and a slowing of bone loss and memory loss.

hospice A program or mode of providing comfort, care, and pain relief to persons dying of cancer or other terminal illness and comfort to the relatives of the patient. Care may be conducted in a hospice center or in the patient's home.

human genome A map of the genetic makeup of all the genes on their appropriate chromosomes being studied extensively by researchers in the Human Genome Project.

human growth hormone (HGH) A powerful hormone originally administered to treat children afflicted by dwarfism but is now taken as a trendy antiaging potion by some of the social elite.

humanistic psychology A psychological theory, deriving from Abraham Maslow, Carl Rogers, and others, proposing that humans are different from all other organisms in that they actively intervene in the course of events to control their destinies and shape the world around them.

hypertension High blood pressure.

hypothyroidism An underactive thyroid gland whose symptoms include weight gain, hair loss, fatigue, depression, muscle and joint pain, dry skin, and constipation.

hypothermia A condition in which body temperature falls more than 4 degrees Fahrenheit below normal and persists at this low level for a number of hours.

hypothesis A tentative proposition that can be tested in a research study; forming a hypothesis is one of the initial steps in the scientific method.

hysterectomy Surgical procedure in which a woman's ovaries and possibly uterus are removed.

I

identity According to Erikson, identity is defined as a sense of well-being achieved by being comfortable in one's body, by knowing where one is going, and by being recognized by significant others.

identity achievement One of James Marcia's four identity types. The individual is able to achieve inner stability that corresponds to how others perceive that person.

identity diffusion According to Erikson, an inability to commit to an occupational or ideological position and to assume a recognizable station in life, experienced by some adolescents.

identity foreclosure One of James Marcia's four identity types. Identity foreclosure is characterized by the individual's avoidance of autonomous choice.

identity moratorium One of James Marcia's four identity types that occurs when the adolescent experiments with various roles, ideologies, and commitments.

imaginary audience An adolescent's belief that everyone in the local environment is primarily concerned with her or his appearance and behavior.

imaginary friend An invisible character whom a young child names, refers to in conversations, and plays with.

implantation The process in which the blastocyst completely buries itself in the wall of the uterus.

impotence A male's inability to have or sustain an erection.

imprinting A process of attachment that occurs only during a relatively short period and is so resistant to change that the behavior appears to be innate.

in vitro fertilization (IVF) Fertilization that occurs outside the body, typically in a petri dish in a medical lab environment, followed by implantation of a fertilized egg into a woman's uterus in an attempt to accomplish pregnancy.

inclusion The integration of students with special needs within the regular classroom programs of the school.

independent variable The variable that is manipulated by the researcher during an experiment in order to observe its effects on the dependent variable. This is often referred to as the treatment variable.

individualism View that individual autonomy is paramount.

Individuals with Disabilities Education Act (IDEA) Legislation providing early intervention services which seeks to enhance the development of infants and toddlers with disabilities and their families' ability to meet their needs.

individualized education plan (IEP) A plan developed in a collaborative effort by the school psychologist, the child's teachers, an independent child advocate, and the parent(s) or guardian that is a legal document ensuring that the child with special learning needs will be provided with educational support services in the least restrictive learning environment.

industry versus inferiority The fourth stage of Erikson's psychosocial model of development in which children either work industriously and are rewarded or fail and develop a sense of inferiority.

infancy The period of child development during the first two years of life.

infant mortality The death of an infant within the first year of life.

information processing The application of mental operations that we use in tackling intellectual tasks in a step-by-step fashion.

informed consent An ethical standard, established by the American Psychological Association, that requires the researcher to inform each subject about the research study and obtain from each subject his or her voluntary, written consent to participate in a research study.

initiative versus guilt According to Erikson, the psychosocial stage in early childhood (about ages 3 to 6) when children strive exuberantly to do things and to test their developing abilities, sometimes reaching beyond their competence.

inner cell mass The internal disc or cluster of cells that compose the blastocyst, which produces the embryo.

insecure/avoidant infants (pattern A attachments) Infants that ignored or avoided their mother when she returned.

insecure/resistant infants (pattern C attachments) Infants that were reluctant to explore a new setting and would cling to their mothers and hide from a stranger.

instrumental tie A social link that is formed when cooperating with another person to achieve a limited goal.

integrity versus despair Erikson's psychosocial stage of late adulthood in which individuals recognize they are reaching the end of life. People take satisfaction in having led a full and complete life, or view their lives with feelings of loss, disappointment, and purposelessness—depending on how they navigated the previous stages of development.

intelligence According to Wechsler, a global capacity to learn exhibited by an understanding of the world, rational thought, and resourceful coping with the challenges of life.

intelligence quotient (IQ) A single number derived from tests of intelligence.

interference theory The theory that retrieval of a cue becomes less effective as more and newer items come to be classed or categorized in terms of it.

interpersonal intelligence The ability to understand other people: what motivates them, how they work, and how to work cooperatively with them.

intimacy The ability to experience a trusting, supportive, and tender relationship with another person.

intimacy versus isolation Erikson's stage of psychosocial development when young adults reach out and attempt to make close connections with other people. Failure to do so can lead to more isolated lives devoid of meaningful bonds.

intrapersonal intelligence Correlative ability turned inward, the capacity to form an accurate, veridical model of oneself, and to be able to use that model to operate effectively in life.

intrinsic motivation The motivation at work when activity is undertaken for its own sake.

in vitro fertilization Fertilization of an egg with sperm outside a woman's body to create a zygote, which will be grown into an embryo and then transplanted into the woman's uterus.

J

job burnout Feelings of dissatisfaction and lack of fulfillment regarding work that once was fulfilling and satisfying.

joint custody A legal custody arrangement where both parents share equally in significant child-rearing decisions and share in regular child-care responsibilities.

K

kinesics Communication by body language.

kinship care An arrangement in which a relative or someone else emotionally close to the child takes primary responsibility for rearing a child.

L

labor In childbirth, the stage when the strong muscle fibers of the mother's uterus rhythmically contract and push the infant downward toward the birth canal.

language A structured system of sound patterns (words and sentences) that have socially standardized meanings that enable people to categorize objects, events, and processes in their environment and communicate with each other about them.

language acquisition device (LAD) An inborn language-generating mechanism in humans, hypothesized by Chomsky. Central to Chomsky's theory of language development is the idea that young children, just from having heard words and sentences spoken, can produce speech.

language reception The quality of receiving or taking in communication.

learning The more or less permanent change in behavior that results from the individual's experience in the environment across the entire life span.

learning disabilities (LDs) The classification used for children, adolescents, and college students who encounter difficulty with school-related material, despite the fact that they appear to have normal intelligence and lack a demonstrable physical, emotional, or social impairment.

life events Turning points at which individuals change direction in the course of their lives.

life review A reminiscence and sharing of family history from one generation to another.

lifestyle The overall pattern of living whereby one attempts to meet biological, social, and emotional needs.

lightening The repositioning of the infant that occurs a few weeks prior to birth, shifting the infant downward and forward in the uterus to lighten the mother's discomfort and ensure that the baby will be born head first.

limited English proficiency (LEP) The legal educational term used to describe students who were not born in the United States and/or whose native language is not English and who cannot participate effectively in the regular school curriculum because they have difficulty speaking, understanding, reading, and writing English.

living will A legal document that states the individual's wishes regarding medical care in case the individual becomes incapacitated and unable to participate in medical care decisions (such as a refusal of heroic measures to prolong her or his life in the event of terminal illness).

locomotion The infant's ability to walk, which typically evolves between 11 and 15 months of age, and is the climax of a long series of early motor development preceded by crawling and creeping.

locus of control An individual's perception regarding who or what is responsible for the outcome of events and behaviors in her or his life. An important moderator of an individual's experience of stress.

longitudinal design   A research approach in which scientists study the same individuals at different points in their lives to assess developmental changes that occur with age.

long-term memory   Information retained in memory over an extended period of time.

M

macrosystem   Bronfenbrenner's fourth level of environmental influence, consisting of the overarching cultural patterns of a society that find expression in family, educational, economic, political, and religious institutions.

macular degeneration   A thinning of the layers of the retina and/or rupturing of tiny blood vessels in the eye, producing faded, distorted, or blurred central vision; more common in late adulthood.

marriage   A legally, socially, and/or religiously sanctioned union between a woman and a man with the expectation that they will perform the mutually supportive roles of wife and husband.

maternal blood sampling   A blood test that can detect birth defects by analyzing fetal cells shed into the pregnant woman's bloodstream.

maternal serum alpha-fetoprotein (MSAFP) test   A maternal blood test used to detect certain fetal disorders that analyzes the concentration of two major blood proteins: albumin and alpha-fetoprotein (AFP) produced by the fetus.

maturation   A component of development that involves the more or less automatic unfolding of biological potential in a sequence of physical changes and behavior patterns.

maturity   In human beings, the capacity to undergo continual change in order to adapt successfully and cope flexibly with the demands and responsibilities of life.

mechanistic model   A model of development that represents the universe as a machine composed of elementary particles in motion. Human development is portrayed as a gradual, chainlike sequence of events.

meiosis   The process of cell division in reproductive cells that produces gametes with half of the organism's normal number of chromosomes.

melanoma   A more serious skin cancer which could be life threatening.

memory   The cognitive capacity to retain information that has been experienced.

menarche   The first menstrual period.

menopause   The normal aging process that culminates in the cessation of female menstrual activity. In Western countries, the typical age range of menopause is from 45 to 55 years old.

menstrual cycle   A series of hormonal changes within a woman, beginning with menstruation and ovulation, typically about 28 days per cycle.

menstruation   The maturing of an ovum and the process of ovulation and eventual shedding of the uterine lining and expulsion of an unfertilized ovum from the body through the vagina.

mental retardation (MR)   The classification of having below average mental functioning and limitations in adaptive skills, and such a diagnosis must occur before the age of 18.

mentor   A teacher, experienced co-worker, boss, or the like who shares expertise and guides someone in new learning.

mesoderm   The cells of the embryo which give rise to the skeletal, muscular, and circulatory systems and the kidneys.

mesosystem   Bronfenbrenner's second level of environmental influences, consisting of the interrelationships among the various settings in which the developing person is immersed.

metacognition   An individual's awareness and understanding of his or her own mental processes.

metamemory   An individual's awareness and understanding of her or his memory processes.

methylphenidate   A mild stimulant of the central nervous system used to treat ADD or ADHD behavior disorders (brand name Ritalin).

microsystem   Bronfenbrenner's first level of environmental influence, which consists of the network of social relationships and the physical settings in which a person is involved each day.

midwifery   The legalized provision of prenatal care and delivery by midwives.

miscarriage   Expulsion of the zygote, embryo, or fetus from the uterus before it can survive outside the mother's womb.

mitosis   The process of ordinary cell division, which results in two new cells identical to the parent cell.

modernization theory   The theory that the status of the elderly tends to be high in traditional societies and lower in urbanized, industrialized societies.

monozygotic (identical twins)   Conception of multiple, identical siblings from one fertilized egg.

moral development   The process by which children adopt principles and values that lead them to evaluate behaviors as "right" or "wrong" and to govern their own actions in terms of these principles.

moral exemplars   Individuals dedicated to acts of morality.

morphology   The study of word formation and changes, as when a child learns to say "Jim's and mine" instead of "Jim's and mines."

motherese (parentese)   The speech adults tend to use with infants and young children; language that characteristically is simplified, redundant, and highly grammatical.

motivation   The inner emotional or cognitive states and processes that prompt, direct, and sustain a person's activity.

mourning   The culturally or socially established manner of expressing sorrow over a person's death.

multifactorial transmission   The interaction of environmental factors with genetic factors to produce traits. For example, a child's inborn predisposition for musical talent can be nurtured or deterred by environmental forces, such as parents or teachers.

multiinfarcts   "Little strokes" that destroy small areas of brain tissue.

multiple intelligences (MIs)   Nine distinctive intelligences that interact: verbal-linguistic, logical-mathematical, visual-spatial, musical, bodily-kinesthetic, interpersonal, naturalist, intrapersonal, and existentialist.

multiple mothering   An arrangement in which responsibility for a child's care is dispersed among several caregivers.

N

natural childbirth   A form of childbirth in which the woman is awake, aware, and unmedicated during labor and delivery.

natural selection   Darwin's evolutionary theory that organisms best adapted to their environment survive and pass on their genetic characteristics to offspring.

naturalistic observation   A research method that involves carefully watching and recording behavior as it occurs in natural settings. The researchers must be careful not to disturb or affect the events under investigation.

near-death experience (NDE)   An experience such as having spiritually left one's body, having undergone otherworldly experiences, and having been "told to come back"—commonly reported by person's experiencing a medical illness, a traumatic accident, a surgical operation, childbirth, or drug ingestion.

negative identity   A diminished self-image, often associated with a diminished social role.

neglect   A type of abuse committed by a caretaker in failing to provide adequate social, emotional, and physical care to maintain the health or safety of a vulnerable person.

neonate   A newborn baby in the first month of life.

neonatology intensive care unit (NICU)   A special medical unit staffed with perinatologists and neonatologists who specialize in managing complicated, high-risk pregnancies, birth, and postbirth experience.

nonnormative life events   In the timing-of-events model, a set of unique turning points at which people change some direction in their life.

normative age-graded influences   In the timing-of-events model, a set of influences that include physical, cognitive, and psychosocial changes at predictable ages.

normative history-graded influences   In the timing-of-events model, historical events, such as wars, epidemics, and economic depressions, that affect large numbers of individuals about the same time.

norms   In child development, standards used for evaluating a child's developmental progress relative to the average for the child's age group.

nuclear family   A family arrangement consisting of a mother, a father, and their biological or adopted children.

O

obesity   Being at least 20 percent over the recommended weight for one's sex, height, and body structure.

object permanence   The understanding that objects continue to exist when they are out of sight; Piaget said this cognitive capacity is mastered by the end of infancy.

obstetrician   Physician who specializes in reproduction, prenatal development, birth, and the woman's postbirth care.

occupational therapist   A therapist who helps children improve basic motor function and reasoning abilities and also learn to compensate for permanent loss of function.

operant conditioning   A type of learning in which the consequences of a behavior alter the strength of that behavior.

oral-sensory stage   Erikson's first stage of psychosocial development in which an infant develops trust in others if a caregiver is responsive and consistent in feeding, comforting, and caring for the infant.

organismic model   A model of development that views human beings as an organized configuration. Human development is characterized by discrete, steplike states.

osteoporosis   A serious bone-thinning disorder that is a "silent" disease, but most evident in late adulthood. An adult's bones typically begin thinning during the midthirties, but weight-bearing exercise and calcium in the diet can prevent or slow its progression.

otitis media   A painful ear infection in young children that causes fluid buildup in the middle ear with the potential for hearing loss if left untreated.

ovaries   The ovaries are a pair of almond-shaped structures that lie in the pelvis that are the primary female reproductive organs. The ovaries produce mature ova and the female sex hormones, estrogen and progesterone.

ovulation   The discharge of a mature ovum from a follicle in the ovary into the fallopian tube.

ovum   The female gamete (sex cell), or egg.

P

paralanguage   The stress, pitch, and volume of vocalizations by which we communicate expressive meaning.

parentese (motherese)   A simplified, redundant, highly grammatical type of language caretakers use with infants.

parent-infant bonding   A process of interaction and mutual attention that occurs over time that builds an emotional bond between parent and infant.

peers   Individuals of approximately the same age.

penis   A man's external reproductive organ.

perimenopause   The period of two to four years before the cessation of menstruation, with sometimes heavy flow and the extension of intervals between periods.

period of concrete operations   Piaget's cognitive stage of middle childhood during which children demonstrate a qualitative change in cognitive functioning and develop a set of rules or strategies for examining the world.

period of formal operations   Piaget's highest stage in the development of cognitive functioning characterized by the ability to think abstractly and to plan for the future, generally reached during adolescence by a majority of people. Adults with cognitive disabilities might never reach the stage of formal operations.

periodontal disease   Condition where the gums of the teeth begin to recede.

permissive parenting   A style of parenting distinguished by a nonpunitive, accepting, and affirmative environment in which the child regulates her or his own behavior as much as possible.

persistent vegetative state   The state in which the functions of the brainstem, such as breathing and circulation, remain intact, but the person loses the higher functioning of the cerebral cortex.

person permanence   The notion that an individual exists independently of immediate visibility.

personal fable   Romantic imagery in which adolescents tend to view themselves as somehow unique and even heroic—as destined for unusual fame and fortune.

phenotype   The observable (expressed) characteristics of an organism.

phobia   An excessive, persistent, and maladaptive fear response—usually to benign or ill-defined stimuli.

phonemes   The smallest units of language such as the long A in bake.

phonology   The study of the sounds involved in a given language.

physical development   Changes that occur in a person's body, including changes in weight and height; in the brain, heart, and other organ structures and processes; and in skeletal, muscular, and neurological features that affect motor, sensory, and coordination skills.

placenta   A structure formed from uterine tissue and the trophoblast of the blastocyst. It functions as an exchange terminal, permitting entry of food materials, oxygen, and hormones into the fetus and allowing exit of carbon dioxide and metabolic wastes.

placenta previa   A condition when the placenta is lower in the uterus than the fetus's head, partially or fully covering the cervix, and may lead to hemorrhaging of the placenta or prevent vaginal delivery, thus leading to a cesarean delivery. Such a serious condition can be detected by ultrasound.

play   Enjoyable voluntary activities that are performed for their own sake.

polygenic inheritance   The determination of traits by a large number of genes in combination and not by a single gene. Examples include personality, intelligences, aptitudes, and abilities.

post-formal operational thought   A fifth stage of cognitive development proposed by neo-Piagetians that is characterized by three features: Adults come to realize that knowledge is not absolute but relativistic, contradiction is inherent in life, and they must find some encompassing whole by which to organize their experience.

postmature infant   A baby delivered more than 2 weeks after the usual 40 weeks of gestation in the womb.

postmenopause   Time period in a woman's life after she no longer menstruates for one year.

postpartum depression (PPD)   Symptoms of depression experienced by some new mothers, such as feeling unable to cope, thoughts of not wanting to take care of the baby, or thoughts of wanting to harm the baby. Also called postportum blues.

post-traumatic stress disorder (PTSD)   A person's delayed response to severe or prolonged stress. Symptoms might include numbing and helplessness, increased irritability and aggressiveness, extreme anxiety, panic and fears, exaggerated startle response, sleep disturbances, and bed-wetting.

pragmatics   Rules governing the use of language in different social contexts.

preeclampsia   A serious disorder a small percent of women experience during pregnancy that causes high blood pressure and the presence of protein in the blood—affecting both the mother and the fetus.

prejudice   A system of negative conceptions, feelings, and actions regarding the members of a particular religious, racial, or ethnic group.

premature infant   By common standards, a baby weighing less than 5 pounds 8 ounces at birth or having a gestational age of less than 37 weeks.

premature menopause   Early menopause (before age 40) often brought about by a hysterectomy.

prenatal diagnosis   A determination of the health and condition of an unborn fetus.

prenatal period   The period of development from conception to birth.

preoperational period   Piaget's stage of cognitive development of children aged 2 to 7. The principal achievement of this stage is the developing capacity to represent the external world internally through the use of symbols.

presbycusis   The inability to hear high-pitched sounds, which is more common in elderly adults.

presbyopia   A normal condition in which the lens of the eye starts to harden with age, losing its ability to accommodate as quickly as it did in younger years.

primary relationships   Social interactions based on significant expressive ties, such as with parents, spouse, siblings, and children.

private speech   Speech commonly used by toddlers and older children that is directed toward one's self or nobody in particuliar.

prosocial behavior   Being sympathetic, cooperative, helpful, rescuing, comforting, and generous; learning such behavior is considered to be an aspect of moral development.

prostate gland   A small gland in males at the base of the urethra that produces prostate fluid for semen. It generally enlarges as males reach their fifties or sixties, creating urinary difficulties.

prostatitis   An inflammation of the prostate gland.

proximodistal development (proximodistal principal)   Development that proceeds outward from the central axis of the body toward the extremities.

PSA test   Medical test that measures a substance called prostate-specific antigen, which is made by the prostate.

psychoanalytic theory   Theory based on Freud's view that personality is fashioned progressively as the individual passes through various psychosexual stages of development.

psychoprophylactic method   A preparatory technique in childbirth used to encourage women to relax and concentrate on their breathing when a contraction occurs during labor.

psychosexual stages   The stages of personality development that Freud believed all human beings pass through: oral, anal, phallic, latency, and genital.

psychosocial development   An individual's development within a social context over the life course.

puberty   The period during early adolescence when sexual and reproductive maturation become evident.

puberty rites   Cultural initiation ceremonies that socially symbolize an adolescent's transition from childhood to adulthood.

R

random sampling   A sample for which each member of the population has an equally likely probability of being chosen; a technique to ensure that the sample under study represents the larger population.

rape   Sexual relations obtained through physical force, threats, or intimidation.

reactive attachment disorder (RAD)   A clinical diagnosis that includes disturbed and developmentally inappropriate social relatedness with peers (autistic-like behaviors, hyperactivity).

recall   Act of remembering something previously learned.

receptive vocabulary   An understanding of spoken words, exhibited by infants before they have developed an expressive vocabulary (speaking their first words).

recessive character   A gene that can determine a trait in an individual only if the other member of that gene pair is also recessive, as in *aa*.

reciprocity   A process that leads to each child's valuing the other person in a way that allows the child to remember the values that their interactions bring about. Piaget asserts that reciprocity of attitudes and values is the foundation of social interchange in children.

recognition   A feeling of familiarity or perceiving something that was previously encountered.

recreational therapist   A physical therapist that works with children to help restore function, improve mobility, relieve pain, and prevent or limit permanent physical disabilities of patients.

reflex   A relatively simple, involuntary, and unlearned physiological response to a stimulus.

rehearsal   A type of memory process in which we repeat information to ourselves to retain information.

reinforcement   One event's strengthening the probability of another event's occurrence. A concept of behavioral theory popularized by B. F. Skinner.

releasing stimuli   Biologically preadapted behaviors and features in infants that activate parenting.

reproduction   The process by which organisms create more organisms of their own kind.

resource dilution hypothesis   The theory that in large families resources get spread thin, to the detriment of all the offspring.

response   A term used by behavioral theorists to break down behavior into units.

retrieval   The cognitive process by which information is gathered from memory when it is required for recall or recognition.

reversibility of operations   The child's failure to recognize that operations can be done in reverse to regain to an earlier state. According to Piaget, it is the most distinguishing characteristic of preoperational thought.

rheumatoid arthritis   An inflammatory disease most common in the elderly that causes pain, swelling, stiffness, and loss of function of the joint.

right to privacy   An ethical standard established by the American Psychological Association requiring that researchers keep confidential all their records of behaviors or information about research participants.

role conflict   A type of stress that occurs when people experience pressures within one role that are incompatible with the pressures that arise within another role (for example, having to be at work and also having to take care of a sick child).

role exit theory of aging   A theory that views retirement and widowhood as life events terminating the participation of the elderly in the principal institutional structures of society—the job and the family.

role overload   A type of stress that occurs when people have too many role demands and too little time to fulfill them.

romantic love   Typically what we think of when we say we are "in love" with someone.

rooming in   An arrangement in a hospital whereby the newborn stays in a bassinet beside the mother's bed, allowing the mother and other family members to care for and to become acquainted with the newborn.

S

sandwich generation   People in middle adulthood who are caring for growing children at the same time as they are helping elderly parents and relatives.

scaffolding   Helping the child to learn through intervention and tutoring that is geared to the child's current level of functioning.

schemas   Piaget's term for mental structures that people evolve to deal with events in their environment.

scientific method   A systematic and formal process for conducting research, including selecting a researchable problem, formulating a hypothesis, testing the hypothesis, arriving at conclusions, and making the findings public.

secondary relationships   Social interactions based on instrumental ties, such as a relationship with a mechanic, or a teacher in a classroom, or a clerk at a store.

securely attached infants (pattern B attachments)   Infants who would greet their mothers warmly, show little anger, or indicate a desire to be picked up and comforted.

selective attrition   Theory that individuals who drop out of a study tend to be different from those who remain in a study.

selective optimization with compensation   The life-span model endorsed by Paul and Margret Baltes. Older people cope with aging through a strategy that involves focusing on the skills most needed, practicing those skills, and developing ways to compensate for other skills.

self   The system of concepts we use in defining ourselves; the awareness of ourselves as separate entities who think and initiate action. The self provides us with the capacity to observe, respond to, and direct our behavior.

self-actualization   Maslow's concept from humanistic psychology that each person needs to fulfill his or her unique potential to the fullest.

self-concept (self-image)   The image a person has of herself or himself.

self-esteem   An overall dimension of one's sense of self-worth or self-image.

self-image   The overall view people have of themselves, which can be positive or negative.

semantics   The rules of meaning in a language, by which words have meaning and are combined to express complete thoughts.

senescence   The process of growing old, which affects a person both physically and cognitively.

senility   A deterioration in cognitive functioning in late adulthood characterized by a lack of consistency in personality and/or behavior.

sensorimotor period   Piaget's first stage of cognitive development, lasting from birth to about two years. Infants use actions—looking, grasping, and so on—to learn about their world. The major tasks of the period revolve around coordinating motor activities with sensory inputs.

sensory integration   A normal developmental process that allows one to take in, process, and organize sensations one receives from one's body and the environment.

sensory information storage   The preservation of sensory information in the sensory register just long enough to permit the stimuli to be scanned for processing, generally less than 2 seconds.

separation anxiety   An infant's fear of being separated from the caregiver, demonstrated by distress behaviors.

sequential designs   A combination of the longitudinal and cross-sectional methods of research.

sex chromosomes The 23rd pair of chromosomes, either XX or XY, which determine the baby's sex.

sex-linked traits Traits other than gender that are affected by genes found on the sex chromosomes. For example, hemophilia is a sex-linked characteristic carried on the X chromosome.

sexual abuse of children Sexual behavior between a child and an older person that the older person brings about through force, coercion, or deceit.

sexually transmitted infections (STIs) Infections transmitted through sexual intercourse or in some cases oral sex (e.g., gonorrhea, syphilis, chlamydia, HIV). Using condoms greatly reduces the risk of contracting an STI.

shaken baby syndrome (SBS) Serious brain damage or death that occurs when a baby's head is violently shaken back and forth or strikes something, resulting in bruising or bleeding of the brain, spinal cord injury, and eye damage.

short-term memory The retention of information in memory for a very brief period, usually no more than 30 seconds.

sleep apnea A sleep disorder in which the person occasionally stops breathing during sleep.

small-for-term infant A low-birth-weight infant that has developed over the usual 40 weeks of gestation in the womb but is born weighing less than is expected.

social aging Changes in an individual's assumptions and roles as she or he ages.

social clock A set of social concepts regarding the appropriate ages for reaching milestones of the adult years.

social convoy The company of other people who travel with us from birth to death.

social exchange theory of aging The theory that people enter into social relationships in order to derive rewards (economic, social, emotional). People also incur costs in social relationships. Relationships persist as long as both parties profit.

social norms Standards and expectations that specify what constitutes appropriate and inappropriate behavior for individuals at various periods in the life span.

social referencing The practice whereby an inexperienced person relies on a more experienced person's interpretation of an event to regulate his or her own behavior.

social relationships Bonds forged with other people in relatively stable social circumstances.

social survey method A research method used to study the incidence of specific behaviors, attitudes, or beliefs in a large population of people.

socialization The process of transmitting culture to children in order to transform them into well-functioning members of society.

sociocultural theory The theory that psychological functions as thinking, reasoning, and remembering are facilitated through language and anchored in the child's interpersonal relationships.

sociogram A type of graph depicting the patterns of peer friendships and relationships existing among members of a group at a given time.

spatial ability The ability to mentally manipulate images in different dimensions.

sperm The male gamete (sex cell).

spontaneous abortion The medical term for miscarriage, which is usually preceded by cramping or bleeding.

states In child development, an infant's continuum of alertness ranging from sleep to vigorous activity, and including such behaviors as crying, sleeping, eating, and eliminating. By regulating their internal states, infants shut out certain stimuli or set the stage to actively respond to their environment.

stem cells Cells that have the capacity to reproduce themselves and to produce distinct differentiated tissues.

stereotypes Exaggerated cultural understandings that guide us in identifying the mutual set of expectations that will govern the social exchange.

stimuli A term used by behavioral theorists to break down the environment into units.

storage The retention of information in memory until it is needed.

storm and stress Hall's notion that adolescence is a stage of inevitable turmoil, maladjustment, tension, rebellion, dependency conflicts, and exaggerated peer-group conformity.

Strange Situation A research technique consisting of a series of eight episodes in which researchers observe infants in an unfamiliar playroom in order to study attachment with a mother.

stranger anxiety A wariness or fear of strangers first exhibited by infants at about 8 months, peaking around 13 to 15 months, and decreasing thereafter.

stroke A life-threatening blockage of blood flow to the brain.

substance abuse The harmful use of drugs or alcohol, lasting over a prolonged period, that can harm the user or others.

sudden infant death syndrome (SIDS) Sudden death of an infant during sleep, due to unknown causes, also called "crib death." One of the leading causes of infant death during the first several months of life. Babies should sleep on their backs to reduce the risk of SIDS.

syntax Rules governing the proper ordering of words to form sentences.

systolic pressure Blood pressure when the heart contracts and is pumping blood.

T

telegraphic speech The use of two- or three-word utterances to express complete thoughts, characteristic of young children's speech.

temperament The relatively consistent, basic dispositions inherent in people that underlie and modulate much of their behavior.

teratogen Any agent that contributes to birth defects or anomalies.

teratology The study of teratogens and birth defects.

testes A pair of primary male reproductive organs, normally lying outside the body in a pouchlike structure called a scrotum.

testosterone Male sex hormone.

thanatology The study of death and dying.

theory A set of interrelated statements intended to explain a class of events.

theory of mind In child development, research that probes children's developing conceptions of major components of mental activity.

time sampling An observational technique that involves counting the occurrences of a specific behavior over systematically spaced intervals of time.

total immersion programs   The instructional approach placing children of all language backgrounds together in regular classrooms and using English for all instruction (with or without support in their first language).

traditional marriage   The style of marriage in which women are homemakers and men are providers.

transition points   Periods in development when the individual relinquishes familiar roles and assumes new ones.

triangular theory of love   Sternberg's theory that different stages and types of love can be explained as combinations of the three elements of intimacy, passion, and commitment.

trophoblast   Outer layer of cells of the blastocyst; this layer is responsible for embedding the embryo in the uterine wall.

two-factor theory of intelligence   Spearman's view that intelligence is a general intellectual ability employed for abstract reasoning and problem solving.

two-way bilingual programs   The instructional approach in which both native-speaking students and nonnative speakers receive instruction in English and in another language; participation is voluntary and instruction is equally divided between two languages.

U

ultrasonography   A noninvasive diagnostic procedure that allows physicians to see inside the body—for instance, to determine the size and shape of the fetus and placenta, the amount of amniotic fluid, and the appearance of fetal anatomy.

umbilical cord   A connecting lifeline carrying two arteries and one vein linking the embryo to the placenta.

uterus   A hollow, thick-walled, muscular organ in a female that can house and nourish a developing embryo and fetus.

V

vagina   A muscular passageway in the female reproductive system that is capable of considerable dilation, allowing for intercourse or birth of a baby.

values   The criteria individuals use in deciding the relative merit and desirability of things (such as themselves, other people, objects, events, ideas, acts, feelings).

W

wisdom   Expert knowledge about life in general and good judgment and advice about how to conduct oneself in complex, uncertain circumstances.

Y

youth culture   Characteristics of a large body of young people that become standardized ways of thinking, feeling, and behaving.

Z

zone of proximal development (ZPD)   Vygotsky's concept that children develop through participation in activities slightly beyond their competence when helped by a more skilled partner.

zygote   A single fertilized ovum (egg).

References

A genome wide screen for autism: Strong evidence for linkage to chromosomes 2q, 7q, and 16p. (2001). *American Journal of Human Genetics, 69,* 570–581.

Abe, J. A., & Izard, C. E. (1999). A longitudinal study of emotion expression and personality relations in early development. *Journal of Personality and Social Psychology, 77,* 566–577.

Abeles, N., Victor, T. L., & Delano-Wood, L. (2004). The impact of an older adult's death on the family. *Professional Psychology: Research and Practice, 35*(3), 234–239.

Aboud, F. E. (2003, January). The formation of in-group favoritism and out-group prejudice in young children: Are they distinct attitudes? *Developmental Psychology, 39,* 48–60.

Aboulafia, M. (Ed.). (1991). *Philosophy, social theory, and the thought of George Herbert Mead.* Albany: State University of New York Press.

Abramov, I., Gordon, J., Hendrickson, A., Hainline, L., Dobson, V., & LaBossiere, E. (1982). The retina of the newborn human infant. *Science, 217,* 265–267.

Abrams, S., Prodromidis, M., Scafidi, F., & Field, T. (1995). Newborns of depressed mothers. *Infant Mental Health Journal, 16,* 233–239.

Academy for Eating Disorders. (2005). *About eating disorders.* Retrieved February 25, 2005, from http://www.aedweb.org/eating_disorders/index.cfm

Accardo, P., & Blondis, T. A. (2001). What's all the fuss about Ritalin? *The Journal of Pediatrics, 138,* 6–9.

Achenbaum, W. (1998). Perceptions of aging in America. *National Forum: Phi Kappa Phi Journal, 78,* 30–33.

Achieve. (2005, February). *National summary: Education pipeline data profile.* Retrieved March 31, 2005, from http://www.achieve.org/dstore.nsf/Lookup/poll/$file/poll.ppt

Acredolo, L. P., & Hake, J. K. (1982). Infant perception. In B. B. Wolman (Ed.), *Handbook of developmental psychology.* Englewood Cliffs, NJ: Prentice Hall.

Acs, G., & Nelson, S. (2002, July). *The kids are alright? Children's well-being and the rise in cohabitation.* Discussion paper B-48, New Federalism: National Survey of America's Families. Washington, DC: The Urban Institute. Retrieved September 15, 2004, from http://www.urban.org/UploadedPDF/310544_B48.pdf

Adair, J. (1775). *The history of the American Indians.* London: E. D. Dilly.

Adams, C., Labouvie-Vief, G., Hobart, C. J., & Dorosz, M. (1990). Adult age group differences in story recall style. *Journal of Gerontology, 45,* P17–P27.

Adams, R. G., & Blieszner, R. (1998, Spring). Baby boomer friendships. *Generations, 22,* 70–75.

Adams, R. G., Blieszner, R., & de Vries, B. (2000, January). Definitions of friendship in the third age: Age, gender, and study location effects. *Journal of Aging Studies, 14*(1), 117–133.

Adamson, L. (1996). *Communication development during infancy.* Boulder, CO: Westview Press.

Addison, S. (2004). Understanding early intervention services. *The Exceptional Parent, 34*(8), 63–65.

Adelman, K. (1991). The toughest thing. *Washingtonian, 26,* 23.

Adelson, J. (1972). The political imagination of the young adolescent. In J. Kagan & R. Coles (Eds.), *Twelve to sixteen.* New York: Norton.

Adelson, J. (1975). The development of ideology in adolescence. In S. E. Dragastin & G. H. Elder, Jr. (Eds.), *Adolescence in the life cycle: Psychological change and social context.* New York: Wiley.

Adler, L. L. (Ed.). (1989). *Cross-cultural research in human development: Life span perspectives.* New York: Praeger.

Administration on Aging. (2001). *A profile of older Americans: 2001.* Retrieved December 27, 2001, from http://www.aoa.dhhs.gov/aoa/stats/ prolfile/2001/8.html

Adolph, K. E. (2000). Specificity of learning: Why infants fall over a veritable cliff. *Psychological Science, 11,* 290–295.

Adolphs, R., & Damasio, A. (2001). The interaction of affect and cognition: A neurobiological perspective. In J. P. Forgas (Ed.), *The handbook of affect and social cognition.* Mahwah, NJ: Erlbaum.

Adoption Institute. (2005). *Private domestic adoption facts.* Retrieved February 15, 2005, from http://www.adoptioninstitute.org/FactOverview/domestic.html

Ahnert, L., & Lamb, M. (2001). The East German child care system: Associations with caretaking and caretaking beliefs, and children's early attachment and adjustment. *American Behavioral Scientist, 44*(11), 1843–1863.

Ai, A.L., Peterson, C., Bolling, S.F., & Koenig, H,. (2002). Private prayer and optimism in middle-aged and older patients awaiting cardiac surgery. *Gerontologist, 42,* 70–81.

AIDS epidemic update. (December 2001). UNAIDS/WHO. Retrieved January 11, 2002, from http: http://www.unaids.org

AIDS epidemic update: 2004. (2004, December). *Joint United Nations Programme on HIV/AIDS (UNAIDS) and World Health Organization (WHO).* Retrieved December 30, 2004, from http://www.unaids.org

Aiken, L. (1998). *Human development in adulthood.* New York: Plenum.

Ainsworth, M. D. S. (1967). *Infancy in Uganda: Infant care and the growth of attachment.* Baltimore: Johns Hopkins University Press.

Ainsworth, M. D. S. (1983). Patterns of infant-mother attachment as related to maternal care. In D. Magnusson & V. Allen (Eds.), *Human development: An interactional perspective.* New York: Academic Press.

Ainsworth, M. D. S. (1992). A consideration of social referencing in the context of attachment theory and research. In S. Feinman (Ed.), *Social referencing and the social construction of reality in infancy.* New York: Plenum.

Ainsworth, M. D. S. (1993). Attachment as related to mother-infant interaction. *Advances in Infancy Research, 8,* 1–50.

Ainsworth, M. D. S. (1995). On the shaping of attachment theory and research: An interview with Mary Ainsworth (Fall 1994). *Monographs of the Society for Research in Child Development, 60,* 3–21.

Ainsworth, M. D. S., & Wittig, B. A. (1969). Attachment and the exploratory behavior of one-year-olds in a strange situation. In B. M. Foss (Ed.), *Determinants of infant behavior* (Vol. 4). London: Methuen.

Ainsworth, M. D. S., Bell, S. M., & Stayton, D. J. (1974). Infant-mother attachment and social development. In M. P. M. Richards (Ed.), *The integration of a child into a social world.* Cambridge: Cambridge University Press.

Ainsworth, M. D. S., Blehar, M. C., Waters, E., & Wall, S. (1979). *Patterns of attachment: A psychological study of the strange situation.* New York: Halsted.

Ainsworth-Darnell, J. W., & Downey, D. B. (1998). Assessing the oppositional cultural explanation for racial/ethnic differences in school performance. *American Sociological Review, 63,* 536–553.

Akima, H., Kano, Y., Enomoto, Y., Ishizu, M., Okada, M., Oishi, Y., Katsuta, S., & Kuno, S. (2001). Muscle function in 164 men and women aged 20–84 years. *Medicine and Science in Sports and Exercise, 33*(2), 220–226.

Akos, P., & Levitt, D. H. (2002, December). Promoting healthy body image in middle school. *Professional School Counseling, 6*(2), 138–145.

Albert, W. (2003, December 16). *Teens continue to express cautious attitudes toward sex.* Washington, DC: The National Campaign to Prevent Teen Pregnancy.

Albus, K. E., & Dozier, M. (1999). Indiscriminate friendliness and terror of strangers in infancy: Contributions from the study of infants in foster care. *Infant Mental Health Journal, 20*(1), 20–41.

Alch, M. (2000). The echo-boom: A growing force in American society. *The Futurist, 34*(5), 42–46.

Alcohol consumption among women who are pregnant or who might become pregnant: United States, 2002. (2004, December 24). *Morbidity and Mortality Weekly Report, 53*(50), 1178–1181.

Aldous, J. (1987). New views on the family life of the elderly and the near-elderly. *Journal of Marriage and the Family, 49,* 227–234.

Aldous, J., & Mulligan, G. M. (2002, July). Fathers' child care and children's behavior problems. *Journal of Family Issues, 23*(5), 624–647.

Aldous, J., Mulligan, G., & Bjarnason, T. (1998). Fathering over time. *Journal of Marriage and the Family, 60,* 809–820.

Alexander, K. L., Entwisle, D. R., & Olson, L. S. (200l, Summer). Schools, achievement, and inequality: A seasonal perspective. *Educational Evaluation and Policy Analysis, 23*(2), 171–191.

Alexander, M. J., & Higgins, E. T. (1993). Emotional trade-offs of becoming a parent: How social roles influence self-discrepancy effects. *Journal of Personality and Social Psychology, 65,* 1259–1269.

Allen, J. (2001, September 10). *HHS awards adoption bonuses.* U.S. Department of Health and Human Services. The Administration of Children and Families. Retrieved December 31, 2001, from http://www.acf.dhhs. gov/news/press/2001/adoption.html

Allen, P. A., Madden, D. J., Weber, T., & Crozier, L. C. (1992). Age differences in short-term memory: Organization or internal noise? *Journal of Gerontology: Psychological Sciences, 47,* P281–P288.

Allen, S. M. (1994). Gender differences in spousal caregiving and unmet need for care. *Journal of Gerontology: Social Sciences, 49,* S187–S195.

Alley, T. R. (1983). Growth-produced changes in body shape and size as determinants of perceived age and adult caretaking. *Child Development, 54,* 241–248.

Allison, B. N., & Schultz, J. B. (2004). Parent-adolescent conflict in early adolescence. *Adolescence, 39*(153), 101–120.

Allison, J. A., & Wrightsman, L. S. (1993). *Rape: The misunderstood crime.* Newbury Park, CA: Sage.

Allman, W. F. (1991, August 19). The clues in the idle chatter. *U.S. News & World Report,* 61–62.

Allport, G. W. (1961). *Pattern and growth in personality.* New York: Holt, Rinehart & Winston.

Almeida, D. M., & Kessler, R. C. (1998). Everyday stressors and gender differences in daily stress. *Journal of Personality and Social Psychology, 75,* 670–680.

ALS more common in war veterans. (2004). *USA Today, 133,* 11.

Alternatives to abortion. (2004). *National Right-to-Life Committee.* Retrieved November 28, 2004, from http://www.nrlc.org/abortion/ASMF/asmf15.html

Altman, L. K. (1993, December 22). A study on impotence suggests half of men over 40 may have problem. *New York Times,* B7.

Altman, L. K. (2004, March 9). Genital herpes declines 17 percent, surveys show. *New York Times, 153,* A19.

Altschuler, J., Katz, A. D., & Tynan, M. (2004, February). Developing and implementing an HIV/AIDS educational curriculum for older adults. *Gerontologist, 44,* 121–126.

Alzheimer's Association. (2003). *African-Americans and Alzheimer's disease: The silent epidemic.* Retrieved April 11, 2005, 2005, from http://www.alz.org/Meida/newsreleases/2003/AA_ALZ.pdf

Amato, P. R. (1993). Children's adjustment to divorce: Theories, hypotheses, and empirical support. *Journal of Marriage and the Family, 55,* 23–38.

Amato, P. R. (2000). The consequences of divorce for adults and children. *Journal of Marriage and the Family, 62,* 1269–1287.

Amato, P. R. (2001, September). Children of divorce in the 1990s: An update of the Amato and Keith (1991) meta-analysis. *Journal of Family Psychology, 15*(3), 355–370.

Amato, P. R., & DeBoer, D. D. (2000). The transmission of marital instability across generations: Relationship skills or commitment to marriage? *Journal of Marriage and the Family, 63*(4), 1038–1052.

Amato, P. R., & Keith, B. (1991). Parental divorce and the well-being of children: A meta-analysis. *Psychological Bulletin, 110,* 26–46.

American Academy of Family Physicians. (2002, May 15). Information from your family doctor: HIV and pregnancy. *American Family Physician, 65*(10), 2125–2126.

American Academy of Pediatric Dentistry. (2005). *April is national facial protection month.* Retrieved March 22, 2005, from http://www.aapd.org/upload/news/2004/528.pdf

American Academy of Pediatrics and the American Psychological Association. (1996). *Raising children to resist violence: What you can do.* Retrieved February 13, 1999, from http:// www.apa.org/pubinfo/apa-aap.html

American Academy of Pediatrics. (1999). Media education. *Pediatrics, 104,* 341–342.

American Academy of Pediatrics. (2001, February). Policy Statement: Children, adolescents, and television. *Pediatrics, 107,* 423–426.

American Association of University Women (AAUW). (2001a). *Beyond the "gender wars": A conversation about girls, boys, and education.* Washington, DC: AAUW Educational Foundation.

American Association of University Women (AAUW). (2001b). *Hostile hallways: Bullying, teasing, and sexual harassment in school.* Washington, DC: AAUW Educational Foundation.

American Association of University Women Educational Foundation (AAUW). (1992). *How schools shortchange girls: The AAUW report.* Washington, DC: AAUW.

American Cancer Society. (1997). *Cancer facts and figures.* Retrieved March 5, 1999, from http://www. cancer.org/statistics/97cff/97tobacc.html

American Cancer Society. (2005). *Cancer facts and figures 2005.* Atlanta, GA: American Cancer Society. Retrieved April 8, 2005, from http://www.cancer.org/downloads/STT/CAFF2005f4PWSecured.pdf

American Foundation for Suicide Prevention. (2005). *Facts about youth suicide. The truth about suicide: Real stories of depression in college.* Retrieved May 11, 2005, from http://www.afsp.org/home.htm

American Geriatrics Society. (1996). *Measuring quality of care at the end of life: A statement of principles.* Retrieved May 10, 2005, from http://www.americangeriatrics.org

American Heart Association. (1998). *Benefits of daily physical activity.* Retrieved March 6, 1999, from http://www.amhrt.org/health/lifestyle/physical_activity/beneact.html

American Psychiatric Association. (2000). *DSM-IV-TR 2000: Diagnostic criteria for 299.0 autistic disorder.* Washington, DC: Author.

American Psychological Association. (2000). *American Psychiatric Association practice guidelines for the treatment of psychiatric disorders: Compendium 2000.* Washington DC: American Psychological Association.

American Psychological Association. (2003). *Ethical principles of psychologists and code of conduct.* Retrieved September 10, 2004, from http://www.apa.org/ethics/code2002.html

American SIDS Institute. (2004). *Reducing the risk of SIDS.* Retrieved October 25, 2004 from http://www.sids.org/nprevent.htm.

American Speech-Language Association. (2005). *Early hearing detection and action center.* Retrieved January 2, 2005, from http://www.asha.org/about/legislation-advocacy/federal/ehdi/

American Stroke Association. (2005). *What is stroke?* The American Heart Association. Retrieved April 30, 2005, from http://www.strokeassociation.org

Amniotic boost. (2004, January 24). *New Scientist, 181*(2431), 14.

Anand, S., & Krosnick, J. A. (2005, January). Demographic predictors of media use among infants, toddlers, and preschoolers. *American Behavioral Scientist, 48*(5), 539–561.

Anastasi, A. (1958). Heredity, environment, and the question "how?" *Psychological Review, 65,* 197–208.

Ancoli-Israel, S. (1997, January). Sleep problems in older adults: Putting myths to bed. *Geriatrics, 52,* 20.

Anderson, C. A., & Bushman, B. J. (2002, March 29). The effects of media violence on society. *Science, 295,* 2377–2379.

Anderson, D. R., & Pempek, T. A. (2005, January). Television and very young children. *American Behavioral Scientist, 48*(5), 505–522.

Anderson, E. (1994). Sex codes among inner-city youth. In M. Smith (Ed.), *Sexuality, poverty, and the inner city* (pp. 1–36). Menlo Park, CA: Henry J. Kaiser Family Foundation.

Anderson, J. R. (1990). *The adaptive character of thought.* Hillsdale, NJ: Erlbaum.

Anderson, K. E., Lytton, H., & Romney, D. M. (1986). Mothers' interactions with normal and conduct-disordered boys: Who affects whom? *Developmental Psychology, 22,* 604–609.

Anderson, T. B., & McCulloch, B. J. (1993). Conjugal support: Factor structure for older husbands and wives. *Journal of Gerontology: Social Sciences, 48,* S133–S142.

Anderson, W., Chitwood, S., & Hayden, D. (1997). *Negotiating the special education maze: A guide for parents and teachers* (3rd ed.). Bethesda, MD: Woodbine House.

Angier, N. (1992, May 20). Is there a male menopause? Jury is still out. *New York Times,* B1, B7.

Angier, N. (1995, May 9). Scientists mull role of empathy in man and beast. *New York Times,* B7, B9.

Anglin, J. M. (1993). Vocabulary development: A morphological analysis. *Monograph of the Society for Research in Child Development, 58* (Serial No. 238).

Annas, G. J. (2005). "Culture of life" politics at the bedside—The case of Terri Schiavo. *New England Journal of Medicine, 352,* 1710–1715.

Ansbacher, H. L., & Ansbacher, R. R. (1956). *The individual psychology of Alfred Adler.* New York: Basic Books.

Antonucci, T. C. (1985). Personal characteristics, social support, and social behavior. In R. Binstock & E. Shanas (Eds.), *Handbook of aging and the social sciences* (pp. 94–128). New York: Van Nostrand Reinhold.

Antonucci, T. C. (1994). A life-span view of women's social relations. In B. F. Turner & L. E. Trolls (Eds.), *Women growing older: Psychological perspectives.* Thousand Oaks, CA: Sage.

Antonucci, T. C., Okorodudu, C., & Akiyama, H. (2003). Well-being among older adults on different continents. *Journal of Social Issues, 58*(4), 617–626.

Apgar, V. (1953). Proposal for a new method of evaluation of the newborn infant. *Anesthesia and Analgesia, 32,* 260–267.

Apple, D. (1956). The social structure of grandparenthood. *American Anthropologist, 58,* 656–663.

Apple, M. W., & Weis, L. (1983). *Ideology and practice in schooling.* Philadelphia: Temple University Press.

Arditti, J. A., & Keith, T. Z. (1993). Visitation frequency, child support payment, and the father-child relationship post divorce. *Journal of Marriage and the Family, 55,* 699–712.

Arieff, I. (2004, November 19). *U.S.-led drive for U.N. stem-cell ban crumbles.* Reuters News Service. Retrieved November 21, 2004, from http://olympics.reuters.com

Ariès, P. (1962). *Centuries of childhood* (R. Baldick, Trans.). New York: Random House.

Ariès, P. (1978). *Western attitudes toward death: From the Middle Ages to the present.* Baltimore: Johns Hopkins University Press.

Ariès, P. (1981). *The hour of our death.* New York: Knopf.

Armas, G. C. (2005, March 28). Black, Asian women with college degree outearn white women. *Seattle Times.* Retrieved April 8, 2005, from http://seattletimes.nwsource.com/html/nationworld/2002222103_income28.html

Armstrong, C., Salles, J., Alcarez, J., Kolody, B., & McKenzie, T. (1998). Children's television viewing, body fat, and physical fitness. *American Journal of Health Promotion, 12,* 363–368.

Armstrong, S. (2004, March 8). A rights revolution. *Maclean's, 117,* 38–40.

Arnett, J. J. (2000). Emerging adulthood: A theory of development from the late teens through the twenties. *American Psychologist, 55,* 469–480.

Arnst, C. (2003, February 17). Men: Your clocks are ticking. *Business Week, 3820,* 73.

Arnst, C., & Kiley, D. (2004, October 11). The kids are not alright. *Business Week, 3903,* 56.

Arnup, K. (1995). Living in the margins: Lesbian families and the law. In K. Arnup (Ed.), *Lesbian parenting: Living with pride and prejudice* (pp. 378–398). Charlottetown, Canada: Gynergy.

Aron, A., & Westbay, L. (1996). Dimensions of the prototype of love. *Journal of Personality and Social Psychology, 70,* 535–551.

Aronson, E., Brewer, M., & Carlsmith, J. M. (1985). Experimentation in social psychology. In G. Lindzey & E. Aronson (Ed.), *Handbook of social psychology* (3rd ed., Vol. 2). New York: Random House.

Arthritis Foundation. (2004). *Exercise and arthritis.* Retrieved March 20, 2005, from http://www.arthritis.org/conditions/exercise/default.asp

Asendorpf, J. B., Warkentin, V., & Baudonniere, P. M. (1996). Self-awareness and other-awareness: Mirror self-recognition, social contingency awareness, and synchronic imitation. *Developmental Psychology, 32,* 313–321.

Ashenburg, K. (2002). *The mourner's dance: What we do when people die.* New York: Farrar, Strauss & Giroux.

Ashmead, D. H., McCarty, M. E., Lucas, L. S., & Belvedere, M. C. (1993). Visual guidance in infants' reaching toward suddenly displaced targets. *Child Development, 64,* 1111–1127.

Ashton, P. T. (1975). Cross-cultural Piagetian research: An experimental perspective. *Harvard Educational Review, 45,* 475–506.

Associated Press. (2005, January 20). Mom gives birth to 16.7-pound 'giant baby.' *Houston Chronicle.* Retrieved January 22, 2005, from http://www.chron.com

Atchley, R. C. (1999). *Continuity and adaptation in aging: Creating positive experiences.* Baltimore: Johns Hopkins University Press.

Atkins, A. (1996, September). Who ages better—Men or women? *New Choices, 36,* 22–25.

Atkinson, M. P., & Blackwelder, S. P. (1993). Fathering in the 20th century. *Journal of Marriage and the Family, 55,* 975–986.

ATP III classification of LDL, total, and HDL cholesterol (mg/dl). Retrieved March 23, 2005, from http://www.nhlbi.nih.gov/guidelines/cholesterol/atglance.htm

Attention pregnant women: What you can do to keep germs from harming your baby. (1999). Centers for Disease Control and Prevention. Retrieved December 30, 2001, from http://www.cdc.gov/od/spotlight/nwhw/pubs/reprhlth.htm

Attie, I., & Brooks-Gunn, J. (1987). Weight-related concerns in women: A response to or a cause of stress? In R. C. Barnett, L. Biener, & G. K. Baruch (Eds.), *Gender and stress.* New York: Free Press.

Ausubel, D. P., & Sullivan, E. V. (1970). *Theory and problems of child development* (2nd ed.). New York: Grune & Stratton.

Autism Society of America (ASA). (2003). *Autism facts.* Retrieved February 13, 2005, from http://www.autism-society.org

Autism Society of America (ASA). (2005). *Common characteristics of autism.* Retrieved February 13, 2005, from http://www.autism-society.org

Aviezer, O., Sabi, A., & van IJzendoorn, M. (2002, Fall). Balancing the family and the collective in raising children: Why communal sleeping in kibbutzim was predestined to end. *Family Process.* Retrieved February 12, 2005, from http://findarticles.com

Aviezer, O., Van IJzendoorn, M. H., Sagi, A., & Schuengel, C. (1994). "Children of the Dream" revisited: 70 years of collective early child care in Israeli kibbutzim. *Psychological Bulletin, 116,* 99–116.

Ayres, A. J. (1972). *Sensory integration and learning disorders.* Los Angeles, CA: Western Psychological Services.

Azmitia, M. (1988). Peer interaction and problem solving: When are two heads better than one? *Child Development, 59,* 87–96.

Azmitia, M., & Hesser, J. (1993). Why siblings are important agents of cognitive development: A comparison of siblings and peers. *Child Development, 63,* 430–444.

Bachu, A. (2000). *Record share of new mothers in labor force.* U.S. Bureau of the Census. Washington, DC: U.S. Department of Commerce News. Retrieved January 20, 2002, from http://www.census/gov/press-release/www/2000/cb00-175.html

Baerwald, A. R., Adams, G. P., & Pierson, R. A. (2003, May 14). Characterization of ovarian follicular wave dynamics in women. *Biology of Reproduction, 69*(3), 1023–1031.

Bagilhole, B., & Goode, J. (2001). The contradiction of the myth of individual merit, and the reality of a patriarchal support system in academic careers: A feminist investigation. *European Journal of Women's Studies, 8*(2), 161–180.

Bailey, J. M., & Zucker, K. J. (1995). Childhood sex-typed behavior and sexual orientation: A conceptual analysis and quantitative review. *Developmental Psychology, 31,* 43–55.

Bairraro, J., & Tietze, W. (1993). *Early childhood services in the European community.* Commission of the European Community Task Force on Human Resources, Education, Training, and Youth. Retrieved October 15, 1998, from http://futureofchildren.org

Baker College: Effective Teaching and Learning Department. (pp. 25–26). Flint, MI: Baker College. Retrieved April 6, 2005, from http://www.baker.edu/departments/instructech/resources/TAG%20document.doc

Baldwin, D. A., & Markman, E. M. (1989). Establishing word-object relations: A first step. *Child Development, 60,* 381–398.

Baldwin, J. M. (1895). *Mental development in the child and the race: Methods,* and *processes.* New York: Macmillan.

Baldwin, J. M. (1897). *Social and ethical interpretations of mental development: A study in social psychology.* New York: Macmillan.

Baltes, M. M., Neumann, E. M., & Zank, S. (1994). Maintenance and rehabilitation of independence in old age: An intervention program for staff. *Psychology and Aging, 9,* 179–188.

Baltes, P. B., & Baltes, M. M. (1990). Psychological perspectives on successful aging: The model of selective optimization with compensation. In P. B. Baltes & M. M. Baltes (Eds.), *Successful aging: Perspectives from the behavioral sciences.* New York: Cambridge University Press.

Baltes, P. B., & Baltes, M. M. (1998). Savoir vivre in old age: How to master the shifting balance between gains and losses. *National Forum: Phi Kappa Phi Journal, 78,* 13–18.

Baltes, P. B., & Lindenberger, U. (1997). Emergence of a powerful connection between sensory and cognitive functions across the adult life span: A new window

to the study of cognitive aging? *Psychology and Aging, 12,* 12–21.

Baltes, P. B., & Mayer, K. U. (Eds.). (1999). *The Berlin Aging Study: Aging from 70 to 100.* New York: Cambridge University Press.

Baltes, P. B., & Schaie, K. W. (1976). On the plasticity of intelligence in adulthood and old age. *American Psychologist, 31,* 720–725.

Baltes, P. B., & Smith, J. (1997). A systemic-wholistic view of psychological functioning in very old age: Introduction to a collection of articles from the Berlin Aging Study. *Psychology and Aging, 12,* 395–409.

Baltes, P. B., & Smith, J. (2001, October). *New frontiers in the future of aging: From successful aging of the young old to the dilemmas of the Fourth Age.* Keynote Speech: Valencia Forum. Retrieved May 10, 2005, from http://valenciaforum.com/

Baltes, P. B., & Smith, J. (2003). New frontiers in the future of aging: From successful aging of the young old to the dilemmas of the fourth age. *Gerontology, 49*(2), 123–135.

Balz, D. (2005, February 27). Microsoft's Gates urges governors to restructure U.S. high schools. *Washington Post,* A10. Retrieved March 31, 2005, from http://www.washingtonpost.com/wp-dyn/articles/A56466-2005Feb26.html

Bandura, A. (1964). The stormy decade: Fact or fiction? *Psychology in the Schools, 1,* 224–231.

Bandura, A. (1973). *Aggression: A social learning analysis.* Englewood Cliffs, NJ: Prentice Hall.

Bandura, A. (1977). *Social learning theory.* Englewood Cliffs, NJ: Prentice Hall.

Bandura, A. (1986). *Social foundations of thought and action: A social cognitive theory.* Englewood Cliffs, NJ: Prentice Hall.

Bandura, A. (1989a). Human agency in social cognitive theory. *American Psychologist, 44,* 1175–1184.

Bandura, A. (1989b). Regulation of cognitive processes through perceived self-efficacy. *Developmental Psychology, 25,* 729–735.

Bandura, A. (1999). Moral disengagement in the perpetration of inhumanities. *Personality and Social Psychology Review, 3*(3), 193–209.

Bandura, A., Ross, D., & Ross, S. (1963). Imitation of film-mediated aggressive models. *Journal of Abnormal and Social Psychology, 66,* 3–11.

Baney, C. (1998). Wired for sound: The essential connection between music and development. *Early Childhood News.* Retrieved February 12, 1999, from http://www.early-childhoodnews.com/wiredfor.htm

Bangladesh: Acid attacks increase despite death penalty. (2002). *Women's International Network News, 28*(4).

Bank, L., Forgatch, M. S., Patterson, G. R., & Fetrow, R. A. (1993). Parenting practices of single mothers: Mediators of negative contextual factors. *Journal of Marriage and the Family, 55,* 371–384.

Bank, S. P., & Kahn, M. D. (1997). *The sibling bond.* New York, NY: HarperCollins.

Bannon, L. (2000, February 14). Why girls and boys get different toys. *The Wall Street Journal, 235*(32), B1, B4.

Barbett, S. F. (2003, August 13). *Postsecondary education in the United States: Fall 2000, Spring 2001, and degrees conferred 1999–2000.* Washington, DC: National Center for Education Statistics. Retrieved March 16, 2005, from http://nces.ed.gov/programs/digest/d03/tables/pdf/table177.pdf

Barkley, R. (2001). *The statistics of AD/HD.* AdditudeMag.Com. Retrieved December 10, 2001, from http://www.additudemag.com

Barlow, S. E., & Dietz, W. H. (1998, September). Obesity evaluation and treatment: Expert committee recommendations. *Pediatrics, 102,* e29.

Barnes, P. M., Adams, P. F., & Schiller, J. S. (2003). Summary health statistics for the U.S. Population: National Health Survey, 2001. *Vital Health Statistics, 10*(217). 1–90. Washington, DC: National Center for Health Statistics. Retrieved April 7, 2005, from http://www.cdc.gov/nchs/data/series/sr_10/sr10_217.pdf

Barnett, R. C. (1997). Gender, employment, and psychological well-being: Historical and life course perpsectives. In M. E. Lachman & J. B. James (Eds.), *Multiple paths of midlife development* (pp. 325–343). Chicago: University of Chicago Press.

Barnett, R. C., & Rivers, C. (2004). Persistence of gender myths in math. *Education Week, 24*(7), 39–40.

Barnett, R. C., Raudenbush, S. W., Brennan, R. T., Pleck, J. H., & Marshall, N. L. (1995). Change in job and marital experience and change in psychological distress: A longitudinal study of dual-earner couples. *Journal of Personality and Social Psychology, 69,* 839–850.

Barrett, E. J. (2004, Winter). Diabetes epidemic is a worldwide threat. *Clinical Diabetes, 22*(1), 47–49.

Barinaga, M. (1994). A new tool for examining multigenic traits. *Science 264,* 1691.

Barringer, F. (1993, April 25). Measuring sexuality through polls can be shaky. *New York Times,* 12.

Bart, P. B. (1972). Depression in middle-age women. In V. Gornick & B. K. Moran (Eds.), *Women in sexist society.* New York: New American Library.

Bartlett, M. S., Hager, J. C., Ekman, P., & Sejnowski, T. J. (1999). Measuring facial expressions by computer image analysis. *Psychophysiology, 36*(2), 253–263.

Bartoshuk, L. M., Rifkin, B., Marks, L. E., & Bars, P. (1986). Taste and aging. *Journal of Gerontology, 41,* 51–57.

Baruch, G., & Barnett, R. C. (1983). Adult daughters' relationships with their mothers. *Journal of Marriage and the Family, 45,* 601–606.

Basham, P. (2001). *Home schooling: From the extreme to the mainstream.* Cato Institute. Retrieved December 19, 2001, from http://www. fraserinstitute.ca/publications/pps/51/ homeschool.pdf

Baskett, L. M. (1985). Sibling status effects: Adult expectations. *Developmental Psychology, 21*(3), 441–445.

Bass, D., & Bowman, K. (1990). The impact of an aged relative's death on the family. In K. F. Ferraro (Ed.), *Gerontology: Perspectives and issues.* New York: Springer.

Bass, S., Shields, M., Lowe-Webb, R., & Lanz, T. (2004, Winter). Children, families, and foster care: A synopsis. *The Future of Children Organization, 14*(1), The David and Lucile Packard Foundation. Retrieved February 20, 2005, from http://www.future-ofchildren.org

Basseches, M. (1980). Dialectical schemata: A framework for the empirical study of the development of dialectical thinking. *Human Development, 23,* 400–421.

Batabyal, A. (2001). On the likelihood of finding the right partner in an arranged marriage. *Journal of Socioeconomics, 39*(3), 273–287.

Bates, E., Bretherton, I., & Snyder, L. (1988). *From first words to grammar: Individual differences and dissociable mechanisms.* New York: Cambridge University Press.

Bauer, I. (2001, Spring). *The gentle wisdom of natural infant hygiene.* Retrieved November 5, 2001, from http://www.natural-wisdom.com/.

Bauer, P. J. (1993). Memory for gender-consistent and gender-inconsistent event sequences by twenty-five-month-old children. *Child Development, 64,* 285–297.

Bauer, P. J., & Mandler, J. M. (1989). One thing follows another: Effects of temporal structure on 1- to 2-year-olds' recall of events. *Developmental Psychology, 25,* 197–206.

Baum, N. (2004, July). Coping with "absence-presence": Noncustodial fathers' parenting behaviors. *American Journal of Orthopsychiatry, 74*(3), 316–324.

Bauman, K. J. (2001). *Home schooling in the United States: Trends and characteristics.* Working Paper No. 53. U.S. Census Bureau, Population Division. Retrieved December 19, 2001 from http://www.census.gov/population/www/documentation/twps0053.html#abs

Bauman, K. J. (2001). *Working Paper No. 53: Home schooling in the United States: Trends and characteristics:* Population Division, U.S. Census Bureau.

Baumeister, R. F., Smart, L., & Boden, J. M. (1996). Relation of threatened egotism to violence and aggression: The dark side of high self-esteem. *Psychological Review, 103*(1), 5–33.

Baumgardner, A. H. (1990). To know oneself is to like oneself: Self-certainty and self-affect. *Journal of Personality and Social Psychology, 58,* 1062–1072.

Baumrind, D. (1967). Child care practices anteceding three patterns of preschool behavior. *Genetic Psychology Monographs, 75,* 43–88.

Baumrind, D. (1971). Current patterns of parental authority. *Developmental Psychology Monographs, 4,* 1.

Baumrind, D. (1972). Socialization and instrumental competence in young children. In W. W. Hartup (Ed.), *The young child* (Vol. 2). Washington, DC: National Association for the Education of Young Children.

Baumrind, D. (1980). New directions in socialization research. *American Psychologist, 35,* 639–652.

Baumrind, D. (1991). The influence of parenting style on adolescent competence and substance use. *Journal of Early Adolescence, 11,* 56–95.

Baumrind, D. (1994). The social context of child maltreatment. *Family Relations, 43,* 360–368.

Baumrind, D. (1996). The discipline controversy revisited. *Family Relations, 45,* 405–414.

Baumrind, D., & Owens, E. (2001, August 24). *Does causally relevant research support a blanket injunction against disciplinary spanking by parents?* Invited address at the 109th Annual Convention of the American Psychological Association. Retrieved December 2, 2001, from http://ihd.berkeley.edu/BaumrindPaper.pdf

Baumrind, D., Larzelere, R. E., & Cowan, P. A. (2002, July). Ordinary physical punishment: Is it harmful? Comment on Gershoff. *Psychological Bulletin, 128*(4), 580–589.

Baumwell, L., Tamis-LeMonda, C. S., & Bornstein, M. H. (1997). Maternal verbal sensitivity and child language comprehension. *Infant Behavior and Development, 20,* 247.

Bauserman, R. (2002). Child adjustment in joint-custody versus sole-custody arrangements: A meta-analytic review. *Journal of Family Psychology, 16*(1), 91–102.

Baydar, N., & Brooks-Gunn, J. (1991). Effects of maternal employment and child-care arrangements on preschoolers' cognitive and behavioral outcomes: Evidence from the Children of the National Longitudinal Survey of Youth. *Developmental Psychology, 27,* 932–945.

Bayley, N. (1935). The development of motor abilities during the first three years. Washington, DC: Society for Research Development.

Bayley, N. (1936). *The California infant scale of motor development: Birth to three years.* Berkeley: University of California Press.

Bayley, N. (1956). Individual patterns of development. *Child Development, 27,* 45–74.

Bayley, N. (1965). Research in child development: A longitudinal perspective. *Merrill-Palmer Quarterly, 11,* 184–190.

Bearak, B. (2001a). Afghanistan girls fight to read and write. *New York Times, 149*(51322). A1.

Bearak, B. (2001b). Escaping Afghanistan, children pay price. *New York Times, 151*(51922), A1.

Beard, R. M. (1969). *An outline of Piaget's developmental psychology for students and teachers.* New York: New American Library.

Becker, W. C. (1964). Consequences of different kinds of parental discipline. In M. L. Hoffman & L. W. Hoffman (Eds.), *Review of child development research* (pp. 169–208). New York: Russell Sage Foundation.

Beckmann, C. A. (2003, April). The effects of asthma on pregnancy and perinatal outcomes. *Journal of Asthma, 40*(2), 171–180.

Behnke, M., Eyler, F. D., Garvan, C. W., Wobie, K., & Hou, W. (2002, May–June). Cocaine exposure and developmental outcome from birth to 6 months. *Neurotoxicology and Teratology, 24*(3), 283–295.

Behrens, M., & Evans, K. (2002). Taking control of their lives? A comparison of the experiences of unemployed young adults (18–25) in England and the new Germany. *Comparative Education, 38*(1), 17–37.

Beilin, H. (1990). Piaget's theory: Alive and more vigorous than ever. *Human Development, 33,* 362–365.

Beilin, H. (1992). Piaget's enduring contribution to developmental psychology. *Developmental Psychology, 28,* 191–204.

Belkin, L. (1992, March 25). Births beyond hospitals fill an urban need. *New York Times,* A1, A15.

Bell, S. M. (1970). The development of the concept of object as related to infant-mother attachment. *Child Development, 41,* 291–311.

Belluck, P. (1998, April 12). Say black? Not so fast. *New York Times, 9,* 1.

Belsky, J. (1981). Early human experience: A family perspective. *Developmental Psychology, 17,* 6.

Belsky, J. (1984). The determinants of parenting: A process model. *Child Development, 55,* 83–96.

Belsky, J. (1990). Parental and nonparental child care and children's socioemotional development: A decade in review. *Journal of Marriage and the Family, 52,* 885–903.

Belsky, J. (1993). Etiology of child maltreatment a developmental-ecological analysis. *Psychological Bulletin, 114,* 413–434.

Belsky, J. (1996a). Infant attachment, security, and affective-cognitive information processing at age 3. *Psychological Science, 7,* 111–114.

Belsky, J. (1996b). Parent, infant, and social-contextual antecedents of father-son attachment security. *Developmental Psychology, 32,* 905–913.

Belsky, J. (1997). Attachment, mating, and parenting: An evolutionary interpretation. *Human Nature, 8*(4), 361–381.

Belsky, J. (1999). Modern evolutionary theory and patterns of attachment. In J. Cassidy & P. R. Shaver (Eds.), *Handbook of attachment: Theory, research, and clinical applications* (pp. 141–161). University Park, PA: Guilford Press.

Belsky, J. (2001). Marital violence in evolutionary perspective. In A. Booth and A. Crouter (Eds.), *Couples in conflict* (pp. 27–36). Mahwah, NJ: Earlbaum.

Belsky, J., & Barends, N. (2002). Personality and parenting. In M. Bornstein, *Handbook of parenting,* (2nd ed., Vol. 3), *Being and Becoming a Parent* (pp. 415–438). Mahwah, NJ: Erlbaum.

Belsky, J., & Eggebeen, D. (1991). Early and extensive maternal employment and young children's socioemotional development: Children of the National Longitudinal Survey of Youth. *Journal of Marriage and the Family, 53,* 1083–1110.

Belsky, J., & Fearon, R. M. P. (2002, Spring). Infant-mother attachment security, contextual risk, and early development: A moderational analysis. *Development & Psychopathology, 14*(2), 293–310.

Belsky, J., & Rovine, M. (1987). Temperament and attachment security in the strange situation: An empirical rapprochement. *Child Development, 58,* 787–795.

Belsky, J., & Rovine, M. (1990). Patterns of marital change across the transition to parenthood: Pregnancy to three years postpartum. *Journal of Marriage and the Family, 52,* 5–19.

Belsky, J., Crnic, K., & Gable, S. (1995). The determinants of coparenting in families with toddler boys: Spousal differences and daily hassles. *Child Development, 66,* 629–642.

Bem, D., & Allen, A. (1974). On predicting some of the people some of the time: The search for cross-situational consistencies in behavior. *Psychological Review, 81,* 506–520.

Bem, S. L. (1993). *The lenses of gender: Transforming the debate on sexual inequality.* New Haven, CT: Yale University Press.

Bem, S. L. (1998). *An unconventional family.* New Haven, CT: Yale University Press.

Benedict, H. (1976). Language comprehension in 10 sixteen-month-old infants. Unpublished doctoral dissertation, Yale University.

Benenson, J., Apostolen, N., & Parnass, S. (1998). The organization of children's same-sex peer relationships in sociometry, then and now: Building on six decades of measuring children's experiences with the peer group. In W. Bukowski & A. Cillesser (Eds.), *New directions for child development, 80.*

Bengston, V. L., & Schaie, K. W. (Eds.). (1999). *Handbook of theories of aging.* New York: Springer.

Bennett, A. T., & Collins, K. A. (2000). Suicide: A ten-year retrospective study. *Journal of Forensic Sciences, 45*(6), 1256–1258.

Bennett, L., & Gates, G. J. (2004). *The cost of marriage inequality to GLB seniors: A Human Rights Campaign Foundation report.* Retrieved April 13, 2005, from http://www.hrc.org/Template.cfm

Bennett, W., & Gurin, J. (1982). *The dieter's dilemma.* New York: Basic Books.

Benoit, D., & Parker, K. C. H. (1994). Stability and transmission of attachment across three generations. *Child Development, 65,* 1444–1456.

Bereaved parents' outcomes 4 to 60 months after their children's deaths by accident, suicide, or homicide: A comparative study demonstrating differences. (2003). *Death Studies, 27*(1), 39–61.

Berg, C. A., & Sternberg, R. J. (1992). Adults' conceptions of intelligence across the adult life span. *Psychology and Aging, 7,* 221–231.

Berger, E. H. (2004). *Parents as partners in education: Families and schools working together* (6th ed.). Upper Saddle River, NJ: Pearson Prentice Hall.

Berger, R. M. (1996). *Gay and gray: The older homosexual man.* New York: Haworth.

Berk, L. E., & Winsler, A. (1995). *Scaffolding children's learning: Vygotsky and early childhood education. NAEYC research into practice series, vol. 7.* Washington, DC: National Book Association for Young Children.

Berkowitz, L. (1993). *Aggression: Its causes, consequences and control.* New York: McGraw-Hill.

Berman, L., Lazarus-Jaureguy, A., & Santos, M. (2004, January). New perspectives on medical therapy for female sexual dysfunction. *Hospital Physician, 40*(1), 39–48.

Bernstein, E. (2004, November 5). My senior year. *Wall Street Journal,* W1, W10.

Bernstein, I. L. (1990). Salt preference and development. *Developmental Psychology, 26,* 552–554.

Bernstein, N. (2004, March 7). Behind fall in pregnancy, a new teenage culture of restraint. *New York Times, 153,* Section 1, 1.

Best, D. L. (1993). Inducing children to generate mnemonic organizational strategies: An examination of long-term retention and materials. *Developmental Psychology, 29,* 324–336.

Bettes, B. A. (1988). Maternal depression and motherese: Temporal and intonational features. *Child Development, 59,* 1089–1096.

Beutel, M., Willner, H., Deckardt, R., VonRad, M., & Weiner, H. (1996, March). Similarities and differences in couples' grief reactions following a miscarriage: Results from a longitudinal study. *Journal of Psychosomatic Research, 40*(1), 245–253.

Bialystok, E. (2001). *Bilingualism in development: Language, literacy, and cognition.* New York: Cambridge University Press.

Bigler, R. S., & Liben, L. S. (1992). Cognitive mechanisms in children's gender stereotyping: Theoretical and educational implica-

tions of a cognitive-based intervention. *Child Development, 63,* 1351–1363.

Bigler, R., Jones, L. C., & Lobliner, D. B. (1997). Social categorization and the formation of intergroup attitudes in children. *Child Development, 68,* 530–543.

Bijou, S. W., & Baer, D. M. (1965). A social learning model of attachment: Socialization—The development of behavior to social stimuli. In *Child development II.* New York: Appleton-Century-Crofts.

Biller, H. B. (1993). *Fathers and families: Paternal factors in child development.* Westport, CT: Auburn House.

Binet, A. (1905). New methods for the diagnosis of the intellectual level of subnormals. *L'Année Psychologique, 12,* 191–244.

Birnholz, J. (1981) The development of human fetal eye movement patterns. *Science, 213,* 679–681.

Birnholz, J. C., & Benacerraf, B. R. (1983). The development of human fetal hearing. *Science, 222,* 516–518.

Birren, J. E. (1987, May). The best of all stories. *Psychology Today, 21,* 91–92.

Birren, J. E. (2000). Using the gift of long life: Psychological implications of the age revolution. In S. H. Qualls, & N. Abeles (Eds.), *Psychology and the aging revolution: How we adapt to longer life.* Washington, DC: American Psychological Association.

Bischof, L. J. (1976). *Adult psychology* (2nd ed.). New York: Harper & Row.

Bishop, D. V. M., & Leonard, L. B. (2000). *Speech and language impairments in children: Causes, characteristics, intervention, and outcome.* Hove, East Sussex: Psychology Press.

Bishop, D. V. M., Price, T. S., Dale, P. S., & Plomin, R. (2003, June). Outcomes of early language delay: Etiology of transient and persistent language difficulties. *Journal of Speech, Language, and Hearing Research, 46*(3), 561–575.

Bishop, J. E. (1993, September 30). Obese adolescents found less likely to marry, more likely to earn less. *Wall Street Journal,* B16.

Bisping, R., Steingrueber, H. J., Oltmann, M., & Wenk, C. (1990). Adults' tolerance of cries: An experimental investigation of acoustic features. *Child Development, 61,* 1218–1229.

Bjerklie, D. (2003, March 31). Sex on campus. *Time, 162*(7), 66.

Bjorklund, D. F., & Green, B. L. (1992). The adaptive nature of cognitive maturity. *American Psychologist, 47,* 46–54.

Black, S. A., & Markides, K. S. (1994). Aging and generational patterns of alcohol consumption among Mexican Americans, Cuban Americans, and mainland Puerto Ricans. *International Journal of Aging and Human Development, 39,* 97–103.

Blackley, M. (2003, July). Eggs for sale: The latest controversy in reproductive technology. *USA Today Magazine, 132*(2698), 56–59.

Blackson, T. C., Butler, T., Belsky, J., Ammerman, R. T., Shaw, D. S., & Tarter, R. E. (1999). Individual traits and family contexts predict sons' externalizing behavior and preliminary relative risk ratios for conduct disorder and substance use disorder outcomes. *Drug and Alcohol Dependence, 56*(2), 115–131.

Blagg, N. (1991). *Can we teach intelligence? A comprehensive evaluation of Feuerstein's instrumental enrichment program.* Hillsdale, NJ: Erlbaum.

Blair, P. S., Drewett, R. F., Emmett, P. M., Ness, A., & Emond, A. M. (2004, May 20). Family, socioeconomic and prenatal factors associated with failure to thrive in the Avon Longitudinal Study of Parents and Children. *International Journal of Epidemiology, 33*(4), 839–847. Retrieved February 3, 2005, from EBSCO*host.*

Blake, S., Simkin, L., Ledsky, R., Perkins, C., & Calabrese, J. M. (2001). Effects of a parent-child communications intervention on young adolescents' risk for early onset of sexual intercourse. *Family Planning Perspectives, 33*(2), 52–61.

Blakely, K. S. (1994). Parents' conceptions of social dangers to children in the urban environment. *Children's Environments, II,* 16–25.

Blakeslee, S. (1986, June 24). Rapid changes seen in young brain. *New York Times, 17,* 20.

Blass, E. M., & Ciaramitaro, V. (1994). A new look at some old mechanisms in human newborns: Taste and tactile determinants of state, affect, and action. *Monographs of the Society for Research in Child Development, 59* (Serial No. 239).

Blau, F. D., Ferber, M. A., & Winkler, A. E. (1998). *The economics of women, men and work* (3rd ed). Upper Saddle River, NJ: Prentice Hall.

Blaxill, M. (2004). What's going on? The question of time trends in autism. *Public Health Reports, 119,* 536–551.

Blinder, B. J. (2001). *Anorexia nervosa in children.* Eating Disorders Specialist. Retrieved December 15, 2001, from http://www.ltspeed.com/bjblinder/2.htm

Block, J. (1995). A contrarian view of the five-factor approach to personality description. *Psychological Bulletin, 117,* 187–215.

Bloom, L. (1970). *Language development: Form and function in emerging grammar.* Cambridge, MA: MIT Press.

Blos, P. (1962). *On adolescence: A psychoanalytic interpretation.* New York: Free Press of Glencoe.

Blumenthal, K. J. (2004). *A valuable aspect of college and university life.* Recreation Management. National Intramural-Recreational Sports Association. Retrieved April 8, 2005, from http://www.recmanagement.com

Blumstein, P., & Schwartz, P. (1983). *American couples.* New York: Morrow.

Bodnar, J. C., & Kiecolt-Glaser, J. K. (1994). Caregiver depression after bereavement: Chronic stress isn't over when it's over. *Psychology and Aging, 9,* 372–380.

Bohan-Baker, M., & Little, P. M. D. (2004, April). *The transition to kindergarten: A review of current research and promising practices to involve families.* The Harvard Family Research Project. Retrieved March 5, 2005, from http://www.gse.harvard.edu/~hfrp/pubs.html

Bokhorst, C. L., Bakermans-Kranenburg, M. J., Pasco Fearon, R. M., Van IJzendoorn, P. F., & Schuengel, C. (2003). The importance of shared environment in mother-infant attachment security: A behavioral genetic study. *Child Development, 74,* 1769–1782.

Boles, R. E., Roberts, M. C., Brown, K. J., & Mayes, S. (2005, February 23). Children's risk-taking behaviors: The role of child-based perceptions of vulnerability and temperament. *Journal of Pediatric Psychology.* Retrieved February 21, 2005, from http://jpepsy.oupjournals.org

Bolton, F., Jr., Morris, L. A., & MacEachron, A. (1989). *Males at risk: The other side of child sexual abuse.* Newbury Park, CA: Sage.

Bonanno, G. A., & Field, N. P. (2001). Examining the delayed grief hypothesis across 5 years of bereavement. *American Behavioral Scientist, 44*(5), 798–816.

Bonanno, G. A., & Kaltman, S. (2001). The varieties of grief experience. *Clinical Psychology Review, 21*(5), 705–734.

Bonanno, G. A., Wortman, C. B., & Nesse, R. M. (2004). Prospective patterns of resilience and maladjustment during widowhood. *Psychology and Aging, 19*(2), 260–271.

Boomsma, D., Busjahn, A., & Peltonen, L. (2002). Classical twin studies and beyond. *Nature Reviews Genetics, 3,* 872–882.

Boonsong, S. (1968). *The development of concentration of mass, weight, and volume in Thai children.* Unpublished master's thesis, College of Education, Bankok, Thailand.

Booth, A., Johnson, D. R., Granger, D. A., Crouter, A. C., & McHale, S. (2003). Testosterone and child and adolescent adjustment: The moderating role of parent-child relationships. *Developmental Psychology, 39,* 85–98.

Bordieu, P. (1977). Cultural reproduction and social reproduction. In J. Karabel, & Halsey (Eds.), *Power and ideology in education* (pp. 487–511). Oxford: Oxford University Press.

Bornstein, M. H. (1989). Sensitive periods in development: Structural characteristics and causal interpretations. *Psychological Bulletin, 105,* 179–197.

Bornstein, M. H. (1995). Parenting infants. In M. H. Bornstein (Ed.), *Handbook of parenting* (Vol. 1). Hillsdale, NJ: Erlbaum.

Bornstein, M. H., & Marks, L. E. (1982, January). Color revisionism. *Psychology Today,* 64–73.

Bornstein, M. H., & O'Reilly, A. W. (Eds.). (1993). *The role of play in the development of thought.* San Francisco: Jossey-Bass.

Bosman, E. A. (1993). Age-related differences in motoric aspects of transcription typing skills. *Psychology and Aging, 8,* 88–102.

Boss, R. (1998). Retirement and retirement planning. In I. H. Nordhus et al. (Eds.), *Clinical geropsychology* (pp. 155–159). Washington, DC: American Psychological Association.

Bouchard, T. J., & McGue, M. (1981). Familial studies of intelligence: A review. *Science, 212,* 1055–1059.

Bouchard, T. J., Jr., Lykken, D. T., McGue, M., Segal, N. L., & Tellegen, A. (1990). Sources of human psychological differences: The Minnesota study of twins reared apart. *Science, 250,* 223–228.

Boudreaux, E. D., Emond, S. D., Clark, S., & Camargo, C. A. (2003, May). Race/ethnicity and asthma among children presenting to the emergency department: Differences in disease severity and management. *Pediatrics, 111,* 615–621.

Bould, S., & Longino, C. (1997). *Handbook on women and aging.* Westport: Greenwood Press.

Bound, J., Duncan, G. J., Laren, D. S., & Oleinick, L. (1991). Poverty dynamics in widowhood. *Journal of Gerontology, 46,* S115–124.

Bowen, C. (1998). *Developmental phonological disorders.* Caroline Bowen, Ph.D., Home Page. http://members.tripod.com/Caroline_Bowen/home.html

Bowen, C. (2001). *Stuttering: What can be done about it?* Caroline Bowen, Ph.D., Home Page. http://members.tripod.com/Caroline_Bowen/home.html

Bower, B. (1991). Emotional aid delivers labor-saving results. *Science News, 139*(18), 277.

Bower, B. (2004). Mothering malnutrition. *Science News, 166*(12), 79–180.

Bower, T. G. R. (1976, November). Repetitive processes in child development. *Scientific American, 235,* 38–47.

Bowlby, J. (1969). *Attachment.* New York: Basic Books.

Bowlby, J. (1988). *A secure base: Clinical application of attachment theory.* London: Routledge.

Bowler, (2003, September/October). Gender gap widening, experts tell reporters. *Education Reporter, 37*(5), 1–2.

Bowman, J. M. (1992). Maternal alloimmunization and fetal hemolytic disease. In E. A. Reece et al. (Eds.), *Medicine of the fetus and mother.* Philadelphia: J. B. Lippincott.

Bowman, L. (2004, May 16). Teen brains found to develop judgment slowly. *Arizona Daily Star.* Retrieved April 10, 2005, from http://www.azstarnet.com

Bowring, F. (2004, January). Therapeutic and reproductive cloning: A critique. *Social Science Medicine, 58*(2), 401–409.

Boyce, N. (2004, February 23–March 1). The clone is out of the bottle: Now we know the recipe. Can a cloned baby be far behind?" *U.S. News & World Report, 136*(7), 40–43.

Bracey, G. W., & Stellar, A. (2001). Long-term studies of preschool: Lasting benefits far outweigh costs. *Phi Delta Kappan, 84.*

Brach, J. S., Simonsick, E. M., Kritchevsky, S., Yaffe, K., & Newman, A. B. (2004). *The association between physical function and lifestyle activity and exercise in the health, aging and body composition study.* Retrieved May 2, 2004, from http://www,nedscaoe,cin/viewarticle/473066?src=search

Bradford, J. (2001). What causes dyslexia? *Dyslexia Online Magazine.* Retrieved December 12, 2001, from http://www.dyslexia-parent.com/mag24.html

Bradway, D. M., Bamforth, J. S., Contrino, A., Young, R. A., Ginsburg, B. E., & Sarfarazi, M. (1995). An investigation into genetic and behavioral aspects of dyslexia. *American Journal of Human Genetics, 57,* A322.

Brady, M. (1998). Female genital mutilation. *Nursing, 28,* 50–51.

Brain facts: A parent's guide to early brain development. (1999). *I Am Your Child.* Retrieved February 4, 1999, from http://iamyourchild. org/docs/bf-0.html

Braine, M. D. S. (1963). The ontogeny of English phrase structure: The first phase. *Language, 39,* 1–14.

Bramlett, M. D., & Mosher, W. D. (2001, May 31). First marriage dissolution, divorce, and remarriage: United States. *Vital Health Statistics, 323.* Washington, DC: National Center for Health Statistics.

Bramlett, M. D., & Mosher, W. D. (2002, July). Cohabitation, marriage, divorce, and remarriage in the United States. *Vital Health Statistics, 23*(22). Washington, DC: National Center for Health Statistics.

Brand names take a back seat: Teens are now value-conscious. (2004, March 19). *Chain Store Executive Fax, 11*(12).

Brandon, P., & Hofferth, S. (2003). Determinants of out-of-school child care arrangements among children in single-mother and two-parent families. *Social Science Research, 32*(1), 129–147.

Brandtstadter, J., & Rothermund, K. (1994). Self-percepts of control in middle and later adulthood: Buffering losses by rescaling goals. *Psychology and Aging, 9,* 265–273.

Branswell, H. (2001, September 4). *Eating disorders on the rise, affecting more younger teens.* C-Health. Retrieved December 15, 2001, from http://www.canoe.ca/Health0109/04_eating-cp.html

Brasic, J. R. (2004). *Pervasive developmental disorder: Autism.* Retrieved February 13, 2005 from http://eMedicine.com

Braun, K. L., Takamura, J. C., Forman, S. M., Sasaki, P. A., & Meininger, L. (1995). Developing and testing outreach materials on Alzheimer's disease for Asian and Pacific Island Americans. *Gerontologist, 35,* 122–126.

Bray, J. H., & Hetherington, E. M. (1993). Families in transition: Introduction and overview. *Journal of Family Psychology, 7,* 3.

Brazelton, T. B. (1978). Introduction. In A. J. Sameroff (Ed.), Organization and stability of newborn behavior: A commentary on the Brazelton Neonatal Behavior Assessment Scale [Monograph]. *Monographs of the Society for Research in Child Development, 43*(177), 1–13.

Brazelton, T. B. (1998, December 6). Early bonding is important to parents, infants. *Houston Chronicle,* 9.

Brazelton, T. B. (2001). *The clinical neonatal behavioral assessment scale: What is it?* The Brazelton Institute. Harvard Medical School. Retrieved September 27, 2001, from http://www.childrenshospital.org/ brazelton/clnbas.html

Brazelton, T. B., Nugent, J. K., & Lester, B. M. (1987). Neonatal Behavioral Assessment Scale. In J. D. Osofsky (Ed.), *Handbook of infant development* (2nd ed.) New York: Wiley.

Brenner, M. H. (1976). Estimating the social costs of national economic policy: Implications for mental and physical health and criminal aggression (Paper No. 5). *Report to the Congressional Research Service of the Library of Congress and Joint Committee of Congress.* Washington, DC: Government Printing Office.

Brenton, M. (1977). What can be done about child abuse? *Today's Education, 66,* 51–53.

Bricker, D. (2000). Inclusion: How the scene has changed. *Topics in Early Childhood Special Education, 20*(1), 14–20.

Bridgman, M. (1984, December 28). Midlifers accept situations and look ahead. *Columbus (Ohio) Dispatch,* C1.

Brim, G. (1992). *Ambition: How we manage success and failure through our lives.* New York: Basic Books.

Brim, O. G., Ryff, C. D., & Kessler, R. C. (Eds.). (2004). *How healthy are we: A national study of well-being at midlife.* Chicago: University of Chicago Press.

Brink, P. (2001). Violence on TV and aggression in children. *Western Journal of Nursing Research, 23*(1), 5–8.

Brittingham, S. (2005, March 1). Leading high-achieving schools. *No Child Left Behind: The Achiever.* Retrieved March 26, 2005, from http://www.ed.gov/news/newsletters/achiever/2005/030105.html#2

Britton, W., & Bootzin, R. R. (2004). Near-death experiences and the temporal lobe. *Psychological Science, 15*(4), 254–258.

Brocklehurst, P. (2004). Antibiotics for gonorrhea in pregnancy. *The Cochrane Database of Systematic Reviews 2002,* 2. Retrieved October 20, 2004, from http://www.update-software.com/Abstracts/ab000098.htm

Brody, E. M. (1990). *Women in the middle: Their parent-care years.* New York: Springer.

Brody, E. M., Litvin, S. J., Albert, S. M., & Hoffman, C. J. (1994). Marital status of daughters and patterns of parent care. *Journal of Gerontology: Social Sciences, 49,* S95–S103.

Brody, G. H., Stoneman, Z., Flor, D., McCrary, C., Hastings, L., & Conyers, O. (1994). Financial resources, parent psychological functioning, parent co-caregiving, and early adolescent competence in rural two-parent African-American families. *Child Development, 65,* 590–605.

Brody, J. E. (1981, May 27). Planning to prevent retirement "shock." *New York Times,* 13.

Brody, J. E. (1992a, November 5). Adolescent obesity linked to ailments in adults. *New York Times,* A8.

Brody, J. E. (1992b, February 5). Maintaining friendships for the sake of good health. *New York Times,* B8.

Brody, J. E. (1994a, October 26). New research on postpartum depression holds hope for the mothers caught in its grip. *New York Times,* B7.

Brody, J. E. (1994b, November 8). Restraints for elderly. *New York Times,* B17.

Brody, J. E. (1995a, June 15). New clues in balancing the risks of hormones after menopause. *New York Times,* A1, A12.

Brody, J. E. (1995b, April 19). Study says exercise must be strenuous to add to lifespan. *New York Times,* A1, B7.

Brody, J. E. (1997, August 27). Diet may become one reason complaints about menopause are rare in Asia. *New York Times Health,* C8.

Brody, N. (1992). *Intelligence* (2nd ed.). New York: Academic Press.

Brodzinsky, D. M., Schechter, M. D., & Henig, R. M. (1992). *Being adopted: The lifelong search for self.* New York: Doubleday.

Brogan, P. (2005, March 15). Social security holds high stakes for women. *USA Today.* Retrieved April 25, 2005, from http://www.usatoday.com/news/washington/2005-03-15-socsec-women_x.htm

Bromberger, J. T. (1997). A hot flash. *Heart and Soul, 23,* 21.

Bronfenbrenner, U. (1977, May). Nobody home: The erosion of the American family. *Psychology Today, 10,* 40–47.

Bronfenbrenner, U. (1979). *The ecology of human development: Experiments by nature and design.* Cambridge, MA: Harvard University Press.

Bronfenbrenner, U. (1986, February). Alienation and the four worlds of childhood. *Phi Delta Kappan, 67,* 430–436.

Bronfenbrenner, U. (1995). Developmental ecology through space and time: A future perspective. In P. Moen, G. H. Elder, Jr. & K. Luscher (Eds.), *Examining lives in context: Perspectives on the ecology of human development* (pp. 619–647). Washington, DC: American Psychological Association.

Bronfenbrenner, U. (1997). Systems vs. associations: It's not either/or. *Families in Society, 78,* 124.

Bronfenbrenner, U. (Ed.). (2005). *Making human beings human.* Thousand Oaks, CA: Sage.

Bronfenbrenner, U., & Crouter, A. C. (1983). Evolution of environmental models of developmental research. In P. Mussen and W. Kessen (Eds.), *Handbook of child psychology.* New York: Wiley.

Bronson, G. (1997). The growth of visual capacity: Evidence from infant scanning patterns. *Advances in Infancy Research, 11,* 109–141.

Bronson, G. W. (1972). Infants' reactions to unfamiliar persons and novel objects. *Monographs of the Society for Research in Child Development, 37*(3).

Bronson, G. W. (1994). Infants' transitions toward adult-like scanning. *Child Development, 65,* 1243–1261.

Bronson, W. (1974). Mother-toddler interaction: A perspective on studying the development of competence. *Merrill-Palmer Quarterly, 20,* 275–301.

Bronstein, R. F. (1992). The dependent personality: Developmental, social, and clinical perspectives. *Psychological Bulletin, 112,* 3–23.

Bronston, B. (1998, October 19). Girl power. *Times-Picayoune,* D1.

Brooks-Gunn, J., & Reiter, E. O. (1990). The role of pubertal processes in the early adolescent transition. In S. S. Feldman & G. R. Elliott (Eds.), *At the threshold: The developing adolescent.* Cambridge, MA: Harvard University Press.

Brooks-Gunn, J., Phelps, E., & Elder, G. H., Jr. (1991). Studying lives through time: Secondary data analysis in developmental psychology. *Developmental Psychology, 27,* 899–910.

Brotherson, S. E., Yamamoto, T., & Acock, A. C. (2003, October). Connection and communication in father-child relationships and adolescent child well-being. *Fathering, 1*(3), 191–214.

Browder, S. (1997). Which body parts wear out the fastest . . . and what you can do to prolong their vitality. *New Choices, 37,* 52–55.

Brown, B. B., & Huang, B. H. (1995). Examining parenting practices in different peer contexts: Implications for adolescent trajectories. In L. Crockett & A. C. Crouter (Eds.), *Pathways through adolescence: Individual development in relation to social contexts* (pp. 151–174). Hillsdale, NJ: Erlbaum.

Brown, L. M., & Gilligan, C. (1992). *Meeting at the crossroads: Women's psychology and girls' development.* Cambridge, MA: Harvard University Press.

Brown, R. (1973). *A first language.* Cambridge, MA: Harvard University Press.

Brown, R., & Herrnstein, R. J. (1975). *Psychology.* Boston: Little, Brown.

Brown, S. L. (2000). Union transitions among cohabitors: The significance of relationship assessments and expectations. *Journal of Marriage and the Family, 63,* 833–846.

Brown, S. L., & Booth, A. (1996). Cohabitation versus marriage: A comparison of relationship quality. *Journal of Marriage and the Family, 58,* 668–678.

Brown, T. (1996). Values, knowledge, and Piaget. In E. Reed, E. Turiel, & T. Brown (Eds.), *Values and knowledge.* Mahwah, NJ: Erlbaum.

Browne, D. C., Crum, L., & Cousins, D. S. (1997). Minority health. In J. B. Kotch (Ed.), *Maternal and child health: Programs, problems, and policy in public health* (pp. 227–252). Gaithersburg, MD: Aspen.

Brownlee, S. (1996). The biology of soul murder: Fear can harm a child's brain. Is it reversible? *U.S. News & World Report, 121*(19), 71–74.

Brownlee, S. (1998, June 15). Baby talk. *U.S. News & World Report, 124*(23), 48–50.

Brownmiller, S. (1993, January 4). Making female bodies the battlefield. *Newsweek,* 37.

Brubaker, T. H. (1990). Families in later life: A burgeoning research area. *Journal of Marriage and the Family, 52,* 959–981.

Brues, A., & Sacher, G. (Eds.). (1965). *Aging and levels of biological organization.* Chicago: University of Chicago Press.

Bruner, J. S. (1970, December). A conversation with Jerome Bruner. *Psychology Today, 4,* 51–74.

Bruner, J. S. (1983). *Child's talk: Learning to use language.* New York: Norton.

Bruner, J. S. (1990). *Acts of meaning.* Cambridge, MA: Harvard University Press.

Bruner, J. S. (1991). *Acts of meaning.* Cambridge, MA: Harvard University Press.

Bruner, J. S., Goodnow, J. J., & Austin, G. A. (1956). *A study of thinking.* New York: Wiley.

Bruner, J. S., Oliver, R. R., & Greenfield, P. M. (1966). *Studies in cognitive growth.* New York: Wiley.

Brushes with death: Scientists validate near-death experiences. (2002). ABCNews.Com. Retrieved January 8, 2002, from http://abcnews.go.comsections/GMA/DrJohnson/SMA020108Near_death_ experiences.html

Bryk, A. S., Lee, V. E., & Holland, P. B. (1993). *Catholic schools and the common good.* Cambridge, MA: Harvard University Press.

Bryson, K., & Casper, L. M. (1999). Coresident grandparents and grandchildren. *Current Population Reports P23–198.* Washington, DC: U.S. Bureau of the Census.

Buchanan, C. M., Eccles, J. S., & Becker, J. B. (1992). Are adolescents the victims of raging hormones: Evidence for activational effects of hormones on moods and behavior at adolescence. *Psychological Bulletin, 111,* 62–107.

Budig, M. J., & England, P. (2001). The wage penalty for motherhood. *American Sociological Review, 66*(2), 204–226,

Buhrmester, D. (1990). Intimacy of friendship, interpersonal competence, and adjustment during preadolescence and adolescence. *Child Development, 61,* 1101–1111.

Buhrmester, D. (1998). Need fulfillment, interpersonal competence, and the developmental contexts of early adolescent friendship. In W. M. Bukowski & A. F. Newcomb (Eds.), *The company they keep: Friendship in childhood and adolescence* (pp. 158–185). Cambridge, UK: Cambridge University Press.

Buhrmester, D., & Furman, W. (1990). Perceptions of sibling relationships during middle childhood and adolescence. *Child Development, 61,* 1387–1398.

Building knowledge for a nation of learners: A framework for education research. (1997). Office of Educational Research and Improvement and the National Educational Research Policy and Procedures Board. Washington, DC: U.S. Department of Education.

Building their futures: How early Head Start programs are enhancing the lives of infants and toddlers in low-income families: Summary report. (2001). Early Head Start Research and Evaluation Project. Commissioner's Office of Research and Evaluation and the Head Start Bureau. Administration on Children, Youth and Families. Washington, DC: U.S. Department of Health and Human Services.

Bukowski, W., & Cillessen, A. (1998). *Sociometry then and now: Building on six decades of measuring children's experiences with the peer group.* San Francisco: Jossey-Bass.

Bukowski, W. M., Gauze, C., Hoza, B., & Newcomb, A. F. (1993). Differences and consistency between same-sex and other-sex peer relationships during early adolescence. *Developmental Psychology, 29,* 255–263.

Bull, R. (2004). Legal psychology in the twenty-first century. *Criminal Behaviour in Mental Health, 4*(3), 167–181.

Bulley, M. (1984, February 6–10) *Early childhood marriage and female circumcision in Ghana.* Report on a seminar on traditional practices affecting the health of women and children in Africa, Dakar, Senegal.

Bullock, M., & Lutkenhaus, P. (1988). The development of volitional behavior in the toddler years. *Child Development, 59,* 664–674.

Bulterys, M., Jamieson, D. J., O'Sullivan, M. J., Cohen, M. H., Maupin, R., Nesheim, S. Webber, M. P., Van Dyke, R., Wiener, J. & Branson, B. M. (2004, July 14). Rapid HIV-1 testing during labor. *Journal of the American Medical Association, 292,* 219–223.

Bumpass, L., Sweet, J., & Martin, T. C. (1990). Changing patterns of remarriage. *Journal of Marriage and the Family, 52,* 747–756.

Bundy, A., Lane, S., & Murray, E. (2002) *Sensory integration theory and practice* (2nd ed.). Philadelphia: F. A. Davis.

Buntaine, R. L., & Costenbader, V. K. (1997, May). Self-reported differences in the experience and expression of anger between girls and boys. *Sex Roles: A Journal of Research, 36*(9), 625–638.

Burhaus, K. K., & Dweck, C. S. (1995). Helplessness in early childhood. *Child Development, 66,* 1717–1738.

Burke, K., & Sutherland, C. (2004, Winter). Attitudes toward inclusion: Knowledge vs. experience. *Education, 125*(2), 163–173.

Burns, B. J., Costello, E. J., Angold, A., Tweed, D., Stangl, D., Farmer, E. M. Z., & Erkanli, A. (1995). Children's mental health service use across service sectors. *Health Affairs, 14*(3), 147–159.

Burton, R. V. (1976). Honesty and dishonesty. In T. Lickona (Ed.), *Moral development and behavior: Theory, research, and social issues.* New York: Holt, Rinehart & Winston.

Bush, G. W. (2001, February 28). *A Blueprint for new beginnings: A responsible budget for America's priorities.* Retrieved January 21, 2005, from http://www.whitehouse.gov/news/usbudget/blueprint/budtoc.html

Bushnell, E. W. (1985). The decline of visually guided reaching during infancy. *Infant Behavior and Development, 8,* 139–155.

Busse, E. W. (1969). Theories of aging. In E. W. Busse & E. Pfeiffer (Eds.), *Behavior and adaptation in late life.* Boston: Little, Brown.

Bussey, K. (1992). Lying and truthfulness: Children's definitions, standards, and evaluative reactions. *Child Development, 63,* 129–137.

Bussey, K., & Bandura, A. (1984). Influence of gender constancy and social power on sex-linked modeling. *Journal of Personality and Social Psychology, 47,* 1292–1302.

Bussey, K., & Bandura, A. (1992). Self-regulatory mechanisms governing gender development. *Child Development, 63,* 1236–1250.

Butler, R. N. (1971, December). The life review. *Psychology Today, 5,* 49–51f.

Butler, R., & Ruzany, N. (1993). Age and socialization effects on the development of social comparison motives and normative ability assessment in kibbutz and urban children. *Child Development, 64,* 532–543.

Byely, L., Archibald, A. B., Graber, J., & Brooks-Gunn, J. (2000). A prospective study of familial and social influences on girls' body image and dieting. *International Journal of Eating Disorders, 28,* 155–164.

Byrd-Bredbenner, C., & Murray, J. (2003). A comparison of the anthropometric measurements of idealized female body images in media directed to men, women, and mixed gender audiences. *Topics in Clinical Nutrition, 18*(2), 117–119.

Byrom, A. (2004, December). Advanced maternal age: A literature review. *British Journal of Midwifery, 12*(12), 779–783.

Cahill, S. E. (1990). Childhood and public life: Reaffirming biographical divisions. *Social Problems, 37,* 390–402.

Cahill, S., South, K., & Spade, J. (2000). *Outing age: Public policy issues affecting gay, lesbian, bisexual and transgender elders.* New York: The Policy Institute of the Gay and Lesbian Task Force.

Cairns, R. B. (1983). The emergence of developmental psychology. In P. H. Mussen (Series Ed.) & W. Kessen (Vol. Ed.), *Handbook of child psychology: Vol. 1. History, theory, and methods* (4th ed., pp. 41–102). New York: Wiley.

Calhoun, G., Jr., & Alforque, M. (1996). Prenatal substance afflicted children: An overview and review of the literature. *Education, 117,* 30–38.

Call, K. T., Mortimer, J. T., & Shanahan, M. J. (1995). Helpfulness and the development of competence in adolescence. *Child Development, 66,* 129–138.

Callum, M. (1996, February). Our boomers-turning-50 happiness index. *New Choices, 24–27.*

Camarata, S. (1996). On the importance of integrating naturalistic language, social intervention, and speech-intelligibility training. In L. Koegel, R. Koegel, & G. Dunlap (Eds.), *Positive behavior support* (pp. 333–351). Baltimore, MD: Brookes.

Campbell, A. (1993). *Men, women, and aggression.* New York: Basic Books.

Campbell, J. J., Lamb, M. E., & Hwang, C. P. (2000). Early child care experiences and children's social competencies between 1.5 and 15 years of age. *Applied Developmental Science: Special Issue: The Effects of Quality Care on Child Development, 4*(3), 166–175.

Campbell, S. B., Pierce, E. W., March, C. L., Ewing, L. J., & Szumowski, E. K. (1994). Hard-to-manage preschool boys: Symptomatic behavior across contexts and time. *Child Development, 65,* 836–851.

Campos, J. J., Mumme, D. L., Kermoian, R., & Campos, R. G. (1993). A functionalist perspective on the nature of emotion. *Monographs of the Society for Research in Child Development, 59* (Nos. 2–3, Serial No. 240).

Camras, L. A., Meng, Z., Ujiie, T., Dharamsi, S., Miyake, K., Oster, H., Wang, L., Cruz, Je., Murdoch, A., & Campos, J. (2002, June). Observing emotion in infants: Facial expression, body behavior, and rater judgments of responses to an expectancy-violating event. *Emotion, 2*(2), 179–193.

Candland, D. K. (1993). *Feral children and clever animals: Reflections on human nature.* New York: Oxford University Press.

Canfield, R. L., Henderson, C. R., Cory-Slechta, D. A., Cox, C., Jusko, T. A., & Lanphera, B. P. (2003, April 17). Intellectual impairment in children with blood lead concentrations below 10 mg per deciliter. *New England Journal of Medicine, 348,* 1517–1526.

Caplan, A. (1999). *The nation waits and watches—Oregon physician-assisted suicide may open Pandora's box.* Retrieved January 27, 1999, from http://www.med.upenn.edu/bioethic/PAS/oregon.html

Caplan, A. (2005, January 24). *How old is too old to have a baby?* Global Action on Aging. Retrieved August 22, 2005, from www.globalaging.org/health/world/2005/old.htm

Caregiving in the U.S. (2004). National Alliance for Caregiving and AARP. Retrieved May 2, 2005, from http://www.caregiving.org/04finalreport.pdf

Carel, J. C., Lahlou, N., & Chaussain, J. L. (2004, March–April). Precocious puberty and statural growth. *Human Reproduction Update, 10*(2), 135–147.

Carey, B. (2004, October 10). Can prayers heal? Critics say studies go past science's reach. *New York Times, 154,* 1, 1.

Carlson, A. C. (1986). What happened to the "family wage"? *Public Interest, 83,* 3–17.

Carlson, M. J., & Corcoran, M. E. (2001). Family structure and children's behavioral and cognitive outcomes. *Journal of Marriage and the Family, 63,* 779–792.

Carpenter, D. G. (1965). Diffusion theory of aging. *Journal of Gerontology, 20,* 191–195.

Carr, M., Borkowski, J. G., & Maxwell, S. E. (1991). Motivational components of underachievement. *Developmental Psychology, 27,* 108–118.

Carson, S. A., & Ware-Branch, D. (2001, February). Management of recurrent early pregnancy loss. ACOG Practice Bulletin, *International Journal of Gynecology and Obstetrics, 78*(2), 179–190.

Carstensen, L. L., Gottman, J. M., & Levenson, R. W. (1995). Emotional behavior in long-term marriage. *Psychology and Aging, 10*(1), 140–149.

Carter, A.S., Garrity-Rokous, F.E., Chazan-Cohen, R., Little, C. & Briggs-Gowan, M.J. (2001). Maternal depression and comorbidity: Predicting early parenting, attachment security, and toddler social-emotional problems and competencies. *Journal of the American Academy of Child and Adolescent Psychiatry, 40*(1), 18–16.

Casamassimo, P. S. (2004, December 1). Oral health in primary care medicine: Practice and policy challenges. *American Family Physician, 70*(11). Editorial.

Case, R. (Ed.). (1991). *The mind's staircase: Exploring the conceptual underpinnings of children's thought and knowledge.* Hillsdale, NJ: Erlbaum.

Caspi, A., Elder, G. H., Jr., & Bem, D. J. (1987). Moving against the world: Life-course patterns of explosive children. *Developmental Psychology, 23,* 308–313.

Caspi, A., Elder, G. H., Jr., & Bem, D. J. (1988). Moving away from the world: Life-course patterns of shy children. *Developmental Psychology, 24,* 824–831.

Cassens, D. (1998). Expanded damages in elder abuse cases. *ABA Journal, 84,* 39.

Cassese, J. (1993). The invisible bridge: Child sexual abuse and the risk of HIV infection in adulthood. *SIECUS Report, 21,* 1–7.

Cassidy, J., & Berlin, L. J. (1994). The insecure/ambivalent pattern of attachment: Theory and research. *Child Development, 65,* 971–991.

Castellanos, L. (1994). *Hispanic/Latina women: Cultural norms and prevention. Just the Facts.* The Florida Alcohol and Drug Abuse Association Resource Center, Tallahassee, Florida. Retrieved November 20, 2001, from http://www.fadaa.org/resource/justfact/!hispani.pdf

Castro, J. (1991, August 26). Watching a generation waste away. *Time,* 10–12.

Catalano, S. M. (2004, September). *Criminal victimization, 2003.* Bureau of Justice Statistics National Crime Victimization Study. NCJ205455. Washington, DC: U.S. Department of Justice.

Cattell, R. B. (1943). The measurement of adult intelligence. *Psychological Bulletin, 40,* 153–193.

Cattell, R. B. (1963). Theory of fluid or crystallized intelligence. *Journal of Educational Psychology, 54,* 1–22.

Cattell, R. B. (1971). *Abilities: Their structure, growth, and action.* Boston: Houghton Mifflin.

Caudron, S. (2001). The myth of job happiness. *Workforce, 80*(4), 32–36.

Cavanaugh, J. C. (1998a). Friendships and social networks among older people. In I. H. Nordhus et al., (Eds.), *Clinical geropsychology* (pp. 137–140). Washington, DC: American Psychological Association.

Cavanaugh, J. C. (1998b). Memory and aging. *National Forum: Phi Kappa Phi Journal, 78,* 34–37.

Celis, W., III. (1991, January 2). Growing talk of date rape separates sex from assault. *New York Times,* A1, B7.

Cellular inflammation precursor to heart disease. (2005, February 2005). *USA Today Magazine, 133,* 8–9.

Center for Biology Evaluation and Research. (2004, June 29). *Xenotransplantation action plan* (FDA Approach to the Regulation of Xenotransplantation). Washington, DC: U.S. Food & Drug Administration.

Centers for Disease Control and Prevention. (1997a). *Atlas of United States Mortality.* Atlanta: USDHHS.

Centers for Disease Control and Prevention. (1997b). *HIV/AIDS and women who have sex with women.* Retrieved June 12, 1998, from http://www.thebody.com/cdc/wsw.html

Centers for Disease Control and Prevention. (1997c). *Youth risk behavior surveillance: United States 1997.* Atlanta: CDC, Division of Media Relations.

Centers for Disease Control and Prevention. (1998). *1993 National Mortality Followback Survey (NMFS).* National Center for Health Statistics. Retrieved October 1, 1998, from http://www.cdc.gov/nchswww/about/major/nmfs/nmfs.htm

Centers for Disease Control and Prevention. (2000a). *School health policies and programs study.* National Center for Chronic Disease Prevention and Health Promotion. Retrieved February 3, 2005, from http://www.cdc.gov/HealthyYouth/shpps/factsheets/index.htm

Centers for Disease Control and Prevention. (2000b). *Semiannual HIV/AIDS Surveillance Report, 12*(1). Retrieved December 31, 2001 from http://www.cdc.gov/std/stats/TOC2000.htm

Centers for Disease Control and Prevention. (2000c). *STD surveillance, 2000.* National Center for HIV, STD and TB Prevention. Division of Sexually Transmitted Diseases. Retrieved December 31, 2001, from http://www.cdc.gov/std/stats/TOC2000.htm

Centers for Disease Control and Prevention. (2000d). *Tracking the hidden epidemics: Trends in STDs in the United States, 2000: Magnitude of the epidemics overall.* U.S. Department of Health and Human Services. Retrieved December 31, 2001, from http://www.cdc.gov/nchstp/od/news/RevBrochure1pdfmag.htm

Centers for Disease Control and Prevention. (2000e). Trends: Cigarette smoking among high school students—United States, 1991–1999. *Morbidity and Mortality Weekly Report, 49,* 755–758.

Centers for Disease Control and Prevention. (2000f). Youth risk behavior surveillance—United States, 1999. *Morbidity and Mortality Weekly Reports, 49*(SS-5), 75.

Centers for Disease Control and Prevention. (2001a). Deaths: Leading causes for 1999. *National Vital Statistics Reports, 49*(11), 1–88.

Centers for Disease Control and Prevention. (2001b). *Health, United States, 2001.* National Center for Health Statistics. Washington, DC: U.S. Government Printing Office.

Centers for Disease Control and Prevention. (2001c). *Health-related quality of life findings.* Retrieved January 14, 2002 from http://www.cdc.gov/nccdphp/hrquol/findings.htm

Centers for Disease Control and Prevention. (2001d). *HIV Prevention Strategic Plan Through 2005.* Retrieved April 4, 2005, from http://www.cdc.gov/nchstp/od/news/prevention.pdf

Centers for Disease Control and Prevention. (2001e). Trends in blood levels among children: Boston, Massachusetts, 1994–1999. *Morbidity and Mortality Weekly Report, 50,* 337–339.

Centers for Disease Control and Prevention. (2001f). Youth tobacco surveillance—United States, 2000. *Morbidity and Mortality Weekly Report, 50,* 1–51.

Centers for Disease Control and Prevention. (2003a). 2001 Assisted reproductive technology success rates. *National Summary and Fertility Clinic Reports.* Retrieved October 18, 2004, from EBSCO*host:* http://www.cdc.gov/reproductivehealth/ART01/PDF/ART2001.pdf

Centers for Disease Control and Prevention. (2003b). *Advancing HIV prevention: The four strategies.* Retrieved March 17, 2005, from http://www.cdc.gov/hiv/partners/ahp_program.htm

Centers for Disease Control and Prevention. (2003c). *STDs in adolescents and young adults.* STD Surveillance 2003. Retrieved April 16, 2005, from http://www.cdc.gov/std/stats/03pdf/SFAdoles.pdf

Centers for Disease Control and Prevention. (2003d). *Teen birth rate continues to decline; African-American teens show sharpest drop.* Retrieved March 21, 2005, from http://www.cdc.gov/nchs/pressroom/03facts/teen

Centers for Disease Control and Prevention. (2004a). *Abortion surveillance-United States, 2001.* Retrieved February 20, 2005, from http://www.cdc.gov/mmwr/PDF/SS/SS5309.pdf

Centers for Disease Control and Prevention. (2004b). *Alzheimer's Disease.* Retrieved April 11, 2005, from http://www.cdc.gov/nchs/fastats/alzheimr.htm

Centers for Disease Control and Prevention. (2004c). *Attention deficit hyperactivity disorder.* National Center on Birth Defects and Developmental Disabilities. Retrieved March 8, 2005, from http://www.cdc.gov/ncbddd/adhd/publichealth.htm

Centers for Disease Control and Prevention. (2004d). Blood mercury levels in young children and childbearing-aged women—United States: 1999–2002. *Morbidity and Mortality Weekly Report, 53*(43), 1018–1020.

Centers for Disease Control and Prevention. (2004e). *Deaths/mortality.* Retrieved April 12, 2005, from http://www.cdc.gov/nchs/fastats/deaths.htm

Centers for Disease Control and Prevention. (2004f). *Health, United States, 2004.* Washington, DC: U.S. Department of Health and Human Services.

Centers for Disease Control and Prevention. (2004g). Recommended childhood and adolescent immunization schedule—United States, July–December 2004. *Morbidity and Mortality Weekly Report, 53*(16) Q1-Q3. Retrieved April 12, 2005, from http://www.cdc.gov/nip/recs/lamincard-instruct.htm#pocketchild

Centers for Disease Control and Prevention. (2004h). Table 70: Overweight children and adolescents 6–19 years of age, according to sex, age, race, and Hispanic origin: United States, selected years 1963–65 through 1999–2002. *Health, United States, 2004.* Washington, DC: National Center for Health Statistics.

Centers for Disease Control and Prevention. (2005a). *Estimated numbers of AIDS cases, by year of diagnosis and selected characteristics of persons, 1999–2003: United States.* Table 3. Retrieved March 17, 2005, from http://www.cdc.gov/hiv/stats/2003SurveillanceReport/table3.htm

Centers for Disease Control and Prevention. (2005b). *Executive summary: Atlas of injury mortality among American Indian and Alaska Native children and youth, 1989–1998.* Retrieved May 10, 2005, from http://www.cdc.gov/ncipc/pub-res/American_Indian_Injury_Atlas/default.htm

Centers for Disease Control and Prevention. (2005c). National Youth Tobacco Survey, United States, 2002 and 2004. *Morbidity and Mortality Weekly Report, 54*(12), 297–301.

Centers for Disease Control and Prevention. (2005d, February 11). *Racial/ethnic differences in the prevalence and impact of doctor-diagnosed arthritis: United States, 2002. Morbidity and Mortality Weekly Report, 54*(5), 119–123. Retrieved May 15, 2005, from http://www.cdc.gov/mmwr/preview/mmwrhtml/mm5405a3.htm

Cerella, J., Rybash, J., Hoyer, W., & Commons, M. L. (Eds.). (1993). *Adult information processing: Limits on loss.* San Diego: Academic Press.

Chaika, G. (2000). *Will higher pay solve the worst teacher shortage ever?* Education World. Retrieved March 17, 2005, from http://www.educationworld.com/a_admin/admin204.shtml

Chaikivsky, A. (1997, June). Getting older will leave a bad taste in your mouth. *Esquire,* 100.

Chamberlain, D. (1998). Pregnancy, birth, and very early parenting. Retrieved July 15, 1998, from http://www.birthpsychology.com/resources/index.html

Chamberlin, J. (2004, November). No desire to fully retire. *Monitor on Psychology, 35*(10), 82–83.

Chan, B. W. H., Chan, K., Koide, T., Yeung, S., Leung, M., et al. (2002, September). Maternal diabetes increases the risk of caudal regression caused by retonic acid. *Diabetes, 51,* 2811–2816.

Chan, J., Edman, J. C., & Koltai, P. J. (2004, March 1). Obstructive sleep apnea in children. *American Family Physician, 69*(5), 1147–1154.

Chance, P., & Fischman, J. (1987, May). The magic of childhood. *Psychology Today, 21,* 48–58.

Chao, E. L., & Utgoff, K. P. (2004, February). *Women in the labor force: A data book.* Bureau of Labor Statistics. Washington, DC: U.S. Department of Labor. Retrieved April 8, 2005, from http://www.bls.gov/cps/wlf-databook.pdf

Chapman, A. R., Frankel, M. S., & Garfinkel, M. S. (1999, November). *Stem cell research and applications: Monitoring the frontiers of biomedical research.* American Association for the Advancement of Science and Institute for Civil Society.

Chapman, M., & Lindenberger, U. (1988). Functions, operations, and decalage in the development of transitivity. *Developmental Psychology, 24,* 542–551.

Charles, S. T., & Pasupathi, M. (2003). Age-related patterns of variability in self-descriptions: Implications for everyday affective experience. *Psychology and Aging, 18,* 524–536.

Charness, N., & Gerchak, Y. (1996). Participation rates and maximal performance: A log-linear explanation for group differences, such as Russian and male dominance in chess. *Psychological Science, 7,* 46–51.

Chartbook on the trends in the health of Americans. (2004). National Center for Health Statistics. *Health, United States: 2004,* Hyattsville, MD: U.S. Department of Health and Human Services. Retrieved April 5, 2005, from http://www.cdc.gov/nchs/data/hus/hus04.pdf

Chase, M. (1995, February 27). Gently guiding the gravely ill to the end of life. *Wall Street Journal,* B1.

Chase-Lansdale, P. L., Cherlin, A. J., & Kiernan, K. E. (1995). The long-term effects of parental divorce on the mental health of young adults: A developmental perspective. *Child Development, 66,* 1614–1634.

Chauncey, G. (1994). *Gay New York: Gender, urban culture, and the making of the gay male world, 1890–1940.* New York: Basic Books.

Check, J. H., Dietterich, C., Graziano, V., Lurie, D., & Choe, J. K. (2004, May). Effect of maximal endometrial thickness on outcome after frozen embryo transfer. *Fertility and Sterility, 81*(5), 1399–1400.

Chen, X., Rubin, K. H., & Sun, Y. (1992). Social reputation and peer relationships in Chinese and Canadian children: A cross-cultural study. *Child Development, 63,* 1336–1343.

Cherlin, A. (2004). The deinstitutionalization of American marriage. *Journal of Marriage and Family, 66,* 848–861.

Cherlin, A. J. (1998). Marriage and marital dissolution among black Americans. *Journal of Comparative Family Studies, 29,* 147–158.

Cherlin, A. J., & Furstenberg, F. F., Jr. (1986). *The new American grandparent: A place in the family, a life apart.* New York: Basic Books.

Chesla, C., Martinson, I., & Muwaswes, M. (1994). Continuities and discontinuities in family members' relationships with Alzheimer's patients. *Family Relations, 43,* 3–9.

Chesler, N. C., & Chesler, M. A. (2002). Gender-informed mentoring strategies for women engineering scholars: On establishing a caring community. *Journal of Engineering Education,* 49–55.

Chess, S., & Thomas, A. (1996). *Temperament: Theory and practice.* New York: Brunner/Mazel.

Chi, M., Hutchinson, J., & Robin, A. (1989). How inferences about novel domain-related concepts can be constrained by structural knowledge. *Merrill Palmer Quarterly, 35,* 27–62.

Chia, R. C., & Poe, E. (2004, Spring). Innovations in international education. *International Psychology Reporter, 8,* 7.

Chieh, L. (2000). Instruction effect and developmental levels: A study on water-level task with Chinese children ages 9–17. *Contemporary Educational Psychology, 25,* 488–498.

Chieh, L., & Nuttall, R. L. (1999). A Test of the Piagetian water-level tasks with Chinese students. *Journal of Genetic Psychology, 160,* 369–381.

Chiesa, M. (1992). Radical behaviorism and scientific frameworks: From mechanistic to relational accounts. *American Psychologist, 47,* 1287–1299.

Child Health USA 2002. (2002). *Maternal and Child Health Bureau,* 1–79. Retrieved February 5, 2005 from http://www.mchb.hrsa.gov/chusa02/

Child poverty fact sheet. (2001). National Center for Children in Poverty. Mailman School of Public Health, Columbia University, New York, New York. Retrieved December 2, 2001, from http://cpmcnet.columbia.edu/dept/nccp/ycpf.html

Child Trends. (2002). *Charting parenthood: A statistical portrait of fathers and mothers in America.* Washington, DC: Child Trends. Retrieved January 16, 2004 from http://www.childtrends.org/files/ParenthoodRpt2002.pdf

Child Trends Data Bank. (2004). *High school dropout rates.* Retrieved March 31, 2005, from http://www.childtrendsdatabank.org/indicators/1HighSchoolDropout.cfm

Children's Defense Fund. (2005). *Protect children not guns.* Retrieved February 21, 2005, from http://www.childrensdefense.org/education/gunviolence/gunreport2005/gunreport2005.pdf

Children's Defense Fund. (2003). *Defining poverty and why it matters to children.* Retrieved December 7, 2004, from http://www.childrensdefense.org/

Children's vision screening. (2003). *Prevent Blindness America.* Retrieved December 15, 2004, from http://www.preventblindness.org/resources/factsheets/ChidrensScreeningsFS78.PDF

China's one child rule risks social problems. (2004, August). *Journal of Medical Ethics, 30*(4), 358.

Choi, Y. (2004, July 2). *Autism statistics: Autism cases and costs on the rise.* Autistic Society. Retrieved February 4, 2005, from http://www.autisticsociety.org/autism-article334.html

Chomsky, N. (1957). *Syntactic structures.* The Hague: Mouton.

Chomsky, N. (1965). *Aspects of a theory of syntax.* Cambridge, MA: MIT Press.

Chomsky, N. (1968). *Language and mind.* New York: Harcourt Brace Jovanovich.

Chomsky, N. (1975). *Reflections on language.* New York: Pantheon Books.

Chomsky, N. (1980). *Rules and representations.* New York: Columbia University Press.

Chomsky, N. (1995). *Language and thought.* Wakefield, RI: Moyer Bell.

Chown, S. M. (Ed.). (1972). *Human aging.* Baltimore: Penguin Books.

Christiansen, S. C. (2000). Day care, siblings, and asthma: Please sneeze on my child. *New England Journal of Medicine, 343*(8), 574–575.

Chu, H. (1978). The Korean learner in an American school. In *Teaching for cross-cultural understanding.* Arlington, VA: Arlington Public Schools.

Chubb, N. H., & Fertman, C. I. (1992). Adolescents' perceptions of belonging in their families. *Families in Society, 73,* 387–394.

Chubb, N. H., Fertman, C. I., & Ross, J. L. (1997). Adolescent self-esteem and locus of control: A longitudinal study of gender and age differences. *Adolescence, 32,* 113–129.

Chugani, H. T., & Phelps, M. E. (1986). Maturational changes in cerebral functions in infants determined by FDG positron emission tomography. *Science, 231,* 840–843.

Chumlea, W. C. (1982). Physical growth in adolescence. In B. B. Wolman (Ed.), *Handbook of developmental psychology.* Englewood Cliffs, NJ: Prentice Hall.

Chumlea, W. C., Schubert, C. M., Roche, A. F., Kulin, H. E., Lee, P. A., Himes, J. H., & Shumei, S. S. (2003, January). Age at menarche and racial comparisons in U.S. girls. *Pediatrics, 111,* 110–113.

Cicchetti, D. (2004). An odyssey of discovery: Lessons learned through three decades of research on child maltreatment. *American Psychologist, 59,* 731–741.

Cicirelli, V. G. (1978). The relationship of sibling structure to intellectual abilities and achievement. *Review of Educational Research, 48,* 365–379.

Cicirelli, V. G. (1992). *Family caregiving: Autonomous and paternalistic decision making.* Newbury Park, CA: Sage.

Cicirelli, V. G. (1994). Sibling relationships in cross-cultural perspective. *Journal of Marriage and the Family, 56,* 7–20.

Cicirelli, V. G. (1995). *Sibling relationships across the life span.* New York: Plenum Press.

Cicirelli, V. G. (1997). Relationship of psychosocial and background variables to older adults' end-of-life decisions. *Psychology and Aging, 12,* 72–83.

Cicirelli, V. G. (2001). Sibling relationships. In G. Maddox (Ed.), *Encyclopedia of Aging* (3rd ed., pp. 928–930). New York: Springer.

Cicirelli, V. G., MacLean, A. P., & Cox, L. S. (2000). Hastening death: A comparison of two end-of-life decisions. *Death Studies, 24*(5), 401–419.

Claman, P. (2004, March). Men at risk: Occupation and male infertility. *Sexuality, Reproduction and Menopause, 2*(1), 19–26.

Clark, A., Oswald, A. & Warr, P. (1996). Is job satisfaction U-shaped in age? *Journal of Occupational and Organizational Psychology, 69*(1), 57–82.

Clark, E. V., Gelman, S. A., & Lane, N. M. (1985). Compound nouns and category structure in young children. *Child Development, 56,* 84–94.

Clark, K., & Shute, N. (2001). The adoption maze. *U.S. News & World Report, 130*(10), 60–66, 69.

Clark, R. D., & Rice, G.A., (1982). Family constellations and eminence: The birth orders of Nobel Prize winners. *Journal of Psychology, 110,* 281–287.

Clarke-Stewart, K. A., & Hevey, C. M. (1981). Longitudinal relations in repeated observations of mother-child interaction from 1 to 2½ years. *Developmental Psychology, 17,* 127–145.

Clarke-Stewart, K. A., McCartney, K., Vandell, D. L., Owen, M. T., & Booth, C. L. (2000). Effects of parental separation and divorce on very young children. *Journal of Family Psychology, 14*(2), 304–326.

Clausen, J. A. (1966). Family structure, socialization and personality. In L. W. Hoffman & M. L. Hoffman (Eds.), *Review of child development research* (Vol. 2). New York: Russell Sage Foundation.

Clausen, J. A. (1993). *American lives: Looking back at the children of the Great Depression.* New York: Free Press.

Clay, E. C., & Seehusen, D. A. (2004, February). A review of postpartum depression for the primary care physician. *Southern Medical Journal, 97*(2), 157–161.

Cleiren, M. P. H. D. (1993). *Bereavement and adaptation: A comparative study of the aftermath of death.* Washington, DC: Hemisphere.

Cleveland, J. (1998). *Ear-splitting music really did split ears.* Senior Connection. Retrieved June 12, 1998, from http://www.seniornews.com/senior-connection/article1032.html

Coall, C., & Chisholm, J. S. (2003). Evolutionary perspectives on pregnancy: Maternal age at menarche and infant birth weight. *Social Science and Medicine, 57*(10), 1771–1781.

Coburn, M. F. (1996). It was scary, but exciting. *New Choices, 36,* 56–58.

Cochran, M., & Niego, S. (1995). Parenting and social networks. In M. H. Bornstein (Ed.), *Handbook of parenting* (Vol. 3). Hillsdale, NJ: Erlbaum.

Cohen, D., Eisdorfer, C., Gorelick, P., Paveza, G., Luchins, D. J., Freels, S., Ashford, J. W., Semla, T., Levy, P., & Hirschman, R. (1993). Psychopathology associated with Alzheimer's disease and related disorders. *Journal of Gerontology: Medical Sciences, 48,* M2555–M260.

Cohen, J. W., Dougherty, D. D., Machlin, S. R., & Spector, W. D. (2001). Who pays for home health care: Shifting burdens past and present [Abstract]. *Gerontologist, 41*(Special Issue 1), 324.

Cohen, S. A. (2004, October). Promoting the "B" in ABC: Its value and limitations in fostering reproductive health. *The Guttmacher Report on Public Policy, 7*(4). Retrieved October 18, 2004, from http://www.guttmacher.org/pubs/tgr/07/4/gr070411.html

Cohen, S. E., & Beckwith, L. (1977). Caregiving behaviors and early cognitive development as related to ordinal position in preterm infants. *Child Development, 48,* 152–157.

Cohn, F., Salmon, M. E., Stobo, J. D. (Eds.). (2002). *Confronting chronic neglect: The education and training of health professionals on family violence* (1st ed.). Washington, DC: National Academy Press.

Cohn, J., & Sugar, J. A. (1991). Determinants of quality of life in institutions: Perceptions of frail older residents, staff and families. In J. E. Birren, J. E. Lubben, J. C. Rowe, & D. E. Deutchman (Eds.), *The concept and measurement of quality of life in the frail elderly.* New York: Academic Press.

Coker, D. M. (1988). The Asian students in the classroom. *Education and Society, 1*(3), 19–20.

Colby, A., & Damon, W. (1992). *Some do care.* New York: Free Press.

Colby, K. M., & Stoller, R. J. (1988). *Cognitive science and psychoanalysis.* Hillsdale, NJ: Erlbaum.

Colditz, G. A. (1992). Economic costs of obesity. *American Journal of Nutrition, 55,* 503–507.

Coldren, J. T., & Colombo, J. (1994). The nature and processes of preverbal learning. *Monographs of the Society for Research in Child Development, 59* (4, Serial No. 241).

Cole, R. A. (1979, April). Navigating the slippery stream of speech. *Psychology Today, 12,* 77–87.

Coleman, M., & Ganong, L. (2004). *Handbook of contemporary families.* London: Sage Publications.

Coley, R. (1998). Children's socialization experiences and functioning in single mother households: The importance of father and other men. *Child Development, 69,* 219–230.

Coley, R. J. (2001). *Differences in the gender gap: Comparisons across ethnic groups in education and work.* Princeton, NJ: Educational Testing Service. Retrieved March 18, 2005, from http://www.ets.org/research/pic/gender.pdf

Coley, R. J. (2003). *Growth in school revisited: Achievement gains from the fourth to the eighth grade.* Princeton, NJ: Educational Testing Service.

Colledge, E., Bishop, D. V. M., Koeppen-Schomerus, G., Price, T. S., Happe, F. G. E., Eley, T. C., Dale, P. S. & Plomin, R. (2002, September). The structure of language abilities at 4 years: A twin study. *Developmental Psychology, 38,* 749–757.

Collier, V. P. (1992). A synthesis of studies examining long-term language minority student data on academic achievement. *Bilingual Research Journal, 16,* 187–212.

Collier, V. P. (1997). Acquiring a second language for school. *Direction in Language and Education, 1,* 4.

Collins, D. E., & Tilson, E. R. (2001). A new generation on the horizon. *Radiologic Technology, 73*(2), 172–176.

Collins, F. S., Green, E. D., Guttmacher, A. E., & Guyer, M. S. (2003, April 24). A vision for the future of genomics research. *Nature, 422,* 1–13.

Collins, G. (1983, October 24). Stepfamilies share their joys and woes. *New York Times,* 21.

Collins, N. L., Dunkel-Schetter, C., Lobel, M., & Scrimshaw, S. C. M. (1993). Social support in pregnancy: Psychosocial correlates of birth outcomes and postpartum depression. *Journal of Personality and Social Psychology, 65,* 1243–1258.

Collins, R., & Ribeiro, R. (2004, Fall). Toward an early care and education agenda for Hispanic children. *Early Childhood Research and Practice (ECRP), 6*(2). Retrieved February 24, 2005, from http://ecrp.uiuc.edu/v6n2/collins.html

Colombo, J. (1993). *Infant cognition: Predicting later intellectual functioning.* Newbury Park, CA: Sage.

Condon, W. S., & Sander, L. W. (1974a). Neonate movement is synchronized with adult speech: Interactional participation and language acquisition. *Science, 183,* 99–101.

Condon, W. S., & Sander, L. W. (1974b). Synchrony demonstrated between movements of the neonate and adult speech. *Child Development, 45,* 456–462.

Conger, R. D., Conger, K. J., Elder, G. H., Jr., Lorenz, F. O., Simons, R. L., & Whitbeck, L. B. (1993). Family economic stress and adjustment of early adolescent girls. *Developmental Psychology, 29,* 206–219.

Congressional Quarterly. (2004). Social Security reform: How should America's retirement system be saved? *CQ Researcher, 14*(33), 781–804.

Conlin, M. (2003a). For Gen X, it's paradise lost. *Business Week, 3839,* 72–73.

Conlin, M. (2003b, May 26). The new gender gap. *Business Week.* Retrieved March 18, 2005, from http://netscape.businessweek.com/magazine/content/03_21/b3834001_mz001.htm

Connidis, I. A., & Campbell, L. D. (2001). Closeness, confiding, and contact among siblings in middle and late adulthood. In A. Walker, M. Manoogian-O'Dell, L. McGraw, & D. L. White (Eds.), *Families in later life* (pp. 149–155). Thousand Oaks, CA: Pine Forge Press.

Conrad, P., & Potter, D. (2004). Human growth hormone and the temptations of biomedical enhancement. *Sociology of Health and Illness, 26*(2), 184–215.

Constantino, J. N., Grosz, D., Saenger, P., Chandler, D. W., Nandi, R., & Earls, F. J. (1993). Testosterone and aggression in children.

Journal of the American Academy of Child and Adolescent Psychiatry, 32(6), 1217–1223.

Cook, G. (2004, November 23). Children's advances stem cell research: News from Boston's medical and scientific community. *The Boston Globe,* E2.

Cook, J. A. (1997, May 4–7). Minority women in U.S. need better access to potent HIV drug regimens. National Conference on Women and HIV. Pasadena, CA: HIV/AIDS Information Center, *Journal of the American Medical Association.*

Cook-Cottone, C. (2004). Childhood post-traumatic stress disorder: Diagnosis, treatment, and school reintegration. *School Psychology Review, 33*(1), 127–140.

Cooksey, E. C., & Craig, P. H. (1998). Parenting from a distance: The effects of paternal characteristics on contact between nonresidential fathers and their children. *Demography, 35,* 187–200.

Cooksey, E. C., & Fondell, M. F. (1996). Spending time with his kids: Effects of family structure on fathers and children's lives. *Journal of Marriage and the Family, 58,* 693.

Cooley, C. H. (1902). *Human nature and the social order.* New York: Scribner's.

Cooley, C. H. (1909). *Social organization.* New York: Scribner's.

Coontz, S. (1992). *The way we never were: American families and the nostalgia trap.* New York: Basic Books.

Coontz, S. (1997). *The way we really are: Coming to terms with America's changing families.* New York: Basic Books.

Coontz, S. (2000). Marriage: Then and now. *National Forum: Phi Kappa Phi Journal, 80,* 10–15.

Coontz, S. (2004). The world historical transformation of marriage. *Journal of Marriage and Family, 66,* 974–979.

Cooper, M. H. (2004, September 24). Social Security reform: How should America's retirement system be saved? *CQ Researcher, 14*(33), 781–804.

Cooper, R. P., & Aslin, R. N. (1990). Preference for infant-directed speech in the first month after birth. *Child Development, 61,* 1584–1595.

Coopersmith, S. (1967). *Antecedents of self-esteem.* San Francisco: Freeman.

Copeland, L. B., Krall, E. A, Brown, L. J., Garcia, R. I., & Streckfus, C. F. (2004, Winter). Predictors of tooth loss in two U.S. adult populations. *Journal of Public Health Dentistry, 64*(1), 31–37.

Corby, B. (2000). *Child abuse: Towards a knowledge base* (2nd ed.). Philadelphia: Open University Press.

Cord blood banking industry flourishes amid controversy. (2004). *Blood Weekly,* 58–60.

Core, J. (2003). Nutrition's role in feeding children's brains. *Agricultural Research. 51*(12), 5–7.

Corey, L., Wald, A., Patel, R., Sacks, S., Tyring, S., & Warren, T., et al. (2004, January 1). Once-daily valacyclovir to reduce

the risk of transmission of genital herpes. *New England Journal of Medicine, 350,* 11–21.

Corr, C. A. (2001). Stage theory of dying. In G. Howarth & O. Leaman (Eds.), *Encyclopedia of death and dying* (pp. 433–434). London: Routledge.

Cosmetic procedures increased by 44% in 2004. (2005, March 14). *Managed Care Weekly Digest,* 50. Retrieved April 21, 2005, from http://search.epnet.com

Costa, P. T., Jr., & McCrae, R. R. (1980). Still stable after all these years: Personality as a key to some issues in adulthood and old age. In P. B. Baltes & O. G. Brim, Jr. (Eds.), *Life-span development and behavior* (Vol. 3, pp. 65–102). New York: Academic Press.

Costa, P. T., Jr., McCrae, R. R., & Arenberg, D. (1980). Enduring dispositions in adult males. *Journal of Personality and Social Psychology, 38,* 793–800.

Costa, P. T., Yang, J., & McCrae, R. (1998). Aging and personality traits: Generalizations and clinical implications. In I. H. Nordhus et al. (Eds.), *Clinical geropsychology.* Washington, DC: American Psychological Association.

Costin, C. (2002). An update on binge eating disorder. *Healthy Weight Journal, 16*(2).

Coulter, D. J. (1995). Music and the making of the mind. *Early Childhood Connections: The Journal of Music and Movement-Based Learning.* Cited in *Early Childhood News.* Retrieved February 12, 1999, from http://earlychildhoodnews.com/wiredfor.htm

Coutinho, M. J., & Oswald, D. P. (2000). Disproportionate representation in special education: A synthesis and recommendations. *Journal of Child and Family Studies, 9*(2), 135–156.

Couzin, J. (2002, June 21). Quirks of fetal environment felt decades later. *Science, 296,* 2167–2169.

Couzin, J. (2004, September 28). Gulf War illness linked to neurotoxins. *Science Now, 3–5.*

Cowan, P. A., & Hetherington, M. (Eds.). (1991). *Family transitions.* Hillsdale, NJ: Erlbaum.

Cowgill, D. O. (1974). Aging and modernization: A revision of the theory. In J. F. Gubrium (Ed.), *Late life.* Springfield, IL: Charles C Thomas.

Cowgill, D. O. (1986). *Aging around the world.* Belmont, CA: Wadsworth.

Cox, C., & Gelfand, D. E. (1987). Familial assistance, exchange and satisfaction among Hispanic, Portuguese, and Vietnamese ethnic elderly. *Journal of Cross-Cultural Gerontology, 2,* 241–255.

Cox, C., & Monk, A. (1993). Hispanic culture and family care of Alzheimer's patients. *Health and Social Work, 18,* 92–100.

Cox, C., & Monk, A. (1996). Strain among caregivers: Comparing the experiences of African American and Hispanic caregivers of Alzheimer's relatives. *International*

Journal of Aging and Human Development, 43(2), 93–105.

Coyle, J. T. (2000). Psychotropic drug use in very young children. *Journal of the American Medical Association, 283*(8), 1059.

Crain, W. C. (1985). *Theories of development.* New York, NY: Prentice Hall.

Crandell, T. L. (1979). The effects of educational cognitive style and media format on reading procedural instruction in picture-text amalgams. *Dissertation Abstracts.* Ann Arbor, MI: University Microfilms International.

Crandell, T. L. (1982, June). Integration of illustrations and text in reading. In B. A. Hutson (Ed.), *Advances in reading language research, Vol. 1.* Greenwich, CT: Jai Press.

Craniosacral therapy for children. (2004). Annex Clinic. Retrieved February 2, 2004, from http://www.annexclinic.com/cst_children.html

CranioSacral Therapy/SomaoEmotional Release. (2004). International Alliance of Healthcare Educators. Retrieved February 2, 2005 from http://www.iahe.com/html/therapies/cst.jps

Crano, W. D. (1998). The leniency contract and persistence of majority and minority influence. *Journal of Personality and Social Psychology, 74,* 1437–1450.

Cratty, B. J. (1970). *Perceptual and motor development in infants and children.* New York: Macmillan.

Cravens H. (1992). A scientific project locked in time: The Terman genetic studies of genius, 1920s–1950s. *American Psychologist, 47,* 183–189.

Crawford, J. (1997). *Best evidence: Research foundations of the Bilingual Education Act.* Washington, DC: Clearinghouse for Bilingual Educators.

Crawford, J. (2004). *No Child Left Behind: Misguided approach to school accountability for English language learners.* Retrieved from http://www.nabe.org/documents/plicy_legislation/NABE_on_NCLB.pdf

Crespo, C. J., Smith, E., Troiano, R. P., Bartlett, S. J., Macera, C. A., & Anderson, R. E. (2001, March). Television watching, energy intake, and obesity in U.S. children. *Archives of Pediatrics and Adolescent Medicine, 155,* 360–365.

Crews, F. C. (1998). *Unauthorized Freud: Doubters confront a legend.* New York: Viking.

Crick, N. R., & Dodge, K. A. (1994). A review and reformulation of social information-processing mechanisms in children's social adjustment. *Psychological Bulletin, 115,* 74–101.

Crick, N. R., & Grotpeter, J. K. (1995). Relational aggression, gender, and social-psychological adjustment. *Child Development, 66,* 710–722.

Critelli, J. W., & Suire, D. M. (1998). Obstacles to condom use: The combination of other forms of birth control and short-term monogamy. *Journal of American College Health, 46,* 215–219.

Crnic, K., & Low, C. (2002). *Everyday stresses and parenting.* Mahwah, NJ: Lawrence Erlbaum Associates

Crockenberg, S., & Litman, C. (1990). Autonomy as competence in 2-year-olds: Maternal correlates of child defiance, compliance, and self-assertion. *Developmental Psychology, 26,* 961–971.

Cronin, A., & Mandich, M. (2005). *Human development and performance: Throughout the lifespan.* Clifton Park, NY: Thomson Delmar Learning.

Crook, C. K., & Lipsitt, L. P. (1976). Neonatal nutritive sucking: Effects of taste stimulation upon sucking rhythm and heart rate. *Child Development, 47,* 518–522.

Cross, S., & Markus, H. (1991). Possible selves across the life span. *Human Development, 34,* 230–255.

Crouter, A. C., & Manke, B. (1994). The changing American workplace: Implications for individuals and families. *Family Relations, 43,* 117–124.

Crume, T. L., DiGuiseppi, C., Byers, T., Sirotnak, A. P., & Garrett, C. J. (2002, August). Underascertainment of child maltreatment facilities by death certificates, 1990–1998. *Pediatrics, 110,* 18.

Crump, W. J. (2001, July). The patient with no prenatal care: Managing an infant whose mother used cocaine. *Family Practice Recertification, 23*(9), 48–50, 53–54.

Csikszentmihalyi, M. (1993). *The evolving self.* New York: HarperCollins.

Csikszentmihalyi, M. (1997). *Creativity: Flow and the psychology of discovery and invention.* New York: HarperPerennial.

Culbertson, J. L., & Willis, D. J. (Eds.). (1993). *Testing young children: A reference guide for developmental, psychoeducational, and psychosocial assessments.* Austin, TX: Pro-Ed.

Cummings, E. M., & Davies, P. T. (1994). *Children and marital conflict: The impact of family dispute and resolution.* New York: Guilford Press.

Cunningham, M. (2001). The influence of parental attitudes and behaviors on children's attitudes toward gender and household labor in early adulthood. *Journal of Marriage and the Family, 63,* 111–112.

Dailard, C. (2002, February). *Abstinence promotion and teen family planning: The misguided drive for equal funding. The Guttmacher Report, 5*(1), 2–3. Retrieved November 30, 2004, from http://www.guttmacher.org/pubs/tgr/05/1/gr050101.pdf

Dailard, C. (2004, October). Courts strike 'partial-birth' abortion ban; decisions presage future debates. *The Guttmacher Report, 7*(4), 1–4. Retrieved November 30, 2004, from http://www.agi-usa.org/

Dailard, C., & Nash, E. (2000, December). State responses to substance abuse among pregnant women. *The Guttmacher Report, 3*(6), 3–6. Retrieved October 19, 2004, from http://www.agi-usa.org

Dainton, M. (1993). The myths and misconceptions of the stepmother identity. *Family Relations, 42,* 93–98.

Daley, S. E., Hammen, C., Davila, J., & Burge, D. (1998). Axis II symptomatology, depression, and life stress during the transition from adolescence to adulthood. *Journal of Consulting and Clinical Psychology, 66,* 595–603.

Damon, W., & Hart, D. (1982). The development of self-understanding from infancy through adolescence. *Child Development, 53,* 841–864.

Daniel, M. (1997). Intelligence testing: Status and trends. *Journal of the American Psychological Association, 52,* 1038–1045.

Daniels, D. (1986). Differential experiences of siblings in the same family as predictors of adolescent sibling personality differences. *Journal of Personality and Social Psychology, 51,* 339–346.

Daniels, D., & Plomin, R. (1985). Origins of individual differences in infant shyness. *Developmental Psychology, 21,* 118–121.

Danner, D. D., Snowdon, D. A., & Friesen, W. V. (2001, May). Positive emotions in early life and longevity: Findings from the nun study. *Journal of Personality and Social Psychology, 80*(5), 804–813.

Darnovsky, M. (2004, January). High-tech sex selection: A new chapter in the debate. *Gene Watch, 17*(1), Center for Genetics and Society. Retrieved February 14, 2005, from http://www.genetics-and-society.org/

Darnovsky, M. (2004, November 2). Center for Genetics and Society calls for tough public oversight of California Stem Cell Institute. *Genetic Crossroads.* (Available from Center for Genetics and Society, Oakland, CA).

Darroch, J., Singh, S., & Frost, J. (2001). Differences in teenage pregnancy rates among five developed countries: The roles of sexual activity and contraceptive use. *Family Planning Perspectives, 34*(1), 56.

Darwin, C. (1872). *The expression of the emotions in man and animals.* New York: D. Appleton.

Dautzenberg, M., Diederiks, J., Philipsen, H., & Stevens, F. (1999). Women of a middle generation and parent care. *Journal of Aging and Human Development, 47*(4), 241–262.

Davey, A., & Szinovacz, M. E. (2004). Dimensions of marital quality and retirement. *Journal of Family Issues, 25*(4), 431–464.

Davidson, J. L. (2001, July 17). *Embryonic stem cell research.* Hearing on Embryonic Stem Cell Research. FDCH Congressional Testimony. Retrieved September 12, 2001, from EBSCOhost database: http://search.epnet.com

Davies, L. (2004, Spring). *Drinking age anniversary is cause to celebrate what's right and fix what's wrong.* MADDonline. Retrieved April 13, 2005, from http://www.madd.org/news/0,1056,8916,00.html

Davies, P. T., & Windle, M. (2000). Middle adolescents' dating pathways and psychosocial adjustment. *Merrill-Palmer Quarterly, 46*(1), 90–100.

Davis, D. M. C. (1990). Portrayals of women in prime-time network television: Some demographic characteristics. *Sex Roles, 23,* 325–332.

Davis, D. S. (2004, July-August). Genetic research and communal narratives. *Hastings Center Report, 34*(4), 40–49.

Davis, K. (1949). *Human society.* New York: Macmillan.

Davison, K. K., & Birch, L. L. (2001). Weight status, parent reaction, and self-concept in five-year-old girls. *Pediatrics, 107,* 46–53.

Dawe, H. C. (1934). The influence of size of kindergarten groups upon performance. *Child Development, 5,* 295–303.

Dawson, G., Ashman, S. B., & Carver, L. J. (2000, Autumn). The role of early experience in shaping behavioral and brain development and its implications for social policy. *Development and Psychopathology, 12*(4), 695–712.

Dawson, G., Frey, K., Panagiotides, H., Yamada, E., Hessl, D., & Osterling, J. (1999, Sept.–Oct). Infants of depressed mothers exhibit atypical frontal electrical brain activity during interactions with mother and with a familiar, nondepressed adult. *Child Development, 70,* 1058–1066.

De Bellis, M. D., Kesshavan, M. S., Beers, S. R., Hall, J., Frustaci, K., Masalehdan, A., Noll, J., & Boring, A. M. (2001). Sex differences in brain maturation during childhood and adolescence. *Cerebral Cortex, 11*(6), 552–557.

de Graaf, C., Polet, P., & van Staveren, W. A. (1994). Sensory perception and pleasantness of food flavors in elderly subjects. *Journal of Gerontology: Psychological Sciences, 49,* P93–P99.

DeAngelis, T. (1997a, June). Psychologists are providing a controversial treatment for reactive attachment disorder. *APA Monitor.* Available: www.apa.org/monitor/jun97/disorder.html.

DeAngelis, T. (1997b, September). There's new hope for women with postpartum blues. *APA Monitor,* American Psychological Association. Retrieved July 31, 1998, from http://www.apa.org/monitor/sep97/hope.html

DeAngelis, T. (2001). Welfare reform and women, five years later. *Monitor on Psychology, 32*(9), 70–81.

DeAngelis, T. (2002a). A genetic link to anorexia. *Monitor on Psychology, 33*(3), 34–36.

DeAngelis, T. (2002b). New data on lesbians, gay, and bisexual mental health. *Monitor on Psychology, 33*(2), 46–47.

DeBard, R. (2004). Millennial characteristics coming to college. In M. D. Coomes & R. DeBard (Eds.), *Serving the millennial generation.* No. 106. New Directions in Student Services. San Francisco: Jossey-Bass.

DeCasper, A. J., Lecanuet, J. P., Busnel, M. C., Granier-Deferre, C., & Maugeais, R. (1994). Fetal reactions to recurrent maternal speech. *Infant Behavior and Development, 17,* 159–164.

Decker, F. H. (2005). *Nursing homes, 1977–1999: What has changed, what has not?* Hyattsville, MD: National Center for Health Statistics.

Deen, D. (2004, June 15). Metabolic syndrome: Time for action. *American Academy of Family Physicians, 69*(12), 2875–2882.

DeFossé, L., Hodge, S., Makris, N., Kennedy, D., Caviness, V., McGrath, L., Steele, S., Ziegler, D., Herbert, M., Frazier, J., Tager-Flusberg, H., & Harris, G. (2004). Language-association cortex asymmetry in autism and specific language impairment. *Annals of Neurology, 56*(6), 757–766. Retrieved February 21, 2005, from http://www.bu.edu/anatneuro/dcn/researchers_and_students/publications.html

DeFrain, J., Millspaugh, E., & Xiaolin, X. (1996). The psychosocial effects of miscarriage: Implications for health professionals. *Families, Systems, and Health, 14,* 331–347.

DeFries, J. C. (1999). *Colorado twin study and reading disability.* Institute for Behavioral Genetics, Boulder, Colorado. Retrieved October 6, 2001 from http://ibg-www.colorado.edu/learning.html

DeHaan, M., Belsky, J., Reid, V., Volein, A., & Johnson, M. (2004, October). Maternal personality and infants' neural and visual responsivity to facial expressions of emotion. *Journal of Child Psychology and Psychiatry and Allied Disciplines, 45*(7), 1209–1219.

DeLaguna, G. (1929). Perception and language. *Human Biology, 1,* 555–558.

Delaney, C. H. (1995). Rites of passage in adolescence. *Adolescence, 30*(120), 891–898.

deLemos, M. M. (1969). The development of conservation in Aboriginal children. *International Journal of Psychology, 4,* 255–269.

Delgadillo, L., Sorensen, S., & Coster, D. C. (2004). An exploratory study of preparation for future care among older Latinos in Utah. *Journal of Family and Economic Issues, 25*(1), 51–78.

DeMaria, A. (2001, February 14). *Georgetown researchers to present evidence of biological cause of dyslexia.* Georgetown University Medical Center. Retrieved December 12, 2001, from http://www.eurekalert.org/pub_releases/2001-02/ GUMC-Grtp-1402101.php

Demetriou, A. (Ed.). (1988). *The Neo-Piagetian theories of cognitive development: Toward an integration.* Amsterdam: North-Holland.

Demetriou, A., Efklides, A., & Platsidou, M. (1993). The architecture and dynamics of developing mind: Experiential structuralism as a frame for unifying cognitive developmental theories. *Monographs of the Society*

for Research in Child Development, 58 (5–6, Serial No. 234).

Demo, D. (1992). Parent-child relations: Assessing recent changes. *Journal of Marriage and the Family, 54,* 104–117.

Demo, D. (2000). *The handbook of family diversity.* Oxford: Oxford University Press.

Demo, D., & Cox, M. (2000). Families with young children: A review of research in the 1990s. *Journal of Marriage and the Family, 62,* 876–895.

DeNavas-Walt, C., Proctor, B. D., & Mills, R. J. (2004, August). Income, poverty, and health insurance coverage in the United States: 2003. *Current Population Reports, P60-226.* Retrieved April 8, 2005, from http://www.census.gov/prod/2004pubs/p60-226.pdf

Denenberg, R. (1997). HIV risks in women who have sex with women. *The Body: An AIDS and HIV Information Resource, 11.* Retrieved September 10, 1998, from http://thebody.com/ gmhc/issues/julaug97/wsw.html

Denham, S., Mason, T., Caverly, S., Schmidt, M., Hackney, R., Caswell, C., & DeMulder, E. (2001, July). Preschoolers at play: Co-socializers of emotional and social competence. *International Journal of Behavioral Development, 25*(4), 290–301.

Denmark, F. L. (2004, Spring). Psychologists working with depression across the life cycle. *International Psychology Reporter, 8,* 14.

Denner, J., & Dunbar, N. (2004). Negotiating femininity: Power and strategies of Mexican American girls. *Sex Roles, 50*(5–6), 301–314.

Denney, N. (1985). A review of lifespan research with the twenty questions task (TQT). *International Journal of Aging and Human Development, 21,* 161–173.

Dennis, W., & Dennis, M. G. (1940). The effect of cradling practices upon the onset of walking in Hopi children. *Journal of Genetic Psychology, 56,* 77–86.

DeNoon, D. (2005, January 19). *Cancer now top killer of Americans under 85: 2005 prediction: 1500 cancer deaths every day.* WebMD. Retrieved April 3, 2005, from http://my.webmd.com/content/article/99/105264.htm

DeRegnier, R. A., Nelson, C. A., Thomas, K. M., Wewerka, S., & Georgieff, M. K. (2000, December). Neurophysiologic evaluation of auditory recognition memory in healthy newborn infants and infants of diabetic mothers. *Journal of Pediatrics, 137,* 777–784.

Despete, A. (2001). Metacognition and mathematical problem solving in grade 3. *Journal of Learning Disabilities, 34*(5), 435–449.

Desrosiers, J., Herbert, R. Bravo, G., & Dutil, E. (August 1996). Hand sensibility of healthy older people. *Journal of the American Geriatric Society, 44*(8), 974–978.

Determinants of health in children. (1996). National Crime Prevention Council of

Canada. Retrieved February 7, 1999, from http://www.crime-prevention.org/ncpc

DeVito, J. A. (1970). *The psychology of speech and language.* New York: Random House.

De Vries, B., & Walker, L. J. (1981). Moral reasoning and attitudes toward capital mental sequelae of maltreatment in infancy. In R. Rizley & D. Cicchetti (Eds.), *Developmental perspectives on child maltreatment.* San Francisco: Jossey-Bass.

DeWeerdt, S. E. (2001). *What's a genome?* Retrieved September 12, 2001, from http://www.celera.com/ genomics/news/whats_a_genome/Chp1_1_1.cfm

DeWitt, P. M. (1993). The birth business. *American Demographics, 15,* 44–49.

DHEA Center. (1997). DHEA Center. Retrieved November 16, 1997, from http://www.dheacenter. com/dheaquo.htm

DHEA prohormone complex. (1997). Be Healthy. Retrieved September 10, 1998, from http://Be-Healthy.simplenet.com/pendo.htm

Dickinson, B. (1997, June). Are you a marked man? *Esquire,* 100.

Dick-Read, G. (1944/1994). *Childbirth without fear.* New York: Harper.

Dietary Guidelines Advisory Committee. (2005, January). *Dietary guidelines for Americans, 2005.* U.S. Department of Health and Human Services and U.S. Department of Agriculture. Washington, DC: U.S. Government Printing Office. Retrieved January 5, 2005, from http://www.health.gov/dietaryguidelines/

Dignan, J., & Sanchez, R. (2004, February 13). San Francisco opens marriage to gay couples. *Washington Post,* A01. Retrieved May 4, 2004, from http://www.washingtonpost.com

Dill, P. L., & Henley, T. B. (1998). Stressors of college: A comparison of traditional and nontraditional students. *Journal of Psychology, 132,* 25–32.

Diller, L. H. (2002). Lessons from three-year-olds. *Journal of Developmental and Behavioral Pediatrics, 23,* S10–S12. Retrieved February 21, 2005, from http://www.jrnldbp.com

DiMarco, M. A., Menke, E. M., & McNamara, T. (May–June 2001). Evaluating a support group for perinatal loss. *American Journal of Maternal/Child Nursing, 26(3),* 135–140.

Dingfelder, S. F. (2003, December). Tibetan Buddhism and research psychology: A match made in Nirvana? *Monitor on Psychology, 34,* 46–48.

Dittmann, M. (2004, November). A new face to retirement: Retirees are shifting interests, reinventing careers, and changing the very definition of "retirement." *Monitor on Psychology, 35(10),* 78–79.

Dix, T. (1991). The affective organization of parenting: Adaptive and maladaptive processes. *Psychological Bulletin, 110,* 3–25.

Dix, T., Ruble, D. N., & Zambarano, R. J. (1989). Mothers' implicit theories of discipline: Child effects, parent effects, and the attribution process. *Child Development, 60,* 1373–1391.

Dobzhansky, T. (1962). *Mankind evolving.* New Haven: Yale University Press.

Dodge, K. A., Bates, J. E., & Pettit, G. S. (1990). Mechanisms in the cycle of violence. *Science, 250,* 1678–1683.

Dolin, E., & Evans, P. (2005, February). Alzheimer's disease: Management in the new millennium. *Family Practice Recertification, 27(2),* 25–45.

Donate-Bartfield, E., & Passman, R. H. (1985). Attentiveness of mothers and fathers to their baby's cries. *Infant Behavior and Development, 8,* 385–393.

Donation or coercion? (2001). *Case 4: Genie, The wild child: Research or exploitation?* Kennedy Institute of Ethics. Georgetown University. Retrieved October 15, 2001, http://bioethics.georgetown.edu/ hsbioethics/unit3_4.htm

Donnelly, D., & Finkelhor, D. (1992). Does equality in custody arrangement improve the parent-child relationship? *Journal of Marriage and the Family, 54,* 837–845.

Donnez, J., Dolmans, M. M., Demylle, D., Jadoul, P., Pirard, C., Squifflet, J., Martinez-Madrid, B., & Van Langendonckt, A. (2004). Live birth after orthotopic transplantation of cryopreserved ovarian tissue. *Lancet, 364(9443),* 1405–1410. Retrieved April 23, 2005, from http://www.saintluc.be/press/commu/tamara_lancet_complet.pdf

Donovan, J. (2002–2003). Changing demographics and generational shifts: Understanding and working with the families of today's college students. *Student Affairs in Higher Education, 12.* Retrieved October 17, 2004, from http://www.sahe.colostate.edu/journal_archive.asp

Donovan, L. (2004, December 21). Smallest baby to live: 8.6 oz. *Chicago Sun-Times.* Retrieved January 16, 2005, from http://www.suntimes.com/output/health/cst-nws-baby21.html

Doolittle, F., & Lynn, S. (1998). *Working with low-income cases: Lessons for the child support enforcement system from parents' fair share.* Manpower Demonstration Research Corporation. Parents' Fair Share Demonstration.

Doress-Worters, P. B., & Siegal, D. L. (1994). *The new ourselves, growing older: Women aging with knowledge and power.* Boston Women's Health Book Collective. New York: Simon & Schuster.

Dorn, L. D., Hitt, S. F., & Rotenstein, D. (1999). Biopsychological and cognitive differences in children with premature vs. on-time adrenarche. *Archives of Pediatrics and Adolescent Medicine, 153(2),* 137–146.

Dorn, L. D., Susman, E., & Ponirakis, A. (2003). Pubertal timing and adolescent adjustment and behavior: Conclusions vary by rater. *Journal of Youth and Adolescence, 32(3),* 157–167.

Douglas, E. (2001). *The ABCs of early child care research: Keeping Congress informed.* APA [Online]. Public Policy Office. Retrieved October 27, 2001, from http://www.apa.org/ppo/issues/skidcaresh.html

Douglas, J. (1990–1991). Patterns of change following parent death in midlife adults. *Omega: Journal of Death and Dying, 22,* 123–138.

Douglass, J. M., Douglass, A. B., & Silk, H. J. (2004, December 1). A practical guide to infant oral health. *American Family Physician, 70(11),* 2113–2120.

Dowd, J. M., & Tronick, E. Z. (1986). Temporal coordination of arm movements in early infancy: Do infants move in synchrony with adult speech? *Child Development, 57,* 762–776.

Dowda, M., Pate, R. R., Gelton, G. M., Saunders, R., Ward, D. S., Dishman, R. K., & Trost, S. G. (2004, December). Physical activities and sedentary pursuits in African American and Caucasian girls. *Research Quarterly for Exercise and Sport, 75(4),* 352–360.

Downey, D. B. (2001, June/July). Number of siblings and intellectual development: The resource dilution explanation. *American Psychologist, 56(6/7),* 497–504.

Drewianka, S. D. (2004, September). How will reforms of marital institutions influence marital commitment? A theoretical analysis. *Review of Economics of the Household, 2(3),* 303–323.

Drexler, K.E. (1986). *Engines of creation: The coming era of nanotechnology.* Retrieved May 10, 2005, from http://www.foresight.org/EOC/index.html#TOC

DSM-IV-TR (2000). Pervasive developmental disorders. In *DSM-IV-TR* (4th ed., Text Revision, pp. 69–75). Washington, DC: American Psychiatric Association.

Duenwald, M. (2003, January). Puzzle of the century. *Smithsonian, 3.* Retrieved April 30, 2005, from http://www.smithsonian-mag.com/smithsonian/issues03/jan03/centenarians.html

Duhaime, A. C., Christian, C. W., Rorke, L. B., & Zimmerman, R. A. (1998). Nonaccidental head injury in infants—The "shaken-baby syndrome." *New England Journal of Medicine, 338,* 1822–1829.

Duke, L. (1999, February 16). Ignorance feeds deadly South African AIDS epidemic: Spurred by myth and social mores, infection reaches crisis proportions. *Washington Post,* A01.

Dunn, J. (1983). Sibling relationships in early childhood. *Child Development, 54,* 787–811.

Dunn, J. (1986). Growing up in a family world: Issues in the study of social development of young children. In M. Richards and P. Light (Eds.), *Children of social worlds:*

Development in a social context. Cambridge, MA: Harvard University Press.

Dunn, J. (1993). *Young children's close relationships: Beyond attachment.* Newbury Park, CA: Sage.

Dunn, J., & Plomin, R. (1990). *Separate lives: Why siblings are so different.* New York: Basic Books.

Dunn, J., Kendrick, C., & MacNamee, R. (1982). The reaction of first-born children to the birth of a sibling: Mothers' reports. In S. Chess & A. Thomas (Eds.), *Annual progress in child psychiatry and child development* (pp. 143–165). New York: Brunner/Mazel.

Dunn, J., Slomkowski, C., & Beardsall, L. (1994). Sibling relationships from the preschool period through middle childhood and early adolescence. *Developmental Psychology, 30,* 315–324.

Dunn, R., Beaudry, J. S., & Klavas, A. (1989). Survey of research on learning styles. *Educational Leadership, 46,* 50–58.

Dunning, D., & Cohen, G. L. (1992). Egocentric definitions of traits and abilities in social judgment. *Journal of Personality and Social Psychology, 63,* 341–355.

Dunson, D. B., Colombo, B., & Baird, D. D. (2002). Changes with age in the level and duration of fertility in the menstrual cycle. *Human Reproduction, 17*(5), 1399–1403.

Durston, S., M., Hilleke, E., Pol, H., Casey, B. J., Giedd, J. N., Buitelaar, J. K., & Van Engeland, H. (2001). Anatomical MRI of the developing human brain: What have we learned? *Journal of the American Academy of Child and Adolescent Psychiatry, 40*(9), 1012–1020.

Eagly, A. H. (1995). The science and politics of comparing women and men. *American Psychologist, 50,* 145–158.

Eamon, M. K. (2001). The effects of poverty on children's social-emotional development: An ecological systems analysis. *Social Work, 46,* 256–267.

Earles, J. L., & Coon, V. E. (1994). Adult age differences in long-term memory for performed activities. *Journal of Gerontology: Psychological Sciences, 49,* P32–P34.

Early child care and self-control compliance and problem behavior at twenty-four and thirty-six months. (1998). The NICHD Early Child Care Research Network, Bethesda, MD: National Institutes of Health.

Eaton, W., Buka, S., Addington, A. M., Bass, A., et al. (2004, June). *Risk factors for major mental disorders: A review of the epidemiologic literature.* Departments of Society, Human Development, and Health and Epidemiology. Cambridge, MA: Harvard School of Public Health. Retrieved April 8, 2005, from http://apps1.jhsph.edu/weaton/MDRF/main.pdf

Ebel, C. (2005, April 5). *Nation failing to curb the spread of STDs among young people.* American Social Health Association.

Retrieved April 10, 2005, from http://www.ashast.org

Eccles, J. S. (1999). The development of children ages 6–14. *The Future of Children, 9,* 30–44.

Eckerman, C. O., & Didow, S. M. (1988). Lessons drawn from observing young peers together. *Acta Paediatrica Scandinavica, 77,* 55–70.

Eckerman, C. O., & Stein, M. R. (1990). How imitation begets imitation and toddlers' generation of games. *Developmental Psychology, 26,* 370–378.

Eder, D. (1995). *School talk: Gender and adolescent culture.* New Brunswick, NJ: Rutgers University Press.

Eder, D., & Hallinan, M. T. (1978). Sex differences in children's friendships. *American Sociological Review, 43,* 237–250.

Edhborg, M., Lundh, W., Seimyr, L., & Widstroem, A. (2001, February). The long-term impact of postnatal depressed mood on mother-child interaction: A preliminary study. *Journal of Reproductive and Perinatal Health Care,* Stockholm, Sweden, *19*(1), 61–71.

Edmonds, M. H. (1976). New directions in theories of language acquisition. *Harvard Educational Review, 46,* 175–198.

Edwards, C. A. (1994). Leadership in groups of school-age girls. *Developmental Psychology, 30,* 920–927.

Edwards, C. P., & Whiting, B. B. (1988). *Children of different worlds.* Cambridge, MA: Harvard University Press.

Egeland, B. (1993). A history of abuse is a major risk factor for abusing the next generation. In R. J. Gelles & D. R. Loeske (Eds.), *Current controversies on family violence.* Newbury Park: Sage.

Egeland, B., Kalkoske, M., Gottesman, N., & Erickson, M. F. (1990). Preschool behavior problems: Stability and factors accounting for change. *Journal of Child Psychology and Allied Disciplines, 31,* 891–909.

Eibl-Eibesfeldt, I. (1989). *Human ethology.* New York: Aldine de Gruyter.

Eimas, P. D. (1985, January). The perception of speech in early infancy. *Scientific American, 252,* 46–52.

Einstein, A. (1949). Autobiography. In P. Schilpp (Ed.), *Albert Einstein: Philosopher-scientist.* Evanston, IL: Library of Living Philosophers.

Eisenberg, J. S. (2003, September 15). The diabetes epidemic: With soaring rates of diabetes and its complications, your role must go beyond your patients' eyes. *Review of Optometry, 40*(9), 78–85.

Eisenberg, N. (1992). *The caring child.* Cambridge, MA: Harvard University Press.

Eisenberg, N., Fabes, R. A., Shepard, S. A., Murphy, B. C., Guthrie, I. K., Jones, S., Friedman, J., Poulin, R., & Maszk, P. (1997). Contemporaneous and longitudinal prediction of children's social functioning from regulation and emotionality. *Child Development, 68,* 642–664.

Eisenberg, N., Gershoff, E. T., Fabes, R. A., Shepard, S. A., Cumberland, A. J., Losoya, S. H., Guthrie, I. K., & Murphy, B. C. (2001). Mothers' emotional expressivity and children's behavior problems and social competence medication through children's regulation. *Developmental Psychology, 37,* 475–490.

Eisenberg, N., Shepard, S. A., Fabes, R. A., Murphy, B. C., & Guthrie, I. K. (1998). Shyness and children's emotionality, regulation, and coping: Contemporaneous, longitudinal, and across-context relations. *Child Development, 69,* 767–790.

Eisner, R. (2000, February 12). *Analysis of human DNA shows fewer genes than expected.* Retrieved September 12, 2001, from http://abcnews.go.com/sections/scitech/DailyNews/genome010212.html

Ekman, P. (1972). Universal in cultural differences in facial expressions of emotion. In J. K. Cole (Ed.), *Nebraska symposium on motivation* (Vol. 19). Lincoln: University of Nebraska Press.

Ekman, P. (1980). *The face of man: Expressions of universal emotions in a New Guinea village.* New York: Garland STPM Press.

Ekman, P. (1994). Strong evidence for universals in facial expressions: A reply to Russell's mistaken critique. *Psychological Bulletin, 115,* 268–287.

Ekman, P. (2003). *Emotions revealed: Recognizing faces and feelings to improve communication and emotional life.* New York: Henry Holt.

Ekman, P., & W. V. Friesen. (2003). *Unmasking the face: A guide to recognizing emotions from facial expressions.* Los Altos, CA: Institute for the Study of Human Knowledge.

Elder, G. H., Jr. (1974). *Children of the great depression.* Chicago: University of Chicago Press.

Elder, G. H., Jr. (1985). Perspectives on the life course. In G. H. Elder, Jr. (Ed.), *Life course dynamics: Trajectories and transitions, 1968–1980.* Ithaca, NY: Cornell University Press.

Elder, G. H., Jr., Shanahan, M. J., & Clipp, E. C. (1994). When war comes to men's lives: Life-course patterns in family, work, and health. *Psychology and Aging, 9,* 5–16.

Elias, M. (1989, August 9). Inborn traits outweigh environment. *USA Today,* 1D, 2D.

Elias, M. (1992). Late-life love. *Harvard Health Letter, 18,* 1–3.

Elias, M. (1993). Mind and menopause. *Harvard Health Letter, 19,* 1–3.

Elias, M. (1995, January 30). Social life and religion boost heart survival. *USA Today,* D1.

Elias, M. (1999, August 24). Midlife divorce lifts women, bums out men. *USA Today, 17*(241), 1D.

Elkind, D. (1970, April). Eric Erikson's eight stages of man. *New York Times Magazine,* 24.

Elkind, D. (1974). *A sympathetic understanding of the child from birth to sixteen.* Boston: Allyn & Bacon.

Elkind, D. (1987, May). Superkids and super problems. *Psychology Today, 21,* 60–61.

Elkind, D. (1995). *Ties that stress: The new family in balance.* Cambridge, MA: Harvard University Press.

Elkind, D. (2001). *The hurried child: Growing up too fast too soon* (3rd ed.) Cambridge, MA: Perseus.

Ellis, B. (2004). Timing of pubertal maturation in girls: An integrated life history approach. *Psychological Bulletin, 130*(6), 920–958.

Ellis, B. J., & Garber, J. (2000, March-April). Psychosocial antecedents of variation in girls' pubertal timing: Maternal depression, stepfather presence, and marital and family stress. *Child Development, 71,* 485–202.

Ellis, D. G. (1992). *From language to communication.* Hillsdale, NJ: Erlbaum.

Ellison, C. G., & Levin, J. S. (1998). The religion-health connection: Evidence, theory, and future directions. *Health Education and Behavior, 25,* 700–720.

Ellison, P. T. (2001). *On fertile ground: A natural history of human reproduction.* Cambridge, MA: Harvard University Press.

Emanuel, L. (1998). Facing requests for physician-assisted suicide: Toward a practical and principled clinical skill set. *Journal of the American Medical Association, 280,* 643–647.

Embryo adoption: Program matches embryos with families. (2001, April 12). ABCNEWS.com. Retrieved September 3, 2001, from http://abcnews.go.com/sections/primetime/2020/PRIMETIME_010412_donatedembryos_feature.html#2

Embryonic stem cell research. (2004, July 14). United States Department of Health and Human Services: Press Release. Retrieved November 21, 2004, from http://www.hhs.gov

Emig, C., Moore, A., & Scarupa, H. J. (2001, October). *School readiness: Helping communities get children ready for school and schools ready for children.* Child Trends research brief. Washington, DC: ChildTrends.Org.

Emslie, G. J., Walkup, J. T., Pliszka, S. R., & Ernst, M. (1999). Nontricyclic antidepressants: Current trends in children and adolescents. *Journal of the American Academy of Child and Adolescent Psychiatry, 38*(5), 517–528.

Engen, T. (1991). *Odor sensation and memory.* New York: Praeger.

Engen, T., Lipsitt, L. P., & Kaye, H. (1963). Olfactory responses and adaptation in the human neonate. *Journal of Physiology and Psychology, 56,* 73–77.

Engen, T., Lipsitt, L. P., & Peck, M. B. (1974). Ability of newborn infants to discriminate sapid substances. *Developmental Psychology, 10,* 741–744.

English heritage. (2005). *Stonehenge.* Retrieved May 20, 2005, from http://www.english-heritage.org.uk/server/show/ConProperty.313/chosenImageId/2

Epstein, S. H. (1983, October). Why do women live longer than men? *Science, 83,* 4, 30–31.

Erdley, C. A., & Dweck, C. S. (1993). Children's implicit personality theories as predictors of their social judgments. *Child Development, 64,* 863–878.

Ericsson, K. A. (2000). How experts attain and maintain superior performance: Implications for the enhancement of skilled performance in older individuals. *Journal of Aging and Physical Activity, 8*(4), 366–372.

Ericsson, K. A., & Charness, N. (1994). Expert performance: Its structure and acquisition. *Journal of the American Psychological Association, 49,* 725–747.

Erikson, E. H. (1959). Identity and the life cycle. *Monograph, Psychological Issues* (Vol. 1). New York: International Universities Press.

Erikson, E. H. (1963). *Childhood and society.* New York: W. W. Norton.

Erikson, E. H. (1964). Inner and outer space: Reflections on womanhood. *Daedalus, 93,* 582–606.

Erikson, E. H. (1968a). *Identity: Youth and crisis.* New York: W. W. Norton.

Erikson, E. H. (1968b). Life cycle. In D. L. Sills (Ed.), *International encyclopedia of the social sciences* (Vol. 9). New York: Free Press and Macmillan.

Erikson, E. H. (1977). *Toys and reasons: Stages in the ritualization of experience.* New York: Norton.

Erikson, E. H. (1982). *The life cycle completed: A review.* New York: W. W. Norton.

Erikson, E. H., & Erikson, J. M. (1997). *The life cycle completed* (Ext. Version). New York: W. W. Norton.

Erikson, E. H., Erikson, J. M., & Kivnick, H. Q. (1986). *Vital involvement in old age.* New York: W. W. Norton.

Erikson, K. (1986). On work and alienation. *American Sociological Review, 51,* 1–8.

Ernst, C., & Angst, A. (1983). *Birth order.* New York: Springer-Verlag.

Ervin, S. L. (2000). Fourteen forecasts for an aging society. *The Futurist.* November–December, 24–28.

Escamilla, K., Shannon, S., Carlos, S., & Garcia, J. (2003). Breaking the code: Colorado's defeat of the anti-bilingual Education Initiative (Amendment 31). *Bilingual Research Journal, 27*(3), 357–372.

Espelage, D. L., & Swearer, S. M. (Eds.). (2004). *Bullying in American schools: A social-ecological perspective on prevention and intervention.* Mahwah, NJ: Lawrence Erlbaum Associates.

Espelage, D. L., Bosworth, K., & Simon, T. S. (2001). Short-term stability and change of bullying in middle school students: An examination of demographic, psychosocial, and environmental correlates. *Violence and Victims, 16*(4), 411–426.

Essex, M. J., Klein, M. H., Miech, R., & Smider, N. A. (2001). Timing of initial exposure to maternal major depression and children's mental health symptoms in kindergarten. *British Journal of Psychiatry, 179,* 151–156

Evans, G. W. (2004, February/March) The environment of childhood poverty. *American Psychologist, 59,* 77–92.

Evans, J. R., Fletcher, A. E., & Wormald, R. P. (2005, May). 28,000 cases of age-related macular degeneration causing visual loss in people aged 75 years and above in the United Kingdom may be attributable to smoking. *British Journal of Ophthalmology, 89*(5), 550–553.

Executive summary of the clinical guidelines on the identification, evaluation, and treatment of overweight and obesity in adults. (1998). *Journal of the American Dietetic Association, 98,* 1178–1191.

Eye M.D.s discuss breakthroughs in treating farsightedness and aging eye. (2001, November 13). American Academy of Ophthalmology. Retrieved April 21, 2005, from http://www.aao.org/news/release/111301e.cfm

Eyer, D. E. (1992, November 24). Infant bonding: A bogus notion. *Wall Street Journal,* A14.

Eyetsemitan, F. (1997). Age, respect and modernization in Africa: Toward a psychosociological understanding. *Western Journal of Black Studies, 21*(2), 142–145.

Fabricius, W. V., & Wellman, H. M. (1983). Children's understanding of retrieval cue utilization. *Developmental Psychology, 19,* 15–21.

Fact sheet. (2005). Universal newborn screening. National Center for Hearing Assessment and Management, Utah State University. Retrieved January 23, 2005, from http://www.infanthearing.org/resources/fact.pdf

Fact sheet: Sudden infant death syndrome. (2003). National Institute of Child Health and Human Development. Retrieved December 15, 2004, from http://www.nichd.nih.gov/publications/pubs/sidsfact.htm

Facts about the DASH eating plan. (2003). National Heart, Lung, and Blood Institute (NHLBI). NIH Publication No. 03-4082. U.S. Retrieved March 15, 2005, from http://www.nhlbi.nih.gov/health/public/heart/hbp/dash/new_dash.pdf

Facts in brief. (2004). *Contraceptive use: Who needs contraceptives?* Alan Guttmacher Institute. Retrieved December 22, 2004, from http://www.agi-usa.org/pubs/fb_contr_use.pdf

Fagot, B. I., & Kavanagh, K. (1993). Parenting during the second year: Effects of children's age, sex, and attachment classification. *Child Development, 64,* 258–271.

Fagot, B. I., Leinbach, M. D., & Hagan, R. (1986). Gender labeling and the adoption of sex-typed behavior. *Developmental Psychology, 22,* 440–443.

Fairstein, L. (1993). *Sexual violence: Our war against rape.* New York: William Morrow & Company.

Falbo, T., & Poston, D. L., Jr. (1993). The academic, personality, and physical outcomes of only children in China. *Child Development, 64,* 18–25.

Family pesticide use suspected of causing child cancers. (1993). *Archives of Environmental Contamination Toxicology, 24*(1), 87–92.

Famularo, R., Kinscherff, R., & Fenton, T. (1992). Parental substance abuse and the nature of child maltreatment. *Child Abuse Neglect, 16,* 475–483.

Farooqi, M. (2003, September 30). A scientific compromise: Ectogenesis may satisfy a long debate. *The Battalion,* Texas A&M. Retrieved November 20, 2004, from http://www.thebatt.com/

Farrar, M. J., & Goodman, G. S. (1992). Developmental changes in event memory. *Child Development, 63,* 173–187.

Farrar, M. J., Raney, G. E., & Boyer, M. E. (1992). Knowledge, concepts, and inferences in childhood. *Child Development, 63,* 673–691.

Farver, J. A. M., & Branstetter, W. H. (1994). Preschoolers' prosocial responses to their peers' distress. *Developmental Psychology, 30,* 334–341.

Farver, J. M., Kim, Y. K., & Lee, Y. (1995). Cultural differences in Korean- and Anglo-American preschoolers' social interaction and play behaviors. *Child Development, 66,* 1088–1099.

Favazza, P. C. (1998, December). Preparing for children with disabilities in early childhood. *Early Childhood Education Journal, 25*(4), 255–258.

Favazza, P. C., & Odom, S. L. (1996). Use of acceptance scale to measure attitudes of kindergarten-age children. *Journal of Early Intervention, 20,* 232.

FDA recommends warning labels for nonoxynol 9. (2003). *Nation's Health, 33*(2), 28.

Feather, N. T. (1990). *The psychological impact of unemployment.* New York: Springer-Verlag.

Federal Bureau of Investigation. (2004, October 27). *Crime in the United States: 2003.* Uniform Crime Reports. Washington, DC: U.S. Department of Justice. Retrieved March 31, 2005, from http://www.fbi.gov/ucr/cius_03/pdf/03sec4.pdf

Federal Interagency Forum on Aging-Related Statistics. (2004, November). *Older Americans 2004: Key indicators of well-being.* Washington, DC: U.S. Government Printing Office. Retrieved April 5, 2005, from http://www.agingstats.gov/chartbook2004/OA_2004.pdf

Federal Interagency Forum on Child and Family Statistics. (2003). *America's children: Key national indicators of well-being, 2003.* Washington, DC: U.S. Government Printing Office.

Federal Interagency Forum on Child and Family Statistics. (2004). *America's children in brief: Key national indicators of well-being, 2004.* Washington, DC: U.S. Government Printing Office.

Fehr, B. (1996). *Friendship processes.* Thousand Oaks, CA: Sage.

Feinlieb, J. A., & Michael, R. T. (1998). Reported changes in sexual behavior in response to AIDS in the United States. *Preventive Medicine, 27,* 400–411.

Feist, G. J., Bodner, T. E., Jacobs, J. F., Miles, M., & Tan, V. (1995). Integrating top-down and bottom-up structural models of subjective well-being: A longitudinal investigation. *Journal of Personality and Social Psychology, 68,* 138–150.

Feldhusen, J. F., Proctor, T. B., & Black, K. N. (1986). Guidelines for grade advancement of precocious children. *Roeper Review, 9,* 25–27.

Feldman, C. F. (1992). The new theory of theory of mind. *Human Development, 35,* 107–117.

Feldman, R., Keren, M., Gross-Rozval, O., & Tyano, S. (2004, September). Mother-child touch patterns in infant feeding disorders: Relation to maternal, child, and environmental factors. *Journal of the American Academy of Child and Adolescent Psychiatry, 43*(9), 1089–1097. Retrieved February 3, 2005, from EBSCOhost.

Feng, J. (1994). *Asian-American children: What teachers should know.* Urbana, IL: ERIC Clearinghouse on Elementary and Early Childhood Education. Retrieved November 20, 2001, from http://www.ed.gov/databases/ERIC_Digests/ed369577.html

Fenson, L., Dale, P. S., Reznick, J. S., Bates, E., Thal, D. J., & Pethick, S. J. (1994). Variability in early communicative development. *Society for Research in Child Development Monograph, 59*(5), 1–173.

Ferenac, M., Polancec, D., Huzak, M., Pereira-Smith, O. M., & Rubelj, I. (2005, July). Early-senescing skin fibroblasts do not demonstrate accelerated telomere shortening. *Journals of Gerontology: Series A. Psychological Sciences and Social Sciences, 60*(7), 820–829.

Fernald, A. (1985). Four-month-old infants prefer to listen to motherese. *Infant Behavior and Development, 8,* 181–195.

Fernald, A. (1990). Intonation and communicative intent in mothers' speech to infants: Is the melody the message? *Child Development, 60,* 1497–1510.

Fernald, A., & Morikawa, H. (1993). Common themes and cultural variations in Japanese and American mothers' speech to infants. *Child Development, 64,* 637–656.

Ferris, T. (1991, December 15). A cosmological event. *New York Times Magazine,* 44.

Feshbach, S. (1970). Aggression. In P. H. Mussen (Ed.), *Carmichael's manual of child psychology* (3rd ed., Vol. 2). New York: Wiley.

Fethers, K., Marks, C., Mindel, A., & Estcourt, C. S. (2000). Sexually transmitted infections and risk behaviors in women who have sex with women. *Sexually Transmitted Infections, 76,* 345–349.

Feyereisen, P., & de Lannoy, J. (1991). *Gestures and speech: Psychological investigations.* New York: Cambridge University Press.

Fiatarone, M. A., & Evans, W. J. (1993). The etiology and reversibility of muscle dysfunction in the aged. *Journal of Gerontology, 48* (Special Issue), 77–83.

Field, D. (1991). Continuity and change in personality in old age: Evidence from five longitudinal studies. *Journal of Gerontology: Psychological Sciences, 46,* P271–P274.

Field, D., & Millsap, R. E. (1991). Personality in advanced old age: Continuity or change? *Journal of Gerontology: Psychological Sciences, 46,* P299–P308.

Field, D., Minkler, M., Falk, R. F., & Leino, E. V. (1993). The influence of health on family contacts and family feelings in advanced old age: A longitudinal study. *Journal of Gerontology: Psychological Sciences, 48,* P18–P28.

Field, T. (1998). *Depressed mothers and their newborns.* Miami: University of Miami School of Medicine.

Fields, C. M. (1981, September 9). Minors found able to decide on taking part in research. *Chronicle of Higher Education, 7.*

Fields, J. (2003, June). *Children's living arrangements and characteristics: March 2002.* P20-547. Washington, DC: U.S. Census Bureau. Retrieved November 15, 2004, from http://www.census.gov/prod/2003pubs/p20-547.pdf

Fields, J. (2004, November). *America's families and living arrangements: 2003.* P20-553. Washington, DC: U.S. Census Bureau. Retrieved March 12, 2005, from http://www.census.gov/prod/2004pubs/p20-553.pdf

Fields, J., & Casper, L. M. (2001). *America's families and living arrangements: March 2000.* Current Population Reports, P20-537. U.S. Census Bureau, Washington, D.C. Retrieved September 26, 2001, from http://www.census.gov/population/www/socdemo/hh-fam/p20-537_00.html

Fiene, R. (2002). *Child Care Bulletin 13 indicators of quality child care: Research update* An annotated bibliography of research conducted since 1992 on thirteen key child care quality indicators used in developing child care licensing regulations. http://childcareresearch.org/location/ccrca818

Fiese, B. H., Tomcho, T. J., Douglas, M., Josephs, K., Poltrock, S., & Baker, T. (2002). A review of 50 years of research on naturally occurring family routines and rituals: Cause for celebration? *Journal of Family Psychology, 16*(4), 381–390.

Final request. (2001, April 23). *American Demographics, 4*(22). Retrieved January 11, 2002, from http://www.demographics.com

Fine, S., & Chance, J. (1998). *Fine beauty: Beauty basics and beyond for African-American women.* New York: Riverhead Books.

Finkelhor, D., & Jones, L. M. (2004, January). *Explanations for the decline in child sexual abuse cases.* Juvenile Justice Bulletin. Washington, DC: Office of Juvenile Justice and Delinquency Prevention. Retrieved February 1, 2005, from http://www.ncjrs.org/pdffiles1/ojjdp/199298.pdf

Finn-Stevenson, M., & Zigler, E. (1999). *Schools of the 21st century: Linking child care and education.* New York, NY: Perseus Books.

Fiscella, K. (1995). Does prenatal care improve birth outcomes? A critical review. *Obstetrics and Gynecology, 85*(3), 468–469.

Fischer, G. J. (1996). Deceptive, verbally coercive college males: Attitudinal predictors and lies told. *Archives of Sexual Behavior, 25*, 5.

Fischer, J. (2001, December 3). The first clone. *U.S. News & World Report, 131*(23), 50–61.

Fisher, B. S., Cullen, F. T., Turner, M. G. (2000). *The sexual victimization of college women.* Bureau of Justice Statistics. Washington, DC: U.S. Department of Justice. Retrieved January 19, 2002, from http://www.ncjrs.org/pdffiles1/nij/182369.pdf

Fisher, S. E., Marlow, A. J., Lamb, J., Maestrini, E., Williams, S. J., Richardson, A. J., Weeks, D. E., Stein, J. F. & Monaco, A. (1999). A quantitative-trait locus on chromosome 6p influences different aspects of developmental dyslexia. *American Journal of Human Genetics, 64*, 146–156.

Fishman, B. (1983). The economic behavior of step-families. *Family Relations, 32*, 359–366.

Flanagan, C. A., & Eccles, J. S. (1993). Changes in parents' work status and adolescents' adjustment at school. *Child Development, 64*, 246–257.

Flavell, J. H. (1992). Cognitive development: Past, present, and future. *Developmental Psychology, 28*, 998–1005.

Flavell, J. H., Flavell, E. R., & Green, F. L. (1983). Development of the appearance of reality distinction. *Cognitive Psychology, 15*, 95–120.

Flavell, J., Freidrichs, A., & Hoyt, J. (1970). Developmental changes in memorization processes. *Cognitive Psychology, 1*, 324–340.

Flower, H. D. (2004). A new look at the safety of breastfeeding during pregnancy. *The Journal of Attachment Parenting International, Annual New Baby Issue.* Retrieved January 22, 2005, from http://www.attachmentparenting.org/apjbaby04.pdf

Focus on obesity. (1998). *Medical Sciences Bulletin.* Retrieved February 7, 1999, from http://www.pharminfo.com/pubs/msb/obesity.html

Fogel, A., & Thelen, E. (1987). Development of early expressive and communicative action: Reinterpreting the evidence from a dynamic systems perspective. *Developmental Psychology, 23*, 747–761.

Folkman, S., & Lazarus, R. S. (1985). If it changes it must be a process: Study of emotion and coping during three stages of a college examination. *Journal of Personality and Social Psychology, 48*, 150–170.

Folven, R. J., & Bonvillian, J. D. (1991). The transition from nonreferential to referential language in children acquiring American Sign Language. *Developmental Psychology, 27*, 806–816.

Foner, A., & Kertzer, D. (1978). Transitions over the life course: Lessons from age-set societies. *American Journal of Sociology, 83*, 1081–1104.

Food additives and hyperactivity: Is there a link? (October, 2004). *Brown University Child and Adolescent Behavior Letter, 20*(10), 1–3.

Forgione, P. D. (1998). *Pursuing excellence: A study of U.S. twelfth-grade mathematics and science achievement in international context.* National Center for Education Statistics (NCES). Retrieved December 10, 1998, from http://www.nces.edu/gov/timss/

Formichelli, L. (2001, Jan/Feb). The male pill. *Psychology Today, 34*, 16.

Forste, R., & Tanfer, K. (1996). Sexual exclusivity among dating, cohabiting, and married women. *Journal of Marriage and the Family, 58*, 33–48.

Foulkes, P. (1996). Eating disorders, families and therapy. *Australian Journal of Psychotherapy, 15*, 28–42.

Fowler, J. (1981). *Stages of faith: The psychology of human development and the quest for meaning.* San Francisco: HarperCollins.

Fowler, J. W. (2001). Faith development theory and the postmodern challenges. *International Journal for the Psychology of Religion, 11*(3), 159–172.

Fowler, J. W., & Dell, M. L. (2004). Stages of faith and identity: Birth to teens. *Child and Adolescent Psychiatric Clinics of North America, 13*(1), 17–33.

Fox, D. J., & Druschel, C. M. (2003, September). Estimating prevalence of fetal alcohol syndrome (FAS): Effectiveness of a passive birth defects registry system. Birth Defects Research, Part A, *Clinical and Molecular Teratology, 67*(9), 604–608.

Fozard, J. L., Vercruyssen, M., Reynolds, S. L., Hancock, P. A. & Quilter, R. E. (1994) Age differences and changes in reaction time: The Baltimore Longitudinal Study of Aging. *Journal of Gerontology: Psychological Sciences, 49*, P179–P189.

Fraiberg, S. H. (1959). *The magic years.* New York: Scribner's.

Frank, D. A., Augustyn, M., Knight, W. G., Pell, T., & Zuckerman, B. (2001, March 28). Growth, development, and behavior in early childhood following prenatal cocaine exposure. *Journal of the American Medical Association, 285*, 1613–1625.

Frankel, N. R. (2004, September). Editorial: Ask your gynecologist. *Sexuality, Reproduction, and Menopause, 2*(3), 131–132.

Fraser, G. E. (2003). *Diet, life expectancy and chronic disease: Studies of Seventh-Day Adventists and other vegetarians.* New York, NY: Oxford University Press.

Fraser, G. E. (2005, March 31). Studies of Adventist health: Does our health message really make a difference in people's lives? *Adventist Review, 182*(13), 36–41.

Fraser, J. (2001). *New research on children who stutter—Situation should not be ignored.* Stuttering Foundation of America. Retrieved November 11, 2001, from http://www. stutteringhelp.org/pressrm/newresrc.htm

Frazier, P. A. (1990). Victim attributions and post-rape trauma. *Journal of Personality and Social Psychology, 59*, 298–304.

Freedman, D. S., Dietz, W. H., Srinivasan, S. R., & Berenson, G. S. (1999). The relation of overweight to cardiovascular risk factors among children and adolescents: The Bogalusa heart study. *Pediatrics, 103*, 1175–1182.

Freeman, C. E. (2004, November). *Trends in Education Equity of Girls and Women: 2004.* National Center for Education Statistics. NCES 2005-016. Washington, DC: U.S. Department of Health and Human Services.

French, D. C. (1984). Children's knowledge of the social functions of younger, older, and same-age peers. *Child Development, 55*, 1429–1433.

Freud, A. (1936). *The ego and the mechanisms of defense.* New York: International Universities Press.

Freud, A. (1958). Adolescence. *Psychoanalytic Study of the Child, 13*, 255–278.

Freud, S. (1930/1961). *Civilization and its discontents.* London: Hogarth Press.

Freud, S. (1940). An outline of psychoanalysis. In J. Strachey (Ed. and Trans.), *The standard edition of the complete psychological works of Sigmund Freud.* London: Hogarth Press.

Frey, W. H. (2003). Married with children. *American Demographics, 25*(2), 17–19.

Fried, S. B., & Mehrotra, C. M. (1998). *Aging and diversity: An active learning experience.* Washington, DC: Taylor & Francis.

Friedberg, L. (1998). Did unilateral divorce raise divorce rates? Evidence from panel data. *American Economic Review, 88*, 608–627.

Friedland, J. (2000, February 15). An American in Mexico champions midwifery as a worthy profession. *Wall Street Journal, 1.*

Friedland, R. B., & Summer, L. (1999, January). *Demography is not destiny.* National Academy on an Aging Society, a policy institute of The Gerontological Society of America. Retrieved May 5, 2005, from http://www.agingsociety.org/agingsociety/pdf/destiny1.pdf

Friedlmeier, W., & Trommsdorff, G. (1999, November). Emotional regulation in early childhood: A cross-cultural comparison between German and Japanese toddlers. *Journal of Cross-Cultural Psychology, 30*(6), 684–711.

Friedman, M. A., & Brownell, K. D. (1995). Psychological correlates of obesity: Moving to the next research generation. *Psychological Bulletin, 117*, 3–20.

Friedman, R. (1998). *Body love—Learning to like our looks and ourselves.* New York: Harper & Row.

Friedrich, M. J. (2001). Women, exercise, and aging: strong message for the "weaker" sex. *Journal of the American Medical Association, 285*(11), 1429–1431.

Friedrich, M. J. (2004, August 18). Researchers make the case for human embryonic stem cell research. *Journal of the American Medical Association, 292*, 791–793.

Friend, T. (1995, January 19). Emotional ties can help heal heart patients. *USA Today,* D1.

Fries, J. F. (1989). The compression of morbidity: Near or far? *Milbank Quarterly, 67*, 208–231.

Fries, J. F. (1997). Can preventive gerontology be on the way? *American Journal of Public Health, 87*, 1591–1593.

Frisch, R. E. (1978, June 30). Menarche and fatness. *Science, 200*, 1509–1513.

Fromm, E. (1941). *Escape from freedom.* New York: Avon.

Frost, J., & McKelvie, S. (2004, July). Self-esteem and body satisfaction in male and female elementary school, high school, and university students. *Sex Roles, 51*(1/2), 45–54.

Fry, D. P. (1993). The intergenerational transmission of disciplinary practices to conflict. *Human Organization, 52*, 176–185.

Fry, P. S. (2003). Perceived self-efficacy domains as predictors of fear of the unknown and fear of dying among older adults. *Psychology and Aging, 18*(3), 474–486.

Fry, R. (2003, June 12). *Hispanic youth dropping out of U.S. schools: Measuring the challenge.* The Pew Hispanic Center.

Fry, D. P., & Björkqvist, K. (Eds.). (1996). *Cultural variation in conflict resolution: Alternatives to violence.* Mahwah, NJ: Erlbaum.

Fu, H., Carroch, J. E., Henshaw, S. K., & Kolb, E. (1998). Measuring the extent of abortion underreporting in the 1995 National Survey of Family Growth. *Family Planning Perspectives, 30*(3), 128–133, 138.

Fuchs-Beauchamp, K. (1996). Preschoolers inferred self-esteem. *Journal of Genetic Psychology, 157*, 204–210.

Fuligni, A. J., & Eccles, J. S. (1993). Perceived parent-child relationships and early adolescents' orientation toward peers. *Developmental Psychology, 29*, 622–632.

Fuligni, A. J., & Pedersen, S. (2002). Family obligation and the transition to young adulthood. *Developmental Psychology, 38*, 856–868.

Fuligni, A. J., & Stevenson, H. W. (1995). Time use and mathematics achievement among American, Chinese, and Japanese high school students. *Child Development, 66*, 830–842.

Fuller-Thomson, E., & Minkler, M. (2001). American grandparents providing extensive child care to their grandchildren: Prevalence and profile. *Gerontologist, 41*, 201–209.

Fullerton, H. N., & Toossi, M. (2001, November). Labor force projections to 2010: Steady growth and changing composition. *Monthly Labor Review.* Retrieved December 27, 2001, from http://www.bls.gov/opub/mlr/2001/11/art2exc.htm.

Funder, D. C., & Colvin, C. R. (1991). Explorations in behavioral consistency: Properties of persons, situations, and behaviors. *Journal of Personality and Social Psychology, 60*, 773–794.

Furstenberg, F. F. (2000). The sociology of adolescence and youth in the 1990s: A critical commentary. *Journal of Marriage and the Family, 62*, 896–910.

Futterman, A., Gallagher, D., Thompson, L. W., Lovett, S., & Gilewski, M. (1990). Retrospective assessment of marital adjustment and depression during the first 2 years of spousal bereavement. *Psychology and Aging, 5*, 277–283.

Gadbow, N. F. & DuBois, D. A. (1998). *Adult learners with special needs: Strategies and resources for postsecondary education and workplace training.* Malabar, FL: Krieger.

Gafner, G., & Duckett, S. (1992). Treating the sequelae of a curse in elderly Mexican Americans. In T. L. Brink (Ed.), *Hispanic aged mental health* (pp. 145–153). New York: Haworth Press.

Gagnon, J. H. (1977). *Human sexualities.* Upper Saddle River, NJ: Scott Foresman and Company.

Galambos, C. (2005). The uninsured: A forgotten population. *Health and Social Work, 30*(1), 3–6.

Gallagher-Thompson, D., Futterman, A., Farberow, N., Thompson, L. W., & Peterson, J. (1993). The impact of spousal bereavement on older widows and widowers. In M. S. Stroebe, W. Stroebe, & R. O. Hansson (Eds.), *Handbook of bereavement: Theory, research, and intervention* (pp. 227–239). New York: Cambridge University Press.

Gallegly, E. (2001a, February 15). *"Manzullo-Gallegly-Shows" bill would provide relief to veterans suffering from Gulf War Illness.* News Release from U.S. House of Representatives. Retrieved September 26, 2001, from http://www.house.gov/gallegly/021501gulfwar.htm

Gallegly, E. (2001b, July 31). *Gallegly Persian Gulf veterans' legislation approved by House.* News Release from U.S. House of Representatives. Retrieved September 26, 2001, from http://www.house.gov/gallegly/073101gulf.htm

Gallup poll monthly. (1991, January). Princeton, NJ: Gallup Organization.

Ganzini, L., Goy, E. R., Miller, L. L., Harvath, T. A., Jackson, A., & Delorit, M. A. (2003). Nurses' experiences with hospice patients who refuse food and fluids to hasten death. *New England Journal of Medicine, 349*, 359–365.

Gao, G. (2001). Intimacy, passion, and commitment in Chinese and U.S. American romantic relationships. *International Journal of Intercultural Relations, 25*(3), 329–342.

Garbarino, J. (1999). *Lost Boys: Why our sons turn violent and how we can save them.* New York, NY: Free Press.

Garces, E., Thomas, D., & Currie, J. (2000, December). Longer-term effects of Head Start: Working mothers and child well-being. *Joint Center for Policy Research Newsletter,* 1–27. Retrieved February 5, 2005, from http://www.jcpr.org/newsletters/VOL6_NO2/articles.html#story_1

Garcia, A. (1993). Income security and elderly Latinos. In M. Sotomayer & A. Garcia (Eds.), *Elderly Latinos: Issues and solutions for the 21st century* (pp. 17–28). Washington, DC: National Hispanic Council on Aging.

Garcia, E. (1994). *Understanding and meeting the challenge of student cultural diversity.* Boston: Houghton Mifflin.

Garcia, J., Kosberg, J., Mangum, W., Henderson, J., & Henderson, C. (1992, November). *Caregiving for and by Hispanic elders: Perceptions of four generations of women.* Paper presented at the annual meeting of the Gerontological Society of America. Washington, DC.

García-Coll, C. T., & Magnuson, K. (2000). Cultural differences as sources of developmental vulnerabilities and resources. In J. P. Shonkoff and S. J. Meisels (Eds.), *Handbook of early childhood intervention* (2nd ed., pp. 94–114). New York: Cambridge University Press.

Gardner, H. (1983). *Frames of mind: The theory of multiple intelligences.* New York: Basic Books.

Gardner, H. (1991). *The unschooled mind: How children think and how schools should teach.* New York: Basic Books.

Gardner, H. (1993a). Lessons in life from creative geniuses: Freud, Einstein, Picasso, Stravinsky, Eliot, Graham and Gandhi. *Boardroom Reports, 22*, 13.

Gardner, H. (1993b). *Multiple intelligences: The theory in practice.* New York: Basic Books.

Gardner, H. (1997). Multiple intelligences as a partner in school improvement. *Educational Leadership, 55*, 20–21.

Gardner, H. (1999). *Intelligence reframed: Multiple intelligences for the 21st century.* New York: Basic Books.

Gardner, H. (2000a). *Intelligence reframed: Multiple intelligences for the 21st Century.* New York: Basic Books.

Gardner, H. (2000b). *The disciplined mind.* New York: Penguin Books.

Gardner, H. (2002, Winter). On the three faces of intelligence. *Daedalus, 131*(1), 139–143.

Gardner, P., & Hudson, B. L. (1996). *Advance report on final mortality statistics, 1993.* Hyattsville, MD: National Center for Health Statistics.

Garner, D. M., & Garfinkel, P. E. (Eds.). (1985). *Handbook of psychotherapy for anorexia nervosa and bulimia.* New York: Guilford Press.

Gartrell, N. Banks, A, Hamilton, J., Reed, N., Bishop, H., & Rodas, C. (1999). The National Lesbian Family Study: 2. Interviews with mothers of toddlers. *American Journal of Orthopsychiatry, 69,* 362–369.

Gartrell, N., Banks, A., Reed, N., Hamilton, J., Rodas, C., & Deck, A. (2000). The National Lesbian Family Study: 3 interviews with mothers of five-year-olds. *American Journal of Orthopsychiatry, 70*(4), 542–548.

Gartrell, N., Hamilton, J., Banks, A., Mosbacher, D., Reed, N., Sparks, C., & Bishop, H. (1996). The National Lesbian Family Study: 1. Interviews with prospective mothers. *American Journal of Orthopsychiatry, 66,* 272–281.

Garvey, C., & Hogan, R. (1973). Social speech and social interaction: Egocentrism revisited. *Child Development, 44,* 562–568.

Gaugler, J. E., Leitsch, S. A., Zarit, S. H., & Pearlin, L. I. (2000). Caregiver involvement following institutionalization: Effects of preplacement stress. *Research on Aging, 22,* 337–359.

Ge, X., Conger, R. D., & Elder, G. H. (2001a). Pubertal transition, stressful life events, and the emergence of gender differences in adolescent depressive symptoms. *Developmental Psychology, 37,* 404–417.

Ge, X., Conger, R. D., & Elder, G. H. (2001b). The relation between puberty and psychological distress in adolescent boys. *Journal of Research on Adolescence, 11*(1), 49–70.

Ge, X., Kim, I. J., Brody, G. H., Conger, R. D., Simons, R. L., Gibbons, F. X., & Cutrona, C. E. (2003, May). It's about timing and change: Pubertal transition effects on symptoms of major depression among African American youths. *Developmental Psychology, 39,* 430–439.

Geber, M., & Dean, R. (1957a). Gesell tests on African children. *Pediatrics, 20,* 1055–1065.

Geber, M., & Dean, R. (1957b). The state of development of newborn African children. *Lancet, 1,* 1216–1219.

Gehri, M., & Stettler, N. (2001, November 19). Marasmus. *eMedicine Journal, 2001, 2*(11). Retrieved December 13, 2001 from http://www. emedicine.com/ped/topic164.htm#sectionpictures

Gehring, J. (2000). Survey: Teens want job security. *Education Week, 19*(28), 10.

Geiger, G., & Lettvin, J. Y. (1987). Peripheral vision in persons with dyslexia. *New England Journal of Medicine, 316,* 1238–1243.

Gelfand, D. E. (1994). *Aging and ethnicity: Knowledge and services.* New York: Springer.

Geller, P. A., Kerns, D., & Klier, C. M. (2004, January). Anxiety following miscarriage and the subsequent pregnancy: A review of the literature and future directions. *Journal of Psychosomatic Research, 56*(1), 35–45.

Gelles, R. J., & Conte, J. R. (1990). Domestic violence and sexual abuse of children: A review of research in the eighties. *Journal of Marriage and the Family, 52,* 1045–1058.

Gellick, M. R. (2004). Terminal sedation: An acceptable exit strategy? *Annals of Internal Medicine, 141*(3), 236–237.

Gelman, D. (1983, November 7). A great emptiness. *Newsweek,* 120–126.

Gelman, R., & Meck, E. (1986). The notion of principle: The case of counting. In J. Hiebert (Ed.), *Conceptual and procedural knowledge: The case of mathematics.* Hillsdale, NJ: Erlbaum.

Gelman, S. (2004, September). Psychological essentialism in children. *Trends in Cognitive Sciences, 8*(9), 404–409.

Gelman, S. A., & Kremer, K. E. (1991). Understanding natural cause: Children's explanations of how objects and their properties originate. *Child Development, 62,* 396–414.

Gendell, M. (1998). Trends in retirement age in four countries, 1965–1995. *Monthly Labor Review, 121,* 20–30.

General facts and stats. (2002). *Teen sexual activity, contraceptive use, pregnancy and childbearing: General facts and stats.* The National Campaign to Prevent Teen Pregnancy. Retrieved February 25, 2005, from http://www.teenpregnancy.org/resources/reading/fact_sheets/genfacts.asp

Gentile, D. A., & Walsh, D. A. (2002, January 28). A normative study of family media habits. *Applied Developmental Psychology, 23,* 157–178.

Gershoff, E. T. (2002, July). Parental corporal punishment and associated child behaviors and experiences: A meta-analytic and theoretical review. *Psychological Bulletin, 128*(4), 539–579.

Gerwitz, J. L. (1972). *Attachment and dependency.* Washington, DC: Winston.

Gesell, A. (1928). *Infancy and human growth.* New York: Macmillan.

Gewertz, C. (2004). Asian students' needs overlooked in N.Y.C., advocacy group says. *Education Week, 23*(42), 15.

Giannarelli, L., & Barsimantov, J. (2000). *Child care expenses of America's families.* Washington, DC: Urban Institute. Retrieved December 11, 2001, from http://newfederalism.urban.org/html/op40/occa40.html

Gibbs, J. C. (2003). *Moral development and reality: Beyond the theories of Kohlberg and Hoffman.* Thousand Oaks: Sage Publications.

Gibbs, J. C., & Schnell, S. V. (1985). Moral development "versus" socialization. *American Psychologist, 40,* 1071–1080.

Gibbs, J. T. (1997). African-American suicide: A cultural paradox. *Suicide and Life-Threatening Behavior, 27,* 68–79.

Gibbs, N. (2002, April 15). Making time for a baby: For years women have been told they could wait until 40 or later to have babies. But a new book argues that's way too late. *Time Magazine, 159*(15), 48–54.

Gibson, E. J. (1969). *Principles of perceptual learning and development.* New York: Appleton-Century-Crofts.

Gibson, E. J., & Walk, R. D. (1960, April). The "visual cliff." *Scientific American, 202,* 64–71.

Gidding, S., Leibel, R. L., Daniels, S., Rosenbam, M., Horn, L. V., & Marx, G. (1996). Understanding obesity in youth. *Circulation, 94,* 33–83.

Gifford-Smith, M. E., & Brownell, C. A. (2003, July/August). Childhood peer relationships: Social acceptance, friendships, and peer networks. *Journal of School Psychology, 41*(4), 235–284.

Gil, R. M., & Vazquez, C. I. (1996). *The Maria paradox: How Latinas can merge old-world traditions with new-world self-esteem.* New York: Putnam.

Gilbert, C. (2004, February). Assessing the factors leading to alcohol abuse in pregnancy. *Journal of Fetal Alcohol Syndrome (JFAS), 2*(4). 1–2.

Gilbert, N. (1997). *Combatting child abuse: International perspectives and trends.* London: Oxford University Press.

Gilewski, M. J., Farberow, N. L., Gallagher, D. E., & Thompson, L. W. (1991). Interaction of depression and bereavement on mental health in the elderly. *Psychology and Aging, 6,* 67–75.

Gilgun, J. F. (1995). We shared something special: The moral discourse of incest perpetrators. *Journal of Marriage and the Family, 57,* 265–281.

Gilinsky, A. S., & Judd, B. B. (1994). Working memory and bias in reasoning across the life span. *Psychology and Aging, 9,* 356–371.

Gilligan, C. (1982a). *In a different voice: Psychological theory and women's development.* Cambridge, MA: Harvard University Press.

Gilligan, C. (1982b, June). Why should a woman be more like a man? *Psychology Today, 16,* 68–77.

Gilligan, C., Rogers, A. G., & Tolman, D. L. (Eds.). (1991). *Women, girls & psychotherapy: Reframing resistance.* New York: Haworth Press.

Gilligan, C., Sullivan, A., & Taylor, J. M. (1995). *Between voice and silence: Women and girls, race and relationship.* Cambridge, MA: Harvard University Press.

Gilmore, D. D. (1990). *Manhood in the making: Cultural concepts of masculinity.* New Haven, CT: Yale University Press.

Gilroy, M. (2002). Bilingual education on the edge. *Education Digest, 67*(5), 50–55.

Ginsburg, G. S., & Bronstein, P. (1993). Family factors related to children's intrinsic/extrinsic motivational orientation and academic performance. *Child Development, 64,* 1461–1474.

Giovannucci, E. (1998). Selenium and risk of prostate cancer. *Lancet, 352,* 755–756.

Giovannucci, E., Rimm, E. B., Colditz, G. A., Stampfer, M. J., Ascherio, A., Chute, C. C., & Willett, W. C. (1993). A prospective study of dietary fat and risk of prostate cancer. *Journal of the National Cancer Institute, 85,* 1571–1579.

Gjerde, P. (2004). Culture, power and experience: Toward a person-centered cultural psychology. *Human Development, 47,* 138–147.

Gjerdingen, D., McGovern, P., Bekker, M., Lundberg, U., & Willemsen, T. (2000). Women's work roles and their impact on health, well-being, and career: Comparisons between the United States, Sweden, and the Netherlands. *Women and Health, 31*(4), 1–20.

Glazer, S. (2003, June 13). Increase in autism. *CQ Researcher, 13*(23), 545–568.

Glazer, S. (2005, January 14). Prayer and healing: Can spirituality influence health? *The CQ Researcher, 15*(2), 1–51.

Gleason, J. B. (1993). *The development of language.* New York: Macmillan.

Glei, D. A. (1999). Measuring contraceptive use patterns among teenage and adult women. *Family Planning Perspectives, 31*(2), 73–81.

Glenn, C. L. (2002). One language or two? *Principal, 82*(2), 28–31.

Glenn, J. (2000, September 27). *Before it's too late: A report to the nation from the National Commission on Mathematics and Science Teaching for the 21st Century.* Washington, DC: U.S. Department of Education, National Commission on Mathematics and Science.

Glenn, N. D. (1990). Quantitative research on marital quality in the (1980)s: A critical review. *Journal of Marriage and the Family, 52,* 818–831.

Gluckman, M. (1955). *Custom and conflict in Africa.* Oxford: Blackwell.

Glueck, S., & Glueck, E. (1957). Working mothers and delinquency. *Mental Hygiene, 41,* 327–352.

Goff, J. (2004, May 7). Make room for daddy: Researchers claim that in one state, paid paternity leave could save employers $89 million in employee-retention costs. *CFO Magazine.* Retrieved February 12, 2005, from http://www.cfo.com

Gogate, L. L, & Bahrick, L. E. (2000). A study of multimodal motherese: The role of temporal synchrony between verbal labels and gestures. *Child Development, 71,* 878–895.

Gohm, C. L., Oishi, O., & Darlington, J. (1998). Culture, parental conflict, parental marital status, and the subjective well-being of young adults. *Journal of Marriage and the Family, 60,* 319–334.

Golant, S. M. (1984). *A place to grow old: The meaning of environment in old age.* New York: Columbia University Press.

Gold, D., Woodbury, M., & George, L. (1990). Relationship classification using grade of membership analysis: A typology of sibling relationships in later life. *Journal of Gerontology: Social Sciences, 45,* S43–S51.

Goldberg, A. E., & Perry-Jenkins, M. (2004). Division of labor and working-class women's well-being across the transition to parenthood. *Journal of Family Psychology, 18*(1), 225–236.

Goldberg, L. R. (1993). The structure of phenotypic personality traits. *American Psychologist, 48,* 26–34.

Goldberg, M. (2001). An interview with Linda Darling-Hammond: Balanced optimism. *Phi Delta Kappan, 82*(9), 687–690.

Goldin-Meadow, S. (2000, Jan–Feb). Beyond words: The importance of gesture to researchers and learners. *Child Development, 71,* 231–239.

Goldin-Meadow, S., & Feldman, H. (1977). The development of language-like communication without a language model. *Science, 197,* 401–403.

Goldin-Meadow, S., & Mylander, C. (1984). Gestural communication in deaf children. *Monographs of the Society for Research in Child Development, 49* (Serial No. 207).

Goldin-Meadow, S., & Mylander, C. (1998, Jan. 15). Spontaneous sign systems created by deaf children in two cultures. *Nature, 391*(6664), 279–281.

Goldscheider, F. K., & Goldscheider, C. (1999). *The changing transition to adulthood: Leaving and returning home.* Thousand Oaks, CA: Sage.

Goldscheider, F. K., Goldscheider, C., St. Clair, P., & Hodges, J. (1999). Changes in returning home in the United States, 1925-1985. *Social Forces, 78*(2), 695–720.

Goldscheider, F. K., Thornton, A., & Yang, L. (2001). Helping out the kids: Expectations about parental support in young adulthood. *Journal of Marriage and Family, 63,* 727–740.

Goldsmith, H. H. (1997). Toddler and childhood temperament. *Developmental Psychology, 33,* 891–905.

Goldstein, A., & Allen, M. (2001, August 10). Bush backs partial stem cell funding. *Washington Post,* p. A1.

Goldstein, M., & West, M. J. (1999). Consistent responses of human mothers to prelinguistic infants: The effect of prelinguistic repertoire size. *Journal of Comparative Psychology, 113,* 52–58.

Goleman, D. (1985, May 28). Spacing of siblings strongly linked to success in life. *New York Times, 17,* 18.

Goleman, D. (1986, December 2). Major personality study finds that traits are mostly inherited. *New York Times, 17,* 18.

Goleman, D. (1989a, February 7). For many, turmoil of aging erupts in the 50's, studies find. *New York Times, 17,* 21.

Goleman, D. (1989b, August 8). New studies find many myths about mourning. *New York Times, 17.*

Goleman, D. (1990b, February 6). In midlife, not just crisis but care and comfort, too. *New York Times, B1, B8.*

Goleman, D. (1990c, January 16). Men at 65: New findings on well-being. *New York Times, 19, 23.*

Goleman, D. (1992, November 24). Anthropology goes looking for love in all the old places. *New York Times, B1.*

Goleman, D. (1995a). *Emotional intelligence: Why it can matter more than IQ.* New York: Bantam Books.

Goleman, D. (1995b, February 14, 1995). For man and beast, language of love shares many traits. *New York Times,* p. C1.

Golombok, S., Perry, B., Burston, A., Murray, C., Mooney-Somers, J., Stevens, M., & Golding, J. (2003, January). Children with lesbian parents: A community study. *Developmental Psychology, 39,* 20–33.

Golsworthy, R., & Coyle, A. (1999). Spiritual beliefs and the search for meaning among older adults following partner loss. *Mortality, 4*(1), 21–40.

Golub, M. S. (1996). Labor analgesia and infant brain development. *Pharmacology, Biochemistry, and Behavior, 55,* 619–628.

Gonzales, P., Guzman, J. C., Partelow, L., Pahlke, E., Jocelyn, L. Kastberg, D., & Williams, T. (2004). *Highlights from the Trends in Mathematics and Science Study (TIMSS) 2003.* U.S. Department of Education, National Center for Education Statistics. Washington, DC: U.S. Government Printing Office. Retrieved March 24, 2005, from http://nces.ed.gov/pubs2005/2005005.pdf

Goode, E. (1991, June 24). Where emotions come from. *U.S. News & World Report,* 54–62.

Goode, E. (2000). Sharp rise found in psychiatric drugs for the very young. *New York Times, 149*(51307), A1, A14.

Goode, E. (2004, January 26). Autism cases up: Cause is unclear. *New York Times,* A1.

Goode, W. J. (1959). The theoretical importance of love. *American Sociological Review, 24,* 38–47.

Goodman, H. S., Macek, M. D., Wagner, M. L., Manz, M. C., & Marrazzo, I. D. (2004, July-August). Self-reported awareness of unrestored dental caries. Survey of the Oral Health Status of Maryland Schoolchildren, 2000–2001. *Pediatric Dentistry, 26*(4), 369–375.

Goodman, M. (1996). Culture, cohort, and cosmetic surgery. *Journal of Women and Aging, 8,* 55–58.

Goodson, P., Suther, S., Pruitt, B. E., & Wilson, K. (2003, March). Defining abstinence. *Journal of School Health, 73*(3), 91–97.

Goran, M. I., Nagy, T. R., Gower, B. A., Mazariegos, M., et al. (1998). Influence of sex, seasonality, ethnicity, and geographic location on the components of total energy expenditure in young children: Implications for energy requirements. *American Journal of Clinical Nutrition, 68,* 675–682.

Gordon, M. (2002, Spring). The benefits of co-sleeping. *The Journal of Attachment Parenting International.* Retrieved January 22, 2005, from http://www.attachmentparenting.org/artbenefitscosleep.shtml

Gormley, M. (2004, July 31). New state law allows schools to hold students until age 17. *Press & Sun-Bulletin,* 5A.

Gosden, R. G. (2000). *Designing babies: The brave new world of reproductive technology.* New York: W. H. Freeman.

Gosselin, P., & Larocque, C. (2000). Facial morphology and children's categorization of facial expressions of emotions: A comparison between Asian and Caucasian faces. *The Journal of Genetic Psychology, 161*(3), 346–358.

Gottlieb, G. (1991). Experiential canalization of behavioral development: Theory. *Developmental Psychology, 27,* 4–13.

Gould, C. G. (1983, April). Out of the mouths of beasts. *Science, 83,* 4, 69–72.

Gould, S. J. (1999). A critique of Heckhausen and Schulz' life-span theory of control from a cross-cultural perspective. *Psychological Review, 106*(3), 597–604.

Graber, J. A., Brooks-Gunn, J., & Petersen, A. C. (1996). *Transitions through adolescence: Interpersonal domains and context.* Mahwah, NJ: Erlbaum.

Graber, J. A., Brooks-Gunn, J., & Warren, M. P. (1995). The antecedents of menarcheal age: Heredity, family environment, and stressful life events. *Child Development, 66,* 346–359.

Graber, J. A., Lewinsohn, P. M., Seeley, J. R., & Brooks-Gunn, J. (1997). Is psychopathology associated with the timing of pubertal development? *Journal of the American Academy of Child and Adolescent Psychiatry, 36*(12), 1768–1776.

Graber, J. A., Lewinsohn P.M., L., Seeley, J. R., & Brooks-Gunn, J. (1997). Is psychopathology associated with the timing of pubertal development? *Journal of the American Academy of Child and Adolescent Psychiatry, 36,* 1768–1776.

Graham, E. (1995, May 9). Working parents' torment: Teens after school. *Wall Street Journal,* B1, B5.

Graham, M. G. (2000). *Sleep needs, patterns, and difficulties of adolescents: Summary of a workshop.* Board on Children, Youth, and Families, Commission on Behavioral and Social Sciences and Education. National Research Council and Institute of Medicine. Washington, DC: National Academy Press.

Graham-Bermann, S., & Levendovsky, A. (1998) Traumatic stress syndrome in children of battered women. *Journal of Interpersonal Violence, 13,* 111–128.

Grail, T. (2000). Child support for custodial mothers and fathers, 1997. *Current Population Reports.* Washington, DC: U.S. Census Bureau.

Gralinski, J. H., & Kopp, C. B. (1993). Everyday rules for behavior: Mothers' requests to young children. *Developmental Psychology, 29,* 573–584.

Grandchildren living in the home of their grandparents, 1970–2002. (2005). In *World Almanac.* New York: World Almanac Books.

Grandin, T. (1995). *Thinking in pictures: And other reports from my life with autism.* New York, NY: Doubleday.

Granrud, C. (Ed.). (1993). *Visual perception and cognition in infancy.* Hillsdale, NJ: Erlbaum.

Gratch, G., and Schatz, J. A. (1988). Evaluating Piaget's infancy books as works-in-progress. *Human Development, 31,* 82–91.

Grayson, B. (2003). Incidence and correlates of near-death experiences in a cardiac care unit. *General Hospital Psychiatry, 25,* 269–276.

Green, N. S. (2004, July). Risks of birth defects and other adverse outcomes associated with assisted reproductive technology. *Pediatrics, 114,* 256–259.

Greenberg, J., Solomon, S., Pyszczynski, T., Rosenblatt, A., Burling, J., Lyon, D., Simon, L., & Pinel, E. (1992). Why do people need self-esteem? Converging evidence that self-esteem serves an anxiety-buffering function. *Journal of Personality and Social Psychology, 63,* 913–922.

Greene, J. G. (1984). *The social and psychological origins of the climacteric syndrome.* Brookfield, VT: Gower.

Greene, J. P., & Winters, M. A. (2005, February). *Public high school graduation and college-readiness rates: 1991–2002.* Education Working Paper No. 8. Manhattan Institute for Policy Research. Retrieved March 31, 2005, from http://www.manhattan-institute.org/html/ewp_08.htm

Greene, M. F., & Ecker, J. L. (2004, January 8). Abortion, health and the law. *New England Journal of Medicine, 350,* 184–187.

Greenfield, P. M. (1966). On culture and conservation. In J. Bruner, R. R. Olver, & P. M. Greenfield (Eds.), *Studies in cognitive growth.* New York: Wiley.

Greenspan, S., & Greenspan, N. T. (1985). *First feelings.* New York: Viking Press.

Greif, J., & Hewitt, W. (1999). Tattooing and body piercings: Body art practices among college students. *Clinical Nursing Research, 8*(4), 368–376.

Greyson, B. (1999). Defining near-death experiences. *Mortality, 4*(1), 7–19.

Griffiths, A. (1999). Work design and management: The older worker. *Experimental Aging Research, 25*(4), 411–420.

Grigorenko, E. L., Sternberg, R. J., Newman, T., Kwiatkowski, J., & Jarvin, L. (2001). *Transitions in the development of giftedness: Learning disabilities and giftedness.* Retrieved December 16, 2001, from http://www.sp.uconn.edu/nrcgt/news/fall01/fall012.html

Grimm, D. (2003, September 14). Ills from the womb. *U.S. News & World Report, 135*(8), 42–45.

Gross, J. (1992, December 7). Divorced, middle-aged and happy: Women, especially, adjust to the 90's. *New York Times,* A8.

Grossman, A. H., D'Augelli, A. R., & Hershberger, S. L. (2000). Social support networks of lesbian, gay, and bisexual adults 60 years of age and older. *Journals of Gerontology Series B: Psychological Sciences and Social Sciences, 55B*(3), 171–179.

Growing up healthy: An overview of the National Children's Study. (2004). *The National Children's Study.* Washington, DC: U.S. Department of Health and Human Services. Retrieved February 10, 2005, from http://www.nationalchildrensstudy.gov

Grunbaum, J., Kann, L., Kinchen, S., Ross, J., Hawkins, J., Lowry, R., Harris, W. A., McManus, T., Chyen, D., & Collins, J. (2004, May 21). Youth Risk Behavior Surveillance—United States, 2003. *Morbidity and Mortality Weekly Report, 53*(SS-2), 1–100. Retrieved March 15, 2005, from http://www.cdc.gov/mmwr/preview/mmwrhtml/ss5302a1.htm

Grusec, J. E. (1992). Social learning theory and developmental psychology: The legacies of Robert Sears and Albert Bandura. *Developmental Psychology, 28,* 776–786.

Grusec, J. E., & Goodnow, J. J. (1994). Impact of parental discipline methods on the child's internalization of values: A reconceptualization of current points of view. *Developmental Psychology, 30,* 4–19.

Grusec, J. E., Kuczysnki, L., Rushton, J. P., & Simutis, Z. M. (1979). Learning resistance to temptation through observation. *Developmental Psychology, 15,* 233–240.

Guan, J., & Wade, M. G. (2000). The effect of aging on adaptive eye-hand coordination. *Journals of Gerontology Series B: Psychological Sciences and Social Sciences, 55B*(3), 151–162.

Guilford, J. P. (1967). *The nature of human intelligence.* New York: McGraw-Hill.

Guillemin, R. (1982). Growth hormone-releasing factor from a human pancreatic tumor that caused acromegaly. *Science, 218,* 583–587.

Guillen, M. A. (1984, April). The I and the beholder. *Psychology Today, 18,* 68–69.

Guinness world records. (2005). *Oldest woman ever: Jeanne Calment.* Retrieved May 4, 2005, from http://www.guinnessworldrecords.com/

Guisinger, S., & Blatt, S. J. (1994). Individuality and relatedness: Evolution of a fundamental dialectic. *American Psychologist, 49,* 104–111.

Gulf War syndrome update. (2003). *VFW Magazine, 90*(11), 12–13.

Gullone, E. (2000). The development of normal fear: A century of research. *Clinical Psychology Review, 20*(4), 429–451.

Gullone, E., King, N. J., & Ollendick, T. H. (2002, March). Self-reported anxiety in children and adolescents: A three-year follow-up study. *Journal of Genetic Psychology, 162*(1), 5–20.

Gunby, P. (1998). 'Life begins' for Baltimore longitudinal study of aging-research group has 40th birthday. (Medical News & Perspectives). *Journal of the American Medical Association, 279*(13), 982(2).

Guo, S., Wu, G., Wang, N., et al. (1994). Follow-up study on children with obesity and hypertension. *Chinese Medical Journal, 77,* 18.

Guoyao, W., Bazer, F. W., Cudd, T. A., Meininger, C. J., & Spencer, T. E. (2004, September). Maternal nutrition and fetal development. *Journal of Nutrition, 134*(9), 2169.

Gupta, A. K., & First, E. R. (1998). Community Outreach Health Information System (COHIS). Boston University Medical Center. Retrieved August 10, 1998, from http://gopher1.bu.edu/COHIS/aids/risks.htm

Guralnick, M. J. (1998, January). Effectiveness of early intervention for vulnerable children: A developmental perspective. *American Journal on Mental Retardation, 102,* 319–345.

Gurian, M. (1996). *The wonder of boys: What parents, mentors, and educators can do to shape boys into exceptional men.* New York: Putnam.

Gutmann, D. L. (1987). *Reclaimed powers: Toward a new psychology of men and women in later life.* New York: Basic Books.

Guttman, J. (1993). *Divorce: Theory and research.* Hillsdale, NJ: Erlbaum.

Haase, A., Steptoe, A., Sallis, J. F., & Wardle, J. (2004). Leisure-time physical activity in university students from 23 countries: Associations with health beliefs, risk awareness, and national economic development. *Preventive Medicine, 39,* 182–190.

Haffner, D. W. (1999, Winter). *Facing facts: Sexual health for American adolescents, 4*(4). Columbus, OH: College of Human Ecology, Ohio State University. Retrieved March 14, 2005, from http://www.hec.ohio-state.edu/famlife/bulletin/volume.4/bull44pd.pdf

Hak, A. E., Huibert, A. P., Pols, M. D., Visser, T. J., Drexhage, H. A., Hofman, A., & Witteman, J. C. M. (2000). Subclinical hypothyroidism is an independent risk factor for atherosclerosis and myocardial infarction in elderly women: The Rotterdam Study. *Annals of Internal Medicine, 132,* 270–278.

Hala, S. (Ed.). (1997). *The development of social cognition.* Hove, UK: Psychology Press/Erlbaum.

Hale-Benson, J. (1990). Visions for children: African-American early childhood education programs. *Early Childhood Research Quarterly, 5,* 199–213.

Halford, G. S., Maybery, M. T., O'Hare, A. W., & Grant, P. (1994). The development of memory and processing capacity. *Child Development, 65,* 1338–1356.

Hall, G. S. (1904). *Adolescence: Its psychology, and its relations to physiology, anthropology, sociology, sex, crime, religion, and education.* New York: Appleton.

Hall, S. E. K, & Geher, G. (2003, March). Behavioral and personality characteristics of children with reactive attachment disorder. *Journal of Psychology, 137*(2), 145–162.

Hall, T. (1987, June 1). Infidelity and women: Shifting patterns. *New York Times,* 20.

Hallinan, M. T., & Williams, R. A. (1989). Interracial friendship choices in secondary schools. *American Sociological Review, 54,* 67–78.

Hallman, W. K., Kipen, H. M., Diefenbach, M., Boyd, K., Kang, H., Leventhal, H., & Wartenberg, D. (2003, April). Symptom patterns among Gulf War registry veterans. *American Journal of Public Health, 93*(4), 624–630.

Hallmayer, J., Glasson, E.J ., Bower. C., Petterson, B., Croen, L., Grether, J., & Risch, N. (2002) On the twin risk in autism. *American Journal of Human Genetics, 71,* 941–946.

Halpern, B. L., Cornell, J. L., Kropp, R. Y., & Tschann, J. M. (2005, April). Oral versus vaginal sex among adolescents: Perceptions, attitudes, and behavior. *Pediatrics, 115,* 845–851.

Halpern, C. T., Joyner, K., Udry, J. R., & Suchindran. (2000). Smart teens don't have sex (or kiss much either). *Journal of Adolescent Health, 26*(3), 213–225.

Halpern, C. T., Udry, J. R., Campbell, B., & Suchindran, C. (1999, May). Effects of body fat on weight concerns, dating, and sexual activity: A longitudinal analysis of black and white adolescent girls. *Developmental Psychology, 35*(3), 721–736.

Halpern, D. (2004, November). Obstacles to female full professorship: Another civil-rights issue. *Monitor on Psychology, 35*(10), 5.

Halpern, D. F. (1992). *Sex differences in cognitive abilities* (2nd ed.). Hillsdale, NJ: Erlbaum.

Halpern, D. F. (1997). Sex differences in intelligence: Implications for education. *American Psychologist, 52,* 1091–1102.

Haltiwanger, J., & Harter, S. (1988). *A behavioral measure of young children's presented self-esteem.* Unpublished manuscript, University of Denver.

Halverson, H. M. (1931). An experimental study of prehension in infants by means of systematic cinema records. *Genetic Psychology Monographs, 10,* 107–286.

Hamer, R. D., & Skoczenski, A. M. (2001). *Milestones in visual development. Infant Vision Lab.* The Eunice Kennedy Shriver Center. University of Massachusetts Medical School, Waltham, MA. Retrieved September 30, 2001, from http://www.shriver.org/research/psychological/infantvision/milestones.htm

Hamilton, B. E., Martin, J. A., & Sutton, P. D. (2003). *Births: Preliminary data for 2003.* Washington, DC: Centers for Disease Control and Prevention.

Hamilton, B. E., Martin, J. A., & Sutton, P. D. (2004, November 23). Births: Preliminary data for 2003. *National Vital Statistics Reports, 53*(9), 1–18.

Hamilton, V. L., Blumenfeld, P. C., & Kushler, R. H. (1988). A question of standards: Attributions of blame and credit for classroom acts. *Journal of Personality and Social Psychology, 54,* 34–48.

Hamilton, V. L., Broman, C. L., Hoffman, W. S., & Renner, D. S. (1990). Hard times and vulnerable people: Initial effects of plant closing on autoworkers' mental health. *Journal of Health and Social Behavior, 31,* 123–140.

Hamilton, V. L., Hoffman, W. S., Broman, C. L., & Rauma, D. (1993). Unemployment, distress, and coping: A panel study of autoworkers. *Journal of Personality and Social Psychology, 65,* 234–247.

Hampton, T. (2004, August 18). Maternal diabetes and obesity may have lifelong impact on health of offspring. *Journal of the American Medical Association, 292,* 789–790.

Han, A. (2001, November). *Chinese mathematics pedagogy and practices: What can we learn?* Mathematics Education Dialogues. National Council of Teachers of Mathematics. Retrieved December 17, 2001 from http://www.nctm.org/dialogues/2001–11/20011116.htm

Hanchette, J. (2004, February 24). *Autism statistics: Precipitous increase in autism cases may be tied to childhood vaccines.* Autistic Society. Retrieved February 4, 2005, from http://www.autisticsociety.org/article437.html

Haney, D. Q. (1985, February 3). Creativity is fragile and easily stifled. *Columbus (Ohio) Dispatch,* C1.

Hankin, B. L., Abramson, L.Y., Moffitt, T. E., & Silva, P. A. (1998). Development of depression from preadolescence to young adulthood: Emerging gender differences in a 10-year longitudinal study. *Journal of Abnormal Psychology, 107,* 128–140.

Hänninen, V., & Aro, S. (1996, November). Sex differences in coping and depression among young adults. *Social Science & Medicine, 43*(10), 1453–1460.

Hansen, B. (2004, October 22). Cloning debate: Should all forms of human cloning be banned? *CQ Researcher, 14*(37), 877–900.

Hansen, G. R. (2002, October). Marijuana abuse. *National Institute on Drug Abuse Research Report,* NIH Publication No. 02-3859. U.S. Department of Health and Human Services.

Hansen, M., Kurinczuk, J. J., Bower, C., & Webb, S. (2002, March 7). The risk of major birth defects after intracytoplasmic sperm injection and in vitro fertilization. *New England Journal of Medicine, 346,* 725–730.

Hanson, M. J., Horn, E., Sandall, S., Beckman, P., Morgan, M., Marquart, J., Barnwell, D., & Chou, H. Y. (2001). After preschool inclusion: Children's educational pathways over the early school years. *Exceptional Children, 68*(1), 65–83.

Hansson, R. O., & Carpenter, B. N. (1994). *Relationships in old age: Coping with the challenge of transitions.* New York: Guilford Press.

Harawa, N. T., Greenland, S., Bingham, T. A., Johnson, D. F., Cochran, S. D., Cunningham, W. E., Celentano, D. D. Koblin, B. A., Valleroy, L. A., et al. (2004, March 15). Associations of race/ethnicity with HIV prevalence and HIV-related behaviors among young men who have sex with men in 7 urban centers in the United States. *Journal of Acquired Immune Deficiency Syndrome, 35*(5), 526–536.

Hardt, M., & Carroll, D. (1999, September/October). *Bereaved parents and divorce.* Bereavement. Retrieved May 11, 2005, from http://www.bereavementmag.com/

Hardy, J. A., & Higgins, G. A. (1992). Alzheimer's disease: The amyloid cascade hypothesis. *Science, 256,* 184–185.

Hardy, L. (2005, February). *Student achievement: Another year of mixed success—Progress on some fronts, not on others.* Education Vital Signs: 2005. Alexandria, VA: National School Boards Association. Retrieved April 14, 2005, from http://www.asbj.com/evs/

Hareven, T. K. (1987). Historical analysis of the family. In M. E. Sussman & S. K. Steinmetz (Eds.), *Handbook of marriage and the family.* New York: Plenum Press.

Harkness, S. (1992). Cross-cultural research in child development: A sample of the state of the art. *Developmental Psychology, 28,* 622–625.

Harkness, S., & Super, C. M. (1996). *Parents' cultural belief systems: Their origins, expressions, and consequences.* New York: Guilford Press.

Harlow, H. F. (1971). *Learning to love.* San Francisco: Albion.

Harnish, J. E., Dodge, K. A., & Valenti, E. (1995). Mother-child interaction quality as a partial mediator of the rules of maternal depressive symptomatology and socioeconomic status in the development of child behavior problems. *Child Development, 66,* 739–753.

Harris, M. J., Milich, R., Corbitt, E. M., Hoover, D. W., & Brady, M. (1992). Self-fulfilling effects of stigmatizing information on children's social interactions. *Journal of Personality and Social Psychology, 63,* 41–50.

Harrison, L. (2001). The use of comforting touch and massage to reduce stress in preterm infants. *Neonatal Intensive Care Unit Newborn and Infant Nursing Reviews, 1*(4), 235–241.

Hart, D., & Chmiel, S. (1992). Influence of defense mechanisms on moral judgment development: A longitudinal study. *Developmental Psychology, 28,* 722–730.

Harter, S. (1983). Causes and consequences of low self-esteem in children and adolescents. In R. Baumeister (Ed.), *Self-esteem: The puzzle of low self-regard* (pp. 87–1170). New York: Plenum Press.

Harter, S. (1998). A model of the effects of perceived parent and peer support on adolescent false self-behavior. *Child Development, 67,* 360.

Harter, S., & Monsour, A. (1992). Developmental analysis of conflict caused by opposing attributes in the adolescent self-portrait. *Developmental Psychology, 28,* 251–260.

Harter, S., & Pike, R. (1984). The pictorial scale of perceived competence and social acceptance for young children. *Child Development, 55,* 1969–1982.

Hartshorne, H., & May, M. A. (1928). *Studies in the nature of character. Vol. 1: Studies in deceit.* New York: Macmillan.

Hartup, W. W., & van Lieshout, C. F. (1995). Personality development in social context. *Annual Review of Psychology, 46,* 655–687.

Harwood, R. L. (1992). The influence of culturally derived values on Anglo and Puerto Rican mothers' perceptions of attachment behavior. *Child Development, 63,* 822–839.

Hashima, P. Y., & Amato, P. R. (1994). Poverty, social support, and parental behavior. *Child Development, 65,* 394–403.

Hasty, P. (2005, January). The impact of DNA damage, genetic mutation and cellular responses on cancer prevention, longevity and aging: observations in humans and mice. *Mechanisms of Aging and Development, 126*(1), 71–77.

Hattie, J. (1992). *Self-concept.* Hillsdale, NJ: Erlbaum.

Haugaard, J. J., & Hazan, C. (2004, May). Recognizing and treating uncommon behavioral and emotional disorders in children and adolescents who have been severely maltreated: Reactive attachment disorder. *Child Maltreatment, 9*(2), 254–161.

Hawley, T. L., & Disney, E. R. (1992, Winter). Crack's children: The consequences of maternal cocaine abuse. *Social Policy Report: Society for Research in Child Development,* 6.

Haworth-Hoeppner, S. (2000, February). The critical shapes of body image: The role of culture and family in the production of eating disorders. *Journal of Marriage and the Family, 62,* 212–228.

Hayes, S. C., & Hayes, L. J. (1992). Verbal relations and the evolution of behavior analysis. *American Psychologist, 47,* 1383–1395.

Hayflick, L. (1980, January). The cell biology of aging. *Scientific American, 242,* 58–65.

Haynes, S. G., Davis, M. K., Grummer-Strawn, L., Malliou, E., Rogan, W., & Lynch, B. (2000). *Breastfeeding: HHS blueprint for action on breastfeeding.* Washington, DC: U.S. Department of Health and Human Services, Office on Women's Health.

Haynie, D. A., Berg, S., Johansson, B., Gatz, M., & Zarit, S. H. (2001). Symptoms of depression in the oldest old: A longitudinal study. *Journals of Gerontology Series B: Psychological Sciences and Social Sciences, 56B*(2), 111–118.

Hays, L. (1995, April 24). PCs may be teaching kids the wrong lessons. *Wall Street Journal,* B1, B7.

Hayslip, B., & Kaminski, P. L. (2005). Grandparents raising their grandchildren: A review of the literature and suggestions for practice. *Gerontologist, 45,* 262–269.

Hayslip, B., Shore, R. J., Henderson, C., & Lambert, P. (1998). Custodial grandparenting and the impact of grandchildren with problems on role satisfaction and role meaning. *Journal of Gerontology, 53B,* S164–S173.

Hayward, C., Killen, J. D., Wilson, D. M., Hammer, L. D., Litt, I. F., Kraemer, H. C., Haydel, F., Varady, A., & Taylor, C. B. (1997). Psychiatric risk associated with early puberty in adolescent girls. *Journal of the American Academy of Child and Adolescent Psychiatry, 36,* 255–262.

Hazen, N. L., & Black, B. (1989). Preschool peer communication skills: The role of social status and interaction context. *Child Development, 60,* 867–876.

Heath, D., & Orthner, D. K. (1999). Stress and adaptation among male and female single parents. *Journal of Family Issues, 20*(4), 557–587.

Hedge, J., Borman, W., & Lammlein, S. (2004). *The aging workforce.* Washington, DC: American Psychological Association.

Hedley, A. A., Ogden, C. L., Johnson, C. L., Carroll, M. D., Curtin, L. R., & Flegal, K. M. (2004). Prevalence of overweight and obesity among US children, adolescents, and adults, 1999–2002. *Journal of the American Medical Association, 291*(23), 2847–2850.

Heer, D. M. (1985). Effects of sibling number on child outcome. *Annual Review of Sociology, 11,* 27–47.

Heffner, L. J. (2004, November 4). Advanced maternal age—How old is too old? *New England Journal of Medicine, 351,* 1927–1930.

Heidrich, S. M., & Ryff, C. D. (1993). Physical and mental health in later life: The self-system as mediator. *Psychology and Aging, 8,* 327–338.

Heinrichs, C., Munson, P. J., Counts, D. R., Cutler, G. B., Jr., & Baron, J. (1995). Patterns of human growth. *Science, 268,* 442–445.

Helfer, R. E., & Kempe, C. H. (Eds.). (1984). *The battered child.* Chicago: University of Chicago Press.

Hellmich, N. (1994, July 13). Size, gender, income linked. *USA Today,* B1.

Helson, R. (1997). The self in middle age. In M. E. Lachman & J. B. James (Eds.), *Multiple paths of midlife development* (pp. 21–43). Chicago: University of Chicago Press.

Helson, R., & Wink, P. (1992). Personality change in women from the early 40s to early 50s. *Psychology and Aging, 7,* 46–55.

Helwig, C. C. (1995). Adolescents' and young adults' conceptions of civil liberties: Freedom of speech and religion. *Child Development, 66,* 152–166.

Hendin, H. (1994, December 16). Scared to death of dying. *New York Times,* A19.

Hendrick, S., & Hendrick, C. (1992). *Romantic love.* Newbury Park, CA: Sage.

Henry, L. (2001, August). What's going on in your baby's mind? *Baby Talk, 66*(6), 46–50.

Henshaw, S. K. (2004, February 19). *U.S. teenage pregnancy statistics with comparative statistics for women aged 20–24.* The Alan Guttmacher Institute. Retrieved October 21, 2004, from http://www.agi-usa.org/pubs/teen_stats.pdf

Herek, G. M. (2002). Gender gaps in public opinion about lesbians and gay men. *American Association for Public Research, 66,* 40–66.

Herman-Giddens, M. E., Slora, E. J., Wasserman, R. C., Bourdony, C. J., Bhapkar, M. V., Koch, G. G., & Hasemeier, C. M. (1997). Secondary sexual characteristics and menses in young girls seen in office practice. *Pediatrics, 99,* 505–512.

Herman-Giddens, M. E., Wang, L., & Koch, G. (2001). Secondary sexual characteristics in boys: Estimates from the national health and nutrition examination survey III, 1988–1994. *Archives of Pediatric and Adolescent Medicine, 155*(9), 1022–1028.

Hernandez, D. J. (1997). Child development and the social demography of childhood. *Child Development, 68,* 149–169.

Herodotus. (1964). *The histories* (A. de Selincourt, Trans.). London: Penguin Books.

Heron, M. P., Schoeni, R. F., & Morales, L. (2003, December). *Health disparities among older immigrants in the United States.* PSC Research Report No. 03-548. Ann Arbor, MI: University of Michigan Population Studies Center. Retrieved April 27, 2005, from http://www.psc.isr.umich.edu

Herrera, N. C., Zajonc, R. B., Wieczorkowska, G., & Cichomski, B. (2003, July). Beliefs about birth rank and their reflection in reality. *Journal of Personality and Social Psychology, 85,* 142–150. Retrieved January 30, 2005, from *PsycArticles.*

Herrnstein, R. J., & Murray, C. (1994). *The bell curve: Intelligence and class structure in American life.* New York: Free Press.

Hershey, J. C., Niederdeppe, J., Evans, W. D., Nonnemaker, J., Blahut, S,, Holden, D., Messeri, P., & Haviland, M. L. (2005, January). The theory of "truth": How counterindustry campaigns affect smoking behavior among teens. *Health Psychology, 24*(1), 22–31.

Hertenstein, M. J., & Campos, J. J. (2004, March-April). The retention effects of an adult's emotional displays of behavior. *Child Development, 75,* 595–613.

Hertsgaard, D., & Light, H. (1984). Anxiety, depression, and hostility in rural women. *Psychological Reports, 55,* 673–674.

Hess, T. M., & Flannagan, D. A. (1992). Schema-based retrieval processes in young and older adults. *Journal of Gerontology: Psychological Sciences, 47,* P52–P58.

Hess, T. M., & Slaughter, S. J. (1990). Schematic knowledge influences on memory for scene information in young and older adults. *Developmental Psychology, 26,* 855–865.

Hess, T. M., Flannagan, D. A., & Tate, C. S. (1993). Aging and memory for schematically vs taxonomically organized verbal materials. *Journal of Gerontology: Psychological Sciences, 48,* P37–P44.

Hetherington, E. M. (1989). Coping with family transitions: Winners, losers, and survivors. *Child Development, 60,* 1–14.

Hetherington, E. M., & Stanley-Hagan, M. (2002). Parenting in divorced and remarried families. In M. Bornstein (Ed.), *Handbook of Parenting* (2nd ed., Vol. 3), *Being and Becoming a Parent* (pp. 287–315). Mahwah, NJ: Lawrence Erlbaum.

Hetherington, E. M., Cox, M., & Cox, R. (1976). Divorced fathers. *Family Coordinator, 25,* 417–427

Hetherington, E. M., Cox, M., & Cox, R. (1977, April). Divorced fathers. *Psychology Today, 10,* 42–46.

Hetherington, E. M., Stanley-Hagan, M., & Anderson, E. R. (1989). Marital transitions: A child's perspective. *American Psychologist, 44,* 303–312.

Hewitt, C. (1998). Homosexual demography: Implications for the spread of AIDS. *Journal of Sex Research, 35*(4), 390–397.

Hewitt, H. (2004, December 2). *Death by committee: What the Groningen Protocol says about our world, and where it might lead next.* The Daily Standard. Retrieved May 9, 2005, from http://www.weeklystandard.com

Heyge, L. L. (1996). Music makes a difference. *Early Childhood Connections: The Journal of Music and Movement-Based Learning.* Cited in *Early Childhood News.* Retrieved February 12, 1999, from http://www.earlychildhoodnews.com/wiredfor.htm

Heymann, S. J., & Phuong, V. (1999). The breast-feeding dilemma and its impact on HIV-infected women and their children. *AIDS Read, 9*(4), 292–299. Retrieved December 29, 2004, from www.medscape.com/

Hibbert, M. (2004, November 20). *Artificial womb technology and the constitutional guarantees of reproductive freedom.* Center for the Study of Law, Science & Technology. The College of Law at Arizona State University. Retrieved November 11, 2004, from http://www.law.asu.edu/?id=8296

Hiedemann, B., Suhomlinova, O., & O'Rand, A. (1998). Economic independence, economic status, and empty nest in midlife marital disruption. *Journal of Marriage and the Family, 60,* 219–231.

Hill, R. (1964). Methodological issues in family development research. *Family Process, 3,* 186–206.

Hill, R. (1986). Life cycle stages for types of single parent families: Of family development theory. *Family Relations, 35,* 19–29.

Hilleras, P., Herlitz, A., Jorm, A., & Winblad, B. (1998). Negative and positive affect among the very old: A survey on a sample age 90 years or older. *Research on Aging, 20,* 593–610.

Himelstein, B. P., Hilden, J. M., Morstad Boldt, A., & Weissman, D. (2004). Pediatric palliative care. *New England Journal of Medicine, 250,* 1752–1762.

Hines, M. (2004). Androgen, estrogen and gender. In A. Eagley, A. Beall & R.J. Sternberg (Eds.), *The Psychology of Gender* (2nd ed.) NY: Guilford Press.

Hirota, A. (2004). Kirishima Yoko and the age of non-marriage. *Women's Studies, 33*(4), 399–411.

Hirshberg, L. M., & Svejda, M. (1990). When infants look to their parents: Infants' social referencing of mothers compared to fathers. *Child Development, 61,* 1175–1186.

HIV infection in women. (2004, May). National Institute of Allergy and Infectious Diseases, National Institutes of Health, Bethesda, MD. Retrieved December 29, 2004, from http://www.niaid.nih.gov/factsheets/womenhiv.htm

HIV/AIDS surveillance report, 2003. (2004, December 1). Centers for Disease Control and Prevention. Atlanta: U.S. Department of Health and Human Services. Retrieved December 31, 2004, from http://www.cdc.gov/hiv/stats/2003SurveillanceReport.pdf

Hoff-Ginsberg, E. (1991, August). Mother-child conversation in different social classes and communicative settings. *Child Development, 62,* 782–96.

Hoff-Ginsberg, E., & Shatz, M. (1982). Linguistic input and the child's acquisition of language. *Psychological Bulletin, 92,* 3–26.

Hofferth, S. L. (1998, November). *Healthy environments, healthy children: Children in families.* Ann Arbor, MI: Institute for Social Research.

Hofferth, S. L., & Anderson, K. G. (2003, February). Are all dads equal? Biology versus marriage as a basis for paternal involvement. *Journal of Marriage and Family, 65,* 213–232.

Hofferth, S. L., & Sandberg, J. F. (2001). How American children spend their time. *Journal of Marriage and the Family, 63,* 295–308.

Hoffman, C.M. (2002). *Federal support for education: Fiscal years 1980 to 2002* (NCES 2003–006). U.S. Department of Education, National Center for Education Statistics. Washington, DC: U.S. Government Printing Office.

Hoffman, M. L. (1971). Father absence and conscience development. *Developmental Psychology, 4,* 400–406.

Hoffman, M. L., & Hoffman, L. W. (1964). *Review of child development research.* Russell Sage Foundation.

Hoffman, W. (2003, November 19). *Stem cells: Human health, global competition and national security.* St. Laboratory Medicine & Pathology and Biomedical Engineering Institute, University of Minnesota. Retrieved November 21, 2004, from www.mbbnet.edu/csbsju.html

Hojat, M., Shapurian, R., Nayerahmadi, H., Farzaneh, M., Foroughi, D., Parsi, M., & Azizi, M. (1999). Premarital sexual, child rearing, and family attitudes of Iranian men and women in the United States and in Iran. *The Journal of Psychology, 133*(1), 19–31.

Holahan, C. K., & Chapman, J. R. (2002). Longitudinal predictors of proactive goals and activity participation at age 80. *Journals of Gerontology, 57B,* 418–425.

Holahan, C. K., Holahan, C. J., & Wonacott, N. L. (1999). Self-appraisal, life satisfaction, and retrospective life choices across one and three decades. *Psychology and Aging, 14*(2), 238–244.

Holahan, C. K., Sears, R. R., & Cronbach, L. J. (1995). *The gifted group in later maturity.* Stanford, CA: Stanford University Press.

Hollander, D. (2004). Over-the-hill childbearing. *Perspectives on Sexual and Reproductive Health, 36*(1), 4.

Hollinger, J. H. (1998). *Adoption law and practice. Volume 1: 1998 supplement.* New York: Matthew Bender.

Holmbeck, G. N., & Hill, J. P. (1991). Conflictive engagement, positive affect, and menarche in families with seventh-grade girls. *Child Development, 62,* 1030–1048.

Honein, M. A., Paulozzi, L. J., & Erickson, J. D. (2001, September). Continued occurrence of Accutane-exposed pregnancies. *Teratology, 64*(3), 142–147.

Hong, E., & Perkins, G. (1997). Children's responses to self-concept questionnaire administered in different contexts. *Child Study Journal, 27,* 111.

Hood, L. (2004). *High school students at risk: The challenge of dropouts and pushouts.* New York: Carnegie Corporation of New York. Retrieved March 31, 2005, from http://www.carnegie.org/pdf/challenge_dropouts.pdf

Hoover, E. (2004, May 28). Alcohol arrests on campuses increased again in 2002. *Chronicle of Higher Education, 50*(38), A33.

Hopkin, M. (2005, January 5). Premature births lead to wide-ranging disabilities. *Nature, 10.* Retrieved January 5, 2005, from http://news.nature.com/news/

Hopson, J. L. (1998). Fetal psychology: Research shows that a 32-week-old fetus can feel and dream. *Psychology Today, 31*(5), 44–49.

Horn, J. L. (1976). Human abilities. A review of research and theory in the early (1970)s. *Annual Review of Psychology, 27,* 437–485.

Horn, T. (1998). Advances in pediatric HIV research. *Community Research Initiative on AIDS (CRIA), 7*(2). Retrieved November 10, 2001, from http://www.thebody.com/cria/ spring98/pediatric.html

Horn, W. (2002, December/2003, January). *Better futures for waiting children.* Children's Bureau Express. Washington, DC: U.S. Department of Health and Human Services. Retrieved March 8, 2005, from http://cbexpress.acf.hhs.gov

Horn, W. F., & Sylvester, T. (Eds.). (2004). *Father facts* (4th ed.). Gaithersburg, MD: National Fatherhood Initiative. Retrieved January 16, 2005, from http://www.fatherhood.org/fatherfacts/late.htm

Horrigan, M. W. (2004, February). Employment projections to 2012. *Concepts and Context 127*(2), 3–22. Retrieved October 23, 2005, from www.bls.gov/opub/mlr/2004/02/artfull.pdf

Hosken, F. P. (1998). *Female genital mutilation: Strategies for eradication.* Retrieved December 22, 1998, from http://www.nocirc.org/symposia/first/hosken.html

Hospice Foundation of America (2005). *What is hospice?* Retrieved April 19, 2005, from http://www.hospicehoundation.org/hospiceInfo/

Hotopf, M., David, A., Hull, L., Nikalaou, V., Unwin, C., & Wessely, S. (2004, May). Risk factors for continued illness among Gulf War veterans: A cohort study. *Psychological Medicine, 34*(4), 747–754.

Houston, D., Jusczyk, P.W., & Jusczyk, A.M. (2003). Memory for bisyllables in 2-month-olds. In D. Houston, A Seidl, G.Hollich, E. Johnson, & A. Jusczyk (Eds.), *Jusczyk Lab Final Report.* Retrieved January 27, 2005, from http://hincapie.psych.purdue.edu/Jusczyk

Howarth, G., & Leaman, O. (Eds.). (2001). *Encyclopedia of death and dying.* New York: Routledge.

Howe, M. L., & Courage, M. L. (1993). On resolving the enigma of infantile amnesia. *Psychological Bulletin, 113,* 305–326.

Howe, N., & Strauss, W. (2000). *Millennials rising: The next great generation.* New York: Random House.

Howe, N., Aquan-Assee, J., & Bukowski, W. M. (2001). Predicting sibling relations over time: Synchrony between maternal management styles and sibling relationship quality. *Merrill-Palmer Quarterly, 47*(1), 121–141.

Howes, C., & Wu, F. (1990). Peer interactions and friendships in an ethnically diverse school setting. *Child Development, 61,* 537–541.

Hoyert, D. L., Kung, H. C., & Smith, B. L. (2005, February 28). Deaths: Preliminary data for 2003. *National Vital Statistics Reports, 53*(15), 1–48. Retrieved April 13, 2005, from http://www.cdc.gov/nchs/data/nvsr/nvsr53/nvsr53_15.pdf

Hsu, F. L. K. (1943). Incentives to work in primitive communities. *American Sociological Review, 8,* 638–642.

Hu, F. B., & Willett, W. (2002). Optimal diets for prevention of coronary heart disease. *Journal of the American Medical Association, 288*(20), 2569–2578.

Hubka, T. A. (2004). Osteoporosis: Exploring new directions. *Women and Wellness, 1*(2), 2.

Huesmann, L. R., & Miller, L. S. (1994). Long-term effects of repeated exposure to media violence in childhood. In L. R. Huesmann (Ed.). *Aggressive behavior.* New York: Plenum Books.

Huggins, C. E. (2001, September 24). *Anorexia, bulimia rates have soared in Japan.* Reuter's Health. Retrieved December 15, 2001, from http://www.reutershealth.com/archive/2001/09/25/professional/links/20010925epid003.html

Hughes, J. N., & Hasbrouck, J. E. (1996). Television violence: Implications for violence prevention. *School Psychology Review, 25*(2), 134–151.

Hultsch, D. F., Hertzog, C., & Dixon, R. A. (1990). Ability correlates of memory performance in adulthood and aging. *Psychology and Aging, 5,* 356–368.

Human organ and tissue transplantation. (2004, May 22). EB113/2004/REC/1, Agenda Item 12.14 §. Fifty-Seventh World Health Assembly. Geneva, Switzerland: World Health Organization.

Humecky, J. (2005, April 28). Tai Chi, a healthy practice for life. *Mendocino Beacon.* Retrieved April 29, 2005, from http://www.mendocinobeacon.com

Humphrey, T. (1978). Function of the nervous system during prenatal life. In U. Stave (Ed.), *Perinatal physiology.* Hillsdale, NJ: Erlbaum.

Humphry, D. (1991). *Final exit: The practicalities of self-deliverance and assisted suicide for the dying.* New York: Dell.

Humphry, D., & Clement, M. (1998). *Freedom to die: People, politics, and the right to die movement.* New York: St. Martin's Press.

Hunt, E. (1983). On the nature of intelligence. *Science, 219,* 141–146.

Hunter, B. T. (June 1998). On nutrition: How fare the elderly? *Consumers' Research Magazine, 81*(6), 10.

Huston, A. C., & Wright, J. C. (1998). Mass media and children's development. In I. E.

Sigel & K. A. Renninger (Eds.), *Handbook of child psychology* (Vol. 4, pp. 999–1058). New York: John Wiley & Sons.

Huston, A. C., Wright, J. C., Rice, M. L., Kerkman, D., & St. Peters, M. (1990). Development of television viewing patterns in early childhood: A longitudinal investigation. *Developmental Psychology, 26,* 409–420.

Huston, T. L., & Geis, G. (1993). In what ways do gender-related attributes and beliefs affect marriage? *Journal of Social Issues, 49,* 87–106.

Hutnik, N. (1991). *Ethnic minority identity: A social psychological perspective.* Oxford, England: Clarendon Press.

Huttenlocher, J., Haight, W., Bryk, A., Seltzer, M., & Lyons, T. (1991). Early vocabulary growth: Relation to language input and gender. *Developmental Psychology, 27,* 236–248.

Hyde, D. M. (1959). *An investigation of Piaget's theories of the development of number.* Unpublished doctoral dissertation, University of London.

Hyde, J. S., Krajnik, M., & Skuldt-Niederberger, K. (1991). Androgyny across the life span: A replication and longitudinal follow-up. *Developmental Psychology, 27,* 516–519.

Hyson, M. C. (1994). *The emotional development of young children: Building an emotion-centered curriculum.* New York: Teachers College Press.

Hyson, M. C. (2004). *The emotional development of young children: Building an emotion-centered curriculum.* New York: Teachers College Press.

Ickes, W. (1993). Traditional gender roles: Do they make, and then break, our relationships? *Journal of Social Issues, 49,* 71–85.

Ikeda, R. M., Crosby, A., Thomas, R. G., Annest, J. L., & Berrios-Torres, S. I. (2004). Suicide among Hispanics—United States, 1997–2001. *MMWR Morbidity and Mortality Weekly Report, 53*(22), 478–481.

Im Thurn, E. F. (1883). *Among the Indians of Guiana.* London: Kegan Paul, Trench & Trubner.

Inagaki, K., & Hatano, G. (1993). Young children's understanding of the mind-body distinction. *Child Development, 64,* 1534–1549.

Induced abortion. (2003). *Facts in brief.* The Alan Guttmacher Institute. Retrieved October 19, 2004, from http://www.agi-usa.org/pubs/fb_induced_abortion.pdf

Information about anaphylaxis. (2005). The Food Allergy and Anaphylaxis Network. Retrieved February 23, 2005, from http://www.foodallergy.org/anaphylaxis.html

Ingersoll-Dayton, B., & Saengtienchai, C. (1999). Respect for the elderly in Asia: Stability and change. *International Journal of Aging and Human Development, 48*(2), 113–130.

Ingrassia, M. (2005, March 21). *Making the brand, MTV-style.* The Daily News.

Retrieved March 1, 2005, from http://www.nydailynews.com/front/v-pfriendly/story/291909p-249939c.html

Inhelder, B., & Piaget, J. (1964). *The early growth of logic in the child.* New York: W. W. Norton.

International Human Genome Sequencing Consortium. (2004, October 21). Finishing the euchromatic sequence of the human genome. *Nature, 431,* 931–945.

Introduction to diabetes. (2004). National Diabetes Information Clearinghouse. Retrieved October 15, 2004, from http://diabetes.niddk.nih.gov/intro/index.htm

Ip, G. (2005, April 11). Wage gap figures in social security's ills. *Wall Street Journal,* A2.

Irwin, H. J. (1985). *Flight of mind: A psychological study of the out-of-body experience.* Metuchen, NJ: Scarecrow Press.

Ishii-Kuntz, M., & Lee, G. R. (1987). Status of the elderly: An extension of the theory. *Journal of Marriage and the Family, 49,* 413–420.

Issacowitz, D. M., & Smith, J. (2003). Positive and negative affect in very old age. *Journals of Gerontology Series B: Psychological Sciences and Social Sciences, 58B*(3), 143–152.

Ivey, P. (2000). Cooperative reproduction in Ituri Forest hunter-gatherers: Who cares for Efé infants? *Current Anthropology, 41*(5), 856–866.

Izard, C. E. (2001). Emotional intelligence or adaptive emotions? *Emotion, 1,* 249–257.

Izard, C. E. (2002a, August). Continuity and change in infants' facial expressions following an unanticipated aversive stimulus. *Behavioral & Brain Sciences, 25*(4), 463–465.

Izard, C. E. (2002b). Translating emotion theory and research into preventive interventions. *Psychological Bulletin, 128,* 796–824.

Izard, C. E. (2004). *The psychology of emotions.* New York: Plenum.

Izard, C. E., & Abe, J. A. (2004, September). Developmental changes in facial expressions of emotions in the strange situation during the second year of life. *Emotion, 4*(3), 251–265.

Izard, C. E., & Malatesta, C. Z. (1987). Perspectives on emotional development: Differential emotions theory of early emotional development. In J. D. Osofsky (Ed.), *Handbook of infant development* (2nd ed.). New York: Wiley.

Izard, C. E., Fantauzzo, C. A., Castle, J. M., Haynes, O. M., Rayias, M. F., & Putnam, P. H. (1995). The ontogeny and significance of infants' facial expressions in the first nine months of life. *Developmental Psychology, 31,* 997–1013.

Izard, C. E., Fine, S. E., Mostow, A. J., Trentacosta, C. J., & Campbell, J. (2002, Fall). Emotion processes in normal and abnormal development and preventive intervention. *Development and Psychopathology, 14*(4), 761–787.

Izard, C. E., Fine, S., Schultz, D., Mostow, A., Ackerman, B., & Youngstrom, E. (2001). Emotion knowledge as a predictor of social behavior and academic competence in children at risk. *Psychological Science, 12*(1), 18.

Izard, C. E., Hembree, E. A., & Huebner, R. R. (1987). Infants' emotion expressions to acute pain: Developmental change and stability of individual differences. *Developmental Psychology, 23,* 105–113.

Jacklin, C. N., & Reynolds, C. (1993). Gender and childhood socialization. In A. E. Beall & R. J. Sternberg (Eds.), *The psychology of gender.* New York: Guilford Press.

Jackson, A., Brooks-Gunn, J., Huang, C., & Glassman, M. (2000). Single mothers in low-wage jobs: Financial strain, parenting, and preschoolers' outcomes. *Child Development, 71*(5), 1409–1423.

Jackson, J. F. (1993). Multiple caregiving among African Americans and infant attachment. The need for an Emic approach. *Human Development, 36,* 87–102.

Jacobs, J. E., & Eccles, J. S. (1992). The impact of mothers' gender-role stereotypic beliefs on mothers' and children's ability perceptions. *Journal of Personality and Social Psychology, 63,* 932–944.

Jacobs, S. (2003). Death by voluntary dehydration—What the caregivers say. *New England Journal of Medicine, 349,* 325–326.

Jacobsen, T., Edelstein, W., & Hofmann, V. (1994). A longitudinal study of the relation between representations of attachment in childhood and cognitive functioning in childhood and adolescence. *Developmental Psychology, 30,* 112–124.

Jacobsson, B., Ladfors, L., & Milsom, I. (2004, October). Advanced maternal age and adverse perinatal outcome. *Obstetrics and Gynecology, 104*(4), 727–733. Retrieved January 2, 2005, from EBSCOhost.

Jaffee, S. R. (2002). Pathways to adversity in young adulthood among early childbearers. *Journal of Family Psychology, 16,* 38–49.

Jaffee, S., Avshalom, C., Moffitt, T. E., Belsky, J., & Silva, P. (2001). Why are children born to teen mothers at risk for adverse outcomes in young adulthood? Results from a 20-year longitudinal study. *Development and Psychopathology, 13*(2), 377–397.

James S. J., Cutler P., Melnyk, S., Hernigan, S., Janak, L., Gaylor, D. W., & Neubrander, J. A. (2004). Metabolic biomarkers of increased oxidative stress and methylation capacity in children with autism. *American Journal of Clinical Nutrition, 80*(6), 1611–1617.

James S. J., Slikker, W., Melnyk, S., New, E., Pogribna, M., Jernigan, S. (2005). Thimerosal neurotoxicity is associated with glutathione depletion: Protection with glutathione precursors. *Neurotoxicology, 26*(1), 1–8.

James, S. L. (1990). *Normal language acquisition.* Boston: Allyn & Bacon.

Jankowiak, W. R., & Fischer, E. F. (1992). A cross-cultural perspective on romantic love. *Ethnology, 31*(2), 149–156.

Jaret, P. (1996, March/April). Think fast: What gives you speedier reactions, quicker recall? Step this way. *Health,* 44–46.

Jeffers, F. C., & Verwoerdt, A. (1969). How the old face death. In E. W. Busse & E. Pfeiffer (Eds.), *Behavior and adaptation in late life.* Boston: Little, Brown.

Jeffrey, N. A. (1995, April 19). More seniors see security in retirement villages. *Wall Street Journal,* C1, C13.

Jellinek, M., & Murphy, J. M. (1999a). *Basic information: Psychosocial problems and screening.* Pediatric Symptom Checklist Homepage. Retrieved October 21, 2001, from http://www.massgeneral.org/psc/

Jellinek, M., & Murphy, J. M. (1999b). *Psychosocial problems, screening, and the pediatric symptom checklist. Pediatric Development and Behavior.* Retrieved October 20, 2001, from http://www.dbpeds.org/pdf/psc.pdf

Jendrek, M. P. (1993). Grandparents who parent their grandchildren: Effects on lifestyle. *Journal of Marriage and the Family, 55,* 609–621.

Jeng, M.S., & Taylor-Thomas, J.T. (1985) *The persistence of adolescent childbearing and socio-cultural influence: An overview of the Gambian experience.* Prepared for the Seminar on Adolescent Fertility, Lome, Togo, December 2–10, 1985.

Jennings, J. M., & Jacoby, L. L. (2003). Improving memory in older adults: Training recollection. *Neuropsychological Rehabilitation, 13,* 417–440.

Jenny, C., Roesler, T. A., & Poyer, K. L. (1994). Are children at risk for sexual abuse by homosexuals? *Pediatrics, 94,* 41–44.

Jensen, A. R. (1972, Summer). The heritability of intelligence. *Saturday Evening Post,* 149.

Jensen, A. R. (1984, March). Political ideologies and educational research. *Phi Delta Kappan, 65,* 460–462.

Jensen, K. (1932). Differential reactions to taste and temperature stimuli in newborn infants. *Genetic Psychological Monographs, 12,* 363–479.

Jessor, R., Turbin, M. S., & Costa, F. M. (1998). Protective factors in adolescent health behavior. *Journal of Personality and Social Psychology, 75,* 788–800.

Johansson, B., & Berg, S. (1989). The robustness of the terminal decline phenomenon: Longitudinal data from the Digit-Span Memory Test. *Journal of Gerontology, 44,* P184–186.

Johnson, C. N. (1990). If you had my brain, where would I be? Children's understanding of the brain and identity. *Child Development, 61,* 962–972.

Johnson, C.Y. (2005, April 28). *Finding meaning in Tai Chi: Teacher's third book focuses on philosophy of martial arts moves. Boston Globe.* Retrieved April 29, 2005, from http://www.boston.com

Johnson, D. (1994, September 21). Study says small schools are key to learning. *New York Times,* B12.

Johnson, J. A., & Williams, E. (2004, August 13). *Stem cell research: CRS Report for Congress.* Washington, DC: Congressional Research Service, The Library of Congress.

Johnson, M. (2001). *Evaluation and treatment of childhood obesity.* ChildObesity.Com. Retrieved December 2, 2001, from http://www.childobesity.com/about.htm

Johnson, M., & Puddifoot, J. (1997). The grief response in the partners of women who miscarry. *British Journal of Medical Psychology, 69,* 313–327.

Johnson, P. B., & Gallo-Treacy, C. (1993). Alcohol expectancies and ethnic drinking differences. *Journal of Alcohol and Drug Education, 38,* 80–88.

Johnson, P. B., & Gurin, G. (1994). Negative affect, alcohol expectancies and alcohol-related problems. *Addiction, 89,* 581–586.

Johnson, R. J., Lund, D. A., & Dimond, M. F. (1986). Stress, self-esteem and coping during bereavement among the elderly. *Social Psychology Quarterly, 49,* 273–279.

Johnson, S. P., Bremner, J. G., Slater, A., Mason, U., Foster, K., & Cheshire, A. (2003, January–February). Infants' perception of object trajectories. *Child Development, 74,* 94–108.

John-Steiner, V. (1986). *Notebooks of the mind: Explorations of thinking.* Albuquerque: University of New Mexico Press.

Johnston, L. (1979, June 17). Artist ends her life after ritual citing "self-termination" right. *New York Times, 1,* 10.

Johnston, L. D., Bachman, J. G., & O'Malley, P. M. (1997). Drug use among American teens shows some signs of leveling after a long rise. *Monitoring the Future Survey: 1997.* University of Michigan Survey Research Center. Retrieved March 6, 1999, from www.health.org/pressrel/dec97/10.htm

Johnston, L. D., O'Malley, P. M., Bachman, J. G., & Schulenberg, J. E. (2004, December 21). *Overall teen drug use continues gradual decline; but use of inhalants rises.* National press release. Ann Arbor, MI: University of Michigan News and Information Services. Retrieved April 13, 2005, from http://www.monitoringthefuture.org/pressreleases/04drugpr_complete.pdf

Jones, A. (2004). Letter from Afghanistan. *Nation, 279*(10), 17–19.

Jones, D. C. (2001). Social comparison and body image: Attractiveness comparisons to models and peers among adolescent girls and boys. *Sex Roles: A Journal of Research, 45*(9–10), 645–664.

Jones, D. C., & Costin, S. E. (1995). Friendship quality during preadolescence and adolescence: The contributions of relationship orientations, instrumentality, and expressivity. *Merrill-Palmer Quarterly, 41,* 517–535.

Jones, H. W., & Cohen, J. (2004, May). IFFS Surveillance, 2004. *Fertility & Sterility, 81*(5), Supplement 4.

Jones, J. (2001). *Around the globe, women outlive men.* Population Reference Bureau. Retrieved January 2, 2002, from http://www.prb.org/Template.cfm?Section=PRB&templa/ContentDisplay.cfm&contentID=367

Jones, M. C. (1957). The later careers of boys who were early- or late-maturing. *Child Development, 28,* 113–128.

Jones, M. C., & Bayley, N. (1950). Physical maturing among boys as related to behavior. *Journal of Educational Psychology, 41,* 129–148.

Jones, S. S. (1985). On the motivational bases for attachment behavior. *Developmental Psychology, 21,* 848–857.

Jónsdóttir, V. (2001). *Early intervention as a framework for music therapy with caretakers and their special-needs infants.* Unpublished thesis. Sognog Fjordane University College, Sandane, Norway. Retrieved January 27, 2005, from http://www.voices.no/mainissues/mi40004000140.html

Josselson, R. (1988). *Finding herself: Pathways to identity development in women.* New York: Jossey-Bass.

Joyner, A. (2003, September). No strings attached: Wireless networks provide students with anytime, anywhere access. *American School Board Journal,* Special Report. Retrieved April 14, 2005, from http://www.asbj.com/specialreports/0903SpecialReports/S5.html

Jung, C. G. (1933). *Modern man in search of a soul.* New York: Harcourt, Brace & World.

Jung, C. G. (1960). The stages of life. In H. Reed, M. Fordham, & G. Adler (Eds.), *Collected works* (Vol. 8). Princeton, NJ: Princeton University Press. (Original work published 1931)

Juster, F. T., Ono, H., & Stafford, F. P. (2004, November). Changing times of American youth: 1981–2003. Ann Arbor, MI: Institute for Social Research, University of Michigan. Retrieved February 13, 2005, from http://www.umich.edu/news/releases/2004/Nov04/teen_time_report.pdf

Jylha, M., & Jokela, J. (1990). Individual experiences as cultural—A cross-cultural study on loneliness among the elderly. *Ageing and Society, 10,* 295–315.

Kadlec, D., Rawe, J., Park, A., Fonda, D., Cole, W., DeQuine, J., et al. (2004). The low-carb frenzy. *Time, 163*(18), 46–53.

Kadlubar, F. F., Berkowitz, G. S., Delongchanip, R. R., Green, B. L., Wang, C., & Wolff, M. S. (2001, March 26). *The putative high activity variant, Cyp3a4*1b, predicts the onset of puberty in young girls*

(Abstract #2198). American Association for Cancer Research 92nd Annual Meeting. Retrieved December 18, 2001, from http://www.aacr.org/1000/1100/1130i.html

Kagan, J. (1972). A conception of early adolescence. In J. Kagan & R. Coles (Eds.), *Twelve to sixteen: Early adolescence.* New York: Norton.

Kagan, J. (1983). Stress and coping in early development. In N. Garmezy & M. Rutter (Eds.), *Stress, coping, and development.* New York: McGraw-Hill.

Kagan, J. (1984). *The nature of the child.* New York: Basic Books.

Kagan, J. (1989). *Unstable ideas: Temperament, cognition, and self.* Cambridge: Cambridge University Press.

Kagan, J. (1993). On the nature of emotion. *Monographs of the Society for Research in Child Development, 59*(2–3, Serial No. 240).

Kagan, J. (1994, October 5). The realistic view of biology and behavior. *Chronicle of Higher Education,* A64.

Kagan, J. (1997). Attention, emotion, and reactivity in infancy and early childhood. In P. J. Lang (Ed.), *Attention and orienting: Sensory and motivational processes.* Mahwah, NJ: Erlbaum.

Kagan, J., & Moss, H. A. (1962). *Birth to maturity.* New York: Wiley.

Kagan, J., & Snidman, N. (1991). Temperamental factors in human development. *American Psychologist, 46,* 856–862.

Kagan, J., Kearsley, R. B. & Zelazo, P. R. (1978). *Infancy: Its place in human development.* Cambridge, MA: Harvard University Press.

Kahn, S., Zimmerman, G., Csikszentmihalyi, M., & Getzels, J. W. (1985). Relations between identity in young adulthood and intimacy at midlife. *Journal of Personality and Social Psychology, 49,* 1316–1322.

Kail, R. (1991). Developmental change in speed of processing during childhood and adolescence. *Psychological Bulletin, 109,* 490–501.

Kaiser, J. (1994). Alzheimer's: Could there be a zinc link? *Science, 265,* 1365.

Kaler, S., & Freeman, B. J. (1997). Analysis of environmental deprivation: Cognitive and social development in Romanian orphans. *Journal of Psychology and Psychiatry and Allied Disciplines, 35,* 769–781.

Kalleberg, A. L., & Loscocco, K. A. (1983). Aging, values, and rewards: Explaining age differences in job satisfaction. *American Sociological Review, 48,* 78–90.

Kallemeyn, L. (1997). Director's Report. *Stepfamilies, 17*(2), 13.

Kallman, D. A., Plato, C. C., & Tobin, J. D. (1990). The role of muscle loss in the age-related decline of grip strength: Cross-sectional and longitudinal perspectives. *Journal of Gerontology, 45,* M82–M88.

Kalter, H. (2004, January–February). Teratology in the 20th century environmental causes of congenital malformations in

humans and how they were established. *Neurotoxicology and Teratology, 26*(1), 1–12.

Kamerman, J. B. (1988). *Death in the midst of life: Social and cultural influences on death, grief, and mourning.* Englewood Cliffs, NJ: Prentice Hall.

Kamin, L. J. (1974). *The science and politics of IQ.* Hillsdale, NJ: Erlbaum.

Kamin, L. J. (1981). Commentary. In S. Scarr (Ed.), *IQ: Race, social class, and individual differences.* Hillsdale, NJ: Erlbaum.

Kamin, L. J. (1994, November 23). Intelligence, IQ tests, and race. *Chronicle of Higher Education,* B5.

Kane, H. (1993). *Child mortality continues to fall.* Retrieved February 11, 1999, from http://www.ai.rcast. u-tokyo.ac.jp/dobashi/workhtml/vi939697.html

Kang, H. K., & Hyams, K. C. (2005, March 31). Mental health care needs among recent war veterans. *New England Journal of Medicine, 352,* 1289.

Kangaroo care. (1998). *Mothering, 86,* 65.

Kantrowitz, B., & Wingert, P. (2001). Unmarried with children. *Newsweek, 137*(22), 46–54.

Kaplan, P. S., Bachorowski, J. & Zarlengo-Strouse, P. (1999, June). Child-directed speech produced by mothers with symptoms of depression fails to promote associative learning in 4-month-old infants. *Child Development, 70,* 560–570.

Kaplowitz P. B., Slora E. J., Wasserman, R. C, Pedlow, S.E., & Herman-Giddens, M. E. (2001, August). Earlier onset of puberty in girls: Relation to increased body mass index and race. *Pediatrics, 108,* 347–353.

Kaplowitz, P. B., & Oberfield, S. E. (1999). Reexamination of the age limit for defining when puberty is precocious in girls in the United States. *Pediatrics, 104,* 936–941.

Kaplowitz, P. B., Slora, E. J., Wasserman, R. C., Pedlow, S. E., Herman-Giddes, M. (2001). Earlier onset of puberty in girls: Relation to increased body mass index and race. *Pediatrics, 108,* 347–353.

Karasik, S. (2000, April 14). *Experts: More latchkey kids means more trouble—High risk behavior increases when parents are gone.* APB News. Retrieved January 1, 2002, from http://www.apbnews.com/safetycenter/ family/2000/04/14/sitter0414_01.html

Karoly, L. A., & Zissimopoulos, J. (2004, July). Self-employment among U.S. older workers. *Monthly Labor Review,* 24–47.

Kasl-Godley, J. E., Gatz, M., & Fiske, A. (1998). Depression and depressive symptoms in old age. In I. H. Nordhus et al. (Eds.), *Clinical geropsychology* (pp. 211–218). Washington, DC: American Psychological Association.

Kastenbaum, R. (1975). Is death a life crisis? On the confrontation with death in theory and practice. In N. Datan & L. H. Ginsburg (Eds.), *Lifespan developmental psychology: Normative life crisis.* New York: Academic Press.

Kastenbaum, R. (1977, September). Temptations from the ever after. *Human Behavior, 6,* 28–33.

Kastenbaum, R. (1979). "Healthy dying": A paradoxical quest continues. *Journal of Social Issues, 35,* 185–206.

Kastenbaum, R. (1991). Where do we come from? What are we? Where are we going? An annotated bibliography of aging and humanities by Donna Polisar, Larry Wygant, Thomas Cole, and Cielo Perdomo. *International Journal of Aging and Human Development, 33,* 247.

Kastenbaum, R. (1993). *Encyclopedia of adult development.* Phoenix, AZ: Onyx Press.

Kastenbaum, R. (1997). Final acts of love: Families, friends; and assisted dying/Life beyond 85 years: The aura of survivorship/ Letting go: Morrie's reflections on living while dying/The psychology of growing old. *Gerontologist, 37,* 698–701.

Kastenbaum, R. (2004a). Death writ large. *Death Studies, 28*(4), 375–392.

Kastenbaum, R. (2004b, Summer). Why funerals? *Generations, 28*(2), 5–10.

Kastenbaum, R. (Ed.). (2003a). *Psychology* (Vol. 1). New York: Macmillan Reference.

Kastenbaum, R. (Ed.). (2003b). *The good death* (Vol. 2). New York: Macmillan Reference.

Kastenbaum, R., & Costa, P. T., Jr. (1977). Psychological perspectives on death. In M. R. Rosenzweig & L. W. Porter (Eds.), *Annual review of psychology* (Vol. 28). Palo Alto, CA: Annual Reviews, Inc.

Katz, P. A. (2003, November). Racists or tolerant multiculturalists? How do they begin? *American Psychologist, 58,* 897–909.

Kaufman, H. G. (1982). *Professionals in search of work: Coping with the stress of job loss and underemployment.* New York: Wiley.

Kaufman, J., & Zigler, E. (1993). The intergenerational transmission of abuse is overstated. In R. J. Gelles and D. R. Loseke (Eds.), *Current controversies on family violence.* Newbury Park, CA: Sage.

Kausler, D. H., & Hakami, M. K. (1983). Memory for topics of conversation: Adult age differences and intentionality. *Experimental Aging Research, 9,* 153–157.

Kausler, D. H., Wiley, J. G., & Lieberwitz, K. J. (1992). Adult age differences in short-term memory and subsequent long-term memory for actions. *Psychology and Aging, 7,* 309–316.

Kazdin, A. (1993). Treatment of conduct disorder: Progress and directions in psychotherapy research. *Development and Psychotherapy, 5,* 277–310.

Kazdin, A. E. (Ed.). (2000). *Encyclopedia of psychology* (Vol. 4). Oxford, UK: Oxford University Press.

Keefer, C. H., Tronick, E., Dixon, S., & Brazelton, T. B. (1982). Special differences in motor performance between Gusii and American newborns and a modification of the neonatal behavioral assessment scale. *Child Development, 53,* 754–759.

Keel, P. K., Mitchell, S. E., Miller, K. B., Davis, T. L., & Crow, S. J. (1999). Long-term outcome of bulimic nervosa. *Archives of General Psychiatry, 56,* 63.

Kegan, R. (1988). *In over our head.* Boston: Harvard University Press.

Keller, B. (2001). Schools seen as out of sync with teens. *Education Week, 20*(33), 17–18.

Keller, H. (2003, September-October). Socialization for competence: Cultural models of infancy. *Human Development, 46,* 288–311.

Keller, M. B., Ryan, N. D., Strober, M., Klein, R. G., Kutcher, S. P., Birmaher, B., Hagino, O. R., Koplewicz, H., Carlson, G. A., et al. (2001). Efficacy of paroxetine in the treatment of adolescent major depression: A randomized controlled trial. *Journal of the American Academy of Child and Adolescent Psychiatry, 40*(7), 762–772.

Kelly, G. A. (1955). *The psychology of personal constructs.* New York: Norton.

Kelly, J. (2004, October 1). The wrong path: Mourning Christopher Reeves. *The National Review.* Retrieved November 20, 2004, from http://www.nationalreview.com/comment/kelly200410210859.asp

Kelly, K. (2001). Looking for meaning in the ruins. *U.S. News & World Report, 131*(14), 52.

Kelsey, J. L., Gammon, M. D., & John, E. M. (1993). Reproductive factors and breast cancer. *Epidemiologic Reviews, 15,* 36–47.

Kendall-Tackett, K. A., Williams, L. M., & Finkelhor, D. (1993). Impact of sexual abuse on children: A review and synthesis of recent empirical studies. *Psychological Bulletin, 113*(1), 164–180.

Kendrick, C., & Dunn, J. (1980). Caring for a second baby: Effects on interaction between mother and firstborn. *Developmental Psychology, 16,* 303–311.

Kennedy, G. J., Haque, M., & Zarankow, B. (1997). Human Sexuality in Late Life. *International Journal of Mental Health, 26,* 35–46.

Kennet, J., McGuire, L., Willis, S. L., & Schaie, K. W. (2000). Memorability functions in verbal memory: A longitudinal approach. *Experimental Aging Research, 26*(2), 121–137.

Kerig, P. K., Cowan, P. A., & Cowan, C. P. (1993). Marital quality and gender differences in parent-child interaction. *Developmental Psychology, 29,* 931–939.

Kessenich, C. R., & Cichon, M. J. (2001). Hormonal decline in elderly men and male menopause. *Geriatric Nursing, 22,* 24–27.

Kieny, M.P., Excler, J., & Girard, M. (November, 2004). Research and development of new vaccines against infectious diseases. *American Journal of Public Health 94*(11), 1931–1935.

Kilborn, P. T. (1993, March 15). New jobs lack the old security in time of "disposable workers." *New York Times,* A1, A6.

Kilbride, H. W., Thorstad, K., & Daily, D. (2004, April). Preschool outcome of less than 801-gram preterm infants compared with full-term siblings. *Pediatrics, 113,* 742–747.

Kileny, P. R., Zwolan, T. A., & Ashbaugh, C. (2001). The influence of age at implantation on performance with a cochlear implant in children. *Otology and Neurotology, 22,* 42–46.

Kilpatrick, M., Ohannessian, C., & Bartholomew, J. B. (1999). Adolescent weight management and perceptions: An analysis of the National Longitudinal Study of Adolescent Health. *Journal of School Health, 69*(4), 148–152.

Kim, J. E., Hetherington, E. M., & Reiss, D. (1999). Associations among family relationships, antisocial peers, and adolescents' externalizing behaviors: Gender and family type differences. *Child Development, 70,* 1209–1230.

Kim, J., & Moen, P. (2000). Late midlife work status and transitions. In M. Lachman (Ed.), *Handbook of midlife development.* New York: John Wiley & Sons.

Kimble, G. A. (1984). Psychology's two cultures. *American Psychologist, 39,* 833–839.

Kimmel, D. C. (1980). *Adulthood and aging: An interdisciplinary, developmental view* (2nd ed.). New York: Wiley.

Kincheloe, J. L., & Steinberg, S. R. (1993). A tentative description of post-formal thinking: The critical confrontation with cognitive theory. *Harvard Educational Review, 63,* 296–320.

Kindlundh, A. M. S., Hagekull, B., Isacson, D. G. L., & Nyberg, F. (2001). Adolescent use of anabolic-androgenic steroids and relations to self reports of social, personality and health aspects. *European Journal of Public Health, 11,* 322–328.

King, H. E., & Webb, C. (1981). Rape crisis centers. *Journal of Social Issues, 37,* 93–104.

King, M. A., Sims, A., & Osher, D. (2001). *How is cultural competence integrated in education?* Center for Effective Collaboration and Practice. Washington, DC. Retrieved November 29, 2001, from http://www.air.org/cecp/cultural/Q_integrated.htm#top

King, R. (2005, April 13). More teens say smoking is a drag, survey says. *The Indianapolis Star.* Retrieved April 13, 2005, from http://www.indystar.com

King, S. M. (2004, August). Evaluation and treatment of the human immunodeficiency Virus-1–exposed infant. *Pediatrics, 114,* 497–506.

Kinsey, A. C., Pomeroy, W. B., & Martin, C. E. (1948). *Sexual behavior in the human male.* Philadelphia: Saunders.

Kinsey, A. C., Pomeroy, W. B., Martin, C. E., & Gebhard, P. H. (1953). *Sexual behavior in the human female.* Philadelphia: Saunders.

Kinsman, S. B., Romer, D., Furstenberg, F. F., & Schwarz, D. F. (1998). Early sexual

initiation: The role of peer norms. *Pediatrics, 102,* 1185–1192.

Kipnis, D. (1994). Accounting for the use of behavior technologies in social psychology. *American Psychologist, 49,* 165–172.

Kirby, D. (2004). Party favors: Pill popping as insurance. *New York Times,* F1.

Kirn, W., & Ressner, J. (2004, July 26). Poker's new face: Hot game in town. *Time, 164*(4), 30.

Kirp, D. L. (2004, November 21). Life way after Head Start. *New York Times Magazine.* Retrieved February 5, 2005, from http://www.nytimes.com/2004/11/21/magazine/21IDEA.html

Kirton, C. (Ed.). (2003). *ANAC's core curriculum for HIV/AIDS nursing* (2nd ed.). Thousand Oaks: Sage.

Kisilevsky, B. S. (1995). The influence stimulus and subject variables on human fetal responses to sound and vibration. In J. P. Lecanuet et al. (Eds.), *Fetal development.* Hillsdale, NJ: Erlbaum.

Kisilevsky, B. S., Hains, S. M. J., Jacquet, A. Y., Granier-Deferre, C., & Lecanuet, J. P. (2004). Maturation of fetal responses to music. *Developmental Science, 7*(5), 550–559.

Kisilevsky, B. S., Hains, S. M. J., Lee, K., Zie, X., Huang, H., Ye, H. H., Zhang, K., & Wang, Z. (2003, May). Effects of experience on fetal voice recognition. *Psychological Science, 14*(1), 220–224.

Kitchener, K. S., Lynch, C. L., Fischer, K. W., & Wood, P. K. (1993). Developmental range of reflective judgment: The effect of contextual support and practice on developmental stage. *Developmental Psychology, 29,* 893–906.

Kitzinger, C., & Wilkinson, S. (1995). Transitions from heterosexuality to lesbianism: The discursive production of lesbian identities. *Developmental Psychology, 31,* 95–104.

Klaus, M. H., & Kennell, J. H. (1976). *Maternal-infant bonding: The impact of early separation or loss on family development.* St. Louis: Mosby.

Klaus, M. H., & Klaus, P. H. (1998). *Your amazing newborn.* Cambridge, MA: Perseus.

Kleinman, R.E. (2004). *Pediatric nutrition handbook.* (5th ed.) Elk Grove Village, IL: American Academy of Pediatrics.

Klinger-Vartabedian, L., & Wispe, L. (1989). Age differences in marriage and female longevity. *Journal of Marriage and the Family, 51,* 195–202.

Kluckhohn, C. (1960). *Mirror for man.* Greenwich, CT: Fawcett.

Knefelkamp, L. L. (1984). *A workbook for the practice-to-theory-to-practice model.* Unpublished manuscript. University of Maryland, College Park.

Knickerbocker, B. (2005, April 7). Ripples spread as states vote on same-sex marriage. *The Christian Science Monitor.* Retrieved April 9, 2005, from http://www.christian-science.monitor.com/2005/

Knight, J. (2004, July 22). Stem-cell specialists split over proposal for a U.S. repository. *Nature, 430,* 389.

Knox, D., Schacht, C., & Zusman, M. E. (1999). Love relationships among college students. *College Student Journal, 33*(1), 149–152.

Kobasa, S. C., Maddi, S. R., & Kahn, S. (1982). Hardiness and health: A prospective study. *Journal of Personality and Social Psychology, 42,* 168–177.

Kobau, R., Safran, M. A., Zack, M. M., Moriarty, D. G., & Chapman, D. (2004). Sad, blue, or depressed days, health behaviors and health-related quality of life, behavioral risk factor surveillance system, 1995–2000. *Health and Quality of Life Outcomes, 2*(40).

Kobre, K. (1998a). *Crack babies in infancy* (Part 1). The Gannett Foundation and San Francisco State University. Retrieved July 29, 1998, from http://www.gigaplex.com/ photo/kobre/ crack/crack1/htm.

Kobre, K. (1998b). *Crack babies in infancy* (Part 2). The Gannett Foundation and San Francisco State University. Retrieved July 29, 1998, from http://www.gigaplex.com/ photo/kobre/ crack/crack2/htm.

Kobre, K. (1998c). *Crack's next generation: How the children of crack addicts grow up.* The Gannett Foundation and San Francisco State University. Retrieved July 29, 1998, from http://www.gigaplex.com/photo/ kobre/ crack/crack1/htm.

Koch, K. (1998, July 10). Encouraging teen abstinence. *CQ Researcher, 8,* 577–600.

Kochanek, K. D., Murphy, S. L., Anderson, R. N., & Scott, C. (2004, October 12). Deaths: Final data for 2002. *National Vital Statistics Reports, 53*(5), 1–116. Retrieved March 22, 2005, from http:// www.cdc.gov/nchs/data/nvsr/nvsr53/ nvsr53_05.pdf

Kochanska, G. (1995). Children's temperament, mothers' discipline, and security of attachment: Multiple pathways to emerging internalization. *Child Development, 66,* 597–615.

Kochanska, G. (2001). Emotional development in children with different attachment histories: The first three years. *Child Development, 72,* 474–490.

Kochanska, G., & Aksan, N. (1995). Mother-child mutually positive affect, the quality of child compliance to requests and prohibitions, and maternal control as correlates of early internalization. *Child Development, 66,* 236–254.

Koerner. B. I. (1997). Is there life after death? *U.S. News & World Report, 122,* 58–64.

Koestner, R., Franz, C., & Weinberger, J. (1990). The family origins of empathic concern: A 26-year longitudinal study. *Journal of Personality and Social Psychology, 58,* 709–717.

Kohlberg, L. (1963). The development of children's orientations toward a moral order. I: Sequence in the development of human thought. *Vita Humana, 6,* 11–33.

Kohlberg, L. (1966). A cognitive-developmental analysis of children's sex-role concepts and attitudes. In E. E. Maccoby (Ed.), *The development of sex differences.* Stanford, CA: Stanford University Press.

Kohlberg, L., & Colby, A. (1990). *Measurement of moral judgment.* New York: Cambridge University Press.

Kohlberg, L., & Gilligan, C. F. (1971). The adolescent as philosopher: The discovery of the self in a postconventional world. *Daedalus, 100,* 1051–1086.

Kohlberg, L., & Ullian, D. Z. (1974). Stages in the development of psychosexual concepts and attitudes. In R. C. Friedman, R. N. Richart & R. L. Vande Wiele (Eds.), *Sex differences in behavior.* New York: Wiley.

Kohn, M. L., Naoi, A., Schoenbach, C., Schooler, C., & Slomczynski, K. M. (1990). Position in the class structure and psychological functioning in the United States, Japan, and Poland. *American Journal of Sociology, 95,* 964–1008.

Kohut, A., & Doherty, C. (2004, February 27). *Gay marriage a voting issue, but mostly for opponents constitutional amendment rates as low priority.* Washington, DC: The Pew Research Center for the People and the Press. Retrieved April 9, 2005, from http://people-press.org/reports/display. php3?ReportID=204

Kolata, G. (1991, September 30). Parents of tiny infants find care choices are not theirs. *New York Times,* A1, A11.

Kolata, G. (1992a, October 30). Baby's growth rate not fast enough? Just wait. *New York Times,* A8.

Kolata, G. (1993, May 3). Family aid to elderly is very strong, study shows. *New York Times,* A16 L.

Kolata, G. (1994a, February 25). Theory on aging is tested, adding 30% to flies' lives. *New York Times,* A8.

Kolata, G. (1994b, July 27). Wrong drugs are given to 1 in 4 of elderly. *New York Times,* B7.

Kolata, G. (1995a, February 28). Man's world, woman's world? Brain studies point to differences. *New York Times,* B5, B8.

Kolata, G. (1995b, February 16). Men and women use brain differently, study discovers. *New York Times,* A1, A8.

Kolata, G. (1997a, April 24). A record and big questions as woman gives birth at 63. *New York Times,* A1.

Kolata, G. (1997b, April 27). Childbirth at 63 says what about life? *New York Times,* A1.

Kolata, G. (2000, October 18). No days off are allowed, experts argue. *New York Times, 150*(51545), A1.

Kolbert, E. (1991, October 11). Sexual harassment at work is pervasive, survey suggests. *New York Times,* A11, A18.

Kolbert, E. (1994, December 14). Television gets closer look as a factor in real violence. *New York Times,* A1, A13.

Koonin, L. M., Strauss, L. T., Chrisman, C. E., & Parker, W. Y. (2000, December 8). *Abortion surveillance: United States, 1997.* National Center for Chronic Disease Prevention and Health Promotion, Centers for Disease Control.

Korner, A. F., Brown, B. W., Jr., Reade, E. P., Stevenson, D. K., Fernbach, S. A., & Thom, V. A. (1988). State behavior of preterm infants as a function of development, individual and sex differences. *Infant Behavior and Development, 11,* 111–124.

Koss-Feder, L. (2003, March 17). Providing for parents: The "sandwich generation" looks for new solutions. *Time, 161*(11), G8.

Koucheravy, E. R. (2004, September 4). Human being, or source of spare parts? *Washington Post,* A30. Retrieved November 20, 2004, from Washingtonpost.com

Kozberg, L. (2001, December 12). *House-Senate Conference Report: No Child Left Behind.* U.S. Department of Education. Retrieved December 16, 2001, from http://www.ed.gov/PressReleases/12-2001/12112001b.html

Kozer, E., & Koren, G. (2001, February). *Effects of prenatal exposure to marijuana.* Motherisk.Org. Retrieved January 5, 2005, from http://motherisk.org

Krach, C. A., & Velkoff, V. A. (1999, July). U. S. Census Bureau. Centenarians in the United States, *Current Population Reports,* P23–199RV. Washington, DC: U.S. Government Printing Office.

Krampe, R. T. (1994). *Maintaining excellence: Cognitive-motor performance in pianists differing in age and skill level.* Berlin, Germany: Edition Sigma.

Krashen, S. D. (1996). *Under attack: The case against bilingual education.* Culver City, CA: Language Education Associates.

Krause, N. (2005, March). God-mediated control and psychological well-being in late life. *Research on Aging, 27*(2), 136–165.

Krause, N., & Goldenhar, L. M. (1992). Acculturation and psychological distress in three groups of elderly Hispanics. *Journal of Gerontology: Social Sciences, 47,* S279–S288.

Krauskopf, L. (2004, February 22). Women continue to get pregnant while taking drug that causes birth defects. Hackensack, NJ: *The Record.*

Kreider, R. M. (2003, October). *Adopted children and stepchildren: 2000.* Washington, DC: U.S. Bureau of the Census. Retrieved April 14, 2005, from http://www.census. gov/prod/2003pubs/censr-6.pdf

Krist, A. H. (2001, January 1). Obstetric care in patients with HIV disease. *American Family Physician, 63,* 107–116, 121–122.

Kronholz, J. (2001, December 18). Dropout rate? Getting one depends on whom is asked. *Wall Street Journal, 238*(119), A18.

Kroska, A. (2004). Divisions of domestic work: Revising and expanding the theoretical explanations. *Journal of Family Issues, 25*, 900–932.

Krueger, J. (1992). On the overestimation of between-group differences. *European Review of Social Psychology, 3*, 31–56.

Kubler-Ross, E. (1969). *On death and dying: What the dying have to teach doctors nurses, clergy and their own families.* New York: Macmillan.

Kübler-Ross, E. (1981). *Living with dying.* New York: Macmillan.

Kübler-Ross, E. (1993). *On death and dying.* New York: Collier.

Kuczynski, A. (1998, April 12). Anti-aging potion or poison? *New York Times, 9,* 1.

Kuczynski, L., & Kochanska, G. (1995). Function and content of maternal demands: Developmental significance of early demands for competent action. *Child Development, 66,* 616–628.

Kuhl, P. K., Williams, K. A., Lacerda, F., Stevens, K. N., & Lindblom, B. (1992). Linguistic experience alters phonetic perception in infants by 6 months of age. *Science, 255,* 606–608.

Kumar, V., & Suryanarayna. (1989). Problems of the aged in the rural sector. In R. N. Pati & B. Jena (Eds.), *Aged in India: Socio-demographic dimensions.* New Delhi: Ashish.

Kunz, J. A. (1991). Reminiscence approaches utilized in counseling older adults. *Illness, Crises and Loss, 4*(1), 48–53.

Kurdek, L. A. (1991). The relations between reported well-being and divorce history, availability of a proximate adult, and gender. *Journal of Marriage and the Family, 53,* 71–78.

Kurdek, L. A. (1994a). Areas of conflict for gay, lesbian, and heterosexual couples: What couples argue about influences relationship satisfaction. *Journal of Marriage and the Family, 56,* 923–934.

Kurdek, L. A. (1994b). Remarriages and stepfamilies are not inherently problematic. In A. Booth & J. Dunn (Eds.), *Stepfamilies: Who benefits? Who does not?* Hillsdale, NJ: Erlbaum.

Kurdek, L. A. (1998). Relationship outcomes and their predictors: Longitudinal evidence from heterosexual married, gay cohabiting, and lesbian cohabiting couples. *Journal of Marriage and the Family, 60,* 553–568.

Kurdek, L. A. (2004, November). Are gay and lesbian cohabiting couples really different from heterosexual married couples? *Journal of Marriage and the Family, 66,* 880–901.

Kurstjens, S., & Wolke, D. (2001). Effects of maternal depression on cognitive development of children over the first 7 years of life. *Journal of Child Psychology and Psychiatry, 42,* 623–636

Kurtz, P. F, Chin, M. D., Huete, J. M., Tarbox, R. S. F., O'Connor, J. T., Paclawskyj, T. R, & Rush, K. S. (2003). Functional analysis and treatment of self-injurious behavior in young children: A summary

of 30 cases. *Journal of Applied Behavior Analysis, 36,* 205–219.

Kutner, L. (1990, February 8). It isn't unusual when the father-to-be wakes up feeling sick. *New York Times,* B8.

Kutner, L. (1993, September 16). Being clumsy. *New York Times,* B4.

Kyle, J., McEntee, L., & Ackerman, J. (1998). *Deaf children developing sign: A guide for parents and teachers.* Bristol, UK: Centre for Deaf Studies.

Labouvie-Vief, G. (1986). Modes of knowledge and the organization of development. In M. L. Commons, L. Kohlberg, F. A. Richards, & J. Sinnot (Eds.), *Models and methods in the study of adult and adolescent thought. Vol. 3: Beyond formal operations.* New York: Praeger.

Labouvie-Vief, G., DeVoe, M., & Bulka, D. (1989). Speaking about feelings: Conceptions of emotion across the life span. *Psychology and Aging, 4,* 425–437.

Lachman, M. E. (2004). Development in midlife. *Annual Review of Psychology, 55,* 305–332.

Lachman, M. E., & James, J. B. (1997). Charting the course of midlife development: An overview. In M. E. Lachman & J. B. James (Eds.), *Multiple paths of midlife development* (pp. 1–17). Chicago: University of Chicago Press.

Lachs, M. S., & Pillemer, K. (2004). Elder abuse. *Lancet, 364*(9441), 1263–1272.

Lachs, M. S., Williams, C. S., O'Brien, S., Hurst, L., Horwitz, L. (1997). Risk factors for reported elder abuse and neglect: A nine-year observational cohort study. *Gerontologist, 37,* 469–474.

Lachs, M. S., Williams, C. S., O'Brien, S., Pillemer, K. A., & Charlson, M. E. (1998). The mortality of elder mistreatment. *Journal of the American Medical Association, 280,* 428–432.

Laderman, G. M. (2003). Funeral industry. In R. Kastenbaum (Ed.), *Macmillan Encyclopedia of Death and Dying* (Vol. 1).

Lagattuta, K., Wellman, H., & Flavell, J. (1997). Preschoolers' understanding of the link between thinking and feeling. *Child Development, 68,* 1081–1104.

Lagercrantz, H., & Slotkin, T. A. (1986, April). The "stress" of being born. *Scientific American, 254,* 100–107.

LaGreca, A. M., & Wasserstein, S. (1995). What do children worry about? Worries and their relation to anxiety. *Child Development, 66,* 671–686.

Lai, C. S. L., Fisher, S. E., Hurst, J. A., Vargha-Khadem, F., & Monaco, A. P. (2001). A forkhead-domain gene is mutated in a severe speech and language disorder. *Nature, 413,* 519–523.

Lamaze, F. (1958). *Painless childbirth: Psychoprophylactic method.* London: Burke.

Lamb, M. E. (1977). Father-infant and mother-infant interaction in the first year of life. *Child Development, 48,* 167–181.

Lamb, M. E., & Bornstein, M. H. (1987). *Development in infancy: An introduction* (2nd ed.). New York: Random House.

Lamb, M.E. (Ed.). (1997). *The role of the father in child development* (3rd ed.). New York, NY: Wiley.

Lamberg, L. (1999, July 21). Safety of antidepressant use in pregnant and nursing women. *Journal of the American Medical Association, 282*(3), 222–224.

Lamborn, S. D., Dornbusch, S. M., & Steinberg, L. (1996). Ethnicity and community context as moderators of the relations between family decision making and adolescent adjustment. *Child Development, 67,* 283–301.

Lambrew, J. (2001). *Diagnosing disparities in health insurance for women: A prescription for change.* The Commonwealth Fund. Retrieved January 15, 2002, from http://www.cmwf.org/programs/ insurance/lambrew_women_493.pdf

Lampl, M., Cameron, N., Veldhuis, J. D. & Johnson, M. L. (1995). Patterns of human growth. *Science, 268,* 445–447.

Landrigan, P. J. (1997). Illness in Gulf War veterans: Causes and consequences. *Journal of the American Medical Association, 277,* 259–261.

Lang, F. R., & Heckhausen, J. (2001). Perceived control over development and subjective well-being: Differential benefits across adulthood. *Journal of Personality and Social Psychology, 81*(3), 509–523.

Lang, S. S., & Patt, R. B. (1994). *You don't have to suffer: A complete guide to relieving cancer pain for patients and their families.* New York: Oxford University Press.

Langer, E. J., & Rodin, J. (1976). The effects of choice and enhanced personal responsibility for the aged: A field experiment in an institutional setting. *Journal of Personality and Social Psychology, 34,* 191–198.

Langmeier, J., & Matejcĕk, Z. (1974). *Psychological deprivation in childhood.* New York: Halsted Press.

Langway, L. (1982, November 1). Growing old, feeling young. *Newsweek,* 56–65.

Lansford, J. E., Ceballo, R., Abbey, A., & Stewart, A. J. (2001). Does family structure matter? A comparison of adoptive, two-parent biological, single-mother, stepfather, and stepmother households. *Journal of Marriage and Family, 63,* 840–841.

Larson, J. H., Wilson, S. M., & Beley, R. (1994). The impact of job insecurity on marital and family relationships. *Family Relations, 43,* 138–143.

Larson, R. W. (2000). Toward a psychology of positive youth development. *American Psychologist, 55,* 170–183.

Larson, R. W. (2001). How U.S. children and adolescents spent time: What it does (and doesn't) tell us about their development. *Current Directions in Psychological Science, 10*(5), 16–164.

Larson, R. W., & Verma, S. (1999). How children and adolescents spend time across the world: Work, play, and developmental opportunities. *Psychological Bulletin, 125*(6), 701–736.

Larson, R. W., Richards, M. H., Sims, B., & Dworkin, J. (2001). How urban African American young adolescents spend their time: Time budgets for locations, activities, and companionship. *American Journal of Community Psychology, 29*(4), 565–597.

Larzelere, R. E. (2001). Combining love and limits in authoritative parenting. In J. D. Westman (Ed.), *Parenthood in America* (pp. 81–89). Madison, WI: University of Wisconsin Press.

Lashbrook, J. T. (2000). Fitting in: Exploring the emotional dimension of adolescent peer pressure. *Adolescence, 35*(140), 747–757.

Lasky, R. E., Klein, R. E., Yarbrough, C., Engle, P. L., Lechtig, A., & Martorell, R. (1981). The relationship between physical growth and infant behavior development in rural Guatemala. *Child Development, 52,* 219–226.

Laslett, B. (1973). The family as a public and private institution: An historical perspective. *Journal of Marriage and the Family, 35,* 480–492.

Lau, R. R., Quadrel, M. J., & Hartman, K. A. (1990). Development and change of young adults' preventive health beliefs and behavior: Influence from parents and peers. *Journal of Health and Social Behavior, 31,* 240–259.

Lauenborg, J., Mathiesen, E., Ovesen, P., Westergaard, J. G., Ekbom, P., Molsted-Pedersen, L., & Damm, P. (2003, May). Audit on stillbirths in women with pregestational type 1 diabetes: Epidemiology/health services/ psychosocial research. *Diabetes Care, 26*(5), 1385–1390.

Lauer, J. C., & Lauer, R. H. (1985, June). Marriages made to last. *Psychology Today, 19,* 22–26.

Laumann, E. O., Gagnon, J. H., Michael, R. T., & Michaels, S. (1994). *The social organization of sexuality: Sexual practices in the United States.* Chicago: University of Chicago Press.

Lavoie, J. C., & Looft, W. R. (1973). Parental antecedents of resistance-to-temptation behavior in adolescent males. *Merrill-Palmer Quarterly, 19,* 107–116.

Laws, E. R., & Bertram, E. H. (1996, November). Epilepsy surgery in children and adolescents. *Neurosurgical Focus.* Retrieved December 12, 2001, from http://www.neurosurgery.org/focus/nov96/1-5-1.html

Layden, T. (2004, November 15). Get out and play! *Sports Illustrated, 101*(19), 80–93.

Leach, P. (1998). *Your baby and child from birth to age five.* New York: Knopf.

Lead poisoning. (2005). California Poison Control System. Retrieved February 23, 2005, from http://www.calpoison.org/public/lead.html

Learning disabilities roundtable. (2005, February). *Comments and recommendations on regulatory issues under the Individuals with Disabilities Education Improvement Act of 2004: Public Law 108–446.* 1–21. Retrieved March 25, 2005, from http://www.cec.sped.org/pdfs/APPENDIX2004LDRoundtableRecs.pdf

Learning to see the inevitable signs of aging eyes. (1998). Better Vision Institute. Retrieved from http://www.visionsite.org/press/ageeyes.htm

Leboyer, F. (1975). *Birth without violence.* New York: Knopf.

Lecanuet, J. P., Granier-Deferre, C., & Busnel, M. C. (1995). Human fetal auditory perception. In: J. P. Lecanuet et al. (Eds.), *Fetal development.* Hillsdale, NJ: Erlbaum.

LeCanuet, J. P., Graniere-Deferre, C., Jacquet, A. Y., & DeCasper, A. J. (2000, January) Fetal discrimination of low-pitched musical notes, *Developmental Psychobiology, 36*(1), 29–39.

Lecca, P. J., Quervalu, I., Nunes, J. V., & Gonzales, H. F. (Eds). (1998). *Cultural competency in health, social, and human services: Directions for the twenty-first century.* New York: Garland.

Lee, K., & Chen, L. (1996, September). The development of metacognitive knowledge of basic motor skill: Walking. *Journal of Genetic Psychology,* 361–365.

Lehr, R., & MacMillan, P. (2001). The psychological and emotional impact of divorce. The noncustodial father's perspective. *Families in Society, 82*(4), 373–383.

Leleszi, J. P., & Lewandowski, J. G. (2005, March). Pain management in end-of-life care. *Journal of the American Osteopathic Association, 105*(3), S6–S11.

Leman, H. C. (1953). *Age and achievement.* Princeton, NJ: Princeton University Press.

Leman, K. (2004). *The birth order book: Why you are the way you are.* Grand Rapids, MI: Baker.

Lemonick, M. D. (1997, December 1). The new revolution in making babies. *Time, 150,* 40–46.

Lemonick, M. D. (2000). Teens before their time. *Time, 156*(18), 66–70, 73–74.

Lenneberg, E. H. (1967). *Biological foundations of language.* New York: Wiley.

Lenneberg, E. H. (1969). On explaining language. *Science, 164,* 635–643.

Lennon, M. C. (1982). The psychological consequences of menopause. The importance of timing of a life stage event. *Journal of Health and Social Behavior, 23,* 353–366.

Leo, J. (1999). Gender wars redux. *U.S. News & World Report, 126*(7), 24.

Lepper, M. R., & Greene, D. (1975). Turning play into work: Effects of adult surveillance and extrinsic rewards on children's intrinsic motivation. *Journal of Personality and Social Psychology, 31,* 479–486.

Lerman, R. I. (2002). *Marriage and the economic well-being of families with children:*

A review of the literature. Washington, DC: Urban Institute.

Lerner, R. M., Castellino, D. R., Terry, P. A., Villarruel, F. A., & McKinney, M. H. (1995). A developmental contextual perspective on parenting. In M. H. Bornstein (Ed.), *Handbook of parenting* (Vol. 2). Hillsdale, NJ: Erlbaum.

Lester, B. (1997). Database of studies on prenatal cocaine exposure and child outcome. *Journal of Drug Issues, 27,* 487–499.

Lester, B. M., Kotelchuck, M., Spelke, E., Sellers, M. J., & Klein, R. E. (1974). Separation protest in Guatemalan infants: Cross-cultural and cognitive findings. *Developmental Psychology, 10,* 79–85.

Leventhal, T., & Brooks-Gunn, J. (2004, July). A randomized study of neighborhood effects on low-income children's education outcomes. *Developmental Psychology, 40,* 488–507.

Levin, I., & Druyan, S. (1993). When sociocognitive transaction among peers fails: The case of misconceptions in science. *Child Development, 64,* 157.

Levin, J. S. (1996). How religion influences morbidity and health: Reflections on natural history, salutogenesis and host resistance. *Social Science Medicine, 43*(5), 849–864.

Levine, L. J. (1995). Young children's understanding of the causes of anger and sadness. *Child Development, 66,* 697–709.

Levine, M. P. (2000). Mass media and body image: A brief review of the research. *Healthy Weight Journal, 14*(6).

Levine, R. (2004). *Aging with attitude: Growing older with dignity and vitality.* Westport, CT: Praeger.

Levine, S. (1998). *Sexuality in mid-life.* New York: Plenum Press.

Levinson, D. J. (1986). A conception of adult development. *American Psychologist, 41,* 3–13.

Levinson, D. J. (1996). *The seasons of a woman's life.* New York: Knopf.

Levinson, D. J., Darrow, C. M., Klein, E. B., Levinson, M. H., & McKee, B. (1978). *The seasons of a man's life.* New York: Knopf.

Levinson, H. (1964, March 9). Money aside, why spend life working? *National Observer, 20.*

Levy, D. S. (1999). Your family. *Time, 153*(22), 86.

Levy-Shiff, R. (1994). Individual and contextual correlates of marital change across the transition to parenthood. *Developmental Psychology, 30,* 591–601.

Lewin, R. (1981). Is longevity a positive selection? *Science, 211,* 373.

Lewin, T. (1995, May 11). Study says more women earn half their household income. *New York Times,* A13.

LeWine, H. (2005). Another culprit to watch. *Newsweek, 145*(3), 48.

Lewis, C. C. (1988). Cooperation and control in Japanese nursery schools. In G. Handel (Ed.), *Childhood socialization* (pp. 125–142). New York: Aldine de Gruyter.

Lewis, C., & Lamb, M. E. (2003, June). Fathers' influence on children's development: The evidence from two-parent families. *European Journal of Psychology of Education, 18*(2), 212–230. Retrieved January 25, 2005, from EBSCO*host.*

Lewis, J. S. (1985, April 3). Fathers-to-be show signs of pregnancy. *New York Times,* 13.

Lewis, M. (1995). Developmental change in infants' responses to stress. *Child Development, 66,* 657–670.

Lewis, M. (1998). The development and structure of emotions. In M. Mascolo (Ed.), *What develops in emotional development? Emotions, personality, and psychotherapy.* New York: Plenum Press.

Lewis, M. D. (1993). Early socioemotional predictors of cognitive competency at 4 years. *Developmental Psychology, 29,* 1036–1045.

Lewis, M. M. (1936/1951). *Infant speech: A study of the beginnings of language.* London: Routledge & Kegan Paul.

Lewis, M., & Starr, M. D. (1979). Developmental continuity. In J. D. Osofsky (Ed.), *Handbook of infant development.* New York: Wiley.

Lewis, M., Young, G., Brooks, J., & Michalson, L. (1975). The beginning of friendship. In M. Lewis & L. A. Rosenblum (Eds.), *Friendship and peer relations.* New York: Wiley.

Li, C. (2000). Instruction effect and developmental levels: A study on water-level task with Chinese children ages 9–17. *Contemporary Educational Psychology, 25*(4), 488–498.

Li, D. K., Daling, J. R., Mueller, B. A., Hickok, D. E., Fantel, A. G., & Weiss, N. S. (1995). Oral contraceptive use after conception in relation to the risk of congenital urinary tract anomalies. *Teratology, 51*(1), 30–36.

Li, R., Zhao, Z., Mokdad, A., Barker, L., & Grummer-Strawn, L. (2003). Prevalence of breastfeeding in the United States: The 2001 national immunization survey. *Pediatrics, 111,* 1198–1201.

Lickona, T. (1976). Research on Piaget's theory of moral development. In T. Lickona (Ed.), *Moral development and behavior theory, research, and social issues.* New York: Holt, Rinehart & Winston.

Lieberman, M. A., & Coplan, A. S. (1970). Distance from death as a variable in the study of aging. *Developmental Psychology, 2,* 71–84

Lieberson, S. (1992). Einstein, Renoir, and Greeley: Some thoughts above evidence in sociology. *American Sociological Review, 57,* 1–15.

Liebow, E. (1967). *Tally's corner: A study of negro streetcorner men.* Boston: Little, Brown.

Liebowitz, M. R. (1983). *The chemistry of love.* Boston: Little, Brown.

Lifton, B. J. (1994). *Journey of the adopted self: A quest for wholeness.* New York: Basic Books.

Lillo-Martin, D. (1997). In support of the language acquisition device. In M. Marschark and P. Siple (Eds.), *Relations of language and thought: The view from sign language and deaf children.* New York: Oxford University Press.

Limber, S. P. (2002). *Bullying among children and youth.* Proceedings of the educational forum on adolescent health: Youth bullying. Chicago, IL: American Medical Association.

Linebarger, D. L., & Walker, D. (2005, January). Infants and toddlers' television viewing and language outcomes. *American Behavioral Scientist, 48*(5), 624–645.

Linnell, Z. M. (2002). Thinking about thinking about 'thinking about thinking'. *Psychoanalytic Study of the Child, 57,* 93–117.

Lingren, H. G. (1996). *The sandwich generation: A cluttered nest.* NebGuide, Cooperative Extension, University of Nebraska–Lincoln. Retrieved November 5, 1998, from http://www.ianr.unl.pubs/family/ g1117.htm

Link between neurodevelopmental disorders and thimerosal remains unclear. (2001). National Academies of Science. Message posted to news@nas.edu electronic mailing list, archived at http://www4.nationalacademiew.org/news.nsf

Link, B. G., Lennon, M. C., & Dohrenwend, B. P. (1993). Socioeconomic status and depression: The role of occupations involving direction, control, and planning. *American Journal of Sociology, 98,* 1351–1387.

Linn, M. C., Lewis, C., Tsuchida, I., & Songer, N. B. (2000). Beyond fourth grade science: Why do U.S. and Japanese students diverge? *Educational Researcher, 29*(3), 4–14.

Lipset, S. M. (1989, May 24). Why youth revolt. *New York Times,* 27.

Liu, X., Liu, L., Owens, J. A., & Kaplan, D. L. (2005, January). Sleep patterns and sleep problems among schoolchildren in the United States and China. *Pediatrics, 115,* 241–249.

Livesley, W. J., & Bromley, D. B. (1973). *Person perception in childhood and adolescence.* New York: Wiley.

Livingston, A., & Wirt, J. (Eds.). (2004, June 1). *The condition of education 2004 in brief.* National Center for Education Statistics, U.S. Department of Education and Institute of Education Sciences NCES 2004-076.

Livingston, M. M., Burley, K., & Springer, T. P. (1996). The importance of being feminine: Gender, sex role, occupational and marital role commitment, and their relationship to anticipated work-family conflict. *Journal of Social Behavior and Personality, 11,* 179–192.

Lobel, T. E., & Menashri, J. (1993). Relations of conceptions of gender-role transgressions and gender constancy to gender-typed toy preferences. *Developmental Psychology, 29,* 150–155.

Lock, M. (1998). Deconstructing the change: Female maturation in Japan and North America. In R. A. Shweder (Ed.), *Welcome to middle age! And other cultural fictions* (pp. 45–74). Chicago: University of Chicago Press.

Loeber, R., & Farrington, D. P. (2000). Young children who commit crime: Epidemiology, developmental origins, risk factors, early interventions, and policy implications. *Development and Psychopathology, 12,* 737–762.

Loehlin, J. C., Lindzey, G., & Spuhler, J. N. (1975). *Race differences in intelligence.* San Francisco: Freeman.

Loewy, J. (2004, March 1). *Integrating music, language and the voice in music therapy.* Voices: A World Forum for Music Therapy. Retrieved January 26, 2005, from http://www.voices.no/mainissues/mi40004000140.html

Loftus, J. (2001). America's liberalization in attitudes toward homosexuality, 1973 to 1998. *American Sociological Review, 66*(5), 762–783.

Longmore, M. A., Manning, W. D., & Giordano, P. C. (2001). Preadolescent parenting strategies and teens' dating and sexual initiation: A longitudinal analysis. *Journal of Marriage and the Family, 63,* 322–336.

Lopata, H. Z. (1981). Widowhood and husband satisfaction. *Journal of Marriage and the Family, 43,* 439–450.

Lord, M. G. (1994, October 25). What that survey didn't say. *New York Times,* A17.

Lorenz, K. Z. (1935). Imprinting. In R. C. Birney & R. C. Teevan (Eds.), *Instinct.* London: Van Nostrand.

Lou, H. C., Hansen, D., Nordentoft, M., Pryds, O., Jensen, F., Nim, J. & Hemmingsen, R. (1994). Prenatal stressors of human life affect fetal brain development. *Developmental Medicine of Child Neurology, 37,* 185.

Love, D. O., & Torrence, W. D. (1989). The impact of worker age on unemployment and earnings after plant closings. *Journal of Gerontology, 44,* S190–195.

Love, S. (2003). *Dr. Susan Love's menopause and hormone book: Making informed choices/Susan M. Love with Karen Lindsey.* New York: Three Rivers Press.

Love, S. (2005). *HRT update: What do we know? What do we need to learn?* Retrieved March 21, 2005, from http://www.sosanlovemd.org/community/flashes/hrt_update04708.htm

Lovecky, D. V. (1994). Exceptionally different children: Different minds. *Roeper Review, 17,* 116–120.

Lovern, E. (2001, January 29). New kids on the block: Here comes the next generation of workers. *Modern Healthcare, 31,* 28–29.

Lowy, J. (2004, January 2). *Autism statistics: Autism reaching "epidemic" levels.* Autistic Society. Retrieved February 4, 2005, from http://www.autisticsociety.org/autism-article298.html

Luo, Y., Baillargeon, R., Brueckner, L., & Munakata, Y. (2003, July). Reasoning about a hidden object after a delay: Evidence for robust representations in 5-month-old infants. *Cognition, 88*(3), B23–32.

Luster, T., & Small, S. A. (1994a). Adolescent sexual activity: An ecological, risk-factor approach. *Journal of Marriage and the Family, 56,* 181–192.

Luster, T., & Small, S. A. (1994b). Factors associated with sexual risk-taking behaviors among adolescents. *Journal of Marriage and the Family, 56,* 622–632.

Lykken, D. T., Bouchard, T. J., Jr., McGue, M., & Tellegen, A. (2004). *Minnesota Twin Family Registry: Some initial findings.* Retrieved November 10, 2004, from http://www.psych.umn.edu/psylabs/mtfs/mtrf2.htm

Lykken, D. T., McGue, M., Tellegen, A., & Bouchard, T. J., Jr. (1992). Emergencies: Genetic traits that may not run in families. *American Psychologist, 47,* 1565–1577.

Lyman, K. A. (1993). *Day in, day out with Alzheimer's: Stress in caregiving relationships.* Philadelphia: Temple University Press.

Lynch, E. W., & Hansen, M. J. (1992). *Developing cross-cultural competence: A guide for working with young children and their families.* Baltimore: Paul H. Brookes.

Lyndon-Rochelle, M. T. (2004). Minimal intervention nurse-midwives in the United States. *New England Journal of Medicine, 351,* 1929–1931.

Lyon, G. R. (2000, January 18). *Learning disabilities: Multidisciplinary research centers.* National Institute of Child Health and Human Development (NICHD), National Institute of Mental Health (NIMH). Retrieved December 18, 2001, from http://grants.nih.gov/grants/guide/ rfa-files/RFA-HD-00-003.html

Lyon, L. (2002, July 23). The future of marriage: Part I. *Gallup Poll Tuesday Briefing,* 1–4.

Lyon, T. D., & Flavell, J. H. (1994). Young children's understanding of "remember" and "forget." *Child Development, 65,* 1357–1371.

Lyons-Ruth, K., Alpern, L., & Repacholi, B. (1993). Disorganized infant attachment classification and maternal psychosocial problems as predictors of hostile-aggressive behavior in the preschool classroom. *Child Development, 64,* 572–585.

Lytton, H. (1979). Disciplinary encounters between young boys and their mothers and fathers: Is there a contingency system? *Developmental Psychology, 15,* 256–268.

Lytton, H., & Romney, D. M. (1991). Parents' sex-differentiated socialization of boys and girls: A meta-analysis. *Psychological Bulletin, 109,* 267–296.

Maccoby, E. E. (1961). The taking of adult roles in middle childhood. *Journal of Abnormal and Social Psychology, 63,* 493–503.

Maccoby, E. E. (1980). *Social development: Psychological growth and the parent-child relationship.* New York: Harcourt Brace Jovanovich.

Maccoby, E. E. (1983). Social-emotional development and responses to stressors. In N. Garmezy & M. Rutter (Eds.), *Stress, coping, and development in children.* New York: McGraw-Hill.

Maccoby, E. E. (1988). Gender as a social category. *Developmental Psychology, 24,* 755–765.

Maccoby, E. E. (1990). Gender and relationships: A developmental account. *American Psychologist, 45,* 513–520.

Maccoby, E. E. (1991). Different reproductive strategies in males and females. *Child Development, 62,* 676–681.

Maccoby, E. E. (1992). The role of parents in the socialization of children: An historical overview. *Developmental Psychology, 28,* 1006–1017.

Maccoby, E. E. (1999). The uniqueness of the parent-child relationship. In W. A. Collins and B. Laursen (Eds.), *Minnesota Symposium on Child Psychology, 29,* Relationships as Developmental Contexts, pp. 157–176. London: Lawrence Erlbaum.

Maccoby, E. E., & Jacklin, C. N. (1974). *The psychology of sex differences.* Stanford, CA: Stanford University Press.

Maccoby, E. E., & Jacklin, C. N. (1987). Gender segregation in childhood. In H. W. Reese (Ed.), *Advances in child development and behavior* (Vol. 20). New York: Academic Press.

Maccoby, E. E., & Lewis, C. C. (2003). Less day care or different day care. *Child Development, 74,* 1069–1076.

Maccoby, E. E., & Maccoby, N. (1954). The interview: A tool of social science. In G. Lindzey (Ed.), *Handbook of social psychology.* Reading, MA: Addison-Wesley.

Maccoby, E. E., & Masters, J. C. (1970). Attachment and dependency. In P. H. Mussen (Ed.), *Carmichael's manual of child psychology* (3rd ed.). New York: Wiley.

MacDonald, K. (1992). Warmth as a developmental construct: An evolutionary analysis. *Child Development, 63,* 753–773.

MacDonald, S. G. (2001). The real and the researchable: A brief overview of the contribution of John Bowlby (1907–1990). *Perspectives in Psychiatric Care, 37*(1), 60.

MacDorman, M. F., Martin, J. A., Mathews, T. J., Hoyert, D. L., & Ventura, S. J. (2005, January 24). Explaining the 2001–02 infant mortality increase: Data from the linked birth/infant death data set. *National Vital Statistics Reports, 53*(12), 1–23. Hyattsville, MD: National Center for Health Statistics.

Macklem, G. L. (2003). *Bullying and teasing: Social power in children's groups.* New York: Kluwer.

Macmillan, M. (1991). *Freud evaluated: The completed arc.* Amsterdam: North-Holland.

MacNair, R. M. (2001, July–September). Focusing on hope: How emphasizing falling abortion rates enhances pro-life education efforts. *The Post-Abortion Review, 9*(3), The Elliot Institute. Retrieved October 18, 2004, from http://www.afterabortion.info/ PAR/V9/n3/cognitivediss.html

MacNeilage, P. F., & Davis, B. L. (2000, April 21). On the origin of the internal structure of word forms. *Science, 288,* 527–531.

Madden, D. J. (1990). Adult age differences in the time course of visual attention. *Journal of Gerontology, 45,* P9–P16.

Magder, L. S., Mofenson, L., Paul, M. E., Zorrilla, C. D., et al. (2005, January 1). Risk factors for in utero and intrapartum transmission of HIV. *Journal of Acquired Immune Deficiency Syndromes, 38*(1), 887–95.

Magnuson, K. A., & Waldfogel, J. (2005, Spring). Early childhood care and education: Effects on ethnic and racial gaps in school readiness. *The Future of Children, 15*(1), 169–188.

Main, M., & Solomon, J. (1986). Discovery of an insecure-disorganized/disoriented attachment pattern. In T. B. Brazelton & M. Yogman (Eds.), *Affective development in infancy* (pp. 95–124). Norwood, NJ: Ablex.

Maine, M. (2000). *Body wars: Making peace with women's bodies.* Carlsbad, CA: Gurze Books.

Makarenko, A. S. (1967). *The collective family: A handbook for Russian parents.* New York: Doubleday.

Makros J., & McCabe, M. P. (2001). Relationships between identity and self-representations during adolescence. *Journal of Youth and Adolescence, 30*(5), 623–639.

Malcolm, A. H. (1990, June 9). Giving death a hand: Rending issue. *New York Times,* 6A.

Malinak, D. P., Hoyt, M. F., & Patterson, V. (1979). Adults' reactions to the death of a parent: A preliminary study. *American Journal of Psychiatry, 136,* 1152–1156.

Mallett, P., Apostolidis, T., & Paty, B. (1997). The development of gender schemata about heterosexual and homosexual others. *Journal of General Psychology, 124,* 91–104.

Malt, B. C., Sloman, S. A., & Gennari, S. P. (2003). *Language in mind: Advances in the study of language and thought.* Cambridge, MA: MIT Press.

Mantyla, T. (1994). Remembering to remember: Adult age differences in prospective memory. *Journal of Gerontology: Psychological Sciences, 49,* P276–P282.

Many black men go untreated for depression. (2005, February 25). IntelliHealth. Com. Atlanta, GA: *The New York Times News Service.*

March of Dimes. (2003). *Distribution of birthweight categories: US, 2002.* Retrieved October 25, 2004, from http://www.marchofdimes.com/peristats

March of Dimes. (2004a). Infant mortality overview. In *Quick facts.* Retrieved October 25, 2004, from http://www.marchofdimes.com/peristats

March of Dimes. (2004b). *On an average week.* Retrieved October 25, 2004, from http://www.marchofdimes.com/files/data

March of Dimes. (2004c). PeriStats. *Born too soon and too small in the United States.* Retrieved October 22, 2004, from http://www.marchofdimes.com/peristats/prematurity

March of Dimes. (2004d). PeriStats. *Infant mortality.* Retrieved October 25, 2004, from http://www.marchofdimes.com/peristats

March of Dimes. (2004e). PeriStats. *Quick facts.* Retrieved October 25, 2004, from http://www.marchofdimes.com/peristats

March of Dimes. (2004f). Delivery method overview. In *Quick facts.* Retrieved October 25, 2004, from http://www.marchofdimes.com/peristats

March of Dimes. (2005). *Complications: Preeclampsia/high blood pressure.* Retrieved January 19, 2005, from http://www.marchofdimes.com

Marchant, J. (2004). Cell suicide is behind prenatal brain damage. *New Scientist, 18*(2435), 1.

Marcia, J. E. (1966). Development and validation of ego identity status. *Journal of Personality and Social Psychology, 3,* 551–558.

Marcia, J. E. (1991). Identity and self-development. In R. M. Lerner, A. C. Peterson, & J. Brooks-Gunn (Eds.), *Encyclopedia of adolescence* (Vol. 1). New York: Garland.

Marini, Z., & Case, R. (1994). The development of abstract reasoning about the physical and social world. *Child Development, 65,* 147–159.

Marks, N. (1998, April). Women and HIV: *Treatment strategies for women examined at physicians' forum.* Positive Living Newsletter. Retrieved June 11, 1998, from http://www.apla.org/apla/9804/womenandhiv.html

Marks, N., & Lambert, J. D. (1998). Marital status continuity and change among young and midlife adults. *Journal of Family Issues, 19,* 652–686.

Markus, H. (1977). Self-schemata and processing information about the self. *Journal of Personality and Social Psychology, 35,* 63–78.

Marlow, N., Wolke, D., Bracewell, M. A., & Samara, M. (2005, January 6). Neurologic and developmental disability at six years of age after extremely preterm birth. *New England Journal of Medicine, 352,* 9–19.

Marlow-Ferguson, R. (Ed.). (2002). *World education encyclopedia: A survey of education systems worldwide.* (2nd ed.). New York: Thomson Learning.

Marshall, T. C., Slate, J., Kruuk, J., & Pemberton, J. M. (1998, May). Statistical confidence for likelihood-based paternity inference in natural populations. *Molecular Ecology, 7*(5), 639–655.

Marshall, W., & Tanner, J. M. (1970, February), Variations in pattern of pubertal changes in boys. *Archives of Disease in Childhood, 45*(239), 13–23.

Martin, J. A., Hamilton, B. E., Sutton, P. D., Ventura, S. J., Menacker, F., & Munson, M. L. (2003, December 17). Births: Final data for 2002. *National Vital Statistics Reports.* Washington, DC: U.S. Department of Health and Human Services. Retrieved October 18, 2004, from http://www.cdc.gov/nchs/data/nvsr/nvsrr52/nvsr52_10.pdf

Martin, L. R., & Friedman, H. S. (2000). Comparing personality scales across time: An illustrative study of validity and consistency in life-span archival data. *Journal of Personality, 68,* 85–110.

Martin, N. K., & Dixon, P. N. (1986). Adolescent suicide: Myths, recognition, and evaluation. *School Counselor, 33,* 265–271.

Martin, T. (1998). Of statistics, single mothers, and the politics of language. *Father Magazine.* Retrieved July 30, 1998, from http://www.fathermag.com/htmlmodules/Jan97/xTrev1.html

Martinson, K. (2000, December). *The national evaluation of welfare-to-work strategies: The experiences of welfare recipients who find jobs.* U.S. Department of Health and Human Services, Administration for Children and Families. Retrieved December 2, 2001, from http://www.mdrc.org/Reports2001/NEWWS_PE_Experiences/NEWWS-PE-Experiences.pdf

Marx, J. L. (1988). Sexual responses are "almost" all in the brain. *Science, 241,* 903–904.

Marx, J. L. (1992). Familial Alzheimer's linked to chromosome 14 gene. *Science, 258,* 550.

Marx, J. L. (1993). Alzheimer's pathology begins to yield its secrets. *Science, 259,* 457–458.

Maslow, A. H. (1954). *Motivation and personality* (3rd ed.). New York: Harper & Row.

Maslow, A. H. (1968). *Toward a psychology of being* (2nd ed.). New York: Van Nostrand.

Maslow, A. H. (1970). *Motivation and personality* (2nd ed.). New York: Harper & Row.

Masters, W. H., & Johnson, V. E. (1966). *Human sexual response.* Boston: Little, Brown.

Matanda, M., Jenvey, V., & Philips, J. G. (2004). Internet use in adulthood: Loneliness, computer anxiety and education. *Behaviour Change, 21*(2), 103–114.

Maternal T3 and T4 levels in early pregnancy affect fetal brain development. (2004). *Heath and Medicine Week,* 942–943.

Matheson, D. M., Killen, J. D., Wang, Y., Varady, A., & Robinson, T. N. (2004, June). Children's food consumption during television viewing. *American Journal of Clinical Nutrition, 79*(6), 1088–1094.

Mathis, W. (2003). No Child Left Behind: Costs and benefits. *Phi Delta Kappan, 84*(9), 679–686.

Matthews, D. A, & Clark, C. (1998). *The faith factor: Proof of the healing power of prayer.* New York: Penguin Putnam.

Mau, W. C., & Kopischke, A. (2001). Job search methods, job search outcomes, and job satisfaction of college graduates: A comparison of race and sex. *Journal of Employment Counseling, 38*(3), 141–149.

Mauther, N. S. (1999). 'Feeling low and feeling really bad about feeling low,' Women's experiences of motherhood and postpartum depression. *Canadian Psychology, 40*(2), 143–161.

Maxwell, E. (1998). Exceptionally gifted children. *Gifted Child Quarterly, 39,* 245.

Mayer, J. D. & Salovey, P. (1997). What is emotional intelligence? In P. Salovey & D. Sluyter (Eds). *Emotional development and emotional intelligence: Implications for educators* (pp. 3–31). New York: Basic Books.

Mayer, J. D., Ciarrochi, J., & Forgas, J. P. (2001). Emotional intelligence and everyday life: An introduction. In J. Ciarrochi, J. P. Forgas, & J. D. Mayer (Eds.), *Emotional intelligence and everyday life* (pp. xi–xviii). New York: Psychology Press.

Mayer, R. E. (1996). Learners and information processors: Legacies and limitations of educational psychology's second metaphor. *Educational Psychologist, 31,* 151–161.

Maynard, A., & Greenfield, P. (2003). Implicit cognitive development in cultural tools and children: Lessons from Maya Mexico. *Cognitive Development, 18,* 489–510.

McAdams, D. P., & de St. Aubin, E. (1992). A theory of generativity and its assessment through self-report, behavioral acts, and narrative themes in autobiography. *Journal of Personality and Social Psychology, 62,* 1003–1015.

McAdams, D. P., de St. Aubin, E., & Logan, R. L. (1993). Generativity among young, midlife, and older adults. *Psychology and Aging, 8,* 221–230.

McAdoo, M. (1995, March 20). For your child, public or private school? *Investor's Business Daily,* A1, A2.

McAuley, E., Katula, J., Mihalko, S. L., Blissmer, B., Duncan, T. E., Pena, M., & Dunn, E. (1999). Mode of physical activity and self-efficacy in older adults: A latent growth curve analysis. *Journal of Gerontology, 54B*(5), 283–292.

McCabe, M. P., & Ricciardelli, L. A. (2004, Spring). A longitudinal study of pubertal timing and extreme body change behaviors among adolescent boys and girls. *Adolescence, 39*(153), 145–166.

McCandless, B. R. (1970). *Adolescents: Behavior and development.* New York: Holt, Rinehart & Winston.

McClelland, D. C., Constantian, C. A., Regalado, D., and Stone, C. (1978, June). Making it to maturity. *Psychology Today, 12,* 42.

McClelland, D. E., & Katz, L. G. (2001). *Assessing young children's social competence.* ERIC Clearinghouse on Elementary and

Early Childhood Education, University of Illinois, Champaign, IL.

McClelland, S. (2002). The mail-order bride business. *MacLean's, 115*(43), 48–51.

McComb, C. (2001, May). Few say it's ideal for both parents to work full time outside of home. *Gallup Poll Monthly, 428,* 24–27.

McCoy, E. (1982, May 6). Children of single parents. *New York Times, 19,* 21.

McCrae, R. R., & Costa, P. T., Jr. (1990). *Personality in adulthood.* New York: Guilford Press.

McCrae, R. R., & Costa, P.T. Jr. (1993). Psychological resilience among widowed men and women: A 10-year follow-up of a national sample. In M. S. Stroebe, W. Stroebe, & R. O. Hansson (Eds.), *Handbook of bereavement: Theory, research, and intervention* (pp. 196–207). New York: Cambridge University Press.

McDonald, K. A. (1994, September 14). Biology and behavior. *Chronicle of Higher Education,* A10.

McDonald, R. B., & Ruhe, R. C. (2003). The progression from physiological aging to disease: The impact of nutrition. In Bales, C. A. and C. S. Ritchie (Eds.), *Handbook of Clinical Nutrition and Aging,* (pp. 49–62). Towata, NJ: Humana Press.

McDowd, J. M., & Filion, D. L. (1992). Aging, selective attention, and inhibitory processes: A psychophysiological approach. *Psychology and Aging, 7,* 65–71.

McGee, J., & Wells, K. (1982). Gender typing and androgyny in later life: New directions for theory and research. *Human Development, 25,* 116–139.

McGovern, C. (2003, March 17). The Raëlians come up with the Babytron. *Citizens Centre Report, 30*(6), 51.

McGowan, R., Kim, J., Chomitz, V., & Kramer, E. (2000). *Obesity and fitness in urban school children (age 10–14).* Cambridge Public Schools. Cambridge, MA: Cambridge Health Alliance, Cambridge Public Health Department.

McGraw, M. B. (1935). *Growth: A study of Johnny and Jimmy.* New York: Appleton-Century.

McGuire, S., Neiderhiser, J. M., Reiss, D., Hetherington, E. M., & Plomin, R. (1994). Genetic and environmental influences on perceptions of self-worth and competence in adolescence: A study of twins, full siblings, and step-siblings. *Child Development, 65,* 785–799.

McHale, S. M., Crouter, A. C., McGuire, S. A., & Updegraff, K. A. (1995). Congruence between mothers' and fathers' differential treatment of siblings: Links with family relations and children's well-being. *Child Development, 66,* 116–128.

McHugh, P. R. (2004, July 15). Zygote and "clonote"—The ethical use of embryonic stem cells. *New England Journal of Medicine, 351,* 209–212.

McKeever, P. S. (2004, November 24). Current good tissue practice for human cell, tissue, and cellular and tissue-based product establishments; inspection and enforcement; final rule. Rockville, MD: U.S. Food and Drug Administration.

McKenna, J. (1996). Sudden infant death syndrome in cross cultural perspective: Is infant-parent co-sleeping protective. *Annual Review of Anthropology, 25,* 201–216.

McKenzie, B. E., Skouteris, H., Day, R. H., Hartman, B., & Yonas, A. (1993). Effective action by infants to contact objects by reaching and leaning. *Child Development, 64,* 415–429.

McKeown, R. E., Garrison, C. Z., Cuffe, S. P., Waller, J., et al. (1998). Incidence and predictors of suicidal behaviors in a longitudinal sample of young adolescents. *Journal of the American Academy of Child and Adolescent Psychiatry, 37,* 612–619.

McLaughlin, D. K., Gardner, E. L., & Lichter, D. T. (1999). Economic restructuring and changing prevalence of female-headed families. *Rural Sociology, 64*(3), 394–417.

McLeod, V. C. (2004). Linking race and ethnicity to culture: Steps along the road from inference to hypothesis testing. *Human Development, 47,* 185–191.

McNamera, M. (2004). *Latina teen pregnancy: Problems and prevention.* Population Resource Center. Retrieved December 10, 2004, from http://www.prcdc.org/summaries/latinapreg04/latinapreg04.html

Mcneil, D. G. (2004, August 17, 2004). Facing middle age and AIDS. *New York Times,* F1.

McWright, D. (2002). African American grandmothers' and grandfathers' influence in the values socialization of grandchildren. In H. P. McAdoo (Ed.), Second edition. *Black children: Social, educational, and parental environments* (pp. 27–46). Thousand Oaks, CA: Sage.

Mead, G. H. (1934). *Mind, self, and other.* Chicago: University of Chicago Press.

Medawar, P. B. (1977, February 3). Unnatural science. *New York Review of Books, 24,* 13–18.

Mederer, H. (1993). Division of labor in two-earner homes: Task accomplishment versus household management as critical variables in perceptions about family work. *Journal of Marriage and the Family, 55,* 133–145.

MedicineNet. (1997). *Fetal alcohol syndrome.* Retrieved July 8, 1998, from http://www.medicinenet.com/mainmenu/encyclop/article/art_a/alcohol.htm

Medina, A. (2001). *Cultural roles.* The Something Fishy Website on Eating Disorders. Retrieved December 15, 2001, http://www.something-fishy.org/cultural/roles.php

Meer, J. (1986, June 20). The reason of age. *Psychology Today,* 60–64.

Mehta, K. M. (1997, Summer). The impact of religious beliefs and practices on aging: A cross-cultural comparison. *Journal of Aging Studies, 11*(2), 101–116.

Mehta, K. M., Yaffee, K., & Covinsky, K. E. (2002). Cognitive impairment, depressive symptoms, and functional decline in older people. *Journal of the American Geriatrics Society, 50*(6), 1045–1050.

Meier, B. (1987, February 5). Companies wrestle with threats to workers' reproductive health. *Wall Street Journal,* 21.

Meier, D. (1998). A national survey of physician assisted suicide and euthanasia in the United States. *New England Journal of Medicine, 338,* 1193–1201.

Meltzoff, A. N., & Moore, M. K. (1977). Imitation of facial and manual gestures by human neonates. *Science, 198,* 75–78.

Meltzoff, A. N., & Moore, M. K. (1983). Newborn infants imitate adult facial gestures. *Child Development, 54,* 702–709.

Meltzoff, A. N., & Moore, M. K. (1997). Explaining facial imitation: A theoretical model. *Early Development and Parenting, 6,* 179–192.

Menacker, F., Martin, J. A., MacDorman, M. F., & Ventura, S. J. (2004, November 15). Births to 10–14 year-old mothers, 1990–2002: Trends and health outcomes. *National Vital Statistics Reports, 53*(7), 1–19.

Menaghan, E. G., & Parcel, T. L. (1990). Parental employment and family life: Research in the 1980s. *Journal of Marriage and the Family, 52,* 1079–1098.

Mendes de Leon, D. F., Kasl, S. V., & Jacobs, S. (1994). A prospective study of widowhood and changes in symptoms of depression in a community sample of the elderly. *Psychological Medicine, 23,* 613–624.

Menken, K., & Antunez, B. (2001). An overview of the preparation and certification of teachers working with limited English proficient (LEP) students. Washington, DC: U.S. Department of Education, Office of Bilingual Education and Minority Languages Affairs in cooperation with ERIC Clearinghouse on Teaching and Teacher Education.

Menten, T. (1991). *Gentle closings: How to say goodbye to someone you love.* Philadelphia: Running Press.

Meredith, H. V. (1973). Somatological development. In B. B. Wolman (Ed.), *Handbook of general psychology.* Englewood Cliffs, NJ: Prentice Hall.

Merriam, S. B. (1993). Butler's life review: How universal is it? *International Journal of Aging and Human Development, 37*(3), 163–175.

Merrill, A. M. (1996). *Report on intercountry adoption.* Boulder, CO: International Concerns for Children.

Mertz, K. J., Ransom, R. L., St. Louis, M. E., Groseclose, S. L., Hadgu, A., Levine, W. C., & Hayman, C. (2001). Decline in the prevalence of genital chlamydia infection in young women entering a national job training program, 1990–1997. *American Journal of Public Health, 91,* 1287–1290.

Merz, B. (1992, October). Why we get old. *Harvard Health Letter* (Special Supp.), 9–12.

Meschke, L. L., & Silbereisen, R. K. (1997). The influence of puberty, family processes, and leisure activities on the timing of first sexual experience. *Journal of Adolescence, 20,* 403–418.

Messick, S. (1976). Personality consistencies in cognition and creativity. In S. Messick et al. (Eds.), *Individuality in learning* (pp. 4–22). San Francisco: Jossey-Bass.

Messick, S. (1984). The nature of cognitive styles: Problems and promises in educational practice. *Educational Psychologist, 19,* 59–74.

Metabolic syndrome: What is it and what can I do about it? (2004). *American Family Physician, 69*(12), 1–2.

Meyer, J. W., Ramirez, F. O., & Soysal, Y. N. (1992). World expansion of mass education, 1870–1980. *Sociology of Education, 65,* 128–149.

Midanik, L. T., Soghikian, K., Ransom, L. J., & Tekawa, I. S. (1995). The effect of retirement on mental health and health behaviors: The Kaiser Permanente Retirement Study. *Journal of Gerontology: Social Sciences, 508,* S59–S61.

Middlekoop, H. A., Smilde-van den Doel, D. A., Neven, A. K., Kamphuisen, H. A., & Springer, C. P. (1996). Subjective sleep characteristics of 1,485 males and females aged 50–93: Effects of sex and age, and factors related to self-evaluated quality of sleep. *Journal of Gerontology and Biological Science Medical Science, 51,* M108–M115.

Midlife passages. (1998a). *Causes of death or impaired health.* Retrieved October 12, 1998, from http://www.midlife-passages.com/newpage2.htm

Midlife passages. (1998b). *What is menopause?* Retrieved May 14, 1998, from http://www.midlife-passages.com/page33.html

Miles, C. (1993). Ethnic and linguistic minority children with special needs: A critical review of educational language and culture. In F. Albrecht & G. Weigt (Eds.), *Obstructed humans at the edge of the societies: Problem definitions and solution strategies of Sonderpaedagogik "Third World."* Frankfurt: pp. 175–199. Verlag.

Milgrom, J., Westley, D. T., & Gemmill, A. W. (2004). The mediating role of maternal responsiveness in some longer term effects of postnatal depression on infant development. *Infant Behavior and Development, 27,* 443–454.

Miller, B., & McFall, S. (1991). The effect of caregiver's burden on change in frail older persons' use of formal helpers. *Journal of Health and Social Behavior, 32,* 165–179.

Miller, B. M. (1995). *Out-of-school time: Effects on learning in the primary grades.* National Institute on Out-of-School Time. Wellesley, MA: Wellesley College, Center for Research on Women.

Miller, J. B. (1991). Relations between young adults and their parents. *Journal of Adolescence, 14,* 179–194.

Miller, J. B., & Striver, I. P. (1997). *The healing connection: How women form relationships in therapy and in life.* Boston: Beacon Press.

Miller, K. (2001). Video games, TV and aggressive behavior in kids. *American Family Physician, 64*(5), 863.

Miller, M. W. (1985, January 17). Study says birth defects more frequent in areas polluted by technology firms. *Wall Street Journal,* 6.

Miller, M. W. (1994, January 14). Survey sketches new portrait of the mentally ill. *Wall Street Journal,* B1.

Miller, P. M., Gorski, P. A., Borchers, D. A., Jenista J. A., Johnson, C. D., Kaufman, N. D., Levitzky, S. E., Palmer, S. D., Poole, & J. M. (2000). Developmental issues for young children in foster care. *Pediatrics, 106,* 1145–1151.

Miller, R. A. (1989). The cell biology of aging: Immunological models. *Journal of Gerontology, 44,* B4–8.

Miller, W. R., & Thoresen, C. E. (2003). Spirituality, religion, and health: An emerging research field. *American Psychologist, 58,* 24–35.

Minkler, M., & Fuller-Thomson, E. (2005). African American grandparents raising grandchildren: A national study using the Census 2000 American Community Survey. *Journals of Gerontology Series B: Psychological Sciences and Social Sciences, 60B*(2), S82–92.

Mirowsky, J. (1995). Age and the sense of control. *Social Psychology Quarterly, 58,* 31–43.

Mirowsky, J., & Ross, C. E. (1989). *Social causes of psychological distress.* New York: Aldine de Gruyter.

Mirowsky, J., & Ross, C. E. (2003). *Education, social status, and health.* New York, NY: Aldine de Gruyter.

Mischel, W. (1969). Continuity and change in personality. *American Psychologist, 24,* 1012–1018.

Mischel, W. (1973). Toward a cognitive social learning reconceptualization of personality. *Psychological Review, 80,* 252–283.

Mischel, W. (1977). On the future of personality measurement. *American Psychologist, 32,* 246–254.

Mischel, W. (1985). *Diagnosticity of situations.* Paper presented at the October meeting of the Society for Experimental Social Psychology, Evanston, IL.

Mitchell, V., & Helson, R. (1990). Women's prime of life. *Psychology of Women Quarterly, 14,* 451–470.

Mitka, M. (2004). Guidelines: New lows for LDL target levels. *Journal of the American Medical Association, 292*(8), 911–913.

Mjoseth, J. (2004, October 26). *NIA establishes new demography centers to enhance knowledge about older Americans.* National Institute on Aging (NIA), National Institutes of Health. Retrieved April 28, 2005, from http://www.nia.nih.gov/

Moen, P. (2003). *It's about time: Couples and careers.* Ithaca, NY: Cornell University Press.

Moen, P., & Roehling, P. (2005). *The career mystique.* Boulder, CO: Rowman & Littlefield.

Moen, P., Dempster-McClain, D., & Williams, R. M., Jr. (1992). Successful aging: A life-course perspective on women's multiple roles and health. *American Journal of Sociology, 97,* 1612–1638.

Moen, P., Kim, J. E., & Hofmeister, H. (2001, March). Couples' work/Retirement transitions, gender and marital quality. *Social Psychology Quarterly, 64*(1), 55–71.

Moffatt, G. K. (2003). *Wounded innocents and fallen angels: Child abuse and child aggression.* Westport, CT: Praeger.

Moffitt, T. E., Caspi, A., Belsky, J., & Silva, P. A. (1992). Childhood experience and the onset of menarche: A test of a sociobiological model. *Child Development, 63,* 47–58.

Mogul, K. M. (1979). Women in midlife: Decisions, rewards, and conflicts related to work and careers. *American Journal of Psychiatry, 136,* 1139–1143.

Mohler, B., & Earls, F. (2001). Trends in adolescent suicide: Misclassification bias? *The American Journal of Public Health, 91,* 150.

Mohler-Kuo, M., Dowdall, G. W., Koss, M., & Wechsler, H. (2004). Prevalence of rape higher in heavy drinking college environments. *Journal of Studies on Alcohol, 65*(1), 37–45.

Moneta, G. B., Schneider, B., & Csikszentmihalyi, M. (2001). A longitudinal study of the self-concept and experiential components of self-worth and affect across adolescence. *Applied Developmental Science, 5*(3), 125–142.

Money, J., & Tucker, P. (1975). *Sexual signatures: On being a man or a woman.* Boston: Little, Brown.

Montagu, A. (1964). *Life before birth.* New York: New American Library.

Montagu, A. (1978). *Touching: The human significance of the skin.* New York: Harper & Row.

Montagu, A. (1986). *Touching: The human significance of the skin* (3rd ed.). New York: Perennial Library.

Montgomery, R. J. V., & Kosloski, K. (1994). A longitudinal analysis of nursing home placement for dependent elders cared for by spouses vs adult children. *Journal of Gerontology: Social Sciences, 49,* S62–S74.

Moody, R. (1976). *Life after life.* New York: Bantam Books.

Moore, C., Bryant, D., & Furrow, D. (1989). Mental terms and the development of certainty. *Child Development, 60,* 167–171.

Moore, D. (1983, January 30). America's neglected elderly. *New York Times Magazine,* 30–35.

Moore, D. W. (2002). Eyes wide open: Americans, sleep and stress. *Gallup Poll Tuesday Briefing,* 1–3.

Moore, E., & Yzaguirre, R. (2004, June 9). Head Start's national reporting system fails our children: Here's why. *Education Week, 23*(39), 40–41.

Moore, K. A., Miller, B.C., Sugland, B.W., Morrison, D.R., Glei, D.A., and Blumenthal, C. (1995). *Beginning too soon: Adolescent sexual behavior, pregnancy, and parenthood.* Executive Summary. Washington, DC: ChildTrends.

Moore, M. R., & Chase-Lansdale, P. L. (2001). Sexual intercourse and pregnancy among African American girls in high-poverty neighborhoods: The role of family and perceived community environment. *Journal of Marriage and the Family, 63,* 1146–1168.

Mor, V., Branco, K., Fleishman, J., Hawes, C., Phillips, C., Morris, J., & Fries, B. (1995). The structure of social engagement among nursing home residents. *Journal of Gerontology: Psychological Sciences, 50B,* P1–P8.

Morabia, A., & Costanza, M. C. (1998). International variability in ages at menarche, first livebirth, and menopause. *American Journal of Epidemiology, 148,* 195–205.

Moreau, R., & Yousafzai, S. (2004, October 11). 'Living dead' no more. *Newsweek, 144*(15), 37–38.

Morel, F., Douet-Guilbert, N., Le Bris, M. J., Amice, V., et al. (2004, June). *International Journal of Andrology, 27*(3), 178.

Morelli, G., Rogoff, B., Oppenheim, D., Goldsmith, D. (1992). Cultural variation in infants' sleeping arrangements. *Developmental Psychology, 28,* 604–613.

Moretti, M. M., Odgers, C. L., & Jackson, M. (Eds.). (2004). *Girls and aggression: Contributing factors and intervention principles.* New York: Kluwer Academic Plenum Publishers.

Morgan, G. A., & Ricciuti, H. N. (1969). Infants' responses to strangers during the first year. In B. M. Foss (Ed.), *Determinants of infant behavior* (Vol. 4). New York: Wiley.

Morokoff, P. J. (1985). Effects of sex guilt, repression, sexual "arousability," and sexual experience on female sexual arousal during erotica and fantasy. *Journal of Personality and Social Psychology, 49,* 177–187.

Morris, A. M., & Katzman, D. K. (2003). *The impact of the media on eating disorders in children and adolescents.* Retrieved March 25, 2004, 2004, from http://www.pulsus.com/Paeds/08_05/morr_ed.htm

Morris, M. R. (1998). Elder abuse: What the law requires. *RN, 61,* 52–54.

Morrongiello, B. A., & Rennie, H. (1998). Why do boys engage in more risk-taking than girls? The role of attributions, beliefs and risk appraisals. *Journal of Pediatric Psychology, 23,* 3–44.

Morse, M. (1992). *Transformed by the light.* New York: Villard.

Morse, N. C., & Weiss, R. S. (1955). The function and meaning of work and the job. *American Sociological Review, 20,* 191–198.

Mothers Against Drunk Driving (MADD). (2001). *Stats and resources.* Retrieved December 31, 2001, from http://www.madd.org/stats/0,1056,1112,00.html

Morton, S. B. (1998). Lesbian divorce. *American Journal of Orthopsychiary 3,* 410–418.

Mosher, W. D., & Bachrach, C. A. (1996). Understanding U.S. infertility: Continuity and change in the National Survey of Family Growth. *Family Planning Perspectives, 28,* 4–12.

Mosher, W. D., Martinez, G. M., Chandra, A., Abma, J. C., & Willson, S. J. (2004, December 10). Use of contraception and use of family planning services in the United States, 1982–2002. *Advance Data from Vital and Health Statistics:* No. 350. Hyattsville, MD: National Center for Health Statistics. Retrieved April 8, 2005, from http://www.cdc.gov/nchs/data/ad/ad350.pdf

Mosier, C., & Rogoff, B. (2003, November). Privileged treatment of toddlers: Cultural aspects of individual choice and responsibility. *Developmental Psychology, 39*(6), 1047–1060.

Moskowitz, B. A. (1978, November). The acquisition of language. *Scientific American, 239,* 92–108.

Moss, M., & Moss, S. (1983–1984). The impact of parental death on middle aged children. *Omega: Journal of Death and Dying, 14,* 65–75.

Moss, S. Z., Rubinstein, R. L., & Moss, M. S. (1997). Middle-aged son's reactions to father's death. *Omega: Journal of Death and Dying, 34*(4), 259–277.

Mott, F. L. (1994). Sons, daughters, and fathers' absence: Differentials in father-leaving probabilities and in home environments. *Journal of Family Issues, 15,* 97–128.

Mowsesian, R. (1987). *Golden goals, rusted realities.* New York: New Horizon/Macmillan.

Moyer, P. (2001). *Engineered endometrial tissue may provide new infertility therapies. Reuters Health Medical News.* Retrieved November 18, 2004, from http://www.g-o-c.org/newsArchived/Reut2.asp

Moyer, S. & Oliveri, C. (1996). *Strengthening families and communities by sharing life stories.* Ohio State University Extension Factsheet, Family and Consumer Sciences, Columbus, Ohio. Retrieved September 23, 1998, from http://www.ag.ohio-state.edu/ohioline/hyg-fact/5000/5227.html

Moynihan, D. P. (1985). *Family and nation.* Cambridge, MA: Harvard University Press.

Muha, L. (June 1999) A new career? At my age? *Good Housekeeping, 228*(6), 92.

Muhle, R., Trentacoste, S. V., & Rapin, I. (2004, May). The genetics of autism. *Pediatrics, 113,* 472–487.

Mulder, E. J., Robles de Medina, P. G., Huizink, A.C., Van den Bergh, B. R., Buitelaar, J. K., & Visser, G. H. (2002, December). Prenatal maternal stress: Effects on pregnancy and the unborn child. *Early Human Development, 70*(1–2), 3–14.

Muller, R. T., Hunter, J. E., & Stollack, G. (1995). The intergenerational transmission of corporal punishment: A comparison of social learning and temperament models. *Child Abuse and Neglect, 19,* 1323–1335.

Mulrine, A. (2001). Unveiled threat. *U.S. News & World Report, 131*(15), 32–34.

Munnell, A. H. (2004a). *A bird's eye view of the Social Security debate.* (No. 25): Center for Retirement Research at Boston College.

Munnell, A. H. (2004b). *Why are so many older women poor?* Retrieved April 11, 2005, from http://www.bc.edu/center/crr/facts/jtf_10.pdf

Murdock, G. P. (1935). Comparative data on the division of labor by sex. *Social Forces, 15,* 551–553.

Murdock, G. P. (1949). *Social structure.* New York: Macmillan.

Murdock, G. P. (1957). Anthropology as a comparative science. *Behavioral Science, 2,* 249–254.

Murphy, S. A., Das Gupta, A., Cain, K. C., Johnson, L. C., et al. (1999). Changes in parents' mental distress after the violent death of an adolescent or young adult child: A longitudinal prospective analysis. *Death Studies, 23,* 129–159.

Murphy, S. A., Johnson, L. C., & Weber, N. A. (2002). Coping strategies following a child's violent death: How parents differ in their responses. *Omega: Journal of Death and Dying, 45*(2), 99–118.

Murphy, T. W. (1997). Guatemalan hot/cold medicine and Mormon words of wisdom: Intercultural negotiation of meaning. *Journal for the Scientific Study of Religion, 36*(2), 297–308.

Murray, T. H. & Baily, M.A. (2002–2005). *Ethical decision-making for newborn screening.* The Hastings Center. Retrieved January 5, 2005, from http://www.thehastingscenter.org/research/prog2/healthcarepolicy_4.asp

Mussen, P. H., & Jones, M. C. (1957). Self-conceptions, motivations, and interpersonal attitudes of late- and early-maturing boys. *Child Development, 28,* 243–256.

Musun-Miller, L. (1993). Sibling status effects: Parents' perceptions of their own children. *The Journal of Genetic Psychology, 154,* 189–198.

Nadel, S. F. (1951). *The foundations of social anthropology.* New York: Free Press.

Naglieri, J. A., Drasgow, F. Schmit, M., Handler, L., Prifitera, A., Margolis, A., & Velasquez, R. (2004, April). Psychological testing on the Internet: New problems, old issues. *American Psychologist, 59,* 150–162.

Nano, S. (2004, March 3). Harvard's new stem cells offered to other researchers. *The Arizona Daily Star.* Retrieved November 20, 2004, from http://www.azstarnet.com/sn/health/12372.php

Nansel, T. R., Overpeck, M. D., Haynie, D. L., Ruan, W. J., & Scheidt, P. C. (2003). Relationships between bullying and violence among U.S. youth. *Archives of Pediatric Adolescent Medicine, 157,* 348–353.

Nansel, T. R., Overpeck, M., Pilla, R. S., Ruan, J., Simons-Morton, B., & Scheidt, P. (2001). Bullying behaviors among U.S. youth: Prevalence and association with psychosocial adjustment. *Journal of the American Medical Association, 285,* 2094–2100.

Nather, D. (2000). Senate clears reauthorization of 1965 Older Americans Act in states-vs.-nonprofits compromise. *CQ Weekly, 58*(42), 2537.

National Adoption Information Clearinghouse. (1996). *Adoption statistics for 1996.* Retrieved December 9, 1998, from http://www.naicinfo.com/stats.htm

National Association of School Psychologists. (2001, September 24). *Children and fear of war and terrorism: Tips for parents and teachers.* Retrieved December 27, 2001, from http://www.nasponline.org/ NEAT/children_war.html

National Board for Professional Teaching Standards. (2004). *Early and middle childhood/English as a new language overview.* Retrieved March 26, 2005, from http://www.nbpts.org/candidates/guide/2_certglance.html

National Cancer Institute. (1998a). *National Cancer Institute initiatives applicable to prostate cancer research.* Retrieved November 30, 1998, from http://www.nci.nih.gov/prostate.html

National Cancer Institute. (1998b). *Screening for prostate cancer.* Retrieved June 12, 1998, from http://cancernet.nci.nih.gov/clinpdq/screening_for_prostate_cancer_physician.html

National Center for Children in Poverty. (2004). *Low-income children in the United States.* Retrieved February 3, 2005, from http://www.nccp.org/pub_cpf04.html

National Center for Education Statistics. (2002). *Supplemental notes: Students with disabilities.* Retrieved March 26, 2005, from http://nces.ed.gov/programs/coe/2002/notes/n10.asp

National Center for Education Statistics. (2003a). *Language Minority Students.* Retrieved February 2, 2005, from http://nces.ed.gov/programs/coe/2003/section1/indicator04.asp

National Center for Education Statistics. (2003b, October). *Projections of education statistics to 2013.* Retrieved March 17, 2005, from http://nces.ed.gov/programs/projections/

National Center for Education Statistics. (2003c). *Status and Trends in the education of Hispanics: Language spoken at home.* Retrieved February 7, 2005, from http://nces.ed.gov/pubs2003/hispanics/Section11.asp

National Center for Education Statistics. (2004, December 23). Chapter 2: Elementary and secondary education. *Digest of Education Statistics,* p. 72, Table 52. Children 3 to 21 years old served in federally supported programs for the disabled, by type of disability: Selected years, 1976–77 to 2001–02. Retrieved March 26, 2005, from http://nces.ed.gov/pubs2005/2005025b1.pdf

National Center for Health Statistics. (2001a, July 24). *New CDC report shows teen birth rate hits record low: U.S. births top 4 million in 2000.* Retrieved September 25, 2001, from http://www.cdc.gov/nchs/releases/01news/newbirth.htm

National Center for Health Statistics. (2003a). *New CDC report shows record low infant mortality rate, SIDS rate drops 11 percent in one year.* Retrieved October 22, 2004, from http://www.cdc.gov/nchs/pressroom/03facts/lowinfant.htm

National Center for Health Statistics. (2003b). *Deaths: Leading causes for 2001 (National Vital Statistics Reports Nov. 7, 2003).* Retrieved October 27, 2004, from http://www.cdc.gov/nchs/data/nvsr52

National Center for Health Statistics. (2004a). *Health United States, 2004, with Chartbook on Trends in the Health of Americans.* Centers for Disease Control and Prevention. Hyattsville, MD: U.S. Department of Health and Human Services. Retrieved March 19, from http://www.cdc.gov/nchs/data/hus/hus04.pdf

National Center for Health Statistics. (2004b). Table 70. Overweight children and adolescents 6–19 years of age according to sex, age, race, and Hispanic origin: United States. *Health, United States: 2004, with Chartbook on trends on the health of Americans.* Hyattsville, MD: U. S. Department of Health and Human Services. Retrieved April 5, 2005, from http://www.cdc.gov/nchs/data/hus/hus04.pdf

National Center for Health Statistics. (2004c). *Teens delaying sexual activity: Using contraception more effectively.* Washington, DC: Centers for Disease Control and Prevention.

National Cholesterol Education Program. (2005, June). *High blood cholesterol: What you need to know.* Retrieved April 18, 2005, from www.nhlbi.nih.gov/health/public/heart/chol/wyntk.pdf

National Clearinghouse on Child Abuse and Neglect Information. (2003). *Child fatalities resource listing.* Retrieved January 20, 2005, from http://nccanch.acf.hhs.gov/pubs/reslist/rl_dsp.cfm?subjID=19

National Coalition on Health Care. (2004). *Facts on health insurance coverage.* Washington, DC: National Coalition on Health Care. Retrieved April 7, 2005, from http://www.nchc.org/facts/coverage.pdf

National Commission on Excellence in Education. (1983). *A nation at risk: The imperative for educational reform.* Washington, DC: U.S. Department of Education.

National Committee to Prevent Child Abuse. (1996a, December). *Child sexual abuse, 19.* Retrieved August 17, 1998, from http://www.childabuse.org/fs19.html

National Council on Aging. (1998). *Healthy sexuality and vital aging.* Retrieved September 28, 1998, from http://www.ncoa.org/news/archives/sexsurvey.htm

National Council on Elder Abuse. (2005). *Fact sheet: Elder abuse prevalence and incidence.* Retrieved April 12, 2005, 2005, from http://www.elderabusecenter.org/pdf/publication/FinalStatistics050331.pdf

National Down Syndrome Society (NDSS). (1998). *Parent and professional information.* Retrieved July 10, 1998, from http://www.ndss.org/information/general_info.html

National Down Syndrome Society (NDSS). (2004). General information. Retrieved October 15, 2004, from http://www.ndss.org/content.cfm?fuseaction=InfoRes.General

National Eating Disorders Screening Program. (2001). *Fact sheet on eating disorders.* Retrieved December 19, 2001, from http://www.mentalhealthscreening.org/eat/eat-fact.htm

National Fatherhood Initiative. (2004, March 11). *Family structure, father closeness, and drug abuse.* Gaithersburg, MD: National Fatherhood Initiative. Retrieved February 12, 2005, from http://www.fatherhood.org/research.asp

National Heart, Lung, and Blood Institute. (2003, May). The DASH eating plan. From http://www.nhlbi.nih.gov/health/public/heart/hbp/dash/index.htm

National Hispanic Council on Aging. (2004). *The voice of the elderly Hispanic community.* Retrieved March 17, 2005, from http://www.nhcoa.org/html/news.html

National Hospice and Palliative Care Organization. (2004). *Hospice facts and figures.* Retrieved April 19, 2005, from http://www.nhpco.org/files/public/Hospice_Facts_110104.pdf

National Human Genome Research Institute. (1998a). *From maps to medicine: About the Human Genome Research Project.* Retrieved July 9, 1998, from http://www.nhgri.nih.gov/policy_and_publications/maps_to_medicine/about.html

National Human Genome Research Institute. (1998b). *How to conquer a genetic disease.* Retrieved July 9, 1998, from http://www.nhgri.nih.gov/policy_and_publications/maps_to_medicine/how.html#key

National Institute of Allergy and Infectious Diseases. (1997). *Pediatric AIDS fact sheet.* National Institutes of Health. Retrieved July 29, 1998, from http://www.intelli-health.com

National Institute of Allergy and Infectious Diseases. (2004a, July). *Facts and figures: HIV/AIDS statistics.* Retrieved October 28, 2004, from http://www.niaid.nih.gov/factsheets/aidsstat.htm

National Institute of Allergy and Infectious Diseases. (2004b, July). Human papillomavirus and genital warts. *Health Matters.* Retrieved December 21, 2004, from http://niaid.nih.gov

National Institute of Allergy and Infectious Disease. (2005). *International trial of two microbicides begins.* Retrieved March 23, 2005, from http://www2.niaid.nih.gov/Newroom/Releases/2microbicides.htm

National Institute of Child Health. (2003, July 16). *Child care linked to assertive, noncompliant, and aggressive behaviors: Vast majority of children within normal range.* Early Child Care Research Network. NIH News Release. Retrieved February 10, 2005, from http://www.nichd.nih.gov

National Institute of Environmental Health Sciences. (November 17, 2000). *Study of normal women demonstrates: There are few "safe" days in menstrual cycle.* National Institute of Environmental Health Sciences Press Release. Retrieved October 10, 2004 from www.niehs.nih.gov/oc/news/2fertil.htm

National Institute of Mental Health. (1993). *Learning disabilities.* Retrieved February 13, 1999, from http://www.nimh.gov/publicat/learndis.htm

National Institute of Mental Health. (2001, January 1). *Teenage brain: A work in progress.* Retrieved December 17, 2001, from http://www.nimh.gov/publicat/teenbrain.cfm.

National Institute of Mental Health. (2003, April). *In harm's way, suicide in America: A brief overview of suicide statistics and prevention.* NIH Publication No. 03-4594. Retrieved May 11, 2005, from http://www.nimh.nih.gov/publicat/harmaway.cfm

National Institute of Mental Health (2004). *Autism Spectrum Disorders Research at the National Institute of Mental Health.* Retrieved February 9, 2005, from http://www.nimh.nih.gov/publicat/autismresfact.cfm

National Institute of Neurological Disorders and Stroke. (NINDS). (2004). *Brain basics: Preventing stroke.* Retrieved March 22, 2005, from http://www.ninds.nih.gov/disorders/stroke/preventing_stroke.htm

National Institute of Neurological Disorders and Stroke. (NINDS). (2005). *NINDS Parkinson's disease information page.* Retrieved March 22, 2005, from http://www.ninds.nih.gov/disorders/parkinsons_disease/parkinsons_disease_pr.htm

National Institute on Aging. (1996a). *Osteoporosis: The silent bone thinner.* Retrieved June 10, 1998, from http://www.nih.gov/nia/health/pubpub/osteo.htm

National Institute on Aging. (1996b). *Skin care and aging.* Retrieved June 10, 1998, from http://www.nih.gov/nia/health/pubpub/skin.htm

National Institute on Aging. (1998). *Aging and alcohol abuse.* Retrieved June 10, 1998, from http://www.silk.nih.gov/silks/niaaa1/publication/agepage.htm

National Institute on Out-of-School Time. (2001, March). *Fact sheet on school-age children's out-of-school time.* Center for Research on Women, Wellesley College.

National Institutes of Health. (1996). *How to prevent high blood pressure.* National Heart, Lung, and Blood Institute. Retrieved June 10, 1998, from http://www.nih.gov/health/htp-hbp/index.htm

National Institutes of Health. (1998). *How rheumatoid arthritis develops and progresses.* Retrieved February 10, 1999, from http://www.nih.gov/niams/healthinfo/rahandout/how.html

National Institutes of Health. (2004a). *Stem cell basics.* Stem Cell Information. Bethesda, MD. Retrieved November 20, 2004, at stemcells.nih.gov

National Institutes of Health. (2004b). *What is high blood pressure?* Retrieved March 22, 2005, from http://www.nhlbi.nih.gov/health/dci/Diseases/Hbp/HBP_All.html

National Institutes of Health. (2004c, November 15). *Stem cell research offered free.* Medline Plus, Bethesda, MD. Retrieved November 20, 2004, from http://www.nlm.nih.gov/medlineplus/news/fullstory_21299.html

National Institutes of Health. (2005). *HIV infection and AIDS: An overview.* Retrieved April 18, 2005, 2005, from http://www.niaid.nih.gov/factshets/hivinf.htm

National Library of Medicine. (1998). *Cesarean section—A brief history.* Retrieved July 27, 1998, from http://www.nlm.hih.gov.exhibition/cesarean/cesarean_4.html

National Mental Health Association. (2003, November 11). *Depression among women in the workplace.* Retrieved April 8, 2005, from http://www.nmha.org/newsroom/womenWorkplaceDepression.pdf

National Organization on Fetal Alcohol Syndrome. (2004a). Fact Sheet. In *Ask me about FASD.* Retrieved October 27, 2004, from http://media.shs.net/nofa.FASDFactSheetFinal.pdf

National Organization on Fetal Alcohol Syndrome. (2004b). Frequently Asked Questions at NOFAS. In *FAQs.* Retrieved October 27, 2004, from http://www.nofas.org/faq

National Organization on Fetal Alcohol Syndrome. (2004c). *Educators. What teachers need to know about FASD.* Retrieved November 16, 2004, from http://www.nofas.org/educator

National Parkinson Foundation. (2005). *About Parkinson disease.* Retrieved May 2, 2005, from http://www.parkinson.org

National Public Radio. (1998, January 6). *Human cloning plans. All Things Considered.* Retrieved July 9, 1998, from http://www.npr.org/news/health/980106.cloning.html.

National Research Council. (1998). *Political debate interferes with research on educating children with limited English proficiency.* Retrieved August 10, 1998, from http://www2.nas.edu/whatsnew/2652.html

National Society of Genetic Counselors. (2004). *Career in genetic counseling.* Retrieved October 10, 2004, from http://www.nsgc.org/careers/index.asp

National Women's Health Resource Center. (2004, April). *Menopause: Hormone therapy and other options.* Retrieved February 15, 2005, from http://www.healthywomen.org/

Nazario, S. L. (1989, December 6). Mormon rules aid long life, study discloses. *Wall Street Journal,* B4.

Needham, A., & Baillargeon, R. (1998). Effects of prior experience on 4.5-month-old infants' object segregation. *Infant Behavior and Development, 21,* 1–24.

Neergaard, L. (2005, April 12). Advisers oppose silicone breast implants. *San Francisco Chronicle.* Retrieved April 12, 2005, from http://www.sfgate.com

Neisser, U. (1967). *Cognitive psychology.* New York: Appleton-Century-Crofts.

Neisser, U. (1991). Two perceptually given aspects of the self and their development. *Psychological Review, 11,* 197–209.

Neisser, U. G., Boodoo, T. J., Bouchard, A. W., Boykin, N., Brody, S., et al. (1996). Intelligence: Knowns and unknowns. *American Psychologist, 51,* 77–101.

Nelson, B. (1982, December 7). Early memory: Why is it so elusive? *New York Times,* 17.

Nelson, B. (1983, April 2). Despair among jobless is on rise, studies find. *New York Times,* 8.

Nelson, K. (1973). Structure and strategy in learning to talk. *Monographs of the Society for Research in Child Development, 38* (No. 149).

Nelson, K. E., Aksu-Ko, A., & Johnson, C. E. (2001). *Children's language: Developing narrative and discourse competence* (Vol. 10). Mahwah, NJ: Erlbaum.

Nelson, K., Rescorla, L., Gruendel, J., & Benedict, H. (1978). Early lexicons: What do they mean? *Child Development, 49,* 960–968.

Nelson, N. M., Enkin, M. W., Saigal, S., Bennett, K. J., Milner, R., & Sackett, D. L. (1980). A randomized clinical trial of the Leboyer approach to childbirth. *New England Journal of Medicine, 302,* 655–660.

Nelson, T. F., Naimi, T. S., Brewer, R. D., & Wechsler, H. (2005, March). The state sets the rate: the relationship among state-specific college binge drinking, state binge drinking rates, and selected state alcohol control policies. *American Journal of Public Health, 95*(3), 441–446.

Neubauer, D. N. (1999, May 1). Sleep problems in the elderly. *American Family Physician, 59*(9), 2551–2560.

Neugarten, B. L., & Datan, N. (1974). The middle years. In S. Arieti (Ed.), *The foundations of psychiatry* (pp. 592–608). New York: Basic Books.

Neugarten, B. L. (1968). The awareness of middle age. In B. L. Neugarten (Ed.), *Middle age and aging.* Chicago: University of Chicago Press.

Neugarten, B. L. (1973). Personality change in later life: A developmental perspective. In C. Eisdorfer & W. P. Lawton (Eds.), *The psychology of adult development and aging.* Washington, DC: American Psychological Association.

Neugarten, B. L. (1982a). Age or need? *National Forum: Phi Kappa Phi Journal, 42,* 25–27.

Neugarten, B. L. (1982b). The aging society. *National Forum: Phi Kappa Phi Journal, 42,* 3.

Neugarten, B. L., & Neugarten, D. A. (1987, May). The changing meanings of age. *Psychology Today, 21,* 29–33.

Neugarten, B. L., Havighurst, R. J., & Tobin, S. S. (1968). Personality and patterns of aging. In B. L. Neugarten (Ed.), *Middle age and aging.* Chicago: University of Chicago Press.

Neuharth, A. (1997, August 8). What did she prove by living to be 122? *USA Today,* A15:1.

Neuman, M. G. (2001). *Emotional infidelity: How to avoid it and 10 other secrets to a great marriage.* New York: Crown.

Neville, H. A., Heppner, M. J., Oh, E., Spanierman, L. B., & Clark, M. (2004). General and culturally specific factors influencing black and white rape survivors' self-esteem. *Psychology of Women Quarterly, 28*(1), 83–94.

Neville, K. (2001). EN's guide to all the latest on heart-smart supplements and foods. *Environmental Nutrition, 24*(8), 1–2.

New research demonstrates unique effects of quantity, quality, and type of child care experienced from birth through age 4.5: Symposium to present the most recent findings from the NICHD Study of Early Child Care. (2001, April 19). Press Release. Office for Policy and Communications. Society for Research in Child Development. Retrieved October 27, 2001, from http://www.srcd.org/pp1.html

New wedding ceremony includes children. (2000, August 31). *New York Amsterdam News,* p. 36. Retrieved December 30, 2001, from Ethnic NewsWatch database.

Newbury, D. F., Bonora, E., Lamb, J. A. Fisher, S. E., Lai, C. S. L., Baird, G., Jannoun, L., Slonims, V., Stott, C. M., Merricks, M. J., Bolton, P. F., Bailey, A. J., Monaco, A. P. (2002). FOXP2 is not a major susceptibility gene for autism or specific language impairment. *American Journal of Human Genetics 70*(5), 1318–1327.

Newcomb, A. F., & Bagwell, C. L. (1995). Children's friendship relations: A meta-analytic review. *Psychological Bulletin, 117,* 306–347.

Newcomb, A. F., Bukowski, W. M., & Pattee, L. (1993). Children's peer relations: A meta-analytic review of popular, rejected, neglected, controversial, and average sociometric status. *Psychological Bulletin, 113,* 99–128.

Newcombe, N., & Fox, N. A. (1994). Infantile amnesia: Through a glass darkly. *Child Development, 65,* 31–40.

Newcombe, N., & Huttenlocher, J. (1992). Children's ability to solve perspective-taking problems. *Developmental Psychology, 28,* 635–643.

Newel, M. L., Cortina-Borja, M., Thorne, C., & Peckham, C. (2003, January). Height, weight, and growth in children born to mothers with HIV-1 infection in Europe. *Pediatrics, 111,* 52–61.

Newport, E. L. (1990). Maturational constraints on language learning. *Cognitive Science, 14,* 11–28.

NICHD Early Child Care Research Network. (2003, May). Does quality of child care affect child outcomes at age 4½? *Developmental Psychology, 39*(3), 451–469.

NICHD Early Child Care Research Network. (2004, February). Are child developmental outcomes related to before-and after-school care arrangements? Results from the NICHD Study of Early Child Care. *Child Development, 75,* 280–295.

Nickel, C. (1997, November). *Repetitive prostate massage works.* Urology Times. Retrieved June 12, 1998, from http://www.prostate.org/nickelarticle97.html

Nickerson, A. B., & Nagle, R. J. (2004). The influence of parent and peer attachments on life satisfaction in middle childhood and early adolescence. In A. Dannerbeck, F. Casas, M. Sadurni, & G. Coenders (Eds.), *Quality-of-life research on children and adolescents* (pp. 35–60). Boston, MA: Kluwer.

Nielsen, L. (2001, June). Fathers and daughters: Why a course for college students? *College Student Journal,* 280–316. Retrieved October 27, 2001, from http://www.findarticles.com

Niemeyer, D. (2005, March 10). *Seventh annual report on Oregon's Death with Dignity Act.* Portland, OR: Department of Human Services. Retrieved May 9, 2005, from http://egov.oregon.gov/DHS/ph/pas/docs/year7.pdf

Nilsson, L. (1993). *How was I born?* New York: Dell.

Nilsson, L., & Hamberger, L. (1990). *A child is born.* New York: Dell.

Nilsson, L., & Hamberger, L. (2004). *A child is born.* (4th ed.). New York: Random House.

Nogas, C. (2005, February 27). Forging new friendships: Social activities help build healthy bonds for early teens. *Press & Sun Bulletin,* 1A, 8A.

Nolen-Hoeksema, S. (October 2001). Gender differences in depression. *Current Directions in Psychological Science, 10*(5), 173–176.

Nolen-Hoeksema, S., Morrow, J., & Frederickson, B. L. (1993). Response styles and the duration of episodes of depressed mood. *Journal of Abnormal Psychology, 102,* 20–28.

Nopola-Hemmi. J., Myllyluoma, B., Haltia, T., Taipale, M., Ollikainen, V., Ahonen, T., Voutilainen, A., Kere, J., & Widen, E. (2001). A dominant gene for developmental dyslexia on chromosome 3. *Journal of Medical Genetics, 38,* 658–664.

Nora, J. J., & Nora, A. H. (1975). A syndrome of multiple congenital anomalies associated with teratogenic exposure. *Archives of Environmental Health, 30,* 17–21.

Norris, F. H., & Murrell, S. A. (1990). Social support, life events, and stress as modifiers of adjustment to bereavement by older adults. *Psychology and Aging, 5,* 429–436.

North American Menopause Society. (2001). *Definitions/epidemiology.* Retrieved July 30, 2001, from http://www.menopause.org/aboutmeno/cca.pdf

North American Menopause Society. (2004, October). Recommendations for estrogen and progestogen use in peri- and postmenopausal women: October 2004 Position Statement of The North American Menopause Society. *Menopause, 11*(6), 589–600.

North, P. (1998). *Hospice care ring.* Retrieved October 31, 1998, from http://www.cp-tel.net/pamnorth/hosring.htm

Novak, J., & Gowin, D. (1989). *Learning to learn.* Cambridge: Cambridge University Press.

Nucci, L. (1998). *Moral development and moral education: An overview.* Retrieved November 11, 2001, from http://tigger.uic.edu/lnucci/MoralEd/overview.html

Nugent, J. K., Lester, B. M., & Brazelton, T. B. (Eds.). (1991). *The cultural context of infancy. Vol. 2: Multicultural and interdisciplinary approaches to parent-infant relations.* Norwood, NJ: Ablex.

Nuland, S. B. (1994). *How we die: Reflections on life's final chapter.* New York: Alfred A. Knopf.

Nursing homes: When a loved one needs care. (1995). *Consumer Reports, 60,* 518–528.

Nyman, L. (1995). The identification of birth order personality attributes. *The Journal of Psychology, 129,* 51–59.

O'Bannon, G. (2001). Managing our future: The generation X factor. *Public Personnel Management, 30*(1), 95–109.

O'Brien, M. (2001). *Selective reduction: A painful choice.* Baby Zone. Retrieved September 5, 2001, from http://www.babyzone.com/pregnancy/selective_reduction.asp

O'Brien, N., Albert, S. M., Muller, C., & Butler, R. N. (2001). *Myths and realities of aging.* Gerontological Society of America. A presentation at the 2001 Annual Scientific Meeting in Chicago, November 15–18, 2001.

O'Connor, P. (1992). *Friendships between women: A critical review.* New York: Guilford Press.

O'Connor, R. D. (1969). Modification of social withdrawal through symbolic modeling. *Journal of Applied Behavior Analysis, 2,* 15–22.

O'Maria, N. S., & Santiago, L. (1998). PTSD in children: Move in the rhythm of the child. *Journal of Interpersonal Violence, 13,* 421.

O'Neill, M. (1995, November 11). So it may be true after all: Eating pasta makes you fat. *New York Times,* A8.

Oakes, L. M. (1994). Development of infants' use of continuity cues in their perception of causality. *Developmental Psychology, 30,* 869–879.

Oaks, J., & Ezell, G. (1993). *Death and dying: Coping, caring and understanding,* (2d ed.) Scottsdale, AZ: Gorsuch Scarisbrick.

Obeidallah, D., Brennan, R. T., Brooks-Gunn, J., & Earls, F. (2004). Links between pubertal timing and neighborhood contexts: Implications for girls' violent behavior. *Journal of the American Academy of Child and Adolescent Psychiatry, 43*(12), 1460.

Obesity and your child: Know the facts. (2005). *Brown University Child and Adolescent Behavior Letter, 21*(2), 9–10.

Occupational Outlook Handbook. (2004). *Child care workers: Earnings.* Retrieved February 1, 2005, from http://www.bls.gov/oco/ocos170.htm#earnings

O'Connor, T. G., Marvin, R. S., Rutter, M., Olrick, J. T, & Britner, P. A. (2003, Winter). English and Romanian Adoptees Study Team: Child-parent attachment following early institutional deprivation. *Developmental Psychopathology, 15*(1), 19–38.

Oden, S., Schweinhart, L., Weikart, D., Marcus, S., & Xie, Y. (2000). *Into adulthood: A study of the effects of Head Start.* Ypsilanti, MI: High/Scope Press.

Oeppen, J, & Vaupel, J. W. (2002, May 10). Broken limits to life expectancy. *Science, 296,* 1029–1031.

Offer, D., & Offer, J. B. (1975). *From teenage to young manhood.* New York: Basic Books.

Offer, D., Ostrov, E., & Howard, K. I. (1981). *The adolescent: A psychological self-portrait.* New York: Basic Books.

Offer, D., Ostrov, E., Howard, K. I., & Atkinson, R. (1988). *The teenage world: Adolescents' self-image in ten countries.* New York: Plenum.

Office of Management and Budget. (2005) Budget of the United States Government: Fiscal Year 2006. Retrieved April 26, 2005, from http://www.gpoaccess.gov/usbudget/

Ogbu, J. (2003). *Black American students in an affluent suburb: A study of academic disengagement.* Mahwah, NJ: Lawrence Erlbaum Associates.

Okie, S. (2005). Physician-assisted suicide—Oregon and beyond. *New England Journal of Medicine, 352,* 1627–1629.

Oliker, S. (2000). Family care after welfare ends. *National Forum: Phi Kappa Phi Journal, 80,* 29–33.

Olshansky, S. J., & Carnes, B. A. (2001). *The quest for immortality: Science at the frontiers of aging.* New York: Norton.

Olshansky, S. J., Passaro, D. J., Hershow, R. C., Layden, J., Carnes, B. A., Brody, J., et al. (2005). A potential decline in life expectancy in the United States in the 21st century. *New England Journal of Medicine, 352,* 1138–1145.

Olson, S. L., Bates, J. E., & Bayles, K. (1984). Mother-infant interaction and the development of individual differences in children's cognitive competence. *Developmental Psychology, 20,* 166–179.

Olweus, D. (1993). *Bullying at school: What we know and what we can do.* New York, NY: Blackwell.

Ono, H. (2003). Women's economic standing, marriage timing, and cross-national contexts of gender. *Journal of Marriage and the Family, 65,* 275–286.

Opinion Roundup. (1980, December/ January). Work in the 70's. *Public Opinion, 3,* 36.

Oppenheimer, J. R. (1955). *The open mind.* New York: Simon & Schuster.

Opsahl, M. S., Thorsell, L. P., Geltinger, M. A., Iwaszko, M. A., Blauer, K. L., & Sherins. R. J. (2002, February). Donor oocyte cytoplasmic transfer did not enhance implantation of embryos of women with poor ovarian reserve. *Journal of Assisted Reproduction and Genetics, 19*(2), 113–117.

Oregon Department of Human Services. (2005). *Seventh Annual Report of Oregon's Death with Dignity Act.* Retrieved April 19, 2005, from http://www.egov.oregon.gov/DHS/ph.pas/docs/year7.pdf

Osgood, C. (2004, June 9). *Ectogenesis: Scientific advancements in neonatal medicine may one day lead to the development of a fetus outside the womb.* American Communications Foundation: CBS Radio Network, The Osgood File. Retrieved November 14, 2004 from http://www.acfnewsource.org

Overend, T. J., Cunningham, D. A., Kramer, J. F., Lefcoe, M. S., & Paterson, D. H. (1992). Knee extensor and knee flexor strength: Cross-sectional area ratios in young and elderly men. *Journal of Gerontology: Medical Sciences, 47,* M204–M210.

Owen, J. D. (1995). *Why our kids don't study: An economist's perspective.* Baltimore: Johns Hopkins University Press.

Owen, P. R. (1998) Fears of Hispanic and Anglo children: Real-world fears in the

1990s. *Hispanic Journal of Behavioral Sciences, 20,* 483–491.

Owen, R. (2001, July 24). Pope chastises Bush over death penalty, stem cell research, globalization and . . . *The Times of London.* Retrieved October 19, 2004, from http://www.mindfully.org/Reform/Pope-Chastises-Bush.htm

Owens, J., Maxim, R., McGuinn, M., Nobile, C., Msall, M., & Alario, A. (1999, September). Television-viewing habits and sleep disturbance in school children. *Pediatrics, 104,* e27.

Paden, S. L., & Buehler, C. (1995). Coping with the dual-income lifestyle. *Journal of Marriage and the Family, 57,* 101–110.

Padian, N. S., Shiboski, S. C., Glass, S. O., & Vittinghoff, E. (1997). Heterosexual transmission of human immunodeficiency virus (HIV) in Northern California: Results from a ten-year study. *American Journal of Epidemiology, 146,* 350–357.

Paikoff, R. L., & Brooks-Gunn, J. (1991). Do parent-child relationships change during puberty? *Psychological Bulletin, 110,* 47–66.

Painter, K. (1992, August 12). Over 60 and still in the mood for love. *USA Today,* D1.

Palmer, B. W., Heaton, R. K., Gladsjo, J. A., Evans, J. D., Patterson, T. L., Golshan, S., and Jeste, D. V. (2002). Heterogeneity in functional status among middle-aged and older patients with schizophrenia: Employment history, living situation, and driving. *Schizophrenia Research, 55,* 205–215.

Palmer, L. F. (2002). Bonding matters: The chemistry of attachment. *Attachment Parenting International, 5*(2). Retrieved January 22, 2005, from http://www.babyreference.com/BondingMatters.htm

Palmer, L. F. (2004). The chemistry of attachment. *The Journal of Attachment Parenting International, Annual New Baby Issue.* Retrieved January 22, 2005 from http://www.attachmentparenting.org/apjbaby04.pdf

Paludi, M. A. (Ed.). (2002). *Human development in multicultural contexts: A book of readings.* Englewood Cliffs, NJ: Prentice Hall.

Pang, V. O., & Cheng, L. R. L. (1998). *Struggling to be heard: The unmet needs of Asian Pacific American children.* Albany, NY: State University of New York Press.

Papousek, M., Papousek, H., & Symmes, D. (1991). The meanings of melodies in motherese in tone and stress languages. *Infant Behavior and Development, 14,* 415–440.

Parcel, T. L., & Menaghan, E. G. (1994a). Early parental work, family social capital, and early childhood outcomes. *American Journal of Sociology, 99,* 972–1009.

Parens, E., & Asch, A. (Eds.). (2000). *Prenatal testing and disability rights.* Washington, DC: Georgetown University Press.

Parenting Empowerment Project: African American Culture. (2001). National Black Child Development Institute. Washington,

DC. Retrieved December 1, 2001, from http:// www.nbcdi.org/PEP_CULTURE. htm

Parenting teens. (2000). *Focus adolescent services.* Retrieved March 21, 2005, from http://www.focusas.com/Parenting.html

Parents' Research Institute for Drug Education (PRIDE). (2004, September 16). *PRIDE questionnaire report for grades 6 thru 12: 2003–04 PRIDE national summary.* Retrieved March 2, 2005, from http://www. pridesurveys.com/main/freeoffer/national-summary/us03ns.pdf

Park, K. A., Lay, K. L., & Ramsay, L. (1993). Individual differences and developmental changes in preschoolers' friendships. *Developmental Psychology, 29,* 264–270.

Park, J. Y., Su, Y. Q., Ariga, M., Law, E., Jin, S. C., & Conti, M. (2004, January 30). EGF-like growth factors as mediators of LH action in the ovulatory follicle. *Science, 303,* 682–685.

Parke, R. D. (1974). Rules, roles, and resistance to deviation: Recent advances in punishment, discipline, and self-control. In A. D. Pick (Ed.), *Minnesota symposia on child psychology* (Vol. 8). Minneapolis: University of Minnesota Press.

Parke, R. D. (1979). Perspectives on father-infant interaction. In J. D. Osofsky (Ed.), *Handbook of infant development.* New York: Wiley.

Parke, R. D. (1995). Fathers and families. In M. H. Bornstein (Ed.), *Handbook of parenting* (Vol. 3). Hillsdale, NJ: Erlbaum.

Parke, R. D. (1996). *Fatherhood.* Cambridge, MA: Harvard University Press.

Parke, R. D., & Deur, J. L. (1972). Schedule of punishment and inhibition of aggression in children. *Developmental Psychology, 7,* 266–269.

Parker, S. (1987, June 25). Mom's troubles affect the kids. *USA Today,* D1.

Parkinson, G. (2005). What to do about allergies. In J. P. Arm & K. C. Allison (Eds.), *Special Health Reports* (Harvard Medical School SR81000, pp. 19–26). Boston, MA: Harvard Medical School.

Parks, C. A. (1998). Lesbian parenthood: A review of the literature. *American Journal of Orthopsychiatry, 68*(3), 376–390.

Parnes, H. S., & Summers, D. G. (1994). Shunning retirement: Work experiences of men in their seventies and early eighties. *Journal of Gerontology: Social Sciences, 49,* S117–S124.

Parpal, M., & Maccoby, E. E. (1985). Maternal responsiveness and subsequent child compliance. *Child Development, 56,* 1326–1334.

Parsons, T. (1955). Family structure and the socialization of the child. In T. Parsons & R. Bales (Eds.), *Family, socialization and interaction process.* New York: Free Press.

Parten, M. B. (1933). Social play among preschool children. *Journal of Abnormal and Social Psychology, 28,* 136–137.

Pascual-Leone, J. (1988). Organismic processes for neo-Piagetian theories: A dialectical causal count of cognitive development. In A. Demetriou (Ed.), *The neo-Piagetian theories of cognitive development: Toward an integration.* Amsterdam: North-Holland (Elsevier).

Pasley, K., & Ihinger-Tallman, M. (Eds.). (1994). *Stepparenting: Issues in theory, research, and practice.* Westport, CT: Greenwood Press.

Paternoster, R., Bushway, S., Brame, R., & Apel, R. (2003). The effect of teenage employment on delinquency and problem behaviors. *Social Forces, 82*(1), 297–335.

Paul, P. (2003). *The PermaParent trap.* Retrieved from http://cms.psychologyto-day.com/articles/pto-20030902-000002.html

Paulson, R. J., Boostanfar, R., Saadat, P., Mor, E., Tourgeman, D. E., Slater, C. C., et al. (2002). Pregnancy in the sixth decade of life: Obstetric outcomes in women of advanced reproductive age. *Journal of the American Medical Association, 288*(18), 2320–2323.

Paus, T., Zijdenbos, A., Worsley, K., Collins, L., Blumenthal, J., Giedd, J. N., Rapoport, J. L., & Evans, A. C. (1999). Structural maturation of neural pathways in children and adolescents: In vivo study. *Science, 283,* 1908–1911.

Peacock, J. R. (2000). Gay male adult development: Some stage issues of an older cohort. *Journal of Homosexuality, 40*(2), 13–29.

Pearson, H. (2004, May 19). *Test could boost IVF success: Molecule from embryo may signal its health.* Nature. Retrieved October 19, 2004, from www.nature.com/nsu/040510/040510-7.html

Peate, I. (2003). The male menopause: Possible causes, symptoms and treatment. *British Journal of Nursing, 12*(2), 80–84.

Peck, R. C. (1968). Psychological developments in the second half of life. In B. L. Neugarten (Ed.), *Middle age and aging.* Chicago: University of Chicago Press.

Peck, R. L. (2000). Does Europe have the answers? *Nursing Homes, 49*(6), 54–57.

Peddle, N., & Wang, C. T. (2001). *Current trends in child abuse prevention, reporting, and fatalities: The 1999 fifty state survey.* Working Paper No. 808, Revised August 28, 2001. National Center on Child Abuse Prevention Research. Chicago, IL: Prevent Child Abuse America.

Peddle, N., Wang, C., Diaz, J., & Reid, R. (2002, September). *Current trends in child abuse prevention and fatalities: The 2000 fifty state survey.* Chicago, IL: Prevent Child Abuse America. Retrieved December 7, 2004, from http://www. preventchildabuse.org/

Perani, D., Paulesu, E., Galles, N. S., Dupoux, E., Dehaene, S., Bettinardi, V., Cappa, S. F., Fazio, F., & Mehler, J. (1998, October). The bilingual brain. Proficiency and age of acquisition of the second language. *Brain, 121*(10), 1841–1852.

Perdue, C. W., Dovidio, J. F., Gurtman, M. B., & Tyler, R. B. (1990). Us and them: Social categorization and the process of intergroup bias. *Journal of Personality and Social Psychology, 59,* 475–486.

Perkins, D. F., Luster, T., Villarruel, F. A., & Small, S. (1998). An ecological, risk-factor examination of adolescents' sexual activity in three ethnic groups. *Journal of Marriage and the Family, 60,* 660–673.

Perlmutter, M., & Myers, N. A. (1976). Recognition memory in preschool children. *Developmental Psychology, 12,* 271–272.

Perloe, M,, & Sills, E. S. (1999). *An overview of infertility.* In OB/GYN Net. Retrieved November 14, 2004, from EBSCOhost, http://www.obgyn.net/infertility/infertility.asp?page=/infertility/articles/infertility_perloesills

Perls, T. (1995, January). The oldest old. *Scientific American,* 70–75.

Perls, T. T. (2004, October). Centenarians who avoid dementia. *Trends in Neurosciences, 27*(10), 633–636.

Perner, J., Ruffman, T., & Leekam, S. R. (1994). Theory of mind is contagious: You catch it from your sibs. *Child Development, 65,* 1228–1238.

Perozynski, L., & Kramer, L. (1999). Parental beliefs about managing sibling conflict. *Developmental Psychology, 35,* 489–499.

Perry, B. D. (2002). Childhood experience and the expression of genetic potential: What childhood neglect tells us about nature and nurture. *Brain and Mind, 3,* 79–100. New York: Kluwer.

Perry, C. L., Bishop, D. B., Taylor, G., Murray, D. M., et al. (1998). Changing fruit and vegetable consumption among children: The 5-a-day Power Plus program in St. Paul, Minnesota. *American Journal of Public Health, 88,* 603–609.

Perry, W. G., Jr. (1968). *Forms of intellectual and ethical development in the college years: A scheme.* New York: Holt, Rinehart & Winston.

Perry, W. G., Jr. (1981). Cognitive and ethical growth: The making of meaning. In A. W. Chickering & Associates (Eds.), *The modern American college: Responding to the new realities of diverse students and a changing society* (pp. 76–116). San Francisco: Jossey-Bass.

Pescitelli, D. (1998). Women's identity development: Out of the inner space and into new territory. *Psybernetika, 3* (Spring). Retrieved August 9, 1998, from http://www. sfu.ca/wwwpsyb/98spring/pescitel.htm

Peter, K., Horn, L., & Carroll, C. D. (2005, February). Gender differences in participation and completion of undergraduate education and how they have changed over time. *Postsecondary education descriptive analysis reports.* NCES 2005-169. National

Center for Education Statistics. Washington, DC: U.S. Department of Education.

Petersen, S., & Rafuls, S. E. (1998). Receiving the scepter: The generational transition and impact of parent death on adults. *Death Studies, 22,* 493–524.

Peterson, B. E., & Klohnen, E. C. (1995). Realization of generativity in two samples of women at midlife. *Psychology and Aging, 10,* 20–29.

Peterson, C. (2003, April 9). *Molecular manufacturing: Societal implications of advanced nanotechnology.* Address to the U.S. House of Representatives Committee on Science. Retrieved May 10, 2005, from http://www.house.gov/science/hearings/full03/apr09/peterson.htm

Peterson, K. S. (1993, April 23). Divorce needn't leave midlife women adrift. *USA Today,* 7D.

Peterson, L., & Brown, D. (1994). Integrating child injury and abuse-neglect research: Common histories, etiologies, and solutions. *Psychological Bulletin, 116,* 293–315.

Petitto, L. A., Holowka, S., Sergio, L. & Ostry, D. (2001, September 6). Language rhythms in babies' hand movements. *Nature, 413,* 35–36.

Petitto, L. A., & Marentette, P. F. (1991). Babbling in the manual mode: Evidence for the ontogeny of language. *Science, 251,* 1493–1496.

Petraitis, J., Flay, B. R., & Miller, T. Q. (1995). Reviewing theories of adolescent substance use: Organizing pieces in the puzzle. *Psychological Bulletin, 117,* 67–86.

Pett, M. A., Long, N., & Gander, A. (1992). Late-life divorce: Its impact on family rituals. *Journal of Family Issues, 13,* 526–552.

Phares, V., Steinberg, A. R., & Thompson, J. K. (2004, October). Gender differences in peer and parental influences: Body image disturbance, self-worth, and psychological functioning in preadolescent children. *Journal of Youth and Adolescence, 33*(5), 421–429.

Phelps, C. K. (2000). In Volz, J. Successful aging: The second 50. *Monitor on Psychology, 31*(1), 24–28.

Phillips, D., & Adams, G. (2001, Spring/Summer). Child care and our youngest children. *The Future of Children.* The David and Lucile Packard Foundation. Retrieved September 14, 2002, from http://www.futureofchldren.org

Phillips, D., Mekos, D., Scarr, S., McCartney, K., & Abbott-Shim, M. (2000). Within and beyond the classroom door: Assessing quality in childcare centers. *Early Childhood Research Quarterly, 15,* 475–496.

Phillips, H. (2004, July 24). The concepts are there even if the words aren't. *New Scientist, 183*(2457), 8.

Piaget, J. (1932). *The moral judgment of the child* (M. Gaban, Trans.). London: Kegan Paul, Trench, & Trubner.

Piaget, J. (1952). *The origins of intelligence in children* (M. Cook, Trans.). New York: International Universities Press.

Piaget, J. (1962). *Play, dreams and imitation in childhood.* New York: Norton.

Piaget, J. (1963). *The child's conception of the world.* Patterson: Littlefield.

Piaget, J. (1965). *The child's conception of number.* New York: Norton. (Original work published 1941)

Piaget, J. (1967). *Six psychological studies.* New York: Random House.

Piaget, J. (1970, May). *Conversations. Psychology Today, 3,* 25–32.

Piaget, J. (1981/1976). *The moral judgment of the child.* New York: Free Press.

Picard, A. (1993, July 1). Women unprepared for labour pain, psychologist says. *Globe and Mail,* A4.

Pienta, A. M., Burr, J. A., & Mutchler, J. E. (1994). Women's labor force participation in later life: The effects of early work and family experiences. *Journal of Gerontology: Social Sciences, 49,* S231–S239.

Pillemer, K., & Finkelhor, D. (1988). The prevalence of elder abuse: A random sample survey. *Gerontologist, 28,* 51–57.

Pillemer, K., & Suitor, J. J. (1998, Spring). Baby boom families: Relations with aging parents. *Generations, 22,* 65–69.

Pillemer, K., Moen, P., Wethington, E., & Glasgow, N. (Eds.). (2000). *Social integration in the second half of life.* Baltimore, MD: Johns Hopkins University Press.

Pincus, T., & Callahan, L. F. (1994). Associations of low formal education level and poor health status: Behavioral, in addition to demographic and medical explanations? *Journal of Clinical Epidemiology, 47,* 355.

Pines, M. (1979, June). Good Samaritans at age two? *Psychology Today, 13,* 66–77.

Pines, M. (1983, November). Can a rock walk? *Psychology Today, 17,* 46–54.

Pinker, S. (1994). *The language instinct: How the mind creates language.* New York: William Morrow.

Pinker, S. (2001, October). Talk of genetics and vice versa. *Nature, 413,* 465–466.

Pinquart, M., & Soerensen, S. (2000). Influences of socioeconomic status, social network, and competence on subjective well-being in later life: A meta-analysis. *Psychology and Aging, 15*(2), 187–224.

Pipher, M. (1994). *Reviving Ophelia: Saving the selves of adolescent girls.* New York: Putnam.

Pipp-Siegel, S., & Foltz, C. (1997). Toddlers' acquisition of self/other knowledge: Ecological and interpersonal aspects of self and other. *Child Development, 68,* 69–79.

Pittet, B., Montandon, D., & Pittet, D. (2005, February). Infection in breast implants. *Lancet Infectious Disease, 5*(2), 94–106

Plaut, V. C., Markus, H. R., & Lachman, M. E. (2002). Place matters: Consensual features and regional variation in American well-being and self. *Journal of Personality and Social Psychology, 83*(1), 160–184.

Plomin, R., & Colledge, E. (2001). Genetics and psychology: Beyond heritability. *European Psychologist, 6,* 229–240.

Plomin, R., & Dale, P. S. (2000). Genetics and early language development: A UK study of twins. In D. V. M. Bishop & B. E. Leonard (Eds.), *Speech and language impairments in children: Causes, characteristics, intervention and outcome* (pp. 35–51). Hove, UK: Psychology Press.

Plomin, R., & Daniels, D. (1987). Why are children in the same family so different from one another? *Behavioral and Brain Sciences, 10,* 1–16.

Plomin, R., & Spinath, F. M. (2004). Intelligence: Genetics, genes, and genomics. *Journal of Personality and Social Psychology, 86,* 112–129.

Plomin, R., Asbury, K., Dip, P. G., & Dunn, J. (2001). Why are children in the same family so different? Nonshared environment a decade later. *Canadian Journal of Psychiatry, 46,* 2001.

Plomin, R., DeFries, J. C., & Fulker, D. W. (1988). *Nature and nurture during infancy and childhood.* New York: Cambridge University Press.

Polatnick, M. R. (2000). Working parents: Issues for the next decade. *National Forum: Phi Kappa Phi Journal, 80,* 38–41.

Pollack, W. (2000). *Real boys' voices: Rescuing our sons from the myths of boyhood.* New York: Penguin Putnam.

Pollitt, K. (2001). Where are the women? *Nation, 273*(12), 10–11.

Polymeropoulos, M. H., Higgins, J. J., Golbe, L. I. (1997). Mapping of a gene for Parkinson's disease to chromosome 4q21–q23. *Science, 274,* 1197–1199.

Ponzetti, J. J. (Ed.) (2003). *International encyclopedia of marriage and family.* New York: Macmillan.

Popkin, B. M., & Udry, R. (1998, April). Adolescent obesity increase significantly in second and third generation U.S. immigrants. *Journal of Nutrition, 128,* 701–706.

Portman, M. V. (1895). Notes on the Andamanese. *Anthropological Institute of Great Britain and Ireland, 25,* 361–371.

Posada, G., Carbonell, O. A., Alzate, G., & Plata, S. J. (2004). Through Columbian lenses: Ethnographic and conventional analyses of maternal care and their associations with secure base behavior. *Developmental Psychology, 40*(4), 508–518.

Postsecondary education. (2003). *Digest of Education Statistics, 2003.* National Center for Education Statistics. Retrieved March 5, 2005, from http://nces.ed.gov/programs/digest/d03/#5

Potts, A., Grace, V., Gavey, N., & Vares, T. (2004). Viagra stories: Challenging erectile dysfunction. *Social Science and Medicine, 59*(3), 489–499.

Poulin, F., & Boivin, M. (2000). The role of proactive and reactive aggression in the formation and development of boys' friendships. *Developmental Psychology, 36,* 233–240.

Poulin-Dubois, D., Serbin, L. A., Kenyon, B., & Derbyshire, A. (1994). Infants' intermodal knowledge about gender. *Developmental Psychology, 30,* 436–442.

Powell, D. H., & Whitla, D. K. (1994). *Profiles in cognitive aging.* Cambridge, MA: Harvard University Press.

Powell, L. H., Shahabi, L., & Thoresen, C. E. (2003). Religion and spirituality: Linkages to physical health. *American Psychologist, 58,* 36–52.

Prasse, J. E., & Kikano, G. E. (2004, November/December). An overview of dysphagia in the elderly. *Advanced Studies in Medicine, 4*(10), 527–533.

Pratt, C. C., Walker, A. J., & Wood, B. L. (1992). Bereavement among former caregivers to elderly mothers. *Family Relations, 41,* 278–283.

Pratt, K. T. (2004, July). Inconceivable: Deducting the costs of infertility treatments. *Cornell Law Review, 89*(5), 1121–1200.

Pratt, M. W., Diessner, R., Hunsberger, B., Pancer, S. M., & Savoy, K. (1991). Four pathways in the analysis of adult development and aging: Comparing analyses of reasoning about personal-life dilemmas. *Psychology and Aging, 4,* 666–675.

Pratt, M. W., Kerig, P., Cowan, P. A., & Cowan, C. P. (1988). Mothers and fathers teaching 3-year-olds: Authoritative parenting and adult scaffolding of young children's learning. *Developmental Psychology, 24,* 832–839.

Prenatal diagnosis. (1998). Spencer S. Eccles Health Sciences Library. Retrieved October 21, 2004, from http://www-medlib.med.utah.edu/WebPath/TUTORIAL/PRENATAL/PRENATAL.html

Prenda, K. M., & Lachman, M. E. (2001). Planning for the future: A life management strategy for increasing control and life satisfaction in adulthood. *Psychology and Aging, 16*(2), 206–216.

Presidential Advisory Commission on Educational Excellence for Hispanic Americans. (2003, March 21). *From risk to opportunity: Fulfilling the educational needs of Hispanic Americans in the 21st century.* Retrieved March 17, 2005, from http://www.yesican.gov/paceea/finalreport.pdf

Prevalence of overweight among children and adolescents: United States, 1999–2002. (2005). Retrieved April 1, 2005, from http://www.cdc.gov/nchs/products/pubs/pubd/hestats/overwght99.htm

Previti, D., & Amato, P. R. (2004). Is infidelity a cause or a consequence of poor marital quality? *Journal of Social and Personal Relationships, 21*(2), 217–230.

Price, J. L., Davis, P. B., Morris, J. C., & White, D. L. (1991). The distribution of tangles, plaques, and related immunohistochemical markers in healthy aging and Alzheimer's disease. *Neurobiology of Aging, 12,* 295–312.

Princiotta, D., Bielick, S., & Chapman, C. (2004, July). (Issue Brief No. NCES 2004-115): *1.1 million homeschooled students in the United States in 2003.* National Center for Educational Statistics. Retrieved March 17, 2005, from http://nces.ed.gov/pubs2004/2004115.pdf

Profile of older americans. (1998). Administration on Aging. Retrieved January 14, 1999, from http://www.aoa.dhhs.gov/aoa/stats/profile/

Profile of older americans. (2001). Administration on Aging. Retrieved December 27, 2001, from http://www.aoa.dhhs.gov/aoa/stats/prolfile/2001/8.html

Prohibition of Human Cloning. (2003, February 23). *Human Cloning Prohibition Act of 2003. HR534.* Retrieved October 19, 2004, from http://thomas.loc.gov/cgi-bin/bdquery/z?d108:HR00534

Prosecutors focusing on pregnant women. (2003, November 25). *Join together online: Take action against substance abuse and gun violence.* Boston University School of Public Health. Retrieved January 19, 2005, from http://www.jointogether.org/

Provenzo, E. G., Jr. (1991). *Video kids: Making sense of Nintendo.* Cambridge, MA: Harvard University Press.

Pruchno, R. A., Peters, N. D., Kleban, M. H., & Burant, C. J. (1994). Attachment among adult children and their institutionalized parents. *Journal of Gerontology: Social Sciences, 49,* S209–S218.

Pruett, K. D. (1987). *The nurturing father.* New York: Warner Books.

Public Affairs Committee. (2000). Teratology Society Public Affairs Committee position paper: Thalidomide. *Teratology, 62,* 172–173.

Public Agenda Online. (2001). *Understanding the issue: Social Security.* Retrieved January 2, 2002 from http://www.publicagenda.org/issuesfactfiles

Public Health Service Task Force. (2004, December 17). *Recommendations for use of antiretroviral drugs in pregnant HIV-1-infected women for maternal health and interventions to reduce perinatal HIV-1 transmission in the United States.* Perinatal HIV Guidelines Working Group. Retrieved December 29, 2004 from http://AIDSinfo.nih.gov

Pugliesi, K. (1995). Work and well-being: Gender differences in the psychological consequences of employment. *Journal of Health and Social Behavior, 36,* 57–71.

Pulkkinen, L., & Ronka, A. (1994). Personal control over development, identity formation, and future orientation as components of life orientation: A developmental approach. *Developmental Psychology, 30,* 260–271.

Qualls, S. H., & Abeles, N. (Eds.). (2000) *Psychology and the aging revolution: How we adapt to longer life.* Washington, DC: American Psychological Association.

Quam, J. K. (2004). Issues in gay, lesbian, bisexual, and transgender aging. In W. Swan (Ed.), *Handbook of gay, lesbian, bisexual, and transgender administration and policy.* New York: Marcel-Dekker, Inc.

Quam, J. K, & Whitford, G. S. (1992). Adaptation and age-related expectations of older gay and lesbian adults. *Gerontologist, 32,* 367–374.

Quatman, T., & Watson, C. M. (2001). Gender differences in adolescent self-esteem: An exploration of domains. *The Journal of Genetic Psychology, 162*(1), 93–117.

Quill, T. (1993). *Death and dignity: Making choices and taking charge.* New York: W. W. Norton.

Quill, T. E. (2004). Dying and decision making—Evolution of end-of-life options. *New England Journal of Medicine, 350,* 2029–2032.

Quinlan, R. J. (2003). Father absence, parental care, and female reproductive development. *Evolution and Human Behavior, 24,* 376–390.

Radcliffe-Brown, A. R. (1940). On joking relationships. *Africa, 13,* 195–210.

Rahman, A., & Toubia, N. (2000). *Female genital mutilation: A guide to laws and policies worldwide.* New York: Zed Books.

Rahman, A., Harrington, R., & Bunn, J. (2002, January). Can maternal depression increase infant risk of illness and growth impairment in developing countries? *Child: Care, Health and Development, 28*(1), 51–56.

Rajkumar, S. V. (2004, July). Thalidomide: Tragic past and promising future. *Mayo Clinic Proceedings, 79*(7), 899–904.

Raloff, J. (1996, August 10). Vanishing flesh: Muscle loss in the elderly finally gets some respect—sarcopenia. *Science News, 150*(6). Retrieved April 10, 2005, from http://www.sciencenews.org/pages/sn_arch/8_10_96/bob1.htm

Raloff, J. (2004). Counting carbs. *Science News, 166*(3), 40–42.

Ramey, S. L., & Ramey, C. T. (1999). *Going to school.* New York: Goddard Press.

Ramirez, J. M. (2003). Hormones and aggression in childhood and adolescence. *Aggression and Violent Behavior, 8,* 621–644.

Ramsey, P. G. (1995). Changing social dynamics in early childhood classrooms. *Child Development, 66,* 764–773.

Ramus, F. (2002). Language discrimination by newborns: Teasing apart phonotactic, rhythmic, and intonational cues. *Annual Review of Language Acquisition, 2,* 85–115.

Ramus, F., Hauser, M. D., Miller, C., Morris, D., & Mehler, J. (2000). Language discrimination by human newborns and by cottontop tamarin monkeys. *Science, 288,* 349–351.

Ramus, F., Nespor, M. & Mehler, J. (1999). Correlates of linguistic rhythm in the speech signal. *Cognition, 73,* 165–292.

Randerson, J. (2003, April 12). Unique vaccine halts spread of herpes. *New Scientist, 178*(2390), 23.

Rapid HIV testing of women in labor and delivery. (2003, June 18). *The body: The complete HIV/AIDS resource.* Centers for Disease Control and Prevention. Retrieved December 30, 2004, from http://www.the-body.com/cdc/labor_rapid_test.html

Rausch, M. L. (1977). Paradox, levels, and junctures in person-situation systems. In D. Magnusson & N. S. Endler (Eds.), *Personality at the crossroads.* Hillsdale, NJ: Erlbaum.

Rauscher, F. (1996). The power of music. *Early Childhood News.* Retrieved December 10, 1998, from http://www.earlychild-hood.com/music.htm

Ray, B. D. (2003). *Homeschooling grows up.* Salem, OR: National Home Education Research Institute. Retrieved March 17, 2005, from http://www.hslda.org/

Ray, D., & Bratton, S. (2001). *What the research shows about play therapy.* Association for Play Therapy, Inc. Retrieved November 26, 2001, from http://www.iapt.org/research.html

Raymo, J. M. (2003). Educational attainment and the transition to first marriage among Japanese women. *Demography, 40*(1), 83–103.

Reaction time studies of lexical production in young second language learners. (2005). Center for Research in Language. Retrieved January 22, 2005, from http://crl.ucsd.edu/bilingual/children/html.

Reber, A. S. (1993). *Implicit learning and tacit knowledge: An essay on the cognitive unconscious.* New York: Oxford University Press.

Recognizing and screening for postpartum depression in mothers of NICU infants. (2003, March 24). *Advances in Neonatal Care, 3*(1). 37–46. Retrieved January 22, 2005, from http://www.medscape.com/viewarticle/450938

Recognizing stress in children: Helping children cope with disaster. (2001). North Carolina State University Cooperative Extension, College of Agriculture and Life Sciences. Retrieved December 27, 2001, from http://www.ces.ncsu.edu/depts/fcs/humandev/disas1.html

Recommendations on ethical issues in obstetrics and gynecology by the FIGO Committee for the Study of Ethical Aspects of Human Reproduction and Women's Health. (2000, August). International Federation of Gynecology and Obstetrics. Retrieved September 5, 2001, from http://www.figo.org/default.asp?id=6001#1

Recommended childhood and adolescent immunization schedule. (2005, January 7). *Morbidity and Mortality Weekly Report, 53*(51), Q1-Q3. Retrieved February 5, 2005, from http://www.cdc.gov/mmwr/preview/mmwrhtml/mm5351-Immunizationa1.htm

Reeder, H. M. (1996). The subjective experience of love through adult life. *International Journal of Aging and Human Development, 43,* 325–340.

Rees, D. (1996). *Death and bereavement: The psychological, religious and cultural interfaces* (2nd ed). London: Whurr Publishers.

Rees, D. (1997). *Death and bereavement: The psychological, religious, and cultural interfaces.* London: Whurr.

Rees, N. S. (1998, January). The self-esteem fraud. *USA Today, 126*(2632), 66–68.

Reichman, J. (1996). *I'm too young to get old: Health care for women over forty.* New York: Random House.

Renshaw, P. D., & Brown, P. J. (1993). Loneliness in middle childhood: Concurrent and longitudinal predictors. *Child Development, 64,* 1271–1284.

Report to the Congress on Kinship Foster Care. (2000, June; updated 2004). U.S Department of Health and Human Services, Administration for Children and Families. Retrieved February 12, 2005, from http://aspe.hhs.gov/hsp/kinr2c00/index.htm#execsum

Rescorla, L. (1976). *Concept formation in word learning.* Unpublished doctoral dissertation, Yale University.

Resendes, B. L., Williamson, R. E., & Morton, C. C. (2001, September 27). At the speed of sound: Gene discovery in the auditory system. *American Journal of Human Genetics, 69,* 923–935.

Restak, R. (1984). *The brain.* New York: Bantam.

Reynolds, A. J., & Temple, J. A. (1998). Extended early childhood intervention and school achievement: Age thirteen findings from the Chicago Longitudinal Study. *Child Development, 69,* 231–246.

Reynolds, A. J., Suh-Ruu, O., & Topitzes, J. W. (2004). Paths of effects of early childhood intervention on educational attainment and delinquency: A confirmatory analysis of the Chicago child-parent centers. *Child Development, 75,* 1299–1329.

Reynolds, C. (2004). Gen X: The unbeholden. *American Demographics, 26*(4), 8–9.

Rheingold, H. L. (1968). Infancy. In D. Sills (Ed.), *International encyclopedia of the social sciences.* New York: Macmillan.

Rheingold, H. L. (1969a). The effect of a strange environment on the behavior of infants. In B. M. Foss (Ed.), *Determinants of infant behavior* (Vol. 4). New York: Wiley.

Rheingold, H. L. (1969b). The social and socializing infant. In D. A. Goslin (Ed.), *Handbook of socialization theory and research.* Chicago: Rand McNally.

Rheingold, H. L. (1985). Development as the acquisition of familiarity. *Annual Review of Psychology, 36,* 105–130.

Rheingold, H. L., & Adams, J. L. (1980). The significance of speech to newborns. *Developmental Psychology, 16,* 397–403.

Rheingold, H. L., Hay, D. F., & West, M. J. (1976). Sharing in the second year of life. *Child Development, 47,* 1148–1158.

Rice, D. P., & Fineman, N. (2004). Economic implications of increased longevity in the United States. *Annual Review of Public Health, 25*(1), 457–473.

Richards, M. H., Viegas-Miller, B., O'Donnell, P. C., Wasserman, M. S., & Colder, C. (2004, June). Parental monitoring mediates the effects of age and sex on problem behaviors among African American urban young adolescents. *Journal of Youth and Adolescence, 33*(3), 221–233.

Richardson, D., Tyra, J., & McCray, A. (1992). Attenuation of the cutaneous vasoconstrictor response to cold in elderly men. *Journal of Gerontology: Medical Sciences, 47,* M211–M214.

Rickman, M. D., & Davidson, R. J. (1994, May). Personality and behavior in parents of temperamentally inhibited and uninhibited children. *Developmental Psychology, 30*(3), 346–354.

Ricks, D. (1979). Making sense of experience to make sensible sounds. In M. Bulowa (Ed.), *Before speech* (pp. 245–268). Cambridge, MA: Cambridge University Press.

Rideout, V. J., Vandewater, E., A., & Wartella, E. A. (2003). *Zero to six: Electronic media in the lives of infants, toddlers, and preschoolers.* Menlo Park: CA: Henry J. Kaiser Foundation.

Rideout, V., Roberts, D. F., & Foehr, U. G. (2005, March). *Generation M: Media in the lives of 8–18 year olds.* Menlo Park, CA: Henry J. Kaiser Family Foundation. Retrieved March 10, 2005, from http://www.kff.org/entmedia/entmedia030905pkg.cfm

Rieser, J., Yonas, A., & Wikner, K. (1976). Radial localization of odors by human newborns. *Child Development, 47,* 856–859.

Riger, S. (1992). Epistemological debates, feminist voices. *American Psychologist, 47,* 730–740.

Riley, J., & Staimer, M. (1993, October 25). Young (old) as you feel. *USA Today,* D1.

Riley, J. W., Jr. (1983). Dying and the meanings of death: Sociological inquiries. *Annual Review of Sociology, 9,* 191–216.

Rimer, S. (1998, December 23). For aged, dating game is numbers game. *New York Times,* Late Edition, A1.

Rimer, S. (1999, November 27). Study details sacrifices in caring for elderly kin. *New York Times, 149*(51719), A9.

Rimer, S. (2000, January 9). A lost moment recaptured: Over 40, dorm food, a 9-by-9 room. What could be better? Education Life, *New York Times, 149*(51261), 21.

Rinaldi, C., & Howe, N. (1998). Siblings' reports of conflict and the quality of their relationships. *Merrill-Palmer Quarterly, 44*(3), 404–422.

Ritter, C., Hobfoll, S. E., Lavin, J., Cameron, R. P., & Hulsizer, M. R. (2000). Stress: Psychosocial resources, and depressive symptomatology during pregnancy in low-income, inner-city women. *Health Psychology, 19*(6), 576–585.

Rivers, W. H. R. (1906). *The Todas.* New York: Macmillan.

Rivkees, S. A. (2003, August). Developing circadian rhythmicity in infants. *Pediatrics, 112,* 373–381.

Roach, M. (1983, January 16). Another name for madness. *New York Times Magazine,* 22–31.

Roazen, P. (1990). *Encountering Freud: The politics and histories of psychoanalysis.* New Brunswick, NJ: Transaction.

Robbins, M. A. (2004, August 3). Law targets pregnant woman using cocaine. *The Legal Intelligencer.* Retrieved October 19, 2004 from InfoTrac One File.

Roberts, D. F., Foehr, U. G., & Rideout, V. (2005, March). *Generation M: Media in the lives of 8–18 year olds.* Menlo Park, CA: The Kaiser Family Foundation. Retrieved April 10, 2005, from http://www.kff.org/entmedia/7251.cfm

Roberts, J. E., Burchinal, M. R., & Clarke-Klein, S. M. (1995). Otitis media in early childhood and cognitive, academic, and behavior outcomes at 12 years of age. *Journal of Pediatric Psychology, 20*(5), 645–660.

Roberts, J. E., Burchinal, M., & Durham, M. (1999). Parents' report of vocabulary and grammatical development of African American preschoolers: Child and environmental associations. *Child Development, 70*(1), 92–106.

Roberts, J. E., Medley, L. P., Swarzfager, J. L., & Neebe, E. C. (1997). Assessing the communication of African American one-year-olds using the Communication and Symbolic Behavior Scales. *American Journal of Speech-Language Pathology, 6*(2), 59–65.

Roberts, K. (1988). Retrieval of a basic-level category in prelinguistic infants. *Developmental Psychology, 24,* 21–27.

Roberts, J. R., Hulsey, T. C., Curtis, G. B., & Reigart, J. R. (2003). Using geographic information systems to assess risk for elevated blood lead levels in children. *Public Health Report, 118,* 221–229.

Roberts, L., Ahmed, I., & Hall. S. (2005). *Intercessory prayer for the alleviation of ill health.* Oxford: The Cochrane Library.

Roberts, T. A., & Ryan, S. A. (2002). Tattooing and high-risk behavior in adolescents. *Pediatrics, 110,* 1058–1063.

Robinson, P. (1993). *Freud and his critics.* Berkeley, CA: University of California Press.

Robinson, R. (1998). Single moms: Raising successful kids. *Parenting, 12,* 171.

Robinson, T. N. (1999). Reducing children's television viewing to prevent obesity: A randomized controlled trial. *Journal of the American Medical Association, 282*(16), 1561–1567.

Robinson, T. N. (2001). Television viewing and childhood obesity. *Pediatric Clinics of North America, 48,* 1017–1025.

Rochat, P., & Striano, T. (1998). Primary action in early ontogeny. *Human Development, 41,* 112–115.

Rodgers, J. L., & Buster, M. (1998). Social contagion: Adolescent sexual behavior and pregnancy: A nonlinear dynamic. *Developmental Psychology, 34,* 1096–2014.

Rodkin, P. C., & Hodges, E. V. E. (2003). Bullies and victims in the peer ecology: Four questions for psychologists and school professionals. *School Psychology Review, 32,* 384–400.

Rodkin, P. C., Farmer, T. W., Pearl, R., Van Acker, R. (2000). Heterogeneity of popular boys antisocial and prosocial configurations. *Developmental Psychology, 36,* 14–24.

Rodriguez, B. (1998). "It lets the sad out": Using children's art to express emotions. *Early Childhood News.* Retrieved December 12, 1998, from http://www.earlychildhoodnews.com/sad.htm

Rogan, W. J., & Ware, J.H. (2003). Exposure to lead in children—How low is low enough? *New England Journal of Medicine, 348,* 1515–1516.

Rogers, A. (1998, December 7). The brain: Thinking differently. *Newsweek,* 60.

Rogers, C. R. (1970). *On becoming a person: A therapist's view of psychotherapy.* Boston: Houghton Mifflin.

Rogers, R. G. (1995). Marriage, sex, and mortality. *Journal of Marriage and the Family, 57,* 515–526.

Rogoff, B. (1990). *Apprenticeship in thinking.* Oxford: Oxford University Press.

Rogoff, B. (2003). *The cultural nature of human development.* New York: Oxford University Press.

Rohner, R. P., & Pettengill, S. M. (1985). Perceived parental acceptance-rejection and parental control among Korean adolescents. *Child Development, 56,* 524–528.

Rohner, R. P., & Rohner, E. C. (1981). Parental acceptance-rejection and parental control: Cross-cultural codes abstract. *Ethnology, 20,* 245–260.

Rohner, R. P., & Veniziano, R. A. (2001). The importance of father love: History and contemporary evidence. *Review of General Psychology, 5*(4), 382–405.

Rohr, C. I., Sarkar, A., Barber, K. R., & Clements, J. M. (2004). Prevalence of prevention and treatment modalities used in populations at risk of osteoporosis. *Journal of the American Osteopathic Association, 104*(7), 281–287.

Rokach, A. (1998). The relation of cultural background to the causes of loneliness. *Journal of Social and Clinical Psychology, 17,* 75–88.

Romanoff, B. D., & Terenzio, M. (1998). Rituals and the grieving process. *Death Studies, 22,* 697–711.

Romer, D., Stanton, B., Galbraith, J., Feigelman, S., Black, M. M., & Li, X. (1999). Parental influence on adolescent sexual behavior in high-poverty settings. *Archives of Pediatric and Adolescent Medicine, 153,* 1055–1062.

Romero, E. (2001, March 23, 2001). The name of the game; teens, and 20-somethings gravitate toward status symbols as they aspire to the good life. *Daily News Record,* 16.

Romero, R., Kuivaniemi, H., & Tromp, G. (2002). Functional genomics and proteomics in term and preterm parturition. *The Journal of Clinical Endocrinology and Metabolism, 87*(6), 2431–2434.

Rosales-Ruiz, J., & Baer, D. M. (1997). Behavioral cusps: A developmental and pragmatic concept for behavior analysis. *Journal of Applied Behavior Analysis, 30,* 533–544.

Rosenberg, E. B. (1992). *The adoption life cycle: The children and their families through the years.* New York: Free Press.

Rosenberg, E. L., & Ekman, P. (2003). Emotion, facial expression. In G. Adelman & B. H. Smith (Eds.), *Encyclopedia of Neuroscience* (3rd ed.), New York: Elsevier Science.

Rosenberg, T. (2004, July 5). Mutilating Africa's daughters: Laws unenforced, practices unchanged. *New York Times, 153*(52901), A14.

Rosenblatt, P. C., & Skoogberg, E. H. (1974). Birth order in cross-cultural perspective. *Developmental Psychology, 10,* 48–54.

Rosenbloom, C. A., & Whittington, F. J. (1993). The effects of bereavement on eating behaviors and nutrient intakes in elderly widowed persons. *Journal of Gerontology: Social Sciences, 48,* S223–S229.

Rosenfeld, A., & Stark, E. (1987, May). The prime of our lives. *Psychology Today, 21,* 62–70.

Rosenstein, K. D. & Oster, H. (1988). Differential facial responses to four basic tastes in newborns. *Child Development, 59,* 1555–1568.

Rosensweig, B. (1999, April 21). *A new way of seeing dyslexia.* Child Development Institute.

Rosenthal, E. (1992, August 18). Troubled marriage? Sibling relations may be at fault." *New York Times,* C-1 and C-9.

Rosenthal, T. L., & Zimmerman, B. J. (1978). *Social learning and cognition.* New York: Academic Press.

Rosinski, R. R., Pellegrino, J. W., & Siegel, A. W. (1977). Developmental changes in the semantic processing of pictures and words. *Journal of Experimental Child Psychology, 23,* 282–291.

Rosner, M. (2000). Future trends of the kibbutz—An assessment of recent changes.

University of Haifa: Insititute for Study and Research of the Kibbutz. Publication No. 83, 2000.

Ross, A. O. (1992). *The sense of self: Research and theory.* New York: Springer.

Rossi, A. S. (1968). Transition to parenthood. *Journal of Marriage and the Family, 30,* 26–39.

Rossi, A. S. (1977). A biosocial perspective on parenting. *Daedalus, 106,* 1–31.

Rossi, S., & Wittrock, M. C. (1971). Developmental shifts in verbal recall between mental ages two and five. *Child Development, 42,* 333–338.

Rovee-Collier, C. (1987). Learning and memory in infancy. In J. D. Osofsky (Ed.), *Handbook of infant development* (2nd ed.). New York: Wiley.

Rowland, A. S., Baird, D. D., Shore, D. L., Weinberg, C. R., Savitz, D.A., & Wilcox, A. J. (1995). Nitrous oxide and spontaneous abortion in female dental assistants. *American Journal of Epidemiology, 141*(6), 531–538.

Rowland, C. J., & Vasquez, C. (2002, April). Toward a strategic approach for reducing disparities in infant mortality. *American Journal of Public Health, 92*(4), 553–557.

Rubenstein, C. (1989, October 8). The baby bomb: Research reveals the astonishingly stressful social and emotional consequences of parenthood. *New York Times Magazine,* 34–41.

Rubin, D. M., Evaline, A., Alessandrini, C., Feudtner, D. S., Mandell, A., Russell, L., & Hadley, T. (2004, September). Placement stability and mental health costs for children in foster care. *Pediatrics, 113,* 1336–1341.

Rubin, J. Z., Provenzano, F. J., & Luria, Z. (1974). The eye of the beholder: Parents' views on sex of newborns. *American Journal of Orthopsychiatry, 43,* 720–731.

Rubin, K. H., Stewart, S. L., & Chen, X. (1995). Parents of aggressive and withdrawn children. In M. H. Bornstein (Ed.), *Handbook of parenting* (Vol. 1). Hillsdale, NJ: Erlbaum.

Rubin, R. (2004, November 10). 56-year-old woman delivers twins. *USA Today,* 9D.

Ruble, D. N., Brooks-Gunn, J., Fleming, A. S., Fitzmaurice, G., Stangor, C., & Deutsch, F. (1990). Transition to motherhood and the self: Measurement, stability, and change. *Journal of Personality and Social Psychology, 58,* 450–463.

Rudman, D., Feller A. G., Cohn, L., Shetty, K. R., Rudman, I. W., & Draper. W. W. (1991). Effects of human growth hormone on body composition in elderly men. *Hormone Resources, 36,* 73–81.

Rudner, L. M. (1999). Scholastic achievement and demographic characteristics of home school students in 1998. *Education Policy Archives, 7*(8). Retrieved December 19, 2001, from http://epaa.asu.edu/epaa/v7n8 and http://www.hslda.org/docs/study/ rudner1999/Rudner0.asp

Rue, V. M., Coleman, P. K., Rue, J. J., & Reardon, D. C. (2004). Induced abortion and traumatic stress: A preliminary comparison of American and Russian women. *Medical Science Monitor, 10*(10), 5–16.

Rush, F. (1996). Freudian coverup. *Feminism and Psychology, 6,* 261–276.

Russell, R. M. (April 2001) Factors in aging that affect the bioavailability of nutrients. *The Journal of Nutrition, 131*(4), 1359S.

Russell, S. T., & Joyner, K. (August 2001). Adolescent sexual orientation and suicide risk: Evidence from a national study. *American Journal of Public Health, 91,* 1276–1281.

Russia confronts the threat of AIDS. (2004). *Lancet, 364*(9450), 2007–2008.

Rutherford, M. (2001, March). What did you say? More folks are losing their hearing—and many don't even realize how much they're missing. *Time Bonus Section Generations,* G7–G10.

Rutter, D. R., & Kurkin, K. (1987). Turn-taking in mother-infant interaction: An examination of vocalizations and gaze. *Developmental Psychology, 23,* 54–61.

Rutter, M. (1974). *The qualities of mothering.* New York: Jason Aronson.

Rutter, M. (1998). Developmental catch-up, and deficit, following adoption after severe global early privation. English and Romanian Adoptees (ERA) Team. *Journal of Child Psychology and Psychiatry, 39*(4), 465–476.

Rutter, M., Andersen-Wood, L., Beckett, C., Bredenkamp, D., Castle, J., Groothues, C., Kreppner, J., Keaveney, L., Lord, C., & O'Connor, T. G. (1999). Quasi-autistic patterns following severe early global privation. English and Romanian Adoptees (ERA) Study Team. *Journal of Child Psychology and Psychiatry, 40*(4), 537–549.

Rutter, M., Caspi, A., Fergusson, D., Horwood, L. J., Goodman, R., Maughan, B., Moffitt, T. E., Meltzer, H., & Carroll, J. (2004). Sex differences in developmental reading disability: New findings from 4 epidemiological studies. *Journal of the American Medical Association, 291*(16), 2007–2212.

Ryan, A. M. (2001). The peer group as a context for the development of young adolescent motivation and achievement. *Child Development, 72,* 1135–1150.

Ryan, B. (2004, June 8). Bordering on equality. *Advocate, 916,* 13.

Ryff, C. (1982). Successful aging: A developmental approach. *Gerontologist, 22,* 209–214.

Saarni, C. (1979). Children's understanding of display rules for expressive behavior. *Developmental Psychology, 15,* 424–429.

Sachs, J. (1987). Preschool boys' and girls' language use in pretend play. In S. U. Phillips, S. Steele, & C. Tanz (Eds.), *Language, gender and sex in comparative perspective.* Cambridge: Cambridge University Press.

Sachs, J., Bard, B., & Johnson, M. (1981). Language learning with restricted input: Case studies of two hearing children of deaf parents. *Applied Psycholinguistics, 2,* 33–54.

Sacker, I., & Zimmer, M. (1987). *Dying to be thin.* New York: Warner Books.

Sadler, L. S., Anderson, S. A., & Sabatelli, R. M. (2001). Parental competence among African American adolescent mothers and grandmothers. *Journal of Pediatric Nursing, 16*(4), 217–233.

Sadler, W. A. (1978). Dimensions in the problem of loneliness: A phenomenological approach in social psychology. *Journal of Phenomenological Psychology, 9,* 157–187.

Sadler, W. A. (2000). *The third age: Six principles of growth and renewal after forty.* Cambridge, MA: Perseus Books.

Safe Motherhood Initiative. (2004). *Facts & figures: Global data.* Safe Mother-hood.Org. Retrieved December 21, 2004, from http:// safemotherhood.org

Saffran, J. R., & Thiessen, E. D. (2003). Pattern induction by infant language learners. *Developmental Psychology, 39,* 484–494.

Sahlstein, E., & Allen, M. (2002). Sex differences in self-esteem: A meta-analytic assessment, In M. Allen, R. W. Preiss, B. M. Gayle, and N. A. Burell (Eds.), *Interpersonal communication research: Advances through meta-analysis* (pp. 79–152). Mahwah, NJ: Erlbaum.

Salthouse, T. (1991). *Theoretical perspectives on cognitive aging.* Hillsdale, NJ: Erlbaum.

Salthouse, T. A., & Babcock, R. L. (1991). Decomposing adult age differences in working memory. *Developmental Psychology, 27,* 763.

Salthouse, T. A., Schroeder, D. H., & Ferrer, E. (2004). Estimating retest effects in longitutdinal assessments of cognitive functioning in adults between 18 and 60 years of age. *Developmental Psychology, 40*(5), 813–822.

Saltz, R. (1973). Effects of part-time "mothering" on IQ and SQ of young institutionalized children. *Child Development, 44,* 166–170.

Sameroff, A. J. (1968). The components of sucking in the human newborn. *Journal of Experimental Child Psychology, 6,* 607–623.

Sameroff, A. J., & Cavanagh, P. J. (1979). Learning in infancy: A developmental perspective. In J. D. Osofsky (Ed.), *Handbook of infant development.* New York: Wiley.

Sampson, R. J., & Laub, J. H. (1990). Crime and deviance over the life course: The salience of adult social bonds. *American Sociological Review, 55,* 609–627.

Samuels, S. C. (1997). Midlife crisis: Helping patients cope with stress, anxiety, and depression. *Geriatrics, 52,* 55–63.

Sandel, M. J. (2004, July 15). Embryo ethics—The moral logic of stem-cell research. *New England Journal of Medicine, 351,* 207–210.

Sanderson, S. K. (2001). Explaining monogamy and polygyny in human societies: Comment on Kanazawa and Still. *Social Forces,* *80*(1), 329–336.

Sanderson, S. L. (2004). Could your food be hurting you? *Exceptional Parent, 3*(2), 20–21.

Sandomir, R. (2005, February 13). Please don't call the customers dead. *New York Times,* BU1.

Sanson, A., & Rothbart, M. K. (1995). Child temperament and parenting. In M. H. Bornstein (Ed.), *Handbook of parenting* (Vol. 4). Hillsdale, NJ: Erlbaum.

Santelli, J. S., Brener, N. D., Lowry, R., & Robin, L. (2000). The association of sexual behaviors with socioeconomic status, family structure, and race/ethnicity among U.S. adolescents. *The American Journal of Public Health, 90,* 1582–1588.

Satter, E. M. (1998). *Secrets of raising a healthy eater.* Chelsea, MI: Kelcy Press.

Savage-Rumbaugh, E. S., Murphy, J., Sevcik, R. A., Brakke, K. E., Williams, S. L., and Rumbaugh, D. M. (1993). Language comprehension in ape and child. *Monographs of the Society for Research in Child Development, 58* (3–4, Serial No. 233).

Save the children. (2004). *Children having children: Where young mothers are most at risk. State of the World's Mothers 2004.* Retrieved January 15, 2005, from http://www.savethechildren.org/mothers/report_2004/images/pdf

Savin-Williams, R. C., & Ream, G. (2003). Suicide attempts among sexual-minority male youth. *Journal of Clinical Child and Adolescent Psychology, 32*(4), 509–522.

Scarcella, C. A., Ehrle, J., & Geen, R. (2003, August). Identifying and addressing the needs of children in grandparent care. Urban Institute: No. B-55 in Series. *New Federalism: National Survey of America's Families.*

Scarlett, W. G., Naudeau, S., Ponte, I. & Salonius-Pasternak, D., & Ponte, I. (2004). *Children's play.* Thousand Oaks, CA: Sage.

Scarr, S. (1985). An author's frame of mind [Review of *Frames of Mind* by H. Gardner]. *New Ideas in Psychology, 3,* 95–100.

Scarr, S. (1997). Why child care has little impact on most children's development. *Current Directions in Psychological Science, 6,* 143–148.

Scarr, S., & McCartney, K. (1983). How people make their own environments: A theory of genotype-environment effects. *Child Development, 54,* 424–435.

Schaal, B., Tremblay, R. E., Soussignan, R., & Susman, E. J. (1996). Male testosterone linked to high social dominance but low physical aggression in early adolescence. *Journal of the American Academy of Child and Adolescent Psychiatry, 35*(10), 1322–1330.

Schacter, D. L., & Tulving, E. (Eds.). (1994). *Memory systems.* Cambridge, MA: MIT Press.

Schaefer, E. S. (1959). A circumplex model for maternal behavior. *Journal of Abnormal and Social Psychology, 59,* 232.

Schaffer, H. R. (1971). *The growth of sociability.* Baltimore: Penguin Books.

Schaffer, H. R. (1996). *Social development.* Cambridge, MA: Blackwell.

Schaffer, H. R., & Emerson, P. E. (1964). The development of social attachments in infancy. *Monographs of the Society for Research in Child Development, 29*(3).

Schaie, K. W. (1989). Perceptual speed in adulthood: Cross-sectional and longitudinal studies. *Psychology and Aging, 4,* 443–453.

Schaie, K. W. (1994). The course of adult intellectual development. *American Psychologist, 49,* 304–313.

Schaie, K. W. (1995). Brain-astics: Mind exercises to keep you sharp. *New Choices for Retirement Living, 35,* 22–24.

Schaie, K. W. (1996). *Intellectual development in adulthood: The Seattle Longitudinal Study.* New York: Cambridge University Press.

Schaie, K. W., & Willis, S. L. (1986). Can decline in adult intellectual functioning be reversed? *Developmental Psychology, 22,* 223–232.

Schaie, K. W., & Willis, S. L. (1993). Age difference patterns of psychometric intelligence in adulthood: Generalizability within and across ability domains. *Psychology and Aging, 8,* 44–55.

Schaie, K. W., Willis, S. L., & O'Hanlon, A. M. (1994). Perceived intellectual performance change over seven years. *Journal of Gerontology: Psychological Sciences, 49,* P108–P118.

Schaie, K. W., Willis, S. L., Caskie, G., & Grace, I. L. (2004). The Seattle longitudinal study: Relationship between personality and cognition. *Aging, Neuropsychology and Cognition, 11*(2–3), 304–324.

Schaps, E., Schaeffer, E. F., & McDonnell, S. N. (2001, September 12). What's right and wrong in character education today. *Education Week, American Education's Online Newspaper.* Retrieved December 18, 2001, from http://www.edweek.org/ew/newstory.cfm?slug=02schaps.h21

Scharlach, A. E. (1987). Relieving feelings of strain among women with elderly mothers. *Psychology and Aging, 2,* 9–13.

Scheck, A. (1994, October 28). The anti-aging effects of physical fitness. *Investor's Business Daily, 1,* 2.

Scheinfeld, N. S., & Davis, A. (2004, April 11). Teratology and drug use during pregnancy. *E-Medicine Continuing Education.* Retrieved January 6, 2005, from http://www.emedicine.com/med/topic3242.htm

Scherer, K. R. (1979). Nonlinguistic vocal indicators of emotion and psychopathology. In C. E. Izard (Ed.), *Emotions in personality and psychopathology* (pp. 495–529). New York: Plenum.

Schieve, L. A., Meikle, S. F., Ferre, C., Peterson, H. B., Jeng, G., & Wilcox, L. S. (2002, March 7). Low and very low birth weight in infants conceived with use of assisted reproductive technology. *New England Journal of Medicine, 346,* 731–737.

Schlegel, A., & Barry, H., III. (1991). *Adolescence: An anthropological inquiry.* New York: Free Press.

Schlesinger, B. (1998). Separating together: How divorce transforms families. *Family Relations, 47,* 308.

Schlossberg, N. (2004). *Retire smart, retire happy: Finding your true path in life.* Washington, DC: American Psychological Association.

Schmeck, B., Gross, R., Dje N'Guessan, P., Hocke, A. C., Hammerschmidt, S., Mitchell, T., Rosseau, S., Suttorp, N., & and Hippenstiel, S. (2004, September). *Streptococcus pneumoniae*-induced caspase 6-dependent apoptosis in lung epithelium. *Infection and Immunity, 72*(9), 4940–4947.

Schmeck, H. M., Jr. (1983, March 22). U.S. panel calls for patients' right to end life. *New York Times, 1,* 18.

Schmit, J. (2005, February 2). Impotence drugs selling slowly. *USA Today.* Retrieved March 5, 2005, from http://www.usatoday.com

Schneider, B. H. (1993). *Children's social competence in context: The contributions of family, school, and culture.* Oxford: Pergamon Press.

Schneider, K., Bugental, J. F. T., & J. F. Pierson. (Eds.). (2002). *Handbook of humanistic psychology: Leading edges in theory, research, and practice.* Thousand Oaks, CA: Sage.

Schneider, M. E. (2003, November 15). President signs ban on partial-birth abortion: legal challenges underway. *Family Practice News, 33*(22), 42.

Schor, J. (1998). *The overspent American: Upscaling, downsizing, and the new consumer.* New York: Basic Books.

Schrader, D. (1988). *Exploring metacognition: A description of levels of metacognition and their relation to moral judgment.* Unpublished dissertation: *Dissertation Abstracts.*

Schrof, J. M. (1993, October 25). Tarnished trophies. *U.S. News & World Report,* 52–59.

Schrof, J. M. (1994, November 28). Brain Power. *U.S. News & World Report,* 89–97.

Schulenberg, J., Wadsworth, K. N., & O'Malley, P. M., et al. (1997). Adolescent risk factors for binge drinking during the transition to young adulthood: Variable- and pattern-centered approaches to change. In G. A. Marlatt and G. R. VandenBox (Eds.), *Addictive behaviors: Readings on etiology, prevention, and treatment* (pp. 129–165). Washington, DC: American Psychological Association.

Schulman, K., & Blank, H. (2004, September). *Child care assistance policies 2001–2004: Families struggling to move forward, states going backward.* Washington, DC: National Women's Law Center. Retrieved

September 26, 2005, from http://www.nwlc.org/pdf/childcaresubsidyfinalreport.pdf

Schulman, S. (1986, February). Facing the invisible handicap. *Psychology Today, 20,* 58–64.

Schultz, D., Izard, C.E., & Bear, G. (2004). Children's emotion processing: Relations to emotionality and aggression. *Development and Psychopathology, 16,* 371–387.

Schultz, R. M., & Williams, C. J. (2002, June 21). The science of ART. *Science, 296,* 2188–2190.

Schulz, R., & Heckhausen, J. (1996). A life span model of successful aging. *American Psychologist, 51,* 702–714.

Schulz, R., & Salthouse, T. (1999). *Adult development and aging: Myths and emerging realities.* Upper Saddle River, NJ: Prentice Hall.

Schulz, R., Heckhausen, J., & Locher, J. L. (1991). Adult development, control, and adaptive functioning. *Journal of Social Issues, 47,* 177–196.

Schwanenflugel, P. J., Fabricius, W. V., & Alexander, J. (1994). Developing theories of mind: Understanding concepts and relations between mental activities. *Child Development, 65,* 1546–1563.

Schwartz, J., & Estrin, J. (2005). New openness in deciding when and how to die. *New York Times, 154,* A1, 2p.

Schwarz, N., & Knaeuper, B. (2000) Cognition, aging, and self-reports. In D. C. Park & N. Schwarz (Eds.), *Cognitive aging: A primer* (pp. 233–252). Philadelphia: Psychology Press.

Schweinhart, L. J., Montie, J., Xiang, Z., Barnett, W. S., Belfield, C. R., & Nores, M. (2005). *Lifetime effects: The High/Scope Perry Preschool Study through age 40.* Ypsilanti, MI: High/Scope Press.

Scott, J. (1994, June 4). Another legacy of Onassis: Facing death on own terms. *New York Times, 1,* 8.

Search Institute. (1994). *Growing up adopted: A portrait of adolescents and their families.* Minneapolis: Author.

Searight, H. R., & Gafford, J. (2005). Cultural diversity at the end of life: Issues and guidelines for family physicians. *American Family Physician, 71*(3), 518–525.

Sears, R. R. (1963). Dependency motivation. In M. Jones (Ed.), *Nebraska symposium on motivation.* Lincoln: University of Nebraska Press.

Sears, R. R. (1972). Attachment, dependency, and frustration. In J. L. Gewirtz (Ed.), *Attachment and dependency.* Washington, DC: Winston.

Sears, R. R., Maccoby, E. E., & Levin, H. (1957). *Patterns of child rearing.* New York: Harper & Row.

Sears, W., & Sears, M. (1994). *The birth book.* Boston: Little, Brown.

Sebald, H. (1977). *Adolescence: A social psychological analysis* (2nd ed.). Englewood Cliffs, NJ: Prentice Hall.

Seely, R. (2004, November 18). State will aid stem-cell institute: Research facility will be built at UW-Madison. *Wisconsin State Journal,* p. A1.

Seeman, T. E., & Adler, N. (1998). Older Americans: Who will they be? *National Forum: Phi Kappa Phi Journal, 78,* 22–25.

Segal, D. L., Mincic, M. S., Coolidge, F. L., & O'Riley, A. (2004). Attitudes toward suicide and suicidal risk among younger and older persons. *Death Studies, 28*(7), 671–678.

Segal, N. L. (1993). Twin, sibling, and adoption methods: Tests of evolutionary hypotheses. *American Psychologist, 48,* 943–956.

Segal, S. J., & Mastroianni, L. (2003). *Hormone use in menopause and male andropause: A choice for women and men.* New York: Oxford University Press.

Seger, C. A. (1994). Implicit learning. *Psychological Bulletin, 115,* 163–196.

Seidman, E., Allen, L., Aber, J. L., Mitchell, C., & Feinman, J. (1994). The impact of school transitions in early adolescence on the self-system and perceived social context of poor urban youth. *Child Development, 65,* 507–522.

Seldin, T. (1996). *Every parent's question: Is Montessori worth it? Communication builds trust and confidence.* The Montessori Foundation. Retrieved July 25, 1998, from http://www.montessori.org/library/ismontworthit.htm

Selevan, S. G., Rice, D. C., Hogan, K. A., Euling, S. Y., Pfahles-Hutchens, A., & Bethel, J., (2003, April 17). Blood lead concentration and delayed puberty in girls. *New England Journal of Medicine, 348,* 1527–1536.

Selman, R. L. (1980). *The youth of interpersonal understanding: Developmental and clinical analyses.* New York: Academic Press.

Seltzer, J. A. (2004). Cohabitation in the United States and Britain: Demography, kinship, and the future. *Journal of Marriage and Family, 66*(4), 921–928.

Selye, H. (1956). *The stress of life.* New York: McGraw-Hill.

Senate Special Committee [Canada] on Euthanasia and Assisted Suicide. (1997). Retrieved November 29, 1997, from http://www.rights.org/ deathnet/senate.html

Seppa, N. (1997, June). Children's TV remains steeped in violence. *APA Monitor, 28,* 36.

Sessler, D. I., & Badgwell, J. M. (1998, November). Exposure of postoperative nurses to exhaled anesthetic gases. *Anesthesia and Analgesia, 87*(5), 1083–1088.

Setterlund, M. B., & Niedenthal, P. M. (1993). "Who am I? Why am I here?": Self-esteem, self-clarity, and prototype matching. *Journal of Personality and Social Psychology, 65,* 769–780.

Settersten, R. A., Jr., Furstenberg, F. F., Jr., & Rumbaut, R. G. (Eds.). (2005). *On the frontier of adulthood: Theory, research, and public policy.* Chicago: University of Chicago Press.

Severy, L., Thapa, S., Askew, I., & Glor, J. (1993). Menstrual experiences and beliefs. *Women and Health, 20,* 1–20.

Sewell, W. H. (1981). Notes on educational, occupational, and economic achievement in American society. *Phi Delta Kappan, 62,* 322–325.

Sewell, W. H., & Mussen, P. H. (1952). The effects of feeding, weaning, and scheduling procedures on childhood adjustment and the formation of oral symptoms. *Child Development, 23,* 185–191.

Shades of the baby blues. (2004, December). *Nursing, 34*(12), 56.

Shaffer, D., Fisher, P., Dulcan, M. K., Davies, M., Piacentini, J., Schwab-Stone, M.E., Lahey, B.B., Bourdon, K., Jensen, P.S., Bird, H.R., Canino, G., & Regier, D.A. (1996). The NIMH Diagnostic Interview Schedule for Children Version 2.3 (DISC-2.3): Description, acceptability, prevalence rates and performance in the MECA Study. Methods for the Epidemiology of Child and Adolescent Mental Disorders Study. *Journal of the American Academy of Child and Adolescent Psychiatry, 35*(7), 865–877.

Shahidullah, S., & Hepper, P. G. (1992). Hearing in the fetus: prenatal detection of deafness. *International Journal of Prenatal and Perinatal Studies, 4,* 235–240.

Shahidullah, S., Scott, D., & Hepper, P. (1993, July–September). Newborn and fetal response to maternal voice. *Journal of Reproductive and Infant Psychology, 11,* 147–153.

Shapiro, A. (2003). Later-life divorce and parent-adult child contact and proximity: A longitudinal analysis. *Journal of Family Issues, 24*(2), 264–285.

Shapiro, J. P. (2001). Growing old in a good home. *U.S. News & World Report, 130*(20), 56–61.

Shapiro, L. (1990, May 28). Guns and dolls. *Newsweek,* 56–65.

Shastry, B. S. (2003). Molecular genetics of autism spectrum disorders. *Journal of Human Genetics, 48*(10), 495–502.

Shaywitz, B. A., Shaywitz, S. E., Pugh, K. R., Mencl, W. E., Fulbright, R. K., Skudlarski, P., Constable, T., Marchione, K.E., Fletcher, J.M., Lyon, G.R., & Gore, J.C., (2002). Disruption of posterior brain systems for reading in children with developmental dyslexia. *Biological Psychiatry, 52,* 101–110.

Sheehan, G., Darlington, Y., Noller, P., & Feeney, J. (2004). Children's perceptions of their sibling relationships during parental separation and divorce. *Journal of Divorce and Remarriage, 41*(1/2), 69–94.

Sheehy, G. (1976). *Passages.* New York: Dutton.

Sheehy, G. (1992). *The silent passage: Menopause.* New York: Random House.

Sheehy, G. (1995). *New passages: Mapping your life across time.* New York: Random House.

Sheehy, G. (1998). *Understanding men's passages: Discovering the new map of men's lives.* New York: Random House.

Sheff, D. (1993). *How Nintendo zapped an American industry, captured your dollars, and enslaved your children.* New York: Random House.

Sheldon, T. (2005). Dutch committee approves euthanasia for a patient with Alzheimer's disease. *British Medical Journal, 330,* 1041.

Sheler, J. L. (1997, March 31). Heaven in the age of reason. *U.S. News & World Report, 122,* 65–66.

Shellenbarger, S. (1997, October 15). Work-life issues are starting to plague teenagers with jobs. *Wall Street Journal,* B1.

Shen, W., & Mo, W. (1990). *Reaching out to their cultures: Building communication with Asian American families.* ERIC abstracts. Retrieved November 20, 2001, from http://eric-web.tc.columbia.edu/abstracts/ed351435.html

Sherman, M. (2004, November 25). *Bush seeks funds for abstinence education.* Yahoo News. Retrieved November 25, 2004, from http://story.news.yahoo.com

Sherman, S. R. (1997). Images of middle-aged and older women: Historical, cultural, and personal. In J. Coyle (Ed.), *Handbook on women and aging* (pp. 14–28), Westport, CT: Greenwood Press.

Sherrid, P. (2000). Retired? Fine. Now get back to work. *U.S. News & World Report, 128*(22), 64–72.

Shimizu, Y. (2001, November). *Why mathematics performance of Japanese students is higher than that of students in Western countries: Listening to the voices from inside.* National Council of Teachers of Mathematics. Retrieved December 17, 2001, from http://www.nctm.org/dialogues/2001-11/ 20011104.htm

Ship, J. A., & Weiffenbach, J. M. (1993). Age, gender, medical treatment, and medication effects on smell identification. *Journal of Gerontology: Medical Sciences, 48,* M26–M32.

Ship, J. A., Pearson, J. D., Cruise, L. J., Brant, L. J., & Metter, E. J. (1996). Longitudinal changes in smell identification. *Journals of Gerontology: Medical Sciences, 51A,* 86–91.

Shneidman, E. (1989). The Indian summer of life: A preliminary study of septuagenarians. *American Psychologist, 44,* 684–694.

Shomon, M. (2005). *Living well with hypothyroidism: What your doctor doesn't tell you . . . that you need to know.* New York: Harper Collins.

Shonkoff, J. P., & Phillips, D. A. (Eds.). (2000). *From neurons to neighborhoods: The science of early childhood development.* National Academy of Sciences: National Research Council, Washington, DC: National Academy Press.

Shore, C. (1986). Combinatorial play, conceptual development, and early multiword speech. *Developmental Psychology, 22,* 184–190.

Shorter, E. (1975). *The making of the modern family.* New York: Basic Books.

Shure, M. B. (1996). *Raising a thinking child. Help your young child to resolve everyday conflicts and get along with others.* New York: Pocket Books.

Shute, N. (1997, August 18–25). Why do we age? *U.S. News & World Report, 123,* 55–57.

Shweder, R. A. (Ed.). (1998). *Welcome to middle age! (And other cultural fictions).* Chicago: University of Chicago Press.

Sicherer, S. H. (1999). Manifestations of food allergy: Evaluation and management. *American Family Physician, 59*(2), 415–425.

Sidani, M. (2001, February). Thyroid disorders in the elderly. *The Female Patient, 26*(2), 52–57.

Siegel, R. K. (1981, January). Accounting for "afterlife" experiences. *Psychology Today, 15,* 65–75.

Signing with your baby. (2005). *Signing babies network.* Retrieved January 23, 2005, from http://www.signingbabies.net

Silverman, L. K. (2002). *Upside-down brilliance: The visual-spatial learner.* Denver: DeLeon.

Silverman, P. (1983, November 14). Coping with grief—It can't be rushed. *U.S. News & World Report,* 65–68.

Silverman, W. K., LaGreca, A. M., & Wasserstein, S. (1995). What do children worry about? Worries and their relation to anxiety. *Child Development, 66,* 671–686.

Silverstein, M., & Marenco, A. (2001). How Americans enact the grandparent role across the family life course. *Journal of Family Issues, 22*(4), 493–522.

Silverstein, M., Parrott, T. M., & Bengtson, V. L. (1995). Factors that predispose middle-aged sons and daughters to provide social support to older parents. *Journal of Marriage and the Family, 57,* 465–475.

Simon, S. (1991, July 15). Joint custody loses favor for increasing children's feeling of being torn apart. *Wall Street Journal,* B1, B2.

Simonton, D. K. (1988). Age and outstanding achievement: What do we know after a century of research? *Psychological Bulletin, 104,* 251–267.

Simonton, D. K. (1991). Emergence and realization of genius: The lives and works of 120 classical composers. *Journal of Personality and Social Psychology, 61,* 829–840.

Sinaki, M. (1996). Effect of physical activity on bone mass. *Current Opinions in Rheumatology, 8,* 376–383.

Singer, T., Verhaeghen, P., Ghisletta, P., Lindenberger, U., & Baltes, P. B. (2003). The fate of cognition in very old age: Six-year longitudinal findings in the Berlin Aging Study (BASE). *Psychology and Aging, 18*(2), 318–331.

Sinkkonen, J., Anttila, R., & Siimes, M. A. (1998). Pubertal maturation and changes in self-image in early adolescent Finnish boys. *Journal of Youth and Adolescence, 27,* 209–218.

Skegg, K., Nada-Raja, S., Dickson, N., Paul, C., & Williams, S. (2003). Sexual orientation and self-harm in men and women. *American Journal of Psychiatry, 160*(3), 541–546.

Skinner, B. F. (1957). *Verbal behavior.* New York: Appleton-Century-Crofts.

Slaby, R. G. (1994, January 5). Combating television violence. *Chronicle of Higher Education,* B1, B2.

Slater, A., Mattock, A., Brown, E., & Bremner, J. G. (1991). Form perception at birth: Cohen and Younger (1984) revisited. *Journal of Experimental Child Psychology, 51,* 395–406.

Slater, S. (1995). *The lesbian family life cycle.* New York: Free Press.

Slay, H. A., Hayaki, J., Napolitano, M. A., & Brownell, K. D. (1998). Motivations for running and eating attitudes in obligatory versus nonobligatory runners. *International Journal of Eating Disorders, 23*(3), 267–275.

Sleep problems: Nightmares. (2001). National Sleep Foundation. Retrieved November 4, 2001, from http://www.sleepfoundation.org/nightmares.html

Slipp, S. (1993). *The Freudian mystique: Freud, women, and feminism.* New York: New York University Press.

Slobin, D. I. (1972, July). They learn the same way all around the world. *Psychology Today, 6,* 71–82.

Sluckin, W., Herbert, M., & Sluckin, A. (1983). *Maternal bonding.* Oxford, England: Blackwell.

Small, B. J., Fratiglioni, L., von Strauss, E., & Backman, L. (2003). Terminal decline and cognitive performance in very old age: Does cause of death matter? *Psychology of Aging, 18,* 193–202.

Small, M. (1998). *Our babies, ourselves: How biology and culture shape the way we parent.* New York: Doubleday/Anchor.

Smetana, J. G. (1986). Preschool children's conceptions of sex-role transgressions. *Child Development, 57,* 862–871.

Smetana, J. G., Metzger, A., & Campione-Barr, N. (2004, June). African American late adolescents' relationships with parents: Developmental transitions and longitudinal patterns. *Child Development, 75,* 932–947.

Smiley, P. A., & Dweck, C. S. (1994). Individual differences in achievement goals among young children. *Child Development, 65,* 1723–1743.

Smith, A. D., Park, D. C., Cherry, K., & Berkovsky, K. (1990). Age differences in memory for concrete and abstract pictures. *Journal of Gerontology, 45,* P205–209.

Smith, D. (2003, January). What you need to know about the new code. *Monitor on Psychology.* Retrieved October 6, 2004, from http://www.apa.org/monitor/Jan03/new-code.html

Smith, D. B. (2000). Postretirement intentions among 50- to 64-year-old workers. *Gerontologist, 401,* 288–289.

Smith, D. B., & Moen, P. H. (2004, March). Retirement satisfaction for retirees and their spouses: Do gender and the retirement decision-making process matter? *Journal of Family Issues, 25*(2), 262–285.

Smith, G. A. (1998). Injuries to children in the United States related to trampolines. *Pediatrics, 101,* 406–412.

Smith, J., Borchelt, M., Maier, H., & Jopp, D. (2002). Health and well-being in the young old and oldest old. *Journal of Social Issues, 58*(4), 715–732.

Smith, L. B., & Thelan, E. (2003). Development as a dynamic system: *Trends in Cognitive Sciences, 7*(8), 343–348.

Smith, P. K. (Ed.). (1991). *The psychology of grandparenthood: An international perspective.* New York: Routledge, Chapman & Hall.

Smith, R. P. (1957). *"Where did you go?" "Out." "What did you do?" "Nothing."* New York: Norton.

Smith, W. J. (1997). *Forced exit: The slippery slope from assisted suicide to legalized murder.* New York: Random House.

Smith. R. (1999, March). The timing of birth. *Scientific American, 280*(3), 68–76.

Smoking linked to childhood asthma. (2001, November 6). 67th annual meeting of the American College of Chest Physicians in Philadelphia, Pennsylvania, November 4–8, 2001. Retrieved November 9, 2001, from http://www.healthanswers.com/HealthTopics/Apps/GUI_TopicHome.asp?tName=Asthma&topicName=asthma

Smolowe, J. (1990, November 5). To grandma's house we go. *Time,* 86–90.

Snarey, J. (1993). *How fathers care for the next generation: A four decade study.* Cambridge, MA: Harvard University Press.

Snider, M., & Hasson, J. (1993, May 19). Halt urged to "futile" health care. *USA Today,* 1A.

Snow, C. E. (1977). The development of conversation between mothers and babies. *Journal of Child Language, 4,* 1–22.

Snowdon, D. (2001). *Aging with grace: What the Nun study teaches us about leading longer, healthier and more meaningful lives.* New York: Bantam Books.

Snyder, H., & Sickmund, M. (1999). *Juvenile offenders and victims: 1999 national report.* Office of Juvenile Justice and Delinquency Prevention. Washington, DC: U.S. Department of Justice.

Snyder, L., & Quill, T. E. (2001). *Physician's guide to end-of-life care.* American College of Physicians-American Society of Internal Medicine.

Snyder, T. D., & Hoffman, C. M. (2002). *Digest of Education Statistics 2001* (NCES 2002-130). U.S. Department of Education, National Center for Education Statistics. Washington, DC: U.S. Government Printing Office.

Sobotka, T. (2004, June). Is lowest-low fertility in Europe explained by the postponement of childbearing? *Population and Development Review, 30*(2), 195–220.

Social Security Administration. (2004). *Women and Social Security.* Retrieved April 11, 2005, from http://www.ssa.gov/pressoffice/factsheets/women-alt.htm

Soja, N. N. (1994). Young children's concept of color and its relation to the acquisition of color words. *Child Development, 65,* 918–937.

Soken, N. H., & Pick, A. D. (1992). Intermodal perception of happy and angry expressive behaviors by seven-month-old infants. *Child Development, 63,* 787–795.

Sokolov, J. L. (1993). A local contingency analysis of the fine-tuning hypothesis. *Developmental Psychology, 29,* 1008–1023.

Soldz, S. (1988). The construction of meaning: Kegan, Piaget and psychoanalysis. *Journal of Contemporary Psychology, 18,* 46–59.

Soloman, S. E., Rothblum, E. D., & Balsam, K. F. (2004). Pioneers in partnership: Lesbian and gay couples in civil unions compared with those not in civil unions and married heterosexual siblings. *Journal of Family Psychology, 18*(2), 275–286.

Sommers, C. H. (1994). *School girls: Young women, self-esteem and the confidence gap.* New York: Doubleday.

Sonfield, A., Benson-Gold, R., Frost, & Darroch, J.E. (2004). U.S. insurance coverage of contraceptives and the impact of contraceptive coverage mandates, 2002. *Perspectives on Sexual and Reproductive Health, 36*(2), 72–79.

Sorensen, E. S. (1993). *Children's stress and coping: A family perspective.* New York: Guilford Press.

Sorensen, R. C. (1973). *Adolescent sexuality in contemporary America.* New York: World.

Soules, M. R. (2001). Human reproductive cloning: Not ready for prime time. *Fertility and Sterility, 76,* 232–234.

Spangler, G., & Grossmann, K. E. (1993). Biobehavioral organization in securely and insecurely attached infants. *Child Development, 64,* 1439–1450.

Speakman, J. R. (2004, August). Obesity: The integrated roles of environment and genetics. *Journal of Nutrition, 134,* 2090–2105.

Spearman, C. (1904). "General intelligence" objectively determined and measured. *American Journal of Psychology, 15,* 201–293.

Spearman, C. (1927). *The abilities of man.* New York: Macmillan.

Speicher, B. (1994). Family patterns of moral judgment during adolescence and early adulthood. *Developmental Psychology, 30,* 624–632.

Spelke, E. S., von Hofsten, C., & Kestenbaum, R. (1989). Object perception in infancy: Interaction of spatial and kinetic information for object boundaries. *Developmental Psychology, 25,* 185–196.

Spelman, E. V. (1988). *Inessential woman: Problems of exclusion in feminist thought.* Boston, MA: Beacon Press.

Spencer, B., & Gillen, F. J. (1927). *The Arunta* (Vol. 1). London: Macmillan.

Spencer, G., & Sherwood, J. (2004, October 20). *International Human Genome Sequencing Consortium describes finished human genome sequence: Researchers trim count of human genes to 20,000–25,000.* Human Genome Project Information. Retrieved November 17, 2004, from http://www.ornl.gov

Sperling, D. (1990, July 5). Summer cools off sperm. *USA Today,* 1A.

Sperry, R. W. (1993). The impact and promise of the cognitive revolution. *American Psychologist, 48,* 878–885.

Spilton, D., & Lee, L. C. (1977). Some determinants of effective communication in four-year-olds. *Child Development, 48,* 968–977.

Spinath, F. B., Price, T. S., Dale, P. S., & Plomin, R. (2004, March/April). The genetic and environmental origins of language disability and ability. *Child Development, 75,* 445–454.

Spinillo, A. G., & Bryant, P. (1991). Children's proportional judgments: The importance of "half." *Child Development, 62,* 427–440.

Spiro, M. E. (1947). *Ifaluk: A South Sea culture.* Unpublished manuscripts, Coordinated Investigation of Micronesian Anthropology, Pacific Science Board, National Research Council, Washington, DC.

Spitz, R. A. (1957). *No and yes: On the genesis of human communication.* Madison, CT: International Universities Press.

Sporting Goods Manufacturers Association (SGMA) International. (2001, May 1). *New survey: 54 percent of U.S. youngsters play organized sports.* Retrieved March 9, 2005, from http://www.sgma.com

Spotlight on the baby milk industry. (1998). McSpotlight Organization. Retrieved July 10, 1998, from http://www.mcspotlight.org/beyond/ nestle.html

Sprecher, S., & Chandak, R. (1992). Attitude about arranged marriages and dating among men and women from India. *Free Inquiry in Creative Sociology, 20,* 1–11.

Stacey, J., & Biblarz, T. (2001, April). How does the sexual orientation of parents matter? *American Sociological Review, 66,* 159–183.

Stack, S. (1990). New micro-level data on the impact of divorce on suicide,1959–1980: A test of two theories. *Journal of Marriage and the Family, 52,* 119–127.

Stack, S. (2001). Occupation and suicide. *Social Science Quarterly, 82*(2), 384–396.

Stack, S., & Eshleman, J. R. (1998). Marital status and happiness: A 17-nation study. *Journal of Marriage and Family, 60*(2), 527–536.

Staff, J., & Uggen, C. (2003). The fruits of good work: Early work experiences and adolescent deviance. *Journal of Research in Crime and Delinquency, 40*(3), 263–290.

Stamler, B. (2004, June 21, 2004). Now that there are choices, how to choose? *New York Times,* F10.

Stams, G. J., Juffer, F., & van IJzendoorn, M. H. (2002, September). Maternal sensitivity, infant attachment, and temperament in early childhood predict adjustment in middle childhood: The case of adopted children and their biologically unrelated parents. *Developmental Psychology, 38*(5), 806–821.

Stanley, B., & Sieber, J. E. (Eds.). (1992). *Social research on children and adolescents: Ethical issues.* Newbury Park, CA: Sage.

Stanley, J. (1998). Reflex action. *Parents, 5*(24), 5.

Stattin, H., & Magnusson, D. (1990). *Pubertal maturation in female development.* Hillsdale, NJ: Erlbaum.

Staudinger, U. M. (2001). Life reflection: A social-cognitive analysis of life review. *Review of General Psychology, 5*(2), 148–160.

Staudinger, U. M., Smith, J., & Baltes, P. B. (1992). Wisdom-related knowledge in a life review task: Age differences and the role of professional specialization. *Psychology and Aging, 7,* 271–281.

Steele, B. G., & Pollock, C. B. (1968). A psychiatric study of parents who abuse infants and small children. In R. E. Helfer & C.H. Kempe (Eds.), *The battered child.* Chicago: University of Chicago Press.

Steelman, L. C., & Powell, B. (1989). Acquiring capital for college: The constraints of family configuration. *American Sociological Review, 54,* 844–855.

Stein, N. L., & Jewett, J. L. (1986). A conceptual analysis of the meaning of negative emotions: Implications for a theory of development. In C. E. Izard & P. B. Read (Eds.), *Measuring emotions in infants and children.* New York: Cambridge University Press.

Stein, S. P., Holzman, S., Karasu, T. B., & Charles, E. S. (1978). Mid-adult development and psychopathology. *American Journal of Psychiatry, 135,* 676–681.

Steinberg, L., Elmen, J. D., & Mounts, N. S. (1989). Authoritative parenting, psychosocial maturity, and academic success among adolescents. *Child Development, 60,* 1424–1436.

Steinberg, L., Lamborn, S. D., Darling, N., Mounts, N. S., & Dornsbusch, S. M. (1994). Over-time changes in adjustment and competence among adolescents from authoritative, authoritarian, indulgent, and neglectful families. *Child Development, 65,* 754–770.

Steinbock, B. (2005, April). The case for physician assisted suicide: Not (yet) proven. *Journal of Medical Ethics, 31*(4), 235–241.

Steinfels, P. (1992, April 3). Bishops warn against withdrawing life supports. *New York Times,* A7.

Steinhauer, J. (1995, July 6). Living together without marriage or apologies. *New York Times,* A9.

Stek, M. L., Vinkers, D. J., Gussekloo, J., Beekman, A., van der Mast, R. C., & Westendorp, R. G. (2005). Is depression in old age fatal only when people feel lonely? *American Journal of Psychiatry, 162*(1), 178–180.

Stem cell research regulations in the European Union. (2003, October 17). International Society for Stem Cell Research: Northbrook, Illinois. Retrieved November 21, 2004, from http://www.isscr.org/scientists/legislative.htm

Stephens, M. A. P., & Franks, M. M. (1995). Spillover between daughters' roles as caregiver and wife: Interference or enhancement? *Journal of Gerontology: Psychological Sciences, 50B,* P9–P17.

Stephenson, J. (1985). *Death, grief, and mourning: Individual and social realities.* New York: Free Press.

Stephenson, J. (2004). Asia's growing HIV/AIDS epidemics in spotlight at international conference. *Journal of the American Medical Association, 292*(10), 1161–1162.

Steptoe, A., Wardle, J., Fuller, R., Holte, A., Justo, J., Sanderman, R., & Wichstrom, L. (1997). Leisure-time physical exercise: Prevalence, attitudinal correlates, and behavioral correlates among young Europeans from 21 countries. *Preventive Medicine, 26,* 845–854.

Steptoe, A., Wardle, J., Weiwei, C., Bellisle, F., Zotti, A., Baranyai, R., et al. (2002). Trends in smoking, diet, physical exercise, and attitudes toward health in European university students from 13 countries, 1990–2000. *Preventive Medicine, 35,* 97–104.

Stern, A. (2001, June 17). Single dad: Popular but misunderstood. *New York Times, 150*(51787), 9(1).

Stern, D. N. (1985). *The interpersonal world of the infant.* New York: Basic Books.

Stern, G. M. (2004, February). Hispanic students ambushed again. *Education Digest, 69*(6), 47–51.

Sternberg, R. J. (1984). *Beyond IQ: A triarchic theory of human intelligence.* New York: Cambridge University Press.

Sternberg, R. J. (1986a, March/April). Inside intelligence. *American Scientist, 74,* 137–143.

Sternberg, R. J. (1986b). *Intelligence applied.* San Diego: Harcourt Brace Jovanovich.

Sternberg, R. J. (1988). *The triangle of love: Intimacy, passion, commitment.* New York: Basic Books.

Sternberg, R. J. (1990). *Metaphors of mind: Conceptions of the nature of intelligence.* Cambridge, England: Cambridge University Press.

Sternberg, R. J. (1997). Educating intelligence. In R. Sternberg (Ed.), *Intelligence, heredity, and environment.* Cambridge; University of Cambridge.

Sternberg, R. J. (1998). Principles of teaching for successful intelligence. *Educational Psychologist, 33,* 65–72.

Sternberg, R. J. (2001). What is the common thread of creativity? Its dialectical relation to intelligence and wisdom. *American Psychologist, 56,* 360–362.

Sternberg, R. J., & Downing, C. J. (1982). The development of higher-order reasoning in adolescence. *Child Development, 53,* 209–221.

Sternberg, R. J., & Grigorenko, E. L. (1997). Are cognitive styles still in style? *American Psychologist, 52,* 700–712.

Sternberg, R. J., & Hojjat, M. (Eds.). (1997). *Satisfaction in close relationships.* New York: Guilford Press.

Sterns, H., & Kaplan, J. (2003). Self-management of career and retirement. In G. A. Adams & T. A. Beehr (Eds.), *Retirement: Reasons, processes and results.* (pp. 188–233). New York: Springer.

Stevens, C. (1996, November 21). Study: Poverty, death rates linked. *Detroit News,* A4.

Stevens, G. (1999). Age at immigration and second language proficiency among foreign-born adults. *Language in Society, 28,* 555–578.

Stevens, J. C., Cruz, L. A., Marks, L. E., & Lakatos, S. (1998). A multimodal assessment of sensory thresholds in aging. *Journals of Gerontology: Psychological Sciences and Social Sciences, 53,* 263–272.

Stevens, L. M., & Glass, R. M. (2001). Adolescent suicide. *Journal of the American Medical Association, 286*(24), 3194.

Stevenson, H. W., Chen, C., & Lee, S. Y. (1993). Mathematics achievement of Chinese, Japanese, and American children: Ten years later. *Science, 259,* 53–58.

Stevenson-Hinde, J., & Shouldice, A. (1995). Maternal interactions and self-reports related to attachment classifications at 4.5 years. *Child Development, 66,* 583–596.

Stevens-Simon, C., Beach, R. K., & McGregor, J. A. (2002, June). Does incomplete growth and development predispose teenagers to preterm delivery: A template for research. *Journal of Perinatology, 22*(4), 315–324.

Steward, D. K., Moser, D., K., & Ryan-Wenger, N. A. (2001, June). Biobehavioral characteristics of infants with failure to thrive. *Journal of Pediatric Nursing, 16*(3), 162–171.

Stewart, R. B., Jr. (1990). *The second child: Family transitions and adjustments.* Newbury Park, CA: Sage.

Stice, E., Prenell, K., & Bearman, S. K. (2001). Relation of early menarche to depression, eating disorders, substance abuse, and comorbid psychopathology among adolescent girls. *Developmental Psychology, 17,* 608–619.

Stipek, D., Recchia, S., & McClintic, S. (1992). Self-evaluation in young children. *Monographs of the Society for Research in Child Development, 57*(1, Serial No. 226).

Stocker, C., & Dunn, J. (1994). Sibling relationships in childhood and adolescence. In J. C. DeFries and R. Plomin (Eds.), *Nature and nurture during middle childhood* (pp. 214–232). Oxford, England: Blackwell.

Stodghill, R. (2002, August 12). Camp Heartland. *Time, 160*(7), 48–52.

Stoneman, B. (1998). Beyond rocking the ages. *Demographics, 20,* 44–49.

Storm, D. S., Boland, M. G., Gortmaker, S. L., He, Y., Skurnick, J., Howland, L., & Oleske, J. M. (2005, January 3). Protease inhibitor combination therapy, severity of illness, and quality of life among children with perinatally acquired HIV-1 infection. *Pediatrics* (epub, ahead of print). Retrieved January 16, 2005, from http://pediatrics.aappublications.org

Strack, S., & Feifel, H. (Eds.). (2003). *Death and the quest for meaning: Essays in honor of Herman Feifel.* Northvale, NJ: Jason Aronson.

Straus, M. A. (2001). *Beating the devil out of them: Corporal punishment in American families and its effects on children* (2nd Ed.). New Brunswick, NJ: Transaction Publishers.

Strauss, L. T., Herndon, J., Chang, J., Parker, W.Y., Bowens, S. V., Zane, S. B., & Berg, C. J. (2004, November 26). Abortion surveillance–United States: 2001. *Morbidity and Mortality Weekly Report, 53*(SS09), 1–32.

Strauss, R. S. (2002, February). Childhood obesity. *Pediatric Clinics of North America, 49*(1), 175–201.

Stuart, M., & Weinrich, M. (2001). Home- and community-based long-term care: Lessons from Denmark. *Gerontologist, 41,* 474–480.

Studies of feral children. (2001). Department of Linguistics and Modern Language. Lancaster University, United Kingdom. Retrieved October 18, 2001, from http://www.ling.lancs.ac.uk/monkey/ihe/linguistics/LECTURE4/4feral.htm

Study finds living to be 100 isn't a major goal for average American: Reaching 91 is enough. (1999). *Jet, 96*(2), 33.

Study: Foster kids face mental illnesses in adulthood. (2005, April 7). IntelliHealth.Com. *New York Times* News Service.

Stunkard, A. S. (1990). The body mass index of twins who have been reared apart. *New England Journal of Medicine, 322,* 1483–1487.

Styne, D. M. (2001). Childhood and adolescent obesity. Prevalence and significance.

Pediatric Clinics of North America, 48(4), 823–854.

Styne, D. M. (2004). Puberty, obesity and ethnicity. *Trends in Endocrinology and Metabolism, 15*(10), 472–478.

Sudden infant death syndrome. (2004). SHANDS Health Care. Retrieved October 22, 2004, from http://www.shands.org/copyright.htm

Sue, S., & Okazaki, S. (1990). Asian-American educational achievements: A phenomenon in search of an explanation. *American Psychologist, 45,* 913–920.

Suedfeld, P., & Bluck, S. (1993). Changes in integrative complexity accompanying significant life events: Historical evidence. *Journal of Personality and Social Psychology, 64,* 124–130.

Sugar, J. A., & Marinelli, R. D. (1997). Healthful aging: A social perspective. Activities, *Adaptation and Aging, 21*(4), 1–12.

Sugarman, S. (1987). *Piaget's construction of the child's reality.* New York: Cambridge University.

Sugisawa, H., Liang, J., & Liu, X. (1994). Social networks, social support, and mortality among older people in Japan. *Journal of Gerontology: Social Sciences, 49,* S3–S13.

Sugiyama, Y. (2001, November). On students' mathematics achievement in Japan. *Mathematics Education Dialogues.* National Council of Teachers of Mathematics. Retrieved December 17, 2001, from http://www.nctm.org/dialogues/2001-11/20011103.htm

Suh, E., & Diener, E. (1998). Events and subjective well-being: Only recent events matter. *Journal of Personality and Social Psychology, 70,* 1091–1102.

Suitor, J. J. (1991). Marital quality and satisfaction with the division of household labor across the family life cycle. *Journal of Marriage and the Family, 53,* 221–230.

Sulak, P. J. (2004). Adolescent sexual health. *Journal of Family Practice Supplement,* S3–4.

Sullivan, H. S. (1947). *Conceptions of modern psychiatry.* Washington, DC: William A. White Psychiatric Foundation.

Sullivan, H. S. (1953). *The interpersonal theory of psychiatry.* New York: Norton.

Sullivan, M. (1998, February 24). *Study finds U.S. high school seniors lag behind global peers in math and science.* Boston College. Retrieved December 10, 1998, from http://www.bc.edu/

Sum, A., Fogg, N., Harrington, P., Khatiwada, I., Palma, S., Pond, N., & Tobar, P. (2003, May). *The growing gender gaps in college enrollment and the degree attainment in the U.S. and their potential economic and social consequences.* Boston, MA: Northeastern University Center for Labor Market Studies. Retrieved March 18, 2005, from http://www.nupr.neu.edu/6-03/gender_gap_report.pdf

Survey says . . . (2005). *Gay and Lesbian Review Worldwide, 12*(1), 17–21.

Svare, G. M., Jay, S., & Mason, M. A. (2004). *Stepparents on stepparenting: An exploratory study of stepparenting approaches.* New York: Haworth.

Swallen, K. C., Reither, E. N., Haas, S. A., & Meier, A. M. (2005, February). Overweight, obesity, and health-related quality of life among adolescents: The National Longitudinal Study of Adolescent Health. *Pediatrics, 115,* 340–347.

Swan, S. H., Brazil, C., Drobnis, E. A., Liu, F., Kruse, R. L., Hatch, M., Redmon, J. B., Wang, C.H., & Overstreet, J. W. (2003, April). Geographic differences in semen quality of fertile U.S. males. *Environmental Health Perspectives, 111*(4), 414–420.

Swan, S. H., Elkin, E. P., & Fenster, L. (2000, October). The question of declining sperm density revisited: An analysis of 101 studies published 1934–1996. *Environmental Health Perspectives, 108*(10), 961–966.

Sweeney, J. F. (2001). *The day care scare again.* Salon.Com. Retrieved December 1, 2001, from http://www.salon.com/mwt/feature/2001/04/20/day_care/index.html

Swensen, C. H., & Trahaug, G. (1985). Commitment and the long-term relationship. *Journal of Marriage and the Family, 47,* 939–945.

Sylvester, K. (2001, Spring/Summer). Caring for our youngest: Public attitudes in the United States. *The Future of Children.* Retrieved September 20, 2002, from http://www.futureofchildren.org

Sylvester, T. (2001, Summer). The most important story of the year. *Fatherhood Today,* 4.

Syphilis: What happens. (2004). *MD health.* Retrieved December 28, 2004, from http://my.webmd.com/hw/sexual_conditions/hw195181.asp

Szinovacz, M. E. (1998). Grandparents today: A demographic profile. *Gerontologist, 38,* 37–52.

Szinovacz, M. E. (1999). Effects of surrogate parenting on grandparents' well-being. *Journals of Gerontology Series B: Psychological Sciences and Social Sciences, 54B*(6), S376–388.

Szinovacz, M. E. (2005). Retirement and marital decision making: Effects on retirement satisfaction. *Journal of Marriage and the Family, 67,* 387–398.

Szinovacz, M. E., & Davey, A. (2004). Retirement transitions and spouse disability: Effects on depressive symptoms. *Journals of Gerontology Series B: Psychological Sciences and Social Sciences, 59B*(6), S333–339.

Tager-Flusberg, H., Joseph, R., & Folstein, S. (2001). Current directions in research on autism. *Mental Retardation and Developmental Disabilities Research Reviews, 7,* 21–29. Retrieved February 21, 2005, from http://www.bu.edu/anatneuro/dcn/researchers_and_students/publications.html

Tahmincioglu, E. (2001). For richer or poorer: Mail-order brides make for big business online. *ZDNet.* Retrieved March

3, 2005, from http://www.evetahmincioglu.com/mailorderbride.html

Tajani, E., & Ianniruberto, A. (1990). The uncovering of fetal competence. In M. Papini, A. Pasquinelli, & E. A. Gidoni (Eds.), *Development handicap and rehabilitation: Practice and theory* (pp. 3–8) Amsterdam: Elsevier Science.

Talbot, M. (2001, February 4). A desire to duplicate. *New York Times Magazine, 150,* 40–45, 67–68.

Tamis-LeMonda, C. S., & Cabrera, N. (Eds.). (2002). *Handbook of father involvement: Multidisciplinary perspectives.* Mahwah, NJ: Lawrence Erlbaum Associates.

Tamis-LeMonda, C. S., Bornstein, M. H., & Baumwell, L. (2001). Maternal responsiveness and children's achievement of language milestones. *Child Development, 72,* 748–767.

Tan, R. S., & Shou-Jin Pu, R. S. (2004). Is it andropause? Recognizing androgen deficiency in aging men preview. *Postgraduate Medicine, 115*(1), 62–66.

Tan, T. X., & Yang, Y. (2005, February 1). Language development of Chinese adoptees 18–35 months old. *Early Childhood Research Quarterly, 20* (in press). Retrieved February 21, 2005, from http://www.sciencedirect.com

Tang, C. S., Yeung, D. Y., & Lee, A. M. (2003). Psychosocial correlates of emotional response to menarche among Chinese adolescent girls. *Journal of Adolescent Health, 33,* 193–201.

Tanne, J. H. (2000). Body art: Marks of identity. *British Medical Journal, 320,* 64.

Tanne, J. H. (2004, May 8). U.S. universities get around regulations on stem cell research. *BMJJournals, 328*(7448), 1094.

Tannen, D. (1994). *Talking from 9 to 5.* New York: William Morrow.

Tanner, J. M. (1970). Physical growth. In P. H. Mussen (Ed.), *Carmichael's manual of child psychology* (3rd ed.). New York: Wiley.

Tanner, J. M. (1971, Fall). Twelve to sixteen: Early adolescence. *Daedalus, 100,* 4.

Tanner, J. M. (1972). Sequence, tempo, and individual variation in growth and development of boys and girls aged twelve to sixteen. In J. Kagan & R. Coles (Eds.), *Twelve to sixteen: Early adolescence.* New York: Norton.

Tanner, J. M. (1973, September). Growing up. *Scientific American, 229,* 34–43.

Tapia, J. (1998). The schooling of Puerto Ricans: Philadelphia's most impoverished community. *Anthropology and Education Quarterly, 29,* 297–323.

Tappan, M. B. (1997). Interpretive psychology: Stories, circles, and understanding lived experiences. *Journal of Social Issues, 53,* 645–656.

Tauer, C. A. (2004). International policy failures: Cloning and stem-cell research. *Lancet, 364,* 209–214.

Taylor, M., & Gelman, S. A. (1989). Incorporating new words into the lexicon: Preliminary evidence for language hierarchies in two-year-old children. *Child Development, 60,* 625–636.

Taylor, M., Carlson, S. M., Maring, B. L., Gerow, L., & Charley, C. M. (2004). The characteristics and correlates of fantasy in school-age children: Imaginary companions, impersonation, and social understanding. *Developmental Psychology, 40*(6), 1173–1187.

Taylor, S. S. (2001, January 12). Educators urge end to classroom "gender wars." *Women's eNews.* Retrieved January 12, 2002, from the http://www.womensenews.org/article.cfm?aid=502&mode=today

Teaching across generations. (2005, January 28). Baker College Effective Teaching and Learning Department. Retrieved March 10, 2005, from http://www.baker.edu/departments/etl/resources/TAG%20document.doc

Teachman, J. D., Tedrow, L. M., & Crowder, K. D. (2000). The changing demography of America's families. *Journal of Marriage and the Family, 62,* 1234–1246.

Team up for youth. (2005). *Youth sports promote youth and community health.* Retrieved March 9, 2005, from http://www.teamupforyouth.org

Teaster, P. B. (2002). *A response to the abuse of vulnerable adults: The 2000 Survey of Adult Protective Services.* The National Center on Elder Abuse, National Committee for the Prevention of Elder Abuse, and The National Association of Adult Protective Services Administrators. Retrieved May 5, 2005, from http://www.elderabusecenter.org/pdf/research/apsreport030703.pdf

Temple, M., & Polk, K. (1986). A dynamic analysis of educational attainment. *Sociology of Education, 59,* 79–84.

Ten leading causes of death, United States, 1998, all races, both sexes. (2001). National Center for Injury Protection and Control. Retrieved November 4, 2001, from http://webapp.cdc.gov/cgi-bin/broker.exe

Tenenbaum, H. R., & C. Leaper, C. (2002). Are parents' gender schemas related to their children's gender-related cognitions? A meta-analysis. *Developmental Psychology, 38*(4), 613–630.

Terkel, S. (1987, April 5). Hero of the life cycle. *New York Times Book Review,* 36–37.

Terkel, S. (2001). *Will the circle be unbroken? Reflections on death, rebirth, and hunger for a faith.* New York: The New Press.

Terkel, S. (2003). Sociable technologies: Enhancing human performance when the computer is not a tool but a companion. M. C. Roco & W. S. Bainbridge (Eds.), In *Converging technologies for improving human performance.* The Netherlands: Kluwer Academic Publishers.

Terman, L. M., & Merrill, M. A. (1937). *Measuring intelligence.* Boston: Houghton Mifflin.

Terry, D. J. (1994). Determinants of coping: The role of stable and situational factors. *Journal of Personality and Social Psychology, 66,* 895–910.

Teti, D. M., & Ablard, K. E. (1989). Security of attachment and infant-sibling relationships: A laboratory study. *Child Development, 60,* 1519–1528.

Thacker, P. D. (2004). Biological clock ticks for men, too: Genetic defects linked to sperm of older fathers. *Journal of the American Medical Association, 291*(14), 1683–1685.

The 2005 Annual Report of the Board of Trustees of the Federal Old-Age and Survivors Insurance and Disability Insurance (OASDI) Trust Funds Report. (2005, March 23). Social Security Online. Retrieved May 2, 2005, from http://www.ssa.gov/OACT/TR/TR05/

The boy who lived with monkeys. (1999, October 13). BBC Online. Retrieved October 15, 2001, from http://www.bbc.co.uk/qed/monkeys.shtml

The case for elementary school recess. (2001). The American Association for the Child's Right to Play. Retrieved November 26, 2001, from http://www.ipausa.org/recesshandbook.htm

The convention on the rights of the child. (2001). The United Nations Convention on the Rights of the Child: Article 31. Retrieved November 26, 2001, from http://www.unicef.org/CRCpamphlet/pamphlet.htm

The facts about breast augmentation. (2005, March 27). *The Today Show.* Retrieved April 12, 2005, from http://www.breastenlargementmagazine.com/news_today.html

The horrible exception. (2001). *Economist, 361*(8250), 41–42.

The standards: What teachers should know. (1998). National Board for Professional Teaching Standards. Retrieved February 7, 1999, from http://www.nbpts.org

Thelen, E. (1981). Rhythmical behavior in infancy: An ethological perspective. *Developmental Psychology, 17,* 237–257.

Thelen, E. (1986). Treadmill-elicited stepping in seven-month-old infants. *Child Development, 57,* 1498–1506.

Thelen, E. (1995). Motor development: A new synthesis. *American Psychologist, 50,* 79–95.

Thernstrom, A., & Thernstrom, S. (2003). *No excuses: Closing the racial gap in learning.* New York: Simon & Schuster.

Thiedke, C. C. (2001, January 15). Sleep disorders and sleep problems in childhood. *American Family Physician, 63*(2), 277–284.

Thiedke, C. C. (2003, April 1). Nocturnal enuresis. *American Family Physician, 67*(7), 1499–1506. Retrieved February

24, 2005, from http://www.aafp.org/afp/20030401/1499.pdf

Thoits, P. A. (1986). Multiple identities: Examining gender and marital status differences in distress. *American Sociological Review, 51*, 259–272.

Thomas, A., & Chess, S. (1987). Roundtable: What is temperament? *Child Development, 58*, 505–529.

Thomas, A., Chess, S., & Birch, H. G. (1970, August). The origin of personality. *Scientific American, 223*, 102–109.

Thomas, A., Chess, S., Birch, H. G., Hertzig, M. E., & Korn, S. (1963). *Behavioral individuality in early childhood.* New York: New York University Press.

Thomas, C. (1996, August 31). Olajuwon says his marriage was arranged. *Houston Chronicle,* 1.

Thomas, E., Johnson, D., Gesalman, A., Smith, V. E., Pierce, E., Peraino, K, & Murr. A. (2001, July 2). Motherhood and murder. *Newsweek, 138*(1), 20–25.

Thompson, G. (1998, December 14). With obesity in children rising, more get adult type of diabetes. *New York Times,* A1.

Thompson, K., & Haninger, K. (2001). Violence in e-rated video games. *Journal of the American Medical Association, 286*(5), 591–598.

Thompson, R. A. (1990). Vulnerability in research: A developmental perspective on research risk. *Child Development, 61*, 1–16.

Thompson, R. A. (2001). Development in the first years of life. Caring for Infants and Toddlers. The Future of Children. *The David and Lucile Packard Foundation, 11*(1). Spring-Summer 2001. Retrieved September 30, 2001, from http://www.futureofchildren.org/ pubs-info2825/pubs-info.htm?doc_id=79324

Thorne, B. (1993). *Gender play: Girls and boys in school.* New Brunswick, NJ: Rutgers University Press.

Thornton, A., & Young-DeMarco, L. (2001). Four decades of trends in attitudes toward family issues in the United States: The 1960s through the 1990s. *Journal of Marriage and Family, 63*, 1009–1037.

Tibbits-Kleber, A. L., & Howell, R. J. (1985). Reactive attachment disorder in infancy (RAD). *Journal of Clinical Child Psychology, 14*(4), 304–310.

Tiedje, L. B., Wortman, C. B., Downey, G., Emmons, C., Biernat, M., & Lang, E. (1990). Women with multiple roles: Role-compatibility perceptions, satisfaction, and mental health. *Journal of Marriage and the Family, 52*, 63–72.

Tikoo, M. (1996). An exploratory study of differences in developmental concerns of middle-aged men and women in India. *Psychological Reports, 78*, 883–887.

Tobacco use among middle and high school students: United States, 2002. (2003). *Morbidity and Mortality Weekly Report, 52*(45), 1096–1098.

Tolan, P. H., Gorman-Smith, D., & Henry, D. B. (2003). The developmental ecology of urban males' youth violence. *Developmental Psychology, 32*, 274–291.

Tomasello, M. (1992). *First verbs: A case study of early grammatical development.* New York: Cambridge University Press.

Tomasello, M. (1995). Joint attention as social cognition. In C. Moore & P. Dunham (Eds.), *Joint attention: Its origins and role in development.* Hillsdale, NJ: Erlbaum.

Tomison, A. M. (1996, Winter). *Intergenerational transmission of maltreatment.* Melbourne, Australia: National Child Protection Clearinghouse. Issues in Child Abuse Prevention.

Tomkins, S. S. (1986). Script theory. In J. Aronoff, R. A. Zucker, & A. I. Rabin (Eds.), *Structuring personality.* Orlando, FL: Academic Press.

Tonti-Filippini, N. (2003 Spring). The embryo rescue debate: Impregnating women, ectogenesis, and restoration from suspended animation. *National Catholic Bioethics Quarterly, 3*(1), 111–137.

Torrey, E. F. (1992). *Freudian fraud: The malignant effect of Freud's theory on American thought and culture.* New York: HarperCollins.

Toussaint-Commeau, M. (2003). Changing Hispanic demographics: Opportunities and constraints in the financial market. *Chicago Fed Letter,* (192). Retrieved April 5, 2005, from http://www.chicagofed.org/publications/fedletter/2003/cflaug2003_192.pdf

Tout, K., Zaslow, M. Papillo, A. R., & Vandivere, S. (2001, September). *Early care and education: Work support for families and developmental opportunity for young children.* Washington, DC: The Urban Institute. Retrieved February 10, 2005, from http://www.urban.org/UploadedPDF/occa51.pdf

Trachtenberg, S., & Viken, R. J. (1994). Aggressive boys in the classroom: Biased attributions or shared perceptions? *Child Development, 65*, 829–835.

Tramont, E. C. (2000). *Treponema pallidum* (syphilis). In G. L Mandell et al. (Eds.), *Principles and practice of infectious diseases* (5th ed., Vol. 2, pp. 2474–2490). New York: Churchill Livingstone.

Travis, E. H. (2005, March). Psychotropic drug use in nursing homes. *Global Action on Aging.* Retrieved April 27, 2005, from http://www.globalaging.org/

Travis, J. (2000, July 1). Human genome work reaches milestone. *Science News, 158*(1), 4.

Travis, N. (1993). New piece in Alzheimer's puzzle. *Science, 261*, 828–829.

Treffert, D. A. (2001). *The savant syndrome: Islands of genius.* State Medical Society of Wisconsin. Retrieved November 11, 2001, from http://www.wismed.org/foundation/islands.htm

Trends in the well-being of America's children and youth 2003. (2003). U.S. Department of Health and Human Services. Retrieved February 7, 2004 from http://aspe.hhs.gov/hsp/03trends/

Trevarthen, C. (1977). Descriptive analysis of infant communicative behavior. In H. R. Schaffer (Ed.), *Studies in mother-infant interaction.* London: Academic Press.

Trickett, P. K., & Susman, E. J. (1988). Parental perceptions of child-rearing practices in physically abusive and nonabusive families. *Developmental Psychology, 24*, 270–276.

Tronick, E. Z., Morelli, G. A., & Ivey, P. K. (1992). The Efé forager infant and toddler's pattern of social relationships. *Developmental Psychology, 28*, 568–577.

Trotter, R. J. (1987, May). You've come a long way, baby. *Psychology Today, 21*, 34–45.

Trueba, H. T., Cheng, L. L., & Ima, K. (1993). *Myth or reality: Adaptive strategies of Asian Americans in California.* Washington, DC: Falmer.

Truglio, R. T., Murphy, K. C., Oppenheimer, S., Huston, A. C., & Wright, J. C. (1996). Predictors of children's entertainment television viewing: Why are they tuning in? *Journal of Applied Developmental Psychology, 17*, 474–494.

Trumbull, E., Carrie Rothstein-Fisch, C., & Greenfield, P. M. (2000). *Bridging cultures in our schools: New approaches that work.* A WestEd Knowledge Brief. Retrieved November 29, 2001, from http://www.wested.org/online_pubs/bridging/welcome.shtml

Truog, R. D. (2004, August). Brain death: At once "Well Settled" and "Persistently Unresolved." *Policy Forum of American Medical Association, 6*(8). Retrieved May 10, 2005, from http://www.ama-assn.org/ama/pub/category/print/12715.html

Trustees of the Social Security and Medicare Programs. (2005, March 23). *Status of the Social Security and Medicare programs.* Retrieved April 10, 2005, from http://www.ssa.gov/OACT/TRSUM/trsummary.html

Tsitouras, P. D., Martin, C. E., & Harman, S. M. (1982). Relationship of serum testosterone to sexual activity in healthy elderly men. *Journal of Gerontology, 37*, 288–293.

Tucker, J. S., Schwartz, J. E., Clark, K. M., & Friedman, H. S. (1999, December). Age-related changes in the associations of social network ties with mortality risk. *Psychology and Aging, 14*, 564–571.

Tuller, D. (2004, June 21, 2004). Gentlemen, start your engines? *New York Times,* F1.

Tulving, E. (1968). Theoretical issues in free recall. In T. R. Dixon & D. L. Horton (Eds.), *Verbal behavior and general behavior theory.* Englewood Cliffs, NJ: Prentice Hall.

Tulving, E. (1997). What are memory disorders disorders of? *Brain and Cognition, 35,* 299–301.

Tulving, E., & Craik, F. (2000). *Oxford handbook of memory.* Oxford: Oxford University Press.

Turnbull, J. E., & Mui, A. C. (1995). Mental health status and needs of black and white elderly: Differences in depression. In D. K. Padgett (Ed.), *Handbook on ethnicity, aging, and mental health* (pp. 73–112). Westport, CT: Greenwood Press.

Turner, A. (1996). A comparison of self-initiated coping behaviors in premature and low-birthweight infants—Toddlers with and without prenatal cocaine exposure. *Dissertation Abstracts, 57*(3-A), 1009.

Turner, L., Conway, A. J., Jimenez, M., Liu, P. Y., Forbes, E., McLachlan, R. I., & Handelsman, D. J. (2003, October). Contraceptive efficacy of a depot progestin and androgen combination in men. *The Journal of Clinical Endocrinology and Metabolism, 88*(10), 4659–4667.

Turner, P. J. (1991). Relations between attachment, gender and behavior with peers in preschool. *Child Development, 62,* 1475–1488.

Turner, R. J., Wheaton, B., & Lloyd, D. A. (1995). The epidemiology of social stress. *American Sociological Review, 60,* 104–125.

Tzeng, J. & Mare, R. D. (1995). Labour market and socioeconomic effects on martial stability. *Social Science Research, 24*(3), 329–351.

Ulick, J. (2004, October 25). How to make a stem cell. *Newsweek, 144*(17), 46–48.

U.S. AID Health. (2005, February 11). HIV/AIDS Frequently asked questions. Retrieved April 19, 2005, from http://www.usaid.gov/

U.S. Bureau of Justice Statistics. (2003). *Prison statistics Summary findings.* Washington, DC: U.S. Department of Justice. Retrieved February 15, 2005, from http://www.ojp.usdoj.gov/bjs/prisons.htm

U.S. Bureau of Justice Statistics. (2004). *Teens experience the highest rates of violent crime.* Washington, DC: U.S. Department of Justice. Retrieved February 21, 2005, from http:www.ojp.usdoj.gov/bjs/glance/vage.htm

U.S. Bureau of Labor Statistics. (1998). *Employment status of the civilian population by sex and age.* Retrieved February 10, 1999, from http://stats.bls.gov/news.release/empsit.t01.htm

U.S. Bureau of Labor Statistics. (2004a, February 27). Table 1. Fastest growing occupations and occupations projected to have the largest numerical increases in employment between 2002 and 2012, by level of education or training. *Occupational Outlook Handbook.* Retrieved May 5, 2005, from http://bls.gov/oco/print/ocotjt1.htm

U.S. Bureau of Labor Statistics. (2004b, April 20). *Employment characteristics of families' summary.* Washington, DC: United States Department of Labor. Retrieved February 10, 2005, from http://www.bls.gov/news.release/famee.nr0.htm

U.S. Bureau of Labor Statistics. (2004c, December 16). Volunteering in the United States, 2004. Washington, DC: U.S. Department of Labor. Retrieved April 25, 2005, from http://www.bls.gov/news.release/volun.nr0.htm

U.S. Bureau of Labor Statistics. (2005, March 25). *College enrollment and work activity of 2004 high school graduates.* Washington, DC: U.S. Department of Labor. Retrieved April 8, 2005, from http://www.bls.gov/news.release/hsgec.nr0.htm

U.S. Bureau of the Census. (2000a). *International database.* Retrieved December 27, 2001, from http://www.census.gov/cgi-bin/ipc/idbsum?cty

U.S. Bureau of the Census. (2000b). No. 655: Families with own children—employment status of parents: 1995 and 1999. *Statistical Abstract of the United States: 2000,* 410.

U.S. Bureau of the Census. (2000c). (NP-D1-A) *Projections of the resident population by age, sex, race, and Hispanic origin: 1999 to 2100.* Retrieved December 27, 2001, from http://www.census.gov/population/www/projections/natdet-D1A.html

U.S. Bureau of the Census. (2001). The 65 years and over population: 2000. *Census 2000 Brief.* Retrieved December 27, 2001, from http://www.census.gov/prod/2001pubs/c2kbr01.10.pdf

U.S. Bureau of the Census. (2002). 2000 Census of Population and Housing. *Summary File 3: Technical Documentation, 2002.* Washington, DC: U.S. Department of Commerce. Retrieved September 15, 2004, from http://www.census.gov/prod/cen2000/doc/sf3.pdf

U.S. Bureau of the Census. (2003a). *Children's living arrangements and characteristics: March 2002* (P20-547). Retrieved October 28, 2004, from http://www.census.gov/prod/2003pubs/p20-547.pdf

U.S. Bureau of the Census. (2003b). No. 13, Resident Population Projections by Sex and Age: 2005–2050. *Statistical Abstract of the United States: 2003.*

U.S. Bureau of the Census. (2004a). *Census Bureau projects tripling of Hispanic and Asian populations in 50 years; non-Hispanic whites may drop to half of the total population.* News release, March 18, 2004.

U.S. Bureau of the Census. (2004b). *Characteristics of Male-Female Unmarried and Married couples: 2003.* Retrieved November 10, 2004, from http://www.census.gov/prod/2004pubs/p20-553.pdf

U.S. Bureau of the Census. (2004c). Families by size and presence of children: 1980 to 2003. *Statistical Abstract of the United States: 2004–2005.* Tables 60 and 61.

Retrieved February 13, 2005, from http://www.census.gov/prod/2004pubs/04statab/labor.pdf

U.S. Bureau of the Census. (2004d). Families with own children—Employment status of parents: 1995 and 2003. *Statistical Abstract of the United States: 2004–2005.* No. 581. Retrieved February 13, 2005, from http://www.census.gov/prod/2004pubs/04statab/labor.pdf

U.S. Bureau of the Census. (2004e). *IDB Summary demographic data.* Retrieved November 16, 2004, from http://www.census.gov/ipc/www/idbsum.html

U.S. Bureau of the Census. (2004f). *Moving to America—Moving to homeownership: 1994 to 2002.* Retrieved March 2, 2005, from http://www.census.gov/prod/2003pubs/h121-03-1.pdf

U.S. Bureau of the Census. (2004g). *Projected population of the United States, by age and sex: 2000 to 2050.* Retrieved April 12, 2005, from http://www.census.gov/ipc/www/usinterimproj/natprojtab02a.pdf

U.S. Bureau of the Census. (2004h). Table 13. Resident population projections by sex and age: 2005 to 2050. *Statistical Abstract of the United States, 2004.* Retrieved February 13, 2005, from http://www.census.gov/prod/2004pubs/04statab/labor.pdf

U.S. Bureau of the Census. (2004i). Table 27. Life expectancy at birth, at 65 years of age, and at 75 years of age, according to race and sex: United States, selected years 1900–2002. *Chartbook on Trends in the Health of Americans, 2004.* Washington, DC: National Center on Health Statistics.

U.S. Bureau of the Census. (2004j). Table 46. Death rates for suicide, according to sex, race, and Hispanic origin, and age: United States, selected years 1950–2002. *Chartbook on Trends in the Health of Americans, 2004.* Washington, DC: National Center on Health Statistics.

U.S. Bureau of the Census. (2004–2005). *Statistical Abstract of the United States: 2004–2005* (124th edition). Washington, DC. Economics and Statistics Administration.

U.S. Bureau of the Census. (2005a). *Older Americans month celebrated in May. Facts for features.* Retrieved April 10, 2005, from http://www.census.gov/Press-Relaease/www/releases/archives/cb05-ff.07.pdf

U.S. Bureau of the Census. (2005b, September 19). *Normal retirement age.* Social Security Administration. Retrieved October 15, 2005, from http://www.ssa.gov/OACT/ProgData/nra.html

U.S. Congress. (2001, June 7). *Economic growth and tax relief reconciliation act of 2001: Public Law 107–16., Sec. 202: Expansion of Adoption Credit and Adoption Assistance Programs.* Washington, DC: 107th Congress.

U.S. Department of Commerce. (1998). *Cohabitation. Current population reports.*

(October). Washington, DC: U.S. Government Printing Office.

U.S. Department of Education Annual Reports to Congress. In Yazbak, F. E. (2003, Winter). Autism in the United States. *Journal of American Physicians and Surgeons, 8*(4). 103–107.

U.S. Department of Education. (1999). Table 53: Children 0 to 21 years old served in federally supported programs for the disabled by type of disability: 1976–77 to 1997–98. *Digest of Education Statistics, 1999.* Chapter 2. Elementary and Secondary Education. Retrieved December 18, 2001, from http://nces.ed.gov/pubs2000/ digest99/d99t053.html

U.S. Department of Education. (2000). *Bilingual professional development.* Retrieved December 16, 2001, from http://www.ed.gov/offices/OBEMLA/fy2000.html

U.S. Department of Education, National Center for Education Statistics. (2000). The Condition of Education 2000, NCES 2000-602, Washington, DC: U.S. Government Printing Office.

U.S. Department of Education. (2001). *No child left behind: Executive summary.* Retrieved December 17, 2001, from http://www.ed.gov/inits/nclb/part2.html

U.S. Department of Education. (2002). *To assure the free appropriate public education of all children with disabilities: Individuals with Disabilities Education Act, Section 618.* Retrieved January 15, 2005, from http://www.ed.gov/about/reports/annual/osep/1998/20thar.pdf

U.S. Department of Education. (2003). *Projections of education statistics to 2013* (NCES 2004-013). Digest of Education Statistics 2003. Retrieved March 17, 2005, from http://nces.ed.gov/

U.S. Department of Education. (2005, March 15). *Biennial evaluation report to Congress on the implementation of the state formula grant program, 2002–2004: English Language Acquisition, Language Enhancement and Academic Achievement Act (ESEA, Title III, Part A).* Washington, DC: Office of English Language Acquisition, Language Enhancement and Academic Achievement for Limited English Proficient Students. Retrieved March 25, 2005, from http://www.ncela.gwu.edu/oela/biennial05/full_report.pdf

U.S. Department of Health and Human Services, Children's Bureau. (2001, April). *Preliminary estimates as of April 2001.* AFCARS. Administration for Children and Families. Retrieved December 13, 2001, from http://www.acf.dhhs.gov/programs/cb/dis/afcars/cwstats.html

U.S. Department of Health and Human Services. (1998). *Profile of older Americans: 1998.* Administration on Aging. Retrieved January 14, 1999, from http://www.aoa.dhhs.gov/aoa/stats/profile

U.S. Department of Health and Human Services. (2003a). *Births: Final data for 2002*

(Vol. 52, No. 10). Washington, DC: U.S. Government Printing Office.

U.S. Department of Health and Human Services. (2003b). *Deaths: Leading causes for 2001* (Vol. 52, No. 9). Washington, DC: U.S. Government Printing Office.

U.S. Department of Health and Human Services. (2003c). *Infant mortality statistics from the 2001 period linked birth/infant death data set.* (Vol. 52, No. 2). Washington, DC: U.S. Government Printing Office.

U.S. Department of Health and Human Services. (2003d). Table 40. Live births by method of delivery and rates of cesarean delivery and vaginal birth after previous cesarean delivery, by age and race and Hispanic origin of mother: United States, 2002. (Vol. 52, No. 10). Washington, DC: U.S. Government Printing Office.

U.S. Department of Health and Human Services. (2003e). Table 41. Rates of cesarean delivery and vaginal birth after previous cesarean delivery, by race and Hispanic origin of mother: United States and territory, 2002. (Vol. 52, No. 10). Washington, DC: U.S. Government Printing Office.

U.S. Department of Health and Human Services. (2003f). *Trends in the well-being of America's children and youth 2003.* Retrieved February 7, 2004 from http://aspe.hhs.gov/hsp/03trends/

U.S. Department of Health and Human Services. (2004a). *How many children were adopted in 2000 and 2001?* Washington, DC: National Adoption Information Clearinghouse.

U.S. Department of Health and Human Services. (2004b). *SIDS deaths by race and ethnicity.* Retrieved October 27, 2004, from http://www.sidcenter.org

U.S. Department of Health and Human Services. (2004c). *Table 32: Leading causes of death and numbers of deaths, according to age United States, 1980 and 2002.* Retrieved December 29, 2004 from http://www.cdc.gov/nchc/data/hus/hus04trend.pdf#topic

U.S. Department of Health and Human Services and U.S. Department of Agriculture. (2005, January). Dietary guidelines for Americans, 2005. Washington, DC: U.S. Government Printing Office.

U.S. Department of Housing and Urban Development. (2000, February). *Eliminating childhood lead poisoning: A federal strategy targeting lead paint hazards.* President's Task Force on Environmental Health Risks and Safety Risks to Children. Retrieved February 22, 2005, from http://www.hud.gov/offices/lead/reports/fedstrategy2000.pdf

U.S. Department of Justice. (2001). *Teens experience the highest rates of violent crime.* Bureau of Justice Statistics. Retrieved January 8, 2002, from http://www.ojp.usdoj.gov/bjs/glance/vage.htm

U.S. Department of Justice. (2003). *Criminal victimization in the United States, 2002: Personal crimes, 2002: Victimization rates for persons 12 and over, by type of crime and age of victims.* Retrieved April 11, 2005, from http://www.ojp.usdoj.gov/bjs/pub/pdf/cvus/current/cv0203.pdf

U.S. Department of Labor. *Question: What is women's labor force participation rate?* Retrieved April 22, 2005, from http://www.dol.gov/wb/faq38.htm

U.S. Department of Social and Health Services (2004). *Infant toddler early intervention program (ITEIP).* Retrieved November 17, 2004, from http://www1.dshs.wa/iteip

U.S. Food and Drug Administration. (2004 January–February). Joint effort to improve the health of older Hispanic Americans. *FDA Consumer, 38*(1). Retrieved May 5, 2005, from www.fda.gov/fdac/features/2004/104_old.html

U.S. Public Health Service Task Force. (2002, November 22). U.S. Public Health Service Task Force Recommendations for Use of Antiretroviral Drugs in Pregnant HIV-1 Infected Women for Maternal Health and Interventions to Reduce Perinatal HIV-1 Transmission in the United States. *Morbidity and Mortality Weekly Report, 51*(RR18), 1–38.

U.S. Surgeon General Rolls Out 2005 Agenda: The Year of the Healthy Child. (2005, January 24). U.S. Department of Health and Human Services. News Release. Retrieved February 21, 2005, from http://www.surgeongeneral.gov/pressreleases/sg01242005.html

Udry, J. R. (1988). Biological predispositions and social control in adolescent sexual behavior. *American Sociological Review, 53,* 709–722.

Umberson, D., & Chen, M. D. (1994). Effects of a parent's death on adult children: Relationship salience and reaction to loss. *American Sociological Review, 59,* 152–168.

UNAIDS. (2004, June). *2004 Report on the Global AIDS Epidemic; 4th Global Report.* Joint United Nations Programme on HIV/AIDS (UNAIDS). Retrieved February 16, 2005, from http://www.unaids.org/bangkok2004/report_pdf.html

UNAIDS/UNIFEM/UNFPA. (2004). *Women and HIV/AIDS: Confronting the crisis.* Retrieved February 16, 2005, from http://www.unfpa.org/hiv/women/report/index.htm

UNAIDS/WHO. (2004, December). *AIDS Epidemic, 2004: Follow-up to the 2001 United Nations General Assembly Special Session on HIV/AIDS.* Retrieved April 8, 2005, from http://www.unaids.org/wad2004/EPI_1204_pdf_en/EpiUpdate04_en.pdf

Underage drinking. (2005, April). *SADD statistics.* Retrieved April 13, 2005, from http://www.saddonline.com/

Understanding allergy and asthma. (2001). Retrieved November 9, 2001, from http://

www.aaaai.org/ public/publicedmat/tips/default. stm#English

United Nations Demographic Yearbook: 2001. (2003). *Early motherhood in the industrialized world.* New York: United Nations.

Updegraff, K. A., Helms, H. M., McHale, S. M., Crouter, A. C., Thayer, S. M., & Sales, L. H. (2004, October). Who's the boss? Patterns of perceived control in adolescents' friendships. *Journal of Youth and Adolescence, 33*(5), 403–420.

Updegraff, K. A., McHale, S. M., Crouter, A. C., & Kupanoff, K. (2001). Parents' involvement in adolescents' peer relationships: A comparison of mothers' and fathers' roles. *Journal of Marriage and Family, 63*(3), 655–668.

Upledger, J. E. (2001). Craniosacral therapy and attention deficit disorder. *Massage Today, 1*(8). Retrieved February 2, 2005, from http://www.massagetoday.com

Upledger, J. E. (2003a). Applications of craniosacral therapy in newborns and infants, Part I. *Massage Today, 3*(5). Retrieved February 2, 2005, from http://www.massagetoday.com

Upledger, J. E. (2003b). Applications of craniosacral therapy in newborns and infants, Part II. *Massage Today, 3*(6). Retrieved February 2, 2005, from http://www.massagetoday.com

Upledger, J. E. (2004, August). A look inside the craniosacral system and how CST helps. *Massage Today, 4*(8). Retrieved February 2, 2005, from http://www.massagetoday.com/

Uskul, A. K. (2004). Women's menarche stories form a multicultural sample. *Social Science and Medicine, 59,* 667–679.

Utz, R. L., Reidy, E. B., Carr, D., Nesse, R., & Wortman, C. (2004, July). The daily consequences of widowhood: The role of gender and intergenerational transfers on subsequent housework performance. *Journal of Family Issues, 25,* 683–712.

Uzgiris, I. C., & Raeff, C. (1995). Play in parent-child interactions. In M. H. Bornstein (Ed.), *Handbook of parenting* (Vol. 4). Hillsdale, NJ: Erlbaum.

Vail, K. (2005, April). Math that adds up: What schools can do to make U.S. students more competitive in the global marketplace. *American School Board Journal.* Retrieved April 14, 2005, from http://www.asbj.com/achievement/0405asbjvail.pdf

Vaillant, C. O., & Vaillant, G. E. (1993). Is the U-curve of marital satisfaction an illusion? A 40-year study of marriage. *Journal of Marriage and the Family, 55,* 230–239.

Vaillant, G. (2002). *Aging well: Surprising guideposts to a happier life from the Landmark Harvard Study of Adult Development.* Boston: Little, Brown and Company.

Vaillant, G. E., & Milofsky, E. (1980). Natural history of male psychological health. IX: Empirical evidence for Erikson's model of the life cycle. *American Journal of Psychiatry, 37,* 1348–1359.

Valins, M. (1995). Western Europe turns to group housing. *Contemporary Longterm Care, 18*(4), 78.

Van Asselt, K. M., Kok, H. S., Pearson, P. L., Dubas, J. S., Peeters, P. H. M., te Velde, E. R., & van Noord, A. H. (2004, November). Heritability of menopausal age in mothers and daughters. *Fertility and Sterility, 82*(5), 1348–1351.

Van Collie, S. C. (1998). Moving up through mentoring. *Workforce, 77,* 36–42.

Van IJzendoorn, M. H., & Hubbard, F. O. A. (2000). Are infant crying and maternal responsiveness during the first year related to infant-mother attachment at 15 months? *Attachment and Human Development, 2*(3), 371–391.

Van IJzendoorn, M. H., & Kroonenberg, P. M. (1988). Cross-cultural patterns of attachment: A meta-analysis of the strange situation. *Child Development, 59,* 147–156.

Van IJzendoorn, M. H., & Sagi, A. (1999). Cross-cultural patterns of attachment. In Cassidy, J. and Shaver, P. H. (Eds.), *Handbook of attachment theory, research, and clinical applications.* (pp. 713–734). New York/London: Guilford Press.

Van IJzendoorn, M. H., & Sagi, A. (2001, October). Cultural blindness or selective inattention? *American Psychologist, 56,* 824–825.

Van Mechelen, W., Twisk, J., Molendijk, A., Blom, B., Snel, J., & Kemper, H. C. (1996). Subject-related risk factors for sports injuries: A one-year prospective study in young adults. *Medicine and Science in Sports and Exercise,* 1171–1178.

Van Vuuren, C. J., & de Jongh, M. (1999). Rituals of manhood in South Africa: Circumcision at the cutting edge of critical intervention. *South African Journal of Ethnology, 22*(4) 142–157.

Van Willigen, M. (2000). Differential benefits of volunteering across the life course. *Journal of Gerontology: Series B: Psychological Sciences and Social Sciences, 55B*(5), S308–S318.

VandenBos, G. R. (1998). Life-span developmental perspectives on aging: An introductory overview. In I. H. Nordhus et al., (Eds.), *Clinical geropsychology.* Washington, DC: American Psychological Association.

Vander Zanden, J. W. (1987). *Social psychology* (4th ed.). New York: Random House.

Vander Zanden, J. W. (1990). *The social experience* (2nd ed.). New York: McGraw-Hill.

Vander Zanden, J. W., & Pace, A. (1984). *Educational psychology* (2nd ed.). New York: Random House.

Vandewater, E. A., & Lansford, J. E. (1998). Influences of family structure and parental conflict on children's well-being. *Family Relations, 47,* 323–330.

Vandewater, E. A., & Stewart, A. J. (1997). Women's career commitment patterns and personality development. In M. E. Lachman & J. B. James (Eds.), *Multiple paths of midlife development* (pp. 375–410). Chicago: University of Chicago Press.

Vandewater, E. A., Bickham, D. S., Lee, J. H., Cummings, H. M., Wartella, E. A., & Rideout, V. J. (2005, January). When the television is always on: Heavy television exposure and young children's development. *American Behavioral Scientist, 48*(5), 562–577.

Vasan, R., & Sullivan, L. M. (2005). Relative importance of borderline and elevated levels of coronary heart disease risk factors. *Annals of Internal Medicine, 142*(6), 393–406.

Vasquez, J. A. (1998). Distinctive traits of Hispanic students. *Prevention Researcher, 5,* 1.

Vaughn, B. E., Block, J. H., & Block, J. (1988). Parental agreement on child rearing during early childhood and the psychological characteristics of adolescents. *Child Development, 59,* 1020–1033.

Venkatraman, M. M. (1995). A cross-cultural study of the subjective well-being of married elderly persons in the United States and India. *Journal of Gerontology: Social Sciences, 50B,* S35–S44.

Ventura, S. J., Abma, J. C., Mosher, W. D., & Henshaw, S. (2004). Estimated pregnancy rates for the United States, 1990–2000: An update. *National Vital Statistics Reports, 53*(23). Hyattsville, MD: National Center for Health Statistics.

Verba, M. (1994). The beginnings of collaboration in peer interaction. *Human Development, 37,* 125–139.

Verbrugge, L. M. (1989). The twain meet: Empirical explanations of sex differences in health and mortality. *Journal of Health and Social Behavior, 30,* 282–304.

Verderber, S., & Song, J. H. (2005). Environment and aging in Japan: A review of recent research. *Environment and Behavior, 37*(1), 43–80.

Verhaeghen, P., Marcoen, A., & Goossens, L. (1993). Facts and fiction about memory aging: A quantitative integration of research findings. *Journal of Gerontology: Psychological Sciences, 48,* P157–P171.

Verhagen, E., & Sauer, P. J. (2005, March 10). The Groningen protocol—Euthanasia in severely ill newborns. *New England Journal of Medicine, 352,* 959–962.

Verstraeten, T. (2004). Thimerosal. The Centers for Disease Control and Prevention and GlaxoSmithKline. *Pediatrics, 113,* 932.

Vidaeff, A. C., & Mastrobattista, J. M. (2003). In utero cocaine exposure: A thorny mix of science and mythology. *American Journal of Perinatology, 20,* 165–172.

Viding, E., Spinath, F. M. Price, T. S., Bishop, D.V.M., Dale, P. S., & Plomin, R. (2004). Genetic and environmental influence on language impairment in 4-year-old same-sex and opposite-sex twins. *Journal of Child Psychology and Psychiatry and Applied Disciplines 45*(2), 315–325.

Villa, R. F., & Jaime, A. (1993). La fe de la gente. In M. Sotomayer & A. Garcia (Eds.), *Elderly Latinos: Issues and solutions for the 21st century* (pp. 129–142). Washington, DC: National Hispanic Council on Aging.

Villareal, D. T., & Holloszy, J. O. (2004). Effect of DHEA on abdominal fat and insulin action in elderly women and men. *Journal of the American Medical Association, 292*(18), 2243–2248.

Villarosa, A. (2004, July). Exercise express. *Essence, 35*(3), 90–92.

Vining, E. P. G., Freeman, J. M., Pillas, D. J., Uematsu, S., Carson, B. S., Brandt, J., Boatman, D., Pulsifer, M. B., & Zuckerberg, A. (1997). Why would you remove half a brain? The outcome of 58 children after hemispherectomy—The Johns Hopkins Experience: 1968 to 1996. *Pediatrics, 100,* 1.

Visible embryo project. (1998). *The visible embryo.* University of California at San Francisco. Retrieved from http://visembryo.ucsf.edu/week1/week1.html

Vitale, B. M. (1986). *Free flight: Celebrating your right brain.* Rolling Hills, CA: Jalmar Press.

Volling, B. L., & Belsky, J. (1992). The contribution of mother-child and father-child relationships to the quality of sibling interaction: A longitudinal study. *Child Development, 63,* 1209–1222.

Volz, J. (2000). Successful aging: the second 50. *Monitor on Psychology, 31*(1), 24–28.

von Goethe, J. W. (1809). *Elective affinities.* London: Penguin Books.

von Hofsten, C. (1982). Eye-hand coordination in the newborn. *Developmental Psychology, 18,* 450–461.

Vondra, J. I., Shaw, D. S., Swearingen, L., Cohen, M., & Owens, E. B. (2001, March). Attachment stability and emotional and behavioral regulation from infancy to preschool age. *Development and Psychopathology, 13*(1), 13–33.

Votipka, J. (1997). Misoprostol for cervical ripening and labor induction. *Journal of Family Practice, 45*(1), 20.

Voydanoff, P. (2004, May). The effects of work demands and resources on work-to-family conflict and facilitation. *Journal of Marriage and Family, 66*(2), 398–412.

Vuchinich, S., Bank, L., & Patterson, G. R. (1992). Parenting, peers, and the stability of antisocial behavior in preadolescent boys. *Developmental Psychology, 28,* 510–521.

Vygotsky, L. S. (1962). *Thought and language.* Cambridge, MA: MIT Press.

Vygotsky, L. S. (1978). *Mind in society.* Cambridge, MA: Harvard University.

Wadden, T. A., & Van Itallie, T. B. (Eds.). (1992). *Treatment of the seriously obese patient.* New York: Guilford Press.

Wahl, H. W., Becker, S., Burmedi, D., & Schilling, O. (2004, March). The role of primary and secondary control in adaptation to age-related vision loss: A study of older adults with macular degeneration. *Psychology and Aging, 19*(1), 235–239.

Wainright, J. L., Russell, St. T., & Patterson, C. J. (2004, November/December). Psychosocial adjustment, school outcomes, and romantic relationships of adolescents with same-sex parents. *Child Development, 75,* 1886–1899.

Wainryb, C. (2004). The study of diversity in human development: Culture, urgencies, and perils. *Human Development, 45,* 131–137.

Waite, L. J., Haggstrom, G. W., & Kanouse, D. E. (1985). The consequences of parenthood for the marital stability of young adults. *American Sociological Review, 50,* 850–857.

Waldrop, D. P., & Weber, J. A. (2001). From grandparent to caregiver: The stress and satisfaction of raising grandchildren. *Families in Society: The Journal of Contemporary Human Services, 82*(5), 461–472.

Walker, E., Downey, G., & Bergman, A. (1989). The effects of parental psychopathology and maltreatment on child behavior: A test of the diathesis-stress model. *Child Development, 60,* 15–24.

Walker, H., Colvin, G., & Ramsey, E. (1995). *Antisocial behavior in school: Strategies and best practices.* Pacific Grove, CA: Brooks/Cole.

Walker, L. J., de Vries, B., & Bichard, S. L. (1984). The hierarchical nature of stages of moral development. *Developmental Psychology, 20,* 960–966.

Walker, N., Grassly, N. C., Garnett, G. P., Stanecki, K. A., & Ghys, P. D. (2004, June 26) Estimating the global burden of HIV/AIDS: What do we really know about the HIV pandemic? *Lancet, 363*(9427), 2180–2185.

Wallace, D. B., Franklin, M. B., & Keegan, R. T. (1994). The observing eye: A century of baby diaries. *Human Development, 37,* 1–29.

Wallerstein, J. (1987). Children of divorce. *American Journal of Orthopsychiatry, 57,* 199–211.

Wallerstein, J. S., & Kelly, J. B. (1980). *Surviving the breakup: How children actually cope with divorce.* New York: Basic Books.

Wallman, K. (1998). *America's children: Key national indicators of well-being.* Interagency Forum on Child and Family Statistics. Retrieved July 22, 1998, from http://www.ChildStats.gov/ac1998/HIGHLITE.HTM

Wallman, K. (2001). *America's children: Key national indicators of well-being.* Washington, DC: U.S. Government Printing Office, Federal Interagency Forum on Child and Family Statistics.

Walsh, D. (2001). *Talking with children when disaster strikes. Talking to kids about terrorism and violence.* PBS: America Responds. Retrieved December 27, 2001, from http://www.ktca.org/TPTspecial_edition/walsh2.html

Walters, J. (1991, March 11). Hospice care lets patients die in comfort of home. *USA Today,* 5D.

Walters, R. H., Leat, M., & Mezei, L. (1963). Inhibition and disinhibition of responses through empathetic learning. *Canadian Journal of Psychology, 17,* 235–243.

Walton, G. E., Bower, N. J. A., & Bower, T. G. R. (1992). Recognition of familiar faces by newborns. *Infant Behavior and Development, 15,* 265–269.

Wang, H., & Amato, P.R. (2000). Predictors of divorce adjustment: stressors, resources, and definitions. *Journal of Marriage and the Family, 62,* 655–668.

Wang, S. S., Brownell, K. D., & Wadden, T. A. (2004, October). The influence of the stigma of obesity on overweight individuals. *International Journal of Obesity Related Metabolism Disorders. 28*(10), 1333–1337.

Wang, Y. (2002). Is obesity associated with early sexual maturation? A comparison of the association in American boys versus girls. *Pediatrics, 110,* 903–910.

Wang, Y. (2003). Chinese ethical views on embryo stem (ES) cell research. In S. Y. Song, Y. M. Koo, & D. R. Macer (Eds.), *Bioethics in Asia in the 21st century* (pp. 49–55). Tsukuba Science City, Ibaraki, Japan: Eubios Ethics Institute.

Warner, H. R., & Price, A. R. (1989). Involvement of DNA repair in cancer and aging. *Journal of Gerontology, 44,* 45–54.

Wasik, B. H., Ramey, C. T., Bryant, D. M., & Sparling, J. J. (1990). A longitudinal study of two early intervention strategies: Project CARE. *Child Development, 61,* 1682–1696.

Watch, N. H., & Update, M. (2005, February). *Gum disease further linked to heart disease.* Retrieved March 22, 2005, from http://www.neighborhood-heart-watch.org/newsletter/article_278.shtml

Waterman, A. S. (1993). Two conceptions of happiness: Contrasts of personal expressiveness (eudaimonia) and hedonic enjoyment. *Journal of Personality and Social Psychology, 64,* 678–691.

Waters, E., Matas, L., & Sroufe, L. A. (1975). Infants' reactions to an approaching stranger: Description, validation, and functional significance of wariness. *Child Development, 46,* 348–356.

Weatherley, D. (1964). Self-perceived rate of physical maturation and personality in late adolescence. *Child Development, 35,* 1197–1210.

Webster-Stratton, C. (1989). The relationship of marital support, conflict, and divorce to parent perceptions, behaviors, and childhood conduct problems. *Journal of Marriage and the Family, 51,* 417–430.

Wechsler, D. (1975). Intelligence defined and undefined. *American Psychologist, 30,* 135–139.

Wechsler, H., Seibring, M., Liu, I-C., & Ahl, M. (2004, January/February). Colleges respond to student binge drinking: Reducing student demand or limiting access. *Journal of American College Health, 52,* 159–168.

Weigel, C., Wertlieb, D., & Feldstein, M. (1989). Percepts of control, competence, and contingency as influences on the stress-behavior symptom relation in school-age children. *Journal of Personality and Social Psychology, 56,* 456–464.

Weinberg, M. K., & Tronick, E. Z. (1994). Beyond the face: An empirical study of infant affective configurations of facial, vocal, gestural, and regulatory behaviors. *Child Development, 65,* 1503–1515.

Weinberg, M. S., Williams, C. J., & Pryor, D. W. (1994). *Dual attraction: Understanding bisexuality.* New York: Oxford University Press.

Weiner, B. (1993). On sin versus sickness: A theory of perceived responsibility and social motivation. *American Psychologist, 48,* 957–965.

Weinraub, M., Clemens, L. P., Sockloff, A., Ethridge, T., Gracely, E., & Myers, B. (1984). The development of sex role stereotypes in the third year. *Child Development, 55,* 1493–1503.

Weinstock, H., Berman, S., & Cates, W. (2004). Sexually transmitted disease among American youth: Incidence and prevalence estimates, 2000. *Perspectives on Sexual and Reproductive Health, 36,* 6–10.

Weiss, B. (1988). *Many lives, many masters.* New York: Simon & Schuster.

Weiss, C. O., Gonzalez, H. M., Kabeto, M. U., & Langa, K. M. (2005). Differences in amount of informal care received by non-Hispanic whites and Latinos in a nationally representative sample of older Americans. *Journal of the American Geriatrics Society, 53*(1), 146–151.

Weiss, R. (2004a, June 10). Stem cells an unlikely therapy for Alzheimer's: Reagan-inspired zeal for study continues. *Washington Times,* A03.

Weiss, R. (2004b, October 14). Harvard team seeks to clone embryos for stem cells. *Washington Times,* A1.

Weiss, R. S. (1990). *Staying the course: The emotional and social lives of men who do well at work.* New York: Free Press.

Weisser, C. (2004, December). The big squeeze. *Money, 33*(12), 112–118.

Weisz, J. R., Roghbaum, F. M., & Blackburn, T. C. (1984). Standing out and standing in: The psychology of control in America and Japan. *American Psychologist, 39,* 955–969.

Weitzman, E. R. (2004). Poor mental health, depression, and associations with alcohol consumption, harm, and abuse in a national sample of young adults in college. *The Journal of Nervous and Mental Disease, 192*(4), 269–277.

Welin, S. (2004). Reproductive ectogenesis: The third era of human reproduction and some moral consequences. *Science and Engineering Ethics, 10*(4), 615–626.

Wellman, H. M. (1977). The early development of intentional memory behavior. *Human Development, 20,* 86–101.

Wellman, H. M. (1990). *The child's theory of mind.* Cambridge, MA: MIT Press.

Wellman, H. M., Ritter, K., & Flavell, J. H. (1975). Deliberate memory behavior in the delayed reactions of very young children. *Developmental Psychology, 11,* 780–787.

Welsch, M. C., Pennington, B. F., Ozonoff, S., Rouse, B., & McCabe, E. R. B. (1990). Neuropsychology of early-treated phenylketonuria: Specific executive function deficits. *Child Development, 61,* 1697–1713.

Wenz-Gross, M., & Siperstein, G. N. (1998). Students with learning problems at risk in middle school: Stress, social support, and adjustment. *Exceptional Children, 65,* 91–100.

Werker, J. F., & Stager, C. L. (1997, July 24). Infants listen for more phonetic detail in speech perception than in word-learning tasks. *Nature, 388,* 381–382.

Werker, J. F., & Tees, R. C. (1999). Influences on infant speech processing: Toward a new synthesis. *Annual Review of Psychology, 50*(1), 509–536.

Werner, E. E. (1989). High-risk children in young adulthood: A longitudinal study from birth to 32 years. *American Journal of Orthopsychiatry, 59,* 72–81.

Werner, E. E. (1990). Protective factors and individual resilience. In S. J. Meisel & J. Shonkoff (Eds.), *Handbook of early childhood intervention.* New York: Cambridge University Press.

Westervelt, K., & Vandenberg, B. (1997). Parental divorce and intimate relationships of young adults. *Psychological Reports, 80,* 923–926.

Wetzstein, C. (2004, May 3). Federal marriage initiatives seen as cost effective. *The Washington Times.* Retrieved February 12, 2005, from http://washingtontimes.com

What is dyslexia? (2000). International Dyslexia Association. Retrieved January 5, 2005, from http://www.interdys.org/servlet/compose?section_id=5&page_id=95

What parents need: Work and caregiving options. (2001). The Future of Children. Retrieved February 10, 2005, from http://www.futureofchildren.org/usr_doc/foc11-1g2.pdf

What teens want. (2000, June). The National Campaign to Prevent Teen Pregnancy. Retrieved January 16, 2002, from http://www.teenpregnancy.org/teenwant.htm

Wheeler, I. (2001). Parental bereavement: The crisis of meaning. *Death Studies, 25*(1), 51–66.

When does the brain go blank? (2005). *Time,* 26–27.

Wherry, L., & Finegold, K. (2004, September). Marriage promotion and the living arrangements of black, hispanic, and white children. *New Federalism,* Series B, No. B-61. Washington, DC: The Urban Institute. Retrieved April 19, 2005, from http://www.urban.org/UploadedPDF/311064_B-61.pdf

Whisman, M. A., & Kwon, P. (1993). Life stress and dysphoria: The role of self-esteem and hopelessness. *Journal of Personality and Social Psychology, 65,* 1054–1060.

Whitaker, C. (2001). Why are young black men killing themselves? *Ebony, 56*(6), 142–144.

Whitbeck, L. B., Hoyt, D. R., Simons, R. L., Conger, R. D., Elder, G. H., Jr., Lorenz, F. O., & Huck, S. (1992). Intergenerational continuity of parental rejection and depressed affect. *Journal of Personality and Social Psychology, 63,* 1036–1045.

White, B. L. (1969). Child development research: An edifice without a foundation. *Merrill-Palmer Quarterly, 15,* 49–79.

White, L. (1994). Growing up with single parents and stepparents: Long-term effects on family solidarity. *Journal of Marriage and the Family, 56,* 935–948.

White, L., & Gilbreth, W. (2001, February). When children have two fathers: Effects of relationships with stepfathers and noncustodial fathers on adolescent outcomes. *Journal of Marriage and the Family, 63,* 155–167.

White, L., & Rogers, S. J. (2000). Economic circumstances and family outcomes: A review of the 1990s. *Journal of Marriage and the Family, 62,* 1035–1051.

White, L. A. (1949). *The science of culture: A study of man and civilization.* New York: Farrar, Straus.

White, L. K. (2001). Sibling relationships over the life course: A panel analysis. *Journal of Marriage and the Family, 63,* 555–568.

White, L. K., & Booth, A. (1985). The quality and stability of remarriages: The role of stepchildren. *American Sociological Review, 50,* 689–698.

White, N., & Cunningham, W. R. (1988). Is terminal drop pervasive or specific? *Journal of Gerontology, 43,* P141–P144.

Whitehead, B. D., & Popenoe, D. (2004, June). The state of our unions: The social health of marriage in America 2004. In *The social indicators of marital health and well-being: Trends of the past four decades.* Rutgers, NJ: The National Marriage Project.

Whitehead, B. D., Wilcox, B. L., & Rostosky, S. S. (2001, September). *Keeping the faith: The role of religion and faith communities in preventing teen pregnancy.* Washington, DC: The National Campaign to Prevent Teen Pregnancy.

Whiting, B. B., & Edwards, C. P. (1988). *Children of different worlds: The formation of social behavior.* Cambridge, MA: Harvard University Press.

Whorf, B. L. (1956). *Language, thought, and reality.* Cambridge, MA: MIT Press.

Wiatrowski, W. J. (2001, April). Changing retirement age: Ups and downs. *Monthly Labor Review, 124*(4), 1–7.

Wichstrom, L. (2000, May). Predictors of adolescent suicide attempts: A nationally representative longitudinal study of Norwegian adolescents. *Journal of the American Academy of Child and Adolescent Psychiatry, 39*(5), 603–610.

Wideman, M. V., & Singer, J. E. (1984). The role of psychological mechanisms in preparation for childbirth. *American Psychologist, 39*, 1357–1371.

Widom, C. S., & Maxfield, M.G. (2001). *An update on the "cycle of violence."* Washington, DC: National Institute of Justice. *Research in brief* (No. NCJ184894). Washington, DC: National Institute of Justice. Retrieved December 7, 2004, from http://www.ncjrs.org/pdffiles1/nij/184894.pdf

Wiebe, D. J. (1991). Hardiness and stress moderation: A test of proposed mechanisms. *Journal of Personality and Social Psychology, 60*, 89–99.

Wiederman, M. W. (1997). Extramarital sex: Prevalence and correlates in a national survey. *Journal of Sex Research, 34*, 167–174.

Wilde Matthews, A., Anand, G., & Davies, P. (2005, February 11, 2005). Why U.S., Canada differ on safety of attention-deficit drug. *Wall Street Journal*, B1.

Wilens, T. E., Fararone, S., & Biederman, J. (2004). Attention-deficit/hyperactivity disorder in adults. *Journal of the American Medical Association, 292*(5), 619–624.

Wiley, D., & Bortz, W. M. (1996). Sexuality and aging—Usual and successful. *Journals of Gerontology: Series A, Biological Sciences and Medical Sciences, 51*, M142–M146.

Wilfert, C. M., Kline, M. W., Futterman, D., Havens, P. L., King, S., Mofenson, L. M., Scott, G. B., Wara, D. W., & Whitley-Williams, P. N. (2000a). Education of children with human immunodeficiency virus infection (RE9950). *Pediatrics, 105*, 1358–1360.

Wilfert, C. M., Kline, M. W., Futterman, D., Havens, P. L., King, S., Mofenson, L. M., Scott, G. B., Wara, D. W., & Whitley-Williams, P. N. (2000b). Identification and care of HIV-exposed and HIV-infected infants, children, and adolescents in foster care (RE9836). *Pediatrics, 106*, 149–153.

Willcox, B. J., Willcox, D. C., & Suzuki, M. (2000). *Evidence-based extreme longevity: The case of Okinawa, Japan.* Okinawa Centenarian Study. Retrieved April 15, 2005, from http://okinawaprogram.com/evidence.html

Willems, E. P., & Alexander, J. L. (1982). The naturalistic perspective in research. In B. B. Wolman (Ed.), *Handbook of developmental psychology.* Englewood Cliffs, NJ: Prentice-Hall.

Willett, J. B., Singer, J. D., & Martin, N. C. (1998). The design and analysis of longitu-

dinal studies of development and psychopathology in context: Statistical models and methodological recommendations. *Development and Psychopathology, 10*, 395–426.

Willi, J. (1997). The significance of romantic love for marriage. *Family Process, 36*, 171–182.

Williams, C. C. (1998). *Reasons to grow old: Elders: Explorers without maps.* Aging and Spirituality. Retrieved January 15, 1999, from http://www.asaging.org/networks/forsa/a&s102.html

Williams, D. A., LoLordo, V. M., & Overmier, J. B. (1992). A reevaluation of Rescorla's early dictums about Pavlovian conditioned inhibition. *Psychological Bulletin, 111*, 275–290.

Williams, D., Ishikawa-Brush, Y., Cleak, J., & Monaco, A. P. (2001). *The genetics of specific language impairment.* The Cambridge Language and Speech Project. Retrieved October 6, 2001, from http://www.well.ox.ac.uk/monaco/slidianne.html

Williams, N., & Torrez, D. J. (1998). Grandparenthood among Hispanics. In M. Szinovacz (Ed.), *Handbook on grandparenthood* (pp. 87–96). Westport, CT: Greenwood Press.

Williamson, D., Netemeyer, R., Jackman, L., Anderson, D., Funsch, C., & Rabalais, J. (1995). Structural equation modeling of risk factors for the development of eating disorder symptoms in female athletes. *International Journal of Eating Disorders, 17*, 387–393.

Willingham, D. T. (2004/05, Winter). Understanding ADHD. *American Educator*, 36–41.

Willis, S. L., & Nesselroade, C. S. (1990). Longterm effects of fluid ability training in old-old age. *Developmental Psychology, 26*, 905–910.

Wilson B., & Gottman, J. (1995). Marital interaction and parenting. In M. Bornstein (Ed.), *Handbook of parenting.* Mahwah, NJ: Lawrence Erlbaum Associates.

Wilson, B., & Gottman, J. (2002). Marital conflict, repair and parenting. In M. Bornstein (Ed.), *Handbook of parenting* (Vol. 4.). Mahwah, NJ: Lawrence Erlbaum Associates.

Wilson, D., & Truman, C. (2004). Evaluating institutionalization by comparing the use of health services before and after admission to a long-term-care facility. *Evaluation and the Health Professions, 27*(3), 219–236.

Wilson, J. Q. (1993). *The moral sense.* New York: Free Press.

Wilson, M., & Daly, M. (1997). Life expectancy, economic inequality, homicide, and reproductive timing in Chicago neighborhoods. *British Medical Journal, 314*, 1271–1274.

Wilson, S. (2001). Attachment disorders: Review and current status. *Journal of Psychology, 135*(1), 37–52.

Wincze, J. P. (1999, September). Viagra can be a useful adjunct in treating psychogenic

problems. *Brown University GeroPsych Report, 3*(9), 1–4.

Wineberg, H., & Werth, J. L. (2003). Physician-assisted suicide in Oregon: What are the key factors? *Death Studies, 27*(6), 501–518.

Winik, M. (2004). The time of my life. *Health, 18*(3), 98–100.

Wink, P., & Helson, R. (1993). Personality change in women and their partners. *Journal of Personality and Social Psychology, 65*, 597–605.

Winsborough, H. H., Bumpass, L. L., & Aquilino, W. S. (1991). *The death of parents and the transition to old age* (Working Paper 39). Madison: University of Wisconsin, Center for Demography and Ecology.

Winslow, R. K. (1990, January 4). Nursing homes get more sick patients due to U.S. policy. *Wall Street Journal*, B3.

Winslow, R. K. (1999, January 6). Medication and psychotherapy help elderly fight depression. *Wall Street Journal*, B4.

Wintre, M. G., & Vallance, D. D. (1994). A developmental sequence in the comprehension of emotions: Intensity, multiple emotions, and valence. *Developmental Psychology, 30*, 509–514.

Wirt, J., Choy, S., Rooney, P. Provasnik, S., Sen, A., & Tobin, R. (2004). *The Condition of Education 2004* (NCES 2004-077). U.S. Department of Education, National Center for Education Statistics. Washington, DC: U.S. Government Printing Office.

Wisborg, K., Kesmodel, U., Bech, B. H., Hedegaard, M., & Henriksen, T. B. (2003, June). Maternal consumption of coffee during pregnancy and stillbirth and infant death in first year of life: A prospective study. *British Medical Journal, 326*(7401), 1268–1269.

Wiseman, R. (2002). *Queen bees and wannabes: Helping your daughter survive cliques, gossip, boyfriends, and other realities of adolescence.* New York, NY: Crown.

Wisner, K. L., & Wheeler, S. B. (1994). Prevention of recurrent postpartum onset major depression. *Hospital and Community Psychiatry, 45*, 1191–1196.

Witkin, H. A. (1964). Origins of cognitive style. In C. Sheerer (Ed.), *Cognition: Theory, research, promise.* New York: Harper & Row.

Witkin, H. A. (1975). Some implications of research on cognitive style for problems of education. In J. M. Whitehead (Ed.), *Personality and learning.* London: Hodder & Stoughton.

Woerlee, G. M. (2004). Darkness, tunnels, and light. *Skeptical Inquirer, 28*(3), 28–32.

Wolf, A. W., Lozoff, B., Latz, S., & Paludette, R. (1996). Parental theories in the management of young children's sleeping in Japan, Italy, and the United States. In S. Harkness and C. M. Super (Eds.), *Parents' cultural belief systems* (pp. 364–384). New York: Guilford Press.

Wolf, S., & Bruhn, J. G. (1993). *The power of clan: The influence of human relationships on heart disease.* New Brunswick, NJ: Transaction.

Wolfe, E. L., Davis, T., Guydish, J., & Delucchi, K. L. (2004, October 21). Mortality risk associated with perinatal drug and alcohol use in California. *Journal of Perinatology, 24,* 93–100.

Wolff, M. S., Berkowitz, G. S., Forman, J., Leleiko, N., Larson, S., Godbold, G. K., Kabat, G., Kase, N. Hochman, S., Britton, J., & Kadlubar, F. (2001, July 12). *1999 Progress report: Environmental exposures related to early puberty.* Mount Sinai Medical Center. Retrieved December 18, 2001, from http://www.es.epa.gov/ncerqa/progress/ grants/97/hhrisk/wolff99.html

Wolff, P. H. (1966). The causes, controls, and organizations of behavior in the neonate. *Psychological Issues, 5,* 1–105.

Wolff, P. H. & Fesseha, G. (1999). The orphans of Eritrea: A five-year follow-up study. *Journal of Child Psychology and Psychiatry, 40*(8), 1231–1237.

Wolinsky, F. D., Callahan, C. M., Fitzgerald, J. F., & Johnson, R. J. (1992). The risk of nursing home placement and subsequent death among older adults. *Journal of Gerontology: Social Sciences, 47,* S173–S182.

Women, children, and HIV. (2004). *New and noteworthy.* Retrieved December 29, 2004, from http://www.womenchildrenhiv.org/

Women's Health Initiative Study Group. (2004, April). Dietary adherence in the Women's Health Initiative Dietary Modification Trial. *Journal of the American Dietetic Association, 104*(4), 654–658.

Wong, E. H., Weiss, D. J., & Cusick, L. B. (2002, Summer). Perceptions of autonomy support, parent attachment, competence and self-worth as predictors of motivational orientation and academic achievement: An examination of sixth- and ninth-grade regular education students. *Adolescence, 37,* 255–266.

Wong, M. M., & Csikszentmihalyi, M. (1991). Affiliation motivation and daily experience: Some issues on gender differences. *Journal of Personality and Social Psychology, 60,* 154–164.

Wood, P. (2003). *Homeschooling and higher education:* ERIC Clearinghouse on Higher Education.

Woodruff, T. J., Axelrod, D. A., Kyle, A. D., Nweke, O., & Miller, G. G. (2003). *America's children and the environment: Measures of contaminants, body burdens, and illnesses.* Washington, DC: United States Environmental Protection Agency.

Woodward, E. H., & Gridina, N. (2000). *Media in the home 2000: The fifth annual survey of parents and children.* Philadelphia: The Annenberg Public Policy Center of the University of Pennsylvania.

Woodward, K. L. (1994). Erik Erikson: Teaching others how to see. *America, 171,* 6–8.

Woodward, K. L. (2001, July 9). A question of life or death. *Newsweek, 138,* 31.

Woollacott, M. H. (1993). Age-related changes in posture and movement. *Journals of Gerontology, 48* (Special issue), 56–60.

Woolley, J. D., & Wellman, H. M. (1993). Origin and truth: Young children's understanding of imaginary mental representations. *Child Development, 64,* 1–17.

Workowski, K. A., & Levine, W. C. (2002, May 10). Sexually transmitted diseases treatment guidelines. *Morbidity and Mortality Weekly Report, 51*(RR6), 1–78.

World Health Organization. (2004). Violence against women and HIV/AIDS: Critical intersections. *Information Bulletin Series* (2).

Worldwide HIV and AIDS epidemic statistics. (2004, December). AVERT Organization. Retrieved January 18, 2005, from http://www.avert.org

Wright, H. (1967). *Recording and analyzing child behavior.* New York: Harper & Row.

Wright, H., & Barker, R. C. (1950). *Methods in psychological ecology, a progress report.* Oxford, UK: Oxford University Press.

Wright, J. C., & Huston, A. C. (1995). *Effects of educational TV viewing of lower-income preschoolers on academic skills, school readiness, and school adjustment one to three years later.* (Report to Children's Television Workshop.) Lawrence, KS: University of Kansas, Center for Research on the Influences of Television on Children.

Wright, J. C., Huston, A. C., Reitz, A. L., & Piemyat, S. (1994). Young children's perceptions of television reality: Determinants and developmental differences. *Developmental Psychology, 30,* 229–239.

Wright, J. D., & Hamilton, R. F. (1978). Work satisfaction and age: Some evidence of the "job change" hypothesis. *Social Forces, 56,* 1140–1158.

Wright, M. A. (1998). *I'm chocolate, you're vanilla: Raising healthy black and biracial children in a race-conscious world.* San Francisco: Jossey-Bass.

Wright, R. (1994). *The moral animal: Evolutionary psychology and everyday life.* New York: Pantheon.

Wrosch, C., & Heckhausen, J. (2002). Perceived control of life regrets: Good for young and bad for old adults. *Psychology and Aging, 17*(2), 340–350.

Wrosch, C., Schulz, R., & Heckhausen, J. (2002). Health stresses and depressive symptomatology in the elderly: The importance of health engagement control strategies. *Health Psychology, 21,* 340–348.

Wu, L. L., & Thomson, E. (2001). Race differences in family experience and early sexual initiation: Dynamic models of family structure and family change. *Journal of Marriage and Family, 63*(3), 682–697.

Wu, T., Mendola, P., & Buck, G. M. (2002). Ethnic differences in the presence of secondary sex characteristics and menarche among US girls: The third national health and nutrition examination survey, 1988–1994. *Pediatrics, 110,* 752–757.

Wu, Z., & Penning, M. J. (1997). Marital instability after midlife. *Journal of Family Issues, 18,* 459–478.

Wu, Z., & Pollard, M. S. (2000). Economic circumstances and the stability of nonmarital cohabitation. *Journal of Family Issues, 21*(3), 303–328.

Wu, Z., & Schimmele, C. M. (2005). Repartnering after first union disruption. *Journal of Marriage and Family, 67*(1), 27–36.

Wulfert, E., & Biglan, A. (1994). A contextual approach to research on AIDS prevention. *Behavior Analyst, 17,* 353–363.

Wyman, L. C. (1970). *Blessingway.* Tucson: University of Arizona Press.

Wyshak, G., & Frisch, R. E. (1982). Evidence for a secular trend in age of menarche. *New England Journal of Medicine, 306,* 1033–1035.

Yaffe, K., Kanaya, A., Linquist, K., Simonsick, E., Harris, T., Shorr, R. I., et al. (2004). The metabolic syndrome, inflammation and risk of cognitive decline. *Journal of the American Medical Association, 292*(18), 2237–2242.

Yang, C., & Hahn, H. (2002, June). Cosleeping in young Korean children. *Journal of Developmental and Behavioral Pediatrics, 23,* 151–157.

Yankelovich, D. (2000). What grown-ups understand about child development: A national benchmark survey. CIVITAS Initiative, *Zero to Three,* BRIO Corporation. Researched by DYG, Inc.

Yarrow, L. J., MacTurk, R. H., Vietze, P. M., McCarthy, M. E., Klein, R. P., & McQuiston, S. (1984). Developmental course of parental stimulation and its relationship to mastery motivation during infancy. *Developmental Psychology, 20,* 492–503.

Yazbak, F. E. (2003, Winter). Autism in the United States. *Journal of American Physicians and Surgeons, 8*(4). 103–107.

Yeoh, B. S. A., & Chang, T. C. (Eds.). (2003, May). Fertility decline in Asia: Trends, implications, and futures. *Journal of Population Research, 20*(1). iii–x.

Yeung, W. J., Sandberg, J. F., Davis-Kearn, P. E., & Hofferth, S. L. (2001). Children's time with fathers in intact families. *Journal of Marriage and the Family, 63,* 136–154.

Yi, Z., & Vaupel, J. W. (2002, December). Functional capacity and self-evaluation of health and life of oldest old in China. *Journal of Social Issues, 58*(4), 733–748.

Yonas, A., Granrud, C. E., & Pettersen, L. (1985). Infants' sensitivity to relative size information at distance. *Developmental Psychology, 21,* 161–167.

Yoo, I. S. (2003, July 8). Infant hearing screenings rise: But goal of 100% is still far off. *USA Today,* 8D.

Yoon, K. (1992). New perspective on intra-sentential code switching. *Applied Linguistics, 13,* 433–449.

Yoshinaga-Itano, C. (1999, November). Development of audition and speech: Implications for early intervention with infants who are deaf or hard of hearing. *Volta Review, 5,* 213–235.

Young, K. T. (1990). American conceptions of infant development from 1955 to 1984: What the experts are telling parents. *Child Development, 61,* 17–28.

Young, T. M., Martin, S. S., Young, M. E., & Ting, L. (2001). Internal poverty and teen pregnancy. *Adolescence, 36*(142), 289–315.

Younger, B. (1992). Developmental change in infant categorization: The perception of correlations among facial features. *Child Development, 63,* 1526–1535.

Youngstrom, E., Wolpaw, J. M., Kogos, J. L., Schoff, K., Ackerman, B., & Izard, C. (2000). Interpersonal problem-solving in preschool and first grade: Developmental change and ecological validity. *Journal of Clinical Child Psychology, 29*(4), 589–602.

Youniss, J., & Smollar, J. (1985). *Adolescent relations with mothers, fathers, and friends.* Chicago: University of Chicago Press.

Zachary, G. P. (1995, February 9). Parents' gifts to adult children studied. *Wall Street Journal,* A2.

Zachry, W. (1978). Ordinality and interdependence of representation and language development in infancy. *Child Development, 49,* 681–687.

Zahn-Waxler, C. (1990). The ABCs of morality: Affect, behavior, and cognition. *Contemporary Psychology, 35,* 25–26.

Zaidi, A., & Shuraydi, M. (2002). Perceptions of arranged marriages by young Pakistani Muslim women living in a Western society. *Journal of Comparative Family Studies, 33*(4), 495–514.

Zajonc, R. B. (1976). Family configuration and intelligence. *Science, 192,* 227–236.

Zajonc, R. B. (1986, February). Mining new gold from old research. *Psychology Today, 20,* 47–51.

Zajonc, R. B., Markus, G. B., Berbaum, M. L., Bargh, J. A., & Moreland, R. L. (1991). One justified criticism plus three flawed analyses equals two unwarranted conclusions: A reply to Retherford and Sewell. *American Sociological Review, 56,* 159–165.

Zamanian, K., Thackery, M., Starrett, R. A., Brown, L. G., Lassman, D. K., & Banchard, A. (1992). Acculturation and depression in Mexican American elderly. In T. L. Brink (Ed.), *Hispanic aged mental health* (pp. 109–121). New York: Haworth Press.

Zanjani, F. A. K., Schaie, K. W. & Willis, S. L. (2001, October 15). Predicting health behaviors using developmental predictors. *Gerontologist,* 10.

Zarit, S. H., Dolan, M., & Leitsch, S. (1998). Interventions in nursing homes and other alternative living settings. In I. H. Nordhus et al. (Eds.), *Clinical geropsychology* (pp. 329–343). Washington: American Psychological Association.

Zaslow, J. (2005, February 3). What if Einstein had taken Ritalin? ADHD's impact on creativity. *Wall Street Journal, 245*(24), D1.

Zautra, A. J., Reich, J. W., & Guarnaccia, C. A. (1990). Some everyday life consequences of disability and bereavement for older adults. *Journal of Personality and Social Psychology, 59,* 550–561.

Zayas, L. H., Rojas, M., & Malgady, R. (1998). Alcohol and drug use, and depression among Hispanic men in early adulthood. *American Journal of Community Psychology, 26,* 425–438.

Zeanah, C. H., Scheeringa, M., Boris, N. W., Heller, S. S., Smyke, A. T., & Trapani, J. (2004). Reactive attachment disorder in maltreated toddlers. *Child Abuse and Neglect, 28,* 877–888.

Zebrowitz, L. A., Olson, K., & Hoffman, K. (1993). Stability of babyfaceness and attractiveness across the life span. *Journal of Personality and Social Psychology, 64,* 453–466.

Zehr, M. A. (2003). Massachusetts legislators override anti-bilingual-education law vetoes. *Education Week, 22*(43), 26.

Zeiss, A. M., & Kasl-Godley, J. (2001). Sexuality in older adults' relationships. *Generations, 25*(2), 18–25.

Zeller, S. (1998). Fetal abuse laws gain favor. *National Journal, 30,* 1758.

Zeman, J., Penza, S., Shipman, K., & Young, G. (1997). Preschoolers as functionalists: The impact of social context on emotion regulation. *Child Study Journal, 27,* 41–67.

Zhan, C., Sangl, J., Bierman, A. S., Miller, M. R., Friedman, B., Wickizer, S. & Meyer, G. S. (2001). Potentially inappropriate medication use in the community-dwelling elderly: Findings from the 1996 medical expenditure panel survey. *Journal of the American Medical Society, 286*(22), 2823–2830.

Zhang, C., & Bennett, T. (2001). Multicultural views of disability: Implications for early intervention professionals. *The Transdisciplinary Journal, 11*(2), 143–154.

Zhang, S. Y. (1995). *Chinese parents' influence on academic performance.* New York

State Association for Bilingual Education, 10, 46–53.

Zigler, E. F. (1970). The environmental mystique: Training the intellect versus development of the child. *Childhood Education, 46,* 402–412.

Zigler, E. F. (1994). Foreword. In M. Hyson, *The emotional development of young children: Building an emotion-centered curriculum.* New York: Teachers College Press.

Zigler, E. F., & Gilliam, W., & Jones, S. (Eds.). (2004). *The case for universal preschool education.* New York: Cambridge University Press.

Zigler, E. F., & Styfco, S. J. (2004, September). Head Start's national reporting system: A work in progress. *Pediatrics, 114,* 858–859.

Zimmer, M. H., & Zimmer, M. (1998). Socioeconomic determinants of smoking behavior during pregnancy. *Social Science Journal, 35,* 133–142.

Zimmerman, M. A., Copeland, L. A., Shope, J. T., & Dielman, T. E. (1997). A Longitudinal Study of Self-Esteem: Implications for Adolescent Development. *Journal of Youth and Adolescence, 26*(2), 117–141.

Zito, J. M., Safer, D. J., dosReis, S., Gardner, J. F., Magder, L., Soeken, K., Boles, M., & Lynch, F. (2002, May). Rising prevalence of antidepressants among U.S. youths. *Pediatrics, 109,* 721–727.

Zito, J. M., Safer, D. J., dosReis, S., Gardner, J. F., Magder, L., Soeken, K., Boles, M., Lynch, F., & Riddle, M. A. (2003, January). Psychotropic practice patterns for youth: A 10-year perspective. *Archives of Pediatrics and Adolescent Medicine, 157,* 17–25. Retrieved February 21, 2005, from http://archpedi.ama-assn.org/

Zito, J. M., Safer, D. J., Zuckerman, I. H., Gardner, J. F., & Soeken, K. (2005, February). Effect of Medicaid eligibility category on racial disparities in the use of psychotropic medications among youths. *Psychiatric Services, 56*(2), 157–163.

Zoba, W. (1999). *Generation 2K: What parents and others need to know about the Millennials.* Downers Grove, IL: InterVarsity Press.

Zsembik, B. A., & Singer, A. (1990). The problem of defining retirement among minorities: The Mexican Americans. *Gerontologist, 30,* 749–757.

Zube, M. (1982). Changing behavior and outlook of aging men and women: Implications for marriage in the middle and later years. *Family Relations, 31,* 147–156.

Photo Credits

Name Index

Subject Index

Career and College Major Application Matrix

Chapter, Page Number, & Description	Education (including Early Childhood, Primary, Secondary & Special Education)	Healthcare (including nursing, physical, speech, & occupational therapy)	Psychology & Sociology	Mental Health & Human Services
Ch.9, pp.333–335: Characteristics of effective schools.	X			
Ch.9, pp.339–340: How to promote prosocial behavior in children.	X		X	X
Ch.10, pp.344–345: Teaching implications for Erikson's stage of industry vs. inferiority.	X			
Ch.10, pp.345–346: Gender and age trends in self esteem.	X			X
Ch.10, p.347: How children express anger.	X			X
Ch.10, pp.351–355: Diverse family structures and their effects on a child's well-being.	X		X	X
Ch.10, p.352, Box: How to Help children cope with disaster and fear.	X			X
Ch.10, pp.356,359: How divorce affects children's development.	X			X
Ch.10, pp.357–358, Box: Adoption—Issues and concerns.				X
Ch.10, p.361: Developmental functions of peer groups during preadolescence.	X		X	
Ch.10, p.365: Behavioral characteristics of children in relation to peer acceptance or rejection.	X		X	X
Ch.10, p.365: Examples of school bullying behaviors.	X			
Ch.10, pp.367–369: The developmental function of schools.	X			
Ch.10, p.368, Box: Consequences of out-of-school childcare programs.	X			X
Ch.10, pp.369–370: Effects of extrinsic vs. intrinsic motivation on school performance.	X		X	
Ch.11, pp.381–382: Effects of early pubertal maturation in girls.	X	X		X
Ch.11, pp.386–388: How early or late maturation impacts children's development.	X			X
Ch.11, pp.389–390, Box: Health risks of female genital mutilation.		X		X
Ch.11, pp.392,394–395: Causes, health risks, and ways to prevent childhood obesity.		X		
Ch.11, pp.393–394, Box: Understanding anorexia and bulimia.		X		X
Ch.11, pp.396–399: Sexually transmitted diseases and HIV.		X		
Ch.11, p.399: Health risks of body art and tattooing.		X		
Ch.11, pp.404–405: Examples of effective classroom instruction in high school.	X			
Ch.12, pp.415–416: Differences between adolescent girls and boys in their struggle for positive self-esteem.	X		X	X
Ch.12, p.418: Characteristics of the millennial generation (largest cohort in American history).	X		X	
Ch.12, pp.419,421–422: Examples of how parent-child relationships change during puberty.			X	X
Ch.12, p.420, Box: The online world of young teens.	X			X
Ch.12, p.423: Environmental factors that influence adolescent sexual behavior.	X			X
Ch.12, pp.427–428: Why teenagers become pregnant.	X			X
Ch.12, p.431: What schools can do to help students prepare for post-secondary education.	X			
Ch.12, pp.434–435, Box: How to determine whether someone you know has an alcohol or drug problem.	X	X		X
Ch.12, p.435: Suggestions for preventing suicide.		X	X	X
Ch.12, p.437, Box: How to protect youths from guns and violence.	X			X
Ch.13, pp.445–447: Traits and values of Generation X and the Millennial generation.			X	
Ch.13, p.450: Cultural differences in societies with age-grade systems.	X		X	
Ch.13, p.454: Nurse practitioner, profile.		X		
Ch.13, pp.457–458: Contraceptive methods to help prevent pregnancy, STI's, and HIV.	X	X		
Ch.13, pp.460–461: Changes in drug and alcohol use over time.				X
Ch.13, pp.462: Mental health concerns for young adults with cross-cultural examples.			X	X
Ch.13, p.464: How stress affects our self-esteem and quality of life.				X
Ch.13, pp.464–465: Stress differences in college students.				X
Ch.13, pp.464–465: The major risk factors of suicide in young adulthood.				X
Ch.13, pp.469–470: Real-world applications of Kohlberg's theory on morality.			X	
Ch.14, p.478: Developmental differences between men and women in their 30's.		X	X	
Ch.14, pp.478–481: New social definition for contemporary women.			X	X
Ch.14, pp.481–482: Defining friendships and love.			X	X
Ch.14, pp.485–486: Implications for young adults who return home to live.				X
Ch.14, pp.486–488: Differences between cohabiters and married couples.				X
Ch.14, pp.489–491: Issues concerning the national debate on same-sex marriages.				X
Ch.14, pp.492–493, Box: Examples of arranged marriages around the world.			X	X
Ch.14, p.494, Box: Research findings on choosing a marriage partner.			X	X
Ch.14, pp.497–499: How becoming a parent impacts a marriage.			X	X
Ch.14, p.499: Factors affecting lesbian parenthood.			X	X
Ch.14, pp.500–503: Effects of separation and divorce on the family.			X	X
Ch.14, pp.503–505: How work affects one's self-respect and self-worth.			X	X
Ch.15, pp.512–514: Examples of sensory changes in Middle adulthood.		X		
Ch.15, pp.513 Box: Occupational/physical therapist, profile.		X		
Ch.15, pp.518–519: Preventive measures of osteoporosis and rheumatoid arthritis.		X		